D1833164

FLORA OF MAURITIUS AND THE SEYCHELLES

FLORA OF MAURITIUS AND THE SEYCHELLES

A DESCRIPTION OF

THE FLOWERING PLANTS AND FERNS OF THOSE ISLANDS.

BY

J. G. BAKER, F.L.S.,

FIRST ASSISTANT IN THE HERBARIUM OFTHE ROYAL GARDENS, KEW.

PUBLISHED UNDER THE AUTHORITY OF THE COLONIAL GOVERNMENT OF MAURITIUS.

GYAN

Published by

GYAN

Gyan Publishing House
5, Ansari Road
Daryaganj, New Delhi-110002
Phone: 011-47034999, 9811692060
E-mail: books@gyanbooks.com

Distribution Network
gyanbooks.com
India, USA, Canada, UK, Australia, France

© **Publisher**

All rights reserved. No part of this work may be reproduced, stored, adapted, or transmitted in any form or by any means, electronic, mechanical, photocopying, micro-filming, recording or otherwise, or translated in any language, without the prior written permission of the copyright owner and the publisher.

ISBN : 978-81-212-3381-1 (PB)
First Published, 1877

2nd Impression 2020

Printed at: Gyan Press, Delhi.

The book is sold subject to the condition that it shall not, by way of trade or otherwise, be lent, resold, hired out, or otherwise circulated without the prior publisher's written consent.

Flora of Mauritius and the Seychelles
Author: J. G. Baker

FLORA OF MAURITIUS AND THE SEYCHELLES:

A DESCRIPTION OF

THE FLOWERING PLANTS AND FERNS

OF THOSE ISLANDS.

BY

J. G. BAKER, F.L.S.,

FIRST ASSISTANT IN THE HERBARIUM OF THE ROYAL GARDENS, KEW.

PUBLISHED UNDER THE AUTHORITY OF THE COLONIAL GOVERNMENT OF MAURITIUS.

LONDON:
L. REEVE & CO., 5, HENRIETTA STREET, COVENT GARDEN.
1877.

CONTENTS.

CONTENTS

PREFACE.

THIS flora has been drawn up under the authority and at the expense of the colonial government. It forms one of a series of floras which have been prepared at Kew, of which those for Hong Kong by Mr. Bentham, of New Zealand by Dr. Hooker, and of the British West Indies by Dr. Grisebach, are completed; and those of Australia by Mr. Bentham, assisted by Baron von Mueller, of India edited by Dr. Hooker, of Tropical Africa by Professor Oliver, and of the Cape, begun by Harvey and Sonder, and intended to be continued by Mr. Thistleton Dyer, are begun, but still unfinished.

The following are the principal books and collections from which our knowledge of the botany of Mauritius and its dependencies is derived:—

1. *Commerson*. An extensive collection, made between 1770 and 1780. Commerson, after his voyage round the world as naturalist to the expedition commanded by Bougainville (1766–1769), settled for five years in Mauritius, during the governorship of M. Poivre, who founded the Botanic Garden at Pamplemousses, and attempted unsuccessfully to make Mauritius a great centre of nutmeg- and clove-cultivation. Commerson visited both Madagascar and Bourbon, and took back with him to France as the result of his whole expedition a herbarium of 3000 numbers. His collections were never regularly reported upon in systematic order, but were distributed to various herbaria, and a large number of his plants were described in the general works published at the end of the 18th and the beginning of the 19th century, especially the 'Encyclopédie' of Lamarck and Poiret, and the 'Species Plantarum' of Willdenow, and he may be fairly considered to be the father of Mauritian botany.

2. *Willemet*, 'Hortus Mauritianus,' a duodecimo of 64 pages, published at Leipsic, after the death of the author, in 1796, with a preface by Professor Millin. Willemet was a native of Nancy, and was born in 1762. He visited the island about 1790, and made a small collection, but in the absence of type specimens it is impossible to recognise many of the species from his brief descriptions.

3. *Colonel Bory de Saint Vincent.* 'Voyage dans les quatres principales îles des Mers d'Afrique, 1801–2,' three volumes octavo, with an atlas in quarto, published at Paris in 1804. Bory de Saint Vincent was a native of Agen in France, and was born in 1780. In his nineteenth year he accompanied as naturalist an expedition sent by the French government to Australia under the command of Capt. Baudin. In consequence of a disagreement with the captain he and several of the other officers left the ship at Mauritius, where he was employed for some time on the staff of the governor in surveying the French possessions in that part of the world. His principal attention was directed to Bourbon, of which he constructed an excellent map. After his return to Europe he saw much service both as a naturalist and a soldier, and highly distinguished himself. He died in 1846.

4. *Chevalier Aubert du Petit Thouars.* Two works entitled respectively 'Histoire des Végétaux recueillis sur les îles de France, la Réunion, et de Madagascar," a quarto of 48 pages with 10 plates, published along with a paper on Cycas, at Paris in 1804, and again with considerable additions (80 pages and 24 plates) in 1805; and 'Histoire particulière des plantes Orchidées recueillis sur les trois îles australes d'Afrique, de France, de Bourbon, et de Madagascar," an octavo of 32 pages and 110 plates, published at Paris in 1822. The second of these is a monograph of the Orchids of the Mascarene group, with figures of each species, and the first contains descriptions and figures of several of the most curious endemic Mascarene genera. Besides these, Du Petit Thouars made a large general collection in Mauritius, which, like that of Commerson, was distributed to various herbaria, especially that of Willdenow at Berlin, but never fully reported upon.

5. *Carmichael.* A small collection made by Capt. Carmichael, F.L.S., the monographer of the island of Tristan d'Acunha. This collection contains several species and varieties I have not elsewhere seen, but unfortunately they are not specially localised. Carmichael was an officer of the 73rd regiment of the British Army. He came to Mauri-

tius from the Cape in 1810, and also visited Bourbon. He died in 1826.

6. *Sieber.* Two sets of dried specimens, gathered with Zeyher in 1822–1823. Many sets were gathered and the collection is distributed widely in herbaria. It is often cited in De Candolle's Prodromus and general monographs, but it contains a great many introduced plants as well as the genuine natives of the island, and as no distinction is made between the two, it has led to many species being regarded as Mauritian, which are simply taken from gardens there, and have no claim to be considered even as naturalised. Sieber collected many similar sets of dried specimens in other parts of the world.

7. *Achille Richard.* 'Monographie des Orchidées des îles de France et de Bourbon,' 1828, quarto, 83 pages, 11 plates.

8. *Bojer.* 'Hortus Mauritianus, ou énumeration des plantes exotiques et indigènes qui croissent à l'île Maurice,' an octavo of 456 pages, published in Mauritius in 1837. M. Bojer was professor of botany for many years at the Royal College of St. Louis, and secretary and curator of the Natural History Society, or, as it was afterwards called, the Royal Society of Arts and Sciences of Mauritius. He explored the botany of the island so thoroughly that he left very little for his successors to discover, and this work contains a complete enumeration of both the wild and garden plants of the island, with the special localities of the former. If Bojer had not drawn with a firm hand more than a generation ago the line of demarcation between the indigenous and introduced species, it could not have been done satisfactorily now, and in this important matter I have every reason to consider him thoroughly trustworthy. Unfortunately the book contains names only, and he never lived to publish the descriptions of the many new species which he named, and, as might be expected, in many cases fell into error in identifying plants of Mauritius with those of other countries, or more often in supposing species to be new and endemic which were known and already named from other countries. He sent large collections to Sir Wm. Hooker, and through the instrumentality of Sir H. Barkly the whole herbarium of the Royal Society of Arts and Sciences, which he formed, was forwarded to Kew, with permission to keep specimens of the duplicates. So that with these and the help of Messrs. Bouton and Horne, we know more or less certainly what is intended by a great majority of the names used in this work, but there are a certain number of which no specimens have been kept, and to

which consequently, in the entire absence of descriptions, we have no clue.

9. *Telfair*. A small collection sent to Sir W. Hooker, by Mr Telfair, a resident landed proprietor, and many Mauritian plants contributed by the same gentleman to Wallich's great Indian herbarium.

10. *Neraud*. A collection of about 800 numbers, of which the first set is in the Delessert herbarium, now at Geneva.

11. *Bouton, L.* 'Plantes Médicinales de Maurice,' our copy, the second edition, an octavo of 147 pages, published at Port Louis in 1864. Next to Bojer, M. Bouton has been the most active resident botanist of the colony. He has filled, since Bojer's death, the post of curator and librarian of the Royal Society of Arts and Sciences, has edited its transactions, of which eight parts of the new series, containing many valuable notes on botany and other departments of natural history, have appeared, and has sent large collections to Kew and other European herbaria.

12. *Ayres, Dr. P. B.* Dr. Ayres, who occupied the post of Superintendent of Quarantine, at St. Louis, from 1856 to 1863, had already before leaving England, established a reputation as a cryptogamic botanist. On his arrival in Mauritius he interested himself greatly in the botany of the colony. He intended to publish a flora of the island, and drafted out a synonymic catalogue, into which he inserted from time to time elaborate descriptions drawn up from living specimens of the species which he was able to procure. Unfortunately his professional work tied him down to the city and allowed him little leisure, so that at his lamented death in the prime of life, after a residence of six years in the island, his task was not far advanced. His papers and collections were presented to Kew, after his death, by Mrs. Ayres, and have been of great use for this present work.

13. *Duncan, Jas.* "Catalogue of the Plants in the Royal Botanic Garden, Mauritius, 1863," 4to, 104 pages, with supplement, and catalogue of colonial names. Duncan was the predecessor of Mr. Horne, in the curatorship of the Botanic Garden, at Pamplemousses, and died lately in Scotland.

14. *Sir Henry and Lady Barkly*. Sir Henry Barkly was governor of the island from 1863 to 1870, and amidst all the responsibilities that devolved upon them during a time of unusual difficulty and anxiety, Lady Barkly and he both took great interest in the botany of the

colony, and by their collections and notes materially increased our knowledge of many of its plants, especially the Ferns and Pandani.

15. *Dupont.* A catalogue of the Flowering Plants of Mauritius, contained in the 7th volume of the Transactions of the Royal Society of Arts and Sciences, pages 116 to 161.

16. *Madame Moon.* A collection of beautiful coloured water colour drawings of plants, made during a residence of many years in the colony by Madame Moon, kindly sent to Kew by Mr. Caldwell, to be used in preparing this work.

For our principal supply of material from the Seychelles we are indebted to Mr. John Horne, F.L.S., the present director of the Botanic Garden, at Pamplemousses, who went out from Kew. He has paid two visits to the group, one in 1871 and the other in 1874, during which he specially devoted himself to the task of exploring its botany. His collections amount to nearly 700 numbers, and of these he has sent a complete set to Kew, accompanied by copious notes on the habit and special stations of the plants. His second collection, the largest of the two, only arrived after the present work was nearly all written. We had previously received smaller collections of Seychelles plants from M. Bojer, Dr. Kirk, Dr. Percival Wright, and the Paris Museum, the latter gathered by M. Auguste Pervillé, about 1840. Dr. Wright, who visited the group in 1867, has published in the Transactions of the Royal Irish Academy three papers, in two of which I have co-operated, in which he has given illustrations of several of the more interesting endemic plants of the group.

On Rodriguez a collection of about 100 species was made several years ago, during short visits by Messrs. Bouton and Duncan; and more recently the island has been thoroughly explored by Dr. I. B. Balfour, who accompanied as naturalist the Transit of Venus expedition and remained upon it in 1874, from August to December. Dr. Balfour's plants reached Kew just as we were beginning to print, and his explorations and those of Mr. Horne have given this work a much greater degree of completeness than was anticipated when it was planned four years ago. Dr. Balfour's collection has been divided between Kew, the British Museum, and the Edinburgh Botanic Garden, and a full account of the plants, with figures of the new genera and most of the new species, will shortly be published in his report to the Royal Society.

The keys and descriptions of orders aud genera have been drawn up with special though not exclusive reference to their Mauritian representatives. It is only the indigenous orders, genera, and species that are numbered, the names of the indigenous species being printed in thick roman type, and those of the introduced species in italics, with the descriptions drawn up in a different form, so as to show at a glance to what class of citizenship any given plant belongs. It is only the introduced species that may fairly claim to be regarded as naturalised, that are described, the mere casuals being simply mentioned by name. Under every indigenous species known to occur in the island or group the words "Mauritius," "Rodriguez," and "Seychelles" are repeated in capital letters in the paragraph that follows the description. A note of admiration after the name of a collector means that I have seen one of the specimens which he gathered; and where the name of a collector is given, and there is no note of admiration, a confirmation of the record is desirable, and we shall be glad to have specimens forwarded. It is also most desirable that the attention of future visitors to Rodriguez and the Seychelles should be specially directed to the numerous plants from those islands mentioned in this flora which cannot be fully determined without further material than has been yet procured. In the botanical exploration of the smaller dependencies of Mauritius there is still a wide field for investigation, as we know nothing or next to nothing of the botany of the St. Brandon Isles, Galega, Diego Garcia, Cortivy, Providence, and St. Pierre Islands, and the Amirauté and Cosmoledo groups.

My best thanks are due to my colleague, Mr. Spencer Le Marchant Moore, F.L.S., for his Synopsis of the Orchids, to Dr. I. B. Balfour for having undertaken to describe the Palms and Pandani, and to Mr. Horne for the help he has given in hunting out information about many of Bojer's doubtful species, and to Dr. Hooker for the trouble he has taken in revising the proof-sheets, which has been the means of correcting many imperfections that would otherwise have escaped attention.

Kew Herbarium, April, 1877.

GENERAL REMARKS ON THE PHYSICAL GEOGRAPHY AND BOTANY OF THE ISLANDS.

Mauritius is situated a couple of degrees within the Tropic of Capricorn, at a distance of 500 miles from Madagascar and of above 100 miles from Bourbon. Its area is 700 square miles, its greatest length from north to south being 39 miles and its breadth from east to west 35 miles. It is a little smaller than the county of Surrey, and the whole area embraced by the present flora is under 850 square miles. The northern quarter of the island, the tract between Port Louis, Pamplemousses and Flacq, is a low plain covered with sugar plantations. The centre consists of a cultivated plateau, which rises to a height of about 1500 feet above sea-level. The great mass of rock is entirely volcanic, but no active volcano has been known within the memory of man. Raised beds of coral, clay, and gravel are found scattered through the island at various elevations, showing that, although many craters remain in almost complete condition, there has been great general elevation since the main volcanic mass was laid down. On the outside of the central plateau, within a short distance of the sea, rise the three principal mountain-ranges which the island contains. Of the north-western-range the highest peaks, the Pouce (2707 feet) and Pieterboth (2874 feet), are within a few miles of Port Louis, and it sends out several short ridges to the west, and two longer spurs (Montagne Longue and the Callebasses hills) to the east. The south-western range is the most considerable of the three. At its north end the isolated mountain of Corps de Garde reaches 2525 feet. The range of the Black River Mountains forms a continuous ridge near the shore of the south-western corner of the island, running north and south for a length of above a dozen miles. Its peaks are the Trois Mamelles (2340 feet), Rampart Mountain (2710 feet), and Piton de la Rivière Noire (2902 feet). At its south end the peak of Morne Brabant forms a bold headland on the very coast, rising to a height of 1937 feet. From the south-west corner of the island, separated from the end of the Black River range by only a narrow gulley, the Savanne range of hills strikes due east, and runs parallel with the shore at a short distance from it for a length of ten miles, reaching a height of 2429 feet. The third range is an irregularly-branched small group of hills situated on the opposite or east side of the central plateau, north of Grandport, the second largest town of the island. This range reaches a height of 2404 feet. Besides these there are many isolated rounded peaks, like the Piton du Milieu de l'Isle, which rises from the very middle of the central plateau. There are two small lakes on the central plateau, called the Grand Bassin and Mare aux Vacoas. There are half-a-dozen streams that reach a length of ten or twelve miles, and run from the central plateau to the sea in the broad open spaces between the three main hill-ranges and innumerable rivulets that break down the short steep mountain-valleys and are often entirely destitute of water in the dry season. At Port Louis and in the low country the average annual temperature is 78° Fahr. The average daily range is from 70° at sunrise to 86° in the middle of the afternoon. The extremes in the shade registered during many years are 61½° and 90°. The general vegetation of the island is consequently of a decidedly tropical character, the south temperate element being only faintly represented on the peaks by such plants as *Phylica mauritiana*, the *Philippia* heaths, *Pellæa hastata*, and the three species of *Helichrysum*. Amongst more widely-spread indigenous temperate types we may mention *Nephrodium Filix-mas, Pteris longifolia and cretica, Cardamine hirsuta, Juncus effusus, Cerastium glomeratum, Convolvulus arvensis, Plantago major and lanceolata.* In orography and botany Mauritius offers a decided contrast to both Bourbon and Madagascar, where the highest peaks are in the centre of the island, rising to a height of 10,000 or 12,000 feet, with the snow lying upon them for many months. The warmest and wettest season of the year is from November to April, the time of the north-west monsoon, the comparatively cool and dry season being from May to October, when the wind blows from the south-east. The rain is very irregular from year to year and very different in quantity in different parts of the island. The average rainfall at Grandport, on the east coast, is said to be 146 inches, at Labourdonnais 63 inches, and at Port Louis only 38 inches. The difference between the longest and shortest days is 2½ hours. Unfortunately so far as botany is concerned the value of land in Mauritius for sugar cultivation has been so great that the forests, which at the time when it was named by the Dutch, in 1598, covered it to the water's edge, have been by degrees cut down till now they are almost entirely destroyed. The cultivation of sugar was introduced by Governor Labourdonnais in 1740, and in ten years we are told it had almost entirely supplanted the useful vegetable products previously grown, which were cloves, indigo, cotton, and coffee. In 1761 the aboriginal forests had already been cut down to such an extent that the French East India Company sent out directions to the Governor to stop their destruction, but the value of the land had become so great that these directions were of very little avail. From 467 tons, in 1812, the amount of sugar exported increased till it reached a maximum of 131,000 tons in 1860, so that it was calculated at that time that this island, with an area of 700 square miles, produced about a tenth of the exported sugar of the whole world. The consequence is that the indigenous flora of the island, as we have it now, is a mere wreck of what it was a hundred years ago, that the remains of the aboriginal forests now linger only in the recesses of the hills, that many of the Orchids, Ferns, Pandani, and other shade- and damp-loving plants, and the interesting endemic trees and shrubs, such as *Fœtidia, Psiloxylon, Labourdonnaisia, Colophania, Stadtmannia, Fissilia, Hornea, Ludia, Quivisia, Aphloia, Monimia, and Tambourissa* have either been entirely exterminated or become very rare, and that a crowd of introduced trees, shrubs, and weeds have replaced the original vegetation to a greater extent than in any other part of the world except St. Helena. Our estimate of the number of these introduced plants which have become established is 269 species, which will be found described in their systematic position intermingled with the indigenous types in the body of the work. The number of wild flowering plants and ferns, which we know with more or less certainty as inhabitants of the island, is 869. Trees are now being extensively planted in the neighbourhood of Port Louis with marked advantage to the health of the town.

The Seychelles are situated 900 miles to the north-east of Mauritius in 3–6° south latitude. There are altogether upwards of 30 islands in the group, but most of them are very small. They rest upon a raised platform of coral and sand, which is about 200 miles long from north to south, and 30–40 miles broad from east to west. They differ from Mauritius, Bourbon, and Madagascar in the rock of which they are composed being entirely granitic. The largest islands of the group are

Mahé (30,000 acres), Praslin (8000 acres), Silhouette (5700 acres), La Digue, the best cultivated and most densely populated of the group (2000 acres), and Curieuse (1000 acres). The length of Mahé is 17 miles. The mountains of the interior reach a height of 3000 feet, and those of Silhouette a height of 2500 feet, but none of the others rise above 1500 feet above sea-level. The seasons are similar to those of Mauritius, the average highest daily temperature in the shade being stated to range from 80° to 87° Fahr., and the lowest from 70° to 74°. The annual rainfall is given by Mr. Horne at 96 inches, by far the greater part of which falls from October to April, during the north-west monsoon. The principal exports of the islands at the present time are cocoa-nut oil and cocoa-nut fibre. In 1862, above £10,000 worth of cocoa-nut oil was exported. Between 1814 and 1827, cotton was cultivated to a large extent, and for its sake many of the aboriginal forests were destroyed, but since the abolition of slavery in the British possessions, America has gradually occupied the European markets, and its cultivation in the Seychelles has dwindled away. The larger islands rise steeply from the sea, and are often bordered by precipices of several hundred feet in height. In Praslin and Silhouette the soil is very poor. In Mahé it is rich in the ravines and forests, but has been much washed away since the principal woods were cut down, and at the present time large trees are only to be found in the more inaccessible parts of the mountains. The entire vegetation is of a distinctively tropical character, the few temperate types that reach Mauritius being here entirely absent. The number of wild flowering plants and ferns with which we are now acquainted in the group is 338. Of these, six genera are endemic: *Medusagyne*, *Deckenia*, *Nephrosperma*, *Roscheria*, *Verschaffeltia*, *Lodoicea*, and *Stevensonia*; all but the first-named of which are Palms. The total number of endemic species is 60, of which 14 are Rubiaceæ, 8 Vascular Cryptogams, and 3 Pandani. Most of the 54 species which do not belong to the monotypic endemic genera just named, are members of large widely-spread genera. Before the botany of the group was worked out, it was expected, from the isolated position of the islands, their granitic soil, and peculiar palms, that their flora would be much richer in individuality of character than has proved to be the case. Besides the 60 endemic species, between 20 and 30 are characteristically Mascarene types, and the remaining 250 mostly plants of wide dispersion.

Rodriguez is situated east, and a little north of Mauritius, at a distance from it of 300 miles, in between 19° and 20° south latitude. It measures eleven miles in length by five miles in breadth, and the hills of the interior reach a little over 1000 feet above sea-level. The climate is completely similar to that of Mauritius, and the subjacent rock is entirely volcanic. The general character presented by the surface of the island is a dry parched volcanic soil, with many deeply-excavated stream-courses, now for the most part dried up. The highest ground and deepest ravines are on the east, and their slopes are covered with a thick scrub, mixed with ferns and weeds, and scattered over them are a considerable number of shrubs and trees, especially Pandani. On the west side the altitude is lower, the ravines are not so deep, and the ground slopes gradually towards the south. The land is covered with stones, and nearly destitute of trees and shrubs, and the ground over wide areas is covered with a scant coating of grasses and *Cyperaceæ*, mixed with social weeds. At the south-west end of the island is a low plain of coralline limestone, which yields several of the endemic species, as *Nesogenes*, *Abrotanella*, and the two species of *Hypoestes*. Here, as in Mauritius, our earliest records of the island, which go back to 1691, report it as richly wooded. Now the forests have been all cut down, and flocks of goats and herds of cattle graze over its surface and nip the young shoots of everything they can reach. Through Dr. Balfour's explorations we now know in the island 202 wild species of Flowering Plants and Ferns. Of these, 36 are peculiar to the island, and three represent monotypic endemic genera, *Mathurinia*, *Scyphochlamys*, and *Tanulepis*. Notably the proportions of Ferns and Orchids is smaller than in Mauritius.

The following table shows the number of species in each systematic subdivision which our flora includes. In looking at this table, it must be borne in mind that all numerical statements which have been hitherto made in regard to the flora of Mauritius have rested upon the data of Bojer, and that by using the standard of what constitutes a species which has been employed in the Kew colonial floras, Bojer's figures are materially reduced. For instance, in the 'Hortus Mauritianus' the vascular Cryptogams of the island are counted at 218, whilst our estimate of their number is 164, and it is probable that a reduction of 25 per cent. will represent a fair average of the difference between the two standards:—

	Total Native.	Native in Mauritius.	Native in Seychelles.	Native in Rodrigues.	Naturalised.	Total.
Thalamifloræ . . .	110	95	32	30	50	160
Calycifloræ	120	89	52	29	70	190
Monopetalæ	244	183	68	49	76	320
Incompletæ	112	93	28	19	35	147
Florideæ	149	124	32	18	24	173
Glumiferæ	131	121	46	31	14	145
Vascular Cryptogams.	192	164	80	26	—	192
Total . . .	1058	869	338	202	269	1327

The following table shows the distribution of the native species. By Mascarene types, we mean plants confined to Bourbon, Mauritius, Madagascar, and the Comoros; not using the term, as has been done recently by Grisebach, to cover the two former islands alone. It will be noted, that half the wild plants of this flora are restricted to the Mascarene archipelago, and that it contains an appreciable percentage, both of plants, which are African, without reaching Asia, and Asiatic without reaching Africa:—

	Endemic.	Mascarene.	African, but not Asian.	Asian, but not African.	Common to Asia and Africa.	Common to the Old and New World.
Thalamifloræ . . .	39	30	4	2	10	25
Calycifloræ	29	20	12	14	20	25
Monopetalæ	97	46	16	20	29	36
Incompletæ	40	32	5	10	13	12
Florideæ	64	57	4	7	8	9
Glumiferæ	14	9	9	12	35	52
Vascular Cryptogams.	21	38	16	21	80	66
Total Number .	304	232	66	86	145	225
Per Centage . .	29	22	6	8	14	21

The following is the rotation as regards the number of species which they contain, in which come the nine orders of the flora which are represented by 20 species or more.

1	Filices . . .	168 species.	6	Euphorbiaceæ .	45 species.
2	Orchideæ . .	79 „	7	Compositæ . .	43 „
3	Gramineæ . .	69 „	8	Leguminosæ .	41 „
4	Cyperaceæ . .	62 „	9	Myrtaceæ . .	20 „
5	Rubiaceæ . .	57 „			

The 1058 wild species belong to 110 natural orders and 440 genera, so that the proportion of species to a genus in this flora is between 2 and 3, and of species to an order between 9 and 10.

OUTLINES OF BOTANY.

FROM MR. BENTHAM'S BRITISH AND COLONIAL FLORAS.

CHAP. I. DEFINITIONS AND DESCRIPTIVE BOTANY.

1. The principal object of a **Flora** of a country is to afford the means of *determining* (*i.e.*, ascertaining the name of) any plant growing in it, whether for the purpose of ulterior study or of intellectual exercise.

2. With this view, a Flora consists of descriptions of all the wild or native plants contained in the country in question, so drawn up and arranged that the student may identify with the corresponding description any individual specimen which he may gather.

3. These descriptions should be *clear*, *concise*, *accurate*, and *characteristic*, so as that each one should be readily adapted to the plant it relates to, and to no other one; they should be as nearly as possible arranged under *natural* (184) divisions, so as to facilitate the comparison of each plant with those nearest allied to it; and they should be accompanied by an *artificial key* or index, by means of which the student may be guided step by step in the observation of such peculiarities or *characters* in his plant as may lead him, with the least delay, to the individual description belonging to it.

4. For descriptions to be clear and readily intelligible, they should be expressed as much as possible in ordinary well-established language. But, for the purpose of accuracy, it is necessary not only to give a more precise technical meaning to many terms used more or less vaguely in common conversation, but also to introduce purely technical names for such parts of plants or forms as are of little importance except to the botanist. In the present chapter it is proposed to define such *technical* or *technically limited* terms as are made use of in these Floras.

5. At the same time mathematical accuracy must not be expected. The forms and appearances assumed by plants and their parts are infinite. Names cannot be invented for all; those even that have been proposed are too numerous for ordinary memories. Many are derived from supposed resemblances to well-known forms or objects. These resemblances are differently appreciated by different persons, and the same term is not only differently applied by different botanists, but it frequently happens that the same writer is led on different occasions to give somewhat different meanings to the same word. The botanist's endeavours should always be, on the one hand, to make as near an approach to precision as circumstances will allow; and, on the other hand, to avoid that prolixity of detail and overloading with technical terms which tends rather to confusion than clearness. In this he will be more or less successful. The aptness of a botanical description, like the beauty of a work of imagination, will always vary with the style and genius of the author.

§ 1. *The Plant in General.*

6. The **Plant** in its botanical sense, includes every being which has *vegetable life*, from the loftiest tree which adorns our landscapes, to the humblest moss which grows on its stem, to the mould or fungus which attacks our provisions, or the green scum that floats on our ponds.

7. Every portion of a plant which has a distinct part or *function* to perform in the operations or phenomena of vegetable life is called an **Organ.**

8. What constitutes *vegetable life*, and what are the functions of each organ, belong to *Vegetable Physiology;* the microscopical structure of the tissues composing the organs, to *Vegetable Anatomy;* the composition of the substances of which they are formed, to *Vegetable Chemistry;* under *Descriptive* and *Systematic Botany* we have chiefly to consider the forms of organs, that is, their *Morphology*, in the proper sense of the term, and their general structure so far as it affects classification and specific resemblances and differences. The terms we shall now define belong chiefly to the latter branch of Botany, as being that which is essential for the investigation of the Flora of a country. We shall add, however, a short chapter on Vegetable Anatomy and Physiology, as a general knowledge of both imparts an additional interest to and facilitates the comparison of the characters and affinities of the plants examined.

9. In the more perfect plants, their organs are comprised in the general terms **Root, Stem, Leaves, Flowers,** and **Fruit.** Of these the three first, whose function is to assist in the growth of the plant, are *Organs of Vegetation;* the flower and fruit, whose office is the formation of the seed, are the *Organs of Reproduction.*

10. All these organs exist, in one shape or another, at some period of the life of most, if not all, *flowering plants*, technically called *phænogamous* or *phanerogamous plants:* which all bear some kind of flower and fruit in the botanical sense of the term. In the lower classes, the ferns, mosses, fungi, moulds or mildews, seaweeds, etc., called by botanists *cryptogamous plants*, the flowers, the fruit, and not unfrequently one or more of the organs of vegetation, are either wanting, or replaced by organs so different as to be hardly capable of bearing the same name.

11. The observations comprised in the following pages refer exclusively to the flowering or phænogamous plants. The study of the cryptogamous classes has now become so complicated as to form almost a separate science. They are therefore not included in these introductory observations, nor, with the exception of ferns and their allies, in the present Flora.

12. **Plants** are

Monocarpic, if they die after one flowering-season. These include *Annuals*, which flower in the same year in which they are raised from seed; and *Biennials*, which only flower in the year following that in which they are sown.

Caulocarpic, if, after flowering, the whole or part of the plant lives through the winter and produces fresh flowers another season. These include *Herbaceous perennials*, in which the greater part of the plant dies after flowering, leaving only a small perennial portion called the Stock or Caudex, close to or within the earth; *Undershrubs*, *suffruticose* or *suffrutiscent* plants, in which the flowering branches, forming a considerable portion of the plant, die down after flowering, but leave a more or less prominent perennial and woody base; *Shrubs* (*frutescent* or *fruticose plants*), in which the perennial woody part forms the greater part of the plant, but branches near the base, and does not much exceed a man's height; and *Trees* (*arboreous* or *arborescent plants*) when the height is greater and forms a woody *trunk*, scarcely branching from the base. *Bushes* are low, much branched shrubs.

13. The terms *Monocarpic* and *Caulocarpic* are but little used, but the other distinctions enumerated above are universally attended to, although more useful to the gardener than to the botanist, who cannot always assign to them any precise character. Monocarpic plants, which require more than two or three years to produce their flowers, will often, under certain circumstances, become herbaceous perennials, and are generally confounded with them. Truly perennial herbs will often commence flowering the first year, and have then all the appearance of annuals. Many tall shrubs and trees lose annually their flowering branches like undershrubs. And the same botanical species may be an annual or a perennial, a herbaceous perennial or an undershrub, an undershrub or a shrub, a shrub or a tree, according to climate, treatment, or variety.

14. Plants are usually *terrestrial*, that is, growing on earth, or *aquatic*, *i.e.*, growing in water; but sometimes they may be found attached by their roots to other plants, in which case they are *epiphytes* when simply growing upon other plants

without penetrating into their tissue, *parasites* when their roots penetrate into and derive more or less nutriment from the plant to which they are attached.

15. The simplest form of the perfect plant, the annual, consists of

(1) The **Root**, or descending axis, which grows downwards from the stem, divides and spreads in the earth or water, and absorbs food for the plant through the extremities of its branches.

(2) The **Stem**, or ascending axis, which grows upwards from the root, branches and bears first one or more leaves in succession, then one or more flowers, and finally one or more fruits. It contains the tissues or other channels (217) by which the nutriment absorbed by the roots is conveyed in the form of *sap* (192) to the leaves or other points of the surface of the plant, to be *elaborated* or *digested* (218), and afterwards redistributed over different parts of the plant for its support and growth.

(3) The **Leaves**, usually flat green, and horizontal, are variously arranged on the stem and its branches. They *elaborate* or *digest* (218) the nutriment brought to them through the stem, absorb carbonic acid gas from the air, exhaling the superfluous oxygen, and returning the assimilated sap to the stem.

(4) The **Flowers**, usually placed at or towards the extremities of the branches. They are destined to form the future seed. When perfect and complete they consist: 1st, of a *pistil* in the centre, consisting of one or more *carpels*, each containing the germ of one or more seeds; 2nd, of one or more *stamens* outside the pistil, whose action is necessary to *fertilize* the pistil or enable it to ripen its seed; 3rd, of a *perianth* or *floral envelope*, which usually encloses the stamens and pistil when young, and expands and exposes them to view when fully formed. This complete perianth is double: the outer one, called *Calyx*, is usually more green and leaf-like; the inner one, called the *Corolla*, more conspicuous, and variously coloured. It is the perianth, and especially the corolla, as the most showy part, that is generally called the flower in popular language.

(5) The **Fruit**, consisting of the pistil or its lower portion, which persists or remains attached to the plant after the remainder of the flower has withered and fallen off. It enlarges and alters more or less in shape or consistence, becomes a *seed-vessel*, enclosing the seed until it is ripe, when it either opens to discharge the seed or falls to the ground with the seed. In popular language the term *fruit* is often limited to such seed-vessels as are or look juicy and eatable. Botanists give that name to all seed-vessels.

16. The herbaceous perennial resembles the annual during the first year of its growth; but it also forms (usually towards the close of the season), on its *stock* (the portion of the stem and root which does not die), one or more *buds*, either exposed, and then popularly called *eyes*, or concealed among leaves. These buds, called *leaf-buds*, to distinguish them from *flower-buds* or unopened flowers, are future branches as yet undeveloped; they remain dormant through the winter, and the following spring grow out into new stems bearing leaves and flowers like those of the preceding year, whilst the lower part of the stock emits fresh roots to replace those which had perished at the same time as the stems.

17. Shrubs and trees form similar leaf-buds either at the extremity of their branches or along the branches of the year. In the latter case these buds are usually *axillary*, that is, they appear in the *axil* of each leaf, *i.e.*, in the angle formed by the leaf and the branch. When they appear at any other part of the plant, they are called *adventitious*. If these buds by producing roots (19) become distinct plants before separating from the parent, or if adventitious leaf-buds are produced in the place of flowers or seeds, the plant is said to be *viviparous* or *proliferous*.

§ 2. *The Root.*

18. **Roots** ordinarily produce neither buds, leaves, nor flowers. Their branches, called *fibres* when slender and long, proceed irregularly from any part of their surface.

19. Although roots proceed usually from the base of the stem or stock, they may also be produced from the base of any bud, especially if the bud lie along the ground, or is otherwise placed by nature or art in circumstances favourable for their development, or indeed occasionally from almost any part of the plant. They

are then often distinguished as *adventitious*, and this term is by some applied to all roots which are not in prolongation of the original radical.

20. **Roots** are

fibrous, when they consist chiefly of slender fibres.

tuberous, when either the main root or its branches are thickened into one or more short fleshy or woody masses called *tubers* (25).

taproots, when the main root descends perpendicularly into the earth, emitting only very small fibrous branches.

21. The stock of a herbaceous perennial, or the lower part of the stem of an annual or perennial, or the lowest branches of a plant, are sometimes underground and assume the appearance of root. They then take the name of *rhizome*. The rhizome may always be distinguished from the true root by the presence or production of one or more buds, or leaves, or scales.

§ 3. *The Stock.*

22. The **Stock** of a herbaceous perennial, in its most complete state, includes a small portion of the summits of the previous year's roots, as well as of the base of the previous year's stems. Such stocks will increase yearly so as at length to form dense tufts. They will often preserve through the winter a few leaves, amongst which are placed the buds, which grow out into stems the following year, whilst the under side of the stock emits new roots from or amongst the remains of the old ones. These perennial stocks only differ from the permanent base of an undershrub in the shortness of the perennial part of the stems and in the texture, usually less woody.

23. In some perennials, however, the stock consists merely of a branch, which proceeds in autumn from the base of the stem either aboveground or underground, and produces one or more buds. This branch, or a portion of it, alone survives the winter. In the following year its buds produce the new stem and roots, whilst the rest of the plant, even the branch on which these buds were formed, has died away. These *annual stocks*, called sometimes *hybernacula*, *offsets*, or *stolons*, keep up the communication between the annual stem and root of one year and those of the following year, thus forming altogether a perennial plant.

24. The stock, whether annual or perennial, is often entirely underground or root-like. This is the *rootstock*, to which some botanists limit the meaning of the term *rhizome*. When the stock is entirely root-like, it is popularly called the *crown* of the root.

25. The term *tuber* is applied to a short, thick, more or less succulent rootstock or rhizome, as well as to a root of that shape (20), although some botanists propose to restrict its meaning to the one or to the other. An Orchis tuber, called by some a *knob*, is an annual tuberous rootstock with one bud at the top. A potato is an annual tuberous rootstock with several buds.

26. A *bulb* is a stock of a shape approaching to globular, usually rather conical above and flattened underneath, in which the bud or buds are concealed, or nearly so, under *scales*. These scales are the more or less thickened bases of the decayed leaves of the preceding year, or of the undeveloped leaves of the future year, or both. Bulbs are annual or perennial, usually underground or close to the ground, but occasionally buds in the axils of the upper leaves become transformed into bulbs. Bulbs are said to be *scaly* when their scales are thick and loosely imbricated, *tunicated* when the scales are thinner, broader, and closely rolled round each other in concentric layers.

27. A *corm* is a tuberous rootstock, usually annual, shaped like a bulb, but in which the bud or buds are not covered by scales, or of which the scales are very thin and membranous.

§ 4. *The Stem.*

28. **Stems** are

erect, when they ascend perpendicularly from the root or stock; *twiggy* or *virgate*, when at the same time they are slender, stiff, and scarcely branched.

sarmentose, when the branches of a woody stem are long and weak, although scarcely climbing.

decumbent or *ascending*, when they spread horizontally, or nearly so, at the base, and then turn upwards and become erect.

procumbent, when they spread along the ground the whole or the greater portion of their length; *diffuse*, when at the same time very much and rather loosely branched.

prostrate, when they lie still closer to the ground.

creeping, when they emit roots at their nodes. This term is also frequently applied to any rhizomes or roots which spread horizontally.

tufted or *cæspitose*, when very short, close, and many together from the same stock.

29. Weak climbing stems are said to *twine*, when they support themselves by winding spirally round any object; such stems are also called *voluble*. When they simply climb without twining, they support themselves by their leaves, or by special clasping organs called *tendrils* (169), or sometimes, like the Ivy, by small root-like excrescences.

30. *Suckers* are young plants formed at the end of creeping, underground rootstocks. *Scions*, *runners*, and *stolons*, or *stoles*, are names given to young plants formed at the end or at the nodes (31) of branches or stocks creeping wholly or partially aboveground, or sometimes to the creeping stocks themselves.

31. A *node* is a point of the stem or its branches at which one or more leaves, branches, or leaf-buds (16) are given off. An *internode* is the portion of the stem comprised between two nodes.

32. **Branches** or **leaves** are

opposite, when two proceed from the same node on opposite sides of the stem.

whorled or *verticillate* (in a *whorl* or *verticel*), when several proceed from the same node, arranged regularly round the stem; *geminate*, *ternate*, *fascicled*, or *fasciculate* when two, three, or more proceed from the same node on the same side of the stem. A tuft of fasciculate leaves is usually in fact a leafy branch, so short that the leaves appear to proceed all from the same point.

alternate, when one only proceeds from each node, one on one side and the next above or below, though usually not in the same vertical line.

decussate, when opposite, but each pair placed at right-angles to the next pair above or below it; *distichous*, when regularly arranged one above another in two opposite rows, one on each side of the stem; *tristichous*, when in three rows, etc. (92).

scattered, when irregularly arranged round the stem; frequently, however, botanists apply the term *alternate* to all branches or leaves that are neither opposite nor whorled.

secund, when all start from or are turned to one side of the stem.

33. **Branches** are *dichotomous*, when several times forked, the two branches of each fork being nearly equal; *trichotomous*, when there are three nearly equal branches at each division instead of two; but when the middle branch is evidently the principal one, the stem is usually said to have two opposite branches; *umbellate*, when divided in the same manner into several nearly equal branches proceeding from the same point. If however the central branch is larger than the two or more lateral ones, the stem is said to have opposite or whorled branches, as the case may be.

34. A *culm* is a name sometimes given to the stem of Grasses, Sedges, and some other Monocotyledonous plants.

§ 5. *The Leaves.*

35. The ordinary or perfect **Leaf** consists of a flat *blade* or *lamina*, usually green, and more or less horizontal, attached to the stem by a stalk called a *footstalk* or *petiole*. When the form or dimensions of a leaf are spoken of, it is generally the blade that is meant, without the petiole or stalk.

36. The end by which a leaf, a part of the flower, a seed, or any other organ, is attached to the stem or other organ, is called its *base*, the opposite end is its *apex* or summit, excepting sometimes in the case of anther-cells (115).

37. **Leaves** are

sessile, when the blade rests on the stem without the intervention of a petiole.

amplexicaul or *stem-clasping*, when the sessile base of the blade clasps the stem horizontally.

perfoliate, when the base of the blade not only clasps the stem, but closes round it on the opposite side, so that the stem appears to pierce through the blade.

decurrent, when the edges of the leaf are continued down the stem so as to form raised lines or narrow appendages, *called wings*.

sheathing, when the base of the blade, or of the more or less expanded petiole, forms a vertical sheath round the stem for some distance above the node.

38. Leaves and flowers are called *radical*, when inserted on a rhizome or stock, or so close to the base of the stem as to appear to proceed from the root, rhizome, or stock; *cauline*, when inserted on a distinct stem. Radical leaves are *rosulate* when they spread in a circle on the ground.

39. **Leaves** are

simple and *entire*, when the blade consists of a single piece, with the margin nowhere indented, *simple* being used in opposition to *compound*, *entire* in opposition to *dentate*, *lobed*, or *divided*.

ciliate, when bordered with thick hairs or fine hair-like teeth.

dentate or *toothed*, when the margin is only cut a little way in, into what have been compared to teeth. Such leaves are *serrate*, when the teeth are regular and pointed like the teeth of a saw; *crenate*, when regular and blunt or rounded (compared to the battlements of a tower); *serrulate*, and *crenulate*, when the serratures or crenatures are small; *sinuate*, when the teeth are broad, not deep, and irregular (compared to bays of the coast); *wavy* or *undulate*, when the edges are not flat, but bent up and down (compared to the waves of the sea).

lobed or *cleft*, when more deeply indented or divided, but so that the incisions do not reach the midrib or petiole. The portions thus divided take the name of *lobes*. When the lobes are narrow and very irregular, the leaves are said to be *laciniate*. The spaces between the teeth or lobes are called *sinuses*.

divided or *dissected*, when the incisions reach the midrib or petiole, but the parts so divided off, called *segments*, do not separate from the petiole, even when the leaf falls, without tearing.

compound, when divided to the midrib or petiole, and the parts so divided off, called *leaflets*, separate, at least at the fall of the leaf, from the petiole, as the whole leaf does from the stem, without tearing. The common stalk upon which the leaflets are inserted is called the *common petiole* or the *rhachis*; the separate stalk of each leaflet is a *petiolule*

40. Leaves are more or less marked by *veins*, which, starting from the stalk, diverge or branch as the blade widens, and spread all over it more or less visibly. The principal ones, when prominent, are often called *ribs* or *nerves*, the smaller branches only then retaining the name of *veins*, or the latter are termed *veinlets*. The smaller veins are often connected together like the meshes of a net, they are then said to *anastomose*, and the leaf is said to be *reticulate* or *net-veined*. When one principal vein runs direct from the stalk towards the summit of the leaf, it is called the *midrib*. When several start from the stalk, diverge slightly without branching, and converge again towards the summit, they are said to be *parallel*, although not mathematically so. When 3 or 5 or more ribs or nerves diverge *from the base*, the leaf is said to be *3-nerved*, *5-nerved*, etc., but if the lateral ones diverge from the midrib a little above the base, the leaf is *triplinerved*, *quintuplinerved*, etc. The arrangement of the veins of a leaf is called their *venation*.

41. The **Leaflets, Segments, Lobes**, or **Veins** of leaves are

pinnate (feathered), when there are several succeeding each other on each side of the midrib or petiole, compared to the branches of a feather. A pinnately lobed or divided leaf is called *lyrate* when the terminal lobe or segment is much larger and broader than the lateral ones, compared, by a stretch of imagination, to a lyre; *runcinate*, when the lateral lobes are curved backwards towards the base of the leaf; *pectinate*, when the lateral lobes are numerous, narrow, and regular, like the teeth of a comb.

palmate, or *digitate*, when several diverge from the same point, compared to the fingers of the hand.

ternate, when three only start from the same point, in which case the distinction between the palmate and pinnate arrangement often ceases, or can only be determined by analogy with allied plants. A leaf with ternate lobes is called *trifid.* A leaf with three leaflets is sometimes improperly called a ternate leaf: it is the leaflets that are ternate; the whole leaf is *trifoliate.* Ternate leaves are leaves growing three together.

pedate, when the division is at first ternate, but the two outer branches are forked, the outer ones of each fork again forked, and so on, and all the branches are near together at the base, compared vaguely to the foot of a bird.

42. Leaves with pinnate, palmate, pedate, etc., leaflets, are usually for shortness called *pinnate, palmate, pedate,* etc., *leaves.* If they are so cut into segments only, they are usually said to be *pinnatisect, palmatisect, pedatisect,* etc., although the distinction between segments and leaflets is often unheeded in descriptions, and cannot indeed always be ascertained. If the leaves are so cut only into lobes, they are said to be *pinnatifid, palmatifid, pedatifid,* etc.

43. The teeth, lobes, segments, or leaflets may be again toothed, lobed, divided, or compounded. Some leaves are even three or more times divided or compounded. In the latter case they are termed *decompound.* When twice or thrice pinnate (*bipinnate* or *tripinnate*), each primary or secondary division, with the leaflets it comprises, is call a *pinna.* When the pinna of a leaf or the leaflets of a pinna are in pairs, without an odd terminal pinna or leaflet, the leaf or pinna so divided is said to be *abruptly pinnate;* if there is an odd terminal pinna or leaflet, the leaf or pinna is *unequally pinnate* (*imparipinnatum*).

44. The number of leaves or their parts is expressed adjectively by the following numerals derived from the Latin:—

uni-,	bi-,	tri-,	quadri-,	quinque-,	sex-,	septem-,	octo-,	novem-,	decem-,	multi-,
1-,	2-,	3-,	4-,	5-,	6-,	7-,	8-,	9-,	10-,	*many-*,

prefixed to a termination, indicating the particular kind of part referred to. Thus—

unidentate, bidentate, multidentate, mean one-toothed, two-toothed, many-toothed, etc.

bifid, trifid, multifid, mean two-lobed, three-lobed, many-lobed, etc.

unifoliolate, bifoliolate, multifoliolate, mean having one leaflet, two leaflets, many leaflets, etc.

unifoliate, bifoliate, multifoliate, mean having one leaf, two leaves, many leaves, etc.

biternate and *triternate,* mean twice or thrice ternately divided.

unijugate, bijugate, multijugate, etc., pinnæ or leaflets, mean that they are in one, two, many, etc., pairs (*juga*).

45. **Leaves** or their parts, when **flat** or any other flat organs in plants, are

linear, when long and narrow, at least four or five times as long as broad, falsely compared to a mathematical line, for a linear leaf has always a perceptible breadth.

lanceolate, when about three or more times as long as broad, broadest below the middle, and tapering towards the summit, compared to the head of a lance.

cuneate, when broadest above the middle, and tapering towards the base, compared to a wedge with the point downwards; when very broadly cuneate and rounded at the top, it is often called *flabelliform* or *fan-shaped.*

spathulate, when the broad path near the top is short, and the narrow tapering part long, compared to a spathula or flat ladle.

ovate, when scarcely twice as long as broad, and rather broader below the middle, compared to the longitudinal section of an egg; *obovate* is the same form with the broadest part above the middle.

deltoid, triangular, in the form of the Greek letter Δ.

orbicular, oblong, elliptical, rhomboidal, etc., when compared to the corresponding mathematical figures.

transversely, oblong, or *oblate* when conspicuously broader than long.

falcate, when curved like the blade of a scythe.

46. Intermediate forms between any two of the above are expressed by combining two terms. Thus, a *linear-lanceolate* leaf is long and narrow, yet broader below the middle, and tapering to a point; a *linear-oblong* one is scarcely narrow enough to be called linear, yet too narrow to be strictly oblong, and does not conspicuously taper either towards the summit or towards the base.

47. The *apex* or *summit* of a leaf is

acute or *pointed*, when it forms an acute angle or tapers to a point.

obtuse or *blunt*, when it forms a very obtuse angle, or more generally when it is more or less rounded at the top.

acuminate or *cuspidate* when suddenly narrowed at the top, and then more or less prolonged into an *acumen* or *point*, which may be acute or obtuse, linear or tapering. Some botanists make a slight difference between the *acuminate* and *cuspidate* apex, the acumen being more distinct from the rest of the leaf in the latter case than in the former; but in general the two terms are used in the same sense, some preferring the one and some the other.

truncate, when the end is cut off square.

retuse, when very obtuse or truncate, and slightly indented.

emarginate or *notched*, when more decidedly indented at the end of the midrib; *obcordate*, if at the same time approaching the shape of a heart with its point downwards.

mucronate, when the midrib is produced beyond the apex in the form of a small point.

aristate when the point is fine like a hair.

48. The base of the leaf is liable to the same variations of form as the apex, but the terms more commonly used are *tapering* or *narrowed* for acute and acuminate, *rounded* for obtuse, and *cordate* for emarginate. In all cases the petiole or point of attachment prevents any such absolute termination at the base as at the apex.

49. A leaf may be *cordate* at the base whatever be its length or breadth, or whatever the shape of the two lateral lobes, called *auricles* (or *little ears*), formed by the indenture or notch, but the term *cordiform* or *heart-shaped* leaf is restricted to an ovate and acute leaf, cordate at the base with rounded auricles. The word auricles is more particularly used as applied to sessile and stem-clasping leaves.

50. If the auricles are pointed, the leaf is more particularly called *auriculate*; it is moreover said to be *sagittate* when the points are directed downwards, compared to an arrow-head; *hastate*, when the points diverge horizontally, compared to a halbert.

51. A *reniform* leaf is broader than long, slightly but broadly cordate at the base, with rounded auricles, compared to a kidney.

52. In a *peltate* leaf, the stalk, instead of proceeding from the lower edge of the blade, is attached to the under surface, usually near the lower edge, but sometimes in the very centre of the blade. The peltate leaf has usually several principal nerves radiating from the point of attachment, being, in fact, a cordate leaf, with the auricles united.

53. All these modifications of division and form in the leaf pass so gradually one into the other that it is often difficult to say which term is the most applicable —whether the leaf be toothed or lobed, divided or compounded, oblong or lanceolate, obtuse or acute, etc. The choice of the most apt expression will depend on the skill of the describer.

54. **Leaves,** when **solid, Stems, Fruits, Tubers,** and other parts of plants, when not flattened like ordinary leaves, are

setaceous or *capillary*, when very slender like bristles or hairs.

acicular, when very slender, but stiff and pointed like needles.

subulate, when rather thicker and firmer like awls.

linear, when at least four times as long as thick; *oblong*, when from about two to about four times as long as thick, the terms having the same sense as when applied to flat surfaces.

ovoid, when egg-shaped, with the broad end downwards, *obovoid* if the broad end is upwards; these terms corresponding to *ovate* and *obovate* shapes in flat surfaces.

globular or *spherical*, when corresponding to *orbicular* in a flat surface. *Round* applies to both.

turbinate, when shaped like a top.

conical, when tapering upwards; *obconical*, when tapering downwards, if in both cases a transverse section shows a circle.

pyramidal, when tapering upwards; *obpyramidal*, when tapering downwards if in both cases a tranverse sections shows a triangle or polygon.

fusiform, or spindle-shaped, when tapering at both ends; *cylindrical* when not tapering at either end, if in both cases the transverse section shows a circle, or sometimes irrespective of the transverse shape.

terete, when the transverse section is not angular; *trigonous*, *triquetrous*, if the transverse section shows a triangle, irrespective in both cases of longitudinal form.

compressed, when more or less flattened laterally; *depressed*, when more or less flattened vertically, or at any rate at the top; *obcompressed* (in the achenes of *Compositæ*), when flattened from front to back.

articulate or *jointed*, if at any period of their growth (usually when fully formed and approaching their decay, or in the case of fruits when quite ripe) they separate, without tearing, into two or more pieces placed end to end. The joints where they separate are called *articulations*, each separate piece an *article*. The name of *joint* is, in common language, given both to the articulation and the article, but more especially to the former. Some modern botanists, however, propose to restrict it to the article, giving the name of *joining* to the articulation.

didymous, when slightly two-lobed, with rounded obtuse lobes.

moniliform, *torulose*, or beaded, when much contracted at regular intervals, but not separating spontaneously into articles.

55. In their consistence **Leaves** or other organs are

fleshy, when thick and soft; *succulent* is generally used in the same sense, but implies the presence of more juice.

coriaceous, when firm and dry, or very tough, of the consistence of leather.

crustaceous, when firm and brittle.

chartaceous, or *papyraceous*, when of the consistence of paper.

membranous, when thin and not stiff.

scarious, or *scariose*, when very thin, more or less transparent and not green, yet rather stiff.

56. The terms applied botanically to the consistence of solids are those in general use in common language.

57. The mode in which unexpanded leaves are disposed in the leaf-bud is called their *vernation* or *præfoliation*; it varies considerably, and technical terms have been proposed to express some of its varieties, but it has been hitherto rarely noticed in descriptive botany.

§ 6. *Scales, Bracts, and Stipules.*

58. **Scales** (*Squamæ*) are leaves very much reduced in size, usually sessile, seldom green or capable of performing the respiratory functions of leaves. In other words, they are organs resembling leaves in their position on the plant, but differing in size, colour, texture, and functions. They are most frequent on the stock of perennial plants, or at the base of annual branches, especially on the buds of future shoots, when they serve apparently to protect the dormant living germ from the rigour of winter. In the later case they are usually short, broad, close together, and more or less *imbricated*, that is, overlapping each other like the tiles of a roof. It is this arrangement as well as their usual shape that has suggested the name of *scales*, borrowed from the scales of a fish. Imbricated scales, bracts, or leaves, are said to be *squarrose*, when their tips are pointed and very spreading or recurved.

59. Sometimes, however, most or all the leaves of the plant are reduced to small scales, in which case they do not appear to perform any particular function. The name of *scales* is also given to any small broad scale-like appendages or reduced organs, whether in the flower or any other part of the plant.

60. **Bracts** (*Bractæ*) are the upper leaves of a plant in flower (either all those of the flowering branches, or only one or two immediately under the flower), when different from the stem-leaves in size, shape, colour, or arrangement. They are generally much smaller and more sessile. They often partake of the colour of the flower, although they very frequently also retain the green colour of the leaves. When small they are often called *scales*.

61. *Floral leaves* or *leafy bracts* are generally the lower bracts or the upper leaves at the base of the flowering branches, intermediate in size, shape, or arrangement, between the stem-leaves and the upper bracts.

62. *Bracteoles* are the one or two last bracts under each flower, when they differ materially in size, shape, or arrangement from the other bracts.

63. **Stipules** are leaf-like or scale-like appendages at the base of the leaf-stalk, or on the node of the stem. When present there are generally two, one on each side of the leaf, and they sometimes appear to protect the young leaf before it is developed. They are however exceedingly variable in size and appearance, sometimes exactly like the true leaves except that they have no buds in their axils, or looking like the leaflets of a compound leaf, sometimes apparently the only leaves of the plant; generally small and narrow, sometimes reduced to minute scales, spots, or scars, sometimes united into one opposite the leaf, or more or less united with, or *adnate* to the petiole, or quite detached from the leaf, and forming a ring or sheath round the stem in the axil of the leaf. In a great number of plants they are entirely wanting.

64. *Stipellæ*, or secondary stipules, are similar organs, sometimes found on compound leaves at the points where the leaflets are inserted.

65. When scales, bracts, or stipules, or almost any part of the plant besides leaves and flowers are stalked, they are said to be *stipitate*, from *stipes*, a *stalk*.

§ 7. *Inflorescence and its Bracts.*

66. The **Inflorescence** of a plant is the arrangement of the flowering branches, and of the flowers upon them. *An Inflorescence*, is a flowering branch, or the flowering summit of a plant above the last stem-leaves with its branches, bracts, and flowers.

67. A single flower, or an inflorescence, is *terminal* when at the summit of a stem or leafy branch, *axillary* when in the axil of a stem-leaf, *leaf-opposed* when opposite to a stem-leaf. The inflorescence of a plant is said to be *terminal* or *determinate* when the main stem and principal branches end in a flower or inflorescence (not in a leaf-bud), *axillary* or *indeterminate* when all the flowers or inflorescences are axillary, the stem or branches ending in leaf-buds.

68. A *Peduncle* is the stalk of a solitary flower, or of an inflorescence; that is to say, the portion of the flowering branch from the last stem-leaf to the flower, or to the first ramification of the inflorescence, or even up to its ramifications; but the portion extending from the first to the last ramifications or the axis of inflorescence is often distinguished under the name of *rhachis*.

69. A *Scape* or *radical Peduncle* is a leafless peduncle proceeding from the stock, or from near the base of the stem, or apparently from the root itself.

70. A *Pedicel* is the last branch of an inflorescence, supporting a single flower.

71. The branches of inflorescence may be, like those of stems, opposite, alternate, etc. (32, 33), but very often their arrangement is different from that of the leafy branches of the same plant.

72. **Inflorescence** is

centrifugal, when the terminal flower opens first, and those on the lateral branches are successively developed.

centripetal, when the lowest flowers open first, and the main stem continues to elongate, developing fresh flowers.

73. Determinate inflorescence is usually centrifugal. Indeterminate inflorescence is always centripetal. Both inflorescences may be combined on one plant, for it often happens that the main branches of an inflorescence are centripetal, whilst the flowers on the lateral branches are centrifugal; or *vice versâ*.

74. **An Inflorescence** is

a *Spike*, or *spicate*, when the flowers are sessile along a simple undivided axis or rhachis.

a *Raceme*, or *racemose*, when the flowers are borne on pedicels along a single undivided axis or rhachis.

a *Panicle*, or *paniculate*, when the axis is divided into branches bearing two or more flowers.

a *Head*, or *capitate*, when several sessile or nearly sessile flowers are collected into a compact head-like cluster. The short, flat, convex, or conical axis on which the flowers are seated, is called the *receptacle*, a term also used for the torus of a single flower (135). The very compact flower-heads of *Compositæ* are often termed *compound flowers*.

an *Umbel*, or *umbellate*, when several branches or pedicels appear to start from the same point and are nearly of the same length. It differs from the head, like the raceme from the spike, in that the flowers are not sessile. An umbel is said to be *simple*, when each of its branches or *rays* bears a single flower; *compound* when each ray bears a *partial umbel* or *umbellule*.

a *Corymb*, or *corymbose*, when the branches and pedicels, although starting from different points, all attain the same level, the lower ones being much longer than the upper. It is a flat-topped or *fastigiate* panicle.

a *Cyme*, or *cymose*, when branched and centrifugal. It is a centrifugal panicle, and is often corymbose. The central flower opens first. The lateral branches successively developed are usually forked or opposite (dichotomous or trichotomous), but sometimes after the first forking the branches are no longer divided, but produce a succession of pedicels on their upper side, forming apparently unilateral centripetal racemes; whereas if attentively examined, it will be found that each pedicel is at first terminal, but becomes lateral by the development of one outer branch only, immediately under the pedicel. Such branches, when in bud, are generally rolled back at the top, like the tail of a scorpion, and are thence called *scorpioid*.

a *Thyrsus*, or *thyrsoid*, when cymes, usually opposite, are arranged in a narrow pyramidal panicle.

75. There are numerous cases where inflorescences are intermediate between some two of the above, and are called by different botanists by one or the other name according as they are guided by apparent or by theoretical similarity. A spike-like panicle, where the axis is divided into very short branches forming a cylindrical compact inflorescence, is called sometimes a spike, sometimes a panicle. If the flowers are in distinct clusters along a simple axis, the inflorescence is described as an *interrupted* spike or raceme, according as the flowers are nearly sessile or distinctly pedicellate; although when closely examined the flowers will be found to be inserted not on the main axis, but on a very short branch, thus, strictly speaking, constituting a panicle.

76. The *catkins* (*amenta*) of *Amentaceæ*, the *spadices* of several Monocotyledons, the *ears* and *spikelets* of Grasses are forms of the spike.

77. **Bracts** are generally placed singly under each branch of the inflorescence, and under each pedicel; bracteoles are usually two, one on each side, on the pedicel or close under the flower, or even upon the calyx itself; but bracts are also frequently scattered along the branches without axillary pedicels; and when the differences between the bracts and bracteoles are trifling or immaterial, they are usually all called bracts.

78. When these bracts appear to proceed from the same point, they will, on examination, be found to be really either one bract and two stipules, or one bract with two bracteoles in its axil. When two bracts appear to proceed from the same point, they will usually be found to be the stipules of an undeveloped bract, unless the branches of the inflorescence are opposite, when the bracts will of course be opposite also.

79. When several bracts are collected in a whorl, or are so close together as to appear whorled, or are closely imbricated round the base of a head or umbel, they are collectively called an *Involucre*. The bracts composing an involucre are described under the names of *leaves*, *leaflets*, *bracts*, or *scales*, according to their appearance. *Phyllaries* is a useless term, lately introduced for the bracts or scales of the involucre of *Compositæ*. An *Involucel* is the involucre of a partial umbel.

80. When several very small bracts are placed round the base of a calyx or of an involucre, they have been termed a *calycule*, and the calyx or involucre said to be *calyculate*, but these terms are now falling into disuse, as conveying a false impression. When the bracts are whorled and inserted upon the calyx, they form what is frequently called an *epicalyx*.

81. A *Spatha* is a bract or floral leaf enclosing the inflorescence of some Monocotyledons.

82. *Paleæ*, *pales*, or *Chaff*, are the inner bracts or scales in *Compositæ*, *Gramineæ*, and some other plants, when of a thin yet stiff consistence, usually narrow and of a pale colour.

83. *Glumes* are the bracts enclosing the flowers of *Cyperaceæ* and *Gramineæ*.

§ 8. *The Flower in General*

84. A *complete* **Flower** (15) is one in which the calyx, corolla, stamens, and pistil are all present; a *perfect* flower, one in which all these organs, or such of them as are present, are capable of performing their several functions. Therefore, properly speaking, an *incomplete* flower is one in which any one or more of these organs is wanting; and an *imperfect* flower, one in which any one or more of these organs is so altered as to be incapable of properly performing its functions. These imperfect organs are said to be *abortive* if much reduced in size or efficiency, *rudimentary* if so much so as to be scarcely perceptible. But in many works, the term *incomplete* is specially applied to those flowers in which the perianth is simple or wanting, and *imperfect* to those in which either the stamens or pistils are imperfect or wanting.

85. A **Flower** is

dichlamydeous, when the perianth is double, both calyx and corolla being present and distinct.

monochlamydeous, when the perianth is single, whether by the union of the calyx and corolla, or the deficiency of either.

asepalous, when there is no calyx.

apetalous, when there is no corolla.

naked, or *achlamydeous*, when there is no perianth at all.

hermaphrodite or *bisexual*, when both stamens and pistil are present and perfect.

male or *staminate*, when there are one or more stamens, but either no pistil at all or an imperfect one.

female or *pistillate*, when there is a pistil, but either no stamens at all, or only imperfect ones.

neuter when both stamens and pistil are imperfect or wanting.

barren or *sterile*, when from any cause it produces no seed.

fertile, when it does produce seed. In some works the terms *barren*, *fertile*, and *perfect*, are also used respectively as synonyms of *male*, *female*, and *hermaphrodite*.

86. The flowers of a plant or species are said collectively to be *unisexual* or *diclinous* when the flowers are all either male or female.

monœcious, when the male and female flowers are distinct, but on the same plant.

diœcious, when the male and female flowers are on distinct plants.

polygamous, when there are male, female, and hermaphrodite flowers on the same or on distinct plants.

87. A head of flowers is *heterogamous* when male, female, hermaphrodite, and neuter flowers, or any two or three of them, are included in one head: *homogamous*, when all the flowers included in one head are alike in this respect. A spike or head of flowers is *androgynous* when male and female flowers are mixed in it. These terms are only used in the case of very few Natural Orders.

88. As the scales of buds are leaves undeveloped or reduced in size and altered in shape and consistence, and bracts are leaves likewise reduced in size, and occasionally altered in colour; so the parts of the flower are considered as leaves still further altered in shape, colour, and arrangement round the axis, and often more or less combined with each other. The details of this theory constitute the comparatively modern branch of botany called *Vegetable Metamorphosis* or *Homology*, sometimes improperly termed *Morphology* (8).

89. To understand the arrangement of the floral parts, let us take a *complete* flower, in which moreover all the parts are *free* from each other, *definite* in number, *i.e.*, always the same in the same species, and *symmetrical* or *isomerous*, *i.e.*, when each whorl consists of the same number of parts.

90. Such a complete symmetrical flower consists usually of either four or five whorls of altered leaves (88), placed immediately one within the other.

The **Calyx** forms the outer whorl. Its parts are called *sepals*.

The **Corolla** forms the next whorl. Its parts, called *petals*, usually *alternate* with the sepals; that is to say, the centre of each petal is immediately over or within the interval between two sepals.

The **Stamens** form one or two whorls within the petals. If two, those of the outer whorl (the *outer stamens*) alternate with the petals, and are consequently opposite to, or over the centre of the sepals; those of the inner whorl (the *inner stamens*) alternate with the outer ones, and are therefore opposite to the petals. If there is only one whorl of stamens, they most frequently alternate with the petals; but sometimes they are opposite the petals and alternate with the sepals.

The **Pistil** forms the inner whorl; its carpels usually alternate with the inner row of stamens.

91. In an axillary or lateral flower the *upper* parts of each whorl (sepals, petals, stamens, or carpels) are those which are next to the main axis of the stems or branch, the *lower* parts those which are furthest from it; the intermediate ones are said to be *lateral*. The words *anterior* (front) and *posterior* (back) are often used for lower and upper respectively, but their meaning is sometimes reversed if the writer supposes himself in the centre of the flower instead of outside of it.

92. The number of parts in each whorl of a flower is expressed adjectively by the following numerals derived from the Greek:—

mono-,	di-,	tri-,	tetra-,	penta-,	hexa-,	hepta-,	octo-,	ennea-,	deca-, etc.,	poly-,
1-,	2-,	3-,	4-,	5-,	6-,	7-,	8-,	9-,	10-,	*many*-,

prefixed to a termination indicating the whorl referred to.

93. Thus, a **Flower** is

disepalous, *trisepalous*, *tetrasepalous*, *polysepalous*, etc., according as there are 2, 3, 4, or many (or an indefinite number of) sepals.

dipetalous, *tripetalous*, *polypetalous*, etc., according as there are 2, 3, or many petals.

diandrous, *triandrous*, *polyandrous*, etc., according as there are 2, 3, or many stamens.

digynous, *trigynous*, *polygynous*, etc., according as there are 2, 3, or many carpels.

And generally (if symmetrical) *dimerous*, *trimerous* *polymerous*, etc., according as there are 2, 3, or many (or an indefinite number of) parts to each whorl.

94. Flowers are *unsymmetrical* or *anisomerous*, strictly speaking, when any one of the whorls has a different number of parts from any other; but when the carpels alone are reduced in number, the flower is still frequently called symmetrical or isomerous, if the calyx, corolla, and staminal whorls have all the same number of parts.

95. Flowers are *irregular* when the parts of any one of the whorls are unequal in size, dissimilar in shape, or do not spread regularly round the axis at equal distances. It is however more especially irregularity of the corolla that is referred to in descriptions. A slight inequality in size or direction in the other whorls does not prevent the flower being classed as *regular*, if the corolla or perianth is conspicuous and regular.

9. *The Calyx and Corolla, or Perianth.*

96. The **Calyx** (90) is usually green, and smaller than the corolla; sometimes very minute, rudimentary, or wanting, sometimes very indistinctly whorled, or not whorled at all, or in two whorls, or composed of a large number of sepals, of which the outer ones pass gradually into bracts, and the inner ones into petals.

97. The **Corolla** (90) is usually coloured, and of a more delicate texture than the calyx, and, in popular language, is often more specially meant by the *flower*. Its petals are more rarely in two whorls, or indefinite in number, and the whorl more rarely broken than in the case of the calyx, at least when the plant is in a natural state. *Double flowers* are in most cases an accidental deformity or monster in which the ordinary number of petals is multiplied by the conversion of stamens, sepals, or even carpels into petals, by the division of ordinary petals, or simply by the addition of supernumerary ones. Petals are also sometimes very small, rudimentary, or entirely deficient.

98. In very many cases, a so-called *simple perianth* (15) (of which the parts are usually called *leaves* or *segments*) is one in which the sepals and petals are similar in form and texture, and present apparently a single whorl. But if examined in the young bud, one half of the parts will generally be found to be placed outside the other half, and there will frequently be some slight difference in texture, size, and colour indicating to the close observer the presence of both calyx and corolla.

Hence much discrepancy in descriptive works. Where one botanist describes a simple perianth of six segments, another will speak of a double perianth of three sepals and three petals.

99. The following terms and prefixes, expressive of the modifications of form and arrangement of the corolla and its petals, are equally applicable to the calyx and its sepals, and to the simple perianth and its segments.

100. The Corolla is said to be *monopetalous* when the petals are united, either entirely or at the base only, into a cup, tube, or ring; *polypetalous* when they are all free from the base. These expressions, established by a long usage, are not strictly correct, for *monopetalous* (consisting of a single petal) should apply rather to a corolla really reduced to a single petal, which would then be on one side of the axis; and *polypetalous* is sometimes used more appropriately for a corolla with an indefinite number of petals. Some modern botanists have therefore proposed the term *gamopetalous* for the corolla with united petals, and *dialypetalous* for that with free petals; but the old established expressions are still the most generally used.

101. When the petals are partially united, the lower entire portion of the corolla is called the *tube*, whatever be its shape, and the free portions of the petals are called the *teeth*, *lobes*, or *segments* (39), according as they are short or long in proportion to the whole length of the corolla. When the tube is excessively short, the petals appear at first sight free, but their slight union at the base must be carefully attended to, being of importance in classification.

102. The **Æstivation** of a corolla is the arrangement of the petals, or of such portion of them as is free, in the unexpanded bud. It is

valvate, when they are strictly whorled in their whole length, their edges being placed against each other without overlapping. If the edges are much inflexed, the æstivation is at the same time *induplicate*; *involute*, if the margins are rolled inward; *reduplicate*, if the margins project outwards into salient angles; *revolute*, if the margins are rolled outwards; *plicate*, if the petals are folded in longitudinal plaits.

imbricate, when the whorl is more or less broken by some of the petals being outside the others, or by their overlapping each other at least at the top. Five-petaled imbricate corollas are *quincuncially* imbricate when one petal is outside, and an adjoining one wholly inside, the three others intermediate and overlapping on one side; *bilabiate*, when two adjoining ones are inside or outside the three others. Imbricate petals are described as *crumpled* (*corrugate*) when puckered irregularly in the bud.

twisted, *contorted*, or *convolute*, when each petal overlaps an adjoining one on one side, and is overlapped by the other adjoining one on the other side. Some botanists include the twisted æstivation in the general term *imbricate*; others carefully distinguish the one from the other.

103. In a few cases the overlapping is so slight that the three æstivations cannot easily be distinguished one from the other; in a few others the æstivation is variable, even in the same species, but, in general, it supplies a constant character in species, in genera, or even Natural Orders.

104. In general shape the **Corolla** is

tubular, when the whole or greater part of it is in the form of a tube or cylinder.

campanulate, when approaching in some measure the shape of a cup or bell.

urceolate, when the tube is swollen or nearly globular, contracted at the top, and slightly expanded again in a narrow rim.

rotate or *stellate*, when the petals or lobes are spread out horizontally from the base, or nearly so, like a wheel or star.

hypocrateriform or *salver-shaped*, when the lower part is cylindrical and the upper portion expanded horizontally. In this case the name of *tube* is restricted to the cylindrical part, and the horizontal portion is called the *limb*, whether it be divided to the base or not. The orifice of the tube is called its *mouth* or *throat*.

infundibuliform or *funnel-shaped*, when the tube is cylindrical at the base, but enlarged at the top into a more or less campanulate limb, of which the lobes often spread horizontally. In this case the campanulate part, up to the commencement of the lobes, is sometimes considered as a portion of the tube, sometimes as a portion of the limb, and by some botanists again described as independent of either, under the name of *throat* (*fauces*). Generally speaking, however, in campanulate, infundibuliform, or other corollas, where the lower entire part passes gradually into the upper divided and more spreading part, the distinction between the *tube* and the *limb* is drawn either at the point where the lobes separate, or at the part where the corolla first expands, according to which is the most marked.

105. Irregular corollas have received various names according to the more familiar forms they have been compared to. Some of the most important are the

bilabiate, or *two-lipped* corolla, when, in a four- or five-lobed corolla, the two or three upper lobes stand obviously apart, like an *upper lip*, from the two or three lower ones or *under lip*. In *Orchideæ* and some other families the name of lip, or *labellum*, is given to one of the divisions or lobes of the perianth.

personate, when two-lipped, and the orifice of the tube closed by a projection from the base of the upper or lower lip, called a *palate*.

ringent, when very widely two-lipped, and the orifice of the tube very open.

spurred, when the tube or the lower part of a petal has a conical hollow projection, compared to the spur of a cock; *saccate*, when the spur is short and round like a little bag; *gibbous*, when projecting at any part into a slight swelling; *faveolate*, when marked in any part with a slight glandular or thickened cavity.

resupinate or *reversed*, when a lip, spur, etc., which in allied species is usually lowest, lies uppermost, and *vice versâ*.

106. The above terms are mostly applied to the forms of monopetalous corollas, but several are also applicable to those of polypetalous ones. Terms descriptive of the special forms of corolla in certain Natural Orders will be explained under those Orders respectively.

107. Most of the terms used for describing the forms of leaves (39, 46) are also applicable to those of individual petals; but the flat expanded portion of a petal, corresponding to the blade of the leaf, is called its *lamina*, and the stalk corresponding to the petiole, its *claw* (*unguis*). The stalked petal is said to be *unguiculate*.

§ 10. *The Stamens.*

108. Although in a few cases the outer stamens may gradually pass into petals, yet, in general, **Stamens** are very different in shape and aspect from leaves, sepals or petals. It is only in a theoretical point of view (not the less important in the study of the physiological economy of the plant) that they can be called altered leaves.

109. This usual form is a stalk, called the *filament*, bearing at the top an *anther* divided into two pouches or *cells*. These anther-cells are filled with *pollen*, consisting of minute grains, usually forming a yellow dust, which, when the flower expands, is scattered from an opening in each cell. When the two cells are not closely contiguous, the portion of the anther that unites them is called the *connectivum*.

110. The filament is often wanting, and the anther sessile, yet still the stamen is perfect; but if the anther, which is the essential part of the stamen, is wanting, or does not contain pollen, the stamen is imperfect, and is then said to be *barren* or *sterile* (without pollen), *abortive* or *rudimentary* (84), according to the degree to which the imperfection is carried. Imperfect stamens are often called *staminodia*.

111. In unsymmetrical flowers, the stamens of each whorl are sometimes reduced in number below that of the petals, even to a single one, and in several Natural Orders they are multiplied indefinitely.

112. The terms *monandrous* and *polyandrous* are restricted to flowers which have really but one stamen, or an indefinite number respectively. Where several stamens are united into one, the flower is said to be *synandrous*.

113. **Stamens** are

monadelphous, when united by their filaments into one cluster. This cluster either forms a tube round the pistil, or, if the pistil is wanting, occupies the centre of the flower.

diadelphous, when so united into two clusters or *phalanges*. The term is more especially applied to certain *Leguminosæ*, in which nine stamens are united in a tube slit open on the upper side, and a tenth, placed in a slit, is free. In some other plants the stamens are equally distributed in the two clusters.

triadelphous, *pentadelphous*, *polyadelphous*, when so united into three, five, or many clusters or *phalanges*.

syngenesious, when united by their anthers in a ring round the pistil, the filaments usually remaining free.

didynamous, when (usually in a bilabiate flower) there are four stamens in two pairs, those of one pair longer than those of the other.

tetradynamous, when (in *Cruciferæ*) there are six, four of them longer than the two others.

exserted when longer than the corolla, or even when longer than its tube, if the limb be very spreading.

114. An **Anther** (109) is

adnate, when continuous with the filament, the anther-cells appearing to lie their whole length along the upper part of the filament.

innate, when firmly attached by their base to the filament. This is an adnate anther when rather more distinct from the filament.

versatile, when attached by their back to the very point of the filament, so as to swing loosely.

115. Anther-cells may be *parallel* or *diverging* at a less or greater angle; or *divaricate*, when placed end to end so as to form one straight line. The end of each anther-cell placed nearest to the other cell is generally called its *apex* or *summit*, and the other end its *base* (36); but some botanists reverse the sense of these terms.

116. Anthers have often, on their connectivum of cells, appendages termed *bristles* (setæ), *spurs*, *crests*, *points*, *glands*, etc., according to their appearance.

117. Anthers have occasionally only one cell: this may take place either by the disappearance of the partition between two closely contiguous cells, when these cells are said to be *confluent*; or by the abortion or total deficiency of one of the cells, when the anther is said to be *dimidiate*.

118. Anthers will open or *dehisce* to let out the pollen, like capsules, in *valves*, *pores*, or *slits*. Their dehiscence is *introrse*, when the opening faces the pistil; *extrorse*, when towards the circumference of the flower.

119. Pollen (109) is not always in the form of dust. It is sometimes collected in each cell into one or two little wax-like masses. Special terms used in describing these masses or other modification of the pollen will be explained under the Orders where they occur.

§ 11. *The Pistil.*

120. The carpels (91) of the **Pistil,** although they may occasionally assume, rather more than stamens, the appearance and colour of leaves, are still more different in shape and structure. They are usually sessile; if stalked, their stalk is called a *podocarp*. This stalk, upon which each separate carpel is supported above the receptacle, must not be confounded with the *gynobasis* (143), upon which the whole pistil is sometimes raised.

121. Each carpel consists of three parts:

(1) the **Ovary,** or enlarged base, which includes one or more cavities or *cells* containing one or more small bodies called *ovules*. These are the earliest condition of the future seeds.

(2) the **Style,** proceeding from the summit of the ovary, and supporting—

(3) the **Stigma,** which is sometimes a point (or *punctiform* stigma) or small head (a *capitate* stigma) at the top of the style or ovary, sometimes a portion of its surface more or less lateral and variously shaped, distinguished by a looser texture, and covered with minute protuberances called *papillæ*.

122. The style is often wanting, and the stigma is then sessile on the ovary, but in the perfect pistil there is always at least one ovule in the ovary, and some portion of stigmatic surface. Without these the pistil is imperfect, and said to be *barren* (not setting seed), *abortive*, or *rudimentary* (84), according to the degree of imperfection.

123. The ovary being the essential part of the pistil most of the terms relating to the number, arrangement, etc., of the carpels, apply specially to their ovaries. In some works each separate carpel is called a pistil, all those of a flower consti-

tuting together the *gynæcsum*; but this term is in little use, and the word *pistil* is more generally applied in a collective sense. When the ovaries are at all united, they are commonly termed collectively a compound ovary.

124. The number of carpels or ovaries in a flower is frequently reduced below that of the parts of the other floral whorls, even in flowers otherwise symmetrical. In a very few genera, however, the ovaries are more numerous than the petals, or indefinite. They are in that case either arranged in a single whorl, or form a head or spike in the centre of the flower.

125. The terms *monogynous*, *digynous*, *polygynous*, etc. (with a pistil of one, two, or more parts), are vaguely used, applying sometimes to the whole pistil, sometimes to the ovaries alone, or to the styles or stigmas only. Where a more precise nomenclature is adopted, the flower is

monocarpellary, when the pistil consists of a single simple carpel.

bi-, *tri-*, etc., to *poly-carpellary*, when the pistil consists of two, three, or an indefinite number of carpels, whether separate or united.

syncarpous, when the carpels or their ovaries are more or less united into one compound ovary.

apocarpous, when the carpels or ovaries are all free and distinct.

126. A *compound* ovary is

unilocular or *one-celled*, when there are no partitions between the ovules, or when those partitions do not meet in the centre so as to divide the cavity into several cells.

plurilocular or *several-celled*, when completely divided into two or more cells by partitions called *dissepiments* (*septa*), usually vertical and radiating from the centre or axis of the ovary to its circumference.

bi-, *tri-*, etc., to *multi-locular*, according to the number of these cells, two, three, etc., or many.

127. In general the number of cells or of dissepiments, complete or partial, or of rows of ovules, corresponds with that of the carpels, of which the pistil is composed. But sometimes each carpel is divided completely or partially into two cells, or has two rows of ovules, so that the number of carpels appears double what it really is. Sometimes again the carpels are so completely combined and reduced as to form a single cell, with a single ovule, although it really consists of several carpels. But in these cases the ovary is usually described as it appears, as well as such as it is theoretically supposed to be.

128. In apocarpous pistils the styles are usually free, each bearing its own stigma. Very rarely the greater part of the styles, or the stigmas alone, are united, whilst the ovaries remain distinct.

129. Syncarpous pistils are said to have

several styles, when the styles are free from the base.

one style, with several branches, when the styles are connected at the base, but separate below the point where the stigmas or stigmatic surfaces commence.

one simple style, with several stigmas, when united up to the point where the stigmas or stigmatic surfaces commence, and then separating.

one simple style, with a branched, lobed, toothed, notched, or entire stigma (as the case, may be), when the stigmas also are more or less united. In many works, however, this precise nomenclature is not strictly adhered to, and considerable confusion is often the result.

130. In general the number of styles, or branches of the style or stigma, is the same as that of the carpels, but sometimes that number is doubled, especially in the stigmas, and sometimes the stigmas are dichotomously or pinnately branched, or *penicillate*, that is, divided into a tuft of hair-like branches. All these variations sometimes make it a difficult task to determine the number of carpels forming a compound ovary, but the point is of considerable importance in fixing the affinities of plants, and, by careful consideration, the real as well as the apparent number has now in most cases been agreed upon.

131. The *Placenta* is the part of the inside of the ovary to which the ovules are attached, sometimes a mere point or line on the inner surface, often more or less thickened or raised. *Placentation* is therefore the indication of the part of the ovary to which the ovules are attached.

132. Placentas are

axile, when the ovules are attached to the axis or centre, that is, in plurilocular ovaries, when they are attached to the inner angle of each cell; in unilocular simple ovaries, which have almost always an excentrical style or stigma, when the ovules are attached to the side of the ovary nearest to the style; in unilocular compound ovaries, when the ovules are attached to a central protuberance, column, or axis rising up from the base of the cavity. If this column does not reach the top of the cavity, the placenta is said to be *free* and *central*.

parietal, when the ovules are attached to the inner surface of the cavity of a one-celled compound ovary. Parietal placentas are usually slightly thickened or raised lines, sometimes broad surfaces nearly covering the inner surface of the cavity, sometimes projecting far into the cavity, and constituting partial dissepiments, or even meeting in the centre, but without cohering there. In the latter case the distinction between the one-celled and the several-celled ovary sometimes almost disappears.

133. Each **Ovule** (121), when fully formed, usually consists of a central mass or *nucleus* enclosed in two bag-like *coats*, the outer one called *primine*, the inner one *secundine*. The *chalaza* is the point of the ovule at which the base of the nucleus is confluent with the coats. The *foramen* is a minute aperture in the coats over the *apex* of the nucleus.

134. **Ovules** are

orthotropous or *straight*, when the chalaza coincides with the base (36) of the ovule, and the foramen is at the opposite extremity, the axis of the ovule being straight.

campylotropous or *incurved*, when the chalaza still coinciding with the base of the ovule, the axis of the ovule is curved, bringing the foramen down more or less towards that base.

anatropous or *inverted*, when the chalaza is at the apex of the ovule, and the foramen next to its base, the axis remaining straight. In this, one of the most frequent forms of the ovule, the chalaza is connected with the base by a cord, called *rhaphe*, adhering to one side of the ovule, and becoming more or less incorporated with its coats, as the ovule enlarges into a seed.

amphitropous or *half-inverted*, when the ovule being as it were attached laterally, the chalaza and foramen at opposite ends of its straight or curved axis are about equally distant from the base or point of attachment.

§ 12. *The Receptacle and Relative Attachment of the Floral Whorls.*

135. The **Receptacle** or *torus* is the extremity of the peduncle (above the calyx), upon which the corolla, stamens, and ovary are inserted. It is sometimes little more than a mere point or minute hemisphere, but it is often also more or less elongated, thickened, or otherwise enlarged. It must not be confounded with the receptacle of inflorescence (74).

136. A *Disk*, or *disc*, is a circular enlargement of the receptacle, usually in the form of a cup (*cupular*), of a flat disk or quoit, or of a cushion (*pulvinate*). It is either immediately at the base of the ovary within the stamens, or between the petals and stamens, or bears the petals or stamens or both on its margin, or is quite at the extremity of the receptacle, with the ovaries arranged in a ring round it or under it.

137. The disk may be *entire*, or *toothed*, or *lobed*, or *divided* into a number of parts, usually equal to, or twice that of the stamens or carpels. When the parts of the disk are quite separate and short, they are often called *glands*.

138. *Nectaries* are either the disk, or small deformed petals, or abortive stamens, or appendages at the base of petals, or stamens, or any small bodies within the flower which do not look like petals, stamens, or ovaries. They were formerly supposed to supply bees with their honey, and the term is frequently to be met with in the older Floras, but is now deservedly going out of use.

139. When the disk bears the petals and stamens, it is frequently adherent to, and apparently forms part of, the tube of the calyx, or it is adherent to, and apparently forms part of, the ovary, or of both calyx-tube and ovary. Hence the three following important distinctions in the relative insertion of the floral whorls.

140. *Petals*, or as it is frequently expressed, flowers, are

hypogynous (*i.e.*, under the ovary), when they or the disk that bears them are entirely free both from the calyx and ovary. The ovary is then described as *free* or *superior*, the calyx as *free* or *inferior*, the petals as being *inserted on the receptacle*.

perigynous (*i.e.*, round the ovary), when the disk bearing the petals is quite free from the ovary, but is more or less combined with the base of the calyx-tube. The ovary is then still described as *free* or *superior*, even though the combined disk and calyx-tube may form a deep cup with the ovary lying in the bottom; the calyx is said to be *free* or *inferior*, and the petals are described as *inserted on the calyx*.

epigynous (*i.e.*, upon the ovary), when the disk bearing the petals is combined both with the base of the calyx-tube and the base outside of the ovary; either closing over the ovary so as only to leave a passage for the style, or leaving more or less of the top of the ovary free, but always adhering to it above the level of the insertion of the lowest ovule (except in a very few cases where the ovules are absolutely suspended from the top of the cell). In epigynous flowers the ovary is described as *adherent* or *inferior*, the calyx as *adherent* or *superior*, the petals as *inserted on* or *above the ovary*. In some works, however, most epigynous flowers are included in the perigynous ones, and a very different meaning is given to the term *epigynous* (144), and there are a few cases where no positive distinction can be drawn between the epigynous and perigynous flowers, or again between the perigynous and hypogynous flowers.

141. When there are no petals, it is the insertion of the stamens that determines the difference between the hypogynous, perigynous, and epigynous flowers.

142. When there are both petals and stamens,

in hypogynous flowers, the petals and stamens are usually free from each other, but sometimes they are combined at the base. In that case, if the petals are distinct from each other, and the stamens are monadelphous, the petals are often said to be *inserted on* or *combined with the staminal tube;* if the corolla is gamopetalous and the stamens distinct from each other, the latter are said to be *inserted in the tube of the corolla*.

in perigynous flowers, the stamens are usually inserted immediately within the petals, or alternating with them on the edge of the disk, but occasionally much lower down within the disk, or even on the unenlarged part of the receptacle.

in epigynous flowers, when the petals are distinct, the stamens are usually inserted as in perigynous flowers; when the corolla is gamopetalous, the stamens are either free and epigynous, or combined at the base with (inserted in) the tube of the corolla.

143. When the receptacle is distinctly elongated below the ovary, it is often called a *gynobasis*, *gynophore*, or *stalk of the ovary*. If the elongation takes place below the stamens or below the petals, these stamens or petals are then said to be *inserted on the stalk of the ovary*, and are occasionally, but falsely, described as *epigynous*. Really epigynous stamens (*i.e.*, when the filaments are combined with the ovary) are very rare, unless the rest of the flower is epigynous.

144. An *epigynous disk* is a name given either to the thickened summit of the ovary in epigynous flowers, or very rarely to a real disk or enlargement of the receptable closing over the ovary.

145. In the relative position of any two or more parts of the flower, whether in the same or in different whorls, they are

connivent, when nearer together at the summit than at the base.

divergent, when further apart at the summit than at the base.

coherent, when united together, but so slightly that they can be separated with little or no laceration; and one of the two coherent parts (usually the smallest or least important) is said to be *adherent* to the other. Grammatically speaking, these two terms convey nearly the same meaning, but require a different form of phrase; practically however it has been found more convenient to restrict *cohesion* to the union of parts of the same whorl, and *adhesion* to the union of parts of different whorls.

connate, when so closely united that they cannot be separated without laceration. Each of the two connate parts, and especially that one which is considered the smaller or of the least importance, is said to be *adnate* to the other.

free, when neither coherent nor connate.

distinct is also used in the same sense, but is also applied to parts distinctly visible or distinctly limited.

§ 13. *The Fruit.*

146. The **Fruit** (15) consists of the ovary and whatever other parts of the flower are *persistent* (*i.e.*, persist at the time the seed is ripe), usually enlarged, and more or less altered in shape and consistence. It encloses or covers the seed or seeds till the period of maturity, when it either opens for the seed to escape, or falls to the ground with the seed. When stalked, its stalk has been termed a *carpophore*.

147. Fruits are, in elementary works, said to be *simple* when the result of a single flower, *compound* when they proceed from several flowers closely packed or combined in a head. But as a fruit resulting from a single flower, with several distinct carpels, is compound in the sense in which that term is applied to the ovary, the terms *single* and *aggregate*, proposed for the fruit resulting from one or several flowers, may be more appropriately adopted. In descriptive botany a fruit is always supposed to result from a single flower unless the contrary be stated. It may, like the pistil, be syncarpous or apocarpous (125); and as in many cases carpels united in the flower may become separate as they ripen, an apocarpous fruit may result from a syncarpous pistil.

148. The involucre or bracts often persist and form part of aggregate fruits, but very seldom so in single ones.

149. The receptacle becomes occasionally enlarged and succulent; if when ripe it falls off with the fruit, it is considered as forming part of it.

150. The adherent part of the calyx of epigynous flowers always persists and forms part of the fruit; the free part of the calyx of epigynous flowers or the calyx of perigynous flowers, either persists entirely at the top of or round the fruit, or the lobes alone fall off, or the lobes fall off with whatever part of the calyx is above the insertion of the petals, or the whole of what is free from the ovary falls off, including the disk bearing the petals. The calyx of hypogynous flowers usually falls off entirely or persists entirely. In general a calyx is called deciduous if any part falls off. When it persists it is either enlarged round or under the fruit, or it withers and dries up.

151. The corolla usually falls off entirely; when it persists it is usually withered and dry (*marcescent*), or very seldom enlarges round the fruit.

152. The stamens either fall off, or more or less of their filaments persists, usually withered and dry.

153. The style sometimes falls off or dries up and disappears; sometimes persists, forming a point to the fruit, or becomes enlarged into a wing or other appendage to the fruit.

154. The *Pericarp* is the portion of the fruit formed of the ovary, and whatever adheres to it exclusive of and outside of the seed or seeds, exclusive also of the persistent receptacle, or of whatever portion of the calyx persists round the ovary without adhering to it.

155. Fruits have often external appendages called *wings* (alæ), *beaks*, *crests*, *awns*, etc., according to their appearance. They are either formed by persistent parts of the flower more or less altered, or grow out of the ovary or the persistents part of the calyx. If the appendage be a ring of hairs or scales round the top of the fruit, it is called a *pappus*.

156. Fruits are generally divided into *succulent* (including *fleshy*, *pulpy*, and *juicy* fruits) and *dry*. They are *dehiscent* when they open at maturity to let out the seeds, *indehiscent* when they do not open spontaneously but fall off with the seeds. Succulent fruits are usually indehiscent.

157. The principal kinds of succulent fruits are

the *Berry*, in which the whole substance of the pericarp is fleshy or pulpy, with the exception of the outer skin or rind, called the *Epicarp*. The seeds themselves are usually immersed in the pulp; but in some berries, the seeds are separated from the pulp by the walls of the cavity or cells of the ovary, which form as it were a thin inner skin or rind called the *Endocarp*.

the *Drupe*, in which the pericarp, when ripe, consists of two distinct portions, an outer succulent one called the *Sarcocarp*, or *Mesocarp* (covered like the berry by a skin or epicarp), and an inner dry endocarp called the *Putamen*, which is either *cartilaginous* (of the consistence of parchment) or hard and woody. In the latter case it is commonly a *stone*, and the drupe a *stone-fruit*. When the putamen consists of several distinct stones or nuts, each enclosing a seed, they are called *pyrenes*, or sometimes *kernels*..

158. The principal kinds of dry fruits are

the *Capsule* or *Pod*,* which is dehiscent. When ripe the pericarp usually splits longitudinally into as many or twice as many pieces, called *valves*, as it contain cells or placentas. If these valves separate at the line of junction of the carpels, that is, along the line of the placentas or dissepiments, either splitting them or leaving them attached to the axis, the dehiscence is termed *septicidal;* if the valves separate between the placentas or dissepiment, the dehiscence is *loculicidal*, and the valves either bear the placentas or dissepiments along their middle line, or leave them attached to the axis. Sometimes also the capsule discharges its seeds by *slits*, *chinks*, or *pores*, more or less regularly arranged, or bursts irregularly, or separates into two parts by a horizontal line; in the latter case it is said to be *circumscise*.

the *Nut* or *Achene*, which is indehiscent and contains but a single seed. When the pericarp is thin in proportion to the seed it encloses, the whole fruit (or each of its lobes) has the appearance of a single seed, and is so called in popular language. If the pericarp is thin and rather loose, it is often called a *Utricle*. A *Samara* is a nut with a wing at its upper end.

159. Where the carpels of the ovary are distinct (125) they may severally become as many distinct berries, drupes, capsules, or achenes. Separate carpels are usually more or less compressed, laterally, with more or less prominent inner and outer edges, called *sutures*, and, if dehiscent, the carpel usually opens at these sutures. A *Follicle* is a carpel opening at the inner suture only. In some cases where the carpels are united in the ovary they will separate when ripe; they are then called *Cocci* if one-seeded.

160. The peculiar fruits of some of the large Orders have received special names, which will be explained under each Order. Such are the *siliqua* and *silicule* of Cruciferæ, the *legume* of Leguminosæ, the *pome* of *Pyrus* and its allies, the *pepo* of Cucurbitaceæ, the *cone* of Coniferæ, the *grain* or *caryopsis* of Gramineæ, etc.

§ 14. *The Seed.*

161. The **Seed** is enclosed in the pericarp in the great majority of flowering plants, called therefore *Angiosperms*, or *angiospermous plants*. In *Coniferæ* and a very few allied genera, called *Gymnosperms*, or *gymnospermous plants*, the seed is naked, without any real pericarp. These truly gymnospermous plants must not be confounded with *Labiatæ*, *Boragineæ*, etc., which have also been falsely called gymnospermous, their small nuts having the appearance of seeds (158).

162. The seed when ripe contains an *embryo* or young plant, either filling or nearly filling the cavity, but not attached to the outer skin or the seed, or more or less immersed in a mealy, oily, fleshy, or horn-like substance, called the *albumen*, or *perisperm*. The presence or absence of this albumen, that is, the distinction between *albuminous* and *exalbuminous* seeds, is one of great importance. The embryo or albumen can often only be found or distinguished when the seed is quite ripe, or sometimes only when it begins to germinate.

163. The shell of the seed consists usually of two separable *coats*. The outer coat, called the *testa*, is usually the principal one, and in most cases the only one attended to in descriptions. It may be hard and *crustaceous*, woody or bony, or thin and *membranous* (skin-like), dry, or rarely succulent. It is sometimes expanded into *wings*, or bears a tuft of hair, cotton, or wool, called a *coma*. The inner coat is called the *tegmen*.

164. The *funicle* is the stalk by which the seed is attached to the placenta. It is occasionally enlarged into a membranous, pulpy or fleshy appendage, sometimes spreading over a considerable part of the seed, or nearly enclosing it, called an *aril*.

* In English descriptions, *pod* is more frequently used when it is long and narrow; *capsule* or sometimes *pouch*, when it is short and thick or broad.

A *strophiole* or *caruncle* is a similar appendage proceeding from the testa by the side of or near the funicle.

165. The *hilum* is the scar left on the seed where it separates from the funicle. The *micropyle* is a mark indicating the position of the foramen of the ovule (133).

166. The **Embryo** (162) consists of the *Radicle* or base of the future root, one or two *Cotyledons* or future seed-leaves, and the *Plumule* or future bud within the base of the cotyledons. In some seeds, especially where there is no albumen, these several parts are very conspicuous, in others they are very difficult to distinguish until the seed begins to germinate. Their observation, however, is of the greatest importance, for it is chiefly upon the distinction between the embryo with one or with two cotyledons that are founded the two great classes of phænogamous plants, *Monocotyledons* and *Dicotyledons*. Cotyledons are said to be *conduplicate* when folded once lengthwise; *contortuplicate* when variously folded or twisted; *conferruminate* when so united that no line of separation can be traced.

167. Although the embryo lies loose (unattached) within the seed, it is generally in some determinate position with respect to the seed or to the whole fruit. This position is described by stating the direction of the radicle next to or more or less remote from the *hilum*, or it is said to be *superior* if pointing towards the summit of the *fruit*, *inferior* if pointing towards the base of the *fruit*.

§ 15. *Accessory Organs.*

168. Under this name are included, in many elementary works, various external parts of plants which do not appear to act any essential part either in the vegetation or reproduction of the plant. They may be classed under four heads: *Tendrils* and *Hooks*, *Thorns* and *Prickles*, *Hairs* and *Glands*.

169. **Tendrils** (*cirrhi*) are usually abortive petioles, or abortive peduncles, or sometimes abortive ends of branches. They are simple or more or less branched, flexible, and coil more or less firmly round any objects within their reach, in order to support the plant to which they belong. *Hooks* are similar holdfasts, but of a firmer consistence, not branched, and less coiled.

170. **Thorns** and **Prickles** have been fancifully called the weapons of plants. A *Thorn* or *Spine* is the strongly pointed extremity of a branch. or abortive petiole, or abortive peduncle. A *Prickle* is a sharply pointed excrescence from the epidermis and is usually produced on a branch, on the petiole or veins of a leaf, or on a peduncle, or even on the calyx or corolla. When the teeth of a leaf or the stipules are pungent, they are also called *prickles*, not *thorns*. A plant is *spinous* if it has thorns, *aculeate* if it has prickles.

171. **Hairs,** in the general sense, or the *indumentum* (or clothing) of a plant include all those productions of the epidermis which have, by a more or less appropriate comparison, been termed *bristles*, *hairs*, *down*, *cotton*, or *wool*.

172. Hairs are often branched. They are said to be *attached by the centre*, if parted from the base, and the forks spread along the surface in opposite directions; *plumose*, if the branches are arranged along a common axis, as in a feather; *stellate*, if several branches radiate horizontally. These stellate hairs have sometimes their rays connected together at the base, forming little flat circular disks attached by the centre, and are then called *scales*, and the surface is said to be *scaly* or *lepidote*.

173. The *Epidermis*, or outer skin, of an organ, as to its surface and indumentum, is

smooth, when without any protuberance whatever.

glabrous, when without hairs of any kind.

glabrescent, *glabrate*, becoming glabrous.

striate, when marked with parallel longitudinal lines, either slightly raised or merely discoloured.

furrowed (*sulcate*) or *ribbed* (*costate*) when the parallel lines are more distinctly raised.

rugose, when rinkled or marked with irregular raised or depressed lines.

umbilicate, when marked with a small round depression.

umbonate, when bearing a small boss like that of a shield.

viscous, *viscid*, or *glutinous*, when covered with a sticky or clammy exudation.

scabrous, when rough to the touch.

tuberculate or *warted*, when covered with small, obtuse, wart-like protuberances.

muricate, when the protuberances are more raised and pointed but yet short and hard.

echinathe, when the protuberances are longer and sharper, almost prickly.

setose or *bristly*, when bearing very stiff erect straight hairs.

glandular-setose, when the setæ or bristles terminate in a minute resinous head or drop. In some works, especially in the case of Roses and *Rubus*, the meaning of *setæ* has been restricted to such as are glandular.

glochidiate, when the setæ are hooked at the top.

pilose, when the surface is thinly sprinkled with rather long simple hairs.

hispid, when more thickly covered with rather stiff hairs.

hirsute when the hairs are dense and not so stiff.

downy or *pubescent*, when the hairs are short and soft; *puberulent*, when slightly pubescent.

strigose, when the hairs are rather short and stiff, and lie close along the surface all in the same direction; *strigillose* when slightly strigose.

tomentose or *cottony*, when the hairs are very short and soft, rather dense and more or less intricate, and usually white or whitish.

woolly (*lanate*), when the hairs are long and loosely intricate, like wool. The wool or tomentum is said to be *floccose* when closely intricate and readily detached, like fleece.

mealy (*farinose*), when the hairs are excessively short, intricate and white, and come off readily, having the appearance of meal or dust.

canescent or *hoary*, when the hairs are so short as not readily to be distinguished by the naked eye, and yet give a general whitish hue to the epidermis.

glaucous, when of a pale bluish-green, often covered with a fine bloom.

glaucescent, subglaucous or becoming glaucous.

174. The meanings here attached to the above terms are such as appear to have been most generally adopted, but there is much vagueness in the use practically made of many of them by different botanists. This is especially the case with the terms *pilose*, *hispid*, *hirsute*, *pubescent*, and *tomentose*.

175. The name of **Glands** is given to several different productions, and principally to the four following:—

1. Small wart-like or shield-like bodies, either sessile or sometimes stalked, of a fungous or somewhat fleshy consistence, occasionally secreting a small quantity of oily or resinous matter, but more frequently dry. They are generally few in number, often definite in their position and form, and occur chiefly on the petiole or principal veins of leaves, on the branches of inflorescences, or on the stalks or principal veins of bracts, sepals, or petals.

2. Minute raised dots, usually black, red, or dark-coloured, of a resinous or oily nature, always superficial, and apparently exudations from the epidermis. They are often numerous on leaves, bracts, sepals, and green branches, and occur even on petals and stamens, more rarely on pistils. When raised upon slender stalks they are called *pedicellate* or (*stipitate*) *glands*, or *glandular hairs*, according to the thickness of the stalk.

3. Small, globular, oblong or even linear vesicles, filled with oil, imbedded in the substance itself of leaves, bracts, floral organs, or fruits. They are often very numerous, like transparent dots, sometimes few and determinate in form and position. In the pericarp of *Umbelliferæ* they are remarkably regular and conspicuous, and take the name *vittæ*.

4. *Lobes* of the disk (137), or other small fleshy excrescences within the flower, whether from the receptacle, calyx, corolla, stamens, or pistil.

CHAP. II. CLASSIFICATION, OR SYSTEMATIC BOTANY.

176. It has already been observed (3) that descriptions of plants should, as nearly as possible, be arranged under natural divisions, so as to facilitate the comparison of each plant with those most nearly allied to it. The descriptions of plants here

alluded to are descriptions of *species*; the natural divisions of the Flora refer to natural *groups of species*.

177. A **Species** comprises all the individual plants which resemble each other sufficiently to make us conclude that they are all, or *may have been* all, descended from a common parent. These individuals may often differ from each other in many striking particulars, such as the colour of the flower, size of the leaf, etc., but these particulars are such as experience teaches us are liable to vary in the seedlings raised from one individual.

178. When a large number of the individuals of a species differ from the others in any striking particular they constitute a **Variety**. If the variety generally comes true from seed, it is often called a *Race*.

179. A *Variety* can only be propagated with certainty by grafts, cuttings, bulbs, tubers, or any other method which produces a new plant by the development of one or more buds taken from the old one. A *Race* may with care be propagated by seed, although seedlings will always be liable, under certain circumstances, to lose those particulars which distinguish it from the rest of the species. A real *Species* will always come true from seed.

180. The known species of plants (now near 100,000) are far too numerous for the human mind to study without classification, or even to give distinct single names to. To facilitate these objects, an admirable system, invented by Linnæus, has been universally adopted, viz., one common substantive name is given to a number of species which resemble each other more than they do any other species; the species so collected under one name are collectively called a **Genus**, the common name being the *generic* name. Each species is then distinguished from the others of the same genus by the addition of an adjective epithet or *specific name*. Every species has thus a botanical name of two words. In Latin, the language usually used for the purpose, the first word is a substantive and designates the genus; the second, an adjective, indicates the species.

181. The genera thus formed being still too numerous (above 6,000) for study without further arrangement, they have been classed under the same principles, viz., genera which resemble each other more than they do any other genera have been collected together into groups of a higher degree called **Families** or **Natural Orders**, to each of which a common name has been given. This name is in Latin an adjective plural, usually taken from the name of some one *typical* genus, generally the best known, the first discovered, or the most marked (e.g., *Ranunculaceæ* from *Ranunculus*). This is however for the purpose of study and comparison. To speak of a species, to refer to it and identify it, all that is necessary is to give the generic and specific names.

182. Natural Orders themselves (of which we reckon near 200) are often in the same manner collected into **Classes**; and where Orders contain a large number of genera, or genera a large number of species, they require further classification. The genera of an Order are then collected into minor groups called *Tribes*, the species of a genus into *Sections*, and in a few cases this intermediate classification is carried still further. The names of these several groups the most generally adopted are as follows, beginning with the most comprehensive or highest:—

Classes.	*Subtribes.*	Sections.
Subclasses or *Alliances.*	*Divisions.*	*Subsections.*
Natural Orders or Families.	*Subdivisions.*	Species.
Suborders.	Genera.	Varieties.
Tribes.	*Subgenera.*	

183. The characters (3) by which a species is distinguished from all other species of the same genus are collectively called the *specific character* of the plant; those by which its genus is distinguished from other genera of the Order, or its Order from other Orders, are respectively called the *generic* or *ordinal* character, as the case may be. The *habit* of a plant, of a species, a genus, etc., consists of such general characters as strike the eye at first sight, such as size, colour, ramification, arrangement of the leaves, inflorescence, etc., and are chiefly derived from the organs of vegetation.

184. Classes, Orders, Genera, and their several subdivisions, are called *natural* when, in forming them, all resemblances and differences are taken into account, valuing them according to their evident or presumed importance; *artificial*, when resemblances and differences in some one or very few particulars only are taken into account independently of all others.

185. The number of species included in a genus, or the number of genera in an Order, is very variable. Sometimes two or three or even a single species may be so different from all others as to constitute the entire genus; in others, several hundred species may resemble each other so much as to be all included in one genus; and there is the same discrepancy in the number of genera to a Family. There is moreover, unfortunately, in a number of instances, great difference of opinion as to whether certain plants differing from each other in certain particulars are varieties of one species or belong to distinct species; and again, whether two or more groups of species should 'constitute as many sections of one genus, or distinct genera, or tribes of one Order, or even distinct Natural Orders. In the former case, as a species is supposed to have a real existence in nature, the question is susceptible of argument, and sometimes of absolute proof. But the place a group should occupy in the scale of degree is very arbitrary, being often a mere question of convenience. The more subdivisions upon correct principles are multiplied, the more they facilitate Order and the Genus, are comprehensive and distinct. But if every group into the study of plants, provided always the main resting-points for constant use, the which a genus can be divided be erected into a distinct genus, with a substantive name to be remembered whenever a species is spoken of, all the advantages derived from the beautiful simplicity of the Linnæan nomenclature are gone.

CHAP. III. VEGETABLE ANATOMY AND PHYSIOLOGY.

§ 1. *Structure and Growth of the Elementary Tissues.*

186. If a very thin slice of any part of a plant be placed under a microscope of high magnifying power, it will be found to be made up of variously shaped and arranged ultimate parts, forming a sort of honeycombed structure. These ultimate parts are called *cells*, and form by their combination the *elementary tissues* of which the entire plant is composed.

187. A cell in its simplest state is a closed membranous sac, formed of a substance permeable by fluids, though usually destitute of visible pores. Each cell is a distinct individual, separately formed and separately acting, though cohering with the cells with which it is in contact, and partaking of the common life and action of the tissue of which it forms a part. The membranes separating or enclosing the cells are also called their *walls*.

188. Botanists usually distinguish the following tissues:—

(1) *Cellular tissue*, or *parenchyma*, consists usually of thin-walled cells, more or less round in form, or with their length not much exceeding their breadth, and not tapering at the ends. All the soft parts of the leaves, the pith of stems, the pulp of fruits, and all young growing parts, are formed of it. It is the first tissue produced, and continues to be formed while growth continues, and when it ceases to be active the plant dies.

(2) *Woody tissue*, or *prosenchyma*, differs in having its cells considerably longer than broad, usually tapering at each end into points and overlapping each other. The cells are commonly thick walled; the tissue is firm, tenacious, and elastic, and constitutes the principal part of wood, of the inner bark, and of the nerves and veins of leaves, forming, in short, the framework of the plant.
notion that their functions are analogous to those of the vessels (veins and arteries)

(3) *Vascular tissue*, or the *vessels* or *ducts* of plants, so called from the mistaken of animals. A *vessel* in plants consists of a vertical row of cells, which have their transverse partition-walls obliterated, so as to form a continuous tube. All phænogamous plants, as well as ferns and a few other cryptogamous plants, have vessels, and are therefore called *vascular plants;* so the majority of cryptogams having only cel-

lular tissue are termed *cellular plants*. Vessels have their sides very variously marked; some, called *spiral vessels*, have a spiral fibre coiled up their inside, which unrolls when the vessel is broken; others are marked with longitudinal slits, cross bars, minute dots or pits, or with transverse rings. The size of vessels is also very variable in different plants; in some they are of considerable size and visible to the naked eye in cross sections of the stem, in others they are almost absent or can only be traced under a strong magnifier.

189. Various modifications of the above tissues are distinguished by vegetable anatomists under names which need not be enumerated here as not being in general practical use. *Air-vessels*, *cysts*, *turpentine-vessels*, *oil-reservoirs*, etc., are either cavities left between the cells, or large cells filled with peculiar secretions.

190. When tissues are once formed, they increase, not by the general enlargement of the whole of the cells already formed, but by *cell-division*, that is, by the division of young and vitally active cells, and the enlargement of their portions. In the formation of the embryo, the first cell of the new plant is formed not by division, but around a segregate portion of the contents of a previously existing cell, the embryo-sac. This is termed *free cell-formation*, in contradistinction to cell-division.

191. A young and vitally active cell consists of the *outer wall*, formed of a more or less transparent substance called *cellulose*, permeable by fluids, and of ternary chemical composition (carbon, hydrogen, and oxygen); and of the *cell-contents*, usually viscid or mucilaginous, consisting of *protoplasm*, a substance of quaternary chemical composition (carbon, hydrogen, oxygen, and nitrogen), which fills an important part in cell-division and growth. Within the cell (either in the centre or excentrical) is usually a minute, soft, subgelatinous body called the *nucleus*, whose functions appear to be intimately connected with the first formation of the new cell. As this cell increases in size and its walls in thickness, the protoplasm and watery cell-sap become absorbed or dried up, the firm cellulose wall alone remaining as a permanent fabric, either empty or filled with various organized substances produced or secreted within it.

192. The principal organized contents of cells are

sap, the first product of the digestion of the food of plants; it contains the elements of vegetable growth in a dissolved condition.

sugar, of which there are two kinds, called *cane-sugar* and *grape-sugar*. It usually exists dissolved in the sap. It is found abundantly in growing parts, in fruits, and in germinating seeds.

dextrine, or vegetable mucilage, a gummy substance, between mucilage and starch.

starch or *fecula*, one of the most universal and conspicuous of cell-contents, and often so abundant in farinaceous roots and seeds as to fill the cell-cavity. It consists of minute grains called *starch-granules*, which vary in size and are marked with more or less conspicuous concentric lines. The chemical constitution of starch is the same as that of cellulose; it is unaffected by cold water, but forms a jelly with boiling water, and turns blue when tested by iodine.

chlorophyll, very minute granules, containing nitrogen, and coloured green under the action of sunlight. These granules are most abundant in the layers of cells immediately below the surface or epidermis of leaves and young bark. The green colouring matter is soluble in alcohol, and may thus be removed from the granules.

chromule, a name given to a similar colouring-matter when green.

wax, *oils*, *camphor*, and *resinous* matter are common in cells or in cavities in the tissues between the cells, also various mineral substances, either in an amorphous state or as microscopic crystals, when they are called *Raphides*.

§ 2. *Arrangement of the Elementary Tissues, or Structure of the Organs of Plants.*

193. Leaves, young stems, and branches, and most parts of phænogamous plants, during the first year of their existence consist anatomically of

1, a *cellular system*, or continuous mass of cellular tissue, which is developed both vertically as the stem or other parts increase in length, and horizontally or laterally as they increase in thickness or breadth. It surrounds or is intermixed with the fibro-vascular system, or it may exist alone in some parts of phænogamous plants, as well as in cryptogamous ones.

2, a *fibro-vascular system*, or continuous mass of woody and vascular tissue, which is gradually introduced vertically into, and serves to bind together, the cellular system. It is continued from the stem into the petioles and veins of the leaves, and into the pedicels and parts of the flowers, and it is never wholly wanting in any phænogamous plant.

3, an *epidermis*, or outer skin, formed of one or more layers of flattened (horizontal), firmly coherent, and usually empty cells, with either thin and transparent or thick and opaque walls. It covers almost all parts of plants exposed to the outward air, protecting their tissues from its immediate action, but is wanting in those parts of aquatic plants which are constantly submerged.

194. The epidermis is frequently pierced by minute spaces between the cells, called *Stomates*. They are oval or mouth-shaped, bordered by *lips*, formed of two or more elastic cells so disposed as to cause the stomate to open in a moist, and to close up in a dry state of the atmosphere. They communicate with intercellular cavities, and are obviously designed to regulate evaporation and respiration. They are chiefly found upon leaves, especially on the under surface.

195. When a phænogamous plant has outlived the first season of its growth, the anatomical structure of its stem or other perennial parts becomes more complicated and very different in the two great classes of phænogamous plants called *Exogens* and *Endogens*, which correspond with very few exceptions to the two classes Dicotyledons and Monocotyledons (167), founded on the structure of the embryo. In Exogens (Dicotyledons) the woody system is placed in concentric layers between a central *pith* (198, 1), and an external separable *bark* (198, 5). In Endogens (Monocotyledons) the woody system is in separate small bundles or fibres running through the cellular system without apparent order, and there is usually no distinct central pith, nor outer separable bark.

196. The anatomical structure is also somewhat different in the different organs of plants. In the **Root**, although it is constructed generally on the same plan as the stem, yet the regular organization, and the difference between Exogens and Endogens, is often disguised or obliterated by irregularities of growth, or by the production of large quantities of cellular tissue filled with starch or other substances (192). There is seldom, if ever, any distinct pith, the concentric circles of fibro-vascular tissue in Exogens are often very indistinct or have no relation to seasons of growth, and the epidermis has no stomates.

197. In the **Stem** or branches, during the first year or season of their growth, the difference between Exogens and Endogens is not always very conspicuous. In both there is a tendency to a circular arrangement of the fibro-vascular system, leaving the centre either vacant or filled with cellular tissue (pith) only, and a more or less distinct outer rind is observable even in several Endogens. More frequently, however, the distinction is already very apparent the first season, especially towards its close. The fibro-vascular bundles in Endogens usually anastomose but little, passing continuously into the branches and leaves. In Exogens the circle of fibro-vascular bundles forms a more continuous cylinder of network, emitting lateral offsets into the branches and leaves.

198. The Exogenous stem, after the first year of its growth, consists of

1, the *pith*, a cylinder of cellular tissue, occupying the centre or longitudinal axis of the stem. It is active only in young stems or branches, becomes dried up and compressed as the wood hardens, and often finally disappears, or is scarcely distinguishable in old trees.

2, the *medullary sheath*, which surrounds and encases the pith. It abounds in spiral vessels (188, 3) and is in direct connexion, when young, with the leaf-buds and branches, with the petioles and veins of leaves, and other ramifications of the system. Like the pith, it gradually disappears in old wood.

3, the *wood*, which lies immediately outside the medullary sheath. It is formed of woody tissue (188, 2), through which, in most cases, vessels (188, 3) variously disposed are interspersed. It is arranged in annual concentric circles

(211), which usually remain active during several years, but in older stems the central and older layers become hard, dense, comparatively inactive, and usually deeper coloured, forming what is called *heart-wood* or *duramen*, the outer, younger, and usually paler-coloured living layers constituting the *sapwood* or *alburnum*.

4, the *medullary rays*, which form vertical plates, orginating in the pith, and, radiating from thence, traverse the wood and terminate in the bark. They are formed of cellular tissue, keeping up a communication between the living portion of the centre of the stem and its outer surface. As the heart-wood is formed, the inner portion of the medullary rays ceases to be active, but they usually may still be seen in old wood, forming what carpenters call the *silver grain*.

5, the *bark*, which lies outside the wood, within the epidermis. It is, like the wood, arranged in annual concentric circles (211), of which the outer older ones become dry and hard, forming the *corky layer* or *outer bark*, which, as it is distended by the thickening of the stem, either cracks or is cast off with the epidermis, which is no longer distinguishable. Within the corky layer is the *cellular*, or *green*, or *middle bark*, formed of loose thin-walled pulpy cells containing chlorophyll (192); and which is usually the layer of the preceding season. The innermost and youngest circle, next the young wood, is the *liber* or *inner bark*, formed of long tough woody tissue called *bast-cells*.

199. The endogenous stem, as it grows old, is not marked by the concentric circles of Exogens. The wood consists of a *matrix* of cellular tissue irregularly traversed by vertical cords or bundles of woody and vascular tissue, which are in connexion with the leaves. These vascular bundles change in structure and direction as they pass down the stem; losing their vessels, they retain only their bast- or long wood-cells, usually curving outwards towards the rind. The old wood becomes more compact and harder towards the circumference than in the centre. The epidermis or rind either hardens so as to prevent any increase of diameter in the stem or it distends, without increasing in thickness or splitting or casting off any outer layers.

200. In the **Leaf**, the structure of the petioles and principal ribs or veins is the same as that of the young branches of which they are ramifications. In the expanded portion of the leaf the fibro-vascular system becomes usually very much ramified, forming the smaller veins. These are surrounded and the interstices filled up by a copious and very active cellular tissue. The majority of leaves are horizontal, having a differently constructed upper and under surface. The cellular stratum forming the upper surface consists of closely set cells, placed vertically, with their smallest ends next the surface, and with few or no stomates in the epidermis. In the stratum forming the under surface, the cells are more or less horizontal, more loosely placed, and have generally empty spaces between them, with stomates in the epidermis communicating with these intercellular spaces. In vertical leaves (as in a large number of Australian plants) the two surfaces are nearly similar in structure.

201. When leaves are reduced to scales, acting only as protectors of young buds, or without taking any apparent part in the economy of vegetable life, their structure, though still on the same plan, is more simple; their fibro-vascular system is less ramified, their cellular system more uniform, and there are few or no stomates.

202. Bracts and floral envelopes, when green and much developed, resemble leaves in their anatomical structure, but in proportion as they are reduced to scales or transformed into petals, they lose their stomates, and their systems, both fibro-vascular and cellular, become more simple and uniform, or more slender and delicate.

203. In the stamens and pistils the structure is still nearly the same. The fibro-vascular system, surrounded by and intermixed with the cellular tissue, is usually simple in the filaments and style, more or less ramified in the flattened or expanded parts, such as the anther-cases, the walls of the ovary, or capillary leaves, etc. The pollen consists of granular cells variously shaped, marked or combined, peculiar forms being constant in the same species, or often in large genera, or even Orders. The stigmatic portion of the pistil is a mass of loosely cellular substance, destitute of epidermis, and usually is in communication with the ovary by the channel running down the centre of the style.

204. Tubers, fleshy thickenings of the stem or other parts of the plant, succulent

leaves or branches, the fleshy, woody, or bony parts of fruits, the albumen, and the thick fleshy parts of embryos, consist chiefly of largely developed cellular tissue, replete with starch or other substances (192), deposited apparently in most cases for the eventual future use of the plant or its parts when recalled into activity at the approach of a new season.

205. Hairs (171) are usually expansions or processes of the epidermis, and consist of one or more cells placed end to end. When thick or hardened into prickles, they still consist usually of cellular tissue only. Thorns (170) contain more or less of a fibro-vascular system, according to their degree of development.

206. Glands, in the primary sense of the word (175, 1), consist usually of a rather loose cellular tissue without epidermis, and often replete with resinous or other substances.

§ 3. *Growth of the Organs.*

207. Roots grow in length constantly and regularly at the extremities only of their fibres, in proportion as they find the requisite nutriment. They form no buds containing the germ of future branches, but their fibres proceed irregularly from any part of their surface without previous indication, and when their growth has been stopped for a time, either wholly by the close of the season, or partially by a deficiency of nutriment at any particular spot, it will, on the return of favourable circumstances, be resumed at the same point, if the growing extremities be uninjured. If during the dead season, or at any other time, the growing extremity is cut off, dried up, or otherwise injured, or stopped by a rock or other obstacle opposing its progress, lateral fibres will be formed on the still living portion; thus enabling the root as a whole to diverge in any direction, and travel far and wide when lured on by appropriate nutriment.

208. This growth is not however by the successive formation of terminal cells attaining at once their full size. The cells first formed on a fibre commencing or renewing its growth, will often dry up and form a kind of terminal cap, which is pushed on as cells are formed immediately under it; and the new cells, constituting a greater or lesser portion of the ends of the fibres, remain some time in a growing state before they have attained their full size.

209. The roots of Exogens, when perennial, increase in thickness like stems by the addition of concentric layers, but these are usually much less distinctly marked; and in a large number of perennial Exogens and most Endogens the roots are annual, perishing at the close of the season, fresh adventitious roots springing from the stock when vegetation commences the following season.

210. The stem, including its branches and appendages (leaves, floral organs, etc.), grows in length by additions to its extremity, but a much greater proportion of the extremity and branches remains in a growing and expanding state for a much longer time than in the case of the root. At the close of one season, leaf-buds or seeds are formed, each containing the germ of a branch or young plant to be produced the following season. At a very early stage of the development of these buds or seeds, a commencement may be found of many of the leaves it is to bear; and before a leaf unfolds, every leaflet of which it is to consist, every lobe or tooth which is to mark its margin, may often be traced in miniature, and thenceforth, till it attains its full size, the branch grows and expands in every part. In some cases however the lower part of a branch and more rarely (*e.g.*, in some *Meliaceæ*) the lower part of a compound leaf attains its full size before the young leaves or leaflets of the extremity are yet formed.

211. The perennial stem, if exogenous (198), grows in thickness by the addition every season of a new layer or ring of wood between the outermost preceding layer and the inner surface of the bark, and by the formation of a new layer or ring of bark within the innermost preceding layer and outside the new ring of wood, thus forming a succession of concentric circles. The sap elaborated by the leaves finds its way, in a manner not as yet absolutely ascertained, into the *cambium-region*, a zone of tender thin-walled cells connecting the wood with the bark, by the division and enlargement of which new cells (190) are formed. These cells separate in layers, the inner ones constituting the new ring of wood, and the outer ones the new

bark or liber. In most exogenous trees, in temperate climates, the seasons of growth correspond with the years, and the rings of wood remain sufficiently distinct to indicate the age of the tree; but in many tropical and some evergreen trees, two or more rings of wood are formed in one year.

212. In endogenous perennial stems (199), the new wood or woody fibre is formed towards the centre of the stem, or irregularly mingled with the old. The stem consequently either only becomes more dense without increasing in thickness, or only increases by gradual distension, which is never very considerable. It affords therefore no certain criterion for judging of the age of the tree.

213. Flowers have generally all their parts formed, or indicated by protuberances or growing cells at a very early stage of the bud. These parts are then usually more regularly placed than in the fully developed flower. Parts which afterwards unite are then distinct, many are present in this rudimentary state which are never further developed, and parts which are afterwards very unequal or dissimilar are perfectly alike at this early period. On this account flowers in this very early stage are supposed by some modern botanists to be more *normal*, that is, more in conformity to a supposed type; and the study of the early formation and growth of the floral organs, called *Organogenesis*, has been considered essential for the correct appreciation of the affinities of plants. In some cases, however, it would appear that modifications of development, not to be detected in the very young bud, are yet of great importance in the distinction of large groups of plants, and that Organogenesis, although it may often assist in clearing up a doubtful point of affinity, cannot nevertheless be exclusively relied on in estimating the real value of peculiarities of structure.

214. The flower is considered as a *bud* (*flower-bud*, *alabastrum*) until the perianth expands, the *period of flowering* (*anthesis*) is that which elapses from the first expanding of the perianth till the pistil is set or begins to enlarge, or, when it does not set, until the stamens and pistil wither or fall. After that, the enlarged ovary takes the name of *young fruit*.

215. At the close of the season of growth, at the same time as the leaf-buds or seeds are formed containing the germ of future branches or plants, many plants form also, at or near the bud or seed, large deposits, chiefly of starch. In many cases—such as the tubers of a potato or other root-stock, the scales or thickened base of a bulb, the albumen or the thick cotyledons of a seed—this deposit appears to be a store of nutriment, which is partially absorbed by the young branch or plant during its first stage of growth, before the roots are sufficiently developed to supply it from without. In some cases, however, such as the fleshy thickening of some stems or peduncles, the pericarps of fruits which perish long before *germination* (the first growth of the seed), neither the use nor the cause of these deposits has as yet been clearly explained.

§ 4. *Functions of the Organs.*

216. The functions of the Root are,—1. To fix the plant in or to the soil, or other substance on which it grows. 2. To absorb nourishment from the soil, water, or air, into which the fibres have penetrated (or from other plants in the case of parasites), and to transmit it rapidly to the stem. The absorption takes place through the young growing extremities of the fibres, and through a peculiar kind of hairs or absorbing organs which are formed at or near those growing extremities. The transmission to the stem is through the tissues of the root itself. The nutriment absorbed consists chiefly of carbonic acid and nitrogen or nitrogenous compounds dissolved in water. 3. In some cases roots secrete or exude small quantities of matter in a manner and with a purpose not satisfactorily ascertained.

217. The Stem and its branches support the leaves, flowers, and fruit, transmit the crude sap, or nutriment absorbed by the roots and mixed with previously organized matter, to the leaves, and retransmit the assimilated or elaborated sap from the leaves to the growing parts of the plant, to be there used up, or to form deposits for future use (204). The transmission of the ascending crude sap appears to take place chiefly through the elongated cells associated with the vascular tissues, passing from one cell to another by a process but little understood, but known by the name of *endosmose*.

218. Leaves are functionally the most active of the organs of vegetation. In them is chiefly conducted digestion or *Assimilation*, a name given to the process which accomplishes the following results:—1. The chemical decomposition of the oxygenated matter of the sap, the absorption of carbonic acid, and the liberation of pure oxygen at the ordinary temperature of the air. 2. A counter-operation by which oxygen is absorbed from the atmosphere and carbonic acid is exhaled. 3. The transformation of the residue of the crude sap into the organized substances which enter into the composition of the plant. The exhalation of oxygen appears to take place under the influence of solar heat and light, chiefly from the under surface of the leaf, and to be in some measure regulated by the stomates; the absorption of oxygen goes on always in the dark, and in the day time also in certain cases. The transformation of the sap is effected within the tissues of the leaf, and continues probably more or less throughout the active parts of the whole plant.

219. The Floral Organs seldom contribute to the growth of the plant on which they are produced; their functions are wholly concentrated on the formation of the seed with the germ of a future plant.

220. The Perianth (calyx and corolla) acts in the first instance in protecting the stamens and pistils during the early stages of their development. When expanded, the use of the brilliant colours which they often display, of the sweet or strong odours they emit, has not been adequately explained. Perhaps they may have great influence in attracting those insects whose concurrence has been shown in many cases to be necessary for the due transmission of the pollen from the anther to the stigma.

221. The pistil, when stimulated by the action of the pollen, forms and nourishes the young seed. The varied and complicated contrivances by which the pollen is conveyed to the stigma, whether by elastic action of the organs themselves, or with the assistance of wind, of insects, or other extraneous agents, have been the subject of numerous observations and experiments of the most distinguished naturalists, and are yet far from being fully investigated. Their details, however, as far as known, would be far too long for the present outline.

222. The fruit nourishes and protects the seed until its maturity, and then often promotes its dispersion by a great variety of contrivances or apparently collateral circumstances, *e.g.*, by an elastic dehiscence which casts the seed off to a distance; by the development of a pappus, wings, hooked or other appendages, which allows them to be carried off by winds, or by animals, etc., to which they may adhere; by their small specific gravity, which enables them to float down streams; by their attractions to birds, etc., who taking them for food drop them often at great distances, etc. Appendages to the seeds themselves also often promote dispersion.

223. Hairs have various functions. The ordinary indumentum (171) of stems and leaves indeed seems to take little part in the economy of the plant besides perhaps some occasional protection against injurious atmospheric influences, but the root-hairs (216) are active absorbents, the hairs on styles and other parts of flowers appear often materially to assist the transmission of pollen, and the exudations of glandular hairs (175, 2) are often too copious not to exercise some influence on the phenomena of vegetation. The whole question, however, of vegetable exudations and their influence on the economy of vegetable life, is as yet but imperfectly understood.

Chap. IV. Collection, Preservation, and Determination of Plants.

224. Plants can undoubtedly be most easily and satisfactorily examined when freshly gathered. But time will rarely admit of this being done, and it is moreover desirable to compare them with other plants previously observed or collected. *Specimens* must, therefore, be selected for leisurely observation at home, and preserved for future reference. A collection of such specimens constitutes a *Herbarium*.

225. A botanical **Specimen**, to be perfect, should have *root*, *stem*, *leaves*, *flowers* (both open and in bud), and *fruit* (both young and mature). It is not, however, always possible to gather such complete specimens, but the collector should aim at completeness. Fragments, such as leaves without flowers, or flowers without leaves, are of little or no use.

226. If the plant is small (not exceeding 15 in.) or can be reduced to that length by folding, the specimen should consist of the whole plant, including the principal part of the root. If it be too large to preserve the whole, a good flowering branch should be selected, with the foliage as low down as can be gathered with it; and one or two of the lower stem-leaves or radical leaves, if any, should be added, so as to preserve as much as possible of the peculiar aspect of the plant.

227. The specimens should be taken from healthy uninjured plants of a medium size. Or if a specimen be gathered because it looks a little different from the majority of those around it, apparently belonging to the same species, a specimen of the more prevalent form should be taken from the same locality for comparison.

228. For bringing the specimens home, a light portfolio of pasteboard, covered with calico or leather, furnished with straps and buckles for closing, and another for slinging on the shoulder, and containing a few sheets of stout coarse paper, is better than the old-fashioned tin box (except, perhaps, for stiff prickly plants and a few others). The specimens as gathered are placed between the leaves of paper, and may be crowded together if not left long without sorting.

229. If the specimen brought home be not immediately determined when fresh, but dried for future examination, a note should be taken of the time, place, and situation in which it was gathered; of the stature, habit, and other particulars relating to any tree, shrub, or herb of which the specimen is only a portion; of the kind of root it has; of the colour of the flower; or of any other particulars which the specimen itself cannot supply, or which may be lost in the process of drying. These memoranda, whether taken down in the field, or from the living specimen when brought home, should be written on a label attached to the specimen or preserved with it.

230. To dry specimens, they are laid flat between several sheets of bibulous paper, and subjected to pressure. The paper is subsequently changed at intervals, until they are dry.

231. In laying out the specimen, care should be taken to preserve the natural position of the parts as far as consistent with the laying flat. In general, if the specimen is fresh and not very slender, it may be simply laid on the lower sheet, holding it by the stalk and drawing it slightly downwards; then, as the upper sheet is laid over, if it be slightly drawn downwards as it is pressed down, it will be found, after a few trials, that the specimen will have retained a natural form with very little trouble. If the specimen has been gathered long enough to have become flaccid, it will require more care in laying the leaves flat and giving the parts their proper direction. Specimens kept in tin boxes will also often have taken unnatural bends, which will require to be corrected.

232. If the specimen is very bushy, some branches must be thinned out, but always so as to show where they have been. If any part, such as the head of a thistle, the stem of an *Orobanche*, or the bulb of a Lily, be very thick, a portion of what is to be the under side of the specimen may be sliced off. Some thick specimens may be split from top to bottom before drying.

233. If the specimen be succulent or tenacious of life, such as a *Sedum* or an *Orchis*, it may be dipped in boiling water *all but the flowers*. This will kill the plant at once, and enable it to be dried rapidly, losing less of its colour or foliage than would otherwise be the case. Dipping in boiling water is also useful in the case of Heaths and other plants which are apt to shed their leaves during the process of drying.

234. Plants with very delicate corollas may be placed between single leaves of very thin unglazed tissue-paper. In shifting these plants into dry paper the tissue-paper is not to be removed, but lifted with its contents on to the dry paper.

235. The number of sheets of paper to be placed between each specimen or sheet of specimens, will depend, on the one hand, on the thickness and humidity of the specimens; on the other hand, on the quantity and quality of the paper one has at command. The more and the better the paper, the less frequently will it be necessary to change it, and the sooner the plants will dry. The paper ought to be coarse, stout, and unsized. Common blotting-paper is much too tender.

236. Care must be taken that the paper used is well dried. If it be likewise hot,

all the better; but it must then be very dry; and wet plants put into hot paper will require changing very soon, to prevent their turning black, for hot damp without ventilation produces fermentation, and spoils the specimens.

237. For pressing plants, various more or less complicated and costly presses are made. None is better than a pair of boards the size of the paper, and a stone or other heavy weight upon them if at home, or a pair of strong leather straps round them if travelling. Each of these boards should be double, that is, made of two layers of thin boards, the opposite way of the grain, and joined together by a row of clenched brads round the edge, without glue. Such boards, in deal, rather less than half an inch thick (each layer about 2½ lines), will be found light and durable.

238. It is useful also to have extra boards or pasteboards the size of the paper, to separate thick plants from thin ones, wet ones from those nearly dry, etc. Open wooden frames with cross-bars, or frames of strong wire-work lattice, are still better than boards for this purpose, as accelerating the drying by promoting ventilation.

239. The more frequently the plants are shifted into dry paper the better. Excepting for very stiff or woody plants, the first pressure should be light, and the first shifting, if possible, after a few hours. Then, or at the second shifting, when the specimens will have lost their elasticity, will be the time for putting right any part of a specimen which may have taken a wrong fold or a bad direction. After this the pressure may be gradually increased, and the plants left from one to several days without shifting. The exact amount of pressure to be given will depend on the consistence of the specimens, and the amount of paper. It must only be borne in mind that too much pressure crushes the delicate parts, too little allows them to shrivel, in both cases interfering with their future examination.

240. The most convenient specimens will be made, if the drying-paper is the same size as that of the herbarium in which they are to be kept. That of writing demy, rather more than 16 inches by 10½ inches, is a common and very convenient size. A small size reduces the specimens too much, a large size is both costly and inconvenient for use.

241. When the specimens are quite dry and stiff, they may be packed up in bundles with a single sheet of paper between each layer, and this paper need not be bibulous. The specimens may be placed very closely on the sheets, but not in more than one layer on each sheet, and care must be taken to protect the bundles by sufficient covering from the effects of external moisture or the attacks of insects.

242. In laying the specimens into the herbarium, no more than one species should ever be fastened on one sheet of paper, although several specimens of the same species may be laid side by side. And throughout the process of drying, packing, and laying in, great care must be taken that the labels be not separated from the specimens they belong to.

243. To examine or dissect flowers or fruits in dried specimens it is necessary to soften them. If the parts are very delicate, this is best done by gradually moistening them in cold water; in most cases, steeping them in boiling water or in steam is much quicker. Very hard fruits and seeds will require boiling to be able to dissect them easily.

244. For dissecting and examining flowers in the field, all that is necessary is a penknife and a pocket-lens of two or three glasses from 1 to 2 inches focus. At home it is more convenient to have a mounted lens or simple microscope, with a stage holding a glass plate, upon which the flowers may be laid; and a pair of dissectors, one of which should be narrow and pointed, or a mere point, like a thick needle, in a handle; the other should have a pointed blade, with a sharp edge, to make clean sections across the ovary. A compound microscope is rarely necessary, except in cryptogamic botany and vegetable anatomy. For the simple microscope, lenses of ¼, ½, 1, and 1½ inches focus are sufficient.

245. To assist the student in *determining* or ascertaining the name of a plant belonging to a Flora, analytical tables should be prefixed to the Orders, Genera, and Species. These tables should be so constructed as to contain, under each bracket, or equally indented, two (rarely three or more) alternatives as nearly as possible contradictory or incompatible with each other, each alternative referring to another bracket, or having under it another pair of alternatives further indented. The stu-

dent having a plant to determine, will first take the general table of Natural Orders, and examining his plant at each step to see which alternative agrees with it, will be led on to the Order to which it belongs, he will then compare it with the detailed character of the Order given in the text. If it agrees, he will follow the same course with the table of the genera of that Order, and again with the table of species of the genus. But in each case, if he finds that his plant does not agree with the detailed description of the genus or species to which he has thus been referred, he must revert to the beginning and carefully go through every step of the investigation before he can be satisfied. A fresh examination of his specimen, or of others of the same plant, a critical consideration of the meaning of every expression in the characters given, may lead him to detect some minute point overlooked or mistaken, and put him into the right way. Species vary within limits which it is often very difficult to express in words, and it proves often impossible, in framing these analytical tables, so to divide the genera and species, that those which come under one alternative should absolutely exclude the others. In such doubtful cases both alternatives must be tried before the student can come to the conclusion that his plant is not contained in the Flora, or that it is erroneously described.

246. In those Floras where analytical tables are not given, the student is usually guided to the most important or prominent characters of each genus or species, either by a general summary prefixed to the genera of an Order or to the species of the genus, for all such genera or species; or by a special summary immediately preceding the detailed description of each genus or species. In the latter case this summary is called a *diagnosis*. Or sometimes the important characters are only indicated by italicizing them in the detailed description.

247. It may also happen that the specimen gathered may present some occasional or accidental anomalies peculiar to that single one, or to a very few individuals, which may prevent the species from being at once recognized by its technical characters. It may be useful here to point out a few of these anomalies which the botanist may be most likely to meet with. For this purpose we may divide them into two classes, viz.:

(1) *Aberrations from the ordinary type or appearance of a species for which some general cause may be assigned.*

A bright, light, and open situation, particularly at considerable elevations above the sea, or at high latitudes, without too much wet or drought, tends to increase the size and heighten the colour of flowers, in proportiou to the stature and foliage of the plant.

Shade, on the contrary, especially if accompanied by richness of soil and sufficient moisture, tends to increase the foliage and draw up the stem, but to diminish the number, size and colour of the flowers.

A hot climate and dry situation tend to increase the hairs, prickles, and other productions of the epidermis, to shorten and stiffen the branches, rendering thorny plants yet more spinous. Moisture in a rich soil has a contrary effect.

The neighbourhood of the sea, or a saline soil or atmosphere, imparts a thicker and more succulent consistence to the foliage and almost every part of the plant, and appears not unfrequently to enable plants usually annual to live through the winter. Flowers in a maritime variety are often much fewer, but not smaller.

The luxuriance of plants growing in a rich soil, and the dwarf stunted character of those crowded in poor soils, are too well-known to need particularizing. It is also an everyday observation how gradually the specimens of a species become dwarf and stunted as we advance into the cold damp regions of the summits of high mountain-ranges, or into high northern latitudes; and yet it is frequently from the want of attention to these circumstances that numbers of false species have been added to our Enumerations and Floras. Luxuriance entails not only increase of size to the whole plant, or of particular parts, but increase of number in branches, in leaves, or leaflets of a compound leaf; or it may diminish the hairiness of the plant, induce thorns to grow out into branches, etc.

Capsules which, while growing, lie close upon the ground, will often become larger, more succulent, and less readily dehiscent, than those which are not so exposed to the moisture of the soil.

Herbs eaten down by sheep or cattle, or crushed underfoot, or otherwise checked in their growth, or trees or shrubs cut down to the ground, if then exposed to favourable circumstances of soil and climate, will send up luxuriant side-shoots, often so different in the form of their leaves, in their ramification and inflorescence, as to be scarcely recognisable for the same species.

Annuals which have germinated in spring, and flowered without check, will often be very different in aspect from individuals of the same species, which, having germinated later, are stopped by summer droughts or the approach of winter, and only flower the following season upon a second growth. The latter have often been mistaken for perennials.

Hybrids, or crosses between two distinct species, come under the same category of anomalous specimens from a known cause. Frequent as they are in gardens, where they are artificially produced, they are probably rare in nature, although on this subject there is much diversity of opinion, some believing them to be very frequent, others almost denying their existence. Absolute proof of the origin of a plant found wild, is of course impossible; but it is pretty generally agreed that the following particulars must always co-exist in a *wild hybrid*. It partakes of the characters of its two parents; it is to be found isolated, or almost isolated, in places where the two parents are abundant; if there are two or three, they will generally be dissimilar from each other, one partaking more of one parent, another of the other; it seldom ripens good seed; it will never be found where one of the parents grows alone.

Where two supposed species grow together, intermixed with numerous intermediates bearing good seed, and passing more or less gradually from the one to the other, it may generally be concluded that the whole are mere varieties of one species. The beginner, however, must be very cautious not to set down a specimen as intermediate between two species, because it appears to be so in some, even the most striking characters, such as stature and foliage. Extreme varieties of one species are connected together by transitions in all their characters, but these transitions are not all observable in the same specimens. The observation of a single intermediate is therefore of little value, unless it be one link in a long series of intermediate forms, and, when met with, should lead to the search for the other connecting links.

(2) *Accidental aberrations from the ordinary type, that is, those of which the cause is unknown.*

These require the more attention, as they may sometimes lead the beginner far astray in his search for the genus, whilst the aberrations above mentioned, as reducible more or less to general laws, affect chiefly the distinction of species.

Almost all species with coloured flowers are liable to occur occasionally with them all white.

Many may be found even in a wild state with double flowers, that is, with a multiplication of petals.

Plants which have usually conspicuous petals will occasionally appear without any at all, either to the flowers produced at particular seasons, or to all the flowers of individual plants, or the petals may be reduced to narrow slips.

Flowers usually very irregular, may, on certain individuals, lose more or less of their irregularity, or appear in some very different shape. Spurs, for instance, may disappear, or be produced on all instead of one only of the petals.

One part may be occasionally added to, or subtracted from, the usual number of parts in each floral whorl, more especially in regular polypetalous flowers.

Plants usually monœcious or diœcious may become occasionally hermaphrodite, or hermaphrodite plants may produce occasionally unisexual flowers by the abortion of the stamens or of the pistils.

Leaves cut or divided where they are usually entire, variegated or spotted where they are usually of one colour, or the reverse, must also be classed amongst those accidental aberrations which the botanist must always be on his guard against mistaking for specific distinctions.

INDEX OF TERMS, OR GLOSSARY.

The figures refer to the Paragraphs of the Outlines.

	Par.
Foveolate	105
Free . . 89, 132, 140,	145
Fruit . . . 15, 146,	222
Frutescent, fruticose	12
Function	7
Funicle (funiculus)	164
Funnel-shaped	104
Furrowed	173
Fusiform = spindle-shaped	54
Gamopetalous	100
Geminate	32
Genus, genera	180
Germ, germination	215
Gibbous	105
Glabrate	173
Glabrescent	173
Glabrous	173
Glands 175,	206
Glandular-setose	173
Glaucescent	173
Glaucous	173
Globose, globular	54
Glochidiate	173
Glume	83
Glutinous	173
Grain	160
Gymnospermous	161
Gynobasis, gynophore	143
Habit	183
Hairs . . 171, 205,	223
Hastate	50
Head	74
Heart-wood	198
Hepta- (7 in composition)	92
Herbaceous perennials	12
Herbarium	224
Hermaphrodite	85
Heterogamous	87
Hexa- (6 in composition)	92
Hilum	165
Hirsute	173
Hispid	173
Hoary	173
Homogamous	87
Hooks	169
Hybernaculum	23
Hybrids	247
Hypocrateriform (salver-shaped)	104
Hypogynous	140
Imbricate, imbricated 58,	102
Imparipinnate	43
Imperfect	84
Incomplete	84
Indefinite	92
Indehiscent	156
Indeterminate	67
Indumentum	171
Induplicate	102
Inferior	140
Inferior radicle	167
Inflorescence	66
Infundibuliform (funnel-shaped)	104
Innate anther	114
Insertion	140
Internode	31
Interrupted spike or raceme	75
Introrse	118
Involucre, involucel	79
Involute	102
Irregular	95
Isomerous	89
Joint, joining	54
Jugum, juga = pairs	44
Kernel	167
Knob.	25
Labellum	105
Laciniate	39
Lamina 35,	107
Lannate = woolly	173
Lanceolate	45
Lateral	91
Leaf, leaves 15, 35, 200,	218
Leaf-bud	16
Leaflet	39
Leaf-opposed	67
Legume	160
Lepidote	172
Liber 198,	211
Ligulate = strap-shaped.	
Limb	104
Linear 45,	54
Lip, lipped	105
Lobe, lobed	39
Loculicidal	158
Lower	91
Lunate = crescent-shaped.	
Lyrate	41
Male	85
Marcescent	151
Mealy	173
Medullary rays and sheath	198
Membranous	55
Meniscoid = in the form of a watch-glass.	
Mesocarp	157
Micropyle	165
Midrib	40
Monadelphous	113
Monandrous	112
Moniliform	54
Mono- (1 in composition)	92
Monocarpellary	125
Monocarpic	12
Monochlamydeous	85
Monocotyledonous plants	167
Monœcious	86
Monogynous	125
Monopetalous	100
Morphology . . . 8,	88
Mucronate	47
Multi- (*many*, or an indefinite number, in composition)	44
Muricate	173
Naked 85,	161
Natural divisions and characters	184
Natural Order	181
Navicular = boat-shaped.	
Nectary	138
Nerve	40
Net-veined	40
Neuter	85
Node	31
Novem- (9 in composition)	44
Nucleus of a cell	191
Nucleus of the ovule	233
Nut	158
Obcompressed	54
Obconical	54
Obcordate	47
Oblate	45
Oblong 45,	54
Obovate	45
Obovoid	54
Obpyramidal	54
Obtuse	47
Oct- or octo- (8 in composition) 44,	92
Offset	23
Opposite	32
Orbicular	45
Order	181
Organ	7
Organogenesis	213
Organs of vegetation and reproduction	9
Orthotropous	134

KEY TO THE NATURAL ORDERS.

Sub-kingdom PHANEROGAMIA.

Reproduction effected by means of stamens and ovules, the latter growing into seeds which contain a distinct embryo.

Class I. DICOTYLEDONS or EXOGENS.

Embryo with two cotyledons, the radicle growing out into a root. Stems when perennial with a central pith, regular rings of wood and a distinct bark. Leaves net-veined.

Series I. THALAMIFLORÆ. Flowers furnished with both a calyx and a corolla, the petals of the latter free down to the base. Stamens hypogynous.

Exceptions: Monochlamydeous, *Clematis, Ludia, Aphloia, Stadtmannia, Doratoxylon, Dodonæa.* Petals united, *Cissampelos, Leea.* Petals and stamens adnate to the torus, *Nymphæa.* Stamens perigynous, *Drymaria.* Stamens epipetalous, *Olax.* Ovary inferior and stamens epigynous, *Gouania, Phylica.*

* *Torus not expanded into a disk.*

I. **Ranunculaceæ.** Carpels many, distinct. Stamens indefinite. Petals in a single row (absent in the only Mauritian genus).—Herbs or shrubs; leaves usually alternate, palmately cut (page 1).

II. **Dilleniaceæ.** Carpels many, usually distinct, but connate in the only Mauritian genus. Stamens indefinite. Petals in a single row.—Trees or shrubs, with alternate entire leaves (page 2).

III. **Anonaceæ.** Carpels many, usually distinct, but cohering in *Anona.* Petals usually in two rows of 3 each. Stamens indefinite. Albumen ruminated.—Trees or shrubs, with alternate entire leaves (page 2).

IV. **Menispermaceæ.** Flowers in the single Mauritian genus irregular and dioicous, and carpel solitary. Stamens definite.—Twining shrubs, with minute flowers and alternate entire leaves (page 4).

Papaveraceæ. Flowers regular. Stamens indefinite, free. Ovary 1-celled; placentas parietal; seeds many, albuminous.—Herbs, with alternate leaves and milky juice (page 5).

Fumariaceæ. Flowers irregular. Stamens in two bundles of 3 each. Ovary 1-celled; seed in our plant solitary, albuminous.—Herbs, with alternate much-divided leaves (page 5).

V. **Nymphæaceæ.** Petals and stamens indefinite, in the single Mauritian genus adnate to the torus, in which the carpels are sunk.—Aquatic herbs, with large entire leaves (page 5).

VI. **Cruciferæ.** Ovary 2-celled; parietal placentas 2, joined by a false dissepiment. Stamens 6, the two outer shorter. Seeds exalbuminous.—Herbs, with alternate leaves (page 6).

VII. **Capparidaceæ.** Ovary 1-celled; placentas 2–4, parietal. Stamens many. Seeds exalbuminous.—Herbs or shrubs, with alternate leaves (page 8).

MORINGACEÆ. Ovary 1-celled; placentas 3, parietal. Stamens 10, 5 without anthers. Seeds exalbuminous.—Shrubs, with alternate compound leaves (page 9).

VIOLACEÆ. Flowers irregular, spurred. Ovary 1-celled; placentas 3, parietal; seeds albuminous. Stamens 5.—Herbs or shrubs, with alternate stipulate leaves (page 10).

VIII. **Bixaceæ.** Flowers regular. Ovary 1-celled; placentas 1 or more, parietal; seeds albuminous. Stamens definite or indefinite.—Trees or shrubs, with alternate simple leaves (page 10).

IX. **Pittosporaceæ.** Flowers regular. Ovary 1-celled; placentas 2-3, parietal; seeds albuminous. Stamens 5.—Shrubs, with alternate entire leaves (page 12).

X. **Caryophyllaceæ.** Ovary 1-celled; placentation free-central; seeds albuminous. Stamens definite.—Herbs, with tumid nodes and opposite sessile entire leaves (page 13).

XI. **Hypericaceæ.** Stamens many, polyadelphous; anthers 2-celled. Ovary 3–5-celled; placentation axile; styles distinct; seeds exalbuminous.—Shrubs or herbs, with opposite entire leaves (page 14).

XII. **Guttiferæ.** Sepals imbricate or decussate. Stamens many, free or connate; anthers 2-celled. Ovary 1- or many-celled; placentation axile; style 0 or short; seeds exalbuminous.—Trees or shrubs with opposite entire leaves and yellow juice (page 15).

XIII. **Ternstrœmiaceæ.** Sepals imbricate. Stamens many, free or connate; anthers 2-celled. Ovary 2- or many-celled; placentation axile; styles distinct; seeds usually exalbuminous.—Trees or shrubs, with simple usually alternate leaves (page 16).

XIV. **Dipterocarpeæ.** Sepals imbricate, usually accrescent. Stamens definite or indefinite; anthers 2-celled. Ovary usually 3-celled; placentation axile; style entire; seeds exalbuminous.—Trees or shrubs with alternate entire coriaceous leaves (page 17).

XV. **Malvaceæ.** Sepals valvate. Stamens many, monadelphous; anthers reniform, 1-celled. Ovary many-celled; placentation axile; styles distinct at the top.—Herbs or shrubs, with alternate leaves (page 17).

XVI. **Sterculiaceæ.** Sepals valvate. Stamens many, monadelphous; anthers 2-celled. Ovary usually 5-celled; placentation axile; styles distinct.—Trees or herbs, with alternate leaves (page 26).

XVII. **Tiliaceæ.** Sepals valvate. Stamens many, free; anthers 2-celled. Ovary 2–5-celled; placentation axile; styles usually distinct at the top.—Trees or shrubs with alternate leaves (page 31).

** *Torus usually expanded into a more or less conspicuous disk.*

XVIII. **Linaceæ.** Stamens 10, joined at the base. Ovary 3–5-celled; ovules 1–2, pendulous; styles distinct. Fruit a drupe or septicidal capsule.—Herbs or shrubs, with alternate stipulate simple leaves (page 33).

MALPIGHIACEÆ. Stamens 5, some often imperfect. Ovary usually 3-celled;

ovule solitary; styles distinct. Fruit various, often capsular, winged.—Shrubs, with entire opposite leaves (page 35).

XIX. **Zygophyllaceæ.** Stamens 5–10, free. Ovary 4–5-celled; ovules 2 or more; style simple. Fruit a septicidal capsule.—Herbs or shrubs, with opposite compound leaves (page 35).

XX. **Geraniaceæ.** Flowers regular or irregular. Stamens definite; filaments free or united. Ovary 3–5-celled; ovules 1 or many. Fruit usually capsular.—Herbs or shrubs, with opposite or alternate leaves (page 36).

XXI. **Rutaceæ.** Flowers regular. Stamens usually definite, free. Carpels 4–5, united or free at the base and joined by the style only; ovules usually 2, superposed. Fruit capsular or baccate.—Usually trees or shrubs, with opposite gland-dotted leaves, often compound (page 38).

XXII. **Simarubeæ.** Flowers regular. Stamens definite, free. Carpels 2–5 free or connate in the lower part; ovules usually solitary. Fruit dry or drupaceous.—Trees or shrubs; leaves usually alternate, not dotted (page 41).

XXIII. **Ochnaceæ.** Flowers regular. Stamens indefinite, free. Carpels 2–10, connate; ovules 1 or many in a cell; styles united. Fruit various.—Shrubs or trees, with alternate simple leaves (page 42).

XXIV. **Burseraceæ.** Flowers regular. Stamens definite, free. Ovary 3–5-celled, not lobed; ovules 2 in a cell; style simple.—Fruit dry or drupaceous.—Balsamiferous trees or shrubs with alternate pinnate leaves (page 43).

XXV. **Meliaceæ.** Flowers regular. Stamens definite, monadelphous. Ovary 4–5-celled; ovules 2 in a cell; style simple. Fruit various.—Trees or shrubs; leaves alternate, pinnate or simple (page 44).

XXVI. **Olacineæ.** Flowers regular. Stamens definite, usually free. Ovary 1-celled, or imperfectly 3-celled; ovules usually 2–3; style 0 or simple. Fruit a 1-seeded drupe.—Trees or shrubs, with alternate entire leaves (page 47).

XXVII. **Celastraceæ.** Flowers regular. Stamens 4–5, free, opposite the sepals. Ovary 1–4-celled; ovules usually 2 in a cell, erect; style simple. Fruit various.—Trees or shrubs, with opposite or alternate simple leaves (page 48).

XXVIII. **Rhamnaceæ.** Flowers regular. Stamens 4–5, free, opposite the petals, which are often hooded. Ovary usually 3-celled, sometimes inferior; ovules solitary, erect. Fruit capsular or drupaceous.—Shrubs or trees, with opposite or alternate simple leaves (page 50).

XXIX. **Ampelideæ.** Flowers regular. Stamens 4–5, opposite the petals, free or monadelphous. Ovary 2–5-celled; ovules 1–2 in a cell; style 0 or simple. Fruit a berry.—Shrubs, usually climbers with tendrils, with alternate simple or compound leaves (page 53).

XXX. **Sapindaceæ.** Flowers regular or irregular. Stamens usually 8, free. Ovary 2–3-celled; ovules usually 1 or 2 in a cell; style entire in the lower part. Fruit dry or fleshy.—Trees or shrubs, with leaves usually alternate and compound (page 55).

XXXI. **Anacardiaceæ.** Flowers regular. Stamens usually definite, free. Ovary 1- or many-celled; ovules solitary, pendulous; stigmas as many as the cells. Fruit fleshy.—Trees, with alternate compound or simple leaves (page 61).

SERIES II. **CALYCIFLORÆ.** Flowers furnished with both a calyx and a corolla, the petals of the latter free down to the base. Stamens perigynous or epigynous.

Exceptions: Gamopetalous, *Mimosea*, *Roussea*, *Bryophyllum*, *Cucumis*, *Citrullus*,

Cucurbita. Loranthus, Monochlamydeous, *Begonia, Terminalia, Fœtidia, Tetrataxis, Casearia, Passiflora suberosa, Sesuvium, Viscum.*

* *Ovary superior. Stamens perigynous.*

XXXII. **Connaraceæ.** Flowers regular. Stamens 5–10. Carpels 5, distinct. Fruit a follicle.—Trees or shrubs with alternate usually compound leaves (page 63).

XXXIII. **Leguminosæ.** Flowers irregular (except in *Mimoseæ*). Stamens usually 10. Carpel solitary. Fruit a pod.—Herbs, shrubs or trees, with alternate stipulate usually compound leaves (page 65).

XXXIV. **Rosaceæ.** Flowers regular. Stamens indefinite. Carpels 1 or many, distinct or connate. Fruit various.—Herbs or shrubs, with alternate stipulate usually compound leaves (page 94).

XXXV. **Saxifragaceæ.** Flowers regular. Stamens definite. Carpels 2–5, connate or free. Fruit various.—Herbs or shrubs, with alternate or opposite exstipulate leaves (page 96).

XXXVI. **Crassulaceæ.** Flowers regular. Stamens definite. Carpels as many as the sepals, free. Fruit follicular.—Fleshy herbs, with opposite leaves (page 98).

XXXVII. **Lythraceæ.** Flowers regular. Stamens definite. Ovary 3–4-celled, immersed in the calyx-tube; placentation axile. Fruit capsular or baccate.—Herbs or shrubs with opposite entire leaves (page 99).

XXXVIII. **Samydaceæ.** Flowers regular Stamens definite. Ovary 1-celled; placentas 3–5, parietal. Fruit capsular or baccate.—Shrubs or trees with alternate entire leaves (page 102).

XXXIX. **Turneraceæ.** Flowers regular. Stamens 5. Ovary 1-celled; placentas 3, parietal. Fruit a loculicidal capsule.—Herbs or shrubs with alternate leaves (page 104).

XL. **Passifloraceæ.** Flowers regular. Stamens definite. Ovary 1-celled, stalked; placentas 3, parietal. Fruit various.—Climbing herbs or shrubs with alternate leaves (page 105).

XLI. **Ficoideæ.** Flowers regular. Stamens definite or indefinite. Ovary in ours 3-celled; placentation axile. Fruit capsular.—Herbs or shrubs with opposite leaves (page 107).

** *Ovary inferior. Stamens epigynous.*

XLII. **Haloragaceæ.** Flowers polygamous, minute. Stamens 4. Ovary 1-celled. Fruit a 1-seeded nut.—Aquatic herbs (page 108).

XLIII. **Rhizophoraceæ.** Flowers hermaphrodite. Stamens twice as many as the petals. Fruit coriaceous, indehiscent, 1-seeded, the radicle taking root before it falls.—Trees with coriaceous entire opposite leaves (page 108).

XLIV. **Combretaceæ.** Flowers hermaphrodite or polygamous. Stamens 8–10. Ovary 1-celled. Fruit dry or fleshy.—Trees or shrubs with entire leaves (page 110).

XLV. **Myrtaceæ.** Flowers hermaphrodite. Stamens indefinite. Ovary 2- or many-celled; placentation axile. Fruit fleshy or dry.—Trees or shrubs, with leaves usually opposite and gland-dotted (page 111).

XLVI. **Melastomaceæ.** Flowers hermaphrodite. Stamens definite, often irregular. Ovary 5-celled, with axile placentation, or 1-celled. Fruit fleshy or dry.—Herbs or shrubs, with opposite entire leaves (page 120).

XLVII. **Onagraceæ.** Flowers hermaphrodite Stamens definite. Ovary 4–5 celled; placentation axile. Fruit capsular.—Herbs, with alternate entire leaves (page 123).

XLVIII. **Portulaceæ.** Flowers hermaphrodite. Sepals 2. Stamens definite or indefinite. Ovary 1-celled; placentation free-central. Fruit capsular.—Herbs, with fleshy entire leaves (page 125).

XLIX. **Araliaceæ.** Flowers hermaphrodite or polygamous. Stamens as many as petals. Ovary many-celled; placentation axile. Fruit baccate.—Shrubs, with alternate leaves (page 126).

L. **Begoniaceæ.** Flowers unisexual. Stamens indefinite. Ovary usually 3-celled, with axile placentation. Fruit capsular.—Succulent shrubs, with alternate leaves (page 128).

LI. **Cucurbitaceæ.** Flowers unisexual. Stamens usually 3. Ovary 3-celled. Fruit fleshy.—Herbs, with tendrils and alternate leaves (page 129).

LII. **Umbelliferæ.** Flowers hermaphrodite or polygamous. Stamens 5. Ovary 2-celled; ovules solitary. Fruit-carpels indehiscent.—Herbs, with alternate divided leaves (page 131).

LIII. **Cactaceæ.** Flowers hermaphrodite. Stamens indefinite. Ovary 1-celled; placentas parietal. Fruit a berry.—Fleshy leafless shrubs (page 133).

LIV. **Loranthaceæ.** Flowers hermaphrodite or unisexual. Stamens definite. Ovary 1-celled; ovule solitary. Fruit baccate.—Parasitic shrubs, leafy or leafless (page 134).

SERIES III. **GAMOPETALÆ** or **MONOPETALÆ.** Flowers furnished with both a calyx and corolla, the petals of the latter more or less united to one another.

* *Ovary inferior.*

LV. **Rubiaceæ.** Flowers regular in all the Mauritian genera. Stamens as many as petals, free. Ovary 2- or many-celled; ovules 1 or many in a cell. Fruit various.—Trees, shrubs or herbs, with opposite entire stipulate leaves (page 136).

LVI. **Compositæ.** Flowers crowded into a head which is surrounded by an involucre, all tubular, all ligulate or both kinds mixed. Stamens as many as petals, syngenesious. Ovary 2-celled; ovules solitary. Fruit an achene, usually crowned with a pappus.—Herbs or shrubs, with alternate or opposite exstipulate leaves (page 160).

LVII. **Goodeniaceæ.** Flowers irregular. Stamens 5. Ovary 1–4-celled; stigma surrounded by a cup. Fruit dry or fleshy.—Herbs or shrubs, with alternate exstipulate leaves (page 182).

LVIII. **Campanulaceæ.** Flowers regular or irregular. Stamens 5. Ovary 2–5-celled; placentation axile; stigma not surrounded by a cup. Fruit dry or fleshy.—Herbs, with alternate exstipulate leaves (page 183).

** *Ovary superior. Corolla regular.*

* *Leaves alternate.*

LIX. **Ericaceæ.** Stamens twice as many as corolla-lobes, hypogynous; anthers dehiscing by terminal pores. Ovary 4–5-celled; placentation axile. Fruit capsular.—Shrubs (page 185).

PLUMBAGINACEÆ. Stamens as many as corolla-lobes. Ovary 1-celled; ovule 1, with a long funiculus. Fruit dry.—Herbs or shrubs (page 187).

LX. **Plantagineæ.** Stamens 4; anthers dehiscing longitudinally. Ovary

1-4-celled. Fruit dehiscent or indehiscent.—Scapose herbs, with flowers in spikes (page 187).

PRIMULACEÆ. Stamens as many as corolla-lobes; anthers dehiscing longitudenally. Ovary 1-celled; placentation free-central. Fruit capsular.—Herbs (page 188).

LXI. **Myrsinaceæ.** Stamens as many as corolla-lobes; anthers dehiscing longitudinally. Ovary 1-celled; placentation free-central. Fruit drupaceous, often 1-seeded.—Shrubs, with entire dotted leaves (page 188).

LXII. **Sapotaceæ.** Flowers hermaphrodite. Fertile stamens 1–3 times as many as the corolla-lobes, often alternating with staminodia. Ovary many-celled; placentation axile. Fruit baccate, usually by abortion 1-seeded.—Trees or shrubs, with milky juice and entire coriaceous leaves (page 191).

LXIII. **Ebenaceæ.** Flowers dioicous. Stamens indefinite. Ovary 3- or more-celled; placentation axile. Fruit indehiscent. — Trees or shrubs, with entire coriaceous leaves (page 196).

LXIV. **Boraginaceæ.** Stamens 5. Carpels 4. Ovules solitary. Fruit drupaceous or 4 dry nucules.—Herbs, with leaves usually rough (page 199).

LXV. **Convolvulaceæ.** Stamens 5. Ovary 1- 4-celled. Ovules 1–2 in a cell. Fruit usually capsular.—Herbs or shrubs, usually twiners, with bell-shaped corollas. (page 204).

LXVI. **Solanaceæ.** Stamens 5. Ovary usually 2-celled; placentation axile. Ovules numerous. Fruit fleshy or dry.—Herbs or shrubs (page 213).

** *Leaves opposite.*

LXVII. **Oleaceæ.** Stamens 2. Ovary 2-celled; placentation axile. Fruit various.—Shrubs, with exstipulate leaves (page 218).

LXVIII. **Apocynaceæ.** Stamens 5, not adnate to the stigma. Carpels 2, free or connate. Fruit drupaceous or follicular.—Shrubs, with exstipulate leaves and milky juice (page 221).

LXIX. **Asclepiadaceæ.** Stamens 5, adnate to the stigma. Carpels 2. Fruit two divaricating follicles.—Shrubs or herbs, with exstipulate leaves and milky juice (page 225).

LXX. **Loganiaceæ.** Stamens 4–5. Ovary 2-celled; placentation axile. Fruit dry or fleshy.—Shrubs with entire leaves with intrapetiolar stipules (page 229).

LXXI. **Gentianaceæ.** Stamens 4–5. Carpels 2; placentation parietal. Fruit usually capsular.—Herbs, with entire exstipulate leaves (alternate in *Limnanthemum*) (page 235).

** *Ovary superior. Corolla irregular. Stamens usually 4, didynamous.*

LXXII. **Scrophulariaceæ.** Ovary 2-celled; placentation axile. Ovules numerous.—Herbs or shrubs. Leaves usually opposite (page 236).

LXXIII. **Lentibulariaceæ.** Ovary 1-celled; placentation free-central. Ovules numerous.—Acaulescent pond or swamp herbs (page 242).

LXXIV. **Bignoniaceæ.** Ovary generally 2-celled, with two placentas in each cell adnate to the septum. Ovules numerous.—Shrubs, often climbers. Leaves usually compound (page 243).

PEDALINEÆ. Ovary in our plant 1-celled, with 2 parietal placentas. Fruit a rostrate capsule, with many seeds (page 244).

LXXV. **Acanthaceæ.** Ovary 2-celled; placentation axile. Ovules 2 or more in a cell. Fruit a capsule with elastic valves. Seeds usually borne on distinct spiny processes.—Herbs or shrubs, with simple opposite leaves (page 245).

LXXVI. **Myoporaceæ.** Ovary 2–4-celled. Ovules 2 in a cell. Fruit a drupe with bony endocarp; radicle superior.—Shrubs, with alternate gland-dotted leaves (page 250).

LXXVII. **Verbenaceæ.** Ovary 2–4-celled, not lobed. Ovules 1–2 in a cell. Fruit dry or fleshy; radicle inferior.—Herbs or shrubs, with opposite leaves (page 250).

LXXVIII. **Labiatæ.** Ovary 4-lobed. Fruit of 4 dry 1-seeded nucules; radicle inferior.—Herbs or shrubs, with opposite leaves (page 257).

SERIES IV. **INCOMPLETÆ.** Flowers with at most only a single wrapper, not both calyx and a corolla. *Exceptions:*—Dichlamydeous, *Rumex, Croton, Aleurites.*

* *Ovary superior 1-celled.* (See also *Rivina, Antidesma and Macaranga.*)

† *Monochlamydeous. Anthers dehiscing longitudinally.*

Flowers usually hermaphrodite.

LXXIX. **Nyctaginaceæ.** Perianth gamophyllous, green or coloured. Stamens hypogynous. Fruit indehiscent.—Shrubs, trees or herbs, with exstipulate simple opposite or alternate leaves (page 262.)

BASELLACEÆ. Perianth gamophyllous. Stamens inserted at the throat of the perianth-tube. Fruit baccate.—Climbing fleshy herbs (page 265).

THYMELACEÆ. Perianth gamophyllous, green or coloured. Stamens inserted in the perianth-tube. Fruit fleshy.—Shrubs, with alternate entire exstipulate leaves (page 265).

LXXX. **Amaranthaceæ.** Perianth scariose, 3–5-partite. Stamens hypogynous. Fruit in our genera a 1-seeded utricle.—Herbs, with simple entire alternate or opposite leaves (page 265.)

CHENOPODIACEÆ. Perianth green, 5-partite. Stamens hypogynous or perigynous. Fruit a 1-seeded utricle.—Herbs, with alternate exstipulate leaves (page 270).

LXXXI. **Polygonaceæ.** Perianth 5–6-partite, usually coloured. Stamens 5–8, hypogynous or perigynous. Fruit a lenticular or triquetrous 1-seeded nut.—Herbs or shrubs, with alternate simple leaves and membranous sheathing stipules (page 271.)

Flowers usually unisexual.

LXXXII. **Urticaceæ.** Perianth green, 3–4-lobed or 3–4-fid, rarely absent. Stamens as many as the perianth-lobes. Fruit usually an achene.—Trees, shrubs or herbs, with opposite or alternate stipulate leaves and watery juice (page 272).

LXXXIII. **Ulmaceæ.** Perianth green, 4–5-lobed. Stamens as many as the perianth-lobes. Fruit dry or fleshy.—Shrubs or trees, with alternate simple stipulate leaves (page 280).

LXXXIV. **Moreæ.** Perianth green, 3–6-lobed or 3–6-fid. Stamens 1–6. Fruit dry or fleshy.—Trees or shrubs, with milky juice, alternate leaves and large stipules rolled together and leaving a scar when they fall (page 282).

LXXXV. **Monimiaceæ.** Perianth saccate, with the numerous stamens spread over its face. Ovaries many in each flower. Fruit dry or fleshy.—Trees or shrubs, with entire usually opposite leaves (page 286).

†† *Monochlamydeous. Anthers dehiscing by flaps* (except in Hernandia).

LXXXVI. **Lauraceæ.** Perianth subcorolline,—deeply 4–10 lobed. Stamens usually definite. Fruit indehiscent.—Trees or shrubs, with coriaceous entire exstipulate leaves (absent in *Cassytha*) (page 290.)

††† *Achlamydeous.*

CASUARINEÆ. Flowers monoicous, unisexual.—Trees with jointed leafless branchlets (page 294).

LXXXVII. **Piperaceæ.** Flowers minute, hermaphrodite or unisexual, spicate, subtended by peltate scales. Stamens usually 2–3.—Shrubs or herbs, with simple exstipulate succulent leaves (page 294.)

** *Ovary superior, syncarpous.*

PHYTOLACCACEÆ. Flowers hermaphrodite. Perianth 5-partite. Fruit baccate; seeds solitary.—Herbs or shrubs, with simple alternate exstipulate leaves.

LXXXVIII. **Nepenthaceæ.** Flowers dioicous. Perianth 4-partite. Capsule 3–4-celled; seeds numerous.—Shrubs, with alternate leaves dilated at the end into a pitcher (page 299).

LXXXIX. **Podostemaceæ.** Flowers hermaphrodite. Perianth 3–5-lobed. Fruit a minute crustaceous capsule; seeds numerous.—Aquatic herbs of moss-like habit (page 300).

XC. **Euphorbiaceæ.** Flowers usually unisexual and monochlamydeous, sometimes achlamydeous or dichlamydeous. Perianth 3–5-lobed. Fruit usually a 3-coccous capsule; seeds 1–2 in a cell.—Trees, shrubs or herbs, with alternate or opposite stipulate or exstipulate leaves (page 301).

*** *Ovary inferior, syncarpous.*

ARISTOLOCHIACEÆ. Perianth gamophyllous, hermaphrodite, with an oblique limb. Anthers adnate in a whorl to the style.—Climbing herbs or shrubs, with alternate leaves (page 322).

CLASS II. MONOCOTYLEDONS OR ENDOGENS.

Embryo with one cotyledon, the radicle not usually growing into a root. Stems, when perennial, with the vascular bundles scattered irregularly through the pith, and no distinct bark. Leaves usually narrow and parallel-veined (net-veined in *Aroideæ*, *Smilaceæ*, and *Dioscoreaceæ*).

SERIES I. **FLORIDEÆ.** Perianth distinctly whorled or if absent the flowers not placed in the axils of dry bracts.

* *Perianth distinctly dichlamydeous.*

XCI. **Commelynaceæ.** Petals fugitive, bright-coloured. Stamens 6, hypogynous, some often imperfect. Ovary free, 3-celled; seeds with abundant fleshy albumen.—Herbs with membranous entire leaves with sheathing bases (page 323).

XCII. **Xyridaceæ.** Sepals glumaceous. Petals bright-coloured. Stamens 3, alternating with 3 staminodes, hypogynous. Ovary free, 1–3-celled. Seeds with abundant albumen.—Perennial acaulescent herbs, with narrow leaves in a basal rosette (page 324).

BROMELIACEÆ. Sepals coriaceous. Petals bright-coloured. Ovary 3-celled, in our plant inferior.—Epiphytic, with coriaceous leaves and copious lepidote pubescence (page 325).

XCIII. **Scitamineæ.** Flowers very irregular. Stamen 1, petaloid, the other anthers represented by petaloid staminodes. Ovary inferior, 3-celled. Seeds with 2 layers of albumen.—Herbs, with large membranous leaves (page 326).

** *Monochlamydeous, with a petaloid perianth.*

XCIV. **Orchideæ.** Perianth very irregular. Stamen combined with the style and stigma. Ovary inferior, 1-celled, with 3 parietal placentas. Seeds minute, exalbuminous.—Herbs, with fibrous often fleshy roots (page 327).

IRIDACEÆ. Perianth regular or irregular. Stamens 3; anthers extrorse. Ovary inferior, 3-celled. Seeds with embryo in the axis of abundant albumen.—Herbs with narrow dry leaves, persistent bracts and rootstocks often bulbous (page 364).

XCV. **Amaryllidaceæ.** Perianth regular. Stamens 6; anthers introrse. Ovary inferior, 3-celled. Seeds with embryo in the axis of abundant albumen.—Bulbous herbs or shrubby with fleshy leaves (page 365).

XCVI. **Hypoxidaceæ.** Perianth regular. Stamens 6; anthers extrorse. Ovary inferior, 3-celled. Seeds albuminous.—Herbs, with dry usually pilose leaves (page 368).

DIOSCOREACEÆ. Flowers small, dioicous. Stamens 6. Ovary inferior, 3-celled. Seeds abundantly albuminous.—Twining herbs or shrubs, with broad reticulated leaves (page 369).

TACCACEÆ. Flowers hermaphrodite. Stamens 6, with hooded petaloid filaments. Ovary 1-celled, inferior, with 3 parietal placentas. Fruit baccate.—Acaulescent herbs with umbellate flowers (page 370).

MUSACEÆ. Flowers irregular. Stamens 6, or some abortive. Ovary inferior, 3-celled. Seeds with abundant albumen. — Gigantic herbs or trees, with large petioled oblong leaves (page 370).

XCVII. **Liliaceæ.** Flowers regular, usually hermaphrodite. Stamens 6; anthers in all ours introrse. Ovary superior, 3-celled. Seeds with copious albumen. Fruit capsular or baccate.—Herbs or shrubs; rootstock often bulbous; leaves dry or fleshy (page 372).

XCVIII. **Smilaceæ.** Flowers polygamo-dioicous. Stamens, 6. Ovary superior, 3-celled. Fruit baccate.—Climbing shrubs, with broad reticulated leaves (page 378).

*** *Monochlamydeous, with a regular sepaloid perianth.*

XCIX. **Palmæ.** Flowers unisexual, arranged on spadices enclosed in spathes. Stamens 6 or many, rarely 3. Carpels 3, distinct or united; ovule usually solitary. Fruit indehiscent, dry or succulent. Seed with small embryo outside the bony albumen.—Trees or shrubs (page 379).

C. **Juncaceæ.** Flowers hermaphrodite. Stamens 6. Ovary 1–3-celled; ovules many or 1. Fruit capsular or baccate. Seed albuminous.—Herbs, with dry persistent leaves, sometimes reduced to sheaths (page 389).

CI. **Eriocauloneæ.** Flowers monoicous, in dense heads. Stamens 4–6, the alternate ones often sterile. Ovary 2–3-celled; ovules solitary. Fruit capsular. Seed albuminous.—Usually acaulescent herbs, with leaves in a dense basal rosette (page 390).

CII. **Naiadaceæ.** Flowers hermaphrodite or monoicous. Stamens 1–4. Carpels 1-4 1-celled; ovules usually solitary. Fruit indehiscent. Seed usually exalbuminous.—Water-plants (page 391.)

CIII. **Typhaceæ.** Flowers monoicous. Perianth of threads or scales. Stamens 2 or more. Ovary usually 1-celled; ovule solitary. Fruit various. Seeds albuminous.—Marsh plants, with minute flowers in dense heads or spikes (page 394).

*** *Achlamydeous* (at any rate in Mauritian genera). See also *Ruppia*, *Zannichellia*.

CIV. **Pandaneæ.** Flowers dioicous, in oblong or globose heads enclosed in spathes. Stamens many. Ovary 1- or many-celled; ovule solitary. Fruit drupaceous. Seed albuminous.—Trees or shrubs, with large linear coriaceous spiny leaves (page 395).

AROIDEÆ. Flowers on a cylindrical spadix enclosed in a spathe, in Mauritian genera monoicous. Stamens various. Fruit baccate. Seed albuminous.—Herbs with broad net-veined leaves (page 403).

CV. **Lemnaceæ.** Flowers minute, hermaphrodite, 1–3 in a spathe from a cleft at the edge of a floating frond. Stamens solitary. Ovary 1-celled. Seed albuminous (page 404).

SERIES II. **GLUMIFERÆ.** Flowers produced in the axils of dry persistent bracts, with perianth absent or represented by minute scales or bristles.

CVI. **Cyperaceæ.** Bracts 1 to each flower. Anthers basifixed. Leaf-sheaths closed (page 405).

CVII. **Gramineæ.** Bracts 2 to each flower. Anthers versatile. Leaf-sheaths open (page 428).

SUB-KINGDOM CRYPTOGAMIA.

Reproduction effected without stamens, ovules, or seeds which contain a distinct embryo.

SERIES I. Capsules of all one kind. Spores falling to the ground to give rise to a prothallus on which antheridia and archegonia are developed.

CVIII. **Filices.** Capsules aggregated in clusters on the back or edge of leafy fronds, rarely forming spikes or panicles. Spores without elaters (page 458).

CIX. **Equisetaceæ.** Capsules placed on the underside of stalked peltate scales, which are aggregated into a cone at the end of a distinctly-jointed leafless stem. Spores with elaters (page 518).

CX. **Lycopodiaceæ.** Capsules solitary in the axils of small closely-placed 1-nerved leaves. Spores without elaters (page 518.)

SERIES II. Capsules of two kinds, one containing macrospores which give rise to a prothallus which bears archegonia and the other microspores which produce antheridia.

CXI. **Selaginellaceæ.** Capsules of both kinds solitary in the axils of small closely-placed 1-nerved leaves (page 522).

CXII. **Marsiliaceæ.** Capsules of both kinds contained in one common receptacle, which arises from a filiform rootstock or petiole (page 525).

FLORA OF THE MAURITIUS AND THE SEYCHELLES.

FLORA OF THE MAURITIUS AND THE SEYCHELLES.

ORDER I. RANUNCULACEÆ.

Sepals 5 or fewer, petaloid when the petals are absent. Petals in a single row, absent in *Clematis*. Stamens indefinite, free, hypogynous. Carpels indefinite. Ovules anatropous, solitary or many. Fruit apocarpous, usually dry, of few or many achenes or follicles, rarely a berry. Seeds small, with copious albumen and a minute embryo.—Commonly herbs with alternate palmate or 3-foliolate leaves. *Clematis* is exceptional by its shrubby habit, and opposite leaves. DISTRIB. Species variously estimated from 600 to 1200, chiefly inhabitants of the north temperate zone.

1. CLEMATIS, Linn.

Sepals 4, petaloid, valvate-induplicate. Petals 0. Stamens indefinite; anthers small, oblong, adnate. Carpels indefinite, in a dense sessile head. Fruit of small achenes, with usually long beautifully feathered tails.—Shrubs with opposite petioled, usually compound leaves, climbing habit, solitary or panicled axillary or terminal flowers, with a tendency to become polygamous. DISTRIB. All temperate countries, rarer in the tropics. Species about 100.

1. **C. mauritiana,** *Lam.; DC. Prod.* i. 6. A glabrous climbing shrub. Leaves petioled; leaflets ternate, ovate, acute, stalked, dentate. Flowers 3–5, on long lax pedicels on axillary peduncles as long as the petiole. Sepals oblong, ½ in. long, dull purple, with a matted grey border where they incurve in bud. Achenes with a feathered tail 1½ in. long.—Deless. Ic. Sel. t. 2. C. triflora, *Vahl.* C. Sonneratii, *Pers.*

MAURITIUS. Common in woods and thickets, from the sea level to a height of 2000 feet. Also Bourbon and Madagascar. *Vigne Vierge.*

ORDER II. DILLENIACEÆ.

Sepals 5, much imbricated, persistent. Petals 2–7, usually 5, Stamens many, free or connate at base; anthers adnate, dehiscing variously. Carpels indefinite, typically free, but in *Wormia* cohering, 1-celled with 1 or more ovules; styles divergent; stigmas capitate. Fruit dry, follicular or capsular. Seeds one or few, thick, arillate.—Trees or shrubs, often climbers, with alternate entire leaves, varied inflorescence, showy yellow or white hermaphrodite or polygamous flowers. DISTRIB. Species 200, spread round the world in or near the tropics; also temperate Australian.

1. WORMIA, Rottb.

Sepals 5, round, leathery. Petals 5, broad, obtuse. Stamens nearly free; filaments not dilated at apex; anthers long, dehiscing by terminal pores. Carpels 5–10, in our plant joined by their inner borders; ovules many; styles spur-like, divergent; stigmas capitate. Fruit dry, follicular.—Trees with large entire alternate closely penninerved leaves, petioles with deciduous wings and flowers in terminal racemes or panicles. DISTRIB. Trop. Asia, reaching Australia. Species 10.

1. **W. ferruginea**, *Baill. Adans.* vi. 268, vii. 343. An erect tree, 30–40 feet high; young branches silky. Leaves oblong, usually ½–1 ft. long, rigidly coriaceous, at first silky, becoming glabrous above, thinly grey-tomentose beneath, with close spreading raised veins and a silky midrib. Racemes ½–1 ft. long; pedicels densely pilose. Sepals ½ in. long, round; 3 outer silky; 2 inner glabrous. Petals whitish, oblong, twice length of sepals. Carpels 7–10, connate in a round coriaceous head into a syncarpous fruit with axile placentation. *Wright in Trans. Roy. Irish Acad.* xxiv. 573. *t.* 27.

Mountain woods of the SEYCHELLES, *Bouton! Pervillé! Wright! Horne!* Endemic. *Bois rouge, bois marré blanc.*

ORDER III. ANONACEÆ.

Sepals 3, deltoid, persistent, distinct or connate. Petals usually in two rows of 3 each, usually valvate, the inner row sometimes absent. Stamens many, distinct, crowded on a prominent torus; filaments short or absent; anthers adnate, the connective mostly overtopping the cells. Carpels many, becoming dry or fleshy, free or in *Anona* united into a mass. Seeds 1 or more in each carpel, with abundant ruminated albumen.—Trees or erect or climbing shrubs with alternate entire exstipulate leaves. Flowers terminal or axillary. DISTRIB. Species about 400, cosmopolitan in tropics.

Carpels united in a mass . . . . 1. ANONA.
Carpels separate from one another.
  Petals unequal . . . . 2. XYLOPIA.
  Six petals subequal.
    Ovules 2 basal . . . . * ARTABOTRYS.
    Ovules biserial . . . . * CANANGA.

1. ANONA, Linn.

Sepals small, connate. Petals in one or two valvate series, concave on the face, caducous, the inner like the outer or different. Stamens very numerous; anthers narrow, the connective forming an ovoid knob above the cells. Carpels numerous; ovules solitary, erect; style oblong. Fruit of fleshy carpels, united in a large round or oblong mass.—Trees with 1-flowered short axillary peduncles. DISTRIB. Species about 50, mostly American; three (*A. reticulata, squamosa*, and *Cherimolia*) now widely cultivated in the Old World.

Inner 3 petals suppressed . . . . * A. SQUAMOSA.
Inner 3 petals much smaller than outer three.
  Leaves sessile, cordate-amplexicaul . . . . 1. A. AMPLEXICAULIS.
  Leaves short-petioled, rounded at base . . . . 2. A. GRANDIFLORA.
Six petals subequal.
  Climbing shrub . . . . 3. A. PYRIFORMIS.
  Erect tree . . . . * A. MURICATA.

1. **A. amplexicaulis,** *Lam.; DC. Prod.* i. 86. A glabrous erect shrub. Leaves close, rigidly coriaceous, glaucous, rather shining, oblong, obtuse or acute, deeply cordate-amplexicaul, 4–6 in. long. Free part of sepals as broad as long. Outer petals oblong, obtuse, 1½ in. long; inner much shorter, lanceolate, with a triquetrous beak-like point. *Dunal, Monog. Anon.* 76, t. 7.

Mountain woods of MAURITIUS, at Nouvelle Découverte and La Savanne. Also Madagascar.

2. **A. grandiflora,** *Lam.; DC. Prod.* i. 86. A glabrous climbing shrub. Leaves close, nearly sessile, green, rigidly coriaceous, rather shining, oblong, acuminate, rounded at the base, ½ ft. long. Sepals joined halfway up. Outer petals oblong, flat, 1–2 in. long; inner shorter, lanceolate, triquetrous. Fruit the size of an egg. *Dunal, Monog. Anon.* 75, *tab.* 6 *et* 6 a.

Mountain woods of MAURITIUS, at Nouvelle Découverte and Piton du Milieu de l'isle. Also Madagascar.

3. **A. pyriformis,** *Bojer, Hort. Maur.* 5 (name only). A glabrous climbing shrub. Leaves nearly oblong, obtuse or subacute, rigidly coriaceous, rather shining, glaucous, 3–6 in. long. Sepals joined halfway up. Petals subequal, oblong-spathulate, 1½–2 in. long, all broad, obtuse and flat, the outer cucullate at the top.

Mountain woods of MAURITIUS, at Nouvelle Découverte, *Bojer!* Endemic.

* Besides the three indigenous species, two others are commonly planted and have become established; viz. *A. muricata*, Linn., a native of the West Indies, a low tree with large oblong glossy coriaceous leaves, six subequal broad ovate petals, and a yellow-green oblong fruit 6–8 in. long, with the areoles produced into recurved spines. *Corossol. A. squamosa*, Linn., Bot. Mag. t. 3095 (Custard apple); also Tropical American, a low erect tree, with oblong membranous glaucous leaves, greenish petals an inch long, the inner three suppressed, and a globose fruit 3 inches thick, with roundish tubercles. *Attier.*

2. XYLOPIA, Linn.

Sepals three, small, deltoid, valvate, connate at the base. Petals 6, valvate, in two sets of three each, triquetrous. Stamens oblong, indefinite, with the connective produced beyond the cells. Carpels numerous, free, inserted in cavities of the torus; ovules 2–6, ventral; style elongated. Carpels cylindrical, often dehiscent.—Trees, with coriaceous leaves, the flowers solitary or fascicled in their axils. DISTRIB. Round the world in the tropics. Species 30.

1. **X. Richardi,** *Boiv. MSS.* A glabrous tree, with crowded terete flexuose branches. Leaves alternate, short-petioled, obovate-oblong, 2–3 in. long, coriaceous, shining, green above, finely venulose beneath, cuneate at the base. Flowers solitary in the axils of the leaves, on short stout pedicels. Outer petals ⅝ in. long, clothed with whitish-brown silky pubescence. Ripe carpels 15–20, sausage-shaped, 1¼ in. long, dark brown, glabrous, marked with flexuose vertical lines. Seeds 4–5, oblong, tightly packed, bright chestnut-brown, with a cupular fleshy-membranous aril at the base. Anona aromatica, *Bojer*, *Hort. Maur.* 6, *non DC.*

MAURITIUS, in hilly woods of Grandport; also Bourbon.

Of the genera with entirely distinct carpels

* *Cananga odorata*, Hk. fil. and Thoms. Fl. Ind. 130 (Unona odorata, DC.; Deless. Ic. t. 88), a common Indian species, has been gathered by Horne in the Seychelles, but is probably planted. It is a tall tree, with fascicled axillary flowers, 6 subequal spreading long petals, ovoid anther-tips, long-stalked fleshy ripe carpels and many biserial ovules.

* *Artabotrys odoratissima*, R. Br. in Bot. Reg. t. 453 (Unona uncinata, Dun. Monog. Anon. p. 105, t. 12), another common Indian species, with 1–2 flowers from a curious hooked peduncle, and 2-seeded yellow oblong fleshy ripe carpels, given by Dunal and others as Mauritian, is planted only.

ORDER IV. MENISPERMACEÆ.

Flowers minute, dioicous or polygamous. Sepals usually 6, distinct much imbricated. Petals usually 6, free or connate. Male flowers, with stamens equal in number to the petals, and opposite to them, distinct or connate, 2-celled adnate anthers and sometimes rudimentary carpels. Female flowers with 3 (1–12) carpels, becoming fleshy in fruit; stigma terminal. Seed concave on the inner face, curved round an intruded point of the endocarp (condyle); albumen ruminate or uniform or absent.—Climbing shrubs with alternate exstipulate entire leaves. DISTRIB. Everywhere in the tropics; species estimated by Benth. and Hk. fil. at about 80.

1. CISSAMPELOS, Linn.

Dioicous, the male and female flowers very different; the male with 4 oblong free sepals, 2–4 petals, united into a cup, and anthers joined into a peltate disk; the female with two small free or connate petals, one large sepal and a single ovoid carpel opposite the petal with a trifid stigma. Fruit fleshy, filled with a single sparingly albuminous seed curved round the condyle.—Slender climbers, with very minute cymose male and racemose female flowers. DISTRIB. Everywhere in the tropics. Species estimated by Hooker and Bentham at 18, by Miers at 70.

1. **C. Pareira,** *Linn.;* var. MAURITIANA. *Hk. fil. and Thoms. Fl. Ind.* i. 198. A wide-climbing slender shrub, densely pilose on all the foliar organs, branches, and even ovary. Leaves long-petioled, round, deeply cordate, 2–4 in. broad, with a conspicuous mucro. Male flowers in densely-fascicled peduncled lateral cymes; female in long solitary flexuose racemes, in nearly sessile distant clusters, each hidden by a persistent bract, like a reduced leaf. Female flowers with two distinct round petals between the sepal and ampullæform ovary. Cissampelos mauritiana, *Thouars*; *DC. Prod.* i. 101. Dissopetalum mauritianum, *Miers, Contrib.* iii. 203, *t.* 117.

MAURITIUS, in woods and thickets. *Cissampelos Bojeriana, madagascariensis, mucronata* (A. Rich.), and *cordifolia* (Bojer), Miers, Cont. iii. 181-4, to my eyes are simply forms of *C. Pareira* with the two petals connate.—Everywhere in the tropics, as here understood, but this considered by Miers to include some 50 distinct species. *Pareira brava.*

ORDER IV. *PAPAVERACEÆ.

**Argemone mexicana*, Linn.; *D.C. Prod.* i. 120, now a common weed in the tropics, of American origin, an erect robust branched prickly annual with milky juice, sessile amplexicaul large sinuated leaves variegated green and white, 2–3 caducous sepals, 4–6 large obovate bright yellow petals, indefinite stamens, short prickly capsule with 4-7 sessile radiant stigmas, is frequent through the islands. *Chardon du pays.*

ORDER IV. *FUMARIACEÆ.

**Fumaria officinalis*, Linn., the common European fumitory, a much branched annual weed, with alternate bipinnate leaves with small linear lobes, small red irregular flowers in simple racemes, two minute scale-like sepals, 4 connivent petals, one outer spurred at base, two inner spoon-shaped at the tip, 6 stamens in two bundles, and small round dry 1-seeded indehiscent green fruit, is frequent in Mauritius. *Fumeterre.*

ORDER V. NYMPHÆACEÆ.

Sepals 3–5. Petals and stamens mostly indefinite, free and hypogynous, or adnate to the torus. Anthers 2-celled, adnate. Carpels many, free or immersed in the receptacle, so as to form a spuriously syncarpous pistil; ovules many, parietal; stigmas radiating.

Seeds with a double albumen.—Aquatic herbs, with a perennial rhizome, long-petioled usually round and floating leaves and showy flowers. DISTRIB. Cosmopolitan. Species 30–40.

1. NYMPHÆA, Linn.

Sepals 4. Petals many, multiserial, adnate to the torus, like the stamens, into which they gradually pass. Anther-cells long; filaments petaloid. Carpels sunk in the fleshy disk, so as to form a globose many-celled pistil, crowned by the radiant stigmas. Fruit spongy. Seeds immersed in pulp, enclosed in a fleshy arillus.—Flowers white, or coloured, often odorous. DISTRIB. Cosmopolitan. Species 20.

1. **N. stellata,** *Willd.;* var. MADAGASCARIENSIS, *Ayres.* Leaves round, 3–4 in. broad, irregularly crenate, lobed at the base nearly to the petiole. Sepals 1½–2 in. long. Petals 6–8, lanceolate, white tinged with blue. Anthers ¼–⅓ in. long; connective produced beyond the cells in a linear process. Stigmatic rays 8–10, short, clavate. N. madagascariensis, *DC. Prod.* i. 114.

MAURITIUS, in streams and lakes. The species spread through the tropics of old world; very variable. *Nenuphar étoilé.*

ORDER VI. CRUCIFERÆ.

Sepals 4, free. Petals 4, obtuse, clawed, cruciate, rarely 0. Stamens 6, hypogynous; 2 outer shorter. Ovary 2-celled; style short or 0; ovules 1 or many in each cell on parietal placentas. Fruit a long or short pod, with two valves usually separating from a central framework (replum). Seeds exalbuminous, with radicle enclosed by the cotyledons or recurved so as to press against their back (incumbent) or edges (accumbent). —Annual or perennial herbs with racemed usually ebracteate flowers, and radical leaves often in a dense rosette. DISTRIB. Temperate regions, chiefly of northern hemisphere; species 1200.

Pods long (Siliquosæ).
  Flowers white; radicle accumbent; cotyledons flat.
    Pod compressed; seeds uniserial . . . . 1. CARDAMINE.
    Pod terete; seeds biserial . . . . 2. NASTURTIUM.
  Flowers yellow; radicle incumbent; cotyledons conduplicate *BRASSICA.
Pods round or oblong (Siliculosæ).
  Valves of pod smooth, dehiscent . . . . 3. LEPIDIUM.
  Valves of pod rugose, not dehiscing . . . . * SENEBIERA.

1. CARDAMINE, Linn.

Sepals not saccate at the base. Petals clawed, longer than the calyx. Pod linear, compressed, narrowed to both ends, the valves not keeled. Seeds uniserial, oblong, compressed, wingless; radicle accumbent.—Annual or perennial herbs; leaves mostly pinnate; flowers small, white or purple. DISTRIB. Everywhere in temperate regions. Species 60.

1. **C. hirsuta**, *Linn.; DC. Prod.* i. 152. A small glabrous annual, with slender cœspitose stems. Leaves petioled, pinnate, with 1–3 small roundish stalked entire or repand leaflets. Flowers minute, whitish, in lax terminal racemes; pedicels ascending, longer than the calyx. Pod about ½ in. long, narrowed to the base, and a short beak. Seeds 6–8, with a space between them. C. borbonica, *Bojer, Hort. Maur.* 11, *non Pers.*

MAURITIUS, in cool elevated situations. Cosmopolitan in temperate regions. *C. borbonica*, Pers., is *C. africana*, Linn, a totally different plant, which is widely spread through Africa and Asia, reaching Bourbon, but not found in Mauritius.

2. NASTURTIUM, R. Br.

Sepals not saccate at the base. Petals clawed, exceeding the calyx. Pod sausage-shaped, rarely short, the valves rounded on the back. Seeds biserial, globose; radicle accumbent.—Annual or perennial herbs; leaves often pinnate; flowers white or yellow or purplish. DISTRIB. Cosmopolitan; species 20–30.

1. **N. barbareæfolium,** *Baker.* A stemless glabrous annual. Leaves all radical, in a dense rosette, petioled, pinnate, with a large oblong obtuse cordate end, and 1–2-jugate small round adnate side lobes. Racemes very lax, ½ ft. long; pedicels flexuose, ¾ to 1½ in. long. Petals purplish-white, twice the length of the oblong sepals. Pod subterete, ½–1 in. long; style short; stigma capitate. Seeds very numerous, minute, globose.

MAURITIUS, in cultivated ground at Pamplemousses, *Bouton!* Moka, *Ayres!* Near the common tropical *N. indicum*, Linn., and Cape *N. fluviatile*, E. Meyer. Endemic.

* *N. officinale*, R. Br., the common European water-cress, a robust glabrous floating perennial, with pinnate leaves, many pairs of oblong leaflets, small white flowers in dense terminal racemes, and cylindrical pods ½–¾ in. long, is established in some of the streams in Mauritius and Rodriguez. It is said to have been introduced about 1760, by Aublet, the author of the Flora of Guiana. *Cresson de fontaines.*

* *Brassica Sinapistrum*, Boiss. (*Sinapis arvensis*, Linn), the common European wild mustard, a hispid annual, with dense yellow flowers, long torulose pods with a deciduous beak and conduplicate cotyledons, is a frequent weed in cultivated ground in Mauritius. *Moutarde sauvage.*

* *B. juncea*, Hk. fil. and Thoms. Fl. Ind. i. 157, (*Sinapis juncea*, Linn.), commonly cultivated through tropical Asia, distinguished by its

entire upper leaves and slender torulose pod, with a flattened beak and 3 ribs on each valve, is in Dr. Balfour's Rodriguez collection.

* *B. nigra*, Koch, (*Sinapis*, Linn.) and *B. alba*, Hk. fil. and Thoms. (*Sinapis*, Linn.) the commonly cultivated black and white mustard, are both grown in Mauritius, and casually subspontaneous.

3. LEPIDIUM, Linn.

Sepals oblong, convex. Petals minute, sometimes absent. Stamens 2–6. Pod round or oblong, compressed laterally, with a narrow replum, often deeply emarginate. Seeds 1 to a cell, pendulous; radicle usually incumbent.—Annuals or perennials, with minute white flowers in long racemes. DISTRIB. Cosmopolitan. Species 60–80.

1. **L. ruderale**, *Linn.; DC. Prod.* i. 205. An erect, glabrous, much-branched annual weed. Radical leaves divided; upper linear, entire. Racemes finally 3–4 in. long. Flowers minute, usually apetalous and diandrous. Pod oblong, $\frac{1}{12}$ inch long, scarcely emarginate. L. iberoides, *Desv.; DC. Prod.* i. 206.

MAURITIUS, in waste ground. Cosmopolitan weed, originating from old World.

* *Senebiera didyma*, Pers. (*S. pinnatifida*, DC.), a cosmopolitan weed, occurs in cultivated ground in Mauritius. It is a diffuse procumbent annual, with leaves cut down to a winged rachis into entire or trifid pinnæ, copious sessile axillary racemes, minute flowers mostly apetalous and diandrous, and a minute pod laterally compressed with 2 globose 1-seeded indehiscent valves.

ORDER VII. CAPPARIDACEÆ.

Sepals 4, free or connate. Petals 4, obtuse, clawed. Stamens numerous or indefinite, hypogynous; filaments sometimes adhering to a gynophore. Ovary 1-celled, sessile or stalked; style short or 0; stigma capitate; ovules many, on 2–4 parietal placentas. Fruit in the Mauritian genera a cylindrical or compressed capsule, the two dry valves separating from a framework as in *Cruciferæ*. Seeds uniform, exalbuminous.—Herbs or shrubs; leaves simple or digitate, leaflets entire; flowers racemose or axillary, often showy. DISTRIB. Species 300, nearly all tropical in both hemispheres.

Capsule long-stalked; filaments few, united in a tube . . 1. GYNANDROPSIS.
Capsule sessile; filaments many, free . . . . 2. POLANISIA.

1. GYNANDROPSIS, DC.

Sepals 4, free, lanceolate. Petals 4, with very long claws. Stamens 4–6, the bases of the filaments forming a tube round the lower part of a gynophore, then spreading; ovary stalked; ovules many, on 2 placentas. Pod cylindrical, narrowed to both ends, the two valves separating from the central framework.—Annual herbs, with digitate leaves and ample bracteated lax terminal racemes. DISTRIB. Everywhere in tropics. Species 10.

1. **G. pentaphylla**, *DC. Prod.* i. 238. A tall branched, almost shrubby, shortly pilose annual. Lower leaves long-petioled; leaflets 5, oblong-cuneate, sessile. Fruiting racemes 6–9 in. long and broad; pedicels spreading; bracts minute, tripartite. Gynophore finally 1–1½ in. long. Petals purple or white, with a claw equalling or exceeding the blade. Pod terete, 2–3 in. long, narrowed to both ends. G. denticulata, *DC. loc. cit.*

MAURITIUS, frequent in waste ground. RODRIGUEZ, a few plants near Mathurin, *Balfour*. A cosmopolitan weed. *Brède Caya. Mosambé.*

2. POLANISIA, Rafin.

Sepals 4, free, lanceolate or oblong. Petals 4, obscurely clawed. Stamens 6–8, or more numerous, hypogynous; filaments free, often some without anthers. Ovary sessile, without a gynophore; style short; stigma capitate. Capsule long, cylindrical or compressed; placentas 2; seeds many.—Annual herbs, mostly hispid-glandulose; leaves simple or digitate; flowers in ample bracteated racemes. DISTRIB. Cosmopolitan in tropics. Species 14. Scarcely distinct from *Cleome.*

1. **P. viscosa**, *DC. Prod*, i. 242. A robust branched viscose-hispid annual. Leaves petioled, digitate; leaflets 3–5, oblong-cuneate, sessile. Raceme ½–1 ft. long, with large leaves bracteating the ascending pedicels. Stamens 8–20. Corolla whitish, ½ in. deep. Pod 2–4 in. long, narrowed to a short style, hispid and marked with parallel vertical grooves. Cleome viscosa, and icosandra, *Linn.*

MAURITIUS and SEYCHELLES, a common weed, especially near the sea. Cosmopolitan in tropics. *Brède Caya.*

ORDER VII. *MORINGACEÆ.

**Moringa pterygosperma*, Gaertn., a native of Tropical Asia, is found sometimes about abandoned plantations in Mauritius, and was gathered by Dr. Balfour in Rodriguez, near Port Mathurin, and on Frigate Island. It is a much-branched shrub, 10–15 feet high, with ample alternate 2–3-pinnate petioled glabrous or puberulent leaves; small oblong membranous entire obtuse leaflets; flowers in small deltoid panicles; 5 oblong imbricated spreading sepals; 5 unequal oblong obtuse petals ½ inch long; 10 declinate included hypogynous stamens, 5 alternate without anthers; anthers 1-celled; a trigonous pod more than a foot long, with three grooved valves; parietal placentas and abundant seeds with three winged angles. *Brède Morongue. Horse-radish tree.*

ORDER VII. *VIOLACEÆ.

* *Viola Patrinii*, DC. (*V. betonicæfolia*, Bojer, non Smith), a common Indian species, is established by roadsides at Ville Bague, Vacquois and Moka, Mauritius. It is a stemless glabrous perennial, with long-petioled deltoid-cordate crenate leaves in a basal rosette; long pedicels; flowers often apetalous; corolla violet blue, ¾ in. long, with an oblong obtuse spur; petals veined at base, and a flattened style.

ORDER VIII. BIXACEÆ.

Flowers regular, hermaphrodite or in *Flacourtia* dioicous. Sepals usually 5, obtuse, imbricate. Petals as many or 0. Stamens hypogynous, 5 or indefinite. Ovary 1-celled; placentas usually 2 or more, one in *Aphloia;* ovules parietal. Fruit baccate or capsular, dehiscing into as many valves as there are placentas. Seeds few or many, albuminous.—Trees or shrubs, with alternate exstipulate entire leaves; the flowers solitary or in peduncled racemes in the axils of the leaves. DISTRIB. Cosmopolitan in tropics; also Cape. Species 160.

Flowers hermaphrodite	
Petals 5; stamens indefinite	* BIXA.
Petals and stamens 5–6 each	1. ERYTHROSPERMUM.
Petals 0; stamens very numerous	
Placentas 2–4; style produced	2. LUDIA.
Placenta 1; stigma sessile, peltate	3. APHLOIA.
Flowers dioicous	* FLACOURTIA.

* *Bixa Orellana*, Linn., the Arnotto, a native of Tropical America, is established in the Seychelles, and commonly planted in Mauritius. It is a low tree, with large petioled alternate cordate-ovate cuspidate entire membranous leaves; large red or white flowers in terminal corymbs; 5 petals; indefinite stamens; long simple flexuose style, and a large ovoid densely prickly capsule, with 2 parietal placentas, which splits into two coriaceous valves. *Roucou.*

1. ERYTHROSPERMUM, Lam.

Sepals 5–6, obovate, much imbricated. Petals 5–6, like the sepals, but smaller. Stamens as many, hypogynous; filaments subulate; anthers lanceolate-sagittate. Ovary globose, sessile; placentas 3–4; ovules many; style short; stigma obscurely lobed. Fruit globose, hard, finally dehiscing. Seeds few, large, turgid.—Erect shrubs with large alternate nearly sessile leaves and small flowers in racemes from their axils. DISTRIB. One other species in Ceylon.

1. **E. mauritianum**, *Baker*. A glabrous erect shrub or small tree. Leaves alternate, subcoriaceous, obtuse or acute, cuneate or rounded at the base, short-petioled or sessile, green, subcoriaceous, exstipulate. Flowers in racemes or corymbs about as long as the leaves; pedicels

spreading or ascending, ½–1 in., with a minute bract at the base. Perianth and stamens caducous. Sepals obovate, ⅛–⅙ in. long. Stamens included. Ovary usually grey-canescent. Fruit globose, hard, rugose, ½–1 in. thick, finally dehiscing.

MAURITIUS, in mountain woods. Also Madagascar, if not a distinct species. *Bois Manioc. Bois Cochon.* A variable plant, of which the following are the principal varieties, connected by intermediate forms,

1. *pyrifolium* (E. pyrifolium, *Lam. Ill. t.* 274, fig. 1. E. ellipticum and paniculatum, *Poir.* E. pauciflorum, *Thouars.* E. polymorphum, *Clos*). Leaves all alternate, 2–4 in. long, obtuse or acute, oblong or obovate-oblong, short-petioled. Racemes 4–8-flowered, subcorymbose. E. laxiflorum, *Clos*, is a form with naked ovary.

2. *erythryoxyloides* (Bojer, Hort. Maur. 19, as a species). Leaves all alternate, small, at most 2–3 in. long, thinner in texture than in the last, distinctly petioled. Flowers 3–4 in a lax corymb, shorter than the leaves.

3. *amplexicaule* (E. amplexicaule, *DC.*) inflorescence of var. 1, but leaves closer, oblong, sessile, obscurely cordate-amplexicaul.

4. *amplifolium* (E. amplifolium, *Thouars*; E. macrophyllum, *Poir*; E. longifolium, *Bojer*). A luxuriant sylvestral form, with alternate short-petioled obovate-oblong leaves 6–9 in. long, long-cuneate at the base, and many flowers in lax racemes 3–4 in. long. E. acuminatum, *Bojer*, connects this with var. 1.

5. *verticillatum* (E. verticillatum, *Lam.*; E. monticolum, *Thouars*). A much-branched form of exposed places, with small obtuse rigid subsessile leaves, congested at the nodes, and few corymbose or subumbellate flowers.

6. *Carmichaelii.* Leaves oblong, acute, in 2–6-nate spaced spreading groups, obscurely cordate-amplexicaul; flowers in short sparse racemes. Discovered by Capt. Carmichael.

2. LUDIA, Lam.

Sepals 5–6, oblong, imbricated. Petals 0. Stamens very numerous, hypogynous; filaments long, filiform; anthers minute, oblong, 2-celled. Ovary sessile, ampullæform; placentas 2–4; style produced; stigmas 2–4; ovules numerous. Fruit many-seeded, hard, usually indehiscent. Seeds few, albuminous. DISTRIB. A single species, confined to the Mascaren Isles and Zanguebar.

1. **L. sessiliflora,** *Lam.*; *DC. Prod.* i. 261. An erect glabrous shrub, 8–12 feet high. Leaves alternate, short-petioled, entire, 1–3 in. long, oblong or lanceolate, rigidly coriaceous, green, rather shining, venulose; base cuneate. Flowers 1 or many, sessile or short-pedicelled in the axils of the leaves. Sepals ⅛ in., reflexed. Stamens longer than the sepals, persistent. Style $\frac{1}{12}$ in., straight or oblique, as long as ovary. Fruit globose, ¼–⅓ in. thick, tipped with the persistent style. L. myrtifolia, *Lam.*; *DC. loc. cit.*

MAURITIUS and SEYCHELLES, in woods. RODRIGUEZ, only on the coralline limestone of the south-west and east ends of the island, *Dr. Balfour.* Also Zanguebar and Bourbon.—The Bourbon *L. myrtifolia*, Lam., is identical with the Mauritian plant. *L. heterophylla*, Lam., seems founded on specimens with abnormal leaves, some entire and obovate, others spinose-dentate; and *L. bivalvis*, Clos, in Ann. Sc. Nat. ser. iv. vol. 8, p. 244, on specimens in which the fruit has split open into two valves. *Prunier Marron* (Seych.), like *Flacourtia Ramontchi.*

3. APHLOIA, Benn.

Sepals 5, round, distinct, much imbricated, the two outer smaller and firmer in texture. Petals 0. Stamens very numerous, hypogynous; filaments filiform; anthers minute, oblong, 2-celled. Ovary oblong, with a single parietal placenta and many ovules; stigma sessile, peltate. Fruit an indehiscent berry. Seeds tightly packed; albumen thin.—Shrubs with alternate leaves and small flowers, solitary or fascicled from the branches. DISTRIB. Endemic in the Mascaren isles. Species 2.

1. **A. mauritiana,** *Baker*. A glabrous much-branched erect shrub. Leaves of the young shoots often deeply pinnatifid (var. *laciniata*, Poir), with 1–3 pairs of ascending obtuse lobes; of the mature branches oblong, obtuse or acute, entire or toothed or crenate, 1–4 in. long, subcoriaceous, green, cuneate or rounded at the base. Flowers yellowish, ¼–½ in. broad, on deciduous ascending pedicels ¼–⅓ in. long, from the axils of the leaves, solitary or fascicled in umbels. Sepals and very numerous stamens persistent. Fruit ovoid-ampullæform, ¼–⅓ in. long, crowned by the large peltate stigma, 10–12-seeded. Ludia heterophylla, *Bory Voy.* ii. *t.* 24, *non Lam.*

MAURITIUS, SEYCHELLES, and RODRIGUEZ, frequent in woods. Also Madagascar. *Bois Goyave, Bois Vilian* (Seych.). The following are the principal varieties:—

1. *integrifolia* (Aphloia integrifolia, *Benn.*; Prockia integrifolia, *Willd*). Mature leaves distinctly petioled, subentire, obovate-oblong, 2–4 in. long. Flowers 1–3 together. Inner sepals ¼ in. broad—Mauritius only.

2. *theæformis* (Aphloia theæformis, *Benn.*; Prockia theæformis, *Willd.*; P. serrata, *Poir, non Willd.* Aphloia madagascariensis, var. seychellensis, *Clos*, in Ann. Sc. Nat. ser. iv. vol. 8, 274). Leaves petioled, distinctly crenate or inciso-crenate. Flowers smaller, sometimes densely fascicled. Inner sepals ⅙ in. broad.—Mauritius, Seychelles, and Rodriguez, the commonest form; also Madagascar.

3. *sessilifolia*. Leaves crowded, oblong, rounded at the base, sessile, subamplexicaul. Flowers solitary, as large as in var. 1.—Mauritius, on the top of the Pouce, *Gardner! Horne!*

* *Flacourtia Ramontchi*, L'Herit, Stirp. 59 t. 30–1; Wight, Ic. t. 85; common in the tropics of the old world, is sometimes planted in Mauritius. It may be wild in the Seychelles, where the unarmed form is called (like Ludia) *Prunier Marron*, and the spiny one *Prunier de Madagascar*, as it is said by Mr. Horne to be common in Mahé, Praslin, and Silhouette, on poor rocky soils at an elevation of from sea-level to 800 feet. It is a small tree, sometimes thorny, with slender branches marked with grey dots; oblong, alternate, petioled, crenate, glabrous, moderately firm obtuse or acute leaves 3–4 in. long; copious, minute, diœcious flowers in sessile racemes and corymbs in the axils of the leaves; 4–5 minute obtuse ciliated sepals; no petals; indefinite stamens, and an oblong fruit the size of a cherry, with 6–10 one-seeded cells, and as many sessile radiant stigmas.

ORDER IX. PITTOSPORACEÆ.

Flowers regular, hermaphrodite. Sepals 5, nearly or quite distinct. Petals 5, regular, imbricated, free or connate below. Stamens 5, hypogynous, free, alternate with the petals; filaments filiform; anthers versatile, 2-celled. Ovary usually 1-celled, with usually 2 parietal placentas; style simple; stigma capitate; ovules many. Fruit capsular or baccate. Seeds albuminous; embryo minute.—Erect or climbing shrubs, with alternate exstipulate mostly entire leaves; inflorescence various. DISTRIB. Australian, except *Pittosporum*. Species 90.

1. PITTOSPORUM, Banks.

Sepals lanceolate, slightly connate below. Petals 5, oblanceolate, free or connate below, much exceeding the calyx. Stamens 5; filaments subulate; anthers dehiscing by two slits. Ovary sessile or short-stalked; placentas 2–3; style short; stigma obscurely lobed. Fruit dehiscing readily into 2–3 coriaceous valves. Seeds not winged, imbedded in pulp.—Erect glabrous shrubs with flowers mostly in dense corymbs. DISTRIB. Polynesia to Trop. Africa. Species 50.

1. **P. Senacia,** *Putterl.; Walp. Rep.* i. 250. A much-branched glabrous shrub. Leaves subcoriaceous, obovate-oblong, 2–5 in. long, cuneate at base, acute or obtuse, short-petioled, crowded at the nodes. Flowers in dense terminal corymbs. Petals yellowish, $\frac{1}{4}$–$\frac{1}{3}$ in. long. Ovary short-stalked; placentas 2. Fruit with two spreading round persistent coriaceous valves, $\frac{1}{4}$–$\frac{1}{3}$ in. broad, tipped with the persistent style. P. mauritianum, *Sieber*. Senacia undulata, *Lam.*

MAURITIUS, in the forests of the Pouce, etc. SEYCHELLES, in Mahé and Silhouette, in rocky places at 800–1500 feet above sea-level, *Dr. Wright! Horne*, 434! RODRIGUEZ, tolerably abundant in the valleys, *Balfour!* Also Bourbon. *Senacia lanceolata*, DC., is a mere form with narrower leaves. *Bois de Joli Cœur, Bois Malabar.*

ORDER X. CARYOPHYLLACEÆ.

Sepals mostly 5, in the Mauritian genera free to the base. Petals the same number, often bifid. Stamens as many as the petals, or twice as many, usually hypogynous; filaments filiform; anthers 2-celled, dehiscing longitudinally. Ovary 1-celled, sessile or stalked; placentation free-central; ovules many, campylotropal; styles free or connate. Capsule membranous, splitting variously. Seeds usually many, reniform; embryo curved round a central mass of albumen.—Herbs, with opposite entire rarely stipulate leaves and hermaphrodite flowers in terminal cymes. DISTRIB. Mainly temperate regions of the northern hemisphere. Species 800.

Stamens hypogynous; stipules none.
  Capsule ovoid, with 6 deep valves . . . . * STELLARIA.
  Capsule cylindrical, with 10 minute teeth . . . . 1. CERASTIUM.
Stamens perigynous; stipules bristly . . . . 2. DRYMARIA.

* *Stellaria media*, Vill., the common European chickweed, is established in Mauritius as a weed in some places. It is a tufted annual, with weak stems, marked by a hairy line; opposite short-

petioled ovate leaves; few small white flowers in lax terminal cymes; 3 styles; and an ovoid membranous capsule, splitting to the base into 6 valves.

There is in the Kew herbarium, from the Bentham collection, an indifferent specimen of a Stellaria marked "S. gracilis, Fenzl; Mauritius, Cambessedes, which is probably identical with the Ceylon *S. drymarioides*, Thwaites; Hook. fil. Flor. Brit. Ind. i, 229. It is a weak straggling annual, with the habit of large forms of S. media, fragile ascending slender stems with a few pairs of short-petioled glabrous ovate membranous leaves ½–1 inch long, few flowers in a lax long-peduncled dichotomous cyme, pedicels ⅛–¼ in. long, pilose, deflexed in fruit, oblong-lanceolate persistent membranous sepals under ¼ inch long, and included bifid petals and stamens.

1. CERASTIUM, Linn.

Sepals free. Petals 5, bifid, in the Mauritian plant absent. Stamens usually 10, hypogynous. Ovary 1-celled, many ovuled; styles 5. Capsule cylindrical, rather curved, exceeding the calyx, dehiscing at the apex, with 10 minute equal teeth.—Pilose annual or perennial herbs, with small white flowers in copious strictly dichotomous terminal cymes. DISTRIB. Cosmopolitan; mainly in temperate regions. Species 40–50.

1. **C. glomeratum,** *Thuill.* var. MAURITIANUM, *Baker.* Annual, densely tufted. Stems weak, with dense short spreading hairs. Leaves small, oblong, obtuse. Cymes not so dense as in the common typical European form, which suggested the name *glomeratum;* bracts herbaceous; pedicels shorter than the calyx. Sepals viscose, half as long as the slightly curved capsule, green with a narrow membranous border. Petals 0 in the specimens seen. C. mauritianum, *Bouton MSS.* C. tomentosum, *Bojer, Hort. Maur.* 24, *non Linn.*

MAURITIUS, frequent in the higher parts of the island. Totally different from the European *C. tomentosum*, which has a matted white pubescence, and large white flowers. Cosmopolitan. *Oreille de Souris.*

2. DRYMARIA, Willd.

Sepals 5, free. Petals minute, white, bifid. Stamens usually 5, distinctly perigynous. Ovary 1-celled, with few ovules; styles 3. Capsule oblong, splitting to the base into 3 lanceolate valves.—Dichotomously branched, stipulate annuals, with copious minute flowers, in terminal cymes. DISTRIB. Species 16, all but two American.

1. **D. cordata,** *Willd.*; *DC. Prod.* i. 395. A glabrous annual weed, with much-branched diffuse slender stems. Stipules of several minute bristles. Leaves ovate or round, small, short-stalked, obtuse or cuspidate. Cymes lax, few-flowered. Sepals ⅛ in. long, lanceolate, very acute, green with a narrow white border, exceeding the petals and stamens, as long as the capsule. Holosteum cordatum, *Linn.*

MAURITIUS, in waste places. Everywhere within the tropics.

ORDER XI. HYPERICACEÆ.

Flowers regular, hermaphrodite. Sepals and petals each 5, distinct, alternate, imbricate in bud. Stamens many, united in several hypogynous bundles; anthers versatile, 2-celled. Ovary 3–5-celled; placentation axile; styles 5, distinct; stigmas capitate. Fruit a drupe or septicidal capsule. Seeds exalbuminous.—Herbs or shrubs with exstipulate opposite entire often gland-dotted leaves, and yellow flowers in terminal corymbose panicles. DISTRIB. Cosmopolitan, both temperate and tropical. Species 200.

1. HARONGA, Thouars.

Sepals 5, lanceolate. Petals 5, villose on the face. Hypogynous scales 5, alternate with the petals. Stamens in 5 bundles, opposite the petals. Ovary 5-celled; ovules 2–4 in a cell, axile; styles 5, distinct, long, diverging; stigmas capitate. Fruit a drupe, each carpel with a hard endocarp.—A single species.

1. **H. madagascariensis**, *Choisy*; *DC. Prod.* i. 541. A shrub, 10–15 feet high; branches, leaves beneath, and sepals clothed with pale brown lepidote pubescence. Leaves petioled, oblong, entire, acute, firm, green and glabrous above, rounded at the base, 4–6 long. Flowers very numerous, minute, $\frac{1}{12}$ in. broad, in leafless corymbose terminal panicles. Drupe globose, $\frac{1}{8}$–$\frac{1}{6}$ in. thick. H. paniculata, *Spach*.

MAURITIUS, common in woods. Also Bourbon, Madagascar, and widely spread in Tropical Africa. *Bois Harongue*.

ORDER XII. GUTTIFERÆ.

Flowers regular, hermaphrodite, polygamous or dioicous. Sepals 2, decussate, or 3–6 imbricated. Petals 0–6, contorted or imbricated. Stamens very many, hypogynous, free or connate in bundles, or in one mass; anthers 2-celled, adnate. Ovary 1- or many-celled; ovules 1 or several from the inner angle or base of the cells; style 0 or short; stigmas as many as the cells. Fruit usually an indehiscent berry. Seeds exalbuminous.—Trees or shrubs with abundant yellow or greenish juice, opposite, coriaceous, entire, closely penninerved leaves, and showy white, yellow, or rose-red flowers. DISTRIB. Cosmopolitan in tropics, few African. Species 230.

1. CALOPHYLLUM, Linn.

Flowers polygamous. Sepals passing into petals, 4 biserial, or many multiserial, outer obtuse, convex on the back. Stamens very numerous, free or connate at the base; anthers dehiscing laterally. Ovary 1-celled; ovule 1, erect; style filiform; stigma 1, peltate. Fruit a drupe, with a crustaceous endocarp and 1 large seed with a brown membranous testa, surrounded by spongy cellular tissue; embryo with thick fleshy cotyledons, and a small radicle.—Trees with opposite shining leaves, with close distinct spreading veins, and copious flowers in axillary racemes. DISTRIB. Tropics of both hemispheres, mainly of Old World; species 25.

Fruit globose . . . . 1. C. INOPHYLLUM.
Fruit oblong-rostrate . . . . 2. C. PARVIFLORUM.

1. **C. Inophyllum,** *Linn.*; *Planch. et Triana, Monog. Guttif.* 254. A tall tree, glabrous in all its parts, with a trunk 4 feet in diameter. Leaves oblong or obovate-oblong, usually obtuse, 3–6 in. long, thick, rigid, shining, green, with close, distinct, spreading parallel venules; base cuneate; petiole very short, channelled. Flowers in sparse broad axillary racemes, which are shorter than the leaves; pedicel ½–1⅓ in. long. Sepals obovate, obtuse, ¼–⅓ in. long, decussate, 2 outer firmer. Petals 4–6, whitish, oblong or lanceolate-spathulate, unequal. Fruit globose, an inch thick.

MAURITIUS, common in forests of the sea-shore. SEYCHELLES, *Horne!* RODRIGUEZ, *Bouton! Balfour!* Common in Tropical Asia and Polynesia; also Madagascar, Bourbon, and Comoros, but not continental Africa.—*C. Tacamaha,* Willd; Planch. and Trian, Mon. 258, is a variety with a pear-shaped drupe. *Bois Tatamaka.*

The Indian *C. spectabile* and *spurium,* recorded by Bojer as Mauritian, both belong to another group, characterised by want of petals.

2. **C. parviflorum,** *Bojer.* Habit and infloresence of *C. Inophyllum,* but leaves and flowers much smaller. Leaves 2–3 in. long, very rigid, obovate with a cuneate base and very short petiole. Sepals obovate, under ¼ in. long, broadly imbricated in bud. Petals 4, oblanceolate, obtuse, rather longer than the sepals. Fruit oblong, ¾ in. long, with a very distinct beak. C. spurium, *Bojer, Hort. Maur.* 52, *non Choisy.*

MAURITIUS, in the forests of Grandport and Savanne. Endemic. *Tatamaka à petites feuilles.*

ORDER XIII. TERNSTRŒMIACEÆ.

Flowers regular, hermaphrodite, usually pentamerous. Sepals imbricated, free or shortly connate. Petals hypogynous, imbricated. Stamens indefinite, hypogynous, free or connate; anthers 2-celled, basifixed, dehiscing laterally. Ovary free, 2- or many-celled; placentation axile; ovules 1, 2, or many in a cell; styles as many as the cells of the ovary; stigmas capitate. Fruit a berry or capsule, dehiscing variously. Seeds few or many; albumen mostly none or scanty.—Shrubs or trees; leaves usually alternate, exstipulate; the flowers lateral or terminal. DISTRIB. Round the world in the tropics, few African. Species 300.

1. MEDUSAGYNE, Baker.

Sepals 5, small, round, shortly joined at the base, persistent, reflexing. Petals 5, oblong, obtuse, alternate with the sepals, imbricated and contorted in bud. Stamens hypogynous, indefinite; filaments free, filiform, shorter than the petals; anthers small, round-oblong, basifixed. Ovary depresso-globose, many-(17–24)-celled; ovules 2, fixed at the middle of the placenta, one ascending, the other pendulous; styles as many as the cells; stigmas capitate. Fruit not seen. The only species.

1. **M. oppositifolia,** *Baker*. A wide-spreading erect shrub, 3–6 feet high, glabrous in all its parts. Leaves opposite, short-petioled, oblong, 1½–2 in. long, obtuse or emarginate, rigidly coriaceous, obscurely toothed, shining and minutely venulose above. Flowers in lax deltoid terminal panicles, 1½–2 in. long, which scarcely overtop the leaves; pedicels slender, curved, ⅓–¾ in. long, articulated at the base. Sepals subcoriaceous, 1/12 in. long. Petals oblong, rose-red, obtuse, ¼ in. long. Stamens and styles included, the latter as long as the ovary, ascending or rather curved.

SEYCHELLES, in exposed places in Mahé, at an elevation of 1800 feet, *Horne*, 587! Endemic.

ORDER XIV. DIPTEROCARPEÆ.

Flowers regular, hermaphrodite. Sepals 5, persistent, 2 or more usually growing out very much to accompany the fruit. Petals 5, contorted. Stamens very various in number and position, the two lobes often unequal and the connective protruded. Ovary 3-celled; ovules 2 in a cell; style entire or nearly so. Fruit dry, indehiscent, or at last splitting into valves. Seed thick, exalbuminous.—Shrubs or trees, with alternate simple stipulate coriaceous leaves, the fragrant flowers in axillary and terminal panicles. DISTRIB. Nearly all east tropical Asian; 3 known in tropical Africa. Species nearly 200.

This order is represented in the Seychelles by a tree of which we have neither flowers nor fruit, but which in habit and leaf comes very near to *Vateria ceylanica*. Wight Ill. i. 88, a native of Ceylon. It has short terete branches, marked all round by the scars of the fallen stipules, terete petioles 2–3 inches long, obovate-oblong obtuse or cuspidate glabrous coriaceous leaves 6–8 in. long, 4–5 inches broad at the middle, broadly rounded at the base, with about 20 strongly marked erecto-patent primary veins. The genus *Vateria* is marked in the order by a calyx, the lobes of which become reflexed, and do not augment as the fruit developes and by its numerous stamens. The following is Mr. Horne's note upon the plant. "A large lofty-growing tree, which in sheltered ravines frequently attains a height of from 80 to 100 feet; trunk from 4 to 6 feet in diameter, and often 40 to 60 feet to the first branch. When wounded, the sap forms an exceedingly inflammable resin, which was formerly used for incense. The tree yields a valuable timber, like that of Sal. in grain and colour. The tree is now becoming scarce, and large ones are only found near Port Glean, in very inaccessible parts of the forest, at elevations of 600 to 1000 feet above sea-level.

ORDER XV. MALVACEÆ.

Flowers regular, hermaphrodite. Calyx mostly subtended by an epicalyx of few or many bracts. Sepals 5, connate downwards, valvate in æstivation. Petals 5, hypogynous, adnate at the base to the staminal column, obtuse, twisted in æstivation. Stamens numerous, united in a long tube, which either bears anthers or is only toothed at the tip; anthers reniform, 1-celled. Ovary many-celled, the carpels in a single whorl round the beaked centre of the torus;

ovules 1 or few in a cell; style usually branched at the top; stigmas capitate or decurrent on the style-branches, carpels dry, usually separating from each other and the axis when ripe. Seeds reniform; albumen mostly scanty.—Herbs or shrubs or trees; leaves alternate, stipulate, usually broad, entire or lobed; flowers showy, solitary, or fascicled in the axils of the leaves. DISTRIB. Cosmopolitan. Species 700.

Staminal column bearing stalked anthers at the top.
  Epicalyx 3-cleft; ovule 1, erect; stigma decurrent . . * MALVA.
  Epicalyx 3-cleft; ovule 1, erect; stigma capitate . . . 1. MALVASTRUM.
  Epicalyx 0; ovule 1, pendulous; stigma capitate . . . 2. SIDA.
  Epicalyx 0; ovules many; stigma capitate . . . . . 3. ABUTILON.
Staminal column merely toothed at the top.
  Style-branches distinct.
    Carpels 5; ovules solitary.
      Flowers aggregated in heads with a common involucre . . . . * MALACHRA.
      No involucre; carpels muricated on back . . . . 4. URENA.
      No involucre; carpels only hairy on back . . . . 5. PAVONIA.
    Carpels many; ovules several . . . . 6. HIBISCUS.
  Style-branches united.
    Seeds pilose only . . . . 7. THESPESIA.
    Seeds wrapped in thick cotton . . . . * GOSSYPIUM.

* *Malva sylvestris*, L., the common European Mallow, is established in Mauritius at Cannonier point. It is a much-branched biennial, with palmately lobed reniform leaves, copious large purple flowers, calyx subtended by 3 leafy bracteoles, 10 rugose awnless uniserial glabrous 1-seeded carpels and styles stigmatic for some distance down the inner side. *Mauve de France.*

1. MALVASTRUM, A. Gray.

Bracteoles 3, linear, minute. Calyx 5-fid; teeth deltoid. Staminal column without any barren teeth. Ovary 5–10-celled; ovules solitary, erect; style filiform, with a capitate stigma. Carpels uniserial, separating when ripe from the axis, small, hard; apex muticous or beaked.—Herbs or undershrubs, with petioled entire or cut leaves and flowers often large and showy. DISTRIB. Species 60, mostly Cape and American, 2 widely-spread tropical weeds.

1. **M. tricuspidatum,** *A. Gray, Pl. Fendl.* 16. An erect branching herb, with copious adpressed bristly hairs. Leaves distant, petioled, ovate-rhomboid, toothed, both sides bristly; base deltoid, entire. Flowers short-peduncled, fascicled in the axils of the leaves. Corolla yellow, ½ in. long. Calyx-teeth deltoid, bristly on the back and edge. Carpels 10, reniform, with an awn at the tip and centre, and many bristles between. Malva borbonica, *Willd.*; *DC. Prod.* i. 430. Sida carpinoides, *DC. Prod.* i. 461.

MAURITIUS, roadsides at Port Louis, etc. FLAT ISLAND, *Horne!* RODRIGUEZ, abundant all over the island, *Balfour.* Cosmopolitan in the tropics. *Mauve sauvage, Herbe à balais.*

2. SIDA, Linn.

Bracteoles 0. Calyx 5-toothed to middle; lobes deltoid. Staminal column without any barren teeth. Ovary 5–10 celled; ovules solitary, pendulous; style filiform, with a capitate stigma. Carpels small, hard, dry, uniserial, separating from the axis when ripe, usually awned.—Herbs or undershrubs with entire leaves and small yellowish or white flowers, solitary or fascicled in the axils of the leaves. Distrib. Species 80, mostly American, several universal tropical weeds.

Leaves cordate about as broad as long.
  Leaves thick; pedicels short . . . . 1. S. cordifolia.
  Leaves thin, very small; pedicels short . . . . 2. S. diffusa.
  Leaves thin; pedicels long.
    Prostrate; carpels muticous . . . . 3. S. humilis.
    Erect; carpels awned . . . . 4. S. glutinosa.
Leaves several times longer than broad.
  Leaves large, thin; both sides green . . . . 5. S. carpinifolia.
  Leaves firmer, small, grey beneath.
    Leaves rounded at the base . . . . 6. S. spinosa.
    Leaves cuneate at the base . . . . 7. S. rhombifolia.

1. **S. cordifolia,** *Linn.; DC. Prod.* i. 464. A biennial shrubby herb softly pilose all over. Leaves cordate, round or ovate, 1–2 in. long, thick, soft, crenate, obtuse; petiole 1–1½ in. long, with dense spreading hairs. Pedicels short. Calyx thick, softly pilose. Carpels 8–10, with rugose borders, tipped with 2 long awns, ciliated with deflexed hairs. S. rotundifolia and borbonica, *Cav.* S. altheifolia, *Sw.* S. waltheriæfolia and ciliosa, *Bojer.*

Mauritius, Rodriguez, and Seychelles, common. A universal tropical weed. *Mauve à feuilles veloutées.*

2. **S. diffusa,** *H.B.K.; DC. Prod.* i. 463. Stems densely tufted, wiry, wide-trailing, thinly pilose upwards. Leaves round, obtuse, slightly cordate, thin, inciso-crenate, ¼ in. each way, greenish, with a thin coating of stellate hairs beneath; stipules setaceous; petiole $\frac{1}{12}$ in. long. Flowers solitary from the axils, on pedicels about as long as the leaves. Calyx ⅛ in. deep, thinly pilose; teeth deltoid, as long as the tube. Petals bright yellow, ¼ in. deep. Carpels 5, glabrescent, truncate at the top, obovoid-trigonous, not so long as the calyx.

Seychelles, amongst grass on the shores of Praslin and Silhouette, *Horne,* 433! Trop. America and Polynesia.

3. **S. humilis,** *Willd.; DC. Prod.* i. 463. A biennial, with trailing slender thinly-bristly branches. Leaves round-cordate, cuspidate, thin, green on both sides, sparsely hairy, inciso-crenate, 1–2 in. long and broad; petiole ½ in. long, clothed with fine spreading hairs. Pedicels long. Upper leaves of the branches often much reduced. Calyx-teeth green, thin, sparsely bristly. Carpels 5, small, not awned, much shorter than the calyx, not furrowed down the back. S. unilocularis, *L'Hérit. Stirp. t.* 56. S. calycina, *Cav.*

MAURITIUS; Champ de Mars, Cannonier Point, and other places near Port Louis. Cosmopolitan in tropics. *S. morifolia*, Cav. is a form with carpels slightly mucronate; and *S. veronicæfolia*, Lam., with carpels tipped with two distinct awns.

4. **S. glutinosa,** *Cav.; DC. Prod.* i. 464. An erect shrubby biennial, with slender puberulous branches. Leaves cordate-round, cuspidate, thin, green on both surfaces, inciso-crenate, puberulent, 1–3 in. long and broad; petiole 1–3 in. Pedicels long; the upper flowers of the branches close and their bract-leaves minute. Calyx-teeth thin, green, minutely downy. Carpels 5, glabrous, as long as the calyx, each with one short awn.

MAURITIUS; roadsides at Port Louis, Mahébourg, Réduit, etc. Also Bourbon.

5. **S. carpinifolia,** *Linn. fil.; DC. Prod.* i. 460. A copiously-branched erect shrubby nearly glabrous biennial. Leaves thin, green on both sides, lanceolate or oblong-lanceolate, acute, rounded at the base, 3–4 in. long, inciso-crenate; petiole very short. Flowers few or many, crowded in the axils of the leaves. Calyx-teeth thin, green, glabrous. Capels 5–10, with two long awns, naked, equalling or exceeding the calyx. *Jacq. Ic. t.* 135. S. stipulata, *Cav.*

MAURITIUS, SEYCHELLES and RODRIGUEZ. Plentiful everywhere in the tropics. FLAT ISLAND, *Horne!* *S. acuta*, Burm. is the form with lanceolate leaves. *Herbe à paniers.*

6. **S. spinosa,** *Linn.; DC. Prod.* i. 460. A much-branched biennial, with leaves beneath and branches hoary. Leaves oblong, firm, crenate, rounded at the base, obtuse or subacute, 1–1½ in. long, always broadest below the middle; petiole ½–1 in. long, with sometimes a hard tubercle on each side at the base. Pedicels short. Calyx-teeth grey, hoary or shortly pilose. Carpels 5–10, pilose, distinctly awned, as long as the calyx. S. alba and alnifolia, *Linn.* S. frutescens, *Cav.*

MAURITIUS, RODRIGUEZ, and SEYCHELLES, common. Everywhere in the tropics. *S. angustifolia*, Lam., is a form with narrow leaves, and *S. pusilla*, Cav., a decumbent form of the coast sandhills with smaller flowers and very small leaves ¼–½ in. long, densely tomentose beneath.

7. **S. rhombifolia,** *Linn.; DC. Prod.* i. 462. A much-branched erect biennial, with shrubby branches, hoary upwards. Leaves firm, rhomboid-lanceolate, inciso-crenate except at the base, green above, hoary beneath, obtuse or subacute, 1–2 in. long; petiole very short. Pedicels ½–1 in. long. Calyx-teeth thin, nearly naked. Carpels 5–10, glabrous, distinctly awned, as long as the calyx. S. rhomboidea, *Roxb.*; *Bojer, Hort. Maur.* 33.

MAURITIUS, by roadsides, frequent. Everywhere in the tropics. *S. retusa*, Linn., is a variety with obovate-oblong leaves, cuneate and entire below the middle, and *S. microphylla*, Cav., a form with small leaves more hoary beneath. *Herbe à balais, herbe balié, faux thé.*

8. ABUTILON, Gærtn.

Epicalyx 0. Calyx with 5 deltoid teeth. Staminal column bearing anthers at the top. Cells of ovary many, uniserial, containing several ovules; styles as many as carpels; stigmas capitate. Ripe carpels membranous, usually beaked, finally breaking away from the axis. Seeds usually 3 in each carpel.—Robust biennials or perennials with round-cordate leaves and middle-sized yellow axillary flowers. DISTRIB. Everywhere in warmer regions. Species 70.

1. **A. indicum,** *G. Don. Gen. Syst.* i. 504. A tall erect branching biennial, with stems and leaves beneath grey-hoary, not otherwise pilose. Leaves long-petioled, thin, round-cordate, cuspidate, 2–4 in. long, irregularly inciso-repand. Flowers 1 or few, long-peduncled, in the leaf-axils. Calyx small, tomentose. Corolla ½ in. long. Carpels about 20, densely tomentose at first, when old naked dehiscing, with short diverging points, 3–4 times the length of the calyx. Sida indica, *Linn.* S. mauritiana, *Jacq. Ic. t.* 137. Abutilon mauritianum, *G. Don.* Sida populifolia, *Lam.*

MAURITIUS, SEYCHELLES, and RODRIGUEZ, common in waste ground. Native of old world, common in tropical Asia, now spread in both hemispheres. *Mauve du pays.*

* Two other common tropical species are now naturalised in Mauritius near Port Louis; *A. asiaticum*, G. Don, distinguished by its larger flowers (2 inches broad when expanded) and hispid carpels, with erect points scarcely exceeding the calyx; and *A. graveolens*, W. and A., with abundant loose hairs, larger flowers, and awnless pilose carpels, scarcely exceeding the calyx. The latter has been confounded in Mauritius with *Sida glutinosa*, Cav. It was gathered by Dr. Balfour in Rodriguez at Oyster Bay.

* *Malachra capitata*, Linn. (mistaken by Bojer for *Pavonia urens*), a native of tropical America, now widely spread in the old world, is established in Mauritius about Port Louis, even in some of the streets. It is a strong hispid biennial, with large palmately-lobed leaves, very numerous small yellow flowers in dense heads subtended by a general involucre, calyx very hispid, five 1-seeded carpels breaking away from the axis when mature, capitate stigmas, and a staminal column truncate at the tip. *Mauve à fleurs jaunes.*

4. URENA, Linn.

Epicalyx of 5 large bracteoles. Calyx 5-toothed. Staminal column not bearing anthers at its top. Ovary 5-celled; ovules solitary, ascending; styles two to each carpel; stigmas capitate. Ripe carpels dry, indehiscent, breaking away from the axis, covered on the back with firm hooked bristles.—Shrubby herbs, with small pink flowers, fascicled in the axils of broad leaves. DISTRIB. Everywhere in the tropics. Species 4–5.

1. **U. lobata,** *Linn.; DC. Prod.* i. 441. A strong much-branched erect shrubby herb, with shortly-pilose young branches. Leaves short-petioled, 3–4 in. broad and long, firm, pale green and finely pilose beneath, inciso-crenate, shallowly palmately 3–5-lobed in the upper half. Pedicels very short; bracteoles linear, exceeding the calyx.

Corolla ½–¾ in. long. Carpels exceeding the bracteoles, armed all over the back with hard prickles. U. tricuspis, *Cav. Diss. t.* 183, *fig.* 1. U. Sieberi, *Colla, Hort. Rip. t.* 39.

MAURITIUS, RODRIGUEZ, and SEYCHELLES, common on borders of forests, from the sea-level to the hill-tops. Cosmopolitan in tropics. *U. sinuata*, Linn. (*U. multifida*, Cav. Diss. t. 184, fig. 2), is a variety with leaves lobed below the middle, and each lobe again pinnatifid. *Herbe à paniers.*

5. PAVONIA, Cav.

Epicalyx of 8–10 linear bracteoles. Calyx 5-lobed. Staminal column not bearing anthers at the top. Ovary 5-celled; ovules solitary, erect; styles 10; stigmas capitate. Carpels separating from the axis when mature, indehiscent, not muricated.—Herbs or shrubs, with lobed leaves and small or middle-sized flowers, various in colour. DISTRIB. Species 60, mostly American.

1. **P. urens,** *Cav. Diss.* iii. *t.* 49, *fig.* 1. A robust biennial, with stems clothed densely with spreading hairs. Leaves long-petioled, densely pilose on both surfaces, 3–4 in. broad, palmately many-lobed; lobes incised. Flowers in dense fascicles, subsessile in the axils of the leaves. Calyx densely hispid. Corolla pinkish, 1 in. long. Carpels 5, each with 3 retrorsely ciliated awns. *Jacq. Ic. t.* 552.

Reported by De Candolle and others from MAURITIUS, but unknown to Bojer and Ayres. We possess wild Bourbon specimens, and have therefore retained it. Bojer's plant so called is *Malachra capitata*.

* *P. zeylanica*, Willd. (Hibiscus zeylanicus, *Linn.*), widely spread in the tropics of old world, is naturalised on the Ile aux Tonneliers. It is a low densely viscoso-pilose biennial, with rigid branches, small long-petioled 3–5-lobed leaves, small pinkish corolla, an epicalyx of 8–10 linear gland-ciliated bracteoles and 5 small hard reniform muticous carpels.

6. HIBISCUS, Linn.

Bracteoles 5 or more, free or connate. Calyx 5-fid, or in § *Abelmoschus* spathaceous, toothed at the top only, and often slit off at the base when the flower opens. Ovary 5- or in § *Paritium* incompletely 10-celled; ovules 3 or more in a cell; styles 5; stigmas capitate. Staminal column only toothed at the top. Ripe carpels dehiscing loculicidally, not breaking away from the axis. Seeds naked or hairy.—Herbs or trees, with broad often lobed leaves and large showy flowers. DISTRIB. Cosmopolitan in the tropics. Species 150, many American.

Section 1. EUHIBISCUS. Calyx 5-cleft, persistent. Bracteoles free or connate at the base only. Stems not prickly.

Shrubby, glabrous.

Leaves entire or toothed, not lobed . . . . 1. H. LILIIFLORUS.

Leaves cordate, deeply lobed . . . . 2. H. COLUMNARIS.

Pilose annuals or biennials.
  Bracteoles 5–6, subulate . . . . 3. H. HORNEI.
  Bracteoles 8–10, linear-spathulate . . . . . . 4. H. PANDURÆFORMIS.
Section 2, PARITIUM. Calyx 5-cleft, persistent. Capsule 10-celled. Leaves entire. Bracteoles connate into a toothed cup.
  The only species . . . . 5. H. TILIACEUS.
Section 3, FURCARIA. Calyx 5-cleft, persistent. Bracteoles narrow, free, leafy. Stems with hooked prickles.
  Prostrate; flowers small . . . . • H. SURATTENSIS.
  Erect; flowers large . . . . • H. RADIATUS.
Section 4, ABELMOSCHUS. Annuals with a deciduous spathaceous calyx, toothed at the tip only.
  Bracteoles 6–12, linear . . . . • H. ABELMOSCHUS.
  Bracteoles 5, large, lanceolate.
    Branches scabrous with hard tubercles; leaf-lobes broad . . . . • H. FICULNEUS.
    Branches naked or faintly bristly; leaf-lobes long, linear . . . . • H. MANIHOT.

1. **H. liliiflorus,** *Cav.; DC. Prod.* i. 446. A glabrous shrub. Leaves distinctly petioled, ovate, 2–4 in. long, entire or crenate, or young deeply trifid, obtuse or acute, firm, rounded at the base. Flowers few, long-peduncled, solitary from the axils of the upper leaves; bracteoles 5, linear, connate at the very base. Sepals lanceolate, 1–1½ in. long, connate above the middle. Corolla large, funnel-shaped, bright red. Stamens as long as the corolla or rather exserted. Carpels dry, firm, as long as the calyx. H. fragilis, *DC. Prod.* i. 446. H. Genevii, *Bojer; Bot. Mag. t.* 3144.

MAURITIUS, in hilly woods of Pouce, Grand Bassin, etc. RODRIGUEZ, not common, *Balfour! Bouton!* SEYCHELLES, in several places in Mahé, but perhaps introduced, *Horne*, 428! Also Bourbon. *Var. hybridus*, Bot. Mag. t. 2891, is a form raised from this, fertilised by pollen of the East Indian *H. mutabilis. Mandrinette*, or *Augerine.*

2. **H. columnaris**, *Cav.; DC. Prod.* i. 448. A glabrous shrub. Leaves long-petioled, round-cordate, firm, green, 3–4 in. broad, acute, shallowly 3-lobed in the upper half; lobes repand. Pedicels short, few, solitary from the axils of upper leaves; bracteoles 5, linear, distinct. Sepals lanceolate, leathery, naked, connate in the upper third. Corolla large, (2–3 in. long), yellow, with a dark eye, silky on the outside. Stamens exserted.

MAURITIUS, in ravines of the Pouce, *Bojer*. Also Bourbon.

3. **H. Hornei**, *Baker*. A low branched annual, with stems clothed with long spreading pungent hairs. Leaves distinctly petioled, small, round-cordate, shallowly 5-lobed, with a lanceolate or deltoid point, inciso-crenate, nearly glabrous above, tomentose beneath. Flowers few, distant, solitary, long-peduncled; bracteoles 5 to 6, small, free, subulate, ciliated. Calyx ½ in. deep, densely pilose; teeth lanceolate, connate halfway up. Corolla 1–1½ in. long, white with a purple eye. Carpels as long as calyx, densely pilose. Seeds naked, tubercled.

SEYCHELLES, in a maize-field in Ile Praslin, *Horne*, 356! 429! Endemic. Near the East Indian *H. vitifolius*, Linn.

4. **H. panduræformis**, *Burm. Fl. Ind. t.* 47, *fig.* 2. A robust, erect biennial, with stems clothed with dense spreading hairs. Leaves petioled, round-cordate, large, shallowly 5-lobed, irregularly crenate, pilose above, tomentose beneath. Bracteoles 8 to 10, linear-spathulate, connate at the very base. Sepals lanceolate, connate in the lower third. Corolla 1½–2 in. long, yellow or purple, hairy outside. Carpels densely pilose, as long as the calyx. H. tubulosus, *Cav.*; *DC. Prod.* i. 447.

MAURITIUS, by roadsides near Port Louis. Australia to tropical Africa.

5. **H. tiliaceus**, *Linn.*; *DC. Prod.* i. 454. A tree, much branched, with branches and leaves beneath hoary. Leaves long-petioled, firm, round-cuspidate, entire, deeply cordate, 4–6 in. long and broad. Flowers many, on short erecto-patent peduncles. Epicalyx a deep persistent cup, with 8–10 lanceolate teeth. Sepals lanceolate, 1 in. long, firm, hoary. Corolla large, bright orange, with a dark eye. Carpels triquetrous, acute, as long as the sepals, each with a central dissepiment and 3 naked reniform seeds in each cell. Paritium tiliaceum. *Wight. Ic. t.* 7.

Coast marshes, MAURITIUS, especially at the mouth of the Petite Rivière Noire.. SEYCHELLES, common in all the islands. RODRIGUEZ. Everywhere in the tropics. *Vau* or *Vaur* (Seych).

* *H. radiatus*, Willd. (H. Lindleyi, *Wall. Pl. Asiat. Rar. t.* 4; *Bot. Reg. t.* 1395), a native of tropical Asia, was introduced by Mr. Telfair, in 1831, and became naturalized. It is a robust erect biennial with branches and petioles armed with small hooked prickles, long-petioled glabrous leaves with 5 deep lanceolate toothed palmate lobes, many short-stalked axillary flowers, 8–10 long leafy linear bristle-ciliated sometimes pinnate bracteoles, 3-nerved lanceolate acuminate bristly sepals, large corolla purple or yellow with a purple eye, and densely hispid carpels.

* *H. surattensis* Linn.; D.C. Prod. i. 449, universal in the tropics of the Old World, is naturalised in Mauritius, at Bois Rouge, in waste ground, and is not uncommon in the Seychelles. It is a trailing branched biennial, with nearly glabrous stems, armed, as are the petioles, with copious small hooked prickles, long-petioled glabrous leaves with 3–5 deep toothed palmate lobes, many peduncled solitary axillary flowers, 10 long narrow sometimes pinnate leafy bracteoles, long-pointed bristly 3-nerved sepals, corolla 1 in. long, yellow, with a purple eye, and carpels thinly bristly.

* *H. Abelmoschus*, Linn.; D.C. Prod. i. 252. (Abelmoschus moschatus, *Moench*), universally cultivated in the tropics, its origin not clearly known, is established in Mauritius, at Grandport, *Dr. Ayres*. It is a tall robust annual, with large long-petioled palmate 5–7-lobed thin pilose leaves, 6–12 linear bristle-ciliated bracteoles, calyx oblong minutely toothed at the top, corolla 2–3 in. long, deep yellow with a crimson eye, and pilose narrow-triquetrous carpels 2–3 in. long.

* *H. ficulneus*, Linn. D.C. Prod. i. 448, (Lagunea aculeata, *Cav.*), a native of India, is established in Mauritius, in marshy ground at Pamplemousses. It is a robust erect annual, with branches scabrous with hard tubercles, not otherwise pilose, long-petioled glabrous round-cordate leaves with 5 deltoid or oblong lobes, 5 lanceolate caducous bracteoles, pilose sepals, connate nearly througnout, large white corolla with a rosy eye, and carpels 1½ in. loug, pilose, triquetrous, with a beak.

* *H. Manihot*, Linn.; D.C. Prod. i. 448, a native of China, is naturalised in Mauritius, round Mont Plaisir. It is a tall robust annual, with thinly bristly stems, long-petioled cordate leaves, glabrous, with 5–7 deep linear lobes, 5–6 large oblong-lanceolate bristly persistent bracteoles, a spathaceous calyx faintly toothed at the top, petals obovate, 2–3 in. long and broad, yellow, with a purple eye, and beaked hairy narrow triquetrous carpels 1½ in. long.

7. THESPESIA, Corr.

Epicalyx of 5 lanceolate deciduous bracteoles. Calyx large, nearly entire. Staminal column only toothed at top. Ovary 5-celled; ovules few in a cell; styles clavate, stigmas connate. Fruit hard, dry, obscurely 5-angled indehiscent. Seed obovoid; cotyledons crumpled; albumen thin.—Trees or shrubs, with entire or lobed leaves, and large showy yellow flowers. DISTRIB. Tropics of Old World. Species 6.

1. **T. populnea**, *Corr.; DC. Prod.* i. 456. A shrub or low tree, with branches, leaves below, calyx and outside of corolla clothed with minute brownish lepidote scales, not otherwise pilose. Leaves long-petioled, large, firm, entire, round, deeply cordate. Flowers many, solitary, axillary, peduncled. Petals obovate, 2–3 in. long and broad, yellow, with a purple spot. Fruit 1 in. or more thick, umbilicate at the apex. Hibiscus populneus, *Linn.*

Moist places near the sea-coast. SEYCHELLES, *Pervillé!* MAURITIUS, Ile aux Tonneliers, *Bojer;* about Port Louis, *Dr. Ayres.* Regarded by Bojer as introduced. RODRIGUEZ, all round the island. *Balfour!* Polynesia to tropical Africa. *Porcher.*

* *Gossypium barbadense*, Linn. (G. vitifolium, *Lam.*) is reported by Dr. Ayres as naturalised on Flat Island. It is the commonly-cultivated fruticose species, and may be known from *G. arboreum* by the cotton separating readily from the seeds. In the Mauritius it is called *Cotonier des Seychelles.* Both this and *G. herbaceum*, Linn, are established in Rodriguez, covering the Pierrot almost entirely.

Eriodendron anfractuosum, *DC.* (*Ouat*) is in Dr. Balfour's Rodriguez herbarium, from two trees seen near the station of the oldest inhabitants. It is a native of the West Indies, and commonly planted in Mauritius and through the tropical zone of the Old World.

ORDER XVI. STERCULIACEÆ.

Flowers regular, usually hermaphrodite. Sepals 5, lanceolate, united at the base, valvate in æstivation. Petals 5, hypogynous; æstivation twisted or imbricated. Stamens monadelphous; staminodes present or absent; anthers 2-celled, dehiscing longitudinally. Ovary 5- or, in *Waltheria*, 1-celled; ovules 1 or many; styles as many as the cells, free or joined downwards. Fruit indehiscent or dehiscing longitudinally; placentation axile. Seeds usually albuminous.—Herbs or trees with alternate simple stipulate petioled leaves and varied inflorescence. DISTRIB. Round the world in the tropics. Species 500–600.

Trees or shrubs.
  Staminodes 0.
    Stamens 5 . . . . 1. HERITIERA.
    Stamens 20 . . . . 2. ASTIRIA.
  Staminodes present.
    Sepals 5.
      Flowers in dense umbels or cymes; ovules two in a cell 3. DOMBEYA.
      Flowers 2–3 together axillary; ovules many in a cell 4. TROCHETIA.
    Sepals 2–3 . . . . * GUAZUMA.
Herbs.
  Cells of capsule and styles 5 . . . . 5. MELOCHIA.
  Cells of capsule and styles 1 . . . . 6. WALTHERIA.

1. HERITIERA, Ait.

Flowers monoicous. Calyx campanulate, 5-toothed. Petals 0. Column of stamens cylindrical, shorter than the calyx, bearing 5 adnate anthers in a ring round its top. Carpels 5, nearly free; ovules solitary; style short, with 5 thickened stigmas. Fruit woody, indehiscent, keeled down the back. Seed exalbuminous; cotyledons very thick—Trees with undivided leaves, lepidote beneath and copious small pilose flowers in axillary panicles. DISTRIB. Tropics of Old World on shores. Species 3.

1. **H. littoralis,** *Ait; DC. Prod.* i. 484. A tree 50–60 feet high, with lepidote branches. Leaves short-petioled, oblong, entire, subcoriaceous, penninerved, acute, or subobtuse, ½–1 ft. long, clothed with persistent brownish-white lepidote scales beneath. Flowers in copious axillary panicles, much shorter than the leaves, with slender branches clothed with brown pubescence. Calyx ⅛ in. deep; teeth deltoid, as long as the tube. Fruit hard, woody, glabrous, oblong, pointed, 2–3 in. long.

SEYCHELLES, common in Mahé and Silhouette, in marshy ground, *Horne,* 421! Polynesia to East Africa. *Bois de Table.*

2. ASTIRIA, Lindl.

Epicalyx of 3 reflexed deciduous bracteoles. Calyx divided nearly to the base into 5 lanceolate segments. Petals 5, obovate, clawed, contorted, marcescent. Staminal cup short, bearing 20 fertile anthers and no staminodes. Ovary 5-celled; ovules 2 in each cell; styles 5, free, clavate. Capsule loculicidal, with one seed in each cell.—A single endemic species, with the habit of *Dombeya*.

1. **A. rosea,** *Lindl. Bot. Reg*, 1844, *t*. 49. A shrub 12–15 feet high, with thick quadrangular branches. Leaves round, deeply cordate, 6–9 in. long and broad, subentire, obscurely 3-lobed, firm, thin, pubescent beneath; tip deltoid; petiole 3–5 in. long, rough with short ferruginous bristly hairs, like the peduncles, pedicels, and sepals. Peduncles as long as petioles. Inflorescence a bifid cyme; pedicels once or twice the length of calyx, very rough, as are the lanceolate sepals. Petals ½ in. long, obovate, rather exceeding the sepals. Styles free to the base. Ovary densely clothed with brown bristly hairs. Dombeya astrapæoides, *Bojer, Hort. Maur.* 40.

MAURITIUS, in forests of Grand Bassin and Trou aux Cerfs, *Bojer; Bouton!* Endemic.

3. DOMBEYA, Cav.

Epicalyx unilateral, of 3 unequal bracteoles. Calyx divided nearly to base into 5 lanceolate segments. Petals 5, obversely deltoid, persisting and becoming scariose. Staminal column bearing 5 ligulate staminodes, with usually 3 fertile anthers between each; anthers 2-celled. Ovary 5-celled; ovules 2, ascending; styles 5, free or connate downwards. Capsule 5-lobed, hard, 5-celled, umbilicate at the apex.—Shrubs with alternate petioled leaves and flowers in peduncled axillary umbels or bifid cymes. DISTRIB. Species 20–25. Confined to continental Africa and the Mascaren Isles.

Flowers in bifid cymes.
- Corolla large . . . . 1. D. ACUTANGULA.
- Corolla small. Peduncles naked . . . . 2. D. POPULNEA.
- Corolla small. Peduncles tomentose . . . . 3. D. FERRUGINEA.

Flowers in simple umbels.
- Corolla large. Leaves smooth above . . . . 4. D. UMBELLATA.
- Corolla small. Leaves scabrous above . . . . 5. D. PUNCTATA.

1. **D. acutangula,** *Cav.; DC. Prod.* i. 498. A low tree or shrub, with leaves crowded at the end of the branches Leaves thin, round-cordate, subglabrous, 3–4 in. broad, with 3–5 incised shallow broad or deep narrow palmate lobes; petiole 2–3 in. long, glabrous or pilose. Peduncles as long as the petioles, densely pilose as are the pedicels, bracts, and calyx. Inflorescence a bifid cyme; pedicels shorter or longer than calyx; bracteoles large, ovate, caducous. Sepals ¼–⅓ in. long, reflexed when the flower opens. Petals ½ in. long, oblique-obovate, white or reddish. Stamens 18, shorter than the ligulate staminodes. Ovary densely tomentose; styles free at the top only.

MAURITIUS, frequent on the Pouce. RODRIGUEZ, in the valley of the Rivière de l'Est, *Balfour!* Also Bourbon. *D. palmata*, Cav., Wall. Pl. Asiat. Rar. t. 235, is only a shade-loving form of the same species, with less pubescence and deeper narrower leaf-lobes. *D. angulata*, Cav., DC. Prod. i. 498, appears to be founded on specimens in which the forking of the inflorescence is obliterated; and *D. tiliæfolia*, Cav. Diss. tab. 39, fig. 2, to be same as *D. cordifolia*, DC. (D. angulata, Bot. Mag. t. 2905), and to be a variety in which the leaves are not at all lobed, running into *palmata* by insensible transitions.

2. **D. populnea,** *Baker*. A tree 20–25 feet high, glabrous throughout, with slender terete branches. Leaves thin, round-cordate, acute or acuminate, 3–4 in. long, shallowly inciso-crenate; petiole slender, as long as the blade. Peduncles as long as the petioles; pedicels 1–3 times length of calyx; bracteoles minute, deltoid, naked, persistent. Sepals $\frac{1}{4}$ inch long, lanceolate, reflexed. Petals $\frac{1}{4}$–$\frac{1}{3}$ in. long, oblanceolate or obversely deltoid. Anthers 3–4 between each staminode. Capsule glabrous, depresso-globose, $\frac{1}{6}$ in. thick. Assonia populnea, *Cav. Diss. tab.* 42, *fig.* 1; *DC. Prod.* i. 498. Dombeya globosa, *Bojer MSS.*

MAURITIUS, in dry and rocky soil at Bois Rouge and Montagne Longue. Also Bourbon. *Bois de senteur bleu.*

3. **D. ferruginea,** *Cav. Diss. tab.* 42, *fig.* 2. A much-branched shrub, 5–10 feet high, with branchlets and leaves beneath clothed with ferruginous or whitish tomentum. Leaves firm, ovate, shortly cordate, smooth and green above, 3–5 in. long, acute, inciso-crenate; petiole 1–2 in. long. Peduncles longer than the petioles, sulcate, clothed with brown or white tomentum; pedicels very short; bracteoles linear, minute; inflorescence a dense bifid cyme. Sepals $\frac{1}{8}$ in. long, tomentose. Expanded corolla whitish, $\frac{1}{4}$–$\frac{1}{3}$ in. broad. Fertile stamens about 15. Styles free to the base. Capsule depresso-globose, tomentose, $\frac{1}{8}$ in. thick.

MAURITIUS, in exposed woods of the Pouce, Grand Bassin, etc. Also Bourbon. M. Bouton sends a variety with subentire leaves, broader and more deeply cordate, which Dr. Balfour also found in several places in RODRIGUEZ. *Bois pipe.*

4. **D. umbellata,** *Cav. Diss. tab.* 41, *fig.* 1. A tree with branchlets, peduncles, and pedicels densely clothed with spreading hairs. Leaves firm, smooth, round, deeply cordate, acute, 3–4 in. long, obscurely crenate; petiole 1–1$\frac{1}{2}$ in. long. Peduncles 2–3 times length of the petioles; inflorescence an umbel of 10–20 flowers on pedicels $\frac{1}{2}$–1 in. long; bracteoles minute, linear, caducous. Sepals linear-lanceolate, $\frac{1}{4}$ in. long, sharply reflexed, tomentose on the back. Petals rather longer than the sepals, obversely deltoid. Ovary densely tomentose; styles free to base. *DC. Prod.* i. 499.

MAURITIUS, at Flacq and Bois Rouge, *Bojer*. We have it at Kew from Bourbon only.

5. **D. punctata,** *Cav. Diss. tab.* 40, *fig.* 1. A much-branched shrub, with branches, leaves beneath, peduncles, and sepals, rough with short grey bristly hairs. Leaves thick, rigid, scabrous above, round-cordate, subacute, dentate, 1–3 in. long and broad; petiole $\frac{1}{4}$–1 inch long. Peduncles 3–4 times the length of the petioles; flowers in dense

umbels, on pedicels $\frac{1}{4}$–$\frac{1}{3}$ in. long. Sepals $\frac{1}{3}$ in. long, thick, tomentose. Petals little longer than sepals, obovate. Styles free to the base. *DC. Prod.* i. p. 499.

MAURITIUS, near the summit of the Pouce, *Bojer*. We have it at Kew only from Bourbon.

4. TROCHETIA, DC.

Bracteoles 0. Calyx divided to the base into 5 lanceolate segments. Petals 5, obovate, marcescent. Stamens monadelphous, the short or long column bearing 5 ligulate staminodes, with 2–4 fertile anthers between each. Ovary 5-celled; ovules many in a cell; style divided at the top into 5 stigmatic points. Capsule hard, globose, finally splitting into 5 valves. — Shrubs with crowded petioled oblong leaves, abundant scurfy pubescence and peduncled axillary flowers. DISTRIB. Two other species in St. Helena, and one in Madagascar.

Flowers large; peduncles deflexed.
  Flowers 3; stamen-column cylindrical . . . . 1. T. TRIFLORA.
  Flowers solitary; stamen-column campanulate.
    Leaves small, densely furfuraceous beneath . . . 2. T. UNIFLORA.
    Leaves large, naked on both surfaces . . . . . . 3. T. BLACKBURNIANA.
Flowers small; peduncles ascending . . . . 4. T. PARVIFLORA.

1. **T. triflora,** *DC. in Mem. Mus. Par.* x. 106, *t.* 8. A shrub, with petioles, peduncles, leaves below and sepals clothed with dense brown scurfy pubescence. Leaves oblong, crowded near the end of the branches, 4–6 in. long, acute, subentire or dentate, broadly rounded at the base, coriaceous, green and scabrous above, covered with brown tomentum beneath; petiole erect, 1–2 in. long. Peduncles much deflexed, exceeding the petioles, 3-flowered. Sepals acuminate, an inch long. Petals obovate, half as long again as the sepals. Staminal column cylindrical, the stalked anthers overtopped by the ligulate staminodes. Styles reaching the top of the petals. Fruit hard, oblong, furfuraceous. T. grandiflora, *Lindl. Bot. Reg.* 1844, *t.* 21; *Bojer, Hort. Maur.* 41.

MAURITIUS, in high exposed woods of Pouce, Grand Bassin, etc. Endemic.

2. **T. uniflora,** *DC. in Mem. Mus. Par.* x. 106, *t.* 7. A low shrub, with petioles, peduncles, and leaves below, clothed with dense brown scurfy pubescence. Leaves oblong, 2–3 in. long, obscurely crenate or entire, firm, rounded at the base, obtuse or subacute; petiole $\frac{1}{3}$–1 inch, ascending or curved. Peduncles one-flowered, deflexed, exceeding the petioles. Sepals lanceolate, $\frac{3}{4}$ inch long, densely furfuraceous. Petals obovate, rather exceeding the sepals. Staminal column cup-shaped, the staminodes overtopping the ten anthers, reaching halfway up the petals. Stigmas overtopping the staminodes. Capsule hard, globose, furfuraceous, $\frac{1}{4}$–$\frac{1}{3}$ inch thick. T. Candolleana, *Bojer, Hort. Maur.* 41.

MAURITIUS, in exposed places of the Pouce, Piton de la Rivière Noire, etc. Endemic.

3. **T. Blackburniana,** *Bojer, Hort. Maur.* 41 (*name only*.) A low branched shrub, with petioles, peduncles, and sepals clothed with grey

or brownish tomentum. Leaves broad-oblong or obovate-oblong, entire or obscurely crenate, 3–6 inches long, firm, smooth, subacute, rather cordate at the base; petiole ½–1 inch long. Peduncles much deflexed, longer than the petioles, 1-flowered. Sepals lanceolate, an inch long. Petals very broad, rather longer than the sepals. Staminal-column ½ inch long, the anthers sessile at its top.

MAURITIUS, in dense forests round Grand Bassin and Trois Mamelles, *Blackburn!* Endemic.

4. **T. parviflora,** *Bojer, Hort. Maur.* 41 (*name only*). A much-branched low shrub, with lepidote brown pubescence, much thinner than in *T. uniflora* and *T. triflora*. Leaves oblong, entire, 1–1½ inch long, firm; obtuse, scabrous above, rather rounded at the base, thinly scurfy beneath; petiole ¼ inch long. Peduncles erect, 3-flowered, longer than the petioles. Sepals lanceolate, ¼–⅓ inch long, densely scurfy on the back. Petals broad, not longer than the sepals. Staminal cup very short; staminodia not overtopping the 10 stalked anthers. Ovary globose, densely lepidote.

MAURITIUS, in high woods of the Pouce, *Bojer; Ayres!* Endemic.

* *Guazuma tomentosa*, H.B.K; DC. Prod. i. 485, a native of tropical America, now widely spread in the Old World, is established near Port Louis and in other parts of Mauritius. It is a shrub, with branches, calyx, petioles, peduncles and leaves below clothed with thick pale brown tomentum, petioled alternate serrate ovate-cuspidate simple leaves, with a very unequal cordate base, copious minute flowers in axillary cymes, 2–3 deltoid sepals, 5 obovate petals bifid at the tip, staminal cup with 5 barren lobes and 3 fertile filaments in each sinus, and a hard oblong rugose capsule, as large as a hazel-nut.

5. MELOCHIA, Linn.

Sepals lanceolate, united at the base. Petals 5, oblong-spathulate, exceeding the sepals. Stamens 5, opposite the petals, connate at the base; anthers 2-celled; staminodes 0. Ovary 5-celled; ovules 2; styles 5, diverging. Capsule membranous, dehiscing loculicidally, the carpels separating from the axis. Seed solitary in each cell.—Annuals (our species) with thin leaves and clustered small flowers. DISTRIB. Species 50, mostly American.

1. **M. corchorifolia,** *Linn.* A simple or branched annual herb, 1–3 feet high, with nearly glabrous stems and petioles. Leaves thin, green, ovate, acute, inciso-crenate, 1–3 inches long. Flowers in dense mostly terminal heads, mixed with copious linear densely ciliated bracteoles. Sepals ⅛ inch, lanceolate. Petals twice as long as the sepals, white or reddish. Capsule fragile, pilose, ⅙ inch thick. Riedleia corchorifolia, *DC. Prod.* i. 491. R. capitata, *Bojer, Hort. Maur.* 38.

MAURITIUS, a common weed by roadsides and in cultivated ground. Everywhere in tropics of Old World. *Herbe à balais.*

* *M. pyramidata,* Linn, a native of tropical America, is naturalised

in Mauritius about Port Louis, and is common in the Seychelles and Rodriguez. It is a glabrous annual, with thin toothed ovate or lanceolate leaves, few minute flowers in short-peduncled axillary clusters, acuminate sepals, and acute conical inflated membranous glabrous capsules, with deltoid valves with a tooth on each side at the base.

6. WALTHERIA, Linn.

Calyx cup-shaped, with 5 lanceolate teeth. Petals 5, oblong-spathulate, deciduous. Stamens 5, opposite to the petals, united at the base; staminodes 0. Ovary sessile, 1-celled; ovules 2; style eccentric. Capsule 1-seeded, 2-valved. Pilose herbs or shrubs, with dense clusters of small flowers in the axils of the leaves. Distrib. Species 16, mostly tropical America.

1. **W. indica,** *Linn.; DC. Prod.* i. 493. A villose shrubby branched perennial. Leaves short-petioled, soft, ovate or oblong, toothed, obtuse or acute, 1–3 inches long, plicate. Flowers in dense axillary fascicles; bracts abundant, minute, lanceolate, villose. Calyx $\frac{1}{12}$ inch long, densely villose. Petals yellow, twice as long as the sepals. *Jacq. Ic. t.* 130. W. americana, *Linn.*

Mauritius, in the plains about Réduit, Pamplemousses, etc. Seychelles, common on St. Anne and Ile aux Cerfs, but not in the larger islands, *Horne*, 420! Everywhere in the Tropics. *Guimauve.*

Three species of *Ruizia* are mentioned in Bojer's Catalogue, but he had not seen Mauritian specimens. We have the genus at Kew from Bourbon only, and Cavanilles expressly restricts it to that island. The genus is like *Dombeya* in habit and flower, but all the stamens bear anthers.

Cheirolæna linearis, Benth. Gen. Plant. 222. There is a specimen labelled as Mauritian in the Kew herbarium, but as the plant has been refound lately in Madagascar by Gerrard, there is probably a mistake in the first record. It is a branched, erect, slender, shrubby perennial, 1–2 feet high, with alternate entire firm sessile linear 1-nerved leaves 2–3 inches long, clothed on both sides, like the branches and sepals with pale scurfy pubescence; flowers 1–3 on ascending pedicels from the axils of the upper leaves; 3 persistent small palmate bracteoles; 5 lanceolate sepals $\frac{1}{4}$ inch long; obovate reddish petals rather longer than the sepals, and stamens and pistil like those of *Trochetia triflora.*

Order XVII. TILIACEÆ.

Flowers regular, hermaphrodite. Sepals 4–5, valvate in æstivation, free or joined at the base. Petals 4–5, hypogynous, imbricated. Stamens indefinite, hypogynous; filaments free, filiform; anthers 2-celled; staminodes 0. Ovary sessile, 2–5-celled; ovules 1 or many, axile; style filiform, usually cleft at the tip into as many stigmas as there are cells in the ovary. Fruit 2- or many-celled, dry or drupaceous. Seeds albuminous.—Usually trees or shrubs, with alternate stipulate leaves; flowers axillary or terminal, small, often cymose. Distrib. Species 300–350. Cosmopolitan, mostly tropical.

Pilose herbs or under shrubs with entire petals.
  Fruit a naked cylindrical-trigonous pod . . . . * Corchorus.
  Fruit a globose prickly capsule . . . . 1. Triumfetta.
Glabrous trees with fringed petals . . . . 2. Elæocarpus.

* *Corchorus trilocularis*, Linn., (C. triflorus, Bojer in Ann. Sc. Nat. ser. 2, xx. p. 100), a common weed through the tropics of the Old World, is established in Mauritius at Port Louis, especially round the eastern suburb, *Bojer! Dr. Ayres*; and was gathered by Dr. Balfour in Rodriguez. It is an erect annual, with slender pilose or glabrescent branches, petioled toothed simple lanceolate or ovate-lanceolate leaves, 1-3-flowered very short leaf-opposed peduncles, small yellow flowers, a cylindrical 3-valved pod 2–3 inches long, with a short beak, and transverse membranous partitions between the seeds.

1. TRIUMFETTA, Linn.

Sepals 5, valvate, ligulate-cuspidate. Petals 5, oblanceolate, caducous, rather protruded. Stamens definite or indefinite, inserted upon an elevated torus bearing with 5 glands; filaments filiform; anthers minute. Ovary 2–5-celled; styles filiform, united to the top. Fruit a small globose prickly dehiscent or indehiscent capsule.—Weedy downy herbs or shrubs, with dense axillary clusters of minute yellowish flowers. DISTRIB. Round the world in the tropics. Species about 40.

1. **T. rhomboidea,** *Jacq. Ic. Sel. Amer. t.* 90. A branched shrubby perennial, 2–3 feet high, with stems, leaves and calyx covered with dense short rough pubescence. Leaves short-petioled, in the typical form entire, oblong, with a cuneate base, irregularly distinctly crenate, acute, 1–2 inches long. Flowers in dense axillary sessile or short-peduncled fascicles, the upper approximated and their subtending leaves often small: buds cylindrical, $\frac{1}{6}$–$\frac{1}{4}$ inch long, densely pilose. Stamens 10–15, as long as the petals. Capsule the size of a pea, indehiscent, pilose, covered with dense hooked spines $\frac{1}{8}$–$\frac{1}{4}$ inch long, 3-celled.

Var. GLANDULOSA, (*Lam.*). Leaves larger, with longer petioles, round with a cusp, rounded at the base, either thin with soft grey hairs, or thicker with dense white tomentum beneath. T. glandulosa, *Lam. Encycl.* iii. 421. T. velutina, *Vahl.* T. Vahlii, *Poir.*

Var. ANGULATA, (*Lam.*). Leaves deeply or shallowly 3-lobed in the upper half, with deltoid segments. T. angulata, *Lam. Encyc.* iii. 421; *Wight. Ic. t.* 320. T. semitriloba, *Bojer, Hort. Maur.* 43.

MAURITIUS, RODRIGUEZ, SEYCHELLES, the type rare, the two varieties common in waste ground, and by roadsides. Everywhere in the tropics. *Herbe à panier.*

* *T. procumbens*, Forst.; DC. Prod. i. 508, a native of the shores of Polynesia and Australia, has been found by Horne in one station in the Seychelles (and by Bojer in Galega island). It is a perennial herb with trailing woody stems sending out short erect branches, distinctly petioled toothed roundish-cordate leaves tomentose beneath, mostly deeply 3-lobed, flowers 1–3 together in peduncled axillary umbels, linear pilose sepals $\frac{1}{4}$–$\frac{1}{3}$ inch long, oblanceolate bright yellow petals as long as the sepals, fruit an indehiscent glabrous ball $\frac{1}{3}$ inch thick, armed with stout prickles.

2. ELÆOCARPUS, Linn.

Sepals 4–5, persistent, free nearly to the base. Petals the same number, broad, fimbriated, induplicate in æstivation, inserted round a raised disk with 4–5 large glands. Stamens indefinite; filaments filiform, inserted on the top of the disk; anthers linear, innate, dehiscing by terminal pores. Ovary 2–5-celled; ovules 2 or many in a cell; style entire. Fruit a drupe, with a stone holding 2–5 one-seeded cells. —Trees with alternate or opposite leaves, usually glabrous; the flowers, which are usually hermaphrodite, rarely polygamous, in axillary racemes. DISTRIB. Species about 50; warmer zones of the Old World, mostly Indian. Not known in trop. Africa, but one discovered lately in Natal.

Flowers tetramerous; petals silky . . . . 1. E. INTEGRIFOLIUS.
Flowers pentamerous; petals glabrous . . . . 2. E. GRANDIFLORUS.

1. **E. integrifolius**, *Lam.; DC. Prod.* i. 519. A tree 20 feet high. Leaves alternate, crowded on the branches, nearly sessile, oblong, entire, rigid, shining, 3–4 in. long, cordate at base, penninerved, glabrous on both surfaces. Flowers in axillary racemes as long as the leaves, on short drooping pedicels, which are finely silky. Sepals 4, lanceolate, silky. Petals 4, silky on both sides, white, fimbriated. Stamens about 30.

MAURITIUS, in the forests of the south-western range of hills. Endemic.

2. **E. grandiflorus**, *Bojer, Hort. Maur.* 45 (*name only*). A tree, glabrous in all its parts. Leaves alternate, crowded near the end of the branches, oblong, entire, firm, green on both surfaces, 3–6 in. long, obtuse or acute; base cuneate or rounded; petiole ½–1 inch. Racemes few-flowered, shorter than the leaves, with cernuous pedicels ½–1 inch long. Sepals 5, naked, glabrous, rugose, lanceolate, ⅓ inch long. Petals rather longer than the sepals, broad, much fringed, deciduous. Stamens about 30; anthers ⅛ in. long, equalling the filaments in length.

MAURITIUS, in hill woods of the Pouce. Endemic.

ORDER XVIII. LINACEÆ.

Flowers regular, hermaphrodite. Sepals 5, imbricated, free or joined at the base. Petals 5, hypogynous, imbricated, often contorted. Stamens 10, joined in a cup round the ovary; filaments free above the cup; anthers versatile, 2-celled. Ovary free, 3–5-celled; ovules 1–2, pendulous, axile, anatropal; styles distinct, as many as the cells; stigmas capitate. Fruit in our genera drupaceous; but more usually a capsule with septicidal dehiscence. Seeds albuminous.—Herbs or shrubs with alternate stipulate mostly entire leaves; inflorescence various; petals fugacious, often showy. DISTRIB. Species 150; cosmopolitan, both tropical and temperate.

Climbers, with hooked tendrils; styles 5; drupe 5-celled 1. HUGONIA.
Erect shrubs with 3 styles and drupes 1-celled by abortion . . . . 2. ERYTHROXYLON.

1. HUGONIA, Linn.

Sepals 5, imbricated, persistent, joined at the very base. Petals obovate, unguiculate, deciduous, contorted in bud. Stamens 10, the filaments unequal, joined in a cup at the base round the ovary. Ovary 5-celled; 2 collateral ovules in a cell; styles 5, stigmatose at the apex. Fruit a fleshy drupe, enclosing 5 triquetrous bony cells.—Woody climbers, with curious opposite spirally curved woody tendrils and flowers in panicled corymbs. DISTRIB. Species 11; 2 tropical Asian, the rest tropical African.

Leaves toothed, glabrous, except a tuft of hairs in the axil of veins beneath . . . . 1. H. SERRATA.
Leaves subentire, silky all over . . . . 2. H. TOMENTOSA.

1. **H. serrata,** *Lam.; DC. Prod.* i. 522. A woody climber, with branchlets and sepals densely clothed with bright brown silky hairs. Leaves short-petioled, obovate-oblong, cuneate at the base, 3–4 in. long, obtuse or acute, glabrous, except tufts of hairs in the axils of the main veins beneath; stipules lanceolate, deciduous. Corymbs closely many-flowered, mixed with small oblong-spathulate bracts. Curved tendrils mainly at the base of tufts of leaves of the year. Sepals $\frac{1}{4}$ inch long. Petals bright yellow, $\frac{1}{2}$–$\frac{3}{4}$ inch broad. Drupe the size of a large pea, brown, pulpy.

MAURITIUS, in forests of the Pouce, Moka, Nouvelle Découverte, etc. Also Bourbon. *Liane à Crochet.*

2. **H. tomentosa,** *Cav.; DC. Prod.* i. 522. General habit, tendrils, inflorescence and flower-structure just as in *H. serrata*. Leaves 4–6 inches long, broader, obtuse or cuspidate, entire or obscurely crenulate, persistently clothed all over below and thinly at first above with brown silky pubescence. Sepals very silky, lanceolate, $\frac{1}{4}$–$\frac{1}{3}$ inch long. Drupe the size of a cherry.

MAURITIUS, in woods of Nouvelle Découverte. Endemic.

2. ERYTHRYOXYLON, Linn.

Sepals 5, minute, lanceolate, persistent. Petals 5, hypogynous, deciduous, with a scale on the face. Stamens 10, united in a cup round the ovary; filaments filiform; anthers minute, roundish. Ovary 3-celled; styles 3, distinct. Fruit a drupe, 1-celled by abortion, with a single seed in a tough thin endocarp.—Glabrous shrubs with entire alternate leaves, persistent brown acute stipules and small whitish flowers, solitary or fascicled from their axils. DISTRIB. Species 50, all tropical, mostly American.

Leaves small; flowers solitary, on filiform pedicels . . 1. E. HYPERICIFOLIUM.
Leaves large; flowers fascicled on stout crowded pedicels . . . . 2. E. LAURIFOLIUM.

1. **E. hypericifolium,** *Lam.; DC. Prod.* i. 573. A very-much-branched shrub 10–15 feet high, glabrous in all its parts, with slender flexuose nodulose twigs. Leaves obovate, short-petioled, moderately

firm, $\frac{1}{4}$–1 inch long, truncate or emarginate at the apex, cuneate at the base; stipules linear, brown, $\frac{1}{12}$–$\frac{1}{8}$ in. long. Flowers few, always solitary, on filiform ascending pedicels $\frac{1}{8}$ inch long. Petals $\frac{1}{12}$ inch long. Drupe oblong, bright red, juicy, pendulous, 1-seeded. *Cav. Diss. t.* 230.

MAURITIUS, common on mountains all through the island; Pouce, Peter Botte, etc. Also Bourbon. *Bois des Dames. Bois à balais. Bois d'huile.*

2. **E. laurifolium,** *Lam.; DC. Prod.* i. 573. A much-branched shrub, 10–15 feet high, glabrous in all its parts. Leaves short-petioled, alternate, oblong, 2–4 inches long, firm, shining, obtuse or acute, narrowed to the base; stipules minute, lanceolate. Flowers copious, 1–6 together from the stipulate nodes of the leafy branches, or crowded on short leafless shoots, on stout ascending pedicels $\frac{1}{8}$ inch long thickened upwards. Sepals $\frac{1}{24}$ inch long, becoming indurated. Petals 4 times the length of the calyx, oblong, white, with a plicate scale on the face. Drupe $\frac{1}{2}$ inch long, oblong, obtusely trigonous, reddish, juicy. E. sideroxyloides and longifolium, *Lam. and DC. loc. cit.*

MAURITIUS and SEYCHELLES, common in woods. Also Bourbon. *E. sideroxyloides* is a hill form with 2–3-nate flowers and obovate-oblong leaves; and *E. longifolium*, a form with leaves under half an inch broad. *Bois de Ronde. Bois à flambeaux.*

Linum usitatissimum, the common flax, is cultivated in Mauritius, and casually subspontaneous, and **Reinwardtia trigyna** (Linum trigynum, *Planch. Roxb.; Bot. Mag. t.* 1100), of the East Indies, is given in Dupont's Catalogue as an introduced species.

ORDER XVIII.* MALPIGHIACEÆ.

* *Hiptage Madablota*, Gærtn.; DC. Prod. i. 583, common in Tropical Asia, is established in many places in woods in Mauritius. It is a woody climber, with large shining oblong acute entire opposite leaves, copious white fragrant flowers in ample axillary racemes, calyx with 5 large adnate glands, petals round with a distinct claw and fringed edge, and a dry fruit of 1–3 carpels produced each into three hard dry linear-oblong wings 1–2 inches long. *Liane de Cythère. Liane de fleurs d'orange.*

ORDER XIX. ZYGOPHYLLACEÆ.

Flowers regular, hermaphrodite. Sepals 5, free, imbricated. Petals 5, free, hypogynous. Disk convex or depressed. Stamens 1–2 times the number of the petals; filaments free; anthers versatile, 2-celled. Ovary 4–5-celled; style simple; stigma capitate or lobed. Fruit of dry separable cocci, or a capsule with septicidal dehiscence. Seeds usually pendulous, solitary; embryo in ours exalbuminous.—Herbs or shrubs, with opposite compound leaves, persistent often spiny stipules and solitary or geminate axillary pedicels. DISTRIB. Widely spread in both hemispheres, mostly tropical; species 100.

1. TRIBULUS, Linn.

Sepals 5, free, deciduous. Petals 5, fugacious, obovate, imbricated. Stamens 10, free, the filaments filiform, those alternate with the petals with a basal gland. Ovary sessile, 5-celled; ovules 1 or few in a cell; style short; stigmas as many as the cells. Fruit of dry hard separable cocci, with a horn at the corners and setose on the back.—Branched herbs with abruptly pinnate leaves and small solitary fugacious flowers. DISTRIB. Species 15; cosmopolitan, mainly tropical.

1. **T. terrestris,** *Linn.; DC. Prod.* i. 703. Annual or perennial, much branched at the crown of the root, with trailing stems, clothed like the leaves and sepals with white adpressed hairs. Leaves short-petioled, in opposite pairs, one smaller than the other; leaflets 5–7-jugate, oblong, sessile; stipules linear, persistent. Flower ½ inch across. Fruit of 5 triquetrous cocci, with a large spiny horn at each corner, containing 2–3 transverse septa with a seed between each. T. lanuginosus, *Linn.*

MAURITIUS and SEYCHELLES, in sandy ground near the sea, not common. Cosmopolitan in and near the tropics.

ORDER XX. GERANIACEÆ.

Tribe 1. OXALIDEÆ.

Flowers regular, hermaphrodite. Sepals 5, persistent, imbricated. Petals 5, obovate, hypogynous, spirally twisted in the bud. Stamens 10; filaments usually joined at the base, biserial, those opposite the petals longer; anthers 2-celled, dehiscing longitudinally. Ovary 5-celled; placentation axile; ovules few or many, anatropal. Fruit a membranous capsule, rarely a drupe. Seeds albuminous.—Herbs, shrubs or rarely trees, with compound acid often sensitive leaves and fugacious often showy axillary or radical solitary, corymbose or umbellate flowers. DISTRIB. Species 200–250. Mostly Cape and trop. American.

1. OXALIS, Linn.

Sepals 5, lanceolate, free. Petals 5, obtuse, contorted. Stamens and pistil often trimorphic, as in *Lythrum*. Stamens 10, in two rows, the inner longer; filaments joined at the base; anthers minute, oblong. Ovary 5-celled; ovules many in a cell; styles distinct, falcate, short. Fruit an oblong or cylindrical membranous capsule, with loculicidal dehiscence.—Herbs or shrubs; leaves digitate or pinnate; peduncles axillary or radical; flowers sometimes dimorphic, some apetalous as in *Viola*. DISTRIB. Species 220; preponderant at the Cape and in South America.

Acaulescent; leaflets ternate . . . . * O. CORYMBOSA.
Caulescent; leaflets ternate . . . . 1. O. CORNICULATA.
Leaves abruptly pinnate; leaflets 6–9-jugate . . . . . 2. O. SENSITIVA.

* *O. corymbosa,* DC. Prod. i. 696 (O. Martiana, Zucc.; Bot. Mag. t. 3938; O. bipunctata, Graham in Bot. Mag. t. 2781), a native of South America, is cultivated in gardens and established in Mauritius by roadsides near Moka and Plaines Wilhems, and was gathered by Mr. Balfour in Rodriguez. It is acaulescent, with a tuberous root with brown membranous coats, pilose peduncles and petioles ½–1 foot long, three sessile leaflets 1–1½ inch broad deeply obcordate at the apex cuneate at the base, 10–20 flowers in a lax corymb, sepals lanceolate under ¼ inch long, red petals three times as long as the calyx and an oblong many-seeded downy capsule. *Alléluia à fleurs roses.*

1. **O. corniculata,** *Linn.; DC. Prod.* i. 692. A much-branched caulescent annual, with trailing stems, the branches, leaves and sepals pilose. Stipules minute, lanceolate; petioles 1–2 inches long; leaflets ternate, sessile, ⅓–¾ inch broad, deeply emarginate, with obtuse lobes. Flowers 1–4, from the axils of the leaves, on long peduncles. Sepals ⅛ in. long. Petals yellow, not much longer than the sepals. Capsule cylindrical, ½–¾ inch long. O. repens, *Thunb.*

MAURITIUS, RODRIGUEZ, and SEYCHELLES, a common weed in cultivated ground. One of the commonest and most widely-spread annual weeds of tropical and temperate countries. *Alléluia à fleurs jaunes.*

2. **O. sensitiva,** *Linn. Sp. Plant.* 622. Annual. Leaves in a dense rosette, sessile on the ground or on a naked wiry stem, abruptly pinnate, the midrib ending in a bristle; leaflets very sensitive, 6–9-jugate, sessile, round or oblong-rhomboid, membranous, slightly pilose. Flowers many, in sessile or peduncled umbels from the centre of the rosette; pedicels none or very short. Sepals ⅛ inch long, lanceolate-acuminate, ribbed. Petals yellow, twice the length of the sepals. Capsule oblong, included in the calyx. Biophytum sensitivum, *DC. Prod.* i. 630.

MAURITIUS, on mountains of Nouvelle Découverte, not seen of late years. Spread through tropics of the Old World.

Averrhoa Carambola, *Linn.* (*Carambolier*) and **A. Bilimbi,** *Linn.* (*Bilimbi*), natives of tropical Asia, are both commonly cultivated in Mauritius and the Seychelles.

Tribe 2. BALSAMINEÆ.

Differs from the last by its irregular spurred flowers, 5 stamens with connate anthers, sessile stigmas and exalbuminous seeds.

2. IMPATIENS, Linn.

Sepals three; two upper smaller green, lower petaloid and hollowed out into a basal spur. Petals 3; upper (standard) erect; two lateral spreading, often two-lobed. Stamens 5; filaments short, broad; anthers connate, united over the stigma. Ovary 5-celled; ovules many in a cell; stigma sessile. Fruit a loculicidal capsule, with 5 elastic valves.—Herbs or shrubs with fleshy stems, alternate or opposite leaves, and axillary solitary or fascicled showy flowers. DISTRIB. Warmer regions chiefly of Old World, especially India. Species 150.

1. **I. Gordoni,** *Horne MSS.* A succulent glabrous annual or biennial herb, 2–3 feet high. Leaves alternate; petiole 1–5 in. long, glandless; blade oblanceolate-oblong, acute or acuminate, 3–4 in. long, cuneate at the base, furnished with cuspidate teeth. Flowers in pairs, on a common peduncle as long as the petiole; pedicels 1–1½ in. long, with two subulate bracts at the base. Flowers 2 inches in diameter; sepals green, deltoid, half as long as the petals, the lower one contracted suddenly into a spur 2–3 inches long. Petals white, running into rose-pink at the base; standard ¾–1 inch broad, emarginate, keeled on the back; wings deltoid, an inch long, lobed nearly down to the base. Capsule glandular, ½ inch long, narrowed from the middle to both ends, equal-sided or the lower side more produced.

SEYCHELLES, on the edge of forests in rich soil in Mahé and Silhouette, *Horne*, 439! Endemic.

ORDER XXI. RUTACEÆ.

Flowers regular, hermaphrodite or polygamous. Sepals 4–5, free or connate at the base. Petals 4–5, hypogynous, imbricate or valvate. Disk mostly annular. Stamens hypogynous, definite or indefinite; anthers 2-celled, versatile. Carpels 4–5, united or free; styles joined; ovules usually 2, superposed. Fruit permanently syncarpous or carpels separating. Seeds usually solitary; albumen none or fleshy.—Shrubs or trees with exstipulate compound usually gland-dotted leaves; flowers in ours copious, small. DISTRIB. Concentrated in Australia and at the Cape; many tropical, very few African. Species 600–700.

Fruit separating into two-valved cocci.
Leaves opposite . . . . 1. EVODIA.
Leaves alternate . . . . 2. ZANTHOXYLUM.
Fruit permanently syncarpous.
Pericarp thin; stamens definite, free . . . . 3. TODDALIA.
Pericarp thick; stamens indefinite, polyadelphous . . . * CITRUS.

1. EVODIA, Forst.

Flowers hermaphrodite or polygamous. Sepals 4, minute, imbricated, patent. Petals 4, valvate. Disk tumid, lobed. Stamens 4, inserted on the disk; filaments subulate; anthers oblong. Ovary 4-celled; ovules 2; style short; stigma 4-lobed. Fruit of 4 1-seeded dry cocci, which split into two valves from the top to the bottom.—Leaves opposite, gland-dotted, simple, digitate or imparipinnate; flowers small, whitish, in axillary panicles. DISTRIB. Species above 20; Australia, tropical Asia, 1 Madagascar, none Continental African.

Leaves with three digitate gland-dotted leaflets . . 1. E. OBTUSIFOLIA.
Leaves simple, not gland-dotted . . . . 2. E. ? ELÆODENDROIDES.

1. **E. obtusifolia,** *DC. Prod.* i. 724. A glabrous erect shrub, 6–12 feet high. Leaflets ternate, subsessile, subcoriaceous, obovate-oblong, cuneate at the base, 3–5 inches long, obtuse, sometimes emarginate, penninerved, minutely gland-dotted, side ones rather oblique; petiole 1–2 inches long. Panicles sessile, as long as the petiole; branches spreading; pedicels very short. Flower hermaphrodite. Calyx minute, spreading. Petals deltoid, $\frac{1}{8}$ inch long. Stamens included. Cocci $\frac{1}{4}$ inch long, 1–4 maturing, splitting from the top to the bottom like a bivalve shell, with a single shining black pendulous seed. Zanthoxylum obtusifolium, *G. Don, non Poir.*

MAURITIUS; mountains of Grand Bassin and Nouvelle Découverte. Endemic. *Patte de Poule* (like Toddalia).

2. **E. ? elæodendroides,** *Baker.* A tree, glabrous in all its parts, with thick straight branches. Leaves opposite, oblong, firm, obtuse, entire, 4–5 inches long, cuneate at base; main veins 8–9-jugate, spreading, connected by distinct intramarginal arches; no glandular dots; petiole under $\frac{1}{2}$ inch long, thick, channelled. Flowers campanulate, in peduncled panicles shorter than the leaves; branches spreading; pedicels very short. Calyx minute, with 4 deltoid teeth. Petals 4, $\frac{1}{8}$ inch long, deltoid. Disk thick. Stamens 4, inserted outside the disk; flattened filament, as long as the anther. Ovary 4-lobed, discoid, pilose; ovules 2 in a cell; styles 4, with capitate stigmas. Fruit unknown.

MAURITIUS, *Captain Carmichael!* (One specimen in Kew herbarium from R. Brown, and a second from Grand Bassin in the collection of the late Judge Blackburn). Habit of *Elæodendron orientale.* Endemic.

2. ZANTHOXYLUM, Linn.

Flowers hermaphrodite or polygamous. Sepals 4, minute, spreading, imbricate. Petals 4, imbricated. Disk thin. Stamens hypogynous, as many as the petals; filaments short; anthers oblong. Carpels 4, 1-celled; styles connate or free; stigmas capitate. Fruit in our plants just like that of *Evodia.*—Trees or shrubs, often prickly, with imparipinnate leaves and small white flowers in copious panicles, the fruit aromatic or pungent, with a gland-dotted pericarp. DISTRIB. Belts the world in the tropics. Species 80.

Leaflets of mature leaves 9–11, acute . . . . 1. Z. HETEROPHYLLUM.
Leaflets of mature leaves 15–19, obtuse . . . . . . 2. Z. PANICULATUM.

1. **Z. heterophyllum,** *Smith; DC. Prod.* i. 726. A tree, glabrous in all its parts, with branches and leaf-rachises often armed with hard hooked spines. Leaves petioled, the young ones remarkably different from the old ones, with a rachis a foot long, and 40–60-jugate oblong firm veined gland-dotted leaflets, $\frac{1}{4}$–$\frac{1}{2}$ inch long. Old leaves unarmed, their leaflets only 4–5-jugate, oblong, sessile, acute, 1–3 inches long, the end one close to the uppermost pair. Panicles peduncled, shorter than the leaves; branches ascending; pedicels very short. Petals $\frac{1}{8}$ inch long, oblong, whitish. Cocci the size of a pea, splitting down to the base,

mostly only one maturing. Fagara heterophylla, *Lam. Encycl.* ii. p. 445.

MAURITIUS, in littoral woods of Grandport, Flacq, etc. Also Bourbon.

2. **Z. paniculatum,** *Balf. fil.* A tree, with stout terete branchlets, armed with a few hooked black prickles. Bud-scales glutinous. Leaves crowded near the top of the branchlets, downy on the short unarmed petiole and rachis and midrib beneath, 6–8 in. long; leaflets 15–19, oblong, obtuse, sessile, subcoriaceous, glossy above, paler beneath, with raised veins, unequally cordate at the base. Panicle shorter than the leaves, subsessile; branches short, spreading, downy; pedicels very short. Calyx $\frac{1}{24}$ inch long, of 4 deltoid sepals. Corolla and stamens not seen. Capsule the size of a small pea, splitting down to the base into two valves, dark brown, glabrous, strongly minutely tubercled, furnished with a very short stalk.

RODRIGUEZ, only in Anse Ouitoze, *Balfour!* Endemic. Near *Z. Budrunga* and *Avicennæ* of Tropical Asia. *Bois Pasuer.*

3. TODDALIA, Juss.

Flowers polygamous. Sepals 4–5, minute. Petals 4–5, valvate or imbricate. Stamens as many or twice as many as petals; filaments filiform; anthers oblong. Disk thin. Ovary 4–5-celled; stigma peltate, subsessile. Fruit hard, coriaceous, permanently syncarpous, globose.—Erect trees or climbers; leaflets ternate, shining, coriaceous, venulose, gland-dotted, with a wavy vein within the edge; flowers copious, small, in dense panicles. DISTRIB. Species 6–8, spread through the tropics of the Old World and Cape.

Subgenus TODDALIA PROPER. Petals valvate. Stamens as many as petals . . . . 1. T. ACULEATA.
Subgenus VEPRIS. Petals imbricate. Stamens twice as many as petals.
Stamens exserted . . . . 2. T. LANCEOLATA.
Stamens included . . . . 3. T. PANICULATA.

1. **T. aculeata,** *Pers.; DC. Prod.* ii. 83. A climbing shrub, with branches often armed with hooked prickles. Petioles an inch long, flattened upwards; leaflets oblanceolate-oblong, acute, $\frac{1}{2}$–1 inch broad, entire or obscurely crenate; edge wrinkled. Panicles shorter than the leaves, copious, many-flowered, with pilose rachises; flowers crowded towards the end of branchlets; pedicels $\frac{1}{12}$–$\frac{1}{8}$ inch. Petals $\frac{1}{8}$ inch, lanceolate, nearly valvate. Stamens as many as the petals, exserted. Fruit orange-yellow, the size of a pea, 4–5-lobed, pellucid with fragrant oil vesicles. T. floribunda, *Vahl.* T. lanceolata, *Lam.; DC. Prod. loc. cit.*

MAURITIUS, frequent in forests, especially of the Pouce range. RODRIGUEZ, *Balfour! T. lanceolata* is a mere form, with narrow leaves and unarmed branches. Common through tropical Asia, but not African. Also Bourbon. *Bambara* or *Bois Patte de Poule.*

2. **T. lanceolata,** *Lam.; DC. Prod.* ii. 83. An entirely glabrous erect shrub or small tree, without prickles. Petioles 1–2 inches long, not flattened; leaflets oblong-lanceolate, 2–3 inches long, acute, entire, waved at the edge, $\frac{3}{4}$–1 inch broad. Panicles many-flowered, axillary and terminal, thrysoid; rachises not pilose; pedicels short, flower-bud round. Petals oblong, $\frac{1}{12}$ inch long, imbricated. Stamens 8, in the male flowers exserted. Fruit the size of a pea, 4-lobed, fleshy, gland-dotted. Vepris lanceolata, *A. Juss.* Zanthoxylum undulatum, *Wall. Cat. No.* 1208. Boscia undulata, *Thunb.*

MAURITIUS, on the eastern slope of the Pouce. Also Cape and Mosambique. *Patte de Poules.*

3. **T. paniculata,** *Lam.; DC. Prod.* ii. 83. An erect tree, 20–30 feet high, without prickles, glabrous in all its parts. Petioles 1–1$\frac{1}{2}$ inch long, subterete; leaflets obovate-oblong, obtuse or subacute, 1–1$\frac{1}{2}$ inch broad, bright green. Flowers in copious deltoid terminal panicles, with spreading or ascending branches, the pedicels $\frac{1}{8}$–$\frac{1}{4}$ inch long. Petals 4, greenish-white, $\frac{1}{12}$ inch long, oblong, much imbricated. Stamens 8, included. Capsule the size of a pea, 4-lobed. Vepris obovata, *G. Don.*

MAURITIUS; woods of the Pouce and Quartier Militaire. RODRIGUEZ, not common, *Balfour!* Endemic.

* *Citrus Hystrix,* DC. Prod. i. 539, the Porcupine orange, a native of the East Indies, is used in Mauritius for hedges, and has become naturalised. It becomes when developed a tree 30 feet high, with branches furnished with erecto-patent spines, leaves densely dotted with an ovate, oblong or lanceolate blade, petiole with a broad leafy wing often larger than the blade truncate at the top cuneate at the base, flowers $\frac{1}{2}$ inch across in crowded sessile corymbs, and fruit round, orange-like, 2–3 inches diam. *Citron Combara.*

C. medica, *Linn.* (The Citron) and **C. vulgaris,** *Risso* (the bitter or Seville orange), are mentioned as wild plants in Dupont's Mauritian Catalogue, but of course are naturalised only. **C. vulgaris, C. Limonum, C. Aurantium,** and **Triphasia trifoliata,** *DC.* are in Dr. Balfour's collection as subspontaneous in Rodriguez.

ORDER XXII. SIMARUBEÆ.

Flowers regular, usually dioicous or polygamous. Sepals 3–5, imbricated, joined at the very base. Petals 3–5, hypogynous. Disk annular. Stamens as many or twice as many as petals; filaments free; anthers oblong, 2-celled, slitting down the side. Ovary 2–5-lobed, or of 5 free carpels; styles distinct; stigmas capitate; ovules usually solitary. Fruit dry or drupaceous. Seeds with or without albumen.—Trees or shrubs; bark usually bitter; leaves not dotted, exstipulate, usually compound; inflorescence mostly axillary. DISTRIB. Round the world in the tropics. Species 110–120.

Flowers trimerous, polygamo-dioicous . . . . 1. SOULAMEA.
Flowers pentamerous, hermaphrodite . . . . 2. SURIANA.

1. SOULAMEA, Lam.

Flowers polygamo-dioicous. Calyx minute; sepals 3, imbricated, deltoid. Petals 3, lingulate. Disk 3-lobed, plate-shaped. Stamens 6, inserted under the disk; filaments naked, subulate. Ovary 2-3-celled; ovules solitary in the cells; styles adnate to the top of the carpels, short, reflexed. Fruit indehiscent, with a broad wing to each carpel.—Trees with alternate entire leaves and minute flowers in axillary racemes. DISTRIB. One other species, which is Malayan and Polynesian.

1. **S. terminalioides,** *Baker.* An erect tree 20–25 feet high, with the leaves and branchlets at first brown-silky, but soon becoming glabrous. Leaves oblong, obtuse, subcoriaceous, 4–6 in. long, deltoid at the base, with numerous fine parallel veins; petioles 2–3 in. Flowers in copious short-peduncled silky axillary racemes, 2–3 in. long, on pedicels as long as the calyx. Calyx $\frac{1}{12}$ inch, densely brown-silky. Petals reflexed when expanded, little longer than the sepals. Stamens included. Fruit under an inch long, brown, glabrous, deeply emarginate, the coriaceous rounded wings quite as broad as the cells.

SEYCHELLES, common in poor soil in the island of Mahé, *Wright*, 109! *Horne*, 440! Bark intensely bitter. Endemic. *Bois des montagnes petit qualité.*

2. SURIANA, Linn.

Flowers hermaphrodite. Sepals 5, persistent, joined at the very base, imbricate. Petals 5, oblong-unguiculate, not longer than calyx. Stamens 10, hypogynous, included. Carpels 5, free, hairy; ovules 2, collateral, basal; styles filiform, distinct, issuing from the base of carpel on the inner side, hooked at the stigmatose tip. Fruit dry, indehiscent, pilose, included in the calyx, attached to the torus by a narrow base. A single species.

1. **S. maritima,** *Linn.; DC. Prod.* ii. 291. A much-branched shrub, 5–10 feet, with finely downy branches and leaves. Leaves oblanceolate, an inch long, thick, alternate, crowded. Flowers few, in corymbs at the end of the branches, half-hidden by leaves. Sepals lanceolate, coriaceous, $\frac{1}{3}$ inch long. Petals bright yellow. Cocci obovoid, hard, pilose, $\frac{1}{8}$ inch thick.

MAURITIUS, RODRIGUEZ, SEYCHELLES, frequent on the shores. FLAT ISLAND, *Horne!* Cosmopolitan within the tropics. Littoral. Rare in Continental Africa.

ORDER XXIII. OCHNACEÆ.

Flowers, regular, hermaphrodite. Sepals 5, free imbricate. Petals 5, free, broad, deciduous, imbricate. Stamens hypogynous, indefinite; filaments free, filiform; anthers 2-celled, basifixed. Ovary deeply lobed; ovules 1 or many in a cell; styles united; stigmas capitate. Torus thickened after flowering. Fruit variable, dry or drupaceous.

Seeds albuminous or exalbuminous.—Shrubs or trees, with alternate simple stipulate glabrous not dotted shining leaves; flowers usually panicled, often showy. Distrib. Tropical, mostly American. Species 140.

1. OCHNA, Schreb.

Sepals 5, oblong, persistent, free, imbricate. Petals 5, hypogynous, obovate-cuneate. Torus thick, 5-lobed. Stamens indefinite, hypogynous; filaments filiform; anthers basifixed, splitting at the top of the sides. Ovary deeply 5-lobed; ovules solitary; styles united below, free at the tip; stigmas capitate. Carpels indehiscent in fruit, dry or fleshy, seated on the tumid torus.—Trees or shrubs, with alternate simple coriaceous glabrous leaves and corymbose showy white or yellow flowers. Distrib. Tropics of Old World and Cape. Species 25.

1. **O. mauritiana,** *Lam.; DC. Prod.* i. 935. An erect tree, 15–20 feet high, glabrous in all its parts. Leaves short-petioled, oblong, denticulate or subentire, 3–4 inches long, acute, shining; stipules ovate, acuminate, deciduous. Flowers in copious ample corymbs, before the leaves appear or contemporary with the young leaves; pedicels $\frac{1}{2}$–$\frac{3}{4}$ inch long, articulated at the middle. Sepals coriaceous, oblong, obtuse, under $\frac{1}{4}$ inch long. Petals whitish, twice as long as the sepals. Stamens 20–30, as long as the calyx. Cocci ovoid, coriaceous, usually only 1 or 2 out of the 5 developed into fruit.

Mauritius; woods of Pouce, Montagne Ory, Rivière Noire, etc. Endemic. *Bois Bouquet. Bois Jasmin.*

Order XXIV. BURSERACEÆ.

Flowers regular, hermaphrodite or polygamous. Sepals 3–5, deltoid, joined at the base or higher. Petals 3–5, free, hypogynous, valvate or imbricate. Disk prominent, annular. Stamens twice as many as the petals; filaments free; anthers oblong, 2-celled, slit down the side. Ovary 3–5-celled; style entire; stigma capitate: ovules 2 in a cell. Fruit dry or drupaceous; 1–5 cells with horny endocarp and 1 seed in each. Seed pendulous with a membranous testa; albumen none.—Balsamiferous trees or shrubs, with large petioled exstipulate alternate imparipinnate leaves and copious small panicled flowers. Distrib. Round the world in the tropics. Species 150.

Sepals and petals 4–5 each . . . . 1. Bursera.
Sepals and petals 3 each . . . . 2. Canarium.

1. BURSERA, Linn.

Flowers in our plant hermaphrodite. Calyx minute, 4–5-partite. Petals 4–5, lanceolate, hypogynous. Disk prominent, annular. Stamens 8–10, inserted at the base of the disk; filaments short, flattened; anthers minute, oblong. Ovary 3–5-celled, style very short; stigma capitate; ovules 2 in a cell. Fruit a hard capsule, finally dehiscing, the pericarp full of cavities containing volatile oil. Seed solitary.—Trees or shrubs, with alternate imparipinnate leaves and copious small whitish panicled flowers. DISTRIB. Tropical, mostly American. Species 40, none Continental African.

1. **B. obtusifolia,** *Lam. Encycl.* ii. 768. A straggling bush, sometimes growing into a tree 20–30 feet high, with a trunk a foot thick. Petioles terete, 2–3 inches long; leaflets 2–5-jugate, oblong, stalked, obtuse, rarely acute, 2–4 inches long, coriaceous, shining, penninerved, oblique at the base. Flowers in copious fascicled axillary panicles shorter than the leaves; pedicels very short; bracts minute, persistent. Sepals minute, deltoid, persistent. Petals $\frac{1}{12}$ inch long, falcate when expanded. Stamens included. Capsule $\frac{1}{3}$–$\frac{1}{2}$ inch long and thick, pointed, sometimes 1–2-celled and 1–2-seeded by abortion. Marignia obtusifolia, *DC. Prod.* ii. 79. *Delese. Ic. Sel.* iii. *t.* 55. M. acutifolia, *Bojer, Hort. Maur.* 83.

MAURITIUS, in the hill-forests, plentiful on the Pouce. Endemic. *Bois Colophane bâtard. Gomart. Bois de Marigni.*

2. CANARIUM, Linn.

Flowers polygamous. Calyx a cup, with 3 valvate deltoid teeth. Petals 3, oblong, hypogynous, valvate. Disk prominent, annular. Stamens 6, inserted at the base of the disk; filaments short; anthers minute, oblong. Ovary flask-shaped, 3-celled; ovules 2 in a cell; style very short; stigma 3-lobed. Fruit a drupe, with thin flesh and a bony endocarp, 1-celled and 1-seeded by abortion. Seed solitary.—Balsamiferous trees with ample alternate imparipinnate leaves and small flowers in ample panicles. DISTRIB. Species 50, nearly all tropical Asian, 2 Continental African.

1. **C. Colophania,** *Baker.* An erect tree, 30 to 50 feet high. Petioles 2–3 inches long, alternate; leaflets 5–9, distinctly stalked, oblong, 4–6 inches long, acute, cordate at the base, glabrous, moderately firm, penninerved, the distant main veins connected by intramarginal arches. Panicles ample, axillary and terminal; branches curved, angular, brown-velvety; flowers clustered towards the end of the branchlets, on very short pedicels. Calyx $\frac{1}{8}$ inch long, brown-velvety, with 3 short teeth. Petals little longer than the calyx. Stamens included. Bursera paniculata, *Lam. Encycl.* iii. 768. Colophania mauritiana, *DC. Prod.* ii. 79; *Delese. Ic. Sel.* iii. *t.* 56.

MAURITIUS, in the forests of the interior, as of the Pouce and about Curepipe. Endemic. *Bois Colophane.*

ORDER XXV. MELIACEÆ.

Flowers regular, hermaphrodite. Sepals 4–5, deltoid, free or joined in a cup. Petals 4–5, valvate or imbricate, hypogynous, deciduous.

Stamens twice as many as the petals, the filaments united in a campanulate or cylindrical cup or tube round the ovary; anthers 2-celled, splitting longitudinally. Ovary 4–5-celled; ovules 2 in a cell; style long, entire; stigma capitate. Fruit in Mauritian genera a round lobed capsule, with loculicidal dehiscence. Seeds 1–2 in each cell, albuminous.—Trees or shrubs with simple or pinnate exstipulate usually alternate leaves and copious small flowers. DISTRIB. Round the world in the tropics. Species 270.

Leaves simple.
  Anthers stalked at the top of the tube . . . . 1. TURRÆA.
  Anthers sessile at the top of the tube . . . . 2. QUIVISIA.
Leaves compound . . . . * CARAPA.

1. TURRÆA, Linn.

Flowers hermaphrodite. Calyx campanulate, with 5 deltoid teeth. Petals 5, strap-shaped, valvate, hypogynous. Stamens 10, the filaments connate in a long tube, free at the top; anthers oblong. Ovary 5-celled; ovules 2 in a cell; style long, filiform; stigma capitate. Fruit a 5-celled capsule, finally dehiscing.—Trees with alternate petioled entire leaves and flowers in axillary cymes. DISTRIB. Tropics of Old World. Species 16.

1. **T. rigida,** *Vent. Choix, t.* 48. A bush or tree glabrous throughout. Leaves alternate, short-petioled, entire, firm, obtuse or acute, 4–6 inches long, penninerved. Flowers in sessile fascicles from nodes of branches or old wood; pedicels $\frac{1}{8}$–$\frac{1}{4}$ inch. Calyx $\frac{1}{12}$ in. long, campanulate, shortly toothed, slightly silky. Corolla $\frac{3}{4}$–1 inch long, tubular, at first silky on outside. Stamens nearly as long as petals, the filaments free $\frac{1}{3}$ down. Capsule 3–4-celled by abortion. *DC. Prod.* i. 620. Quivisia chilosantha, *Bojer, Hort. Maur.* 58.

MAURITIUS; forests of the interior about Moka, etc. Endemic.

2. QUIVISIA, Comm.

Flowers hermaphrodite. Calyx campanulate or discoid, with 4–5 small deltoid teeth. Petals 4–5, obtuse, valvate. Stamens twice as many as the petals; filaments united in a tube up to the top. Ovary globose, 4–5-celled; 2 collateral ovules in a cell; style long, entire; stigma capitate. Fruit a hard globose capsule splitting loculicidally into 4–5 valves. Seeds oblong with a large lateral hilum.—Shrubs, with leaves alternate entire, or upper opposite. DISTRIB. Confined to Mauritius, Bourbon, and Rodriguez. Species 3.

Filaments joined in a cylindrical tube . . . . 1. Q. MAURITIANA.
Filaments joined in a short cup.
  Pedicels $\frac{1}{8}$ inch long . . . . 2. Q. LACINIATA.
  Pedicels $\frac{1}{4}$–$\frac{1}{2}$ inch long . . . . 3. Q. FILIPES.

1. **Q. mauritiana,** *Baker*. A much-branched glabrous shrub, reaching a height of 10 or 15 feet. Leaves short-petioled, alternate or upper opposite, obovate or oblong, 1–3 inches long, cuneate at the base, firm, penninerved, obtuse or subacute, entire or in one variety

shallowly or deeply lobed pinnatifidly. Flowers 4–8, in copious subsessile or short peduncled axillary cymes; pedicels stout, $\frac{1}{8}$–$\frac{1}{4}$ inch long. Calyx $\frac{1}{12}$ inch deep, thinly silky, nearly truncate. Petals 4–5, lingulate, densely grey-silky on the outside, $\frac{1}{8}$–$\frac{1}{4}$ inch long. Stamens 8–10, the filaments united in a tube at least half as long as the petals. Fruit a globose or pyriform hard tomentose capsule $\frac{1}{4}$–$\frac{1}{3}$ inch thick, splitting halfway down into 4–5 valves.

MAURITIUS, common in the hill forests. Also Bourbon. *Bois Quivi* or *Café Marron.* A variable plant of which the following forms are figured and described as species by Cavanilles.

1. *Q. ovata*, Cav. Diss. t. 212. Hill form, with firm obtuse obovate alternate leaves, and 3–4 tetramerous flowers in a sessile umbel.

2. *Q. heterophylla*, Cav. Diss. t. 213. Like the last, but some of the leaves entire, the others pinnatifid, with 2–3 deep or shallow obtuse lobes on each side.

3. *Q. decandra*, Cav. Diss. t. 211. Forest form, with larger alternate acute leaves, and 8–12 pentamerous racemose flowers.

4. *Q. oppositifolia*, Cav. Diss. t. 214. Forest form, with large subobtuse oblong leaves, many opposite, and tetramerous flowers in peduncled cymes.

2. **Q. laciniata,** *Balf. fil.* A small much-branched low shrub, glabrous in all its parts. Leaves alternate or opposite, nearly sessile, obovate-cuneate, obtuse, $\frac{3}{4}$–1 inch long, very glossy, strongly veined, entire or shallowly or deeply pinnatifid with a few erecto-patent obtuse lobes. Flowers 2–4 in sessile or nearly sessile cymes in the axils of the leaves on pedicels $\frac{1}{8}$ inch long. Calyx discoid, under $\frac{1}{12}$ inch broad; teeth 4, short. Bud globose, nearly or quite glabrous. Petals 4, obovate, $\frac{1}{12}$ inch long. Stamens 8; cup of united filaments short.

RODRIGUEZ, abundant over the island. *Bouton! Balfour!* Endemic. *Bois Balais.*

3. **Q. filipes,** *Baker.* A small much-branched shrub, glabrous throughout, or ultimate branches slightly pilose. Leaves alternate or uppermost opposite, short-petioled, obovate, obtuse, cuneate in the lower half, entire, firm, bright green, reticulato-venulose, $\frac{1}{2}$–$\frac{3}{4}$ inch long. Flowers 2–4 in short peduncled axillary cymes; pedicels filiform, spreading, $\frac{1}{4}$–$\frac{1}{2}$ inch long. Bud oblong, glabrous. Calyx minute, glabrous, with 4 deltoid teeth. Petals 4, oblong, $\frac{1}{12}$ inch long, widespread in the expanded flower. Stamens 8, the cup of the joined filaments very short. Q. trichopoda, *Baill. Adans.* xi. 255?

MAURITIUS on the Pouce, *Gardner! Ayres!* Endemic.,

* *Carapa moluccensis*, Lam.; DC. Prod. i. 626 (Xylocarpus Granatum, Koen.), a common plant on muddy shores from East Tropical Africa to Australia, has been gathered by Mr. Horne in the Seychelles at St. Annes Bay, Praslin, where it is called *Manglier*. It is a glabrous tree 30–40 feet high, with alternate equally pinnate leaves, 1–2-jugate large sessile obovate-oblong entire obtuse coriaceous leaflets, few flowers in lax axillary panicles shorter than the leaves, 4–5-merous calyx and corolla, the latter $\frac{1}{4}$ inch long, 8–10 anthers inside a toothed tube, large peltate stigma, and a 4–5-celled capsular fruit as large as a child's head finally dehiscing loculicidally, with few very large angular seeds with a thick corky testa.

Melia Azederach, Linn., a native of Tropical Asia, is commonly planted. *Lilas de l'Inde.*

A small tree, seen by Mr. Horne on the border of a swamp near the sea north of Port Victoria, Mahé, Seychelles, is most likely a *Trichilia;* but the specimen is too imperfect to be certain. It is glabrous in all its parts, with alternate imparipinnate leaves, membranous short-stalked oblong acute leaflets 2–3 inches long, the side ones oblique, flowers in axillary panicles shorter than the leaves, spreading pedicels $\frac{1}{4}$–$\frac{1}{3}$ in. long, a minute calyx with 5 deltoid teeth, 5 oblong obtuse petals $\frac{1}{8}$ inch long, a campanulate calyx-tube with 10 square emarginate teeth at the top with an anther to each, a cylindrical style, a 2–3-celled ovary and large capitate stigma.

ORDER XXVI. OLACINEÆ.

Flowers regular, in our genera hermaphrodite. Calyx minute, campanulate, truncate, or 4–5-toothed. Petals 4–5, lingulate, valvate. Stamens hypogynous, or adnate to the base of petals, as many or twice as many as the petals; several in *Olax* anantherous (staminodes); anthers linear or oblong, dorsifixed or basifixed, 2-celled, slitting down the side. Ovary 1-celled throughout or 3-celled at the base; ovules 2–3, pendulous; style produced or absent; stigma capitate. Fruit a 1-seeded drupe, with a hard endocarp. Seed pendulous, mostly solitary; albumen abundant.—Trees or shrubs with alternate entire exstipulate leaves; flowers small, in axillary or terminal cymes, or panicles. DISTRIB. Round the world in warm climates. Species 170.

Stamens (including staminodes) twice as many as the petals.
  Staminodes many. Calyx truncate, accrescent . . . . . . 1. OLAX.
  Staminodes 0. Calyx toothed, not accrescent . . . . . . 2. XIMENIA.
Stamens (without staminodes) as many as the petals . . . . 3. APODYTES.

1. OLAX, Linn.

Calyx truncate, campanulate, enlarging after the petals fall. Petals 5, valvate, caducous. Stamens with staminodes 9–12, the 3 bearing anthers inserted between the petals and connecting them, the barren ones adnate to the petals. Ovary free, 1-celled or 3-celled at the base; ovules 3, pendulous from a central placenta; style entire; stigma capitate. Fruit a drupe, half-included in the accrescent calyx.—Glabrous trees or shrubs, with alternate entire leaves and minute flowers in axillary racemes or corymbs. DISTRIB. Through the tropics of the Old World. Species 20–25.

1. **O. psittacorum,** *Vahl, Enum.* ii. 33. A shrub, glabrous throughout. Leaves alternate, short-petioled, 1–1$\frac{1}{2}$ inch long, ovate or ovate-lanceolate, acute, moderately firm, pale green, 1-nerved. Flowers few, in axillary peduncled corymbs. Petals 5, whitish, united by the stamens. Stamens included. Staminodia filiform, adnate halfway up to the petals, marked at the base with a black blotch. Drupe larger than a pea, half immersed in the cup-shaped truncate calyx. Fissilia psittacorum, *Lam. Encycl. t.* 28; *DC. Prod.* i. 532.

MAURITIUS, in the thick forests of Quartier Militaire, especially about Bois Chéri. Endemic. *Bois Perroquets.*

2. XIMENIA, Linn.

Calyx minute, spreading, persistent, with 4–5 not accrescent teeth.

Petals 4–5, hypogynous, valvate bearded on the face. Stamens twice as many as the petals; filaments free, filiform; anthers linear, basifixed. Ovary 3-celled; ovules 3, pendulous from a central placenta; style long, entire; stigma capitate. Fruit a 1-seeded drupe, with a bony endocarp.—Trees or shrubs, often spinose; leaves alternate, entire; flowers in axillary cymes. DISTRIB. Three other species, Cape, Polynesian, and Mexican.

1. **X. americana,** *Linn.; DC. Prod.* i. 533. A much-branched glabrous shrub 10–15 feet high. Spines in the axils of the leaves, subulate, spreading, often absent. Leaves short-petioled, obovate or oblong, 1–2 inches long, obtuse, firm, entire. Flowers in copious nearly sessile axillary cymes; pedicels shorter than the flower, ascending. Petals $\frac{1}{4}$–$\frac{1}{3}$ inch long, lingulate, falcate when expanded, clothed with long dense hairs on the face. Stamens included. Drupe as large as a plum, oblong, scarlet, edible.

SEYCHELLES, near the sea at Praslin, *Horne!* Round the world in the tropics; rare in Africa.

3. APODYTES, E. Meyer.

Calyx minute, with 5 deltoid teeth joined in a cup. Petals 5, caducous, lingulate, valvate. Stamens 5, alternate with the petals; filaments short, rather flattened; anthers oblong, dorsifixed. Ovary 1-celled; ovules 2, pendulous, superposed; style filiform, oblique; stigma capitate. Fruit a 1-seeded drupe, with a crustaceous endocarp.—Trees with alternate entire leaves and minute fragrant flowers in dense very compound panicles. DISTRIB. Tropics of the Old World. Species 9.

1. **A. mauritiana,** *Planch. in Herb. Kew.* A tree 30–40 feet high. Leaves alternate, short-petioled, glabrous, oblong, entire, obtuse or subacute, 2–3 inches long, moderately firm. Flowers in short-peduncled deltoid terminal panicles 2–3 inches long; branches with short brown pubescence; pedicels very short; bracts minute, deltoid. Calyx very small, pilose. Petals caducous, glabrous, $\frac{1}{12}$ inch long. Stamens included; filament as long as the oblong anther. Ovary villose, shorter than the oblique style. Icacina mauritiana, *Miers, Cont.* i. 56.

MAURITIUS, in woods of the Pouce, Moka, Colville Bridge, etc. Endemic.

Dr. Wright and Mr. Horne send from the Seychelles as common on the hills of Mahé and other islands specimens of a tree 50–60 feet high, of which we need to have flowers to decide whether it belong to *Gomphandra* or *Lasianthera.* It has oblong entire obtuse coriaceous short-petioled leaves 4–6 inches long, inflorescence a dense short-peduncled axillary cyme, pedicels very short, calyx minute with 6–7 oblong ciliated imbricated teeth, ovary 1-celled oblong pilose with a sessile capitate stigma, drupe oblong one-seeded $\frac{1}{2}$–$\frac{3}{4}$ inch long. *Bois Marie.*

ORDER XXVII. CELASTRACEÆ.

Flowers regular, hermaphrodite. Calyx small, spreading, persistent, with 4–5 deep teeth. Petals the same number, short, spreading, imbricate. Disk broad, annular. Stamens as many as the petals, alternate with them, inserted outside the base of the disk; filaments short; anthers minute, 2-celled, splitting lengthwise. Ovary 1–4-celled; ovules 2 in a cell, erect; style short, entire; stigma capitate. Fruit capsular or drupaceous. Seeds albuminous, often arillate.—Trees or shrubs, with opposite or alternate simple leaves, usually exstipulate, and copious small wide-opening cymose flowers. DISTRIB. Cosmopolitan. Species 400.

Leaves opposite.
  Fruit a 1-celled indehiscent capsule . . . . 1. PLEUROSTYLIA.
  Fruit a 2–4-celled drupe with thick bony endocarp . . 2. ELÆODENDRON.
Leaves alternate . . . . 3. GYMNOSPORIA.

1. PLEUROSTYLIA, Wt. and Arn.

Calyx minute, spreading, with 4–5 deltoid spreading teeth. Petals 4–5, oblong, spreading. Stamens 4–5, inserted outside the large annular disk; filaments short, rather flattened; anthers oblong. Ovary 1-celled, confluent with the disk; style short, oblique; stigma capitate. Fruit a turbinate 1-seeded indehiscent capsule.—Glabrous shrubs, with opposite entire simple leaves and minute flowers in axillary cymes. DISTRIB. East Indies and Madagascar. Species 3.

1. **P. leucocarpa,** *Baker.* A much-branched shrub 12–15 feet high, glabrous throughout, with quadrangular branchlets. Leaves short-petioled, obovate-oblong, coriaceous, shining, venulose, obtuse or emarginate, 1–1½ in. long; base cuneate. Flowers in short peduncled axillary cymes; pedicels very short. Petals oblong, whitish, $\frac{1}{12}$ in. deep. Capsule rather fleshy, ⅙ in. long, obliquely tipped by the short persistent style, containing one large dark brown obovoid seed. Euonymus leucocarpus, *Bojer, Hort. Maur.* 68. Boottia obovata, *Ayres MSS.*

MAURITIUS; hill forests of the Pouce and near Moka, *Bojer, Bouton!* Endemic, but very near the E. Indian and Ceylonese *P. Wightii.*

2. ELÆODENDRON, Jacq. fil.

Sepals 4–5, round, persistent. Petals 4–5, round, spreading. Stamens 4–5, inserted outside the large annular disk; filaments short, subulate; anthers globose. Ovary depresso-globose, confluent with the disk, 2–4-celled; ovules 2, erect; style thick, short; stigma capitate. Fruit a 2–4-celled drupe with a thick bony endocarp.—Trees or shrubs, with simple opposite leaves and copious minute flowers in axillary cymes. DISTRIB. Species 30; mostly Cape and E. Indian, a few tropical American.

1. **E. orientale,** *Jacq. Ic. Rar. t.* 48; *D.C. Prod.* ii. 10. A shrub or tree, 10–30 feet high, glabrous in all its parts. Leaves opposite, short-petioled, obovate, coriaceous, obtuse, crenate, 2–3 inches long, cuneate at the base. Flowers in copious close axillary cymes, shorter than the

leaves; pedicels equalling or exceeding the corolla. Expanded flower under ¼ inch across. Calyx lobed down nearly to the base. Petals glabrous, yellowish-green. Disk plate-shaped, with a broad rim outside the ovary. Drupe oblong, the size of an olive, usually 2-celled with one seed in each cell.

MAURITIUS, frequent in the hill-forests. RODRIGUEZ, perhaps the commonest tree of the island, *Bouton!* *Balfour!* Also Bourbon and Madagascar. *Bois d'Olive.* Young leaves dimorphic, linear, acute, half a foot long, passing into the mature by gradual transition stages.

3. GYMNOSPORIA, Wt. and Arn.

Calyx minute, with 4–5 round teeth. Petals 4–5, hypogynous, oblong, spreading. Disk large, cupular. Stamens as many as the petals, inserted in the edge of the disk; filaments short, subulate; anthers oblong. Ovary 3-celled, confluent with the disk; style very short; stigma capitate, 3-lobed; ovules 2 in a cell, basal. Fruit a 3-lobed capsule, with loculicidal dehiscence. Seed with a fungoid arillus at the base.—Shrubs, often spinose, with alternate leaves and copious minute cymose flowers. DISTRIB. Old World, from Australia to the Cape, Spain, and Canaries. Species 55.

1. **G. trigyna,** *Baker.* A glabrous shrub, 6–12 feet high, with straggling branches, without spines. Leaves short-petioled, alternate, often fascicled on short branches, oblanceolate-oblong, 3–4 inches long, firm, obtuse, crenate, narrowed at the base. Flowers in copious peduncled often fascicled cymes shorter than the leaves; pedicels slender, 2–4 times the length of the flowers. Calyx minute, with 4–5 round fimbriated teeth. Petals white, denticulate, ⅛ inch long. Capsule the size of a large pea, with 3 firm persistent divaricating valves bearing the septum down the middle. Seeds 1–3 maturing. Celastrus trigynus. *Lam.; D.C. Prod.* ii. 6. Catha trigyna, *Presl.* Celastrus pyreus, *Willem.* Ilex salicifolia, *Jacq. Coll.* v. 56, *tab.* 2, *fig.* 2.

MAURITIUS, woods of Pouce, Moka, etc. Endemic. *Bois à poudre.*

ORDER XXVIII. RHAMNACEÆ.

Flowers regular, hermaphrodite or polygamous. Calyx with a cupular usually free tube and 4–5 deltoid valvate teeth. Petals the same number as the sepals, minute, often hooded. Stamens 4–5, often hidden in the folded or concave petals; filaments subulate; anthers 2-celled, splitting down the side. Disk lining the calyx, with a free border, in *Gouania* and *Phylica* epigynous. Ovary free (inferior in *Gouania* and *Phylica*), usually 3-celled; ovules solitary, erect, anatropal; style simple or trifid. Fruit capsular or drupaceous. Seeds albuminous.—Shrubs or trees, often climbers; leaves simple, alternate or opposite, stipulate; flowers minute, copious, cymose or racemose. DISTRIB. Cosmopolitan. Species 430.

Tendrils none. Flowers in axillary cymes. Ovary superior.
  Leaves alternate. Fruit a drupe . . . . * ZIZYPHUS.
  Leaves opposite. Fruit a drupe . . . . 1. SCUTIA.
  Leaves alternate. Fruit a capsule . . . . 2. COLUBRINA.
Tendrils spiral. Flowers in terminal racemes. Ovary inferior . . . . 3. GOUANIA.
Tendrils none. Flowers in terminal clusters. Ovary inferior 4. PHYLICA.

* *Zizyphus Jujuba*, Lam.; DC. Prod. ii. 21, widely spread through the tropics of the Old World and extensively cultivated for its fruit, is plentifully established in Mauritius round Port Louis and in other parts of the island and in Rodriguez. It is a tree 15–30 feet high, with branches leaves beneath and outside of the flower densely matted with whitish pubescence, stipulary spines small hooked or straight often abortive, short-petioled rather oblique minutely toothed oblong or roundish obtuse simple tripli-nerved leaves, copious minute pentamerous flowers in sessile axillary cymes, and a yellow drupe as large as a cherry, with a bony endocarp containing 1–3 (usually 2) 1-seeded cells. *Z. rotundata*, DC. Prod. ii. 21, and *Z. mauritiana*, Lam. Ency. iii. 319, are Mauritian forms of the plant. *Masson.*

1. SCUTIA, Brongn.

Flowers hermaphrodite. Calyx campanulate, with 5 lanceolate teeth, which fall off after flowering. Petals 5, oblong unguiculate. Disk filling the tube, with a free undulated border. Stamens 5, opposite the petals; filaments subulate; anthers round. Ovary free, immersed in the calyx-tube, 2–3-celled; style short, simple; stigmas 2–3. Fruit rather fleshy, containing 2–3 triquetrous pyrenes.—Glabrous spiny shrubs, with small coriaceous opposite leaves and small flowers in axillary cymes. DISTRIB. Round the world in the tropics, also Cape. Species 8.

1. **S. Commersoni,** *Brong. in Ann. Sc. Nat.* x. 363. A climbing glabrous shrub, 6–10 feet high. Spines in the axils of leaves, hooked, often abortive. Leaves opposite, short-petioled, coriaceous, obtuse, 1–2 inches long, finely penninerved, cuneate at the base. Flowers in copious sessile or short-peduncled axillary cymes. Calyx glabrous, $\frac{1}{12}$ in. deep; teeth deciduous. Petals white, shorter than the calyx-lobes. Drupe the size of a pea, oblong, aromatic. S. indica, *Brong. loc. cit.* Rhamnus circumscissus, *Linn.* R. capensis, *Thunb.*

MAURITIUS and RODRIGUEZ, common in woods, annoying from its hooked spines. Also Cape, Bourbon, and Tropical Asia. *Bambara. Bois Senti.*

2. COLUBRINA, Rich.

Flowers polygamous. Calyx tube campanulate; teeth 5, deltoid, caducous. Petals 5, minute, hooded, enclosing the 5 stamens. Disk filling up the calyx-tube. Ovary confluent with the disk, 3-celled;

style trifid. Fruit a 3-celled capsule, with septicidal dehiscence and one large triquetrous seed in each cell.—Erect or climbing unarmed shrubs, with alternate leaves and copious minute flowers in axillary cymes. DISTRIB. Species 10, the others all American.

1. **C. asiatica,** *Brong. in Ann. Sc. Nat.* x. 369. An erect or trailing unarmed shrub, with glabrous terete branches. Leaves short-petioled, alternate, ovate, acute, membranous, 2–3 in. long, faintly toothed, rounded at the base. Flowers in copious sessile axillary cymes. Calyx $\frac{1}{12}$ in. deep; teeth as long as the tube. Petals not exceeding the calyx-teeth. Fruit a glabrous capsule, as large as a pea, finally splitting into three valves, with membranous septa and three large triquetrous seeds. Ceanothus asiaticus, *Linn.; DC. Prod.* ii. 30.

Common in the SEYCHELLES. Flat Island, *Horne!* Mauritius, on the seashore at the bay of the Petite Rivière Noire, etc., introduced. Polynesia, Tropical Asia.

Horne's 586, from the Seychelles, frequent in woods in Mahé, with alternate short-petioled membranous entire acute leaves half a foot long, of which the flowers have not yet been procured, may be a second species of *Colubrina.*

3. GOUANIA, Linn.

Flowers polygamous. Calyx-tube obconical, adnate to the ovary; teeth 5, deltoid. Petals 5, oblong unguiculate, hooded, not exceeding the calyx-teeth. Stamens 5, enfolded in the petals. Ovary inferior, 3-celled; stigma trifid; stigmas capitate. Disk epigynous, pentagonal. Fruit a three-winged capsule, the valves finally separating septicidally from the axis.—Climbing shrubs, with alternate penninerved leaves, woody spirally-curved tendrils from the axils of the upper leaves and minute flowers in long racemes. DISTRIB. Round the world in the tropics. Species 30.

Leaves only silky when young on the main veins beneath . . . 1. G. TILIÆFOLIA.
Leaves persistently silky on both surfaces . . . . . . 2. G. MAURITIANA.

1. **G. tiliæfolia,** *Lam.; DC. Prod.* ii. 40. A climbing shrub, with young branches only and veins of the leaf below rusty-pilose. Stipules and bracts similar, minute, brown, lanceolate, caducous. Leaves short-petioled, cordate-ovate, 2–4 in. long, inciso-crenate, soon naked on both sides. Flower-raceme close, 2–4 in long, with a densely pilose axis; pedicels fascicled, $\frac{1}{12}$–$\frac{1}{8}$ in. long. Expanded flower $\frac{1}{8}$ in. broad; sepals deltoid, pilose on the outside. Disk acutely pentagonal. Petals whitish, shorter than sepals. Ovary globose, naked, crowned by the persistent disk. Capsule hard, naked, $\frac{1}{2}$–$\frac{3}{4}$ in. broad, deeply triquetrous, with thick wings $\frac{1}{4}$ in. broad. G. retinaria, *DC. Prod.* ii. 40. G. Stadtmanni, *Willd.* Retinaria scandens, *Gærtn.*

MAURITIUS, in woods of Grandport, Savanne, etc. RODRIGUEZ, not common, *Balfour!* Also Bourbon. *Liane Charretiers.*

2. **G. mauritiana,** *Lam.; D.C. Prod.* ii. 40. A shrubby climber, with branches densely and persistently clothed with rusty pubescence. Leaves short-petioled, alternate, cordate-ovate, acute, distantly toothed, 2–3 in. long, clothed thinly above and densely beneath with grey silky pubescence. Racemes dense, 2–3 in. long, and also a few cymes in the axils of the upper leaves. Sepals deltoid, densely pilose, as long as the tube. Petals shorter than the sepals. Capsule $\frac{3}{8}$ in. broad, persistently silky, with rather thinner broader wings than in *G. tiliæfolia.*

MAURITIUS, *Carmichael!* Also Bourbon, Madagascar, and Comoros. There may be some mistake in this being Mauritian, as all the specially-localised specimens of Mauritian Gouanias I have seen belong to *G. tiliæfolia.*

4. PHYLICA, Linn.

Flowers hermaphrodite. Calyx superior, densely pilose; tube campanulate; teeth 5, lanceolate. Petals 5, minute, hooded. Stamens 5, hidden by the petals; filaments short, incurved; anthers small, roundish. Ovary inferior, 3-celled; style short, trifid. Fruit globose, areolate at the apex, coriaceous, finally breaking up into three cocci. —Heath-like shrubs, with crowded rigid leaves and small flowers in dense clusters. DISTRIB. Cape, with outlying representatives also in Madagascar, Bourbon, St. Helena, Tristan d'Acunha, and Amsterdam Island. Species 60–70.

1. **P. mauritiana,** *Bojer, Hort. Maur.* 70 (name only). A much-branched shrub, with slender wiry ascending stems, the old ones nodulose with the scars of fallen leaves, the young ones clothed with whitish tomentum. Leaves spreading at a right angle from the top of short pilose petioles, which are adpressed to the branchlets; blade ligulate, $\frac{3}{8}$–$\frac{1}{2}$ in. long, rigidly coriaceous, naked above, pilose below, 1-nerved with strongly revolute borders. Flowers very minute, crowded in sessile terminal heads. Calyx campanulate, $\frac{1}{24}$ in. deep, densely clothed with grey silky hairs, the teeth as long as the tube. Fruit not seen.

MAURITIUS, in the hilly forests of Grand Bassin. Endemic.

ORDER XXIX. AMPELIDEÆ.

Flowers regular, hermaphrodite or polygamous. Calyx-tube cupular; teeth 4–5, obscure or distinct. Petals 4–5, valvate. Stamens 4–5, opposite the petals, free or monadelphous; anthers 2-celled, splitting down the side. Ovary 2–5-celled; ovules 1–2 in a cell, anatropal; style none, or short, entire; stigma capitate. Fruit a 1- or many-celled berry. Seeds 1–2, bony, albuminous.—Shrubs or trees, usually climbers; leaves alternate, simple or compound; flowers copious, minute, mostly cymose. DISTRIB. Cosmopolitan, mainly tropical. Species 270.

Sepals, petals and free stamens 4; carpels 2 . . . . 1. VITIS.
Sepals, petals, carpels, and monadelphous stamens 5 . . . . 2. LEEA.

1. VITIS, Linn. § Cissus.

Flowers hermaphrodite. Calyx-tube obconic; limb obscurely 4-toothed. Petals 4, valvate, cohering by their tips. Stamens 4, free, opposite the petals. Ovary 2-celled; ovules 2 in a cell; style short, erect; stigma capitate. Fruit a berry, often by abortion 1-celled and 1-seeded.—Climbing, rarely suberect shrubs with copious leaf-opposed spiral tendrils, simple or compound leaves and copious minute flowers, usually in cymes. DISTRIB. Round the world, mostly in the tropics. Species 250.

Leaves digitately 5-foliolate . . . . 1. V. COMMERSONI.
Leaves digitately 3-foliolate or pinnately 5-foliolate . . . 2. V. MAPPIA.

1. **V. Commersoni,** *Baker*. Branches climbing, glabrous, tetragonous, moderately slender. Leaves digitate; leaflets 5, sessile, lanceolate, 3–4 inches long, $\frac{1}{3}$ in. broad, narrowed to both ends; teeth distant, setiferous; petioles cylindrical. Flowers and fruit unknown. Cissus palmata, *Poir. Encyc. Suppl.* i. 107.

MAURITIUS, *Commerson*. Escarped rocks of Montagne Ory, *Bojer*. Endemic. I have not seen any specimens.

2. **V. Mappia,** *Baker*. An erect tree, 12–30 feet high, glabrous in all its parts, with very soft wood and brittle thick fleshy terete zigzag branches. Leaves petioled, palmately 3-foliolate, or pinnately 5-foliolate, or upper simple; leaflets 2–4 in. long, acute, rather thick and fleshy, entire, cuneate at the base; stipules deltoid, membranous, caducous. Flowers in lax peduncled leafless or leaf-opposed cymes 2–3 in. broad; pedicels short. Petals 5, greenish, $\frac{1}{12}$ in. long. Berry ovoid, purple, fleshy, 1-celled, 1-seeded. Cissus Mappia, *Lam.; DC. Prod.* i. 632.

MAURITIUS, formerly abundant on the Pouce range, and still found in the old forests of the Great Bay and in the part of the island called Mapou, to which it has given its name. Endemic. *Mapou.*

Mr. Horne has sent us from amongst Bojer's Mauritian gatherings the leaves of a third species, which are glabrous, membranous, pinnately trifoliolate, the two side leaflets with a short and the end one with a long petiolule, ovate cuspidate, 3–4 in. long, broadly rounded at the base, crenato-repand, with minute cusps to the crenations. It is probably an unnamed plant.

2. LEEA, Linn.

Flowers hermaphrodite. Calyx-tube obconic; teeth 5, distinct, deltoid. Petals 5, valvate, joined at the base to the staminal tube, reflexed when expanded. Stamens 5; filaments united in a tube to the top; anthers united by their margins inside the tube. Ovary 5-celled; style short; ovules solitary. Fruit a depresso-globose berry.—Erect shrubs, with alternate compound leaves and copious minute cymose flowers. DISTRIB. Tropics of Old World. Species 20.

1. **L. sambucina,** *Willd.; DC. Prod.* i. 635. A suberect shrub, glabrous in all its parts. Leaves ample, alternate, 3–5-partite, each

division pinnate; leaflets short-petioled, opposite, oblong, acute, 1–8 in. long, penninerved, membranous, deeply inciso-crenate; base cuneate, entire. Flowers in sessile or short-peduncled axillary cymes 3–6 in. broad; branches rough with glands; pedicels short, thickened at the tip so as to enlarge gradually into the calyx. Calyx $\frac{1}{8}$ in. deep; teeth deltoid. Petals $\frac{1}{8}$ in. long, yellow or reddish, finally spreading. Tube of filaments nearly as long as the petals. Berry depresso-globose, umbilicate, under $\frac{1}{2}$ inch thick. L. coccinea, *Bojer, Hort. Maur.* 61. L. arborea, *Bojer loc. cit.*

MAURITIUS, common in the forests. Everywhere in the tropics of Old World. *L. arborea* is said to be more of a tree and to have whitish flowers, but quite agrees with the type in structure. *Bois de Sureau. Bois de Bœuf. Bois de Source.*

ORDER XXX. SAPINDACEÆ.

Flowers usually polygamous, regular or irregular. Sepals usually 5 and free. Petals 5, or 4 with the place of the fifth vacant, or absent, often crested with a scale on the face, or villose. Disk prominent, centrical or oblique. Stamens usually 8, in *Hornea* many; filaments free, hypogynous; anthers 2-celled, slitting down the side. Ovary 2–3-celled; ovules 1 or 2, rarely more; placentation axile; style entire at the base, entire or 2–3-fid at the stigmatose apex. Fruit dry or fleshy, often 1-celled and 1-seeded by abortion. Seed flat or turgid, usually exalbuminous.—Usually trees or shrubs, with alternate, usually extipulate and compound leaves and small flowers, variously arranged. DISTRIB. Cosmopolitan. Species 700–800.

Flowers with petals, irregular (the fifth petal being absent and disk unilateral).	
Cirrhose herbs with ternate peduncles	1. CARDIOSPERMUM.
Shrubs; flowers racemed; petals not crested	2. SCHMIDELIA.
Tree with panicled flowers; petals crested on the face .	* DITTELASMA.
Flowers with petals, regular.	
Stamens 5–8.	
Fruit, a loculicidal capsule; seeds solitary	3. CUPANIA.
Fruit a loculicidal capsule; seeds in a cell 2–3 . .	4. COSSIGNYA.
Fruit a saponiferous drupe	* SAPINDUS.
Stamens 20–24	5. HORNEA.
Flowers without petals.	
Leaves pinnate; sepals connate	6. STADTMANNIA.
Leaves pinnate; sepals free, imbricated	7. DORATOXYLON.
Leaves simple	8. DODONÆA.

1. CARDIOSPERMUM, Linn.

Flowers irregular, polygamous. Sepals 4, obovate, imbricated, 2 alternate ones much larger. Petals 4, obovate, unguiculate, crested with a scale at the base, 2 large and 2 small. Disk unilateral, with two large glands. Stamens 8, eccentric; filaments unequal, subulate, pilose. Ovary sessile, 2-celled; ovules solitary; style short, trifid. Frut a large membranous inflated capsule dehiscing loculicidally.—Shrubby herbs, with slender climbing stems, alternate 2–3-ternate leaves, flowers in trifid umbels, and peduncles with a pair of spiral tendrils at the top. DISTRIB. Round the world in the tropics. Species 15.

Capsule 1–1½ inch broad and long . . . . 1. C. HALICACABUM.
Capsule ½ inch broad and long . . . . 2. C. MICROCARPUM.

1. **C. Halicacabum,** *Linn.; DC. Prod.* i. 601. A wide-climbing annual, with slender groved stems, at first finely downy. Leaves long-petioled, 2–3-ternate, membranous; first divisions long-stalked; ultimate rhomboid, acute, deeply pinnatifid. Flowers in axillary long-peduncled trifid umbels, with a pair of spiral tendrils at the top of the peduncle. Petals whitish, ⅛ in. long; largest pair of sepals as long as the petals. Capsules stalked, 1–1½ in. broad and long, finely pilose. *Bot. Mag.* t. 1049. C. Corindum, *Bojer*, *Hort. Maur.* 55.

MAURITIUS, common, especially in cultivated ground. Round the world in tropics. *Pokepoke. Bonnet de Prêtre.*

2. **C. microcarpum,** *H.B.K.; DC. Prod.* i. 601. Scarcely more than a variety of *C. Halicacabum*, with which it agrees precisely in habit, leaves and flower, differing only in the size of its capsule, which is not more than half an inch broad and long.

SEYCHELLES, *Perville! Horne!* RODRIGUEZ, abundant, *Dr. Balfour!* Round the world in tropics. No doubt will be found also in Mauritius if looked for.

2. SCHMIDELIA, Linn.

Flowers irregular, polygamous Sepals 4, round, obtuse, convex, much imbricated. Petals 4, lingulate, hairy on the face. Disk unilateral, lobed. Stamens 8, eccentric; filaments subulate; anthers round, minute. Ovary 2-lobed, 2-celled; ovules solitary; style subulate, with two deep falcate branches. Fruit globose, rather fleshy, indehiscent, 1-celled by abortion.—Erect shrubs or trees, with alternate exstipulate 1–3-foliolate leaves and minute flowers in simple or panicled racemes. DISTRIB. Species 80. Cosmopolitan in the tropics. *Allophylus*, Linn., an older name for the genus, is used by Hiern in Flora Indica.

Leaves trifoliate . . . . 1. S. RACEMOSA.
Leaves simple . . . . 2. S. MONOPHYLLA.

1. **S. racemosa.** *Linn.; DC. Prod.* i. 610. An erect shrub or small tree. Petioles 1–1½ in. long; leaflets 3, glabrous, subcoriaceous, oblong, penninerved, acute, 2–3 in. long, obscurely repand, the central one short-petioled, deltoid at the base, the side ones oblique, nearly sessile. Racemes short-peduncled, mostly simple, shorter than the leaves.

Flowers fascicled; pedicels as long as the calyx. Sepals obovate, glabrous $\frac{1}{24}$ in. long. Expanded flower greenish-white, $\frac{1}{12}$ in. broad. Stamens much exserted. Ovary glabrous. Fruit a globose red berry, as large as a pea. Ornitrophe mauritiana, *Bojer*. Schmidelia Bojeriana, *Camb.*; *DC. loc. cit.*

Var. INTEGRIFOLIA (*DC. Prod.* i. 610, as a species). Habit more arborescent, leaflets larger subentire often 4–6 inches long, racemes often copiously panicled, ovary villose. Ornitrophe integrifolia, *Willd.*; *Lam. Ill.* t. 309, fig. 1.

MAURITIUS, common in the woods, the type principally on the Pouce range. SEYCHELLES, *Wright!* RODRIGUEZ, *Balfour!* Also Tropical Asia, Madagascar, and Bourbon. *Bois Merles. Bois trois feuilles.*

2. **S. monophylla**, *Presl, Bot. Bemerk.* 40. A tree 20–30 feet high. Leaves simple, oblong, acute, subcoriaceous, shining, entire or obscurely repand, 3–4 in. long, cuneate at the base; petiole $\frac{1}{2}$ inch long. Racemes simple, dense, short peduncled, 2–3 in. long; pedicels spreading, as long as the calyx. Sepals $1\frac{1}{2}$ in. long, glabrous, obovate. Petals as long as the sepals, pilose on the face and edge. Stamens not exserted. Ovary 2-celled, villose. Fruit globose, fleshy, the size of a pea. S. Dregeana, *Sonder*. Rhus monophylla, *E. Meyer*.

SEYCHELLES, not uncommon in the mountain woods of Mahé and Praslin, *Horne! Wright!* Also Natal, Madagascar, Comoros. *Bois Maris.*

* *Dittelasma Rarak*, Hook. fil. Gen. Plant. i. 396 (Sapindus Rarak, *DC. Prod.* i. 608), a native of Tropical Asia, has been found by Mr. Horne in the Seychelles in several places in Mahé, but is perhaps an introduction. It is a tree with silky branchlets, large alternate exstipulate pinnate leaves, numerous alternate or opposite entire oblique acuminate lanceolate leaflets, very copious small polygamous flowers in ample terminal panicles, very short pedicels, 5 oblong silky imbricated sepals, 4 villose petals crested on the face with a large scale and a fleshy saponiferous fruit as large as a cherry 1-celled by abortion.

3. CUPANIA, Linn.

Flowers regular, polygamous. Sepals 5, free, oblong, much imbricated. Petals 5, oblong, pilose, without scales. Disk conspicuous, symmetrical. Stamens usually 8, placed inside the disk, exserted in the male flowers, rudimentary in the females; filaments subulate, villose; anthers round, minute. Ovary stipitate, 3-celled; ovules solitary; style short, entire. Fruit a stalked 3-celled obversely deltoid coriaceous capsule, dehiscing loculicidally.—Trees or shrubs, with alternate exstipulate, equally pinnate leaves, and small flowers in copious panicles. DISTRIB. Round the world in the tropics. Species 30.

Panicle dense, its branches and the thick sepals silky . . 1. C. LÆVIS.
Panicle lax, its branches and the thin sepals naked . . 2. C. VENULOSA.

1. **C. lævis**, *DC. Prod.* i. 613. A bush or small tree, 12–30 feet high. Leaves petioled, alternate; leaflets 6–8, usually opposite, sessile, coriaceous, obovate-oblong, obtuse or subacute, glabrous, venulose shining, 2–4 in. long; base much narrowed. Flowers in dense axillary panicles, shorter than the leaves, with brown silky branches; pedicels as long as calyx. Sepals $\frac{1}{8}$ in. broad, oblong, obtuse, silky, coriaceous persistent. Petals round, with a claw, not longer than the sepals. Filaments slightly villose. Capsule $\frac{1}{2}$–$\frac{3}{4}$ in. broad, narrowed suddenly into a stalk $\frac{1}{4}$ inch long; valves hard, venulose; style persistent. Molinæa lævis, *Lam. Ill.* tab. 305, fig. 1.

MAURITIUS, hill forests of the Pouce, Savanne range, Montagne Longue, etc. Also Bourbon. *Molinæa alternifolia*, Lam., Pers., is a mere form with the leaflets thrown out of their usual opposite arrangement. *Bois de Goulettes.*

2. **C. venulosa**, *DC. Prod.* i, 613. A much-branched bush or low tree. Leaves short-petioled, alternate; leaflets 2–4, sessile, obovate-oblong, obtuse, rather oblique, cuneate at the base, sessile, 2–5 in. long, thinner than in *C. lævis*, venulose, glabrous. Panicles copious, from the axils of the upper leaves, which they usually overtop; branches angular, naked; pedicels exceeding the flowers. Expanded flower broadly bell-shaped. Sepals $\frac{1}{8}$ in. long, roundish, thin, reflexing. Filaments densely villose in the lower part. Capsule exactly as in *C. lævis*.

MAURITIUS, frequent in the forests, Pouce, Montagne Longue, etc. Also Bourbon. *Bois de Goulettes.*

4. COSSIGNYA, Comm.

Flowers irregular, polygamous. Sepals 5, distinct, oblong, imbricated. Petals 4, round with a claw, longer than the sepals, caducous. Stamens 5–6, eccentric; filaments filiform. Ovary sessile, obovoid, 3-lobed, 3-celled; style long, filiform, persistent; stigma trifid. Fruit a coriaceous loculicidal 3-celled capsule, with 2–3 seeds in a cell.—The only species.

C. pinnata, *Lam. Encyc.* ii. 132, *Illust.* t. 236. A much-branched erect shrub, with branchlets rough with stellate pale brown tomentum. Leaves petioled, alternate, exstipulate; leaflets 3–5, obovate-oblong, obtuse, entire, coriaceous, penninerved, 2–4 in. long, cuneate at the lower half, pale and scabrous with pubescence like that of the branches below. Flowers in dense terminal corymbose panicles. Sepals $\frac{1}{8}$ in. long, reflexing. Expanded flower $\frac{1}{2}$ in. broad, white. Ovary densely brown-tomentose; style $\frac{1}{4}$–$\frac{1}{3}$ in. long. Stamens included. Capsule as large as a cherry. Seeds round, black, axile. *Wall. Cat.* 8484. C. borbonica, *DC. Prod.* i. 614. C. ternata, *Lam. loc. cit.* Ruizia aurea, *Hort.*

MAURITIUS, common on the Pouce range, and at Trou-aux-Cerfs. Also Bourbon, teste DC. *Bois de Judas.*

* *Sapindus emarginatus*, Vahl; DC. Prod. i. 607, a native of Tropical Asia, is planted in Mauritius, and naturalised on the seashore of Rodriguez, near Mathurin, *Bouton! Balfour!* It is a tree with large alternate petioled imparipinnate leaves, 5–7 short-petioled coriaceous oblong obtuse or emarginate entire leaflets 2–4 in. long, small flowers in ample terminal deltoid panicles, 5 oblong silky much imbricated coriaceous sepals, 5 villose narrow petals, 8 villose exserted stamens, a densely hairy 3-lobed 3-celled ovary, with a short entire style, and 1-3 large fleshy saponiferous carpels. *Bois Savon. Savonnier.*

5. HORNEA, Baker.

Flowers polygamous. Sepals 5, round, much imbricated, silky on the back, naked on the face, the two outer smallest. Petals 5, just like the inner sepals in shape and vestiture, but with a densely pilose emarginate scale at the claw. Disk cup-shaped, irregularly lobed, enclosing the stamens and ovary. Stamens 20–24, inserted inside the disk, glabrous; filaments short, filiform; anthers minute, oblong. Ovary sessile, densely pilose, 2-celled, with a single ovule in each cell from the axis below the middle; style short, simple, pilose; stigma capitate. Fruit a 2-lobed velvety samara, with a broad wing. Seed globose, black. Endemic and monotypic.

1. **H. mauritiana**, *Baker.* A shrub or tree, with branchlets clothed with brownish silky hairs. Leaves short-petioled, equally pinnate; leaflets 4, sessile, oblong, obtuse, glabrous, coriaceous, venulose, 2–4 in. long, oblique at the base. Flowers in axillary and terminal panicles with silky ascending branches; pedicels very short. Petals and inner sepals $\frac{1}{4}$ in. long. Lobes of samara rhomboid, erecto-patent, an inch long, above $\frac{1}{2}$ in. broad, brown-velvety, rigidly coriaceous, the wing as broad as the cell. Thouinia? Mauritiana, *Bojer, Hort. Maur.* 56 (*name only*).

MAURITIUS, in the forests of Flacq, near Pierre-font, *Bojer!* Endemic. *Arbre à l'huile.*

6. STADTMANNIA, Lam.

Flowers regular, polygamous. Calyx a deep cup, with 5 obscure deltoid teeth. Petals 0. Disk thick, elevated, lobed. Stamens 8, regular, exserted; filaments filiform; anthers oblong. Ovary deeply 3-lobed, 3-celled; ovules solitary in each cell; style short; stigma capitate. Fruit usually 1-celled by abortion, large, dry, round, indehiscent. Monotypic.

1. **S. Sideroxylon,** *DC. Prod.* i. 615. A large tree with hard heavy reddish wood. Leaves alternate, petioled, abruptly pinnate; leaflets 8–12, opposite, oblong, short-stalked, obtuse, coriaceous, entire, oblique at the base. Panicles dense, cylindrical, 3–4 in. long; branches corymbose, rather silky; pedicels $\frac{1}{12}$–$\frac{1}{8}$ in. Calyx $\frac{1}{12}$ in. long, coriaceous. Stamens twice as long as the calyx. Fruit a hard globe nearly an inch thick. S. oppositifolia, *Poir. Encyc.* vii. 376.

MAURITIUS, once frequent in the primeval woods, but now becoming scarce. Endemic. *Bois de Fer.*

7. DORATOXYLON, Thouars.

Flowers polygamous, regular. Sepals 5, oblong, free, much imbricated, persistent. Petals 0. Disk minute, annular. Stamens 5–8, much exserted; filaments filiform; anthers round, minute. Ovary 2-celled; ovules 2, axile; stigma nearly sessile, capitate. Fruit fleshy, indehiscent, 1–2-celled; cells by abortion 1-seeded. Seeds ovoid, exalbuminous, with a membranous testa. Monotypic.

1. **D. mauritianum,** *Thouars; Hook. fil. Gen. Plant.* i. 408. A much-branched shrub, 6–8 feet high. Leaves alternate, short-petioled, exstipulate, imparipinnate; leaflets 2–8, opposite, sessile, oblique, oblong or obovate, obtuse or subacute, entire, shining, coriaceous, venulose. Flowers in dense sessile crowded panicles in the axils of the leaves; pedicels very short. Sepals $\frac{1}{12}$ in. long, oblong, coriaceous, silky. Stamens 2–3 times as long as the calyx. Fruit oblong, purplish, juicy, the size of a cherry. Melicocca diversifolia, *Juss. in Mem. Mus.* iii. 178, t. 7; *DC. Prod.* i. 615. M. apetala, *Poir. Encycl. Suppl.* iii. 224.

MAURITIUS, in woods of the Pouce range, Plaines-Wilhelms, Rivière Noire, etc. Also Bourbon. *M. diphylla,* Bojer, Hort. Maur. 56, is a form with large unijugate obovate leaflets. *Bois de goulettes. Bois de joilettes. Bois de Sagai.*

8. DODONÆA, Linn.

Flowers unisexual or polygamous. Sepals 4, ovate-lanceolate. Petals 0. Stamens usually 8; anthers nearly sessile, not exceeding the sepals. Ovary sessile, 3–4-lobed and -celled; ovules 2 in each cell; stigmas as many as the lobes. Fruit a 2–3-lobed and -celled dry septicidal capsule, each lobe with a broad wing. Seeds exalbuminous, solitary.—Shrubs or trees, with alternate exstipulate viscose simple or abruptly pinnate leaves and inconspicuous panicled flowers. DISTRIB. Species 80. Many Australian; a few extending round the world in the tropics.

1. **D. viscosa,** *Linn.; DC. Prod.* i. 617. A small shrub, with glabrous viscose leaves and triquetrous branchlets. Leaves nearly sessile, fragrant, simple, oblanceolate, firm, entire, obtuse or acute, 2–4 in. long. Flowers in small dense terminal panicles; pedicels ¼ in. long. Sepals thin, green, $\frac{1}{12}$ in. long. Valves of capsule 2–3, ¼–⅜ in. broad, samara-like, rounded at the base and apex, with a wing encircling the outside of the cell. D. salicifolia and microcarpa, *DC. loc. cit.*

MAURITIUS, in woods of the Pouce, Piton de Rivière Noire, etc. RODRIGUEZ, common on hill-slopes, *Balfour!* All round the world in the tropics. *Bois de Reinette.*

ORDER XXXI. ANACARDIACEÆ.

Flowers regular, hermaphrodite or polygamous. Calyx 3–5-fid; sepals free. Petals the same number as the sepals, small, obtuse. Disk usually annular. Stamens twice as many as the petals, in *Sclerocarya* indefinite; filaments free, subulate, inserted on or outside the disk; anthers minute, round, 2-celled, slitting down the side. Ovary free, placed inside the disk, 1- or several-celled; ovules solitary; styles present or absent, stigmas as many as the cells. Fruit fleshy, with a bony endocarp. Seed with albumen 0 or thin.—Trees with alternate exstipulate imparipinnate or simple leaves, juice often glutinous, and small flowers in axillary racemes or panicles. DISTRIB. Cosmopolitan.

Fruit 1-celled. Leaves entire . . . . 1. CAMPNOSPERMA.
Fruit with several cells. Leaves imparipinnate.
  Stamens 8–10. Styles joined above . . . . 2. SPONDIAS.
  Stamens 12–18. Styles free from the base . . . . . 3. SCLEROCARYA.

1. CAMPNOSPERMA, Thwaites.

Flowers regular, hermaphrodite. Calyx persistent, 3–5-lobed; lobes ovate-deltoid. Petals 3–6, round, slightly longer than the calyx. Disk prominent, cup-shaped. Stamens 6–10, inserted outside the disk; filaments filiform; anthers round, minute. Ovary immersed in the disk, 1-celled, with one pendulous ovule; style 0; stigma peltate. Fruit a fleshy drupe, with a bony endocarp.—Trees, with entire leaves, and minute flowers in axillary panicles. DISTRIB. Species 6, 4 Indian, 1 Madagascar.

1. **C. seychellarum,** *March. Rev. Anac.* 173. A tree 30 feet high, with thick straight branches. Leaves alternate, exstipulate, oblong, subobtuse, entire, coriaceous, glabrous, petioled, 4–6 in. long, cuneate at the base, with crowded anastomosing veins raised on the under surface. Flowers minute, in dense nearly sessile panicles shorter than the leaves; bracts minute, deltoid; pedicels very short. Flower $\frac{1}{12}$ in. broad when expanded. Sepals and petals 3 each. Stamens rather exserted. Drupe purple, the size of a small cherry.

SEYCHELLES, common in all the islands from the shore to the hilltops. Wood used for making canoes. Endemic, but very near *C. zeylanicum*, Thwaites, of Ceylon. *Bois des Montagnes.*

2. SPONDIAS, Linn.

Flowers polygamous. Calyx small, deciduous, 4–5-cleft. Petals the same number, nearly valvate, spreading when expanded. Disk prominent, cupshaped, with a raised crenate border. Stamens 8–10, inserted with the petals beneath the disk. Ovary sessile, free, 4–5-celled; ovules solitary, pendulous; styles 5, short, free at the base, joined upwards. Fruit a fleshy drupe, with a 1–5-celled bony endocarp.—Large trees, with alternate exstipulate imparipinnate leaves, numerous opposite leaflets, minute whitish flowers and yellow eatable fruit as large as a plum. DISTRIB. All round the world in the tropics. Species 8.

Leaves and peduncles densely pubescent . . . . 1. S. PUBESCENS.
Leaves and peduncles glabrous . . . . 2. S. BORBONICA.

1. **S. pubescens,** *Baker.* A tree, with stout terete branchlets. Leaves crowded at the end of the branchlets, imparipinnate, 5–6 in. long; leaflets 9–11, ovate, acute, membranous, 2–3 in. long, pilose on both surfaces, opposite, nearly sessile; petiole densely pilose, 1–1½ in. long. Panicles almost racemose, crowded at the end of the branches, 2–3 in. long, with a densely pilose rachis, distinctly peduncled, with the flowers crowded on very short distant spreading branches. Calyx nearly sessile, glabrous, campanulate, under $\frac{1}{24}$ in. long, with 5 obtuse oblong teeth as long as the tube. Petals lanceolate, twice as long as the sepals: Anthers 10, oblong, included. Fruit not seen. Shakua pubescens, *Bojer, Hort. Maur.* 82.

MAURITIUS, in the dense forests of Quartier Militaire and Savanne. Endemic. *Bois Blanc.*

2. **S. borbonica,** *Baker.* A tree, glabrous in all its parts, with stout terete branches. Leaves imparipinnate, crowded near the end of the branches; petiole 2–3 in. long; blade half a foot long; leaflets 7–9, sessile, opposite, membranous, 2–3 in. long, oblong or lanceolate acuminate. Panicles crowded at the end of the branches, short-peduncled, 3–4 in. long, almost racemose, the flowers crowded on very short spreading branchlets. Buds globose. Calyx nearly sessile, under $\frac{1}{24}$ in. long; teeth 5, ovate, obtuse, longer than the tube. Petals twice as long as the sepals. Stamens 10, included. Fruit not seen. Poupartia borbonica, *Lam. Encyc. v.* 606; *Bojer, Hort. Maur.* 82.

MAURITIUS, on woody hills at Flacq and Trois Ilots. Also Bourbon. *Bois Poupart.*

The Polynesian *S. dulcis*, Forst. is commonly cultivated both in Mauritius and the Seychelles. *Fruit de Cythère. Hévi.*

3. SCLEROCARYA, Hochst.

Flowers regular, polygamous. Sepals 4–5, free, oblong, imbricated. Petals 4–5, broad-oblong, imbricated. Disk prominent, cup-shaped, with a spreading border. Stamens 12–18, inserted under the disk; filaments filiform; anthers round, minute. Ovary subglobose, 2-5-celled; styles spreading from the base. Fruit a large fleshy drupe, with a 2–3-celled endocarp.—Large trees, with imparipinnate leaves and small flowers in dense short axillary racemes. DISTRIB. Entirely African. Species 4.

Leaflets distinctly petioled . . . . 1. S. SHAKUA.
Leaflets sessile . . . . 2. S. CASTANEA.

1. **S. Shakua,** *Baker.* A tall tree, glabrous in all its parts, with thick stiff branchlets. Leaflets 9–11, opposite, moderately firm, oblong, acute or cuspidate, $1\frac{1}{2}$–2 in. long; petiole slender, $1\frac{1}{2}$–2 in. long. Racemes short-peduncled, 2–3 in. long, close or interrupted; pedicels very short; bracts minute, deltoid, navicular. Calyx campanulate, $\frac{1}{12}$ in. long. Petals 2–3 times as long as the sepals. Stamens 15–16, rather exserted. Female flowers and fruit not seen. Spondias Chakoua, *Bojer in Herb. Kew.*

MAURITIUS, *Newman!* This may be *Shakua excelsa*, Bojer, Hort. Maur. 82 (name only), which is a native of Madagascar and in Mauritius cultivated only. Dr. Kirk has found it in Zanguebar.

2. **S. castanea,** *Baker.* A tree, glabrous in all its parts, with very thick terete branchlets. Leaves crowded, imparipinnate; petiole 1–$1\frac{1}{2}$ in. long; leaflets 7–9, opposite, sessile, oblong, acute, 2–4 in. long, moderately firm, obscurely crenulate, unequally rounded at the base, the lowest pair shorter and broader than the rest. Flowers in dense sessile axillary racemes, withered and badly shown in our only specimen. Expanded corolla $\frac{1}{8}$ in. across, exceeding the calyx; petals oblong, stellate. Styles 5, diverging.

Island of RODRIGUEZ, in the valleys of Rivière Palmiste and Rivière Mouruc. *Bouton! Balfour! Figue Marron.* Endemic.

* The Cashew-nut, *Anacardium occidentale*, Linn., a native of the West Indies, is commonly planted both in Mauritius and is now the commonest of all trees in the Seychelles. It is a tree 15–20 feet high, with crowded petioled large entire obtuse obovate-cuneate leaves with very distinct spreading main veins, small polygamous pentamerous flowers in terminal panicles with corymbose branches, silky linear petals and an oblique reniform indehiscent fruit on a thickened clavate red or yellow pedicel. *Noix d'acajou. Cajou.*

The Mango, *Mangifera indica*, Linn., is also commonly planted and subspontaneous. *Manguier.*

ORDER XXXII. CONNARACEÆ.

Flowers regular, hermaphrodite or polygamous. Sepals 5, free or connate at the base, coriaceous, persistent. Petals 5, obovate or lingulate, with a short claw. Disk obscure. Stamens 5–10, obscurely perigynous; filaments subulate, free; anthers minute, 2-celled, slit down the side. Carpels 5, distinct, villose, each narrowed into a short style, usually only one maturing; ovules 2, collateral, ascending; stigma capitate. Fruit an oblique rugose coriaceous follicle, dehiscing down the dorsal suture. Seed solitary, often arillate.—Trees or shrubs, with alternate usually compound leaves, entire coriaceous opposite leaflets and minute flowers in panicles or racemes. DISTRIB. Round the world in the tropics. Species 140.

Leaflets 3; flowers in ample terminal panicles; stamens 5 . . . 1. AGELÆA.
Leaflets numerous, flowers in fascicled racemes from the old wood; stamens 10 . . . . 2. CNESTIS.

1. AGELÆA, Soland.

Flowers regular, hermaphrodite. Sepals 5, oblong-lanceolate, distinct, slightly imbricated in bud. Petals 5, free, lanceolate. Disk minute. Stamens in our plant 5, included; filaments filiform; anthers oblong. Carpels 5, pilose, narrowed gradually into the style, generally only one maturing. Fruit a coriaceous rugose oblique follicle, opening down the lower half of the dorsal suture.—Climbing shrubs, with trifoliolate leaves, broad entire leaflets, and very copious minute flowers in ample terminal panicles. DISTRIB. Tropics of the Old World. Species 9.

1. **A. Lamarckii,** *Planch. in Linn.* xxiii. 438. A woody climber, without tendrils. Leaves long-petioled, alternate, exstipulate; leaflets 3, orbicular or ovate-cuspidate, 2–4 in. long, entire, coriaceous, glabrous; side ones stalked, opposite, rather oblique. Panicle ½–¾ foot long, with dense erecto-patent thyrsoid branches; pedicels very short. Sepals ⅛ in. long, persistent, silky on the back, coriaceous. Petals a little longer. Follicle obliquely turbinate, ½ in. long, rugose, finely brown-velvety. Cnestis obliqua, *Bojer, Hort. Maur.* 84, *non Beauv.* Connarus pinnatus, *Lam.* Omphalobium pentagynum, *D.C. Prod.* ii. 86.

MAURITIUS, in the woods of Flacq and the Savanne range. Also Madagascar and Zambesi land. *Bois Haricot.*

2. CNESTIS, Juss.

Flowers polygamous. Sepals 5, lanceolate, connate at the base, reflexing, persistent. Petals 5, lingulate with a claw. Stamens 10, hypogynous; filaments subulate; anthers globose, minute. Carpels 5, distinct, sessile, villose, narrowed into a short style, usually only one maturing; stigma terminal. Fruit a silky coriaceous follicle.—Woody climbers, with imparipinnate leaves, the flowers in small fascicled racemes from the old wood. DISTRIB. Spread through the tropics of the Old World. Species 10.

Leaflets large, flat, glabrous, cuneate at the base . . . . 1. C. GLABRA.
Leaflets smaller, bullate, downy below, cordate at the base . 2. C. POLYPHYLLA.

1. **C. glabra,** *Lam. Ill.* t. 387. A robust woody climber, without tendrils, reaching to the top of high trees; branchlets and leaves entirely glabrous. Leaves ½–1 foot long, distinctly petioled; leaflets 9–

15, oblong, short-stalked, obtuse, flat, coriaceous, entire, 2–4 in. long, cuneate at the base. Flowers in dense short-peduncled racemes 1–3 in. long from the old branchlets, rarely panicled; the rachis grey-downy; pedicels very short. Calyx $\frac{1}{12}$ in. long, reflexing, villose on the outside. Petals shorter than the sepals, yellowish-white. Carpels 5, diverging, densely villose. Follicles an inch long, finely brown-silky, lined with a coat of bristles inside. Seed with a whitish cupular arillus. *DC. Prod.* ii. 87.

Mauritius, woods of the Pouce, Montagne Longue and Savanne ranges. Also Bourbon. *Liane des Rats. Mort aux Rats.*

2. **C. polyphylla,** *Lam. Ill. t.* 387, *fig.* 2. A woody climber, with silky branchlets. Leaves 3–4 in. long, petioled; leaflets 11–17, oblong, cordate, opposite, short-stalked, 1–1½ in. long, rather bullate, coriaceous, downy beneath. Flowers in densely fascicled racemes 1–2 in. long from the old branches, with a densely brown-silky rachis; pedicels very short. Petals lingulate, $\frac{1}{8}$ in. long, exceeding the lanceolate reflexed sepals. Stamens as long as the petals. Follicles not seen. *DC. Prod.* ii. 86.

Mauritius, in forests of the Savanne range and gorges of the Rivière Noire. *Bojer.* We have it only from Madagascar. *Liane des Rats. Liane à Paniers.*

Order XXXIII. LEGUMINOSÆ.

Flowers irregular, except in Acacieæ, usually hermaphrodite. Calyx gamosepalous, with 5 teeth, subequal or more or less fully joined into two lips. Petals 5, unequal or equal, occasionally some absent. Stamens 10, rarely indefinite or 1 or more absent or imperfect; anthers 2-celled, usually slit down the side. Ovary monocarpellary, sessile or stalked; ovules 1 or many; style and stigma various. Fruit a pod, in most of the Mauritian representatives splitting down both sutures. Seeds usually exalbuminous.—Herbs, shrubs or trees; leaves alternate, stipulate, usually pinnate; inflorescence various. Distrib. The second largest of all the known natural orders. Cosmopolitan. Species 7000–8000.

Sub-order I. Papilionaceæ. Corolla papilionaceous, the upper petal (standard) outermost in bud.

Tribe I. Genisteæ. Stamens monadelphous. Leaves digitately trifoliolate. Pod not jointed.

Spiny shrub with bilabiate calyx . . . . * Ulex.
No spines; calyx 5-cleft . . . . 1. Crotalaria.

Tribe II. Trifolieæ. Stamens diadelphous. Leaves pinnately trifoliolate, with toothed leaflets. Pod not jointed.

The only genus . . . . * Melilotus.

Tribe III. Galegeæ. Stamens diadelphous. Leaves usually imparipinnate, with entire leaflets. Pod not jointed.

Pod small, globose, one-seeded . . . . * PSORALEA.
Pod cylindrical, terete . . . . 2. INDIGOFERA.
Pod flat, with thin sutures . . . . 3. TEPHROSIA.
Pod large, torulose, with thick sutures . . . . * SESBANIA.

Tribe IV. HEDYSAREÆ. Pod splitting up into one seeded joints. Stamens and leaves various.

Stamens diadelphous, 9 and 1; joints flat . . . . . . 4. DESMODIUM.
Stamens diadelphous, 9 and 1; joints turgid . . . . . 5. ALYSICARPUS.
Stamens diadelphous, 5 and 5 . . . . 6. ÆSCHYNOMENE.
Stamens monadelphous . . . . 7. ZORNIA.

Tribe V. VICIEÆ. Leaves pinnate, ending in a tendril. Pod not jointed.

Herb with 10 diadelphous stamens . . . . * VICIA.
Shrubby climber with 9 monadelphous stamens . . . . 8. ABRUS.

Tribe VI. PHASEOLEÆ. Stamens various. Pod not jointed. Leaves pinnately trifoliolate. Usually climbers.

Climbers with monadelphous stamens.
Pod small, linear, subcompressed . . . . 9. TERAMNUS.
Pod large, square, with four crisped wings . . . . . . * PSOPHOCARPUS.
Pod large, ensiform, with a rib down each valve . . . . 10. CANAVALIA.
Climbers with diadelphous stamens.
Ovules more than two. Leaves not gland-dotted.
Petals very unequal in length.
Standard very large. Pod thin, flat . . . . 11. CLITORIA.
Standard very large. Pod torulose. . . . . 12. ERYTHRINA.
Standard small . . . . 13. MUCUNA.
Petals equal in length.
Keel spiral . . . . * PHASEOLUS.
Keel beaked . . . . 14. DOLICHOS.
Keel obtuse.
Pod small, oblong, turgid, depressed between seeds . 15. ATYLOSIA.
Pod large, oblong, turgid, depressed between seeds . * PACHYRHIZUS.
Pod small, terete. uniform . . . . 16. VIGNA.
Pod small, flat, linear . . . . 17. GALACTIA.
Ovules two. Leaves gland-dotted . . . . 18. RHYNCHOSIA.
Erect shrubs with diadelphous stamens
Bracts large, persistent, hiding the flowers . . . . . . * FLEMINGIA.
Bracts caducous . . . . * CAJANUS.

Tribe VII. DALBERGIEÆ. Stamens monadelphous or diadelphous. Pod indehiscent. Trees or shrubs with imparipinnate leaves and entire leaflets.

The only genus . . . . 19. PONGAMIA.

Sub-order II. CÆSALPINEÆ. Petals rather unequal, all obovate, the uppermost inside in bud.

Stamens ten, all present, free.
Pod thin flat, splitting down the valves . . . . * HÆMATOXYLON.
Pod turgid moniliform . . . . * PARKINSONIA.
Pod oblong, flattish, dehiscent or indehiscent . . . . * CÆSALPINIA.
Pod large, oblong, coriaceous, rough . . . . 20. TRACHYLOBIUM.
Stamens, some of the ten absent or imperfect.
Pod thin, flat, sharp-shaped . . . . 21. CASSIA.
Pod flat, oblong . . . . 22. AFZELIA.
Pod thick, strap-shaped, with a pulpy mesocarp . . . * TAMARINDUS.

Sub-order III. **Mimoseæ.** Petals regular, strap-shaped, valvate in bud.

Stamens definite (10).
  Flowers in spikes.
    Pod very large, woody, jointed . . . . * Entada.
    Pod large, curved, coriaceous, not jointed . . . . . * Adenanthera.
    Pod small, with a wing down each suture . . . . . 23. Gagnebina.
  Flowers in round heads.
    Pinnæ of leaf digitate . . . . * Mimosa.
    Pinnæ of leaf pinnate.
      Pod small, subsessile, linear . . . . * Desmanthus.
      Pod large, flat, stalked . . . . * Leucæna.
Stamens indefinite
    Stamens free . . . . 24. Acacia.
    Stamens connate
      Pod straight, flat . . . . * Albizzia.
      Pod spirally curved . . . . * Pithecolobium.

* *Ulex europæus*, Linn., the common European furze, is naturalised in Mauritius on the hills of Nouvelle Découverte. It is a bush, with abundant rigid spiny branchlets, leaves of seedling plants trifoliolate, of mature branchlets simple or abortive, bright yellow flowers with the structure of *Genisteæ*, calyx with two deep obscurely-toothed lips, and a small oblong flattened few-seeded pod, scarcely protruded from the calyx.

1. CROTALARIA, Linn.

Calyx-tube campanulate; teeth 5, distinct, subequal. Corolla papilionaceous; petals equal in length; standard round or oblong unguiculate; keel narrowed into a long upcurved beak. Ovary sessile or stalked, 2- or many-ovuled; style abruptly bent upwards near the base, bearded down the inner side; stigma terminal. Stamens all united in a tube slit down the top; anthers of two kinds. Pod oblong or cylindrical, continuous within. Seeds globose, few or many.—Herbs or shrubs, with simple or digitate leaves, and flowers in axillary or terminal peduncled racemes. Distrib. Round the world in the tropics. Species 200–300.

Leaves simple.
  Pod much protruded from the glabrous calyx.
    Stipules large, foliaceous, persistent . . . . 1. C. verrucosa.
    Stipules minute, setaceous, deciduous . . . . . . 2. C. retusa.
  Pod not protruded from the very silky calyx . . . . . * C. fulva.
Leaves 3-foliolate.
  Pod oblong or cylindrical, many-seeded.
    Stems clothed with spreading brown hairs . . . . . * C. incana.
    Stems with a few adpressed minute white silky hairs . * C. striata.
  Pod globose, few-seeded . . . . * C. vasculosa.
Leaves 5-foliolate. . . . . * C. quinquefolia.

1. **C. verrucosa**, *Linn.*; *DC. Prod.* ii. 125. A robust erect subglabrous annual, 2–3 feet high, with acutely quadrangular branches,

Leaves short-petioled, green, membranous, 2–3 in. long, obtuse or acute, ovate or oblong-rhomboid; stipules round, obtuse, leafy, persistent. Flowers 10–15 in close peduncled terminal racemes. Calyx $\frac{1}{4}$–$\frac{3}{8}$ in. long, glabrous; teeth linear, longer than the tube. Corolla slightly exceeding calyx; standard round, white veined with blue; wing lilac-blue; keel yellowish, veined. Pod oblong, 1–1$\frac{1}{2}$ in. long, silky, short-stalked; seeds 6–8. *Jacq. Ic. t.* 144. *Bot. Mag. tab.* 3034.

MAURITIUS, in dry ground at Pamplemousses, and on the hills round Port Louis. All round the world in the tropics. *C. acuminata*, G. Don, is a variety with rhomboid acute leaves. *Cascarelle à fleurs bleues*, and a white variety, *Cascarelle à fleurs blanches*.

2. **C. retusa,** *Linn.; DC. Prod.* ii. 125. An erect shrubby annual 2–3 feet high, with terete branches. Leaves nearly sessile, oblanceolate-oblong, obtuse, moderately firm, 2–4 in. long, cuneate at the base, obscurely grey-silky below; stipules minute, setaceous, deciduous. Flowers 10–20 in lax terminal racemes leafy up to the base. Calyx $\frac{1}{2}$ in. long, glabrous; teeth lanceolate. Corolla bright yellow, $\frac{3}{4}$ in. deep; standard with a round limb, veined with purple. Pod glabrous, stalked, 1$\frac{1}{2}$ in. long, obling-cylindrical; seeds 15–20. *Bot. Mag. t.* 2561. *Bot. Reg. t.* 253.

MAURITIUS, on plains and hills all over the island. SEYCHELLES, common in all the islands, *Horne!* RODRIGUEZ, frequent, *Balfour!* All round the world in the tropics. *Cascarelle jaune.*

* *C. fulva*, Roxb. Fl. Ind. iii. 266, a native of the East Indies, is naturalised plentifully in Mauritius and the Seychelles. It is a much branched shrub 4–5 feet high, densely silky over the stems and leafy parts, with nearly sessile simple oblanceolate leaves 3–4 inches long, flowers in an ample panicle with the lower bracts of the branches flowerless, calyx $\frac{1}{2}$ in. long, clasped by a pair of persistent bracteoles, upper teeth oblong, lower lanceolate, corolla large yellow silky on the outside, and a thinly silky oblong 2-seeded pod as long as the calyx.

* *C. incana*, Linn; DC. Prod. ii. 132 (*C. purpurascens*, Lam.; DC. Prod. ii. 131; *C. affinis*, DC. Prod. ii. 132) is sent from Mauritius by M. Bouton. It seems to be a native of America, but is now established, both in Tropical Asia and Africa. It is an erect much-branched annual, clothed all over with fine spreading soft brown hairs, with minute setaceous stipules, petioled trifoliolate leaves, obtuse obovate-cuneate leaflets, flowers 6–12 together in lax terminal and lateral racemes, calyx $\frac{1}{4}$ in. long with lanceolate teeth, corolla bright yellow little exserted and a subsessile oblong-cylindrical pod with 15–20 seeds.

* *C. striata*, DC. Prod. ii. 131; Bot. Mag. t. 3200 (*C. Saltiana*, Andr. Bot. Rep. t. 648), spread all round the world in the tropics, is established in Mauritius in fields at Moka and Pamplemousses, *Bouton!* It is a shrubby obscurely grey-silky annual, with minute setaceous stipules, petioled trifoliolate leaves, large obovate-cuneate leaflets,

flowers 20–60 in dense terminal racemes, calyx ¼ in. long with lanceolate teeth, bright yellow much exserted corolla, and a cylindrical glabrous rather recurved pod with 15–20 seeds.

* *C. vasculosa*, Wall. Cat. No. 5427, is said to be a plant of Mauritius, but we have it only from the Calcutta Garden. It is shrubby, with stems and foliage densely clothed with short brown spreading silky hairs, 3 oblanceolate or oblong leaflets, short petioles, minute setaceous stipules, flowers 30–60 in dense terminal racemes leafy up to the base, calyx subsessile silky ⅙ in. long with lanceolate teeth, corolla twice the length of the calyx, pod small round sessile densely clothed with long dense dark brown silky hairs.

* *C. quinquefolia*, Linn.; DC. Prod. ii. 131; Wight Ill. t. 16, a native of Tropical Asia, is established in Mauritius on the banks of the waterfall at Reduit and in plains round Fort Blanc. It is an erect branched annual, 3–4 feet high, with obscurely grey-silky branches and foliage, linear stipules, 5 linear leaflets 2–3 in. long, like those of a Lupine, flowers in lax terminal racemes with persistent lanceolate bracts, calyx naked ½ in. long with lanceolate teeth, large veined petals, standard ¾ inch broad, and a distinct stalked large oblong pod with 30–40 seeds.

A plant found by Mr. Horne in the Seychelles in several parts of Mahé, is perhaps an endemic species near **C. zanzibarica**, Benth., but we have not yet seen either flowers or pod. It is a shrub with virgate branches, shortly pilose when young, trifoliolate petioled leaves with obtuse oblanceolate leaflets 1⅓ in. long, flowers in lax peduncled terminal racemes, minute linear bracts, and pedicels shorter than the calyx, which is campanulate, glabrous, ⅙ in. deep, with lanceolate teeth shorter than the tube.

* *Melilotus parviflora*, Desf.; DC. Prod. ii. 187 (*M. indica*, All.; *M. officinalis*, Bojer, Hort. Maur. 89, non Willd.), of European origin, now widely spread as a weed of cultivation, is sometimes found in Mauritius. It is a glabrous erect slender annual, fragrant when dried, with three oblanceolate obtuse toothed leaflets, the central one stalked, copious flowers in long narrow racemes, calyx $\frac{1}{24}$ in. long with deltoid teeth, corolla pale yellow twice as long as the calyx, diadelphous stamens, uniform anthers, and an oblong one-seeded pod $\frac{1}{12}$ in. long, obscurely reticulated.

* *Psoralea corylifolia*, Linn.; DC. Prod. ii. 218; Bot. Mag. t. 665, a native of the East Indies, is established in Mauritius on the seashore round Fort Blanc. It is an erect robust branched thinly pilose annual, with branches and leafy parts marked with copious glandular dots, large simple petioled membranous toothed ovate leaves, flowers in copious dense peduncled axillary racemes, calyx nearly sessile ⅛ inch long with 5 deep lanceolate teeth, yellow little exserted petals, upper stamen connate or free, anthers uniform, and a small globose one-seeded black glabrous pod.

2. INDIGOFERA, Linn.

Calyx tube campanulate; teeth 5, variable in shape, upper often shorter. Corolla papilionaceous; standard oblong-unguiculate; wings oblique oblong, adhering a little to the keel, which is obtuse or acute. Stamens diadelphous, the anthers uniform and apiculate. Ovary sessile, many-ovuled; style glabrous, short, upcurved; stigma terminal. Pod terete, cylindrical, continuous within. Seeds many.—Herbs or shrubs, clothed with adpressed silky bristles fixed by the middle, the leaves in all ours imparipinnate and flowers in peduncled racemes. DISTRIB. All round the world in the tropics, also many Cape. Species 300–400.

Racemes few-flowered, lax . . . . 1. I. COMPRESSA.
Racemes many-flowered, dense.
Shrubs with opposite leaflets.
Very silvery; pod much recurved; seeds 3–5 . . . 2. I. ARGENTEA.
Slightly silvery; pod nearly straight; seeds 6–8 . * I. TINCTORIA.
Annual herb, with alternate leaflets . . . . 3. I. ENDECAPHYLLA.

1. **I. compressa,** *Lam.; DC. Prod.* ii. 226. An erect shrub, 1–1½ feet high; branchlets remarkably flattened, the young ones thinly silky. Leaflets 3–5, very small, ovate or lanceolate, acute, at first thinly silky. Peduncles axillary, exceeding the leaves, bearing 5–6 small flowers in a lax raceme. Pod linear-cylindrical, nearly glabrous, ¾ in. long.

MAURITIUS, on the mountains of the Rivière Noire, *Bojer*. Also Madagascar, gathered by Commerson. I have not seen this and have made an abstract of Lamarck's description. It seems to be near *I. pentaphylla*, L.

2. **I. argentea,** *Linn.; DC. Prod.* ii. 224. A much-branched shrub, 5–6 feet high, with woody silvery branches. Stipules minute, setaceous; leaflets usually 9, obovate, obtuse, the same size but thicker and more silvery than in *I. tinctoria*; side ones opposite. Racemes many-flowered, nearly sessile, shorter than the leaves. Calyx silvery, $\frac{1}{12}$ in. long; teeth lanceolate, as long as the tube. Corolla yellow, much exserted. Pods sausage-shaped, much recurved, silvery, ½–¾ in. long; seeds 3–5. I. cinerascens, *DC. Prod.* ii. 226. I. cærulea, *Roxb.*; *Wight. Ic. t.* 366. I. glauca, *Lam. Encyc.* iii. 246.

MAURITIUS, on the dry slopes of the Peter-Botte and Montagne Longue. RODRIGUEZ, in many places, *Balfour!* SEYCHELLES, common in waste ground, *Horne*, 479. Also Tropical Asia and Africa. *Indigotier sauvage.*

* *I. tinctoria*, Linn.; D.C. Prod. ii. 224, the most valuable officinal species, a native of Tropical Africa, is naturalised in many places in Mauritius and Rodriguez. It is a shrub 4–6 feet high, with minute setaceous stipules, imparipinnate short-petioled leaves with 4–8 pairs of obtuse short-stalked oblong opposite leaflets ½–¾ in. long membranous subglaucous and thinly silvery on both sides, flowers in dense subsessile racemes in the axils of the leaves, minute calyx with lanceolate teeth as long as the tube, yellow corolla ⅛ in. long, and slender glabrous slightly recurved cylindrical pods 1–1½ in. long containing 8–12 seeds. *I. oligophylla*, Lam. Ill. tab. 626, fig. 2, is a form with not more than 4 pairs of leaflets. *Indigotier*.

3. **I. endecaphylla,** *Jacq. Ic. t.* 570. An annual herb, with suberect or trailing slender stems, only thinly silvery when young.

Stipules lanceolate, persistent; leaflets 7–9, short-stalked, alternate, obovate-oblong, obtuse, $\frac{1}{4}$–$\frac{1}{2}$ in. long, thinly silvery. Racemes peduncled, many-flowered, exceeding the leaves. Calyx $\frac{1}{12}$–$\frac{1}{8}$ in. long; teeth setaceous, exceeding the tube. Corolla purple, twice as long as the calyx. Pod linear, deflexed, straight glabrous, under an inch long; seeds 6–8. *Beauv. Fl. Owar. t.* 84; *Bot. Reg. t.* 789. I. anceps, *Vahl.* I. Schimperiana, *Hochst.* I. pusilla, *Lam. Encyc.* iii. 248.

MAURITIUS, in grassy places round Port Louis, as Champ de Mars and Ile aux Tonneliers. Through the Tropics of Old World, also Cape. *I. pusilla*, Lam. is a trailing shore form with 3–5 very small leaflets. *I. enneaphylla*, Bojer, Hort. Maur. 91, seems to be this species, not the true plant of Linnæus.

3. TEPHROSIA, Pers.

Calyx-tube campanulate; teeth distinct, subequal, deltoid or lanceolate. Petals clawed; standard suborbicular; keel incurved, not rostrate. Stamens diadelphous; anthers obtuse, uniform. Ovary sessile, linear, many-ovuled; style much incurved, filiform or flattened, glabrous or bearded; stigma capitate, often penicillate. Pod linear, flattened, many-seeded, two-valved, continuous within.—Herbs or shrubs, with imparipinnate silky leaves, entire narrow subcoriaceous leaflets and flowers in peduncled leaf-opposed racemes. DISTRIB. All round the world in the tropics. Species 100.

Undershrub with large narrow oblong leaflets . . . . * T. TINCTORIA.
Herbs with oblanceolate leaflets.
 Pod glabrescent . . . . 1. T. PURPUREA.
 Pod clothed with minute spreading hairs . . . . . 2. T. HOOKERIANA.

* *T. tinctoria*, Pers.; DC. Prod. ii. 252 (*T. nervosa*, Pers.; *T. hypargyræa*, DC.), a native of the East Indies, is naturalised in Mauritius on plains round Moka. It is an erect undershrub, with woody branches, densely clothed with grey or brown velvety pubescence, leaflets 5–9 casually solitary firm linear-oblong 1–4 in. long, the end one much the largest, very silky below, flowers few in long-peduncled close racemes, calyx $\frac{1}{8}$ in. long with deep setaceous teeth, corolla silky three times as long as the calyx, pod glabrescent 2–2$\frac{1}{2}$ inches long 10–12-seeded, and bearded flattened style.

1. **T. purpurea,** *Pers.*; *DC. Prod.* ii. 251. A copiously-branched suberect perennial herb 1–2 feet high. Branches slender, firm, terete a little silvery. Stipules linear-lanceolate; leaflets 13–21 oblanceolate, obtuse or subacute, $\frac{1}{2}$–1 inch long, opposite, nearly sessile. Racemes lateral, peduncled, many or few-flowered. Calyx $\frac{1}{8}$ in. long; teeth linear-subulate, as long as the tube. Corolla twice as long as the calyx. Pod ensiform, 1$\frac{1}{2}$–2 in. long, glabrous; seeds 6–10; style flattened, subglabrous, penicillate at the apex. Galega purpurea, *Linn.* T. leptostachya, *DC.* T. lanceæfolia, *Link.*

Common on hills and plains through MAURITIUS, RODRIGUEZ, SEYCHELLES. All round the world in the tropics. *Indigo sauvage.* **T. pumila,** Pers.; DC. Prod. ii. 254 (T. timoriensis, *DC.*; T. diffusa, *Wt. and Arn.*), is a dwarf much-branched diffuse littoral variety with more silvery leaves and branches, fewer leaflets and smaller flowers and pods.

2. **T. Hookeriana,** *Wt. and Arn. Prod.* 212. Scarcely more than a variety of *T. purpurea*, from which it principally differs by having the pod clothed with minute spreading soft brown hairs. Stems suberect, 2–3 feet high, finely pubescent. Leaflets 13–19, oblanceolate, ¾–1 in. long, thinly silvery. Calyx densely silky, ⅛ in. long. Pod 1½–2 in. long, ⅙ in. broad, slightly recurved. Galega hirta, *Hamilt. in Trans. Linn. Soc.*, xiii. 546.

MAURITIUS, at Pailles, *Bouton!* SEYCHELLES, common in Mahé and the other islands, *Horne!* Also East Indies.

* *Sesbania aculeata*, Pers.; DC. Prod. ii. 265, widely spread through the tropics of the Old World, is established in many places in Mauritius and Seychelles in swampy ground. It is an erect glabrous shrubby annual, 3–4 feet high, with branchlets and leaf-rachises furnished with weak minute prickles, imparipinnate leaves ½–1 foot long, 20–40 pairs of linear-oblong membranous glaucous mucronate leaflets, bright yellow papilionaceous flowers in lax axillary racemes, diadelphous stamens, campanulate membranous calyx with short deltoid teeth, slender cylindrical torulose pods 6–9 in. long with thickened sutures and distinct septa between the very numerous seeds. The plants given in Bojer's Catalogue as *S. ægyptiaca* and *cannabina* both belong here.

4. DESMODIUM, Desv.

Calyx campanulate; teeth longer than the tube, the two upper often subconnate. Corolla papilionaceous; wings adhering to the obtuse keel. Stamens diadelphous; anthers uniform. Ovary sessile or stalked; ovules 3–6; style incurved; stigma minute, capitate. Pod composed of several indehiscent joints, with one seed in each, flattened on the face, the sutures slender, one or both wavy.—Shrubs or herbs, with trifoliolate or simple stipellate leaves and small red flowers, usually in racemes. DISTRIB. Round the world in the tropics, also Cape and United States. Species 100–120.

Leaves simple, with a conspicuously winged petiole . . 1. D. TRIQUETRUM.
Leaves trifoliolate; petiole not winged.
  Erect, with flowers in ample peduncled racemes.
    Pod stalked; joints rhomboid.
      Racemes very lax, few-flowered . . . . 2. D. SCALPE.
      Racemes dense, many-flowered . . . . * D. CAJANIFOLIUM.
    Pod sessile; joints square.
      Lower suture deeply indented.
        Leaflets large, downy below . . . . 3. D. INCANUM.
        Leaflets small, subglabrous . . . . 4. D. MAURITIANUM.
      Lower suture little indented.
        Leaflets acute . . . . 5. D. OXYBRACTEUM.
        Leaflets obtuse . . . . 6. D. POLYCARPUM.

Prostrate, with flowers most or all without peduncles in the axils of the leaves . . . . 7. D. TRIFLORUM.
Erect shrub, with flowers in short peduncled umbels . 8. D. UMBELLATUM.

1. **D. triquetrum,** *DC. Prod.* ii. 326. An erect much-branched shrubby perennial. Branches acutely triquetrous, thinly pilose. Leaves simple, firm, oblong-lanceolate, acute, 4–6 in. long, finely hairy on the ribs below; stipules large, lanceolate, scariose; petioles ½–1 in. long, broadly winged. Racemes ½–1 ft. long, peduncled, axillary and terminal; pedicels ⅛–¼ in. long, spreading; bracts minute. Calyx ⅛ in. long; upper teeth deltoid, lower linear. Corolla red, twice the length of the calyx. Pod 1–2 in. long, pilose or glabrescent; joints 6–8, square; both sutures nearly straight. D. auriculatum, pseudo-triquetrum and alatum, *DC. loc. cit.* Pteroloma triquetrum, *Benth. in Pl. Jungh.* 220.

SEYCHELLES; common in Mahé and the other islands, *Wright! Horne!* MAURITIUS, naturalised at Les Pailles, between Port Louis and Moka. Through Tropical Asia, not African.

2. **D. Scalpe,** *DC. Prod.* ii. 334. A shrubby erect perennial, with slender sulcate finely downy stems. Leaves long-petioled; leaflets 3, thin, firm, 2–4 in. long, acute, rather repand; central one round or ovate, acute; stipules large, scariose, lanceolate. Flowers in long very lax mostly terminal racemes; pedicels erecto-patent, very slender, ½–1 in. long. Calyx ⅛ in. long, downy; teeth lanceolate, as long as the tube. Corolla deep red, ½ in. long. Pod distinctly stalked; joints 3–4, pilose, ¼–⅜ in. long, semicircular, with the upper suture nearly straight and lower deeply indented. D. abyssinicum and repandum, *DC.* D. strangulatum, *Wight, Ic. t.* 985.

MAURITIUS, in the woods of the Pouce range. Through Tropical Asia and Africa. Also Natal and Kaffraria.

* *D. cajanifolium*, DC. Prod. ii. 331 (*Hedysarum*, H.B.K. Nov. Gen. t 598), a native of Tropical America, introduced in Ceylon, is sent by Mr. Horne from the Seychelles from hills near Port Victory in Mahé. It is a tall pilose erect perennial, with 3 oblong obtuse sub-coriaceous leaflets, hairy on both sides, an ample terminal panicle with long rather dense racemose branches, slender ascending pedicels ¼ in. long, a minute deeply-cut calyx, a bright lilac corolla ¼–⅓ in. long, and a short-stalked glabrescent pod under an inch long, slightly indented at the upper, deeply at the lower suture, of 3–4 very oblique joints that easily fall away.

3. **D. incanum**, *DC. Prod.* ii. 332. A shrubby erect branched perennial, 2–3 ft. high, with thinly pilose branches. Stipules lanceolate; petioles short, pilose, channelled; leaflets oblong, obtuse, or subacute, 3–4 in. long, glaucous and finely pilose all over beneath. Racemes ample, peduncled, moderately close, terminal and lateral; pedicels ¼–⅓ in.

long. Calyx minute; teeth lanceolate or deltoid. Corolla red, ¼ in. long. Pod an inch long, densely pilose; joints 5–6; upper suture straight, lower deeply waved. D. sparsiflorum, *G. Don.*

MAURITIUS, in dry places on the mountains, chiefly round Port Louis. Coin de Mire, *Horne!* RODRIGUEZ, common, *Balfour!* SEYCHELLES, common in Mahé and Praslin, etc., *Bouton! Horne!* Also Tropical Africa and America, not Asia.

4. **D. mauritianum,** *DC. Prod.* ii. 334. A much-branched perennial, 1–3 ft. high, with woody wiry branches, pilose only towards the top. Leaves short-petioled; leaflets 3, obovate, firm, obtuse, ¼–¾ in. long, greenish and obscurely silky beneath; stipules minute, lanceolate, scariose. Racemes peduncled, 2–3 in. long, moderately dense, mostly terminal; pedicels ⅛–¼ in. long, slender, glabrous. Calyx 1/12 in. long; teeth deep, linear. Corolla red, twice the length of the calyx. Pod straight, pilose, ½–¾ in. long; joints 4–5; upper suture straight, lower deeply waved.

MAURITIUS and RODRIGUEZ, frequent in dry soil. Madagascar and through Tropical Africa.

5. **D. oxybracteum,** *DC. Prod.* ii. 334. An erect perennial herb, 3–4 ft. high, with sulcate branches, finely pilose upwards. Leaves long-petioled; leaflets 3, stipellate, oblong-lanceolate, acute, subglabrous, glaucous beneath, 4–6 in. long; stipules large, lanceolate, persistent. Racemes copious, dense, peduncled, axillary and terminal; bracts ¼ in. long, lanceolate acuminate; pedicels short. Calyx 1/12 in long; teeth deep, linear. Corolla red, twice as long as the calyx. Pod sessile, ½–¾. in long, pubescent; joints 4–5, twice as long as broad; upper suture straight, lower little indented. D. paleaceum, *Guill. and Per. Fl. Seneg.* 209. D. grande, *E. Meyer.*

Described by De Candolle from MAURITIUS, but not seen there lately. It is spread from Senegambia to Natal, and we have it from Madagascar, Bourbon, and Johanna Island.

6. **D. polycarpum,** *DC. Prod.* ii. 334. An erect perennial, 2–3 ft. high, with firm pilose branches. Leaves distinctly petioled, subcoriaceous, naked above, thinly grey-silky below; leaflets obovate, obtuse, the end one largest, 1½–2 in. long; stipules lanceolate, acuminate, persistent. Flowers in dense terminal and lateral racemes, hidden at first by the large lanceolate bracts; pedicels ⅛–⅙ in. long, glabrous. Calyx 1/12 in. deep; teeth long, acuminate. Corolla reddish, under ¼ in. long. Pod strapshaped, downy, under an inch long; joints 6–8; lower suture little indented. D. spectabile, *Bojer, Hort. Maur.* 99 (name).

SEYCHELLES, common in Mahé on the beaches, *Horne*, 489! A common Asian and Polynesian species found by Bojer in Zanzibar, but not known on the African continent.

7. **D. triflorum,** *DC. Prod.* ii. 334. A perennial herb, with diffuse

procumbent wiry much branched stems, finely pilose upwards. Leaves short-petioled; leaflets 3, obovate, $\frac{1}{8}$–$\frac{1}{2}$ in. long, truncate or emarginate; stipules lanceolate, persistent. Flowers 1–3 together in the axils of the leaves, on slender pedicels $\frac{1}{4}$–$\frac{1}{3}$ in. long. Calyx $\frac{1}{12}$–$\frac{1}{8}$ in. long; teeth deep, setaceous. Corolla red, small, little exserted. Pod $\frac{1}{8}$–$\frac{1}{2}$ in. long, sessile, glabrescent, recurved; joints 3–4, square; upper suture straight, lower little indented. Hedysarum triflorum, *Linn.* Sagotia triflora, *Walp.*

MAURITIUS, frequent in dry soil. Champ de Mars, Pouce, hills of the Rivière Noire, etc. RODRIGUEZ, on the shore in one or two places, *Balfour!* Praslin and other islands of the SEYCHELLES, *Horne!* Round the world in the tropics.

Var. D. HETEROPHYLLUM, *DC. Prod.* ii. 334. A more robust variety, with larger leaves, joints of pod 4–5 and flowers produced both from the axils of the leaves and also from upper nodes which do not bear leaves. D. cæspitosum, *DC. Prod.* ii. 333.

MAURITIUS, frequent through the island in dry ground, ascending high up the hills. SEYCHELLES, *Bojer!* Also Tropical Asia. *Tréfle. Petit tréfle.*

8. **D. umbellatum**, *DC. Prod.* ii. 325. A shrub, 6–10 ft. high, with densely silky branches. Stipules lanceolate, deciduous; petioles 1–1$\frac{1}{2}$ in. long; leaflets 3, distinctly stalked, broad oblong, obtuse or subacute, 3–4 in. long, firm, very glaucous, thinly silky beneath. Flowers 6–12, in dense nearly sessile umbels in the axils of the leaves; pedicels $\frac{1}{8}$–$\frac{1}{4}$ in., pilose. Calyx $\frac{1}{8}$ in.; teeth lanceolate, as long as the turbinate tube. Corolla $\frac{1}{4}$ in., red. Pod sessile, with 1–4 pilose deeply indented joints, each $\frac{1}{4}$–$\frac{3}{8}$ in. long.

MAURITIUS, naturalised on the shore at Grandport, *Ayres!* SEYCHELLES, common on the shore of Praslin, *Horne! Pervillé!* Also Zanzibar, Bourbon, Madagascar, and Tropical Asia.

Mr. Horne has gathered in Mahé and Dr. Balfour in Rodriguez flowerless specimens of a Desmodium that is most likely **D. ascendens**, Sw. It is a trailing finely pilose herb, with small lanceolate stipules, lower leaves trifoliolate, upper simple, leaflets broad obovate obtuse rounded or slightly cordate at the base, under an inch long, green and glabrous above, glaucous and finely pilose beneath. **D. ascendens** has very lax terminal racemes, pedicels half an inch long, large ovate-cuspidate densely hairy bracts, a minute calyx with linear teeth, and a small pilose pod of 4–5 joints, straight on the upper, deeply indented on the lower suture.

* *Bremontiera Ammoxylon*, DC.. in Ann. Sc. Nat. Ser. 1, iv. 93, which we have from Bourbon, from Dr. Cordemoy, is reported by Bojer from the shores of Mauritius, but the plant sent under the name from the Mauritian herbarium is *Desmodium mauritianum*. *Bremontiera* is a shrub with the habit of an Indigofera, nearly sessile simple coriaceous oblong-lanceolate leaves above an inch long clothed with short grey bristly hairs, flowers in dense spike-like racemes, a silvery campanulate calyx $\frac{1}{12}$ in. long with 5 small acute teeth, a corolla three times as long as the calyx, and a pod with 12 or 14 rather compressed joints, which finally separate from one another.

5. ALYSICARPUS, Neck.

Calyx dry, with a turbinate tube, and 5 deep, often imbricated teeth. Corolla papilionaceous, not exserted from the calyx; keel obtuse, adhering to the wings. Stamens 9 and 1, diadelphous; anthers uniform. Ovary sessile or short-stalked; ovules 4–8; styled incurved; stigma capitate. Pod turgid, composed of 4–8 indehiscent joints.—Diffuse dry wiry annuals, with dry persistent stipules, simple leaves and copious flowers in lax racemes. Distrib. Species 15, common weeds through the tropics of the Old World.

Calyx not longer than the first joint of the pod.
  Pod not constricted between the joints . . . . . 1. A. nummularifolius.
  Pod distinctly constricted between the joints . . * A. monilifer.
Calyx nearly or quite including the whole pod . . 2. A. bupleurifolius.

1. **A. nummularifolius,** *DC. Prod.* ii. 353. A much-branched glabrous annual, with trailing wiry stems, ½–1 ft. long. Leaves short-petioled, oblong, obtuse, or the lower nearly round, firm, venose, ¼–1½ in. long; stipules lanceolate, persistent. Racemes 2–3 in. long, 6–12-flowered; pedicels shorter than the calyx. Calyx ⅛ in. long; teeth linear, exceeding the tube. Pod ½–¾ in. long, cylindrical, not constricted between the 5–6 joints, which are longer than thick, and rather wrinkled.

Mauritius, in grassy places at Pamplemousses, etc.. Also Tropical Africa and Asia. A mere variety of *A. vaginalis*, D.C. (*Hedysarum*, Linn).

* *A. monilifer*, DC. Prod. ii. 353, which is common in Tropical Asia, rare in Tropical Africa, is said by Bojer to be a Mauritian plant, but I have not seen specimens. It is just like *A. nummularifolius* in habit, and has the same short calyx, but the pod is distinctly constricted between the smooth joints, which are not longer than thick.

2. **A. bupleurifolius,** *DC. Prod.* ii. 352. A much-branched glabrous annual, with ascending wiry stems a foot long. Leaves short-petioled, simple, firm, oblong or lanceolate or linear, acute, 1–2 in. long. Flowers in long very lax terminal and lateral racemes, in 10–20 distant pairs on very short ascending pedicels. Calyx ¼ in. long, the ciliated lanceolate teeth twice as long as the funnel-shaped tube. Pod stalked, ⅜–½ in. long; joints 4–6, slightly moniliform, as long as broad, quite smooth. Hedysarum bupleurifolium, *Linn.*

Mauritius, frequent in dry soil, ascending the Pouce. Common through Tropical Asia, but not African.

6. ÆSCHYNOMENE, Linn.

Calyx deeply 2-lipped, the lips subentire. Corolla papilionaceous, exserted; keel obtuse. Stamens in two bundles of 5 each; anthers uniform. Ovary stalked, linear, with 4–6 ovules; style filiform, incurved; stigma capitate. Pod linear, distinctly stalked, dividing into 3–6 square indehiscent flattened joints, with the seed raised in the middle. —Herbs or shrubs with close sensitive imparipinnate leaflets, and few flowers in lax racemes. DISTRIB. Round the world in the tropics. Species 30.

Leaflets few, firm. Stipules firm, not spurred, persistent . . . . 1. Æ. MICRANTHA.
Leaflets many, membranous. Stipules membranous, spurred, deciduous . . . . * Æ. SENSITIVA.

1. **Æ. micrantha,** *DC. Prod.* ii. 321. A low perennial, with slender wiry branched stems obscurely hairy upwards. Leaves short-petioled; leaflets 4–5, oblong, sessile, obtuse, sensitive, $\frac{1}{4}$ in. long, firm, glabrous; stipules minute, lanceolate, striated, not spurred. Flowers few, in very lax axillary peduncled racemes; pedicels short, ascending. Calyx $\frac{1}{12}$ in. long, glabrous, striated, with two deep lanceolate lips. Corolla pale yellow, $\frac{1}{4}$ in. long. Pod stalked, $\frac{1}{2}$–$\frac{3}{4}$ in. long, straight; joints 3–4, square; upper suture slightly, lower deeply indented. *Harv. and Sond. Fl. Cap.* ii. 224.

MAURITIUS, in damp savannas near Maison Blanche. Also Natal, not Tropical Africa. *Tréfle a fleurs jaunes.*

* *Æ. sensitiva,* Sw.; DC. Prod. ii. 320, (*Æ. patula,* Poir.; Bojer, Hort. Maur. 96), common in Tropical America, rare in tropical Africa, is said by Bojer to be naturalized in Mauritius, round Mont Plaisir, and in other places. It is a branched shrubby perennial, with glandulose branchlets, large lanceolate membranous spurred deciduous stipules, short-petioled imparipinnate leaves with 20 or more pairs of sessile ligulate obtuse membranous sensitive leaflets $\frac{1}{2}$ in. long, flowers 3–4 in lax terminal corymbs, deeply bilibiate calyx $\frac{1}{6}$ in. deep, pale yellow middle-sized corolla, a straight pod $1\frac{1}{2}$–2 in. long, with 4–6 glabrescent square joints, deeply waved along the lower suture.

7. ZORNIA, Gmel.

Calyx minute; upper teeth short, connate; lowest shorter than the two side ones. Corolla papilionaceous, much exserted; keel incurved, acute. Stamens monadelphous; anthers dimorphic. Ovary sessile, many-ovuled; style filiform, incurved; stigma capitate. Pod of several small round flattened indehiscent 1-seeded muricated joints.—Annuals with large persistent coriaceous bracts in pairs, and leaves with a single pair of sessile leaflets. DISTRIB. Species 10, all but two American.

1. **Z. diphylla,** *Pers.; Benth. in Mart. Fl. Bras.* xv. 82, t. 21-22. Stems wiry, ascending or spreading, much-branched, $\frac{1}{2}$–1 ft. long,

Leaves petioled; leaflets lanceolate or ovate, sessile, acute, firm, glabrous, ½–1 ft. long, dotted with black glands; stipules persistent, lanceolate, with a long spur. Racemes lax, few-flowered; bracts ovate, acute, nearly or quite hiding the pod. Joints 2–6, densely muricated. Hedysarum diphyllum, *Linn.* Z. angustifolia, *Lam.*: *Bojer*, *Hort. Maur.* 96.

MAURITIUS, frequent in dry soil. Everywhere in the tropics. *Z. zeylonensis*, Pers. DC. Prod. ii. 317, is a variety with ovate leaflets and pod exceeding the shorter bracts.

* VICIA, Linn.

Calyx-tube obliquely campanulate; teeth 5, subequal. Corolla papilionaceous. Stamens diadelphous; anthers uniform; tube of filaments very oblique at the mouth. Ovary sessile; ovules at least two; style filiform or slightly flattened. Pod subcompressed, two-valved.—Annual or perennial herbs with equally pinnate leaves with rachis produced into a tendril.

* *V. sativa*, Linn., the vetch commonly grown for forage, is sometimes seen in Mauritius in cultivated ground. It is a glabrous erect annual, 1–2 feet high, with persistent sagittate stipules, retuse ligulate 4–5-jugate leaflets, middle-sized red flowers solitary or in pairs in the axils of the leaves, and a linear pod 1–1½ in. long, with 6–8 seeds.

* *V. hirsuta*, Koch. (Ervum hirsutum, *Linn.*), a common European weed in cultivated fields, is rarely seen in Mauritius. It is a scrambling climber, with very slender downy stems, minute linear-lanceolate toothed stipules, leaflets 8–16 distant very narrow, flowers minute 4–8 together in peduncled secund racemes, calyx ⅛ in. long, with linear teeth, pod oblique-oblong torulose pubescent ¼ in. long two-seeded, style slightly flattened.

8. ABRUS, Linn.

Calyx campanulate, with 4 very obscure teeth, the two upper coalescing. Corolla papilionaceous, much exserted. Stamens only 9, connate in a sheath slit down the top; anthers uniform. Ovary subsessile, with several ovules; style short, incurved, beardless; stigma capitate. Pod oblong or linear, somewhat flattened, with two coriaceous valves, slightly septate between the large seeds.—Shrubby climbers, with abruptly pinnate leaves not ending in a tendril, and flowers in dense peduncled racemes. DISTRIB. Round the world in the tropics. Species 5.

Pod half to a third as broad as long, with 4–5 seeds . . 1. A. PRECATORIUS.
Pod a fourth as broad as long, 7–9 seeded . . . . 2. A. PULCHELLUS.

1. **A. precatorius,** *Linn.*; *DC. Prod.* ii. 381. A glabrous shrub, with tough flexible branches, climbing trees to a height of 20 feet.

Leaves short-petioled, 2–3 in. long; leaflets 20–40, crowded, oblong membranous, $\frac{1}{2}$ in. long, deciduous, mucronate; stipules minute, lanceolate, deciduous. Racemes peduncled, dense, axillary and terminal. Calyx $\frac{1}{12}$ in. long, obscurely 4-toothed. Corolla under $\frac{1}{2}$ in. long, whitish. Pod oblong, rugose, an inch long, with 4–5 round seeds as large as a pea, which are bright scarlet, with a black spot round the hilum, and often used for necklaces.

MAURITIUS, everywhere common in the woods, but said by Bojer to be not truly wild. SEYCHELLES, common in dry waste ground in Mahé, *Horne*, 473! RODRIGUEZ, near Mathurin, *Balfour!* Coin de Mire, *Horne!* Everywhere in the tropics. *Reglisse.*

2. **A. pulchellus,** *Wall.; Thwaites, Enum. Pl. Zeyl.* 91. Very near A. *precatorius*, with which it quite agrees in flowers, seeds, and general habit, differing only by the leaflets being fewer (10–20), and the pod longer, not rugose, 7-9-seeded. A. lævigatus, *E. Meyer*. A. acutifolius, *Blume*.

SEYCHELLES, in woods in Mahé, *Horne!* Tropical Asia, Tropical Africa, and Natal.

9. TERAMNUS, Sw.

Calyx-tube turbinate; teeth lanceolate, as long as the tube. Corolla little exserted; petals about equal in length. Stamens monadelphous; alternate anthers small, abortive. Ovary sessile, many-ovuled; style short, curved, beardless; stigma capitate, Pod linear, subcompressed, recurved, septate between the seeds.—Twining herbs with stipellate trifoliolate leaves and copious minute flowers in lax racemes. DISTRIB. Round the world in the tropics. Species 4.

1. **T. labialis,** *Spreng. Syst.* ii. 235. Stems wide-climbing, perennial, thinly pilose. Leaves petioled, trifoliolate; leaflets obscurely stipellate, oblong or lanceolate, obtuse, 2–4 in. long, subcoriaceous, glaucous and clothed with obscure adpressed hairs beneath; stipules minute, lanceolate. Flowers in lax axillary racemes overtopping the leaves; pedicels short, geminate. Calyx $\frac{1}{8}$ in., silky; teeth as long as the tube. Corolla red, scarcely exserted. Pod linear, reflexed, glabrescent, $1\frac{1}{4}$ to $1\frac{1}{2}$ in long, brown; seeds 8–12. Galactia sericea and diversifolia, *Bojer, Hort. Maur*, 92, according to our specimens. Glycine parviflora, *Lam.*

MAURITIUS and SEYCHELLES, spread through the islands in savannas and on the hillsides. RODRIGUEZ, on the shore in one or two places, *Balfour!* Round the world in the Tropics.

* *Psophocarpus tetragonolobus*, DC. Prod. ii. 403, (*Dolichos tetragonolobus*, Linn.), cultivated through Tropical Asia, the native country

not clearly known, is cultivated and casually subspontaneous in Mauritius. It is a subglabrous perennial twiner, with a large tuberous root, spurred lanceolate stipules, 3 large rhomboid membranous acute stipellate leaflets, lax few-flowered long-peduncled axillary racemes, ovate bracteoles shorter than the calyx, short calyx-teeth, rather large white and blue corolla, monadelphous stamens, a large square pod with 4 crisped coriaceous wings, septate between the seeds, and style long much recurved penicillate round the terminal stigma.

10. CANAVALIA, DC.

Calyx-tube deeply campanulate, with two lips, the upper largest, the short lower one obscurely 3-toothed. Corolla papilionaceous, much exserted; petals about equal in length. Stamens monadelphous; anthers uniform. Ovary short-stalked; ovules several; style incurved, beardless; stigma terminal. Pod large, ensiform, turgid, with a distinct rib down each valve near the upper suture, septate between the large beanlike seeds.—Herbaceous twiners, with stipellate trifoliolate leaves, and few flowers in lax axillary racemes, with tumid nodes. DISTRIB. Round the world in the tropics, mostly American. Species 10–12.

Leaflets thin, acute . . . . 1. C. ENSIFORMIS.
Leaflets thicker, obtuse . . . . 2. C. OBTUSIFOLIA.

1. **C. ensiformis,** *DC. Prod.* ii. 404. Stems wide-twining, glabrous, biennial or perennial. Leaves distinctly petioled; leaflets distinctly stalked, oblong, thin, acute, 3–6 in. long; stipules minute, deciduous. Peduncles and racemes each 3–6 in. long; pedicels geminate, very short; bracteoles minute, ovate, caducous. Calyx $\frac{3}{8}$–$\frac{1}{2}$ in. deep, glabrous, the upper lip a third of the length of the tube. Corolla more than twice as long as the calyx, red or white. Pod 6–9 in. long, rather recurved, 8–12-seeded. C. gladiata and incurva, *DC.*

SEYCHELLES, *Dr. Wright!* RODRIGUEZ, in the Rivière Cascade Valley, *Dr. Balfour!* In Mauritius planted only. Everywhere in the tropics. *Pois Sabre. Dolic.*

2. **C. obtusifolia,** *DC. Prod.* ii. 404. A glabrous perennial, climbing or trailing. Leaflets thicker than in *C. ensiformis*, obovate, obtuse, often emarginate, 3–4 in. long. Racemes overtopping the leaves, the flowers few and distant; pedicels $\frac{1}{8}$–$\frac{1}{4}$ in. long, springing from fleshy tubercles. Calyx $\frac{3}{8}$ in. deep, the upper lip shorter than in the other species. Corolla red, fragrant, an inch long. Pod 4–6 in. long, rather recurved; seeds 6–10, compressed $\frac{1}{2}$–$\frac{3}{4}$ in. broad, chesnut-brown. C. emarginata, *DC.*

MAURITIUS and SEYCHELLES, common on the shores. RODRIGUEZ, on the shore at English Bay, *Dr. Balfour!* Round the world in the tropics. Also Natal.

11. CLITORIA, Linn.

Calyx large, funnel-shaped, with a pair of persistent bracteoles at the base; teeth lanceolate. Corolla papilionaceous, with a large obovate standard, much exceeding in size, and hiding the wings and incurved acute keel. Stamens diadelphous; anthers uniform. Ovary subsessile, linear, many-ovuled; style flattened, bearded down the inner face; stigma terminal. Pod linear, thin, flat.—Herbaceous twiners, with imparipinnate leaves with flowers solitary in their axils. DISTRIB. Round the world in the tropics. Species 27.

Bracteoles large, round, obtuse . . . . 1. C. TERNATEA.
Bracteoles small, ovate, acute . . . . 2. C. HETEROPHYLLA.

1. **C. Ternatea,** *Linn.; DC. Prod.* ii. 223. A wide-climbing perennial herb, with glabrous or finely downy slender stems. Leaves petioled, imparipinnate; leaflets 5–7, large, oblong, obtuse, membranous, short-stalked, stipellate; stipules minute, lanceolate. Flowers solitary, on very short pedicels in the axils of the leaves. Calyx with a pair of round persistent bracteoles at the base, $\frac{1}{2}$–$\frac{3}{4}$ in. long; teeth lanceolate, shorter than the tube. Standard $1\frac{1}{2}$ in. long, nearly as broad, bright blue, sometimes white, with an orange spot at the throat. Pod 3–4 in. long, flat, glabrescent; seeds 8–10. *Bot. Mag. tab.* 1542.

MAURITIUS, in woods at Morne, Brabant, etc. Coin de Mire, *Horne!* SEYCHELLES, rare in Mahé, *Pervillé! Horne!* RODRIGUEZ, on the shore at English Bay, *Dr. Balfour.* Round the world in the tropics. *Liane Madame. Liane Ternate.*

2. **C. heterophylla,** *Lam.; DC. Prod.* ii. 223. A glabrous annual, with very slender copiously twining stems. Leaves distinctly petioled; leaflets 3–7, very variable in shape, ligulate, oblong, or even round, $\frac{1}{4}$–$1\frac{1}{2}$ in. long, rather firm, obtuse. with a mucro; stipules minute, linear. Flowers distinctly peduncled, solitary in the axils of the leaves. Calyx with a pair of small ovate acute bracteoles at the base, under $\frac{1}{2}$ in. long; teeth lanceolate, shorter than the tube. Standard $\frac{3}{4}$ in. long, bright blue, with a white throat. Pod glabrous, 1–$1\frac{1}{2}$ in. long; seeds 5–6.

MAURITIUS, roadsides at Flacq, Moka, and Pamplemousses. Also Bourbon and Madagascar.

12. ERYTHRINA, Linn.

Calyx oblique, spathaceous in our plant, splitting down to the base. Petals very unequal in length, the standard being much longer than the wings and keel; upper stamen nearly or quite free; anthers all alike. Ovary stalked; ovules numerous; style incurved, beardless, with a capitate stigma. Pod large, linear, turgid, torulose.—Trees with prickly branches and dense racemes of large coral-red flowers; leaves trifoliolate. DISTRIB. Warmer zones of the Old and New World. Species 25–30.

1. **E. indica,** *Lam.; DC. Prod.* ii. 412. A tall tree with stout branchlets, armed with minute hard prickles. Petiole 4–6 in. long; leaflets membranous, the end one pointed, 4–6 in. long and broad. Racemes dense, 6–9 in. long, on spreading stout woody peduncles; pedicels tomentose, $\frac{1}{4}$–$\frac{1}{3}$ in. long. Calyx an inch or more long, minutely 5-toothed at the very oblique mouth, splitting to the base down the upper side. Standard 2–2$\frac{1}{2}$ in. long. Pod $\frac{1}{2}$–1 ft. long, distinctly torulose.

MAURITIUS, naturalised in several places. SEYCHELLES, frequent in Mahé and Praslin, apparently indigenous, *Horne*, 468! RODRIGUEZ, common, especially in Anse Mourouc, *Balfour!* Polynesia and Tropical Asia, not African. *Mourouc*.

13. MUCUNA, Adans.

Calyx-tube campanulate; teeth 4, the two upper connate. Corolla papilionaceous; standard not more than half as long as the beaked keel, which slightly exceeds the wings. Stamens diadelphous; anthers dimorphous, like those of *Genisteæ*. Ovary sessile, many-ovuled; style incurved, beardless; stigma capitate. Pod oblong, variously winged and armed on the faces.—Herbs or shrubby climbers, with pinnately trifoliolate leaves; flowers large, showy, purple, turning black when dried. DISTRIB. Species 20; round the world in the tropics.

Pod without wings at the sutures, but with ridges on the faces, 1. M. ATROPURPUREA.
Pod without ridges on the faces, but with wings at the sutures, 2. M. GIGANTEA.

1. **M. atropurpurea,** *DC. Prod.* ii. 406. A woody climber, with slender glabrous branches. Leaves long-petioled; leaflets 3, stipellate, membranous, glabrous, 4–6 in. long, central one oblong-cuspidate. Flowers in long-peduncled axillary racemes; bracts small, ovate, deciduous; bracteoles obtuse, oblong-spathulate, $\frac{1}{4}$ in. long. Calyx $\frac{1}{2}$ in. long, deeply bilabiate. Corolla large, dark purple. Pod sessile, oblong, coriaceous, 3 in. long, not winged, the faces traversed by oblique waved ridges, two-seeded. Carpopogon atropurpureum, *Roxb*.

SEYCHELLES, common in Mahé, *Pervillé, Horne!* Also East Indies. In Mauritius cultivated in gardens under the name of *Pois Evêque*.

2. **M. gigantea,** *DC. Prod.* ii. 406. A woody climber, with slender glabrous branches. Leaflets 3, membranous, glabrous, 3–4 in. long, stipellate; end one oblong-cuspidate. Flowers in long peduncled drooping crowded racemes; bracts oblong, wrapping up the buds. Calyx campanulate, $\frac{1}{3}$ in. long and broad; upper lip subentire; lower with 3 small deltoid teeth. Corolla yellow, 1–1$\frac{1}{2}$ in. long; keel twice as long as the standard. Pod stalked, oblong, flat, 4–5 in. long, with two broad rigid wings to each suture, clothed on the ridgeless faces with deciduous stinging bristles.

SEYCHELLES, common in all the islands at low levels, *Horne*, 496! RODRIGUEZ, in several of the valleys, *Dr. Balfour!* Tropical Asia and Polynesia.

* Amongst Professor Wright's Seychelles and in Dr. Balfour's Rodriguez collections are specimens of *Phaseolus lunatus*, Linn.; DC. Prod. ii. 393, widely spread and cultivated through the tropics of both hemispheres. It is an annual climber, with thinly pilose stems, long-petioled membranous stipellate trifoliolate leaves, central leaflet ovate-deltoid acute 2–3 in. long, flowers in axillary racemes, campanulate calyx ⅛ in. long with very short teeth, greenish much-recurved bud, corolla under ½ in. deep with a circinate keel, and a half-oblong pod ½–¾ inch broad with 2–4 large compressed purple or white pea-like seeds.

14. DOLICHOS, Linn.

Calyx tube campanulate; teeth small, deltoid. Corolla papilionaceous, much exserted; keel beaked, not spiral. Stamens diadelphous; anthers uniform. Ovary short-stalked, with several ovules; style cylindrical or flattened; stigma terminal. Pod flat, linear or oblong, rather recurved, smooth, not torulose, the valves readily dehiscing.—Climbing herbs, with stipellate trifoliolate leaves, flowers in racemes or in the axils of the leaves, and small persistent bracts and stipules. Like Phaseolus, but the keel not spiral. DISTRIB. Round the world in the tropics, etc. Species 20.

Style flattened; flowers in long lax racemes . . . . . 1. D. LABLAB.
Style cylindrical; flowers 2–3 together in the axils of the leaves without any common peduncle . . . . . . 2. D. AXILLARIS.

1. **D. Lablab,** *Linn.; Roxb. Fl. Ind.* iv. 305. A subglabrous wide-twining annual. Stipules lanceolate, basifixed; leaflets as broad as long, (3–6 in.) acute, membranous. Peduncles and lax racemes each 6–9 in. long; pedicels densely fascicled, ⅛–¼ in.; bracteoles oblong, sometimes as long as the calyx. Calyx broadly campanulate, under ¼ in. long. Corolla ½–¾ in. long, reddish or white. Pod oblong, much recurved, flat, glabrous, 2 in. long, ½–¾ in. broad, tipped with the persistent flattened style. Seeds 2–4, as large as a pea, black, red, or purple. Lablab vulgaris, *Savi; DC. Prod.* ii. 401.

Commonly cultivated through the tropics of the Old World. Planted only in Mauritius. Wild or naturalised on the shore of Mahé, Seychelles, *Wright! Horne! Haricot Rouge.*

2. **D. axillaris,** *E. Meyer Comm. Pl. Afr. Austr.* 144. A wide-climbing perennial, with slender subglabrous branches. Leaves distinctly petioled; leaflets 3, oblong, entire, membranous, subacute, ½–2 in. long; stipules small, lanceolate. Flowers 2–3 together on short pedicels in the axils of the leaves, without a common peduncle. Calyx broadly campanulate; teeth short. Corolla ¾ in. long, greenish-yellow. Pod short-stalked, linear, flat, glabrous, nearly straight, narrowed to

both ends; style filiform. Seeds 6–8. Clitoria viridiflora, *Bouton in Hook. Ic. t.* 152; *Bojer, Hort. Maur.* 92.

MAURITIUS, in thickets at Flacq. Also Tropical Africa, Madagascar and Cape.

15. ATYLOSIA, Wt. and Arn.

Calyx tube short; teeth 5, linear. Corolla papilionaceous; keel not beaked. Stamens diadelphous; anthers uniform. Ovary sessile; ovules 4–6; style filiform, incurved, glabrous; stigma capitate. Pod oblong, turgid, marked with conspicuous depressed lines between the arillate seeds.—Twining herbs, with trifoliolate leaves, gland-dotted beneath, and flowers in axillary racemes. DISTRIB. Tropics of the Old World. Species 20.

1. **A. scarabœoides,** *Benth. in Pl. Jungh*, 243. An annual twiner, with slender densely pilose stems. Leaves petioled, trifoliolate, exstipellate; leaflets oblong or obovate, subobtuse, subcoriaceous, silky, 1–1½ in. long; stipules minute caducous. Corymbs few-flowered, short-peduncled. Calyx ¼ in. long, densely silky; teeth deep, linear. Corolla yellow, half as long again as the calyx. Pod sessile, oblong, ¾–1 in. long, with distinct depressed oblique lines between the 4–6 seeds. Dolichos scarabœoides, *Linn.* Rhynchosia scarabœoides, *DC. Prod.* ii. 387.

MAURITIUS, frequent in grassy places, especially on the Pouce. RODRIGUEZ, not unfrequent, *Balfour!* Through Tropical Asia, Madagascar, and Bourbon; not African.

* *Pachyrhizus angulatus*, Rich.; DC. Prod. ii. 402. (Dolichos bulbosus, *Linn.*), universally cultivated in the tropics, the native country not clearly known, is subspontaneous in Mauritius round the Baie du Cap. It is a half shrubby pilose perennial climber, with a large eatable tuber like a turnip, linear stipellæ, 3 large membranous leaflets cuneate at the base with three shallow palmate lobes, lax racemes ½–1 foot long, sometimes panicled below, a bilabiate calyx with the lower lip deeply 3-cleft, large reddish corolla, an obtuse keel, diadelphous stamens, a linear turgid pod 6–9 in. long deeply depressed between the 8–12 seeds, a long style circinate at the top and very oblique stigma.

16. VIGNA, Savi.

Calyx-tube campanulate; teeth deltoid. Corolla papilionaceous, much exserted; petals equal in length; keel hemispherical, not at all beaked. Stamens diadelphous; anthers uniform. Ovary sessile, many-ovuled; style long filiform; stigma oblique. Pod linear, subterete, subseptate.—Twining herbs or shrubs with the habit of *Phaseolus*, from which the flowers differ by their truncate keel. DISTRIB. Round the world in the tropics. Species 40–50.

Leaflets acute; stipules large . . . . * V. SINENSIS.
Leaflets obtuse; stipules small . . . . 1. V. LUTEA.

* *V. sinensis*, Endl. (Dolichos sinensis, *Linn.; DC. Prod.* ii. 399,) universally cultivated in the tropical zone, is frequent in waste and cultivated ground in the Seychelles. It is a glabrous twining or suberect annual, with persistent lanceolate striated stipules, large long-petioled membranous trifoliolate leaves, the end leaflet ovate cuspidate with a slight rhomboid tendency, flowers 6–12 in corymbose racemes with persistent bracts resembling the stipules, calyx $\frac{1}{8}$ in. long with deltoid-acuminate teeth, corolla large red or yellow, pod cylindrical glabrous $\frac{1}{2}$–1 ft. long 10–15 seeded.

1. **V. lutea,** *A. Gray, Bot. Amer. Expl. Expedit.* i. 454. A glabrous perennial twiner. Leaves petioled, trifoliolate, stipellate; leaflets rather fleshy, oblong or obovate, 3–4 in. long, obtuse, entire; stipules small, lanceolate. Flowers few, in corymbose long-peduncled axillary racemes; pedicels short, unequal. Calyx $\frac{1}{8}$ in. long; teeth short, deltoid. Corolla $\frac{1}{2}$ in. long, yellowish. Pod 2–3 in. long, glabrous, terete, reflexed, rather torulose, turning black. Seeds 6–8, oblong, brown, the size of a pea. V. anomala and retusa, *Walpers.*

SEYCHELLES, on the shores of Praslin and Curieuse, *Horne!* Trop. Africa, Natal, Australia, America.

17. GALACTIA, P. Br.

Calyx-tube short; teeth long, lanceolate, the two upper connate. Corolla little exserted, its petals nearly equal in length; keel obtuse. Stamens diadelphous; anthers uniform. Ovary subsessile, with few ovules; style long, filiform, beardless; stigma capitate. Pod flat, linear.—Twining herbs, with trifoliolate leaves and middle-sized flowers in racemes with slightly tumid nodes. DISTRIB. Species 45, mostly tropical American.

1. **G. tenuiflora,** *W. and A. Prod.* 206. A perennial twiner, with slender stems clothed with short dense pubescence. Stipules minute, linear, persistent; petioles 1–1$\frac{1}{2}$ in. long, pilose like the branches; leaflets 3, oblong, obtuse, 1–1$\frac{1}{2}$ in. long, sometimes emarginate, rather firm in texture, clothed thinly above, densely below, with short whitish pubescence. Flowers few, in condensed peduncled axillary racemes. Calyx $\frac{1}{4}$ in. long, silky; teeth deep, lanceolate. Corolla reddish, little exserted. Pod 1$\frac{1}{2}$ in. long, flat, glabrous. Seeds 4–5. G. villosa. *W.* and *A. Prod.* 207.

MAURITIUS, on Coin de Mire Island, *Horne!* Also from Australia to Natal.

18. RHYNCHOSIA, Lour.

Calyx tube campanulate; upper teeth more or less connate. Corolla papilionaceous; standard round or obovate-unguiculate; wings narrow; keel incurved at the tip. Stamens diadelphous; anthers uniform. Ovary subsessile, 2-ovuled; style incurved at the top; stigma capitate. Pod compressed, oblong, 2-valved, continuous within. Seeds 1–2, with a central funiculus.—Twining herbs, with pinnately trifoliolate leaves gland-dotted on the under side and flowers in axillary racemes. DISTRIB. Everywhere in the tropics. Species 70–80.

1. **R. minima,** *DC. Prod.* ii. 385. A twining herb, with slender nearly glabrous stems. Leaves distinctly petioled; central leaflet roundish or broad ovate, ¾–1 in. broad and long; stipules minute, setaceous. Flowers in lax 6-12-flowered racemes, 2–4 in. long, on short axillary peduncles; bracts and bracteoles minute, setaceous, deciduous. Calyx ⅛–⅙ in. long; teeth linear, longer than the tube. Corolla yellowish, twice the length of the calyx. Pod under an inch long, ¼ in. broad, soon glabrous. R. nuda, medicaginea, rhombifolia, ervoidea and punctata, *DC. loc. cit.*

RODRIGUEZ, frequent on dry banks, *Balfour!* Warmer regions of both hemispheres.

* *Flemingia strobilifera*, R. Br.; DC. Prod. ii. 351, Wt. Ic. t. 267, common in Tropical Asia, is established in Mauritius on plains at Moka, Réduit and Pamplemousses; and Mr. Horne sends it from the Seychelles. It is an erect shrub, 6–10 feet high, with slender densely pilose branches, large caducous stipules, short-petioled large simple firm oblong glabrescent subacute leaves, flowers in close racemes with a pilose zigzag rachis, each hidden in a large round membraneous persistent bract, calyx ¼ in. long with lanceolate teeth, corolla purple, little exserted, pod oblong downy turgid ¼–⅓ in. long two-seeded.

* *Cajanus indicus*, Spreng, Syst. iii. 248, now spread everywhere within the tropics, probably a native of the Old World, is often seen in Mauritius, Rodriguez and the Seychelles about abandoned plantations. It is a shrub, 6–12 feet high with slender sulcate silky branches, petioled trifoliolate leaves, oblong lanceolate subcoriaceous indistinctly gland-dotted leaflets, flowers in sparse corymbose racemes uniting to form a terminal panicle, silky calyx ¼ in. deep with lanceolate teeth, middle-sized corolla with the standard yellow (C. flavus, *DC.*) or veined with red (C. bicolor, *DC.* C. striatus, *Bojer*), diadelphous stamens and linear straight torulose pod 2–3 in. long narrowed to both ends with distinct oblique furrows between the 3–5 seeds. *Ambrevète. Ambrevade.*

19. PONGAMIA, Vent.

Calyx campanulate, nearly truncate. Corolla much exserted; standard broad; keel obtuse, its petals cohering at their tips. Stamens monadelphous, the upper filament free low down; anthers oblong, versatile. Ovary subsessile, 2-ovulate; style incurved, glabrous; stigma capitate. Pod sublignose, flat, oblong, indehiscent, neither winged nor thickened at the sutures. A single species.

1. **P. glabra,** *Vent.; DC. Prod.* ii. 416. A large robust climber with glabrous branches and leaves. Leaflets 5–7, the side ones opposite, subcoriaceous, 2–4 in. long, oblong or acute, pointed, stalked. Flowers in lax simple racemes 3–6 in. long on the end of the branches or from the axils; pedicels 2–4-nate, spreading, silky, with a pair of minute bracteoles at the middle. Calyx $\frac{1}{8}$ in. long. Corolla reddish, silky, 3–4 times as long as the calyx. Pod $1\frac{1}{2}$–2 in. long, $\frac{1}{8}$–$\frac{1}{4}$ in. thick, sublignose, glabrous, with a short decurved point. Robinia mitis, *Linn*. Galedupa indica, *Lam*.

SEYCHELLES, not uncommon in the shore-marshes of Mahé, *Horne*, 482! Common in Tropical Asia; not African.

* *Hæmatoxylon campeachianum*, Linn.; DC. Prod. ii. 485; Hayne Arzn. ix. t. 44, the tree that yields Logwood, a native of Central America, is half-wild in Rodriguez round Mathurin and in Mauritius on the lower part of the Pouce range, and used for hedges. It is a much-branched tree 15–20 feet high with a smooth bark, abruptly pinnate leaves with 3–4 pairs of small obovate obtuse rigid veined leaflets, fragrant flowers in copious dense axillary racemes, calyx with a short cup and 5 subequal lingulate lobes, 5 bright yellow small equal oblanceolate petals, 10 free stamens with filaments hairy at the base and a flat thin nearly sessile membranous pod narrowed to both ends splitting not by the sutures but the middle of the valves. *Bois de Campêche.*

* *Parkinsonia aculeata*, Linn.; DC. Prod. ii. 485, a native of America, now spread everywhere in the tropics, is often seen in Mauritius in hedges. It is a glabrous shrub, 6–10 feet high, armed with sharp woody spines which represent the primary axils of a bipinnate leaf, and bear 2–6 crowded pinnæ, which are often a foot long, with a flattened rachis and very numerous minute obovate leaflets. The flowers are in lax racemes, with a membranous calyx cleft nearly to the base into obtuse valvate lobes, large yellow obovate-unguiculate subequal petals, 10 free stamens and a 1–6-seeded dry moniliform pod, which finally splits open. *Genêt épineux.*

* CÆSALPINIA, Linn.

Calyx deeply cleft, with 5 imbricated lobes, the lowest the largest, cucullate. Petals spreading, obovate-unguiculate, the uppermost the smallest of the five. Stamens 10, free, declinate; anthers oblong, uniform, versatile. Ovary nearly sessile, with several ovules; style filiform; stigma capitate. Pod few-seeded, variable, oblong, dehiscent or indehiscent.—Robust woody prickly climbers with very large bipinnate leaves, abruptly pinnate pinnæ and copious flowers in axillary racemes. DISTRIB. Round the world in the tropics. Species 40

Pod dehiscing, the valves armed with dense prickles . . * C. BONDUCELLA.
Pod indehiscent, the valves unarmed.

Pod turgid, veined, ¾ inch broad . . . . * C. SEPIARIA.
Pod flat, smooth, ¼ inch broad . . . . * C. SAPPAN.

* *C. Bonducella*, Fleming, Asiat. Res. xi. 159 (Guilandina Bonducella, *Linn. DC. Prod.*, ii. 480; G. Bonduc, *Bojer, Hort. Maur.* 117), spread everywhere in the tropics, is often seen in Mauritius about plantations, and is common in many parts of Mahé and in Rodriguez. It is a shrubby climber, armed with very copious firm prickles, very large bipinnate leaves with 6–8 pinnæ, each with 8–10 pairs of oblong membranous downy leaflets an inch long, flowers in dense peduncled axillary racemes with a downy rachis, squarrose persistent acute bracts, yellow flowers ½ inch long, and a short-stalked rigid oblong pod 2–3 in. long with the valves armed all over with unequal straight prickles. *Cadoque.*

* *C. sepiaria*, Roxb. Fl. Ind. ii. 360, common in Tropical Asia, is often used in Mauritius for hedges, and is in Dr. Balfour's Rodriguez collection from Anse Baleine. It is a shrubby climber with pilose branches armed with copious small hooked prickles, bipinnate leaves a foot long, with 6–10 pairs of stalked pinnæ, 8–12-jugate small close oblong membranous leaflets ½–1 inch long, long simple peduncled racemes, middle-sized bright yellow flowers, densely pilose filaments and a hard turgid veined oblong pod 3–4 inches long with thick sutures and 4–8 seeds. *Sappan liane. Mysore thorn. Cassie.*

* *C. Sappan*, Linn.; DC. Prod. ii. 482, a native of Tropical Asia, is now naturalised through Mauritius. It is a shrubby climber, armed with few small prickles, branchlets clothed with short ferruginous hairs, bipinnate leaves a foot or more long with 8–12-pairs of pinnæ, 10–15-jugate close articulated membranous leaflets square on the inner, rounded on the outer edge, ample panicles often as long as the leaves, middle-sized bright yellow flowers, densely pilose filaments and a woody indehiscent flattish brown oblong pod 3 inches long with a short recurved beak. *Bois Sappin* or *Sappan.*

20. TRACHYLOBIUM, Hayne.

Calyx-tube very short; sepals 4, broad, much imbricated. Petals 5, two lower or all reduced to mere scales. Stamens 10, free from the base of the ovary; filaments filiform, pilose; anthers uniform. Ovary short-stalked; ovules few; style filiform; stigma minute. Pod oblong, large, rigid, rough, indehiscent.—Apparently one species only, clearly a native of Madagascar, now widely spread in Tropical Asia and Africa.

1. **T. verrucosum,** *Lam. Ill. t.* 330 *fig.* 2 (*as a Hymenæa*). A tall unarmed tree, with terete branches. Leaves short-petioled, consisting of a single pair of oblique oblong rigidly coriaceous glabrous pointed leaflets, 2–3 in. long, cuneate at the base on the inner, rounded on the outer side. Flowers in an ample corymbose panicle, the lower branches of which often spring from the axils of the leaves; branchlets pilose. Calyx-limb ½ in. long; segments oblong, obtuse, tomentose on

the back. Petals white, the three upper often exserted from the calyx rounded, with a distinct claw. Pod oblique, oblong, warty, obtuse, 2 in. long. T. Hornemannianum, *Hayne, Arzneg. t.* 18. T. Gærtnerianum, *Hayne, l. c. t.* 19. T. mossambicense, *Klotzsch in Peters Mossam. Bot.* 21, *t.* 2.

SEYCHELLES, in Mahé near Port Victoria, *Horne*, 476! Hayne's t. 18 is drawn from a Mauritian specimen, but it is only cultivated in the island for the sake of its Gum Copal. Also Madagascar and East Tropical Africa. *Copalier.*

21. CASSIA, Linn.

Calyx-tube very short; teeth lanceolate or lingulate, unequal or subequal. Petals 5, imbricated, subequal, obovate. Stamens normally ten, often some imperfect, usually basifixed, dehiscing by terminal pores or the slit continued down the side. Ovary sessile or stalked, many-ovuled; style incurved; stigma terminal. Pod in our species dehiscent, flattened or rather turgid. Seeds numerous, albuminous.—Herbs or shrubs, with equally pinnate leaves, inflorescence variable, flowers showy, mostly yellow. DISTRIB. Round the world in warm regions. Species 340. Monographed by Bentham, Trans. Linn. Soc. xxvii. 503, tab. 60–63.

Flowers in corymbose racemes.
  Leaflets 3–5-jugate, ovate-oblong . . . . * C. OCCIDENTALIS.
  Leaflets 6–12-jugate, oblong-lanceolate . . . . * C. SOPHERA.
Flowers in axillary pairs.
  Leaflets 3-jugate, large, obovate-oblong . . . . * C. TORA.
  Leaflets 12–15-jugate, crowded, small, firm, ligulate . . * C. GLANDULOSA.
  Leaflets 30–50-jugate, crowded small, firm, ligulate . . . 1. C. MIMOSOIDES.

* *C. occidentalis*, Linn.; DC. Prod. ii. 497; Bot. Reg. t. 83, widely-spread in the tropics, is frequent in Mauritius, Rodriguez, and Seychelles, but introduced. It is a robust shrubby annual 3–5 feet high, with long-stalked abruptly pinnate leaves with a single gland placed just above the base of the petiole, 4–5-jugate large ovate or oblong acute leaflets, flowers in axillary and terminal corymbs, oblong membranous nearly free sepals, middle-sized yellow petals, 7 perfect and 3 barren stamens, and an ensiform curved glabrous torulose pod 4–5 inches long with 20–30 seeds. *Casse puante.*

* *C. Sophera*, Linn.; DC. Prod. ii. 492 (C. chinensis, *Jacq. Ic.* t. 73), a native of Tropical Asia, is established in Mauritius in plains at Moka and Plaines-Wilhelms. It is very near *C. occidentalis*, but differs by its more shrubby habit, more numerous narrower leaflets, and shorter broader more turgid pods which are scarcely at all torulose.

* *C. Tora*, Linn.; DC. Prod. ii. 493 (C. obtusifolia, *Linn.*), spread round the world in the tropics, is naturalised in Mauritius in waste ground and fields near Port Louis and other parts of the island. It is an erect shrubby glabrous annual, with petioled abruptly-pinnate leaves, 3-jugate sessile obovate-oblong glaucous membranous leaflets 1-1½ in. long, flowers in nearly sessile pairs in the axils of the leaves,

small bright yellow corolla, 7 fertile and 3 barren stamens and narrow square recurved pods ½–¾ foot long with 30–40 square shining pale brown seeds.

* *C. glandulosa*, Linn.; DC. Prod. ii. 453 (C. Chamæcrista, *Bojer, Hort. Maur.* 122, *non Linn.*), a native of Tropical America, is naturalised in Mauritius on the Pouce and in plantations round Mont Plaisir. It is a shrubby glabrous biennial, with linear persistent stipules, sensitive leaves with a single stalked peltate gland on the short petiole, 12–15-jugate close sessile ligulate firm cuspidate leaflets, flowers solitary or in pairs distinctly stalked in the axils of the leaves, linear sepals, bright yellow obovate petals ⅓ inch long, 10 perfect stamens with anthers very unequal in length and a linear flat pod 1–1½ inch long narrowed to the base, with 10–12 seeds.

1. **C. mimosoides,** *Linn.; DC. Prod.* ii. 505. A shrubby perennial, 2–3 feet high, with downy branches. Leaves 1–3 in. long, with a solitary sessile gland on the short petiole; leaflets 30–50-jugate, linear, rigidly coriaceous, ⅛–¼ in. long, obliquely pointed, sensitive; stipules linear, persistent. Flowers 1–2 in the axils of the leaves on short pedicels. Petals yellow, ½ in. deep, rather exceeding the lanceolate downy sepals. Pod flat, thin, dehiscent, downy, 1½–2 in. long; seeds 15–20, small, oblong.

SEYCHELLES, common in waste lands in many parts of Mahé, *Horne*, 475! Round the world in the tropics.

22. AFZELIA, Smith.

Calyx with a long cylindrical tube, and 4 oblong imbricated subequal segments. Upper petal only produced, round with a long claw. Perfect stamens declinate, with very long anthers; imperfect 5-6, filiform. Ovary with a stalk rather protruded from the disk at the top of the tube, linear with few ovules and a long curved filiform style. Pod large, flat, oblong, subindehiscent.—Unarmed trees, with abruptly pinnate leaves, large rigid leaflets and copious flowers in corymbose panicles. DISTRIB. Tropics of the Old World. Species 10.

1. **A. bijuga,** *A. Gray, Bot. Amer. Expl. Expedit.* 467, *t.* 51. An unarmed tree, with petioled abruptly pinnate leaves. Leaflets bijugate, short-stalked, oblique oblong, subacute, glabrous, firm, 3–4 in. long, the lower pair distant smaller. Flowers in ample corymbose terminal panicles; pedicels ascending, bibracteolate, articulated at the middle. Petal exserted, roundish, with a long claw. Fertile stamens above an inch long, with much recurved slender pilose filaments. Pod firm, flat, oblong, 6–8 inches long. Outea bijuga, *DC. Prod.* ii. 511. Macrolobium bijugum, *Coleb. in Trans. Linn. Soc.* xii. 359, t. 17. Intsia madagascariensis, *Thouars; Bojer, Hort. Maur.* 422.

Said to have been once common in the SEYCHELLES, but now rare. Also Malay peninsula and isles, Galega and Madagascar. *Gayac* or *Faux Gayac*.

* *Tamarindus indica*, Linn.; DC. Prod. ii. 488, of which the native country is not clearly known, is often seen in Mauritius and Rodriguez in a half-wild condition. It is a tree with short-stalked abruptly pinnate leaves with 10–20 pairs of crowded firm reticulated articulated leaflets, copious flowers in lax terminal racemes with pedicels jointed at the top, calyx split down nearly to the base into imbricated oblanceolate teeth, petals only 3 developed the uppermost hooded, stamens monadelphous only 3 bearing anthers and a curved ligulate 3–10-seeded pod ¼–½ foot long with a thin crustaceous epicarp and a thick pulpy stringy edible mesocarp. *T. occidentalis*, Gærtn., and *T. officinalis*, Hook. Bot. Mag. tab. 4363, are the same species. *Tamarinier.*

* *Entada scandens*, Benth. in Hook. Journ. Bot. 1842, 332 (Mimosa scandens, *Linn.*; Entada Pursætha, *DC. Prod.* ii. 425), spread round the world in the tropics, is established in Mauritius near the sea at La Savanne, and in ravines round the Baie du Cap. It is a large glabrous woody climber, with slender terete branches, bipinnate leaves with rachis ending in a tendril, 3–4-jugate oblong firm large leaflets, polygamous minute flowers in slender peduncled axillary spikes nearly a foot long, a minute campanulate 5-toothed calyx, 5 equal narrow spreading petals, 10 free slightly exserted stamens, and a flat curved woody pod 1–2 feet long, composed of many discoid deltoid one-seeded joints, the endocarp of which persists round the large flat discoid seeds. *Liane sabre.*

* *Adenanthera pavonina*, Linn.; DC. Prod. ii. 446, widely spread in Tropical Asia, is common in the Seychelles, where the timber is used for houses, but is not clearly indigenous. It is an erect unarmed tree, with large bipinnate leaves, 4–6-jugate pinnæ, 6–9-jugate oblong obtuse glabrous membranous leaflets ¾–1½ in. long, minute yellow flowers in spike-like mostly axillary racemes, 10 free stamens, a strap-shaped torulose coriaceous pod 6–9 inches long, with 10–12 bright scarlet seeds and a dry glossy endocarp. *Bois noir à la graine. Bois noir de Bourbon.*

23. GAGNEBINA, Neck.

Calyx campanulate, 5-toothed. Petals 3–4 times as long as the calyx, 5, equal, lingulate, valvate. Stamens 10, free, much exserted; filaments filiform; anthers crowned with a gland. Ovary short-stalked; ovules numerous; style long, filiform; stigma capitate. Pod flat, firm, oblong, indehiscent, with a broad firm wing to each suture, septate between the seeds. Monotypic.

1. **G. tamariscina**, *DC. Prod.* ii. 432. A much-branched shrub, 6–12 feet high, with wrinkled brown bark, and rather hairy branchlets. Leaves abruptly bipinnate, 3–6 in. long; petiole jointed at the base, square, with a large discoid gland below the pinnæ, and a smaller one between each pair; pinnæ 10–20-jugate, 1–2 in. long; leaflets 30–50-

jugate, close, firm, ligulate, $\frac{1}{8}$ in. long, sessile, deciduous. Spikes 1–3, peduncled in the axils of the leaves, 1–2 in. long. Petals whitish, $\frac{1}{12}$ in. long. Pod firm, 1–2 in. long, with a rigid persistent wing to each suture. G. axillaris, *DC. loc. cit.*

MAURITIUS in woods of the Pouce, Bois Rouge, and Montagne Longue. Coin de Mire, *Horne !* Also Madagascar.

* *Mimosa pudica*, Linn.; DC. Prod. ii. 426, the well-known Sensitive plant, a native of America, now spread widely in the Old World, occurs occasionally as a weed in Mauritius, and is common in the Seychelles, in Mahé. It is a shrubby perennial, with branches armed with small prickles and spreading hairs, petioled digitate leaves, each with 3–4 pinnæ with 12–20 pairs of small close linear-oblong membranous leaflets, minute polygamous tetramerous flowers in small round peduncled heads, 10 free stamens, flat linear pods armed with copious spreading stramineous bristles, which split up into 4–5 one-seeded joints, like a Desmodium, and fall away from the sutures. *Sensitive.*

* *Leucæna glauca*, Benth. in Hook. Lond. Journ. iv. 416, (Acacia frondosa, glauca, biceps, and leucocephala, *DC.*), probably a native of America, but now diffused through the Old World, is common throughout Mauritius, the Seychelles, and Rodriguez. It is a low spineless tree with bipinnate leaves, with rachises ending in a bristle, 4–8-jugate pinnæ, 10–15-jugate linear acute glaucous membranous leaflets deltoid at the base, minute pentamerous hermaphrodite flowers in dense peduncled round heads, 10 free much exserted stamens, and a flat flexible glabrous strap-shaped pod 4–6 inches long, with 15–20 small seeds and a long stalk. *Cassie blanc. L'Acacie.*

24. ACACIA, Willd.

Flowers hermaphrodite or polygamous, usually pentamerous. Calyx campanulate or funnel-shaped, shortly toothed. Petals exserted, united towards the base. Stamens free, indefinite, much exserted; anthers minute, not gland-crested. Ovary sessile or stalked, many-ovuled; style filiform; stigma minute, capitate. Pod ligulate or oblong, not articulated, usually compressed and dry, rarely turgid; sutures straight or wavy, not thickened.—Prickly or unarmed trees, the leaves bipinnate or often represented only by flattened petioles (phyllodia), the minute flowers in dense peduncled rounded heads. DISTRIB. Tropics and Australia. Species 430.

Pod thick, with a fleshy mesocarp.
  Erect with spines in stipular pairs . . . . 1. A. FARNESIANA.
  Climber with copious scattered spines, none stipular * A. CONCINNA.
Pod thin, flat, flexible.
  No spines; petioles flattened into phyllodia, some only bearing leaves . . . . 2. A. HETEROPHYLLA.
  Petioles terete; spines in stipular pairs . . . . . * A. EBURNEA.

1. **A. Farnesiana**, *Willd.; DC. Prod.* ii. 461. A shrub, 6–15 feet high, with zigzag brown slender branches, marked with grey dots. Spines stipular only, spreading, subulate. Leaves bipinnate, with a petiolar gland; pinnæ 4–8-jugate; leaflets 10–20-jugate, minute, firm, linear-oblong, crowded. Flowers in dense peduncled heads $\frac{1}{2}$ inch thick; peduncles 1–3-nate, with a ring of bracts near the top. Pod cylindrical, curved, 2–3 in. long, with straight sutures, biserial seeds and a pulpy mesocarp, the valves marked with fine horizontal striations. Mimosa Farnesiana, *Linn.* A. indica, *Desv.; DC. Prod.* ii. 462.

MAURITIUS, forming a great part of the underwood of the savannas. SEYCHELLES, in Mahé, not common, *Horne*, 469! RODRIGUEZ, a few shrubs near Mathurin and in Oyster Bay, *Dr. Balfour!* Cosmopolitan in the tropics, but often planted. *Cassie.*

* *A. concinna*, DC. Prod. ii. 464, (A. polycephala, *DC.*; A. habbasoides, *Bojer*, *Hort. Maur.* 116), common in Tropical Asia, is naturalised in various places in Mauritius, the pods being used by the Indians like soap, and sold in the bazaars. It is a shrubby climber, with branches armed with abundant small irregular prickles, 6–8-jugate pinnæ, 15–25-jugate ligulate obtuse leaflets $\frac{1}{8}$–$\frac{1}{2}$ in. long, flowers in copiously-panicled small round heads, thick succulent strap-shaped pods 3–4 inches long much shrivelled when dry, narrowed into a short stalk, and the valves depressed between the 6–8 seeds. *Chickakai.*

2. **A. heterophylla**, *Willd.; DC. Prod.* ii. 452. An unarmed tree, with slender glabrous quadrangular branchlets. Phyllodia some with, some without leaves, strap-shaped, narrowed to both ends, 3–4 in. long, coriaceous, strongly closely veined. Leaves bipinnate, with 1–4-jugate erecto-patent pinnæ, each with 10–11 pairs of oblong obtuse leaflets $\frac{1}{4}$–$\frac{1}{3}$ in. long. Flowers in short peduncled round heads in the axils of the leaves. Pod sessile, strap-shaped, flat, thin, rather curved, 3–4 in. long, 6–8-seeded, with both sutures straight. *Benth. in Trans. Linn. Soc.* XXX. 402.

MAURITIUS, in the cantons of Flacq and La Savanne. Also Bourbon. Extremely near Sandwich Islands *A. Koa*, A. Gray Bot. Amer. Expl. Exped. i. 380.

* *A. eburnea*, Willd.; DC. Prod. ii. 461, a native of Tropical Asia, is naturalised in Mauritius, near Port Louis and La Riviere des Lataniers. It is a shrub, 10–15 feet high, with the habit of the Gum Acacia, a pair of spreading subulate pungent stipular spines at the base of each leaf, 2–5-jugate pinnæ, minute 6–8-jugate oblong grey-green pilose leaflets, flowers in small round peduncled axillary heads, calyx $\frac{1}{24}$ in. long, corolla scarcely exserted, and thin flat strap-shaped pod rather waved at the sutures, with 6–10 seeds. *Cassie à piquants blancs.*

* *Desmanthus virgatus*, Willd.; DC. Prod. ii. 445, a native of Tropical America, is naturalised in Mauritius in gardens and plantations round

Port Louis, and has been gathered by Mr. Horne in the Seychelles, on Ile St. Anne, and was found several times by Dr. Balfour in Rodriguez. It is a glabrous shrubby perennial, with virgate branches, unequally bipinnate leaves with rachises ending in a small bristle, 3–4-jugate pinnæ with a gland beneath the lowest, 15–20-jugate small obtuse oblong membranous leaflets, minute pentamerous polygamous flowers in small round peduncled axillary heads, 10 free stamens, narrow linear flat coriaceous smooth 2-valved pods with 20–30 small seeds.

* *Albizzia Lebbek*, Benth. in Hook. Lond. Journ. 1844, 87 (Acacia Lebbek, *Willd.; Bojer, Hort. Maur.* 116), spread through the tropics of the Old World, is naturalised throughout Mauritius, Rodriguez, and the Seychelles, both in the plains and on the hills. It was brought from Bengal by Cossigny in 1767. It is an unarmed tree, 20–40 feet high, with a round head, thick trunk and rugged bark, abruptly bipinnate leaves, 2–4-jugate pinnæ, 4–9-jugate large obtuse oblique-oblong membranous leaflets, flowers in dense round heads, downy calyx $\frac{1}{8}$ in. long, gamopetalous corolla, indefinite monadelphous very long stamens, and a large firm flat coriaceous pod $\frac{1}{2}$–1 foot long, 1–1$\frac{1}{2}$ inch broad, 6–10-seeded, with straight sutures. *Bois noir.*

* *Pithecolobium dulce*, Benth. in Hook. Lond. Journ. 1844, 199, (Inga dulcis, *Willd.*; *DC. Prod.* ii. 436), a native of Tropical America, now widely spread in the Old World, is naturalised in Mauritius on the Pouce and in other places. It is an erect tree, 30–50 feet high, with a pair of erecto-patent stipular thorns, bipinnate leaves, with pinnæ and leaflets both unijugate, the latter oblique-oblong rather firm obtuse 1–2 in. long, flowers in small round peduncled heads panicled on elongating branchlets, gamophyllous corolla, indefinite monadelphous stamens, and a spirally-curved flat strap-shaped pod 3–4 in. long with thick sutures, veined valves, rather turgid over the 6–8 seeds, which are enveloped in a white fleshy aril, which is eaten by the negro boys.

Order XXXIV. ROSACEÆ.

Flowers regular, hermaphrodite. Calyx free; sepals 5, imbricated, joined in a tube at the base, Petals 5, obovate, with a short claw, inserted at the throat of the calyx. Stamens free, indefinite, inserted at the throat of the calyx; filaments filiform; anthers minute, didymous. Carpels 1 or many; ovules in the Mauritian genera two, erect or pendulous; style sometimes basilar. Fruit dry or fleshy. Seeds exalbuminous.—Our plants shrubby; leaves alternate, stipulate, simple or compound; flowers in panicled racemes. Distrib. Cosmopolitan. Species about 1000.

Carpel solitary, style basal . . . . 1. Grangeria.
Carpels numerous, style terminal . . . . * Rubus.

1. GRANGERIA, Comm.

Flowers hermaphrodite. Calyx-tube short, turbinate; teeth 5, oblong, obtuse, imbricated. Petals 5, round, inserted at the throat of the calyx, minute, caducous. Stamens 15, inserted in a regular ring with the petals at the throat of the calyx; filaments filiform; anthers round, minute. Ovary immersed in the tube, woolly, one-celled; style short, basilar, glabrous. Drupe trigonous, nearly dry, with a bony endocarp, woolly inside, 1-seeded. The only species.

1. **G. borbonica**, *Lam.; DC. Prod.* ii. 527. A much-branched glabrous shrub, 10–15 feet high. Leaves crowded, alternate, nearly sessile, obtuse, entire, coriaceous, shining, 1–2 in. long. Racemes 1–2 in. long, dense, copious, short-peduncled, axillary, or forming a terminal panicle; pedicels downy, erecto-patent, exceeding the calyx, with a minute linear persistent bract at the base. Calyx $\frac{1}{8}$ in. long, downy, coriaceous; sepals reflexed, persistent, exceeding the tube. Ring of stamens erect, longer than the sepals, persisting round the minute white ovary. Drupe turbinate, $\frac{1}{2}$ in. long. G. buxifolia, *Smith*.

MAURITIUS, universal in woods. Also Bourbon. *Faux Buis.*

* RUBUS, Linn.

Calyx cleft nearly to the base into 5 acute teeth. Petals 5, obovate-unguiculate, inserted at the throat of the calyx. Stamens indefinite, inserted with the petals; filaments filiform; anthers minute. Carpels numerous, crowded on a prominent torus, with 2 pendulous ovules; style subterminal. Fruit a drupel, with a single bony seed.—Prickly shrubs, with simple or compound leaves and panicled flowers. DISTRIB. One of the most cosmopolitan of genera; but none of the species are truly wild within our limits. Species 100–200.

Leaves simple . . . . * R. MOLUCCANUS.
Leaves digitately compound . . . . * R. BERGII.
Leaves pinnately compound . . . . * R. ROSÆFOLIUS.

* *R. moluccanus*, Linn.; DC. Prod. ii. 566 (R. rugosus, *Smith*; R. Hamiltonianus, *Seringe*), very common in Tropical Asia, is established in Mauritius at Moka. It is a sarmentose shrub, with densely pilose branches, minute hooked prickles, deeply cordate large rugose 5-lobed minutely toothed leaves densely matted with whitish tomentum beneath, a dense panicle with distant lower branches in the axils of the leaves, acute very silky permanently ascending sepals $\frac{1}{2}$ inch long, broad included petals and a dense rounded head of numerous minute drupels. *Framboisier de Java.*

* *R. Bergii*, Eckl. and Zeyh. (R. fruticosus, *var.* Bergii, *Cham. and Schlecht.; Harv. and Sond. Fl. Cap.* ii. 228), the common bramble of the Cape (mistaken by Bojer, Hort. Maur. 127, for the European

R. cæsius), is established abundantly in Mauritius at Moka and Crêvecœur. It is a shrub with glabrous angular branches, large equal hooked prickles, digitately compound leaves with 5–7 ovate-cuspidate sharply toothed subglabrous leaflets, crowded panicle with distant lower branches, short deltoid sepals matted on the back especially at the edges, and copious small drupels in a round head.

* *R. rosæfolius*, Smith, Icon. Inedit. t. 60; DC. Prod. ii. 559; Bot. Mag. tab. 556, common in Tropical Asia, is established abundantly in Mauritius, Rodriguez and Seychelles. It was brought from the Malay Isles by Commerson, about 1780. It is a bush, with slender pilose branches, few small distant prickles, pinnate leaves with 5–7 oblong-lanceolate opposite membranous doubly-toothed slightly pilose leaflets, lax few-flowered corymbose panicles, pilose sepals lengthened out into long points which exceed the round petals, and very numerous small red drupels in an oblong head. *Framboisier*.

The Almond, *Amygdalus communis*, Linn., is in Dr. Balfour's Rodriguez collection as a naturalised species. *Amandier*.

Fragaria vesca, Linn., the common European Strawberry, is included in Dupont's Catalogue as a species naturalised in Mauritius. *Fraisier*.

Rosa semperflorens, Curt. Bot. Mag. t. 284, is also included in Dupont's Mauritian Catalogue. *Rosier de Chine*.

ORDER XXXV. SAXIFRAGACEÆ.

Flowers regular, hermaphrodite or polygamous. Sepals 4–5, minute; joined at the very base. Petals the same number, much larger, oblong, caducous. Stamens definite, perigynous; filaments filiform, anthers didymous, splitting down the side. Ovary free, ampullæform, 2–5-celled; ovules many; styles free or joined; stigmas capitate. Fruit indehiscent or dehiscing septicidally. Seeds usually small, with a minute embryo and copious albumen, but *Brexia* is an exception. DISTRIB. A truly cosmopolitan order of very various habit. Species 500–600.

Petals free.
- Fruit large, subdrupaceous, indehiscent, 5-celled . . . 1. BREXIA.
- Fruit minute, dry, 2-celled, the carpels soon dehiscing septicidally . . . . 3. WEINMANNIA.

Petals united in the lower third or quarter. . . . . . . 3. ROUSSEA.

1. BREXIA, Thouars.

Calyx small, with 5 round imbricated sepals, connate at the base. Petals 5, oblong, imbricated, deciduous. Stamens 5, arising from a thick perigynous disk, which is produced into teeth (staminodia) between them; filaments subulate; anthers oblong, versatile. Ovary ampullæform, 5-celled, narrowed into the style; ovules indefinite; stigma capitate, 5-lobed. Fruit large, drupaceous, oblong, 5-lobed. Seeds horizontal, obovoid-oblong, black, with a large embryo, with amygdaloid cotyledons and very thin albumen. The only species.

1. **B. madagascariensis,** *Thouars; Ker, Bot. Reg. t.* 730. A glabrous shrub, 10–20 ft. high, with terete grey virgate branchlets. Leaves alternate, short-petioled, oblanceolate-oblong, 4–6 in. long, coriaceous, obtuse, reticulato-venose, usually entire. Flowers 6–20 in peduncled axillary umbels; pedicels exceeding the flowers, bractless, articulated at the base. Calyx spreading, patellæform. Petals oblong, ½ in. deep, twisted in æstivation. Stamens nearly as long as the petals; filaments fleshy; anthers ⅛ in. long. Fruit oblong-cuspidate, ¼ in. long. Venana, *Lam. Ill. t.* 131.

SEYCHELLES, not uncommon in Mahé, rare in Praslin, *Horne! Wright!* Also Madagascar and East Tropical Africa. *B. spinosa*, Lindl. Bot. Reg. t. 872, is a variety with toothed, and *B. chrysophylla*, Sweet, a form with long oblanceolate subentire leaves.

2. WEINMANNIA, Linn.

Flowers polygamous or hermaphrodite. Calyx minute, cut down nearly to the base into 4–5 teeth. Petals the same number, alternate with the sepals. Stamens 8–10, perigynous, exserted when fully developed; filaments filiform; anthers didymous. Ovary sessile, ampullæform, 2-celled; ovules many; styles two, filiform, falcate; stigmas capitate. Fruit a dry capsule, soon dehiscing septicidally.—Trees with opposite simple or compound coriaceous leaves and abundant small racemose flowers. DISTRIB. All round the world in the tropics, but none in continental Africa. Species 50.

1. **W. tinctoria,** *Smith in Rees' Cyclop.* A small much-branched tree with terete straight branchlets. Leaves 2–4 in. long; leaflets 5–15, oblong, obtuse, coriaceous, 1–1½ in. long, sessile, inciso-crenate, with the rachis broadly winged between them; stipules broad, short, reflexed, truncate or emarginate. Racemes copious, peduncled, axillary, 2–6 in. long, with a pilose axis and very numerous flowers in dense fascicles; pedicels 3–4 times the flower. Petals oblong, $\frac{1}{24}$ in. long. Valves of the capsule dry, $\frac{1}{12}$ in. long, persistent, tipped with the hooked styles. W. macrostachya, *DC. Prod.* iv. 10. W. glabra, *Lam. Ill. t.* 313, *fig.* 1, *non Linn. fil.* W. Boiviniana, *Tulasne.*

MAURITIUS, common in the hill forests. Also Bourbon. *Arbre Mouche à miel.* In Bourbon, *Tan Rouge.*

3. ROUSSEA, Smith.

Calyx-tube broadly obconic, short, adnate to the base of the ovary; teeth 5, large, lanceolate, valvate. Petals 5, lanceolate, united near the base into a campanulate tube, thick and pilose on the outside, reflexing. Stamens 5, erect, inserted between the lobes of the disk; filaments subulate; anthers basifixed, lanceolate-sagittate. Ovary ampullæform, superior, 5-celled, narrowed into a stout cylindrical style; stigma peltate. Fruit baccate, girt with the persistent calyx; septa fleshy; cells filled with pulp. A single species.

1. **R. simplex,** *Smith, Icon. Inedit. t.* 6. A glabrous shrubby climber with stout terete branchlets. Leaves opposite, short-petioled, crowded near the end of the branchlets, coriaceous, oblanceolate-oblong, cuneate at the base, simple, penninerved, 4–6 in. long, glanduloso-serrate. Flowers solitary on short cernuous peduncles in the axils of the leaves. Calyx accrescent, finally 1–1½ in. long. Corolla yellow. Petals and sepals ¼–⅓ in. broad. Stamens rather overtopping the petals and stigma. *Endlich. Icon. t.* 107.

MAURITIUS, frequent in dense forests. Also Bourbon.

ORDER XXXVI. CRASSULACEÆ.

Flowers regular, hermaphrodite. Calyx free, persistent; sepals usually 4–5, in our plant joined in a long tube. Petals as many as the sepals, joined in a long tube. Stamens usually twice as many as the petals, in our plant epipetalous; filaments filiform; anthers minute, didymous. Carpels free or nearly so, apocarpous, as many as the sepals, narrowed into a long style; stigma capitate; ovules numerous, attached to the ventral suture. Fruits follicular, dehiscing by the dorsal suture. Seeds numerous, minute.—Herbs with exstipulate fleshy leaves and cymose flowers. DISTRIB. Cosmopolitan in dry climates. Species 400.

1. BRYOPHYLLUM, Salisb.

Calyx large, membranous, with an oblong tube, and 4 deltoid teeth. Corolla longer than the calyx, with a long tube much constricted above the ovaries and 4 lanceolate teeth. Stamens 8, in two rows, springing from the corolla-tube; filaments filiform; anthers small. Carpels 4, nearly free, with very long connivent styles, reaching to the top of the corolla tube; ovules numerous; stigmas capitate. Fruit follicular. —Large almost shrubby succulent perennial herbs, with ample lax terminal panicles. DISTRIB. Two other species inhabit Madagascar and one Cape Colony.

1. **B. calycinum,** *Salisb. Parad. t.* 3; *DC. Prod.* iii. 396. Stems 3-6 feet high, stout, glabrous, angular. Leaves opposite, petioled, proliferous from the edges, crowded near the base of the stem; lower compound, with 3–5 obovate-cuneate deeply crenate obtuse fleshy leaflets; upper simple, larger, oblong. Panicle 2–3 feet long, made up of opposite lax long-peduncled cymes with divaricated slender flexuose pedicels. Calyx 1–1½ in. long, green streaked with red. Corolla-tube

greenish, 4-angled at the base, urceolate above the constriction, with purplish spreading teeth. Hypogynous scales square, nearly free. Follicles 4, fusiform; seeds minute, very numerous. *Bot. Mag. t.* 1409. Cotyledon pinnata, *Lam.*

MAURITIUS, on dry hills of Rivière Noire, Signal Mountain, etc. RODRIGUEZ, not frequent, *Balfour*. SEYCHELLES, in Mahé about abandoned dwellings, *Horne*, 464! Cosmopolitan in the tropics.

ORDER XXXVII. LYTHRACEÆ.

Flowers regular, mostly hermaphrodite. Calyx-tube campanulate, often ribbed; teeth 4-6, usually with a small horn in each sinus. Petals the same number as the calyx-teeth or absent. Stamens inserted in the calyx-tube, definite; filaments filiform; anthers oblong, didymous, splitting down the side. Ovary free, but usually immersed in the persistent calyx-tube, 3–4-celled, or the septa obliterated; style and stigma, except in *Psiloxylon*, simple. Fruit usually a fragile capsule. Seeds numerous, minute, exalbuminous. — Herbs or shrubs with opposite entire leaves, the branches often square, the flowers solitary or cymose in the axils of the leaves. DISTRIB. Cosmopolitan, mostly tropical. Species 250.

Annual herbs.
  Stamens 4 . . . . 1. AMMANNIA.
  Stamens 8–12 . . . . 2. NESÆA.
Shrubs.
  Fruit capsular.
    Petals none. Stamens 4 . . . . 3. TETRATAXIS.
    Petals 6. Stamens 12 . . . . 4. PEMPHIS.
  Fruit baccate.
    Stamens 10; ovary superior . . . . 5. PSILOXYLON.
    Stamens indefinite; ovary almost inferior . . . . . 6. SONNERATIA.

1. AMMANNIA, Linn.

Calyx campanulate, with 4 small teeth and a horn in the sinuses. Petals absent, or fugacious and very minute. Stamens 4, inserted in the calyx-tube; filaments filiform; anthers didymous. Ovary free, immersed in the calyx-tube, 1- or imperfectly 2–3-celled; ovules many; style filiform; stigma entire. Fruit a membranous fragile capsule, bursting irregularly.—Annual herbs, with opposite sessile leaves and very minute flowers in axillary cymes. DISTRIB. Round the world in the tropics. Species 30.

Cymes lax . . . . 1. A. BACCIFERA.
Cymes congested . . . . 2. A. SALICIFOLIA.

1. **A. baccifera,** *Linn. Sp. Plant.* 175. A much-branched glabrous annual, $\frac{1}{2}$–1 foot high, with tetragonal branches. Leaves linear or lanceolate, 1–2 in. long, narrowed from the middle to both ends. Flowers

8–12 in sessile or nearly sessile cymes in the axils of most of the leaves; pedicels as long as calyx. Calyx campanulate, $\frac{1}{24}$ in. broad, with 4 deltoid teeth and a small horn in each of the sinuses. Petals none. Stamens 4. Capsule 1- or imperfectly 2-celled, membranous, splitting transversely. A. indica, *Lam.* A. vesicatoria, *Roxb.*

MAURITIUS, in damp ground at Pamplemousses and Nouvelle Découverte. Spread through the tropics of Old World.

2. **A. salicifolia,** *Monti Comm. Bonon.* i. 112. A glabrous annual, $\frac{1}{2}$–1 ft. high, with stoutish quadranglar branches. Leaves firmer than in the last, lanceolate, deflexed, sessile, rounded at the base. Flowers many, in dense glomerules in the axils of most of the leaves; pedicels mostly none. Calyx campanulate, under $\frac{1}{12}$ in. broad, with 4 obscure teeth. Petals mostly absent. Stamens 4. Capsule globose, membranous, brown, twice as large as the calyx, 1-celled with a triquetrous central placenta. A. ægyptiaca, *Willd.* A. verticillata, *Lam.* A. glauca, *Wall.*

MAURITIUS, in damp ground at Flacq and Pamplemousses. Spread through the tropics of the Old World.

2. NESÆA, Comm.

Calyx-tube campanulate, with 4 short teeth, and a small horn in each sinus. Petals 4, inserted at the throat of the calyx. Stamens 8–12, inserted in the tube; filaments filiform; anthers small, oblong. Ovary free, globose, immersed in the calyx-tube, 4-celled; ovules many; style filiform, curved; stigma entire. Fruit a small globose membranous capsule splitting at the top.—Herbs with opposite entire leaves and small purplish flowers in axillary cymes. DISTRIB. Tropics of Africa and America. Species 12.

1. **N. triflora,** *Kunth.*; *DC. Prod.* iii. 90. A slender annual, glabrous throughout, branched at the base, with quadrangular stems a foot long. Leaves nearly sessile, oblong or lanceolate, an inch long. Flowers 3 together in peduncled cymes from the axils of the leaves, subtended by a pair of lanceolate bracts. Calyx-tube $\frac{1}{8}$ in. broad and long, 8-ribbed. Petals very fugacious. Style as long as the calyx. Stamens scarcely exserted from the calyx-tube; filaments purple; anthers minute, yellow. Capsule round, fragile, immersed in the calyx-tube.

MAURITIUS, frequent by streamsides. Also Bourbon and Madagascar.

3. TETRATAXIS, Hook. fil.

Calyx large, campanulate, acutely tetragonal, with 4 acute teeth. Petals absent. Stamens 4, springing from the base of the calyx; filaments filiform, exserted; anthers oblong. Ovary 4-lobed, 4-celled, many-ovuled; placentation axile; style filiform, long; stigma capitate,

Capsule 4-celled, with the valves breaking away from the placentas. Seeds many, minute, linear-oblong. A single species

1. **T. salicifolia,** *Baker.* A shrub, glabrous in all its parts, with quadranglar branches. Leaves opposite, short-petioled, ovate-lanceolate, acute, 2–3 in. long, rigidly subcoriaceous, penninerved. Flowers 1–3, on erect axillary peduncles an inch long, with a pair of linear-oblong caducous bracteoles to each. Sepals ovate, ½ inch broad, the tube 4-winged and wings decurrent down the pedicel. Style exceeding the stamens. Tetradia salicifolia, *Thouars; Tulasne in Ann. Sc. Nat. ser.* iv, *vol.* 6, 137.

Mauritius, in the woods of the Rivière Noire, *Thouars.* Endemic. The generic name used by Du Petit Thouars is pre-occupied by Robert Brown.

4. PEMPHIS, Forst.

Calyx-tube campanulate, with 12 distinct ribs; teeth 6, deltoid with a spur in each sinus. Petals 6, inserted at the throat of the calyx. Stamens 12, biseriate, inserted low down in the calyx-tube; filaments filiform; anthers oblong. Ovary globose, included in the calyx-tube, short-stalked, 3-celled at the base; style filiform; stigma capitate. Capsule globose, hidden in the persistent calyx, splitting round near the base; placenta basilar. Seeds numerous. A single species.

1. **P. acidula,** *Forst.*; *DC. Prod.* 3, 89. A much-branched shrub, 2-4 feet high, with terete branchlets. Leaves crowded, short-petioled, oblong or lanceolate, ½–1 in. long, subcoriaceous, 1-nerved, rather silky. Flowers solitary, from the axils of the leaves, on short hairy pedicels. Calyx ⅛ in. long, prominently grooved. Petals white, crumpled, obovate-unguiculate, as long as the calyx, deciduous. Capsule crustaceous, fragile, as large as the calyx-tube. P. angustifolia, *Roxb.*

Mauritius, on the shore at Baie du Cap, Canonier point, etc. Flat and Amber Islands, *Horne!* Rodriguez, common on the limestone cliffs of the shore, *Balfour!* Spread through the tropics of the Old World.

5. PSILOXYLON, Thouars.

Flowers polygamous, regular. Calyx-tube hemispherical; lobes 5, round, slightly imbricated. Petals 5, round, unguiculate, perigynous. Stamens 10, springing from the edge of a broad pentagonal disk; filaments filiform; anthers oblong, bilocular. Ovary entirely superior, oblong, 3-celled; ovules indefinite in each cell; stigma large, 3-lobed, subsessile. Fruit a small globose berry. Seeds minute, exalbuminous; embryo straight, fleshy. A single species.

1. **P. mauritianum,** *Baill. Adans* x. 41. A shrub, glabrous in all its parts, with terete branchlets. Leaves alternate, short-petioled,

oblong or obovate-oblong, obtuse or subacute, cuneate at the base, 3–6 in. long, coriaceous, bright green above, paler below and minutely gland-dotted with fine laurel-like venation. Flowers 3–6 in the axils of the leaves or from the branch below them on short separate pedicels. Bud globose, ⅛ in. thick. Pentagonal disk ⅛ in. broad. Petals whitish, ⅛ in. broad and long. Stamens rather exceeding the petals. Berry ½ in. deep, girt with the persistent calyx, and crowned with the persistent 3-lobed stigma. Psiloxylon, *Thouars*; *Tulasne, Ann. Sc. Nat. ser.* iv. *vol.* 6, 138. Fropiera mauritanica, *Bouton*; *Hook. fil. in Journ. Linn. Soc.* v. 2, *tab.* 1.

MAURITIUS, in dense woods. *Bois Maigre. Bois sans écorce.* Also Bourbon.

6. SONNERATIA, L. fil.

Calyx coriaceous; tube campanulate; teeth about 6, valvate, persistent. Petals the same number as the calyx-teeth, small, caducous, sometimes absent. Stamens very numerous, inserted in 2–3 rows at the throat of the calyx; filaments filiform, curled up in the bud as in *Myrtaceæ*; anthers small, reniform. Ovary almost entirely adhering to the calyx-tube; cells 14–16; ovules many, on axillary placentas; style long, filiform; stigma capitate. Fruit broad-turbinate, with an umbilicate apex, girt by the persistent calyx.—Shore shrubs with entire opposite leaves. DISTRIB. Tropics of the Old World. Species 2–3.

1. **S. acida,** *Linn. fil.; DC. Prod.* iii. 231. A small pyramidal tree, 12–20 feet high, with terete naked branchlets. Leaves short-petioled, oblong, obtuse, fleshy-coriaceous, penninerved, 3–4 in. long. Flowers about three together at the end of the branchlets; bracts small, caducous. Calyx an inch long, the teeth much exceeding the tube. Filaments twice as long as the sepals and style still longer. Fruit with a flat top above an inch broad, splitting irregularly from the base. *Wt. Ic. t.* 340.

SEYCHELLES, in shore-marshes with mangroves, *Horne* 449! Australia to Mozambique.

The Pomegranate, **Punica Granatum,** Linn., is commonly cultivated, and is in Dr. Balfour's Rodriguez collection as an established plant. *Grenadier. Grenade.*

ORDER XXXVIII. SAMYDACEÆ.

Flowers regular, hermaphrodite. Calyx-tube short; teeth broad or narrow. Petals as many as the sepals, absent in *Casearia*. Stamens as many or twice as many as the sepals, in *Casearia* monadelphous and alternating with staminodia. Ovary 1-celled, superior or half-inferior; placentas 3–5, parietal; ovules few or many to each placenta; stigmas separate. Fruit capsular or baccate, many-seeded; albumen copious. —Shrubs or trees with alternate simple petioled often dotted or lineolate leaves; inflorescence various; flowers copious, minute. DISTRIB. Round the world in the tropics. Species 150.

Petals none; ovary free . . . . 1. CASEARIA.
Petals present; ovary half inferior . . . . 2. HOMALIUM.

1. CASEARIA, Jacq.

Calyx-tube very short; lobes 5, round, imbricated. Petals none. Stamens 10, united in a short tube, alternating with square truncate staminodes. Ovary free, ampullæform, narrowed gradually into a short style; stigma three-lobed; placentation parietal; ovules numerous. Fruit subbaccate, with many small seeds.—Trees or shrubs with alternate simple leaves and small flowers in axillary cymes. DISTRIB. Round the world in the tropics. Species 80.

1. **C. fragilis,** *Vent.; DC. Prod.* ii. 50. A shrub 6–8 feet high, glabrous in all its parts, with rugose lenticellate branchlets. Leaves petioled, alternate, oblong or obovate, subcoriaceous, penninerved, 2–4 in. long, obtuse or subacute, cuneate or rather rounded at the base. Flowers 3–6 from the swollen nodes; pedicels as long or longer than the calyx. Calyx $\frac{1}{12}$–$\frac{1}{8}$ in. long, persistent. Stamens and staminodes included, the latter shortly ciliated. Fruit oblong-lanceolate, an inch long, pointed. C. fasciculata, *Bojer, Hort. Maur,* 71.

MAURITIUS, woods of the Pouce, Grand Bassin, Nouvelle Découverte, etc. Leaves vary from 1½ to 4 times as long as broad. *C. fasciculata,* Bojer, is a form with very obtuse obovate leaves. Also Bourbon. *Bois Callant. Bois Maigre.*

2. HOMALIUM, Jacq.

Calyx-tube obconic, adnate to the base of the ovary; teeth 8–12, linear. Petals inserted at the throat of the calyx, the same shape and number as the sepals. Stamens inserted with the petals, in § *Blackwellia* one opposite each; filaments filiform, pilose; anthers small, globose. Ovary 1-celled, half inferior; placentation parietal. Styles 5, slender, spreading; ovules about 4 to each placenta. Fruit capsular, opening at the top.—Trees or shrubs with alternate petioled leaves, the flowers minute, pilose, in simple or panicled racemes. DISTRIB. Round the world in the tropics. Species 30.

1. **H. paniculatum,** *Benth. in Journ. Linn. Soc.* iv. 34. A tree with all parts except the flower glabrous. Leaves distinctly petioled, broad oblong, glaucous, subcoriaceous, distinctly penninerved, subentire or inciso-crenate, 3–4 in. long, rounded at the base. Flowers whitish, in copious fascicled racemes or panicles from the nodes of old leafless branches; pedicels very short. Calyx $\frac{1}{8}$–$\frac{1}{6}$ in. long; the petals, sepals, stamens, and ovary densely ciliated; the stamens and styles rather exserted. Placentas and styles 5. Blackwellia integrifolia and paniculata, *Lam.; DC. Prod.* ii. 54. B. glauca, *Vent. Choix. t.* 55.

MAURITIUS, frequent through the island in shaded woods. Endemic. *Bois de Source des hauts. Bois à écorce blanche.*

ORDER XXXIX. TURNERACEÆ.

Flowers regular, hermaphrodite. Calyx-tube campanulate; teeth 5, imbricated. Petals 5, membranous, obovate-unguiculate. Stamens 5, inserted low down in the calyx-tube; filaments rather flattened; anthers oblong, splitting down the sides. Ovary free, 1-celled; placentas 3, parietal; ovules many, horizontal; styles 3, subulate, free from the base; stigmas terminal. Fruit a loculicidal capsule; seeds numerous, minute, albuminous.—Herbs or shrubs, with alternate petioled exstipulate simple leaves, with flowers usually solitary in their axils. DISTRIB. Mainly tropical American. Species 70-80.

Herbaceous; seeds not crested with a tuft of hairs. . . . * TURNERA.
Tree; seeds crested with a tuft of hairs . . . . 1. MATHURINA.

* *Turnera ulmifolia*, Linn.; DC. Prod. iii. 246, (T. angustifolia, *Bot. Mag. t.* 281), a native of Tropical America, is a frequent weed in Mauritius and the Seychelles. It is an erect biennial, with large alternate petioled simple lanceolate acute deeply toothed slightly hairy leaves, flowers solitary from the upper axils on peduncles connate with the petioles, calyx an inch long with 5 lanceolate teeth and a funnel-shaped tube, 5 obovate bright yellow large fugacious petals, 5 stamens inserted with the petals in the calyx-tube, a 1-celled ovary with 3 parietal placentas, 3 filiform styles and a loculicidal many-seeded capsule.

1. MATHURINA, Balf. fil.

Sepals 5, lanceolate-cuspidate, with a tubercle on the face at the base, imbricated in æstivation. Petals 5, obovate, membranous, fugacious, about as long as the sepals. Stamens 5, exserted, inserted at the base of the sepals; filaments long, slightly flattened; anthers oblong. Ovary oblong, sessile, 1-celled; placentas 3, parietal; styles subulate; stigmas capitate. Fruit a triquetrous 3-valved capsule. Seeds minute, bottle-shaped, crested with a tuft of hairs.—The only known species. Closely allied to the monotypic Central American genus *Erblichia*, Seem., of which the fruit is unknown.

1. **M. penduliflora,** *Balf. fil. in Journ. Linn. Soc.* xv. 160. A small tree, glabrous in all its parts, with stout terete branchlets marked in the lower part with the scars of the fallen leaves. Leaves crowded, shortly petioled, oblanceolate, acute, 3–4 in. long, an inch broad, deeply crenate, cuneate and entire at the base, varying in young plants to ligulate, ¼ in. broad, subcoriaceous, the fine distinct veinlets connected by intramarginal arches. Flowers pendulous, solitary in the axils of the leaves, on peduncles 1–2 in. long, with a pair of linear bracts at the middle. Sepals and petals an inch long. Stamens and styles nearly twice as long. Capsules oblong-triquetrous, an inch long, the valves nearly flat on the back.

RODRIGUEZ, frequent in the higher parts of the interior of the island, *Balfour!* Endemic. *Bois Gandine.*

ORDER XL. PASSIFLORACEÆ.

Flowers regular, hermaphrodite or dioicous. Calyx-tube in ours short; lobes mostly 5. Petals the same number and shape as the calyx-lobes or absent. Stamens isomerous; anthers linear-oblong, versatile, slit down the side. Ovary free, stalked, one-celled; placentas 3, parietal; ovules indefinite; styles or stigmas free when they leave the ovary. Fruit baccate or capsular. Seeds albuminous, with a fleshy arillus or testa.—Herbs or shrubs with alternate stipulate leaves, axillary flowers and copious axillary spiral tendrils. DISTRIB. Round the world in the tropics, mostly American. Species 250.

Flowers hermaphrodite, with a crown of barren filaments between the petals and stamens . . . . * PASSIFLORA.
Flowers dioicous, without any crown . . . . 1. OPHIOCAULON.

* PASSIFLORA. Linn.

Flowers hermaphrodite, regular. Calyx-tube campanulate; lobes usually 5, similar to the petals in size and shape. Petals 5, lanceolate or oblong-lanceolate sometimes absent. Crown simple or double, the outer of numerous spreading filaments often as long as the flower-wrappers. Stamens the filaments adnate, except at the tip, to a long gynophore; anthers large, versatile, linear-oblong. Ovary long-stalked, 1-celled; placentas 3, parietal; styles 3, spreading, thickest at the tip; stigmas capitate. Fruit usually baccate.—Climbing herbs or shrubs with copious spiral axillary tendrils. DISTRIB. Species above 100, nearly all American none truly wild within our bounds.

Section *Cicca*. Petals none . . . . * P. SUBEROSA.
Section *Dysosmia*. Petals present. Bracts and stipules cut up into filiform lobes . . . . * P. FŒTIDA.
Section *Granadilla*. Petals present; flowers large and showy. Bracts and stipules entire, foliaceous.
Leaf entire . . . . * P. ALATA.
Leaf 3-lobed, with broad segments . . . . * P. STIPULATA.
Leaf deeply 5-7-lobed, with narrow segments . . . . . * P. CÆRULEA.

* *P. suberosa*, Linn.; DC. Prod. iii. 325; Jacq. Vind. t. 163, spread through tropical America, is now a troublesome weed in Mauritius in plantations. It is a climber, with very slender naked or pilose stems, minute subulate stipules, short petioles with a pair of small glands, shallowly or deeply three-lobed leaves with a deltoid base, minute apetalous flowers with a crown not more than half as long as the calyx, and a glaucous purple baccate fruit as large as a cherry.

* *P. fœtida*, Linn.; DC. Prod. iii. 331; Bot. Mag. t. 2619, a native of tropical America, now widely spread in the old world, is occasionally subspontaneous in Mauritius. It is a slender herbaceous climber, with a fœtid scent, branches and leaves clothed with fine spreading hairs, stipules and bracts cut up into innumerable gland-tipped filiform segments, a solitary middle-sized very fugacious whitish flower, and a nearly dry fruit as large as a plum.

* *P. alata*, Aiton; Bot. Mag. t. 66, (P. mauritiana, *Thouars*), a native of Brazil, is established in Mauritius near Moka, and also in the Seychelles in several places in Mahé. It is a glabrous woody climber, with stout acutely-angular branches, large ovate-lanceolate deciduous stipules, short petioles with several large glands, large entire cuspidate cordate-ovate leaves of rather firm texture, large solitary fragrant flowers with petals and sepals on the inside bright red, a crown nearly as long as the petals with stout filaments variegated with red and white, and a large baccate fruit. *Grenadille.*

* *P. stipulata*, Aublet; DC. Prod. iii. 329; (P. glauca, *Ait.*), a native of tropical America, is said by Bojer to be established in Mauritius in fields round Mont Plaisir. It is a glabrous woody climber, with slender terete stems, large half-round cordate persistent stipules, long petioles with 2–4 conspicuous sessile glands, large membranous leaves with 3 deep broad palmate lobes, a fragrant flower 2½–3 inches broad with whitish petals, a crown nearly as long as the petals with rays purple at the base, and an involucre of three small ovate bracts. *Grenadille sauvage.*

* *P. cærulea*, Linn.; DC. Prod. iii. 330; Bot. Mag. t. 28, a native of South Brazil and Uruguay, the most hardy of all the showy Passion-flowers, is subspontaneous in Mauritius near Moka and Réduit. It is a glabrous climber, with slender angular stems, large persistent half-cordate ovate stipules, petioles with a few minute sessile glands, leaves deeply palmately cut into 5–7 lanceolate or linear lobes, expanded flower 2½–3 inches broad with blue oblong-lanceolate petals, aristate sepals, a crown decidedly shorter than the petals with rays purple at the bottom white in the middle and blue at the tip, and a yellow baccate fruit the size of a plum. *Grenadille bleue.*

1. OPHIOCAULON, Hook. fil.

Flowers regular, dioicous. Calyx-tube very short; teeth 5, lanceolate, acute. Petals 5, minute, linear, alternate with the sepals. Corona none. Stamens 5; filaments very short, almost hypogynous, represented by minute staminodes in the female flower; anthers long, linear. Ovary oblong, stalked, 1-celled; placentas 3, parietal; ovules many; stigmas 3, sessile, flabellate. Fruit a membranous capsule.—Scandent shrubs, with petioled broad alternate leaves, copious tendrils and minute green flowers in axillary cymes. DISTRIB. Species 3–4. Tropical Africa, Natal, Madagascar.

1. **O. cissampeloides,** *Hk. fil. Gen. Plant.* i. 814. A glabrous woody climber, with slender terete branchlets. Leaves alternate, distinctly petioled, membranous, deltoid or roundish, subacute, cordate or truncate at the base, subentire or repand, very glaucous below, 3–4 in. broad. Tendrils representing barren peduncles, axillary, firm, many times spirally curved above the middle. Cymes lax, axillary, and terminal; pedicels equally or exceeding the calyx. Calyx green, ⅙–¼

in. long. Capsule oblong, fragile, an inch long. Modecca cissampeloides, *Planch. in Hook. Fl. Nigrit.* 365.

SEYCHELLES, common in hill woods of Mahé and Silhouette, *Dr. Percival Wright! Horne*, 459! Sap drunk by the negroes. Through Tropical Africa. *Liane blanc.*

The Papaw, **Carica Papaya**, Linn. is commonly cultivated and is now subspontaneous both in Mauritius and Rodriguez. *Papaye. Papayer.*

ORDER XLI. FICOIDEÆ.

Flowers regular, hermaphrodite. Calyx 4–5-toothed, mostly free. Petals as many as the sepals or absent. Stamens perigynous, definite or indefinite; filaments filiform; anthers oblong, didymous, slit down the side. Ovary 2- or many-celled; ovules one or many in a cell; styles filiform, as many as the cells. Fruit usually capsular, dehiscing variously. Seeds with embryo curved round a central nucleus of albumen.—Herbs or undershrubs; leaves very variable, often fleshy; inflorescence, if compound, centrifugal. DISTRIB. Mainly Cape. Species 450.

Dehiscence of capsule loculicidal . . . . 1. MOLLUGO.
Dehiscence of capsule circumscissile . . . . 2. SESUVIUM.

1. MOLLUGO, Linn.

Calyx-tube very short; teeth 5, persistent, subequal, membranous at the edge. Petals absent. Stamens 5–10, inserted at the base of the calyx. Ovary free, 3-celled; ovules many in a cell; placentation axile; stigmas minute, sessile. Fruit a loculicidal capsule.—Annual herbs, with whorled or opposite leaves, the flowers in lateral or terminal umbels or cymes. DISTRIB. Spread round the world in the tropics. Species 12.

1. **M. Spergula**, *Linn.; DC. Prod.* i. 391. A diffuse much-branched low annual. Leaves 3–6 in a whorl, oblanceolate, entire, subsessile, acute, rather fleshy, ½–1 in. long. Flowers solitary or 2–6 in a whorl from the same nodes as the leaves, on spreading pedicels much shorter than the leaves. Sepals ⅛ in. long, oblong, imbricated. Capsule oblong, as long as the sepals. Seeds chesnut-brown, tubercled. Glinus Mollugo, *Fenzl.*

SEYCHELLES, in waste marshy ground at La Digue, *Horne!* Spread through the tropics of the Old World.

2. SESUVIUM, Linn.

Calyx-tube obconic: teeth 5, equal, lanceolate, coloured on the inside. Petals absent. Stamens indefinite, inserted in the calyx-tube; filaments filiform; anthers minute, oblong. Ovary free, 3-celled; styles 3, filiform, free; ovules many in a cell. Fruit an ovoid capsule with circumscissile dehiscence.—Herbs or undershrubs with opposite entire fleshy leaves, the flowers in our species solitary in their axils. DISTRIB. Cosmopolitan. Species 6–7.

1. **S. Portulacastrum,** *Linn.; DC. Prod.* iii. 453. A glabrous wide-trailing littoral herb, the whole plant often red. Leaves oblanceolate, obtuse, entire, very fleshy, 1–2 in. long, with a membranous deltoid clasping stipule adnate to the narrowed base. Flowers solitary, peduncled or nearly sessile in the axils of many of the leaves. Calyx ¼ in. long, green outside, red within. Stamens about 12, included.

MAURITIUS, on sand round salt-water pools, near Fort William, *Ayres!* Coin de Mire and Amber island, *Horne!* RODRIGUEZ, *Balfour!* Cosmopolitan on tropical shores.

ORDER XLII. HALORAGACEÆ.

Flowers in our plant monoicous or polygamous, tetramerous. Calyx adnate to the ovary in the female flowers, 4-toothed. Petals 4, free or absent. Anthers 4, subsessile, basifixed, strap-shaped, two-celled, dehiscing longitudinally. Ovary ovoid, inferior, 1-celled; stigmas 4, sessile. Fruit a minute 1-seeded nut. Seeds albuminous.—Herbs, usually aquatic; leaves alternate or opposite; flowers minute, in axillary clusters. DISTRIB. Cosmopolitan. Species 80.

1. SERPICULA, Linn.

Flowers monoicous or polygamous. Sepals 4, lanceolate, free to the base in the male, deltoid with a tube adnate to the ovary in the female flowers. Petals 4 or absent. Stamens 4, large, linear, subsessile. Ovary inferior, 1-celled, with 4 pendulous ovules; stigmas 4, sessile, spreading. Fruit a dry one-seeded nut. Many species described, but they seem all varieties of one.

1. **S. repens,** *Linn.; DC. Prod.* iii. 65. Rootstock wiry, perennial, wide-creeping; stems simple, ascending, nearly glabrous. Leaves sessile, oblanceolate, alternate or opposite, entire, glabrous, 1-nerved in the common Mauritian form (*S. repens*, Bojer; *S. brasiliensis*, Camb.) under ½ inch long. Flowers in dense clusters in the axils of the upper leaves; males pedicellate, with 4 strap-shaped anthers $\frac{1}{12}$ in. long; females sessile, the ovoid nut with 8 tubercled grooves and crowned with the erect persistent deltoid calyx-teeth.

MAURITIUS, in swamps at Pamplemousses, Mare aux Vacouas, etc. Cosmopolitan in the tropics; also Cape. *S. veronicæfolia*, Bory.; DC. Prod. *loc. cit.*, is a variety with opposite obovate toothed glabrous leaves.

ORDER XLIII. RHIZOPHORACEÆ.

Flowers regular, hermaphrodite. Calyx-tube more or less adnate to the ovary; teeth few or many, coriaceous, persistent. Petals as many as the calyx-teeth, inserted at their base, entire or bifid. Stamens twice as many as the petals, inserted with them at base of the calyx-teeth; filaments filiform; anthers at first many, finally two-celled. Ovary partly or entirely inferior; style entire. Fruit indehiscent, coriaceous, one-seeded. Seeds exalbuminous; the radicle growing very large, hard, and cylindrical, and taking root without falling.—Trees of muddy shores, with coriaceous entire opposite leaves. DISTRIB. Cosmopolitan in the tropics. Species 50.

Calyx-teeth 4. Petals entire, not setose . . . . 1. RHIZOPHORA.
Calyx-teeth 5. Petals setose, obscurely toothed at tip . . . 2. CERIOPS.
Calyx-teeth 8-14. Petals bifid, setose . . . . 3. BRUGIERA.

1. RHIZOPHORA, Linn.

Calyx-tube short, adnate to the lower part of the ovary; teeth 4, lanceolate, coriaceous, persistent, reflexed. Petals 4, deciduous, entire, inserted in the disk. Stamens 8, inserted with the petals; filaments short; anthers connivent, oblong-accuminate. Ovary half-inferior, 2-celled, produced in a large cone beyond the calyx, narrowed into the style; ovules 2. Fruit large, coriaceous, ovoid, 1-seeded, the long cylindrical radicle protruding from the apex, and taking root without the fruit falling.—Trees inhabiting muddy shores, with crowded petioled oblong entire very coriaceous leaves, and trunks sending out roots above the base. DISTRIB. Cosmopolitan in the tropics. Species 3–4.

1. **R. mucronata,** *Lam.; DC. Prod.* iii. 32. An erect tree, 12–16 feet high, with leaves crowded at the end of the thick branches. Leaves petioled, oblong, very coriaceous, mucronate, 4–5 in. long; stipules large, lanceolate, convolute, deciduous. Flowers 2–4 together in peduncled axillary drooping cymes; pedicels short, with a pair of persistent small deltoid connate bracteoles clasping the calyx. Flower-calyx ½ in. long, with a short tube. Petals oblong-navicular, silky. Fruit hard, 1–1½ in. long, girdled near the base with the reflexed sepals, the radicle issuing from the top.

SEYCHELLES and MAURITIUS, common on muddy shores. Spread through the tropics of the Old World. *Manglier.*

2. CERIOPS, Arnott.

Calyx-tube obconic, adnate to the base of the ovary; teeth 5, lanceolate, coriaceous, valvate, finally patent. Petals as many as the sepals, truncate, with 2–3 minute bristles from the tip. Stamens 10, in pairs opposite the petals; filaments filiform; anthers linear-oblong. Ovary partly inferior, imperfectly 3-celled; ovules 2 in each cell, pendulous; style filiform; stigma simple. Fruit small, conical, girt near the base with the spreading calyx-teeth, by abortion 1-celled and 1-seeded, the clavate radicle protruding as in *Rhizophora.*—Small trees with the habit and leaves of *Rhizophora.* DISTRIB. Tropics of the Old World. Species 2–3.

1. **C. Candolleana,** *Arn. in Ann. Sc. Nat.* 1838, 364. A small tree,

glabrous in all its parts, with straight terete branchlets. Leaves distinctly petioled, 3–4 in. long, obovate-oblong, obtuse, rigidly coriaceous, cuneate at the base. Flowers in dense cymes on short cernuous peduncles from the axils of the leaves; pedicels very short, with a pair of persistent round connate bracteoles at the tip. Calyx ¼ in. long. Petals shorter than the calyx-teeth. C. mossambicensis, *Klotzsch.* Rhizophora timorensis, *DC. Prod.* iii. 32.

SEYCHELLES, common on the shores of Mahè and Praslin, *Horne!* Australia to Zambesi land.

3. BRUGIERA, Lam.

Calyx-tube turbinate, adnate to the ovary; teeth 8–14, as long as the tube, linear, permanently erect. Petals as many as the sepals, deeply bifid, the sinus and horns setigerous, the claw holding a pair of stamens. Stamens 16–28; filaments filiform, as long as the claw of the petals; anthers linear. Ovary inferior, 2-4-celled; ovules 2–4 in a cell, axile; style filiform, with 2–4 small cusps at the stigmatose apex. Fruit turbinate, coriaceous, crowned with the calyx-teeth, one-seeded, the clavate radicle protruded as in *Rhizophora.*—Trees with leaves and habit of *Rhizophora.* DISTRIB. Tropics of the Old World. Species few.

1. **B. gymnorhiza,** *Lam. Ill. t.* 397. A much-branched low tree, with leaves crowded at the end of the branches. Leaves petioled, oblong, entire, subacute, very coriaceous, 3–4 in. long, cuneate at the base; stipules large, convolute, caducous. Flowers solitary, on short ebracteate nutant pedicels in the axils of the leaves. Calyx 1–1½ in. long, the coriaceous teeth as long as the grooved tube. Petals shorter than the calyx-teeth, bifid nearly half down, the lobes erect, linear, with a conspicuous bristle, or more than one from the point, and a large one in the sinus. Rhizophora gymnorhiza, *Linn.; DC. Prod.* iii. 33. B. capensis and cylindrica, *Blume.*

SEYCHELLES, in marshes near the sea, in Mahé, *Pervillé! Horne!* MAURITIUS, on the shore at Grandport, *Bojer.* Tropics of the Old World.

ORDER XLIV. COMBRETACEÆ.

Flowers regular, hermaphrodite or polygamous. Calyx-tube adnate to the ovary, not produced above it in the Mauritian plant; limb 4–5 toothed. Petals often present, but not so in our genus. Stamens epigynous, 8–10, filaments filiform, inflexed in bud; anthers versatile, slit down the side. Ovary 1-celled; ovules one or few, pendulous from the apex. Style and stigma simple. Fruit dry or drupaceous. Seed solitary, exalbuminous.—Trees or shrubs, often climbers; leaves alternate, entire, exstipulate; flowers small, racemose, spicate or cymose. DISTRIB. Round the world in the tropics. Species 240.

1. TERMINALIA, Linn.

Flowers regular, polygamous. Calyx campanulate, with 5 deltoid teeth. Petals none. Stamens 10, biseriate, exserted; filaments filiform; anthers minute, globose. Ovary inferior, one-celled; ovules 2, pendulous from the apex; style subulate; stigma capitate. Fruit in our plant a hard triquetrous nut, with a coriaceous wing all round.—Erect trees or shrubs with alternate leaves and minute flowers in simple racemes. DISTRIB. Cosmopolitan in the tropics. Species 80–90.

Racemes as long as the leaves. Fruit-wing broad . . . 1. T. BENZOIN.
Racemes much shorter than the leaves. Fruit-wing narrow 2. T. CATAPPA.

1. **T. Benzoin,** *Linn. fil. Suppl.* 434, (*excl. syn. and loc.*) A tree 30–40 feet high, with leaves crowded at the thickened tips of the branches, which are tessellated with the scars of the fallen petioles. Leaves oblong-spathulate, crenate, obtuse or cuspidate, glabrous, subcoriaceous, 3–4 in. long, narrowed into a glandular petiole. Racemes axillary, petioled, as long as the leaves; pedicels exceeding the calyx. Calyx greenish, glabrous, $\frac{1}{12}$ in. broad. Stamens twice as long as the calyx. Fruit an inch long, round, emarginate, with a broad firm persistent wing. T. angustifolia, *Jacq. Vind.* 3, *t.* 100. T. mauritiana, *Lam.; DC. Prod.* iii. 11.

MAURITIUS, in the woods of the Savanne range and in the plains of Poudre d'Or; now rare. RODRIGUEZ, common. *Bouton! Balfour!* Also Bourbon. *Bois Benzoin. Bon Charon.*

2. **T. Catappa,** *Linn.; DC. Prod.* iii. 11. A tree 60–80 feet high, with a trunk 3–6 feet in diameter and stout branchlets, marked with the scars of fallen leaves. Leaves crowded near the end of the branchlets, short-petioled, obovate, obtuse, entire, membranous, $\frac{1}{2}$–1 ft. long, glabrous or pilose beneath, with two glands near the base of the midrib. Flowers in short peduncled slender spike-like racemes from the axils of the leaves. Calyx $\frac{1}{12}$ in. long, silky outside and inside, with five lanceolate reflexing teeth. Stamens exserted. Anthers round, minute. Fruit oblong, woody, $1\frac{1}{2}$–2 in. long, with a narrow wing and an edible kernel. *Jacq. Ic. t.* 197; *Bot. Mag. t.* 197.

SEYCHELLES, in Felicité and Marie Anne Isles forming two-thirds of the woody vegetation, in the other islands only near houses, *Horne,* 451! RODRIGUEZ, frequent, *Balfour!* Also much planted in MAURITIUS. *Badamier.* Common in Tropical Asia.

ORDER XLV. MYRTACEÆ.

Flowers regular, hermaphrodite. Calyx-tube adnate to the ovary, sometimes produced beyond it; limb 2–5-lobed, sometimes entire in bud. Petals usually 4, absent in *Fœtidia.* Stamens epigynous, very numerous; filaments filiform; anthers minute, 2-celled. Ovary inferior, 2- or many-celled; placentation axile; ovules 2 or many; style long, filiform; stigma mostly entire. Fruit dry or fleshy, 1-2- or few-celled. Seeds many or solitary, exalbuminous.— Trees or shrubs; leaves mostly opposite and gland-dotted, exstipulate; inflorescence various. DISTRIB. Tropical and subtropical round the world. Species 1800.

Leaves opposite, gland-dotted.
Ovary 4–6-celled. Radicle elongated . . . . PSIDIUM.

Ovary 2-celled. Radicle short . . . . 1. EUGENIA.
Leaves alternate, not gland-dotted.
Petals present. Stamens connate at the base . . . . . 2. BARRINGTONIA.
Petals absent. Stamens free . . . . 3. FŒTIDIA.

* *Psidium pomiferum*, Linn.; DC. Prod. iii. 234, the Guava, a native of tropical America, is subspontaneous in many places in Mauritius, Rodriguez and the Seychelles. It is a much-branched shrub, 10–15 feet high, with angular puberulent branchlets, nearly sessile oblong coriaceous obtuse strongly penninerved leaves 3–6 in. long finely downy below, solitary stalked flowers in the axils of the leaves, small globose calyx-tube constricted at the neck, ovoid entire calyx-limb which splits when the flower expands into four unequal lobes, expanded corolla an inch broad, many-celled ovary, filiform style, entire stigma, and large round fleshy yellow or reddish edible fruit. *P. pyriferum*, Linn.; DC. loc. cit., is a variety with fruit shaped like a pear. *Goyavier.*

* *P. Cattleyanum*, Sabine, Bot. Reg. t. 622. (P. indicum, *Bojer, Hort. Maur*, 139; P. variabile, *Berg.*; P. obovatum and coriaceum, *Mart.*), a native of Brazil, was introduced into Mauritius about 1830, and is now widely spread and subspontaneous both there and in the Seychelles and Rodriguez. It is readily distinguished by its distinctly petioled obovate-leaves with a cuneate base, which have not the strong erecto-patent parallel ribs of those of the other species. The peduncles are much shorter, and the corolla smaller. The fruit is globose or ovoid, red or yellow, 1–2 in. thick, with a more acid taste than that of the common Guava. *Goyavier de China.*

1. EUGENIA, Linn.

Flowers regular, sometimes undeveloped and abortive. Calyx-tube turbinate or campanulate; lobes 4, obtuse, usually broader than deep. Petals 4, spreading or in § *Syzygium* not expanding and falling away in an early stage. Stamens very numerous, epigynous; anthers minute, versatile. Ovary 2-celled; ovules many in a cell; style filiform, simple. Fruit more or less fleshy, globose, crowned with the persistent calyx-lobes. Embryo thick and fleshy, with a short radicle.—Shrubs or low trees, with opposite simple leaves, the flowers in the axils of the leaves or in lateral or terminal trichotomous cymes. DISTRIB. Round the world in the warmer zones. Species 500 or more.

Subgenus 1. JOSSINIA. Pedicels one-flowered, one or several from a node. Petals free, spreading.
Sepals oblong, thin, reflexed . . . . * E. UNIFLORA.
Sepals round, coriaceous, erect.
Petioles $\frac{1}{4}$–$\frac{3}{4}$ in. long . . . . 1. E. MESPILOIDES.
Petioles $\frac{1}{8}$–$\frac{1}{4}$ in. long.
Pedicels none or short . . . . 2. E. COTINIFOLIA.
Pedicels elongated . . . . 3. E. BUXIFOLIA.
Subgenus 2. JAMBOSA. Flowers in terminal and lateral trichotomous cymes. Petals free, spreading and falling separately.

Flowers large, Leaves lanceolate . . . . * E. JAMBOSA
Flowers middle-sized. Leaves oblong.
  Leaves nearly sessile, rounded or cuneate at the base.
    Calyx-teeth as deep as broad . . . . 4. E. BOJERI.
    Calyx-teeth twice as long as deep . . . . * E. MALACCENSIS.
  Leaves sessile, cordate at the base . . . . 5. E. VENOSA.
Flowers middle-sized. Leaves large, obovate . . . . . . 6. E. DUPONTII.
Subgenus 3. SYZYGIUM. Flowers in terminal and lateral trichotomous cymes. Petals cohering and falling in a cap together.
Leaves oblong, acute.
  Flowers small; developed stamens $\frac{1}{8}$–$\frac{1}{4}$ inch long.
    Leaves petioled.
      Flowers many at the end of the branchlets . . . . * E. JAMBOLANA.
      Flowers 1–3 at the end of the branchlets . . . . 7. E. BALFOURII.
    Leaves sessile . . . . 8. E. RAMPANS.
  Flowers middle-sized; developed stamens $\frac{3}{8}$–$\frac{1}{2}$ inch long.
    Leaves subcoriaceous, their veinlets not raised . . . 9. E. CYMOSA.
    Leaves coriaceous, their veinlets raised.
      Leaves cuneate at both ends . . . . 10. E. SECHELLARUM.
      Leaves rounded at base, cuspidate at point . . . . 11. E. WRIGHTII.
Leaves obovate or round, obtuse. Flowers in all small.
    Stamens $\frac{1}{12}$–$\frac{1}{8}$ in. long.
  Leaves small (1–1$\frac{1}{2}$ in. long.) . . . . 12. E. GLOMERATA.
  Leaves middle-sized (1$\frac{1}{2}$–3 in. long)
    Leaves as long as broad.
      Leaves nearly sessile . . . . 13. E. NUMMULARIA.
      Leaves distinctly petioled . . . . 14. E. POPULIFOLIA.
    Leaves half as long again as broad . . . . 15. E. SCANDENS.
  Leaves large (4–9 inches long) . . . . 16. E. OBOVATA.

* *E. uniflora*, Linn. Sp. Plant, 673, (E. Michelii, *Lam.; DC. Prod.* iii. 263; Plinia pedunculata, *Linn. fil. Suppl.* 253, *Bot. Mag. t.* 473; P. rubra, *Linn. Mant.* 243; Myrtus brasiliana, *Linn. Sp. Plant.* 674), a native of Tropical America, now widely spread in the Old World, is naturalised in Mauritius, Rodriguez and Seychelles. It is an erect glabrous shrub or small tree, with slender terete branchlets, short-petioled distant thin flexible ovate acute leaves 1$\frac{1}{3}$–2 in. long, flowers up to 6–8 in sessile axillary umbels on very slender pedicels $\frac{1}{2}$–1 inch long, very small campanulate calyx-tube, reflexed oblong calyx-teeth $\frac{1}{8}$ in. long, obovate petals exceeding the sepals and equalling the expanded stamens, and a bright red subacid aromatic fruit the size of a cherry. *Roussailler. Brazil Cherry.*

1. **E. mespiloides,** *Lam. Ency.* iii. 205. A bush or small tree, with stout sulcate branchlets clothed with ferruginous pubescence. Leaves not close, very thick and rigid, shining above, opaque, and more or less clothed with fine brown tomentum below, only the erecto-patent main ribs conspicuous, ovate, subobtuse or acute, broadly rounded at the base, 3–4 in. long, 1$\frac{1}{2}$–2 in. broad; petioles $\frac{1}{2}$–$\frac{3}{4}$ in. long. Pedicels solitary, from the axils of the leaves, 1–2 in. long, densely puberulent, simple or forked. Calyx $\frac{3}{8}$ in. long, turbinate, tomentose, with a pair of persistent deltoid bracteoles at the base, the lobes broader than deep.

Expanded flower above an inch broad, the developed stamens shorter than the petals. Fruit as large as a crab, crowned with the persistent accrescent calyx-lobes. E. tinifolia, *Lam. Encyc.* iii. 204. Jossinia mespiloides and tinifolia, *DC. Prod.* iii. 238. J. revoluta and ferruginea, *Bojer, Hort. Maur.* 140–1.

MAURITIUS, frequent in the mountain woods. *J. revoluta,* Bojer, is a mountain form with obtuse very rigid lucid leaves, and *J. ferruginea,* Bojer, a form with both sides at first clothed with brown tomentum. Endemic. *Bois de Nèfle.*

2. **E. cotinifolia,** *Jacq. Obs.* 3, *t.* 53. A much-branched shrub, with moderately slender grey terete obscurely downy branchlets. Leaves rigidly coriaceous, obtuse, variable in size and shape, round, obovate or oblong, 1–3 in. long, green and shining above, pale and opaque beneath, with only the erecto-patent main veins visible, glabrous or slightly canescent; petioles very short. Pedicels one or several from the axils of the leaves, very short, canescent, Calyx turbinate, ¼ in. long, densely clothed with brown tomentum, the rounded lobes broader than deep. Expanded flowers ¾–1½ in. broad, the stamens rather shorter than the obovate white petals. Fruit globose, an inch thick, crowned with the persistent calyx-lobes.

MAURITIUS, spread throughout the island. RODRIGUEZ, not uncommon, *Dr. Balfour!* Also Bourbon and Ceylon. *Bois de Clous.* The following are the principal varieties.

1. *E. orbiculata,* Lam. Ency. iii. 204 (Jossinia, *DC.*). Leaves rigidly coriaceous, round-obovate, broadly cuneate or rounded at the base, 1½–2 in. long, glabrous below, only the main veins raised. Flowers up to 5–6 from a node, on very short pedicels.

2. *J. cordifolia,* Bojer, Hort. Maur. 141. Leaves round, 2–3 in. long and broad, broadly rounded or even cordate at the base, thinner and more flexible than in the last, glabrous below, with the veinlets more visible. Flowers larger, an inch broad when expanded, mostly solitary.

3. *Gardneri,* Baker. Leaves obovate-cuneate, 1½–2 in. long, thinly clothed beneath with bright brown tomentum, only the main veins raised. Flowers mostly solitary.

4. *E. lucida,* Lam. Ency. iii. 205 (Jossinia, *DC.*). Leaves obovate-cuneate, 1½–2 in. long, glabrous below. Pedicels very short, mostly solitary.

5. *E. elliptica,* Lam. Ency. iii. 206 (Jossinia elliptica, *DC.;* J. lanceolata, *Bojer, Hort. Maur.* 141). A mountain form with shining elliptical leaves 1–1½ in. long, glabrous beneath, cuneate at the base. Flowers smaller, sessile or short-pedicelled, often several from a node.

3. **E. buxifolia,** *Lam. Encyc.* iii. 204. A much-branched erect shrub 10–12 feet high, with slender terete glabrous pale brown branchlets. Leaves oblong, short-petioled, very thick and rigid, shining above, quite glabrous with raised veinlets beneath, 1–1½ in. long, obtuse, slightly rounded at the base. Pedicels solitary or geminate, glabrous, rigid, erecto-patent, ½–¾ in. long. Calyx ¼ in. long; tube campanulate, canescent; teeth as deep as broad and as long as the tube. Petals round, ¼ in. long. Developed stamens not exceeding the petals. Jos-

sinia buxifolia, *DC. Prod.* iii. 237. Myrtus borbonica, *Spreng. Syst.* ii. 481.

MAURITIUS, on the mountains. *Jossinia terminalis*, Bojer, Hort. Maur. 141, which grows in the damp woods of Trois Ilots, is a variety with lanceolate leaves, ¼–⅜ in. broad, and rather longer pedicels. Endemic.

* *E. Jambosa*, Linn. Sp. 672; Bot. Mag. t. 1696, (Jambosa vulgaris, *DC. Prod.* iii. 286), common in Tropical Asia, is established in Mauritius, Rodriguez and the Seychelles. It is a tree 20–30 feet high, with terete virgate branches, short-petioled firm shining prominently-veined lanceolate acuminate leaves 6–9 in. long, large flowers 3–4 together in lateral or terminal cymes, broadly turbinate short calyx-tube, rounded sepals twice as broad as deep, round white petals ¾ inch broad, very numerous stamens an inch long, pear-shaped rose-coloured fruit as large as a crab with 1-3 seeds, not so palatable as that of *E. malaccensis. Jam-rosa.*

4. **E. Bojeri,** *Baker.* A creeping shrub with ultimate branchlets like ash twigs, angular, ¼ in. thick, with wrinkled drab bark. Leaves short-petioled, oblong, 1–1½ foot long, 4–5 in. broad at the middle, acute, cuneate or rounded at the base, coriaceous, with copious raised erecto-patent venules meeting in a prominent intramarginal vein. Cymes few-flowered, sessile, lateral, sometimes copiously branched, and bearing only rudimentary flowers; pedicels with a pair of bracteoles near the top. Calyx middle-sized, the turbinate tube pilose, the lobes as deep as broad. Petals ⅛ inch deep, quite free, shorter than the stamens. Berry purple, size of a small pear. Jambosa macrophylla, *Bojer, Hort. Maur.* 143, *non DC.*

MAURITIUS, in dense woods at Grandport and in the centre of the island.

**E. malaccensis*, Linn. Sp. 672; Sm. Exot. Bot. t. 61, (E. macrophylla, *Lam. Ency.* iii. 196; Jambosa malaccensis, macrophylla, purpurea and domestica, *DC.*), common in Tropical Asia, is often planted, and sometimes naturalised in Mauritius and the Seychelles. It is a low tree, with slender terete branchlets, oblong nearly sessile moderately firm acute leaves 6–9 in. long rounded at the base, middle-sized flowers 6-15 together in lateral or terminal cymes, with divaricate branches, broadly turbinate calyx-tube ⅜ in. thick narrowed at the base, imbricated rounded sepals twice as broad as deep, round white or pink petals ½ inch broad, stamens ½ inch long, rose-scented, and turbinate red or white fleshy fruit 1½ inch thick. *Jamalac.*

5. **E. venosa,** *Lam. Ency.* iii. 200. A low tree, with slender terete branchlets. Leaves spaced, oblong, sessile, cordate at the base, acute or subacute, 3–4 in. long, rigidly coriaceous, with divaricating raised venules. Flowers 3–6, middle sized, in short-peduncled terminal and

lateral cymes with erecto-patent branches. Calyx-tube ¼ in. broad, narrowed at the base, the teeth very shallow. Petals round, caducous. Stamens ⅓ in. long. Fruit globose, fleshy, nearly an inch thick, crowned with a rim formed by the produced calyx-tube. Jambosa venosa, *DC. Prod.* iii. 286.

MAURITIUS, in shaded woods of Grandport, Savanne, and Mahé. Also Madagascar.

6. **E. Dupontii,** *Baker.* A bush, with very thick angular straight branches and crowded leaves. Leaves obovate or obovate-oblong, 4–6 in. long, 3 in. broad above the middle, obtuse, broadly rounded at the base, very thick, rigid and shining, with the veinlets conspicuous. Flowers in terminal cymes ½ ft. broad with thick erecto-patent branches; pedicels very short. Calyx glabrous, turbinate, ½ in. long; lobes twice as broad as deep. Petals round, ⅜ in. broad. Stamens very numerous, ½–¾ in. long.

MAURITIUS, in the woods of the Rivière de la Cascade. *Dupont! Bouton!*

* *E. Jambolana,* Lam. Ency. iii. 198; Wt. Ic. t. 535 and 624, (Syzygium Jambolanum, *DC. Prod.* iii. 259), common in tropical Asia, is established in Mauritius on the Pouce and elsewhere, and in Rodrigues in Oyster Bay. It is a tall tree, with flexuose branchlets, distinctly petioled oblong acute rigidly coriaceous leaves 4–6 in. long, small flowers in copious deltoid lateral panicles 3–6 in. long with spreading branches, sessile flowers 4–10 together at the end of the branchlets, turbinate glabrous calyx ⅛ in. long with very obscure teeth, corolla $\frac{1}{12}$ in. long soon falling, stamens ⅛ in. long, and a subglobose one-seeded drupe as large as a grape. *Jamlongue.*

7. **E. Balfourii,** *Baker.* A much branched shrub, with glabrous terete branchlets. Leaves oblong, acute, 2½–3 in. long, cuneate at the base, rigidly subcoriaceous, with close fine ribs. Flowers in copious peduncled lateral panicles as long as the leaves, 1½–2 in. broad, only 2 or 3 at the end of the branchlets, which spread from the rachis at a right angle, sessile or the end one obscurely pedicelled. Calyx ¼ in. long; teeth obscure, deltoid. Stamens ¼ in. long.

RODRIGUEZ, *Balfour!* Near *E. Jambolana,* from which it differs by its smaller leaves, with much closer veining and fewer larger flowers. Endemic.

8. **E. rampans,** *Baker.* A creeping shrub, with stems 20–25 ft. long and square branchlets. Leaves not close, sessile or subsessile, cordate-oblong, acute or cuspidate, 2–3 in. long, 1–1½ in. broad, rigidly coriaceous, with the veinlets in relief. Panicles lateral and terminal, peduncled, sometimes forming an end panicle 6–8 in. long and broad, the main branches spreading, acutely 4-angled. Calyx hemispherical, ⅛ in. broad, short-pedicelled, nearly truncate. Corolla

so short that the unexpanded flower is broader than deep. Expanded stamens $\frac{1}{12}$–$\frac{1}{8}$ in. long.

MAURITIUS, near Colville Bridge and Grand Bassin, *Newman! Bojer!* Endemic.

9. **E. cymosa,** *Lam. Ency.* iii. 199. An erect tree, with straight terete brown branchlets. Leaves distinctly petioled, oblong, acute, rounded at the base, 2–4 in. long, 1–2 in. broad, not so rigid and thick in texture as in its allies and the veinlets immersed. Flowers in crowded small trichotomous short-peduncled or sessile cymes 1–2 in. broad, which are usually lateral from old branches; pedicel above the joint often as long as the calyx, which is $\frac{1}{8}$ in. broad and deep, with teeth twice as broad as deep. Rounded cap formed by the united petals broader than deep. Developed stamens $\frac{1}{2}$ in. long. Fruit globose, an inch thick, the tube not produced above it, crowned by the accrescent persistent calyx-teeth. Syzygium cymosum, *DC. Prod.* iii. 259.

MAURITIUS, frequent on the Pouce and in other hill-woods. *E. paniculata,* Lam. Ency. iii. 199, (Syzygium paniculatum, *DC. Prod. loc. cit.*) seems to be only a variety of the same species with terminal cymes. Endemic. *Bois à écorce blanche.*

10. **E. sechellarum,** *Baker.* Branches terete, moderately slender. Leaves distant, distinctly petioled, oblong, acute, or acuminate, cuneate at the base, 4–5 in. long, 1$\frac{1}{2}$–2 in. broad, rigid, with the veinlets raised. Panicles short-peduncled, terminal or lateral, 3–4 in. broad, with the flowers sessile at the end of the branchlets and spreading main branches. Calyx $\frac{1}{2}$ in. long, turbinate, narrowed into a short pedicel above the joint, the lobes twice as broad as deep. Expanded stamens $\frac{1}{2}$–$\frac{3}{4}$ in. long.

SEYCHELLES. Described from a specimen in the Herbarium of Judge Blackburn, now in the Kew collection. Resembles *E. Jambolana* in general habit, but differs entirely in its flowers. Endemic.

11. **E. Wrightii,** *Baker.* A small tree with branches straight, grey, terete, moderately thick. Leaves distant, distinctly petioled, ovate or oblong, 4–6 in. long, 2$\frac{1}{2}$–3 in. broad, cuspidate, broadly rounded at the base, rigidly coriaceous, shining, with all veinlets conspicuous. Cymes copious, lax, peduncled, lateral and terminal, 4–6 in. broad, with ascending main branches; flowers pedicelled or sessile. Calyx $\frac{3}{8}$–$\frac{1}{2}$ in. long, narrowed into a false pedicel in the lower half above the joint; lobes twice as broad as deep; tube not produced beyond the ovary. Petals round, $\frac{1}{4}$ in. long. Stamens and style $\frac{1}{2}$ in. long. Fruit not seen.

SEYCHELLES, common in Mahé and Praslin, *Prof. Wright! Horne!* Endemic.

12. **E. glomerata,** *Lam. Ency.* iii. 199. A much-branched erect shrub, with grey branches and crowded leaves. Leaves obovate, short-petioled, 1–1$\frac{1}{2}$ in. long, obtuse, rarely cuspidate, rigidly coria-

ceous, glabrous, with immersed veinlets. Cymes small, crowded, usually terminal, short-peduncled, with main branches erecto-patent, rarely spreading; pedicels very short. Calyx glabrous, broadly turbinate, truncate, $\frac{1}{12}$ in. deep. Unexpanded flower globose. Stamens not longer than the calyx. Berry as large as a pea. Syzygium glomeratum, *DC. Prod.* iii. 209.

MAURITIUS, frequent in the mountain-woods. Also Madagascar. *Bois de Pomme.*

13. **E. nummularia,** *Baker.* An erect shrub, with straight terete moderately stout ashen-grey branches. Leaves quite or nearly sessile, not close, round, 2–3 in. long and broad, truncate or emarginate at the apex, rigidly coriaceous, the veinlets raised. Panicles small, crowded, lateral and terminal, short-peduncled, the branches quadrangular, all erecto-patent. Calyx not more than $\frac{1}{12}$ in. long, sessile or short-pedicelled, the teeth minute, deltoid. Unexpanded corolla hemispherical. Expanded stamens not more than $\frac{1}{12}$ in. long.

MAURITIUS, in the forests at Moka and Savanne, *Bouton! Dupont!* Endemic.

14. **E. populifolia,** *Baker.* An erect tree; branches straight, terete, moderately stout, ashen-grey. Leaves nearly round, obtuse or obscurely cuspidate, 3–4 in. long, 3 in. broad, broadly rounded at the base, rigidly coriaceous, not so thick as in *E. nummularia* and *obovata*, the veinlets fine and scarcely raised; petiole $\frac{1}{4}$–$\frac{1}{3}$ in. long. Panicles crowded, short-peduncled, terminal, all the branches erecto-patent. Calyx-tube $\frac{1}{8}$ in. long, with a short pedicel above the joint, the rounded lobes twice as broad as long. Unexpanded corolla hemispherical. Expanded stamens $\frac{1}{6}$ in. long.

MAURITIUS, in the forests of Mahé and Savanne, *Bouton!* Endemic.

15. **E. scandens,** *Baker.* A woody climber, with trailing moderately stout terete grey branches. Leaves not crowded, short-petioled, obovate-oblong or oblong, obtuse or cuspidate, broadly cuneate at the base, 3–4 in long, 2 in. broad, very thick and rigid, with raised venules. Flowers in copious peduncled lateral and terminal panicles 1–2 in. broad, with cymes crowded at the end of the branchlets, as in *E. Jambolana.* Calyx broadly turbinate, subsessile, $\frac{1}{12}$ in. long, the teeth minute, deltoid. Stamens not longer than the calyx. Petals very small. Berry depresso-globose, purple, $\frac{1}{3}$ in. thick. Syzygium scandens, *Bojer, Hort. Maur.* 143 (name only).

MAURITIUS, in woods of Grand Bassin and Bassin blanc. Endemic.

16. **E. obovata,** *Poir. Ency. Suppl.* iii. 124. An erect bush, with thick straight branchlets. Leaves close, subsessile, obovate, obtuse, 6–9 in. long, 3–4 in. broad, rounded at base, very thick and rigid, opaque, the veinlets distinct. Flowers in crowded cymose terminal panicles with erecto-patent main branches, subtended by reduced leaves. Calyx sessile, turbinate, glabrous, $\frac{1}{6}$ in. long; lobes very short.

Petals $\frac{1}{12}$ in. long. Expanded stamens not longer than the calyx. Berry globose, purple, an inch thick. Syzygium obovatum, *DC. Prod.* iii. 259. Calyptranthes pollicina, *Willem.*

MAURITIUS, in the hill-woods of the Pouce and other ranges. Endemic. *S. latifolium*, DC. loc. cit., is founded on leaves of this, mixed with flowers of *E. cymosa. Bois Bœuf.*

2. BARRINGTONIA, Forst.

Flowers regular, hermaphrodite. Calyx-tube obconical; lobes of limb 2–4, either free from the first or united in bud and splitting free as the flower expands. Petals 4–5, adnate to the base of the united stamens. Stamens epigynous, very numerous, multiserial; filaments long, filiform, joined at the very base; anthers minute. Ovary inferior, 2–4-celled; ovules 2 or few in a cell; style long filiform; stigma capitate. Fruit large, sublignose, oblong, terete or angled, sometimes by abortion 1-celled and 1-seeded; embryo thick, fleshy, undivided.—Tall trees, with large alternate undotted leaves, the flowers mostly in pendulous long racemes or spikes. DISTRIB. Tropics of Old World. Species 20.

Subgenus BUTONICA, *Juss.* Calyx-limb entire in bud, splitting as the flower expands into 2–3 valvate lobes.
The only species . . . . 1. B. SPECIOSA.
Subgenus STRAVADIUM, *Juss.* Calyx-limb from the first divided into imbricated lobes.
Expanded flower 2–2½ in. broad . . . . 2. B. RACEMOSA.
Expanded flower ½ in. broad . . . . 3. B. ACUTANGULA.

1. **B. speciosa,** *L. fil.; DC. Prod.* iii. 288. A tall tree, glabrous in all its parts, with thick branches marked by the large round scars of the fallen leaves. Leaves sessile, subcoriaceous, shining, entire, obovate-oblong, a foot or more long. Flowers few, in terminal cymes on pedicels above an inch long. Calyx-limb 2 in. long, entire in bud, splitting to the base into 2 or 3 valvate coriaceous lobes. Petals broad, obtuse, exceeding the stamens. Stamens very numerous, 3–4 in. long. Fruit tetragono-pyramidal, with a distinct separable epicarp and endocarp. Butonica speciosa, *Lam. Ill. t.* 590 and 591, fig. 1. Mammea asiatica, *Linn.* Agasta asiatica, *Miers in Trans. Linn. Soc. ser.* 2, *vol.* i, *part* 261.

SEYCHELLES, on the seashore, *Bojer, Horne!* Common on the Mahé side of Praslin, *Dr. Wright.* Polynesia to Comoro isles; not continental Africa.

2. **B. racemosa,** *Roxb.; DC. Prod.* iii. 288. A tall tree, glabrous in all its parts. Leaves crowded at the end of the branches, oblanceolate-oblong, thin, subcoriaceous, penninerved, obscurely dentate, subobtuse or subacute, narrowed through the lower half, reaching a foot or more long. Flowers in lax pendulous peduncled racemes reaching 2 feet in length; pedicels very short. Sepals 3–4, finally ½ in. long. Expanded flower 2–2½ in. broad, the stamens rather exceeding the petals. Fruit ovoid, obsoletely quadrangular. *Gaud. in Frey. Voy.* 483, *t.* 107.

SEYCHELLES, on the sea-shore, common, *Horne!* Tropical Asia and Africa.

3. **B. acutangula,** *Gærtn. Fruct.* ii. 97, *t.* 101. A tall tree, glabrous in all its parts. Leaves crowded towards the end of the branches, oblanceolate-oblong, thin, subcoriaceous, penninerved, distinctly toothed, 4–8 in. long, sessile, narrowed through the lower half. Flowers in lax pendulous peduncled racemes reaching a foot long; pedicels sometimes exceeding the calyx, which is $\frac{1}{8}$ in. long, with 4 obtuse teeth exceeding the ribbed obconic tube. Expanded flower $\frac{1}{2}$ in. broad, the stamens not longer than the sepals. Fruit oblong, $1\frac{1}{2}$ in. long, acutely quadrangular. Stravadium album, rubrum, and coccineum, *DC.*

SEYCHELLES, *Bojer.* Not seen by Mr. Horne. Australia and Tropical Asia.

8. FŒTIDIA, Comm.

Flowers hermaphrodite, regular. Calyx-tube obconic, 4-angled; limb large, slit to the base into four valvate acute coriaceous persistent lobes. Petals none. Stamens very numerous, epigynous; filaments filiform; anthers oblong. Ovary inferior, 4-celled, with 2 ovules in a cell; style filiform; stigma 4-cleft. Fruit obconic, woody, with a large square flat disk at the top, crowned by the accrescent spreading calyx teeth. Seeds subglobose, 1–2 in a cell.—Trees with alternate undotted coriaceous leaves and solitary flowers in the axils of the leaves. DISTRIB. Endemic in the Mascaren isles. Species 3.

1. **F. mauritiana,** *Lam. Ill. t.* 419. A tree 20–40 feet high, glabrous in all its parts, with stout terete branches marked with the scars of fallen leaves. Leaves crowded, sessile, obovate or oblanceolate-oblong, 4–6 in. long, obtuse or cuspidate, coriaceous, with immersed veins and a broad flat midrib. Flowers solitary, on short pedicels in the axils of the leaves. Square flat disk of the top of the fruit $\frac{1}{2}$–$\frac{3}{4}$ in. broad; spreading coriaceous lanceolate-deltoid acute calyx teeth $\frac{3}{4}$–1 in. long. Stamens shorter than the calyx-teeth. *DC. Prod.* iii. 295.

MAURITIUS, once frequent in the woods, now becoming rare. RODRIGUEZ, common. *Bouton! Balfour! Bois puant.*

ORDER XLVI. MELASTOMACEÆ.

Flowers regular, hermaphrodite. Calyx wholly or partially adnate to the ovary; limb entire or 4–5-lobed. Petals 4–5. Stamens twice as many as the petals; anthers often dissimilar, with the connective variously produced and spurred, 2-celled, basifixed, opening by 1 or 2 pores at the tip. Ovary usually 5-celled, with axile placentation and indefinite ovules, in *Memecylon* 1-celled, with free central placentation and few ovules; style filiform; stigma simple. Fruit baccate or capsular, splitting irregularly or loculicidally. Seeds exalbuminous.—Herbs or shrubs, with opposite exstipulate entire leaves, usually distinctly nerved from tip to base; inflorescence various; flowers often showy, purple. DISTRIB. Round the world in the tropics, especially in America. Species 1800.

Leaves and calyx bristly. Fruit 5-celled, with indefinite minute seeds.
  Stamens of two kinds, in one of which the connective is much produced below the anther cells . . . . 1. MELASTOMA.
  Stamens all alike . . . . 2. TRISTEMMA.
Leaves and calyx naked. Fruit with a single large seed.
  The only genus . . . . 3. MEMECYLON.

1. MELASTOMA, Linn.

Calyx densely scaly, adnate to the lower part of the ovary; tube globose; teeth 5, lanceolate. Petals 5, rather unequal, round-unguiculate, springing from high up in the calyx-tube. Stamens 10, very unequal, the smaller erect with cells as long as the connective, the larger curved, with the cells confined to the upper half of the connective, which has two spurs in front at the bottom. Ovary half-inferior, 5-celled; ovules very numerous; style filiform; stigma simple. Fruit subbaccate, bursting irregularly.—Shrubs with opposite entire bristly 3-5-nerved leaves, and large showy flowers in terminal corymbs. DISTRIB. Polynesia and Tropical Asia, not Africa. Species 40.

1. **M. malabathricum,** *Linn.; DC. Prod.* iii. 145. A shrub, 6–8 feet high, with slender quadrangular scabrous branchlets. Leaves distinctly petioled, oblong, acute, 3–4 in. long, with 5 distinct ribs from top to bottom, densely clothed on both sides with firm short bristles. Flowers 3–6, in sessile corymbs at the end of the branchlets, with short pedicels and deciduous rather large lanceolate bracts. Calyx-tube globose, ⅜ in. thick; teeth lanceolate, deciduous. Petals purple or nearly white, an inch long, rather exceeding the stamens. Anthers usually 5 of each kind. M. sechellarum, *Naudin*.

SEYCHELLES, common by streamsides at all levels. Tropical Asia, and Polynesia; not Continental Africa.

2. TRISTEMMA, Comm.

Calyx tube tubuloso-campanulate, angular, girt with three rings of bristles; teeth 5, erect, lanceolate. Petals 5, round-unguiculate. Stamens 10, subequal; connective not produced at the base below the cells, spurred in front with two tubercles. Ovary half-inferior, 5-celled; ovules numerous; style filiform; stigma capitate. Fruit capsular, bursting irregularly; seeds numerous, minute.—Shrubs, with opposite entire bristly 5–7 nerved leaves, the flowers solitary or in clusters from the end of the branchlets. DISTRIB. All the rest Continental African. Species 12.

1. **T. virusanum,** *Comm.; DC. Prod.* iii. 144. A shrub, 2–3 feet high, with quadrangular bristly branchlets. Leaves opposite, distinctly petioled, ovate-oblong, acute, membranous, thinly bristly on both sides, 4–6 in. long, with 5–7 distinct ribs from tip to base. Flowers 4–8, in dense sessile or nearly sessile heads from the end of the branchlets, hidden by reduced leaves and persistent coriaceous round-

cuspidate bracts. Calyx sessile, $\frac{3}{8}$ in. deep, the erect teeth shorter than the tube. Petals $\frac{1}{4}$ in. deep, whitish or purple. Stamens shorter than the petals. *Vent. Choix. t.* 35. T. mauritianum, *Pers.*

MAURITIUS, in shaded woods of the centre of the island. Also Madagascar and Comoros.

3. MEMECYLON, Linn.

Calyx naked, with a small obconic adnate tube and an entire or obscurely 4-toothed collar-like limb. Petals 4, deltoid. Stamens 8, equal, included or exserted; filaments filiform; anthers small, oblong, the connective dilated on the back, spurred minutely at the base behind. Ovary 1-celled; ovules few, whorled round a central placenta; style filiform; stigma entire. Fruit a globose berry with one large seed.—Shrubs with opposite entire leaves, entirely destitute of bristles or hairs, the copious minute bluish or white flowers in axillary cymes. DISTRIB. Tropics of the Old World. Species 100.

- Leaves triplinerved . . . . 1. M. TRINERVE.
- Leaves penninerved.
  - Branchlets quadrangular.
    - Leaves 1½–2 as long as broad. Flowers copiously cymose . . . . 2. M. ANGULATUM.
    - Leaves 3 times as long as broad. Pedicels solitary or forked . . . . 3. M. ELÆAGNI.
  - Branchlets terete.
    - Leaves sessile, cordate . . . . 4. M. CORDATUM.
    - Leaves petioled, cuneate at the base . . . . . 5. M. SPHÆROCARPUM.

1. **M. trinerve,** *DC. Prod.* iii. 5. A shrub, 10–15 feet high with quadrangular branchlets. Leaves short-petioled, oblong, usually 2–3 in. long, obtuse or subacute, in one specimen acuminate, 4–5 in. long, subcoriaceous, with 3 distinct ribs from tip to base, cuneate or rather rounded at the base; transverse venules obvious. Flowers in dense sessile cymes in the axils of the leaves; pedicels equalling or exceeding the calyx, which is under $\frac{1}{12}$ in. long, with a faintly toothed spreading limb longer than the tube. Petals as long as the calyx. Stamens and style much exserted. Berry the size of a small pea.

MAURITIUS, frequent in the hill-woods. Endemic.

2. **M. angulatum,** *Reich.; DC. Prod.* iii. 5. A shrub, 10–12 feet high, with slender quadrangular branchlets. Leaves short-petioled, oblong, obtuse, rigidly subcoriaceous, 2–4 in. long, cuneate at the base, with only the midrib visible. Flowers in sessile or short-peduncled solitary or fascicled many-flowered cymes from the swollen nodes; pedicels equalling or exceeding the calyx. Calyx truncate, campanulate, $\frac{1}{12}$ in. broad and deep. Petals white, deltoid, as long as the calyx. Stamens not exserted. Berry $\frac{1}{2}$ in. long.

MAURITIUS, frequent in woods. Endemic. *M. sparsifolium*, Bojer, Hort. Maur. 132, is known to me by name only.

3. **M. Elæagni,** *Blume, Mus. Bot.* i. 356. A small tree or large

shrub, with slender tetragonal branchlets, the hard wood used to make pestles for the mills of cocoa-nut-oil. Leaves short-petioled, oblong, obtuse, rigidly coriaceous, cuneate at the base, 2–3 in. long, with only the midrib visible. Flowers solitary or two from a short peduncle in the axils of the leaves; pedicels straight, $\frac{1}{4}$–$\frac{1}{3}$ in. long. Calyx-tube with a short spreading obscurely toothed limb. Mature berry globose, black, the size of a pea. M. Pervilleanum, *Naudin.*

SEYCHELLES, in woods of Mahé and Praslin and the other islands at an elevation of 400 to 800 feet above the sea. *Pervillé! Horne! Bois Caleau* or *Bois Caloo.*

4. **M. cordatum,** *Desv.; DC. Prod.* iii. 6. A much-branched shrub, with slender terete branchlets. Leaves sessile, rigidly coriaceous, shining, penninerved, 3–6 in. long, acute or subobtuse, cordate at the base, the basal lobes sometimes imbricating. Flowers in distinctly peduncled cymes from the swollen nodes; pedicels exceeding the calyx. Calyx $\frac{1}{8}$–$\frac{1}{10}$ in. long and broad, obconic, narrowed at the base, truncate. Petals deltoid, as long as the calyx. Stamens and style included. M. latifolium, *Bojer, Hort. Maur.* 133.

MAURITIUS, frequent in woods. Also Bourbon. *M. latifolium*, Bojer, is a shade form, with large leaves scarcely cordate at the base.

5. **M. sphærocarpum,** *DC. Prod.* iii. 6. A much-branched shrub, with slender terete branchlets. Leaves short-petioled, oblong, obtuse, often emarginate at the point, cuneate at the base, 1–3 in. long, rigidly coriaceous, with only the midrib visible. Flowers in sparse sessile or short peduncled fascicled cymes from the swollen nodes; pedicels as long as the calyx. Calyx obconic, $\frac{1}{12}$ in. long, distinctly 4-toothed. Petals deltoid, as long as the calyx. Stamens and style not exserted. Unripe berries green, globose, the size of a pea. M. ramiflorum, *Bojer, Hort. Maur.* 132, *non Lam.* M. tinctorium, *Sieber.* M. ligustrinum and rhamnoideum, *Naud.*

MAURITIUS, frequent in the forests. Also Bourbon.

ORDER XLVII. ONAGRACEÆ.

Flowers regular, hermaphrodite Calyx-tube adnate to the ovary, long and slender; teeth 4–5, persistent. Petals 4–5, obovate, epigynous. Stamens inserted with the petals, definite; filaments filiform; anthers oblong, didymous, slit down the side. Ovary inferior, 4–5-celled; ovules many; placentation axile; style filiform; stigma capitate. Fruit capsular. Seeds numerous, minute, exalbuminous.—Herbs, with alternate entire exstipulate leaves and solitary flowers in the axils of the leaves. DISTRIB. Cosmopolitan. Species 300.

Stamens twice as many as the sepals . . . . 1. JUSSIÆA.
Stamens as many as the sepals . . . . 2. LUDWIGIA.

1. JUSSIÆA, Linn.

Calyx-tube adnate, cylindrical, 8–10-ribbed; teeth 4–5, persistent.

Petals 4–5, obovate-unguiculate, perigynous. Stamens twice as many as the petals, included; filaments filiform: anthers oblong. Ovary inferior, 4–5-celled; placentation axile; ovules many; style short, filiform; stigma capitate, 4–5-lobed. Capsule cylindrical, at last splitting between the ribs. Seeds many, minute.—Herbs, with alternate entire leaves and solitary yellow flowers in the axils of the leaves. DISTRIB. Everywhere in the tropics. Species 30.

Stems trailing naked; flowers pentamerous . . . . . . 1. J. REPENS.
Stems erect pilose; flowers mostly tetramerous . . . . 2. J. SUFFRUTICOSA.

1. **J. repens,** *Linn.; DC. Prod.* iii. 58. A perennial, with trailing glabrous stems, rooting copiously from the lower nodes. Leaves petioled, obovate-oblong, obtuse, cuneate at base, 1–2 in. long, membranous, glabrous. Pedicels 1–2 in. long, with a pair of minute bracteoles at tip. Sepals 5, linear, ¼ in. long. Petals bright yellow, twice as long as the sepals. Fruit cylindrical, 10-ribbed, 1–1½ in. long, mostly glabrous. J. stolonifera, *G. and P.* J. Swartziana, *DC.*

MAURITIUS, in brooks near Port Louis, etc. *J. diffusa*, Forsk., is a form with oblanceolate acute leaves. Round the world in tropical and subtropical regions.

2. **J. suffruticosa,** *Linn.; DC. Prod.* iii. 58. An almost shrubby perennial, with pilose stems, 2–4 feet high, tetragonal upwards. Leaves subsessile, oblanceolate-oblong, acute, membranous, pilose, distinctly penninerved, 2–4 in. long. Flowers sessile or subsessile. Calyx-lobes 4, ovate-lanceolate, ⅓ in. long, rather shorter than the petals. Capsule cylindrical, 1½–2 in. long, 8-ribbed. J. villosa, *Lam.* J. scabra, *Willd.* J. fruticosa, *DC.*

MAURITIUS and SEYCHELLES, common in swamps. Round the world in the tropics.

2. LUDWIGIA, Linn.

Calyx-tube adnate, prismatico-cylindrical; teeth 4, lanceolate, persistent. Petals 4, roundish, epigynous. Stamens 4; filaments short, filiform; anthers oblong. Ovary inferior, 4-celled; placentation axile; ovules many; style short, simple; stigma capitate. Fruit a long membranous capsule splitting between the ribs; seeds very many, minute.—Herbs with the habit of *Jussiæa*. DISTRIB. Wide-spread, mostly North American. Species 20.

1. **L. jussiæoides,** *Linn.; DC. Prod.* iii. 58. An erect much-branched half-shrubby perennial, 3–4 feet high, glabrous throughout. Leaves short-petioled, alternate, lanceolate, membranous, 2–3 in. long, narrowed to both ends. Flowers copious, short-petioled, solitary. Sepals lanceolate, erect, ¼–⅓ in. long, rather shorter than the fugacious yellow petals. Capsule membranous, naked, cylindrical, 1–1¼ in. long *DC. Mem. Onagr. t.* 3.

SEYCHELLES and MAURITIUS, frequent in damp places. Also Natal and Zanzibar.

ORDER XLVIII. PORTULACEÆ.

Sepals always only two, in our plants adnate at the base to the ovary. Petals 4–5, entire. Stamens perigynous, definite or indefinite; anthers bilocular, dehiscing longitudinally. Ovary free or half-inferior, 1-celled; ovules many; placentation free-central; styles joined at the base, free above; stigmas decurrent. Capsule membranous, splitting round the middle or into valves at the top. Seeds like these of *Caryophyllaceæ.*—Herbs with fleshy entire alternate or opposite leaves, varied inflorescence and fugacious petals. DISTRIB. Species 125, mostly American.

1. PORTULACA, Linn.

Sepals 2, adnate to the ovary at the base. Petals 4–5, free, inserted where the calyx leaves the ovary. Stamens 8–20, inserted with the petals. Ovary adnate to the calyx at the base, 1-celled, many-ovuled; styles 3–8. Capsule membranous, dehiscing round by a horizontal line where it is free from the calyx. Seeds reniform; embryo peripheric. —Annuals, with fleshy leaves and stems and small flowers in terminal clusters, surrounded by a whorl of ordinary leaves mixed with scariose bracts. DISTRIB. Cosmopolitan in the tropics; much cultivated. Species 16.

Robust, with broad obtuse exstipulate leaves . . . . . 1. P. OLERACEA.
Small, with narrow acute leaves and stipules cut to the base into bristles.
Flowers tetramerous, yellow . . . . 2. P. QUADRIFIDA.
Flowers pentamerous, purple. . . . . 3. P. PILOSA.

1. **P. oleracea,** *Linn.; DC. Prod.* iii. 353. A much-branched fleshy glabrous annual. Internodes long. Leaves exstipulate, alternate, or subopposite, sessile, obovate, obtuse, $\frac{1}{2}$–1 in. long, cuneate at the base. Flower-clusters at the end, and sessile in the forks of the branches, surrounded by 2–5 ordinary leaves, and a few minute entire bracts. Petals 5, yellow, as long as the sepals. Stamens 8–12.

MAURITIUS and RODRIGUEZ, common in waste ground. Cosmopolitan in the tropics. The common cultivated Purslane. *Pourpier.*

2. **P. quadrifida,** *Linn.; DC. Prod.* iii. 354. Much less robust than *P. oleracea,* with trailing stems and shorter internodes. Leaves linear or lanceolate, acute, $\frac{1}{4}$–$\frac{1}{2}$ in. long; persistent stipules cut down to the base into many slender bristly hairs. Heads of flowers involucred by several ordinary leaves, mixed with minute bracts just like the stipules. Petals 4, yellow. Stamens usually 8. P. meridiana, *Linn.*

MAURITIUS, frequent in cultivated ground. Cosmopolitan in the tropics. *Pourpier marron.*

3. **P. pilosa,** *Linn. DC. Prod.* iii. 334. An annual, with many spreading fleshy branches with close nodes. Leaves minute, linear, acute; persistent stipules cut down to the base into very slender hairs. Heads

of flowers terminal on the branches, involucred by several ordinary leaves and minute densely pilose bracts. Petals 5, purple. Stamens about 20. *Bot. Reg. t.* 792.

MAURITIUS, in cultivated ground; now spread in the tropics of the Old World, but probably native only in America. *Petit Pourpier marron.*

ORDER XLIX. ARALIACEÆ.

Flowers regular, hermaphrodite or often polygamous in the Mauritian species. Calyx-tube adnate to the short ovary; limb narrow, cupular, persistent, subentire. Petals numerous, epigynous, valvate, cohering long in a hemispherical cap; filaments short, inflexed; anthers oblong, didymous, dorsifixed. Ovary many-celled; placentation axile; ovules solitary in each cell, pendulous; styles as many as the cells, free or connate at the base in a cone. Fruit baccate, with the bony endocarp investing the seeds; albumen copious, often ruminate.—Shrubs, with simple or pinnate or palmate shining coriaceous stipulate leaves, and small copious greenish often umbellate flowers. DISTRIB. Cosmopolitan. Species 350.

1. POLYSCIAS, Forst.

Flowers regular, hermaphrodite. Calyx-tube adnate to the ovary, campanulate; limb narrow, coriaceous, collar-like. Petals 6-16, cohering in a hemispherical cap, finally spreading. Stamens as many as the petals, included. Ovary inferior, 6–12-celled; styles the same number, short, distinct, falcate. Fruit baccate, subglobose, with a triquetrous pyrene in each cell; albumen horny, not ruminate.—Erect glabrous shrubs, with shining coriaceous pinnate leaves and varied inflorescence. DISTRIB. Species about a dozen, the rest tropical Asian and Polynesian, none African.

Flowers in dense simple subspicate racemes . . . . 1. P. PANICULATA.
Flowers in panicles with spicate branches . . . . . 2. P. DICHROOSTACHYA.
Flowers in panicles with racemose branches, the end ones umbelled.
  Petals and stamens about 14 . . . . 3. P. CUPULARIS.
  Petals and stamens 6–8 . . . . 4. P. AYRESII.
Flowers in panicles with branches most or all umbelled.
  Styles and cells of ovary 10–12 . . . . 5. P. CUTISPONGIA.
  Styles and cells of ovary 6–8.
    Branches of panicle short, simple . . . . . . 6. P. REPANDA.
    Branches of panicle elongated, compound . . . 7. P. SECHELLARUM.

1. **P. paniculata**, *Baker*. An erect glabrous shrub, with stout terete branchlets. Leaves long-petioled; blade 6–9 in. long; leaflets usually 7, short-stalked, oblong, obtuse, shining, subcoriaceous, deltoid or rather rounded at base, 4–6 in. long. Flowers in dense subspicate peduncled racemes 2-4 in. long, with a rosette of lanceolate bracts at the base before expansion; pedicels very short and thick, not arti-

culated, with a distinct cupule clasping the calyx. Corolla hemispherical; petals and stamens about 16. Fruit hemispherical, with 6 falcate styles and 6 deep grooves. Gilibertia paniculata, *DC. Prod.* iv. 255. Grotefendia paniculata and cuneata, *Seem. Revis. Hed.* 13.

MAURITIUS, in shaded woods of the mountains. The specific name is misleading, as it is the only species of the seven that is *not* panicled. *G. cuneata*, Seem., seems to be a luxuriant form, with 11 leaflets and 10-merous ovary. Endemic.

2. **P. dichroostachya,** *Baker*. An erect glabrous shrub, with stout sulcate branches. Leaves above a foot long, petioled; leaflets 11, narrow, oblong, obtuse, subcoriaceous, 3–4 in. long, petioled, rounded or subdeltoid at the base. Panicles peduncled, as long as the leaves, with numerous small sessile flowers often in interrupted clusters on short spreading slender flexuose branches. Calyx-tube hemispherical, $\frac{1}{24}$–$\frac{1}{16}$ in. deep; limb very narrow, crispato-crenulate. Receptacle prominent. Styles and ovary-cells usually six. Petals and stamens not seen. Gilibertia dichroostachya, *Bojer, Hort. Maur.* 162, (name only).

MAURITIUS, in forests of Mahé and Savanne. Endemic.

3. **P. cupularis,** *Baker*. A glabrous shrub, with stout terete branches. Leaflets oblong, distinctly stalked, subcoriaceous, shining, obtuse, 3–5 in. long, deltoid or truncate at the base. Flowers in a peduncled panicle a foot long, with a stout angular multisulcate rachis, and many lax ascending racemose branches 2–4 in. long, with a large clasping persistent hemispherical scariose bract at the base; pedicels $\frac{1}{12}$–$\frac{1}{16}$ in. long, not articulated, with a large cupule clasping the base of the calyx. Calyx-limb $\frac{1}{24}$ in broad, crisped; tube obconic. Styles about 8. Corolla hemispherical when unexpanded; petals and stamens about 14.

MAURITIUS, described from a single specimen in Rottler's Herbarium, now at Kew. *Endemic.*

4. **P. Ayresii,** *Baker*. An erect glabrous shrub with terete branches. Leaves a foot long, petioled; leaflets many, oblong, coriaceous, shining, obtuse, ½ foot long, broadly rounded at the base, nearly sessile. Panicle above a foot long, with a stout sulcate rachis and many deflexed racemose branches 1–4 in. long, with the flowers copiously scattered down the sides and crowded into umbels at the end; pedicels $\frac{1}{12}$ in. long, articulated, obscurely cupulate at the tip. Calyx-tube hemispherical, $\frac{1}{8}$ in. long; limb very narrow, crenulate. Petals, stamens, ovary-cells and styles 6–8 each.

MAURITIUS, on the left of the Moka Road before coming to Bagatelle, from Port Louis. *Dr. Ayres.* Endemic.

5. **P. cutispongia,** *Baker*. An erect glabrous shrub, with terete branches. Leaves petioled, above a foot long; leaflets 3–4-jugate, sometimes 3–4-nate, oblong, shining, coriaceous, stalked, obtuse, 5–6 in. long, deltoid or rounded at the base. Panicles a foot long, with a very

stout angular multisculate rachis, the flowers in umbels at the end of the crowded erecto-patent branches; pedicels $\frac{1}{8}$–$\frac{3}{4}$ in. long, neither articulated nor cupulate at the tip. Calyx-tube oblong or hemispherical, $\frac{1}{8}$–$\frac{1}{4}$ in. long; limb $\frac{1}{12}$ in. broad, spreading, subentire. Petals, stamens, styles and cells of ovary each 10–12. Gastonia cutispongia, *Lam.; DC. Prod.* iv. 256; *Seem. Revis. Hed*, 12. G. spongiosa, *Pers.*

MAURITIUS and SEYCHELLES, in dense woods. Also Bourbon. *Bois d'éponge. Bois Papaye.*

6. **P. repanda**, *Baker.* An erect glabrous shrub, with terete branches. Leaves above a foot long, long-petioled; leaflets 5–9, oblong, obtuse, shining, coriaceous, distinctly petioled, 4–6 in. long, rounded or deltoid at the base. Inflorescence a peduncled panicle as long as the leaves, with most of the flowers in umbels at the end of short spreading slender branches, but some scattered or whorled below the ends; pedicels $\frac{1}{4}$–$\frac{1}{3}$ in. long, articulated, not cupulate at the tip. Calyx-tube obconic, $\frac{1}{12}$ in. long; limb very narrow. Styles and petals each 6–8. Fruit globose, under $\frac{1}{4}$ in. thick. Gilibertia repanda, *DC. Prod.* iv. 256. Grotefendia repanda, *Seem. Revis, Hed.* 14.

MAURITIUS and RODRIGUEZ, in dense woods. Also Bourbon. *Bois Papaye. Bois Blanc.*

7. **P. sechellarum**, *Baker.* An erect glabrous shrub 10–15 feet high. Leaves long-petioled, reaching $1\frac{1}{2}$ ft. long; leaflets 11–13, oblong, obtuse, subcoriaceous, 4–6 in. long, unequally rounded at base, short-stalked. Panicle 2 ft. long, with long flexuose ascending branches, with most of the flowers in umbels at the tip of short-spreading branchlets; pedicels $\frac{1}{4}$ in. long, neither articulated nor cupular at the tip. Calyx-tube oblong, $\frac{1}{8}$ in. long; limb very narrow. Styles and cells of ovary usually 6. Receptacle prominent. Flowers not seen.

SEYCHELLES, in Frigate Island, Praslin, Mahé and Curieuse, *Sir A. H. Gordon! Horne!* Endemic.

ORDER L. BEGONIACEÆ.

Flowers unisexual, monoicous or dioicous. Perianth-segments two or many, the two outer (sepals) firmer. Stamens indefinite; filaments short, free or joined; anthers basifixed, erect, slit introrsely down the side. Ovary inferior, 1–3 celled; ovules numerous; placentation mostly axile; styles 3, distinct, twisted, branched. Fruit usually a triquetrous capsule, with loculicidal dehiscence. Seeds minute, very numerous; albumen little or none.—Succulent caulescent or acaulescent herbs or undershrubs, with cymose flowers. DISTRIB. Tropical, mostly American. Species about 350.

1. BEGONIA, Linn.

Flowers unisexual. Perianth of two outer, and many inner petaloid segments, the latter sometimes absent. Stamens many, the filaments free or joined in a column; anthers ligulate, basifixed. Ovary inferior, 3-celled; placentas simple or forked, axile, rarely parietal; ovules numerous; styles three, forked or multifid, the branches often twisted. Fruit usually a triquetrous capsule, with unequal wings; but the wings in our plant quite absent.—Herbs or shrubs, with fleshy usually oblique leaves and cymose flowers. DISTRIB. Round the world in the tropics, mostly American. Species 330.

1. **B. aptera,** *Roxb. Fl. Ind.* iii. 650. A branched fleshy undershrub, 3–4 feet high. Leaves distinctly petioled, oblong, very oblique, acute, 4–6 inches long, simple, repand, thin, fleshy, bright metallic green; stipules large, lanceolate, caducous. Flowers in lax bisexual peduncled cymes from the axils of the leaves; bracts opposite, lanceolate-navicular, caducous; pedicels short, erect. Sepals round, reddish, ½ in. broad. Petals 2, much narrower, or absent. Stamens free; strap-shaped anthers twice as long as the filaments. Styles short, thick, with 2–3 papillose forks. Fruit oblong, under an inch long, terete and wingless, three-celled with forked placentas. Meziera salaziensis, *Gaudich. Atl. Bon. t.* 32; *A. DC. Prod.* xv. 407.

MAURITIUS, in thick forests of Quartier Militaire and Nouvelle Découverte. Also Bourbon, Timor, Philippines. In the SEYCHELLES in the damp forests of Mahé, and other islands, a variety is common with broader and less oblique sometimes subequal leaves reaching nearly a foot broad. *Oseille marron*, (Maur.) *Oseille des forêts* (Seyc.)

B. mascariensis, Bojer, Hort. Maur. 271, I know only by an imperfect specimen of old date sent by Mr. Horne, who believes it to be acaulescent. It has a cordate-palmatifid naked leaf, equal at the base, half a foot broad, with seven lanceolate-deltoid lobes reaching halfway down to the top of the petiole, and a laxly corymbose monoicous inflorescence half a foot broad, on a long peduncle, with abundant pairs of small spreading obovate bracts from the nodes, ¼-½ in. pedicels, an apetalous male flower with two round sepals ½ inch broad, obtuse ligulate anthers twice as long as the free filaments, and a broad-oblong capsule half an inch deep, with one narrow wing, and another one triangular half an inch broad, with bipartite placentas, and a style as long as the three spreading corrugated subulate stigmatic lobes. It was gathered by Bojer in Mauritius in the deep forests of Quartier Militaire, and is said by him to be also an inhabitant of Bourbon.

ORDER LI. CUCURBITACEÆ.

Flowers monoicous or dioicous. Calyx-tube adnate to the ovary in the females; limb 5-toothed. Petals 5, free or joined below. Stamens usually 3, perigynous, free or monadelphous. Anther-cells in ours contorted. Ovary inferior, 3-celled; placentas three, fleshy, often joining in the axis; ovules very numerous; style simple or lobed; stigmas various. Fruit usually fleshy and indehiscent. Seeds exalbuminous. — Climbing herbs, with tendrils and alternate leaves. DISTRIB. Cosmopolitan in warmer regions. Species 470.

Fruit a small soft globose berry . . . . 1. BRYONOPSIS.
Fruit large, fleshy, gourd-like.
Petals free; male flowers in racemes.
Petals fringed . . . . * TRICHOSANTHES.
Petals not fringed . . . . * LUFFA.
Petals connate; flowers direct from leaf axils.
Male flowers fascicled . . . . * CUCUMIS.
Males and females both solitary.
Petals connate low down . . . . * CITRULLUS.
Petals connate high up . . . . * CUCURBITA.

1. BRYONOPSIS, Arn.

Flowers monoicous. Male flower with a campanulate calyx-tube, 5 minute linear teeth, 3 short filaments arising from the base of the calyx, one of the anthers 1-celled, the other two 2-celled, with flexuose cells and a broad round connective. Female flower with an ovoid ovary, surrounded by 5 staminodes, numerous ovules and a slender trifid style. Petals 5, lanceolate, arising from the top of the calyx-tube. Fruit a naked globose berry the size of a small crab-apple. DISTRIB. Spread through the tropics of the Old World; the only species.

1. **B. laciniosa,** *Arn. in Hook. Journ.* iii. 274. A climbing herb with a perennial root and slender stems much twisted spirally and forked tendrils. Leaves very thin, slightly pilose beneath, round-cordate, 3–6 in. broad, with 5–7 deep or shallow palmate lobes. Flowers fascicled at the nodes, one female and two or three males in a cluster on short pedicels. Corolla yellowish, ¼ in. deep. Fruit an inch thick, green striped with yellow. Bryonia laciniosa, *Linn.*; *Wt. Icon. t.* 500. B. dioica, *Bojer, Hort. Maur.* 148, *non Linn.*

MAURITIUS, in woods on the banks of the stream at Moka. SEYCHELLES, climbing to the top of trees in woods near the Cascade in Mahé, *Horne*, 460! *Calebasse marron.*

In Mauritius, several of the commonly-cultivated gourds are casually subspontaneous, of which the following are the principal, viz.,

* *Trichosanthes anguina*, Linn.; DC. Prod. iii. 314; Bot. Mag. t. 472. A native of Tropical Asia. Annual, leaves round-cordate deeply 3–5-lobed, tendrils trifid, petals small white fringed free spreading, male flowers in stalked corymbs from the axils of the leaves, female flowers solitary from the same axils, fruit hispid spindle-shaped nearly a foot long, with a long beak. *Patole.*

* *Luffa acutangula*, Seringe; DC. Prod. iii. 302 (Cucumis, *Linn.*; Luffa fœtida, *Cav.; DC. Prod. loc. cit.; Bot. Mag. t.* 1638), a native of Tropical Asia. Stems slender glabrous, tendrils simple or forked, leaves round-cordate with 5 deltoid lobes, petals large free obovate spreading yellow, male flowers in long or short racemes from the axils of the leaves, female flowers solitary, fruit clavate a foot long 2–3 inches thick with ten sharp angles dry dehiscing by a terminal lid. *Papangaye. Pipengaye.*

* *Cucumis Anguria*, Linn.; DC. Prod. iii. 301 (C. echinatus, *Moench, Mill. Ic. t.* 33), a native of Tropical America. Stems slender sulcate densely hispid, tendrils short simple, leaves small deeply palmately 5-lobed with divisions spathulately narrowed at base, corolla under ⅓ in. broad, with lanceolate petals joined at base, flowers direct from leaf axils, males 1–6, females solitary, fruit fleshy, the size and shape of a hen's egg, bristly, obtuse, indehiscent. *Concombre marron.*

* *Citrullus vulgaris*, Schrad. (Cucumis Citrullus, *DC.; Cucurbita, Linn.*), a native of the Old World. Stems and petioles densely pilose, tendrils mostly forked, leaves cordate-deltoid cut up into many broad or narrow spathulate obtuse lobes, flowers of both sexes solitary on stalks in the axils of the leaves, corolla yellow middle-sized with segments joined below the middle, fruit large globose indehiscent smooth with starry spots and abundant yellow or reddish fleshy. *Water melon, Citrouille, Melon d'eau.*

* *Cucurbita Pepo*, Linn.; DC. Prod. iii. 317, a native of the Orient. Stems stout, scabrous, tendrils much branched, leaves very large with five deltoid lobes, flowers of both sexes solitary, corolla very large with deltoid ascending segments shorter than the funnel-shaped tube, fruit large smooth round or oblong indehiscent. *Pumpkin, Pompion, Giraumon.*

Dr. Balfour's Rodriguez collection contains **Lagenaria vulgaris**, Seringe; **Citrullus vulgaris**, Schrad., and **Momordica balsamina**, Linn.

Order LII. UMBELLIFERÆ.

Flowers regular or irregular, hermaphrodite or polygamous. Calyx-tube adnate to the ovary; teeth 5 or obsolete. Petals 5, epigynous, often emarginate. Stamens 5, inserted with the petals; filaments inflexed; anthers oblong, didymous, slit down the side. Ovary inferior 2-celled; ovules solitary, pendulous, anatropous; epigynous disk flat or prominent; styles 2, distinct, falcate. Fruit separating into two indehiscent halves (mericarps), which are sometimes compressed dorsally and sometimes laterally, with a broad or narrow plane of junction (commissure) and 5 or 10 unarmed or prickly sometimes winged ribs.—Herbs, well-marked by their umbellate inflorescence. Distrib. Temperate and subtemperate regions, especially of the northern hemisphere. Species 1300.

Trailing perennials with entire leaves . . . . 1. Hydrocotyle.
Erect annuals or biennials with decompound leaves with linear lobes.
Involucre none. Fruit not prickly . . . . * Carum.
Involucre of compound bracts. Fruit prickly . . . . * Daucus.

1. HYDROCOTYLE, Linn.

Calyx-teeth obsolete. Petals entire. Disk flat. Styles filiform from the base. Fruit broader than long, flattened laterally, with a narrow commissure; 5 primary ribs distinct, especially the dorsal one; carpophore undivided.—Prostrate perennial herbs of swampy ground, with entire leaves, small lanceolate bracts and simple or irregularly compound umbels. DISTRIB. Cosmopolitan. Species 70.

Leaves not peltate. Flowers in simple heads.
  Heads one from each node . . . . 1. H. SIBTHORPIOIDES.
  Heads several from each node . . . . 2. H. ASIATICA.
Leaves peltate. Flowers in compound whorls . . . 3. H. BONARIENSIS.

1. **H. sibthorpioides,** *Lam.; DC. Prod.* iv. 66. Stems very slender, wide-trailing, glabrous. Leaves orbicular or rather broader than long, ¼–⅜ in. broad, membranous, glabrous, shallowly lobed, the lobes crenate; petiole ½–2 in. long, from a narrow deep basal sinus. Heads solitary, dense, globose, on slender peduncles as long as the petioles, 8–10-flowered; pedicels 0. Fruit $\frac{1}{24}$ in. broad and deep, only the 5 primary ribs distinct. *A. Rich. Monog. Hydrocot. t.* 8.

MAURITIUS, in marshy ground, *Bouton!* Endemic.

2. **H. asiatica,** *Linn.; DC. Prod.* iv. 62. Stems in dense rosettes, wide-trailing, and producing rosettes of leaves and peduncles at the often rooting nodes, usually glabrous. Leaves round, petioled from a deep basal sinus, crenate, ½–2 in. broad; petioles 1–8 in. long. Flowers 1–4 in dense heads on copious short peduncles from the nodes, each cluster subtended by a pair of lanceolate bracts; pedicels none. Fruit $\frac{1}{12}$ in. deep, corky; mericarps rounded on the back, with both secondary and primary ribs developed as slender lines. H. ficarioides and nummularioides, *DC. Prod. loc. cit.*

MAURITIUS and SEYCHELLES, common in swampy places. Cosmopolitan in warmer regions. *Bevilaqua.*

3. **H. bonariensis,** *Lam.; DC. Prod.* iv. 60. Stems slender, wide-trailing, glabrous, rooting at the distant nodes. Leaves round, peltate, glabrous, crenulate or subentire, 1–4 in. broad; petioles reaching ½ ft. long. Peduncle 4–24 in. long; umbel with many rays, bearing lateral and terminal whorls of flowers and one from the centre; pedicels finally ¼–½ in. long; bracts linear, shorter than the pedicels. Fruit $\frac{1}{12}$–⅛ in. broad, the mericarps acutely keeled and showing only the distinct primary ribs. H. petiolaris, *DC. Prod. loc. cit.*

MAURITIUS and RODRIGUEZ, in swampy ground. Spread through Tropical Africa and common in Tropical America.

* *Carum (Trachyspermum) dichotomum,* Benth. Gen. Plant. i. 891 (Pimpinella dichotoma, *Linn.; DC. Prod.* iv. 123), a commonly cultivated Anise from Spain, has become subspontaneous in some places in Mauritius. It is a slender erect glabrous annual, 1–1½ feet high, with decompound leaves with minute linear lobes, compound umbels without either involucre or involucel, emarginate petals with an inflexed point and minute laterally-compressed mericarps with five equal ribs. *Anis sauvage.*

* *Daucus Carota*, Linn.; DC. Prod. iv. 251, the common European carrot, has strayed from cultivation in some places in Mauritius; and in Rodriguez is found on hill-slopes all over the island. It may be readily known by its fusiform biennial root, decompound leaves with linear acute lobes, deeply-cut general bracts, and small ten-ribbed mericarps armed with hooked prickles. *Carotte sauvage.*

Fœniculum vulgare, *Gærtn.*, the common cultivated Fennel, is given in Dupont's Mauritian List as a naturalised species. *Fenouil.*

Anethum graveolens, *Linn.*, the commonly cultivated Anise, or Dill, is also casually subspontaneous in Mauritius. *Anis sauvage.*

ORDER LIII. CACTACEÆ.

Flowers regular, hermaphrodite. Calyx-tube adnate to the ovary, often produced beyond it; lobes indefinite, scaly, leafy or petaloid. Petals indefinite, mostly numerous and passing gradually into sepals. Stamens indefinite, inserted at the throat of the calyx; filaments filiform; anthers minute, oblong. Ovary inferior, one-celled; placentation parietal; ovules very numerous; style single, filiform; stigmas 2 or several, spreading. Fruit a berry.—Fleshy leafless shrubs of very characteristic habit. DISTRIB. All American, except *Rhipsalis Cassytha*. Species reckoned in gardens about 1000.

Stems slender, terete, unarmed . . . . 1. RHIPSALIS.
Stems of large flattened prickly joints . . . . * OPUNTIA.

1. RHIPSALIS, Gærtn.

Calyx-tube not produced above the ovary; teeth 5–6, minute. Petals 5–6, oblong, spreading. Stamens 12–14; filaments subequal; anthers short. Ovary inferior; style filiform; rays of stigma 3. Berry subglobose, smooth, one-celled, many-seeded.—Fleshy shrubs with articulated terete or flattened branches, and minute scale-like leaves, with copious small flowers sessile in their axils. DISTRIB. Species 30, all the rest Tropical American.

1. **R. Cassytha,** *Gærtn.; DC. Prod.* iii. 476. Stems slender, shrubby, terete, firm, erect or pendulous, branched in dense whorls, and branches again branched in whorls or forked. Joints rare, except at the branching. Flowers abundant on the sides of the branchlets, often crowded. Calyx teeth 5–6, small, unequal, acute. Petals 5–6, ovate, obtuse, greenish-white. Stamens 12–14, shorter than the petals. Berry waxy white, like that of the Mistletoe, the size of a small pea. *Bot. Mag. t.* 3080. Cactus pendulinus, *Sieber*.

MAURITIUS, on rocks of the Pouce, Montagne Longue, etc. SEYCHELLES, in one place on a rock near the south end of Mahé, *Horne*, 461! Also Ceylon, Tropical Africa and America.

* *Opuntia Tuna*, Miller; DC. Prod. iii. 472, a native of South America, has been planted for fences in Rodriguez and Mauritius, and is now spread through the islands. It has dichotomous stems, 3–6 feet high, with flattened oblong joints 6–12 in. long,

beset with bundles of large hard yellow spines with a tuft of short wool at the base, solitary sessile flowers, numerous imbricated acute reddish-green sepals, 8 or more yellow or reddish petals above an inch long, indefinite included irritable stamens and a juicy fruit the size and shape of a small pear. *Raquette.*

ORDER LIV. LORANTHCAEÆ.

Flowers perfect or diclinous. Perianth simple in *Viscum* (double in *Loranthus*); segments 4–5, valvate. Stamens inserted on the perianth-segments and opposite to them. Ovary 1-celled; ovule solitary, erect, orthotropous, adnate to the cell-wall; style simple or absent; stigma simple. Fruit a one-seeded berry. Seed with an embryo in copious fleshy albumen.—Parasitic shrubs, leafy or leafless. DISTRIB. Cosmopolitan in warmer regions. Species 500.

Flowers unisexual; perianth single . . . . 1. VISCUM.
Flowers bisexual; perianth double . . . . 2. LORANTHUS.

1. VISCUM, Linn.

Flowers unisexual. Calyx-tube adnate to the ovary; sepals 4, valvate. Petals 0. Stamens adnate to the petals; anthers many-celled, opening by many pores. Ovary inferior; stigma sessile, peltate. Fruit a one-seeded berry.—Parasitic shrubs, leafy or leafless. DISTRIB. Old World. Species 50.

Stems not jointed, furnished with leaves . . . . 1. V. TRIFLORUM.
Stems without leaves, distinctly jointed at the nodes.
Joints $\frac{1}{12}$ in. broad . . . . 2. V. CAPENSE.
Joints $\frac{1}{6}$–$\frac{1}{4}$ in. broad . . . . 3. V. TÆNIOIDES.

1. **V. triflorum,** *DC. Prod.* iv. 279. Glabrous, leafy, much-branched, a foot or more long, with slender sulcate angular branchlets. Leaves opposite, ovate or oblong, obtuse, 1–2½ in. long, obscurely 3–5-nerved, deltoid at the base, short-petioled, thick and rigid. Flowers 3 together on copious short erecto-patent solitary rarely 2–3-nate peduncles, with a pair of small deltoid bracts at the tip; pedicels none. Sepals 4, minute, lanceolate. Berry yellow, the size of a pea. V. venosum, *DC. loc. cit.* V. rotundifolium, *Bory, Iter* i. 320, *non Linn.* V. nervosum, *Hochst.*

MAURITIUS and SEYCHELLES, frequent in the woods. Also Bourbon and Abyssinia. Mr. Horne sends also two plants from the Seychelles which may be varieties of this or distinct species. 572. Leaves smaller, more rigid, 1–1½ in. long, obovate, very obtuse, with a deltoid base, the 3 ribs only perceptible at the very base of the leaf when dried. 573. Leaves with texture and nerving of type, 1¼–1½ in. long, oblong-lanceolate, deltoid at the base, narrowed from the middle to a subobtuse point. In both, the flowers seem quite to match those of the type. *Gui du pays.*

2. **V. capense,** *Linn. fil.*; *DC. Prod.* iv. 282. A leafless parasite, with stems jointed like those of a *Salicornia*, 3–4 in. long, densely fascicled, tripinnately branched with spreading branchlets; joints glabrous,

flattened, $\frac{1}{4}$–$\frac{1}{2}$ in. long, $\frac{1}{12}$ in. broad, dilated into a minute cupule at the top, from which spring 2–6 minute flowers. Perianth-segments minute, deltoid, caducous. Ovary subsessile, turbinate, $\frac{1}{12}$ in. deep.

MAURITIUS, in woods of the Pouce, chiefly on *Nuxia*. SEYCHELLES, on *Sideroxylon*, rare, *Horne*, 539! Also Bourbon, Cape.

3. **V. tæniolides,** *Comm. DC.; Prod.* iv. 282. Very near the last, of which it is scarcely more than a variety, differing by its much more robust broader joints, which are flattened and nearly $\frac{1}{4}$ inch broad. Flowers just the same, both in size and arrangement.

MAURITIUS, in woods of the Pouce, etc., on *Nuxia* and *Eugenia*. RODRIGUEZ, on *Fernelia buxifolia* in the valley of Rivière Baleine, *Balfour!* Endemic.

2. LORANTHUS, Linn.

Flowers hermaphrodite. Calyx-tube adnate to the ovary; limb campanulate, truncate or obscurely toothed. Petals 4–6, joined together in a long tube that slits down the side, or finally separating low down. Stamens as many as the petals and opposite to them; filaments adnate to the tube; anthers erect, 2-celled. Ovary 1-celled; style filiform; stigma entire. Fruit a one-seeded berry.—Parasites, with alternate or opposite entire leaves and varied inflorescence. DISTRIB. Round the world in the tropics. Species 300.

Lobes of corolla oblong . . . . 1. L. BOJERI.
Lobes of corolla lanceolate . . . . 2. L. SECHELLENSIS.

1. **L. Bojeri,** *Baker*. Glabrous; branches grey, terete with short internodes. Leaves upper opposite, lower alternate, short-petioled, oblong, obtuse, cuneate at base, 1$\frac{1}{2}$–3 in. long, very thick and rigid, obscurely triplinerved. Flowers in copious dense subsessile umbels in the axils of the leaves. Calyx $\frac{1}{8}$ in. long, nearly cuneate, with a cupular bracteole at the base. Corolla under an inch long, naked, clavate, scarlet, with a green top, not gibbous at the base, splitting down one side to the base; lobes 5, short, oblong. Anthers erect, oblong, $\frac{1}{12}$ in. long. L. indicus, *Bojer, Hort Maur.* 163, *non Lam.*

MAURITIUS, in dense woods of Grand Bassin, Savanne, etc., parasitic on *Eugenia*. Near the Mascaren *L. clavatus*, Lam. Endemic.

2. **L. sechellensis,** *Baker*. Glabrous; branches grey, terete, dotted with rough raised spots; internodes an inch or more long. Leaves oblong, very thick and rigid, 3–4 in. long, obtuse, obscurely penninerved, cuneately narrowed into a short petiole. Flowers few together in the axils of leaves, without common peduncle; pedicel $\frac{1}{8}$ in. long. Calyx $\frac{1}{4}$ in. deep, oblong-pentagonal, minutely bracteolate; limb very short, entire, collar-like. Corolla bright red, 1$\frac{1}{4}$–1$\frac{1}{2}$ in. long; tube strongly pentagonal; lobes lanceolate, $\frac{1}{4}$ in. long. Anthers ligulate, obtuse, $\frac{1}{8}$ in. long.

SEYCHELLES, frequent in woods above 800 feet, *Horne*, 571! Endemic.

We have imperfect specimens of a third species from Mauritius, gathered by Bojer. It has thick rigid obscurely 3-nerved oblanceolate-oblong obtuse leaves 3 in. long, narrowed into a short petiole, and flowers 2–3 together from the lower part of the virgate branches without a common peduncle. I have not seen the corolla.

ORDER LV. RUBIACEÆ.

Flowers hermaphrodite or polygamous, in all the Mauritian genera regular. Calyx-tube adnate to the ovary; teeth 4–5, long or short. Corolla funnel-shaped or hypocrateriform; tube short or long; lobes usually 4 or 5, valvate or imbricated in bud. Stamens numerous, inserted at the throat of the corolla; filaments short or none; anthers 2-celled, slit down the side, basifixed or versatile. Ovary inferior, two or many-celled; ovules one or many in a cell; style simple below, mostly branched above. Fruit and seeds very various; albumen mostly copious.—Trees, shrubs or herbs with opposite entire leaves and connate interpetiolar stipules; inflorescence various. DISTRIB. Cosmopolitan, mostly in warm countries. Species 4000.

SERIES A. Ovules more than one in each cell.

Fruit capsular.
  Shrubs . . . . 1. DANAIS.
  Herbs . . . . 2. OLDENLANDIA.
Fruit indehiscent. (All shrubby.)
  Flowers in terminal corymbs.
    Flowers small, seeds few . . . . 3. WEBERA.
    Flowers large; seeds numerous . . . . 4. MUSSÆNDA.
  Flowers in terminal panicles with cymose branches . . 5. BERTIERA.
  Flowers in clusters in the axils of the leaves . . . . 6. RANDIA.
  Flowers solitary in the axils of the leaves.
    Shrubs with naked fruit.
      Flowers small, polygamous . . . . 7. FERNELIA.
      Flowers large hermaphrodite . . . . 8. GARDENIA.
    Minute herb with bristly fruit . . . . * DENTELLA.

SERIES B. Ovules solitary in each cell. Radicle superior.

Albumen absent or very scanty.
  Lobes of corolla imbricate.
    Corolla large hypocrateriform 4–10-lobed . . . . 9. GUETTARDA.
    Corolla small funnel-shaped 4-lobed . . . . . . 10. ANTIRRHŒA.
  Lobes of corolla valvate . . . . 11. TIMONIUS.
Albumen abundant.
  Fruit a berry with a single seed . . . . 12. CRATERISPERMUM.
  Fruit a drupe with 2–3 pyrenes . . . . 13. PLECTRONIA.
  Fruit a drupe with several pyrenes.
    Flowers in dichotomous cymes . . . . * VANGUERIA.
    Flowers one or few clustered within a pair of bracts . . . . 14. PYROSTRIA.
    Flowers many clustered within a pair of large bracts 15. SCYPHOCHLAMYS.

SERIES C. Ovules solitary in each cell. Radicle inferior.

Erect shrubs.
  Æstivation of corolla-lobes twisted.
    Fruit a berry with a single seed . . . . 16. RUTIDEA.
    Fruit a drupe with many pyrenes . . . . 17. MYONIMA.
    Fruit a drupe with two pyrenes.
      Flowers in terminal corymbs . . . . 18. IXORA.
      Flowers axillary . . . . 19. COFFEA.
  Æstivation of corolla-lobes valvate.
    Flowers united in a globose head . . . . 20. MORINDA.
    Flowers distinct.
      Stamens inserted at the throat of the corolla-tube.
        Pyrenes two; tube long . . . . 21. CHASALIA.
        Pyrenes two; tube short . . . . 22. PSYCHOTRIA.
        Pyrenes 5–6 . . . . 23. PSATHURA.
      Stamens inserted low down in the corolla-tube . * SERISSA.
Climbing shrub . . . . 24. PÆDERIA.
Annual herbs . . . . 25. SPERMACOCE.

1. DANAIS, Comm.

Flowers polygamous. Calyx-tube campanulate; teeth 5, minute, deltoid, persistent. Corolla funnel-shaped; tube cylindrical, villose at the throat; teeth 5, lanceolate, valvate. Stamens inserted at the throat of the tube; filaments filiform Ovary 2-celled; ovules numerous; style filiform, deeply 2-forked in the female flower. Fruit a small crustaceous capsule, splitting down the middle from the top to the bottom. Seeds peltate, winged, attached to a central placenta.—Climbing shrubs with copious axillary or terminal corymbs of minute flowers. DISTRIB. Mascaren Isles also. Species 4.

Corymbs terminal . . . . 1. D. CORYMBOSA.
Corymbs axillary . . . . 2. D. FRAGRANS.

1. **D. corymbosa,** *Balf. fil.* A woody climber with slender glabrous branches. Leaves short-petioled, oblong or lanceolate, subcoriaceous, glabrous, $1\frac{1}{2}$–3 in. long, $\frac{1}{2}$–1 in. broad, acute or acuminate, cuneate at the base; stipules deltoid, minute. Flowers in dense terminal corymbs $1\frac{1}{2}$–2 in. broad; pedicels erect, slender, puberulent, $\frac{1}{12}$–$\frac{1}{8}$ in. long. Calyx under $\frac{1}{12}$ in. long; tube campanulate; teeth 5 lanceolate. Corolla under $\frac{1}{4}$ in. long; segments oblong-spathulate, as long as the tube; throat densely villose. Stamens exserted. Fruit globose, glabrous, $\frac{1}{6}$ in. long, dry, splitting to the bottom into two halves.

RODRIGUEZ, scattered through the island, but not plentiful. *Balfour!* Endemic.

2. **D. fragrans,** *Comm.; DC. Prod.* iv. 361. A wide-climbing shrub with slender branches. Leaves short-petioled, oblong or obovate, obtuse or subacute, cuneate at the base, 2–4 in. long, glabrous, penninerved. Corymbs copious, axillary, often fascicled, much shorter than the leaves; bracts very minute; pedicels ascending, slender, often

puberulous, exceeding the calyx. Calyx $\frac{1}{14}$ in. long. Corolla fragrant, red-orange, $\frac{1}{3}$ in. long; teeth shorter than the tube, reflexed when expanded. Capsule fragile, glabrous, the size of a small pea. D. rotundifolia and sulcata, *DC. Prod. loc. cit.* D. laxiflora, *Bojer an DC.*? Malanea verticillata, *Sieber*.

MAURITIUS, frequent in woods. Also Madagascar. We have a monster without petals or stamens with very large calyx-teeth. *Liane de bois jaune.*

2. OLDENLANDIA, Linn.

Flowers hermaphrodite. Calyx-tube campanulate; teeth 4–5, small, lanceolate. Corolla funnel-shaped; tube long or short; teeth 4–5, valvate. Stamens 4–5, inserted at the naked throat of the corolla, included; filaments very short. Ovary 2-celled; ovules many; styles slender, with two short forks. Capsule minute, globose, membranous, splitting from top to bottom down the centre. Seeds many, very small. —Much-branched slender herbs with small flowers in terminal or axillary cymes. DISTRIB. Tropics, nearly all of Old World. Species 150.

Flowers tetramerous.
  Flowers solitary in the axils of the leaves, on $\frac{1}{4}$-$\frac{1}{3}$ in. pedicels.
    Stems short, with leaves mostly congested . . . . 1. O. CONGESTA.
    Stems trailing, with distant leaves . . . . 2. O. SIEBERI.
  Flowers fascicled, pilose, nearly sessile . . . . . . 3. O. TRINERVIA.
Flowers pentamerous.
  Leaves oblong or lanceolate . . . . 4. O. MACROPHYLLA.
  Leaves minute, linear . . . . 5. O. HORNEI.

1. **O. congesta,** *Balf. fil.* Perennial, densely cæspitose, glabrous. Stems generally so short that the leaves are congested into a rosette at the surface of the soil, sometimes slender, trailing to a length of 2–3 inches. Leaves obovate-oblong, glossy, rigid, 1-nerved, $\frac{1}{12}$–$\frac{1}{8}$ in. long, narrowed to a short petiole. Flowers few, solitary in the axils of the leaves, on $\frac{1}{4}$–$\frac{1}{3}$ in. pedicels. Flower-calyx $\frac{1}{12}$ in. long; tube campanulate; teeth 4, lanceolate-deltoid. Petals not seen. Capsule turbinate, $\frac{1}{8}$ in. long, opening at the top.

RODRIGUEZ, on the shore. *Dr. Balfour!* Endemic.

2. **O. Sieberi,** *Baker*. A diffuse glabrous annual, with very numerous stems, $\frac{1}{4}$–$\frac{1}{2}$ ft. long, spreading from the crown of the root. Leaves distant, oblanceolate, obtuse, subsessile, 1-nerved, spreading, $\frac{1}{4}$ in. long. Flowers copious, solitary, on slender curved pedicels $\frac{1}{4}$–$\frac{1}{3}$ in. long from the axils of the leaves. Corolla minute, funnel-shaped, with a short tube. Capsule turbinate, fragile, glabrous, $\frac{1}{12}$–$\frac{1}{8}$ in. long; teeth 4, linear, minute. Hedyotis repens, *Bojer, Hort. Maur.* 167, *non DC.*

MAURITIUS, by roadsides and in damp ground. *Sieber!* (Fl. Maur. ii. 207). *Ayres!* Endemic.

3. **O. trinervia,** *Retz. Obs.* iv. 23. A much-branched annual, with slender trailing stems, $\frac{1}{2}$–1 ft. long, hairy upwards, Leaves distant, oblong, $\frac{1}{2}$–$\frac{3}{4}$ in. long, subtriplinerved, spathulate at the base, acute, membranous, nearly sessile. Flowers 4–10, in whorls in the axils of the leaves, on very short pedicels. Calyx-tube globose, $\frac{1}{12}$ in. long, densely pilose; teeth linear-lanceolate, often falcate. Corolla white, fugacious, minute; tube short. Hedyotis rotundifolia, *Spreng.; DC. Prod.* iv. 420.

MAURITIUS and SEYCHELLES, a frequent weed. Through the tropics of the Old World.

4. **O. macrophylla,** *DC. Prod.* iv. 427. A glabrous annual or perennial herb, with trailing stems 1–2 feet long. Leaves sessile, acute, oblong or oblong-lanceolate, membranous, 1–2 in. long; stipules short, broad, entire or ciliated. Flowers in lax peduncled corymbs or racemes from the axils of the leaves, which they much exceed; bracts minute, lanceolate; pedicels spreading, as long or longer than the flowers. Calyx $\frac{1}{8}$ in. long and broad. Corolla under $\frac{1}{4}$ in. long, regularly funnel-shaped. Pentodon abyssinicus, *Hochst.* Oldenlandia laxiflora, *Benth. Fl. Nigr.* 404. Pentodon decumbens, *Hochst. in Flora,* 1844, 552.

SEYCHELLES, by the side of swamps and in damp places, common in all the islands. *Horne! Wright!* Through Tropical Africa; also Natal.

5. **O. Hornei,** *Baker.* A much-branched glabrous perennial, with slender trailing stems 1–2 feet long. Leaves in rather distant pairs, linear, acute, 1-nerved, $\frac{1}{2}$–$\frac{3}{4}$ in. long; stipules minute, deltoid aristate. Flowers in pairs from the nodes on a common peduncle as long as the leaf; pedicels $\frac{1}{8}$–$\frac{1}{4}$ in. long, reflexing after flowering. Corolla white, caducous. Fruit-calyx membranous, globose, $\frac{1}{12}$ in. long, crowned by the 5 minute erect linear teeth.

SEYCHELLES, in Ile Silhouette in holes in the rocks, *Horne,* 251! Endemic.

3. WEBERA, Schreb.

Calyx-tube campanulate or turbinate; teeth 4–5, minute, erect, persistent. Corolla funnel-shaped; tube long; lobes 4–5, ligulate, obtuse, twisted in bud. Stamens 4–5, inserted at the throat of the corolla; filaments very short; anthers linear. Ovary 2-celled; ovules in a cell few; style elongated, with two flattened forks. Fruit small, globose, indehiscent, coriaceous or fleshy.—Shrubs or trees, with small or middle-sized flowers, in dense terminal corymbs. DISTRIB. Through the tropics of the Old World. Species 40. Habit of *Pavetta,* from which it only differs in the number of ovules.

1. **W. sechellensis,** *Baker.* An erect glabrous shrub 8–12 feet high, with slender terete branches. Leaves petioled, oblong-lanceolate,

acute, 4–5 in. long, cuneate at the base, moderately firm in texture; stipules small, lanceolate, connate, deciduous. Flowers in lax sessile terminal corymbs, with minute bracts and elongated slender pedicels. Calyx $\frac{1}{16}$ in. long; teeth 4, minute. Corolla white, $\frac{1}{4}$–$\frac{1}{3}$ in. long; lobes rather longer than the tube. Anthers rather shorter than the corolla lobes. Berry the size of a pea, 3-seeded.

SEYCHELLES, common in all the islands in dry soil at a low elevation, *Pervillé*, 33 *Wright! Horne*, 258! 261! Endemic.

4. MUSSÆNDA, Linn.

Calyx-tube clavate; teeth 5, lanceolate, deciduous, in the Mauritian species subequal. Corolla hypocrateriform; tube long, clavate; lobes 5, oblong. Stamens 5, inserted low down in the tube; filaments short; anthers linear, included in the tube. Ovary 2-celled; ovules very numerous; placentas fleshy; styles long, filiform, with two short lobes. Fruit fleshy, indehiscent, oblong or clavate, 2-celled. Seeds numerous, minute.—Shrubs with rather large flowers in terminal corymbs. DISTRIB. Species 40, spread through the tropics of the Old World.

Erect shrub, with silky leaves and flowers . . . . . 1. M. LANDIA.
Climber, with leaves and flowers glabrous, except the inside of the tube . . . . 2. M. ARCUATA.

1. **M. Landia,** *Lam.; DC. Prod.* iv. 372. An erect shrub, 4–6 feet high, with stout silky branchlets. Leaves petioled, ovate or lanceolate, acuminate, 4–9 in. long, subcoriaceous, glabrescent above, silky all over or only on the ribs beneath; stipules lanceolate, silky. Flowers in lax deltoid short-peduncled terminal corymbs; bracts small, linear; pedicels erect. Calyx-tube silky, clavate, $\frac{1}{3}$–$\frac{1}{2}$ in. long; teeth lanceolate, $\frac{1}{3}$–$\frac{1}{2}$ in. long. Corolla white, silky within and without, 2–3 in. long; teeth oblong-aristate, $\frac{1}{3}$–$\frac{1}{4}$ as long as the tube. Fruit ribbed, clavate, above an inch long. M. Stadtmanni, *Mich.; DC. loc. cit.*

MAURITIUS, in forests through the island. *M. Stadtmanni* is a mere shade form, with long sepals and leaves silky only on the ribs below. Endemic. *Quinquina indigéne.*

2. **M. arcuata,** *Lam.; DC. Prod.* iv. 372. A twining shrub, with glabrous stem and leaves. Leaves distinctly petioled, subcoriaceous, oblong, acute, shining, 3–4 in. long; stipules short, ciliated, 2–3-partite, usually glabrous, caducous, leaving a hairy rim above the scar. Flowers in lax terminal corymbs, the main branches of which spring from the axils of large leaves; upper bracts small, linear. Calyx glabrous, $\frac{1}{4}$–$\frac{1}{3}$ in. long, clavate; teeth linear, rather shorter than the tube. .Corolla bright yellow, $1\frac{1}{3}$ in. long, glabrous on the outside of and face of the lobes; tube villose internally; segments oblong, not

aristate, half as long as the tube. Berry oblong, crowded by the disk; teeth deciduous.

MAURITIUS, in shaded woods through the island. Also Madagascar and Tropical Africa. *Liane caca poule.*

5. BERTIERA, Aublet.

Calyx-tube small, subglobose; teeth 5, minute, deltoid. Corolla funnel-shaped; teeth 5, lanceolate, imbricated, shorter than the tube. Stamens 5, included, inserted at the throat of the corolla-tube; filaments very short; anthers oblong, with the connective produced beyond the cells in an awn. Ovary 2-celled; ovules many; style fusiform, entire. Fruit a small dry indehiscent capsule. Seeds numerous, minute.—Shrubs with large connate stipules and small flowers in terminal panicles with cymose branches. DISTRIB. Trop. Africa and America. Species about a dozen.

1. **B. Zaluzania,** *Gærtn.; DC. Prod.* iv. 392. A low erect shrub, with silky branchlets. Leaves short-petioled, oblong, acute, subcoriaceous, distinctly penninerved, 4–6 in. long, glabrous above, glabrescent or obscurely silky below; stipules large, membranous, connate, breaking away and leaving a cup. Flowers in peduncled terminal drooping panicles ½ foot long; cymes many, lax, 3–4 times dichotomously forked, with a flower sessile in each fork. Calyx very silky, $\frac{1}{12}$ in. long; teeth minute, erect, persistent. Corolla silky, ¼ in. long; teeth shorter than the tube. Berry dry, size of a small pea. B. rufa and borbonica, *DC. loc. cit.* B. bistipulata, *Bojer, Hort. Maur.* 166.

MAURITIUS, in woods through the island. Also Bourbon. *B. bistipulata* is a shade form, with a broad almost deltoid panicle and oblong stipules an inch long.

6. RANDIA, Linn.

Calyx-tube funnel-shaped or turbinate; limb usually nearly truncate. Corolla hypocrateriform; tube funnel-shaped; throat naked or villose; lobes 5, contorted and imbricated in bud. Stamens 5, sessile at the throat of the corolla; anthers acute. Ovary 2-celled; ovules many in a cell; style entire or forked. Fruit a two-celled many-seeded berry. —Trees or shrubs, erect or scandent, sometimes spinose; flowers usually white or yellow, one or several together in the axils of the leaves. DISTRIB. Tropics, mainly of the Old World. Species 90.

1. **R. heterophylla,** *Balf. fil.* A shrub, glabrous in all its parts with angular branches. Leaves short-petioled, subcoriaceous, oblong, rounded at both ends, obtuse or emarginate, 3–4 in. long by half as broad, varying to lanceolate, narrowed to both ends, ½–1 foot long, an inch or less broad; stipules short, truncate, connate, forming a persistent ciliated ring. Flowers 1–4 together in copious axillary cymes on ½–1 in. peduncles arising from a little above the node. Calyx ¼ in. long,

narrowly funnel-shaped; teeth obscurely deltoid, ciliated. Corolla tube ¾ in. long, narrowly funnel-shaped; throat pilose; expanded limb 1¼–1½ in. broad; lobes oblong-lanceolate. Anthers protruding from the throat, ⅓ in. long, ligulate, acute. Fruit oblong, coriaceous, 1½–1¾ in. long, narrowed from the middle to both ends.

RODRIGUEZ, in the most unfrequented part of the island, at the head of the valleys. *Dr. Balfour!* Endemic. *Café marron.*

7. FERNELIA, Comm.

Flowers polygamous, girt with a cupular calycule. Calyx-tube obconic; teeth 4, lanceolate, persistent, pilose on the inside. Corolla hypocrateriform; tube funnel-shaped; lobes 4, lanceolate, imbricated in bud, spreading when fully expanded. Stamens 4, inserted in the corolla-tube; anthers ligulate, included. Ovary 2-celled, with an imperfect dissepiment; ovules many; style short-branched. Fruit a small glabrous dry many-seeded berry, crowned with the persistent calyx-teeth.—Shrubs with copious small flowers, solitary in the axils of the leaves. Endemic and Monotypic.

1. **F. buxifolia,** *Lam.; DC. Prod.* iv. 398. A much-branched shrub, 4–5 feet high, with slender branchlets, at first a little downy. Leaves short-petioled, shining, glabrous, subcoriaceous, obtuse, obovate or oblong, ¼–½ in. long; stipules minute, deltoid. Flowers copious, solitary, sessile in the axils of the leaves. Calycule minute, campanulate, obscurely toothed. Calyx ⅛ in. long; teeth linear-lanceolate. Corolla whitish, under ¼ in. long, the lobes exceeding the tube. Berry deep red, juiceless, the size of a pea, sessile inside the calycule.

Var. F. PEDUNCULATA, *Gærtn.; DC. loc. cit.* Taller and laxer in habit. Leaves 1–1½ in. long, broad, oblong, or nearly round, more distinctly petioled. Calycule larger, sessile. Calyx-tube obconic, distinctly stalked within the calycule; teeth lanceolate-acuminate. F. obovata, *Lam.; DC. Prod. loc. cit.*

Var. F. OVATA, *Ayres MSS.* Leaves thinner, 1–1½ in. long, obovate-oblong with a deltoid base. Calycule funnel-shaped, ¼ in. long, with the tube sessile inside it. Berries larger, more oblong.

MAURITIUS, in woods, through the island; the type in more exposed mountainous situations. Round island, *Sir H. Barkly!* Frequent in RODRIGUEZ, *Bouton! Dr. Balfour!* The three forms are completely connected by intermediate links, and we have a specimen called "*F. biflora*" just like var. *ovata*, but with sometimes a pair of flowers in the axil of a leaf. Endemic. *Bois Chauve Souris. Bois de Buis.*

8. GARDENIA, Linn.

Flowers hermaphrodite. Calyx-tube clavate, produced considerably beyond the ovary; teeth 5, linear, small, deciduous. Corolla broadly funnel-shaped, with 5 deltoid imbricated lobes. Stamens 5, sessile, included; anthers very long and narrow. Ovary 1-celled, with 2 parietal placentas and numerous ovules; style long, included, fusiform, entire. Fruit large, baccate, with pulpy placentas and numerous seeds filling up the cavity.—Erect shrubs, with large solitary axillary flowers. DISTRIB. Tropics of the Old World. Species 60.

1. **G. Annæ,** *Wright in Trans. Roy. Irish Acad.* xxiv. 575. *t.* 28. An erect glabrous shrub, 10–12 feet high, with slender terete branchlets. Leaves short-petioled, oblong-lanceolate, acute, cuneate at the base, 3–4 in. long, membranous, shining, turning black in drying; stipules minute, deciduous. Flowers solitary, subsessile in the axils of the leaves. Calyx naked, narrowly funnel-shaped, $\frac{1}{2}$–$\frac{3}{4}$ in. long; teeth small, linear, from a broad base. Corolla $1\frac{1}{2}$ in. long, whitish, spotted with red; tube broadly dilated directly after leaving the calyx; lobes much shorter than the tube, spreading. Berry smooth, globose, 3 in. long, cuspidate, the base turbinate.

SEYCHELLES, in the woods of Mahé and Praslin, Ile Aride and Ile Félicité. *Wright! Horne!* A variety from Zambesi Land, *Meller*. *Calabassier.*

* *Dentella repens*, Forst.; DC. Prod. iv. 418, widely-spread in Tropical Asia and Polynesia, is included in Dupont's Mauritian catalogue, but I have not seen specimens. It is a very slender much-branched trailing perennial herb, with small oblanceolate membranous nearly sessile leaves, solitary subsessile axillary flowers, an oblong calyx-tube with lanceolate teeth, a funnel-shaped white corolla $\frac{1}{6}$ in. long, and a many-seeded globose dry indehiscent fruit $\frac{1}{12}$ in. thick covered with hooked bristles.

9. GUETTARDA, Linn.

Flowers polygamous. Calyx coriaceous, campanulate; mouth obscurely repand. Corolla hypocrateriform; tube long, cylindrical; lobes 4–9, short, obtuse, imbricate. Anthers sessile at the throat of the corolla, as many as the lobes. Ovary 4–9-celled, with one ovule in each cell; style filiform; stigma entire or obscurely two-lobed. Fruit a drupe, with a thin fleshy epicarp, fibrous mesocarp and thick woody endocarp.—Shrubs with flowers crowded in unilateral bifid axillary cymes. DISTRIB. Mostly Tropical American. Species 40–50.

1. **G. speciosa,** *Linn.; DC. Prod.* iv. 455. A low tree, with stout pubescent branchlets. Leaves petioled, large, oblong, obtuse, membranous, rounded at the base, finely grey-downy below; stipules large, lanceolate, deciduous. Flowers in copious axillary long-peduncled cymes, sessile, crowded, unilateral. Calyx silky, coriaceous, $\frac{1}{6}$ in. long. Corolla $1\frac{1}{2}$–2 in. long, white, fragrant, silky on the outside; expanded limb an inch broad. Drupe globose, an inch thick. Seeds much curved. *Lindl. Bot. Reg. t.* 1393.

SEYCHELLES, on the shores of Mahé, Praslin, and La Digue, *Bojer*, *Wright! Horne!* Zanguebar to Australia.

10. ANTIRRHŒA, Comm.

Flowers polygamous. Calyx small, with a funnel-shaped tube and short 4-toothed erect persistent limb. Corolla funnel-shaped, with a cylindrical tube and 4 short obtuse imbricated lobes. Stamens 4, nearly sessile at the throat of the corolla-tube. Ovary 2–3-celled, with a single ovule in each cell; style with as many branches as there are cells. Fruit a small indehiscent berry, with a bony endocarp.—Shrubs with small flowers in copious peduncled axillary bifid scorpioid cymes. DISTRIB. Tropics of both hemispheres, but not continental African. Species 20.

Drupe cylindrical. Corolla $\frac{1}{4}$–$\frac{1}{3}$ in. long . . . . . . 1. A. VERTICILLATA.
Drupe globose. Corolla $\frac{1}{8}$–$\frac{1}{6}$ in. long . . . . 2. A. FRANGULACEA.

1. **A. verticillata,** *DC. Prod.* iv. 459. An erect shrub, 10–15 feet high, much-branched, with slender terete branchlets. Leaves opposite or ternate, crowded towards the end of the branchlets, oblanceolate-oblong, acute, cuneate at the base, 3–6 in. long, subcoriaceous, glabrescent or slightly pilose below; stipules moderately large, lanceolate, deciduous. Cymes much shorter than leaves, with flowers crowded on slender spreading silky branches. Calyx $\frac{1}{8}$ in. long; teeth obscure. Corolla whitish, $\frac{1}{4}$–$\frac{1}{3}$ in. long, silky on the outside. Ovary 2-celled. Drupe cylindrical, red, juicy. A. dioica, *Bory; DC. loc. cit.*

MAURITIUS, in woods through the island. Also Bourbon. *Bois Lousteau.*

2. **A. frangulacea,** *DC. Prod.* iv. 460. A much-branched shrub, 4–6 feet high, with slender branchlets. Leaves opposite, crowded towards the end of the branchlets, petioled, oblanceolate-oblong, 2–3 in. long, subcoriaceous, glabrous, acute, cuneate at the base; stipules small, lanceolate, deciduous. Peduncles slender, glabrous, $\frac{1}{2}$–1 in. long, the flowers not crowded and branchlets slightly silky. Calyx $\frac{1}{24}$ in. long, silky; teeth 4, deltoid. Corolla nearly glabrous, yellowish, $\frac{1}{8}$–$\frac{1}{6}$ in. long. Ovary 3-celled. Drupe globose, the size of a small pea, containing 3 pyrenes.

MAURITIUS and RODRIGUEZ, in woods of the high hills. Endemic.

11. TIMONIUS, Rumph.

Flowers polygamous. Calyx-tube campanulate; teeth 4, deltoid, erect, persistent. Corolla funnel-shaped, with 4 short thick ligulate obtuse valvate lobes. Stamens 4, sessile at the throat of the corolla. Ovary many-celled; ovules 1 in each cell; style short, in our plant with four branches. Fruit a small globose drupe, with the minute pyrenes radiating in four bundles from the centre.—Shrubs with the flowers mostly in axillary bifid cymes. DISTRIB. Tropical Asia. Species 20.

1. **T. flavescens,** *Baker*. A much-branched shrub, with rather stout glabrous branchlets. Leaves petioled, oblong, subcoriaceous,

bright green, acute, deltoid at the base, 4–5 in. long, at first obscurely silky beneath; stipules lanceolate, deciduous. Flowers solitary or 3, crowded together on short axillary peduncles, with a pair of small persistent deltoid bracts at the tip. Calyx ⅛ in. long, silky, coriaceous. Corolla ¼ in. long, very silky. Drupe glabrous, globose, the size of a pea, containing 20–24 pyrenes in four radiating bundles. Helospora flavescens, *Jack; DC. Prod.* iv. 391. Guettarda? peduncularis, *Wall. Cat.* 6222.

SEYCHELLES, common in all the islands from sea-level up to 3000 feet, *Pervillé*, 152! *Wright! Horne!* Also Malay isles and peninsula.

12. CRATERISPERMUM, Benth.

Calyx-tube oblong; limb campanulate, 5-toothed. Corolla hypocrateriform; tube as long as the calyx; teeth 5, lanceolate, induplicate-valvate. Stamens 5, inserted at the throat of the corolla; filaments very short; anthers oblong, shorter than the corolla-limb. Ovary 2-celled; ovules solitary in the cells, pendulous; style long, clavate, bifid at the top. Fruit a pea-shaped berry, with usually a single seed, with fleshy albumen.—Glabrous erect shrubs, with oblong petioled leaves, the flowers small, in congested peduncled axillary cymes. DISTRIB. Species 5, the others Continental African.

1. **C. microdon,** *Baker.* An erect tree 25–35 feet high, glabrous in all its parts, with slender terete branches. Leaves distinctly petioled, oblong, acute, cuneate at the base, subcoriaceous, green on both sides, 4–5 in. long. Flowers in congested cymes, on very short erecto-patent axillary peduncles; bracts minute, deltoid-cuspidate; pedicels none. Calyx ⅛ in. long; campanulate limb as long as the oblong tube, with 5 small distant deltoid teeth. Corolla-tube as long as the calyx; lobes lanceolate. Fruit white, ovoid, the size of a pea.

SEYCHELLES, in the woods of Mahé and Praslin. Endemic. *Bois doux.*

13. PLECTRONIA, Linn.

Flowers hermaphrodite or polygamous. Calyx-tube globose or turbinate; teeth short, 4–5. Corolla hypocrateriform; lobes 4–5, valvate, about as long as the tube. Ovary 2–3-celled, with a single ovule in each cell; style filiform; stigma capitate or bilobed. Fruit a 2–3-celled drupe with a bony pyrene in each cell.—Shrubs, with small flowers in axillary fascicles. DISTRIB. Tropics of Old World. Species 70.

Umbels peduncled . . . . 1. P. BIBRACTEATA.
Umbels sessile.
  Leaves sessile . . . . 2. P. VIBURNOIDES.
  Leaves petioled.
    Leaves rounded at the base . . . . 3. P. CELASTROIDES.

Leaves deltoid at the base.
Umbels from the axils of the leaves.
Corolla ⅛ in. long . . . . 4. P. ACUMINATA.
Corolla $\frac{1}{12}$ in. long . . . . 5. P. CARINATA.
Umbels from leafless nodes . . . . 6. P. TRILOCULARIS.

1. **P. bibracteata,** *Baker.* A much-branched shrub, with glabrous terete branchlets. Leaves turning black in drying, distinctly petioled, oblong, acute, subcoriaceous, 3–4 in. long, rounded or cuneate at the base; stipules lanceolate acuminate, firm. Flowers in dense short peduncled axillary umbels, subtended by a pair of small linear bracts; pedicels exceeding the calyx. Calyx minute, turbinate, with an obscurely-toothed limb. Corolla ⅛ in. long; lobes 4, oblong-lanceolate, thick; throat densely pilose. Stamens minute, with a short filament. Stigma capitate. Fruit not seen.

MAURITIUS, *Sieber*, ii. 247! SEYCHELLES, in the woods of Mahé, *Pervillé*, 82! *Wright*, 58! *Horne*, 255, 520! We have it also from Johanna Island, from Bojer, under the unpublished name of *Pyrostria comorensis*, and from Madagascar as *Psathura macrophylla*; and it is closely allied to the Mascaren *Pyrostria umbellata*, Bojer, Hort. Maur. 170, which is cultivated in Mauritius. Also Zanzibar. *Bois dur*, (Seych).

2. **P. viburnoides,** *Baker.* A glabrous shrub, with slender terete branches. Leaves sessile, subcoriaceous, shining, subacute, 2–3 in. long, broadly rounded or subcordate at the base; stipules small, deltoid. Flowers in dense sessile axillary fascicles. Calyx broadly funnel-shaped, ⅛ in. long; teeth deltoid, acute, as long as tube. Corolla hypocrateriform, ⅛ in. long; lobes 4, spreading, lanceolate, rather shorter than the tube; throat very hairy. Anthers subsessile at the throat of the corolla, with the connective produced beyond the top of the cells. Stigma slightly lobed. Fruit not seen.

MAURITIUS. Four specimens in the Kew herbarium, two from Mr. Duncan marked "Native," and two from the herbarium of Judge Blackburn. Dr. Balfour gathered a closely allied species in Bourbon.

3. **P. celastroides,** *Baker.* An erect shrub 10–12 feet high, glabrous in all its parts, with slender terete branches. Leaves ovate-oblong, 3–5 in. long, 2–3½ in. broad below the middle, obtuse or subacute, rounded or broad-deltoid at the base, subcoriaceous, with 4–5-jugate very distinct erecto-patent main veins; stipules deciduous; petioles channelled, ¼–⅓ in. long. Flowers 6–10 together in umbels which are sessile in the axils of the leaves, on raised nodules; pedicels slender, flexuose, under ½ in. long. Calyx $\frac{1}{24}$ in. long, campanulate, obscurely toothed. Corolla ⅛ in. long, white, the 5 lanceolate lobes much exceeding the tube. Fruit a 2-3-lobed obovoid naked horny capsule under ½ in. long, with rugose horny valves, depressed at the apex and with a linear keel between the lobes.

SEYCHELLES, common in the damp shady forests of Mahé at an elevation of about 2000 feet, *Horne*, 403! 508! Endemic.

4. **P. acuminata,** *Baker*. An erect shrub, 12–15 feet high, glabrous in all its parts, with spreading terete branches. Leaves oblong-lanceolate, 3–4 in. long, acuminate, cuneate at the base, subcoriaceous, with distant slender erecto-patent main ribs, flat, pale green; petioles $\frac{1}{2}$–$\frac{3}{4}$ in. long; stipules minute, deltoid-cuspidate, caducous. Flowers 2–4 together in umbels, sessile in the axils of the leaves, on slender pedicels $\frac{1}{4}$–$\frac{1}{3}$ in. long. Calyx $\frac{1}{24}$ in. long, campanulate, nearly truncate. Corolla white, $\frac{1}{6}$ in. long, the 5 lanceolate lobes as long as the tube. Fruit obovoid, naked, with 2–3 obtuse lobes, not seen fully mature.

SEYCHELLES, common in the mountain woods of Mahé and Praslin, *Horne*, 504! Endemic.

5. **P. carinata,** Baker. Very near *P. acuminata*, with which it quite agrees in general habit, in the shape and texture of the leaves, in inflorescence and structure, but the leaves dark green, the borders raised from the keel, the petioles and pedicels shorter, and flowers not above half the size.

SEYCHELLES, common in the mountain forests of Mahé and Silhouette, at an elevation of above 1000 feet above sea-level, *Horne*, 503! Endemic.

6. **P? trilocularis,** Baker. A much-branched low shrub, glabrous in all its parts. Leaves oblong, very coriaceous, glossy, 2–4 in. long, $\frac{3}{4}$–$1\frac{1}{2}$ in. broad, varying to linear, 1–$1\frac{1}{2}$ in. by $\frac{1}{8}$–$\frac{1}{4}$ in. broad; petiole $\frac{1}{4}$–$\frac{3}{8}$ in; stipules deltoid-cuspidate, connate, deciduous, the cusp as long as the lamina. Flowers 2–3 in sessile axillary umbels, usually produced from the nodes below the leafy part of the branch; pedicels $\frac{1}{8}$–$\frac{1}{4}$ in.; bracts minute, rigid, lanceolate. Corolla not seen. Fruit globose $\frac{3}{8}$ in. thick and deep, usually three but sometimes two-celled.

RODRIGUEZ, *Dr. Balfour!* Endemic.

* *Vangueria edulis*, Lam.; DC. Prod. iv. 454 (V. Commersoni, *Jacq. Hort. Schoen.* t. 44), widely spread in the tropics of the Old World, is commonly naturalised in Mauritius, Rodriguez, and the Seychelles. It is a glabrous shrub, 10–15 feet high, with very large short-petioled oblong membranous obtuse or acute leaves, flowers in copious peduncled axillary dichotomous cymes with compound branches, short pedicels, a minute obconic calyx with 5 spreading deltoid teeth, funnel-shaped corolla $\frac{1}{4}$ in. long with 5 spreading deltoid teeth, 5 included stamens subsessile at the throat of the corolla, a capitate stigma, and a globose drupe $1\frac{1}{2}$ in. thick with five large bony pyrenes. *Vavangue.*

A second species, which is also subspontaneous in the Seychelles (Horne, 518), is *V. velutina*, Hook. B. M. t. 3014 (V. infausta, *Burch.*), of the Cape and Tropical Africa, which is marked by its pilose branches and large densely pilose flowers.

14. PYROSTRIA, Comm.

Flowers polygamous. Calyx-tube campanulate; teeth 4–5, deltoid. Corolla hypocrateriform; lobes 4–5, thick, lanceolate, valvate, nearly as long as the tube. Stamens 4–5; anthers nearly sessile at the villose throat of the corolla, included. Ovary 4–10-celled; style filiform; stigma capitate, with 2–6 lobes. Fruit a drupe, with 4–10 pyrenes.—Shrubs, with flowers solitary or fascicled in the axils of the leaves, subtended by a pair of small coriaceous persistent bracts. DISTRIB. Confined to the Mascaren Isles. Species 6.

Stigma with many lobes. Bracts larger, lanceolate . . 1. P. MACROPHYLLA.
Stigma with two lobes. Bracts minute, deltoid.
Leaves and flowers distinctly stalked . . . . 2. P. POLYMORPHA.
Leaves and flowers subsessile . . . . 3. P. FASCICULATA.

1. **P. macrophylla,** *A. Rich.; DC. Prod.* iv. 464. A branched shrub, with stems clothed with ferruginous pubescence. Leaves nearly sessile, broad-oblong, obtuse or subacute, broadly rounded or rather cordate at the base, 3–4 in. long, 2–3 in. broad, subcoriaceous. Flowers solitary in the axils of the leaves, subtended by coriaceous lanceolate persistent bracts ¼ in. long. Calyx ⅛ in. long; teeth distinct, deltoid. Corolla three times as long as the calyx; lobes lanceolate. Stigma capitate, with several minute distinct lobes. Cells of ovary 8–10. Fruit not seen. P. cordifolia and orbicularis, *A. Rich.; DC. loc. cit.*

MAURITIUS, in the forests of Flacq, Nouvelle Découverte, etc. Also Bourbon.

2. **P. polymorpha,** *A. Rich.; DC. Prod.* iv. 464. A much-branched glabrous shrub, 8–12 feet high, with slender angular branchlets. Leaves distinctly petioled, obovate or oblong, obtuse, rounded at the base, 1½–2 in. long, subcoriaceous; stipules small, deltoid. Flowers solitary or in pairs, on short distinct axillary peduncles, subtended by a pair of very minute deltoid bracts. Calyx $\frac{1}{12}$ in. long; teeth minute, deltoid. Corolla ⅜ in. long, whitish; lobes 4, lanceolate nearly as long as the cylindrical tube. Ovary 4-celled; stigma capitate, two-lobed. Fruit turbinate, with 8 ribs and 4 pyrenes.

MAURITIUS, on the Pouce and Montagne Longue. Endemic.

3. **P. fasciculata,** *Bojer in Herb. Kew.* A much-branched shrub, with ultimate branchlets clothed with a little ferruginous pubescence. Leaves nearly sessile, obovate-oblong, rather oblique at the base, obtuse, 2–3 in. long, subcoriaceous, shining. Flowers solitary or several subsessile in the axils of the leaves, subtended by a pair of minute coriaceous persistent deltoid bracts. Calyx campanulate, $\frac{1}{12}$ in. long; teeth 4, deltoid. Corolla ¼ in. long; lobes lanceolate, nearly as long as the funnel-shaped tube. Stigma distinctly two-lobed. Mature drupe 1½ in. long, narrowed to both ends, with 10 ribs and 5 woody pyrenes.

MAURITIUS, in the forests of the centre of the island and the Savanne range. This may be *P. oleoides*, Bojer, Hort. Maur. 170, but differs from the Bourbon plant named by Lamarck, figd. Ill. t. 68, by its broader oblique leaves and want of peduncle or pedicel. A plant called *Pyrostria obliqua*, by Bojer, is simply a form with solitary flowers and leaves rather more oblique than usual. Of *P. lancifolia*, Bojer, MSS., which has sessile flowers and lanceolate leaves 3–4 inches long, narrowed to both ends, we have only a flowerless scrap.

15. SCYPHOCHLAMYS, Balf. fil.

Calyx with a campanulate coriaceous obscurely 4–5-toothed limb above the ovary. Corolla funnel-shaped, with a campanulate tube, and 4–5 thick lanceolate triquetrous segments, valvate in æstivation. Anthers 4–5, sessile at the villose throat of the corolla tube, lanceolate, acute. Ovary 4–5-celled; ovules one in a cell; style simple, cylindrical. Fruit large, oblong, fleshy, not seen mature. Flowers in dense peduncled axillary heads enclosed in a persistent cup-shaped coriaceous involucre. Endemic. The only species.

1. **S. revoluta,** *Balf. fil.* A much-branched glabrous shrub, with moderately stout terete branchlets. Leaves shortly petioled, glossy, coriaceous, normally broad-oblong, 3–4 in. long, 1½–3 in. broad, rounded at both ends, but varying to lanceolate or linear, narrowed to both ends, 3–4 in. long, ¼–½ in. broad; stipules coriaceous, deltoid, persistent, forming a complete ring. Clusters of flowers on short erecto-patent peduncles from the axils of the leaves, 6–10 flowers crowded in a cup-shaped persistent truncate coriaceous involucre ½ in. broad and long; pedicels very short and stout. Calyx campanulate, ⅓ in. long. Corolla-tube half as long again as the calyx; segments ⅛ in. long, spreading horizontally when expanded. Anthers ⅙ in. long, reaching halfway up the limb, and conniving over the stigma. Fruits in the specimen seen only one ripening in an involucre, oblong, an inch long, crowded by the persistent coriaceous calyx.

RODRIGUEZ, in the higher parts of the island, along with *Randia heterophylla*, *Dr. Balfour!*

16. RUTIDEA, DC.

Calyx-tube campanulate; teeth 5, minute, obtuse. Corolla funnel-shaped, with a short tube and 5 lingulate lobes, contorted and imbricated in bud. Stamens 5, inserted at the throat of the tube; filaments very short. Ovary 2-celled; ovules solitary in the cells; style filiform, with two branches. Fruit a small pea-like berry with a single seed. —Erect or climbing shrubs, pilose or glabrous, with small flowers in dense terminal corymbs. DISTRIB. Africa. Species about 10.

1. **R. coriacea,** *Baker.* An erect shrub, 20–30 feet high, with short stout erect branchlets. Leaves distinctly petioled, glabrous, shining, subcoriaceous, spotted and ribbed with red when young, broad-oblong, subacute, deltoid at the base, 4–6 in. long; stipules large, connate, lanceolate. Flowers in dense sessile or short-peduncled terminal corymbs 2–3 in. broad, with puberulent branches and short erect pedicels. Calyx campanulate, $\frac{1}{14}$ in. long with 5 erect obtuse teeth.

Corolla $\frac{1}{4}$–$\frac{1}{3}$ in. long; lobes as long as the tubes. Berry the size of a small pea. Pavetta coriacea and diversifolia, *Bojer, Hort. Maur.* 172 (names only.)

MAURITIUS, in the woods of Moka, Pieter Both, and Nouvelle Découverte. Also Bourbon.

17. MYONIMA, Comm.

Flowers polygamous. Calyx campanulate, with an obscurely-toothed limb. Corolla hypocrateriform; tube short, cylindrical; lobes 4, obtuse, spreading, twisted in bud. Ovary 4–6-celled, with a single ovule in a cell; style filiform; stigma clavate, forked. Fruit indehiscent, dry or fleshy, containing 2–6 pyrenes.—Glabrous shrubs with flowers in terminal corymbs. The only species.

Flowers very many in a dense corymb . . . . . . 1. M. MULTIFLORA.
Flowers few in a very lax corymb.
  Fruit the size of a pea . . . . 2. M. MYRTIFOLIA.
  Fruit the size of a hazel nut . . . . 3. M. OBOVATA.

1. **M. multiflora,** *A. Rich. DC.; Prod.* iv. 463. An erect glabrous shrub, 4–8 feet high, with stout terete branchlets. Leaves quite sessile, coriaceous, shining, venose, oblong, obtuse, 4–6 in. long, broadly rounded or cordate at the base; stipules short, broad, obtuse. Flowers in dense terminal corymbs; pedicels $\frac{1}{8}$–$\frac{1}{4}$ in., pilose. Calyx turbinate, $\frac{1}{8}$ in. long. Corolla tube very short; lobes obovate, $\frac{1}{6}$ in. long, white inside, red without. Fruit a glabrous drupe, as large as a pea, with 2–4 pyrenes. *Hook. Bot. Misc. t.* 87. M. latifolia, *Bojer, Hort. Maur.* 169. Ixora parviflora, *Lam. Ill. t.* 66. I. mauritiana, *Bojer olim.*

MAURITIUS, in the woods of the Pouce and Savanne ranges, etc. Endemic.

2. **M. myrtifolia,** *Lam.; DC. Prod.* iv. 463. A much-branched shrub, with slender glabrous branchlets. Leaves nearly sessile, oblong or oblanceolate-oblong, subacute, or subobtuse, cuneate in the lower half, 1–1$\frac{1}{2}$ in. long, coriaceous, shining; stipules minute, deltoid, deciduous. Flowers 5–10, in lax terminal corymbs, with minute bracts; pedicels ascending, $\frac{1}{4}$–$\frac{1}{2}$ in. long. Calyx obconic, $\frac{1}{12}$ in. long. Corolla white, $\frac{1}{3}$ in. across when expanded; lobes obtuse, oblanceolate. Fruit fleshy, the size of a small pea; pyrenes 4–5. M. lanceolata, *Willd.*

MAURITIUS, in the woods of the Pouce range, etc. Also Bourbon. *M. heterophylla*, Bojer, Hort. Maur. 169, is a form with some of the leaves linear and 1-nerved.

3. **M. obovata,** *Lam.; DC. Prod.* iv. 463. A much-branched glabrous shrub. Leaves nearly sessile, obovate, obtuse, shining, venose, coriaceous, 1–2 in. long, cuneate in the lower half; stipules minute, deltoid, deciduous. Flowers few, in lax terminal corymbs with minute bracts; pedicels slender, $\frac{1}{2}$–1 in. long. Calyx campanulate, $\frac{1}{12}$ in. long, with four obscure teeth. Corolla $\frac{1}{4}$–$\frac{1}{3}$ in. long; lobes oblong; expanded limb $\frac{1}{2}$ in. across. Fruit indehiscent, depresso-globose, $\frac{1}{2}$ in. thick; pyrenes 4.

MAURITIUS, in the gorges of the Rivière Noire and at Tamarin. Also Bourbon. *Bois de Rat.*

18. IXORA, Linn.

Calyx-tube campanulate; teeth 4–5, minute, persistent. Corolla hypocrateriform, with a cylindrical tube and 4–5 spreading lobes, contorted and imbricated in bud. Stamens 4–5, inserted in the tube; filaments none or very short. Ovary 2-celled; style filiform, with two branches. Fruit small, globose, coriaceous, indehiscent, the two seeds in bony pyrenes.—Trees or shrubs, with large opposite entire leaves and often showy abundant flowers in terminal corymbs. DISTRIB. Round the world in the tropics, principally in the Old World. Species 100.

Flowers small, naked, tetramerous . . . . 1. I. PUDICA.
Flowers large, silky, pentamerous . . . . 2. I. SERICEA.

1. **I. pudica**, *Baker*. An erect shrub, 8–12 feet high, glabrous in all its parts, with rather stout terete branches. Leaves short-petioled, oblong, subcoriaceous, acute, cuneate at the base, 5–6 in. long, 2–3 in. broad, with many wide-spreading distinct main veins; stipules deltoid-cuspidate, caducous. Flowers in crowded terminal corymbs 2–3 in. broad, with straight naked branches; pedicels erect, $\frac{1}{24}$–$\frac{1}{4}$ in. long. Calyx naked, $\frac{1}{24}$ in. with 4 minute deltoid teeth. Corolla $\frac{1}{4}$ in. long, white, fragrant; the lanceolate reflexing lobes as long as the tube. Anthers strap-shaped, $\frac{1}{24}$ in. long, with a short filament. Drupe the size of a pea, naked, with two large pyrenes, channelled down the face and rounded on the back as in *Coffea*.

SEYCHELLES; in the woods of Mahé, at about 600 feet above sea-level. *Horne*, 292! 514! *Wright*, 97! Leaf, general habit, inflorescence and fruit of the Malayan *I. coriacea*, R. Br., from which it differs in leaf-veining, and by its smaller flowers. Endemic.

2. **I. sericea**, *Baker*. A small tree, glabrous beyond the inflorescence, with wide-spreading branches. Leaves short-petioled, oblong, deltoid at both ends, 4–6 in. long, 2–2$\frac{1}{2}$ in. broad at the middle, very glossy above, very rigid in texture, and minutely beautifully reticulato-venose on both sides; stipules deltoid, caducous. Flowers in terminal corymbs $\frac{1}{2}$ foot or more broad, with flattened almost winged stout ascending peduncles; pedicels $\frac{1}{12}$–$\frac{1}{8}$ in. long, silky upwards. Calyx $\frac{1}{8}$ in. long, with a campanulate grey-silky tube, and 5 small erect deltoid teeth. Corolla-tube 1$\frac{1}{2}$–1$\frac{3}{4}$ in. long, densely grey-silky on the outside; lobes 5, lanceolate, acute, silky on the back, cream-coloured on the face, spotted with black at the base. Anthers and emarginate stigma just exserted from the tube. Drupe small, globose, silky, with 2 pyrenes.

SEYCHELLES, in Mahé and Silhouette, only on the mountains above 1800 feet, associated always with *Nepenthes*, *Horne*, 510! Endemic.

19. COFFEA, Linn.

Flowers hermaphrodite. Calyx-tube hemispherical; teeth 5, deltoid, minute, persistent. Corolla funnel-shaped; tube long or short; lobes 5, oblanceolate-oblong, obtuse, twisted. Stamens 5, nearly sessile at the throat of the corolla; anthers long and narrow. Ovary 2-celled; ovules solitary in the cells; style deeply forked. Drupe oblong, containing two large pyrenes, with flattened channelled faces.—Glabrous erect shrubs, with white flowers in axillary fascicles. DISTRIB. Tropics of the Old World. Species 20.

Leaves sessile, or scarcely petioled, cuneate in the lower third. Corolla-tube short.
- Leaves very coriaceous, 5–6 in. long . . . . 1. C. MACROCARPA.
- Leaves subcoriaceous, 2-3 in. long . . . . 2. C. MAURITIANA.

Leaves distinctly petioled, not cuneate at the base.
- Corolla tube long . . . . * C. ARABICA.

1. **C. macrocarpa,** *A. Rich.; Bojer, Hort. Maur.* 173. A shrub, 5–6 feet high, with stout nodulose branches, glabrous in all its parts. Leaves sessile, oblong-spathulate, acute, 5–6 in. long, very coriaceous and shining; stipules deltoid, subpersistent. Flowers 1–3, sessile in the axils of the leaves, very fragrant. Calyx $\frac{1}{8}$ in. long, subtended by a pair of deltoid coriaceous persistent entire bracteoles; teeth obscure. Corolla $\frac{1}{2}$ in. long; lobes oblong, exceeding the tube. Anthers $\frac{1}{4}$–$\frac{1}{3}$ in. long. Drupe an inch long, oblong, narrowed to both ends. C. grandifolia, *Bojer, MSS.*

MAURITIUS, in woods of the Pouce and Savanne ranges. Endemic.

2. **C. mauritiana,** *Lam.; DC. Prod.* iv. 498. A much-branched shrub, glabrous in all its parts, with slender terete branches. Leaves with a very short flattened petiole, oblong, shining, subcoriaceous, subobtuse, 2–3 in. long, cuneate at the base; stipules minute, deltoid. Flowers 1–4 together, sessile in the axils of the leaves. Calyx $\frac{1}{12}$ in. long, subtended by a pair of small deltoid fimbriated bracteoles; teeth 5, distinct, deltoid. Corolla white, $\frac{1}{4}$ in. long; tube short. Anthers $\frac{1}{6}$ in. long. Drupe oblong, narrowed to the base.

MAURITIUS, in woods of the Pouce, rare. Also Bourbon.

* *C. arabica*, Linn., the cultivated Coffee, which is sometimes found where it has been cultivated, may be known by its thinner acuminate oblong distinctly petioled leaves and corolla nearly an inch long, with a cylindrical tube as long as the lobes. *Cafeyer.*

20. MORINDA, Linn.

Flowers hermaphrodite, fused by the union of the calyces into a globose head. Calyx-tube campanulate; limb very short, truncate

Corolla funnel-shaped, with a long tube and 5 spreading valvate lobes. Stamens 5, inserted at the throat of the corolla; filaments very short. Ovary 2–4-celled; ovules solitary in the cells; style with two branches. Fruits fleshy, combined into a round head, each containing 2–4 pyrenes. —Shrubs or low trees, with heads solitary, opposite or umbellate. DISTRIB. Round the world in the tropics. Species 40.

Glabrous, with short corolla-lobes . . . . 1. M. CITRIFOLIA.
Pubescent, with corolla-lobes half as long as the tube . . . 2. M. PUBESCENS.

1. **M. citrifolia,** *Linn.; DC. Prod.* iv. 446. A low tree, glabrous in all its parts, with stout quadrangular branchlets. Leaves large, petioled, oblong, acute, glabrous, membranous; stipules deltoid, persistent. Heads ½ in. thick before expansion, consisting of 20–30 flowers, solitary or opposite, axillary or terminal, on short ascending peduncles. Corolla ¾ in. long, whitish; lobes short, lanceolate. Drupes white.

SEYCHELLES, in Mahé and other islands, common chiefly on the shore, *Bojer, Horne!* Through the tropics of the Old World. *Mûrier de Java.*

2. **M. pubescens,** *Smith; DC. Prod.* iv. 447. A shrub with slender flexuose tomentose branchlets. Leaves short-petioled, oblanceolate-oblong, acute, cuneately narrowed in the lower half, membranous, thinly pilose beneath, 3–4 in. long, 1–1½ in. broad above the middle; stipules small, deltoid. Heads ¼ in. thick before expansion, solitary, on short ascending peduncles, one terminal and one each from the axil of many of the leaves. Corolla ¾ in. long; lobes lanceolate, half as long as the broadly funnel-shaped tube. Anthers reaching halfway up the limb.

MAURITIUS, in the forests of Grandport, *Bojer.* Described from the type specimen in Smith's Herbarium, sent by Thouin to the younger Linnæus.

21. CHASALIA, Comm.

Calyx-tube campanulate; teeth 5, minute or nearly obsolete. Corolla hypocrateriform, with a long slender tube and 5 spreading lanceolate or deltoid lobes. Stamens 5; anthers nearly sessile at the throat of the corolla. Ovary 2-celled; ovules solitary in the cells; style filiform, forked. Fruit a small fleshy oblong drupe, containing two bony pyrenes.—Shrubs, with leaves sometimes ternate, the flowers in terminal heads or corymbose panicles. DISTRIB. Tropics of Old World. Species about 10. Confused by Bojer and others with *Gærtnera,* which it exactly resembles, except that the ovary is inferior.

Flowers in a single globose terminal head . . . . . . 1. C. CAPITATA.
Flowers in a terminal corymbose panicle, not pedicellate.
  Stipules small. Petiole 1–1½ in. long . . . . 2. C. BORYANA.
  Stipules as long as the petioles.
    Calyx under $\frac{1}{12}$ in. long, nearly truncate at the mouth 3. C. GRANDIFOLIA.
    Calyx ⅛ in. long, with distinct deltoid cuspidate teeth. 4. C. DIVARICATA.
Flowers in a lax terminal corymbose panicle and pedicellate 5. C. MOONII.

1. **C. capitata,** *DC. Prod.* iv. 531. A glabrous shrub, with rather stout terete branches. Leaves short-petioled, obovate-oblong, 3–4 in. long, minutely cuspidate, subcoriaceous, cuneately narrowed from the middle to the base, turning black in drying; stipules membranous, deltoid, $\frac{1}{3}$ in. long. Flowers 20–30 in a dense globose sessile terminal head; pedicels none. Calyx campanulate, $\frac{1}{8}$ in. long; teeth lanceolate, $\frac{1}{3}$–$\frac{1}{2}$ as long as the tube. Corolla nearly an inch long; lanceolate lobes $\frac{1}{4}$–$\frac{1}{5}$ as long as the slender nearly cylindrical tube. Drupe oblong, $\frac{1}{2}$ in. long, crowned by a deep cup.

MAURITIUS, in shaded woods of the Pouce range, etc. *Sieber*, ii. 66! etc. Endemic. This is not the plant figured by Bojer, Nouv. Mem. Soc. Helv. viii. t. 2, as *Gærtnera capitata*, which has a superior ovary, but it appears to be included by him under that name in Hort. Maur. 216.

2. **C. Boryana,** *DC. Prod.* iv. 532. A much-branched glabrous shrub, 3–4 feet high, with rather stout angular branchlets. Leaves obovate-oblong, often ternate, 3–4 in. long, 1$\frac{1}{2}$–2 in. broad at the middle, subacute with a deltoid base; stipules deltoid, subpersistent, $\frac{1}{4}$–$\frac{1}{3}$ in. long; petiole slender, 1–1$\frac{1}{2}$ in. long. Flowers in an ample terminal corymbose panicle, 3–6 in. broad, usually fascicled 3–6 together at the end of the branchlets. Calyx $\frac{1}{24}$ in. long; teeth minute, deltoid. Corolla $\frac{1}{2}$ in. long, whitish; lobes lanceolate-deltoid, $\frac{1}{3}$–$\frac{1}{4}$ as long as the tube. Drupe oblong, $\frac{1}{4}$ in. long, purple, not crowned by a cup. C. borbonica, *A. Rich.; Bojer, Hort. Maur.* 173. Gærtnera cymiflora, *Bojer, Hort. Maur.* 218.

MAURITIUS, in woods through the island, frequent. *Sieber*, ii. 2–3, etc. Endemic. What we have from M. Bouton as *Gærtnera lanceolata*, DC. Prod. 933, is in part this and in part *C. divaricata*.

3. **C. grandifolia,** *DC. Prod.* iv. 532. A low glabrous shrub, with stout terete branches. Leaves 2–3-nate, obovate-oblong, acute, subcoriaceous, 4–6 in. long, cuneately narrowed in the lower half; stipules deltoid, $\frac{3}{8}$–$\frac{1}{2}$ in. long, persistent; petiole $\frac{1}{4}$–$\frac{1}{2}$ in. long. Flowers in an ample corymbose terminal panicle, 3–4 in. broad, sessile in clusters of 3–6 at the end of the branchlets. Calyx under $\frac{1}{12}$ in. long, campanulate, the teeth very obscure. Corolla $\frac{3}{4}$ in. long, the deltoid spreading lobes $\frac{1}{5}$–$\frac{1}{3}$ the length of the tube. Drupe oblong, whitish or black, $\frac{1}{2}$ in. long, not crowned with a cup. Gærtnera cærulea, *Bojer, Hort. Maur.* 217. Psychotria grandifolia, *Sieber.*

MAURITIUS, frequent in the mountain woods. *Sieber*, ii. 55! etc. Endemic.

4. **C. divaricata,** *DC. Prod.* iv. 532. A low erect glabrous shrub, with stout terete branches. Leaves obovate-oblong, 4–6 in. long, sometimes ternate, acute, cuneately narrowed in the lower half; stipules $\frac{1}{2}$–$\frac{1}{4}$ in. long, deltoid, persistent; petiole $\frac{1}{2}$–1 in. long. Flowers in a corymbose terminal panicle, sessile in clusters of 2–6 at the end of the branchlets. Calyx $\frac{1}{8}$ in. deep, campanulate; teeth deltoid-cuspidate. Developed corolla $\frac{3}{4}$ in. long; lobes lanceolate, $\frac{1}{3}$ as long as the tube. Drupe ovoid-oblong, $\frac{1}{2}$ in. long, rather 4-angular, crowned with a dis-

tinct cup. C. stipulacea, *DC. loc. cit.* C. coffeoides, *DC. loc. cit.?* Gærtnera incarnata, *Bojer, Hort. Maur.* 217.

MAURITIUS, in woods about Moka, etc. *Sieber*, ii. 271! etc. Endemic.

5. **C. Mooniæ,** *Baker*. A glabrous shrub, with terete branchlets. Leaves oblong, subcoriaceous, 3–6 in. long, acute, cuneate at the base, subcoriaceous, with 7–8 distinct erecto-patent pairs of main veins; petiole $\frac{1}{2}$–1 in. long; stipules $\frac{1}{4}$ in. long, truncate, caducous. Corymb very lax, 3–6 in. broad, with divaricate branches and branchlets, all the flowers pedicelled; pedicels sometimes $\frac{1}{2}$ in. or more long. Calyx campanulate, $\frac{1}{6}$ in. long, truncate or obscurely 5-toothed. Corolla pure white; tube $\frac{1}{2}$–$\frac{2}{3}$ in. long; lobes $\frac{1}{4}$–$\frac{1}{3}$ in. long, lanceolate, acute.

MAURITIUS, in mountain woods, *Bouton! Blackburn!* and a beautiful coloured drawing by Madame Moon in a collection of sketches kindly sent by Mr. Caldwell. Endemic.

22. PSYCHOTRIA, Linn.

Calyx-tube campanulate; teeth 5, deltoid. Corolla small, funnel-shaped; lobes 5, lanceolate, valvate, as long as the tube. Stamens 5, inserted at the throat of the corolla, included; filaments very short. Ovary 2-, rarely 3-celled; ovules solitary in the cells; style filiform, with two branches. Fruit a small globose drupe with 2 or rarely 3 pyrenes.—Shrubs, with opposite leaves, the flowers small, either terminal, in dense panicles, or axillary. DISTRIB. The largest genus of the order, cosmopolitan in the tropics, including some 500 species.

Flowers in dense terminal corymbose panicles.
  Lobes of the corolla as long as the tube . . . . 1. P. PERVILLEI.
  Lobes of the corolla not half as long as the tube . . . 2. P. AFFINIS.
Flowers in axillary umbels . . . . 3. P. LANCEOLATA.
Flowers 2–3 in congested axillary clusters . . . . 4. P. WRIGHTII.
Flowers solitary in the axils of the leaves . . . . 5. P. FERRUGINEA.

1. **P. Pervillei,** *Baker*. A glabrous shrub, with moderately stout terete branches. Leaves short-petioled, oblanceolate-oblong, acute, subcoriaceous, 3–4 in. long, 1–1$\frac{1}{2}$ in. broad at the middle, cuneate at the base; stipules small, deltoid, soon withering. Flowers in dense corymbose terminal panicles 2–3 in. broad, shorter than the leaves; pedicels very short. Calyx broadly campanulate, $\frac{1}{24}$ in. deep; teeth minute, deltoid. Corolla under $\frac{1}{4}$ in. long; throat densely pilose; lobes lanceolate, spreading, as long as the tube. Drupe globose, $\frac{1}{8}$ in. thick, crowned by a nearly truncate rim; pyrenes 2–3.

SEYCHELLES, in the woods of Mahé and Praslin. *Pervillé*, 154! *Horne*, 267! 269! Very near *P. obtusifolia*, Lam. Ill. tab. 161, fig. 4, of Madagascar. Endemic.

2. **P. affinis,** *Baker*. Very near the last, with which it quite agrees in general habit and also very near the Mascaren *P. obtusifolia*, Lam. Ill. tab. 161, fig. 4. From *P. Pervillei* it differs by its oblong leaves, 3–4 in. long by 2 in. broad, shorter petioles, more congested corymbs,

but principally by its corolla, the funnel-shaped tube of which is ¼ in. long, with 5 lanceolate spreading lobes a third as long as the tube. From *P. obtusifolia* it differs by its pointed leaves and flowers twice as large.

SEYCHELLES, in the damp shady forests of Mahé and Silhouette, *Horne*, 298! 507! A shrub 6–8 feet high, with white flowers.

3. **P. lanceolata,** *Balf. fil.* A much-branched shrub, with glabrous stems and leaves. Internodes very short. Leaves lanceolate, subcoriaceous, 3–4 in. long, ¾–1 in. broad at the middle, acute, narrowed very gradually into a short petiole; stipules minute, deltoid. Umbels from the axils of the upper leaves on ½–1 in. peduncles, ebracteate; pedicels very short. Calyx broadly campanulate, under $\frac{1}{12}$ in. broad, not so deep, obscurely 5-toothed. Corolla ⅛ in. long; lobes lanceolate, longer than the tube; throat densely pilose. Fruit not seen.

RODRIGUEZ, *Dr. Balfour!* Endemic.

4. **P. Wrightii,** *Baker.* A glabrous shrub, with moderately stout terete branches swollen at the nodes. Leaves subsessile, oblong, obtuse, very coriaceous, 5–6 in. long, cuneate at the base; stipules soon falling. Flowers 2–3 together in the axils of the leaves on a very short stout terete common peduncle; pedicel as long as the calyx, with deltoid bracts at the base. Calyx ⅛ in. long; limb very narrow, broadly campanulate, with 4 obscure cusps. Corolla ½ in. long; lobes lanceolate, rather shorter than the narrowly funnel-shaped tube. Ovary 2-celled. Fruit not seen.

SEYCHELLES, *Wright*, 45! Endemic.

5. **P. ferruginea,** *Baker.* A much-branched shrub, with slender terete branches, clothed with short brown pubescence. Leaves lanceolate, nearly sessile, membranous, narrowed gradually from the middle to both ends, 2–3 in. long, glabrous above, ciliated on the ribs, especially the midrib below; stipules membranous, brown, deltoid, persistent, each with 1–3 awns. Flowers solitary, nearly sessile in the axils of the leaves. Corolla not seen. Drupe the size of a small pea, crowned by the minute lanceolate ciliated calyx-teeth. Pyrenes two.

SEYCHELLES, in woods of Mahé. *Horne*, 253! Endemic.

I have no means of identifying *P. psathuroides*, DC. Prod. iv. 518, described from imperfect specimens gathered in Mauritius by Bory de Saint Vincent.

23. PSATHURA, Comm.

Calyx-tube broadly funnel-shaped; teeth 5, small, deltoid, persistent. Corolla funnel-shaped, pilose at the throat; lobes 5, lanceolate, as long as the tube; anthers 5, small, oblong, nearly sessile at the throat of the corolla-tube. Ovary 5–6-celled; style filiform, with 5–6 short lobes at the tip. Fruit a small globose drupe, with 4–6 dry triquetrous pyrenes.—Shrubs, with small whitish flowers in axillary cymes or terminal panicles. DISTRIB. Zanguebar, Mascaren Isles and Seychelles. Species 5–6.

Flowers in an ample terminal panicle . . . . 1. P. SECHELLARUM.
Flowers many, in peduncled axillary cymes . . . . . 2. P. BORBONICA.
Flowers 2–3 together in the axils of the leaves.
Calyx-teeth small, deltoid . . . . 3. P. TERNIFLORA.
Calyx-teeth large, leafy, lanceolate . . . . 4. P. MYRTIFOLIA.

1. **P. sechellarum,** *Baker.* A glabrous shrub, with stout sulcate angular branches. Leaves short-petioled, obovate-oblong, obtuse, cuneate at the base, 4–6 in. long, very coriaceous, shining, finely venulose below; stipules small, deltoid, persistent. Flowers in a lax deltoid terminal panicle, as long as the leaves, with spreading central deflexed lower branches; branches corymbose; bracts small, deltoid, persistent. Calyx $\frac{1}{12}$ in. long, broadly campanulate; teeth deltoid. Corolla under $\frac{1}{4}$ in. long; teeth as long as the tube. Fruit a drupe, the size of a small pea, crowned by the persistent calyx-teeth.

SEYCHELLES, common in woods of Mahé, *Horne* 264, 535! *Wright* 120! Endemic.

2. **P. borbonica,** *Gmel.; DC. Prod.* iv. 463. A much-branched glabrous shrub, 4–5 feet high, with fragile slender branches, swollen at the nodes. Leaves short-petioled, oblong, acute, subcoriaceous, $1\frac{1}{2}$–2 in. long, deep green, very smooth, cuneate at the base; stipules small, lanceolate, deciduous. Flowers 6–12, in short-peduncled axillary cymes. Calyx $\frac{1}{24}$ in. long, campanulate; teeth minute, deltoid. Corolla broadly funnel-shaped, whitish, $\frac{1}{12}$ in. long, with teeth exceeding the tube. Fruit a globose whitish drupe, smaller than a pea, crowned by the minute persistent calyx-teeth. P. corymbosa, *Gærtn. Fruct. t.* 194, *fig.* 4.

MAURITIUS, in forests through the island. Also Bourbon. Var. *grandiflora*, Baker, is a form with flowers as long as those of *P. terniflora*. *Bois Cassant.*

3. **P. terniflora,** *A Rich.; DC. Prod.* iv. 462. A much-branched shrub 5–6 feet high, just like *P. borbonica* in habit and leaf. Flowers 1-3, from the axils of the leaves, without any common peduncle; pedicels straight, ascending, $\frac{1}{8}$–$\frac{1}{4}$ in. long. Calyx $\frac{1}{8}$–$\frac{1}{6}$ in. long, broadly funnel-shaped; teeth deltoid. Corolla white, fragrant, $\frac{1}{4}$ in. long; lobes lanceolate, as long as the tube. Drupe like that of *P. borbonica.*

MAURITIUS, in woods of Moka, etc. Endemic.

4. **P. myrtifolia,** *A. Rich.; DC. Prod.* iv. 463. A much-branched glabrous low shrub, with slender fragile branches with swollen nodes. Leaves short-petioled, oblong, obtuse, smooth, subcoriaceous, cuneate at the base, 1–$1\frac{1}{2}$ in. long; stipules minute, deltoid. Flowers 2–3, on short pedicels from a very short common peduncle in the axil of the leaves. Calyx $\frac{1}{6}$ in. long, the lanceolate leafy teeth much exceeding the tube. Corolla funnel-shaped, $\frac{1}{4}$ in. long; teeth as long as the

tube. Drupe globose, the size of a small pea, crowned by the persistent leafy lobes, which become ¼ in. long.

MAURITIUS, in dense woods of Curepipe, Grand Bassin, etc. Endemic. *Bois Cassant à petites feuilles.*

* *Serissa fœtida*, Comm.; DC. Prod. iv. 575, widely-cultivated in gardens, probably a native of Tropical Asia, is established in Mauritius in plains at Moka. It is an erect shrub, with very abundant slender glabrous or downy branches, small nearly sessile oblong acute coriaceous small leaves often fascicled at the end of short branchlets, prominently bristly persistent stipules, sessile usually solitary flowers, a funnel-shaped calyx with 4–6 lanceolate teeth, a funnel-shaped whitish corolla ½ in. long with 4–6 oblong cuspidate lobes, included stamens inserted low down in the tube, and a 2-celled ovary with solitary basal ovules. *Niclande.*

24. PÆDERIA, Linn.

Calyx minute, with a campanulate tube and 5 deltoid teeth. Corolla funnel-shaped, dilated from the base, hairy within, glandular on the outside, with 5 obtuse spreading minute crisped lobes. Stamens 5; anthers nearly sessile at the hairy throat of the corolla. Ovary free at the top, 2-celled; ovules solitary in the cells; style with two deep filiform forks. Fruit small, globose, with a dry fragile epicarp, a pulpy yellow mesocarp and a pair of bony 1-seeded pyrenes.—Climbing shrubs, with copious small flowers in axillary cymes or panicles. DISTRIB. Round the world in the tropics. Species 5–6.

1. **P. fœtida,** *L. var. sessiliflora* (*Poir.; DC. Prod.* iv. 474, as a species). A copiously-branched shrubby climber, with slender glabrous branches. Leaves distinctly petioled, fœtid when bruised, varying from lanceolate to cordate-ovate, membranous, glabrous, acute, 2–4 in. long; stipules minute, deltoid. Flowers in axillary cymes or panicles with cymose branches, distant, secund in our plant, sessile on the scorpioid forks. Calyx under $\frac{1}{12}$ in. long. Corolla $\frac{1}{3}$–$\frac{1}{2}$ in. long, white-mealy externally, the purple throat closed with long white glandular hairs, the crisped lobes yellowish. Berry brown, the size of a small pea.

MAURITIUS, in forests through the island, used for lotions for horses. Common through Tropical Asia, not African. *Liane K.K.*

25. SPERMACOCE, Linn.

Calyx small, with a campanulate tube and 2–4 rarely 5 unequal persistent teeth. Corolla small, funnel-shaped; lobes 4, spreading, valvate. Stamens 4; anthers nearly sessile at the throat of the corolla. Ovary 2-celled; ovules solitary in the cells; style forked or simple. Fruit a septicidal capsule, the dissepiment entire, or dividing into two.

—Herbs, with sheathing fringed stipules and minute flowers, which, in our species are clustered in axillary whorls. DISTRIB. Abundant tropical weeds, mostly American. Species 100–150.

Section 1, SPERMACOCE PROPER. Dissepiment of the capsule not divided between the two cocci when they separate.

The only species . . . . 1. S. HISPIDA.

Section 2, BORRERIA. Dissepiment of capsule split into two membranes when it opens, one to each coccus.

Fruit pilose all over; leaves linear or lanceolate . . . . 2. S. STRICTA.
Fruit not pilose; leaves obovate or oblong . . . . . . 3. S OCYMOIDES.

1. **S. hispida,** *Linn.; DC. Prod.* iv. 555. A branched annual, a foot or more high, with rather stout more or less hairy quadrangular branches. Leaves narrowed to the base, stout, and more or less hairy, varying in shape from obtuse obovate-spathulate to acute lanceolate; stipules $\frac{1}{8}$–$\frac{1}{6}$ in. long, fringed with bristles quite as long as the blade. Flowers 2–6, crowded in the axils of each of the leaves. Capsule oblong, $\frac{1}{8}$ in. long, pilose; teeth lanceolate, persistent, as long as the capsule. Corolla $\frac{1}{8}$ in. long; lobes as long as the tube. *Burm. Zeyl. t.* 20, *fig.* 3. S. articularis, *Linn. fil.* S. scabra, *Willd.*

MAURITIUS, frequent in waste grounds through the island. Spread through the tropics of the Old World. Also Cape.

2. **S. stricta,** *Linn. fil.; DC. Prod.* iv. 554. Stems a foot or more high, simple or branched, erect, angular, glabrous. Leaves sessile, distant, linear, or lanceolate, firm, 1–3 in. long, acute, narrowed to the base, scabrous on the ribs below; stipules $\frac{1}{8}$ in. long, ciliated by bristles as long as the blade. Flowers in very dense axillary clusters. Capsule subglobose, $\frac{1}{24}$ in. deep, pilose; teeth 4, deltoid, aristate, shorter than the fruit. Corolla purplish, funnel-shaped, $\frac{1}{8}$ in. long; lobes short. S. flagelliformis, *Poir.; DC. Prod. loc. cit.* S. muriculata, *DC. Prod. loc. cit.* Borreria lasiocarpa, *Wt. and Arn.* B. hebecarpa, *Hochst.*

MAURITIUS, frequent in waste ground. Everywhere in the tropics of the Old World. Allied to the common American *Borreria verticillata.*

3. **S. ocymoides,** *Burm. Fl. Ind. tab.* 18, *fig.* 1. A diffuse low annual, with slender quadrangular stems, glabrous throughout or obscurely pilose upwards. Leaves nearly or quite glabrous, oblong, sessile, membranous, acute, 1–1$\frac{1}{2}$ in. long; stipules $\frac{1}{8}$ in. long, ciliated with bristles quite as long as the blade. Flowers in very dense axillary clusters. Capsule globose, not more than $\frac{1}{24}$ in. long, subglabrous; teeth deltoid, aristate, as long as the tube, 4, rarely 5, two often smaller. Corolla purplish, $\frac{1}{8}$ in. long; lobes short. Borreria ocymoides, *DC. Prod.* iv. 544. Spermacoce Roxburghiana, *Wall. Cat. No.* 6186. Borreria ramisparsa, *DC. loc. cit.*

MAURITIUS, in waste ground. Cosmopolitan in the tropics.

ORDER LVI. COMPOSITÆ.

Flowers hermaphrodite, or by abortion unisexual, rarely neuter, many crowded in a head on a flat or conical naked or scaly receptacle surrounded by an involucre of one or many rows of imbricated scale-like bracts. Calyx adnate to the ovary, the limb absent or represented by a pappus of scales or many or few bristles or hairs. Corolla gamopetalous, the limb campanulate or funnel-shaped with 5 regular teeth or slit open or strap-shaped in the outer flowers or all the flowers of the clusters. Stamens 5, epipetalous, with free filiform filaments, but the anthers connate by their edges. Ovary inferior, 2-celled; ovules solitary, basal, anatropal; style filiform, branching into two arms at the stigmatose apex. Fruit a minute dry terete or flattened achenium, crowned by the persistent or caducous pappus. Seed exalbuminous, usually confluent with the pericarp.—Herbs or shrubs, with alternate or opposite exstipulate leaves, the heads usually copious, mostly in terminal corymbs or corymbose panicles. DISTRIB. Cosmopolitan. The largest known natural order, containing 10,000 species.

Flowers all perfect, purple and tubular.
  Leaves alternate.
    Involucre campanulate, with very numerous scales . 1. VERNONIA.
    Involucre cylindrical; scales 8, biserial . . . . . 2. ELEPHANTOPUS.
  Leaves opposite.
    Pappus of 3–5 small gland-tipped bristles . . . . 3. ADENOSTEMMA.
    Pappus of 4–5 long lanceolate scales . . . . . . 4. AGERATUM.
    Pappus of abundant long bristles . . . . * EUPATORIUM.
Heads heterogamous or rarely with flowers all tubular and perfect.
  Anthers produced at the base into tails.
    Herbs.
      Stems winged . . . . * PTEROCAULON.
      Stems not winged.
        Scales herbaceous not cottony . . . . 5. BLUMEA.
        Scales dry cottony . . . . 6. GNAPHALIUM.
    Shrubs.
      Pappus of flattened scales . . . . 7. CYLINDROCLINE.
      Pappus of bristles.
        Involucre a narrow funnel . . . . 8. MONARRHENUS.
        Involucre campanulate . . . . 9. HELICHRYSUM.
  Anthers not tailed.
    Leaves opposite.
      Pappus none or very obscure.
        Outer scales of involucre longest clavate . . . . 10. SIEGESBECKIA.
        Scales of involucre subequal.
          Receptacle conical . . . . 11. SPILANTHES.
          Receptacle rather convex . . . . 12. ECLIPTA.
      Pappus of 2–4 short bristles . . . . 13. BIDENS.
      Pappus of copious long plumose bristles . . . . * TRIDAX.
    Leaves alternate.
      Involucre multiserial with imbricated scales.
        Glutinous shrubs . . . . 14. PSIADIA.
        Dwarf perennial herbs . . . . 15. ABROTANELLA.

Annual herbs.
Heads monoicous . . . . 16. XANTHIUM.
Heads uniform.
All the flowers tubular.
Pappus none . . . . * CENTIPEDA.
Pappus of abundant fine hairs . . . . 17. CONYZA.
Outer flowers ligulate.
Heads few large . . . . * XIMENESIA.
Heads many small . . . . * PARTHENIUM.
Involucre of one long row of scales placed edge to edge with sometimes a few small ones at the base.
Outer flowers female though tubular.
Pappus of rather firm hairs . . . . 18. FAUJASIA.
Pappus of soft white hairs . . . . * ERECHTHITES.
Flowers usually all hermaphrodite, except in the ligulate species of Senecio.
Style arms long subulate . . . . 19. GYNURA.
Style arms with short appendages . . . . 20. EMILIA.
Style arms truncate . . . . 21. SENECIO.
Flowers all perfect, yellow and strap-shaped.
Achenes flattened.
Achenes beaked. . . . . 22. LACTUCA.
Achenes not beaked . . . . 23. SONCHUS.
Achenes cylindrical.
Pappus-hairs free . . . . 24. CREPIS.
Pappus-hairs joined in a ring . . . . 25. MICRORHYNCHUS.

1. VERNONIA, Schreb.

Heads of many uniform perfect tubular purple or whitish flowers. Involucre campanulate; scales very numerous, multiserial, linear, dry. Receptacle nearly flat, naked or fimbrilliferous. Corolla funnel-shaped, with 5 narrow lobes. Anthers sagittate at the base, not tailed. Style-branches long, subulate, pilose. Achenes cylindrical, with 8–10 minute ribs; pappus biserial, as long as the achene.—Herbs or shrubs, with alternate leaves and numerous capitula in terminal corymbs. DISTRIB. Mostly Tropical American. Species 300–400.

Annual, with small obovate-spathulate repand leaves . . 1. V. CINEREA.
Shrubs.
Leaves petioled, tomentose beneath . . . . 2. V. POPULIFOLIA.
Leaves sessile, nearly glabrous . . . . 3. V. SECHELLENSIS.

1. **V. cinerea,** *Less.; DC. Prod.* v. 24. A much-branched erect annual, 2–4 feet high, with slender finely downy branches. Leaves obovate, membranous, obtuse, petioled, 1–2 in. long, narrowed gradually at the base. Heads very numerous, stalked, in lax corymbose panicles. Involucre $\frac{1}{8}$–$\frac{1}{6}$ in. long and broad; scales linear, grey-green, obscurely pilose. Florets 20-30. Receptacle naked, rather convex. Corolla bright purple. Achenes $\frac{1}{24}$ in. long, pilose; outer row of pappus very short; inner of soft white setæ $\frac{1}{6}$ in. long.

MAURITIUS, and SEYCHELLES, common in waste ground. Everywhere through the tropics of the Old World. *Ayapana sauvage.*

2. **V. populifolia,** *Spreng. Syst.* iii. 434. A shrub 3–4 feet high, with woody sulcate tomentose branches. Leaves distinctly petioled,

ovate, acute, rounded at the base, 3–4 in. long, thickly matted below with white tomentum. Heads few or many, in a dense terminal corymb. Involucre ¼ in. long, ⅜ in. broad, broadly campanulate; scales lanceolate, grey, tomentose, reflexed at the tip. Receptacle minutely fimbrilliferous. Florets about 40 in a head. Achenes pilose, ⅛ in. long; pappus yellow-white, twice as long as the achene; the outer row of linear scales a quarter as long as the inner. Distephanus populifolius, *Cass.*; *DC. Prod.* v. 74.

MAURITIUS, on the rocky escarpments of the Pouce, Pieterboth, and Montagne Longue. Endemic.

3. **V. sechellensis**, *Baker*. A shrub 3–4 feet high, with woody rather puberulent branches. Leaves crowded towards the end of the branches, sessile, oblanceolate-oblong, subacute, subcoriaceous, nearly glabrous, 2–3 in. long, narrowly rounded at the base. Heads in a dense corymbose panicle 3–4 in. broad, the stout ascending branches of which are naked, except at the top; pedicels none or very short. Involucre campanulate, under ¼ in. long; scales 4–5-serial, very caducous, dull brown; outer short, obtuse, puberulent; inner lanceolate, acute. Achenes $\frac{1}{12}$ in. long, terete, with 8–10 distinct ribs, persistently pilose; pappus ¼ in. long, of 100 or more firm equal ciliated persistent bristles of a bright salmon-red colour.

SEYCHELLES, in the Black Forest of Mahé, *Horne*, 497! Endemic.

2. ELEPHANTOPUS, Linn.

Heads of 4 uniform tubular purple flowers, many aggregated in a dense cluster. Involucre cylindrical, of two rows of four linear scales each. Receptacle flat, naked. Corolla with 5 narrow lobes, sometimes irregular. Anthers sagittate at the base. Style-branches subulate, minutely pilose. Achenia cylindrical, minutely ribbed; pappus of a few long setæ in a single row.—Perennial herbs with alternate leaves. DISTRIB. Species 10–12, mostly Tropical American.

1. **E. scaber**, *Linn.*; *DC. Prod.* v. 85. A perennial herb 3–6 feet high, with densely pilose stems. Leaves oblong-spathulate, subcoriaceous, crenate, minutely pilose below; lower 4–6 in. long, narrowed into a petiole; upper much reduced. Clusters each containing 30–40 cylindrical heads, bracteated by three small leaves, arranged in a very lax corymb. Involucre ¼–⅓ in. long; scales rigid, lanceolate, shining; outer row half as long as the inner. Achenes with pappus as long as the involucre. E. carolinianus, nudicaulis, mollis, and Martii, *DC. loc. cit.*

MAURITIUS and SEYCHELLES, common in waste ground. Round the world in tropical and subtropical regions.

3. ADENOSTEMMA, Forst.

Heads of numerous uniform perfect purplish flowers. Involucre broadly campanulate; scales biserial, oblanceolate, obtuse, herbaceous, subequal. Receptacle naked, convex. Corolla-limb campanulate, shortly 5-toothed. Anthers truncate at the base and apex. Style-branches long, flattened, recurved, petaloid, clavate. Achenes cylindrical, acutely angular; pappus a ring, with 3–5 short bristles gland-clubbed at the tip.—Herbs with opposite leaves and laxly corymbose heads. DISTRIB. Round the word in the tropics. Species 4–5.

1. **A. viscosum,** *Forst.; DC. Prod.* v. 111. A robust perennial herb, 2–4 feet high, with a creeping root-stock, the upper branches finely downy. Leaves few, opposite, long-petioled, rhomboid, membranous, glabrous, toothed, 3–4 in. long. Heads few, in very lax corymbs; pedicels finely gland-downy. Flowers 20–30 in a head. Involucre ¼ in. long; scales oblanceolate, obtuse, herbaceous, nearly naked. Achenes shorter than the scales of the involucre, stout, distinctly angled, glandular; pappus-rays very short. A. mauritianum and upwards of 20 other species, *DC. Prod. loc. cit.*

MAURITIUS, in shaded and damp places, frequent. Round the world in the tropics.

4. AGERATUM, Linn.

Heads of many uniform tubular purplish flowers. Involucre campanulate, of many scariose linear acute subequal scales. Receptacle convex, alveolate. Corolla-limb cylindrical; teeth 5, short. Anthers obtuse at the base. Style-branches long, falcate, clavate. Achenes minute, cylindrical, angular; pappus of 4–5 lanceolate acuminate scales. —Herbs with opposite petioled leaves and copious small heads in dense corymbs. DISTRIB. Round the world in the tropics, mostly American. Species about 20.

1. **A. conyzoides,** *Linn.; DC. Prod.* v. 108. An erect pilose annual, 2–3 feet high. Leaves few, distinctly petioled, ovate, membranous, crenate, 3–4 in. long. Heads in dense terminal corymbs, with short pedicels. Involucre ⅛ in. long and broad; scales pale green, linear, obscurely pilose. Achenes brown-black, scabrous, slender, angular, $\frac{1}{12}$ in. long; pappus as long as the achene.

MAURITIUS, RODRIGUEZ, and SEYCHELLES, common in waste ground; Round Island, *Sir H. Barkly!* Round the world in the tropics. *Herb de Bouc.*

* EUPATORIUM, Linn.

Heads of numerous uniform tubular flowers. Involucre campanulate; scales linear, numerous, imbricated. Receptacle naked, flat or convex. Anthers obtuse at the base. Style-branches long, clubbed. Achenes cylindrical, angular; pappus of a single row of bristles as long as the achene.—Herbs or undershrubs with opposite leaves. DISTRIB. Nearly all American. Species 400.

Leaves deltoid, finely downy. Receptacle convex . . . * E. CŒLESTINUM.
Leaves linear, glabrous. Receptacle flat . . . . . . * E. TRIPLINERVE.

* *E. cœlestinum*, Linn. (Conoclinium cœlestinum, *DC. Prod.* v. 135), a native of North America, is naturalised in Mauritius on the slopes

and near the summit of the Pouce. It is an erect herbaceous perennial, 2–3 feet high, with slender finely downy stems, few opposite distinctly petioled crenate membranous deltoid leaves, small copious campanulate heads in crowded corymbs, linear equal subglabrous 2–3-serial involucral scales, a conical naked receptacle, flowers purplish about 40 in a head, and minute angular cylindrical scabrous achenes much shorter than the biserial white bristly pappus.

* *E. triplinerve*, Vahl, (E. Ayapana, *Vent.; DC. Prod.* v. 169), a native of the valley of the Amazon, is cultivated and sometimes subspontaneous in Mauritius, to which it was brought by Captain Baudin in 1797, and Rodriguez. It is a slender glabrous erect perennial herb, with nearly sessile subentire linear leaves 2–3 in. long narrowed from the middle to both ends, small heads in very lax corymbose panicles, a flat receptacle and triserial linear involucral scales. *Ayapana.*

* *Pterocaulon Bojeri*, Baker (Monenteles Pterocaulon, *DC. Prod.* v. 455), a native of Madagascar, is said by Bojer to be established in Mauritius in fields round Port Louis. It is a much-branched wiry perennial, with the small distant entire sessile oblanceolate finely silky leaves decurrent as a continuous narrow wing to the branches, heads aggregated in copious round sessile clusters, a minute campanulate involucre of few linear acute pilose scales, flowers all tubular, with slender corollas, the outer female, a few inner hermaphrodite, a naked receptacle, tailed anthers, and very minute flattened pilose achenes with a pappus of copious soft white flexuose bristles.

5. BLUMEA, *DC.*

Heads heterogamous, many outer rows of flowers female, with slender corollas, a few inner hermaphrodite or male, with more open tubes. Involucre campanulate; scales linear, acute, herbaceous, 2–3-serial. Receptacle naked, papillose. Anthers tailed at the base. Style-branches flattened. Achenes very minute, cylindrical-angular; pappus of a single row of soft deciduous bristles.—Herbs with alternate leaves and very copious heads in terminal panicles. Distrib. Tropics of the Old World, principally Asia. Species about 100.

1. **B. lacera,** *DC. Prod.* v. 436. An erect annual, 1–4 feet high, with finely pilose stems. Leaves distinctly petioled, 2–3 in. long, oblong, obtuse, cuneate at the base, rather repand, with abundant minute sharp teeth, finely downy below. Heads in dense panicles, with short glandular-pilose branches; the upper crowded above the leaves, the lower distant, springing from the axils of large leaves. Involucre $\frac{1}{4}$–$\frac{1}{3}$ in. long, scales 2–3-serial, linear, pilose. Achenes $\frac{1}{24}$ in. long, glabrous; pappus $\frac{1}{6}$ in. long, of fine white brittle flexuose setæ. B. axillaris, *DC. Prod.* v. 434. B. Wightiana, *DC. loc. cit.*

Mauritius, in waste ground. Throughout Tropical Asia and Africa.

6. GNAPHALIUM, Linn.

Flowers many in a head, all tubular and fertile, many outer rows female, a few in the centre hermaphrodite. Involucre campanulate; scales 2–3-serial, dry, acute, immersed in cotton, outer broader. Receptacle flat, naked. Anthers tailed at the base. Style-branches subterete. Achenes very minute, oblanceolate, subterete or rather flattened; pappus of one row of very fine flexuose setæ.—Cottony herbs, with crowded entire alternate leaves, the small heads in corymbs or panicles. DISTRIB. Cosmopolitan. Species about 100.

Heads corymbose . . . . 1. G. LUTEO-ALBUM.
Heads in a congested panicle . . . . 2. G. INDICUM.

1. **G. luteo-album,** *Linn.; DC. Prod.* vi. 230. An erect annual 1–2 feet high, with little-branched stems, matted with adpressed cottony pubescence. Leaves not crowded, thinly cottony; lower oblanceolate, very obtuse, 2–3 in long; stem-leaves sessile, not decurrent, little crisped, upper acute. Heads congested in 1–3 dense clusters. Involucre campanulate, $\frac{1}{8}$ in. long; scales pale, acute. Flowers 50 or more in a head. Achenes oblanceolate, subterete, very minute, naked; pappus $\frac{1}{12}$ in. long, of very fine flexuose white bristles.

Var. PALLIDUM (*Lam.; DC. Prod.* vi. 230, as a species). Much-branched. Stem-leaves lanceolate, acute, with crisped edges. Clusters of heads many, forming a corymbose panicle, the lower one in the axils of its forks; scales pale.

Var. ARNICOIDES (*Lam.; DC. Prod.* vi. 227, as a species). Stems short, simple, almost shrubby. Leaves more densely cottony. Clusters of heads many, aggregated in a dense terminal corymb. Involucre larger, with broader less acute scales.

MAURITIUS, the two first varieties in the low ground, the third on the Pouce and other mountains. Cosmopolitan.

2. **G. indicum,** *Linn.; DC. Prod.* vi. 231. An annual herb, with very numerous cottony slender stems $\frac{1}{2}$ foot long, spreading from the crown of the root. Leaves crowded, sessile, linear-spathulate, 1–$1\frac{1}{2}$ in. long, obtuse, with a minute mucro, very cottony, the edges crisped. Heads in spicate terminal panicles, the top congested and leafless, the lower branches arising from the axils of small leaves. Involucre $\frac{1}{8}$ in. long, immersed in cotton; scales linear, brownish or white. Flowers 50 or more in a head, a few in the centre hermaphrodite. Achenes very minute, obovoid, rather flattened; pappus of very fine flexuose whitish setæ.

MAURITIUS, in cultivated fields at Moka and Port Louis. Common throughout the tropics of the Old World.

7. CYLINDROCLINE, Cass.

Heads heterogamous, of many flowers, all tubular with slender corollas, the outer female, the inner hermaphrodite. Involucre oblong, of very numerous dry scales, the inner acute, naked, the outer gradually shorter, obtuse, with a tuft of wool at the top. Receptacle very prominent, with ligulate scales as long as the flowers, the same texture as those of the involucre. Anthers tailed at the base. Style simple or with short obtuse branches. Achenes angular-cylindrical, glabrous; pappus of 10–12 flattened rigid bristles. Endemic.

1. **C. Commersoni,** *Cass.; D.C. Prod.* v. 458. A low shrub, with spreading branches as thick as a man's finger, clothed upwards with long dense whitish cottony hairs. Leaves crowded, oblanceolate, entire, sessile, coriaceous, rugose, 3–4 in. long, obtuse or acute, thinly pilose on the face, densely clothed with white tomentum and long white cottony hairs beneath. Heads crowded at the end of the branches, forming a very dense rounded corymb 3–4 in. broad. Involucre oblong, $\frac{3}{8}$ in. long; scales persistent, pale brown. Pappus $\frac{1}{3}$ in. long, exceeding in length the glabrescent achene. Lepidopogon gnaphalodes and Ponæ, *Tausch.*

MAURITIUS, near the summit of the Pouce and Piton de la Rivière Noire. Endemic.

8. MONARRHENUS, Cass.

Heads of numerous flowers, all discoid with slender corollas, the outer female, the inner hermaphrodite. Involucre funnel-shaped, 2–3 times as long as broad, the outer scales growing gradually shorter. Receptacle small, naked. Anthers tailed. Style-branches filiform. Achenes minute, terete; pappus of a single row of bristles, much longer than the achene.—Shrubs with crowded narrow alternate entire leaves, and minute heads crowded in bundles forming a corymbose panicle. DISTRIB. Endemic in the Mascaren Isles.

Leaves matted with white tomentum beneath . . . . 1. M. SALICIFOLIUS.
Leaves clothed with short spreading grey pubescence beneath . . . . 2. M. RUFESCENS.

1. **M. salicifolius,** *Cass.; DC. Prod.* v. 457. A much-branched shrub, 3–4 feet high. Leaves crowded, linear, sessile, subcoriaceous, 3–4 in. long, $\frac{1}{8}$–$\frac{1}{4}$ in. broad at the middle, narrowed to both ends, green and glabrous above, matted with thin white tomemtum beneath. Heads very numerous, arranged in dense clusters, which form a congested corymbose panicle 3–4 in. broad, funnel-shaped, $\frac{1}{6}$ in. long, half as broad; inner scales dry, lanceolate, acute pale brown; outer obtuse and obscurely tipped with green. Achenes cylindrical; pappus $\frac{1}{12}$ in. long.

MAURITIUS, on dry escarpments of the Pouce. Also Bourbon. *M. pinifolius*, DC. seems a mere form of this, with narrow leaves with inflexed borders. *Bois Senil* or *Bois de Chenille.*

2. **M. rufescens,** *Cass.; DC. Prod.* v. 457. Habit of the last, from which it mainly differs by having the branches and leaves on both sides clothed with short spreading grey pubescence. Leaves sessile, $1\frac{1}{2}$–2 in. long, under $\frac{1}{4}$ in. broad, not clothed with tomentum beneath. Involucre under $\frac{1}{6}$ in. long, the outer scales more distinctly coloured green. Flowers in a head fewer. Achenes at first pilose; pappus under $\frac{1}{12}$ in. long.

MAURITIUS, *Bouton!* Also Madagascar (distributed by Bojer as *Vernonia leptoclada*), and Bourbon.

9. HELICHRYSUM, Vaill.

Heads heterogamous, the flowers all tubular, purplish, a few outer female only, a great many in the centre hermaphrodite. Involucre campanulate, of very numerous gradually imbricated persistent dry scales. Receptacle flattish, foveolate. Anthers tailed. Style-branches terete, purplish, spreading. Achenes very minute, a little compressed; pappus of a single row of firm very caducous ciliated bristles.—Herbs or shrubs, with crowded narrow entire alternate leaves, the heads in congested corymbs. DISTRIB. Dry districts, principally of the south temperate zone. Species 200–300.

Involucral-scales broad. Flowers 50 or more in a head . . . . 1. H. YUCCÆFOLIUM.
Involucral-scales narrow. Flowers 15–20 in a head.
Erect, with acute triplinerved leaves . . . . 2. H. PROTEIFORME.
Dwarf, with obtuse leaves with hidden veins . . . . 3. H. CÆSPITOSUM.

1. **H. yuccæfolium,** *Lam.; DC. Prod.* vi. 173. A much-branched erect shrub, 1–2 feet high, with stems and leaves densely clothed with brownish-white adpressed cottony-silky tomentum, the branches marked closely with scars of old leaves. Leaves crowded, sessile, lanceolate, acute, 1–2 in. long, the veins quite hidden beneath the tomentum. Heads in dense corymbs 1–3 inches broad at the end of the branches. Involucre $\frac{1}{4}$ inch broad and long, immersed in tomentum; the scales in several rows, nearly white, the outer oblong, $\frac{1}{12}$ in. broad. Flowers upwards of 50 in a head. Corolla-tube $\frac{1}{6}$ in. long. Pappus of firm white ciliated scales as long as the corolla. Gnaphalium yuccæfolium, *Lam. Encycl.* ii. 742. H. multicaule, *DC. Prod. loc. cit.* Gnaphalium proteoides, *Sieb. Fl. Maur. Exsic.* ii. 269.

MAURITIUS, in exposed places near the summit of the Pouce and other hills. Endemic. *Immortelle du Pouce.*

2. **H. proteiforme,** *Baker.* A shrub, with exactly the same general habit as *H. yuccæfolium.* Leaves crowded, oblanceolate, sessile, $1\frac{1}{2}$–2 in. long, with the midrib and two long side veins visible through the brownish-white tomentum. Heads dense, congested, forming corymbose panicles. Involucre $\frac{1}{8}$ in. long, the whitish multiserial scales ligulate, not more than $\frac{1}{24}$ in. broad, nearly all reflexing at the tip. Flowers not more than 15–20 in a head. Corolla-tube and pappus $\frac{1}{8}$ in. long, just like those of the last. Gnaphalium proteiforme, *Lam.; DC. Prod.* vi. 227.

MAURITIUS, near the summit of several of the higher mountains. Also Bourbon.

3. **H. cæspitosum,** *DC. Prod.* vi. 173. A shrubby perennial, with densely packed ascending and spreading stems, not more than a few inches long. Leaves very crowded, oblanceolate, obtuse, spreading, under an inch long, the veins quite hidden beneath the whitish-brown tomentum. Heads in a single dense round cluster at the end of each of the branches. Involucre $\frac{1}{8}$ in. long, the ligulate whitish scales soon reflexing at the tip, $\frac{1}{24}$ in. or less broad. Flowers 15–20 in a head.

Corolla and pappus of the last. Gnaphalium cæspitosum, *Lam.*; G. foliosum, *Poir.*

MAURITIUS, on exposed escarpments of the Pouce and Pieterboth. Endemic. *Petite Immortelle.*

10. SIEGESBECKIA, Linn.

Flowers about a dozen in a head, all fertile, the outer obscurely ligulate, the inner funnel-shaped, all yellow and glandular. Involucre campanulate, biserial; the inner scales obianceolate, obtuse, 5 outer twice as long, linear-clavate, densely gland-ciliated. Receptacle small, scaly. Anthers not tailed. Style-branches short, flat. Achenes oblanceolate, turgid, outer curved, externally glandular; pappus none.—Herbs with opposite leaves and small heads in lax corymbs. DISTRIB. One other species, a native of Peru.

1. **S. orientalis,** *Linn.; D.C. Prod.* v. 495. An erect annual, 1–3 feet high, with slender finely-downy branches. Leaves distant, opposite, deltoid, scarcely petioled, acute, membranous, irregularly toothed, 3–6 in. long, narrowed suddenly at the base into a long haft. Heads in lax terminal corymbs, on slender glandular pedicels. Inner scales of the involucre as long as the achenes, outer scales much longer than the rest of the head. Corolla yellow, very minute. Achenes $\frac{1}{8}$ in. long, naked on the side towards the centre of the head. S. triangularis, *Cav.* and sp. 2 to 7, *DC. Prod. loc. cit.*

SEYCHELLES, RODRIGUEZ, and MAURITIUS, a common weed. Everywhere within the tropics. *Herbe de flacq. Herbe grasse.*

11. SPILANTHES, Linn.

Heads with numerous flowers, all fertile and hermaphrodite or the outer row female and ligulate. Involucre campanulate, of two rows of subequal herbaceous scales. Receptacle very prominent, covered with deciduous obtuse scales, which clasp the flowers. Anthers not tailed. Style-arms truncate. Achenes minute, those of the disk compressed, of the ray angular-cylindrical; pappus in our plant none. —Annual or perennial herbs, with simple opposite leaves and few small scattered heads. DISTRIB. Round the world in the tropics. Species 50.

1. **S. Acmella,** *Linn.; DC. Prod.* v. 623. A perennial herb, with slender trailing finely pilose purplish stems 1–2 feet long with assurgent branches. Leaves short-petioled, opposite, ovate, membranous, an inch long, obtusely toothed. Heads solitary, terminal or axillary, on peduncles which exceed the leaves. Involucre $\frac{1}{4}$ in. long; scales herbaceous, lanceolate, subobtuse. Flowers 50–100 in a hemispherical head; ligules 5–10. Achenes $\frac{1}{24}$ in. long, glabrous, oblanceolate-oblong; pappus none. S. africana and caulirhiza, *DC. loc. cit.* S. mauritiana, *DC. Prod.* v. 625 (wrongly placed in § Salivaria). Acmella mauritiana, *Rich.*

MAURITIUS, in damp grassy places on the slope of the Pouce, and at Curepipe, Vacquois, etc. Throughout the tropics of the Old World. *Acmelle.*

12. ECLIPTA, Linn.

Heads heterogamous, the outer flowers ligulate, fertile, those of the disk tubular, hermaphrodite and also fertile. Involucre campanulate, composed of about two rows of lanceolate herbaceous scales of equal length. Receptacle convex, bearing scales as long as the achenes. Anthers not tailed. Style-branches flat, with deltoid appendages. Achenes triquetrous or slightly compressed, scabrous on the face, tipped by a toothed ring, which sometimes bears one or two short bristles.—Herbs, with narrow opposite leaves and inconspicuous heads from the axils of the leaves. DISTRIB. Round the world in the tropics. Species 3 or 4.

1. **E. erecta,** *Linn.; DC. Prod.* v. 490. A branched erect annual, 2–3 feet high, with stems and leaves clothed with short bristly hairs. Leaves rhomboid-lanceolate, 2–3 in. long, obscurely toothed, sessile. Heads one terminal and the rest solitary or in pairs from the axils of the leaves on distinct ascending peduncles. Involucre broadly campanulate; scales few, imbricated, $\frac{1}{4}$ in. long. Flowers 30–40 in a head; rays pale yellow. Achenes $\frac{1}{12}$ in. long, oblanceolate-triquetrous, glabrous. E. alba, *Haenke*.

Var. PROSTRATA (*Linn.; DC. Prod. loc. cit.* as a species). Dwarf, diffuse, with slender stems 3–6 in. long, smaller leaves and fewer flowers in a head.

MAURITIUS, frequent in waste ground and damp places. All the eight species of the section *Eueclipta* enumerated in Decandolle's Prodromus seem mere forms of one, a universal tropical weed.

13. BIDENS, Linn.

Flowers all tubular and hermaphrodite or often the outer row neuter and producing yellow ligules. Involucre campanulate; scales biserial, subequal, linear, herbaceous, connate at the base. Receptacle scaly. Anthers not tailed. Style-branches pilose, tipped with a small cone. Achenes in our plant cylindrical-angular, tipped with 2–4 short bristles, with stiff reflexed barbs.—Annual or perennial herbs, with opposite divided leaves and middle-sized yellow heads in lax corymbs. DISTRIB. Cosmopolitan. Species about 50.

1. **B. pilosa,** *Linn.; DC. Prod.* v. 597. An erect annual, 2–3 feet high, with weak subglabrous, tetragonous stems. Leaves distinctly petioled, opposite, the lower compound, with 3–5 ovate, acute, membranous toothed leaflets, the uppermost simple. Heads few, long-peduncled, laxly corymbose. Involucre $\frac{1}{4}$ in. long; scales about 15, in two rows, linear, herbaceous, ciliated. Flowers in our specimens all tubular. Achenes glabrous, longer than the involucre; bristles 2–4, a third the length of the achene. B. leucantha, *Willd.; DC. Prod.* v. 598. B. tripartita, *Bojer, Hort. Maur.* 183, *non Linn.*

MAURITIUS, RODRIGUEZ, and SEYCHELLES, frequent in waste ground. A cosmopolitan weed. *La Ville-bague.*

* *Tridax procumbens*, Linn.; DC. Prod. v. 679, a native of Mexico and the West Indies, escaped from the Botanic Garden at Pamplemousses about 1840, and is now spread through Mauritius by roadsides, and has reached Flat Island, Rodriguez, and Bourbon. It is a trailing perennial, branched in the lower part, with branches and leaves scabrous with short bristly hairs, opposite petioled rhomboid-deltoid deeply toothed acute simple leaves, few middle-sized many-flowered heads on very long peduncles, scales of the involucre subequal 2–3 serial, outer scabrous ovate-lanceolate acute herbaceous, inner membranous, obtuse ligulate, receptacle scaly, a few outer flowers with yellow ligules, anthers not tailed, receptacle scaly, achenes pilose angular-cylindrical, pappus of a single row of persistent densely plumose bristles. *Herbe Caille.*

14. PSIADIA, Jacq.

Heads heterogamous, the outer flowers female with a short entire or 2–3-cleft ligule, and the inner tubular and often abortive, all yellow. Involucre campanulate; scales linear, 2–3-serial, unequal. Receptacle alveolate. Anthers not tailed. Achenes very minute, glabrous, angulato-cylindrical; pappus of numerous slender bristles, longer than the achene.—Glutinous shrubs, with alternate leaves and copious minute heads in dense terminal corymbs. DISTRIB. Tropical Africa, Madagascar, Bourbon, Cape. Species about a dozen.

Leaves distinctly 3-, or in the broader forms 5-nerved from the base above the middle . . . . 1. P. TRINERVIA.
Leaves penninerved.
  Glabrous and glutinous.
    Leaves oblanceolate, obtuse, entire . . . . 2. P. PENNINERVIA.
    Leaves oblong-lanceolate, acute, inciso-dentate . . * P. GLUTINOSA.
  Pilose, not glutinous . . . . 3. P. RODRIGUESIANA.

1. **P. trinervia,** *Willd. Mag. Berl.* 1807, 139. A low shrub, with glutinose branchlets and leaves. Leaves crowded, oblong, subcoriaceous, obtuse, 1–2 in. long, entire, with two distinct side veins running from the base nearly to the top, narrowed at the base into a petiole $\frac{1}{2}$ in. long. Flowers in dense terminal corymbs, 10–12 in a head. Involucre campanulate, $\frac{1}{4}$ in. long and broad; scales linear, pale green, scariose, outer short. Achenes of outer flowers under $\frac{1}{12}$ in. long; setæ twice as long as the achene. P. integerrima, *DC. Prod.* v. 319.

Var. LINEARIFOLIA, (*DC. Prod. loc. cit.*, as a species). Leaves linear, narrowed to both ends, petioled, entire, 2–3 in. long, under $\frac{1}{2}$ in. broad. Flowers in a head 10–12.

Var. DENTATA (*DC. Prod. loc. cit.*) Leaves petioled, lanceolate, inciso-dentate. Heads rather larger, and flowers in a head more numerous.

Var. LANCEOLATA, *Baker*. Leaves more membranous, lanceolate, entire, 3–4 in. long, an inch broad at the middle, narrowed to both ends. Heads of the type, containing ten or a dozen flowers.

Var. QUINQUENERVIA. Branches stouter. Leaves obovate, 3–4 in. long, subacute, entire, with two prominent ribs on each side of the midrib, 1½–2 in. broad, deltoid, narrowed in the lower third into a distinct petiole. Heads ⅛ in. long and broad, with 30–40 flowers in each. P. integerrima, *var.* quinquenervia, *DC.* P. glauca, *Ayres, MSS. with description.* (Elphegea quinquenervia, *Cass. Dict.* xiv. 363.)

Var. BALSAMICA (*DC. Prod.* v. 319, as a species). Leaves obovate-cuneate, distinctly triplinerved, 1–1½ in. broad, scarcely petioled, furnished with a few distinct acute teeth on each side in the upper half. Heads as large as in the last, with 30–40 flowers in each.

Var. MACRODON, *Baker.* Leaves rigidly coriaceous, oblong, about 2 in. long, distinctly petioled, strongly 3–5-nerved, cuneate at the base, with many large lanceolate or deltoid rather obtuse teeth. Heads as in vars. *balsamica* and *quinquenervia.*

MAURITIUS, common in rocky places and dry ground. The forms are connected by intermediate links. The first is confined to exposed places on the hills, and the two latter are luxuriant lowland varieties, and occur plentifully on the Platte, Flat Island and Gabriol Island. *Var.* MACRODON in Rodriguez, on the south shore and on some of the coral islands, *Balfour !* Also Bourbon. *Baume d'Ile Platte.*

2. **P. penninervia,** *DC. Prod.* v. 319. A glutinous shrub, glabrous in all its parts, with stout terete branches. Leaves crowded, oblanceolate, 2–3 in. long, ½–¾ in. broad above the middle, entire, not at all triplinerved, narrowed from the middle into a winged petiole. Involucre in our specimens ⅛ in. long; scales lanceolate, subequal, with a dark brown midrib and pale edges. Flowers in the form described by De Candolle 10–12, in our plant 30 or more. Achenes $\frac{1}{24}$ in. long, half the length of its bristles.

MAURITIUS, in mountain-woods of La Savanne and Rivière Noire. Endemic.

* *P. glutinosa,* Jacq. Hort. Schoen. t. 152, of which all our specimens are from gardens, is evidently distinct specifically from all the varieties of *P. trinervia.* The leaves are oblong-lanceolate, acute, with regular teeth extending all down the edge except at the tip and cuneate base, and the main veins spread regularly all the way up parallel with one another at a broad angle from the midrib, the involucral-scales are fewer and more oblong than in *trinervia,* the heads being ⅛ in. deep and broad, with about 30 florets. It has always been said to be a Mauritian species, but if so, it seems to be now lost and the name transferred by the island botanists to forms of *P. trinervia.*

3. **P. rodriguesiana,** *Balf. fil.* A low-shrub, with terete woody branches rather densely clothed with adpressed white cottony hairs. Leaves shortly petioled, moderately firm in texture, oblong-rhomboid, acute, cuneate and entire in the lower third, the rest of the edge dentate, thinly pubescent, especially beneath, the midrib with 5–6 ascending ribs on each side, branching from it. Heads about 30-flowered, arranged in a dense corymb on a short pubescent peduncle. Involucre $\frac{1}{12}$ in. long. Achenes glabrous, $\frac{1}{24}$ in. long, rather shorter than the pappus.

RODRIGUEZ, rare in the unfrequented parts of the island, *Dr. Balfour*. Endemic.

Sarcanthemum Coronopus, Cass. DC. Prod. v. 367 (Conyza, *Lam.*), gathered by Commerson in Rodriguez, by Bory in Bourbon, and attributed by Sprengel to Mauritius, may perhaps be one of the varieties of *P. trinervia*. It is said to be a viscose shrub, with alternate crowded linear-lanceolate leaves 2–3 in. long, ¼ in. broad, obscurely triplinerved and toothed near the tip and narrowed to the base, a flat fimbrilliferous receptacle, small flowers crowded in terminal corymbs, and the central tubular flowers as in *Dichrocephala* with an inflated, not a narrowly funnel-shaped mouth. It cannot. I think, be the Bourbon *P. retusa*, DC., as suggested by Cordemoy in the Adansonia, vol. x. p. 24.

15. ABROTANELLA, Cass.

Flowers all tubular, those of the circumference female, those of the disk hermaphrodite. Involucre campanulate; scales few, narrow, imbricated, subequal in length, or 1–2 of the outer ones larger, subherbaceous. Receptacle naked, narrow. Anthers not tailed. Branches of the style short, truncate. Achenes compressed or tetragonal, glabrous, the pappus none or minute and coroniform.—Dense cæspitose minute perennials with alternate leaves and solitary or sparsely corymbose terminal heads. DISTRIB. Species 10, the others Antarctic American or inhabitants of New Zealand and South Australia.

1. **A. rhynchocarpa**, *Balf. fil.* Shrubby, densely cæspitose, glabrous in all its parts, not rising above half an inch above the soil. Leaves in a rosette, oblanceolate, fleshy-coriaceous, subacute, entire or pinnatifid with 1–2 deep lobes on each side, narrowed into a flattened petiole, which is longer than the lamina and dilated at the base. Heads solitary, sessile in the centre of the rosette, few-flowered, $\frac{1}{12}$ in. long. Scales few, irregularly biserial, equal in length, linear, with a herbaceous centre and hyaline obscurely ciliated edge. Achenes as long as the corolla-tube, black when mature, compressed, glabrous, $\frac{1}{24}$ in. long, with 3 distinct ribs on one side and two on the other.

RODRIGUEZ, on the coralline limestone, in small quantity, *Balfour!* Endemic.

16. XANTHIUM, Linn.

Heads of flowers monoicous, the male ones many-flowered, with tubular corollas and an involucre of numerous free spineless bracts, the females without corollas, only two in a head, with a connate involucre armed with toothed spines. Anthers not tailed. Style-branches of female flowers slender. Involucre of female flowers two-celled, with a septum representing the scales of the receptacle.—Coarse annual herbs, with alternate leaves, and copious heads forming terminal and axillary panicles. DISTRIB. Cosmopolitan weeds. Species 4.

Branches spineless. Leaves green, obscurely grey-downy beneath . . . . 1. X. STRUMARIUM.
Branches armed with trifid spines. Leaves clothed with white tomentum beneath . . . . 2. X. SPINOSUM.

1. **X. strumarium,** *Linn.; DC. Prod.* v. 523. A large coarse annual, with spineless branches and leaves beneath obscurely grey-downy. Leaves distinctly petioled, deltoid, three-lobed, irregularly toothed. Heads few together in abundant terminal and axillary panicles, the males uppermost. Corolla of male flowers with a colourless tube and 5 short greenish lobes. Enlarged involucre of females oblong, with a beak on each side of the opening ½ in. long, slightly hairy between the copious firm spreading hooked spines. X. indicum, *Roxb.; D.C. loc. cit.*

MAURITIUS, frequent in waste ground about Port Louis, etc. Cosmopolitan.

2. **X. spinosum,** *Linn.; DC. Prod.* v. 523. Stems finely mealy, much branched, armed with trifid stramineous spines ½–1 inch long. Leaves nearly sessile, lanceolate-rhomboid, acuminate, usually with 1 or 2 deep teeth at the middle, clothed beneath with white mealy tomentum. Heads 2–4 together from the axils of most of the leaves; males about 30 in a head, with clavate yellowish-green corollas, with short lobes. Enlarged involucre of female flowers oblong, ¼–⅓ in. long. X. catharticum, *H.B.K.; DC. loc. cit.*

MAURITIUS, in waste ground near Port Louis, etc. Now cosmopolitan; probably originally American.

* *Centipeda minuta,* Baker, (Myriogyne minuta, *Less.; DC. Prod.* vi. 139; Dichrocephala minima, *Bojer, Hort. Maur,* 179), a common weed of Polynesia and Tropical Asia, is established in Mauritius on the banks of canals in the botanic garden at Pamplemousses. It is an annual, with dense cæspitose trailing stems a few inches long, minute sessile alternate obovate-cuneate leaves often toothed in the upper half, copious subsessile globose heads ⅛ in. thick, a small biserial involucre with oblong bracts with a membranous border, a naked flat receptacle, very numerous yellow tubular flowers, the outer rows female, the inner hermaphrodite and angular achenes without any pappus.

17. CONYZA, Linn.

Heads heterogamous, of very numerous flowers, all tubular, the outer ones female, the central hermaphrodite, all fertile with a slender corolla-tube. Involucre campanulate; scales numerous, imbricated, linear, herbaceous. Receptacle convex, naked. Anthers not tailed. Style-branches flattened, with lanceolate appendages. Achenes very minute, compressed; pappus uniserial, of numerous fine flexuose setæ. —Herbs, with alternate toothed or divided leaves, and numerous corymbose or panicled heads. DISTRIB. Round the world in the warmer zones. Species about 50.

1. **C. leariloba,** *DC. Prod.* v. 385. A little-branched erect annual 2–3 feet high with densely pilose stems. Leaves crowded, the

lower petioled, lanceolate, 2–3 in. long, deeply pinnatifid; upper lobes close, entire, ligulate; lower more distant, sometimes again pinnatifid. Heads numerous, in a long narrow panicle with ascending racemose branches. Involucre $\frac{1}{4}$ in. long; scales linear, acuminate, nearly glabrous. Flowers 100 or more in a head. Receptacle convex, lanceolate. Achene flat, oblanceolate, glabrous, $\frac{1}{48}$ in. long; pappus $\frac{1}{8}$ in. long, of copious very slender flexuose salmon-coloured bristles.

MAURITIUS, in cultivated fields and waste ground. Also Bourbon, Madagascar, and Tropical Africa. Scarcely more than a variety of the widely-spread *C. ægyptiaca*.

* *Ximenesia encælioides*, Cav.; DC. Prod. v. 627, (Verbesina, *Benth.*), a native of Mexico, now widely spread in the Old World, has been long established in Mauritius near the cemetery at Port Louis. It is a robust erect branched annual, with densely pilose stems, large membranous alternate deltoid acute sharply toothed leaves silvery beneath, narrowed suddenly into a sessile auriculate haft, a few long-peduncled showy yellow heads in a terminal corymb, involucre of 2–3 rows of large linear equal herbaceous scales, outer flowers with a large yellow ligule, inner very numerous tubular, tailless anthers, receptacle with large lanceolate scales clasping the flowers, and flattened obovate achenes with a wing on each side and a pair of small bristles at the tip.

* *Parthenium Hysterophorus*, Linn.; DC. Prod. v. 551; a native of Tropical America, is now a common weed in Mauritius and Rodriguez. It is a much-branched annual, 2–3 feet high, with obscurely pilose slender stems, large bipinnatifid petioled alternate lower leaves with narrow segments, copious very small heads in lax corymbose panicles, campanulate involucre with two rows of broad shining scales, the outer acute, the inner obtuse, outer flowers with a minute ligule, many inner tubular, receptacle scaly, anthers not tailed, style of hermaphrodite flowers unbranched, obovoid campanulate shining minute achenes with a pappus of 2–3 lanceolate scales. It has been gathered by Mr. Horne on Flat Island, and is also established in Bourbon. *Herbe Blanche*.

18. FAUJASIA, Cass.

Flowers in a head all tubular, those of the centre perfect, but a few of the outside ones antherless. Involucre funnel-shaped or campanulate, of one row of ligulate herbaceous scales, edge to edge, and a few small outside ones at the base. Receptacle naked or obscurely fimbrilliferous. Anthers not tailed. Style-armed subterete, truncate, penicillate at the tip. Achenes glabrous, cylindrical; pappus of copious white rather firm ciliated bristles.—Shrubs with alternate leaves and copious heads in terminal corymbose panicles. DISTRIB. Endemic in the Mascaren Isles. No other species than these three known.

Flowers few. Leaves linear, 1-nerved . . . . 1. F. PINIFOLIA.
Flowers many. Leaves broad.
  Leaves petioled, ovate or oblong . . . . 2. F. FLEXUOSA.
  Leaves sessile, round-cordate . . . . 3. F. RETICULATA.

1. **F. pinifolia**, *Cass.*; *DC. Prod.* vi. 293. A much-branched glabrous low shrub, with stems clothed with the adherent bases of fallen leaves. Leaves crowded, sessile, subcoriaceous, very narrow, $\frac{1}{24}$ in. broad, 1-nerved, $\frac{3}{4}$ in. long. Heads few, small, in close thyrsoid or corymbose terminal panicles. Involucre funnel-shaped, $\frac{1}{6}$ in. deep, with 8–10 ligulate glabrous scales and 7–8 included flowers. Achenes slender, under $\frac{1}{12}$ in. long; pappus $\frac{1}{12}$ in. long, of copious scabrous white bristles, distinctly shorter than the yellow narrowly funnel-shaped corollas. Senecio pinifolius, *Pers.* Conyza pinifolia, *Bory, non Lam.*

MAURITIUS, in high and damp stations, especially in the neighbourhood of Grand Bassin, *Bouton* ' Also Bourbon.

2. **F. flexuosa,** *Benth. Gen. Plant.* ii. 443. A glabrous shrub, 3–6 feet high, with slender woody branches. Leaves distinctly petioled, ovate or oblong, 2–4 in. long, subcoriaceous, acute, incised or crenate, rounded or narrowed at the base; the veinlets beneath not raised. Heads very numerous, in dense terminal panicles. Involucre campanulate, $\frac{1}{6}$ in. broad and long; scales 10–12, brownish, glabrous, ligulate, with a deltoid tip. Receptacle conical, with a few obscure fibrillæ. Flowers 20-30 in a head. Corollas yellow, the limb almost campanulate. Achenes slender, glabrous, cylindrical, strongly ribbed, $\frac{1}{8}$ in. long; pappus as long as the achene, of copious distinctly ciliated white bristles. Cacalia flexuosa, *Wall.*; *DC. Prod.* vi. 330. Senecio flexuosus, *Less.* Eupatorium flexuosum, *Lam.* Senecio pollicaris, *DC.*; *Bojer, Hort. Maur.* 188.

Var. LANCIFOLIA, *Baker.* Leaves lanceolate, 3 in. long, under $\frac{1}{2}$ in. broad, narrowed gradually to both ends, sharply incised. Heads smaller, with fewer flowers in each.

MAURITIUS, in woods through the island. Also Bourbon and Madagascar. *Senecio subcordatus*, Bojer, MSS. is a form with ovate leaves with a subcordate base. *Bois Cassant. Bois cassem. Zigzag.*

3. **F. reticulata,** *Benth. Gen. Plant.* ii. 443. A glabrous undershrub, 2–3 feet high, with flexuose terete branches. Leaves distant, sessile, round, with a deeply cordate base, 2–4 in. diameter, obtuse or cuspidate, finely regularly toothed, subcoriaceous, with the reticulated veinlets in relief on the under side. Heads 10–30, in crowded terminal corymbs. Involucre campanulate, $\frac{1}{6}$ in. broad and long; scales about a dozen, glabrous, with a cusp. Receptacle conical. Flowers 30–40 in a head. Achenes glabrous, $\frac{1}{8}$ in. long, slender, cylindrical; pappus shorter than the achene, of densely ciliated firm white hairs. Cacalia reticulata, *Vahl*; *DC. Prod.* vi. 330. Senecio penicillatus, *DC.*: *Bojer, Hort. Maur.* 188. Senecio asarifolius, *Bojer, MSS.* Cacalia asarifolia, *Steud.*

MAURITIUS, in the forests of Grand Bassin and the Pitton de la Rivière Noire. Endemic.

* *Erechthites hieracifolia*, Raf.; DC. Prod. vi. 294, (Senecio cacalioides, *Spreng.*; *Bojer. Hort. Maur.* 188), a common American weed,

occurs occasionally in Mauritius. It is an erect obscurely-pilose annual, 2–4 feet high, with fragile sulcate stems, alternate acute lanceolate clasping toothed or runcinate membranous leaves, copious many-flowered heads twice as long as broad in dense corymbose panicles, involucre oblong of about 20 narrow uniserial herbaceous scales with a few small loose ones at the base, corollas all tubular, outer female, receptacle naked, anthers not tailed, minute angular-cylindrical achenes with a long pappus of very fine soft pure white hairs.

19. GYNURA, Cass.

Heads many-flowered, all the corollas tubular, all perfect, or the outer row female. Involucre campanulate, of 15–20 equal ligulate herbaceous scales, placed edge to edge, and a few small ones at the base. Receptacle flat or convex, foveolate. Anthers not tailed. Style-arms long, spreading, subulate, pilose. Achenes glabrous, cylindrical, ribbed; pappus of very numerous long soft white hairs. Large annuals, with alternate membranous often runcinate leaves, and few distant large heads of bright purple tubular flowers. DISTRIB. Tropics of the Old World. Species about 20. *Crassocephalum*, Moench, is an older name for the genus.

Inner scales of involucre 20–25 . . . . 1. G. CERNUA.
Inner scales of involucre 12–15 . . . . 2. G. PSEUDO-CHINA.

1. **G. cernua,** *Benth. in Fl. Nigr.* 437. An erect annual, 2–4 feet high, with slightly pilose fragile sulcate branches. Leaves obovate-oblong, membranous, toothed, 2–4 in. long, entire or runcinate; upper sessile, auricled at the base; lower narrowed into a petiole. Heads cernuous, on peduncles often a foot long, with only a few small leaves, the upper entire, linear-subulate. Involucre ½ in. long and broad; inner scales 20–25, concrete at the base, and an outer circle of minute subulate ones at the base. Flowers above 100, the outer row often antherless. Achenes glabrous, slender, ⅛ in. long, with a caducous pappus nearly ½ in. long, of copious very fine soft white hairs. Senecio cernuus, *Linn. fil.; Bojer, Hort. Maur.* 187. Cremocephalum cernuum, *Cass.; DC. Prod.* vi. 298. Senecio purpureus, *Willemet, Fl. Maur.* 57.

MAURITIUS, through the island in waste ground. Also Bourbon, Madagascar and Tropical Africa.

2. **G. pseudo-china,** *DC. Prod.* vi. 299. An erect annual, 2–3 feet high, with nearly naked or finely downy sulcate stems. Leaves alternate, obovate-oblong, 3–4 in. long, irregularly toothed, the upper sessile, often auricled at the base, the lower narrowed gradually into a short petiole, often densely pilose. Heads several to a branch, erect or cernuous, on much shorter peduncles than in the last and all the flowers perfect. Involucre ⅜ in. broad and long; scales of inner series 12–15, ligulate, with a lanceolate tip, shortly connate at base and a few

minute linear outer ones. Flowers much fewer than in the last and corollas much stouter. Achenes and pappus just the same. Senecio pseudo-china, *Linn.*; *Bojer*, *Hort. Maur.* 188. G. auriculata, *Cass.*; *DC. Prod.* vi. 300. G. ovalis, *DC. loc. cit.* Cacalia ovalis, *Ker*; *Bot. Reg. t.* 101.

MAURITIUS, in waste ground. Through the tropics of the Old World.

20. EMILIA, Cass.

Flowers in a head all tubular and fertile. Involucre oblong-cylindrical, the scales herbaceous, few, ligulate, placed edge to edge, with none outside at the base. Receptacle flat, alveolate. Anthers not tailed. Style-arms subterete, with short appendages. Achenes slender, cylindrical, ribbed; pappus of long copious soft white hairs.—Annuals, with alternate toothed entire or lyrate membranous leaves and middle-sized heads in lax corymbs. DISTRIB. Mostly tropics of the Old World. Species 45.

1. **E. sonchifolia,** *DC. Prod.* vi. 302. A nearly glabrous branched erect annual, 2–3 feet high, with fragile slender stems. Leaves membranous and rather glaucous; lower petioled, lyrate-pinnatifid, 3–4 in. long; lobes toothed, the end ones much the largest; stem-leaves sessile, lanceolate-hastate. Heads few, in a lax terminal corymb, with long peduncles. Involucre $\frac{3}{8}$–$\frac{1}{2}$ in. long; scales 10–12, persistent, reflexing after the flowers fall. Flowers 40–50 in a head, yellow, just exceeding the scales. Achenes glabrous, very slender, $\frac{1}{8}$–$\frac{1}{6}$ in. long; pappus of very soft white hairs three times as long as the achene. Cacalia sonchifolia, *Linn.*

MAURITIUS, in waste grounds; Flat Island, *Dr. Ayres!* *E. rigidula*, DC. loc. cit., is a slender variety with all the leaves narrow simple and lanceolate. A cosmopolitan weed.

21. SENECIO, Linn.

Flowers in a head all tubular and hermaphrodite or the outer ligulate and female. Involucre cylindrical or campanulate; scales narrow, herbaceous, except in *S. appendiculatus* placed edge to edge and usually a few small outer ones at the base. Receptacle flat, foveolate. Anthers not tailed. Style-arms falcate, subterete, truncate. Achenes cylindrical, glabrous, ribbed; pappus of copious slender soft white hairs.—Herbs or shrubs, with alternate simple or compound leaves and heads in terminal corymbs. DISTRIB. Cosmopolitan; one of the largest and widely spread of all known genera. Species 800–900.

Involucral scales imbricated, tomentose . . . . . . 1. S. APPENDICULATUS.
Involucral scales naked, valvate.
  Flowers all perfect and tubular.
    Subacaulescent herb . . . . 2. S. PITHOSILLUM.
    Tall shrub . . . . 3. S. SECHELLENSIS.

Outer flowers of the head ligulate without anthers.
  Herbs, with entire leaves.
    Leaves linear, $\frac{1}{12}$ in. broad . . . . 4. S. BOUTONI.
    Leaves lingulate, $\frac{1}{4}$ in. broad . . . . 5. S. LINGUA.
  Shrub, with lyrate-pinnate leaves . . . . 6. S. AMBAVILLA.

1. **S. appendiculatus,** *DC. Prod.* vi. 376. A much-branched shrub, 6–10 feet high, with branches and leaves beneath clothed with persistent white cottony tomentum. Leaves short-petioled, lyrate-pinnate, subcoriaceous, green above, white beneath with raised parallel branch-veins, the end lobe oblong-lanceolate, acute, 4–5 in. long, cuneate at the base, the side ones minute, spreading, linear, entire. Heads in a crowded terminal corymb, with cottony branches. Involucre campanulate, $\frac{1}{8}$ in. long, composed of about 20 imbricated linear cottony scales. Flowers about 20 to a head, yellow, the outer with an oblong ray $\frac{1}{8}$ in. long, with three teeth at the tip. Achenes under $\frac{1}{12}$ in. long, glabrous, angular-cylindrical; pappus $\frac{1}{8}$ in. long, of caducous soft white hairs. Conyza appendiculata, *Lam.* Synarthrum appendiculatum, *Cass. Dict.* 48, 455.

MAURITIUS, on the higher hills, as the Pouce, Pieter-both, Grand Bassin, and Rivière Noire. Endemic. *Bois de chèvre*, or *chève*. *Bois de chèvre marron.*

2. **S. Pithosillum,** *DC. Prod.* vi. 375. A dwarf glabrous annual herb. Leaves in a radical rosette, lyrato-pinnate, with a large ovate terminal lobe. Stems 2–3 from a root, naked or furnished with a few small linear bracts. Heads 3–4 to a branch, on long peduncles. Involucre cylindrical, with 5–6 inner and no external scales. Flowers all discoid. Achenes whitish, glabrous, striated, shortly beaked; pappus white, very fugacious. Pithosillum lyratum, *Cass. Dict.* 41, 165.

MAURITIUS, on the Pouce, *Bory de St. Vincent.* Endemic. I have not seen specimens.

3. **S. sechellensis,** *Baker.* A glabrous shrub, 4–6 feet high. Leaves distinctly petioled, oblong, membranous, entire, 3–4 in. long, $1\frac{1}{2}$ in. broad, obtuse or subacute, cuneate at the base, rather fleshy, the veins immersed. Heads 12–20 in a lax terminal corymb, each distinctly peduncled. Involucre glabrous, between campanulate and cylindrical; scales about 10, ligulate, firm; outer 2–3 lax, minute. Flowers yellow, about 30 in a head, all tubular. Achenes $\frac{1}{8}$ in. long, glabrous, cylindrical; pappus $\frac{1}{4}$ in. long, of very numerous very fine pure white hairs.

SEYCHELLES, in all the islands in shady damp places from 600 to 3000 feet above sea-level, *Wright*, 92! *Horne*, 316! Endemic.

4. **S. Boutoni,** *Baker.* A much-branched glabrous perennial, $\frac{1}{2}$–1 foot high, with slender terete branches. Leaves sessile, linear, entire or obscurely toothed, 1–$1\frac{1}{2}$ in. long, $\frac{1}{12}$ in. broad, subobtuse, one-nerved, rather fleshy, narrowed to the base. Heads 1–3 to a branch, each on a long peduncle, with minute linear bracts. Involucre campanulate,

$\frac{1}{4}$ in. long; scales about 15, linear, naked; several small lax outer ones at the base. Flowers yellow, about 30 in a head; outer with an oblong ligule $\frac{1}{4}$ in. long. Achenes $\frac{1}{12}$ in long, cylindrical, glabrous; pappus $\frac{1}{4}$ in. long, of pure white soft caducous hairs.

Island of RODRIGUEZ, plentiful, *Bouton! Duncan! Dr. Balfour!* Endemic.

S. linearis, DC. Prod. vi. 375, "ex insulis mauritianis," which I have not seen, must be very near this. It is said to have entire or subdenticulate leaves $\frac{1}{8}$ in. broad, the upper half-amplexicaul, few heads in a lax corymb and involucre without any minute outer basal scales.

5. **S. Lingua,** *Poir.; DC. Prod.* vi. 375. Apparently perennial. Stems firm, branched, terete, glabrous. Leaves petioled, entire, lingulate, obtuse, $\frac{1}{2}$–$\frac{3}{4}$ in. long, $\frac{1}{6}$ in. broad, subacute at the base, rather fleshy. Corymb of few heads on an elongated scaly peduncle. Involucre glabrous, the scales lanceolate with a membranous border. Heads the thickness of those of *S. vulgaris*, but shorter, the outer flowers ligulate, all yellow.

MAURITIUS, gathered by Commerson. Described by Poiret from a specimen of Desfontaines. Unknown to Bojer and the recent resident botanists. Endemic.

6. **S. Ambavilla,** *DC. Prod.* vi. 376 A much-branched glabrous shrub, with very slender crowded ascending branchlets. Leaves sessile, lyrate-pinnate, subcoriaceous, glabrous, with a large linear inciso-dentate terminal lobe an inch or less long, $\frac{1}{4}$ in. broad, subobtuse, cuneate at the base, and 2–3 crowded spreading minute linear entire lobes at the base. Heads in dense terminal corymbs. Involucre funnel-shaped, $\frac{1}{3}$ in. long; scales 8–10, glabrous, linear, with a deltoid tip; outer at base 1–2, minute. Flowers 12–15 to a head, yellow; outer with a ligulate ray $\frac{1}{8}$ in. long. Achenes $\frac{1}{12}$ in. long, angular-cylindrical; pappus as long as the achene, of copious rather firm ciliated white hairs like those of *Faujasia*. Hubertia Ambavilla, *Bory, Voyage*, i. 334, *tab.* 14, *fig.* 1.

MAURITIUS, a specimen in the Kew collection from Baron Delessert, said to have been gathered by Commerson, but there may have been some mistake about the island, as it is a well-known Bourbon species, and has not been seen in Mauritius by Bojer or the recent local botanists.

There is a specimen in the Kew herbarium from Delessert of *Eriothrix lycopodioides*, DC. Prod. vi. 293, labelled as gathered by Commerson in Mauritius, but as it is a plant well-known in Bourbon, and no one else has found it, I fear an error, as in the case *Senecio Ambavilla*. It is a small rigid erect shrub of the hill-tops, much-branched dichotomously, with densely imbricated ascending linear-subulate coriaceous leaves under $\frac{1}{4}$ in. long, heads at the end of the stem without any involucre than a whorl of ordinary ascending leaves and minute heterogamous tubular florets emerging from a dense white woolly mass formed by the multiserial pappus of the cylindrical achenes.

22. LACTUCA, Linn.

Heads of numerous yellow flowers, all ligulate and fertile. Involucre campanulate; scales herbaceous, 2–3-serial, imbricated. Receptacle flat, naked. Anthers sagittate at the base, not tailed. Style-arms terete. Achenes broad, glabrous, flattened, with a distinct beak and a long pappus of copious soft fine simple hairs.—Herbs with milky juice, alternate often compound leaves, and numerous heads in lax panicles. DISTRIB. Mainly north temperate. Species 60.

1. **L. indica,** *Linn.; DC. Prod.* vii. 136. A robust glabrous annual or biennial, 4–6 feet high. Leaves radical and many below the inflorescence, sessile, not sagittate at the base, nor auricled, 4–6 in. long, lanceolate, mostly runcinate, with deep spreading linear lobes; upper entire. Heads in a long narrow panicle with short ascending laxly racemose slender branches. Involucre ½ in. long; scales 3-serial, inner much the longest, lanceolate; outer oblong, obtuse. Flowers about 30 in a head, yellow. Achenes ⅛ in. long, nearly black, obovate-oblong, with a distinct beak; pappus ¼ in. long, of copious fine soft white hairs. L. mauritiana, *Poir.; DC. Prod.* vii. 141.

MAURITIUS and SEYCHELLES, on banks and roadsides, frequent. Also East Indies and Madagascar. *Lastron. Laitron.*

23. SONCHUS, Linn.

Heads of numerous yellow flowers, all ligulate and perfect. Involucre campanulate; scales 2–3-serial, lanceolate, herbaceous, imbricated. Receptacle flat, naked. Anthers sagittate at the base, minutely tailed; style-arms terete. Achenes minute, oblong, compressed, with 3 ribs on each face, not beaked; pappus of copious soft white hairs, caducous in a ring.—Herbs, with milky juice and alternate membranous leaves, the heads in lax terminal corymbs. DISTRIB. Originally Old World, some species now cosmopolitan. Species 20–30.

Auricles of stem-leaves acute. Achenes rough . . . . 1. S. OLERACEUS.
Auricles of stem-leaves rounded. Achenes smooth . . . 2. S. ASPER.

1. **S. oleraceus,** *Linn. ex parte.* An annual weed, 2-3 feet high, with stout subglabrous sulcate stems. Basal leaves petioled, ½ foot long, runcinate-pinnate, with a large deltoid acute terminal and smaller side lobes, repand and irregularly sharply toothed; stem-leaves sessile, clasping, with a deep acute auricle. Heads in a lax corymb. Involucre campanulate, ½ inch long; scales lanceolate, persistent, thin. Achenes pale brown, glabrous, $\frac{1}{12}$ in. long, oblanceolate, with three distinct ribs, which like the interspaces are rugose-scabrous. S. ciliatus, *Lam.; DC. Prod.* vii. 185. S. Royleanus, *DC.*

MAURITIUS and RODRIGUEZ, common in waste places. Cosmopolitan. *Lastron.*

2. **S. asper,** *Vill. Delph.* iii. 158. Habit exactly of the last, but leaves less compound, with longer sharper teeth and firmer texture those of the stem with a rounded auricle. Achenes bordered and marked on the face with three distinct ribs, both ribs and interspaces smooth. S. fallax, *Wall.; DC. Prod.* vii. 185. S. eryngioides, *DC. loc. cit.*

MAURITIUS, equally common with the last and also now a cosmopolitan weed, originating doubtless in the temperate regions of the Old World. *Lastron.*

24. CREPIS, Linn.

Heads of numerous yellow flowers all fertile and ligulate. Involucre between a cylinder and a cup, of one long and one short row of linear herbaceous scales. Receptacle flat, naked. Anthers not tailed. Style-arms terete. Achenes cylindrical, with many fine ribs; pappus of a single row of soft white hairs.—Annual or perennial herbs, with milky juice, alternate leaves, the lower mostly pinnate or pinnatifid and copious heads in terminal corymbs. DISTRIB. Cosmopolitan, mostly Old World. Species 130.

1. **C. japonica,** *Benth. Fl. Austral.* iii. 679. An annual herb, 1–3 feet high, with a few short hairs in the lower part. Leaves in a dense basal rosette, present with the flowers, membranous, pinnate-runcinate, 3–6 in. long, the upper lobes connected, the lower free, deltoid, repand-denticulate. Stem fragile, branched low down, with a few distant reduced leaves. Flowers very numerous, in lax corymbs. Involucre $\frac{1}{4}$ in. long; scales valvate, inner 8, outer 5, minute. Flowers in a head 12–16. Achene $\frac{1}{12}$ in. long, narrowed to the tip; pappus $\frac{1}{8}$ in. long, of copious soft white hairs. Youngia japonica, mauritiana, multiflora, Thunbergiana and fastigiata, *DC.* Y. lyrata, *Cass.*

MAURITIUS, a frequent weed. Japan, Australia, Trop. Asia, Bourbon, etc.

25. MICRORHYNCHUS, Less.

Heads of few yellow flowers, all ligulate and perfect. Involucre cylindrical; scales imbricated in 2–3 rows, lanceolate, thin, persistent. Receptacle flat, naked. Anthers sagittate at the base, not distinctly tailed. Achenes glabrous, tetragono-cylindrical, not beaked; pappus of very abundant soft white hairs, deciduous in a ring. —Perennial herbs, with milky juice, leaves in a rosette at the base and from the nodes of long trailing stems; heads few, scattered. DISTRIB. Warmer parts of the Old World. Species about 20.

1. **M. sarmentosus,** *DC. Prod.* vii. 181. A glabrous perennial herb, with a fusiform milky root. Leaves in a dense basal rosette, oblanceolate, 2–3 in. long, subsessile, deeply pinnatifid, with few or many obtuse or subacute lobes. Stems slender, trailing to a length of a foot or more, rooting and producing smaller tufts of leaves from distant nodes. Heads 1–6 from a node, on short scaly pedicels. Involucre cylindrical, $\frac{3}{8}$–$\frac{1}{2}$ in. long; eight inner scales much the longest. Flowers 10–12 in a head. Achenes glabrous, $\frac{1}{6}$ in. long, not narrowed at all either to tip or base; pappus $\frac{1}{4}$ in. long, of very copious pure white hairs permanently connate at the base. Launæa pinnatifida, *Cass.*; *Bojer, Hort. Maur.* 192.

MAURITIUS, frequent on the sandy sea-shore; Ile aux Tonneliers and Flat Island. Also Tropical Asia, Madagascar, Bourbon, Zambesi-land. *M. bellidifolius*, DC. Prod. loc. cit., is a variety with the leaves nearly entire.

Of the commonly-cultivated plants of this order, *Cichorium Intybus*, *Tagetes patula*, and *Zinnia multiflora* are enumerated amongst the introduced species in Dupont's Mauritian Catalogue.

ORDER LVII. GOODENIACEÆ.

Flowers hermaphrodite. Calyx-tube adnate to the ovary; limb equally 5-toothed, or obsolete. Corolla gamopetalous, slit down the tube, the limb 5-partite, more or less irregular. Stamens 5, epigynous; filaments filiform; anthers free or connate, basifixed, 2-celled, slit longitudinally. Ovary usually 2-celled; ovules one or many in a cell; style simple; stigma fleshy, surrounded by a cup (indusium). Fruit drupaceous or capsular. Seeds albuminous.—Herbs or shrubs, with alternate exstipulate leaves. Allied to *Campanulaceæ*, but differing by its remarkable stigma. DISTRIB. Mostly Australian. Species 200.

1. SCÆVOLA, Linn.

Calyx-tube adnate to the ovary, campanulate; limb 5-toothed or nearly truncate. Corolla secund-hypocrateriform, with a cylindrical tube, slit all down the upper side to the base, and 5 subequal lobes, spreading on the lower side. Stamens 5, epigynous; filaments filiform; anthers shedding their pollen before the flower opens. Ovary inferior, 1–4-celled; ovules solitary in the cells; style filiform, as long as the tube; stigma capitate, surrounded by a densely fringed cup, becoming curved and the cup closing when the flower expands. Fruit a plum-like drupe with a spongy mesocarp and bony endocarp.—Shrubs with alternate entire leaves, the flowers in copious dichotomous axillary cymes. DISTRIB. Mostly Australian. Species 60.

Calyx-teeth as long as the tube . . . . 1. S. KŒNIGII.
Calyx-teeth obsolete . . . . 2. S. PLUMIERI.

1. **S. Kœnigii,** *Vahl; DC. Prod.* vii. 505. A shrub, 4–8 feet high, the longer branches decumbent, sending out long erect soft stout branchlets. Leaves with tufts of white silky hairs in their axils, sessile, obovate, obtuse, entire or slightly repand, 4–9 in. long, narrowed from the middle to the base, subcoriaceous, rather fleshy. Flowers in copious peduncled dichotomous cymes in the axils of the leaves. Branches with many small opposite bracts, those at the base of the calyx caducous. Calyx glabrous, $\frac{1}{4}$–$\frac{1}{3}$ in. long; teeth linear, as long as the tube. Corolla under an inch long, greenish-yellow on the outside; lobes obtuse, as long as the tube, with a crumpled white border. Drupe globose, whitish, $\frac{1}{2}$ in. thick, with a spongy mesocarp and bony 2-celled endocarp. *Bot. Mag. t.* 2732. S. Lobelia, *Linn.* S. sericea, *Forst.*

MAURITIUS and SEYCHELLES, common on the sea-shore. Polynesia to Africa. *Veloutier blanc.*

2. **S. Plumieri,** *Vahl; DC. Prod.* vii. 506. Habit of the other species, but leaves without tufts of hairs in their axils, smaller, more fleshy and more coriaceous, the pair of small bracts at the base of the

calyx persistent, calyx reduced to a mere rim at the top of the ovary and corolla-lobes narrower and more acute, without a distinct crumpled border. S. Thunbergii and senegalensis, *DC. Prod. loc. cit.*

MAURITIUS, on shores, *Sieber*, ii. 122! Abundant on Flat Island, *Bojer*. Tropics of both hemispheres.

ORDER LVIII. CAMPANULACEÆ.

Calyx-tube adnate to the ovary; limb regularly 5-cleft. Corolla gamopetalous, with 5 regular or irregular lobes. Stamens 5, epigynous or epipetalous; filaments free or joined; anthers 2-celled, basifixed. Ovary 2–5-celled; ovules many; placentation axile; style filiform, clothed with a ring of or throughout with collecting hairs; stigmas as many as the ovary-cells. Fruit a capsule, dehiscing variously by slits or pores, or an indehiscent berry. Seeds minute, albuminous, dotted.—Herbs with alternate exstipulate leaves, milky juice, and mostly showy racemed flowers. DISTRIB. Cosmopolitan. Species 1000.

Corolla regular. Anthers free, not bearded . . . . . . 1. HETEROCHÆNIA.
Corolla irregular. Anthers syngenesious, bearded . . . 2. LOBELIA.

1. HETEROCHÆNIA, A. DC.

Calyx-tube oblong-cylindrical; teeth long, lanceolate, acuminate, ciliated, rather imbricated in bud. Corolla campanulate, deeply 5-cleft. Stamens 5, free. Ovary inferior, 3-celled; style cylindrical, as long as the corolla, pilose, with three broad stigmas. Capsule cylindrical, trilocular, at first opening loculicidally by three valves at the top, afterwards by pores at the base between the ten ribs. Seeds abundant, ovoid-trigonous, dotted. The only species.

1. **H. ensifolia,** *A. DC. Prod.* vii. 442. Stems woody, unbranched, terete, 1–2 feet high, as thick as a man's finger, marked with the scars of the fallen leaves. Leaves crowded near the top of the stem, subcoriaceous, glabrous, lanceolate, acute, 4–8 in. long, $\frac{1}{2}$–$\frac{3}{4}$ in. broad at the middle, acute, narrowed to $\frac{1}{4}$ in. above the deltoid clasping base, strongly nerved, conspicuously ciliato-denticulate. Inflorescence a lax panicle a foot long with large leafy bracts and ascending few-flowered corymbose branches. Calyx-teeth $\frac{3}{8}$–$\frac{5}{8}$ in., twice as long as the tube. Corollas pendent, an inch long, yellowish, with 5 purple blotches inside. Capsule erect, glabrous, an inch long. Campanula ensifolia, *Lam. Encyc.* i. 582.

MAURITIUS, on dry slopes of the part of the Pouce called the Fenêtre de Pieter-both, *Bojer!* Also Bourbon, *Balfour!*

2. LOBELIA, Linn.

Calyx-tube adnate to the ovary; teeth 5, linear or lanceolate. Corolla with a cylindrical tube, slit down the upper side; limb

2-lipped; two upper teeth smaller, three larger forming the lower lip. Stamens epigynous; filaments as long as the corolla-tube, joined in the upper part and the basifixed anthers also syngenesious, the two lower bearded. Ovary 2-celled; style filiform, with a ring of collecting hairs; stigma scarcely lobed. Capsule many-seeded, opening above the calyx-tube.—Herbs with alternate leaves, the flowers in terminal racemes. DISTRIB. Cosmopolitan. Species about 200.

Ovary almost completely adnate to the calyx. Bract-leaves like the stem leaves.
  Corolla $\frac{1}{4}$–$\frac{1}{3}$ in. long . . . . 1. L. SERPENS.
  Corolla $\frac{1}{2}$–$\frac{3}{4}$ in. long . . . . 2. L. VAGANS.
Ovary only half-adnate to the calyx. Bract leaves minute * L. CLIFFORTIANA.

1. **L. serpens,** *Lam.; DC. Prod.* vii. 368. A perennial herb, with wide-trailing slender mostly glabrous stems, simple or with ascending branches. Leaves membranous, abundant; lower oblanceolate, short-petioled, the rest linear, sessile, $\frac{1}{12}$–$\frac{1}{8}$ in. broad, obscurely or distinctly toothed, under an inch long, narrowed from the middle to the base and point. Flowers from the axils of the upper leaves in a lax raceme; pedicels $\frac{1}{4}$–$\frac{1}{2}$ in. long, mostly shorter than their subtending leaves. Calyx-teeth linear, $\frac{1}{12}$ in. long, equalling the obconic flower-calyx. Corolla $\frac{1}{3}$ in. long; lobes blue, lower obovate, the throat yellowish, blue spotted. Capsule obovoid, $\frac{1}{4}$ in long, scarcely protruding from the calyx-tube. L. filiformis, *Lam.; DC. Prod. loc. cit.* L. telephioides, *DC.* L. polymorpha, *Bory.* L. bicolor, *Bojer, Hort. Maur.* 193, *non Sims.*

MAURITIUS, frequent in dry soil. Also Bourbon and Madagascar. *L. madagascariensis*, R. and S., seems only a variety of the same species, with larger leaves (lower oblong or obovate-oblong $\frac{1}{8}$–$\frac{1}{4}$ in. broad), grown in richer soil.

2. **L. vagans,** *Balf. fil. MSS.* A tufted perennial, glabrous in all its parts, with trailing branched slender stems a foot or more long, acutely-angled upwards. Leaves oblong or lanceolate, membranous, shortly petioled, $\frac{3}{4}$–$1\frac{1}{2}$ in. long, obtuse, crenate, cuneate and entire at the base. Flowers 6–8 in a lax raceme from the axils of the reduced upper leaves, on ascending pedicels $\frac{1}{2}$–$\frac{3}{4}$ in. long. Calyx-teeth linear, $\frac{1}{8}$ in. long, equalling the obconic tube. Corolla white, $\frac{1}{2}$–$\frac{3}{4}$ in. long, the oblong-ligulate teeth a third as long as the cylindrical tube. Capsule little protruded from the calyx-tube.

RODRIGUEZ, common on the cliffs of the upper part of the valleys, *Dr. Balfour!*

* *L. Cliffortiana,* Willd.; DC. Prod. vii. 372, a native of Tropical America, is now well-established in Mauritius, and has often been distributed as *L. filiformis.* It is a rather robust erect glabrous annual, 1–$1\frac{1}{2}$ in. high, with petioled broad ovate membranous deeply crenate leaves confined to the lower half of the stem, a long ($\frac{1}{2}$–1 ft.) lax panicle, bract-leaves minute linear-subulate, corolla purplish scarcely exceeding the linear calyx teeth, capsule oblong $\frac{1}{4}$ in. long, the upper

half protruding from the calyx-tube. It was found by Dr. Balfour in Rodriguez at the mouth of the Rivière Grande.

ORDER LIX. ERICACEÆ.

Flowers regular, hermaphrodite. Calyx small, inferior, with 4–5 lobes. Corolla-tube campanulate or urceolate, with as many teeth as the sepals. Stamens twice as many as the sepals, hypogynous; anthers 2-celled, dehiscing by a pore at the top of each of the cells. Ovary free, 4–5-celled; placentation axile; ovules many in a cell; style simple; stigma simple. Fruit a small capsule, with regular loculicidal dehiscence. Seeds many, minute, albuminous.—Evergreen shrubs, with exstipulate alternate leaves, the flowers in clusters or racemes. DISTRIB. Temperate regions. Species about 1000.

Corolla campanulate, deeply cleft, tetramerous. Leaves crowded, 1-nerved . . . . 1. PHILIPPIA.
Corolla urceolate, shallowly cleft, pentamerous. Leaves flat, lanceolate or oblong . . . . 2. AGAURIA.

1. PHILIPPIA, Klotzsch.

Calyx minute, 4-fid. Corolla small, campanulate, with 4 teeth about as long as the tube. Stamens 8, included; filaments free or connate; anthers not tailed, opening by two pores at the top. Ovary 4-celled; ovules many in a cell; style filiform; stigma conspicuous, peltate, lobed, Fruit a dry capsule, with loculicidal dehiscence. Seeds minute.—Glabrous heath-like shrubs, with crowded small coriaceous 1-nerved leaves and small campanulate flowers at the end of the branches. DISTRIB. Cape and Mascaren Isles. Species about 20.

Leaves $\frac{1}{4}$–$\frac{1}{3}$ in. long . . . . 1. P. ABIETINA.
Leaves $\frac{1}{12}$–$\frac{1}{8}$ in. long . . . . 2. P. MONTANA.
Leaves $\frac{1}{24}$ in. long . . . . 3. P. BRACHYPHYLLA.

1. **P. abietina,** *Klotzsch; Benth. in DC. Prod.* vii. 696. A much-branched shrub, 2–5 feet high, with crowded erect branches. Leaves $\frac{1}{4}$–$\frac{1}{3}$ long, erecto-patent, densely crowded, glossy on both sides, ligulate, rigidly coriaceous, with revolute edges. Flowers clustered at the end of the branches in the axils of the leaves, on very short pedicels. Calyx with four unequal obtuse lobes. Corolla $\frac{1}{12}$ in. long, campanulate, reddish-brown. Stamens free, glabrous, the anther dilated at the base. Stigma mostly exserted. Salaxis abietina, *Bory; Bojer, Hort. Maur.* 195. S. mauritiana, *Bojer in Wall. Cat. No.* 1525.

Var. ARBORESCENS, *Baker*. Pedicels much longer ($\frac{1}{8}$–$\frac{1}{4}$ in.) so that the clusters of flowers are laxer, rather pilose. Stigma much exserted. Salaxis arborescens, *Willd.; Bojer, Hort. Maur.* 195. Philippia arborescens, *Klotzsch; Benth. loc. cit.*

MAURITIUS, on the higher mountains; Pouce range, Grand Bassin, etc. Endemic. *Bruyère des montagnes.*

2. **P. montana,** *Klotzsch.*; *Benth. in DC. Prod.* viii. 295. Above a foot high, with crowded slender whitish branches. Leaves crowded, $\frac{1}{12}$–$\frac{1}{8}$ in. long, glossy, ligulate, rigidly coriaceous, 1-nerved, ascending and closely imbricated. Flowers 1–3, near the end of the branches in the axils of the leaves, on very short pedicels. Calyx-lobes oblong, rather unequal, the longest about as long as the corolla. Corolla under $\frac{1}{12}$ in. long. Filaments and anthers closely connate. Stigma just exserted.

MAURITIUS; only one small specimen seen in Mr. Bentham's herbarium, received from De Candolle. It is a Bourbon plant (Boivin), and the names of the islands may have been crossed.

3. **P. brachyphylla,** *Benth. in DC. Prod.* vii. 697. Rising a few inches above the soil, producing very crowded erect branched pale branchlets $\frac{1}{48}$ in. thick. Leaves adpressed to the stems, glabrous, imbricated, $\frac{1}{24}$ in. long, 1-nerved, glossy. Flowers 1–3, near the end of the branchlets, on pedicels as long as the corolla. Calyx-lobes obtuse, subequal, shorter than the corolla, which is broadly campanulate, under a $\frac{1}{12}$ in. deep. Stamens not seen.

MAURITIUS, on the highest mountains. Endemic. This (and not P. montana) is most likely *Salaxis montana*, Bojer, Hort. Maur. 195, as we have it from Bojer, Bouton, and Judge Blackburn.

2. AGAURIA, Hk. fil.

Calyx campanulate, small, persistent, with 5 deltoid teeth; æstivation valvate. Corolla ventricose, contracted at the mouth, with 5 short deltoid lobes. Stamens 10; filaments flattened, pilose; anthers adnate, not tailed, each cell opening by a large oblique pore at the top. Ovary free, 5-celled; ovules many in a cell; style filiform; stigma capitate. Fruit a globose capsule, with loculicidal dehiscence, and no central column; placentas basilar. Seeds copious, with the testa produced into a wing beyond the nucleus at each end.—Shrubs with alternate entire coriaceous leaves, the flowers in copious racemes. DISTRIB. Continental Africa and Mascaren Isles. Species 3 or 4.

1. **A. salicifolia,** *Hook. fil. Gen. Plant.* ii. 586. A much-branched glabrous shrub, 4–5 feet high. Leaves distinctly petioled, lanceolate, entire, acuminate, cuneate at the base, green above, pale beneath, 2–3 in. long, $\frac{1}{4}$–$\frac{1}{2}$ in. broad. Flowers in abundant close subsecund axillary and terminal racemes 2–3 in. long; pedicels spreading, $\frac{1}{8}$–$\frac{1}{4}$ in. long. Calyx broadly campanulate. Corolla oblong, purplish, $\frac{1}{4}$–$\frac{1}{3}$ in long. Fruit a globose glabrous capsule the size of a pea, splitting into 5 valves, girt by the persistent clasping calyx. Andromeda salicifolia, *Lam.*; *Bot. Mag. tab.* 3286. Leucothoe salicifolia, *DC. Prod.* vii. 602.

MAURITIUS, in mountain woods of the Pouce, Montagne Ory, etc. *A. pyrifolia*, Pers., is a variety with oblong-lanceolate leaves $\frac{3}{4}$-1 inch broad. Also Madagascar.

Bourbon, Camaroon Mountains. Bojer gives *L. buxifolia*, DC. loc. cit. (Andromeda buxifolia, *Lam.*, *Smith, Ic. ined.* t. 59; *Hook. Bot. Mag.* t. 2660), as a Mauritian species. This has oblong leaves broadly rounded at the base, obtuse or slightly cuspidate, pilose branches and pedicels and larger calyx (finally ⅛ in. deep); but what we have from Mauritius under the name is only the broad-leaved form of *A. salicifolia*, our only specimens of the true plant being from Bourbon.

ORDER LIX.* PLUMBAGINACEÆ.

Of the order *Plumbaginaceæ*, marked in regular pentamerous Monopetalæ by its 1-celled free ovary with 5 long filiform styles and single ovule pendulous from an erect long basal funiculus, we have two subspontaneous species :

Plumbago capensis, Thunb., Bot. Mag. t. 2100, Bot. Reg. t. 417, received from Mauritius from Mr. Telfair, a native of the Cape, a subscandent shrub with oblong-spathulate nearly sessile entire leaves, flowers in dense corymbose spikes, a tubular gland-ciliated calyx, and a hypocrateriform blue corolla with a tube about three times as long as the limb, and limb nearly an inch broad with obovate segments ;

P. zeylanica, Linn., a native of Tropical Asia, found abundantly by Dr. Balfour in Rodriguez, with ovate-spathulate leaves, a more densely glandular-hispid calyx, and a white corolla with tube not more than twice as long as the calyx, and a limb not much over half an inch across.

What "*P. auriculata*, Lam. ?" given by Bojer, Hort. Maur. 263, as wild on the crest of Montagne Longuo, may be, I have no means of ascertaining. Lamarck's *auriculata* is the same as *capensis*.

ORDER LX. PLANTAGINACEÆ.

Flowers regular, in Mauritius hermaphrodite. Sepals 4, free, persistent, imbricated. Corolla-tube campanulate, with 4 spreading lobes. Stamens 4, exserted, epipetalous or hypogynous. Anthers 2-celled, versatile. Ovary superior, 1–4-celled; ovules one or more; style simple, pilose. Fruit dehiscent or indehiscent. Seeds peltate, albuminous.—Scapose annual or perennial herbs, with minute flowers in dense spikes or heads. DISTRIB. Species 50; principally temperate regions.

1. PLANTAGO, Linn.

Sepals 4, free, persistent. Corolla-tube campanulate, persistent, scariose, with 4 spreading lobes. Stamens inserted in the corolla-tube. Ovary 2–4 celled; ovules one or more in a cell. Fruit a small membranous capsule with circumscissile dehiscence.—Annual or perennial herbs with a dense radical rosette of broad or narrow leaves, and small flowers in dense spikes. DISTRIB. All temperate and warm temperate regions. Species 50.

Leaves broad. Ovules 4-8 in a cell . . . . 1. P. MAJOR.
Leaves narrow. Ovules solitary . . . . 2. P. LANCEOLATA.

1. **P. major,** *Linn.; Decne. in DC. Prod.* xiii. 694. Perennial, nearly glabrous. Leaves $\frac{1}{4}$–$\frac{1}{2}$ foot long, ovate or obovate, often repand, 5–9-nerved, with a broad channelled petiole nearly as long as the blade. Peduncle shorter than or as long as the leaves. Spike cylindrical, 3–12 in. long; bracts minute, green, lanceolate. Sepals $\frac{1}{12}$ in. long, oblong, imbricated, with a broad membranous border. Corolla brown, with spreading lanceolate lobes half as long as the tube. Stamens and style little exserted. Capsule 2-celled; seeds 4–8 in a cell, black, rugose. P. asiatica, *Linn.*

MAURITIUS, in fields at Moka, Plaines Wilhelms, Grandport, etc., considered by Bojer as introduced. RODRIGUEZ. Temperate zone of Old World, but now widely diffused.

2. **P. lanceolata,** *Linn.; Decne. in DC. Prod.* xiii. 714. Perennial, with a short oblique rootstock, pilose at the crown. Leaves lanceolate, $\frac{1}{2}$–1 foot long, narrowed to both ends, membranous, 5-nerved, with a short channelled pilose petiole. Peduncles much longer than the leaves. Spikes dense, usually oblong; bracts minute, scariose. Sepals $\frac{1}{12}$ in. long, membranous beyond the keel. Corolla-tube urceolate; lobes deltoid. Stamens and styles much exserted; anthers yellow. Capsule 2-celled; seeds solitary, oblong, brown-black, shining. P. capensis, *Bojer, Hort. Maur.* p. 263, *non Thunb.*

MAURITIUS, common both in the low country and on the peaks. Now widely-spread, but probably originating in the temperate zone of the Old World.

ORDER LX.* PRIMULACEÆ.

* *Anagallis arvensis,* Linn., the common European Pimpernel, now spread widely as a weed of cultivated ground, occurs occasionally in Mauritius. It is a diffuse much-branched annual, with slender square stems, small sessile opposite ovate leaves dotted beneath, flowers 1–3 from the axils of the leaves on long pedicels, 5 free lanceolate sepals $\frac{1}{4}$ in. long, broad, obtuse red or blue petals not longer than the sepals, and a globose capsule the size of a pea which dehisces in a horizontal line round the middle, with many seeds on a free central placenta.

* *Lubinia spathulata,* Vent. Hort. Cels, t. 19 (Lysimachia mauritiana, *Lam.*) which has been attributed to Mauritius, is evidently identical with Lysimachia lineariloba, *Hook. and Arn.* (L. lubinioides, *Sieb. and Zucc.*) a plant of China and Japan. We have lately received it from Bourbon from Dr. Cordemoy.

ORDER LXI. MYRSINACEÆ.

Flowers regular, hermaphrodite or polygamous, usually pentamerous. Calyx minute, persistent, cut halfway down or more. Corolla rotate, cut down to a very short tube. Stamens inserted in the short corolla opposite its lobes; filaments short; anthers basifixed, 2-celled, dehiscing longitudinally. Ovary sessile, 1-celled, with a free central placenta; ovules peltate, few or many; style short cylindrical; stigma capitate or lobed. Fruit a small pea-like drupe, often 1-seeded; albumen horny.—Shrubs with alternate exstipulate entire coriaceous leaves dotted with black glands and terminal or axillary inflorescence. DISTRIB. Tropics of both hemispheres. Species 500.

Climber with terminal inflorescence . . . . 1. EMBELIA.
Erect shrubs with axillary inflorescence.
  Flowers in crowded fascicles from the leafless part of the branches . . . . 2. MYRSINE.
  Flowers in racemes or panicles from the axils of the leaves . . . . 3. ARDISIA.

1. EMBELIA, Burm.

Flowers polygamous or hermaphrodite, mostly pentamerous. Calyx minute, deeply cut. Corolla-lobes oblong, imbricated in bud. Stamens inserted at the bottom of the corolla; filaments very short. Ovary ovoid, 1-celled, with 1–4 ovules on a basilar placenta; style cylindrical, simple; stigma capitate. Fruit a small globose 1-seeded drupe.—Climbers with minute flowers in terminal panicles. DISTRIB. Tropics of the Old World. Species about 50.

1. **E. micrantha,** *A. DC. Prod.* viii. 84. A climbing shrub, with slender terete branches. Leaves distinctly petioled, oblong, 3–4 in. long, obtuse or subacute, cuneate at the base, subcoriaceous, glabrous. Flowers in dense racemes, forming decompound deltoid terminal panicles, with brown tomentose branches; pedicels very short. Calyx pilose, cut down nearly to the base. Bud globose. Corolla $\frac{1}{24}$ in. long, cut down nearly to the base. Badula scandens, *Bojer, Hort. Maur.* 196.

MAURITIUS, in the hill-forests of the southern half of the island. Endemic. *Liane Poilly.*

2. MYRSINE, Linn.

Flowers polygamous or hermaphrodite, usually pentamerous. Calyx minute, with round spreading lobes. Corolla rotate, the lobes oblong, obtuse, imbricated in bud. Stamens 5, inserted in the very short corolla-tube; filaments very short. Ovary globose, 1-celled; ovules few, on a round placenta; style cylindrical, very short; stigma various. Fruit a 1-seeded pea-like drupe.—Shrubs, with alternate entire coriaceous leaves, the flowers in crowded fascicles from the old branches. DISTRIB. Round the world in the tropics. Species 80.

1. **M. capitellata,** *Wall.; A. DC. Prod.* viii. 94. A small tree, 10–20 feet high, with spreading reddish-green branches. Leaves crowded at the end of the branchlets, oblong, coriaceous, sessile, obtuse, cuneate at the base, 2–3 in. long, glabrous, minutely reticulated and black-dotted. Flowers 4–9 together in crowded fascicles on the old wood below the leaves; pedicels $\frac{1}{12}$ in. long. Calyx persistent, with 5 minute round spreading lobes. Corolla caducous, $\frac{1}{12}$ in. long. Drupe small, globose, pea-like, 1-seeded.

SEYCHELLES, on and near the tops of the mountains in Mahé and Silhouette, *Horne*, 442! 588! East Indies and Ceylon, not African.

3. ARDISIA, Swartz.

Flowers hermaphrodite. Calyx minute, campanulate, with 5 deltoid teeth. Corolla rotate, the 5 lobes twisted and imbricated in bud. Stamens 5; filaments very short. Ovary globose, with few ovules on a basal placenta; stigma capitate. Fruit a small coriaceous 1-seeded pea-like drupe.—Shrubs, with alternate entire leaves and abundant flowers in axillary panicles or racemes. DISTRIB. Tropics of both hemispheres. Species 200.

Racemes few-flowered, simple . . . . 1. A. SIEBERI.
Racemes copiously panicled . . . . 2. A. INSULARIS.

1. **A. Sieberi,** *Baker.* A much-branched glabrous erect shrub, 5–6 feet high. Leaves obovate-oblong, obtuse or obtusely cuspidate, 2–3 in. long, 1–1½ in. broad above the middle, deltoid at the base, subcoriaceous, reticulato-venose when mature and distinctly gland-dotted; petiole ¼–½ in. long. Racemes axillary, simple, distinctly peduncled, few-flowered, ½–⅓ as long as the leaves, with spreading pedicels ⅛–¼ in. long. Calyx $\frac{1}{24}$ in. long, the teeth broad and obtuse, with a whitish ciliated edge. Expanded corolla ¼–⅓ in. broad, with obtuse lobes. Drupe globose, ⅓ in. thick. Badula Sieberi, *A. DC. Prod.* viii. 108 Ardisia latifolia, *Sieber, Herb. Maur.* ii. 53.

MAURITIUS, in mountain-woods of Grand Bassin and the Savanne range. Also Madagascar.

2. **A. insularis,** *Baker.* An erect shrub, glabrous in all its parts. Leaves crowded, obovate-oblong, subcoriaceous, obtuse, cuneate at the base, reticulato-venose and gland-dotted, 3–6 in. long, 1½–2 in. broad above the middle; petiole very short, channelled. Flowers in distinctly-peduncled copious axillary panicles as long or half as long as the leaves, with spreading racemose branches; pedicels about as long as the flowers. Calyx $\frac{1}{24}$ in. long, with round ciliated teeth. Bud ovoid or globose. Corolla ⅛ in. long, the lobes subobtuse or subacute. Drupe the size of a small pea. Badula insularis, *A. DC. Prod.* viii. 109. B. Barthesia and micrantha, *Bojer, Hort. Maur.* 196, *non A. DC.*

MAURITIUS, frequent in the mountain-forests. Also Bourbon. Judging from the description, *B. reticulata*, A. DC. Prod. viii. 108, seems a variety of this with larger leaves (6–10 in. long), and panicles as long as the leaves and short pedicels; *B. multiflora*, A. DC. Prod. viii. 109, a variety with rather pointed leaves 5 - 6 in. long, and panicles crowded at the top of the branch, short-peduncled and not more than $\frac{1}{3}$-$\frac{1}{2}$ as long as the leaf; and *B. crassa*, A. DC., a form with thick branches, very thick obtuse leaves, short subsessile congested panicles $\frac{1}{3}$–$\frac{1}{2}$ as long as the leaf and short pedicels. *Bois Pintade.*

Mr. Horne sends from shaded forests in Mahé, Seychelles (No. 541), what is probably a species of this genus, of which he has not been able to procure flowers; and Dr. Balfour found in Rodriguez, in the upper part of the valleys, a plant resembling in leaf the large forms of *A. insularis*, with slightly compound panicles shorter than the leaves, a minute obconic calyx with deltoid teeth, and a depresso-globose glabrous drupe half an inch thick.

ORDER LXII. SAPOTACEÆ.

Flowers regular, hermaphrodite. Calyx persistent, coriaceous, cut nearly to the base into 5–8 lobes. Corolla with a short tube and as many or 2–3 times as many lobes as the sepals. Stamens inserted into the tube of the corolla, the fertile ones 1–3 times the number of the sepals, placed opposite the petals, often alternating with petaloid barren ones (staminodia). Ovary many-celled; placentation axile; ovules solitary in the cells; style and stigma simple. Fruit baccate, mostly by abortion 1-seeded; albumen present or absent. — Trees or shrubs, with copious milky juice, entire coriaceous exstipulate leaves and copious small inconspicuous flowers in lateral fascicles. DISTRIB. Round the world in the tropical zone. Species about 300.

Staminodes none . . . . 1. LABOURDONNAISIA.
Staminodes as many as the sepals.
  Sepals and petals each 5–8 . . . . 2. SIDEROXYLON.
  Petals 18–24.
    Outer petals entire . . . . 3. MIMUSOPS.
    Outer petals deeply laciniated . . . . 4. IMBRICARIA.

1. LABOURDONNAISIA, Bojer.

Calyx divided nearly to the base into 6 oblong-deltoid lobes, of which 3 are external. Petals as long as the calyx, all entire, 12 in one row, or 18, of which the inner 6 form a second inner row. Stamens as many as the petals; anthers as long as the subulate filaments. Staminodia none. Ovary 6-celled; ovules solitary in the cells. Fruit a large 1-seeded berry, with a coriaceous skin. — Trees, with oblong coriaceous leaves, the axillary flowers crowded towards the end of the branches. DISTRIB. Two other species, one in Natal, the other Cuban.

Leaves three times as long as broad, green beneath . 1. L. CALOPHYLLOIDES.
Leaves twice as long as broad, whitish beneath . . 2. L. GLAUCA.

1. **L. calophylloides,** *Bojer, Hort. Maur.* 199 (name only). A tree 30–40 feet high, glabrous in all its parts, with stout branchlets. Leaves crowded towards the end of the branchlets, on petioles $\frac{1}{2}$ in. long, oblong, obtuse, cuneate at the base, 2–4 in. long, very rigid, green beneath, with fine immersed erecto-patent veins. Flowers on solitary or crowded often drooping pedicels $\frac{1}{2}$–$1\frac{1}{2}$ in. long. Calyx $\frac{3}{8}$ in.

long, the divisions ovate-deltoid, naked, the three outer more coriaceous. Petals 12, lanceolate, whitish, as long as or rather longer than the sepals. Stamens 12, as long as the petals, one opposite each. Fruit a 1-seeded brown berry, girt by the persistent calyx, with a gelatinous endocarp. *A. DC. Prod.* viii. 194.

MAURITIUS, in the mountain woods. *L. revoluta*, Bojer, seems to be only a form of exposed places with smaller leaves with revolute edges. *L. sarcophleia*, Bojer, I have not seen, and there is nothing in the description in the Prodromus by which to separate it clearly. Endemic. *Bois de Natte à petites feuilles.*

2. **L. glauca,** *Bojer, Hort. Maur.* 199 (name only). General habit just the same as in the other species. Petioles longer (1–1¼ in.). Leaves obovate-oblong, 2–3 in. long, rounded and emarginate at the tip, deltoid at the base, very rigid, green above, very thinly coated with white tomentum below. Peduncles shorter than the petiole, 1–3-nate. Flowers much smaller than in *L. calophylloides.* Sepals ¼–⅓ in. long, reflexed after flowering. Petals and stamens 12–13 each. Berry oblong, 1–1¼ in. long, tipped with the persistent base of the style. *DC. Prod.* viii. 195.

MAURITIUS, on the Pouce. Endemic.

2. SIDEROXYLON, Linn.

Calyx persistent, of 5 distinct obtuse coriaceous much-imbricated lobes. Corolla rotate; tube very short; lobes 5, lingulate or obovate, obtuse, as long as or rather longer than the calyx. Stamens 5 fertile, opposite the petals, with subulate filaments inserted in the short corolla-tube and versatile anthers and 5 sterile petaloid alternate with the petals. Ovary ovoid, 5-celled; cells with a single ovule in each; style simple, subulate. Fruit a small or large 1-seeded berry.—Trees, with alternate simple coriaceous leaves, the flowers in copious fascicles from nodes lower down the branch. DISTRIB. Round the world in the tropics. Species 60.

Corolla-tube very short.
  Pedicels glabrous, much longer than the calyx.
    Petals narrow-lingulate . . . . 1. S. BOUTONIANUM.
    Petals obovate . . . . 2. S. ATTENUATUM.
  Pedicels ferrugineo-tomentose, at most as long as the calyx.
    Sepals ⅛ in. long . . . . 3. S. BOJERIANUM.
    Sepals ¼ in. long . . . . 4. S. GRANDIFLORUM.
Corolla-tube as long as the lobes . . . . 5. S. LESSERTII.

1. **S. Boutonianum,** *A. DC. Prod.* viii. 179. A tree, glabrous in all its parts, with moderately stout terete rugose branches. Leaves glabrous, coriaceous, obovate-oblong, obtuse, rounded at the base, 3–6 in. long; petiole ¼–½ in. long. Flowers 3–6 in a cluster, on slender flexuose pedicel ¼–⅜ in. long. Sepals ⅛ in. long, glabrous, much

imbricated, the three inner not quite so obtuse as the two outer. Petals lingulate, as long as the sepals. Anthers lanceolate-sagittate, exserted, half as long as the glabrous filaments. S. Corsanii, *Bojer, MSS.*

MAURITIUS, in woods of the Pouce, etc. Endemic.

2. **S. attenuatum,** *A. DC. Prod.* viii. 178. A tree about 20 feet high, glabrous in all its parts, with slender branches. Leaves not crowded at the end of the branches, glossy, obovate-oblong, obtuse, cuneate at the base, 3–5 in. long; petiole $\frac{1}{2}$ in. long. Flowers 6–12 in a fascicle, both from the axils of the leaves and below them on the branch, on glabrous pedicels $\frac{1}{4}$–$\frac{1}{3}$ in. long. Sepals $\frac{1}{8}$ in. long, obtuse, much imbricated. Petals obovate, as long as the sepals. Stamens very short. Drupe glossy, $\frac{1}{2}$ in. long and thick. S. ferrugineum, *Hook. and Arn. Bot. Beech.*, 266, *t.* 25.

SEYCHELLES, not uncommon in the woods of Mahé and Praslin, *Horne*, 406! Tropical Asia, not Africa.

3. **S. Bojerianum,** *A. DC. Prod.* viii. 179. A tall tree, with stout rugose grey branches with close much-raised nodes from which the flowers spring. Leaves obovate-oblong, glabrous, obtuse, cuneate at the bases, rigidly coriaceous, 3–9 in. long, finely reticulato-venulose; petiole 1–1$\frac{1}{2}$ in. long. Flowers 3–12 in a fascicle, on very short ferrugineo-tomentose pedicels. Sepals $\frac{1}{8}$ in. long, all very obtuse, ferrugineo-tomentose. Petals lingulate, as long as the sepals. Stamens included, the obtuse anthers about as long as the filament. Drupe the size of a large pea, naked, 1-seeded. S. cinereum, *Bojer, Hort. Maur.* 197, *an Lam.?*

Var. S. PUBERULUM, *A. DC. Prod.* viii. 179. Petioles and leaves below at first matted with ferruginous tomentum like that which clothes the pedicels and sepals. Petals longer than the sepals.

MAURITIUS, common in forests through the island. I have no material for distinctly separating from this *S. parviflorum*, *longifolium* and *imbricarioides*, A. DC. Prod. viii. 179–184. The same or a very closely allied species occurs in Bourbon. *Bois cendré.*

4. **S. grandiflorum,** *A. DC. Prod.* viii. 180. A tree with stout terete branchlets. Leaves crowded at the end of the branches; petiole $\frac{3}{4}$–1$\frac{1}{4}$ in. long; blade obovate-oblong, cuneate at the base, obtuse or shortly cuspidate, coriaceous, glabrous, with raised veins. Flowers 1–3 together, the nodes little raised; pedicels $\frac{1}{4}$–$\frac{1}{3}$ in. long, ferrugineo-tomentose. Calyx $\frac{1}{4}$ in. long; sepals all broad and very obtuse, ferrugineo-tomentose. Petals lingulate, as long as the sepals. Anthers obtuse, oblong, $\frac{1}{12}$ in. long, equalling the filaments. Drupe the size of

a small apple, with a thick fleshy pericarp. Seed depresso-globose, 1½ in. thick Calvaria major, *Gærtn. Carp. t.* 200.

MAURITIUS, in the forests of Moka and Grand Bassin. A plant gathered by Dr. Balfour in Rodriguez on the banks of the Rivière Baleine agrees with this in habit and leaf, but the specimens are without either flower or fruit.

5. **S. Lessertii,** *Baker.* An unarmed tree with thick rugose branches. Leaves crowded near the end of the branches, obovate-oblong, 2–2½ in. long, coriaceous, glabrous, retuse or emarginate, narrowed to the base; petiole ½–¾ in. long, minutely puberulent. Flowers 1–3 together in the axils of the leaves on pedicels shorter than the petiole. Sepals 5–6, silky on the outside. Corolla glabrous, twice as long as the calyx. Ovary globose, silky, 5–6-celled. Sapota Lessertii, *A. DC. Prod.* viii. 174.

MAURITIUS. Described from a specimen in the Delessert herbarium at Geneva.

The *Capucin* of the Seychelles (Horne, 539) is probably a sixth unnamed species of this genus, but I have not seen flowers. It is a tree 50–60 feet high, with very stout conspicuously nodose branchlets, stout flattened petioles ¾–⅞ in. long, oblong obtuse very thick coriaceous leaves 5–9 inches long glabrous and shining above, ferrugineo-puberulent below, with many close distinct veins (not more than $\frac{1}{12}$ in. apart) spreading from the costa nearly at a right angle and remaining visible to the edge.

3. MIMUSOPS, Linn.

Calyx-lobes 6–8, biseriate, the outer ones valvate, coriaceous. Corolla-tube short; divisions 18–24, all entire, biseriate. Fertile stamens 6–8; filaments short; anthers lanceolate, acute; staminodia 6–8, petaloid, alternate with the stamens. Ovary hairy, 6–8-celled; style simple. Drupe globose or elliptical, usually by abortion 1–2-celled and 1–2-seeded.—Trees, with coriaceous entire leaves and axillary fascicled flowers. DISTRIB. Tropics of both hemispheres. Species 30.

1. **M. Erythryoxylon,** *Bojer, Hort. Maur.* 198 (name only). A tree with stout rugose branchlets. Leaves obovate-oblong, retuse, coriaceous, 1½–3 in. by 1–1½ in., rufo-sericeous below when young; petiole ½–¾ in. long. Pedicels 1–3-nate, shorter than the calyx. Sepals 8, the outer 4 silky on the outside. Corolla slightly exceeding the calyx, the divisions linear, the inner row rather broader. Fertile stamens 8. *A. DC. Prod.* viii. 202.

MAURITIUS, in mountain woods. Endemic. *Bois de Natte rouge. M. angustifolia,* Bojer, Hort. Maur. 198 (name only), is said to be very closely to this species, but to have narrower leaves.

4. IMBRICARIA, Juss.

Calyx-lobes 8, biseriate, the outer valvate, coriaceous, the inner grey, narrower. Corolla with a very short tube, the divisions as long as the calyx, the outer 16 deeply 2–5-cleft with linear lobes, the inner 8 entire. Stamens 8, opposite the inner petals; anthers oblong-lanceolate, acute; staminodes 8, pilose. Ovary globose, pilose, 8-celled. Drupe globose, with mostly only one or two seeds. —Trees, with distinctly-petioled entire shining coriaceous leaves, the flowers on long pedicels in their axils. DISTRIB. Species 4, the other Tropical African.

Leaves oblong, twice as long as broad.
Leaves large . . . . 1. I. MAXIMA.
Leaves small . . . . 2. I. MEDIA.
Leaves round-oblong, not much longer than broad . . . . 3. I. PETIOLARIS.

1. **I. maxima,** *Poir.; A. DC. Prod.* viii. 200. A tree, with stout rugose grey glabrous branches. Leaves oblong, glabrous, shining, rigidly coriaceous, obtuse, 4–6 in. long by half as broad, deltoid at the base; petiole 1–1½ in., brown-silky or glabrescent. Pedicels 1–3-nate, cernuous, rather shorter than the petiole, brown-silky. Calyx ⅝ in. long, the 4 outer lobes coriaceous, lanceolate-deltoid, acute, brown-silky, the 4 inner thinner, whitish. Petals and stamens as long as the calyx, the outer petals 2–4-cleft. Drupe globose, glabrous, the size of a small apple, 1–4 seeded. Mimusops Imbricaria, *Willd.; Bojer, Hort. Maur.* 198. M. retusa, *Willem.; A. DC. Prod.* viii. 207?

MAURITIUS, in the thick woods of the interior. Also Bourbon. *Bois de Natte à grandes feuilles, Nattier, Bardotier.*

2. **I. media,** *Bojer, MSS.* Very near *I. maxima,* and perhaps a mere variety grown in more exposed places. Leaf oblong, 2–2½ in. long by half as broad, obtuse, rounded at both ends, glabrous, shining above, very rigid and coriaceous; petiole 1–1¼ in. long. Pedicels ½ in. long, solitary, cernuous, clothed like the outer sepals with brown-drab tomentum. Flower exactly of *I. maxima.*

MAURITIUS, in mountain woods, *J. Grey!* Endemic.

3. **I. petiolaris,** *A. DC. Prod.* viii. 200. A tree 40–50 ft. high, with stout rugose grey glabrous branchlets. Leaves round-oblong, glabrous, 2–3 in. long and nearly as broad, rather thinner and more flexible than in the other species, obtuse, rounded to both ends; petiole 2–3 in. long, obscurely brown-silky. Flowers 2–3-nate in the axils of the leaves, on cernuous brown-silky pedicels about an inch long. Calyx ⅝ in. long. Petals and stamens as long as the calyx, the outer row of the former deeply 4–5-fid.

MAURITIUS, in mountain woods. Endemic.

The Bois de Natte of the Seychelles (Horne, 361, 362) is probably an unnamed species of *Imbricaria,* but we have no flowers. So far as the specimens go, the habit is just like that of *I. maxima,* but the petioles are shorter and leaves less coriaceous in texture and broader in proportion to the length (3–6 in. by 2–3½ in.). It is a large tree, growing on the mountains of Mahé, with an oblong yellow drupe 1½ in. long by ¾ in. broad. The Madagascar *I. coriacea,* A. DC. Prod. viii. 200 (*Mimusops hexandra,* Bojer), cultivated in Mauritius, belongs to the genus *Labramia,* which differs from *Imbricaria* by the absence of staminodes.

ORDER LXIII. EBENACEÆ.

Flowers regular, polygamous. Calyx campanulate, with 3–6 round lobes. Corolla with an urceolate tube and 3–6 round spreading lobes. Stamens 9–40, epipetalous or hypogynous, represented by staminodes in the female flower; filaments short, often connate; anthers erect, adnate, narrow, 2-celled, dehiscing longitudinally. Ovary sessile, 3-or more-celled, represented by a rudiment in the male flower; styles as many as the cells; placentas axile; ovules 1–2 in a cell, pendulous, anatropous. Fruit indehiscent, fleshy or coriaceous, girt by the persistent accrescent calyx. Seeds large; albumen horny, abundant.—Hard-wooded trees or shrubs, with exstipulate alternate coriaceous leaves, the sessile flowers solitary or cymose or fascicled at the nodes. DISTRIB. Round the world in warmer regions. Species 260. Elaborately monographed lately by Mr. Hiern in vol. xii. of the Transactions of the Cambridge Philosophical Society.

Lobes of calyx and corolla 3 . . . . 1. MABA.
Lobes of calyx and corolla usually 4–5, rarely 6 . . . . . . 2. DIOSPYROS.

1. MABA, Forster.

Flowers polygamous, trimerous. Calyx campanulate, shortly 3-lobed. Corolla 3-lobed, exceeding the calyx, campanulate or tubular. Stamens in the male flower usually 9, glabrous, distinct or joined in pairs; anthers oblong or linear-lanceolate, placed round a rudimentary ovary. Ovary in the female flower 3–6-celled, with 1 or 2 ovules in a cell; styles free or connate below. Fruit globose, or ovoid, dry or baccate.—Shrubs with alternate entire leaves, the flowers solitary or in cymes in their axils. DISTRIB. Round the world in tropics. Species 59.

1. **M. seychellarum,** *Hiern, Mon. Eben.* 130. An erect shrub, of bushy habit, 10–15 feet high, with slender terete rather zigzag branches, clothed with short spreading hairs. Leaves close, distichous, rigidly coriaceous, glossy, nearly sessile, oblong-lanceolate, 1–2 in. long, obtuse or obscurely emarginate, base cuneate. Male flowers unknown. Females 1–3, nearly sessile in the axils of the leaves. Calyx campanulate, $\frac{1}{8}$ in. long and broad, with 3 obscure obtuse erect lobes. Ovary 3-celled; ovules 2 in a cell. Fruit like a small acorn, oblong, mucronate with the persistent base of the style.

SEYCHELLES, in mountain woods of Mahé, Praslin, and Silhouette, *Pervillé*, 36! *Wright! Horne*, 323, 540! Endemic.

2. DIOSPYROS, Linn.

Flowers polygamous, 4–6-merous. Calyx campanulate, with 4–6 short lobes, in fruit persistent and accrescent. Corolla with an urceolate tube, and 4–6 imbricated round spreading lobes. Stamens in the male flowers 12–40, surrounding a rudimentary ovary, hypogynous and rising from the base of the petals; filaments short, often joined in pairs; anthers linear. Ovary in the female flower sessile, mostly 8–12-celled, usually accompanied by staminodes; styles short or obsolete; ovules solitary in the cells. Fruit indehiscent, large, pulpy.—Trees, with alternate entire coriaceous leaves, the flowers solitary or clustered at the nodes. DISTRIB. Round the world in the tropics. Species 150.

Stamens about 12.
  Leaves short-petioled, rounded at the base . . . . 1. D. TESSELLARIA.
  Leaves long-petioled, cuneate at the base . . . . 2. D. CHRYSOPHYLLOS.
Stamens 20–40.
  Leaves subsessile, cordate at the base. . . . . . 3. D. LEUCOMELAS.
  Leaves petioled, rounded at the base.
    Leaves glabrous beneath.
      Lobes of fruit-calyx erect, not winged.
        Leaves large (2–6 in. long) uniform.
          Calyx-lobes very short . . . . 4. D. MAURITIANA.
          Calyx-lobes ⅓ as long as the tube . . . 5. D. NODOSA.
        Leaves small (1½–2 in. long) varying from oblong to narrow linear . . . . 6. D. DIVERSIFOLIA.
      Lobes of fruit-calyx with an erect crisped wing . 7. D. MELANIDA.
    Leaves persistently silky beneath . . . . . . * D. DISCOLOR.

1. **D. tessellaria,** *Poir.; Hiern, Mon.* 176. A shrub or low tree, with nearly straight glabrous branches. Leaves short-petioled, oblong, obtuse, rigidly coriaceous, 3–6 in. long, broadly rounded at the base, with all the little venules beneath distinctly raised so as to make a very fine network. Flowers in copious sessile clusters from the nodes of young branches; bracts small, ovate-navicular. Flower-calyx ⅙ in. long and broad, shortly 4-lobed, densely clothed with brown silky pubescence. Corolla with a ventricose tube as long as the calyx and 4 round spreading lobes silky on the outside. Stamens about 12, glabrous, hypogynous. Fruit-calyx ½ in. broad, quite flat, the lobes reaching halfway down. Fruit broad-oblong, edible, glabrescent, 1¼–1½ in. long. D. reticulata, *Willd.; A. DC. Prod.* viii 225. D. Ebenum, *Bojer, Hort. Maur.* 199, *non Retz.*

MAURITIUS, in the woods of La Savanne, Vacquois, Quartier Militaire, and Cent Gaulettes. Endemic. *Bois d'ebène noir.*

2. **D. chrysophyllos,** *Poir; Hiern, Mon.* 180. A small tree, with glabrous very zigzag slender branchlets. Leaves oblong or oblong-lanceolate, glossy, green above, coriaceous, subacute, deltoid at the base, 3–5 in. long, only the distant branching main veins beneath raised; petiole ½–1 in. long. Flowers 1–4, sessile in the axils of the leaves. Flower-calyx ¼ in. long, tomentose, with 5 short erect lobes. Stamens 12–15. Fruit-calyx glabrescent, plate-shaped, under an inch broad. Fruit nearly globose, pulpy, above an inch long, 7–10-celled.

MAURITIUS, in the forests of Flacq, Nouvelle Découverte, and the Pouce range. Endemic. *Bois d'ebène blanc.*

3. **D. leucomelas,** *Poir.; Hiern. Mon.* 179. A shrub or low tree, with glabrous nearly straight terete branchlets. Leaves nearly sessile, oblong, obtuse, 4–6 in. long, rigidly coriaceous, glossy, cordate at the base, with only the main veins raised below. Flowers 1–3 from the nodes, surrounded by several round dry persistent bracts. Flower-calyx ⅜ in. long, densely brown-tomentose, with 5–6 short erect round lobes. Corolla-tube longer than the calyx, silky on the outside; lobes 5–6, round, spreading, orange-red. Stamens 30–40, epipetalous, cohering in pairs. Ovary 10–12-celled. Fruit-calyx not seen. Fruit globose, smooth, shining, 1¼ in. broad. D. reticulata, *Sieber, Hort. Maur.* ii. 114, *non Willd.*

MAURITIUS, in forests throughout the island; Round Island, *Sir H. Barkly!* Also Madagascar. A variety, with anther tips obtuse and shortly pilose, was sent to Kew from the Mauritius herbarium. *Bois d'ébène à veines noires.*

4. **D. mauritiana,** *A. DC. Prod.* viii. 226. A tree, with virgate terete glabrous branchlets. Leaves oblong, glossy, rigidly coriaceous, obtuse or rather pointed, 3–5 in. long, rounded or subdeltoid at the base, the raised bright coloured purplish veins below anastomosing in broad areoles; petiole ¼–½ in. long. Flowers 1–3, from the distant nodes. Flower-calyx deeply cup-shaped, nearly truncate, glabrous, ⅓ in. long. Corolla twice the length of the calyx, silky on the outside. Stamens 20–30. Fruit-calyx above an inch broad, ½ inch deep, with 5 short erect round lobes. D. macrocalyx, *A. DC. Prod.* viii. 226.

MAURITIUS, in the forests of Moka, Grand Port, Savanne, and Grand Bassin. United by Mr. Hiern with *D. nodosa.* I cannot by the descriptions in any way separate from this *D. anonæfolia, Neraudii,* and *Boutoniana* of A. De Candolle. We have barren specimens of an allied plant gathered by Sir H. Barkly on Round Island with slender zigzag branches, very short petioles, and very glossy strongly veined leaves 3–4 times as broad as long rounded at both ends. Both this and the other Round Island form may likely prove, when fully known, distinct from the Mauritian species. Endemic. *Bois de Chêne.*

5. **D. nodosa,** *Poir.; Hiern, Mon.* 178. A much-branched shrub, with grey glabrous branches with the close nodes much thickened. Leaves oblong, rigidly coriaceous, glossy, obtuse or rather pointed, 2–3 in. long, rounded at the base, the main veins beneath very fine and little raised; petiole ¼–½ long. Flowers 1–2, nearly sessile at the crowded nodes. Flower-calyx ⅜ in. long, glabrous, the 5 half-circular lobes ⅓ as long as the tube. Stamens above 20. "Lobes of the fruit-calyx erect." D. angulata, *Poir. teste Bojer.*

MAURITIUS, in woods of the Pouce range, *Gardner!* and at Pailles, *Dupont!* Of this I have seen neither the fruit-calyx nor developed corolla. A specimen with only 11 stamens and nearly truncate calyx connects this with *D. mauritiana.* Also Bourbon. *Bois d'ebène bâtard à petites feuilles.*

6. **D. diversifolia,** *Hiern.* A small much-branched glabrate tree of about 15 feet, with pale ashy leafy branches. Leaves elliptical rounded at the apex, rigidly coriaceous, dark green and glossy above,

pale green with reddish midrib and delicate reticulation beneath, 1–2 by $\frac{1}{2}$–1 in.; those of the barren bottom-shoots or of young trees linear, $\frac{1}{2}$–2 by $\frac{1}{16}$–$\frac{1}{3}$ in.; petiole $\frac{1}{16}$–$\frac{1}{4}$ in. Fruit sessile, globose or oblong, 1–1$\frac{1}{2}$ in. 12- or fewer-celled, resting at the base on a thick shortly 5–6-lobed appressed calyx.

RODRIGUEZ, on the slopes of hills, *Bouton!* *Balfour!* Endemic.

7. **D. melanida,** *Poir.; Hiern, Mon.* 177. A tree, with slender terete virgate glabrous branchlets. Leaves oblong, obtuse, rigidly coriaceous, glossy, bright green, 3–4 in. long, deltoid or rather rounded at the base, the principal anastomosing veins only raised beneath; petiole $\frac{1}{4}$–$\frac{1}{3}$ in. long. Flowers 1–4 from the crowded nodes, the bracts very minute. Flower-calyx a tomentose nearly truncate deep cup $\frac{1}{3}$ in. long. Corolla lobes 5–6, $\frac{1}{3}$ in. long and broad, round-obovate, densely brown-silky on the outside. Stamens 20–25. Fruit-calyx nearly flat, above an inch broad, the lobes produced at the border into a broad reflexed crisped wing. Fruit glossy, an inch thick, 10-celled. D. pterocalyx, *Bojer, Hort. Maur.* 200; *A. DC. Prod.* viii. 225.

MAURITIUS, in woods of the Savanne range, and at Nouvelle Découverte and head of the Grande Rivière. We have a plant from Round Island, gathered by Sir H. Barkly, with a fruit-calyx just like that described above, but with larger leaves more rounded at the base, and veining more like that of *D. tessellaria.* Endemic. *Bois d'ébène marbré.*

* *D. discolor,* Willd.; Hiern, Mon. 260; (D. melanida, *Sieber, non Poir.* D. Embryopteris, *Bojer, Hort. Maur.* 200. *non Pers*), a native of the Philippines and Malaya, is planted and half wild in Mauritius and the Seychelles. It is a tree 30–40 feet high, with black wood and wide-spreading densely pilose branches, oblong leaves 6–8 in. long silky beneath, a very silky calyx $\frac{1}{3}$ in. long with round much imbricated lobes much longer than the tube, stamens 25–30, and a globose densely pilose fruit 2–4 inches thick. *Mabolo.*

I am informed by Mr. Hiern that the original label of his *D. platycalyx,* Mon. Eben. p. 267, which has been attributed to the Seychelles, shows that it is really a plant of Madagascar.

D. membranacea, A. DC. Prod. viii. 227, is founded on cultivated Mauritian specimens of *D. Ebenaster,* Retz. (*D. decandra,* Bojer, Hort. Maur. 200).

ORDER LXIV. BORAGINACEÆ.

Flowers regular, hermaphrodite, usually pentamerous. Calyx persistent, deeply cleft. Corolla rotate, hypocrateriform or campanulate. Stamens 5, inserted in the corolla-tube, alternate with the lobes; filaments usually short; anthers oblong, 2-celled, slit longitudinally. Carpels 4; ovules usually solitary in the cells, ascending, anatropous; style simple or forked. Fruit a drupe, with bony pyrenes, or of 4 dry nucules.—Herbs or shrubs; leaves mostly alternate, exstipulate, usually rough; flowers in scorpioid spikes or cymes. DISTRIB. Cosmopolitan. Species 1200.

Fruit a drupe with bony pyrenes.
  Calyx large, accrescent, inclosing the fruit . . . . 1. CORDIA.
  Calyx small, not enclosing the fruit.
    Corolla campanulate . . . . 2. EHRETIA.
    Corolla hypocrateriform . . . . 3. TOURNEFORTIA.
Fruit of four dry nucules.
  Leaves opposite. Calyx large . . . . 4. TRICHODESMA.
  Leaves alternate. Calyx small.
    Nucules 4, spreading equally. Flowers racemose.
      Nucules erect. Racemes bracteated . . . . . . * BOTHRIOSPERMUM.
      Nucules spreading. Racemes without bracts . . 5. CYNOGLOSSUM.
    Nucules in two divaricating pairs.
      Flowers in secund spikes . . . . 6. HELIOTROPIUM.

1. CORDIA, Linn.

Calyx funnel-shaped, usually 5-toothed. Corolla funnel-shaped, usually 5-lobed. Ovary 4-celled; ovules solitary in the cells; style filiform, twice forked at the top. Fruit drupaceous, often by abortion 3–1-celled.—Shrubs, with leaves usually alternate, with small or large flowers in terminal or lateral spikes or cymes. DISTRIB. Round the world in the warmer zones. Species about 200.

1. **C. subcordata,** *Lam.; A. DC. Prod.* ix. 477. A low tree, glabrous in all its parts or the branchlets rather downy. Leaves alternate, entire, round or broad-oblong, cuspidate, subcoriaceous, reaching ½ foot long and broad; petiole 1–2 in. long. Flowers few, in short-peduncled lateral cymes; pedicels articulated at the tip. Calyx oblong, not ribbed; teeth 3–5. Corolla white, 1½ in. long and broad, with 6–7 plicate round imbricated lobes. Fruit as large as an acorn, dry, enclosed in the accrescent calyx. C. orientalis, *R. Br.*

SEYCHELLES, common on the shores. Polynesia to Zanzibar and Mozambique.

2. EHRETIA, Linn.

Calyx campanulate, 5-toothed. Corolla campanulate, with 5 short spreading lobes. Stamens 5, included, inserted about the middle of the tube. Ovary 4-celled, seated on a round disk; style filiform, obscurely two-lobed at the apex. Fruit a small drupe, containing 1–4 bony 2-seeded pyrenes.—Shrubs, with alternate leaves and small flowers in dense corymbs. DISTRIB. Round the world in the warmer zones. Species 50.

Leaves serrated . . . . * E. SERRATA.
Leaves entire . . . . 1. E. PETIOLARIS.

* *E. serrata*, Roxb.; DC. Prod. ix. 503; Lindl. Bot. Reg. t. 1097, a native of the East Indies, is naturalised in Mauritius near Moka. It

is a tree 30 feet high, glabrous in all its parts, with slender terete branches, distinctly petioled oblong acute finely serrated subcoriaceous leaves, flowers in copious small axillary and terminal deltoid corymbs, crowded at the end of the branchlets, calyx campanulate $\frac{1}{24}$ in. long with round obtuse much-imbricated ciliated lobes, corolla white with a tube as long as the calyx and 5 spreading lobes and a red drupe the size of a pea. *Telfairia.*

1. **E. petiolaris,** *Lam.; DC. Prod.* ix. 504. A shrub 6–15 feet high, glabrous in all its parts, with slender virgate branches. Leaves alternate, oblong, entire, glabrous, penninerved, acute, membranous, 3-4 in. long; petiole $\frac{1}{2}$–$1\frac{1}{2}$ in. long. Flowers in dense peduncled lateral corymbs with spreading branches; pedicels short, articulated at the apex. Calyx $\frac{1}{8}$ in. long; teeth as long as the tube. Corolla whitish, rather longer than the calyx, with a campanulate tube and 5 spreading deltoid lobes. Drupe red, juicy, the size of a small pea. E. internodis, *L'Herit. Stirp.* i. 47, *t.* 24. Hilsenbergia Ehretia and rugosa, *Dunal in DC. Prod.* xiii. 478.

Mauritius, frequent in the woods. Amber Island, *Horne!* Also Bourbon, Madagascar, and Zanguebar. *E. laxa,* Jacq. Hort. Schoen. t. 41, is a variety with drooping branches and laxer corymbs. *Bois Betel. Bois de Pipe.*

3. TOURNEFORTIA, Linn.

Calyx small, campanulate, with 5 teeth reaching all or part of the way down. Corolla hypocrateriform; lobes 5, short, spreading. Stamens 5, included, inserted in the corolla-tube. Ovary 4-celled; ovules solitary in the cells; style simple or forked. Fruit a drupe, with two 2-seeded pyrenes.—Shrubs, with alternate entire leaves and abundant small flowers in dichotomous cymes with scorpioid branches. Distrib. Round the world in the tropics. Species about 100.

Style forked. Corolla-tube not longer than the calyx . . . 1. T. argentea.
Stigma capitate. Corolla-tube twice as long as the calyx.
  Climber, with oblong leaves rounded at the base . . . . 2. T. sarmentosa.
  Erect, with oblong-lanceolate leaves narrowed at the base . . . . 3. T. Bojeri.

1. **T. argentea,** *Linn. fil.; DC. Prod.* ix. 514. An erect shrub, with stout tessellated branches, clothed like the leaves on both sides with persistent pale brown glossy tomentum. Leaves crowded, oblanceolate-oblong, obtuse, 4–9 in. long, narrowed gradually from the middle to the base. Flowers in ample long-peduncled dichotomous terminal cymes, with abundant crowded scorpioid branches. Calyx sessile, campanulate, $\frac{1}{8}$ in. long, densely tomentose; teeth deltoid. Corolla white, fragrant, pilose on the outside; tube as long as the calyx; lobes round, spreading. Style short, deeply forked. Drupe smooth, yellow, the size of a pea, containing two 2-seeded pyrenes. T. velutina, *Smith, non H.B.K.*

MAURITIUS and SEYCHELLES, frequent on the shores; Coin de Mire and Flat Island, *Horne!* RODRIGUEZ, common on the coral of the shore and the coral islets, *Balfour!* Through tropics of Old World. *Veloutier. Voultie.*

2. **T. sarmentosa,** *Lam.; DC. Prod.* ix. 516. A twining shrub, with young branches and leaves beneath finely pubescent. Leaves oblong, subcoriaceous, acute, 3–6 in. long, glabrous above, glabrescent or finely pubescent beneath; base rounded; petiole an inch long. Flowers in ample peduncled lateral and terminal dichotomous cymes, with many crowded curved pilose scorpioid branches. Calyx $\frac{1}{12}$ in. long, 5-partite; teeth linear. Corolla white; tube twice as long as the calyx; teeth short, obtuse. Stigma large, capitate. Drupe globose, glabrous, the size of a small pea. T. viridiflora, *Wall.; DC. loc. cit.*

MAURITIUS, originally described from specimens gathered by Sonnerat, but not seen lately. SEYCHELLES, common in the forests of Mahé, *Horne*, 247! North Australia and Tropical Asia.

3. **T. Bojeri,** *DC. Prod.* ix. 516. An erect shrub, with branches and leaves below clothed with fine pubescence. Leaves oblong-lanceolate, membranous, 4–6 in. long, narrowed gradually from the middle to the base and a long point, soon glabrous above; petiole 1–1½ in. long. Flowers in long-peduncled terminal dichotomous cymes, with crowded curved branches. Calyx silky, 5-partite, $\frac{1}{12}$ in. long; teeth lanceolate. Corolla silky, twice as long as the calyx; lobes minute, deltoid. Stigma and fruit of *T. sarmentosa*. T. bifida, *Bojer, Hort. Maur.* 234, *non Lam.*

MAURITIUS, in the woods of the Rivière Noire and at Grand Bassin. Endemic.

T. bifida, Lam.; Poir. Encyc. v. 360, gathered in Mauritius by Commerson, is said to be a shrub with wrinkled grey bark, petioled ovate glabrous coriaceous leaves, axillary peduncles bearing two horizontal spikes, a short calyx with 5 obtuse teeth, and a tubular elongated cream-coloured corolla. It does not seem to have been found by any later botanist.

4. TRICHODESMA, R. Br.

Calyx of five distinct large acute foliaceous sepals. Corolla funnel-shaped; lobes deltoid. Stamens inserted in the corolla-tube; anthers persistently connivent in a cone surrounding the stigma, tapering into a long point. Ovary 4-celled; style filiform; stigma capitate. Fruit of 4 dry stony ovoid erect nuts, fitting into the boat-shaped hollows of the receptacle.—Coarse herbs, with rough hairs, opposite leaves, and flowers in lax racemes, each pedicel bracteated by a reduced leaf. DISTRIB. Tropics of the Old World. Species about 10.

Sepals not auricled at the base . . . . 1. T. ZEYLANICUM.
Sepals produced into an auricle on each side at the base . 2. T. INDICUM.

1. **T. zeylanicum,** *R. Br.; DC. Prod.* x. 172. A coarse erect much-branched annual, 3–4 feet high, with stem and leaves with bristly hairs rising from white calcareous tubercles. Leaves sessile

or lanceolate, nearly so, 3–6 in. long. Flowers in terminal corymbs on flexuose densely hairy slender pedicels 1–1½ in. long. Sepals lanceolate, densely ciliated on the edge and keel, finally ½–⅝ in. long, not auricled at the base. Corolla just exserted from the calyx, the expanded limb under ½ in. broad. Anthers straw-coloured, twisted, pilose, ¼ in. long. Nucules ⅛ in. long, ovoid, rather flattened, glossy, brownish on the outside, dull and slightly rugose on the inside. Borago zeylanica, *Linn.; Jacq. Ic. t.* 314.

MAURITIUS, RODRIGUEZ, and SEYCHELLES, frequent everywhere in waste ground. Tropical Asia and Africa. *Bourrache sauvage.*

2. **T. indicum,** *R. Br.; DC. Prod.* x. 172. More slender in habit than *T. zeylanicum*, with lingulate amplexicaul leaves, smaller sepals produced into an auricle on each side at the base, and a larger corolla, anthers, and nucules. Borago indica, *Linn.*

MAURITIUS, frequent in waste ground. Tropical Asia.

* *Bothriospermum tenellum*, F. and M.; DC. Prod. x. 117, (Anchusa zeylanica, *Jacq. fil. Ecl.* i. 47 t. 29), common through Tropical Asia, is found occasionally in Mauritius in cultivated ground. It is a diffuse much-branched annual, half a foot high, with slender bristly stems, small petioled oblong rugose acute alternate leaves, flowers in lax terminal racemes each on a short pedicel from the axil of a reduced leaf, calyx campanulate $\frac{1}{12}$ in. long with lanceolate teeth, corolla minute hypocrateriform with the throat of the tube closed with 5 obtuse scales, nucules oblong-trigonal minute obtuse papillose with an oblong umbilicus in the middle of the inner face.

5. CYNOGLOSSUM, Linn.

Sepals 5, small, distinct. Corolla funnel-shaped, with small round spreading lobes, its throat closed by obtuse scales. Ovary 4-lobed; style short, filiform; stigma capitate. Anthers globose, nearly or quite sessile at the throat of the tube. Nucules 4, spreading, subglobose, prickly.—Herbs, with alternate leaves, the flowers in long lax leafless secund racemes. DISTRIB. Cosmopolitan. Species 40.

Leaves lanceolate; sepals linear . . . . 1. C. ROCHELIA.
Leaves linear; sepals lanceolate . . . . 2. C. BORBONICUM.

1. **C. Rochelia,** *A. DC. Prod.* x. 153. An erect annual, 2–3 feet high, more or less branched, with stems thinly clothed with short hairs. Leaves membranous, glabrescent above, rather bristly below, oblong, acute, narrowed to the base, the largest 4–5 in. long, 1–1½ in. broad. Racemes very lax, bractless, simple or forked, 2–4 in. long; pedicels longer than the calyx, cernuous after flowering. Sepals ligulate, $\frac{1}{16}$ in. long. Corolla whitish, scarcely longer than the calyx. Nucules ovoid-

oblong, scarcely ⅛ in. long. Rochelia borbonica, *Roem. and Schult.* iv. 118; *Bojer, Hort. Maur.* 232.

MAURITIUS, in damp and shaded places, frequent. Also Bourbon.

2. **C. borbonicum,** *Bory; DC. Prod.* x. 151. Annual or biennial, more or less branched, the stems densely clothed with short soft grey hairs. Leaves linear, acute, ⅛ in. broad, the lower narrowed into a petiole. Racemes very lax, simple or forked, 1–4 in. long; pedicels at most as long as the calyx. Sepals oblong-lanceolate, $\frac{1}{12}$ in. long, pilose. Corolla twice as long as the calyx. Nucules ovoid, densely prickly, ⅛–⅙ in. long. Rochelia strigosa, *Roem. and Schult. Syst. Veg.* iv. 782.

MAURITIUS, in grassy places. Also Bourbon.

6. HELIOTROPIUM, Linn.

Calyx 5-partite; teeth lanceolate. Corolla hypocrateriform, the tube constricted at the throat; lobes 5, short, spreading, obtuse. Anthers oblong, sessile in the lower part of the corolla-tube. Ovary 4-celled; style very short; stigma capitate. Fruit of four dry nucules.—Herbs or shrubs, with rough alternate leaves and cymose inflorescence. DISTRIB. Cosmopolitan. Species 100 or more.

1. **H. indicum,** *Linn. Sp.* 187. A coarse erect annual, with stems densely clothed with bristly hairs. Leaves alternate, distinctly petioled, large, ovate, acute, crenate. Flowers in simple or geminate stalked secund scorpioid spikes 3–6 in. long. Sepals $\frac{1}{12}$ in. long, rather unequal. Corolla purple, 3 times as long as the calyx; tube pentagonal, narrowed from the bottom to the top. Nucules twice as long as the calyx, in two divaricating pairs, deeply plicate, with a foliaceous tip. *Bot. Mag. t.* 1837. Heliophytum indicum, *DC. Prod.* ix. 556. Tiaridium indicum, *Lehm.*

MAURITIUS, RODRIGUEZ, and SEYCHELLES, a common weed. Everywhere in the tropics. *Herbe queue de rats. Herbe aux papillons.*

ORDER LXV. CONVOLVULACEÆ.

Flowers regular, hermaphrodite, pentamerous. Calyx inferior, the 5 sepals distinct, usually broad and imbricated, accrescent in fruit. Corolla funnel-shaped or hypocrateriform, contorted in æstivation, with 5 very short lobes. Stamens 5, epipetalous, opposite the sepals; anthers sagittate, 2-celled, basifixed, slit down the sides. Ovary usually simple, 1–4 celled; style filiform; stigmas 2; ovules 1–2 in a cell. Fruit usually a 4-valved capsule. Seeds albuminous.—Twining herbs or shrubs, with alternate exstipulate petioled mostly cordate or hastate leaves and showy flowers on axillary peduncles solitary or corymbose. DISTRIB. Round the world, mostly in the warmer regions. Species 800.

Carpels united.
  Fruit baccate . . . . 1. ARGYREIA.
  Fruit capsular.
    Lobes of stigma globose . . . . 2. IPOMŒA.
    Lobes of stigma falcate, terete . . . . 3. CONVOLVULUS.
    Lobes of stigma flat, ovate . . . . 4. JACQUEMONTIA.
Carpels separate . . . . 5. DICHONDRA.

1. ARGYREIA, Lour.

Sepals 5, round, obtuse, much imbricated. Corolla widening gradually from the top of the calyx to the throat. Stamens inserted low down in the corolla, and not more than half as long. Ovary 4-celled, with a single ovule in a cell; style filiform; stigma of two globose lobes. Fruit baccate, indehiscent.—Shrubby climbers, with large showy flowers. DISTRIB. Round the world in the tropics. Species 20–30.

Leaves beneath obscurely downy . . . . 1. A. TILIÆFOLIA.
Leaves beneath clothed with thick white shining silky tomentum . . . . * A. SPECIOSA.

1. **A. tiliæfolia,** *Benth. Gen. Plant.* ii. 869. A robust shrubby climber with puberulent stems. Leaves round, cuspidate, deeply cordate, membranous, puberulent below, 3–4 inches long and broad; petiole spreading, 2–3 in. long. Flowers usually solitary, rarely 2–3 from the axils of the leaves on a short spreading peduncle. Flower-sepals ½ in. long, obtuse, much imbricated. Corolla white, 3–4 in. long and the throat nearly as broad when expanded. Berry as large as a plum, wrapped round by the accrescent persistent sepals. Seeds as large as a pea. Convolvulus tiliæfolius, *Desr. in Lam. Encycl.* iii. 544. Rivea tiliæfolia, *Choisy in DC. Prod.* ix. 325.

MAURITIUS, on the seashore and in inland woods. RODRIGUEZ, on the shore at Bai Malgache, *Balfour !* SEYCHELLES, in Mahé, *Horne*, 276! Round the world in the tropics.

* *A. speciosa*, Sweet; Choisy in DC. Prod. ix. 328, (Convolvulus speciosus, *Linn.; Smith Ic. Pict. t.* 17), a native of the East Indies, is cultivated in gardens and subspontaneous in Mauritius. It is a shrubby climber, with stems and leaves below coated with dense persistent white silky tomentum, large entire subcoriaceous cordate-ovate leaves glabrous on the upper surface, flowers in axillary corymbs on long peduncles, large deciduous ovate-cuspidate bracts, calyx ½ in. long with broad oblong much imbricated sepals and a purple corolla 3 inches broad and long, with short stamens. *Liane d'argent.*

2. IPOMŒA, Linn.

Sepals 5, usually broad and much imbricated. Corolla broadly or narrowly funnel-shaped, if the latter with a spreading limb. Stamens epipetalous, with long or short filaments. Ovary 2–4 celled; ovules 1–2 in a cell; style filiform; stigma with two capitate lobes. Capsule membranous, splitting up mostly into four valves.—Climbing or trailing herbs or shrubs, with simple or compound leaves and mostly large showy flowers. DISTRIB. Round the world in the warmer regions. Species 300 or more.

Series 1. Corolla broadly funnel-shaped, with short stamens.

Subgenus 1, IPOMŒA PROPER. Ovary 2-celled with two ovules in each cell.

Leaves divided.
  Stems and leaves glabrous.
    Leaflets sessile or joined at the base.
      Sepals above an inch long . . . . * I. TUBEROSA.
      Sepals ¼ inch long . . . . 1. I. CAIRICA.
    Leaflets stalked . . . . 2. I. HORNEI.
  Stems and leaves pilose.
    Flowers 1–3 together stalked . . . . 3. I. SINUATA.
    Flowers many in a dense head . . . . 4. I. PES-TIGRIDIS.
Leaves simple.
  Stems and leaves glabrous.
    Leaves peltate . . . . 5. I. PELTATA.
    Leaves cordate.
      Flowers in cymes . . . . 6. I. CYMOSA.
      Flowers solitary . . . . 7. I. LEUCANTHA.
  Stems and leaves pilose.
    Slender annual herb . . . . 8. I. OBSCURA.
    Suffruticose perennial . . . . 9. I. TURPETHUM.

Subgenus 2, PHARBITIS. Ovary 3- rarely 4-celled; ovules two in a cell.

Leaves entire.
  Stems and leaves finely silky . . . . * I. PURPUREA.
  Stems and leaves densely clothed with thick spreading hairs . . . . 10. I. FRAGRANS.
Leaves 3-lobed . . . . * I. NIL.

Subgenus 3, BATATAS. Ovary 4-celled; ovules one in each cell.

Stems and leaves pilose.
  Annual twiner, with 5 distinct leaflets . . . . . . * I. PENTAPHYLLA.
  Perennial trailer, with entire or little-lobed leaves . . * I. BATATAS.
Stem and leaves glabrous.
  Shrubby climber, with leaves palmately lobed . . . 11. I. PANICULATA.
  Shore trailers.
    Peduncle 1-flowered . . . . 12. I. ACETOSÆFOLIA.
    Peduncle 1–6-flowered . . . . 13. I. PES-CAPRÆ.

Series 2. Corolla hypocrateriform or nearly so, with long stamens.

Subgenus 4, CALONYCTION. Corolla large, white.

Stems unarmed . . . . 14. I. GLABERRIMA.
Stems armed with copious prickles . . . . * I. MURICATA.

Subgenus 5, QUAMOCLIT. Corolla small, bright red.

Leaves entire or slightly lobed, cordate . . . . . 15. I. COCCINEA.
Leaves pinnate, with linear leaflets . . . . * I. QUAMOCLIT.

* *I. tuberosa*, Linn.; Choisy in DC. Prod. ix. 362, (Bot. Reg. t. 768. Batatas tuberosa, *Bojer, Hort. Maur*, 226), spread round the world in the tropics, is naturalised in Mauritius in ravines near Moka and Château d'Eau, and was found by Dr. Balfour in Rodriguez. It is a glabrous perennial, with robust stems, climbing to the top of high trees, long-petioled large leaves with 7 palmate oblong acute leaflets, flowers 3–6 on a long peduncle, sepals above an inch long obtuse much imbricated, corolla twice as long as the calyx bright yellow, and a globose capsule above an inch long, with 2–4 seeds clothed with black tomentum. *Liane de Gondelour.*

1. **I. cairica,** *Sweet, Hort. Brit.* 287. A slender perennial climber, glabrous in all its parts, the branches often tubercled. Leaves 1–3 in. broad and long, deeply cordate, membranous, cut down nearly or quite to the base into 5–7 oblong acute lobes; petiole 1–3 in. long, sometimes furnished at the base with a persistent laciniated stipule. Flowers 3–6, corymbose on a long or short peduncle. Sepals obtuse, imbricated, $\frac{1}{4}$ in. long. Corolla $1\frac{1}{2}$–2 in. long and broad, reddish or white. Capsule globose, $\frac{1}{4}$–$\frac{1}{3}$ in. thick, 2-celled, the cells 2-seeded. Seeds with a grey-brown villose testa. Convolvulus cairicus, *Linn.; Bot. Mag. tab.* 699. I. tuberculata, *R. and S.; Bojer, Hort. Maur.* 228. I. stipulata, *Jacq. Hort. Schoen. tab.* 199. Batatas venosa, *Bojer, Hort. Maur.* 226. I. palmata, *Forst.; Choisy in DC. Prod.* ix. 387.

MAURITIUS, RODRIGUEZ and SEYCHELLES, frequent in bushy places. Round the world in the tropics. *I. venosa* is a variety with the leaflets quite distinct, and *I. tuberculata* with the stems tubercled. *Liane de sept ans.*

2. **I. Hornei,** *Baker.* A robust glabrous creeper, with stems and peduncles tubercled with raised points. Leaves digitately compound, membranous, glabrous, dark green; leaflets 3–7, usually 5, oblong, acute, $1\frac{1}{2}$–2 in. long, deltoid at the base, on petiolules $\frac{1}{4}$–$\frac{1}{3}$ in. long; petiole slender, $1\frac{1}{2}$–2 in. long. Peduncles stout, straight, 4–6 in. long; flowers 12–20, in a crowded corymb, on short pedicels. Sepals $\frac{1}{4}$ in. long, broad, obtuse, much imbricated. Corolla $1\frac{1}{2}$–2 in. long, white, broadly funnel-shaped. Capsule small, 2-celled, with a single seed in each cell.

SEYCHELLES, in Mahé on the top of the hills that separate Anse la Mouche from Anse la Pin, *Horne*, 530! Endemic.

3. **I. sinuata,** *Orteg.; Choisy in DC. Prod.* ix. 362. A perennial climber, with slender stems and petioles densely clothed with fine spreading brown hairs. Leaves 4–6 in. broad, membranous, cut down nearly to the centre into 5–7 oblong acute deeply pinnatifid lobes; petiole 2–3 in. long. Peduncles as long as the petioles, 1–3-flowered. Flower-sepals $\frac{5}{8}$–$\frac{3}{4}$ in. long, glabrous, obtuse, with a minute cusp, much imbricated. Corolla more than twice as long as the calyx, white, with a reddish throat. Capsule globose, glabrous, an inch thick, shorter than the sepals. Convolvulus dissectus, *Linn.; Jacq. Hort. Vind. t.* 159.

SEYCHELLES; roadsides in Mahé near Port Victoria, *Horne*, 531! Cosmopolitan in the tropics.

4. **I. pes-trigidis**, *Linn.; Choisy in DC. Prod.* ix. 363. An annual twiner, with slender stems, and petioles clothed with fine spreading hairs. Leaves 1–3 in. broad, membranous, pilose, mostly deeply palmately 5–7-lobed, with oblong-spathulate acute lobes, the lobes sometimes three only (*I. hepaticifolia*, Linn.), sometimes shallow and deltoid, rarely absent. Flowers in a dense long-peduncled head, surrounded by many oblanceolate obtuse foliaceous bracts. Sepals $\frac{3}{8}$–$\frac{1}{2}$ in. long, lanceolate, densely clothed with bristly hairs. Corolla purplish, 1–1$\frac{1}{2}$ in. long. Capsule small, glabrous, included in the calyx.

MAURITIUS, on the banks of the canal of the Grande Rivière, *Bojer!* Common in Tropical Asia. Also gathered by Dr. Meller and Dr. Kirk in Zambesi-land.

5. **I. peltata,** *Choisy in DC. Prod.* ix. 359. A robust shrubby glabrous climber, with terete stems. Leaves ovate or roundish-cuspidate, 3–12 in. broad, the petiole inserted a third of the way up, the main nerves very distinct to the edge, rather coriaceous, bright green above. Flowers up to a dozen, distinctly pedicelled, on a long common peduncle. Sepals obtuse, much imbricated, $\frac{3}{4}$–1 in. long. Corolla more than twice as long as the calyx, yellowish white, with red spots. Anthers pilose. Capsule large. Seeds pilose. Convolvulus peltatus, *Linn.* Spiranthera peltata, *Bojer, Hort. Maur.* 226.

MAURITIUS, in the forests of Flacq and Grand-port. RODRIGUEZ, abundant in the Rivière Coco Valley, *Balfour!* SEYCHELLES, frequent in the island of Mahé, *Bojer! Sir A. H. Gordon! Dr. Wright!* Polynesia to the Comoro Islands.

6. **I. cymosa,** *R. and S.; Choisy in DC. Prod.* ix. 371. A woody climber, with glabrous or finely pilose terete slender stems. Leaves entire, ovate or oblong, acute, deeply cordate, 1–3 in. long, membranous, glabrous or beneath pilose; petiole 1–1$\frac{1}{2}$ in. long. Flowers 8–12 in a shortly-peduncled cyme. Sepals $\frac{1}{8}$ in. long, much imbricated, obtuse with a distinct cusp. Corolla 1–$\frac{1}{2}$ in. long, pinkish-white. Capsule globose, $\frac{1}{4}$–$\frac{1}{3}$ in. thick. Seeds 4, pilose. Convolvulus cymosus, *Desr. in Lam. Encycl.* iii. 556. C. bifidus, *Vahl.*

SEYCHELLES, common in Mahé near the shore, and also on the table-lands. *Horne,* 526! Common in Tropical Asia.

7. **I. leucantha,** *Jacq. Ic. t.* 318. A glabrous annual, with slender twining stems. Leaves entire, cordate-deltoid, acute, membranous, 1–1$\frac{1}{2}$ in. long; petiole an inch or less long. Flowers without a common peduncle, 1–2 from each node on pedicels $\frac{1}{4}$–1 in. long, thickened in the upper third. Sepals $\frac{1}{8}$ in. long, obtuse, much-imbricated, with a distinct cusp. Corolla reddish, 1–1$\frac{1}{4}$ in. long. Capsule small, globose. *Choisy in DC. Prod.* ix. 382. Convolvulus leucanthus, *Desr. in Lam. Encycl.* iii. 541.

SEYCHELLES; Mahé, in long grass in waste ground on the slope of the Signal Mountain, Port Victoria, *Horne,* 277! RODRIGUEZ, on the shore in several places, *Balfour!* Also Tropical America.

8. **I. obscura,** *Ker, Bot. Reg. t.* 239. An annual climber, with very slender stems, clothed with minute hairs or glabrescent. Leaves entire, cordate-ovate, acute, membranous, 1–3 in. loug and broad; petiole 2–3 in. long. Flowers 1–3 ou a short common peduncle; pedicels thickened, with a pair of small lanceolate persistent bracts at the base. Flower-sepals $\frac{1}{8}$–$\frac{1}{6}$ in. long, ovate, subacute, glabrous. Corolla under an inch long, cream-coloured, with yellow longitudinal bands and a purple throat. Capsule glabrous, $\frac{1}{4}$–$\frac{1}{3}$ in. thick. Seeds 4, pilose. *Choisy in DC. Prod.* ix. 370. Convolvulus obscurus, *Linn.* C. gemellus, *Vahl.* C. gonatodes, *Steud.*

MAURITIUS, round Port Louis and by waysides at Plaines Wilhelms, *Dr. Ayres.* Not native, according to Bojer. RODRIGUEZ, common, *Dr. Balfour!* SEYCHELLES; common in all the islands, *Horne,* 278! 529! Through the tropics of the Old World.

9. **I. Turpethum,** *R. Br.*; *Choisy in DC. Prod.* ix. 360. A woody twiner, with finely pilose angular stems, often furnished with four narrow membranous wings (*I. anceps,* R and S.). Leaves cordate-deltoid, rarely crenate, acute or obtuse, with a minute cusp, 2–6 in. long and broad. Flowers 2–6, on a short peduncle, corymbose, with large membranous subpersistent bracts. Flower-sepals pilose, $\frac{5}{8}$–$\frac{3}{4}$ in. long, obtuse, with a minute cusp, much imbricated. Corolla white, more than twice as long as the calyx. Capsule globose, an inch thick. Seeds 4, glabrous, the size of a pea. Convolvulus Turpothum, *Linn.*; *Bot. Mag. tab.* 2093. Spiranthera Turpethum, *Bojer, Hort. Maur.* 226.

SEYCHELLES, common in damp shady places in the island of Mahé, *Horne,* 279! RODRIGUEZ, not common, *Dr. Balfour!* Subspontaneous in Mauritius at the battery of the Grande Rivière. Through the tropics of the Old World. *Turbith.*

Of the subgenus *Pharbitis,* marked by its trimerous ovary, the two following common garden species are casually subspontaneous.

* *I. purpurea,* Lam. (Convolvulus, *Linn.; Bot. Mag. t.* 113, 1105, 1682; Pharbitis hispida, *Choisy in DC. Prod.* ix. 341), a slender twining perennial, with minutely downy stems, entire round-cordate leaves pilose on both sides, peduncles 3–5-flowered, sepals ovate-acuminate $\frac{1}{2}$ inch long, corolla middle-sized purple red or white.—Rodriguez. *Dr. Balfour.* A native of America.

* *I. Nil,* Roth. (Convolvulus, *Linn.; Bot. Reg. t.* 276), an annual, with longer deflexed hairs, leaves membranous as broad as long deeply three-lobed, peduncles 2–3-flowered, sepals an inch long lanceolate densely bristly near the base, corolla middle-sized blue.—Round the world in the tropics. Found by Dr. Balfour in Rodriguez, and a densely pilose form in the island of Gombrian.

10. **I. fragrans,** *Bojer, MSS.* A shrubby climber, with stems densely clothed with persistent spreading soft grey hairs. Leaves distinctly petioled, cordate-ovate, acute, entire, 2–3 in. long, moderately firm in texture, shortly pubescent above, densely clothed beneath with

soft grey hairs like those of the stem. Peduncles 2 in. long; flowers 5–6 in an umbel, on ¼–½ in. pedicels. Calyx ⅜ in. long; sepals free to the base, oblong, acute, much imbricated. Corolla 1½–2 in. long, bright red-purple. Ovary 3-celled. Pharbitis fragrans, *Bojer, Hort. Maur.* 227; *Choisy in DC. Prod.* ix. 341. Ipomœa Lindleyi, *Choisy in DC. Prod.* ix. 371.

RODRIGUEZ, perhaps introduced, *Dr. Balfour!* Cultivated in Mauritius. Also Madagascar, Johanna Island, and Tropical Africa.

* *I. pentaphylla*, Jacq. Ic. t. 319, (Convolvulus, *Linn.*; Batatas, *Choisy*; Spiranthera, *Bojer*), a native of Tropical America, is casually subspontaneous in Mauritius. It is an annual twiner, with slender stems clothed with deflexed bristly hairs, leaves with 5 oblong membranous distinct leaflets narrowed to both ends, peduncles 4–6-flowered, with long flexuose pedicels, flower-sepals ½ in. long growing out in fruit to 1–1¼ inch outer acute inner obtuse clothed with spreading hairs like those of the stem, corolla white twice as long as the calyx, capsule not exserted from the calyx naked within.

* *I. Batatas*, Lam. (Convolvulus Batatas, *Linn.*; Batatas edulis, *Choisy*), the common tropical sweet potato, is often found about abandoned plantations. It is a perennial, with a large white or red edible tuberous root, trailing pilose stems, long-petioled membranous cordate-deltoid acute entire or shallowly-lobed leaves, peduncles 3–4-flowered, sepals cuspidate ¼–⅓ in. long, corolla purplish, 1–1½ in. long. *Batate* or *Patate*.

11. **I. paniculata,** *R. Br. Prod.* 486. A shrubby perennial climber, glabrous in all its parts. Root thick, tuberous. Leaves as broad as long, 4–6 in. across, cordate, with 5–7 deep acute palmate lobes; petiole 2–3 in. long. Peduncles longer than the petioles, corymbosely 4–12-flowered. Flower-sepals obtuse, ¼–⅓ in. long. Corolla purple, 2 in. long, and the throat as broad when expanded. Stamens reaching halfway up the corolla. Capsule ½ in. long, exceeding the sepals, densely woolly within. *Bot. Reg. t.* 62. Convolvulus paniculatus, *Linn.* Batatas paniculata, *Choisy*. Ipomœa mauritiana, *Jacq. Hort. Schoen. t.* 200. I. insignis, *Andrews, Bot. Rep. t.* 635; *Ker, Bot. Reg. t.* 75; *Bot. Mag. t.* 1790.

MAURITIUS, RODRIGUEZ, and SEYCHELLES, not uncommon in waste lands. Cosmopolitan in the tropics.

12. **I. acetosæfolia,** *Vahl, Ecl.* i. 18. A trailing perennial, glabrous in all its parts. Leaves short-petioled, fleshy, very variable in shape, ligulate or oblong, obtuse or emarginate, entire or palmately 5-lobed. Peduncles 1-flowered, longer than the petioles. Sepals oblong, with a distinct cusp, ¼–⅓ in. long. Corolla white, 1¼–1½ in. long. Capsule ¼–⅓ in. thick, globose, 4-celled. Seeds as large as a pea, densely hairy. Convolvulus littoralis, *Linn.* Batatas littoralis, *Choisy; DC. Prod.* ix. 337.

Given by Dupont as a native of MAURITIUS, but I have not seen specimens. Round the world on shores of the tropical and subtropical zones.

13. **I. pes-capræ,** *Roth; Choisy in DC. Prod.* ix. 349. A glabrous perennial, with woody stems trailing sometimes to a length of 80 or 100 feet on the sands of the seashore. Leaves firm, roundish, broadly deltoid at the base, 1–3 in. long, with two long or short obtuse lobes, with a deltoid sinus between them; petiole ascending, 1–3 in. long. Flowers 1–6, from the axils of the leaves on a long common peduncle. Sepals $\frac{3}{8}$–$\frac{1}{2}$ in. long, much imbricated. Corolla 2–2$\frac{1}{2}$ in. long and broad, reddish. Ovary 4-celled with a single ovule in a cell. Capsules much longer than the calyx, 2-celled, 4-valved. Seeds 2–4, large, covered with brown tomentum. Convolvulus pes-capræ, *Linn.* Ipomœa maritima, *R. Br.; Bot. Reg. t.* 319. Batatas maritima, *Bojer, Hort. Maur.* 225.

MAURITIUS and RODRIGUEZ, common on the shores. Round Island, *Sir H. Barkly!* Round the world in the tropics. Connects *Batatas* and *Ipomœa* proper in the structure of its ovary, in which two of the four septa vanish wholly or partially as it matures. *Batate à Durand* or *Batatrant. Batate ronde.*

14. **I. glaberrima,** *Bojer, in Hook. Journ.* i. 357. A large woody climber, glabrous in all its parts. Leaves round, membranous, cuspidate, 4–5 in. long and broad, entire, deeply cordate; petiole 2–5 in. long. Peduncles 1-flowered, shorter than the petioles, thickened for an inch below the flower. Sepals $\frac{3}{4}$, finally an inch long, obtuse, much imbricated. Corolla white, with a cylindrical tube 3 in. long, and a suddenly spreading limb 3 in. broad. Capsule globose, an inch thick. Seeds densely pilose. Calonyction comesperma, *Bojer, Hort. Maur.* 228.; *Choisy in DC. Prod.* ix. 346.

SEYCHELLES, in bushy places near the shore, *Bojer! Wright!* Polynesia to Zambesi-land.

* *I. muricata*, Jacq. Hort. Schoenb. 340, t. 323, (Convolvulus, *Linn.*), a variety of *I. bona-nox*, Linn, (Calonyction speciosum, *Choisy in DC. Prod.* IX. 345,) universally cultivated or wild in the tropics, is plentiful in Rodriguez, *Dr. Balfour!* It is a shrubby climber, glabrous in all its parts, with copious weak deltoid prickles, long-petioled cordate-ovate membranous large entire or 3-lobed leaves, flowers 3–4 in lax axillary cymes, long pedicels becoming clavate as the fruit ripens, large ovate or lanceolate cuspidate sepals, a spreading purple corolla-limb 2–3 in. broad, and a globose capsule an inch thick.

15. **I. coccinea,** *Linn. Sp. Plant.* 163. An annual glabrous climber, with slender stems. Leaves deltoid, deeply cordate, acute, entire or furnished with a few large teeth or obscurely 3-lobed, bright green, membranous, 3–4 in. long and broad; petiole 1$\frac{1}{2}$–2 in. long. Peduncles $\frac{1}{4}$–$\frac{1}{2}$ foot long, with 6–12 corymbose or racemose flowers on short ascending pedicels. Sepals $\frac{1}{4}$ in. long, obtuse, with a very long cusp. Corolla bright red, 1$\frac{1}{2}$ in. long, with an almost rotate limb under an inch broad, with broad shallow lobes. Stamens distinctly exserted from the corolla tube. Capsule the size of a large pea, 4-seeded,

P 2

4-valved, naked within. *Bot. Mag. t.* 221; *Andr. Bot. Rep. t.* 449. Quamoclit coccinea, angulata, and phœnicea, *Choisy in DC. Prod.* ix. 335–6.

MAURITIUS; roadsides at Pailles and Pamplemousses. Round the world in the tropics. *Amourette à feuilles en cœur.*

* *I. Quamoclit*, Linn.; Bot. Mag. tab. 244, (Convolvulus pinnatus, *Lam.*; Quamoclit vulgaris, *Choisy*; Q. pinnata, *Bojer*), spread through the tropics of both hemispheres and well known in cultivation, is sometimes subspontaneous in Mauritius. (Sieber, ii. 213! etc.) It is a glabrous annual climber, with slender stems, pinnate leaves with numerous parallel 1-nerved very narrow leaflets, flowers 1–3 on long peduncles, sepals ¼ in. long obtuse with a cusp, corolla bright red narrowly tubular an inch long with small spreading deltoid lobes and stamens exserted from the throat, capsule ½ in. long naked within, 4-valved. *Amourette.*

3. CONVOLVULUS, Linn.

Sepals 5, broad, imbricated. Corolla broadly funnel-shaped. Stamens 5, inserted low down in the corolla-tube. Ovary 2-celled, with 2 ovules in each cell; style filiform; stigmas 2, cylindrical. Fruit a small 2-celled capsule.—Twining or erect herbs, with flowers solitary or in cymes in the axils of the leaves. DISTRIB. Temperate and subtropical regions. Species about 150.

1. **C. arvensis**, *Linn.*; *Choisy in DC. Prod.* ix. 406. A perennial herb, with slender tough twining glabrous or hairy stems. Leaves in our plant (*C. auriculatus*, Desr. in Lam. Encyc. iii. 540) linear-sagittate, with acute auricles. Peduncles 1–4-flowered; bracts small, linear. Sepals oblong, obtuse, unequal. Corolla white or reddish, 1 in. broad at the throat. Capsule small, globose.

MAURITIUS, in cultivated fields and by roadsides. Chiefly in the north temperate zone.

4. JACQUEMONTIA, Choisy.

Sepals 5, oblanceolate, free to the base. Corolla small, campanulate. Stamens included. Ovary 5-celled; cells 2-ovuled; style filiform; stigmas two, flat, ovate-lamelliform. Fruit a small membranous dehiscent capsule.—Twining herbs, with leaves usually cordate and flowers in axillary cymes or clusters. DISTRIB. All but this one species out of 36 natives of Tropical America.

1. **J. capitata**, *G. Don, Gard. Dict.* IV. 283. An annual climber, with slender finely pilose stems. Leaves simple, cordate-deltoid, acute, entire, membranous, 2–3 in. long; petiole 1–2 in. long. Peduncles much longer than the petioles; flowers in a dense globose head, bracteated by two large leaves and many smaller one. Sepals ¼ in. long, lanceolate, densely clothed with strong brown hairs. Corolla rather longer than

the calyx, purplish-white, fugacious, ½ in. broad when expanded. Capsule glabrous, the size of a pea glabrous within, 4-seeded. Convolvulus capitatus, *Desr. in Lam. Encyc.* iii. 544. Ipomœa capitata, *Choisy in DC. Prod.* ix. 365.

MAURITIUS, in waste ground, *Telfair !* Through Tropical Africa.

5. DICHONDRA, Forst.

Sepals 5, free, oblanceolate, obtuse. Corolla smaller than the calyx, 5-fid, campanulate. Stamens 5; filaments short, filiform. Carpels 2, distinct, subglobose; styles distinct, short, subulate; stigmas capitate. Capsules 2, small, globose, membranous, 1-seeded.—Small prostrate herbs with minute flowers in the axils of the leaves. DISTRIB. Round the world in warmer regions. Species 4 or 5.

1. **D. repens,** *Forst.; Choisy in DC. Prod.* ix. 451. A perennial, with slender wide-trailing stems. Leaves 1–3 from a node, entire, cordate-reniform, finely silky, ¼–1 in. broad; petiole 1–3 in. long. Flowers 1–2 from a node, on pedicels shorter than the petioles. Sepals finally ⅛–¼ in. long. Corolla minute, yellowish. Capsules pilose, $\frac{1}{12}$ in. thick. Seeds solitary, with a smooth black testa. *Lam. Ill. t.* 183.

MAURITIUS, on the slopes of the Pouce and Trois Mamelles, and a form with very small (⅛–¼ in. broad) leaves densely white-silky below gathered by Dr. Balfour in RODRIGUEZ on the patches of coralline limestone at the S. W. end of the island. Cosmopolitan in sub-tropical regions.

ORDER LXVI. SOLANACEÆ.

Flowers regular, hermaphrodite. Calyx inferior, rotate, funnel-shaped or campanulate, with 5 long or short teeth. Corolla shallowly or deeply 5-lobed, rotate or campanulate. Stamens 5; filaments inserted in the corolla-tube alternate with the lobes; anthers 2-celled, dehiscing by longitudinal slits or terminal pores. Ovary usually 2-celled; placentation axile; ovules numerous; style single, filiform; stigma capitate. Fruit baccate or capsular. Seeds albuminous.—Herbs or shrubs, with alternate exstipulate leaves, the flowers axillary, solitary or cymose. DISTRIB. Cosmopolitan, mostly tropical. Species 1200.

Fruit a berry.
  Anthers dehiscing by terminal pores . . . . . . 1. SOLANUM.
  Anthers dehiscing by slits.
    Calyx remaining small.
      Corolla rotate.
        Calyx toothed. Leaves pinnate . . . . . . * LYCOPERSICUM.
        Calyx truncate. Leaves simple. . . . . . . * CAPSICUM.
      Corolla deeply funnel-shaped . . . . 2. LYCIUM.
    Calyx becoming large and bladdery.
      Ovary 2-celled.
        Herbs with solitary flowers . . . . * PHYSALIS.
        Shrub with clustered flowers . . . . . . 3. WITHANIA.
      Ovary 3–5-celled . . . . * NICANDRA.
Fruit a capsule which slits into four valves . . . . . * DATURA.

1. SOLANUM, Linn.

Calyx rotate, with 5 or 10 teeth. Corolla rotate, with a short tube and 5 spreading lanceolate or deltoid lobes. Stamens 5, inserted in the throat of the corolla; filaments short; anthers linear, permanently conniving round the style, dehiscing by two pores at the tip. Ovary 2-celled, with axile placentation and numerous ovules; style filiform; stigma capitate. Fruit a globose or oblong juicy berry.—Herbs or shrubs, with flowers in axillary cymes. DISTRIB. Cosmopolitan, mostly tropical. Species 500.

Stem unarmed.
  Annual herbs.
    Leaves entire . . . . 1. S. NODIFLORUM.
    Leaves repand . . . . 2. S. NIGRUM.
  Perennials.
    Glabrous, large-fruited . . . . 3. S. MACROCARPUM.
    Tomentose, small-fruited . . . . 4. S. AURICULATUM.
Stem and leaves prickly.
  Flowers and berries small . . . . * S. INDICUM.
  Flowers and berries large.
    Leaf-veins unarmed . . . . * S. MELONGENA.
    Leaf-veins prickly . . . . * S. SANCTUM.

1. **S. nodiflorum,** *Jacq.; Dunal in DC. Prod.* xiii. 46. A tall glabrous annual, reaching several feet in height, rather shrubby in the lower part, with long spreading branches. Leaves ovate, acute, entire, 1–3 in. long, membranous, cuneate or rounded at the base. Flowers in copious short-peduncled axillary cymes. Calyx minute; teeth deltoid. Expanded corolla under ¼ in. broad, nearly white. Berry black, glabrous, the size of a pea. *Jacq. Ic. t.* 326. S. nigrum, *var.* patulum, *Linn.*

MAURITIUS and RODRIGUEZ, in waste places, and cultivated in kitchen-gardens. Cosmopolitan in the tropics. *Brède Malgache.*

2. **S. nigrum,** *Linn.; Dunal in DC. Prod.* xiii. 50. A diffuse annual, 1–2 feet high, with glabrous or pubescent stems. Leaves petioled, rhomboid, acute, membranous, 2–3 in. long, irregularly crenate-sinuated. Flowers in copious short-peduncled lateral cymes; pedicels ¼–⅓ in. long, cernuous. Calyx under $\frac{1}{12}$ in. long; teeth deltoid. Corolla whitish, under ½ in. across when expanded. Berry the size of a pea, shining, glabrous, usually black.

MAURITIUS, frequent in waste ground. A cosmopolitan weed. *S. villosum*, Lam. is a variety with hairy leaves and stems, and *S. miniatum*, Bernh. with red berries. *Brède Martin.*

3. **S. macrocarpum,** *Linn.; Dunal in DC. Prod.* xiii. 353. A robust unarmed shrubby perennial, glabrous in all its parts. Leaves oblong, membranous, subobtuse, cuneate at the base, 6–9 in. long, with long deltoid lobes; petiole 1–3 in. long. Cymes sessile, one fork bear-

ing a single fertile and the other several short-stalked barren flowers. Calyx ½–1 inch long; teeth linear or lanceolate, as long as the tube. Corolla violet, an inch long and broad. Berry yellow, the size of an apple. *Miller, Ic. t.* 294.

MAURITIUS and RODRIGUEZ, in waste ground. Also Madagascar and Comoros. *Grosse Anghive.*

4. **S. auriculatum,** *Ait.: Dunal in DC. Prod.* xiii. 115. A shrubby perennial, 6–10 ft. high, with stems and leaves beneath clothed with dense persistent whitish tomentum. Leaves oblong, acute, entire, cuneate at the base, 6–9 in. long, minutely downy above, venulose and tomentose beneath; petiole 1–2 in. long, with a pair of large oblong persistent stipules like the leaves in texture. Flowers very numerous, in dense long-peduncled dichotomous cymes 3–6 in. broad. Calyx ¼ in. long, densely matted; teeth lanceolate. Corolla ½ in. broad, violet, pilose externally. Berry small, yellow, pilose.

MAURITIUS, frequent by roadsides and on the borders of woods. Round the world in the tropics. *Tabac marron.*

* *S. indicum*, Linn.; Dunal in DC. Prod. xiii. 309; (S. Anguivi, *Bojer in Hook. Fl. Exot. t.* 199), widely spread in the tropics of the Old World, is now common in Mauritius and Rodriguez in waste ground. It is a shrubby perennial, with abundant prickles on the branches, petioles, peduncles, leaf-veins and calyx, oblong distinctly petioled leaves with a few deltoid lobes clothed beneath with white tomentum, flowers few in lax subsessile corymbose cymes on long pedicels, small tomentose calyx with lanceolate teeth, expanded violet corolla ⅓ in. broad, berry orange or red glabrous shining the size of a large pea. *Anghive* or *Bringelle marron. Petite Anghive.*

* *S. Melongena*, Linn; Wt. Ic. t. 166, widely spread through the tropics of the Old World, is commonly cultivated and subspontaneous in Mauritius, Rodriguez, and the Seychelles. It is a shrubby perennial, 2–4 ft. high, with stem and leaves on both sides clothed with persistent whitish tomentum, prickles copious straw-coloured those of the branches ¼ in. long rather hooked, leaves thin broad oblong 4–5 in. long with a few broad lobes, cymes sessile few-flowered with mostly only one flower fertile, flower calyx ½ in. long densely tomentose, expanded corolla violet an inch broad, berry size of a small apple very variable in shape and colour globose or oblong white violet yellow purple or nearly black. Here belong as varieties *S. incanum*, Linn.; *S. edule*, Thonn.; *S. undatum*, Lam.; *S. ovigerum, esculentum* and *heteracanthum*, Dunal. *Gros Bringelle* or *Anghive.*

* *S. sanctum*, Linn. (S. coagulans, *Forsk.; Dunal in DC. Prod.* xv. 319), a native of the warm temperate zone of the Old World from Egypt to China, is in Dr. Balfour's Rodriguez collection. It is a much-

branched low shrub, with zigzag tomentose branches armed with copious straw-coloured straight or slightly hooked pungent spines $\frac{1}{4}$–$\frac{1}{3}$ in. long thick ovate, repand tomentose leaves 3–4 in. long with strong prickles on the ribs, large purple flowers in congested pendulous cymes and a pendulous globose glabrous berry as large as a plum.

* *Lycopersicum Galeni*, Miller, Dict. No. 2, (L. cerasiforme, *Dunal in DC. Prod.* xiii. 26 ; Solanum pseudo-lycopersicum, *Jacq. Vind. t.* 11), the Cherry Tomato, is commonly cultivated and frequent on rubbish heaps. It is a much-branched annual, with puberulent bristly stems, pinnate leaves with stalked ovate acute sinuate or even pinnate leaflets, flowers in axillary cymes, sepals $\frac{1}{2}$ in. long linear joined at the base, a rotate yellow corolla not longer than the calyx, 5 long anthers cohering in a cone and dehiscing down the inner side, and a bright red or yellow rather villose berry as large as a plum.

* Several forms of *Capsicum* are cultivated and have become subspontaneous. Our Mauritian specimens from Dr. Ayres and M. Bouton all belong to *C. fastigiatum*, Blume; Dunal in DC. Prod. xiii. 416, marked by its shrubby zigzag branches, ovate acute membranous leaves cuneate at the base, long often geminate ascending or deflexed pedicels, entire campanulate calyx and clavate scarlet fruit $\frac{1}{2}$–$\frac{3}{4}$ in. long tapering to the point. The same form is established abundantly in Rodriguez. It seems a mere variety of *C. frutescens*, Linn., which yields the common Cayenne pepper. *Piment arbrisseau*.

* Dr. Balfour's Rodriguez collection also contains two forms of *C. cordiforme*, Miller, marked by its shrubby very flexuose stems and large pendulous scarlet fruit. One of them has a globose berry an inch long and thick and the other a larger ovoid-oblong fruit a couple of inches long. *Gros Piment*.

2. LYCIUM, Linn.

Calyx campanulate, 4–5-toothed. Corolla funnel-shaped, 4–5-lobed. Stamens 4–5, inserted at the middle of the tube, included or exserted; filaments filiform ; anthers small, dehiscing longitudinally. Ovary 2-celled ; ovules numerous ; style filiform ; stigma capitate. Fruit a small oblong berry.—Shrubs with alternate or fascicled entire leaves and small purplish solitary or umbellate axillary flowers. DISTRIB. Cosmopolitan. Species 30.

1. **L. tenue,** *Var.* SIEBERI, *Dunal in. DC. Prod.* xiii. 515. A low much-branched glabrous shrub, with pale grey branches and branchlets often copious and spiny. Leaves fascicled, fleshy, glabrous, subsessile, oblanceolate, obtuse, entire, $\frac{1}{4}$–$\frac{1}{3}$ in. long. Flowers solitary from

tufts of leaves on pedicels $\frac{1}{12}$–$\frac{1}{8}$ in. long. Calyx campanulate, under $\frac{1}{8}$ in. long; lobes 5 minute, deltoid. Corolla purplish, $\frac{1}{4}$–$\frac{1}{3}$ in. long; teeth broad, obtuse, $\frac{1}{3}$ the length of the tube.

MAURITIUS, *Sieber.* RODRIGUEZ, usually on the coral near the sea, but found also in the valley of the Rivière de l'est, *Balfour!* Also Cape. *L. capense*, Miller (L. tetrandrum, *Thunb. in Linn. Trans.* ix. 154 t. 15; L. afrum, *Bojer, Hort. Maur.* 241, *non Linn*), which differs mainly from *L. tenue* by its obovate leaves, is naturalised by the sea in Mauritius at the Rivière Noire, and on the Ile aux Tonneliers.

* *Physalis peruviana*, Linn.; Dunal in DC. Prod. xiii. 440; (P. edulis, *Sims, Bot. Mag. t.* 1068), spread round in the world in the warmer zones, is well-established in Mauritius, Rodriguez and the Seychelles, and was gathered by Dr. Ayres on Flat Island. It is a robust diffuse herb, clothed all over with fine grey pubescence, distinctly-petioled ovate acute entire or sinuated geminate membranous leaves, flowers solitary from the axils of the leaves on short pedicels, calyx remarkably accrescent at first $\frac{1}{4}$ inch finally $1\frac{1}{2}$–2 inches long with an inflated globose tube and 5 lanceolate teeth, corolla $\frac{1}{2}$ in. broad and long funnel-shaped obscurely lobed yellowish with 5 large purple blotches at the throat, and globose yellow eatable fruit enclosed in the angled inflated calyx. *Pockepocke. Cape Gooseberry.*

* *P. angulata*, Linn.; Dunal in DC. Prod. xiii. 449, a common tropical weed, also occurs sometimes both in Mauritius and the Seychelles. It is a robust nearly glabrous annual, 2–3 feet high, with petioled ovate membranous acute irregularly toothed leaves, flowers solitary on short pedicels in the axils of the leaves, corolla campanulate yellowish $\frac{1}{3}$ inch long unspotted, fruit-calyx an inch broad and long pentagonal truncate at the base, filled with the large yellowish berry.

3. WITHANIA, Pauquy.

Calyx campanulate, with 5 linear teeth, persistent and accrescent. Corolla funnel-shaped, with 5 small lanceolate teeth. Stamens included; anthers oblong, dehiscing longitudinally. Ovary 2-celled; style subulate; stigma capitate. Fruit a small berry, enclosed in the large inflated calyx tube.—Hoary perennials with entire leaves, the flowers in clusters in the axils of the leaves. DISTRIB. Warmer regions of the Old World. Species 4.

1. **W. somnifera,** *Dunal in DC. Prod.* xiii. 454. A shrubby perennial, 2–3 feet high, with stems clothed with persistent white tomentum. Leaves alternate, distinctly-petioled, ovate, acute, membranous, 2–3 in. long, cuneate at the base. Flowers 4–9, subsessile in the axils of the leaves. Flower-calyx $\frac{1}{4}$ in. long, densely tomentose; teeth minute. Corolla greenish-yellow, with 10 oblong green spots at the throat. Calyx-tube finally $\frac{1}{2}$–$\frac{3}{4}$ in. long and broad. Berry the size of a pea, red, glabrous, shining. Physalis somnifera, *Linn.; Wt. Ic. t.* 853.

MAURITIUS, common in waste ground; Flat Island, *Horne!* Tropics of Old World. *Pocke-pocke sauvage.*

* *Nicandra physaloides*, Gærtn.; Bot. Mag. t. 2438, a native of America well-known in cultivation, is naturalised in Mauritius by roadsides at Plaines Wilhelms and Nouvelle Découverte. It is a much-branched glabrous annual, with large petioled membranous ovate deeply sinuated leaves, flowers solitary in the axils of the leaves, bright blue funnel-shaped corolla above an inch broad with 5 short obtuse imbricating lobes, large accrescent calyx with a broad wing between the united portion of the 5 cordate ovate divisions and a large dry membranous indehiscent capsule with 3–5 cells. *Pocke-pocke à fleurs bleues.*

* *Datura alba*, Nees; Dunal in DC. Prod. xiii. 541; Wt. Icones, t. 852, (D. Stramonium, *Bojer, Hort. Maur.* 236; D. Bojeri, *Delile*), widely-spread through the tropics of the Old World, is a frequent weed in the Mauritius and Rodriguez. It is a robust nearly glabrous shrubby annual, with large petioled deltoid membranous leaves with a few irregular deltoid teeth, solitary flowers from the axils of the leaves, a long tubular calyx, a very large white funnel-shaped corolla with deltoid cuspidate lobes, and an echinate ovoid capsule splitting into four valves. *Feuille du Diable. Herbe du Diable.*

Nicotiana Tabacum, Linn., which is universally cultivated, is in Dr. Balfour's Rodriguez collection as subspontaneous.

ORDER LXVII. OLEACEÆ.

Flowers regular, hermaphrodite. Calyx inferior; tube short, campanulate; teeth long or short, various in number. Corolla hypocrateriform or rotate; lobes spreading, the same number as the calyx-teeth. Stamens 2, included, epipetalous; filaments short, filiform or 0; anthers 2-celled, dehiscing longitudinally. Ovary 2-celled; ovules 2 in each cell; placentation axile; style simple; stigma emarginate. Fruit indehiscent in the Mauritian genera. Seeds solitary in the cells, albuminous or exalbuminous.—Shrubs, with opposite simple or compound exstipulate leaves, scaly buds and abundant flowers in panicles or corymbs. DISTRIB. Almost cosmopolitan. Species 280.

Corolla-tube short; lobes 4 . . . . 1. OLEA.
Corolla-tube long; lobes 5–9 . . . . 2. JASMINUM.

1. OLEA, Linn.

Calyx minute, campanulate, with 4 deltoid teeth. Corolla rotate, with a very short tube, and 4 spreading lanceolate lobes. Stamens 2, included; filaments short, inserted in the tube. Ovary 2-celled; ovules 2, pendulous from the axile placenta; style entire, very short;

stigma capitate or emarginate. Fruit a drupe, with a fleshy mesocarp and bony endocarp. Seed albuminous.—Shrubs, with entire coriaceous opposite small leaves and abundant minute white flowers in axillary or terminal panicles. DISTRIB. Tropical and warm temperate zones of the Old World. Species 35.

Panicles terminal . . . . 1. O. LANCEA.
Panicles lateral.
  Leaves lanceolate, distinctly petioled . . . . 2. O. CHRYSOPHYLLA.
  Leaves obovate, subsessile.
    Leaves cuspidate. Calyx-teeth lanceolate . . . . 3. O. MACROPHYLLA.
    Leaves obtuse. Calyx-teeth deltoid . . . . 4. O. OBOVATA.

1. **O. lancea,** *Lam.; DC. Prod.* viii. 287. A much-branched shrub, 4–12 feet high, glabrous in all its parts. Leaves short-petioled, glossy, rigid, lanceolate or oblong, narrowed to both ends, 2–3 in. long, ½–1 inch broad at the middle, not lepidote beneath. Flowers in deltoid terminal panicles 2–3 in. long, the lower branches from the axils of developed leaves; bud globose. Calyx naked, $\frac{1}{48}$ in. long. Corolla $\frac{1}{12}$ in. long, the teeth oblong-lanceolate. Drupe juicy, ovoid, acuminate, purple with a rugose pointed stone.

MAURITIUS, on dry escarpments of the hills, frequent. RODRIGUEZ, on the higher parts of the island ridge, (the type and a variety with broader (¾–1¼ in.) obtuse, truncate or emarginate leaves), *Duncan! Balfour!* Also Bourbon. *Olivier sauvage. Olivier du pays.*

2. **O. chrysophylla,** *Lam.; DC. Prod.* viii. 285. A much-branched shrub, with exactly the habit of *O. lancea,* except that branches, leaves beneath, and calyx are clothed with bright ferruginous lepidote scales, and the small (½–1 inch long) panicles spring only from the axils of the leaves, the one or two top pairs of the branch being usually, but not always flowerless. Leaves lanceolate, glossy, 2 in. long, ½ in. broad at the middle. "Drupe globose, with a cusp."

MAURITIUS, on dry escarpments of the Pouce and Pieter-both. Also Bourbon and Abyssinia. *Olivier de Bourbon.*

3. **O. macrophylla,** *Baker.* A shrub, with terete branches, glabrous in all its parts except the panicle. Leaves scarcely petioled, obovate, rigidly coriaceous, cuspidate, deltoid at the base, 3–4 in. long, 2–2½ in. broad at the middle, only the erecto-patent main veins visible beneath. Panicles sessile, axillary, ½–¾ in. long, with a hairy rachis and short spreading branches; bracts lanceolate, pilose, $\frac{1}{24}$ in. long. Calyx $\frac{1}{24}$ in. long, pilose, the teeth longer and more lanceolate than in the other species. Corolla twice as long as the calyx. Fruit not seen.

MAURITIUS, *Bouton!* (without special station.) Endemic.

4. **O. obovata,** *Baker.* A shrub, with slender terete branches, glabrous in all its parts. Leaves nearly sessile, obovate, obtuse, coriaceous, bright green, 1½–2½ in. long, 1–1¾ in. broad, with a broad deltoid

base, the veining perceptible when dried. Flowers in sparse sessile axillary panicles $\frac{1}{4}$–$\frac{1}{2}$ in. long. Calyx $\frac{1}{24}$ in. long; teeth deltoid. Corolla $\frac{1}{12}$ in. long. Drupe not seen.

MAURITIUS, *Dr. Ayres*! (special station not stated). Leaves like those of *O. capensis* in shape, but thinner in texture, with more distinct veins, and the inflorescence axillary. Endemic.

O. obtusifolia, Lam.; A. DC. Prod. viii. 285, (O. cernua, *Vahl*), attributed by Lamarck and others to Mauritius, is known there in cultivation only, and is a native of Madagascar.

2. JASMINUM, Linn.

Calyx-tube campanulate; teeth 5–9, long or short. Corolla hypocrateriform, with a long tube and 5–9 horizontal lobes. Stamens 2, included in the corolla-tube, epipetalous. Ovary 2-celled; placentation axile; ovules 2, rarely 3–4, erect; style simple; stigma capitate. Fruit 2-lobed or by abortion simple, membranous or fleshy; lobes usually 1-seeded. Seed exalbuminous.—Shrubs, often climbers, with opposite simple or compound leaves, the flowers in terminal corymbs. DISTRIB. Tropical and warm temperate regions. Species about 100.

Leaves simple. Calyx long, with setaceous teeth . . * J. SAMBAC.
Leaves trifoliolate. Calyx-teeth minute.
  Downy. Corolla lobes 6–8 . . . . 1. J. AURICULATUM.
  Glabrous. Corolla lobes 5 . . . . * J. AZORICUM.

1. **J. auriculatum,** *Vahl; A. DC. Prod.* viii. 309. A wide-climbing shrub with branches densely pilose upwards. Leaves petioled, moderately firm, bright green; leaflets 3, all distinctly stalked, roundish, obtuse or cuspidate, 1–1$\frac{1}{2}$ in. long, the two side ones often smaller, or in the upper leaves not produced. Flowers in copious lax terminal corymbs, with ascending pilose branches. Calyx $\frac{1}{12}$ in. long, campanulate, pilose; teeth deltoid. Corolla white, fragrant, 1–1$\frac{1}{4}$ in. long; lobes 6–8, oblique-lanceolate, obtuse or subacute, half as long as the tube. Fruit fleshy, 2-lobed; lobes the size of a pepper-corn, smooth, dark purple. *Bot. Reg.* t. 264; *Wight, Icones, t.* 700. J. trifoliatum, *Pers.* J. mauritianum, *Bojer, Hort. Maur.* 204. J. mucronatum, *Reich.* J. tettense, *Klotzsch in Peters' Mossamb. Bot.* i. 248.

MAURITIUS, in mountain and valley woods through the island. SEYCHELLES, *Horne*, 538! Also Tropical Asia and Tropical Africa. *Jasmin du pays.*

We have also examples of the two following, which have strayed from cultivation:—

* *J. azoricum*, Linn.; A. DC. Prod. viii. 311; Bot. Reg. t. 89; Bot. Mag. t. 1889, (J. flavum, *Sieber, Fl. Maur.* ii. 255), just like *J. auriculatum* in general habit and leaf, but quite glabrous, the leaflets always acute, the spreading lobes of the corolla regularly five in number. Mauritius, *Sieber!* Seychelles, *Horne*, 355! A native of the Azores.

* *J. Sambac*, Ait., (Bot. Mag. t. 1785. J. undulatum, *Willd.* Nyctanthes Sambac, *Linn.*); branches pilose, leaves nearly sessile simple oblong acute crisped towards the edge, flowers few in crowded corymbs, calyx long with 5–9 setaceous teeth, corolla white with 6–9 lanceolate lobes nearly as long as the tube. Seychelles on waste lands in Praslin, *Horne*, 334! A native of Tropical Asia, now widely spread in cultivation.

ORDER LXVIII. APOCYNACEÆ.

Flowers regular hermaphrodite, pentamerous. Calyx inferior, campanulate, usually small. Corolla usually hypocrateriform; lobes oblique, obtuse or acute, twisted in bud. Stamens 5, inserted high up in the throat, alternate with the petals; filaments 0 or short; anthers 2-celled, dehiscing longitudinally, usually cohering round the stigma. Ovary free, composed of two distinct or combined carpels; ovules 2 or more in each cell; style simple; stigma capitate or emarginate. Carpels becoming more or less distinct in fruit, drupaceous or follicular. Seeds mostly albuminous, not comose in any of our genera.—Shrubs, with opposite leaves, often milky juice, the stipules none or very small, the flowers mostly corymbose. DISTRIB. Round the world in the tropics and warmer zones. Species about 900.

Fruit-carpels drupaceous.
  Calyx large, with foliaceous teeth . . . . 1. CERBERA.
  Calyx minute.
    Corolla-lobes acute . . . . 2. CARISSA.
    Corolla-lobes obtuse . . . . 3. OCHROSIA.
Fruit carpels follicular.
  Flowers cymose. Carpels oblong, pulpy inside . . 4. TABERNÆMONTANA.
  Flowers 1–3, sessile, axillary. Carpels dry, cylindrical . . . . * VINCA.

1. CERBERA, Linn.

Calyx large, divided nearly or quite to the base into 5 oblong acute lobes. Corolla hypocrateriform, the tube furnished with 5 longitudinal folds at the top of the throat, the segments acute, twisted in bud. Stamens 5, inserted above the middle of the throat; anthers sagittate, incumbent on the stigma. Ovary of 2 distinct carpels; style filiform; stigma conical at the top, with 10 ribs, the summit emarginate. Drupe usually of one lobe, large, oblong, with a thick woody endocarp.—Shrubs, with milky juice, oblanceolate prominently veined leaves and showy flowers in lax corymbs. DISTRIB. Tropics of the Old World. Species 4.

1. **C. Odollam,** *Gærtn.*; *A. DC. Prod.* viii. 353. A tall shrub, 20–30 feet high, glabrous in all its parts. Leaves distinctly petioled, oblanceolate, acute, 6–9 in. long, cuneate at the base, subcoriaceous, with very distinct spreading main veins. Flowers in a broad lax terminal corymb; bracts large, ovate, caducous. Calyx $\frac{1}{2}$–$\frac{3}{4}$ in. long, with large foliaceous lobes. Corolla-tube $\frac{3}{4}$ in. long, broadly funnel-shaped at

the top, pilose within; limb an inch across, white with a pink eye. Lobes of drupes oblong, 2 in. long. *Wight, Ic. t.* 441. C. Manghas, *Bot. Mag. t.* 1845.

SEYCHELLES, common in the woods of Mahé, *Kirk! Wright! Horne*, 246! Frequent in Tropical Asia, not African.

2. CARISSA, Linn.

Calyx minute, deeply 5-toothed. Corolla hypocrateriform, with a slender tube internally pilose and 5 pointed lobes, twisted in æstivation. Stamens 5, inserted about the middle of the corolla-tube; filaments short; anthers oblong or lanceolate. Ovary of 2 combined carpels; ovules few or many in a cell; style shorter than the corolla-tube; stigma bifid. Fruit a large or small berry.—Spiny shrubs or trees, with opposite coriaceous leaves, and few-flowered axillary cymes. DISTRIB. Tropics of the Old World. Species 20.

Leaves obtuse. Drupes the size of a plum . . . . . . 1. C. XYLOPICRON.
Leaves acuminate. Drupes the size of a cherry . . . 2. C. SECHELLENSIS.

1. **C. Xylopicron,** *Thouars; A. DC. Prod.* viii. 333. A shrub or low tree, glabrous in all its parts. Leaves short-petioled, oblong, obtuse, glossy, rigidly coriaceous, very variable in size, $\frac{1}{2}$–2 in. long, a pair of sharp erect spines produced from each fork in the small-leaved forms, which do not produce flowers. Cymes from the axils of the upper leaves only, 1–6-flowered; pedicels $\frac{1}{8}$–$\frac{1}{2}$ in. long, bractless. Calyx $\frac{1}{8}$ in. long, the deltoid-acuminate teeth exceeding the tube. Expanded corolla-limb $\frac{3}{4}$ in. broad, the acute lanceolate segments as long as the slender tube. Anthers lanceolate. Fruit an oblong pointed berry an inch long, containing 12–15 seeds. C. coriacea, *Wall. Cat. No.* 1681.

MAURITIUS, in woods of Flacq, Bois Cheri and Corps de Garde Mountain, now scarce. RODRIGUEZ, common, *Bouton! Balfour!* Also Bourbon and Madagascar, if, as seems likely, *C. madagascariensis* of Thouars be conspecific. *Calac* or *Bois Amer* (Maur). *Bois Sandal.*

2. **C. sechellensis,** *Baker.* A tree 30–40 feet high, glabrous in all its parts, with slender terete branches. Spines none in the specimens seen. Leaves short-petioled, oblong, acuminate, rigid, glossy, cuneate at the base, $1\frac{1}{2}$ in. long, with fine immersed veins. Cymes 4–8-flowered, short-peduncled, umbellate or corymbose; pedicels erect, ebracteate, $\frac{1}{4}$ in. long. Calyx under $\frac{1}{12}$ in. long; teeth deltoid-cuspidate. Corolla-tube $\frac{1}{4}$ in. long, reddish, hairy within; teeth lanceolate, acute, whitish, as long as the tube. Anthers small, oblong, sessile at the throat of the tube. Fruit a red or black berry as large as a cherry.

SEYCHELLES; rare, now known only in Silhouette, but said to have once been common in the northern forests of Mahé. Wood like sandal-wood and very beautiful. *Horne*, 511! *Bois Sandal.*

3. OCHROSIA, Juss.

Calyx minute, campanulate; teeth 5, broad, obtuse. Corolla hypocrateriform; lobes 5, obtuse, twisted in bud. Stamens 5, inserted at the middle of the tube; filaments very short. Ovary of 2 distinct carpels; style filiform; stigma bifid. Fruit of 2 distinct drupes, with a very thick woody endocarp, each containing 2 or 3 seeds.—Shrubs, with whorled conspicuously-veined leaves and flowers in very dense terminal trichotomous cymes. DISTRIB. Tropical Asia and Polynesia. Species 12.

1. **O. borbonica,** *Gmel.; A. DC. Prod.* viii. 356. A tree 20–40 feet high, glabrous in all its parts. Leaves 3 rarely 4 in a whorl, distinctly petioled, oblong or oblanceolate-oblong, obtuse or subacute, cuneate at the base, 3–6 in. long, glossy, with numerous parallel distinct spreading veins below. Flowers in dense sessile or short peduncled terminal cymes; pedicels short, with densely imbricated small persistent bracts. Calyx $\frac{1}{12}$ in. long, with coriaceous rounded ciliated lobes. Corolla under $\frac{1}{2}$ in. long, whitish, the obovate obtuse lobes as long as the limb. Drupes ovoid or oblong, pointed, above an inch long. O. maculata, *Jacq. Ic. t.* 321; *A. DC. Prod.* viii. 356. O. undulata, *Bojer, Hort. Maur.* 206. O. platyspermos, *A. DC. loc. cit.*

MAURITIUS, in the shaded hill-forests. SEYCHELLES, in all the islands, principally on the shores, *Wright! Horne*, 534! Also Bourbon. *Bois jaune* or *quinquina du pays* (Maur). *Bois Chauve souris* (Seych).

4. TABERNÆMONTANA, Linn.

Calyx campanulate, persistent, with 5 short broad teeth. Corolla hypocrateriform, the 5 oblique obtuse lobes hairy on the face. Stamens 5, the anthers sessile in the tube near the top. Ovary of 2 distinct carpels; ovules indefinite; style filiform; stigma two-lobed. Fruit of two oblong divaricating capsules, which dehisce down the whole length of the inner side (follicles), and contain numerous seeds imbedded in pulp.—Glabrous shrubs, with opposite prominently-veined entire leaves and abundant flowers in peduncled cymes. DISTRIB. Round the world in the tropics. Species about 100.

Cymes as long as the leaves. Expanded corolla 2 inches broad . . . . 1. T. TELFAIRIANA.
Cymes much shorter than leaves. Expanded corolla $\frac{3}{4}$–1 in. broad.
  Main veins of the leaf about 20 pairs . . . . . . 2. T. PERSICARIÆFOLIA.
  Main veins of the leaf 10–12 pairs.
    Pedicels $\frac{1}{12}$–$\frac{1}{4}$ in. long, bracteate . . . . . . 3. T. MAURITIANA.
    Pedicels $\frac{1}{4}$–$\frac{1}{2}$ in. long, naked . . . . 4. T. COFFEÆFOLIA.

1. **T. Telfairiana,** *Wall.; A. DC. Prod.* viii. 369. A tall erect shrub, glabrous in all its parts. Leaves distinctly petioled, oblong, acute, cuneate at the base, 3–4 in. long, $1\frac{1}{2}$–2 in. broad, membranous, with

about 10 ascending main veins on each side. Cymes as long as the leaves, longer and laxer than in the other species, the peduncle much exceeding the petiole; pedicels $\frac{1}{8}$–$\frac{1}{2}$ in. long, the bracts minute, lanceolate. Calyx $\frac{1}{8}$ in. long, the deltoid teeth as long as the tube. Expanded corolla 2 inches broad, whitish, the oblique obovate lobes as long as the tube. Follicles not seen.

MAURITIUS, in forests of the Pouce and Quartier Militaire, *Telfair!* etc. Endemic. *Bois de Lait.*

2. **T. persicariæfolia,** *Jacq.; A. DC. Prod.* viii. 369. A glabrous shrub, 6–10 feet high, with leaves and flowers crowded near the end of the branchlets. Leaves distinctly petioled, oblong or lanceolate, always acute or acuminate, cuneate at the base, 2–4 in. long, 1–2 in. broad at the middle, membranous, with about 20 distinct spreading main ribs coalescing in arches near the edge. Cymes many-flowered, short-peduncled, not more than $\frac{1}{2}$–$\frac{1}{3}$ as long as the leaves; pedicels $\frac{1}{12}$–$\frac{1}{4}$ in. long, with minute ovate bracts. Calyx $\frac{1}{12}$ in. long, the teeth broad, obtuse, and much imbricated. Corolla greenish-yellow, the expanded limb an inch broad, the segments as long as the tube, $\frac{1}{4}$ inch broad. Follicles ovoid, apiculate, 1–1$\frac{1}{2}$ in. long. *Jacq. Ic. t.* 320. T. amygdalifolia, *Sieber, Exsic.* ii. 84.

MAURITIUS, frequent in woods through the island; Amber Island, *Horne!* Endemic. *Bois de Lait.*

3. **T. mauritiana,** *Poir.; A. DC. Prod.* viii. 370. An erect shrub, with leaves and flowers crowded towards the tips of the slender terete branchlets. Leaves distinctly petioled, oblong, subacute, obtuse, deltoid at the base, 3–4 in. long, 2–2$\frac{1}{2}$ in. broad at the middle, membranous, with 10–12 distinct main veins. Cymes many-flowered, their peduncles scarcely longer than the petioles; pedicels $\frac{1}{12}$–$\frac{1}{4}$ in. long, furnished with several minute persistent bracts. Calyx $\frac{1}{12}$ in. long, with short obtuse teeth. Expanded limb of corolla yellowish, $\frac{3}{4}$–1 in. broad, the oblique oblanceolate-oblong lobes shorter than the tube. Follicles ovoid, pointed, 1$\frac{1}{2}$ in. long. T. squamosa, *Sieber.*

MAURITIUS, in woods through the island. *T. micrantha*, A. DC. Prod. viii. 370. (*T. parviflora*, Bojer, Hort. Maur. 209), is a small-flowered variety. Also Bourbon. *Bois de Lait.*

4. **T. coffeæfolia,** *Bojer, MSS.* Very near *T. mauritiana*, but the leaves firmer in texture and more pointed, the peduncle of the cymes longer, and the pedicels also longer ($\frac{1}{4}$–$\frac{1}{2}$ inch), and without bracts. Venation of leaves, calyx and corolla of *T. mauritiana.*

SEYCHELLES, in the woods of Mahé, *Wright! Herb. Blackburn! Horne*, 249, 537! Also Johanna Island.

* *Vinca rosea*, Linn.; A. DC. Prod. viii. 382, (Bot. Mag. t. 248; Miller, Ic. t. 186; Castharanthus roseus, *G. Don*), now spread universally in the tropics and hothouses, apparently a native of Tropical America, is established plentifully in Mauritius, Rodriguez and the

Seychelles. It is a low half-shrubby glabrous perennial, with short-petioled obovate-oblong obtuse leaves cuneate at the base, flowers 1–3 sessile in the axils of many leaves, calyx small with 5 setaceous teeth, corolla hypocrateriform rose or white with a slender tube and oblique obovate segments, stigma bearded at the top and furnished with a cup-shaped membrane below, and 2 cylindrical vertically-striated follicles about an inch long, containing each 15–20 seeds. *Saponaire. Pervenche.*

ORDER LXIX. ASCLEPIADACEÆ.

Flowers regular, hermaphrodite, pentamerous. Calyx free, campanulate, mostly minute; teeth 5. Corolla rotate; divisions 5, spreading, linear, lanceolate or deltoid. Corona usually present, single or double; stamens 5, connate with the stigma into a mass (gynostegium); anther-cells 2–4; pollen grains connate into 10–20 pendulous or erect granular or waxy masses (pollinia). Pistil free, 2-carpellary; placentation sutural; ovules numerous, pendulous, anatropous; style short, simple; stigma pentagonal. Fruit of two divaricating ovoid or clavate-fusiform acuminate smooth or prickly follicles. Seeds usually furnished with a dense crest of hairs, albuminous.—Shrubs or herbs, with abundant milky juice. Leaves, if present, opposite, entire. Flowers mostly small, umbellate or cymose. DISTRIB. Cosmopolitan; mostly tropical. Species 1300.

Pollinia granular . . . . 1. TANULEPIS.
Pollinia waxy.
  Pollinia 20, erect . . . . 2. SECAMONE.
  Pollinia 10, pendulous.
    Leafless climbers with a double staminal corona.
      Inner row of corona the smallest; scales all cuspidate 3. DECANEMA.
      Inner row of corona the largest; scales not cuspidate . 4. SARCOSTEMMA.
    Erect perennials with a single staminal corona.
      Leaflets of corona with a hooked horn from the face . * ASCLEPIAS.
      Leaflets of corona without any horn . . . . . . 5. GOMPHOCARPUS.
  Pollinia 10, erect or ascending . . . . 6. TYLOPHORA.

1. TANULEPIS, Balf. fil.

Calyx small, deeply 5-fid, with 5 basal glands on the inside. Corolla sub-rotate, deeply 5-cleft; segments subvalvate. Corona single; scales 5, lanceolate, as long as the petals, submembranous, connate in a ring at the base and adhering to the base of the gynostegium; stamens opposite to the lobes of the corona; filaments broad, short; anthers cuspidate; pollinia granular. Stigma 5-angled. Follicles spreading, slender, faintly ribbed. DISTRIB. A single endemic species.

1. **T. sphenophylla,** *Balf. fil.* A climber, glabrous in all its parts, with slender terete branches. Leaves oblong-lanceolate, 2–3 in. long acute, cuneate at the base, membranous; petiole $\frac{1}{4}$–$\frac{1}{3}$ in. long. Cymes

few-flowered, axillary, sessile or short-peduncled; pedicels $\frac{1}{3}$–$\frac{3}{4}$ in. long, flexuose, often bracteolate. Calyx $\frac{1}{24}$ in. long; teeth deltoid, not longer than the campanulate tube. Corolla $\frac{1}{8}$ in. long, greenish, glabrous; segments lanceolate. Gynostegium $\frac{1}{24}$ in. deep and broad; leaves of the staminal corona lingulate, obtuse, as long as the gynostegium. Follicles erecto-patent, smooth, cylindrical, acute, 3 in. long.

RODRIGUEZ, in tolerable abundance both in the valleys and on the hill-slopes, *Duncan! Balfour!* Endemic.

2. SECAMONE, R. Br.

Calyx minute, with 5 long obtuse teeth. Corolla rotate, with long oblong teeth. Staminal corona of 5 lingulate acute simple lobes, which exceed the gynostegium; anthers 4-celled, the 20 pollinia erect. Stigma short or elongated. Follicles clavate, unarmed.—Shrubby leafy climbers, with minute flowers in intrapetiolar cymes. DISTRIB. Tropics of the Old World. Species 24.

1. **S. saligna,** *Dcne. in DC. Prod.* viii. 503. A twining (or suberect?) shrub, with woody terete branches clothed at first with brownish-white tomentum. Leaves short-petioled, linear, 1½–2 in. long, one-nerved, narrowed from the middle to both ends, coriaceous, bright green above, clothed with brownish-white tomentum beneath. Cymes short-peduncled, composed of few flowers on tomentose pedicels. Corolla wide-spreading, $\frac{1}{12}$ in. diam. Stigma elongated, apiculate. Young follicles tomentose.

MAURITIUS, in mountain-forests. Also Bourbon. (We have it from Bourbon only.)

Mr. Horne has found (No. 533) in the Seychelles in the woods of Mahé at an elevation of 2000 feet, an Asclepiadaceous climber of similar habit of which the flowers are at present unknown. It is glabrous in all its parts, with distinctly petioled coriaceous glossy lanceolate acuminate leaves 3–4 in. long cuneate at the base, flowers few in short-peduncled cymes in the axils of the leaves, follicles 3 inches long naked firm clavate acuminate.

3. DECANEMA, Dcne.

Calyx minute, with 5 long deltoid teeth. Corolla rotate; tube short, campanulate; teeth 5, deltoid. Staminal corona double, both rows cup-shaped, 5-toothed, each tooth furnished with a long cusp, the 2-celled anthers terminated by a membrane, the 10 clavate pollinia pendulous from the top of the gynostegium. Stigma obscurely emarginate. Fruit of two large unarmed clavate follicles.—A single species.

1. **D. Bojerianum,** *Decne. in DC. Prod.* viii. 546. Stems shrubby, slender, terete, glabrous, $\frac{1}{8}$ in. thick, twining over bushes to a height of

8 or 10 feet, flexuose and irregularly branched. Bracts at each joint minute, scariose, ovate acuminate. Leaves entirely absent. Flowers few together in distant lateral and terminal umbels on pedicels $\frac{1}{8}$–$\frac{1}{4}$ in. long. Corolla under $\frac{1}{8}$ in. long, the segments fleshy, yellow. Follicles half a foot long.

MAURITIUS; on the Pouce and Montagne Longue, *Bouton*, teste *Decaisne*. We have no specimens, and I suspect some confusion with *Sarcostemma viminale*. Also Madagascar.

4. SARCOSTEMMA, R. Br.

Calyx small, deeply 5-fid, furnished with 5 very minute glands. Corolla subrotate, deeply 5-cleft. Corona usually double; outer cup-like; inner of 5 erect scales adnate to the back of the stamens, with a short free tip; anthers ending in an inflexed membrane; pollinia solitary in the cells, pendulous. Stigma faintly lobed at the top. Follicles spreading, slender or stout.—Climbing leafless shrubs with copious small flowers in lateral or terminal umbels. DISTRIB. Tropics of the Old World. Species 6–8.

Outer corona toothed only	1. S. VIMINALE.
Outer corona 5-lobed nearly down to the base . . .	2. S. ODONTOLEPIS.

1. **S. viminale,** *R. Br.; Dcne. in DC. Prod.* viii. 538. A glabrous leafless fleshy twiner, with terete branches articulated at the nodes. Umbels sessile or peduncled; pedicels puberulent, $\frac{1}{8}$–$\frac{3}{8}$ in. long. Calyx $\frac{1}{16}$ in. long; teeth ovate-oblong, ciliated at the edge. Corolla $\frac{1}{8}$ in. long, deeply cleft; lobes oblong, obtuse, glabrous. Outer corona cup-like, sinuate-dentate; teeth 15, those opposite the stamens the largest; inner scales widely saccate, twice the length of the outer corona, shorter than the gynostegium. Stigma minutely 2–3-lobed.

MAURITIUS and RODRIGUEZ, and probably also Seychelles, but our specimens from the latter are not in flower. Also Cape and Tropical Africa. *Liane Calé.*

2. **S. odontolepis,** *Balf. fil.* Habit and inflorescence exactly of *S. viminale.* Calyx $\frac{1}{24}$ in. long; teeth ovate or suborbicular, slightly keeled, ciliated at the edge. Corolla $\frac{1}{8}$ in. long, deeply cleft; lobes oblong, glabrous. Outer corona deeply 5-partite; lobes with three unequal teeth, the central one the largest; inner scales saccate, thrice the length of the outer corona, nearly as long as the gynostegium. Stigma minutely 2-lobed.

RODRIGUEZ, *Balfour!* May prove a variety of the last, as Dr. Balfour has seen a form which appears to be intermediate. Endemic.

* The large American genus *Asclepias*, which is distinguished from Gomphocarpus by its smooth follicles and the hooded divisions of the

staminal crown furnished with a falcate horn from the inner face, is represented both in the Seychelles and Mauritius by *A. curassavica*, Linn.; Bot. Reg. t. 81, of the West Indies, which is now widely spread in the Old World. It is an erect milky glabrous perennial herb, with opposite petioled lanceolate leaves, flowers in terminal umbels on slender puberulous pedicels, minute calyx with 5 linear teeth, petals much reflexed oblong red, large stalked table-shaped staminal corona and stigma with the horns projecting over its summit.

5. GOMPHOCARPUS, R. Br.

Calyx-tube very short; teeth 5, linear. Corolla rotate, with a very short tube and 5 spreading obtuse oblong teeth. Staminal corona composed of 5 obtuse hooded lobes, with the edges furnished with a single tooth on each side; pollen-masses 10, clavate, pendulous. Stigma flat-topped, pentagonal. Follicles oblong, acuminate, muricated.—Shrubby perennials, with flowers in copious peduncled axillary umbels. DISTRIB. Mainly Cape. Species 80.

1. **G. cornutus**, *Dcne. in DC. Prod.* viii. 557. A shrubby erect perennial, 4–6 feet high, with virgate puberulous stems. Leaves linear, 1-nerved, short-petioled, acuminate, membranous, 3–5 in. long. Flowers in copious distinctly-peduncled axillary umbels with long puberulous pedicels. Sepals linear, nearly as long as the petals. Corolla yellowish, under ¼ in. in diam. Staminal corona of 5 distinct obtuse lobes as long as the pentagonal stigma. Follicles ovoid, acuminate, prickly, 2–3 in. long. G. niveus, *Bojer, MSS.*

MAURITIUS and SEYCHELLES, in waste ground. Also Madagascar and Zambesiland. Probably a mere variety of *G. fruticosus*, R. Br., widely spread in Africa and West Asia. *Asclépiade. La Ouatte.*

6. TYLOPHORA, R. Br.

Calyx minute; teeth 5, linear or deltoid. Corolla rotate, with 5 long lanceolate or deltoid lobes. Staminal corona of 5 flat fleshy distinct lobes adnate to the gynostegium; pollen-masses 10, erect, clavate or subglobose. Stigma obscurely emarginate. Follicles smooth, clavate, acuminate.—Slender leafy climbers, with copious small flowers in axillary cymes. DISTRIB. Tropics of the Old World. Species 40.

Stems glabrous . . . . 1. T. LÆVIGATA.
Stems densely pubescent . . . . 2. T. ASTHMATICA.

1. **T. lævigata,** *Dcne. in DC. Prod.* viii. 602. A slender woody climber, glabrous in all its parts. Branchlets rather angular. Leaves cordate-ovate, membranous, 2–3 in. long, subacute or obtuse, with a

distinct mucro; petiole ¼–½ in. long. Flowers in copious sessile or short-peduncled axillary cymes on pedicels ¼–½ in. long; bracts minute, lanceolate. Calyx with 5 long linear teeth. Corolla ⅛-⅙ in. long, yellowish-green; teeth deltoid. Gynostegium not longer than the calyx. Lobes of staminal corona lanceolate, subacute, as long as the gynostegium. Follicles smooth, clavate-acuminate, ¼–½ in. long. Periploca mauritiana, *Poir.*; *Bojer Hort. Maur.* 212. Cynanchum capense, *Sieber.* C. mauritianum, *Lam.*

MAURITIUS, common in woods and bushy places. Round Island, *Sir H. Barkly!* Flat Island and Coin de Mire, *Horne!* Also Bourbon. *Ipéca or Ipécacuanha du pays.*

2. **T. asthmatica,** *Wt. and Arn.*; *Dcne. in DC. Prod.* viii. 611. A slender shrubby climber, with terete densely pubescent branchlets. Leaves cordate-ovate, 2–3 in. long, membranous, pubescent beneath, obtuse with a distinct mucro; petiole ¼–½ in. long. Flowers in copious peduncled cymes from the axils of the leaves; bracts minute, deltoid, persistent; pedicels slender, ½–1 inch long. Calyx $\frac{1}{12}$ in. long; teeth linear. Corolla ¼ in. long, greenish-yellow; teeth deltoid. Gynostegium $\frac{1}{12}$ in. deep, the lobes of the staminal corona ligulate, distinct, cuspidate, just overtopping the flat-topped stigma. Follicles 3–4 in. long, spreading, smooth, clavate acuminate. Asclepias asthmatica, *Roxb.*

SEYCHELLES, in woods of Mahé, *Horne*, 366! Common in Tropical Asia.

Two other glabrous slender shrubby climbing species were gathered by Dr. Balfour in Rodriguez in Cascade Valley, without flower and fruit, which should be specially looked after by future visitors.

1. Leaves oblanceolate-oblong, distinctly petioled, glossy, subcoriaceous, 2½–3 inches by ¾–1 inch, acute, slightly rounded at the base, with many straight erecto-patent veins branching from the midrib, and distinctly visible on the under side parallel nearly to the edge.

2. Leaves membranous, oblong, acute, cuneate at the base, 1½–2 in. long, ¾–1 in broad, with more irregular fine immersed veins anastomosing in arches just within the edge.

ORDER LXX. LOGANIACEÆ.

Flowers regular, hermaphrodite. Calyx small, persistent, with 4–5 distinct or obscure teeth. Corolla hypocrateriform, with a long or short tube and 4–5 spreading lobes. Stamens 4–5 from the throat of the corolla, alternate with the petals; filaments short; anthers 2-celled, dehiscing longitudinally. Ovary free, sessile, 2-celled; placentation axile; ovules 2 or many in a cell; style simple or forked. Fruit a drupe or berry, or septicidal capsule. Seeds two or many, small; albumen cartilaginous or fleshy.—Shrubs with opposite usually entire leaves, intrapetiolar stipules and flowers axillary or in terminal panicles. Distrib. Round the world in the tropics. Species 350. Very like *Rubiaceæ*, from which it mainly differs by its free ovary.

Ovules 2 in a cell. Corolla-tube long . . . . 1. Gærtnera.
Ovules many in a cell.
  Corolla-tube long. Fruit baccate . . . . 2. Nicodemia.
  Corolla-tube long. Fruit capsular . . . . 3. Buddleia.
  Corolla-tube short. Fruit capsular
    Corolla pentamerous, with contorted æstivation . . . 4. Geniostoma.
    Corolla tetramerous, with imbricated æstivation . . . 5. Nuxia.
  Corolla-tube short. Fruit a large drupe, pulpy inside . . 6. Brehmia.

1. GÆRTNERA, Lam.

Calyx campanulate; teeth 5, distinct or obscure. Corolla hypocrateriform; 5 spreading lobes much shorter than the cylindrical or narrowly funnel-shaped limb. Anthers 5, nearly sessile at the throat of the corolla. Ovary 2-celled, with a single ovule in each cell; style filiform, with two branches. Fruit nearly dry, oblong or obovoid, with two pyrenes.—Low erect shrubs, with the flowers in terminal corymbose panicles, or congested into heads. Distrib. Tropics of the Old World. Species about 20. Just like *Chasalia* except in the superior ovary.

Flowers in congested terminal globose heads.
  Leaves obovate, obtuse . . . . 1. G. rotundifolia.
  Leaves oblanceolate-oblong, acute . . . . . . 2. G. crassiflora.
Flowers in corymbose panicles, not pedicellate.
  Teeth of calyx very obscure . . . . 3. G. edentata.
  Teeth of calyx broad-deltoid.
    Leaves acute . . . . 4. G. vaginata.
    Leaves obtuse . . . . 5. G. psychotrioides.
  Teeth of calyx lanceolate or deltoid, cuspidate . . 6. G. pendula.
Flowers in corymbose panicles, distinctly pedicellate.
  Calyx $\frac{1}{12}$ in. long; teeth obscure . . . . 7. G. longifolia.
  Calyx very large; teeth broad, deltoid . . . . . 8. G. calycina.

1. **G. rotundifolia,** *Bojer.; A. DC. Prod.* ix. 33. A much-branched glabrous shrub, with stout branches. Leaves crowded, nearly sessile, obovate, obscurely cuspidate, coriaceous, 2–4 in. long, the main ribs prominent on both surfaces; lower stipules deltoid; upper lanceolate. Flowers in a dense globose terminal head. Calyx sessile, $\frac{1}{8}$–$\frac{1}{6}$ in. long; teeth distinct, lanceolate. Corolla white, $\frac{1}{4}$ in. long; teeth half as long as the tube. Fruit not seen. *Bojer in Mem. Soc. Helv.* viii. *tab.* 2, (*dissections*).

Mauritius, in woods of Grand-port, Savanne, and Grand Bassin. *G. cuneifolia* Bojer l. c., which I have not seen, judging from the description and plate may well be the same species. Endemic.

2. **G. crassiflora,** *Bojer.*; *A. DC. Prod.* ix. 33. A glabrous shrub, with slender terete branches. Leaves short-petioled, oblanceolate-

oblong, acute, cuneate at the base, subcoriaceous, 4–5 in. long; stipules large, persistent, with 2–4 deciduous awns. Flowers congested into a terminal head, sessile. Calyx campanulate, $\frac{1}{8}$ in. long, with 5 distinct lanceolate teeth. Corolla white, nearly an inch long; teeth lanceolate. Fruit large, obovoid, 4-angular, whitish. *Bojer in Mem. Soc. Helv.* viii. *t.* 2, (*dissections*).

MAURITIUS, in thick damp forests of the centre of the island. Endemic.

3. **G. edentata,** *Bojer.; A. DC. Prod.* ix. 33. A low glabrous shrub with terete branchlets. Leaves obovate-oblong, very coriaceous, cuspidate, 2–4 in. long, deltoid at the base; stipules short, with 1–2 deciduous awns; petiole very short, flattened. Flowers sessile, in dense corymbose terminal panicles 2–3 in. broad; bracts small, deltoid, coriaceous, persistent. Calyx coriaceous, $\frac{1}{8}$ in. long, obscurely toothed. Corolla greenish-white, $\frac{3}{4}$ in. long; teeth lanceolate, half as long as the tube. Fruit oblong, whitish. *Bojer in Mem. Helv.* viii. *t.* 2, (*dissections*). G. truncata, *A. DC. Prod.* ix. 34.

MAURITIUS, in forests of Nouvelle Découverte, Quartier Militaire, and on the mountains of Grand-port. Endemic.

4. **G. vaginata,** *Lam.; A. DC. Prod.* ix. 33. A low erect glabrous shrub, with moderately stout terete branches. Leaves short-petioled, oblong-lanceolate, subcoriaceous, acute, cuneate at the base, 4–6 in. long; stipules clasping the stem, $\frac{1}{4}$ in. long, furnished with 2–4 deciduous awns. Flowers in a corymbose terminal panicle 3–4 in. broad, clustered at the end of the branchlets; bracts oblong, persistent. Calyx $\frac{1}{8}$ in. long; teeth distinct, deltoid. Corolla whitish; $\frac{3}{4}$ in. long; teeth lanceolate, half as long as the tube. *Lam. Ill. t.* 167, *non Bojer, nec Sieber.*

MAURITIUS, in hill-woods. Also Bourbon and Madagascar. Differs from *G. psychotrioides* by its acute leaves and much larger calyx and corolla.

5. **G. psychotrioides,** *Baker.* A much-branched glabrous erect shrub, 4–8 feet high, with moderately stout terete branches. Leaves short-petioled, obovate-oblong, obtuse, subcoriaceous, 3–6 in. long, cuneately narrowed in the lower third; stipules $\frac{1}{4}$ in. long, truncate, clasping the branch, persistent, ciliated with 2–4 deciduous awns. Flowers in corymbose terminal panicles 3–4 in. broad, sessile, clustered at the end of the branchlets; bracts minute, deltoid, persistent. Calyx $\frac{1}{12}$ in. long, campanulate, with 5 small deltoid teeth. Corolla $\frac{1}{2}$ in. long, white, the teeth lanceolate, $\frac{1}{3}$ as long as the tube. Fruit oblong, blue-black, under half an inch long. Chasalia psychotrioides, *A. DC. Prod.* iv. 531. Gærtnera parviflora, *Bojer; A. DC. Prod.* ix. 34. G. quadriseta, *A. DC. Prod. loc. cit.* G. vaginata, *Bojer, Hort. Maur.* 216, *non Lam.* G. bifida, *Bojer in Nouv. Mem. Helv.* viii. *t.* 1; *A. DC. Prod. loc. cit.*

MAURITIUS, frequent in woods through the island. *Sieber*, ii. 57! etc. Endemic. *Bois cafi.*

6. **G. pendula,** *Bojer; A. DC. Prod.* ix. 34. A glabrous shrub, with rather stout branchlets. Leaves distinctly petioled, oblong or oblong-lanceolate, acute, cuneate at the base, 3–5 in. long, subcoriaceous; stipules large, lanceolate, with two deciduous awns. Flowers in terminal crowded peduncled corymbose panicles 2–3 in. broad, sessile in clusters at the end of the branchlets. Calyx ¼ in. long; teeth lanceolate or deltoid-aristate, nearly as long as the tube. Corolla white, an inch long, the lower flowers of the corymb cernuous; teeth ⅓ as long as the tube. Fruit fusiform, black, an inch long.

MAURITIUS, in damp shaded woods of the Pouce range. Endemic.

7. **G. longifolia,** *Bojer; A. DC. Prod.* ix. 34. A shrub 5–6 feet high with pilose branchlets. Leaves oblong, subcoriaceous, acute, cuneate at the base, a foot or more long, 3–4 in. broad at the middle, slightly downy beneath; petiole flattened, 1–1½ in. long. Flowers in corymbose terminal panicles, on short downy pedicels, with minute deltoid bracts. Calyx $\frac{1}{12}$ in. long, irregularly repand at the border. Corolla an inch long; teeth lanceolate, ⅓ as long as the tube. Fruit obovoid-cuspidate, angular, black, an inch long. *Bojer in Mem. Soc. Helv.* viii. *t.* 2, *dissections, (fruit immature).*

MAURITIUS, in dense woods of Nouvelle Découverte and Quartier Militaire. Endemic.

8. **G. calycina,** *Bojer; A. DC. Prod.* ix. 35. A glabrous shrub 3–4 feet high, with stout terete branchlets. Leaves oblong or obovate-oblong, 4–6 in. long, subcoriaceous, cuspidate, deltoid or rather rounded at the base; stipules deltoid, with a single deciduous awn; lower petioles 1–1½ in. long. Flowers in ample corymbose terminal panicles half a foot or more broad, distinctly peduncled, with lanceolate bracts at the base of the pedicels. Calyx very large, broadly campanulate, green, or white variegated with green, finally ½ in. long, with 5 broad unequal deltoid teeth. Corolla ½–¾ in. long; teeth half as long as the tube. Fruit oblong, black, twice as long as the calyx. *Bojer in Mem. Helv.* viii. *t.* 2, *(dissections)*. G. vaginata, *Sieb. non. Poir.* G. æthionoma, *Steudel.*

MAURITIUS, in the forests of Grand Bassin, Nouvelle Découverte, etc. Endemic.

2. NICODEMIA, Tenore.

Calyx small, tubular; teeth 4, linear. Corolla hypocrateriform, with a cylindrical tube and 4 round spreading lobes imbricated in bud. Stamens 4; anthers minute, nearly sessile at the throat of the corolla. Ovary 2-celled; ovules many in a cell; style filiform; stigma entire. Fruit fleshy, 2-celled.—Shrubs with opposite leaves and small flowers in terminal and axillary clusters. DISTRIB. Species 2, the other a plant of the Comoros. Only differs from *Buddleia* by its fleshy fruit.

1. **N. diversifolia,** *Tenore; Walp. Ann.* i. 531. A low shrub, with slender branchlets, clothed at first with thin ferruginous tomentum. Leaves distinctly petioled, oblong or roundish, cuneate at the base, obtuse or acute, entire or repand, membranous, at first ferrugineo-tomentose, but soon glabrescent. Flowers 2–6 in short-peduncled axillary clusters. Calyx ferruginous, $\frac{1}{8}$ in. long; teeth linear, shorter than the tube. Corolla under $\frac{1}{4}$ inch long; lobes nearly round. Drupe roundish, tomentose, $\frac{1}{3}$ in. long. Seeds many, black. Buddleia diversifolia, *Vahl: Benth. in DC. Prod.* x. 445. B. indica, *Lam.*

MAURITIUS, plentiful near Moka, etc. Also Madagascar. *Vigne Malgache.*

3. BUDDLEIA, Linn.

Calyx small, campanulate, 4-toothed. Corolla hypocrateriform, with a cylindrical tube and 4 short obtuse lobes, imbricated in bud. Stamens 4, inserted at the throat of the tube. Ovary 2-celled; ovules many in a cell; style entire, clavate. Fruit a septicidal capsule.—Trees or shrubs, often tomentose, with opposite entire leaves and cymose flowers in the axils of the leaves or terminal panicles. DISTRIB. Round the world in the warmer zones. Species 60–70.

1. **B. madagascariensis,** *Lam.; Benth. in DC. Prod.* x. 447. Stems and leaves below clothed with persistent rusty or white tomentum. Leaves distinctly petioled, oblong, acute, 3–5 in. long, rounded or cordate at the base, subcoriaceous, glossy green and glabrous above. Cymes in a narrow terminal panicle $\frac{1}{2}$–1 foot long, with tomentose branches. Flowers sessile, in two or threes at the end of the branchlets; bracts small, linear. Calyx $\frac{1}{12}$ in. long, campanulate; teeth deltoid. Corolla yellow, $\frac{3}{8}$ in. long, tomentose on the outside; lobes oblong, obtuse, horizontal. *Bot. Mag. t.* 2824. B. heterophylla, *Lindl. Bot. Reg. t.* 1259.

RODRIGUEZ, in the valley of the Rivière Acacie, *Balfour!* Also Madagascar and Bourbon. *Vigne Malgache.*

4. GENIOSTOMA, Forst.

Calyx minute, with a funnel-shaped tube and 5 lanceolate teeth. Corolla broadly funnel-shaped, with a short tube and 5 lanceolate teeth, which are hairy down the face and contorted in æstivation. Stamens 5, inserted on the throat of the corolla; filaments short; anthers linear, with the connective produced beyond the cells. Ovary 2-celled; ovules many in each cell; style short, filiform; stigma capitate. Fruit a fusiform firm capsule, splitting into two valves from top to bottom. Seeds many, ovoid, wingless.—Shrubs, with opposite leaves, small deltoid intrapetiolar stipules and flowers in copious axillary usually sessile fascicles or cymes. DISTRIB. Tropics of the Old World. Species about 10.

Leaves 2–4 inches long . . . . 1. G. BORBONICUM.

Leaves under an inch long.
Pedicels long. Leaves cuneate at the base . . . . 2. G. PEDUNCULATUM.
Pedicels short. Leaves cordate or broadly rounded at the base . . . . 3. G. CORDIFOLIUM.

1. **G. borbonicum,** *Spreng. Syst.* i. 588. A much-branched glabrous shrub, 10–12 feet high, with slender terete branchlets. Leaves confined to the end of the branches, distinctly petioled, obovate-oblong, obtuse or subacute, subcoriaceous, 3–4 in. long, cuneate at the base, turning black in drying. Flowers up to a dozen in copious axillary fascicles or short peduncled cymes with spreading branches; pedicels $\frac{1}{8}$–$\frac{1}{4}$ in. long, with a pair of small persistent lanceolate bracts remote from the calyx. Calyx $\frac{1}{12}$ in. long; teeth lanceolate. Corolla $\frac{1}{8}$–$\frac{1}{6}$ in. long; tube very short; teeth spreading, yellowish-white. Capsule $\frac{1}{2}$–$\frac{3}{4}$ in. long, the valves recurving and leaving the placenta in the axis. G. obovatum, *Bojer; Benth. in Journ. Linn. Soc.* i. 96.

MAURITIUS, frequent in woods through the island. Also Bourbon and Madagascar. *G. ovatum*, Bojer; DC. Prod. ix. 26. is a variety with thinner more acute leaves, and smaller flowers and fruit; and *G. lanceolatum*, Bojer; DC. loc. cit., a similar form with lanceolate leaves narrowed to point and base. *G. angustifolium*, Bojer; DC. loc. cit. of which I have not seen authentic examples, is probably another variety. *Bois Piment.*

2. **G. pedunculatum,** *Bojer*; *A. DC. Prod.* ix. 28. A much-branched low shrub, with very slender shortly pilose branchlets. Leaves distinctly petioled, obovate-cuneate, membranous, obtuse, glabrous, $\frac{1}{2}$–$\frac{3}{4}$ in. long. Flowers up to six in axillary fascicles, rarely with a common peduncle, on drooping thread-like pedicels $\frac{1}{2}$ in. long, with a pair of minute bracts at the middle. Calyx $\frac{1}{12}$ in. long; teeth deltoid; tube narrowed gradually into the pedicel. Corolla $\frac{1}{12}$ in. long and as broad when expanded. Capsule fusiform, $\frac{1}{4}$–$\frac{1}{3}$ in. long, tipped with the persistent style. G. parvifolium, *Bojer; DC. Prod. loc. cit.*

MAURITIUS, in woods of Nouvelle Découverte, Quartier Militaire, etc. Endemic.

3. **G. cordifolium,** *Bojer; A. DC. Prod.* ix. 28. A low much-branched shrub, with slender shortly pilose branchlets. Leaves roundish, obtuse, with a broadly rounded or cordate base, subcoriaceous, $\frac{1}{4}$–$\frac{1}{2}$ in. long and broad; petiole distinct, very short. Flowers 3–6 in the axils of the leaves, on pedicels $\frac{1}{8}$–$\frac{1}{4}$ in. long, rarely with a common peduncle. Calyx $\frac{1}{12}$ in. long; teeth lanceolate. Corolla $\frac{1}{12}$ in. long, and as broad when expanded. Capsule not seen.

MAURITIUS, in woods of Grand Bassin and La Savanne. Endemic.

5. NUXIA, Lam.

Calyx small, campanulate, with 4 lanceolate teeth. Corolla hypocrateriform, with a campanulate tube and 4 minute lobes imbricated in æstivation. Stamens 4, inserted at the throat of the corolla; filaments as long as the lobes; anther-cells divaricating. Ovary globose, 2-celled; ovules many in a cell; style cylindrical; stigma capitate.

Fruit a small ovoid pilose capsule, with septicidal dehiscence. Seeds oblong, very minute.—Shrubs with petioled leaves and very abundant small flowers in ample terminal panicles. DISTRIB. Cape and Tropical Africa. Species 10.

1. **N. verticillata,** *Lam. Ill. t.* 71. A glabrous shrub or low tree, with moderately stout rather angular branches. Leaves 2–4-nate, distinctly petioled, oblong, subcoriaceous, 3–5 in. long, subacute, cuneate at the base; stipules obscure. Flowers in spaced clusters on the branches of a very compound panicle a span long and broad, the lower branches of which are subtended by large leaves; pedicels 0, or very short. Calyx $\frac{1}{12}$–$\frac{1}{8}$ in. long. Corolla twice as long as the calyx, whitish, the tube pilose at the throat. Capsule a little longer than the persistent calyx.

MAURITIUS, in woods of the Pouce, Nouvelle Découverte, etc., ascending to the top of the mountains. Also Bourbon. *Bois Malabar* or *Bois de Bouc.*

6. BREHMIA, Harv.

Calyx with a very short campanulate tube and 5 long setaceous teeth. Corolla small, funnel-shaped, hairy at the throat, with 5 short spreading teeth, valvate in bud. Ovary 1-celled by the vanishing of the septum; style simple; stigma capitate. Stamens 5, included, inserted low down in the tube of the corolla. Fruit a large drupe, with a coriaceous rind and many seeds, imbedded in a pulpy edible mesocarp.—The only species.

1. **B. spinosa,** *Harv.; A. DC. Prod.* ix. 18. A low-growing tree, with horizontal slender virgate branches, armed with short pungent spines from the nodes. Leaves obovate, subcoriaceous, obtuse or subacute, 1–3 in. long, nearly sessile, 5-nerved. Flowers in small dense terminal corymbs, with pilose peduncles. Calyx and corolla each $\frac{1}{8}$ in. long. Fruit the size and colour of an orange. Strychnos spinosa, *Lam.* S. Vuntac, *Bojer, Hort. Maur.* 205. S. madagascariensis, *Spreng.*

SEYCHELLES, common in some parts of Mahé, especially on the waste lands of the west coast, *Horne*, 529! Also Tropical Africa, Natal, and Madagascar.

ORDER LXXI. GENTIANACEÆ.

Flowers regular, hermaphrodite, usually pentamerous. Calyx free, usually 4–5-lobed. Corolla 4–5-lobed, with twisted or induplicate æstivation. Stamens 4–5, inserted in the tube alternate with the corolla-lobes; anthers 2-celled, slit down both sides or opening by pores at the end. Ovary free, 1–2-celled, 2-carpellary; placentation parietal; ovules many, anatropous; style simple; stigma bifid. Fruit usually a 2-valved capsule. Seeds albuminous.—Herbs with exstipulate leaves, usually opposite and entire and varied inflorescence. DISTRIB. Cosmopolitan; mainly temperate. Species 500.

Terrestrial, with opposite leaves . . . . 1. EXACUM.
Aquatic, with alternate leaves . . . . 2. LIMNANTHEMUM.

1. EXACUM, Linn.

Calyx 4–5-partite, with lanceolate winged or keeled divisions. Corolla rotate, with a globose tube, and 4–5-lobed limb. Stamens 4–5, inserted at the throat of the tube; anthers dehiscing by terminal pores. Ovary 2-celled; style declinate; stigma capitate. Fruit a globose membranous 2-valved capsule, with the placentas separating from the valves.—Herbs, usually annual, with flowers in terminal cymes. DISTRIB. Tropics of the Old World. Species 20.

1. **E. quinquenervium,** *Griseb. in DC. Prod.* ix. 46. An erect glabrous annual, with simple or forked stems a foot or more long. Leaves lanceolate or ovate-lanceolate, 1–2 in. long, acute, 3–5-nerved, narrowed to a short flattened petiole. Flowers in dichotomous terminal cymes, on erect $\frac{1}{4}$–1 in. pedicels. Sepals 5, free, lanceolate, acute, $\frac{1}{8}$ in. long, acutely keeled. Corolla blue, half as long again as the calyx, with 5 deltoid lobes. Capsule globose, $\frac{1}{4}$ in. long, splitting into two membranous valves.

MAURITIUS, near Piton du Milieu de l'Isle, *Horne!* Also Madagascar and East Tropical Africa.

2. LIMNANTHEMUM, Gmel.

Calyx 5-partite, persistent. Corolla rotate, deciduous, the segments variously fimbriated. Stamens included, inserted at the throat of the corolla. Ovary sessile, 1-celled, surrounded by 5 hypogynous glands; placentation parietal; ovules numerous; style cylindrical, persistent. Fruit a small membranous capsule.—Aquatic herbs, with floating leaves and umbellate flowers. DISTRIB. Round the world in the Tropics. Species 10–20.

1. **L. indicum,** *Griseb. in DC. Prod.* ix. 139. A floating glabrous aquatic herb. Leaves round-cordate, not peltate, 2–4 in. broad, with a deep basal sinus; petiole varying in length according to the depth of the water. Flowers many, in a sessile umbel from near the top of the petiole; pedicels longer than the flowers. Sepals lanceolate, $\frac{1}{4}$ in. long. Corolla twice as long as the calyx, with whitish segments, covered with white hairs down the face. Capsule globose, $\frac{1}{4}$ in. broad, containing about a dozen white seeds; style $\frac{1}{12}$ in. long. Villarsia indica, *Vent.; Hook. Bot. Misc.* 3, *t.* 30.

MAURITIUS, in the Mare aux Vacouas, Grand Bassin, and other lakes. Through the tropics of the Old World.

ORDER LXXII. SCROPHULARIACEÆ.

Flowers irregular, hermaphrodite. Calyx persistent, inferior, divided part of the way down or to the base into 4–5 lobes. Corolla deciduous, with a cylindrical or funnel-shaped tube and a bilabiate limb. Stamens 4, inserted in the corolla tube, or 2 abortive, or represented by staminodes; anther-cells 2, often divaricated. Ovary 2-celled, with axile placentation; ovules numerous; style filiform; stigma bifid or capitate. Fruit a membranous capsule, the valves mostly separating from the septum. Seeds many, albuminous.—Herbs or shrubs, with leaves usually opposite, exstipulate, the flowers in their axils or terminal racemes. DISTRIB. Cosmopolitan. Species 1800.

Lower lip of corolla outermost in bud.
  Subaphyllous shrub . . . . * RUSSELLIA.
  Small, usually annual, herbs.
    Capsule short, globose or ovoid, 1–2 times length of calyx.
      Calyx divided nearly to the base.
        Stamens 4, all fertile . . . . 1. HERPESTIS.
        Stamens 4, 2 barren . . . . 2. ILYSANTHES.
      Calyx not divided half-way down.
        Calyx-ribs winged . . . . 3. TORENIA.
        Calyx-ribs not winged . . . . 4. VANDELLIA.
    Capsule cylindrical . . . . 5. BONNAYA.
Lower lip of corolla not outermost in bud.
  Shrubby perennials.
    Branches and leaves alternate . . . . * CAPRARIA.
    Branches and leaves ternate . . . . * SCOPARIA.
  Herbaceous.
    Corolla rotate; stamens 2 . . . . * VERONICA.
    Corolla campanulate; stamens 2 . . . . 6. BRYODES.
    Corolla with a funnel-shaped tube and bilabiate limb.
      Calyx-strongly 10-ribbed.
        Calyx-teeth as long as the tube . . . . 7. ALECTRA.
        Calyx-teeth shorter than the tube . . . . 8. STRIGA.
      Calyx faintly 5-ribbed . . . . 9. RADAMÆA.

* *Russellia juncea*, Zucc.; Benth. in DC. Prod. x. 332; Bot. Reg. t. 1773, a native of Mexico, commonly cultivated in gardens, is established in several places in the Seychelles in Mahé (Horne, 542 !). It is a glabrous shrub, 3–4 feet high, with very numerous slender leafless branchlets, sparse flowers 2–3 together on common peduncles, a minute campanulate calyx with deltoid teeth, a tubular scarlet corolla an inch long with a very short limb and a globose capsule the size of a small pea.

1. HERPESTIS, Gærtn. fil.

Calyx cut nearly to the base into 5 unequal leafy lobes, of which the posticous one is the largest. Corolla campanulate, with 5 obovate subequal lobes as long as the tube. Stamens 4, didynamous, included; anthers all fertile. Ovary ovoid; style filiform; stigma capitate. Capsule ovoid, membranous, the valves entirely separating from the central placenta. Seeds minute, numerous.—Small prostrate herbs, with minute flowers, usually solitary in the axils of the leaves. DISTRIB. Species 40, nearly all American.

1. **H. Monnieria,** *H.B.K.; Benth. in DC. Prod.* x. 400. A slender trailing glabrous perennial herb, with much-branched stems rooting at the nodes. Leaves sessile, obovate-cuneate, obtuse, rather fleshy, $\frac{1}{4}$–$\frac{1}{2}$ in. long; pedicels solitary from the axils of the leaves, short. Calyx $\frac{1}{4}$ in. deep, clasped at the base by a pair of lanceolate bracteoles, the

divisions broad, foliaceous, much imbricated, the three outer largest. Corolla pale violet, twice as long as the calyx. Capsule as long as the calyx, ovoid. H. cuneifolia, *Pursh; Bojer, Hort. Maur.* 245.

MAURITIUS and RODRIGUEZ, in swampy places. Amber Island, *Horne!* Cosmopolitan in the tropics. Included in Sieber's Mauritian Herbarium, No. 368, as a *Euphorbia*.

2. ILYSANTHES, Rafin.

Calyx minute, cut nearly to the base into 5 subequal linear teeth. Corolla with a funnel-shaped tube and bilabiate limb, the upper lip short, emarginate, the lower much longer. Stamens 2 fertile, inserted down in the tube, and 2 barren at the throat, which are bilobed at the tip. Ovary ampullæform; style filiform; stigma peltate. Capsule membranous, ovoid, many-seeded, the two valves separating from the placenta.—Annual herbs, with sessile entire leaves, the small flowers solitary, pedicellate in their axils. DISTRIB. Cosmopolitan in the tropics. Species 8.

Erect; leaves oblong or lanceolate. . . . . 1. I. PARVIFLORA.
Trailing; leaves round . . . . 2. I. ROTUNDIFOLIA.

1. **I. parviflora,** *Benth. in DC. Prod.* x. 419. A slender annual herb, with branched erect densely cæspitose stems 4–6 in. high. Leaves sessile, entire, oblong or lanceolate, membranous, cuneate at the base, acute, the upper much reduced. Flowers from the axils of most of the leaves, on erecto-patent slender pedicels. Calyx $\frac{1}{12}$ in. long; teeth equal, linear. Corolla whitish, fugacious, twice as long as the calyx. Capsule oblong, twice as long as the calyx. Gratiola parviflora, *Roxb. Pl. Corom. t.* 204.

MAURITIUS, in damp places at Bois Rouge and Mapou, *Bojer*. Common in East Indies. I have no means of identifying *Gratiola minima*, Bojer, Hort. Maur. 245, said to grow in shaded and damp alleys of the Royal Botanic Garden.

2. **I. rotundifolia,** *Benth. in DC. Prod.* x. 420. A slender trailing glabrous annual herb, with stems $\frac{1}{2}$–1 ft. long. Leaves round, sessile, entire, membranous, $\frac{1}{4}$–$\frac{1}{2}$ in. Flowers from the axils of the upper leaves only, on $\frac{1}{2}$–$\frac{3}{4}$ in. pedicels. Calyx $\frac{1}{12}$ in. long; teeth linear, or lanceolate. Corolla 3–4 times as long as the calyx. Capsule globose, scarcely longer than the calyx. Gratiola rotundifolia, *Linn.; Roxb. Pl. Corom. t.* 203.

MAURITIUS, in damp places, *Telfair!* Also Madagascar and East Indies.

3. TORENIA, Linn.

Calyx bilabiate, with an oblong or clavate tube longer than the 5 teeth, of which three out of the 5 ribs are more or less distinctly winged. Corolla bilabiate, the upper lip emarginate, the lower with three deep rounded lobes. Stamens 4, didynamous, the upper pair furnished with an appendage at the base. Ovary ampullæform; style filiform, arcuate; stigma bilamellate. Capsule membranous, many-seeded, shorter than the calyx.—Small annual herbs, with opposite petioled toothed leaves, with flowers on long pedicels from their axils. DISTRIB. Round the world in the tropics. Species 20.

Corolla twice as long as the calyx . . . . 1. T. CORDIFOLIA.
Corolla scarcely longer than the calyx . . . . 2. T. PARVIFLORA.

1. **T. cordifolia,** *Roxb. Pl. Cor.* ii. 52, t. 161. An annual, with slender stems, trailing and rooting at the base, afterwards erect, glabrous or finely pilose. Leaves petioled, membranous, ½–1 in. long, ovate, acute, dentate, rounded or cordate at the base; pedicels longer than the calyx, 3–4 from the uppermost node, two from the others. Calyx ⅜ in. long; tube oblong, with 3 distinct ciliated wings; teeth of lower lip lanceolate, nearly as long as the tube. Corolla violet, twice as long as the calyx. Tooth of upper filaments minute. *Bot. Mag. t.* 3715.; *Benth. in DC. Prod.* x. 409.

MAURITIUS, in shaded places, *Neraud!* Also East Indian, not African.

2. **T. parviflora,** *Hamilt.; Benth. in DC. Prod.* x. 410. A diffuse annual, with slender glabrous acutely quadrangular stems ½–1 foot long. Leaves petioled, ½–¾ in. long, ovate, toothed, acute, membranous, cuneate at the base. Pedicels as long as or longer than the calyx, 2–6-nate, after flowering spreading or reflexed. Calyx-tube clavate, with three slight wings; teeth minute. Corolla pale purple, scarcely longer than the calyx. Tooth of upper filaments subulate, conspicuous. Nortenia Thouarsii, *Cham. and Schlecht. in Linnæa,* iii. 18.

MAURITIUS, *Du Petit Thouars,* (Herb. Willdenow, No. 11530); roadsides on the Midlands estate, *Horne!* Cosmopolitan in the tropics.

4. VANDELLIA, Linn.

Calyx with a tube which exceeds the 5 subequal lanceolate teeth, the ribs not winged. Corolla with a funnel-shaped tube, a short round emarginate upper lip and a longer deeply 3-lobed lower one. Stamens 4, didynamous, all fertile, included; the filaments of the upper pair appendiculate. Ovary oblong; style filiform, arcuate; stigma 2-lamellate. Capsule globose, membranous, many-seeded, included in the calyx.—Annual herbs, with exactly the habit of *Torenia.* DISTRIB. Cosmopolitan in tropics. Species 30.

1. **V. crustacea,** *Benth. in DC. Prod.* x. 413. A much-branched annual herb, with diffuse quadrangular stems ½–1 foot long. Leaves opposite, petioled, membranous, ovate, acute, ½–¾ in.; base cuneate. Pedicels ½–1 in. long, solitary, erecto-patent. Calyx ⅙ in. long; teeth shorter than obovoid tube. Corolla 2–3 times as long as the calyx. Capsule subglobose, the size of a pea. Capraria crustacea, *Linn. Mant.* 87.

MAURITIUS, according to Bentham. Cosmopolitan in the Tropics.

5. BONNAYA, Link and Otto.

Calyx with a clavate tube and 5 subequal linear teeth. Corolla with a short round emarginate upper lip and deeply trifid larger lower one.

Fertile stamens 2, the upper ones being represented by minute staminodes. Ovary clavate; style filiform; stigma 2-lamellate. Capsule cylindrical, much longer than the calyx.—Glabrous annual herbs, with opposite toothed leaves, the flowers in terminal racemes. Distrib. Tropics of the Old World. Species 10.

1. **B. reptans,** *Spreng.*; *Benth. in DC. Prod.* x. 420. A wide-trailing glabrous annual. Leaves distant, short-petioled, oblong, obtuse, finely serrated, membranous, 1–1½ in. long, narrowed very gradually into the petiole. Flowers 6–10, in a lax peduncled terminal raceme; pedicels spreading, about as long as the calyx, exceeding the lanceolate bracts. Calyx cylindrical, ¼ in. long; teeth linear, shorter than the tube. Corolla half as long again as the calyx. Capsule fusiform, twice as long as the calyx.

Mauritius, in damp and shaded places at Flacq, *Bojer*. Tropical Asian, not African.

* *Capraria peruviana*, Feuill.; Benth. in DC. Prod. x. 430, a native of South America, is naturalized in the Seychelles in the island of Mahé (Horne, 543 !) It is a shrubby perennial, with finely pilose terete branches, alternate entire lanceolate leaves 2–3 inches long, flowers 1–4-nate from their axils on pedicels 3–4 times the length of the calyx, which is campanulate ⅙ in. long slit below the middle into 4–5 lanceolate lobes, corolla greenish-white campanulate with 4–5 long teeth and a 4-valved membranous capsule twice the length of the calyx.

* *Scoparia dulcis*, Linn.; Benth. in DC. Prod. x. 431, cosmopolitan in the tropics, is established in Mauritius in fields at Pamplemousses and other places. It is an erect glabrous shrubby annual, with 3-nate branchlets, small ternate lanceolate toothed leaves, the upper reduced to mere bracts, abundant flowers in the axils of the leaves on short pedicels, minute calyx divided to the base into 4 lanceolate teeth, a minute whitish rotate corolla, and a globose membranous capsule $\frac{1}{12}$ in. long.

* VERONICA, Linn.

Calyx divided to the base into 4 lanceolate lobes. Corolla rotate, with a short tube and 4 unequal lobes. Stamens 2, inserted in the corolla-tube. Ovary obcordate; style short, straight, filiform; stigma capitate. Capsule obcordate, broader than long, laterally compressed. Seeds numerous.—Herbs or shrubs of various habit. Distrib. Temperate regions, mainly of the northern hemisphere. Species 180.

Two common annual species of the northern hemisphere occur occasionally in cultivated fields in Mauritius, viz.

* *V. arvensis*, Linn.; Benth. in DC. Prod. x. 483, with ovate crenate leaves, lax terminal racemes longer than the stems, lanceolate bracts, very short ascending pedicels, ⅛ in. calyx, minute blue corolla, deeply emarginate capsule as long as the calyx, and minute oblong compressed seeds.

* *V. agrestis*, Linn.; Benth. in DC. Prod. x. 487, with diffuse trailing stems, flowers from the axils of similar leaves all down the stem on arcuate pedicels, larger calyx and capsule, and shallowly cup-shaped seeds fastened by one face to the placenta.

6. BRYODES, Benth.

Calyx campanulate, divided to the base into 5 lanceolate segments. Corolla campanulate, with 4 short rounded lobes. Stamens 2, included, inserted low down in the tube; staminodes 0. Ovary ampullæform; style arcuate, filiform; stigma capitate. Capsule globose, membranous, with many minute seeds.—A single endemic species.

1. **B. micrantha,** *Benth. in DC. Prod.* x. 433. A minute glabrous moss-like herb with trailing or suberect stems. Leaves opposite, sessile, linear-oblong, entire, $\frac{1}{12}$ in. long. Flowers solitary, sessile in the axils of the leaves. Calyx $\frac{1}{4}$ line long. Corolla scarcely exserted from the calyx.

MAURITIUS, in watery places, *Bojer!* Endemic.

7. ALECTRA, Thunb.

Calyx campanulate, deeply 5-toothed, 10-ribbed. Corolla with a campanulate tube, and oblique broadly 5-toothed limb. Stamens didynamous, included; anthers often bearded on the back and mucronate at the base. Ovary globose; style filiform, declinate; stigma nearly or quite entire. Fruit a globose capsule, included in the persistent calyx.—Annual parasitic herbs, turning black when dried. DISTRIB. Cape and tropics of both hemispheres. Species 12.

1. **A. indica,** *Benth. in DC. Prod.* x. 339. Stems erect, $\frac{1}{2}$–1 foot high, square, hispid, simple or branched. Leaves subsessile, ovate, toothed, the lower an inch long. Flowers in a lax spike in the upper 3-4 inches of the stem, bracteated by reduced leaves. Calyx under $\frac{1}{4}$ inch long, bristly; teeth deltoid-cuspidate, as long as the campanulate 10-ribbed tube. Corolla yellow, half as long again as the calyx. Capsule black, glabrous, the size of a pea.

MAURITIUS, at the survey camp near Tamarin Falls, growing amongst grass and on logs, *Horne!* Also East Indies.

8. STRIGA, Lour.

Calyx with a strongly-ribbed oblong or cylindrical tube and 5 subequal long teeth. Corolla with a cylindrical curved tube and a bilabiate patulous limb. Stamens 4, didynamous, included in the tube; filaments very short. Ovary oblong; style filiform; stigma capitate. Capsule oblong, emarginate, included in the calyx tube, black, opening elastically.

Seeds numerous, minute.—More or less parasitic herbs, turning black when dried, with entire alternate narrow leaves, and solitary flowers sessile in their axils. DISTRIB. Tropics of the Old World. Species 16.

1. **S. hirsuta,** *Lour.; Benth. in DC. Prod.* x. 502. Annual, erect, much-branched scabrid-pilose, ½–1 ft. high. Leaves except the lowest alternate, linear-ligulate, entire, ½–1½ in. Flowers sessile in the axils of the leaves to below the middle of the stem. Calyx ¼ in. long; tube oblong, with 10 strong ribs and 5 linear teeth shorter than the tube. Corolla-tube longer than the calyx, glandular; limb usually bright scarlet, sometimes yellow, ⅙–¼ in. broad. Capsule black, as long as the calyx-tube. Campuleia coccinea, *Hook. Exot. Flora, t.* 203; *Bojer, Hort. Maur.* 244.

MAURITIUS, a common weed in cultivated fields, especially of maize, regarded by Bojer as an introduced species. SEYCHELLES, common in Mahé and Praslin in dry soils. Through the tropics of the Old World.

9. RADAMÆA, Benth.

Calyx with a funnel-shaped tube and 5 equal lanceolate teeth. Corolla with an exserted funnel-shaped tube and a bilabiate limb, with 5 subequal round lobes. Stamens 4, didynamous, included; filaments short. Ovary ovoid; style filiform; stigma capitate. Capsule small, ovoid. Seeds numerous.—Shrubby perennials, with small opposite entire leaves and axillary flowers. DISTRIB. Species 2, the other a plant of Madagascar.

1. **R. prostrata,** *Benth. in DC. Prod.* x. 509, 597. A much-branched diffuse perennial, about a foot high, with rigid slender minutely pilose stems. Leaves turning black when dried, oblong, acute, entire, short-petioled, coriaceous, cuneate at the base, ⅙–¼ in. long. Flowers few, solitary in the axils of the leaves, on very short pedicels. Calyx ⅙ in. long, narrowed to the base; teeth half as long as the tube. Corolla rose-red, twice the length of the calyx. Centranthera prostrata, *Bojer, Hort. Maur.* 246.

SEYCHELLES, *Bojer*. Also Isle of Galega.

ORDER LXXII.* CYRTANDRACEÆ.

Baa Commersoni, R. Br., given in DeCandolle's Prodromus and other works as a plant of the Seychelles on the supposition that it was gathered by Commerson in the island of Praslin, seems to have been really found at Port Praslin, in New Ireland in Polynesia, as it has been recently refound in the same vicinity by Mr. C. Walter. A full account by Dr. Trimen of the circumstances of the case will be found in the Proceedings of the Linnean Society, vol. xv. p. 163, so that this order has no claim to a place in our flora.

ORDER LXXIII. LENTIBULARIACEÆ.

Flowers irregular, hermaphrodite. Calyx with a very short tube, and bilabiate limb, with entire or toothed lobes. Corolla bilabiate, personate or ringent. Stamens 2, hypogynous or epipetalous; filaments short; anthers 1-celled. Ovary superior, 1-celled; placenta free-central; ovules very numerous; style short; stigma of two unequal plates. Capsule membranous, 2-valved. Seeds numerous, minute, exalbuminous.—Pond or marsh acaulescent herbs, with leaves in a radical rosette and flowers solitary or racemose. DISTRIB. Cosmopolitan. Species 180.

1. UTRICULARIA, Linn.

Calyx with a very short tube and two entire lips. Corolla personate; tube very short; lips subentire, lower spurred. Stamens 2, inserted at the base of the upper lip of the corolla; filaments short, curved; anthers 1-celled. Ovary globose; style erect, very short; plates of stigma mostly unequal. Capsule membranous, dehiscing from the apex.—Aquatic herbs, with leaves usually floating and multifid with capillary segments and copious bladders, the flowers in peduncled lax racemes. DISTRIB. Cosmopolitan. Species 150.

1. **U. stellaris,** *Linn.; DC. Prod.* viii. 4. Stems slender, floating, reaching a length of 2–4 feet or more. Leaves fascicled, 2–3 in. long, decompound, with capillary segments and copious small round bladders. Peduncle furnished below the raceme with a whorl of 4–10 large sessile oblong-cylindrical bladders fringed at the apex. Racemes lax, many-flowered; pedicels longer than the calyx, thickened upwards, minutely bracteated at the base. Calyx-lobes ⅛ in. long, membranous, roundish, after flowering persistent and growing much larger. Corolla ¼ in. long, yellow; upper lip round, erect, with purple longitudinal veins; lower saccate, with reflexed edges. Capsule the size of a pea. *Hook. Bot. Misc. Suppl. t.* 27.

MAURITIUS, in the Grand Bassin, Mare aux Vacouas, etc. Through the tropics of the Old World.

ORDER LXXIV. BIGNONIACEÆ.

Flowers irregular, hermaphrodite. Calyx various, always inferior, campanulate or spathaceous. Corolla gamopetalous, with a funnel-shaped tube and a more or less irregular limb. Stamens didynamous, generally 4, included. Ovary inserted on a glandular disk, generally 2-celled; ovules numerous, horizontal; style long, simple; stigma of two plates. Fruit generally capsular, the dissepiment parallel with or perpendicular to the valves. Seeds exalbuminous, thin, generally winged.—Shrubs, often climbers; leaves opposite, usually compound; flowers large, showy, terminal, corymbose or panicled. DISTRIB. Tropics of both hemispheres. Species 450.

1. COLEA, Bojer.

Calyx campanulate, truncate or obscurely 5-toothed. Corolla with a slightly curved nearly cylindrical tube and 5 short round nearly equal lobes. Stamens 4, didynamous, just exserted from the tube; anthers 1-

or 2-celled. Ovary seated on a prominent glandular disk, cylindrical, 2-celled; ovules very numerous; style filiform; stigma of two minute plates. Fruit rather fleshy, probably indehiscent. Seeds thin, flat, broader than long, narrowly winged.—Our plants erect glabrous shrubs, with the leaves near the top of the stem, and flowers below them from the trunk. DISTRIB. Endemic in the Mascaren Isles. Species 9 or 10.

Flowers red, not peduncled . . . . 1. C. MAURITIANA.
Flowers yellow, on a long common peduncle . . . . . 2. C. PEDUNCULATA.

1. **C. mauritiana,** *Bojer, Hort. Maur.* 220 (*name only*). An erect unbranched shrub, 10–15 feet high, with stipulate erect leaves in threes, crowded near the top of the stem and flowers below them from the trunk. Leaflets 5, oblong, entire, obtuse, short-petioled, subcoriaceous, green, cuneate at the base. Flowers in fascicles of 3-5 from the old wood without a common peduncle. Calyx under ¼ in. long, with 5 obscure teeth. Corolla red, an inch long. Fruit oblong, verrucose. *DC. Prod.* ix. 241. Bignonia Colei, *Hook. Bot. Mag. t.* 2817.

MAURITIUS, in the damp forests of the interior. Endemic.

2. **C. pedunculata,** *Baker.* A small tree, 20–25 feet high, glabrous in all its parts. Leaves a foot long; leaflets 9-11, narrow oblong, obtuse, short-stalked, subcoriaceous, cuneate at the base. Peduncles in fascicles from the old wood, sometimes a foot long, bearing 12–20-flowers in a lax panicle. Calyx ¼–⅓ in. long, truncate. Corolla yellow, 1¼–1½ in. long, the lobes not more than ¼–⅓ as long as the tube. Fruit oblong-cylindrical, smooth, glabrous, narrowed to the base and tipped with the persistent style.

SEYCHELLES, in the woods from the seashore to the top of the hills. Endemic. *Bilimb* ou *Bilimb marron.*

C. cauliflora, DC. Prod. ix. 241, founded on *Bignonia cauliflora*, Sieber, Herb. Maur. No. 284, is identical with *C. floribunda*, Bojer, Hort. Maur. 220, Bot. Reg. vol. xxvii. tab. 69, which is a native of Madagascar, and in Mauritius is cultivated only.

ORDER LXXIV.* PEDALINEÆ.

* *Martynia diandra*, Glox.; A. DC. Prod. ix. 253; Bot. Reg. t. 2001, a native of Tropical America, is casually subspontaneous in Mauritius. It is annual, with stout erect finely glandulose-pilose stems 2–3 feet high, large petioled round-cordate membranous repand leaves, flowers in a short axillary raceme, ½ in. calyx with ovate-lanceolate teeth subtended by 2 large foliaceous bracts, a 2-in. corolla with a whitish ventricose tube spotted with yellow and purple and 5 round purple lobes, two fertile stamens, and an oblique oblong rugose coriaceous fruit with two incurved sharp beaks dehiscing longitudinally by two greenish-brown ferrugineo-tomentose valves.

Order LXXV. ACANTHACEÆ.

Flowers irregular, hermaphrodite. Calyx inferior, persistent, usually 4–5-partite, with unequal divisions. Corolla with a long tube and 5 bilabiate or subequal imbricated or contorted lobes. Stamens 4, didynamous, or the anterior pair abortive; filaments subulate, inserted low down in the corolla-tube; anthers 2-celled, the lobes not always parallel, sometimes one aborted, dehiscing longitudinally. Ovary superior, 2-celled; ovules 2 or more in a cell; style filiform, usually entire. Fruit a capsule, with two loculicidal valves opening elastically from the top. Seeds exalbuminous, usually borne on distinct spine-like processes (retinacula).—Herbs or shrubs with exstipulate opposite simple leaves, the flowers often showy. Distrib. Round the world in the tropics. Species 1300–1400.

Climbers. Capsule without retinacula . . . . * Thunbergia.
Erect. Seeds borne on retinacula.
  Corolla with 5 short obtuse nearly equal lobes.
    Perfect stamens two . . . . * Barleria.
    Perfect stamens four . . . . 1. Asystasia.
  Corolla distinctly bilabiate.
    Anthers 1-celled . . . . 2. Hypoestes.
    Anthers 2-celled.
      Flowers in terminal spikes . . . . 3. Justicia.
      Flowers in axillary umbels . . . . 4. Dicliptera.

* THUNBERGIA, Linn.

Calyx globose, small, persistent, with 12–15 long linear teeth, which become rigid, at first hidden by two large ovate membranous bracts. Corolla with a long funnel-shaped tube and 5 nearly equal spreading obovate lobes. Stamens 4, didynamous, inserted near the base of the corolla-tube; filaments short; anthers 2-celled, oblong, adnate. Ovary ovoid, 2-celled; ovules 2 in a cell. Capsule globose, abruptly beaked, dehiscing by 2 recurved valves; retinacula none.—Twining herbs, with opposite cordate or hastate leaves, the flowers showy, axillary, pedicelled. Distrib. Tropics of the Old World. Species 30.

Petiole terete . . . . * T. fragrans.
Petiole distinctly winged . . . . * T. alata.

* *T. alata*, Bojer in Hook. Flor. Exot. t. 177, a native of Tropical Asia and Madagascar, is naturalised in Mauritius by roadsides at Pamplemousses and in other parts of the island. It is a herbaceous climber, with densely pilose stems and leaves, distinctly winged petioles 1–2 in. long, a membranous cordate or hastate-ovate acute leaf-blade, slender terete pedicels exceeding the petioles, cordate-ovate acute pilose bracts ½–¾ in. long, and a yellowish inodorous flower with an expanded limb 1–1½ inch across.

* *T. fragrans*, Roxb. Pl. Corom. t. 67, widely spread in Tropical

Asia, is naturalised in Mauritius in the ravine of the Grand Rivière. It has very slender glabrous or finely pilose stems, short terete petioles, ovate or lanceolate acute membranous entire or sinuated leaves cordate or hastate at the base, pedicels much longer than the petioles flattened after flowering, ovate-oblong bracts ½–¾ in. long, and a fragrant pure white flower with a tube as long as the bracts and an expanded limb 1½–2 inches across.

* BARLERIA, Linn. (*Barreliera*, Bojer).

Calyx divided to the base into 4 segments, the two outer much larger than the two inner. Corolla with a long funnel-shaped tube and 5 nearly equal obovate spreading lobes, of which one forms an upper, and four a lower lip. Stamens 4, inserted low down the corolla-tube, two with long filaments and oblong equally 2-celled anthers, the two others rudimentary. Ovary 2-celled; cells 2-ovuled; style long, filiform. Capsule oblong or ampullæform, 2-celled, each cell bearing one or two seeds in the lower half, the retinacula large, uncinate.—Tall erect shrubs or perennial herbs, with showy flowers. DISTRIB. Tropics, mainly of the Old World. Species 60.

Spines in axils of the leaves in fours . . . . * B. PRIONITIS.
Spines in axils of the leaves in pairs . . . . * B. LUPULINA.
Spines in axils of the leaves none . . . . * B. CRISTATA.

* *B. Prionitis*, Linn.; Nees in DC. Prod. xi. 237, common in Tropical Asia, is naturalised in Mauritius, Rodriguez, and the Seychelles. It is an erect much-branched shrubby perennial, with stalked quaternate spreading spines in the axils of the leaves, leaves oblong-spathulate acute short-petioled membranous, flowers solitary sessile in the axils of the leaves, the upper crowded with leaves much reduced, calyx ½ in. long, the outer sepals oblong with a spiny point the inner lanceolate, corolla funnel-shaped orange-yellow with 5 obovate lobes of which 4 form the lower lip, capsule ampullæform exceeding the calyx.

* *B. lupulina*, Lindl. Bot. Reg. t. 1483 (B. macrostachya, *Bojer, Hort. Maur.* 260), a native of Madagascar, is now frequent round Port Louis. It is a half-shrubby glabrous perennial 3–4 feet high, with a pair of spreading spines in the axils of the nearly sessile large linear-lanceolate leaves, the flowers aggregated in terminal spikes 2–3 in. long, with large round imbricated clasping obtuse bracts with a minute mucro, calyx hidden by the bracts, corolla 1½ in. long bright yellow with a slender tube and 5 obovate lobes half an inch long and an ampullæform capsule as long as the calyx.

* *B. cristata*, Linn.; Bot. Mag. t. 1615, Wt. Ic. t. 453 (B. dichotoma, *Roxb.*), common in Tropical Asia, is often naturalised in Mauritius and Rodriguez, near abandoned habitations. It is a robust half-shrubby perennial, clothed with short adpressed hairs, spines none in the axils of the petioled oblong-acuminate leaves, flowers in crowded cymes in the axils of the leaves, bracts small linear-pectinate, calyx-

teeth very unequal outer large membranous veined ovate-lanceolate spine-ciliated inner lanceolate, corolla $1\frac{1}{2}$–2 in. long with a broadly funnel-shaped tube three times as long as the roundish lobes and an oblong-clavate capsule shorter than the calyx.

1. ASYSTASIA, Blume.

Calyx funnel-shaped, cut nearly to the base into 5 linear equal segments. Corolla broadly funnel-shaped, with 5 short subequal round lobes. Stamens 4, all fertile, the anthers oblong, with two equal cells spurred at the base. Ovary 2-celled; cells 2-ovuled; style filiform, simple; stigma capitate. Capsule clavate, fertile in the upper half, 2–4-seeded.—Herbs or shrubs, with flowers in lax subspicate racemes with minute bracts. DISTRIB. Tropics of the Old World. Species 20.

1. **A. gangetica,** *T. Anders. in Thwaites' Enum. Pl. Zeyl.* 235. A much-branched herb, 1–4 feet high, with slender weak quadrangular stems. Leaves distant, opposite, petioled, pilose, ovate-lanceolate, 1–3 in. long. Racemes secund, 1–3 in. long, lax; pedicels very short; bracts linear, very minute. Calyx $\frac{1}{8}$–$\frac{1}{4}$ in. long; segments equal, linear, acuminate. Corolla whitish, $\frac{3}{4}$–1 in. long, the broadly funnel-shaped tube dilated above the calyx. Capsule 1–$1\frac{1}{4}$ in. long, cylindrical in the lower, oblong in the upper half. A. capensis, coromandeliana, and Bojeriana, *Nees.* Justicia gangetica, *Linn.*

SEYCHELLES, common in Mahé amongst grass by roadsides, *Horne*, 545! Tropical Asia, Africa, and Natal.

2. HYPOESTES, R. Br.

Calyx funnel-shaped, with 5 narrow acute segments. Corolla with a funnel-shaped tube and short bilabiate limb, the lower lip 3-lobed. Stamens 2, included; anthers 1-celled. Ovary 2-celled; cells 2-ovuled; style filiform, simple. Capsule clavate, 4-seeded in the upper half.—Herbs or shrubs of various habit with flowers usually in axillary clusters or cymes, 4 bracteoles uniting to form an involucre to each. DISTRIB. Tropics of the Old World. Species 40.

Shrub . . . . 1. H. RODRIGUESIANA.
Dwarf procumbent herbs.
  Leaves $\frac{1}{8}$–$\frac{1}{4}$ in. long . . . . 2. H. INCONSPICUA.
  Leaves $\frac{1}{2}$–$\frac{3}{4}$ in. long . . . . 3. H. SERPENS.

1. **H. rodriguesiana,** *Balf, fil.* A much-branched shrub, glabrous in all its parts, except the corolla. Leaf-blade ovate, entire, acute, subcoriaceous, cuneate at the base, 1–$1\frac{1}{2}$ in. long, twice the length of the petiole. Flowers small, in dense terminal and axillary congested racemes, with oblanceolate leafy bracts; pedicels very short; involucre of 4 subequal scariose oblanceolate bracteoles united in the lower half. Calyx $\frac{1}{4}$ in. long, the 5 lanceolate equal segments shorter than the tube. Corolla $1\frac{1}{4}$ in. long, pale sulphur-yellow, pilose on the outside, cleft down to the involucre into two narrow lips, which are as long as the tube. Stamens 2, finally exserted; anthers oblong, $\frac{1}{8}$ in. long.

RODRIGUEZ, on the top of Mount Malartie, *Balfour!* Allied to *H. pulchra* and *Bojeriana*, Nees, of Madagascar. Endemic.

2. **H. inconspicua,** *Balf. fil.* A slender decumbent perennial herb, with tufted wiry slender stems, the young parts thinly clothed with short adpressed hairs. Leaves distant; petiole ¼–⅓ in. long; blade as long as the petiole, oblong or obovate, obtuse, cuneate at the base. Flowers solitary, nearly sessile in the axils of the leaves; involucre densely pilose, under ¼ in. long; segments 4, linear, unequal, herbaceous, the top and bottom ones the largest, exceeding the tube. Calyx very small, with 5 deltoid cuspidate segments. Corolla with a narrowly funnel-shaped tube as long as the involucre and a short limb; upper lip arching, lingulate; lower deflexed.

RODRIGUEZ, only on a patch of coralline limestone, mixed with *Dichondra*, *Balfour!* Endemic.

3. **H. serpens,** *R. Br.; Nees in DC. Prod.* xi. 501. A much-branched perennial herb, with slender wiry spreading puberulent stems half a foot long. Leaves distinctly petioled, distant, ovate or oblong, membranous, obscurely pilose, ½–¾ in. long, obtuse, spathulate at the base. Flowers solitary, sessile in the axils of the leaves; involucre under ½ in. long, of 4 unequal linear or ligulate bracteoles, connate above the base. Calyx not half as long as the involucre; segments lanceolate. Corolla not seen. Capsule ¼ in. long, 4-seeded. H. Alsine, *Nees in DC. Prod.* xi. 502. Justicia serpens, *Vahl, Enum.* i. 112. Calophanes mauritianus, *T. Anders. in Journ. Linn. Soc.* vii. 23 (name only).

MAURITIUS, on the Piton de la Rivière Noire, etc. Endemic.

3. JUSTICIA, Linn.

Calyx funnel-shaped, with 4–5 long segments. Corolla bilabiate, with a long slender tube, an emarginate upper and three-lobed lower lip. Stamens 2; filaments filiform, inserted low down in the tube; anther-cells superposed, the lower cell spurred. Ovary 2-celled; cells 2-ovuled; style filiform, simple; stigma capitate. Capsule 2-valved, contracted at the sterile base.—Herbs, rarely shrubs, with opposite leaves and spicate flowers, with minute bracts. DISTRIB. Tropics of both hemispheres. Species 100.

Glabrous shrub, with cylindrical spikes . . . . 1. J. GENDARUSSA.
Pilose herbs, with ovate or oblong spikes.
  Calyx-segments deltoid-cuspidate . . . . 2. J. BRACHYSTACHYA.
  Calyx-segments subulate . . . . 3. J. PSYCHOTRIOIDES.

1. **J. Gendarussa,** *Linn. Suppl.* 85. A shrub 4–5 feet high, glabrous in all its parts, with slender woody rather quadrangular branches. Leaves distant, short-petioled, lanceolate, subcoriaceous, narrowed to both ends, 3–4 in. long. Flowers in dense terminal spikes 2–4 in. long, the lower in fascicles; bracteoles small, subulate. Calyx ⅛ in. long; segments lanceolate acuminate. Corolla ½ in. long, with a limb less

than half as long as the tube, white, marked with pink. Capsule rarely developed. Gendarussa vulgaris, *Nees in DC. Prod.* xi. 410.

SEYCHELLES, common in all the islands from the shore to a high elevation, *Horne*, 327! Naturalised commonly in Mauritius. Common in Tropical Asia. *Nitchoulli.*

2. **J. brachystachya,** *Willd. Herb. No.* 308. A perennial herb, with stems and leaves on the midrib pubescent. Leaves oblong, narrowed to both ends, short-petioled. Spikes from the axils of the upper leaves, peduncled, 1–3-nate, oblong, with secund flowers; bracts obovate-cuneate, obtuse, subciliated; bracteoles linear, less than half as long as the calyx. Calyx with 4 triangular-subulate segments with membranous edges. Capsule ⅓ in. long, clavate, seedless in the lower half. Rostellularia brachystachya, *Nees in DC. Prod.* xi. 369.

MAURITIUS, described by Nees from a specimen in Willdenow's herbarium, gathered by Du Petit Thouars. Unknown to recent collectors. Endemic.

3. **J. psychotrioides,** *Willd. Herb. No.* 309. Stems and leaves beneath firmly pilose. Leaves petioled, ovate, obtusely cuspidate, somewhat rigid, 1½–2 in. long, narrowed to the petiole. Spikes terminal and axillary, ovate, shorter than the petiole, with secund flowers; bracts cuneate, subacute, somewhat rigid, bristle-ciliated; bracteoles half as long as the calyx. Calyx with 4 subulate carinate immarginate segments. Rostellularia psychotrioides, *Nees in DC. Prod.* xi. 370.

MAURITIUS. Like the last, described from a specimen sent by Du Petit Thouars to Willdenow. Endemic.

4. DICLIPTERA, Juss.

Calyx funnel-shaped, divided nearly to the base into 5 linear equal segments. Corolla bilabiate, the divisions long, oblanceolate, the upper subentire, the lower shortly 3-lobed. Stamens 2; filaments filiform, inserted low down in the tube; anther-cells oblong, superposed, the lower not spurred. Ovary 2-celled; cells 2-ovuled; style exserted, filiform; stigma capitate. Capsule 4-seeded, 2-valved, contracted and sterile in the lower part, the septum separating from the valves.—Herbs or shrubs with large bracteoles. DISTRIB. Tropics of both hemispheres. Species 50.

1. **D. lævigata,** *Juss.; Nees in DC. Prod.* xi. 476. A much-branched shrub, 3–4 feet high, with spreading opposite branches. Leaves petioled, ovate-lanceolate, 2–4 in. long, acute, with a few obscure hairs beneath. Flowers in short-peduncled axillary umbels, subtended by small linear-subulate bracts; pedicels pilose, ⅛–¼ in. long; bracteoles 4; two outer oblong, hiding the calyx, two inner lanceolate. Calyx ¼ in. long. Corolla light-blue, pilose on the outside, 1–1¼ in. long, with lanceolate-spathulate lips exceeding the tube. Stamens as long as the upper lip. Style rather exserted. Justicia falcata, *Lam.*

MAURITIUS, in woods of the Pouce range. Endemic.

ORDER LXXVI. MYOPORACEÆ.

Flowers hermaphrodite, irregular. Calyx persistent, inferior, usually 5-partite. Corolla monopetalous, with 5 subequal or bilabiate divisions. Stamens 4, inserted in the corolla-tube; anthers reniform, finally 1-celled. Ovary 2-celled, with a couple of pendulous anatropal ovules in each cell, or rarely 4-celled; style filiform; stigma capitate, lobed. Fruit a small drupe with a 2–4-celled bony endocarp. Albumen thin, fleshy; radicle superior.—Shrubs, with usually alternate gland-dotted exstipulate leaves with solitary or fascicled flowers in their axils. DISTRIB. Chiefly Australian. Species 80.

1. MYOPORUM, Banks and Sol.

Calyx 5-partite, not accrescent. Corolla campanulate, with 5 subequal rounded lobes. Stamens 4, subequal, included. Ovary 2-4-celled; style filiform; stigma capitate. Fruit a 2–4-celled drupe, with 2–4-seeds.—Shrubs, with gland-dotted simple mostly alternate leaves, the whitish flowers 1 or few, without common peduncles, in their axils. DISTRIB. Species about 20, principally Australian.

1. **M. mauritianum,** *A.DC. Prod.* xi. 711. A much-branched glabrous gland-dotted shrub with viscose branchlets. Leaves crowded towards the end of the branchlets, subcoriaceous, lanceolate, nearly sessile, 2 in. long, acute, narrowed from the middle gradually to both ends, entire or finely serrated. Flowers 1–2 together in the axils of each leaf, on $\frac{1}{4}$–$\frac{1}{3}$ in. pedicels. Calyx $\frac{1}{12}$ in. long, glabrous; segments lanceolate. Corolla campanulate, $\frac{1}{4}$ in. long, conspicuously gland-dotted; lobes round. Style $\frac{1}{48}$ long; stigma 4-lobed. Drupe the size of a small pea.

MAURITIUS, *Sieber, Herb. Maur. No.* 260 (under the name of Bontea daphnoides). RODRIGUEZ, one small patch on the coralline limestone of the shore at the east end of the island, *Balfour!* Endemic.

ORDER LXXVII. VERBENACEÆ.

Flowers more or less irregular, hermaphrodite. Calyx persistent, inferior, campanulate or tubular, 4–5-toothed or truncate. Corolla with a funnel-shaped tube and usually 5 subequal or unequal lobes, the limb often bilabiate, two lobes in the upper and three in the lower lip. Stamens didynamous, inserted in the corolla-tube; anthers 2-celled, with longitudinal dehiscence. Ovary 2–4-celled; ovules 1–2 in a cell; style simple; stigma capitate or forked. Fruit a capsule or drupe, with 2–4-cells. Seeds erect or pendulous; albumen none or scanty; radicle inferior.—Herbs, shrubs or trees, with opposite exstipulate leaves and various inflorescence. DISTRIB. Mainly tropical in both hemispheres. Species 700.

Cotyledons thin; embryo not germinating till the seed falls.
Fruit dry, splitting up into 2–4 pyrenes.
Fertile stamens and pyrenes, 2 each . . . . 1. STACHYTARPHETA.
Fertile stamens 4.
Cocci 4 . . . . * VERBENA.
Cocci 2 . . . . 2. LIPPIA.
Fruit a small dry indehiscent drupe . . . . 3. NESOGENES.
Fruit a drupe, with bony pyrenes.
Stigma capitate . . . . * LANTANA.
Stigma bifid.
Filaments very short . . . . 4. PREMNA.
Filaments long, filiform.
Leaves simple . . . . 5. CLERODENDRON.
Leaves usually digitate . . . . 6. VITEX.
Cotyledons thick; embryo germinating before the seed falls 7. AVICENNIA.

1. STACHYTARPHETA, Vahl.

Calyx tubular, persistent, compressed, oblique at the apex and minutely 4-toothed. Corolla with a long straight or curved cylindrical tube and 5 rounded spreading subequal divisions. Stamens 4, didynamous, included, the upper two without anthers. Ovary 2-celled; cells 1-ovulate; stigma capitate. Fruit included in the persistent calyx-tube, splitting up into two pyrenes.—Herbs, with simple opposite leaves, the flowers in very long spikes inserted in the hollows of a thickened cylindrical rachis. DISTRIB. Species 40, nearly all Tropical American.

Subglabrous, with blue flowers . . . . 1. S. INDICA.
Pilose, with red flowers . . . . * S. MUTABILIS.

1. **S. indica,** *Vahl; Schauer in DC. Prod.* xi. 564. Annual, shrubby at the base, nearly or quite glabrous. Leaves membranous, obovate or oblong, acute or obtuse, sharply serrated, narrowed gradually into a short petiole. Spikes terminal, glabrous, $\frac{1}{2}$–1 foot long, the dilated rachis $\frac{1}{8}$ in. thick; bracts linear or lanceolate, adpressed; flowers inserted in deep hollows of the rachis. Calyx compressed, bifid, indistinctly 4-toothed, $\frac{1}{6}$–$\frac{1}{4}$ in. long. Corolla with a tube slightly longer than the calyx and a blue limb $\frac{1}{6}$–$\frac{1}{4}$ in. across, with a white throat. S. jamaicensis, *Vahl; DC. Prod. loc. cit.*.

MAURITIUS, RODRIGUEZ, and SEYCHELLES, a frequent weed. Cosmopolitan in the tropics. *Vervsine bleue.*

* *S. mutabilis*, Vahl; Schauer in DC. Prod. xi. 565, a native of Tropical America often cultivated, is established in one or two places in the Seychelles in the island of Mahé. It is a more robust plant than *S. indica*, with crenate leaves persistently pilose beneath, stouter pilose spikes with larger lanceolate spreading bracts with a long awn, and larger rose-red flowers inserted in shallower hollows of the rachis. *Verveine à fleurs rouges.*

* *Verbena bonariensis*, Linn.; Schauer in DC. Prod. xi. 541, a native of South Brazil and Buenos Ayres, is naturalised plentifully in Mauritius in fields and by roadsides about Moka, Pamplemousses, etc. It is an erect perennial herb, 2–3 feet high, with rough square stems, distant lanceolate sessile sharply serrated leaves 3–4 in. long, flowers in very numerous short spikes arranged in a deltoid panicle, small bracts, a pilose 5-ribbed tubular hairy calyx $\frac{1}{8}$ in. long with 5 linear teeth, a minute red-purple corolla with a long cylindrical tube and a short nearly regular limb, didynamous included stamens and fruit which splits into 4 cylindrical brown pyrenes included in the persistent calyx-tube. *Verveine sauvage.*

2. LIPPIA, Linn.

Calyx membranous, campanulate; segments 4. Corolla with a cylindrical tube and obscurely bilabiate limb, with 5 rounded lobes. Stamens 4, didynamous. Ovary 2-celled, globose; cells 1-ovulate; style simple; stigma capitate. Fruit ovoid, dry, separating into 2 pyrenes. —Herbs or shrubs, with simple opposite leaves and minute flowers arranged in axillary spikes or capitula. DISTRIB. Species 80, all the rest American.

1. **L. nodiflora,** *Rich.; Schauer in DC. Prod.* xi. 585. A wide-trailing perennial herb, rooting at the joints and more or less clothed with obscure adpressed short whitish hairs. Leaves nearly sessile, obovate or oblanceolate, obtuse, sharply toothed in the upper half, cuneate-spathulate in the lower. Peduncles axillary, ascending, longer than the leaves. Heads $\frac{1}{4}$ in. thick, at first globose, afterwards oblong; bracts small, deltoid, the outer largest. Calyx $\frac{1}{12}$ in. long, hyaline, with two purplish ciliated keels; teeth deltoid. Corolla $\frac{1}{8}$ in. long, the obscurely bilabiate limb $\frac{1}{12}$ in. across. Fruit ovoid, included in the calyx. Zapania nodiflora, *Pers.; Bojer, Hort. Maur.* 254

MAURITIUS and SEYCHELLES, frequent on grassy shores. Cosmopolitan in tropical and warm-temperate regions.

3. NESOGENES, A. DC.

Calyx-tube oblong; teeth 5, large, rather unequal. Corolla-tube funnel-shaped; lobes 5, round, nearly equal. Stamens 4, obscurely didynamous, shorter than the corolla; filaments short. Ovary obovoid, 2-celled; ovules solitary in the cells; style simple; stigma capitate. Fruit a small dry drupe, enclosed in the persistent calyx-tube.—Herbs, or shrubs, with small opposite leaves and flowers solitary or fascicled in their axils. DISTRIB. Species 2, the other one Polynesian.

1. **N. decumbens,** *Balf. fil.* A diffuse perennial herb, much-branched at the crown of the root, with trailing simple or little branched finely downy slender wiry stems 1–2 ft. long. Leaves short-petioled,

membranous, lanceolate or rhomboid, acute, small, entire or sparsely toothed, base cuneate, the upper reduced. Flowers 3–4 in umbels in the axils of the leaves all down the stem, on short downy pedicels. Calyx ⅛ in. long; teeth lanceolate-cuspidate, as long as the tube. Corolla twice as long as the calyx, gradually widening from the base to the top of the tube.

RODRIGUEZ, on a small patch of coralline limestone ¾ mile from the shore, *Balfour!* Endemic.

* LANTANA, Linn.

Calyx minute, campanulate, obscurely 4-toothed. Corolla with a long slender tube and an obscurely bilabiate limb, with small rounded lobes. Stamens 4, didynamous, included in the corolla-tube. Ovary 2-celled; cells 1-ovuled; style simple; stigma capitate. Fruit a small drupe, containing two 1-seeded pyrenes.—Shrubs, with simple opposite or whorled leaves; the flowers in dense heads on axillary peduncles. DISTRIB. Mainly Tropical America. Species 40–50.

Branches prickly . . . . * L. CAMARA.
Branches not prickly.
  Leaves opposite . . . . * L. LILACINA.
  Leaves whorled . . . . * L. TRIFOLIA.

* *L. Camara*, Linn.; Schauer in DC. Prod. xi. 598, (L. aculeata, *Linn.; Bot. Mag. t.* 96), a native of Tropical America, now widely spread in the Old World, is established both in Mauritius and Seychelles. It is a shrub 4–8 feet high, with tetragonous branches, armed with copious small uncinate prickles, hispid short-petioled ovate acute crenate leaves, globose heads on axillary peduncles 1–1½ in. long, linear bracts not more than half as long as the pilose flowers, a slender corolla tube under ½ in. long widening gradually from the base to the top and a ¼ in. limb at first yellow afterwards turning orange and red and a black shining drupe the size of a small pea.

* *L. lilacina*, Desf.; Schauer in DC. Prod. xi. 604, (L. fucata, *Lindl. Bot. Reg. t.* 798), a native of Brazil, often cultivated in gardens, is naturalised in the Seychelles in Mahé and Silhouette. It is a branched undershrub with tetragonal unarmed branches clothed with short spreading bristly hairs, opposite ovate-rhomboid acute crenate rugose leaves, short-peduncled globose heads, and bracts much shorter than the lilac flowers.

* *L. trifolia*, Linn.; Schauer in DC. Prod. xi. 606; Bot. Mag. t. 1449, (L. annua, *Linn.; Bot. Mag. t.* 1022), a native of Tropical America, now widely spread in the old world, is naturalised in the Mauritius on the Pouce range. It is a little-branched undershrub, with pilose unarmed hexagonal branches, 3–4-nate oblong-lanceolate acute crenate membranous hairy leaves, 2–3 in. peduncles, heads at first globose finally cylindrical 1–2 in. long, and lower bracts as long as the flowers, which are lilac with a yellow throat.

L. mixta, Linn. and *L. Sellowiana*, Link, both also American, are included in Dupont's Mauritian Catalogue.

4. PREMNA, Linn.

Calyx minute, campanulate, shortly toothed. Corolla-tube a narrow funnel, with a ring of hairs inside; lobes 4, round, spreading, subequal. Stamens 4, inserted high up in the tube; filaments very short; anthers round, just exserted from the tube. Ovary 4-locellate; ovules solitary; style filiform; stigma bifid. Fruit a small drupe, with a 4-celled bony endocarp.—Shrubs or trees, with opposite simple leaves and copious minute flowers in ample corymbs. DISTRIB. Tropics of the Old World. Species 40.

1. **P. serratifolia,** *Linn.; Schauer in DC. Prod.* xi. 632. A shrub or small tree, glabrous except the panicle, in shaded woods sometimes subscandent (*P. scandens*, Bojer, Hort. Maur. 257). Leaves short-petioled, round or broad-oblong, 4–9 in. long, acute or obtuse, sub-coriaceous, usually entire (*P. integrifolia*, Linn. *P. divaricata*, Wall.; DC. Prod. xi. 633). Flowers numerous, minute, in terminal corymbs 2–4 in. broad, with glabrous or pilose branches; bracts minute, lanceolate. Calyx $\frac{1}{24}$ in. long; limb sometimes obscurely bilabiate; teeth deltoid. Corolla-tube twice the length of the calyx; limb greenish-yellow, with 4 round subequal lobes. Drupe purple, juicy, glabrous, the size of a small pea.

MAURITIUS, RODRIGUEZ and SEYCHELLES, frequent in woods and thickets, both near the shore and amongst the hills. China to Madagascar and Zambesi-land. *Bois Sureau sauvage.*

5. CLERODENDRON, Linn.

Calyx-tube campanulate; teeth 5, usually short, deltoid. Corolla with a narrowly funnel-shaped tube longer than the calyx, and 5 obovate or obovate-oblong subequal or unequal spreading lobes. Stamens 4, didynamous, usually exserted from the corolla. Ovary 4-celled; ovules solitary in the cells; style filiform; stigma bifid. Fruit a small 2–4 lobed drupe, girt by the accrescent calyx, with 2–4 bony pyrenes.—Shrubs or trees, with opposite simple leaves, the copious flowers mostly in terminal corymbs. DISTRIB. Species about 80; tropical, mainly in the Old World.

Inflorescence corymbose.
  Calyx-teeth obscure. Leaves variable, cuneate at the base.
    Corolla-lobes obovate-oblong . . . . 1. C. HETEROPHYLLUM.
    Corolla-lobes obovate . . . . 2. C. LACINIATUM.
  Calyx-teeth large. Leaves round-cordate . . . . * C. FRAGRANS.
Inflorescence a thyrsoid panicle . . . . * C. SERRATUM.

1. **C. heterophyllum,** *R. Br.; Schauer in DC. Prod.* xi. 660. A low much-branched shrub, with puberulent terete ashen-grey branchlets. Leaves petioled, membranous, acute, glabrous, 2–4 in. long, varying from oblong to lanceolate and linear, narrowed at the base. Flowers in close terminal corymbs 2–4 inches across; pedicels $\frac{1}{8}$–$\frac{1}{4}$ in.,

puberulent; bracts minute, subulate. Calyx $\frac{1}{12}$ in. long, campanulate, with 5 minute cusps. Corolla greenish-white, with obovate-oblong divisions quite as long as the tube. Stamens twice long as the limb. Drupe the size of a small cherry, white, spongy, juicy. Volkameria angustifolia, *Andr. Bot. Rep. t.* 554.

MAURITIUS, on dry hills of the Pouce range, etc. Also Bourbon. *Bois Chenilles. Bois Cabri.*

2. **C. laciniatum,** *Balf. fil.* A shrub, with terete ashen-grey branchlets, minutely puberulent at the top. Leaves petioled, membranous, glabrous, 2–3 in. long, varying from oblong entire with a cuneate base, to rhomboid bipinnatifid with distant long ligulate obtuse segments $\frac{1}{12}$–$\frac{1}{8}$ in. broad. Flowers in close terminal corymbs 2–3 inches across; pedicels $\frac{1}{8}$–$\frac{1}{4}$ in. long, puberulent. Calyx $\frac{1}{8}$ in. long, campanulate, truncate, glabrous. Corolla $\frac{1}{2}$ in. long, with subequal obovate lobes, much shorter than the tube. Filaments twice as long as the corolla-limb.

RODRIGUEZ, not uncommon both on the hill-slopes and in the valleys, *Balfour!* Endemic. *Bois Cabri.*

* *C. fragrans*, Vent. Jard. Malm. t. 70; Bot. Mag. t. 1834; Schauer in DC. Prod. xi. 664, a native of China, well known in cultivation, has become subspontaneous both in Mauritius and the Seychelles. It has tomentose square branchlets, round-cordate large toothed membranous leaves pilose on both sides, flowers in dense terminal corymbs, large linear squarrose calyx-teeth, bright rose-red fragrant corollas with 5 round subequal lobes as long as the tube, and short stamens.

* *C. serratum*, Spreng.; Schauer in DC. Prod. xi. 664; (C. macrophyllum, *Bot. Mag. t.* 2536) a native of Tropical Asia, is subspontaneous both in Seychelles and Mauritius. It has very large 2–3-nate sessile glabrous obovate-oblong serrated leaves, copious cymes arranged in a long thyrsoid terminal panicle, a campanulate calyx with 5 short deltoid teeth, a whitish corolla with a blue lip and a tube twice as long as the calyx and a limb with unequal divisions of which the lowest is spreading and twice as long as the tube and stamens an inch long.

6. VITEX, Linn.

Calyx small, campanulate or funnel-shaped, accrescent in fruit, truncate or shortly 5-toothed. Corolla with a funnel-shaped tube and bilabiate limb, with 5 rounded subequal lobes. Stamens 4, didynamous, reaching beyond the corolla-limb. Ovary 4-locellate; ovules solitary in the cells; style filiform, curved; stigma bifid. Fruit a drupe, girt by the persistent calyx, with a 4-celled bony endocarp.—Trees or shrubs, with opposite simple or digitate leaves, the flowers either cymose or panicled. DISTRIB. Tropics of both hemispheres, principally the New World. Species 50.

Leaves beneath and branches whitish. Flowers in ample terminal panicles.
Leaflets 1–3, sessile . . . . * V. TRIFOLIA.
Leaflets 5, stalked . . . . * V. NEGUNDO.
Glabrous. Flowers in simple axillary cymes . . . . 1. V. PERVILLEI.

* *V. trifolia*, Linn.; DC. Prod. xi. 683, a native of Tropical Asia, widely spread in cultivation, is half-naturalised both in Mauritius and Seychelles (Sieber, ii. 283! etc.). It is a shrub, with the leaves beneath and calyx clothed with white tomentum, leaflets 1–3-nate sessile obovate-oblong green above, and abundant small flowers arranged in deltoid panicles.

* *V. Negundo*, Linn.; DC. Prod. xi. 684; Bot. Mag. t. 364, also Tropical Asian, and common in cultivation, is given as Mauritian in the Prodromus on faith of Sieber, ii. 161, but is not even naturalised. It has the copious small tomentose panicled flowers of *V. trifolia*, but the leaflets are 5 in number, on long petiolules, and are merely puberulent, not canescent beneath.

1. **V. Pervillei**, *Baker*. A shrub, glabrous in all its parts, with slender terete branchlets. Leaves digitately trifoliolate, subcoriaceous, glabrous, venulose; leaflets nearly sessile, oblong, 1–1½ in. long, narrowed gradually from the middle to a rather obtuse point, cuneate spathulate at the base; petiole an inch long. Cymes simple, short-peduncled, few-flowered, axillary and terminal, seen in the fruiting stage only; pedicels ¼–⅜ in. long, thickened at the apex. Fruit-calyx ⅙ in. long, broadly campanulate, obscurely toothed. Drupe obovoid, ½ in. long.

SEYCHELLES, *Pervillé*, 686! Also Madagascar, *Pervillé*, 870 bis!

Mr. Horne sends leaves (No. 547!) of a second Seychelles species which is probably unnamed and endemic, which he describes as a large tree common in many parts of Mahé on the shore. It is glabrous, with digitately 5-foliolate leaves, like those of *V. leucoxylon*, Linn, the leaflets long-stalked (1–1½ in.), obovate-oblong, 6–10 in. by 3–3½ in., obtuse with a cuneate base and obscurely crenulate margins, subcoriaceous and flexible in texture with distinct distant erecto-patent main veins.

7. AVICENNIA, Linn.

Calyx campanulate, coriaceous, divided nearly to the base into 5 round obtuse much-imbricated lobes. Corolla with a short tube and 5 round obovate-oblong subequal lobes. Stamens 4, subequal, the anthers just exserted from the corolla-tube. Ovary 2-celled; ovules 2 in a cell, collateral; stigma bifid, subsessile. Fruit ovoid, coriaceous, indehiscent, the thick fleshy embryo germinating before it falls.—Evergreen trees, with wide-creeping roots, small entire coriaceous leaves and minute flowers in terminal and axillary globose heads. DISTRIB. Shores of the Tropical zone. Species 4.

1. **A. officinalis,** *Linn.; Schauer in DC. Prod.* xi. 700. Branchlets and leaves below clothed with whitish tomentum. Leaves opposite, short-petioled, oblong-lanceolate, narrowed to both ends, 2–4 in. long, entire, coriaceous, green and glabrous on the upper surface. Flowers in small round peduncled heads from the end of the branch, and axils of the upper leaves. Calyx $\frac{1}{8}$ in. long; lobes round, coriaceous, densely downy downwards. Corolla-tube as long as the calyx; round lobes silky on the outside. Fruit downy, the size of a small plum.

SEYCHELLES, in the Mangrove swamps of Mahé and Praslin. Tropical shores of the Old World.

ORDER LXXVIII. LABIATÆ.

Flowers irregular, hermaphrodite. Calyx inferior, persistent, with 5 mostly unequal teeth. Corolla deciduous, bilabiate. Stamens inserted in the corolla tube, usually 4, in two equal pairs; anthers 2-celled, dehiscing longitudinally. Ovary 4-lobed; style filiform, curved forked at the end; ovules solitary, erect, anatropous. Fruit of four small dry 1-seeded nucules. Seed usually exalbuminous; radicle inferior.—Herbs or shrubs, with opposite leaves and whorled flowers, either aggregated into racemes or spaced and bracteated with large leaves. DISTRIB. Mostly warm-temperate regions. Species 2500.

Stamens curved downwards.
  Lower lobe of corolla flat.
    Upper tooth of calyx decurrent down the tube . . . * OCYMUM.
    Upper tooth of calyx not decurrent . . . . * MOSCHOSMA.
  Lower lobe of corolla oblong-spathulate, convex . . . 1. PLECTRANTHUS.
  Lower lobe of corolla short, deeply saccate . . . . * HYPTIS.
Stamens curved upwards.
  Calyx-teeth 3. Stamens 2, with anthers 1-celled. . . * SALVIA.
  Calyx-teeth 5, deltoid, not spiny.
    Nucules with a lacunose crest at the top . . . . 2. ACHYROSPERMUM.
    Nucules naked at the top . . . . 3. ANISOMELES.
  Calyx-teeth 5, subulate, spiny . . . . * LEONURUS.
  Calyx-teeth 10.
    Corolla deeply bilabiate . . . . 4. LEONOTIS.
    Corolla shallowly bilabiate . . . . 5. LEUCAS.

* OCYMUM, Linn.

Calyx-tube short; upper tooth much the largest, with decurrent edges. Corolla with a short tube and two subequal lips, the upper 4-toothed, the lower declinate, nearly flat. Stamens 4, the two lower the longest; filaments often with a tooth or tuft of hairs at the base; anthers reniform. Style shortly bifid. Nucules globose, smooth or dotted.—Herbs or shrubs, with small flowers in long narrow racemes, bracteated by minute leaves. DISTRIB. Round the world in the tropics, some species much cultivated. Species 40.

* Several of the species are commonly cultivated, and have become more or less established. Of these the most common is *O. gratissimum*, Linn., (O. frutescens, *Mill.*), which is almost shrubby, much branched, several feet high, with glabrous stems and large petioled ovate-rhomboid nearly glabrous leaves, calyx-tube $\frac{1}{8}$ in. long, upper tooth with an abruptly recurved round point $\frac{1}{12}$ in. broad, the others much shorter minute subulate and the lower lip closed against the upper, and corolla not longer than the calyx. From this *O. suave*, Willd. (O. paniculatum, *Bojer*, *Hort. Maur.* 258, *non Pers.*), differs mainly by its hairy branches and leaves pilose beneath. *O. canum*, Sims, Bot. Mag. t. 2452, is dwarfer and less shrubby in habit, with pilose slender stems, leaves much smaller, pilose beneath, upper lip of calyx round $\frac{1}{4}$ in. broad, not recurved at the point and not longer than the others, and corolla $1\frac{1}{2}$–2 times the length of the calyx. The latter was found by Dr. Balfour in Rodriguez near Mathurin. *Basilic.*

* *Moschosma polystachyum*, Benth. (Ocymum, *Linn.*), the Musk Basil, is also commonly cultivated and usually subspontaneous. It is an erect annual, 2–3 feet high, with a glabrous stem, glabrous ovate acute leaves, very small flowers in copiously panicled racemes, minute bracts, calyx $\frac{1}{12}$ in. long, with teeth nearly equal in length, the upper round obtuse with edges not decurrent down the tube, the side ones deltoid, the lowest linear-cuspidate. It is a native of the tropics of the Old World. *Basilic musqué.*

1. PLECTRANTHUS, L'Herit.

Calyx declinate, with a campanulate tube, the five teeth equal in length, the uppermost broad, obtuse, the others narrow, acute. Corolla bilabiate, 3–4 times the length of the calyx, the lower lip oblong-spathulate, concave, declinate. Stamens 4, nearly as long as the lower lip, didynamous; anthers ovate, with divaricate lobes. Style shortly bifid. Nucules globose.—Herbs or shrubs, with blue flowers in lax long racemes of distant whorls. DISTRIB. Tropical and subtropical regions of the Old World. Species 70.

Leaves and stems densely pilose . . . . 1. P. MADAGASCARIENSIS.
Leaves and stems nearly or quite glabrous . . . . 2. P. ROTUNDIFOLIUS.

1. **P. madagascariensis,** *Benth. in DC. Prod.* xii. 68. A perennial herb, with a procumbent rootstock, from which issue many spreading or erect densely pilose stems 1–2 feet long. Leaves petioled, roundish, crenate, thick, densely pilose, $\frac{1}{2}$–1 in. long. Racemes 3–6 in. long, of many distant dense whorls of 10–12 flowers each, bracteated by lanceolate minute leaves; pedicels very short. Calyx finally $\frac{1}{6}$ in. long, sprinkled with minute glands; teeth as long as the tube, upper roundish, the others lanceolate. Corolla pale blue, pilose, $\frac{1}{2}$ in. long, the upper lip shortly 4-lobed. Ocimum madagascariense, *Pers.* Plectranthus villosus, *Sieb. Fl. Maur. Exsic.* ii. 152. P. mauritianus, *Bojer*, *Hort. Maur.* 254.

MAURITIUS, on mountain rocks of the Pouce, Montagne Longue, Rivière Noire, etc. Also Arabia, Madagascar and Natal. *Omime sauvage* or *Omime bâtard.*

2. **P. rotundifolius,** *Spreng.; Benth in DC. Prod.* x.ii 65. Stems erect from a creeping rootstock, glabrous or nearly so. Leaves petioled, round-ovate, glabrous, turning black when dried, rounded or cuneate at the base. Whorls close, lax, many-flowered. Calyx campanulate, pilose; upper tooth broad, oblong; side ones truncate; lowest broad ovate, subconnate, cuspidate. Corolla 3 times as long as the calyx, blue; throat scarcely inflated. Stamens included. Coleus rugosus, *Benth. in Wall. Pl. Asiat. Rar.* ii. 15. Germanea rotundifolia, *Poir. Dict.* ii. 763.

MAURITIUS, gathered by Commerson, not seen recently. Also perhaps East Indian.

* *Hyptis suaveolens,* Poit.; Benth in DC. Prod. xii. 126, (Ballota suaveolens, *Linn.; Jacq. Hort. Vind.* t. 42), a native of Tropical America, now widely spread in the Old World, is naturalised in Mauritius near Port Louis. It is a robust herb, with square stems densely clothed with firm grey hairs, leaves round-cordate irregularly repand-crenate, flowers in copious lax panicles, calyx-tube $\frac{1}{4}$–$\frac{1}{3}$ in. long funnel-shaped with 10 strong ribs, teeth 5 equal subulate, corolla with a cylindrical tube twice as long as that of the calyx blue with a white throat hairy within, lobes short, four upper flat, lowest saccate abruptly deflexed. *H. pectinata,* Poir., is given by Dupont as a plant introduced in Mauritius.

* The large genus *Salvia,* Linn., marked by its galeate corolla and two ascending stamens, of which the connective is deeply forked and one branch barren, is represented by *S. coccinea,* Linn.; Benth. in DC. Prod. xii. 243, a commonly cultivated American species, which is established in Rodriguez. It is a branched perennial, with small toothed ovate-crenate leaves finely pubescent beneath, scarlet flowers in whorls forming a lax terminal raceme, a strongly-ribbed calyx with 3 deltoid teeth and a corolla about an inch long of which the lower lip is deflexed and deeply 3-lobed.

2. ACHYROSPERMUM, Blume.

Calyx glabrous; tube funnel-shaped, indistinctly ribbed; teeth 5, deltoid, subequal. Corolla with a long slender arching tube, much longer than the calyx; upper lip short, oblong, convex; lower with 3 deltoid lobes, the lowest deflexed. Stamens 4, didynamous, the longest exserted; anthers 1–2-celled Style shortly bifid. Nucules 4, minute, with a coral-like crest.—Herbs or shrubs, with large membranous leaves, the flowers in congested racemes with minute bracts. DISTRIB. Tropics of the Old World. Species 6.

1. **A. sechellarum,** *Baker.* A shrub, 3–5 feet high, glabrous in all its parts. Stems square; main ones tubercled, woody, $\frac{1}{4}$–$\frac{1}{3}$ in. thick. Leaves distinctly petioled, oblong, acute, membranous, inciso-crenate, cuneate at the base; largest 6–9 in. long. Racemes short, dense, sessile, ascending from the distant nodes, with minute foliaceous oblanceolate bracts; pedicels very short. Calyx $\frac{1}{8}$ in. long; teeth $\frac{1}{4}$ as

long as the tube. Corolla white, spotted with light red, $\frac{5}{8}$–$\frac{3}{4}$ in. long. Longer stamens and style exserted from the galea.

SEYCHELLES, in shaded woods of Mahé and Silhouette, *Horne*, 553 ! Endemic.

3. ANISOMELES, R. Br.

Calyx-tube funnel-shaped, 10-ribbed; teeth 5, subequal, lanceolate or deltoid. Corolla arching, deeply bilabiate; upper lip oblong, entire; lower deeply 3-lobed, the lowest lobe deeply emarginate. Stamens 4, didynamous, exserted; anthers of the long ones 1-celled. Style bifid. Nucules ovoid-trigonal, dry, smooth.—Perennial herbs, with flowers in close or subdistant whorls of congested cymes. DISTRIB. Tropics of the Old World. Species probably 2 or 3 only.

Leaves thick, ovate-lanceolate, persistently tomentose on both sides . . . . 1. A. MALABARICA.
Leaves thin, broad ovate . . . . * A. OVATA.

1. **A. malabarica,** *R. Br.; Bot. Mag. t.* 2071. An erect branched perennial, 3–5 feet high, with stem and leaves on both sides matted with persistent soft whitish tomentum. Leaves thick, petioled, ovate-lanceolate, acute, crenate, 2–3 in. long. Racemes 6–9 in. long, the upper whorls close, the lower distant, all the bract-leaves small. Calyx $\frac{1}{3}$ in. long, densely pilose; teeth large, lanceolate, acuminate. Corolla lilac, pilose, the limb $\frac{1}{4}$ in long, exserted from the calyx. *Wight Ic. t.* 864; *Benth. in DC. Prod.* xii. 456. Nepeta malabarica, *Linn.* Stachys mauritiana, *Sieber, Exsic.* 159. Craniotome mauritiana, *Bojer, Hort. Maur.* 249.

MAURITIUS, common about Port Louis and in other parts of the island. Tropical Asia, common.

* *A. ovata*, R. Br.; Jacq. fil. Eclog. t. 86; Hook. Bot. Misc. ii. 358, t. 19, common in Tropical Asia, is naturalised in Mauritius on the slope of the Pouce by the side of the road to Moka. It has the stem and leaves below clothed with short soft spreading pubescence, thin broad ovate leaves, lower whorls of flowers distant and bracteated with large leaves and lanceolate-deltoid calyx-teeth half as long as the tube.

* *Leonurus sibiricus*, Linn. (L. tataricus, *Bojer, Hort. Maur.* 249, *non Linn.*), a native of Asia, is subspontaneous in Mauritius and Rodriguez in cultivated and waste ground. It is a subglabrous erect annual, with leaves deeply palmately cut with pinnatifid lobes, distant dense whorls of flowers bracteated by large leaves, calyx funnel-shaped $\frac{1}{4}$ in. long with 5 subulate teeth nearly as long as the tube, an arching deeply bifid reddish corolla with a tube as long as the calyx naked within, upper lip oblong-spathulate entire, the lower with small side lobes and a large deflexed lower lobe and 4 included stamens.

4. LEONOTIS, R. Br.

Calyx-tube long, narrowly funnel shaped, 8–10-ribbed; teeth 8–10, spine-pointed, the upper much the largest. Corolla arching, twice as long as the calyx, deeply bilabiate; upper lip oblong-spathulate, convex, entire; lower shortly 3-lobed. Stamens 4, included; anthers all 2-celled, the cells divaricating, acute at both ends. Nucules trigonous, with a cup-like concavity at the apex.—Herbs, with the flowers in very dense distant whorls bracteated by large leaves. DISTRIB. Tropical and South Africa. Species 12.

1. **L. nepetæfolia,** *R. Br.; Benth. in DC. Prod.* xii. 535. An annual herb, 3–6 feet high, with finely puberulent square stems. Leaves long-petioled, ovate, membranous, inciso-crenate, 3–4 in. long, cuneate at the base Flowers 100 or more, in very dense distant whorls 3–4 inches thick. Calyx ¾–1 in. long, all the teeth pungent. Corolla twice as long as the calyx, densely coated with bright scarlet pubescence, the lower lip half as long as the upper, the tube with three rings of colourless hairs inside below the insertion of the stamens. *Bot. Reg. t.* 281; *Wight Ic. t.* 867. Phlomis nepetæfolia, *Linn.* Leonotis ovata, *Bojer, Hort. Maur.* 250.

MAURITIUS and SEYCHELLES, frequent in waste ground. Now Cosmopolitan in the tropics.

5. LEUCAS, R. Br.

Calyx-tube long, arching, funnel-shaped, 10-ribbed; teeth 10 minute cusps. Corolla-tube as long as calyx; limb shortly bilabiate; upper lip entire, lower trifid, the central lobe the longest. Stamens 4, didynamous, exserted; all the anthers 2-celled. Nucules 4, smooth, trigonous.—Herbs, with the flowers in a few distant dense whorls, bracteated by large leaves. DISTRIB. Tropics of the Old World. Species 50.

1. **L. aspera,** *Spreng.; Benth. in DC. Prod.* xii. 532. A much-branched annual, ½–1 foot high, with finely pilose stems. Leaves short-petioled, lanceolate or oblong-lanceolate, 1–2 in. long. Flowers 30–40, in a few dense globose whorls bracteated by large leaves; bracteoles linear-subulate. Calyx subsessile, ⅜ in. long, finely pilose. Corolla-limb white, under ¼ in. long, the concave upper lip clothed with dense white hairs, the central lobe of the lower one obovate, retuse, veined and rugulose, the side ones very small. Leucas zeylanica, *Bojer, Hort. Maur.* 250.

MAURITIUS, in cultivated fields and waste ground. Common in Tropical Asia. *Madame Tombé.*

A plant gathered by Dr. Balfour in Rodriguez has the habit and foliage of a *Stachys* of the section Stachiotypus, but flowers are wanting in the only specimen.

Mentha viridis, Linn., the commonly-cultivated mint, is enumerated as an introduced species in Dupont's Mauritian Catalogue.

ORDER LXXIX. NYCTAGINACEÆ.

Flowers hermaphrodite or polygamo-dioicous. Perianth herbaceous or coloured, with a long or short funnel-shaped tube and a shortly 5-toothed or lobed spreading limb. Stamens variable in number, hypogynous; filaments filiform, often connate at the base; anthers 2-celled, dehiscing longitudinally. Ovary superior, 1-celled, 1-ovuled; style filiform; stigma various. Fruit an achene or utricle, usually enclosed in the accrescent usually viscose tube of the perianth. Seed albuminous.—Shrubs, trees, or herbs, with exstipulate simple opposite or alternate leaves, the flowers small or large, various in position and arrangement. DISTRIB. Cosmopolitan in the tropics. Species 100.

Flower enclosed in a calyx-like involucre . . . . * MIRABILIS.
Bracts minute, caducous.
  Shrubs; stamens 5–10 . . . . 1. PISONIA.
  Herbs; stamens 2–3. . . . . 2. BOERHAAVIA.

* *Mirabilis Jalapa*, Linn.; Choisy in DC. Prod. xiii. 2, 427, a commonly-cultivated species of Tropical American origin, is casually subspontaneous in Mauritius (*Sieber*, 221! etc.) It is a subglabrous dichotomously-branched perennial herb, with opposite petioled ovate acute leaves, flowers 3 to 6 together in terminal fascicles expanding at night, red, yellow, white, or variegated, each enclosed in a calyx-like involucre with 5 long lanceolate teeth, a cylindrical perianth-tube 1–1½ in. long, a spreading limb an inch broad with 5 round lobes, 5 stamens incurved at the tip with minute anthers, and an obovoid or subglobose black 10-ribbed fruit surrounded by the indurated base of the perianth. *Belle de Nuit.*

1. PISONIA, Linn.

Flowers polygamo-dioicous, greenish. Male perianth funnel-shaped, with short spreading deltoid lobes. Stamens 5–10, exserted, unequal; filaments filiform; anthers globose. Female perianth longer and narrower, with rudiments of stamens round the elongated ovary; style exserted, usually lateral; stigma bifid or multifid. Fruit surrounded by the indurated clavate pentagonal perianth, which has often a row of small spreading glandular bristles on each rib; achene nearly or quite as long as the perianth and the same shape.—Climbing or erect shrubs or trees, sometimes spiny, with alternate or opposite simple leaves, the numerous small greenish flowers in dense or lax corymbose panicles. DISTRIB. Cosmopolitan in the tropics, mostly American. Species 30.

Fruit-perianth with a row of hard viscid bristles on the five ribs.
  Prickly climber . . . . * P. ACULEATA.
  Unarmed erect trees.
    Pedicels 0 or very short . . . . 1. P. MACROPHYLLA.
    Pedicels distinct . . . . 2. P. VISCOSA.
Fruit-perianth without bristles on the ribs.
  Limb of perianth ⅛ in. across . . . . 3. P. COSTATA.
  Limb of perianth ¼ in. across . . . . 4. P. CALPIDIA.

* *P. aculeata*, Linn.; Choisy in DC. Prod. xiii. 2, 440, a native of Tropical America now widely spread in the Old World, is naturalised in Mauritius. It is a climbing shrub, with slender terete stems armed with large spreading hooked pungent spines in the axils of the leaves, petioled oblong subcoriaceous glabrous acute leaves, male flowers in dense peduncled axillary corymbose panicles with pubescent branches, pedicels none or very short, perianth pubescent $\frac{1}{12}$ in. long and as broad at the throat when expanded, stamens 6–8 distinctly exserted, female flowers in very lax panicles with pedicels an inch or more long, clavate fruit-perianth $\frac{3}{4}$ in. long armed with 5 rows of hard gland-tipped bristles. *Bambaras.*

1. **P. macrophylla,** *Choisy in DC. Prod.* xiii. 2, 446. An erect small tree 15–20 feet high with stout unarmed branchlets. Leaves membranous, $\frac{1}{2}$–1 ft. or more long, acute, rounded or cuneate at the base, with strong erecto-patent ribs, slightly pubescent on the under side when young; petiole 1–1$\frac{1}{4}$ in. long. Male flowers in dense corymbose panicles 2–3 in. broad with downy branches; pedicels none or very short. Perianth $\frac{1}{6}$ in. long, narrowly funnel-shaped, pilose, with minute deltoid lobes. Stamens 8, finally just exserted. Fruit-perianth clavate, with 5 rows of short spreading gland-tipped bristles; not seen fully mature. Calpidia macrophylla, *Bojer, Hort. Maur.* 265.

SEYCHELLES, near the summit of Morne Blanc at a height of 2000 feet, *Horne,* 555! Also Island of Galega, *Bojer!* The Seychelles specimen is in bud only, so that the plant needs comparison with that from Galega, as described, in mature flower and fruit. *Bois Mapou.*

5. **P. viscosa,** *Balf. fil.* An erect unarmed tree with stout branchlets. Leaves obovate, 3–4 in. long, membranous, slightly pubescent at first beneath, deltoid at the base, obtuse or obscurely cuspidate, turning as in the rest nearly black when dried; petiole $\frac{1}{4}$–$\frac{1}{2}$ in. Panicle of male flowers dense, 1$\frac{1}{2}$–2 in. broad, corymbose, as long as the leaves, densely brown-pubescent; pedicels $\frac{1}{12}$–$\frac{1}{8}$ in., with minute subulate bracts. Perianth $\frac{1}{8}$ in. narrowly funnel-shaped, pilose; teeth minute, deltoid. Stamens 10, just exserted. Fruit-panicle half a foot broad, with erecto-patent pedicels $\frac{1}{4}$–$\frac{1}{2}$ in. long. Fruit-perianth under $\frac{1}{2}$ in. long, with 5 rows of spreading short gland-tipped bristles, the seed reaching to the top.

RODRIGUEZ, on the shore, especially at Ile aux Frégates, *Balfour!* Endemic. *Mapou.*

3. **P. costata,** *Choisy in DC. Prod.* xiii. 2, 446. A tree, reaching a height of 30–40 feet, with stout unarmed corky branchlets. Leaves crowded at the end of the branchlets, ferrugineo-pilose on the petiole and ribs beneath till mature, oblong, immature when the flowers are produced, finally $\frac{1}{2}$ foot long, with strong erecto-patent main ribs; petiole 1–1$\frac{1}{2}$ in. long. Male corymbs 2–3 in. broad, very dense, with

brown-pubescent branchlets; pedicels 0 or very short; bracts minute, linear-subulate. Perianth $\frac{1}{12}$–$\frac{1}{8}$ in. long, narrowly funnel-shaped, densely brown-puberulent, with minute deltoid teeth. Stamens 5–6, finally distinctly exserted. Female corymbs much laxer Fruit-perianth clavate, not seen fully mature, the ribs not armed with gland-tipped bristles. Stigma bifid. Calpidia costata, *Bojer*, *Hort. Maur.* 265.

MAURITIUS, in mountain woods of the Pouce range, etc. Endemic.

4. **P. Calpidia,** *Steud. Nomencl. edit.* 2, *p.* 345. A low erect tree, nearly glabrous in all its parts, with corky bark and stout branchlets. Leaves alternate or opposite, crowded near the end of the branchlets, on $\frac{1}{2}$–$1\frac{1}{2}$ in. petioles, the blade oblong, obtuse, 3–4 in. long, rounded or cuneate at the base, subcoriaceous, glabrous, with slender ribs. Male flowers in dense peduncled terminal and axillary corymbose panicles 2–3 in. broad, with stout subglabrous branches; pedicels $\frac{1}{24}$–$\frac{1}{8}$ in. long. Perianth $\frac{1}{4}$ in. long; the expanded mouth $\frac{1}{4}$ in. broad, with distinct deltoid teeth. Stamens 10, shorter than the perianth-lobes. Female corymbs much laxer; pedicels finally $\frac{1}{2}$–1 in. long, erecto-patent. Fruit-perianth 2 inches long, smooth, the seed filling only the lower half, and the fimbriated stigma just exserted from the tip. Calpidia lanceolata, *Thouars, Pl. Afr. Austr.* 37, *t.* 10; *Bojer, Hort. Maur.* 268. C. ovalifolia, *Bojer, loc. cit.* Pisonia ovalifolia and lanceolata, *Choisy in DC. Prod.* xiii. 2, 441–2.

MAURITIUS, in the mountain woods of the Pouce range, etc. *C. lanceolata* and *ovalifolia* represent two extreme forms of leaf, which are connected by intermediate gradations. Endemic. *Bois Cassant* or *Mapou.*

2. BOERHAAVIA, Linn.

Flowers hermaphrodite. Perianth with lower half greenish-black, funnel-shaped, viscose, persistent, the upper half campanulate, corolline, deciduous, with 5 deltoid teeth. Stamens 2–3; filaments filiform, as long as the perianth; anthers globose. Ovary ovoid; style filiform, as long as the stamens; stigma capitate. Fruit enclosed in the enlarged clavate lower half of the perianth, which is united to its testa.—Annual or perennial weedy herbs, with opposite leaves and minute panicled flowers. DISTRIB. Cosmopolitan in the tropics. Species 20.

1. **B. diffusa,** *Linn.*; *Choisy in DC. Prod.* xiii. 2, 452. A perennial herb, with densely tufted glabrous terete diffuse stems 2–3 feet long. Leaves distant, petioled, ovate, membranous, green on both sides, obtuse or acute, $\frac{1}{2}$–$1\frac{1}{2}$ in. long, broadly rounded or subcordate at the base. Flowers in lax panicles with very slender pubescent branches, in clusters of 4–8 together on very short viscose pedicels with minute lanceolate bracts. Perianth $\frac{1}{24}$ in. long, the viscose green calycine and pinkish corolline portion of equal size. Accrescent fruit-perianth $\frac{1}{12}$ in. long, viscose, narrowed to the base. B. periplocifolia,

Sieb. Herb. Maur. No. 145, *non Comm.* B. procumbens and insularis, *Bojer, Hort. Maur.* 264.

MAURITIUS, SEYCHELLES, and RODRIGUEZ, common in waste ground. Through the tropics of the Old World. *Herbe Pintade.*

ORDER LXXIX.* BASELLACEÆ.

Basella rubra, Linn; Moq. in. DC. Prod. xiii. 2, 222, a native of Tropical Asia, commonly cultivated as a potherb, is subspontaneous in Mauritius and Rodriguez. It is a succulent annual herb, with climbing purple stems, large alternate petioled entire ovate acute leaves, rose-purple flowers in lax simple axillary spikes, a campanulate calyx-tube becoming berry-like as it matures, a biserial perianth with two navicular outer lobes and 5 deltoid inner ones, 5 included stamens inserted at the throat of the perianth, a 1-celled 1-ovulate ovary with three stigmas and small black berries with purple juice. *B. alba*, Linn., is a variety with green stems and white flowers and berries. *Brèdes Gandolles* or *Brèdes d'angole.*

ORDER LXXIX.** THYMELACEÆ.

Wikstromia viridiflora, Meisn. in DC. Prod. xiv. 546, (Daphne viridiflora, Wall.; Bojer, Hort. Maur. 276), a native of Tropical Asia and Polynesia, is now established on the hills in Mauritius. It is a much-branched glabrous shrub, with nearly sessile small oblong coriaceous leaves, greenish flowers few together in terminal corymbs, perianth hypocrateriform ¼ in. long with a cylindrical tube dilated into a globe at the base and 4 oblong spreading lobes, 8 stamens nearly sessile in two rows in the upper half of the tube, a superior 1-celled ovary with a single pendulous ovule and nearly sessile capitate stigma and a fleshy fruit the size of a pea. *Herbe à tourterelle.*

ORDER LXXX. AMARANTHACEÆ.

Flowers regular, hermaphrodite or polygamo-monoicous, the lateral ones of the clusters sometimes neuter. Perianth scariose; segments usually 5, sometimes 3, surrounded by 3 equal or unequal bracts, often of similar texture. Stamens 3–5, hypogynous; filaments free or united in a cupule at the base, often alternating with staminodia; anthers 2- or 1-celled. Ovary usually 1-celled and 1-ovuled; style absent or filiform; stigma capitate or 2-3-cleft. Fruit in the Mauritian genera always a utricle, which in *Amaranthus* dehisces horizontally round the middle. Seed solitary, with a peripheric embryo and a round central mass of farinaceous albumen.—Herbs with simple entire opposite or alternate leaves and persistent minute scariose flowers clustered in spikes or round heads. DISTRIB. Tropics of both hemispheres. Species 400.

Anthers 2-celled.
  Abortive lateral flowers none.
    Utricle with circumscissile dehiscence . . . . * AMARANTHUS.
    Utricle indehiscent.
      Flowers woolly . . . . 1. ÆRVA.
      Flowers naked . . . . 2. ACHYRANTHES.
  Lateral flowers represented by hooked spines . . . . 3. CYATHULA.
Anthers 1-celled . . . . 4. ALTERNANTHERA.

* AMARANTHUS, Linn.

Flowers polygamous, each enveloped in three bracts like the perianth-segments. Perianth of 5 or 3 free equal scariose glabrous segments. Filaments free, subulate, as many as the perianth-segments; anthers 2-celled; staminodia none. Ovary 1-celled; ovule solitary; stigmas 2–3, sessile, subulate. Fruit a membranous utricle, with circumscissile dehiscence. Seed shining, lenticular.—Annual herbs, with alternate entire petioled leaves, the numerous minute flowers in axillary and terminal spikes and panicles. DISTRIB. Common tropical weeds; some species widely cultivated. Species about 20.

Perianth-segments and stamens 5.
  Stems spinose . . . . * A. SPINOSUS.
  Stems unarmed.
    Bracts much longer than the perianth . . . . * A. HYBRIDUS.
    Bracts about as long as the perianth . . . . * A. TRISTIS.
Perianth-segments and stamens 3 . . . . * A. GANGETICUS.

* *A. spinosus*, Linn.; Moq. in DC. Prod. xiii. 2, 260, a universal tropical weed, is frequent in Mauritius. It has a comparatively slender branched erect stem armed at the nodes with spreading spines $\frac{1}{4}$–$\frac{1}{2}$ in. long, petioled ovate-rhomboid leaves, flowers in globose clusters in the axils of the lower leaves and spikes in the axils of the upper ones forming a little branched caudate panicle, pentamerous flowers under $\frac{1}{12}$ in. long with ovate scariose obtuse or subacute perianth-segments, unequal subulate bracts equalling or exceeding the perianth, and a utricle as long as the perianth. *Brèdes Malabares à piquans.*

* *A. hybridus*, Linn.; Moq. in DC. Prod. xiii. 2, 259, (A. lætus, *Willd.*), a widely-cultivated species of doubtful origin, is said by Bojer to be naturalised in Mauritius in the streets of Port Louis and other places. It is a stout erect unarmed annual, 3–4 feet high, with large petioled oblong acute leaves, flowers in small panicles from the axils of the leaves and a very large and compound one from the top of the stem, pentamerous flowers $\frac{1}{12}$ in. long with lanceolate acuminate segments scariose with a green keel, lanceolate-subulate bracts usually twice as long as the perianth, and a utricle as long as the perianth. *Brèdes Malabares.*

* *A. tristis*, Linn.; Moq. in DC. Prod. xiii. 2, 260; Wight, Ic. t. 514, 713. (A. caracasanus, *H.B.K.*), a cosmopolitan tropical weed, is plentiful in Mauritius and has been gathered by Dr. Balfour in Rodrigues. It

has comparatively slender unarmed stems 1½–2 feet high, ovate-rhomboid petioled leaves, cylindrical spikes simple in the axils of the leaves, and forming a slightly compound terminal panicle, oblong subacute perianth-segments under $\frac{1}{12}$ in. long, lanceolate-subulate bracts scarcely exceeding the flower, and a utricle as long as the perianth.

* *A. gangeticus*, Linn.; Moq. in DC. Prod. xiii. 2, 261, (A. mangostanus, *Linn.*; A. oleraceus, *Wight, Ic. t.* 715; *Bojer, Hort. Maur.* 266, *non Linn.*), commonly cultivated in the tropics of the Old World, is subspontaneous in Mauritius. It is a stout erect glabrous annual with little-branched stems 2–3 feet high, distinctly petioled ovate or lanceolate acute leaves, trimerous flowers in dense globose clusters in the axils of the leaves, and forming terminal spikes or panicles, perianth-segments ⅛ in. long scariose with a green keel running out into a distinct cusp, stamens 3, bracts and utricle as long as the perianth. *A. melancholicus*, Linn., is a variety with the globose clusters of flowers all axillary, and *A. tricolor*, Linn., a similar form with bright-coloured variegated leaves (red, purple and yellow). *Brèdes Malabares.*

1. ÆRVA, Forsk.

Flowers hermaphrodite. Bracts 3, ovate, shorter than the flower. Perianth-segments 5, oblanceolate, woolly, permanently conniving. Stamens 5; filaments joined at the base; staminodia present; anthers 2-celled. Ovary 1-celled, 1-ovuled; style very short; stigmas 2, minute. Utricle indehiscent. Seed solitary, vertical, very minute.—Annuals or perennials; leaves usually alternate; spikes in the axils of the leaves, solitary or fascicled. DISTRIB. Tropics of the Old World. Species 20.

Perennials.
  Large, with densely woolly flowers . . . . 1. A. LANATA.
  Dwarf, with thinly woolly flowers . . . . 2. A. CONGESTA.
Annual . . . . 3. A. BRACHIATA.

1. **A. lanata,** *Juss.*; *Moq. in DC. Prod.* xiii. 2, 303. Perennial, with much-branched downy stems 1–3 feet long. Leaves ½–1 in. long, opposite or alternate, ovate or obovate, obtuse or acute, membranous, distinctly petioled; base cuneate-spathulate. Spikes ¼–½ in., oblong or cylindrical, sessile, solitary or fascicled in the axils of the leaves. Perianth $\frac{1}{24}$ in. long, white, very woolly, twice as long as the deltoid densely pilose bracts. Staminodes deltoid-cuspidate, shorter than the filaments. *Wight, Ic. t.* 723.

MAURITIUS, on the Pouce and at Grand Bassin, *Bojer!* Through the tropics of the Old World. *Æ. villosa*, Moq. in DC. Prod. xiii. 2, 304, gathered in Mauritius by Coulon, seems to be a shrubby variety of this species with spikes ¼ inch long, and flowers $\frac{1}{12}$ in. long.

2. **A. congesta,** *Balf. fil.* Perennial, the wiry trailing sub-glabrous stems forming a dense tuft 3–4 inches across. Leaves opposite and alternate, obovate-spathulate, subcoriaceous, glabrous, obtuse

or cuspidate, $\frac{1}{12}$–$\frac{1}{8}$ in. long, narrowed into a distinct petiole. Spikes globose or oblong, $\frac{1}{12}$–$\frac{1}{8}$ in. long, from the axils of the congested upper leaves. Perianth-segments $\frac{1}{24}$ in. long, densely pilose, dirty white, oblong-lanceolate, cuspidate, twice as long as the deltoid glabrous bracts.

RODRIGUEZ, only on coral, near the shore, *Balfour !* Endemic.

3. **A. brachiata,** *Mart.*; *Moq. in DC. Prod.* xiii. 2, 304. A much-branched erect glabrous annual, with stems $\frac{1}{4}$–1 foot long. Leaves alternate and opposite, petioled, oblong-spathulate or lanceolate, acute, glabrous, membranous, $\frac{1}{2}$–1 in. long. Spikes $\frac{1}{4}$–1 in. long, oblong or cylindrical, all axillary, sessile, usually fascicled. Perianth white, $\frac{1}{12}$ in. long; segments oblanceolate cuspidate, very woolly, twice as long as the deltoid bracts. Staminodia deltoid, very minute. Æ. chenopodiifolia, *Bojer*, *Hort. Maur.* 268.

MAURITIUS, in sandy soil near the sea. Tropical Asia and Africa.

2. ACHRYANTHES, Linn.

Flowers hermaphrodite. Bracts 2–3, subspinose, subequilateral. Segments of perianth 5, permanently erect, not pilose. Stamens 5; filaments joined at the base, alternating with inflexed staminodes, which are fimbriated at the tip; anthers 2-celled. Ovary 1-celled, 1-ovuled; style filiform; stigma capitate. Utricle indehiscent.—Herbs, with opposite leaves, the flowers in long terminal spikes. DISTRIB. Weeds of the tropical zone of the Old World. Species about a dozen.

1. **A. aspera,** *Linn. Sp.* 295. An erect shrubby annual, with thinly pilose branched stems 2–5 feet high. Leaves opposite, obovate, petioled, entire, 1–3 in. long, obtuse or acute, thinly white-silky beneath. Spikes $\frac{1}{2}$–1 ft. long, cernuous at the top, with a pubescent woody pilose nodose rachis. Flowers except the uppermost deflexed; bracts subulate, from a dilated base, straw-coloured, subspinescent, shorter than the perianth. Perianth-segments $\frac{1}{8}$ in. long, lanceolate, acute, firm, green, with pale edges. Staminodes joined with the dilated bases of the filaments into a cup.

MAURITIUS, SEYCHELLES, and RODRIGUEZ, a common weed. *A. argentea*, Lam., Sibth. and Sm., Flor. Græc. t. 244, probably identical with *A. borbonica*, Bojer, Hort. Maur. 267, is a variety with green flowers, leaves thicker and more densely silvery beneath and spinose bracts nearly or quite as long as the perianth. *A. mauritiana*, Moquin in DC. Prod. xiii. 2, 313, is a herbaceous form with very slender subglabrous stems, acute leaves, short spikes and brownish flowers. Spread through tropics of the Old World, and also naturalised occasionally in the New. *Herbe Sergent.*

3. CYATHULA, Lour.

Flowers in clusters, the fertile ones hermaphrodite, mixed with barren ones represented by copious hooked bristles. Bracts 3 to a flower. Perianth-segments 5, free, lanceolate, connivent. Stamens 5; filaments united at the base, alternating with 5 staminodes; anthers 2-celled. Ovary 1-celled, 1-ovuled; style filiform; stigma capitate. Utricle indehiscent. Seed vertical.—Herbs, with opposite entire leaves, the flowers in terminal spikes or globose heads. DISTRIB. Tropics of both hemispheres. Species about 10.

1. **C. prostrata,** *Blume: Moq. in DC. Prod.* xiii. 2, 326. An annual finely pilose herb, with stems slender and trailing, or more often erect and branched, 2–4 feet high. Leaves short-petioled, membranous, oblong, acute, 1–3 in. long, thinly pilose or glabrous. Spikes peduncled, terminal, 1–3-nate, $\frac{1}{4}$–$\frac{1}{2}$ foot long, dense in the upper half, lax in the lower. Perianth-segments lanceolate, $\frac{1}{12}$ in. long, dull green, cartilaginous, more or less pilose. Unmodified bracts deltoid-cuspidate, much shorter than the perianth. Hooked spines variable in size and length, often very numerous and as long as the perianth. *Achyranthes debilis*, Poir.; Bojer, Hort. Maur. 267. *Desmochæta micrantha*, DC.; Bojer loc. cit.

MAURITIUS and SEYCHELLES, in shaded woody situations. Very variable in habit and hairiness. *C. achyranthoides*, Moq. in DC. Prod. xiii. 2, 326, and *C. geminata*, Moq. loc. cit. 330, are tall erect subglabrous varieties with stouter spikes and larger flowers. Cosmopolitan in the tropics.

4. ALTERNANTHERA, Forsk.

Flowers hermaphrodite, all uniform and fertile, 3-bracteate. Perianth-segments 5, glabrous, lanceolate. Stamens 3; filaments united in a cup; staminodes subulate, entire; anthers 1-celled. Ovary 1-celled, 1-ovuled; style short; stigma capitate. Utricle indehiscent, obcordate, compressed. Seed vertical.—Trailing herbs, with opposite entire leaves, the flowers in small globose heads, sessile in their axils. DISTRIB. Cosmopolitan in the tropics. Species 30.

1. **A. sessilis,** *R. Br.; Moq. in DC. Prod.* xiii. 2, 357. An annual herb, with trailing glabrous or subglabrous jointed stems, rooting at the lower nodes. Leaves nearly sessile, oblanceolate or oblong-spathulate, 1–3 in. long, membranous, glabrous or subglabrous. Flowers in dense globose heads $\frac{1}{8}$–$\frac{1}{4}$ in. broad, in the axils of leaves, sessile or nearly so; bracts deltoid, the same texture as the perianth-segments, not more than a quarter their length. Perianth pure white, under $\frac{1}{12}$ in. long; segments lanceolate, acute, 1-nerved on the back. *A. denticulata*, R. Br.; Moq. in DC. Prod. xiii. 2, 356.

MAURITIUS, SEYCHELLES, and RODRIGUEZ, a common weed. Cosmopolitan in the tropics. *Brède amballage.*

Order LXXX.* CHENOPODIACEÆ.

Flowers hermaphrodite or unisexual. Perianth inferior, calyx-like; segments green, equal, free to the base, usually 5. Stamens 1-5, hypogynous or perigynous; anthers 2-celled, dehiscing longitudinally. Ovary 1-celled; ovule solitary; styles 2-4. Fruit an indehiscent 1-seeded utricle. Seeds with an embryo coiled round a mass of albumen or spiral.—Herbs or shrubs with alternate exstipulate leaves and abundant minute green flowers, variously arranged. Distrib. Temperate regions, both north and south. Species 450.

* CHENOPODIUM, Linn.

Flowers hermaphrodite. Perianth-segments 5, sometimes reduced to 3 in some of the flowers of the cluster. Stamens hypogynous or nearly so; filaments subulate. Disk none. Fruit a depresso-globose utricle, with a very thin pericarp, enclosed in the closed globose perianth. Seed with an embryo forming a ring on the outside of a round mass of flowery albumen.—Annual weeds, with alternate leaves, stems usually striped green and white, and abundant minute flowers in dense clusters. Distrib. Cosmopolitan. Species 50.

Scent aromatic; clusters of flowers forming leafy spikes . * C. ambrosioides.
Scent not aromatic; clusters of flowers forming leafless cymes.
  Upper leaves lanceolate entire . . . . * C. album.
  All the leaves rhomboid and sinuated . . . . * C. murale.

* *C. ambrosioides*, Linn.; Moq. in DC. Prod. xiii. 2, 72, a cosmopolitan weed, probably of Tropical American origin, is now frequent in Mauritius and was gathered by Dr. Balfour in Rodriguez. It is covered with minute glandular pubescence and has a strong aromatic scent. It has much-branched slender stems 1-3 feet high, lanceolate usually sinuated green leaves narrowed to both ends, and the globose clusters of flowers are placed on long branchlets and each is bracteated by a minute entire oblanceolate leaf. *Herbe Pipi. Thé du Mexique.*

* *C. album*, Linn.; Moq. in DC. Prod. xiii. 2, 70, the most abundant of all the species, originating in the temperate regions of the Old World, but now cosmopolitan, is frequent in Mauritius. It has stout much-branched erect stems 2 to 5 feet high, rhomboid slightly sinuated more or less mealy lower leaves and entire lanceolate upper ones, the clusters of flowers forming copious thyrsoid panicles above the leafy part of the stem. *Epinard sauvage.*

* *C. murale*, Linn.; Moq. in DC. Prod. xiii. 2 69, of north temperate Old World origin, has been gathered in Mauritius by Belanger, Dr. Ayres, and others. It resembles *C. album*, but differs by its larger green leaves, all rhomboid and copiously sinuated, cymes laxer and more corymbose and not forming an ample panicle above the leaves.

Order LXXXI. POLYGONACEÆ.

Flowers regular, usually hermaphrodite. Perianth-segments 5–6, free nearly or quite to the base, equal or unequal, usually petaloid. Stamens 5–8, hypogynous or perigynous; filaments subulate; anthers 2-celled, dehiscing longitudinally. Ovary superior, 1-celled; ovule 1, basal, orthotropous; styles 2–3; stigmas capitate. Fruit an indehiscent nut, lenticular or triquetrous. Seed albuminous.—Herbs or shrubs, with alternate simple leaves, sheathing membranous stipules (ochreæ) and small flowers variously arranged. Distrib. Cosmopolitan. Species 500.

Perianth-segments all alike. . . . . 1. Polygonum.
Inner perianth-segments becoming much larger than the outer * Rumex.

1. POLYGONUM, Linn.

Flowers hermaphrodite. Perianth-segments 5, oblong, petaloid, subequal. Stamens 5–8; filaments subulate, hypogynous. Ovary compressed or trigonous; styles 2–3. Fruit triquetrous or lenticular.—Herbs, with alternate leaves, large membranous sheathing stipules (ochreæ) and small flowers either in spikes or clustered in the axils of the leaves. Distrib. Cosmopolitan. Species 150.

Trailing annual with flowers fascicled in the axils of the leaves . . . . 1. P. aviculare.
Erect perennials with flowers in peduncled cylindrical spikes.
Leaves bristle-ciliated . . . . 2. P. Poiretii.
Leaves naked on the edge . . . . 3. P. senegalense.

1. **P. aviculare,** *Linn.* var. P. Dryandri, *Spreng.* A trailing glabrous much-branched annual, with slightly zigzag purple stems. Leaves sessile, spreading, oblanceolate, 1-nerved, $\frac{1}{4}$–$\frac{1}{2}$ in. long, the upper ones crowded; ochreæ small, lanceolate-deltoid, fringed at the tip. Flowers clustered in the axils of the leaves, nearly or quite sessile. Perianth $\frac{1}{12}$ in. long; segments oblong, reddish-white, with a green keel. Nut triquetrous, as long as the perianth. P. Roxburghii, *Meisn. in DC. Prod.* xiv. 93. P. hyssopifolium, *Bojer, Hort. Maur.* 271.

Mauritius, in sandy soil. A very variable cosmopolitan weed.

2. **P. Poiretii,** *Meisn. in DC. Prod.* xiv. 113. An erect perennial with stout nearly simple stems 2–3 feet high. Leaves lanceolate, 6–9 in. long, 1–1$\frac{1}{3}$ in. broad at the middle, acuminate, ciliated with strong bristles on the edge and midrib and on the short petiole; ochreæ

½–1 in. long, clasping all round the stem, the upper ones fringed at the tip. Spikes 2–6 to a stem, peduncled, cylindrical, 2–3 in. long; bracts scariose, obovate-amplexicaul, obtuse. Flowers several to each bract, on pedicels articulated at the tip. Perianth $\frac{1}{12}$ in. long, reddish-white, not glandular. Styles 2. Nut lenticular. P. serratum, *Poir. Ency.* vi. 144.

MAURITIUS, in the swamps of the Mare aux Vacouas, etc. Also Bourbon.

3. **P. senegalense,** *Meisn. in DC. Prod.* xiv. 123. A stout erect perennial, with stems sometimes 6–8 feet high. Leaves membranous, short-petioled, oblong-lanceolate, acuminate, 6–9 in. long, 2–2½ in. broad below the middle, densely glandular, not ciliated at the edge, obscurely pilose on the midrib below; ochreæ membranous, ¾–1 in. long, clasping all round the stem, the uppermost fringed at the tip. Spikes 4–8 to a stem, peduncled, cylindrical, 2–3 in. long; bracts flowers and nut just like those of *P. Poiretii.*

SEYCHELLES, frequent in damp places in Mahé, etc., *Wright! Horne,* 271! 556! Also Bourbon and Tropical Africa.

A dock, gathered by Dr. Balfour in several valleys in the centre of Rodrigues, is either the north temperate *Rumex crispus,* Linn, or a close ally. It has stout erect stems 3–4 feet high, long-petioled oblong root-leaves a foot long, a large dense panicle with ascending branches leafy only at the lowest nodes and round-cordate obscurely denticulate enlarged sepals ⅙ in. long and broad with an oblong tubercle in the centre and a deltoid point.

ORDER LXXXII. URTICACEÆ.

Flowers monochlamydeous, rarely achlamydeous, polygamo-monoicous or dioicous, regular or irregular. Perianth calyx-like, with usually 3 or 4 lobes, which are free or united at the base. Stamens as many as the perianth-lobes; filaments subulate, incurved in bud, and springing back elastically; anthers 2-celled, with longitudinal dehiscence. Ovary superior or rarely united to the perianth, 1-celled; ovule solitary, basal, erect, orthotropous; stigma subulate or penicillate. Seed minute, albuminous.—Herbs or shrubs with watery juice, hairs often stinging, leaves petioled stipulate simple, and minute copious flowers in clusters or cymes. DISTRIB. Cosmopolitan. Species 500.

Female perianth polyphyllous.
  Flowers of both sexes not on a common receptacle.
    Hairs stinging.
      Annual herbs . . . . * URTICA.
      Shrub . . . . 1. OBETIA.
    Hairs none (in the Mauritian species) . . . . 2. PILEA.
  Female flowers only on a discoid receptacle . . . . . . 3. PROCRIS.
  Flowers of both sexes on a discoid receptacle . . . . . 4. ELATOSTEMA.
Female perianth gamophyllous.
  Stigma penicillate . . . . 5. URERA.

Stigma subulate.
Fruit dry, free from the ovary.
Clusters in long spikes . . . . * BOEHMERIA.
Clusters sessile in the axils of the leaves . . . . 6. POUZOLZIA.
Fruit subbaccate and adherent to the ovary . . . 7. PIPTURUS.
Female perianth obsolete.
Stamens 4. Flowers without an involucre . . . . * PHENAX.
Stamens 1. Flowers surrounded by an involucre . . . 8. DROGUETIA.

* *Urtica urens*, Linn.; Wedd. in. DC. Prod. xvi. 40, the second commonest herbaceous stinging nettle of the north temperate zone, is established in some places in Mauritius. It is an annual herb, with small distinctly-petioled deeply toothed leaves as broad as long, flowers in small congested monoicous cymes in the axils of the leaves, 4 free perianth-segments, 4 stamens and a compressed ovate achene as long as the perianth with a sessile penicillate stigma. *Ortie de France.*

1. OBETIA, Gaud.

Flowers polygamo-dioicous. Male perianth 5-partite, with oblong obtuse lobes and 5 stamens round a rudimentary pistil. Female perianth 4-partite, with unequal segments. Ovary at first symmetrical, becoming oblique as it matures; stigma nearly sessile. Fruit an ovoid compressed achene.—Erect shrubs with large free stipules, copious stinging hairs, alternate petioled leaves and flowers in axillary panicles. DISTRIB. One other species in Madagascar.

1. **O. ficifolia**, *Gaud. Bot. Voy. Bon, Atl. t.* 82. Branches rugose, $\frac{1}{4}$–$\frac{1}{2}$ in. thick, with the leaves crowded at the top. Leaves membranous, as broad as long (3–9 in.), deeply cordate, palmatifid with 3–7 deltoid inciso-crenate lobes, green and sparsely hispid above, paler and densely bristly beneath; petiole 2–6 in. long, finely pubescent; stipules large, free, scariose, persistent. Flowers in ample peduncled panicles with bristly branches, with the flowers of both sexes in sessile clusters. Achene $\frac{1}{24}$ in. long, included in the accrescent perianth. Urtica ficifolia, *Poir.*; *Bojer*, *Hort. Maur.* 293.

MAURITIUS, in woods, *Telfair!* RODRIGUEZ, in the upper part of the valleys, not common, *Balfour!* Also Bourbon and Madagascar. *Figue marron.*

2. PILEA, Lindl.

Flowers polygamo-monoicous or dioicous, those of both sexes in cymes without any discoid receptacle. Male perianth 4-partite, with ovate white or reddish segments with usually a mucro below the tip; stamens 4, surrounding a rudimentary ovary. Female perianth 3-partite, with unequal segments. Ovary permanently erect, ovoid, surrounded by rudimentary stamens; stigma subsessile, penicillate. Fruit a compressed achene.—Annual or perennial herbs, with opposite or whorled leaves.

Hairs absent from all the Mauritian species and when present not stinging. Distrib. Round the world in the tropics. Species 150.

Leaves entire . . . . 1. P. articulata.
Leaves toothed.
Cymes peduncled.
Dwarf trailers with small leaves.
Peduncle much shorter than leaves . . . . . . 2. P. lævicaulis.
Peduncle as long as leaves . . . . 3. P. sessilifolia.
Erect, with leaves ½–1½ in. long . . . . 4. P. urticifolia.
Erect, with leaves 3–4 in. long . . . . 5. P. lucens.
Cymes sessile in the axils of the leaves.
Petioles $\frac{1}{12}$–⅛ in. long.
Leaves oblanceolate-rhomboid . . . . 6. P. cuneiformis.
Leaves oblong-rhomboid . . . . 7. P. atroviridis.
Petioles ½–1½ in. long.
Herbaceous, with slender stems . . . . 8. P. Balfourii.
Shrubby, with stout stems . . . . 9. P. verbascifolia.

1. **P. articulata,** *Wedd. in DC. Prod.* xvi. 109. A dioicous perennial, with erect simple stems 1–1½ foot high, with short upper internodes. Leaves ovate-lanceolate, entire, acuminate, rounded at the base, triplinerved, 2–3 in. long; petiole ¼–½ in. long; stipules very small, deltoid, connate beneath the petiole. Male cymes capitate, the size of a pea, on a peduncle as long as the petiole; pedicels very short. Perianth-segments scarcely at all mucronate below the tip.

Mauritius, *Commerson, Du Petit Thouars.* Endemic.

2. **P. lævicaulis,** *Wedd. in DC. Prod.* xvi. 129. A dioicous perennial, with wiry trailing much-branched stems a foot or more long. Leaves opposite or whorled, the upper ones crowded, dark green, subcoriaceous, triplinerved, ovate, rounded at the base, ¼–½ in. long, obtuse, entire or furnished with 1–2 distinct teeth on each side; petiole $\frac{1}{12}$–⅛ in. long; stipules minute, deltoid, persistent. Cymes few, dense, shortly-peduncled, shorter than the leaves. Male perianth $\frac{1}{24}$ in. long, the segments mucronate below the tip.

Mauritius, on damp rocks of the Pouce Mountain, *Boivin, Blackburn!* Both this and *P. sessilifolia* may prove montane varieties of *P. urticifolia*. *P. trilobata*, Weddell loc. cit. (*Urtica*, Poir.) gathered in Mauritius by Commerson, judging from the description, does not differ from this materially.

3. **P. sessilifolia,** *Wedd. in DC. Prod.* xvi. 125. A dioicous perennial, with firm trailing stems ½–1 foot long. Leaves opposite or 4-nate, elliptic or ovate, usually narrowed to both ends, distinctly toothed, obscurely triplinerved, ½–1 in. long; petiole none or very short; stipules minute, deltoid, persistent. Cymes a single cluster on a peduncle longer than the leaves. Male perianth $\frac{1}{12}$ in. long, the segments mucronate below the tip. Achene ovoid, rather longer than its perianth. Urtica sessilifolia, *Poir. Encyc.* iv. 642.

Mauritius, *Commerson.* Endemic.

4. **P. urticifolia**, *Blume, Mus. Bot. Lug. Bat.* ii. 47. A monoicous perennial, with firm erect branched cæspitose stems 1–1½ ft. long, naked in the lower half. Leaves opposite or the upper whorled, ovate or oblong-rhomboid, membranous, acuminate, rounded or cuneate at the base, broadly inciso-crenate, triplinerved or penninerved, ½–1½ in. long, often purplish beneath; petiole ¼–¾ in. long; stipules minute, deltoid. Cymes few-flowered, usually lax and peduncled, sometimes clustered and sessile. Male perianth $\frac{1}{12}$ in. long, with hyaline segments distinctly mucronate below the tip. Achene ovoid, compressed, exceeding the female perianth, wrinkled, distinctly bordered. Urtica pendula *Willd.; Bojer, Hort. Maur.* 293. Bœhmeria urticæfolia, *Spreng.*; *Bojer, Hort. Maur.* 294, Pilea rupipendia, *Wedd. in DC. Prod.* xvi. 123.

MAURITIUS, common in forests throughout the island. Also Bourbon and East Tropical Africa. I have ascertained, by inspection of the type specimen from Bourbon, gathered by Thouin, now in the Smithian herbarium, that this is *Parietaria urticifolia*, Linn. fil. Suppl. 434.

5. **P. lucens,** *Wedd. in DC. Prod.* xvi. 130. A dioicous glabrous perennial, with erect stems 4–5 feet high. Leaves opposite, the upper internodes ½–1 in. long, ovate, membranous, scabrous, acute or acuminate, distinctly triplinerved, 3–4 in. long, with numerous broad teeth; petiole 1-2 in. long; stipules minute, deltoid. Cymes 1–2 in. long, usually in pairs, with lax spreading slender branches bearing small clusters of flowers. Male perianth under $\frac{1}{12}$ in. long, the whitish segments mucronate below the tip. Achene brown, glabrous, compressed, very small Urtica cuspidata, *Willd.; Bojer, Hort. Maur.* 293. U. triplinervia, *Poir.; Bojer, loc. cit.*

MAURITIUS, in the forests of the Pouce range, etc. Also Bourbon and Malay isles.

6. **P. cuneiformis,** *Wedd. in DC. Prod.* xvi. 133. A monoicous glabrous perennial, with densely tufted branched stems, varying from a couple of inches to a foot long. Leaves crowded, opposite, subcoriaceous, oblanceolate-rhomboid, varying from ¼ in. to 3 in. long, distinctly triplinerved, obtuse or acute, toothed in the upper half, cuneate and entire in the lower half; petiole very short; stipules deltoid, very minute. Cymes many-flowered, dense, deltoid, sessile in the axils of the leaves. Male flowers pedicillate, $\frac{1}{12}$ in. long, the segments mucronate below the tip. Achene ovoid, smooth, rather longer than its perianth. Urtica cuneiformis, *Poir.; Bojer. Hort. Maur.* 293.

MAURITIUS, in rocky woods of the Pouce range, etc. Endemic.

7. **P. atroviridis,** *Baker.* An erect monoicous perennial, with tufted wiry branched stems a foot long. Leaves opposite or the upper 4-nate, oblong-rhomboid, subobtuse, dark green, distinctly triplinerved, ¾–1 in. long, inciso-crenate in the upper half, crenate and entire in the

lower half; petiole $\frac{1}{12}$–$\frac{1}{8}$ in. long; stipules minute, deltoid. Cymes few-flowered, glomerate, sessile in the axils of the leaves. Achene $\frac{1}{32}$ in. long, pale brown, smooth, longer than its perianth.

MAURITIUS, in shaded woods, *Carmichael!* Midway between *P. urticifolia* and *cuneiformis*. Endemic.

8. **P. Balfourii,** *Baker*. A monoicous perennial, with densely tufted slender square stems 1–1¼ foot long. Leaves membranous, oblong-rhomboid, 1–3 in. long, acute or acuminate, deeply inciso-crenate, triplinerved from the base nearly to the apex, cuneate and entire at the base; petiole ¼–1 in. long; stipules minute, deltoid. Cymes deltoid, many-flowered, ¼–⅜ in. broad, sessile in the axils of the leaves. Male flowers distinctly pedicellate. Perianth $\frac{1}{24}$ in. long, the segments distinctly mucronate. Achene ovoid, compressed, smooth, acutely margined.

RODRIGUEZ, on the faces of damp cliffs in the highest part of the valleys, *Balfour!* Endemic.

9. **P. verbascifolia,** *Wedd. in DC. Prod.* xvi. 132. A shrubby perennial, with simple or branched erect woody stems 3–4 feet high. Leaves oblanceolate-oblong, distinctly triplinerved from the base to the apex, 4–8 in. long, membranous, acute, obscurely denticulate, cuneate at the base; petiole channelled, ½–1½ in long; stipules large, deciduous, obtuse, oblong-spathulate. Cymes copiously branched, dense, sessile in the axils of the leaves, deltoid, ½–¾ in. broad. Male flowers pedicellate, ⅛ in. long, with reddish acute segments, distinctly mucronate below the tip. Achenes brown, compressed, with an acute edge, as long as their perianth. Urtica longifolia, *Willd.*; *Bojer. Hort. Maur.* 292.

MAURITIUS, in the mountain forests of Grand-port, Savanne, etc. Endemic.

3. PROCRIS, Comm.

Flowers monoicous or dioicous, the females sessile on a fleshy discoid receptacle, the males cymose. Male perianth 5-partite, with obovate-oblong segments; stamens 5, surrounding a rudimentary pistil. Female perianth of 3–4 oblong greenish-white fleshy persistent segments; ovary ovoid; stigma sessile, penicillate. Fruit a compressed achene, sessile on the fleshy receptacle.—Glabrous succulent undershrubs, the leaves alternate or, if opposite, one of the pair large and the other very small; the female heads sessile or peduncled. DISTRIB. Tropics of the Old World. Species 4.

1. **P. pedunculata,** *Wedd. in DC. Prod.* xv. 191. A monoicous undershrub, glabrous in all its parts, with simple or branched stems 1–2 feet long. Leaves oblique, lanceolate, 3–6 in. long, acuminate, unequally cuneate at the base, entire or obscurely toothed, subcoriaceous, penninerved, with the main arcuate-ascending veins only distinct; petiole ¼–½ long. Female flowers in globose sessile heads ¼–⅓ in. thick, not surrounded by an involucre. Male flowers in peduncled

usually simple crowded cymes. Male perianth $\frac{1}{12}$ in. long. P. cephalida, *Comm.; Bojer, Hort. Maur.* 294. P. integrifolia, *Bojer, loc. cit. non D. Don.*

MAURITIUS and SEYCHELLES, in dense woods. Spread through the tropics of the Old World. *P. integrifolia*, Bojer, is simply a form with small entire leaves and quite different from the Himalayan plant of D. Don, which is an *Elatostema.*

4. ELATOSTEMA, Forst.

Monoicous or dioicous, the flowers of both sexes placed on a flat fleshy receptacle surrounded by an involucre, and mixed with linear bracts. Male perianth with 4–5 segments mucronate below the tip, and 4–5 perigynous stamens surrounding a rudimentary pistil. Female perianth usually triphyllous and minute. Ovary oblong, surrounded by rudimentary stamens; stigma sessile, densely penicillate. Fruit a compressed superior achene.—Annual or perennial herbs, with distichous, usually alternate leaves and copious sessile or peduncled heads. DISTRIB. Tropics of the Old world. Species 50.

1. **E. fagifolium,** *Gaud.; Wedd. in DC. Prod.* xvi. 174. A dioicous perennial herb, 1–2 feet high, simple or little branched, glabrous or nearly so in all its parts, with firm suffruticose stems. Leaves 3–9 in. long, oblique, oblanceolate, acuminate, unequally cuneate at the base, inciso-crenate, membranous, bright green, penninerved, with distinct veinlets and copious dots; petiole $\frac{1}{4}$–$\frac{1}{2}$ in. long; stipules linear, $\frac{1}{2}$–1 in. long. Heads numerous, globose, sessile or shortly peduncled, $\frac{1}{4}$–$\frac{1}{2}$ in. broad; bracts of the involucre $\frac{1}{4}$ in. long, lanceolate, acute, similar to the leaves in texture. Segments of the male perianth ovate, with a bristly mucro. Procris fagifolia, *Poir.; Bojer. Hort. Maur.* 294.

MAURITIUS, in dense woods, usually on old trunks. Also Bourbon, Madagascar and Comoros.

5. URERA, Gaud.

Flowers polygamo-dioicous. Male perianth 4–5-partite, with ovate segments, membranous at the tip, and 4–5 stamens round a rudimentary pistil. Female perianth gamophyllous, with 4 unequal lobes. Ovary ovoid, straight or oblique, with a subsessile penicillate stigma. Fruit a compressed achene included in the fleshy cupular perianth, but entirely superior.—Erect or climbing shrubs, sometimes as in our plant glabrous, sometimes furnished with stinging bristles; leaves alternate; flowers in axillary heads or cymes. DISTRIB. Round the world in the tropics. Species 18.

1. **U. acuminata,** *Gaudich.; Wedd. in DC. Prod.* xvi. 96. A subscandent shrub, glabrous in all its parts, with smooth brown branchlets

rugose with the scars of the fallen leaves. Leaves cordate-ovate, green, subcoriaceous, cuspidate, entire, triplinerved, 2–4 in. long; petiole ½–1 in. long; stipules brown, lanceolate, persistent, ¼ in. long. Flowers in copious lax short peduncled compound cymes 1–2 in. long, spreading from the nodes of leafless branches. Female flowers sessile, solitary or clustered. Achene ovoid, compressed, yellowish, nearly $\frac{1}{12}$ in. long, slightly exceeding the campanulate fleshy reddish perianth lobes, the densely penicillate stigma slightly oblique. Urtica acuminata, *Poir.*; *Bojer*, *Hort. Maur.* 283.

MAURITIUS, in woods of Signal Mountain range, etc., *Carmichael! Boston! Ayres!* Also Timor.

* *Bœhmeria platyphylla*, D. Don.; Wedd. in DC. Prod. xvi. 210, a common and variable weed of Tropical Asia, is subspontaneous in Mauritius. It is an erect perennial 3–6 feet high, with glabrous or hispid stems, small free lanceolate stipules, long-petioled large opposite ovate acute toothed membranous subglabrous or pubescent leaves, flowers in lax or close globose clusters on simple or sparsely panicled spikes ½–1 foot long, male perianth 4-partite with 4 stamens, female perianth tubular 4-toothed only at the tip closely investing the compressed oblong achene, which is tipped with a persistent filiform stigma longer than itself. The common Mauritian form is var. *macrostachya*, Wedd. (Urtica caudata, *Poir. Ency.* iv. 640; Splitgerbera macrostachya, *Wight*, *Ic. t.* 1977), with long lax simple spikes and small subglabrous leaves. Var. *molliuscula*, Wedd. (Sieber, 375), is a form with smaller thicker softly pubescent leaves. Dr. Weddell also gives *B. stipularis*, Wedd. in DC. Prod. xvi. 209, as a Mauritian species. This is marked by its very large (an inch or more long) connate intrapetiolar pubescent stipules and copiously-panicled flower spikes.

6. POUZOLZIA, Gaud.

Flowers polygamo-monoicous. Male perianth in our species cut halfway down into 5 lobes. Stamens 5, surrounding a rudimentary ovary. Female perianth gamophyllous, with 5 small teeth at the contracted mouth, including the free ovary. Stigma filiform. Fruit dry, globose.—Undershrubs or herbs; leaves alternate, entire or toothed; flowers of both sexes in small globose clusters, which either form spikes or are placed in the axils of the leaves. DISTRIB. Tropics of both hemispheres. Species 35.

1. **P. lævigata,** *Gaudich.*; *Wedd. in DC. Prod.* xvi. 224. An undershrub, with stout glabrous brown branchlets marked with the scars of the fallen leaves. Leaves oblong-lanceolate, acute, deltoid at the base, entire, glabrous, 2–4 inches long, deep green above, pale green beneath, distinctly triplinerved; petiole ¼–½ in. long; stipules ¼ in. long,

lanceolate, deciduous. Flowers in dense globose clusters $\frac{1}{8}$ in. broad, sessile in the axils of the leaves, which are crowded near the top of the branchlets. Perianth of both sexes $\frac{1}{24}$ in. long, that of the males cut halfway down into deltoid lobes. Fruit perianth rugose, globose, winged and crested. Parietaria lævigata, *Poir. Encyc.* v. 17.

Var. P. CANESCENS, *Gaudich.; Wedd. in DC. Prod.* xvi. 225. Branchlets, leaves on both surfaces and flowers finely pubescent. Parietaria canescens, *Poir.*

MAURITIUS, in woods of the Pouce and Savanne ranges, both varieties. Also Bourbon.

7. PIPTURUS, Wedd.

Flowers polygamo-dioicous. Male perianth with 4 ovate acute lobes and 4 stamens surrounding a rudimentary ovary. Female perianth bottle-shaped, minutely toothed at the contracted mouth, surrounding and adnate to the ovary; style filiform. Fruit subbaccate.—Shrubs with alternate petioled leaves, without any stinging hairs, the flowers of both sexes in globose clusters either forming spikes or sessile in the axils of the leaves. DISTRIB. Tropics of the Old World. Species 8.

Leaves entire, not silvery beneath . . . . 1. P. ROTUNDIFOLIUS.
Leaves inciso-crenate, silvery beneath . . . . 2. P. INCANUS.

1. **P. rotundifolius,** *Wedd. in DC. Prod.* xvi. 235[18]. A climbing shrub, with finely pubescent branchlets. Leaves oblong or round-ovate, rounded or subcordate at the base, acute, entire, glabrous above, with fine adpressed pubescence on the ribs beneath; petiole 1–1½ in. long; stipules ovate-lanceolate, $\frac{1}{6}$–$\frac{1}{4}$ in. long. Clusters of flowers in ternate spikes 2–6 in. long, simple or branched at the very base, the upper bracteated by very small leaves. Fruit-perianth ovoid, pubescent, $\frac{1}{12}$ in. long, much shorter than the stigma. Urtica rotundifolia, *Poir.: Bojer, Hort. Maur.* 293.

MAURITIUS, in damp woods of the Pouce and Quartier Militaire. Endemic. *Bois à gratter.*

2. **P. incanus,** *Wedd. in DC. Prod.* xvi. 235[18]. A much-branched shrub 3–5 feet high, with finely pubescent branches. Leaves membranous, round-cordate, 3–6 in. long, acute, inciso-crenate, green and glabrescent above, silvery beneath; stipules deciduous, deltoid, $\frac{1}{6}$–$\frac{1}{4}$ in. long. Flowers in spaced globose clusters $\frac{1}{8}$ in. thick, in short simple or branched spikes from the axils of the leaves. Female perianth $\frac{1}{24}$ in. long, silvery, shorter than the stigma. P. velutinus, *Wedd. olim.*

SEYCHELLES, on the beach at Grand Anse in the island of Praslin, *Horne*, 562! Also Malaya and Polynesia. We have *P. argenteus*, Wedd., which is probably a mere variety, from Galega Island, *Bojer!* and it is *Bœhmeria frondosa*, Bojer, Hort. Maur. 294, but not of D. Don. *Bois Cendre.*

* *Phenax Sonneratii*, Wedd. in D.C. Prod. xvi. 235[37] (P. vulgaris, Wedd. olim), a native of Tropical America, was gathered by Commerson in Mauritius, no doubt introduced. It is a polygamo-monoicous glabrous perennial, with much-branched shrubby brown stems, alternate middle-sized petioled toothed oblong acute leaves, flowers in dense globose axillary clusters, a gamophyllous male perianth with 4 deltoid mucronate lobes, 4 stamens, an obsolete female perianth and an ovoid ventricose brown achene tipped with a persistent filiform stigma as long as itself and subtended by a scariose bract.

8. DROGUETIA, Gaudich.

Flowers monoicous, placed in a gamophyllous involucre, the females in the centre. Male perianth monophyllous, with a single stamen, its margin lacerated when expanded. Female flower without any perianth. Ovary woolly or glabrous, with a filiform stigma. Fruit an achene.—Nettle-like perennial herbs, with opposite or alternate toothed leaves, the involucres solitary or in clusters, often in the axils of the leaves. DISTRIB. Africa and East Indies. Species 4.

Tall, with leaves 2–3 in. long . . . . 1. D. LEPTOSTACHYS.
Dwarf, with leaves ½ in. long . . . . 2. D. THOUARSIANA.

1. **D. leptostachys,** *Wedd. in DC. Prod.* xvi. 235[37]. A perennial herb, with firm slender finely pilose stems. Leaves ovate, membranous, acute, 1–2 in. long, distinctly toothed, rounded and entire at the base, green and thinly bristly on both sides, distinctly triplinerved; stipules distinct, linear, deciduous; petiole ¼–½ in. long. Involucres many-flowered, campanulate, pubescent, $\frac{1}{12}$ in. long, forming terminal and peduncled axillary spikes and sometimes prolonged down into the axils of the leaves. Female flower solitary in the centre of the cluster, with a flexuose stigma as long as the involucre. Achene densely pilose. D. elliptica, *Gaudich. Bot. Voy. Bonite Atl. t.* 86. D. ovata, *Gaudich.; Wedd. Monog.* 540 *t.* 19. f. 12. Urtica leptostachys, *Juss.; Bojer, Hort. Maur.* 294.

MAURITIUS, in shaded places, *Carmichael!* Also Bourbon.

2. **D. Thouarsiana,** *Gaudich. Bot. Voy. Bonite Atl. t.* 87. Stems pubescent, densely tufted, ½ ft. long. Leaves distinctly petioled, ovate, sharply toothed, ⅛–¼ in. long. Involucres solitary, forming close terminal spikes 1–2 in. long and prolonged into the axils of the upper leaves. *Wedd. in DC. Prod.* xvi. 235[38].

MAURITIUS. Also Bourbon. Probably a mere montane variety of *D. leptostachys.*

ORDER LXXXIII. ULMACEÆ.

Flowers regular, monochlamydeous, polygamo-monoicous or hermaphrodite. Perianth calyx-like, inferior, 4–5-lobed, with imbricate or valvate æstivation. Stamens as many as the perianth-lobes and opposite to them; filaments free, subulate; anthers 2-celled with longitudinal dehiscence. Ovary in the Mauritian genera 1-celled; ovule solitary, pendulous; stigmas 2, sessile. Fruit 1-celled, with a solitary seed, fleshy or dry. Seed exalbuminous.—Shrubs or trees, with alternate petioled stipulate simple leaves and minute clustered or cymose flowers. DISTRIB. Cosmopolitan. Species 140.

Perianth caducous. Stamens incurved in æstivation . . . . 1. CELTIS.
Perianth persistent. Stamens suberect in æstivation . . . . 2. SPONIA.

1. CELTIS, Linn.

Flowers polygamo-monoicous. Perianth 5-partite, the segments imbricate, caducous. Stamens 5, inserted on the pilose disk round a rudimentary ovary; filaments subulate, incurved in æstivation. Ovary 1-celled, 1-ovuled, surrounded by the disk and imperfect stamens; stigmas 2, subulate, deciduous. Fruit a fleshy drupe with a hard endocarp. — Trees or shrubs with triplinerved toothed or entire leaves and axillary inflorescence. DISTRIB. Cosmopolitan. Species 50.

1. **C. mauritiana,** *Planch. in Ann. Sc. Nat.* 1848, 307; *DC. Prod.* xvii. 184. A tree, glabrous in all its parts, with slender terete branches. Leaves oblong, acuminate, entire, subcoriaceous, bright green, subequally deltoid at the base, triplinerved more than halfway up, with reticulated raised veinlets; petiole $\frac{1}{4}$–$\frac{1}{2}$ in. long; stipules small, lanceolate, caducous. Male flowers in small sessile or nearly sessile clusters in the axils of the leaves. Perianth segments $\frac{1}{24}$ in. long, oblong, obtuse, glabrous. Female flowers solitary on short pedicels with a similar perianth. Drupe broad ovoid, $\frac{1}{3}$ in. long.

MAURITIUS, *Commerson! Carmichael!* Also Bourbon.

2. SPONIA, Commers.

Flowers polygamo-monoicous. Perianth 5-partite, persistent, the segments scarcely imbricated. Stamens 5, inserted on the disk round a more or less imperfect ovary; filaments erect in bud, diverging in the expanded flower. Ovary 1-celled, 1-ovuled, surrounded by more or less imperfect stamens; stigmas 2, subulate, diverging. Fruit a small drupe with thin flesh and a firm endocarp.—Trees with triplinerved leaves with an unequal base and minute flowers in axillary cymes. DISTRIB. Tropics of both hemispheres. Species 20.

1. **S. orientalis,** *Planch. in Ann. Sc. Nat.* 1848, 323; *DC. Prod.* xvii. 200. An unarmed tree, reaching a height of 40–50 feet, with strigose terete branchlets. Leaves subcoriaceous, green and scabrous above, clothed with thin white silky pubescence beneath, ovate, acute, 3–4 in. long, denticulate, unequal at the base, broadly cordate on the upper side and merely rounded on the lower, triplinerved more than halfway up with several other distinct ribs parallel with two first side ones; petiole $\frac{1}{4}$–$\frac{1}{3}$ in. long. Flowers in dense subsessile cymes $\frac{1}{8}$–$\frac{1}{4}$ in.

broad in the axils of the leaves, dichotomous with spreading main branches; bracts lanceolate, persistent, as long as the buds. Perianth $\frac{1}{12}$ in. long, green and naked on the outside, pilose within. Drupe ovoid, glabrous, $\frac{1}{8}$ in. long, surrounded by the persistent perianth. S. Wightii, *Planch.*; *Wight, Icones, t.* 1971.

Var. S. COMMERSONII, *Decne.*; *Planch. in DC. Prod.* xvii. 198. Leaves not so firm in texture and the pubescence of the under surface less abundant and not white, sometimes vanished when the leaf is mature. S. guineensis, *Schum.*; *Planch. in DC. Prod.* xvii. 197. Trema Commersonii, *Blume.*

Var. S. AFFINIS, *Planch. in Ann. Sc. Nat.* 1848, 329; *DC. Prod.* xvii. 198. Leaves as coriaceous and scabrous as in the type, clothed below with thicker softer grey pubescence. Celtis madagascariensis, *Bojer, Hort. Maur.* 296.

SEYCHELLES, in Mahé, in elevated rocky woods, *Pervillé! Wright! Horne*, 322! I cannot draw any clear line of demarcation between these four species of Dr. Planchon's. The wild Seychelles plant is a connecting form between vars. 1 and 2. We have typical specimens of vars. 1 (Sieber, 250! Carmichael!) and the extreme glabrescent form of var. 2 (Carmichael!) from Mauritius, where it is probably introduced only. Bojer says var. 3 is established on the heights of Plaines Wilhelms and round the Mare aux Vacouas. Through Tropical Asia, Tropical Africa and Natal. *Andarains.*

ORDER LXXXIV. MOREÆ.

Flowers monochlamydeous, rarely achlamydeous, polygamo-monoicous or dioicous. Perianth calyx-like, 3–6-merous, polyphyllous or gamophyllous, rarely absent. Stamens 1–6; filaments subulate, usually inflexed in bud; anthers 2-celled, dehiscing longtitudinally. Ovary 1-celled; ovule solitary, basal or lateral; style subulate, simple or forked. Fruit dry or fleshy. Seed usually albuminous.—Trees or shrubs, often climbing, with milky juice, alternate petioled leaves, stipules rolled together in vernation, and leaving an annular scar when they fall, and copious minute flowers variously arranged, one or both sexes spicate or clustered, or inserted on an open or closed discoid receptacle. DISTRIB. Warmer regions of both hemispheres. Species 800.

Flowers in unisexual masses outside a cylindrical receptacle . * ARTOCARPUS.
Flowers many males round one female on a plate-shaped receptacle . . . . 1. BOSQUEIA.
Flowers of both sexes crowded inside the same hollow receptacle . . . . 2. FICUS.

* *Artocarpus integrifolia*, Linn. Suppl. 412; Roxb. Cor. Pl. t. 250; Bot. Mag. tab. 2833–4, the Jack-tree, a native of Tropical Asia, is cultivated and casually wild in Mauritius, the Seychelles and Rodriguez. It is a tree, with large coriaceous caducous clasping stipules, large usually entire obovate-oblong alternate petioled coriaceous penninerved leaves, monoicous flowers congested in dense unisexual spikes, male perianth 2–3-cleft, stamen 1, and fusiform concrete fruit-perianths

becoming fleshy, and forming a dense oblong mass half a foot long on a cylindrical receptacle, of which few of the ovaries pass into fruits. *Jacquier.*

1. BOSQUIEA, Thouars.

Flowers male and female crowded on a small open receptacle, many males without any perianth, consisting of a single stamen only, round a single central female flower, consisting of a membranous lacerated perianth or circle of bracts, a 1-celled 1-ovuled ovary immersed in the receptacle with a single ovule pendulous from its apex, and a style with two subulate forks stigmatose on the inner side.—Trees, with alternate entire leaves, caducous fig-like stipules, and receptacles on short peduncles in the axils of the leaves. DISTRIB. Two other species in Madagascar. *Baillon Adansonia* iii. p. 338, *tab.* 10.

1. **B. gymnandra,** *Baker.* A tree, 15–20 feet high, glabrous in all its parts, with slender terete branchlets. Leaves obovate-oblong, distinctly cuspidate, deltoid at the base, subcoriaceous, glossy on both sides, with 15–16 pairs of erecto-patent main veins, which anastomose in abrupt arches just within the border; petiole ½ in. long; stipules small, glutinose, lanceolate, caducous. Receptacles plate-shaped, ¼ in. broad, with an obscurely lobed limb, and short peduncle obconically dilated at the top. Stamens without any bract or perianth; filament and connective slender, the former as long as the oblong anther. Female flower surrounded by about four lacerated lanceolate membranous scales.

SEYCHELLES, at low elevations in all the islands, but not common, *Horne*, 417! and perhaps also 578! of which we have no flowers. Endemic.

2. FICUS, Linn.

Flowers monochlamydeous, monoicous, placed inside a hollow receptacle with a small orifice at the top, usually a few males at the top and the rest females. Perianth in the Mauritian species 2–3-cleft with lanceolate divisions. Stamens 1–2, with adnate 2-celled anthers and a stout filament. Ovary oblique; style simple or forked, subulate. Fruit consisting of the enlarged receptacle; achenes minute, surrounded by the persistent perianth.—Trees or climbing shrubs with copious milky juice, clasping stipules, alternate leaves, and receptacles sessile or peduncled in the axils of the leaves, or on barren branches. DISTRIB. Cosmopolitan in the tropics. Species 300–400.

Sect. *Sycomorus* (Gasp.). Receptacles large, turbinate, usually produced on leafless branches.
Leaves toothed, pilose beneath . . . . 1. F. MAURITIANA.
Leaves entire, glabrous from the beginning.
  Leaves cuneate at the base . . . . 2. F. SAPOTOIDES.
  Leaves cordate at the base . . . . 3. F. AYRESII.
Sect. *Urostigma* (Miq.) Receptacles small, globose, produced on leafy branches.

Receptacles sessile.
Stipules large, persistent . . . . 4. F. RUBRA.
Stipules small, caducous.
Branchlets stout and leaves large . . . . 5. F. NAUTARUM.
Branchlets slender and leaves small.
Leaves oblanceolate-oblong . . . . 6. F. PYRIFOLIA.
Leaves obovate-oblong . . . . 7. F. TEREBRATA.
Receptacles peduncled.
Leaves subcoriaceous, with about 20 pairs of main veins . . . . 8. F. CONSIMILIS.
Leaves membranous, with 6–8 pairs of main veins . . 9. F. BOJERI.

1. **F. mauritiana,** *Lam. Encycl.* ii. 499. An erect tree, 40–60 feet high, with a thick trunk and spreading branches. Leaves cordate ovate, 6–8 in. long, acute, subcoriaceous, toothed or subentire, finely downy all over beneath, with 4–5 pairs of erecto-patent main veins, the lowest springing from the base of the midrib; petiole 1–1½ in. long pilose; stipules an inch long, lanceolate, caducous, hairy on the outside. Fruit-bearing branches usually leafless, springing from the trunk a few feet from the ground. Peduncles ½–1 in. long, with three small deltoid bracts clasping the turbinate pilose brown receptacle, which is finally as large as a walnut or small apple. F. terragena, *Bory, Voy.* ii. 143.

MAURITIUS, in woods of the Pouce, Moka River, etc. Also Bourbon. A plant from Dr. Ayres, with smaller more coriaceous nearly glabrous entire leaves, is probably a montane variety. Sieber's No. 196, mentioned by Miquel, in Hook. Lond. Journ. vii. 115, as a doubtful Sycomorus, is *Artocarpus integrifolia*. *Figuier du pays* or *Figuier sauvage*.

2. **F. sapotoides,** *Baker*. Glabrous in all its parts. Branchlets stout, terete. Leaves coriaceous, obovate-oblong, 3–4 in. long, quite entire, green on both surfaces, cuneate at the base, obtuse or obtusely deltoid at the apex, with 5–6 erecto-patent main veins on a side, and fine raised anastomosing intermediate veinlets; petiole ½–¾ in. long; stipules caducous (not seen). Receptacles produced from thick branches, turbinate, glabrous, blackish, ½ in. thick in an undeveloped state, narrowed into a distinct pedicel ¼–⅓ in. long, at the base of which are 3–4 minute bracts and a very short peduncle.

MAURITIUS, on the Pouce above the plateau, *Dr. Ayres!* Endemic.

3. **F. Ayresii,** *Baker*. Glabrous in all its parts, with slender terete branchlets. Leaves thin, subcoriaceous, ovate or oblong, acute, quite entire, rounded or shortly cordate at the base, with 6–8 pairs of erecto-patent main veins; petiole 1–2 in. long; stipules ½ in. long, lanceolate, acuminate, caducous. Receptacles racemose on barren branches, turbinate, finely pilose, ¾–1 in. long, narrowed into a distinct pilose pedicel ¼–½ long, with three lanceolate-deltoid minute silky bracts at the base, and an ⅛–¼ in. peduncle.

MAURITIUS, in the Pouce woods, *Dr. Ayres!* and also cultivated at Pamplemousses. Also Bourbon.

4. **F. rubra,** *Vahl Enum.* ii. 191. A shrub, glabrous in all its parts. with slender terete branchlets. Leaves obovate-oblong, 2 in. long, coriaceous, obtuse, narrowed through the lower half to a cuneate or slightly-rounded base, green on both surfaces, with 6–8 pairs of distinct erecto-patent main veins; petiole ½–1 in. long; stipules lanceolate, red-brown, persistent, ¼ in. long. Receptacles copious, sessile, glabrous, ¼ in. thick, subtended by 3 small deltoid bracts, and by the persistent stipules. Urostigma rubrum, *Miquel in Hook. Lond. Journ.* vi. 559, in part.

Var. SECHELLENSIS, *Baker.* Leaves equally coriaceous, oblong, deltoid at the apex, with 10–12 distinct pairs of distinct main veins; stipules of the type.

Var. AMBLYPHYLLUM, *Baker.* Leaves the same shape and veining as in the type, but more membranous; stipules ½–1 in. long, lanceolate acuminate, very persistent and conspicuous. Urostigma amblyphyllum, *Miquel in Hook. Lond. Journ.* vi. 569.

The type MAURITIUS, in mountain woods of the Pouce; the second variety gathered in the SEYCHELLES by Dr. Percival Wright; and the third, which matches an East Indian plant, by Dr. Balfour in RODRIGUEZ. *La Fouche.*

5. **F. nautarum,** *Baker.* A large tree, glabrous in all its parts with stout terete branchlets. Leaves obovate-oblong, 6–9 in. long, subcoriaceous, entire, obtuse or deltoid at the tip, narrowed through the middle half to a rounded base, with about half-a-dozen distant distinct erecto-patent main veins on a side, and very fine raised reticulated venules; petiole 1–1½ in. long; stipules ½ in. long, lanceolate, caducous. Receptacles glabrous, sessile, globose, ½ in. thick, red when ripe, subtended by three large persistent roundish bracts

SEYCHELLES, common in the woods in Mahé, *Wright*, 102! *Horne*, 343! Very durable canoes are made from its wood. Near *F. obtusifolia* of Tropical Asia.

6. **F. pyrifolia,** *Lam. Encycl.* ii. 497. Glabrous in all its parts, with moderately stout terete branchlets. Leaves oblanceolate-oblong, very coriaceous, 2–3 in. long, obtuse, narrowed through the lower half to a cuneate base, with 8–10 distinctly impressed erecto-patent main veins on a side, with distinct anastomosing intermediate venules; petiole ¼–1 in. long; stipules minute, lanceolate, caducous. Receptacles copious, globose, sessile, glabrous, ¼ in. thick, clasped by three minute deltoid bracts.

MAURITIUS, in mountain woods, *Commerson, Boivin*, 1517! Also Bourbon, and perhaps Madagascar.

7. **F. terebrata,** *Willd. Sp. Plant.* iv. 1145. A tree 15–25 feet high, glabrous in all its parts, with moderately stout terete branchlets. Leaves 2–4 in. long, oblong or obovate-oblong, obtuse or slightly cuspidate, deltoid or a little rounded at the base, coriaceous, with 10–12 distinct erecto-patent ribs on a side; petiole ½–1 in. long; stipules small, lanceolate, caducous. Receptacles globose, glabrous, sessile,

$\frac{1}{4}$–$\frac{1}{3}$ in. thick, with 3 minute roundish reddish-brown basal bracts. Urostigma terebrata, *Miquel in Hook. Lond. Journ.* vi. 558.

MAURITIUS, in the forests of the Pouce, Grand-port and Savanne. Also Comoros and East Tropical Africa, and very near *F. retusa* of Tropical Asia. *La Fouche bâtard.*

8. **F. consimilis,** *Baker.* A small tree, sometimes epiphytal, glabrous in all its parts, with slender terete branches. Leaves oblong, 3–4 in. long, subcoriaceous, deltoid at the base and apex, with about 20 pairs of distinct ascending main ribs; petiole $\frac{1}{2}$–1 in. long; stipules $\frac{1}{2}$ in. long, lanceolate, deciduous. Receptacles glabrous, globose, $\frac{1}{4}$–$\frac{1}{3}$ in. thick, clasped by 2–3 minute rounded bracts and supported on a $\frac{1}{4}$ in. peduncle.

SEYCHELLES, common in all the islands, *Wright! Horne,* 565! Closely resembling the East Indian *F. nitida,* Roxb.; Wt. Icon. t. 642, except for its distinctly peduncled receptacles. *Horne,* 566, common in the Seychelles, has leaves similar in shape, texture, and veining, but larger, reaching sometimes a foot in length. Mr. Horne describes it as a large tree, with useful timber, the receptacle of which is $\frac{1}{2}$ in. thick, and much eaten by flying foxes; and Dr. Balfour has a plant from RODRIGUEZ precisely like this so far as leaves go, but of which the receptacle is not known.

9. **F. Bojeri,** *Baker.* A small tree, glabrous in all its parts, with slender terete branches. Leaves membranous, green on both surfaces, ovate or oblong, acute, rounded or slightly cordate at the base, 4–6 in. long, obscurely repand, with 6–8 distant pairs of main veins; petiole 1–1$\frac{1}{2}$ in. long; stipules minute, lanceolate, caducous. Receptacles globose, glabrous, $\frac{1}{4}$–$\frac{1}{3}$ in. thick, on a slender $\frac{1}{8}$–$\frac{1}{4}$ in. peduncle.

SEYCHELLES, in the woods of Mahé, at an elevation of 2000 feet, *Horne,* 342! 564! Also Johanna Island, *Bojer! Dr. Meller!*

I cannot make out that there is any ground for regarding *Morus australis,* Poir. Encycl. iv. 380, as a Mauritian plant. A specimen so labelled from Bourbon is not *Broussonetia papyrifera,* to which the synonym is referred by Bureau, but the common Mulberry of Tropical Asia, *Morus indica,* Linn., now regarded as a variety of *M. alba.*

ORDER LXXXV. MONIMIACEÆ.

Flowers usually monoicous. Perianth saccate, that of the male flower splitting up into 4 sometimes 5 or 6 lobes, that reach down nearly to the base when the anthers are mature. Stamens indefinite, spread over the whole face of the perianth, all fertile or some abortive (staminodia); anthers 2-celled, with longitudinal dehiscence. Ovaries many in each flower, 1-celled, 1-ovuled; style simple; stigma capitate. Fruits dry or fleshy, crowded within the accrescent perianth-tube.—Trees or shrubs; leaves entire, usually opposite; inflorescence various. DISTRIB. Tropical American and Asian, none Continental African. Species 120.

Ovaries immersed in the inner face of the perianth and the styles just protruding . . . . 1. TAMBOURISSA.
Ovaries not immersed and the styles reaching up to the narrow throat of the female perianth . . . . 2. MONIMIA.

1. TAMBOURISSA, *Sonnerat.*

Flowers monoicous. Perianth fig-like, at first a closed bag, the female remaining permanently closed, but the male splitting up into 4 or 5 deep lobes when the anthers are mature. Stamens very numerous, spread all over the face of the perianth; filaments short and stout; anther consisting of a stout connective and 2 narrow cells. Ovules very numerous, immersed in the thick substance of the perianth, out of which the style and stigma emerge. Fruits dry, ampullæform, immersed in a layer of pulp, crowded in the accrescent perianth-sac.—Trees with opposite or rarely alternate leaves; flowers large, solitary or racemose. DISTRIB. All Mascarene, except one Javan species. Species 10–12.

Pedicels about as long as the flowers.
Anthers oblong, $\frac{1}{24}$ in. long.
Branches glabrous . . . . 1. T. AMPLIFOLIA.
Branches tomentose . . . . 2. T. SIEBERI.
Anthers ligulate, $\frac{1}{12}$ in. long.
Leaves subcoriaceous, with indistinct venation.
Petiole short; female flower oblong . . . . . . 3. T. QUADRIFIDA.
Petiole long; female flower subdiscoid. . . . . 4. T. PELTATA.
Leaves coriaceous, with very distinct veining . . . 5. T. ELLIPTICA.
Pedicels scarcely any . . . . 6. T. TETRAGONA.
Pedicels elongated . . . . 7. T. PEDICELLATA.

1. **T. amplifolia,** *A. DC. Prod.* xvi. 2, 659. Branchlets stout, glabrous, terete. Leaves alternate, on very short channelled petioles, oblong, cuneate at the base, deltoid or rounded with a cusp at the apex, $\frac{1}{2}$–1 foot long, subcoriaceous, with distinct arcuate-ascending main veins and visible intermediate reticulated venules. Flowers from the axils of the leaves solitary on short pedicels, or said to be sometimes racemed. Male perianth an inch broad, with 4 deep lobes. Anthers oblong, obtuse, $\frac{1}{24}$ in. long. Bud of female perianth black, subdiscoid, apiculate. Accrescent female perianth $1\frac{1}{2}$ in. thick, depresso-globose, with crowded conical fruits half an inch long. Mithridatea amplifolia, *Bojer, Hort. Maur.* 290. Ambora grandifolia, *R. Brown Herb.*

MAURITIUS, in the forests of the Pouce and other mountain ranges. Endemic. *Bois tambour pomme jacot.*

2. **T. Sieberi,** *A. DC, Prod.* xvi. 2, 660. Known only by the male inflorescence, which forms a peduncled deltoid panicle nearly a foot long, with a few spreading branches, which like the rachis and outside of the perianth are densely clothed with short drab-brown pubescence. Pedicels $\frac{1}{15}$ in. long. Perianth coriaceous, $\frac{1}{2}$–$\frac{5}{8}$ in. long, splitting down beyond the middle into four spreading lanceolate-deltoid lobes. Filaments very short and stout; anthers oblong, obtuse, not more than $\frac{1}{24}$ in. long. Ambora tomentosa, *Sieber Herb. Maur.* ii. No. 316, not of *Bory,* (which is Monimia rotundifolia.)

MAURITIUS, *Sieber!* Endemic.

3. **T. quadrifida,** *Sonnerat; A. DC. Prod.* xvi. 2, 658. A tree 20–30 feet high, with slender terete glabrous branchlets. Leaves opposite or casually subalternate; petiole ¼–⅓ in. long; blade obovate obtuse, cuneate at the base, 2–4 in. long, subcoriaceous, deep green above, paler green beneath, with fine just visible erecto-patent main veins. Flowers of both sexes varying from solitary in the axils of the leaves to 10 or 12 in a raceme half a foot long, rarely in cymes at the end of leafy branchlets. Pedicels shorter or not much longer than the flowers. Male perianth oblong, when unexpanded ½ to ¾ in. long, gradually splitting into usually 4 long oblong-lanceolate lobes. Stamens with a short stout purple filament and a ligulate horizontal anther $\frac{1}{12}$ in. long. Female flowers oblong, the same size as the male, with 3-4 short deltoid lobes. Accrescent female perianth as large as a potato, with a rough brown coriaceous cuticle, the crowded fruits half an inch long, only the style emergent from the mass of pulp. Mithridatea Tambourissa, *Bojer, Hort. Maur.* 290. M. quadrifida, *Willd.*

MAURITIUS, formerly frequent in the mountain-woods. Also Bourbon and Madagascar. I cannot by the descriptions separate from this *T. neglecta* and *obovata*, A. D.C. Prod. xvi. 2, 659 and 660. Tulasne attributes Bojer's synonym as cited above to *T. Boivini*, A. D.C. which has large acute coriaceous leaves with a rounded base and subsessile solitary axillary fruits. This is not known to me as a Mauritian plant, and our specimens from Bojer are *T. quadrifida. Ambora racemosa*, R. Brown, MSS. is a slight variety of this species with narrower (1–1⅛ in.) subacute leaves and smaller flowers. *T. alternifolia*, A.DC., may be a form of this with alternate leaves. *Bois Tambour.*

4. **T. peltata,** *Baker*. Branchlets slender, glabrous, terete. Leaves opposite or alternate, obovate or oblong, obtuse or subacute, deltoid at the base, 2–3 in. long, pale green, with only the fine main veins distinctly visible; petiole ¾ to 1 in. long. Flowers solitary from the nodes of the branchlets on pedicels under an inch long. Expanded male perianth 1½ in. broad, thin in texture, glabrous on the outside, with 4 deep lobes. Anthers ligulate, $\frac{1}{12}$ in. long, with a thick connective and very short filament. Unexpanded female perianth depresso-globose, ½ in. broad. Ambora peltata, *R. Brown, Herb.*

MAURITIUS, *Carmichael!* Endemic.

5. **T. elliptica,** *A. DC. Prod.* xvi. 2, 660? Branchlets glabrous, terete or sometimes compressed and dilated near the top. Leaves opposite or casually subalternate, obovate-oblong, obtuse, cuneate at the base, the most coriaceous in texture of any of the species, bright green above, paler green beneath, with veins and venules distinctly visible. petiole ¼–¾ in. long. Flowers solitary, on short pedicels. Expanded male perianth 2–2½ inches broad, glabrous, very thick in texture, splitting into 5–6 long irregular lobes. Stamens horizontal, densely imbricated, with ligulate anthers $\frac{1}{12}$ in. long. Female perianth depresso-globose, with a large open obscurely-lobed throat.

MAURITIUS, on the shoulder of the Pouce, *Capt. Carmichael! Dr. Ayres!* Also Bourbon, *Boivin*, but I have not seen the Bourbon plant, and its stamens are not known.

6. **T. tetragona,** *A. DC. Prod.* xvi. 2, 659. Branchlets quite glabrous, tetragonous, compressed and dilated at the top. Leaves opposite, lanceolate or narrow oblong, shortly pointed, narrowed to the base, shortly petioled, with obscure venation. Male flowers in dense subspicate racemes. Ambora tetragona, *Tulasne, Mon.* 302.

MAURITIUS, in woods near Grandport, *Commerson, Boivin.* Endemic. This I have not seen.

7. **T. pedicellata,** *Baker.* Branches terete, more or less compressed and dilated at the nodes. Leaves oblong, subcoriaceous, acute, deltoid at the base, 3–5 inches long, dark green above, with the veins and reticulated veinlets distinctly visible; petiole $\frac{1}{4}$–$\frac{1}{2}$ in. long. Flowers single or in short racemes from the dilated nodes on slender pedicels 1–1$\frac{1}{2}$ in. long. Male flowers not seen. Female perianth globose, glabrous, in flower $\frac{1}{4}$–$\frac{1}{3}$ in. thick, in fruit 1$\frac{1}{2}$ inch thick, irregularly lobed with a truncate mouth $\frac{1}{4}$–$\frac{1}{3}$ in. broad, which finally becomes lacerated.

MAURITIUS, in mountain woods, *Blackburn! Bouton!* Endemic.

2. MONIMIA, Thouars.

Dioicous. Male perianth when expanded with 4 long spreading lanceolate lobes. Stamens indefinite, clothing the whole face of the perianth; filaments with a stalked capitate gland on each side; anthers ovoid-quadrangular, with longitudinal dehiscence. Female perianth globose, with a small opening at the mouth, not splitting open. Ovaries 6–8, bottle-shaped, free, with long slender styles and capitate stigmas, just protruding from the mouth of the perianth. Fruit with a fleshy pericarp and bony endocarp, included in the accrescent perianth-tube. —Shrubs or low trees, with rough coriaceous opposite leaves and small flowers in lateral or terminal peduncled cymes or panicles. DISTRIB. Confined to Mauritius and Bourbon. Species 3.

Leaves scabrous above, cuneate at the base . . . . . . 1. M. OVALIFOLIA.
Leaves pilose above, broadly rounded at the base . . . 2. M. ROTUNDIFOLIA.

1. **M. ovalifolia,** *Thouars; A. DC. Prod.* xvi. 2, 661. A low tree, with thinly pilose terete branchlets. Leaves opposite, short-petioled, obovate with a cuneate base, cuspidate, 2–3 in. long, very coriaceous pale green and rough with raised points on the upper surface, clothed with thin whitish lepidote tomentum below. Male flowers not seen. Female flowers 3–10 together, on very short pedicels, in peduncled umbels or cymes, 6 or 8 of which sometimes form a lateral or terminal panicle, with small leafy caducous bracts at the base of the short pilose stiff erecto-patent branches. Perianth globose-urceolate, $\frac{1}{12}$ in. long and broad, crenulate at the mouth. Ovaries 5–6 to a flower. Fruit-perianth glabrescent, coriaceous, black, the size of a pea.

MAURITIUS, in woods of the Pouce range. Also Bourbon, *Vesco!*

2. **M. rotundifolia,** *Thouars; A. DC. Prod.* xvi. 2, 661. Habit of *M. ovalifolia*, but the hairs of the branches, petioles and outside of the perianth denser and more spreading. Leaves nearly round, 2–5 in. diam., green and softly pilose above, thinly white tomentose and reticulato-venose beneath. Flowers of both sexes in shortly peduncled lateral cymes; pedicels densely pilose, as long as the obovoid unexpanded female perianth. Expanded male flowers ¼–⅓ in. across, splitting down nearly to the base.

MAURITIUS, in the woods of Flacq, and Savanne. Also Bourbon.

ORDER LXXXVI. LAURACEÆ.

Flowers hermaphrodite, monoicous or polygamo-dioicous. Perianth subcorolline, deeply 4–6-cleft, with imbricate æstivation. Stamens perigynous, usually definite, often abortive (staminodes) and some with 1 or 2 basal glands; anthers 2–4-celled, opening by flaps except in *Hernandia*. Ovary free, 1-celled; ovule solitary, pendulous; style simple; stigma capitate. Fruit indehiscent, fleshy, girt at the base by the persistent perianth-tube. Seed exalbuminous.—Trees or shrubs, with coriaceous entire exstipulate usually alternate leaves (*Cassytha* is a twining leafless parasite), minute panicled or racemose greenish, yellowish or white flowers, which like the bark are usually more or less fragrant. DISTRIB. Cosmopolitan in the tropics. Species 900.

Anthers opening by 2–4 flaps.
  Leafy erect shrubs or trees.
    Flowers not in umbels.
      Fertile stamens 9 and also 3 staminodes present.
        Leaves opposite, triplinerved . . . . * CINNAMOMUM.
        Leaves alternate, feather-veined . . . . * PERSEA.
      Fertile stamens 9; staminodes 0 . . . . 1. MESPILODAPHNE.
    Flowers in umbels surrounded by an involucre . . . * TETRANTHERA.
  Leafless twining parasites . . . . 2. CASSYTHA.
Anthers not opening by flaps . . . . 3. HERNANDIA.

* The true Cinnamon, *Cinnamomum zeylanicum*, Breyn.; Meissn. in DC. Prod. xv. 13; Wight, Ic. t. 123, a native of Ceylon, is now plentifully naturalised both in Mauritius and the Seychelles. It may be recognised by its opposite oblong very coriaceous shining 3-nerved leaves, lax panicles with corymbose branches, silky 6-fid perianth of which the lobes in the fruiting stage break away near the base, 9 antheriferous stamens of which the inner three have a pair of glands at the base, 3 staminodes and small oblong fruit girt by the perianth at the base only. It forms a tree 20 to 30 feet high. *Cannellier.*

* *Persea gratissima*, Gærtn.; Meissn. in DC. Prod. xv. 52; Wight Ic. t. 1823; Bot. Mag. tab. 4580, the well-known Avocado pear, a native of tropical America, is now subspontaneous in Mauritius, Seychelles and Rodriguez. It is a tree 30–40 feet high, with long-petioled

alternate coriaceous oblong leaves usually glaucous beneath with many strong erecto-patent veins, silky deeply 6-fid flowers in congested panicles shorter than the leaves, with persistent lobes, 9 fertile stamens the inner 3 furnished with a couple of glands above the base, 3 staminodes, and a pear-shaped eatable fruit 3–4 inches long. *Avocat, Avocado.*

1. MESPILODAPHNE, Nees.

Flowers exinvolucrate, polygamo-dioicous. Perianth with an obconic tube and 6 equal deciduous oblong lobes. Fertile stamens 9, the three inner extrorse, with two glands at the base, all the anthers 4-celled; staminodes none. Ovary included in the perianth tube; style filiform; stigma capitate. Fruit oblong, girt at the base with the truncate perianth-tube.—Shrubs or trees, with alternate feather-veined leaves and small flowers in lateral or terminal corymbs or panicles. DISTRIB. America and Mascarene Isles. Species 50.

1. **M. cupularis,** *Meissn. in DC. Prod.* xv. 104. A shrub or low tree, 15–20 feet high, with only the youngest branches slightly pilose. Leaves alternate, coriaceous, oblong, green and glabrous on both surfaces, 3–6 in. long, 1¼–4 in. broad, obtuse or acute, deltoid or rounded at the base, with distant erecto-patent main veins with often a pilose gland at the base of the lowest, and more or less distinct reticulated veinlets; petiole ¼–1 in. long, channelled. Corymbs few flowered, 1–2 in. long, peduncled or sessile, fascicled in the axils of the leaves, or from the nodes of pilose young shoots; pedicels as long as or longer than the perianth. Perianth ⅛ in. long, glabrous or thinly pilose, the 6 (rarely 7–8) oblong greenish-yellow lobes as long as the deltoid tube. Stamens half as long as the limb. Fruit oblong, under an inch long, purplish, enclosed at the base in a cup about ¼ in. broad and deep on a lengthened and much-thickened pedicel. M. mauritiana, heteromorpha, Lindleyana, marginata and cymosa, *Meissn. loc. cit.* Calycodaphne cupularis, floribunda and dysoxylon, *Bojer, Hort. Maur.* 273.

MAURITIUS, in the mountain woods, now becoming rare. Also Bourbon and Madagascar. I cannot make out more than one species of the Mauritian plant. The leaves vary greatly in shape, texture, and in the distinctness of the venules. *Bois de Cannelle.*

A Lauraceous plant of which we have a flowerless specimen from Mr. Horne (No. 445!) and which he reports as common on dry soils in Mahé and Praslin, is perhaps a *Mespilodaphne.* It is a shrub 10 feet high, glabrous in all its parts, with slender terete branchlets, short petioles, alternate oblong acute leaves 2–3 in. long with a cuneate base subcoriaceous in texture green and quite glabrous beneath, with fine erecto-patent main veins which anastomose in arches a short distance from the edge and distinctly visible fine veinlets. The relics of the single flower show a slender axillary pedicel 1½ inch long, and a campanulate perianth ¼ in. broad and long, lobed nearly to the base.

* TETRANTHERA, Jacq.

Flowers dioicous, several together in an umbel surrounded by an involucre of 5–6 oblong-navicular bracts. Perianth with a funnel-shaped tube and 6 acute lobes. Stamens in the male flowers about a dozen; anthers 4-celled. Ovary in the female flower surrounded by glandular staminodes. Fruit small, globose, girt at the base only by the plate-shaped relics of the perianth.—Shrubs or trees with alternate penninerved leaves, the umbels on short peduncles, solitary or fascicled in the axils of the leaves. DISTRIB. Cosmopolitan in the tropics, mostly Asiatic. Species 80–90.

Filaments 5–6 times as long as the anthers . . . . . . * T. LAURIFOLIA.
Filaments not more than twice as long as the anthers . . * T. MONOPETALA.

* *T. laurifolia*, Jacq. Hort. Schoen. t. 113; Meissn. in DC. Prod. xv. 178; T. apetala, *Roxb. Cor. Pl. t.* 147, a common plant through Tropical Asia, is now subspontaneous in Mauritius, the Seychelles and Rodriguez. It is a tree 15–30 feet high, with petioled obovate-oblong obtuse leaves 3–6 in. long at first pilose beneath, short axillary peduncles bearing 1–4 small globose umbels surrounded by 5–6 downy oblong concave deciduous bracts, perianth very minute densely pilose 6-cleft, stamens about 12 much exserted, fruit globose purple juicy the size of a large pea. *Bois d'oiseaux. Bois Zozo.*

* *T. monopetala*, Roxb. Cor. Pl. t. 148; Meissn. in DC. Prod. xv. 189; T. villosa, *Bojer, Hort. Maur.* 272, a native of the East Indies, is also subspontaneous in Mauritius. It has thinner leaves than *T. laurifolia*, pubescent beneath, with very distinct numerous parallel erecto-patent main veins, umbels densely fascicled in the axils of the leaves, a densely pilose perianth with 6 acute teeth, stamens 12–14 of which 3–5 are sterile, much less exserted than in *T. laurifolia* and a similar fruit seated on the truncate plate-shaped base of the perianth.

2. CASSYTHA, Linn.

Flowers hermaphrodite, without an involucre. Perianth with a campanulate tube and 6 oblong imbricate erect lobes. Fertile stamens 9, inserted at the throat of the tube; filaments short; anthers 2-celled, oblong, opening by flaps; staminodes 3. Ovary globose, included in the perianth-tube; style cylindrical; stigma capitate. Fruit globose, fleshy, included in the fleshy persistent perianth-tube.—Leafless parasites, with the habit of *Cuscuta*. DISTRIB. Cosmopolitan in the tropics. Species 30.

1. **C. filiformis**, *Linn.; Meissn. in DC. Prod.* xv. 255. Perennial,

flowering all the year, the root soon decaying. Stems copiously branched, extending to a length of 10 or 20 feet, twining round herbs and shrubs and adhering by suckers that penetrate their epidermis. Flowers 6–10, sessile, in short spreading peduncled spikes, with a bract at the base, the rachis flexuose; bracteoles 3, ovate, persistent. Perianth $\frac{1}{12}$ in. long; lobes greenish white, the inner the largest. Fruit the size of a large pea, crowned by the persistent perianth-lobes. *Wight, Ic. t.* 1847.

MAURITIUS, SEYCHELLES and RODRIGUEZ, at all elevations. *Liane jaune. Liane sans fin.*

3. HERNANDIA, Linn.

Flowers monoicous, placed three together in a small involucre of 4 oblong downy bracts, the central flower subsessile, female, enclosed in a cup-shaped nearly truncate involucel, the two outside ones pedicelled, male, without any involucel. Perianth downy, similar in texture to the involucre, with a short funnel-shaped tube, and 6–10 oblong biseriate lobes. Male perianth with a 6-partite limb. Stamens 3 or rarely 4, with monadelphous filaments inserted at the throat of the tube and glandular at the base; anther oblong, 2-celled, dehiscing by the valves breaking away from the connective. Female perianth with an 8–10-partite limb, with the stamens represented only by glands at the throat. Ovary minute; style cylindrical, pilose; stigma irregularly lobed. Fruit globose, indehiscent, enclosed in both the accrescent calyx-tube and involucel, which latter becomes a membranous bag much larger than the fruit.—Trees, with long petioled alternate broad ovate leaves, the small flowers in peduncled corymbose panicles from the axils of the upper leaves. DISTRIB. Cosmopolitan in the tropics. Species 6.

Petiole inserted at the base of the blade . . . . 1. H. OVIGERA.
Petiole inserted above the base of the blade . . . . 2. H. PELTATA

1. **H. ovigera,** *Linn.; Meissn. in DC. Prod.* xv. 262. A tree 30–40 feet high, with stout glabrous branchlets. Leaves broad ovate-cordate, 4–6 in. long, deltoid at the tip, subcoriaceous, green and quite glabrous on both surfaces, with the petiole inserted at the base, and 7 veins radiating from its apex; petiole 3–4 in. long. Peduncle as long as or shorter than the petiole; flowers in corymbose panicles with grey canescent branchlets and minute lanceolate bracts. Lobes of the involucre obovate, obtuse, grey, downy, $\frac{1}{8}$ in. long. Lobes of the perianth oblong, $\frac{1}{8}$ in. long. Filaments each with two glands at the base. Fruit globose, an inch long.

MAURITIUS, on the damp forests of Trois Ilots and Grandport, now become rare, *Bouton!* Tropical Asia and Africa. *Bois Blanc.*

2. **H. peltata,** *Meissn. in DC. Prod.* xv. 263. A large tree, glabrous beyond the panicle. Leaves ovate-deltoid, $\frac{1}{2}$–1 ft. long, deltoid at the apex, truncate or slightly cordate at the base, subcori-

aceous, green on both surfaces, with the petiole attached $\frac{1}{2}$–1 in. above the base, with 7 veins radiating from the point of its insertion. Peduncles as long or longer than the petioles. Inflorescence and flowers just like those of *H. ovigera*. *Seem. Fl. Vit. tab.* 52. H. Sonora, *Linn. in part*. H. ovigera, *Bojer, in part*.

Seychelles, common on the shores of Mahé and Praslin, *Horne*, 331! Polynesia to Madagascar and the Comoro islands. What we have received from Mauritius as *Sassafras mauritiana*, Bojer, Hort. Maur. p. 273, is just like this in general habit, but with some of the leaves deeply three-lobed from the top, and is without flowers. *Bois Blanc*.

Order LXXXVI.* CASUARINEÆ.

* *Casuarina equisetifolia*, Forst.; Miquel in DC. Prod. xvi. 2, 338; (C. muricata, *Roxb.*; C. lateriflora, *Lam.*), a native of the Malay Archipelago, now widely spread through the tropics of the Old World, is one of the commonest trees both in Mauritius and the Seychelles. It is 30–50 feet high, with a straight trunk, crowded slender terete branchlets without leaves, but with 7 ribs and 7 little teeth like those of an *Equisetum* at each distinctly-jointed node, achlamydeous flowers, the males of a single stamen each crowded in cylindrical catkins at the end of the branchlets, the females in globose heads from the same branches on short lateral peduncles, with two long red filiform styles and two hard ovate capsule-valves enclosing a single winged seed. *Filao*.

Order LXXXVII. PIPERACEÆ.

Flowers in hermaphrodite or dioicous spikes, without any perianth, but subtended by a peltate stalked or sessile bract; rachis often fleshy and usually pitted. Stamens 2–3, sometimes more numerous; anthers 2–4-valved, usually sessile, dehiscing longitudinally. Ovary 1-celled, usually sessile; ovule solitary, sessile, basilar, orthotropous; stigma usually sessile, simple or many-lobed. Fruit fleshy or dry; embryo placed outside a large mass of albumen and included in the persistent embryo-sac.—Herbs or shrubs with simple exstipulate petioled more or less succulent leaves variously arranged, and minute flowers packed tightly in the spikes. Fibro-vascular bundles scattered. Distrib. Round the world in the tropics in shady woods. Species 1000.

Shrubs, with 4-valved anthers . . . . 1. Piper.
Herbs, with 2-valved anthers . . . . 2. Peperomia.

1. PIPER, Linn.

Flowers hermaphrodite or unisexual. Bract sessile or stalked. Stamens in our species 2 or 3, the latter posticous; mature anther

4-valved. Ovary stalked or sessile; stigma sessile, peltate or of 3–4 divergent lanceolate lobes. Fruit fleshy, globose or ovoid.—Shrubs, often epiphytic and rooting at the lower nodes, the leaves in all the Mauritian species alternate. DISTRIB. Cosmopolitan in the tropics. Species 600.

Flowers hermaphrodite. Spikes 2–6 in an umbel . . . 1. P. SUBPELTATUM.
Flowers dioicous. Spikes solitary.
  Fruits stalked . . . . 2. P. BORBONENSE.
  Fruits sessile.
    Leaves membranous.
      Leaves not cordate . . . . 3. P. SYLVESTRE.
      Leaves cordate . . . . * P. BETLE.
    Leaves coriaceous . . . . * P. NIGRUM.

1. **P. subpeltatum,** *Willd.; Cas. DC. Prod.* xvi. 333. A little-branched shrub, 3–4 feet high, with stout zigzag woody stems. Leaves alternate, broader than long, ½–1 foot broad, acute, deeply cordate at the base, membranous, bright green above, obscurely pilose beneath, with 11–13 ribs radiating from the apex of the petiole, and a pair of strong ones springing from the midrib a space above; petiole 6–9 in. long, dilated and sheathing at the base. Spikes 2 to 6, short-peduncled, 2–5 in. long, in solitary or geminate peduncled umbels from the axils of the leaves. Flowers minute, hermaphrodite, 12–15 in a row round the spike; bract stalked, nearly round, distinctly ciliated. Stamens 2–3. Fruit turbinate, pilose, not larger than a pin's head. Pothomorphe subpeltata, *Miquel Illust.* 29, *t.* 26; *Wight, Ic. t.* 1925. Piper latifolium, *Bojer, Hort. Maur.* 355, *non Forst.*

MAURITIUS and SEYCHELLES, in shaded woods. Cosmopolitan in the tropics.

2. **P. borbonense,** *Cas. DC. Prod.* xvi. 339. Stems short, dichotomously branched. Leaves alternate, oblong, acute, moderately firm in texture, glabrous on both surfaces, 2–3 in. long, unequal at base, rounded or obscurely cordate, with 4–6 slender secondary ribs branching from the midrib on each side, and anastomosing in arches; petiole ¼–⅓ in. long, slightly pilose. Spikes dioicous, 2–3 in. long, on short leaf-opposed peduncles. Flowers in crowded spiral rows; bract stalked, round, minutely ciliated. Stamens 3; filaments longer than the oblong anthers. Fruits oblong, on stalks twice as long as themselves; stigmas 3. Cubeba borbonensis and costulata, *Miq. Syst. Pip.* 299 and 301. Piper cubeba, *Bojer Hort. Maur.* 355,

MAURITIUS, parasitic on trees in woods on Montagne Ory, etc. Also Bourbon. Our Mauritian examples called *P. pyrifolium* belong here. Vahl's plant of that name belongs to the section with sessile fruit. *Cubebe du pays.*

3. **P. sylvestre,** *Lam.; Cas. DC. Prod.* xvi. 361. A glabrous scandent shrub, with slender stems. Leaves short-petioled, ovate, acuminate, unequally rounded on the two sides, not cordate at the base, 3–5 in. long, membranous, glabrous on both surfaces, 5-nerved from the base. Spikes dioicous, 4–5 in. long, on an ascending peduncle about as long as the petiole (½–1 inch); rachis glabrous; bract attached by the

centre, obovate, glabrous. Stamens 3. Ovary sessile, ovoid; stigmas 3–4, lanceolate, spreading. Fruit the size of a small pea. *Wight, Ic. t.* 1937.

MAURITIUS, in shady humid forests about the Mare aux Vacouas, *Bojer*. Also Bourbon and Tropical Asia. *P. laxum*, Vahl, said to have been gathered in Mauritius by Commerson, differs from *P. sylvestre* by its longer leaves, equally rounded at the base and less crowded flowers. *Poivrier sauvage.*

* *P. Betle*, Linn.; Cas. DC. Prod. xvi. 359, a native of Tropical Asia, is cultivated and subspontaneous in Mauritius and the Seychelles. It is a glabrous scandent shrub rooting at the lower nodes, with alternate short-petioled broad-ovate membranous leaves with an unequally cordate base with 7 ribs radiating from the apex of the petiole, and two strong ones ascending from the midrib a little above it, dioicous spikes ¼–⅓ foot long on short peduncles opposite the upper leaves, round sessile bracts attached by the centre, 2 stamens, 4–5 stigmas, and a globose sessile fruit the size of a small pea. We have a plant with closely similar leaves, not in flower, sent by M. Bouton, as a native of forests of the interior. *Betel.*

* *P. nigrum*, Linn.; Cas. DC. Prod. xvi. 363, the commonly cultivated Black Pepper, a native of Tropical Asia, is casually subspontaneous in Mauritius and the Seychelles. It has terete woody subscandent stems rooting from the lower nodes, subcoriaceous alternate petioled acute roundish or broad ovate leaves ¼–⅓ foot long rounded at the base, with 5 ribs from the base and 2 strong ones rising a little above it, peduncled dioicous or monoicous spikes arising singly opposite the upper leaves, a bract adnate to the rachis but free at the edge, 2 stamens, 3–5 stigmas, and a sessile fruit the size of a pea. *Poivrier.*

P. radicans, *Vahl Enum.* i. 333, said to have been gathered in Mauritius by Commerson and reported by Bojer as growing on old trunks on the Pouce, is described as having trailing pilose stems as thick as a goosequill rooting at the lower nodes, leaves pilose on the petiole and ribs beneath, the lower ones cordate-ovate obscurely 5-nerved, 2 inches long, the upper ones oblong acuminate and peduncled spikes 1½ in. long.

2. PEPEROMIA, R. & P.

Flowers hermaphrodite. Bract sessile or stalked. Stamens always only two, lateral; anthers oblong, subsessile, 2-valved. Ovary sessile, often immersed at the base in the pitted rachis; stigma in all the Mauritian species sessile, peltate. Fruit globose, not larger than a pin's head.—Trailing more or less succulent herbs, the leaves in all our species opposite or whorled, the spikes terminal or leaf-opposed. DISTRIB. Cosmopolitan in the tropics. Species 350.

Leaves opposite, membranous.
  Leaves triplinerved.
    Dwarf, with small leaves . . . . 1. P. SERPYLLIFOLIA.

1. **P. serpyllifolia,** *Dietr; Cas. DC. Prod.* xvi. 445. Stems filiform. Leaves opposite or the lowest alternate, roundish or obovate, obtuse, membranous, glabrous on both surfaces, $\frac{1}{8}$–$\frac{1}{3}$ in. long, obscurely triplinerved, ciliolate with brownish hairs towards the apex; petiole $\frac{1}{8}$–$\frac{1}{4}$ in. long. Spikes terminal, scarcely overtopping the leaves. Fruit ovoid, immersed at the base.

MAURITIUS, *Neraud.* Endemic.

2. **P. portulacoides,** *Dietr.; Cas. DC. Prod.* xvi. 443. Stems terete, succulent, trailing at the base, $\frac{1}{8}$–$\frac{1}{4}$ in. thick, rooting from the lower nodes, $\frac{1}{2}$–1 foot long, copiously branched and ascending in the upper part, glabrous. Leaves opposite, rarely ternate, membranous, glabrous, 1–2 in. long, obovate, obtuse, cuneate in the lower half, distinctly triplinerved from the base three-quarters of the way up, with obscure veinlets between the main ribs; petiole $\frac{1}{4}$–$\frac{1}{2}$ in. long. Spikes 2–3 in. long, on $\frac{1}{2}$–1 in. peduncles, solitary, opposite the upper leaves and 2–3 terminal; bract round, glabrous, short-stalked. Ovary globose, immersed at the base, not narrowed to a point; stigma terminal, penicillate. *Wight, Ic. t.* 1922.

MAURITIUS and SEYCHELLES, frequent in shaded woods. Also Bourbon, Madagascar, and East Indies. *Poivrier à feuilles de pourpier. Pourpier marron.*

Var. P. PEROTTETIANA, *Miq.; Cas. DC. Prod.* xvi. 443. Leaves broader in proportion to their length, nearly as broad as long, glabrous, as are the stems. Spikes 3–4 in. long.

MAURITIUS, in thick woods, *Sieber*, 165! *Bojer! Bouton!* Also Bourbon, *Boivin!*

Var. PILOSA, *Baker.* Stems and leaves clothed with fine pubescence.

SEYCHELLES, *Wright! Horne*, 567! Also East Indies.

3. **P. reticulata,** *Balf. fil.* Stems $\frac{1}{2}$–1 foot long, $\frac{1}{8}$ in. thick at the base, simple or once branched, trailing and rooting from the nodes in the lower half, then ascending. Leaves opposite, rarely ternate at the end node, oblong or obovate-oblong, glabrous, membranous-succulent, obtuse, 1–2 in. long, deltoid at the base, distinctly triplinerved from the base three-quarters of the way up, with distinct anastomosing intermediate veinlets; petiole $\frac{1}{4}$–$\frac{1}{2}$ in. long. Spike terminal, 2–4 in long, generally solitary on a peduncle under an inch long; bract round, sessile, glabrous like the rachis. Fruit globose, slightly immersed at the base, with a peltate terminal stigma.

RODRIGUEZ; *Balfour!* Endemic.

4. **P. elliptica,** *Dietr.; Cas. DC. Prod.* xvi. 440. Stems slender, glabrous, $\frac{1}{2}$ foot long, trailing and rooting at the nodes in the lower part, ascending afterwards. Leaves broad obovate, or nearly round, glabrous, $\frac{1}{3}$–$\frac{3}{4}$ in. long, very obtuse, deltoid or rather rounded at the base, penninerved, with 3–4 slender ribs on each side forming an angle of 45° with the midrib; petiole under $\frac{1}{4}$ in. long. Spikes solitary, under an inch long, shortly peduncled, axillary and terminal; bract round, glabrous, subsessile. Ovary ovoid, immersed at the base, with a terminal penicillate sessile stigma. Piper mauritianum, *Roem. et Schult. Mant.* v. 1245.

MAURITIUS, in the dense woods of the Pouce range, etc. Also Bourbon.

5. **P. penninervia,** *Baker.* Stems under $\frac{1}{12}$ in. thick, trailing and rooting at the nodes in the lower part, $\frac{1}{2}$–1 foot long, simple or branched glabrous. Leaves nearly round, membranous, opposite, obtuse, rounded at the base, $\frac{1}{4}$–$\frac{5}{8}$ in. long, furnished, especially at the base, with fine spreading brownish hairs, penninerved with 3–4 ribs on each side erecto-patent from the midrib; petiole $\frac{1}{8}$–$\frac{1}{4}$ in. long. Spikes solitary, terminal or lateral, under an inch long, on $\frac{1}{4}$–$\frac{1}{2}$ in. ascending peduncles; rachis glabrous, pitted; bract round, sessile, glabrous. Ovary globose, immersed at the base, with a sessile terminal stigma.

MAURITIUS, *Carmichael!* Endemic.

6. **P. reflexa,** *Dietr.; Cas. DC. Prod.* xvi. 451. Stems $\frac{1}{4}$–$\frac{1}{2}$ foot long, once or twice dichotomously forked, slender, glabrous, articulated at the nodes, tetragonous and when dried deeply sulcate. Upper leaves usually 4 in a whorl, horizontal, bright green, coriaceous, obovate, $\frac{1}{4}$–$\frac{1}{2}$ in. long, obtuse, glabrous, slightly rounded at the base, obscurely triplinerved; petiole very short. Lower leaves opposite, on longer petioles. Spikes terminal, solitary, $\frac{1}{2}$–$1\frac{1}{2}$ in. long, distinctly peduncled; rachis pilose, with deep rhomboid pits; bract round, subsessile. Ovary ovoid-ampullæform, with a terminal penicillate stigma. Fruit oblong, narrowed to a point. *Wight, Ic. t.* 1923.

MAURITIUS, in shaded woods of the Pouce, etc. Cosmopolitan in the tropics.

There are two other species in Dr. Balfour's Rodriguez collection, both probably novelties and endemic, but as yet unknown in flower.

7. Stems under a foot long, rooting from the lower nodes, copiously branched, $\frac{1}{12}$ in. thick, with a few short spreading hairs. Leaves opposite, oblong or obovate, with a cuneate base, very obtuse, $\frac{1}{2}$–$\frac{3}{4}$ in. long, membranous, bright green, distinctly triplinerved from the base nearly to the top, with distinct anastomosing intermediate veinlets; petiole pilose, $\frac{1}{4}$–$\frac{1}{3}$ in. long. *Balfour*, 1305!

8. Stems branched or simple, half a foot long, $\frac{1}{12}$ in. thick at the base, rooting from the lower nodes, densely clothed with short spreading whitish hairs. Leaves opposite, obovate or oblong, rather rounded at the base, $\frac{1}{2}$–$\frac{3}{4}$ in. long, membranous, with both surfaces pubescent, distinctly triplinerved from the base nearly to the apex, with very distinct and anastomosing intermediate veinlets; petiole $\frac{1}{4}$–$\frac{1}{3}$ in. long, densely pubescent. *Balfour*, 1279!

ORDER LXXXVII.* PHYTOLACCACEÆ.

Flowers regular, hermaphrodite. Perianth greenish, cut down to the base into 5 rounded segments. Stamens hypogynous, as many or twice as many as the perianth-segments; filaments filiform; anthers 2-celled. Ovary usually of many carpels, of one in *Rivina;* ovules solitary in the cells; styles distinct, if more than one. Fruit baccate. Seeds with peripheric embryo round a central mass of albumen.—Herbs or shrubs, with alternate exstipulate simple leaves and small greenish racemose flowers. DISTRIB. Cosmopolitan. Species about 70.

Carpels solitary . . . . * RIVINA.
Carpels numerous. * PHYTOLACCA.

* *Rivina lævis*, Linn.; Moq. in DC. Prod. xiii. 2, 11, a native of Tropical America, common in gardens, is subspontaneous in Mauritius. It is a glabrous branched perennial, with slender shrubby stems, petioled alternate ovate acuminate membranous leaves, flowers in lax peduncled terminal and axillary racemes, minute greenish calyx-like perianth with 4 free obtuse segments, 4 hypogynous stamens and a bright red one-seeded fruit the size of a small pea. *Petites Groseilles.*

* *Phytolacca decandra*, Linn.; Moq. in DC. Prod. xiii. 2. 32; Bot. Mag. t. 931, a commonly-cultivated plant, originating probably in the warm temperate zone of the Old World, is subspontaneous in Mauritius. It is a stout erect herb several feet high, with petioled alternate oblong acute membranous leaves, peduncled leaf-opposed racemes 4–6 in. long, spreading pedicels furnished with minute linear bracts and bracteoles, a greenish perianth with 5 obovate obtuse segments, stamens, carpels and styles 10–12 each, and a depresso-globose umbilicate purple-black berry with compressed black seeds and abundance of purple juice.

ORDER LXXXVIII. NEPENTHACEÆ.

Flowers dioicous. Perianth of 4 oblong equal coriaceous segments, which in our plant in the female are united a little above the base. Stamens 4–16, monadelphous; anthers oblong, distinctly 2-lobed, with longitudinal dehiscence. Ovary superior, 3–4-lobed, 3–4-celled; ovules many; placentation parietal; stigma sessile, peltate. Fruit a coriaceous capsule, with loculicidal dehiscence. Seeds albuminous, minute, very numerous, clavate.—Shrubs with alternate exstipulate sessile coriaceous leaves produced into pendent pitchers at the end and copious small flowers in peduncled panicles or racemes. DISTRIB. New Caledonia to Madagascar; none Tropical African; concentrated in the Malay isles. Species 30.

1. NEPENTHES, Linn.

Characters and distribution of the order.

1. **N. Pervillei,** *Blume; Hook. fil. in DC. Prod.* xvii. 92. Stems $\frac{1}{4}$–$\frac{1}{3}$ in. thick, woody, prostrate or climbing. Leaves crowded at the end of the

branches, coriaceous, glabrous, oblong-spathulate, obtuse, amplexicaul, 4–10 in. long, the stout midrib produced 1–2 in. beyond the blade and then dilated into a vertical funnel-shaped pitcher 3–6 in. deep, with an oblique revolute closely-ribbed mouth and a round-cordate horizontal lid $1\frac{1}{2}$–3 in. broad. Flowers in peduncled panicles 6–9 in. long, with corymbose branches, which, like the rachis and outside of the perianth, are clothed with dense persistent ferruginous tomentum. Perianth segments $\frac{1}{12}$–$\frac{1}{8}$ in. long. Anthers 6–10 in a globose head as long as the column of filaments. Ovary trigonous, glabrous, 3-celled, obconical. Mature fruit not seen. N. Wardii, *Wright in Trans. Roy. Irish Acad.* xxiv. 576, t. 29–30.

SEYCHELLES, by the side of mountain streams in Mahé at about 1500 feet. Endemic.

ORDER LXXXIX. PODOSTEMACEÆ.

Flowers hermaphrodite, naked or enclosed in a single perianth, usually included before they open in a membranous spathe. Perianth green or coloured, 3–5-lobed. Stamens 1 or more; filaments free or connate; anthers 2-celled, with longitudinal dehiscence; staminodes sometimes present. Ovary free, 2–3- or by abortion 1-celled; placentation axile; ovules numerous; style 0 or very short; stigmas 2–3, subulate. Fruit a minute crustaceous dehiscent capsule. Seeds minute, exalbuminous.—Submerged herbs of moss-like habit with minute flowers variously arranged. DISTRIB. Cosmopolitan in the tropics. Species 100.

1. TRISTICHA, Thouars.

Flowers hermaphrodite. Perianth of 3 oblong obtuse membranous unilateral segments. Stamen 1, hypogynous, unilateral, exserted; filament rather compressed; anther ovate-oblong, purple. Ovary subsessile, 3-celled; ovules many in a cell; stigmas 3, minute, sessile, subulate, diverging. Capsule membranous, oblong, 9-ribbed, septicidally 3-valved.—Submerged herbs of moss-like appearance, with tristichous leaves and pedicellate solitary flowers, not enclosed in a spathe. DISTRIB. Round the world in the tropics. Species 6.

1. **T. hypnoides,** *Spreng.; Weddell in DC. Prod.* xvii. 45. Habit of a large moss, with copiously-branched stems from an inch to a foot long. Leaves oblong, trifarious, $\frac{1}{24}$–$\frac{1}{48}$ in. long, bright green, obtuse, 1-nerved, exceeding the internodes. Flowers terminal on short branches on pedicels usually much longer than themselves. Perianth $\frac{1}{16}$ in. long, of 3 boat-shaped membranous persistent segments free to the base. Capsule oblong, brown, crustaceous, as long as or longer than the perianth. T. bryoides, *Gardn. in Wight, Ic. t.* 1920.

MAURITIUS, in running streams at Moka, Flacq. etc. *T. trifaria*, Tulasne, Weddell, loc. cit., seems to be a mere variety with short stems and smaller densely crowded leaves. Cosmopolitan in the tropics.

ORDER XC. EUPHORBIACEÆ.*

Flowers monoicous or dioicous, usually monochlamydeous, but sometimes dichlamydeous or achlamydeous. Perianth with a short tube and usually 3–5 divisions. Hypogynous disk often present and bordered with glands. Stamens very various in number, central or surrounding a rudimentary ovary; anthers usually 2-celled, and dehiscing longitudinally. Ovary usually 3-celled; ovules solitary or in pairs in the cells, pendulous; styles as many as the cells, simple or divided. Fruit usually a 3-coccous capsule, the cocci breaking away from a persistent central column. Seeds with abundant fleshy albumen, often carunculate.—Herbs or shrubs of very various habit; leaves mostly alternate, often stipulate; flowers numerous, often minute, variously arranged, the bracts or involucres sometimes a conspicuous feature of the inflorescence. DISTRIB. Cosmopolitan. Species 3000.

Achlamydeous, with many males surrounding a single female flower in a cup-shaped involucre . . . . . 1. EUPHORBIA.
Monochlamydeous.
  Ovary 1-celled.
    Ovules in pairs. Fruit indehiscent . . . . 2. ANTIDESMA.
    Ovules solitary. Fruit follicular . . . . 3. MACARANGA.
  Ovary usually 3- rarely 2-celled. Fruit a 3- rarely 2-coccous capsule.
    Ovules in pairs.
      Stamens surrounding a rudimentary ovary . . . . 4. SECURINEGA.
      Stamens in the centre of the flower.
        Glands of the disk alternate with the perianth-lobes . . . . 5. PHYLLANTHUS.
        Glands of the disk opposite the perianth-lobes . . . . 6. AGYNEIA.
    Ovules solitary in the cells.
      Flowers in monoicous racemes without a general involucre.
        Stamens 2–3.
          Leaves round-cuspidate . . . . * EXCÆCARIA.
          Leaves oblanceolate . . . . 7. STILLINGIA.
        Stamens 8. Flowers minute . . . . 8. ACALYPHA.
        Stamens 10. Flowers large . . . . * MANIHOT.
        Stamens very numerous . . . . * RICINUS.
      Flowers in a monoicous cluster with a large 2-leaved general involucre . . . . 9. DALECHAMPIA.
      Flowers in dioicous racemes without a general involucre.
        Disk present . . . . 10. CLAOXYLON.
        Disk absent . . . . 11. MALLOTUS.
One or both sexes dichlamydeous.
    Flowers in racemes . . . . 12. CROTON.
    Flowers in compound corymbs.
      Calyx 5-lobed . . . . * JATROPHA.
      Calyx 2–3-lobed . . . . * ALEURITES.

1. EUPHORBIA, Linn.

Flowers apetalous, monoicous, many male round one female in a campanulate involucre. Male flower consisting of one pedicellate stamen subtended by a ciliated fimbriated bract. Female flower on an exserted usually curved pedicel; ovary 3-celled; cells 1-ovuled; styles 3, bifid. Capsule dehiscing septicidally in 3 dry cocci which fall from the persistent axis.—Herbs or shrubs of very various habit; leaves entire, opposite or alternate, with or without stipules; flower-heads axillary or in terminal bracteated cymes. DISTRIB. Cosmopolitan. Species 700.

Leaves stipulate.
  Annual weeds, with opposite leaves, (Anisophyllum).
    Leaves $\frac{1}{4}$–$\frac{1}{3}$ in. long, with heads of flowers in their axils.
      Leaves obscurely toothed.
        Keel of capsule-lobes not ciliated . . . . . 1. E. HEYNEANA.
        Keel of capsule-lobes ciliated with bristles . 2. E. PROSTRATA.
      Leaves distinctly toothed . . . . 3. E. THYMIFOLIA.
    Leaves 1–1$\frac{1}{2}$ in. long; heads of flowers in dense cymes.
      Stems densely pubescent . . . . 4. E. PILULIFERA.
      Stems nearly glabrous . . . . 5. E. HYPERICIFOLIA.
  Shrub, with crowded alternate leaves . . . . . 6. E. PYRIFOLIA.
Leaves exstipulate.
  Fleshy shrub, with leaves soon deciduous . . . . * E. TIRUCALLI.
  Shrub, with wiry woody branches . . . . 7. E. DAPHNOIDES.
  Annual herbs.
    Leaves sessile, linear . . . . 8. E. DRACUNCULOIDES.
    Leaves petioled obovate . . . . * E. PEPLUS.

1. **E. Heyneana,** *Boiss. in DC. Prod.* xv. 2, 35. A much-branched glaucous annual, with filiform densely tufted trailing stems 3–6 in. long. Leaves oblong, obtuse, $\frac{1}{4}$–$\frac{1}{3}$ in. long, on very short petioles, much more produced and cordate on the lower side at the base; stipules linear, deeply toothed. Heads 1–2 from the axils of the leaves of the main stem and on short congested leafy shoots; peduncle as long as the involucre; involucre $\frac{1}{48}$ in. long, campanulate, glabrous; glands quadrate, obscurely 3-lobed. Capsule $\frac{1}{24}$ in. each way, glabrous; lobes acutely keeled, not ciliated. Seeds acutely tetragonous, rough.

MAURITIUS, teste Boissier. Also Bourbon and tropical Asia.

2. **E. prostrata,** *Ait.; Boiss. in DC. Prod.* xv. 2, 47. A densely tufted annual, with much-branched filiform trailing stems 4–6 in. long, pubescent at first, but soon becoming glabrous. Leaves opposite, glaucous, on very short petioles, oblong, obtuse, $\frac{1}{4}$–$\frac{1}{3}$ in. long, obscurely denticulate, more produced and cordate on the lower side at the base. Heads 1–2 from the axils of the main leaves, and on short branches from the axils of reduced minute leaves; peduncles 3–4 times as long as the involucre; involucre minute, turbinate, glabrous, with deltoid lobes and round glands. Capsule $\frac{1}{24}$ in. long and broad, the

valves with an acute keel on the back ciliated with strong bristles. Seeds grey, acutely tetragonous, deeply sulcate.

MAURITIUS, a frequent weed, *Dr. Ayres !* etc. Tropical Africa and America.

3. **E. thymifolia,** *Burm.; Boiss. in DC. Prod.* xv. 2, 47. An annual herb, with very slender much-branched trailing pilose densely tufted stems ½–1 foot long. Leaves opposite, oblong, obtuse, ¼–⅓ in. long, on very short petioles, distinctly toothed, cuneate-truncate on the upper side, cordate on the lower side at the base; stipules lanceolate, fimbriated. Heads few together in the axils of small densely congested leaves on short shoots. Involucre campanulate, pilose, deeply lobed; glands minute, stalked, roundish, with a 2–3-lobed appendage. Capsule $\frac{1}{16}$ in. long and broad, brown, permanently erect, pilose, obtusely keeled. Seeds reddish, rough. E. Burmanniana, *J. Gay in Webb, Phyt. Can.* iii. 239.

MAURITIUS, and RODRIGUEZ, a common weed. Cosmopolitan in the tropics.

4. **E. pilulifera,** *Linn.; Boiss. in DC. Prod.* xv. 2, 21. An annual weed, with tufted branched erect stems ½–1 foot long, densely clothed in the upper part with spreading brown hairs. Leaves membranous, oblong-rhomboid, 1–1½ in. long, obtuse or subacute, distinctly toothed, very oblique, rounded on the lower side at the base and cuneate on the upper; stipules minute, linear, fimbriated; petiole very short. Heads in congested leafless cymes, ¼–½ in. thick, on short axillary peduncles. Involucre turbinate; lobes deltoid; glands round, with a minute or very narrow appendage. Capsule $\frac{1}{16}$ in. long, pilose. Seeds reddish-brown, rough.

MAURITIUS, SEYCHELLES and RODRIGUEZ, a common weed. Cosmopolitan in the tropics.

5. **E. hypericifolia,** *Linn.;* var. E. INDICA, *Lam.; Boiss. in DC. Prod.* xv. 2, 22. An annual weed, with erect densely tufted stems 1–1½ foot long, slightly pubescent towards the top. Leaves distinctly petioled, oblong, obtuse or minutely cuspidate, glabrous, glaucous, triplinerved, ½–1 in. long, rounded on the lower, cuneate on the upper side at the base. Heads in dense axillary cymes on short peduncles, sometimes subtended by a pair of small leaves. Involucre campanulate; lobes deltoid; glands ovate with a broad appendage. Capsule pubescent, nearly $\frac{1}{12}$ in. broad; valves keeled on the back. Seeds pitted, dull brown. E. hypericifolia, *Bojer, Hort. Maur.* 288. E. cassioides, *Presl.*

MAURITIUS, a frequent weed, regarded by Bojer as an introduction. Spread through the warmer regions of the Old World; and the type in America. *E. parviflora*, Linn., given by Bojer as an introduced Mauritian plant, scarcely differs from this except by its smooth seeds.

6. **E. pyrifolia,** *Lam.; Boiss. in DC. Prod.* xv., 77. A shrub, 10–15 feet high, with dichotomously forked or whorled branches and

smooth stiff woody terete branchlets marked below the rosettes with the scars of the fallen leaves. Leaves crowded at the end of the branchlets, oblanceolate-oblong, short-petioled, cuneate at the base, 3–4 in. long by 1–1½ in. broad, glabrous, subcoriaceous, obtuse; stipules conic, glandular, minute. Cymes of 1–3 heads, several from a rosette of leaves on 1–3 in. peduncles. Involucre ⅙ in. long, campanulate, subtended by a pair of oblong bracts; glands 5, twice as broad as long, exappendiculate. Capsule twice as broad as long, ⅙ in. long, glabrous, deeply 3-lobed. Seeds globose, smooth, glabrous.

MAURITIUS and SEYCHELLES, common in poor soils and the crevices of rocks. Endemic. *Fangame. Tanghin rouge.*

7. **E. daphnoides,** *Balf. fil.* A shrub, with the habit of *Daphne Laureola*, with slender woody terete branchlets. Leaves crowded near the end of the branches, deciduous, scattered, exstipulate, short-petioled, oblanceolate, 2–3 in. long, ⅓–¼ in. broad, glabrous, coriaceous. Heads in a deltoid cyme, 3–4 in. broad; bracts large, obovate, coriaceous, the ultimate ones ¼ in. long. Involucre nearly sessile, campanulate, $\frac{1}{12}$ in. long, glabrous, with 5 round entire glands. Fruit broader (⅙ in.) than long, deeply 3-lobed, glabrous. Seeds obovoid, glabrous, smooth, $\frac{1}{12}$ in. long.

RODRIGUEZ, *Balfour!* Endemic.

* **E. Tirucalli,** *Linn.; Boiss. in DC. Prod.* xv. 2, 96, a native of East Africa, now spread through the tropics of the Old World, is subspontaneous in Mauritius. It is a bush, reaching a height of 20 feet, with copious rod-like green curved branchlets, from which the small scattered exstipulate linear leaves fall in an early stage, deltoid sessile cymes of several heads each from the forks and end of the branchlets, a campanulate pilose involucre $\frac{1}{12}$ in. long, with transversely ovate glands and a pair of bracts at the base of the pedicel, a velvety deeply triquetrous capsule and smooth ovoid seeds. *Tirucalli.*

8. **E dracunculoides,** *Lam.; Boiss. in DC. Prod.* xv. 2, 139. An erect glabrous annual, 1–1½ feet high, with scattered sessile spreading linear glabrous acute leaves 2–3 in. long, narrowed to both ends. Heads in sparse lax dichotomous cymes on long single peduncles from the axils of the upper leaves, and whorled peduncles from the end of the main stem; ultimate bracts ½ in. long, lanceolate, like the leaves in texture. Involucre $\frac{1}{12}$ in. long, subsessile, campanulate, glabrous, with 2-horned glands. Capsule glabrous, rather broader (⅙ in.) than long, with acutely keeled turgid valves. Seeds oblong, mottled, not pitted. *Boiss. Ic. Euphorb. t.* 91.

MAURITIUS, a frequent weed. Also Bourbon and Tropical Asia.

* *E. Peplus*, Linn.; Boiss. in DC. Prod. xv. 2, 141, a common European weed, is now introduced into Mauritius and Rodriguez. It is an erect glabrous annual ¼–½ foot high, with scattered petioled obovate obtuse membranous leaves, heads in an ample corymb first

branching in threes and afterwards in twos, large bracts like the leaves in shape and texture, involucre $\frac{1}{24}$ in. long, campanulate, with 2-horned glands, capsule glabrous $\frac{1}{24}$ long and broad, the valves with two keels on the back and pale oblong deeply pitted seeds. The Rodriguez plant belongs to the Mediterranean subspecies *E. peploides*, Gouan, marked by its capsule and seeds not more than half as large as those of the type.

E. serpyllifolia, Bojer, Hort. Maur. 288, is not the plant of Persoon which is American only, but *E. serpens*, Kunth, which differs from *E. Heyneana* mainly by its broader leaves and smooth seeds. We have it from Galega Islands, but not from the Seychelles, from which Bojer reports it doubtfully.

2. ANTIDESMA, Burm.

Flowers polygamo-dioicous. Perianth calyx-like, with 3–8 long or short lobes. Stamens usually as many as the perianth-lobes, and opposite to them, inserted on a disk surrounding a rudimentary ovary; filaments filiform; anthers opening by slits at the top of the cells, versatile. Perfect ovary 1-celled, with two pendulous ovules; stigmas 3–4, sessile, spreading. Fruit indehiscent, with a solitary seed. Seed albuminous, without either caruncle or aril.—Trees or shrubs, with simple alternate stipulate leaves and numerous minute flowers in axillary or terminal bracteated spikes or racemes. DISTRIB. Tropics of Old World. Species 60.

Leaf-veins with pitted swellings in their axils.
- Leaves subsessile . . . . 1. A. MADAGASCARIENSE.
- Leaves petioled . . . . 2. A. ROTUNDIFOLIUM.

Leaf-veins without pitted swellings in their axils.
- Leaves large, oblong-lanceolate . . . . 3. A. LONGIFOLIUM.
- Leaves small, oblong . . . . 4. A. BOUTONI.
- Leaves small, lanceolate . . . . 5. A. LANCÆFOLIUM.

1. **A. madagascariense,** *Lam.; Mull. Arg. in DC. Prod.* xv. 2, 265. A shrub or small tree, 20–30 feet high, glabrous in all its parts. Leaves oblong, subcoriaceous, bright green, 3–6 in. long, obtuse or acute, rounded or cordate at the base, penninerved with distinct reticulated venules, and a swelling with a circular pore at the base of several of the main veins; petiole scarcely any. Racemes 1–4-nate, cotemporary with the leaves, nearly sessile, 1–2 in. long; pedicels $\frac{1}{24}$–$\frac{1}{12}$ in. long, stouter in the female than the male flower; bracts minute, deltoid. Perianth $\frac{1}{36}$ in. long, broadly campanulate, with 4–5 deltoid lobes. Stamens 4–5, much exserted. Stigmas 3–4, terminal Drupe purple, the size of a small pea, with a large bony endocarp and a solitary oblong seed.

MAURITIUS, on dry and woody hills of the interior, frequent. Also Bourbon and Madagascar.

2. **A. rotundifolium,** *Bojer, Hort. Maur.* 289 (name only). A shrub or small tree. Leaves membranous, obovate, obtuse or emarginate, cuneate or rounded at the base, $1\frac{1}{2}$–2 in. long, with about 4 erecto-patent veins on each side of the midrib, with a swelling with a pore at the base of the lower ones; petiole $\frac{1}{4}$ in. long, finely downy.

Racemes 1–2 in. long, cotemporary with the leaves, crowded on short branchlets; rachis densely pilose; pedicels of the lower flowers as long as the perianth; bracts pilose. Perianth campanulate, densely pilose, $\frac{1}{16}$ in. broad. Stamens 3–5, four times as long as the perianth. Female flowers not seen.

MAURITIUS, on hills of the Montagne du Garde and at the Petite Rivière. Endemic.

3. **A. longifolium,** *Bojer, Hort. Maur.* 289 (name only). General habit exactly of *A. madagascariense.* Leaves oblong-lanceolate, 5–9 in. long, deltoid at the base and apex, subcoriaceous, with many erecto-patent veins with distinct anastomosing venules between them, without any glandular pits in their axils; petiole $\frac{1}{4}$–$\frac{1}{2}$ in. long. Male flowers in crowded sessile racemes under an inch long; bracts deltoid, very minute; pedicels finally as long as the minute glabrous broadly campanulate perianth, which has 4 deltoid teeth. Stamens 4, three or four times as long as the perianth. Female flowers not seen.

MAURITIUS, on the banks of the Moka River and round Bois Chéri. Endemic.

4. **A. Boutoni,** *Baker.* A shrub 8 or 10 feet high. Leaves more oblong, smaller and more coriaceous in texture than in *A. longifolium,* 2–3$\frac{1}{2}$ in. long, very glossy on the face, the main veins erecto-patent, without any glandular pits in their axils; petiole flattened, $\frac{1}{4}$–$\frac{1}{3}$ in. long. Racemes very short; rachis glabrous; pedicels very short; bracts deltoid. Drupe oblique ovoid, $\frac{1}{3}$ in. long when dry, with 3 stigmas.

MAURITIUS, on rocks of the mountains near Port Louis, *Bouton!* Endemic.

5. **A. lanceæfolium,** *Bojer, Hort. Maur.* 289 (name only). A shrub, glabrous in all its parts. Leaves lanceolate, acute, subcoriaceous, rounded at the base, 2–4 inches long, $\frac{3}{4}$–1 inch broad; main veins erecto-patent, without any pitted swellings in their axils. Racemes solitary or in pairs, sessile, above an inch long; rachis glabrous; pedicels and bracts as long as the perianth. Perianth campanulate, $\frac{1}{16}$ in. broad; lobes deltoid. Stamens 4, three times the length of the perianth. Female flowers not seen.

MAURITIUS, in the forests of Moka and Quartier Militaire. Endemic.

3. MACARANGA, Thouars.

Flowers dioicous. Male perianth with 3–4 valvate lobes. Disk absent. Stamens central, very various in number; filaments free; anthers peltate, 3–4 celled. Female perianth with 3 imbricated lobes. Ovary various in structure, in *Eumacaranga*, to which our plant belongs, 1-celled, with a single style; ovules solitary in the cells. Fruit capsular. Seeds not carunculate.—Trees or shrubs, with alternate petioled stipulate leaves and minute clustered flowers. DISTRIB. Tropics of the Old World. Species 80 (including *Mappa*).

1. **M. mauritiana,** *Bojer, Hort. Maur.* 283 (name only). A small tree, 15 to 20 feet high, with stout branchlets marked by the scars of fallen leaves. Young parts clothed with brown tomentum, which entirely disappears from the mature leaves. Leaves subcoriaceous, glabrous, ½–1 foot long, entire, deltoid at the apex, equally rounded at the base, nearly as broad as long, with the petiole attached 1–1½ in. above the base and 7 ribs radiating from it; petiole 3–4 in. long; stipules ½ in. long, lanceolate, caducous. Flowers of both sexes on ascending peduncles from the axils of the crowded leaves. Males in dense clusters, sessile, terminal and lateral on the peduncles, subtended by tomentose foliaceous bracts with large glands near the edge. Male perianth $\frac{1}{12}$ in. long. Stamens 6–12; anthers 4-celled. Female flowers few to a peduncle, with an urceolate perianth-tube. Capsule follicular, glabrous, half an inch long, obliquely globose, crowned by the remains of the cylindrical style and large lanceolate stigma. *Baill. Etud. Euphorb. t.* 21, *fig.* 8–9; *Mull. Arg. in DC. Prod.* xv. 2, 1009.

MAURITIUS, in the woods of the Pouce range and at Vacquois, etc. Endemic. *Bois Violin.*

4. SECURINEGA, Juss.

Flowers dioicous. Perianth calycine, with 5 long lobes, with imbricate æstivation. Stamens usually 5, inserted on the disk round a rudimentary ovary and alternating with glands; filaments free, filiform; anthers oblong, dehiscing longitudinally. Ovary 3-celled; cells 2-ovuled; styles 3, bifid, short, connate. Fruit a septicidal capsule.—Shrubs, with alternate entire minutely stipulate leaves and abundant minute flowers in dense axillary fascicles. DISTRIB. Cosmopolitan in the tropical and subtropical zones. Species 13.

Leaves ovate, acute. Anthers dehiscing introrsely . . . . 1. S. DURISSIMA.
Leaves obovate obtuse. Anthers dehiscing extrorsely . . . 2. S. OBOVATA.

1. **S. durissima,** *Gmel.; Mull. Arg. in DC. Prod.* xv. 2, 447. A much-branched shrub or low tree with slender terete stiff branchlets. Leaves short-petioled, coriaceous, ovate, acute, bright green, glabrous, 1–3 in. long, usually cuneate at the base. Male flowers about 20 in a dense cluster in the axils of the leaves; pedicel finally as long as the perianth. Male perianth $\frac{1}{24}$ in. long; lobes deltoid, green. Stamens twice as long as the perianth. Female flowers fewer in a cluster, with longer (ultimately ¼–⅓ in.) pedicels, and narrower lobes, persistent and reflexed from the fruit. Capsule broader (¼–⅓ in.) than long, obtusely lobed. S. nitida, *Willd.; Bojer, Hort. Maur.* 277.

MAURITIUS, in ravines of the Pouce range, etc. RODRIGUEZ, abundant in the valleys, *Balfour!* Also Bourbon. *Bois dur.*

2. **S. obovata,** *Mull. Arg. in DC. Prod.* xv. 2, 429. A much branched glabrous spineless shrub, with tetragonous branchlets. Leaves short-petioled, obovate, obtuse, membranous, 1–2 in. long. Flowers minute, in copious clusters in the axils of the leaves. Perianth green, $\frac{1}{16}$ in. long, deeply 5-cleft; segments toothed. Female flowers fewer in a cluster, on very short pedicels. Male flowers in denser clusters, on filiform pedicels $\frac{1}{8}$–$\frac{1}{4}$ in. long. Stamens 3–4 times as long as the perianth, surrounding a 2–3-celled rudimentary ovary. Capsule depresso-globose, the size of a pea, at first rather fleshy, finally dry and black. Fluggea comorensis and arborescens, *Bojer, Hort. Maur.* 278.

SEYCHELLES, common in poor soil in all the islands, *Horne*, 583! MAURITIUS, *Telfair!* probably not a native. Spread through the tropics of the Old World.

5. PHYLLANTHUS, Linn.

Flowers monoicous or dioicous. Perianth calycine, 5–6-partite, the segments imbricate. Disk with glands which alternate with the perianth-segments. Male flowers without any rudimentary ovary. Stamens 3–5, the filaments connate or free. Ovary usually 3-celled; ovules in pairs in the cells; styles as many as the cells, usually bifid. Fruit a capsule with septicidal dehiscence. Seeds without either arillus or caruncle. —Herbs or shrubs; leaves short-petioled, entire, usually alternate; flowers minute, in the axils of the leaves, solitary or clustered. DISTRIB. Cosmopolitan in the Tropics. Species 400–500.

Annual or perennial herbs, with flowers 1–2 in the axils of most of the leaves.
  Leaves very narrow, 1-nerved . . . . 1. P. LONGIFOLIUS.
  Leaves broad, penninerved.
    Pedicels scarcely any.
      Annual; sepals oblanceolate-oblong . . . . 2. P. URINARIA.
      Perennial; sepals obovate . . . . 3. P. MADERASPATENSIS.
    Pedicels as long as the perianth . . . . 4. P. NIRURI.
    Pedicels much longer than the perianth . . . . 5. P. TENELLUS.
Low shrub of heath-like habit with narrow 1-nerved leaves . . . . 6. P. DUMETOSUS.
Tall shrubs with broad penninerved leaves.
  Cells of ovary and styles 2 . . . . 7. P. ANOMALUS.
  Cells of ovary and styles 3.
    Flowers 1–4 together in the axils of the leaves . 8. P. CASTICUM.
    Flowers in dense clusters in the axils of the leaves.
      Leaves alternate.
        Leaves ovate or round . . . . 9. P. PHILLYREÆFOLIUS.
        Leaves oblanceolate obtuse . . . . 10. P. LANCEOLATUS.
      Leaves opposite . . . . 11. P. OPPOSITIFOLIUS.
  Cells of ovary 4. Flowers in leafless racemes . . * P. DISTICHUS.

1. **P. longifolius,** *Lam. Ill. tab.* 756, *fig.* 3. A glabrous annual or perennial herb, with densely cæspitose ascending wiry branches $\frac{1}{4}$–$\frac{1}{2}$ foot long. Leaves alternate, nearly sessile, linear, 1-nerved, $\frac{1}{2}$–1 in. long, membranous, glabrous, green above, glaucous beneath; stipules

very minute, deltoid-cuspidate. Female flowers solitary, nearly sessile in the axils of the leaves. Female perianth $\frac{1}{24}$ in. long; segments oblanceolate, obtuse, with a narrow white membranous border. Capsule under $\frac{1}{12}$ in. broad, brown, depresso-globose. Seeds longitudinally striate Male flowers smaller, in pairs in the axils of the upper leaves. Glands of the disk of both sexes free. *Mull. Arg. in DC. Prod.* xv. 2, 361. P. linifolius, *Comm. MSS.* P. simplex, *Bojer, Hort. Maur.* 279, *not of Retz.*

MAURITIUS, on the sands of the seashore, *Commerson!* etc.; Ile aux Tonneliers, *Bory de St. Vincent.* Also Bourbon..

2. **P. Urinaria,** *Linn.; Mull. Arg. in DC. Prod.* xv. 2, 364. A much-branched erect glabrous annual, 1–2 feet high, with acutely tetragonous spreading or ascending branchlets. Leaves nearly sessile, oblong, obtuse, with a mucro, ascending, imbricated, $\frac{1}{4}$–$\frac{1}{2}$ in. long, green above, glaucous beneath, firmer than in *P. Niruri;* stipules very minute, lanceolate, acuminate. Flowers sessile or nearly sessile in the axils of the leaves, usually solitary. Female perianth $\frac{1}{24}$ in. long; segments oblong or lanceolate, with a broad membranous border, persistent. Capsule depresso-globose, $\frac{1}{12}$ in. broad, smooth or rugose. Seeds transversely ribbed. Male flowers in the axils of the upper leaves, very minute. Filaments monadelphous. P. cantoniensis, *Hornem, Hort. Hafn*, 910.

MAURITIUS and SEYCHELLES, a frequent weed at all elevations. Regarded by Bojer as an introduced species. Also Bourbon, Madagascar, and common in Tropical Asia. *P. rubens*, Bojer, MSS. is a common form with deep purple stems.

3. **P. maderaspatensis,** *Linn; Mull. Arg. in DC. Prod.* xv. 2, 362. An erect perennial, 1–3 feet high, with slender glabrous terete woody stems. Leaves nearly sessile, broad-oblanceolate, $\frac{1}{2}$–1 in. long, cuneate in the lower half, moderately firm, obtuse with a mucro; stipules lanceolate, membranous, persistent, ascending. Flowers 1–2 on very short pedicels in the axils of the leaves; the sexes often mixed. Segments of female perianth $\frac{1}{24}$ in. long, obovate with a narrow white edge, persistent. Filaments monadelphous. Glands of both sexes free. Capsule depresso-globose, $\frac{1}{8}$ in. broad. Seeds dotted in longitudinal lines. P. stipulaceus, *Bojer, Hort. Maur.* 280.

SEYCHELLES, on the shore of Praslin at Grand Anse, *Horne*, 582! Island of Diogo Garcia, where it is called *Herbe à balais, Bojer!* Warmer regions of the Old World.

P. simplex, Retz.; Mull. Arg. in DC. Prod. xv. 2, 391, which is given by Bojer as a Mauritian plant, but about which I suspect some mistake, differs from this by its lanceolate acute leaves and female flowers on pedicels $\frac{1}{8}$–$\frac{1}{6}$ in. long. It is spread through Tropical Asia and Polynesia.

4. **P. Niruri,** *Linn.; Mull. Arg. in DC. Prod.* xv. 2, 406. A much-branched erect annual, 1–2 feet high, with slender terete glabrous

branchlets. Leaves nearly sessile, $\frac{1}{4}$–$\frac{1}{3}$ in. long, oblong or obovate-oblong, obtuse with a minute mucro, membranous, pale green above, glaucous beneath; stipules lanceolate, acuminate, very minute. Flowers in the axils of most of the leaves, usually solitary on pedicels twice as long as the perianth. Female perianth $\frac{1}{24}$ in. long; segments oblanceolate-oblong, with a broad membranous border, persistent, reflexing after the capsule falls. Capsule smooth, depresso-globose, under $\frac{1}{12}$ in. broad. Seeds longitudinally ribbed. Male flowers smaller, usually in pairs in the axils of the upper leaves. Stamens 3, with monadelphous filaments.

SEYCHELLES, MAURITIUS, and RODRIGUEZ, a common weed; Coin de Mire, *Horne!* Cosmopolitan in the Tropics. *Castique petite espèce* or *Nuriri.*

5. **P. tenellus,** *Roxb.; Mull. Arg. in DC. Prod.* xv. 338. An erect much-branched glabrous annual with the habit of *P. Niruri*, with filiform terete branchlets. Leaves membranous, nearly sessile, obovate, obtuse, $\frac{1}{4}$–$\frac{1}{2}$ in. long, green above, glaucous beneath; stipules very minute, ascending, lanceolate acuminate. Female flowers solitary in the axils of the lower leaves, on erecto-patent filiform $\frac{1}{8}$–$\frac{1}{4}$ in. pedicels. Female perianth $\frac{1}{36}$ in. long; segments oblanceolate-oblong, obtuse, with a green centre and broad white membranous edge. Capsule under $\frac{1}{12}$ in. broad, depresso-globose, umbilicate. Seeds minutely granular. Male flowers very minute, in pairs in the axils of the upper leaves on shorter pedicels.

SEYCHELLES, in the streets of Port Victoria and other places in Mahé, *Horne*, 311! 584! Said to have been introduced from Mauritius to the Calcutta botanic garden, but I have not seen Mauritian specimens. Also Cape, Natal, and Arabia.

6. **P. dumetosus**, *Poir.; Mull. Arg. in DC. Prod.* xv. 2, 398. A low erect shrub of heath-like habit, with very numerous crowded angular slender glabrous sulcate branchlets. Leaves nearly sessile, subcoriaceous, ascending, 1-nerved, linear or lanceolate, $\frac{1}{4}$ in. long; stipules minute, deltoid-cuspidate. Flowers monoicous, usually solitary in the axils of the leaves; pedicels scarcely as long as the perianth. Female perianth $\frac{1}{36}$ in. long, with 5–6 oblanceolate-oblong obtuse segments with a narrow green centre and broad whitish borders. Capsule depresso-globose, $\frac{1}{24}$ in. broad. Seeds smooth. Filaments nearly free. Glands of the disk of both sexes free. Kirganelia dumetosa, *Spreng.; Bojer, Hort. Maur*, 278.

RODRIGUEZ, *Commerson, Balfour!* Said by Bojer to be also a plant of Mauritius, but I have not seen specimens. Endemic.

7. **P. anomalus,** *Mull. Arg. in DC. Prod.* xv. 2, 418. A much-branched dioicous shrub, with angular branchlets. Leaves distinctly petioled, obovate or oblong, 2–3 in. long, obtuse or acute, subcoriaceous, deltoid at the base; stipules large, lanceolate, membranous, caducous. Female flowers solitary in the axils of the leaves on stout pedicels

finally $\frac{1}{2}$ inch long. Expanded female perianth $\frac{1}{8}$ in. across; segments 4, oblong, obtuse, persistent. Capsule broader ($\frac{1}{4}$ inch) than long, 2-celled; styles 2, short, broad, spreading, bifid. Male flowers in dense clusters on filiform pedicels. Perianth similar to that of the female. Stamens 4, free. Disk of the flowers of both sexes minute. Securinega hysterantha, *Bojer, Hort. Maur.* 282. Bridelia Berryana, *Wall. Cat. No.* 7960. Cicca anomala and Fluggea major, *Baillon*.

MAURITIUS, frequent in mountain woods. Also Comoros, Madagascar, and Zambesi-land.

8. **P. casticum,** *Willem; Mull. Arg. in DC. Prod.* xv. 2, 348. A shrub 10–15 feet high, with very numerous very slender ascending pubescent or glabrescent branches. Leaves distichous, alternate, short-petioled, membranous, obtuse, oblanceolate or oblong, $\frac{1}{4}$–$\frac{3}{4}$ in. long. Flowers monoicous, 1–4 together in the axils of all the leaves, on pedicels $\frac{1}{12}$–$\frac{1}{8}$ in. long, subtended by minute lanceolate persistent bracts. Perianth $\frac{1}{16}$–$\frac{1}{12}$ in. long; segments oblong, purplish-green, imbricated. Stamens twice as long as the perianth, the 3 inner joined in a column, the 2 outer nearly free. Ovary-cells and styles usually 3, sometimes 4 or 5; styles bifid. Fruit obovoid, the size of a small pea, at first reddish, fleshy. P. virgineus, *Pers.* Kirganelia elegans, *Juss.; Bojer, Hort. Maur.* 279.

MAURITIUS, common on dry banks through the island. RODRIGUEZ, only in one or two of the valleys, *Balfour!* There are two varieties, one with pilose branches and smaller leaves, and the other with glabrous branches and larger leaves. Also Bourbon and Madagascar. *Kirganellie* or *Castique*.

9. **P. phillyreæfolius,** *Poir.; Mull. Arg. in DC. Prod.* xv. 2, 376. A dioicous shrub, 5–10 feet high, with numerous erecto-patent angular branchlets. Leaves shortly petioled, coriaceous, bright green above, very variable in size and shape, oblong or ovate or obovate, 2–4 in. long, acute or obtuse, usually deltoid at the base; stipules minute, deltoid. Flowers of both sexes in dense axillary clusters, with masses of cupular bracts; pedicels of the female finally $\frac{1}{4}$–$\frac{1}{2}$ in. long. Expanded female perianth $\frac{1}{12}$ in. across; segments whitish, oblong, obtuse. Male flowers smaller, on shorter pedicels. Stamens 3, monadelphous and the anthers also adhering. Capsule blackish, depresso-globose, $\frac{1}{8}$ in. thick; seeds smooth. P. Commersoni, *Baill. Adans.* ii. 53. P. polymorphus, *Mull. Arg. in Linnæa*, xxxii. 24, in part.

MAURITIUS, frequent in the woods at all elevations. Also Bourbon. A variable plant, of which Dr. Muller in the Prodromus describes and names eleven varieties. Of these, the most striking are *P. subcordatus*, Baill., a high mountain form, with nearly orbicular small obtuse subcordate leaves, and *P. Telfairianus*, Wall. Cat. 7935, with nearly sessile membranous oblong leaves about an inch long, and flowers smaller and fewer in a cluster. *P. consanguineus*, Mull. Arg. in DC. Prod. xv. 2, 378, which differs from typical *phillyreæfolius* by its larger lanceolate-acuminate stipules, is probably another variety.

10. **P. lanceolatus**, *Poir.; Mull. Arg. in DC. Prod.* xv. 2, 378. A dioicous shrub, with numerous erecto-patent angular branchlets. Leaves subcoriaceous, oblanceolate, obtuse, emarginate, 1½–2 in. long, narrowed from the middle to the base; petiole very short; stipules deltoid-cuspidate, persistent. Flowers of both sexes in dense axillary fascicles, with cupular bracts; pedicels finally ⅛–¼ in. long. Expanded female perianth 1/12 in. across; segments oblong, obtuse. Capsule 1/12 in. thick, depresso-globose; seeds smooth. Male flowers not more than 1/48 in. long, broadly campanulate. Stamens 3, with free anthers, but filaments connate towards the base.

Mauritius, in shady forests, frequent. Endemic.

11. **P. oppositifolius**, *Baill.; Mull. Arg. in DC. Prod.* xv. 2, 378. A much-branched dioicous shrub, 10–15 feet high, with a distinct wing on each side running from node to node of the branchlets. Leaves opposite, cordate-ovate, sessile, acute, 1–2 inches long, membranous, green on both surfaces. Flowers of both sexes in dense axillary clusters with cupular bracts; female pedicels finally ¼ in. long. Expanded female perianth 1/12 in. across; segments oblong, obtuse, much imbricated. Capsule brown, depresso-globose, ¼ in. thick. Male perianth smaller than the female, on a filiform pedicel ⅛–⅙ in. long. Stamens 3, with connate anthers. Glands of the disk 5, round, large.

Mauritius, in woods near Moka, Colville bridge, etc. Endemic.

* *P. distichus*, Mull. Arg. in DC. Prod. xv. 2, 413 (Cicca disticha, *Linn.; Bojer, Hort. Maur.* 278), is casually subspontaneous both in Mauritius (Sieber, 301 !) and the Seychelles (Horne, 310 !). It is a shrub with stout branchlets, minute monoicous flowers in nodose racemes from the old wood, ovate membranous acute glabrous leaves 2–3 in. long, segments of the male perianth roundish, and a 4-celled globose black capsule the size of a large pea. The native country is not known clearly. There is a form (*Cicca nodiflora*, Lam.) with small leaves on the floriferous branchlets. *Cherimbolier.*

6. AGYNEIA, Vent.

Flowers monoicous. Perianth calycine, deeply 6-lobed, persistent. Male flower with square emarginate perianth-lobes, 3 stamens with filaments connate in a column, a disk with a gland opposite each sepal and no rudimentary ovary. Female flower with deltoid perianth-lobes. Ovary 3-celled; ovules 2 in each cell; styles 3, spreading, bifid. Capsule membranous. Seed without caruncle or arillus.—A single species.

1. **A. bacciformis**, *A. Juss.; Mull. Arg. in DC. Prod.* xv. 2, 235. A glabrous annual, with wiry tufted branched ascending or spreading

stems 1–2 feet long, the branchlets acutely quadrangular. Leaves oblong, sessile, coriaceous-succulent, $\frac{1}{2}$–$\frac{3}{4}$ in. long, rounded at both ends; stipules minute, spreading, lanceolate, persistent. Flowers placed in the axils of the upper leaves, males and females in different axils; pedicels as long as the perianth, subtended by minute lanceolate acuminate bracts. Perianth $\frac{1}{24}$–$\frac{1}{16}$ in. long, persistent. Capsule glabrous, the size of a pea. A. impubes, *Vent. Hort. Cels, t.* 23; *Bojer, Hort. Maur.* 280, *not Linn.*

MAURITIUS, on the seashore near Port Louis, *Bojer, Dr Ayres!* Also Tropical Asia, Bourbon, and Madagascar, not continental Africa.

* *Excæcaria sebifera*, Mull. Arg. in DC. Prod. xv. 2, 1210 (Croton sebiferus, *Linn.*; Stillingfleetia sebifera, *Bojer, Hort. Maur.* 282), a native of China and Japan, now widely cultivated, is occasionally subspontaneous in Mauritius. It is a tree, glabrous in all its parts, with middle-sized entire round-cuspidate leaves with a pair of glands at the top of the long petiole, monochlamydeous monoicous flowers in dense cylindrical spike-like racemes consisting of one or two females at the base and the very numerous males in fascicles, a minute plate-shaped perianth with usually 3 deltoid lobes, male flower with 2 stamens, disk absent, capsule globose cuspidate smooth black 3-valved with three roundish hard seeds with a white waxy coat. *Arbre à suif.*

7. STILLINGIA, Garden.

Flowers monoicous. Disk 0. Perianth in each sex with 2–3 obtuse broad imbricated lobes. Stamens as many as the perianth-lobes; anthers 2-celled. Ovary 3-celled; ovules solitary in the cells; styles simple, subulate, united below. Fruit a 3-coccous capsule. Seeds carunculate. —Milky glabrous shrubs, with stipulate alternate leaves and flowers in spikes with the females below the males. DISTRIB. Warmer regions of both hemispheres. Species 10–12.

1. **S. lineata,** *Mull. Arg. in DC. Prod.* xv. 2, 1157. A milky shrub, 5–6 feet high, glabrous in all its parts, with stout terete branchlets. Leaves glossy, coriaceous, oblanceolate, bright green, 3–5 inches long, $\frac{3}{4}$–1 in. broad two-thirds of the way up, narrowed to a subobtuse point and very gradually to the base, entire, the distinct contiguous parallel erecto-patent veins anastomosing in arches a space within the border; petiole flattened, $\frac{1}{4}$–$\frac{1}{2}$ in. long. Flowers in lax short-peduncled terminal spikes 2–3 in. long, 1–5 solitary females at the bottom, the rest males, 5–6 flowers together in little pockets formed by the amplexicaul truncate bract, which has a couple of large adnate oblong glands at its base. Male perianth short-stalked, $\frac{1}{36}$ in. long, with 2 rounded lobes. Anthers minute, globose, just exserted. Capsule glabrous, $\frac{1}{3}$ in. broad and long, with three obtuse lobes. Sapium lineatum and lævigatum, *Lam.*; *Bojer, Hort. Maur.* 283–4.

Var. OBTUSIFOLIA, *Mull. Arg. loc. cit.* Leaves obtuse and often emarginate, shorter in proportion to their breadth (2–3 in. by 1–1½ in.) very glossy and coriaceous. Expanded spikes lax. Sapium obtusifolium, *Lam.; Bojer, Hort. Maur.* 284.

Var. TANGUINA, *Mull. Arg. loc. cit.* Leaves 8–10 in. long, under an inch broad, thinner in texture, obscurely crenate, narrowed to both ends from two-thirds of the way up. Stillingia tanguina, *Baill. Adans.* ii. 28.

Var. DENSIFLORA, *Baker.* Leaves longer (4–8 in. long by 2–3 in. broad two-thirds of the way up), very obtuse, thinner in texture than in the two first varieties; veins much more distant. Fully expanded spikes shorter and denser, so that the clusters of flowers nearly hide the rachis. Capsule larger (½–⅝ in. broad).

MAURITIUS, in the mountain woods, the first three varieties, the second the commonest. Var. *densiflora*; SEYCHELLES, in the woods of Mahé at 800–1600 feet, where it is called *Bois Jasmin*, and superstitiously dreaded by the natives, *Horne*. 309! 579! *Wright*, 112! Endemic.

8. ACALYPHA, Linn.

Flowers usually monoicous. Male perianth 4-partite, with valvate divisions. Disk and rudimentary ovary 0. Stamens usually 8; filaments free; anther-cells subulate, free, pendulous. Female perianth with 3–5 slightly imbricated segments. Ovary 3-celled; ovules solitary; styles 3, usually deeply laciniated. Fruit capsular. Seeds carunculate. —Herbs or shrubs with petioled alternate stipulate leaves, the minute flowers in copious axillary spikes, the males at the top in clusters with minute bracts, the females at the bottom subtended by or enveloped in large foliaceous persistent bracts. DISTRIB. Cosmopolitan in the tropics. Species 200.

Annual weeds, with copious female flowers.
  Stems puberulent. Bracts dentate . . . . 1. A. INDICA.
  Stems bristly. Bracts deeply incised . . . . 2. A. POIRETII.
Shrubs, with few female flowers.
  Bracts of female flowers $\frac{1}{12}$–⅛ in. broad.
    Leaves glabrous, short-petioled . . . . 3. A. COLORATA.
    Leaves pubescent, long-petioled . . . . 4. A. MARGINATA.
  Bracts of female flowers ¼–⅓ in. broad . . . . 5. A. RETICULATA.

1. **A. indica,** *Linn.; Mull. Arg. in DC. Prod.* xv. 2, 868. An erect annual, 1–3 feet high, with branchlets and leaves beneath puberulent. Leaves broad, ovate, 5-nerved, membranous, dentate, with a cuneate or rounded base; petiole longer than the blade. Female spikes lax, copious, nearly sessile, 1–2 in. long. Female flowers 3–5 in a cluster, subtended by an amplexicaul leafy bract ¼ in. long, toothed round the outer edge. Capsule bristly, green, membranous, nearly $\frac{1}{12}$ in.

long. Styles deeply laciniated. A. spicata, *Linn.* A. ciliata and canescens, *Wall.*

SEYCHELLES and MAURITIUS, a common weed. Spread through the tropics of the Old World.

2. **A. Poiretii,** *Spreng.; Mull. Arg. in DC. Prod.* xv. 2, 880. An erect annual, 1–3 feet high, with stems clothed with spreading bristly hairs. Leaves middle-sized, membranous, ovate, deeply crenate, entire at the base; petiole bristly, as long as or longer than the blade. Female spikes short, sessile, oblong. Female flowers solitary in the clasping pilose deeply toothed foliaceous bracts. Capsules $\frac{1}{12}$ in. long, the valves splitting into two and rolling up. Styles simple. A. hispida, *Willd.; Bojer, Hort. Maur.* 285.

MAURITIUS, a frequent weed. Probably of American origin, but now widely spread in the Old World.

3. **A. colorata,** *Spreng. Syst.* iii. 879. A shrub, 4 or 6 feet high, with glabrous branchlets. Leaves subcoriaceous, glabrous, oblong-panduriform, very variable in size, usually 3–6 inches long, 1–$2\frac{1}{2}$ inches broad at the middle, rounded at the base, obtuse or obtusely pointed, obscurely crenate or entire, green on the upper surface, concolorous or bright claret-purple beneath; petiole usually $\frac{1}{4}$–$\frac{1}{2}$ in. long, rarely longer. Male flowers in dense clusters on copious sessile or nearly sessile axillary spikes 2–4 in. long. Female flowers few, usually in sessile clusters of 2–4 in the axils of the leaves, subtended by a round coriaceous entire bract $\frac{1}{12}$–$\frac{1}{8}$ inch broad. Ovary pilose, prickly; styles deeply laciniated. Seeds smooth. A. discolor, marginata, and integrifolia, *Bojer, Hort. Maur.* 286. A. Commersoniana, *Baill.; Mull. Arg. in DC. Prod.* xv. 2, 849.

MAURITIUS, common through the island in woods and thickets. A very variable plant. *A. discolor*, Bojer, is a common form with the leaves bright purple beneath; *A. marginata*, Bojer, not Spreng., with the leaves purple beneath except a green edge; *A. integrifolia*, Willd., a form with entire leaves. Var. *parvifolia*, Mull. Arg. (Sieber 369), is a striking variety of dwarf habit with oblong leaves not more than $\frac{1}{2}$–1 inch long. Also Madagascar, Comoros, and perhaps Timor.

4. **A. marginata,** *Spreng.; Mull. Arg. in DC. Prod.* xv. 2, 850, *not Bojer.* A shrub, with finely pubescent tetragonous branchlets. Leaves membranous, oblong, shallowly dentate, deltoid at the apex and base, 4–8 in. long, at first finely pubescent beneath, but nearly or quite glabrous when mature; petiole $\frac{1}{2}$–2 in. long, pubescent. Male spikes 2–4 in. long, sessile in the axils of the leaves; bracts deltoid, densely pilose. Female flowers few, in small clusters, sessile in the axils of the leaves, subtended by a minute obovate coriaceous entire bract. Ovary prickly; styles deeply laciniated. A. tomentosa, *Bojer, Hort. Maur.* 285.

MAURITIUS, on the mountains of Nouvelle Découverte. Also Bourbon. *Bois queue de Rats.*

5. **A. reticulata,** *Mull. Arg. in DC. Prod.* xv. 2, 851. A shrub with slender glabrous terete branchlets. Leaves membranous, always green, glabrous, ovate or oblong, obtuse or acute, 2–4 in. long, crenulate or nearly entire; petiole ¼–1 in. long, glabrous or puberulent; stipules subulate. Male spikes numerous, slender, flexuose, 2–4 in. long, sessile or short-peduncled. Female flowers few, 1–3 sessile or peduncled in the axils of the leaves or at the base of the male spikes, subtended by a round coriaceous entire bract ¼–⅓ in. broad. Ovary prickly; styles short, pectinately laciniated. Capsule glabrous, the size of a pea. Seeds smooth. Tragia reticulata, *Poir. Encycl.* vii. 725. Acalypha lantanæfolia and filiformis, *Bojer, Hort. Maur.* 286.

MAURITIUS, in woods of the Pouce and Piton du Milieu de l'Isle. Also Bourbon, Comoros, Madagascar, and St. Helena.

* *Manihot utilissima,* Pohl Ic. *t.* 24; Mull. Arg. in DC. Prod. xv. 2. 1064); Janipha Manihot, *Kunth; Bot. Mag. t.* 3071; *Bojer, Hort. Maur.* 282), the commonly-cultivated Cassava, is often found in Mauritius, the Seychelles, and Rodriguez, about abandoned plantations. It is an erect perennial, with a stout root reaching a length of 3 feet with abundant farina and milky juice, stems 6–8 feet high, deeply palmate or rarely entire long-petioled glabrous membranous leaves glaucous on the under side, flowers in lax axillary monoicous racemes or panicles, a petaloid 5-partite perianth much larger (⅜–½ in. long) in the female than the male flowers, a disk present in both sexes, 10 biserial included stamens inserted round the disk, a 3-celled ovary surrounded by 10 staminodes, and a capsular fruit half an inch long, with 6 rugose narrowly-winged valves. There are two varieties, one with a red (*Manioc rouge*) and the other with a blue stem (*Manioc bleu*). It is probably a native of South America.

* *Ricinus communis,* Linn.; Mull. Arg. in DC. Prod. xv. 2, 1017, (the castor-oil plant), a native of Tropical Asia, is commonly cultivated and casually subspontaneous in Mauritius, Rodriguez, and the Seychelles. It is an erect glabrous shrubby perennial with long-petioled large peltate palmatifid leaves with toothed acute lobes, monoicous monochlamydeous fascicled flowers in racemes or little-branched panicles, a membranous 5-partite perianth, stamens very numerous (up to 1000) connate in dichotomous fascicles, and a round muricated 3-celled capsule each cell of which contains a smooth oblong mottled copiously oleaginous seed. *Palma Christi.*

9. DALECHAMPIA, Linn.

Flowers of both sexes placed together in a 2-leaved foliaceous involucre. Disk and petals 0. Male perianth of 4–5 entire pieces. Stamens central, usually about 20; filaments connate; anthers 2-celled. Ovary 3–4-celled; ovules solitary in the cells; styles 3–4 connate in a long column dilated at the top. Fruit a 3–4-coccous capsule. Seeds not carunculate.—Twining herbs or shrubs with alternate leaves and long-stalked clusters of flowers concealed by the two leaves of the large leafy involucre. DISTRIB. Cosmopolitan in the tropics. Species 50.

1. **D. tamifolia,** *Lam.; Mull. Arg. in DC. Prod.* xv. 2, 1248. A climbing shrub, with slender finely pilose branches and petioles. Leaves long-petioled, deeply cordate, membranous, as broad as long (4–6 in.), with three deep palmate denticulate acute lobes; stipules reflexed, lanceolate, persistent. Peduncles as long as the petiole, with a whorl of reflexed lanceolate persistent bracts below the involucre; bracts of the involucre $1\frac{1}{2}$–2 inches broad and long, pale rose, acute, entire or 3-lobed, conspicuously veined. Female flowers in threes with the deeply laciniated perianth-segments persistent and accrescent in fruit. Style-column nearly $\frac{1}{2}$ inch long, slightly dilated at the tip. Male flowers numerous, the glabrous globose buds $\frac{1}{8}$ inch thick, splitting open and disclosing a dense head of yellow oblong anthers on a column as long as the lanceolate perianth-segments. D. trilobata, *Sieber, Herb. Maur. No.* 256.

MAURITIUS, *Sieber!* Also Madagascar and the Comoro Islands.

10. CLAOXYLON, A. Juss.

Flowers dioicous. Perianth calycine, the male usually 3-partite, with valvate segments. Stamens numerous, inserted on a thick disk, the glands of which alternate with the perianth-segments; filaments free; anthers of two cells which adhere to one another at the base only. Female perianth 2–3-partite; ovary usually 3-celled; ovules solitary in the cells; styles 3 short, simple, spreading. Fruit a deeply-lobed small capsule. Seeds enveloped in a thin arillus.—Shrubs or trees, with alternate petioled penninerved leaves, the flowers of both sexes in racemes, with minute bracts, usually fascicled in clusters. DISTRIB. Tropics of the Old World. Species 40.

Leaves coriaceous, glabrous.
  Racemes short, dense . . . . 1. C. GRANDIFOLIUM.
  Racemes short, lax . . . . 2. C. PARVIFLORUM.
  Racemes long and slender.
    Leaves oblong or oblanceolate-oblong; male flowers 1–3-nate . . . . 3. C. LINOSTACHYS.
    Leaves obovate; male flowers solitary . . . . . 4. C. NERAUDIANUM.
Leaves membranous, pilose beneath . . . . * C. INDICUM.

1. **C. grandifolium,** *Mull. Arg. in DC. Prod.* xv. 2, 785. A shrub, with stout terete glabrous branchlets. Leaves oblanceolate-oblong, glabrous, subcoriaceous, 6–9 in. long, deltoid at the apex, cuneate at the base, distantly denticulate; petiole $\frac{1}{2}$–1 in. long. Flowers in dense nearly sessile axillary racemes 1–$1\frac{1}{2}$ in. long; bracts minute, deltoid, densely imbricated before the flowers open; pedicels very short. Stamens about 40. Ovary ovoid, tomentose. Capsule

depresso-globose, ⅛ in. broad, with deep round lobes, clothed with whitish brown tomentum. Seeds globose, pitted, with a thin white arillus. Acalypha grandifolia, *Poir. Encyc.* vi. 204. Claoxylon crassifolium, *Baill. Adans.* i. 279.

MAURITIUS, on the hill-woods, *Sieber*, 184! Also Bourbon, *Carmichael!*

2. **C. parviflorum,** *A. Juss.; Mull. Arg. in DC. Prod.* xv. 2, 785. A shrub, with glabrous branchlets. Leaves subcoriaceous, more or less tinged with vinose purple, oblanceolate, obtuse, broadly crenulate, 2–4 in. long, narrowed from the middle to a slightly rounded base; petiole ¼–½ in. long. Racemes lax-flowered, subsessile, little longer than the petioles. Male flowers 3–5-nate. Stamens about 15. Female pedicels as long as the perianth. Bracts and perianth-segments deltoid. Capsule tomentose, ⅛ in. thick. Seeds white, slightly pitted.

RODRIGUEZ, *Balfour!* Included in Dupont's Mauritian catalogue, but I have not seen specimens. Also Bourbon.

3. **C. linostachys,** *Baill.; Mull. Arg. in DC. Prod.* xv. 2, 786. A shrub, 6 to 10 feet high, with terete glabrous branchlets. Leaves oblanceolate-oblong, coriaceous, scabrous on both surfaces, deltoid or obtuse at the tip, cuneate at the base, 4–8 in. long, obscurely crenulate; petiole ⅛–¼ in. long. Flowers in lax racemes 4–6 in. long, on 2–3 inch axillary peduncles. Male flowers 1–3-nate; bracts deltoid, glabrous, very minute. Male pedicels as long as the buds. Stamens 15–30. Capsule glabrous, under ¼ in. broad, deeply 3-lobed. Seeds rugose, purple. C. scabrum, *Bojer, Hort. Maur.* 285.

MAURITIUS, in dense woods of the Pouce range and about Savanne and Bassin blanc. Endemic.

4. **C. Neraudianum,** *Baill.; Mull. Arg. in DC. Prod.* xv. 2, 788. A shrub, with glabrous branchlets. Leaves obovate-oblong, obtuse, cuneate at the base, 3 inches long by half as broad, entire, scabrous, subcoriaceous, tinged with purple; petiole ½–1 in. long. Female racemes slender, with the rachis and short pedicels puberulous. Flowers always solitary. Male flowers unknown. Hypogynous glands round, petaloid, connate at the base. Ovary pubescent; styles plumose.

MAURITIUS. Described by M. Baillon from a specimen in the Delessert herbarium gathered by Neraud. Endemic.

* *C. indicum*, Hassk.; Mull. Arg. in DC. Prod. xv. 2, 782 (C. macrophyllum, *Bojer, Hort. Maur*, 284), a native of China and the Malay isles, is planted and casually subspontaneous in Mauritius, (Sieber, 324, etc.). It is a shrub, with pilose branchlets, long-petioled large oblong membranous dentate leaves acute cuneate at the base green and glabrous above thinly pubescent beneath, flowers of both sexes in clusters on long racemes, short pedicels, minute deltoid tomentose perianth-seg-

ments, a thick disk, about 20 purple stamens and a tomentose depresso-globose capsule under half an inch broad with three deep rounded lobes and short divaricated entire pilose styles.

Of *C. Mezierii*, Bouton in Bojer, Hort. Maur. 283 (name only), I have not seen a specimen. Probably it is either *C. grandifolium* or *Neraudianum*. *C. glandulosum*, which is enumerated in Dupont's Mauritian catalogue, I have seen from Bourbon only.

11. MALLOTUS, Lour.

Flowers usually dioicous. Male perianth with 3–5 valvate lobes. Disk and petals 0. Stamens very numerous, central; anthers 2-celled; filaments free or joined at the base. Female perianth 3–5-partite. Ovary usually 3-celled; ovules solitary in the cells; styles 3, simple, subulate. Fruit capsular. Seeds not carunculate.—Shrubs or trees with alternate or opposite petioled stipulate leaves, the flowers of both sexes racemose. DISTRIB. Tropics of the Old World. Species 70.

1. **M. integrifolius,** *Mull. Arg. in DC. Prod.* xv. 2, 960. A tree 20–25 feet high, with the young parts clothed with thin whitish lepidote tomentum, which disappears as they mature. Leaves alternate, long-petioled, entire, coriaceous, ovate, acute, 4–9 in. long, rounded at the base, the numerous strong ascending main veins connected by distinct transverse venules. Flowers in axillary racemes, the males copious and usually panicled; pedicels very short. Buds round, $\frac{1}{8}$ in. thick, glabrous or lepidote. Male perianth-lobes deltoid. Stamens 200–300. Female racemes few-flowered and simple. Segments of female perianth subulate, $\frac{1}{4}$ inch long. Capsule $\frac{1}{2}$ inch broad, with round carpels each furnished with four firm spreading horns. Styles subulate, $\frac{1}{2}$–$\frac{3}{4}$ in. long. Ricinus integrifolius, *Willd. Sp. Plant.* iv. 567. Boutonia mascariensis, *Bojer, Hort. Maur.* 282. Cordemoya integrifolia, *Baill. Adans*, i. 255.

MAURITIUS, in the dense forests of the centre of the island. Also Bourbon.

No. 577 of Mr. Horne's Seychelles collection, of which a single tree without flowers was seen at the south end of the island of Mahé, may be a second species of *Mallotus*. It is glabrous in all its parts, with slender terete branchlets, short-petioled obovate obtuse entire subcoriaceous leaves 2–3 inches long with a cuneate base, and a tricoccous smooth capsule the size of a pea broader than long, forming part of a lax terminal raceme from which all the flowers have fallen, which is continued into the axils of the upper leaves.

12. CROTON, Linn.

Flowers in monoicous racemes, dichlamydeous or the petals in the females suppressed. Calyx campanulate, with 5 deltoid imbricated lobes. Petals free, ligulate or oblanceolate. Stamens numerous, central; filaments filiform; anthers oblong. Disk bearing 5 glands alternate with the petals. Ovary usually 3-celled; ovules solitary in the cells; styles 3, dichotomously branched. Fruit a 3-coccous capsule. Seeds caruncculate.—Herbs or shrubs, with alternate petioled leaves, the pubescence often lepidote, the racemes axillary and terminal, usually monoicous with the male flowers at the top and the females below. DISTRIB. Cosmopolitan in the tropics. Species 450.

Section ELUTERIA. Flowers of both sexes furnished with petals.

Stamens about 90; petioles long . . . . 1. C. MAURITANICUS.
Stamens 20–30; petioles short . . . . 2. C. BOUTONIANUS.

Section EUCROTON. Petals suppressed in the female flowers.

Leaves with only a few lepidote scales, which often disappear as they mature.
Leaves small oblong . . . . 3. C. GRANGERIOIDES.
Leaves larger obovate . . . . 4. C. FOTHERGILLÆFOLIUS.
Leaves with crowded stellate tufts of hairs . . . 5. C. TILIÆFOLIUS.

1. **C. mauritanicus,** *Lam.; Mull. Arg. in DC. Prod.* xv. 2, 520. A shrub, with the branchlets clothed with soft spreading hairs. Leaves round-cordate, acute, distinctly crenate, membranous, clothed thinly above and more densely below with soft stellate hairs; petiole 1–2 in. long, densely pilose. Racemes 1–4 in. long, with a tetragonous pilose axis and tomentose peduncles; pedicels finally $\frac{1}{2}$–$\frac{3}{4}$ in. long. Expanded female flower $\frac{1}{2}$ in. across, with spreading deltoid tomentose sepals and densely pilose oblanceolate-oblong petals, which are also present in the male flower. Capsule $\frac{3}{8}$ in. broad, matted with dense whitish tomentum; styles twice deeply forked. Stamens about 50; filaments glabrous, 4–5 times as long as the anthers.

MAURITIUS, *Commerson! Bojer!* Also Bourbon.

2. **C. Boutonianus,** *Mull. Arg. in DC. Prod.* xv. 2, 520. A shrub, with crowded short-petioled ovate or elliptical acute entire leaves rounded at the base, 1–2 in. long, penninerved, the hairs of the upper surface distinctly stellate, of the lower surface sublepidote, with a pair of stalked glands at the base. Racemes moderately long, with pedicels as long as the whitish round buds. Sepals deltoid. Ovary matted with tomentum. Styles two or three times forked. Stamens 20–30, with barbate filaments. Petals present in the male flowers. Fruit unknown.

MAURITIUS; described by Dr. Muller from specimens in De Candolle's herbarium gathered by MM. Bojer and Bouton. Endemic.

3. **C. grangerioides,** *Bojer; Mull. Arg. in DC. Prod.* xv. 2, 584. A shrub 3–4 feet high, with densely lepidote slender branchlets. Leaves crowded, oblong, subcoriaceous, $1\frac{1}{2}$–3 in. long, obtuse, obscurely crenu-

late, rounded or deltoid and furnished with a pair of glands at the base, scattered over on both sides at first with copious scales, which often disappear as the leaves mature; petiole $\frac{1}{8}$–$\frac{1}{4}$ in. long. Racemes dense, 1–$1\frac{1}{2}$ in. long, with short pedicels. Expanded female flowers $\frac{1}{8}$ in. broad; sepals deltoid, whitish all over on the outside or at the edges only; petals absent from the female flowers. Stamens about 15, with glabrous filaments. Capsule glabrescent, $\frac{1}{4}$ in. thick; styles thrice forked. *Bojer, Hort. Maur.* 281 (name only).

MAURITIUS, on the dry slopes of the Pouce, etc. Endemic.

4. **C. fothergillæfolius,** *Baill.; Mull. Arg. in DC. Prod.* xv. 2, 582. A shrub, 6–14 feet high, with grooved branchlets, clothed with pale, brown lepidote scales. Leaves crowded, short-petioled, obovate, obtuse, obscurely crenulate, rounded at the base, membranous, with a few scales at first, but quite naked when mature, furnished with a pair of stalked glands at the base, 2–3 in. long. Flowers in crowded terminal racemes not more than an inch long; pedicels at most as long as the calyx. Expanded female flowers $\frac{1}{4}$ in. broad; sepals lepidote on the outside. Petals as long as the sepals, absent from the female flower. Stamens 12–20, with glabrous filaments. Capsule depresso-globose, naked, $\frac{1}{4}$ in. thick; styles with 4–6 subulate lobes. C. muricatus, *Bojer, Hort. Maur.* 281, *non Vahl.*

MAURITIUS, in the woods of Grand Bassin. Endemic.

5. **C. tiliæfolius,** *Lam.; Mull. Arg. in DC. Prod.* xv. 2, 587. A shrub, with slender branchlets, clothed with soft spreading hairs. Leaves membranous, round-cordate, cuspidate or subobtuse, denticulate, subcoriaceous, 2–3 in. long, with a pair of glands at the base, obscurely stellato-tomentose above, densely beneath and whitish; petiole $\frac{1}{4}$–$\frac{1}{3}$ in. long, densely pilose. Racemes dense, an inch long, with a very tomentose rachis, deciduous subulate tomentose bracts and pedicels not longer than the calyx. Expanded flowers $\frac{1}{4}$ inch broad; sepals deltoid, tomentose all over the back. Petals tomentose, as long as the sepals, absent from the female flowers. Stamens 20–30; filaments pilose. Capsule oblong, $\frac{1}{4}$ in. long; styles thrice forked. C. canescens, *Bojer, Hort. Maur.* 281.

MAURITIUS, on the dry slopes of the Pouce, Piton de la Rivière Noire, etc. Also Bourbon, and closely allied to *C. lacciferus* and *aromaticus* of Tropical Asia.

* JATROPHA, Linn.

Flowers dichlamydeous, polygamo-monoicous. Calyx of both sexes with 5 imbricated segments. Petals 5, alternate with the sepals. Disk with glands alternate with the petals. Stamens central, 10–30; filaments connate at the base; anthers 2-celled. Ovary 2–3-celled; ovules solitary in the cells; style-branches once or twice forked. Fruit capsular. Seeds caruncululate.—Shrubs or herbs, with petioled alternate leaves, often deeply lobed, the flowers in dense compound corymbs. DISTRIB. Cosmopolitan in the tropics. Species 60–70.

Leaves shallowly lobed. Petals joined in lower half . . . 1. J. CURCAS.
Leaves palmatifid nearly to base. Petals free . . . . . . 2. J. MULTIFIDA.

* *J. Curcas*, Linn.; Jacq. Hort. Vind. t. 63; Mull. Arg. in DC. Prod. xv. 2, 1080, a native of America, cultivated through the tropics, is casually subspontaneous in Mauritius and Seychelles. It is an erect shrub, reaching a height of 15–20 feet, with stout fleshy branchlets, long-petioled subcoriaceous glabrous cordate-deltoid repand leaves, small caducous lanceolate entire stipules, flowers in dense corymbose panicles shorter than the leaves, calyx of the males ⅛ in. long with oblong segments, petals twice as long as the calyx united in the lower half and pilose within, stamens 10–12 with filaments joined at the base only, and a 2–3-coccous capsule an inch long with large oblong smooth seeds full of purgative oil. *Pignon d'Inde* or *Médicinier*.

* *J. multifida*, Linn.; Mull. Arg. in DC. Prod. xv. 2, 1089, a native of tropical America, is also casually subspontaneous in Mauritius. It is a glabrous shrub, 10–20 feet high, with persistent stipules cut into filiform divisions, long-petioled palmatifid leaves with 11 very deep entire or toothed lobes, flowers in dense peduncled compound corymbs, small membranous calyx with a campanulate tube and 5 deltoid or oblong segments, free scarlet petals, the glands of the male flower connate in a cup and a globose glabrous 3-celled capsule the size of a hazel-nut. *Arbre Corail.*

* *Aleurites moluccana*, Willd.; Mull. Arg. in DC. Prod. xv. 2, 723 (A. triloba, *Forst.*), a native of Polynesia and tropical Asia, is planted and casually subspontaneous in Mauritius. It is a tall tree, with branchlets and calyces clothed with brown lepidote pubescence, long-petioled large ovate or deltoid acute entire or 3–5-lobed leaves, small monoicous flowers in a dense corymbose terminal panicle, calyx splitting irregularly into 2–3 lobes, 5 exserted strap-shaped petals, numerous stamens in a central head, glands of the disk alternate with the petals, a 2-celled ovary with solitary ovules and a depresso-globose fleshy fruit as large as an apple. *Noyer de Bancoul.*

ORDER XC.* ARISTOLOCHIACEÆ.

Aristolochia acuminata, Lam.; Duchartre in DC. Prod. xv. 479, said by Lamarck to be a plant of Mauritius, is known on the island only as an introduction, and is supposed by Bojer to be a native of Madagascar. It is a glabrous herbaceous twiner, with long-petioled middle-sized alternate cordate-ovate entire membranous acuminate leaves, flowers few in lax axillary corymbs with small round leafy bracts at the nodes and a perianth 1¼ in. long with a tube consisting in the lower half of a globe and the upper half of a cylinder and with an oblique panduriform limb as long as the tube, 6 anthers adnate in a whorl to the style and a 6-celled inferior capsule with septicidal dehiscence.

Order XCI. COMMELYNACEÆ.

Flowers dichlamydeous, hermaphrodite. Sepals small, membranous, persistent. Petals bright coloured, equal or unequal, fugitive, deciduous, usually free. Stamens 6, hypogynous, some often imperfect; filaments filiform, often bearded with jointed hairs; anthers 2-celled, usually introrse. Ovary free, 3-celled; ovules usually few; style filiform; stigma capitate. Capsule 3-celled, with loculicidal dehiscence. Seeds with abundant fleshy albumen; embryo in a cavity of the albumen opposite the hilum.—Herbs with membranous leaves with clasping sheathing bases and flowers variously arranged. Distrib. Warmer regions of both hemispheres. Species 200–300.

Flowers irregular, with free sepals and petals . . . . . . 1. Commelyna.
Flowers regular, with united sepals and petals . . . . . 2. Cyanotis.

1. COMMELYNA, Linn.

Flowers irregular. Sepals free, obtuse, cucullate, unequal, membranous, marcescent. Petals roundish, two with a distinct claw, one without. Stamens 6, three of which are fertile with oblong anthers, 3 barren with cruciform abortive anthers; filaments beardless. Ovary sessile, 3-celled, one ovule in one of the cells, one or two in each of the two others; style elongate, filiform. Capsule small, membranous; two cells dehiscing, the other indehiscent.—Herbs with membranous leaves with a sheathing base, the flowers rising out of persistent hooded spathes. Distrib. Warmer regions of both hemispheres. Species 50.

Spathes ovate acute, twice as long as broad . . . . . 1. C. communis.
Spathes deltoid, as long as broad . . . . 2. C. benghalensis.

1. **C. communis,** *Linn.; Kunth, Enum.* iv 36. An annual, with much-branched procumbent stems 1–3 feet long, rooting at the lower joints, glabrous or finely pilose. Leaves lanceolate, acuminate, 2–3 in. long, ½–¾ in. broad, with a membranous veined clasping petiole ½–¾ in. long, finely ciliated principally at the top. Spathes cordate-ovate, acuminate, ¾–1 in. long, horizontal, the two halves folded together, glabrous or pubescent. Peduncles both flower-bearing and exserted, the lower with 2–3, the upper with one perfect and one abortive flower. Sepals ⅛ in. long, unequal, almost colourless. Petals ¼ in. long, bright blue. Capsule oblong, the cell on the back indehiscent and 1-seeded, the two other dehiscing cells containing each two small rugose seeds. *C. B. Clarke, Commelyn. Beng. tab.* 1. C. salicifolia, longifolia, and barbata, *Bojer, Hort. Maur.* 359–360.

Mauritius, Seychelles, and Rodriguez, common in damp places. Spread through the tropics of the Old World and of the New, if, as seems likely, *C. agraria*, Kunth, be conspecific. The true *C. salicifolia* of Roxburgh, which is likely to occur, differs by its stouter habit, longer leaves, and smooth seeds.

2. **C. benghalensis,** *Linn.*; *Kunth, Enum.* iv. 50. Stems trailing, much-branched, 1–3 feet long, usually pubescent. Leaves ovate, acute, 1–3 in. long, often 1–1½ in. broad, strongly ciliated at the base with strong brown hairs and the edges of the pale dilated ½–¾ in. membranous sheath also strongly ciliated. Spathe-valves deltoid-cucullate, ½ in. broad and long, pubescent on the outside. Peduncles both floriferous, one much exserted, with a single flower, the other with two or three. Sepals ⅛ in. long, oblong-cucullate. Petals ¼ in. long, bright blue. Capsule oblong, membranous, the two dehiscing cells each containing two small rugose seeds. *Wt. Icones, t.* 2065; *C. B. Clarke, Comm. Beng. t.* 4. C. cucullata, *Linn.*; *Bojer, Hort. Mar.* 360.

Mauritius, common in damp situations. Also Tropical Asia, Tropical Africa and Cape. *Herbe aux cochons.*

2. CYANOTIS, D. Don.

Flowers nearly regular. Sepals lanceolate, united below. Corolla marcescent, with a funnel-shaped tube and 3 equal segments. Stamens 6, all perfect, the filaments with a tuft of hairs at the top. Ovary sessile, 3-celled; ovules two in each cell; style filiform. Capsule regularly 3-valved, with two seeds in each cell.—Annual herbs, with the habit of *Commelyna*, several spathes usually congested at the end of the stems. Distrib. Tropics of the Old World. Species 15.

1. **C. cristata,** *Roem. and Schultes*; *Kunth, Enum.* iv. 102. A branched annual, with erect or spreading subglabrous stems ½–1 foot long. Leaves distant, spreading, lanceolate, 1–2 in. long, with a short clasping membranous basal sheath. Spathes 6–10, semilunate, glabrous, under ½ in. broad, congested in the axil of a leaf at the top of each branch. Flowers two in a spathe, subsessile. Sepals lanceolate, acute. Corolla bright blue, with lanceolate segments. Filaments long, flexuose, with a tuft of bright blue hairs at the top. Seeds subtrigonal-oblong. *C. B. Clarke, Comm. Beng. t.* 36. Tradescantia cristata, *Jacq. Hort. Vind. t.* 137.

Mauritius, in waste rocky ground near Port Louis, *Sieber*, 143! etc. Tropical Asia, not Tropical Africa.

C. axillaris, R. and S.; Kunth, Enum. iv. 105, is reported doubtfully by Bojer as a Mauritian plant under the name of *Tradescantia axillaris*, and I have seen no specimens. It is an Indian, not an African species, differing conspicuously from the rest in habit by having its flowers congested in the axils of all the narrow linear leaves of the stem and the bracts minute and lanceolate, not spathe-like and folded together.

Order XCII. XYRIDACEÆ.

Flowers dichlamydeous, hermaphrodite, densely capitate. Sepals 3, glumaceous, persistent. Petals 3, bright-coloured, united in a tube or unguiculate. Fertile stamens 3, alternating with 3 staminodes; anthers 2-celled, extrorse. Ovary free, sessile, 1–3-celled; ovules numerous, orthotropous; style trifid at the top. Capsule loculicidally 3-valved. Seeds with a minute embryo placed opposite the hilum, outside the albumen.—Perennial acaulescent herbs, with narrow dry leaves, the flowers in heads, in the axils of dry hard bracts. DISTRIB. Tropics of both hemispheres. Species 50–60.

1. XYRIS, Linn.

Corolla trifid, with oblong unguiculate segments. Stamens 3, short, hypogynous, alternating with 3 penicillate staminodia. Ovary usually 1-celled; placentas parietal or basal. Capsule 3-valved. Seeds very numerous, minute.—Habit as in the order. DISTRIB. Tropics of both hemispheres. Species 50.

Dwarf, with narrow linear leaves . . . . 1. X. HUMILIS.
Tall, with broad linear leaves . . . . 2. X. PLATYCAULIS.

1. **X. humilis,** *Kunth, Enum.* iv. 15. Leaves striate, glabrous, narrow linear, $1\frac{1}{2}$–3 in. long. Scape 2–5 in., filiform, rigid, rather compressed. Heads $\frac{1}{6}$ in. long, turbinate, containing about 3 flowers; bracts roundish, coriaceous, emarginate, keeled upwards, brown on the back, the sides paler. Sepals narrow, keeled, acute, glabrous. Capsule oblong, brown, membranous, rather shorter than the bracts.

MAURITIUS. Described by Kunth from a specimen in Willdenow's herbarium. Also Madagascar.

2. **X. platycaulis,** *Poir.*; *Kunth, Enum.* iv. 18. Acaulescent, densely tufted. Leaves linear, rigid, sheathing the scape at the base, 4–8 in. long, $\frac{1}{8}$–$\frac{1}{4}$ in. broad. Scape a foot or more long, clasped by a leaf for some distance above the base, acutely angled at the top. Head globose, $\frac{1}{4}$–$\frac{1}{3}$ in. broad; bracts hard, shining, deltoid, greenish-white when young, dark brown when mature. Calyx $\frac{1}{8}$ in. long; sepals acutely keeled. Petals nearly twice as long as the calyx. Capsule obovoid, brown, retuse, $\frac{1}{12}$–$\frac{1}{8}$ in. long.

MAURITIUS, *Petit Thouars* in Herb. Willdenow, No. 1070. Also Madagascar and Zanguebar.

ORDER XCII.* BROMELIACEÆ.

* *Ananassa sativa,* Lindl. in Bot. Reg. sub. t. 1068 (Bromelia Ananas, Linn.; Bot. Mag. tab. 1554), the Pine-Apple, a native of Tropical America, is now established in Mauritius, Seychelles, and Rodriguez. It has a fibrous root, a dense sessile rosette of lanceolate coriaceous channelled leaves 2–3 feet long with prickly edges, flowers in a dense peduncled oblong head with a crown of empty bracts at the top, an inferior ovary united to its bract, sepals 3 horny deltoid,

petals 3 purplish-blue lingulate deciduous united for a space above the ovary. *Ananas.*

ORDER XCIII. SCITAMINEÆ.

Flowers hermaphrodite. Perianth distinctly dichlamydeous. Sepals 3, membranous. Petals 3, often irregular. Stamen solitary, petaloid, with a 1- or 2-celled anther. Staminodes petaloid, various in shape and number, the one opposite the fertile stamen (labellum) larger than the rest. Ovary inferior, 3-celled; ovules many in a cell; style filiform; stigma capitate. Fruit capsular or baccate, crowned by the marcescent sepals. Seeds with two layers of albumen, often arillate; embryo axile. — Herbs with often stout creeping root-stocks, large membranous leaves and showy fugitive very irregular flowers. DISTRIB. Tropics of both hemispheres. Species 500.

Anthers 2-celled. Flowers in heads on special stems.
  Posterior petal large and galeate . . . . 1. AMOMUM.
  Petals all small and uniform . . . . * NICOLAIA.
Anthers 1-celled. Flowers in lax branched spikes on leafy stems * CANNA.

1. AMOMUM, Linn.

Calyx spathaceous, 3-toothed. Corolla 3-lobed, the side segments lanceolate, the top one larger and galeate. Staminodes represented by a large labellum with two processes at the base. Filament petaloid; connective produced in a crest beyond the 2-celled anther. Fruit indehiscent or dehiscing by three valves.—Herbs with a creeping root-stock, a long leaf-stem, a short special flower-stem and showy flowers. DISTRIB. Tropics of Old World. Species 30.

1. **A. Daniellii,** *Hook. fil. Bot. Mag. t.* 4764, *fide Hanbury.* Root-stock thick, creeping. Leaf-stem 6–10 feet high, Leaves short-petioled, oblong, acute, membranous, above a foot long. Flower-stem $\frac{1}{2}$–1 foot long, clothed with obtuse, scariose sheathing bracts. Flowers few in a head, each subtended by a membranous bract, which they greatly overtop. Calyx spathaceous, slit and 3-toothed. Corolla 3-lobed, deep red, the side segments lanceolate, the upper one twice as large and galeate. Labellum yellow, obovate-cuneate, $1\frac{1}{2}$–2 in. long. Anther with a 3-lobed crest. Fruit as large as a hen's egg, deep red, obscurely trigonous. Seeds oblong, enveloped in a whitish aril. A. angustifolium, *Hanbury in Linn. Journ.* xiii. 155, not of *Sonnerat.* A. nemorosum, *Bojer, Hort. Maur.* 327 (name only). 'A. Clusii, *Bot. Mag. t.* 5250 (variety with yellow flowers).

MAURITIUS, in swamps of the Pouce range, etc. SEYCHELLES, in marshy ground in the forests of Mahé, *Horne,* 596! Also Madagascar and Tropical Africa. *Longouze, Zedoaire du pays.*

* *Nicolaia imperialis,* Horan. Prod. Scit. 32, t. 1 (Alpinia magnifica.

Roscoe, Scit. Plant. 75; Hook. Bot. Mag. t. 3192), a native of Madagascar, is naturalised in Mauritius on the banks of the stream near Moka and round Bois Chéri, and is contained in Prof. Percival Wright's Seychelles collection. It has a large thick creeping rootstock, leafy stems 10 or 12 feet high, oblong acute subcoriaceous short-petioled leaves 1–1½ feet long, flowers 50–100 in a dense conical head on a much shorter special stem, the head surrounded by several large red bracts with a pale border, and each flower overtopped by a smaller oblong spathulate bract of a similar kind, a curved tubular perianth above an inch long, a densely pilose ovary, a cylindrical membranous calyx with three short lanceolate teeth, three oblanceolate red petals shorter than the calyx, a large protruded oblanceolate bright red labellum enfolding the genitalia, a pilose ligulate filament, a petaloid obtuse emarginate connective slightly produced beyond the separated anther-cells, a cylindrical style with a discoid stigma, and an obovoid capsule 1–1½ in. long.

* *Canna indica*, Linn.; Bot. Reg. t. 776, Rosc. Scit. Plant. t. 1, the Indian Shot, a native of Tropical Asia, is now abundantly established in Mauritius, Seychelles, and Rodriguez. It has leafy stems 4–5 feet high, large membranous oblong leaves on long sheathing petioles, flowers in lax branched terminal spikes each subtended by an oblong membranous bract, a densely papillose ovary, 3 small lanceolate scariose sepals, 3 lanceolate scarlet subequal reflexing petals, 3 still longer oblanceolate-spathulate bright coloured petaloid staminodes, a shorter lingulate petaloid filament with a linear 1-celled anther adnate to one side at the tip, a compressed clavate style and dry rugose capsule containing many globose black seeds. *Safron marron* or *Balisier*.

ORDER XCIV. ORCHIDEÆ.

(By S. LE MARCHANT MOORE, F.L.S.)

Flowers hermaphrodite, except in rare instances irregular. Perianth superior, herbaceous or gaily coloured, of three outer segments (sepals) free from each other or the lateral or all united, equal or the upper or posterior (anterior when the ovary is straight) larger or smaller; inside these are two segments (petals) which are equal or unequal to the sepals and free or united to the upper sepal to form a hood arching over the column, and in the same whorl with these and opposite the upper sepal is found the labellum, usually larger than the other perianth-segments, and often provided with rows of hairs, fleshy crests or spurs. Within the perianth is the column, composed of the combined andrœcium and style and stigma; it is free from or united to the labellum, sometimes produced at its base into a foot-like prolongation, and often bears appendages at the top and sides. Crowning the column, or at its back, or running down its face, is a single anther (double in a very few genera not Mascarene) bursting longitudinally, or provided with a persistent or deciduous lid-like cap; pollen in 2, 4 or 8, waxy granular or pulverulent masses; masses simple or with tail-like prolongations (caudicles) or with the caudicle tipped with a viscid gland, or sessile on a viscid gland. Ovary inferior, more or less cylindrical, usually twisted (so that the upper part of the flower becomes the lower), but occasionally straight, 1- (very rarely 3-) celled, with 3 parietal placentas, on which are borne a vast number of minute ovules; stigma of 2 viscid lobes or a single broad surface variously situated at the front of the column, the third lobe modified into a short or long, entire or divided, occasionally rudimentary structure (rostellum), from the cells composing which the viscid gland is often formed. Fruit in the vast majority of cases a capsule, splitting into 6 valves, 3 of which bear hair-like tufts of minute seeds with a homogeneous embryo. — Perennial herbs, either terrestrial and provided with creeping rhizomes, tubers or fibrous roots, or growing on trees or rocks, and then usually with green bulb-like modified stems (pseudobulbs), and adventitious roots outwardly of corky consistence (aerial roots). Flowers solitary or in spikes, racemes, or panicles, often large and gaily coloured. Theoretically the Orchidean flower consists of 15 parts in 5 whorls of 3 each, of which 2 whorls are perianthial, 2 andrœcial, and 1 gynœcial; the sepals form the first whorl, the petals and part of the labellum the second, two members of the third are combined with the labellum, while the remaining one is present as the single anther; the fourth whorl is variously conjoined with the column, and the fifth appears in the two stigmatic lobes and rostellum. DISTRIB. Cosmopolitan. Species 3000.

Of the 23 genera mentioned in this Flora, 5 are endemic in the Mascarene Archipelago, 3 have eastern connections only, not appearing in the African continent, and 1 is in the same condition in a western sense. The remaining 14 have both eastern and western connections; the eastern element preponderating in 1 case, the western in 4, while 9 are fairly evenly diffused in both directions.

The following arrangement, a modification of that of Lindley, is advocated by Dr. H. G. Reichenbach, of Hamburg, the first of living authorities on the Order.

Tribe 1. OPHRYDEÆ. Anther facing or crowning the column, its cells bursting longitudinally. Pollen-masses granular. Terrestrial herbs.

Lateral sepals saccate or spurred . . . . 1. DISPERIS.
Lateral sepals plane.
  Labellum posticous, 2-spurred . . . . 2. SATYRIUM.
  Labellum anticous.
    Arms of the anther diverging. Stigma at the front of the column.

Labellum large, deeply lobed or incised, with a long clavate spur. Stigmatic lobes projecting downwards at the base of the column . . . . . . 3. HABENARIA.
Labellum small; spur short. Stigmatic lobes on the inner side of the arms of the anther, confluent with the column . . . . 4. PERISTYLUS.
Arms of the anther parallel; stigmatic lobes on their outer side.
Anther-arms elongate, terete; rostellum projecting between them, thick and fleshy . . . . . . 5. CYNORCHIS.
Anther-arms short, flat; rostellum linear, membranous . . . . 6. AMPHORCHIS.
Arms of the anther parallel; stigmatic lobes at the front of the upper part of the column . . . . 7. ARNOTTIA.

Tribe II. OPERCULATÆ. Anther on the top or back of the column; cap lid-like, persistent or cast off by removal of the pollen-masses.

Sub-tribe I. NEOTTIEÆ. Anther-cap persistent; pollen-masses granular or powdery. Terrestrial herbs.

Labellum with calli on the inner face. Column elongate . . . . 8. PLATYLEPIS.
Labellum without calli. Column short . . . . 9. GOODYERA.

Sub-tribe II. EUOPERCULATÆ. Anther-cap cast off by removal of the pulverulent mealy or waxy pollen-masses. Terrestrial, epiphytic, or saxicolous.

Section α. ARETHUSEÆ. Pollen-masses pulverulent or mealy, without any prolongations. Terrestrials.

Small, slender, leafless, 1-flowered. Labellum convolute round the column . . . . 10. APLOSTELLIS.

Section β. MALAXIDEÆ. Pollen-masses waxy, without any prolongations. Epiphytic, rarely terrestrial.

Stem erect or ascending. Column not produced at base.
Leaves distichous. Labellum free from the column . . . 11. OBERONIA.
Leaves not distichous. Labellum adnate to the lower part of the column . . . . 12. LIPARIS.
Stem horizontal, creeping. Labellum tongue-like, adnate to the produced base of the column . . . . 13. BULBOPHYLLUM.

Section γ. EPIDENDREÆ. Pollen-masses waxy, with tail-like prolongations, free or united together into a caudicle or caudicles, but without a viscid gland. Epiphytes or terrestrials.

Labellum convolute round the column. Pollen-masses 8, the tails united to form a short broad caudicle . . . . 14. PHAJUS.

Section 8. VANDEÆ. Pollen-masses waxy, provided with both caudicle and gland Usually epiphytes.

Pollen-masses 2.
 Caudicles 2.
  Petals lobed. Caudicles with cup-like summits, each attached to a gland . . . . 15. CRYPTOPUS.
  Petals entire. Caudicles flat at the summit, each attached to a gland . . . . 16. ARRANTHUS.
  Petals entire. Caudicles flat at the summit; gland single . . . . 17. LISTROSTACHYS.
 Caudicle single.
  Inflorescence axillary or extra-axillary. Labellum more or less like sepals and petals. Column not produced at base . . . . . 18. ANGRÆCUM.
  Inflorescence terminal. Labellum unlike the sepals and petals. Column with a long basal production.
   Labellum spurred . . . . 19. EULOPHIA.
   Labellum not spurred . . . . 20. CYRTOPERA.
Pollen masses 4.
 Labellum adnate to the produced base of the column . . . . 21. POLYSTACHYA.
Pollen-masses 8.
 Leaves distichous. Flowers small, capitate. Labellum saccate . . . . 22. AGROSTOPHYLLUM.
 Leaves not distichous. Flowers rather large, racemed. Labellum usually with a long slender spur . . . . 23. CALANTHE.

1. DISPERIS, Sw.

Lateral sepals broad, spreading, usually more or less connate, but occasionally free, each with a concavity or pouch near the centre; upper sepal connivent with the petals into a hood arching over the column; hood (in Mascarene species) ovate, cuspidate. Labellum small, adnate to the whole front of the column, going off above it as a broad or narrow, entire or variously lobed limb. Column short. crowned by a large anther with short or elongate, straight or twisted, parallel or diverging arms; pollen-masses long and narrow, of few large, almost free granules; gland broad, naked.—Low terrestrial herbs, with small tubers, opposite or alternate membranous leaves and terminal solitary or racemose flowers. DISTRIB. The genus is found mainly at the Cape, and extends through the Mascarene Archipelago to India, where it is represented by two species.

Leaves opposite. Labellum 3-lobed. Lateral sepals united . . . . 1. D OPPOSITIFOLIA.
Leaves alternate. Labellum entire.
 Lateral sepals free, spathulate-oblong. Pulvinus of labellum ovate . . . . 2. D. TRIPETALOIDES.
 Lateral sepals connate halfway up, lanceolate. Pulvinus of labellum transversely elongated . . . 3. D. CORDATA.

1. **D. oppositifolia,** *Smith in Rees' Encyc.* Tubers oblong, about ½ in. in length. Stem slender, erect, 4–9 in. high. Leaves opposite, lanceolate or ovate-lanceolate, subcordate at the base, 1–2 in. long, about ½ in. broad, a solitary pair on each stem at about ⅔ of its distance from the ground, with a basal, cordate, long-petiolate pair which soon withers away. Flowers few together; bracts ovate, leaf-like, ⅛–⅓ in. in length. Lateral sepals spathulate, united for the lower two-thirds, each with a shallow pouch near the point of union. Limb of labellum ascending, broadly-cuneate, 3-lobed, pubescent; lobes linear, subequal, the lateral diverging. Arms of the anther short, parallel. *Lindl. Gen. and Sp. Orch.* 371. Dryopeia oppositifolia, *Thouars, Orch. Afr. t.* 1; *Rich. Orch. Maur.* 35.

MAURITIUS, woods near the summit of the Pouce, *Ayres!* Quartier Militaire and Anse Courtois, *Bojer.* Also Bourbon.

2. **D. tripetaloides,** *Lindl. Gen. and Sp. Orch.* 371 (in part). Tubers oblong-ovoid, less than ½ in. long. Stem 4–6 in. high, ascending. Leaves usually two on each stem, alternate, cordate, somewhat amplexicaul, ¾–1 in. long, ⅓–½ in. broad. Infloresence as in *D. oppositifolia.* Lateral sepals spathulate-oblong, acute or cuspidate, free, with a small pouch near the centre. Limb of labellum clavate, reflexed, with an ovate pulvinus at the point of reflexion; apex shortly 2-lobed, the broad sinus between the lobes pubescent. Arms of the anther as in *D. oppositifolia.* Dryopeia tripetaloides, *Thouars, Orch. Afr. t.* 3; *Rich. Orch. Maur.* 36.

MAURITIUS, the Pouce, *Ayres!* Savanne and Nouvelle Découverte, *Bojer.* Also Bourbon and Galega. The Ceylon plant referred by Lindley to this species is evidently different.

3. **D. cordata,** *Sw. in Köngl. Vatens. Acad.* 1800, p. 220. Very much like *D. tripetaloides*, but the flowers appear to be smaller, the lateral sepals are lanceolate and united halfway up, and the pulvinus on the limb of the labellum is transversely elongated. Dryopeia discolor, *Thouars, Orch. Afr. t.* 2 (?)

MAURITIUS, round Grand Bassin and at the cascade on Rivière Noire, *Bojer.* SEYCHELLES, Mahé, *Pervillé!* Endemic. I have had no flower for examination. Swartz describes in these words the only Mascarene species known in his day; "Caule diphyllo, multifloro, foliis cordatis, glabris, floribus distinctis," which suits well either with this or the last species, and might even be intended for *D. oppositifolia.* It would appear that Lindley was not justified in referring the *Dryopeia discolor* of Thouars to Swartz's plant, since the latter's type was not seen by him; as, however, I am not in a position to solve this doubt, I have thought it better to retain a familiar nomenclature.

2. SATYRIUM, Sw.

Sepals and petals spreading, subequal. Labellum posticous, larger than the other perianth-segments, entire, hooded over the column, 2-saccate or 2-spurred. Column short or elongate. Anther resupinate; arms parallel or diverging, sharply curved upwards; glands naked. Stigma broad, placed just above the anther. Tuberous terrestrial herbs, with or without stems. Flowers usually rather large, in terminal cylindrical spikes. DISTRIB. A considerable genus, with head-quarters at the Cape, whence it wanders to Abyssinia, and through the Mascarene Archipelago to India.

1. **S. amœnum,** *Rich. Orch. Maur.* 31. Plant when full grown about 1 foot high. Tubers ovoid-oblong, fascicled. Leaves twin, radical, unequal, ovate, acute, 2–3 in. long, more than 1 in. broad, with one or two leafy scales below. Scape stoutish, copiously clothed with loose sheathing scales; bracts lanceolate ½–1 in. long; flowers ¼ in. diameter, somewhat crowded, purple. Sepals oblong, obtuse, ⅙ in. long. Petals a little shorter and narrower. Labellum rotundate-ovate, cuspidate, keeled on the back, about the same length as the other perianth-segments; spurs linear, somewhat attenuated at the end, slightly arched forwards, nearly ¾ in. long. Column elongate; arms of the anthers almost parallel; pollen-masses depressed-pyriform, as long as the linear caudicle; glands quadrate. Diplectrum amœnum. *Thouars, Orch. Afr. tt.* 21, 22.

MAURITIUS, forests round marshes and mountains situated towards centre of island, *Bojer.* Also in Bourbon. I have seen no specimen from Mauritius.

3. HABENARIA, Willd.

Sepals subequal, the lateral ascending, patent or recurved, the upper hooded over the column. Petals ascending. Labellum free from the column, usually lobed, with narrow filiform lobes; spur elongate, clavate or vesicular at the apex. Column short; cells of the anther diverging below; glands naked, spheroidal; rostellum rudimentary; stigma 2-lobed; lobes projecting downwards at the base of the column.—Tuberous (occasionally fibrous-rooted) terrestrial herbs. Leaves radical or cauline. Flowers in terminal erect spikes or racemes, green or white, often sweet-scented. DISTRIB. A large genus, found principally in the north temperate zone, and represented more sparingly in the tropics, at the Cape, and in Australia.

Stems leafy.
- Leaves linear-lanceolate, 2–5 in. long. Petals with a long slender basal appendage; spur clavate . . 1. H. LANCIFOLIA.
- Leaves lanceolate, 2–4 in. long. Petals without an appendage; spur pouched at the extremity . 2. H. VESICULOSA.
- Leaves linear-lanceolate, ½ foot long. Petals without an appendage; spur clavate, arching forwards 3. H.? PRÆALTA.
- Leaves ovate-lanceolate, 4–5 in. long. Petals without an appendage; spur obtuse, nearly straight . 4. H.? SIGILLUM.

Leaves all radical, spathulate-oblong, 1½ in. long. Petals lanceolate . . . . 5. H.? MASCARENENSIS.

1. **H. lancifolia,** *Rich. Orch. Maur.* 20, *t.* 1. Root of slender branching fibres. Stem erect, above ½ foot high, leafy, with many loose

sheathing scales clothing its lower portion. Leaves linear-lanceolate, narrowed towards the base, 2–5 in. long, ¼ in. broad, with a short entire sheathing base. Raceme 2 in. long, few-flowered; bracts lanceolate ¼ in. or more in length; pedicel and ovary nearly ⅓ in. long. Sepals about ⅙ in. long, ovate, obtuse. Petals about as long, narrowly spathulate, each with an appendage springing from its base and twice its own length. Labellum about ⅙ in. long, deeply 3-lobed; lobes linear, obtuse, the median one a little the broader; spur clavate, about ⅓ in. long. *Lindl. Gen. and Sp. Orch.* 310.

MAURITIUS, *Commerson* (fide Richard). Description taken from Richard's figure. Endemic.

2. **H. vesiculosa,** *Rich. Orch. Maur.* 20, *t.* 2. Tuber ovoid-oblong, more than ½ in. in length. Stem about ½ foot high, erect, leafy, clothed with numerous sheathing scales below the leaves. Leaves lanceolate, narrowed towards the base, 2–4 in. long, ½–¾ in. broad, with shortly-sheathing bases. Raceme about ½ foot long when full-grown, with numerous sparsely-set greenish flowers; bracts lanceolate, ¼ in. long; pedicel and ovary about $\frac{1}{12}$ in. in length. Upper sepal ovate, about ½ in. long; lateral a little longer, lanceolate. Petals lanceolate. Labellum ⅙ in. long, 5-partite; segments linear, obtuse, the two basal the narrower; mid-lobe somewhat shorter and broader than its lateral fellows; spur ⅓ in. long, dilated at its extremity into a wide pouch. *Lindl. Gen. and Sp. Orch.* 310.

MAURITIUS, Flacq, and Nouvelle Découverte, *Bojer! Herb. Blackburn!* Endemic.

3. **H. ? præalta,** *Rich. Orch. Maur.* 22 (*Habenaria*). Root of numerous unbranched woolly fibres. Stem 2–3 feet high, erect, stout, leafy. Leaves linear-lanceolate, ½ foot long, nearly ½ in. broad, with a long entire sheathing base. Raceme 1 foot long, bearing a dense mass of greenish flowers; bracts ovate-lanceolate, usually about ¾ in. in length. Sepals ovate, obtuse. Petals a little smaller, obovate-oblong. Labellum deeply 3- (occasionally irregularly) 2-lobed; lobes subequal, linear, obtuse; spur clavate, arching forwards, about ⅓ in. long. *Lindl. Gen. and Sp. Orch.* 321. Satyrium præaltum, *Thouars, Orch. Afr. t.* 11.

MAURITIUS, Piton du Milieu de l'Ile, La Savanne, and Rivière Noire, *Bojer.* Also Bourbon. I have had no flower for examination, and have seen no specimen from Mauritius.

4. **H. ? Sigillum,** *Thouars, Orch. Afr. t.* 20. Stem erect, 1½ foot high, leafy near the top, with a few tight sheathing scales below. Leaves ovate-lanceolate, 4–5 in. long, less than 1¼ in. broad, with short, entire sheathing bases. Raceme about 10 in. long, sparsely flowered; bracts ovate, ⅓ in. in length; pedicel and ovary 1 in. long. Upper sepal ovate, cuspidate, about as long as the ovate-lanceolate lateral ones. Petals broadly spathulate, obliquely bifid. Labellum 5-lobed, the two basal lobes short, the lateral terminal ones obtuse; mid-lobe shortly rotundate, with a long, linear cusp; spur ⅔ in. long, almost straight, obtuse.

MAURITIUS, banks of Rivière du Poste and of Grande Rivière sud-est, *Bojer*. Also Bourbon. In Thouars' figure the arms of the anther are represented as turned upwards. As this is not a character of *Habenaria*, the propriety of placing the plant in that genus has been justly questioned by Lindley. I have seen no specimen.

5. **H.? mascarenensis,** *Spreng. Syst. Veg.* iii. 690. Tubers oblong, becoming attenuated and root-like below. Leaves radical, spathulate-oblong, acute, $1\frac{1}{2}$ in. long, about $\frac{1}{2}$ in. broad. Scape erect, nearly 1 foot high, with a few scattered, sheathing scales; flowers rather closely packed; bracts lanceolate, $\frac{1}{3}$ in. long (or less). Sepals subequal, ovate-oblong, acute. Petals shorter, lanceolate. Labellum about the same length as the sepals, 3-lobed; lobes oblong, obtuse; mid-lobe the longest; spur linear, obtuse, arching forwards, about four times as long as the labellum. Satyrium rosellatum, *Thouars, Orch. Afr. t.* 8. Gymnadenia rosellata, *Rich. Orch. Maur.* 27; *Lindl. Gen. and Sp. Orch.* 279.

MAURITIUS, Trois Mamelles, Crève-cœur, and Mare aux Vacouas, *Bojer*. Also Bourbon. I have seen no specimen.

4. PERISTYLUS, Bl.

Characters of *Habenaria*, but the labellum is usually small, the spur very short, and the stigmatic lobes do not project downwards. DISTRIB. A considerable genus, found chiefly in temperate regions of both worlds; there is perhaps one in South Africa.

Flowers about $\frac{1}{2}$ in. diameter. Labellum entire.
Leaves ovate-lanceolate. Labellum with the terminal border entire or toothed; spur linear, straight; ovary glandular-hairy . . . . 1. P. CITRINUS.
Leaves linear. Labellum cuspidate; spur clavate, arching forwards; ovary glabrous . . . . 2. P.? PURPUREUS.
Flowers $\frac{1}{4}$ in. diameter (or less). Labellum 3-lobed.
Leaves lanceolate-oblong, congested near the bottom of the stem. Flowers $\frac{1}{4}$ in. diameter; spur clavate, much shorter than the labellum . . . . 3. P. LATIFOLIUS.
Leaves linear-lanceolate, congested near the bottom of the stem. Flowers $\frac{1}{6}$ in. diameter; spur as in *P. latifolius* . . . . 4. P. SPIRALIS.
Leaves linear-lanceolate, scattered. Flowers $\frac{1}{4}$ in. diameter; spur linear, almost as long as the labellum . 5. P.? GRAMINEUS.
Leaves lanceolate, radical. Flowers $\frac{1}{6}$ in. diameter; spur obtuse, $\frac{1}{16}$ in. long . . . . 6. P. FLEXUOSUS.

1. **P. citrinus,** *Lindl. Gen. and Sp. Orch.* 298. Tubers clavate, fascicled. Leaves ovate-lanceolate, acute or acuminate, about 4 in. long, 1 in. broad, congested near the base of the stem. Stem nearly 1 foot high, erect, terete, with a few scattered lanceolate sheathing scales between leaves and flowers; bracts ovate-lanceolate, about $\frac{1}{4}$ in. long, glandular-hairy; flowers subsessile, somewhat scattered. Sepals oblong, obtuse, as long as the lanceolate petals. Labellum a little larger than the other perianth-segments entire, narrowly cuneate, the

terminal margin entire or toothed; spur straight, linear, obtuse, about ¼ as the long as the labellum. Ovary tapering below, glandular-hairy on the ribs. Habenaria citrina, *Thouars, Orch. Afr. t.* 16; *Bojer, Hort. Maur.* 309; *Rich. Orch. Maur.* 21, *t.* 3.

MAURITIUS, in forests on high mountains towards centre of island, *Bojer*. Also Bourbon. I have seen no specimen.

2. **P.? purpureus,** *S. Moore.* Tubers oblong, fascicled. Leaves few together, linear, acute, 3–4 in. long. ¼ in. broad, loosely imbricate at the base of the stem. Stem erect, terete, more than ½ in. high, clothed with a few scattered scales above the leaves. Spike few- and lax-flowered, about 3 in. long; flowers purple; bracts ovate-lanceolate, less than ½ in. in length. Lateral sepals ovate-lanceolate, spreading; upper sepal and petals oblong. Labellum oblong-obovate, cuspidate, somewhat longer than the other perianth-segments; spur clavate, arching forwards, about ⅓ as long as the labellum. Ovary glabrous. Habenaria purpurea, *Thouars, Orch. Afr. t.* 17; *Lindl. Gen. and Sp. Orch.* 317 (*Habenaria?*).

MAURITIUS, round Grand-Bassin, *Bojer*. Also Madagascar. I have seen no specimen.

3. **P. latifolius,** *Lindl. Gen. and Sp. Orch.* 297. Tubers twin, oblong. Leaves lanceolate-oblong, about 5 in. long, ¾ in. broad, two or three together congested near the bottom of the stem. Stem erect, clothed with a few scattered scales above the leaves, bearing a long dense-flowered cylindrical spike; flowers ¼ in. diam.; bracts lanceolate, acuminate, ½ in. long, becoming shorter above. Sepals subequal, ovate oblong. Petals a little shorter and narrower. Labellum scarcely longer than the other perianth-segments, rotundate, 3-lobed; lobes subequal, oblong, obtuse; spur about $\frac{1}{12}$ in. long. Satyrium latifolium, *Thouars, Orch. Afr. t.* 10. Benthamia latifolia, *Rich. Orch. Maur.* 43, *t.* 7, *f.* 2. Habenaria chlorantha, *Spreng. Syst. Veg.* iii. 691; *Bojer, Hort. Maur.* 309.

MAURITIUS, Flacq, and Quartier Militaire, *Bojer! Bouton!* Also Bourbon.

4. **P. spiralis,** *S. Moore.* Tuber apparently solitary, oblong. Leaves 4–5 in. long, ¼ in. broad, linear-lanceolate, 3–5 congested near the bottom of the stem. Stem erect, usually about 1 foot high, with two or three loose sheaths; flowers ⅙ in. diam., somewhat scattered, secund; bracts lanceolate, ½ in. (or less) in length. Sepals and petals oblong, obtuse, $\frac{1}{12}$ in. long, the lateral sepals adnate to the labellum below. Labellum about the same length as the sepals and petals, ovate, 3-lobed; lateral lobes short, oblong, obtuse; mid-lobe longer, tongue-like, fleshy; spur as in *P. latifolius*. Satyrium spirale, *Thouars, Orch. Afr. t.* 9. Benthamia spiralis, *Rich. Orch. Maur.* 44. Spiranthes africana, *Lindl. fide Spreng. Syst. Veg.* iii. 709.

MAURITIUS, shoulder of the Pouce, abundant, *Ayres!* Nouvelle Découverte, Savanne, etc., *Bouton!* Also Bourbon.

5. **P.? gramineus**, *S. Moore.* Very like *P. spiralis*, but the leaves are scattered, the flowers somewhat larger ($\frac{1}{4}$ in. diam.) and arranged in a short dense spike and the spur is linear, obtuse, arched forwards and about as long as the labellum. Satyrium gramineum. *Thouars, Orch. Afr. t.* 6. Platanthera? graminea, *Lindl. Gen. and Sp. Orch.* 292. Habenaria graminea, *Spreng. Syst. Veg.* iii. 690; *Bojer, Hort. Maur.* 310.

MAURITIUS, banks of Moka river and at Quartier Militaire, *Bojer.* Also Madagascar. I have seen no specimen.

6. **P. flexuosus**, *S. Moore.* Tubers fascicled, attenuated downwards. Leaves twin, radical, equal or unequal, lanceolate, nearly $1\frac{1}{2}$ in. long, $\frac{1}{4}$ in. broad. Scape wiry, ascending, about $\frac{1}{2}$ foot high, with about two sheathing scales; flowers about $\frac{1}{4}$ in. diam., few together, collected at the top of the scape; bracts lanceolate, $\frac{1}{8}$ in. in length. Upper sepal ovate-oblong, obtuse. $\frac{1}{12}$ in. long. Lateral sepals and petals about the same length, oblong. Labellum 3-lobed; lobes oblong, obtuse, the lateral a little the smaller; spur obtuse, $\frac{1}{24}$ in. long. Gymnadenia flexuosa, *Rich. Orch. Maur.* 27; *Lindl. Gen. and Sp. Orch.* 278 (Gymnadenia ?). Satyrium flexuosum, *Thouars, Orch. Afr. t.* 7.

MAURITIUS, at Moka and Quartier Militaire, *Bojer.* Also Bourbon. I have seen no specimen from Mauritius.

5. CYNORCHIS, Thouars.

Sepals and petals connivent, forming a hood over the column, the petals usually narrower than the sepals. Labellum patent, adnate to the lower part of the column, much longer than the other perianth-segments, lobed, usually with a long, slender, almost straight spur. Column short, straight; cells of the anther at the top or hinder part of the column, going off into two long upward- and forward-reaching arms; pollen masses oblong or pyriform; caudicles elongate; glands naked, spheroidal; rostellum fleshy, projecting upwards between the arms of the anther; stigma of two broad foliaceous lobes, one on the outer side of each arm of the anther.—Terrestrial herbs with tuberous roots and radical leaves. Flowers small or rather large, usually in erect racemes or spikes. DISTRIB. The genus consists of a few species endemic in the Mascarene Archipelago.

Sepals and petals nearly $\frac{1}{4}$ in. long. Labellum 4-lobed, nearly 1 in. long; spur elongate. Stigmatic lobes thin and glabrous, placed below the arms of the anther . 1. C. PURPURASCENS.
Sepals and petals $\frac{1}{4}$ in. long. Labellum 4-lobed, less than $\frac{1}{2}$ in. in length; spur elongate. Stigmatic lobes fleshy and warted, ascending above the base of the arms of the anther . . . . 2. C. FASTIGIATA.
Sepals and petals about $\frac{1}{4}$ in. long. Labellum 3-lobed, about $\frac{1}{4}$ in. long; spur short, clavate . . . . . . 3. C. BORYANA.

1. **C. purpurascens,** *Thouars, Orch. Afr. t.* 15, (*Cynosorchis*). Leaves lanceolate, acute or acuminate, 4–9 in. long, ½–1 in. broad, solitary or in unequal pairs. Scape usually about 1 foot high, bearing few or several somewhat scattered flowers; bracts ovate-oblong, acuminate, 1 in. long below, becoming smaller above; pedicel and ovary 1–1¾ in. long. Lateral sepals oblong-falcate, nearly ½ in. long; upper a little shorter, oblong. Petals lanceolate, as long as the upper sepal. Labellum broadly-obovate, nearly 1 in. long; lobes in two opposite pairs, oblong, truncate, crenulate; spur nearly ½ in. long, straight. Anther-cells at the back of the column; rostellum erect, distant from the long tapering arms of the anther, below the base of which are placed the ovate, thin, glabrous stigmatic-lobes. *Lindl. Gen. and Sp. Orch.* 331. Gymnadenia purpurascens, *Rich. Orch. Maur.* 29, *t.* 6, *f.* 1. *Bojer, Hort. Maur.* 311.

MAURITIUS, Plaines Wilhelms, and Moka, *Bojer.* Also Bourbon and Madagascar. I have seen no specimen from Mauritius.

2. **C. fastigiata,** *Thouars, Orch. Afr. t.* 13. Leaves usually two together, 3–6 in. long, ½–1½ in. broad, lanceolate, acute or obtuse. Scape usually about 1 foot high, bearing 8 or fewer somewhat crowded greenish flowers; bracts oblong-ovate, acuminate, ½ in. (or less) in length; pedicel and ovary 1–1½ in. long. Lateral sepals falcate-oblong, rather more than ⅛ in. long; upper sepal and petals a little shorter, oblong, obtuse, green tipped with pink. Labellum obovate, green tinged with white and pink, 4-lobed; lobes in two opposite pairs, oblong, truncate, crenulate; spur slender, straight, about 1 in. long. Anther crowning the column; rostellum erect, placed close behind the broad and not very long arms of the anther; stigmatic lobes broadly oblong, fleshy, warted all over, reaching up beyond the base of the arms of the anther. *Lindl. Gen. and Sp. Orch.* 332; *Bot. Reg. t.* 1998. Gymnadenia fastigiata, *Rich. Orch. Maur.* 25; *Bojer, Hort. Maur.* 310.

MAURITIUS, Moka, Plaines Wilhelms, and Villa Bague, *Bojer!*; shoulder of the Pouce, *Ayres! Bouton!* etc. SEYCHELLES, common in Mahé, *Horne! Salep du pays.*

Var? triphylla. Leaves three together, cordate at the base. Scape 2-flowered. C. tryphylla, *Thouars, Orch. Afr. t.* 14; *Lindl. Gen. and Sp. Orch.* 332. Gymnadenia triphylla, *Rich. Orch. Maur.* 26.—MAURITIUS, high mountains, *Bojer.* Perhaps a distinct species, but I have seen no specimen.

3. **C. Boryana,** *Lindl. Gen. and Sp. Orch.* 331. Leaves solitary, lanceolate, about 4 in. long, nearly 1 in. broad. Scape erect, more than ½ foot in height, several-flowered; bracts ovate, acuminate, about ½ in. long; pedicel and ovary 1 in. in length. Sepals oblong-ovate, obtuse, about ¼ in. long. Petals obovate, obtuse. Labellum more than ½ in. long, obovate, 3-lobed; lobes oblong, truncate, crenulate; spur ⅛ in. long, clavate, curved. Anther apparently dorsal, going out in two long dilated upcurved arms. Gymnadenia Boryana, *Rich. Orch. Maur.* 28, *t.* 5; *Bojer, Hort. Maur.* 311.

MAURITIUS, the Pouce, *fide Richard.* Unseen by me.

6. AMPHORCHIS, Thouars.

Sepals and petals spreading, subequal, the lateral sepals adnate to the base of the labellum. Labellum patent, free from the column, unequally 3-lobed. Anther terminal, its arms short, horizontal, broadly oblong, obtuse; pollen-masses pyriform, attached by straight slender caudicles to thin, oblong, exposed glands; rostellum short, linear, parallel with the arms of the anther, on the outer side of which are placed the stigmatic lobes.—A tuberous terrestrial plant. Leaves lanceolate. Scape erect, bearing many small, spurred flowers. DISTRIB. The genus is monotypic.

1. **A. calcarata,** *Thouars, Orch. Afr. t.* 4. Tubers about 1 in. in length, oblong. Leaves lanceolate, acuminate 4–6 in. long, $\frac{1}{2}$–$\frac{3}{4}$ in. broad, sheathing the scape for a short distance. Scape slender, 6–9 in. high, clothed with a few narrow sheathing scales; flowers numerous, crowded; bracts lanceolate, acuminate, nearly $\frac{1}{4}$ in. long. Sepals and petals subequal, ovate-oblong, about $\frac{1}{8}$ in. in length. Labellum about $\frac{1}{4}$ in. long, broadly cuneate, 3-lobed; lateral lobes short, obtuse; mid-lobe rotundate, cuspidulate, crenulate; spur more than $\frac{1}{8}$ in. long, straight, slender, obtuse. Rostellum almost horizontal; lobes of the stigma cuneate, with a row of black dots round the outer border. Capsule oblong, $\frac{1}{3}$ in. long. Cynorchis squamosa, *Lindl. Gen. and Sp. Orch.* 332. Gymnadenia squamata, *Rich. Orch. Maur.* 24, *t.* 6, *f.* 2. Habenaria Amphorchis, *Spreng. Syst. Veg.* iii. 689; *Bojer, Hort. Maur.* 310.

MAURITIUS, Cure-pipe and Plaines Wilhelms, *Bojer!*; Nouvelle Découverte, *Bouton!* etc. Also in Bourbon.

7. ARNOTTIA, Rich.

Sepals spreading, free, the lateral larger than the upper. Petals ascending, narrow. Labellum free from the column, not much unlike the other perianth-segments, spurless. Anther crowning the column, with two linear, straight arms; pollen-masses ovoid, joined by slender caudicles to a naked, oblong gland; rostellum rudimentary; stigma of two broad, fleshy lobes meeting in the centre, and occupying the whole front of the upper part of the column.—Terrestrial herbs with tuberous roots. Leaves radical, solitary. Scapes erect, bearing numerous small flowers. DISTRIB. Genus endemic in the Mascarene Archipelago.

Leaves ovate-oblong. Lateral sepals spathulate-ovate, $\frac{1}{6}$ in. long. Labellum oblong. Lobes of the stigma fleshy . 1. A. MAURITIANA.
Leaves lanceolate. Lateral sepals broadly oblong, $\frac{1}{8}$ in. long. Labellum lanceolate. Lobes of the stigma membranous 2. A. INERMIS.

1. **A. mauritiana,** *Rich. Orch. Maur.* 33 *t.* 7, *f.* 1. Tubers clustered, narrowly ovoid. Leaves ovate-oblong, acute or shortly apiculate, $\frac{3}{4}$ in. long, 1–1$\frac{1}{2}$ in. broad; base sheathing the scape. Scape 6–10 in. high

clothed with a few broad, loose, scattered, membranous scales; bracts lanceolate, $\frac{1}{4}$–$\frac{1}{2}$ in. in length; pedicel and ovary $\frac{3}{4}$ in. long when full-grown. Lateral sepals spathulate-ovate, $\frac{1}{4}$ in. long; upper sepal and petals shorter, oblong. Labellum oblong, $\frac{1}{6}$ in. in length. Ovary narrowing upwards, pilose on the ribs; lobes of the stigma fleshy, densely warted. *Lindl. Gen. and Sp. Orch.* 333.

MAURITIUS, *Boivin! Bouton!* Also Bourbon.

2. **A. inermis,** *S. Moore.* Tubers clustered, oblong. Leaves lanceolate, narrowed towards the base, 4–6 in. long, $\frac{1}{3}$–$\frac{3}{4}$ in. broad, base sheathing the scape. Scape $\frac{1}{2}$–1 foot high, slender, with several narrow sheathing scales; flowers subsessile in the axils of lanceolate bracts. Lateral sepals broadly oblong, obtuse, about $\frac{1}{6}$ in. long; upper a little narrower and shorter. Petals linear-oblong, a little shorter than the lateral sepals. Labellum lanceolate, oblique or cuspidate at the apex, a little longer than the lateral sepals. Ovary $\frac{1}{3}$ in. long, narrowed above and below, obscurely pilose; stigmatic lobes membranous, crenulate. Amphorchis inermis, *Thouars, Orch. Afr. t.* 5. Arnottia mauritiana? *Rich. Orch. Maur.* 33 (in part); *Lindl. Gen. and Sp. Orch.* 333.

MAURITIUS, *Bouton!* I think Bouton's specimen must be the *Amphorchis inermis* of Thouars. The labellum appears to be very variable, sometimes almost like that of *A. mauritiana*, sometimes very nearly that of Thouars' figure.

8. PLATYLEPIS, Rich.

Sepals and petals connivent, the petals concrete with the upper sepal into a hood. Labellum adnate to the column, entire, concave at base, with two fleshy calli near the bottom on the inner surface. Column elongate, claviform; anther dorsal; pollen-masses 2, subpulverulent, sessile on a small common gland; rostellum bifurcate, erect.—Terrestrial herbs with creeping rhizomes, leafy stems and terminal spikes of inconspicuous flowers. DISTRIB. A very small genus, found also in W. Tropical Africa and Tahiti.

Spike dense-flowered; bracts ovate. Sepals $\frac{1}{3}$ in. long.
  Stigmatic lobes oblong . . . . 1. P. GOODYEROIDES.
Spike lax-flowered; bracts lanceolate. Sepals $\frac{1}{6}$ in.
  long. Stigma rotundate . . . . 2. P.? SECHELLARUM.

1. **P. goodyeroides,** *Rich. Orch. Maur.* 39, *t.* 6, *f.* 4. Glabrous, except for a few short glandular hairs on the upper part of the stem, bracts, ovary and sepals. Stem erect, stoutish, $\frac{1}{2}$–1 foot high. Leaves numerous, 3–4 in. long, about 1 in. broad, ovate-lanceolate, narrowed below, then dilating to form a short loose amplexicaul sheath. Flowers in a short dense spike, partially hidden in the axils of ovate, acute bracts. Sepals oblong, $\frac{1}{3}$ in. in length. Petals as long, linear. Labellum $\frac{1}{4}$ in. long, oblong-spathulate, 3-nerved; lateral nerves bearing the calli. Column about as long as the labellum, slightly arching forwards;

pollen-masses pyriform; stigmatic lobes ascending, oblong. Goodyera occulta, *Thouars, Orch. Afr. t.* 28. Ætheria occulta, *Lindl. Gen. and Sp. Orch.* 491. Notiophrys occulta, *Lindl. in Journ. Linn. Soc.* i. 189.

MAURITIUS, dense woods near summit of the Pouce, *Ayres!*; the Pouce and Quartier Militaire, *Bojer! Bouton!* etc. SEYCHELLES, common in moist shady forests in Mahé, Praslin, and Silhouette, *Horne!* Endemic.

2. **P. ? sechellarum,** *S. Moore.* Stem about $\frac{1}{3}$ foot high, glandular-pubescent above, leafy below, clothed in the upper part with numerous loose, white, imbricate sheathing scales. Leaves as in P. goodyeroides, but lanceolate. Spike 3 in. long, lax-flowered; bracts lanceolate, glandular-pubescent. Sepals oblong, $\frac{1}{8}$ in. long. Petals linear, apparently quite free from the upper sepal. Labellum about as long as the column, and adnate to its base, ovate-oblong, obtuse, with several papilla-like calli near the base. Column slightly curved forwards; pollen-masses subpyriform, longitudinally sulcate; stigma rotundate.

SEYCHELLES, moist shady forests of Mahé, rare, *Horne!* Divergent from the genus by reason of its non-concrete petals and numerous small calli on the labellum.

9. GOODYERA, R. Br.

Sepals and petals ascending, the petals concrete with the upper sepal. Labellum entire, free from or adnate to the column, ventricose or concave at base, without calli. Column short, erect; anther dorsal; pollen-masses 2, sulcate; rostellum bifurcate, erect; stigma broad, occupying the face of the column.—Terrestrial fibrous-rooted herbs, with leafy stems and small flowers in erect terminal spikes. DISTRIB. A genus of several species natives of temperate and tropical regions of both worlds, but absent from Tropical and South Africa.

1. **G. nuda,** *Thouars, Orch. Afr. t.* 29. Stem erect, slender, about $\frac{1}{3}$ foot high. Leaves $\frac{3}{4}$–$1\frac{1}{2}$ in. long, oblong-lanceolate, suddenly narrowed near the base and then dilating to form a loose amplexicaul sheath. Spike $1\frac{1}{2}$ in. long, rather laxly flowered; bracts lanceolate. Sepals about $\frac{1}{12}$ in. long, oblong, obtuse, minutely crenulate. Petals as long, subspathulate. Labellum $\frac{1}{12}$ in. in length, free from the column, unappendaged. Pollen-masses pyriform. Stigma rotundate, occupying the whole front of the column. *Rich. Orch. Maur.* 38, *t.* 6, *f.* 3. *Lindl. Gen. and Sp. Orch.* 494.

MAURITIUS, shoulder of the Pouce, *Ayres! Herb. Blackburn!*; the Pouce and Flacq, *Bojer.* Also Bourbon.

See Monochilus Borge Reichb. f. Linnaea 41: 60

10. APLOSTELLIS, Rich.

Sepals and petals free, spreading, subequal. Labellum erect, free from the column and cucullate round it. Column clavate, shorter than the labellum; anther terminal; pollen-masses 4, in two pairs, pulverulent.—A small erect fibrous-rooted leafless herb. Flowers solitary, terminal. DISTRIB. The genus is monotypic and, as far as known, restricted to Mauritius.

1. **A. ambigua,** *Rich. Orch. Maur.* 41. Scape slender, 2–3 in. high, with a single linear bract near the middle. Sepals and petals linear-lanceolate, apparently about ½ in. long. Labellum about the same length, broadly oblong, the terminal margin truncate, incised. Column rather more than half as long as the labellum; stigma obcordate. Arethusa simplex, *Thouars, Orch. Afr. t.* 24. Haplostellis truncata. *Lindl. Gen. and Sp. Orch.* 411.

MAURITIUS, forests towards centre of the island, *Bojer.* No specimen seen by me. Endemic.

11. OBERONIA, Lindl.

Sepals spreading, usually equal to each other, free. Petals smaller than the sepals, but similar to them. Lip free from the column, generally lobed, hollowed at base. Column very short, with a prominent stigma; anther 2-celled; pollen-masses 4, collateral.—Caulescent or scapigerous herbs without pseudobulbs. Leaves distichous. Flowers minute, in long dense ascending or pendulous racemes, green or yellow. DISTRIB. The genus has its head-quarters in tropical Asia; it extends over the Indian Archipelago, and is represented by two species in Eastern Australia and by three or four in Polynesia.

1. **O. brevifolia,** *Lindl. Gen. and Sp. Orch.* 16; *Fol. Orch. No.* 36. Stem leafy, 1–3 in. long. Leaves closely imbricate, ovate or oblong. Racemes generally about as long as the stem, slender, usually drooping; bracts lanceolate, acuminate, serrulate, loosely investing the pedicel and ovary, about $\frac{1}{24}$ inch long. Sepals broadly ovate. Petals linear. Labellum slightly embracing the column, hollowed at base, usually 2-lobed at apex. Capsule ovoid, with three prominent ribs and as many alternating riblets, $\frac{1}{16}$ inch long. *Brongn. Voy. Coquille, t.* 40 *B.* Cymbidium equitans, *Thouars, Orch. Afr. t.* 92. Pleurothallis disticha, *Rich. Orch. Maur.* 55, *t.* 8, *f.* 1.

MAURITIUS, on the bark of trees in the interior of forests, *Bojer! Bouton!* etc. RODRIGUEZ? *Balfour!* (specimens without flowers). Also Bourbon and Madagascar.

12. LIPARIS, Rich.

Sepals and petals free, spreading or reflexed, the petals usually narrower than the sepals. Labellum adnate to the base of the column, ascending, horizontal or recurved, entire, usually tubercled. Column elongated, bent forwards, winged above; anther 2-celled; pollen-masses 4, in two pairs.—Plants growing in earth or on rocks or trees, with or without pseudobulbs. Leaves few together, usually broad and membranous, or long, narrow and fleshy. Flowers inconspicuous, in terminal racemes. DISTRIB. A large genus, found chiefly in tropical regions of the Old World, and represented by a few species in South Africa, Australia, Polynesia, and the tropics of America. *L. Lœselii*, Rich., is a native of North Europe and eastern North America.

Leaves solitary, narrow and fleshy, crowning a pseudobulb.
- Bracts distichous. Sepals reflexed. Petals erect, twisted . . . . 1. L. GREGARIA.
- Bracts scattered. Sepals and petals reflexed . . . 2. L. CÆSPITOSA.

Leaves broad and membranous, 2-4 together, their bases sheathing the dilated lower portion of the stem.
- Leaves ovate or lanceolate. Labellum ascending, crenulate . . . . 3. L. FLAVESCENS.
- Leaves cordate at the base. Labellum recurved, toothed . . . . 4. L. PURPURASCENS.

1. **L. gregaria,** *Lindl. Gen. and Sp. Orch.* 33. Pseudobulbs oblong-ovoid, narrowed above, when young clothed with sheathing scales. Leaves solitary, ensiform, erect, 3½–9 in. long, ⅓–½ in. broad. Scapes ascending, usually shorter than the leaf and arising side-by-side with it from the crown of the pseudobulb, 2-winged; flowers springing from the axils of distichous keeled bracts imbricate at the top of the scape. Pedicel at length ⅓ in. long. Sepals reflexed, ovate-oblong, crenulate above. Petals narrower than the sepals, erect, twisted, undulate. Labellum horizontal, broadly oblong, truncate, with a bifid callus. Capsule obovoid, ⅓ in. long. L. disticha, *Lindl. Bot. Reg. sub. t.* 882; *Rich. Orch. Maur.* 54. Malaxis disticha, *Thouars, Orch. Afr. t.* 89. Stelis micrantha, *Sieb. Herb. Maur. No.* 168!

MAURITIUS, on rocks in shady places, *Bojer!*; on trees in the forest of Grand Bassin, *Bouton! Ayres!* etc. Also Bourbon, Ceylon, and Tenasserim.

2. **L. cæspitosa,** *Lindl. Bot. Reg. sub. t.* 882. Leaves solitary, oblong or oblanceolate, obtuse, ¾–1½ in. long, ⅛ in. broad, crowning small ovoid pseudobulbs. Scape about as long as the leaves, erect, subterete; flowers distant; pedicels at length ⅛ in. long. Sepals and petals reflexed. Labellum lanceolate, recurved. Capsule obovoid, triquetrous, $\frac{1}{12}$ in. long. *Rich. Orch. Maur.* 53.; *Lindl. Gen. and Sp. Orch.* 32. Malaxis cæspitosa, *Thouars, Orch. Afr. t.* 90.

MAURITIUS, on old trees on mountains covered with wood at the Pouce and at Quartier Militaire, *Bojer*; *Bouton!* Also Bourbon. I have seen no flowering specimen of this plant.

3. **L. flavescens,** *Lindl. Bot. Reg. sub. t.* 882. Stem variable in height, dilated below, sheathed by scales and by the membranous leaf-bases. Leaves usually 3 or 4 together, lanceolate or ovate, acute, 1½–2½ in. long, ½–1⅓ in. broad. Scape terete, flexuous, exceeding the leaves, bearing a several-flowered lax raceme; bracts ovate-lanceolate, acuminate, about half as long as the slender pedicels. Lateral sepals broadly oblong-falcate, obtuse, 5-nerved; upper sepal longer and narrower, 3-nerved. Petals linear, as long as the upper sepal. Labellum rotundate, cuspidate, crenulate, with a small tongue-shaped callus at

base. Column narrowed below. Capsule obovoid, $\frac{1}{3}$ in. long. *Rich. Orch. Maur.* 51; *Lindl. Gen. and Sp. Orch.* 29. Malaxis flavescens, *Thouars, Orch. Afr. t.* 25.

MAURITIUS, in moist shady places on the sides of ravines and cascades in the interior of the island, *Bojer!* SEYCHELLES, common in moist shady forests of Mahé, Praslin, and Silhouette, *Horne!* Also Bourbon and Madagascar. I have seen no specimen from Mauritius.

4. **L. purpurascens,** *Lindl. Bot. Reg. sub. t.* 882. Stem erect, subterete, becoming bulbous below, sheathed with membranous scales. Leaves usually two together, ovate-cordate, acute, 5-nerved, 1–2 in. long, $\frac{3}{4}$–2 in. broad. Raceme few-flowered; bracts about $\frac{1}{12}$ in. long; pedicels thrice the length of the bracts. Sepals spreading, the upper linear-lanceolate, the lateral ovate. Petals linear, longer than the sepals. Labellum subrotund, emarginate, toothed. Capsule nearly $\frac{1}{2}$ in. long. *Rich. Orch. Maur.* 53; *Lindl. Gen. and Sp. Orch.* 27. Malaxis purpurascens, *Thouars, Orch. Afr. tt.* 26 *and* 27.

MAURITIUS, in damp places on high mountains, *Bouton!*; in moist forests and on rocks on the Pouce and at Nouvelle Découverte, *Bojer.* I have seen no flowers of this species.

L. foliosa, Lindl. Bot. Reg. t. 882, Hook. Bot. Mag. t. 2709, given as Mauritian on the authority of Barclay, is, in all probability, not a native of this region. Thouars makes no mention of it, and it was not seen by either Richard or Bojer. On the other hand, careful dissection will, I believe, show that it is identical with the Australian L. reflexa, *Lindl.*

There is at Kew a flowerless specimen gathered in the Seychelles by Mr. Horne, which has the habit of *L. flavescens*, but with smaller bracts, shorter pedicels and smaller fruits. It is probably a new species belonging either to this genus or to its close ally *Microstylis.*

13. BULBOPHYLLUM, Thouars.

Sepals free, or the lateral connate, erect or spreading; lateral sometimes the larger and adnate to the produced base of the column. Labellum hinged on to the top of the produced column-base, or continuous with it, entire, usually tongue-like and fleshy. Column short, with a long basal projection and, on each side, an apical tooth; pollen-masses 4, usually cohering in pairs.—Herbs growing on trees or rocks, with scaly rhizomes, and leaves solitary or twin from the crown of the pseudobulb. Flowers in spikes or umbels, usually small; scapes arising from the side of the base of the pseudobulb, sometimes dilated above, usually more or less densely clothed with sheathing scales below the inflorescence. DISTRIB. A large genus occurring principally in the tropics and subtropics of the Old World; the section *Bulbophyllaria* contains a few species found in Tropical America.

Section I. *Bulbophyllum* proper. Flowers in spikes. Lateral sepals free, equal. Labellum entire, hinged on to the column.

Leaves 9 in. long. Pseudobulb developed after the flowers . . . . 1. B. VARIEGATUM.
Leaves never more than 6 in. long. Scape from the side of the base of the full-formed pseudobulb.
Flowers completely hidden by large imbricate tetrastichous bracts . . . . 2. B. OCCULTUM.
Bracts small.
Leaves twin. Petals oblong . . . . 3. B. NUTANS.
Leaves solitary. Petals linear or spathulate.
Scape stout, nodding. Petals linear . . . . 4. B. INCURVUM.
Scape slender, ascending. Petals broadly spathulate . . . . 5. B. SECHELLARUM.

Section II. *Cirrhopetalum*, Lindl. (Gen.) Flowers in umbels. Lateral sepals much longer than the upper one, free. Labellum entire, hinged on to the column.

The only species . . . . 6. B. LONGIFLORUM.

Section III. *Bulbophyllaria*, Rchb. f. (Gen.) Flowers in spikes. Lateral sepals connate. Labellum entire, hinged on to the column.

Leaves twin, much longer than the pseudobulb.
Scape stout. Labellum cordate at the base.
Scape much dilated above, longer than the leaves . . 7. B. CLAVATUM.
Scape but little dilated above, about as long as the leaves . . . . 8. B. CÆSPITOSUM.
Scape thin, wiry. Labellum truncate at the base.
Scape erect, with few sheathing scales . . . . . . 9. B. DENSUM.
Scape nodding, with many imbricated sheathing scales . . . . 10. B. PENDULUM.
Leaves solitary, scarcely longer than the small globular pseudobulbs . . . . 11. B. PUSILLUM.

Section IV. *Lyræa*, Lindl. (Gen.) Flowers in spikes. Lateral sepals connate. Labellum 2-lobed, continuous with the column.

The only species . . . . 12. B. PRISMATICUM.

1. **B. variegatum,** *Thouars, Orch. Afr. t.* 105. Pseudobulbs ovoid, 1½ in. long, not fully developed until after the flowering. Leaves two together, lanceolate, acute, fleshy, many-nerved, 9 in. long, ¾–1 in. broad, invested below by several broad sheathing scales persistent round the full-formed pseudobulbs. Scape nodding, stout, about as long as the leaves, with a few large sheathing scales; bracts broad, almost as long as the flower. Sepals ovate-lanceolate, acuminate, ½ in. long, yellow-brown with purple spots. Petals broadly oblong-spathulate, crenulate, with a long slender apiculus, purple. Labellum oblong, fleshy, its margins recurved. Column long for the genus, its apical

teeth short and stout. *Lindl. Gen. and Sp. Orch.* 51; *Rich. Orch. Maur.* 64.

MAURITIUS, on trees and moist shaded rocks; Cent Gaulettes, and Grand Port, *Bojer! Ayres!* Also Bourbon.

2. **B. occultum,** *Thouars, Orch. Afr. tt.* 93, 94. Pseudobulbs ovoid, when full grown about 1 in. long. Leaves twin, sometimes unequal, oblong, obtuse, 3 in. long. $\frac{1}{2}$–$\frac{3}{4}$ in. broad. Scape stout, ascending or nodding, copiously clothed with loose, brown, scarious sheaths becoming larger above; spike as long as the lower portion of the scape; flowers completely hidden in the axils of large imbricate tetrastichous bracts. Sepals curved, the upper one a little the longer and narrower. Petals subulate, half as long as the sepals. Labellum oblong, coarsely ciliate. Teeth of the column long and horn-like. Capsule $\frac{1}{3}$ in. long. *Rich. Orch. Maur.* 64. Dendrochilum occultum, *Lindl. Gen. and Sp. Orch.* 34.

MAURITIUS, the Pouce, Quartier Militaire, round Grand Bassin on trees, *Bojer! Bouton! Grey!* Also Bourbon.

3. **B. nutans,** *Thouars, Orch. Afr. t.* 107. Pseudobulbs ovoid, $\frac{1}{4}$–$\frac{1}{2}$ inch long. Leaves twin, oblong, emarginate, $\frac{3}{4}$–$1\frac{1}{3}$ in. long, $\frac{1}{4}$–$\frac{1}{2}$ in. broad, fleshy. Scape longer than the leaves, slender, nodding, with a few sheathing scales. Sepals patent, ovate, acute, about twice as long as the oblong, obtuse petals. Labellum oblong-ovate, somewhat cordate at base. Teeth of the column short. *Lindl. Gen. and Sp. Orch.* 52, *Rich. Orch. Maur.* 63.

MAURITIUS, on trees and rocks, Piton du Milieu de l'Ile, *Bojer!*; summit of the Pouce, *Ayres!* Also Bourbon.

4. **B. incurvum,** *Thouars, Orch. Afr. t.* 95. Pseudobulbs ovoid or subglobular, sulcate, $\frac{1}{2}$–$\frac{3}{4}$ in. long. Leaves solitary, oblong, emarginate, $1\frac{1}{2}$–$2\frac{1}{2}$ in. long, $\frac{1}{4}$–$\frac{1}{2}$ in. broad. Scape stout, wiry, nodding, about twice as long as the leaves, sheathed with a few scattered scales; bracts triangular-deltoid, about $\frac{1}{12}$ in. long. Lateral sepals ovate-falcate; the upper oblong. Petals linear, half as long as the sepals. Labellum oblong, grooved down the centre, ciliolate. Teeth of the column long, thin, curved forwards. Capsule oblong-ovoid, about $\frac{1}{3}$ in. in length. *Lindl. Gen. and Sp. Orch.* 52.

MAURITIUS, windy places near the middle of the island, *Bojer!*; Pouce range to left of Fenestre, *Ayres!* RODRIGUEZ, *Balfour!* Perhaps also Bourbon.

5. **B. sechellarum,** *Rchb. f. MSS.* Pseudobulbs oblong-ovoid, obtusely 4-angled, $\frac{1}{6}$ in. long. Leaves solitary, lanceolate, $\frac{1}{2}$–$\frac{3}{4}$ in. long, $\frac{1}{8}$ in. broad. Scape slender, wiry, ascending, $3\frac{1}{2}$ in. high, with few sheathing scales; flowers scattered, about twice as long as the ovate-lanceolate bracts. Sepals oblong, acute. Petals broadly spathulate,

crenulate, about half as long as the sepals. Labellum lanceolate. fleshy. Column very short, its produced base broad, ⅓ as long as the labellum.

SEYCHELLES, common in forests, *Horne!* Endemic.

6. **B. longiflorum,** *Thouars, Orch. Afr. t.* 98. Pseudobulbs ovoid, 4-gonous, ¾ in. long, surrounded at the base by the persistent ribs of sheathing scales. Leaves solitary, oblong, obtuse, narrowed below, 2½–6 in. long, ¾–1⅓ broad. Scape erect, wiry, terete, 6–9 in. high, with about 3 sheathing scales; flowers few or several together in a secund umbel, the slender pedicels twice or thrice as long as the linear bracts. Upper sepal broadly ovate, apiculate, crenulate, 5-nerved, about ¼ in. long, tawny spotted with red; lateral sepals lanceolate, twisted near the base, 5-nerved, nearly 1⅓ in. long, tawny without, yellow dotted with red-brown within. Petals ovate-lanceolate, apiculate, coarsely and sparsely ciliate, yellow with red spots. Labellum oblong. Teeth of the column long, curving forwards, serrate. Cirrhopetalum Thouarsii, *Lindl. Gen. and Sp. Orch.* 58; *Bot. Reg.* 1838, *t.* 11; *Hook. Bot. Mag. t.* 4237. Cymbidium umbellatum, *Forst. Prod.* 321.

MAURITIUS, on trees, Quartier Militaire, and upper part of Plaines Wilhelms, *Bojer.* Occurs also in Madagascar and the Indian and Pacific Archipelagoes; the type of the old genus *Cirrhopetalum.*

7. **B. clavatum,** *Thouars, Orch. Afr. t.* 99. Pseudobulbs oblong-ovoid, ¾–1 in. long, ½ in. (or less) broad, clothed by a whitish papery scale with one or two smaller scales at the base. Leaves twin, oblong, obtuse or somewhat emarginate, narrowed towards the base, 3–4 times as long as the pseudobulb. Scape stout, longer than the leaves, with several loose sheathing scales, becoming thickened above into a fleshy mass in which the flowers are partially immersed; bracts short and broad, hiding the young buds. Lateral sepals united almost to the very tip; upper sepal narrower, 3-nerved. Petals linear, less than half the length of the sepals. Labellum broadly ovate-cordate, obtuse, papillose. Produced base of column long, curving upwards. Capsule broadly ovoid, nearly ½ in. long. *Rich. Orch. Maur.* 61; *Lindl. Gen. and Sp. Orch.* 55. B. Conitum, *Thouars, Orch. Afr. t.* 100. Bulbophyllaria clavata, *Rchb. f. in Walp. Ann.* vi. 242.

MAURITIUS, on trees in high mountain forests, *Bojer! Bouton! Ayres!* Endemic.

8. **B. cæspitosum,** *Thouars, Orch. Afr. t.* 103. Very like *B. clavatum*, but the scape is shorter, thinner, and but slightly dilated above, the bracts and flowers are considerably smaller, and the capsule is only ⅛ in. long. *Lindl. Gen. and Sp. Orch.* 55.

MAURITIUS, on trees, forests of Grand Port and La Savanne, *Bojer! Ayres!* Also Bourbon. Thouars figures the lateral sepals as free for at least the upper third of their course; I found them exactly as in *B. clavatum.*

9. **B. densum,** *Thouars, Orch. Afr. t.* 108. Pseudobulbs ovoid, $\frac{3}{8}$ in. long. Leaves twin, narrow-oblong, 3 in. long, $\frac{1}{4}$ in. broad. Scape slender, wiry, erect, about twice as long as the leaves, with a few loose scattered sheathing scales. Spike short, crowning the scape; bracts ovate, concealing the buds. Lateral sepals connate throughout; upper one shorter and narrower. Petals subulate. Labellum ovate, acute, truncate at base, thickened in the middle. Teeth of the column directed almost vertically upwards, its produced base short. Capsule ovoid, $\frac{1}{4}$ in. long. *Lindl. Gen. and Sp. Orch.* 52. *Rich. Orch. Maur.* 64.

MAURITIUS, on trees in forests and on high mountains, *Bojer;* Quartier Militaire, *Ayres!* Endemic.

10. **B. pendulum,** *Thouars, Orch. Afr. t.* 104. Pseudobulbs subglobular, sulcate, less than $\frac{1}{8}$ in. in length. Leaves twin, oblong, emarginate, 2 in. long, $\frac{1}{8}$–$\frac{1}{4}$ in. broad. Scape short, nodding, bearing a short dense flower-spike. Sepals ovate, acute, the upper narrower than the lateral. Petals oblong. Labellum broadly ovate, obtuse, truncate at base. *Lindl. Gen. and Sp. Orch.* 52; *Rich. Orch. Maur.* 64.

MAURITIUS, on trees in forests at Quartier Militaire and La Savanne, *Bojer.* I have seen no specimen.

11. **B. pusillum,** *Thouars, Orch. Afr. t.* 102. Pseudobulbs subglobular, scarcely $\frac{1}{4}$ in. long. Leaves solitary, obovate or oblong, emarginate, scarcely longer than the pseudobulbs. Scape much longer than the leaves, clothed with numerous sheathing scales, dilated above; flowers partially immersed in the dilated portion of the scape. Lateral sepals apparently connate about half the way up; upper sepal ovate, acuminate. Petals labellum and column as in *B. clavatum*, but all the floral parts are much smaller than are those of that species. *Lindl. Gen. and Sp. Orch.* 55. *Rich. Orch. Maur.* 64. B. clavatum, var. *Spreng. Syst. Veg.* iii. 732.

MAURITIUS, the Pouce and Peter Both, *Bojer.* Described from Thouars' figure.

12. **B. prismaticum,** *Thouars, Orch. Afr. t.* 109. Pseudobulbs oblong, much laterally compressed, less than $1\frac{1}{2}$ in. long. Leaves twin, oblong, emarginate, nearly $2\frac{1}{2}$ in. long, $\frac{1}{3}$ in. broad. Scape erect, $\frac{1}{2}$ foot high, with a few loose scarious sheaths; bracts ovate, acute, $\frac{1}{8}$ in. long. Upper sepal oblong, acute. Petals about half the length of the sepals. Labellum deeply 2-lobed; tips of the lobes curving outwards, the intervening sinus broad. *Rich. Orch. Maur.* 62, *t.* 8, *f.* 3. Lyræa prismatica, *Lindl. Gen. and Sp. Orch.* 46.

MAURITIUS, on trees in dark forests towards the centre of the island, *Bojer.* Also Bourbon. I have seen no specimen.

Thouars (Orch. Afr. t. 101) has a singular figure of a plant which he calls *Bulbophyllum gracile:* its pseudobulbs are apparently much laterally compressed, the leaves are nearly $5\frac{1}{2}$ in. long, and the scape more than twice that length, with large loose sheathing scales, bears a long sparsely-flowered spike. There is no dissection of the flower given by Thouars, so that it is deemed advisable not to include it in the Flora; the plant was never seen by Bojer.

14. PHAJUS, Lour.

Sepals and petals free, spreading, nearly equal, deciduous. Labellum convolute round and free from the column or adnate to it below, entire or more or less 3-lobed, spurred or saccate at base, usually crested or lanceolate on the inner face. Column elongated, clavate; anther 8-celled; pollen-masses 8, all equal or four smaller, joined to a broad thick caudicle, but without any gland.—Terrestrial herbs, with stems usually swollen into pseudobulbs. Leaves large, membranous, many-nerved. Racemes erect, bearing numerous gaily coloured flowers. DISTRIB. A genus of several species, natives, for the most part, of the Indian and Malayan peninsulas and Archipelago; two are found in Australia, and as many in Polynesia.

Stem 4-angled. Labellum adnate to the lower half of the column . . . . 1. P. TETRAGONUS.
Stem subterete. Labellum free from the column . . . . 2. P. VILLOSUS.

1. **P. tetragonus,** *Rchb. f. in Bonpl.* iii. 221; *Walp. Ann.* vi. 458. Stem a foot or more high, erect, stout, jointed, sharply 4-angled, clothed below with several green scales. Leaves springing from the joints, broadly ovate-lanceolate, acuminate, narrowed towards the base, plicate, about 1 foot long and from 2 in. broad. Raceme axillary, stout, as long as the leaves; peduncles short, ultimately becoming decurved and carrying up the longer sheathing bracts; flowers about 8 or 10 in a lax spike, 2 in. diam., red and yellow. Sepals spathulate-oblong, acute, 1 in. long, ¼ in. broad. Petals a little longer and narrower. Labellum adnate to the lower half of the column, gibbous at base, with three central longitudinal raised lines within, obscurely 3-lobed; mid-lobe acuminate, reflexed. Column winged, dentate at the top, puberulous. Epidendrum tetragonum, *Thouars, Orch. Afr. tt.* 33, 34. Limodorum tetragonum, *Rich. Orch. Maur.* 47, *t.* 7, *f.* 4. Broughtonia tetragona, *R. Br.; Spreng. Syst. Veg.* iii. 734. Pesomeris tetragona, *Lindl. Bot. Mag. t.* 4442.

MAURITIUS, Plaines Wilhelms and round Grand Bassin, *Bojer! Ayres!* SEYCHELLES, forests of Mahé, not common, *Horne!* Endemic.

2. **P. villosus,** *Rchb. f. MSS. in Herb. Kew.* Habit and stem as in *P. tetragonus*, but the latter is subterete and sometimes only 6 in. high. Leaves ovate-lanceolate, rather more than 1 foot long, narrowed towards the base; bracts lanceolate, nearly 1 in. long; flowers 1 in. diam. Sepals broadly lanceolate, ¾ in. long. Petals a little shorter and narrower. Labellum free from the column, ovate-lanceolate, undulate, about ¾ in. long, with a central longitudinal patch of coarse yellow hairs. Column ½ or ¼ in. long, entire at the top; anther-bed prolonged upwards behind. Bletia villosa, *Rich. Orch. Maur.* 42; *Lindl. Gen. and Sp. Orch.* 123. Limodorum villosum, *Thouars, Orch. Afr. t.* 32.

MAURITIUS, Quartier Militaire and Grand Bassin, *Bouton!*; Quartier Militaire, Flacq, Plaines Wilhelms, and La Savanne, *Bojer!*

Var. LONGIBRACTEATA. Bracts 2–5 in. long. Bletia lancifolia, *Ayres MSS.* Shoulder of the Pouce, *Ayres !*; grand Bassin, *Bouton ! Bojer !*

There appear to be two forms of column to this plant, which are probably connected with some peculiar sexual condition. A specimen of Ayres' gathering in which fertilization has been accomplished without opening of the flowers, was called by him *Calanthe inaperta*; see *Trimen Journ. Bot.* 1876, 290.

15. CRYPTOPUS, Lindl.

Sepals spreading, entire. Petals a little larger than the sepals, lobed. Labellum almost free from the column, 4-lobed, with a long slender spur. Column short, terete, with a broad arm on each side; pollen-masses 2, ovoid; caudicles 2, with shallow cup-like summits, villous below; glands oblong; rostellum beaked.—Epiphytes with short leafy stems. Leaves distichous, vaginate, fleshy. Flowers conspicuous, in elegant erect lax racemes. DISTRIB. The genus is monotypic, and restricted to Mauritius and the neighbouring archipelago.

1. **C. elatus,** *Lindl. Bot. Reg. sub. t.* 817. Stem terete, somewhat flexuous, as thick as a goose-quill, closely invested by the sheaths of the leaves and bearing, at almost every internode, a stout, unbranched aerial root. Leaves oblong or oblong-ovate, obliquely emarginate, 1–2$\frac{3}{4}$ in. long, $\frac{1}{2}$–$\frac{3}{4}$ in. broad. Racemes 1–2 feet long, piercing the back of the leaf-sheaths; flowers 1$\frac{1}{2}$ in. diam., yellowish. Sepals spathulate, $\frac{3}{4}$ in. long. Petals unguiculate, the lamina irregularly 4-lobed. Lobes of labellum in two opposite pairs, the lower incurved-falcate, the upper spathulate, retuse; spur nearly 1 in. long. *Hook. Journ. Bot.* i. 45, *t.* 115. Angræcum elatum, *Thouars, Orch. Afr. t.* 79. Beclardia elata, *Rich. Orch. Maur.* 78, *t.* 11. *f.* 3. Epidendrum dipterum, *Sieb. Herb. Maur. No.* 210!

MAURITIUS, the Pouce and Quartier Militaire, *Bojer ! Bouton ! Telfair !* etc. Also Bourbon and Madagascar.

16. AERANTHUS, Lindl.

Sepals subequal, spreading or recurved, the lateral sometimes adnate to the base of the spur. Labellum free from the column, entire, like the other perianth-segments or larger than them and lobed; spur short, straight and obtuse or long, curved and attenuated. Column short, incurved, clavate; pollen-masses 2, each sessile on or joined by a slender caudicle to an oblong gland; rostellum of two broad, obtuse lobes. Habit and distribution of *Angræcum*.

Flowers solitary, axillary or leaf-opposed. Labellum like the sepals and petals.
  Leaves scattered on a slender stem.
    Flowers axillary, subsessile, $\frac{1}{8}$ in. diam.; spur obtuse $\frac{1}{12}$ in. long . . . . 1. A. PECTINATUS.
  Flowers on long slender leaf-opposed peduncles.
    Leaves lanceolate, 1$\frac{1}{2}$–3 in. long. Flowers $\frac{3}{4}$ in. diam.; petals ovate-lanceolate; spur 2–3 in. long . . . . 2. A. GLADIIFOLIUS.

Leaves lorate, emarginate, 4–5 in. long. Flowers ¾ in. diam.; petals linear; spur 1½ in. long . . . 3. A. FRAGRANS.
Leaves linear, emarginate, less than 2 in. long. Flowers over 1 in. diam.; petals lanceolate; spur recurved, ½ in. long. . . . . . . 4. A.? EXPANSUS.
Leaves narrow-linear, emarginate, 2 in. long, 1/12 in. broad. Flowers about 1 in. diam.; petals lanceolate; spur almost straight, 4 in. long . . . . 5. A.? THOUARSII.
Leaves imbricate on a stout erect stem.
Leaves linear-oblong, emarginate. Flowers ½ in. diam.; spur curved, 3 in. long. . . . . 6. A.? RECTUS.
Flowers in racemes.
Labellum unlike the sepals and petals.
Labellum sessile, lobed.
Racemes many-flowered. Leaves imbricate, linear-oblong, marginate, 4–5 in. long . 7. A. MACROSTACHYS.
Racemes few-flowered. Leaves subimbricate, broadly-oblong emarginate, 2–2½ in. long . 8. A.? BRACHYSTACHYS.
Racemes few-flowered. Leaves scattered, ovate-oblong, 1 in. long. . . . . 9. A. VOLUCRIS.
Labellum clawed, entire.
Leaves 4–10 in. long. Lateral sepals ¾–1½ in. in length; upper sepals ovate-lanceolate . 10. A. ARACHNITES.
Labellum like the sepals and petals.
Leaves oblong-oblanceolate. Spur ⅛ in. long . . 11. A.? CALCEOLUS.

1. **A. pectinatus,** *Rchb. f. in Walp. Ann.* vi. 900. Stem straight, stiff, rooting copiously below. Limb of leaf linear-oblong, obtuse, ½–¾ in. long; sheath ⅙ in. in length. Flowers solitary, axillary, subsessile, ⅓ in. diam.; bracts ovate, acute, ⅛ in. long. Sepals oblong, obtuse, ⅙ inch in length. Petals a little narrower and shorter. Labellum like the sepals, but acute; spur almost straight, obtuse, rather more than 1/12 in. long. Pollen-masses sessile each on a short oblong gland. Angræcum pectinatum, *Thouars, Orch. Afr. t.* 51; *Lindl. Gen. and Sp. Orch.* 247; *Rich. Orch. Maur.* 68, *t.* 10, *f.* 5; *Hook. Journ. Bot.* i. 47, *t.* 116.

MAURITIUS, wooded districts towards centre of the island, *Bojer!* near summit of the Pouce, *Ayres!* etc. Also Bourbon and Madagascar.

2. **A. gladiifolius,** *Rchb. f. in Walp. Ann.* vi. 900. Stem stoutish, somewhat flexuous. Limb of leaf lanceolate, 1½–3 in. long; sheath ½ in. (or more) in length. Peduncle leaf-opposed, 1-flowered, slender, together with the ovary 2–3 in. long. Sepals, petals and labellum ovate-lanceolate, acuminate, nearly 1 in. long, milk-white; spur slender, tapering, as long as the peduncle. Pollen-masses attached by slender caudicles to a linear gland. Angræcum gladiifolium, *Thouars, Orch. Afr. t.* 53; *Lindl. Gen. and Sp. Orch.* 246; *Bot. Reg.* 1840, *t.* 68; *Rich. Orch. Maur.* 69. Orchis mauritiana, *Lam. Encyc.* iv. 601 (?)

MAURITIUS, the Pouce, Peter Both, and Crève-cœur, *Bojer! Sieber! Ayres!* etc. Also Bourbon and Madagascar.

3. **A. fragrans,** *Rchb. f. in Walp. Ann.* vi. 899. Stem stoutish, subterete. Limb of leaf lorate, emarginate, 4–5 in. long, less than

$\frac{1}{2}$ in. broad, aromatic; sheaths $\frac{1}{2}$ in. (or less) in length. Peduncles leaf-opposed, 1-flowered, ascending, together with the ovary 3 in. long. Sepals lanceolate-oblong, acute, somewhat recurved, the lateral the narrower. Petals linear. Labellum oblong-spathulate, acute; spur $1\frac{1}{2}$ in. long. Caudicles long and slender. Angræcum fragrans, *Thouars, Orch. Afr. t.* 54; *Lindl. Gen. and Sp. Orch.* 246; *Rich. Orch. Maur.* 69.

MAURITIUS, La Savanne and Grand Port, *Bojer!* Also Bourbon. *Fahame.*

4. **A.? expansus**, *S. Moore.* Stem terete, rather slender and flexuous, about 3 in. long. Leaves linear, obliquely emarginate, $1\frac{1}{3}$–$1\frac{3}{4}$ in. long, $\frac{1}{3}$–$\frac{1}{4}$ in. broad; sheaths $\frac{1}{4}$–$\frac{1}{2}$ in. in length. Peduncles leaf-opposed, 1-flowered, nearly 2 in. long; flowers more than 1 in. diam. Sepals and petals subequal, lanceolate, nearly $\frac{3}{4}$ in. long. Labellum ovate-lanceolate, acuminate, somewhat shorter than the sepals and petals; spur slender, recurved, $1\frac{1}{2}$ in. long. Angræcum expansum, *Thouars, Orch. Afr. t.* 57; *Lindl. Gen. and Sp. Orch.* 246.

MAURITIUS, Plaines Wilhelms, Grand Bassin, and Trou aux Cerfs, *Bojer.* Also Bourbon. I have seen no specimen from Mauritius, nor have I been able to examine the pollen.

5. **A.? Thouarsii**, *S. Moore.* Stem ascending, slender, somewhat flexuous, 4–5 in. high. Leaves narrow-linear, emarginate, about 2 in. long, $\frac{1}{12}$ in. broad; sheaths $\frac{1}{2}$ in. in length. Peduncles leaf-opposed, 1-flowered, $\frac{3}{4}$ in. long; flowers about 1 in. diam. Sepals lanceolate, $\frac{1}{2}$ in. long. Petals a little narrower, spreading. Labellum panduriform, scarcely $\frac{1}{2}$ in. long; spur slender, almost straight, about 4 in. in length. Angræcum filicornu, *Thouars, Orch. Afr. t.* 52; *Lindl. Gen. and Sp. Orch.* 246.

MAURITIUS, Grand Bassin, Curepipe, and La Savanne, *Bojer.* No specimen seen; there is already an *Aeranthus filicornis*, Rchb. f. (*Mystacidium*, Lindl.) from the Cape.

6. **A.? rectus,** *S. Moore.* Leaves linear-oblong, emarginate, 3–4 in. long, $\frac{1}{2}$ in. broad, imbricate on a straight subterete stem about 4 in. in height. Peduncles axillary, ascending, 1-flowered, nearly 3 in. long; flowers $\frac{1}{2}$ in. diam. Upper sepal nearly $\frac{1}{2}$ in. long, lanceolate; lateral sepals and petals a little longer, linear, directed forwards. Labellum lanceolate-spathulate, about $\frac{1}{2}$ in. long; spur about 3 in. long, slender with a sharp curve about a fifth the way down. Angræcum rectum, *Thouars, Orch. Afr. t.* 55; *Rich. Orch. Maur.* 70. A. fragrans, var. *Lindl. Gen. and Sp. Orch.* 246.

MAURITIUS, Moka River, Bois Chéri, and the Pouce, *Bojer.* Also Bourbon.

Var? RECURVUS. Leaves shorter and narrower. Peduncles about $1\frac{1}{4}$ in. long. Spur sharply curved at right angles to the column. Angræcum recurvum, *Thouars, Orch. Afr. t.* 56; *Rich. Orch. Maur.* 70. A. fragrans, var. *Lindl. Gen. and Sp. Orch.* 246. MAURITIUS, in forests towards the centre of the island, *Bojer. Fahame bâtard.* I have seen no specimen either of the typical or supposed varietal form.

7. **A. macrostachys,** *Rchb. f. in Walp. Ann.* vi. 900. Stem thick, terete, giving off very thick, almost straight aerial roots. Leaves imbricate, linear-oblong, emarginate, 4–5 in. long, ½ in. broad. Racemes erect from the inner side of the leaf-base, about 1 foot long, many-flowered; pedicel and ovary about ¾ in. in length. Flowers 1 in. diam. Sepals ovate-oblong, acute. Petals spathulate. Labellum obovate, crenulate, cuspidulate at the sinus between the two truncate terminal lobes; spur parallel to the column, saccate above, narrowed towards the extremity, ¼ in. long. Pollen-masses sessile on ovate-acuminate glands. Epidendrum macrostachys, *Thouars, Orch. Afr. t.* 83. Œonia macrostachya, *Lindl. Gen. and Sp. Orch.* 245. Beclardia macrostachya, *Rich. Orch. Maur.* 79, *t.* 11, *f.* 2.

MAURITIUS, La Savanne, *Bojer.* Also Bourbon. I have seen no specimen from Mauritius.

8. **A.? brachystachyus,** *Bojer, Hort. Maur.* 314 (name only). Leaves subimbricate, broadly oblong, obliquely emarginate, 2–2½ in. long, ½ in. broad. Raceme few-flowered, erect, ½ foot long; bracts ¼ in. in length, ovate-lanceolate. Pedicels and ovary ascending, less than ½ in. long. Sepals and petals ovate-oblong, acute. Labellum ovate, retuse; lateral lobes almost obsolete; spur parallel to the column, saccate above, obtuse, ⅓ in. long. Epidendrum brachystachyum, *Thouars, Orch. Afr. t.* 84. Œonia brachystachya, *Lindl. Gen. and Sp. Orch.* 245. Beclardia brachystachya, *Rich. Orch. Maur.* 80.

MAURITIUS, the Pouce, and Peter Both, *Bojer.* I have seen no specimen.

9. **A. volucris,** *Rchb. f. in Walp. Ann.* vi. 900. Limb of the leaf ovate-oblong, acute, about 1 in. long, ⅓ in. broad; sheaths ¾ in. long. Racemes nearly 1 foot long, few-flowered; flowers 1½ in. diam.; pedicel and ovary nearly 2 in. long. Sepals and petals oblong-lanceolate, acute. Labellum obovate, cuspidulate at the sinus between the two broad truncate terminal lobes; spur straight, saccate ½ in. long. Epidendrum volucre, *Thouars, Orch. Afr. t.* 81. Œonia Auberti, *Lindl. Bot. Reg. sub. t.* 817, *and Gen. and Sp. Orch.* 244.

MAURITIUS, in forests towards centre of the island, *Bojer.* Also Bourbon. I have seen no specimen.

10. **A. arachnites,** *Lindl. Bot. Reg. sub. t.* 817. Leaves imbricate, lorate, obliquely emarginate, 4–8 in. long, ½–¾ in. broad, sheathing the dwarf erect stem for a short distance below. Racemes ascending from the base of the stem, few-flowered, from ½ foot long, copiously clothed with long, narrow scarious sheathing scales; flowers about ½ in. diam.; pedicel about $\frac{1}{12}$ in. in length. Lateral sepals ovate, acuminate, ¾ in. long, adnate to the claw of the labellum; upper sepal ovate-lanceolate, scarcely more than ½ in. long. Petals narrower and shorter than the lateral sepals, adnate to the claw of the labellum. Limb of the labellum cordate, acute, incumbent over the column, ½ in. long; claw broad, channelled, about ⅛ in. in length; spur clavate,

about $\frac{1}{4}$ in. long. Anther-cap pointed in front; pollen-masses spheroidal; caudicles linear, twisted, and rostellum of two broad, obtuse lobes projecting at right angles to the column. *Bot. Mag. t.* 6034. A. grandiflorus, *Lindl. Gen. and Sp. Orch.* 243 (in part). Dendrobium arachnites, *Thouars, Orch. Afr. t.* 88.

MAURITIUS, high parts of the island, *Bojer!*; Mont Rosamond, *Bouton! Ayres!* Endemic.

Var. BALFOURI. Leaves 10 in. long. Lateral sepals $1\frac{1}{4}$ in. in length. RODRIGUEZ. *Balfour!* Described from a living specimen obligingly communicated by its discoverer.

11. **A.? Calceolus,** *S. Moore.* Leaves oblong-lanceolate, obliquely emarginate, 4–$5\frac{1}{2}$ in. long, $\frac{1}{3}$–$\frac{3}{4}$ in. broad, imbricate on a thick, copiously rooting stem. Raceme or panicle erect, wiry, clothed with several loose, sheathing scales; bracts ovate, loose, $\frac{1}{12}$–$\frac{1}{8}$ in. long; flowers $\frac{1}{2}$ in. diam.; pedicels $\frac{1}{8}$–$\frac{1}{4}$ in. long. Sepals lanceolate, nearly $\frac{1}{3}$ in. in length. Petals a little narrower and shorter. Labellum ovate-lanceolate, acuminate, concave round the column; spur slender, clavate, about $\frac{1}{2}$ in. long; pollen-masses ovoid, sessile on oblong glands? Angræcum Calceolus, *Thouars, Orch. Afr. t.* 78; *Rich. Orch. Maur.* 76, *t.* 10, *f.* 4; *Lindl. Gen. and Sp. Orch.* 248. A. carpophorum, *Thouars, Orch. Afr. t.* 76; *Lindl. Gen. and Sp. Orch.* 247 (?).

MAURITIUS, high places towards centre of island, *Bojer!* Moka, *Dupont!* Also Bourbon. After many trials I am unable to place this species definitely; it does not appear to be a true *Angræcum*.

17. LISTROSTACHYS, Rchb. f.

Sepals and petals spreading, equal, or the petals a little the smaller. Labellum more or less unlike the sepals and petals, entire or lobed, with a short and obtuse or long, slender and tapering spur. Column short, terete, straight or incurved; pollen-masses 2, attached each to a tapering caudicle; gland single; rostellum elongate, entire or lobed.—Epiphytes with the habit of *Angræcum*. Leaves usually fleshy. Flowers in dense spikes or erect or pendulous racemes, white, green, or yellow. DISTRIB. The genus would appear to be restricted to Tropical and South Africa and the neighbouring islands.

Spikes axillary, dense-flowered; flowers minute; labellum at right-angles to column, entire . . . . . 1. L. PESCATORIANA.

Racemes leaf-opposed, rather lax-flowered; flowers at least $\frac{1}{2}$ in. diam.; labellum convolute round column, 3-lobed; mid-lobe linear, much smaller than the broad lateral ones.

Leaves oblong, 1–2 in. long; flowers 1 in. diam.; spur nearly $\frac{1}{3}$ in. long; lobes of rostellum directed upwards and forwards . . . . 2. L. POLYSTACHYS.

Leaves linear-oblong, $2\frac{1}{2}$–3 in. long; flowers $\frac{1}{2}$ in. diam.; spur $\frac{1}{12}$ in. long; lobes of rostellum directed vertically upwards . . . . 3. L. APHRODITE.

Racemes from the base of the stem, 3–6-flowered; flowers ⅛ in. diam.; labellum flat, 3-lobed, the lobes subequal . . . . 4. L. PARVIFLORA.

1. **L. Pescatoriana,** *S. Moore.* Leaves probably imbricate on a short thick stem, lorate, obliquely emarginate, nearly 1 foot long. Spikes axillary, about 4 in. long, bearing a number of close-set, minute, bracteate flowers. Sepals ovate, obtuse or cuspidulate, rather more than $\frac{1}{12}$ in. long, the outer surface clothed with short, black, glandular hairs. Petals a little shorter and narrower than the sepals, acute, glabrous. Limb of labellum at right-angles to the column, nearly ¼ in. long, obovate-oblong, truncate and incised at the apex, with a long channelled claw; spur nearly straight, subclavate, about ¼ in. long. Pollen-masses ovoid, attached by short, foliaceous, crenulate, downward-tapering caudicles to a lunate gland. Ovary short, glandular-hairy; rostellum arching upwards, entire, obtuse. Angræcum Pescatorianum, *Lindl. in Journ. Hort. Soc.* iv. 263. Listrostachys pertusa, *var.* Pescatoriana, *Rchb. f. in Walp. Ann.* vi. 909.

MAURITIUS, *Bouton* (fide *Reichenbach*). Also Bourbon. Very near to *L. pertusa*, Rchb. f., from Sierra Leone, but specifically distinct.

2. **L. polystachys,** *Rchb. f. Walp. in Ann.* vi. 909. Stem stout, terete, 3–6 in. high, here and there giving off wiry, leaf-opposed, aerial roots. Leaves subimbricate, oblong, obliquely emarginate, 1–2 in. long, ½ in. (or more) broad. Racemes erect, leaf-opposed, rather laxly flowered, 6 in. (or more) in length, with several close, scattered, sheathing scales; bracts rotundate, loose; pedicel and ovary ⅙ in. long. Sepals linear-lanceolate, acuminate, ⅙ in. long. Petals a little shorter, linear. Labellum about the same length as the petals, ovate-rotundate, 3-lobed; lateral lobes crenulate, convolute round the column below; mid-lobe narrow-linear, entire, ⅛ in. long; spur tapering, nearly ⅛ in. in length. Caudicles linear; rostellun of two fleshy, obtuse lobes directed upwards and forwards. Epidendrum polystachys, *Thouars, Orch. Afr. t.* 82. Angræcum polystachyum, *Rich. Orch. Maur.* 74, *t.* 10, *f.* 2; *Lindl. Comp. Bot. Mag.* ii. 205 (*not Bot. Reg.* 1840, *sub. t.* 68).

MAURITIUS; Grand Port, La Savanne, and Plaines-Wilhelms, *Bojer.* Also Bourbon and Madagascar. I have seen no Mauritian specimen.

3. **L. Aphrodite,** *Balf. f. and S. Moore.* Stems erect, stout, ½–1 foot high. Leaves subimbricate, fleshy, linear oblong, obliquely emarginate, 2½–3 in. long, ⅓ in. (or more) broad. Racemes ascending, leaf opposed, nearly 5 in. long, clothed with several loose, tough, scarious, sheathing scales below the flowers; bracts rotundate, ⅛ in. long. Sepals lanceolate, acuminate, nearly ½ in. long. Petals shorter, linear. Labellum ovate-rotundate, 3-lobed; lateral lobes convolute round the column below, crenulate; mid-lobe narrow-linear, entire, scarcely ⅛ in. long; spur $\frac{1}{12}$ in. in length, almost straight. Pollen-masses oblong-

ovoid; caudicles linear, tapering slightly into an ovate gland; lobes of rostellum directed vertically upwards.

RODRIGUEZ, *Balfour!* Endemic.

4. **L. parviflora,** *S. Moore.* Leaves linear or lanceolate, submembranous, about 2 in. long, $\frac{1}{6}$–$\frac{1}{3}$ in. broad, imbricate on a very short, subterete stem. Racemes $2\frac{1}{2}$–3 in. long, wiry, ascending from the base of the stem, with 4 or 5 scattered, sheathing scales below the flowers; bracts broad, $\frac{1}{12}$ in. long; flowers $\frac{1}{6}$ in. diam., scattered; pedicels patent, together with the ovary $\frac{1}{4}$ in. in length. Lateral sepals oblong, $\frac{1}{12}$ in. long; upper sepal and petals broader and shorter. Labellum ovate, flat; mid-lobe a little longer and broader than the oblong obtuse lateral ones; spur slender, dilated above and below, $\frac{1}{4}$ in. long. Pollen-masses ovoid; gland oblong; rostellum of 2 linear decurrent lobes. Angræcum parviflorum, *Thouars, Orch. Afr. t.* 60; *Rich. Orch. Maur.* 70. Œceoclades parviflora, *Lindl. Gen. and Sp. Orch.* 236.

MAURITIUS; the Pouce, Peter Both, and Plaines-Wilhelms, *Bojer! Grey!* Endemic.

18. ANGRÆCUM, Thouars.

Sepals and petals subequal, usually spreading Labellum entire, free from the column, similar to the other perianth-segments or larger than them, with a usually long, slender, straight or curved spur. Column erect, very short, with an auricle on each side; anther with a membranous appendage in front; pollen-masses 2, fixed on the shoulders of a single caudicle; gland oblong or ovoid; rostellum of two broad, lateral lobes.—Caulescent or subscapigerous (occasionally leafless) epiphytes, without pseudobulbs, but with numerous stout aerial roots. Leaves coriaceous, imbricate or scattered, with persistent stem-sheathing bases. Flowers axillary, solitary or in erect or pendulous racemes or panicles, usually white or greenish. DISTRIB. A genus of many species, native for the most part of Africa and the neighbouring islands, and very sparsely represented in the New World.

Leaves broad, thick and fleshy, more than one foot long. Flowers $2\frac{1}{2}$ inches diam. Labellum much larger than the sepals and petals; spur $2\frac{1}{2}$ inches long . . . . 1. A. EBURNEUM.
Leaves usually oblong or linear, never more than 8 inches long (except in *A. gracile*). Flowers under 1 inch diam. Labellum more or less like the sepals and petals; spur never more than $\frac{1}{2}$ inch in length.
  Racemes few or many-flowered, never more than 5 inches long (except in *A. gracile*).
    Stem 1 foot high, leafless below. Leaves 8 inches long. Flowers 1 inch diam. . . . . 2. A. PALMIFORME.
    Stem short, sometimes almost absent.
      Leaves lorate, $\frac{1}{2}$ foot long. Racemes several-flowered. Flowers $\frac{3}{4}$ inch diam.; spur obtuse, $\frac{1}{2}$ inch in length . . . . 3. A. STRIATUM.

Leaves linear-oblong, 2–3½ inches long. Racemes several-flowered. Flowers ¼ in. diam.; spur $\frac{1}{12}$ inch long . . . . 4. A. CAULESCENS.

Leaves narrow-linear, 1–2 inches long. Racemes 2-flowered. Flowers ⅙ inch diam.; spur $\frac{1}{12}$ inch in length . . . . 5. A. PARVULUM.

Leaves lorate, nearly 1 foot long. Racemes about as long as the leaves. Flowers numerous, ⅙ inch diam.; spur $\frac{1}{12}$ in. in length . . . . 6. A. GRACILE.

Flowers solitary on axillary peduncles.

Leaves lorate, emarginate, 3–4 inches long. Labellum lanceolate; spur straight, ⅓ inch in length . . . . 7. A. TRIQUETRUM.

Leaves linear-falcate, obtuse, 2¼–3½ inches long. Labellum oblong-ovate; spur recurved, ⅛ in. long . . . . 8. A. INAPERTUM.

Leaves oblong, emarginate, ¾ inch long. Labellum broadly ovate; spur almost straight, ⅙ inch in length . . . . 9. A. CUCULLATUM.

Leafless. Flowers minute, in short dense racemes . . . . 10. A. APHYLLUM.

1. **A. eburneum,** *Thouars, Orch. Afr. t.* 65. Leaves oblanceolate-lorate, obliquely emarginate, more than 1 foot long, 1½ in. or more broad, imbricate on a stout stem. Racemes erect, about as long as the leaves, laxly flowered, clothed with numerous large, scattered, sheathing scales; bracts broad, sheathing the pedicel, 1 in. in length; flowers about 2½ in. diam. Sepals and petals linear-lanceolate, acuminate, 1½–2 in. long, reflexed, green. Labellum cordate-rotundate, cuspidate, nearly 1½ in. long, with a median lanceolate plate at its base, white; spur slender, 2½ in. in length, parallel with, then almost at right angles to, the column, green; lobes of rostellum broad, obtuse. *Rich. Orch Maur.* 71; *Lindl. Gen. and Sp. Orch.* 245; *Rchb. f. in Walp. Ann.* vi. 904. A. virens, *Lindl. Bot. Reg.* 1847, *sub. t.* 19; *Paxt. Fl. Gard.* i. 25. Limodorum eburneum *Bory, Voyage, t.* 19.

SEYCHELLES, *Horne! Wright!* Also Bourbon, and perhaps Johanna Island.

2. **A. palmiforme,** *Thouars, Orch. Afr. tt.* 68 *and* 69. Stems 1 foot high, stout, erect, somewhat laterally compressed. Leaves lorate, emarginate, about 8 in. long, imbricate at the top of the stem. Racemes 8–9 in. in length, arising just below the leaf-crown from the axils of dead leaves and making a right angle with the stem; bracts ample; flowers about 1 in. diam.; pedicel and ovary ½ in. long. Sepals lanceolate, acuminate, about 1 in. in length, the lateral ones directed forwards parallel to the labellum. Petals narrower and shorter than the sepals, spreading. Labellum ovate-lanceolate, obscurely 3-lobed, ¾ in. long; spur clavate, ⅓ in. in length. *Rich. Orch. Maur.* 72, *t.* 10, *f.* 1; *Lindl. Gen. and Sp. Orch.* 246.

MAURITIUS, near Crève-cœur, and declivities at Nouvelle Découverte, *Bojer.* I have seen no specimen.

3. **A. striatum,** *Thouars, Orch. Afr. t.* 72. Stems very short, giving off numerous thick branching aerial roots below. Leaves imbri-

cate, lorate, emarginate, ½ foot or more long, ¼ in. broad. Racemes about as long as the leaves, ascending, few-flowered, with a few broad sheathing scales; bracts ovate, sheathing the pedicel; flowers nearly ¼ in. diam. Sepals and petals subequal, broadly oblong, obtuse, about ⅛ in. long. Labellum ovate, obtuse, shorter than the perianth-segments; spur stout, obtuse, ⅓ in. in length. *Rich. Orch. Maur.* 72.

MAURITIUS, round Grand Bassin, on Mount Jacoti, and at Petite Savanne, *Bojer.* Also Bourbon. I have seen no specimen from Mauritius.

4. **A. caulescens,** *Thouars, Orch. Afr. t.* 75. Leaves linear or oblong, obliquely emarginate, 2–3½ in. long, ¼–½ in. broad, imbricate on a stout, copiously rooting stem. Racemes ascending from below the leaves, varying from 1–4 in. in length, wiry, flexuous, clothed with a few scarious sheathing scales; bracts ovate, about $\frac{1}{12}$ in. long; flowers scattered, about ¼ in. diam.; pedicel and ovary ¼–½ in. long. Sepals ⅛ in. in length, lanceolate. Petals as long as, but narrower than, the sepals. Labellum ovate-lanceolate, ⅙ in. long; spur clavate, almost straight, about the same length as the labellum; lobes of rostellum broad, obtuse. *Rich. Orch. Maur.* 73, *t.* 10, *f.* 3; *Lindl. Gen. and Sp. Orch.* 247; *Hook. Lond. Journ. Bot.* 1834, 48, *t.* 117.

MAURITIUS, the Pouce and heights near centre of the island. *Bojer! Telfair! Ayres!*

Var. MULTIFLORUM. Stems elongated. Leaves subimbricate. Racemes about 1½ in. long. A. multiflorum, *Thouars, Orch. Afr. t.* 74; *Rich. Orch. Maur.* 73. Moka and the Pouce, *Bojer.* Also Bourbon.

5. **A. parvulum,** *Ayres MSS.* Leaves narrow-linear, obliquely emarginate, submembranous, 1–2 in. long, rather more than $\frac{1}{12}$ in. broad, about 6 imbricate on a slender, dwarf stem. Racemes about as long as the leaves, wiry, usually 2-flowered, with about three loose sheathing scales; bracts broad, nearly $\frac{1}{12}$ in. in length; flowers subsessile, about ⅙ in. diam. Sepals oblong, obtuse, $\frac{1}{12}$ in. long. Petals linear. Labellum ovate-rotundate, cuspidate, concave, round the column; spur almost straight, obtuse, $\frac{1}{12}$ in. in length. Lobes of rostellum linear, obtuse. Capsule oblong, ¾ in. long.

MAURITIUS, the Pouce, *Ayres!* Endemic.

6. **A. gracile,** *Thouars, Orch. Afr. t.* 77. Leaves lorate, obliquely emarginate, nearly 1 foot long, less than ½ in. broad, subimbricate on a short, rather slender stem. Racemes ascending, about 1 foot long, clothed with a few scattered lanceolate scales, and dilated at the floral nodes; bracts lanceolate, $\frac{1}{12}$ in. long; flowers ⅙ in. diam. Sepals and petals subequal, lanceolate, spreading. Labellum deltoid-ovate; spur recurved near the obtuse extremity, ⅙ in. long. *Rich. Orch. Maur.* 73. Œceoclades? gracilis, *Lindl. Gen. and Sp. Orch.* 237.

MAURITIUS; moist forests towards centre of the island, Plaines-Wilhelms, La Savanne and Quartier Militaire, *Bojer.* I have seen no specimen. Endemic.

7. **A. triquetrum,** *Thouars, Orch. Afr. t.* 49. Leaves very fleshy, lorate, emarginate, 4–9 in. long, about ½ in. broad, imbricate on a short, stout, copiously rooting stem. Peduncles 1-flowered, ascending from the axils of dead leaves, together with the ovary nearly 2 in. long; flowers ½ in. diam. Lateral sepals and petals linear-lanceolate, more than ½ in. long, directed forwards parallel to the labellum; upper sepal a little shorter and broader. Labellum lanceolate, ½ in. in length; spur almost straight, linear, ⅓ in. long. Capsule obovate-oblong, 1¼ in. long. *Lindl. Gen. and Sp. Orch.* 247.

MAURITIUS, at Quartier Militaire, La Savanne, and Grand Bassin, *Bojer.* Also Bourbon. I have seen no specimen from Mauritius.

8. **A. inapertum,** *Thouars, Orch. Afr. t.* 50. Leaves linear-falcate, obtuse, 2½–3½ in. long, ¼–⅓ in. broad, loosely imbricate on a short stem. Peduncles 1-flowered, wiry, ascending, with one loose scale at its base and another a little below the flower. Sepals and petals lanceolate, about ⅙ in. long. Labellum oblong-ovate. Spur recurved, obtuse, ⅙ in. in length. *Lindl. Gen. and Sp. Orch.* 247.

MAURITIUS; the Pouce, Quartier Militaire, and banks of Grand Rivière south-east, *Bojer.* No specimen seen by me. The flowers are probably fertilised while in bud.

9. **A. cucullatum,** *Thouars, Orch. Afr. t.* 48. Leaves oblong, obliquely emarginate, ¾ in. long, four or six subimbricate on a dwarf stem. Flowers solitary, on pedicels ¼ in. long. Sepals oblong, acute, ⅓ in. long. Petals as long, lanceolate. Labellum ⅓ in. in length, broadly ovate, obtuse or cuspidulate, its sides half embracing the column; spur as long as the labellum, wide at the throat, tapering slightly to the obtuse tip. Rostellum of two oblong lobes running down the side of the column far beyond the anther. *Lindl. Gen. and Sp. Orch.* 247; *Rich. Orch. Maur.* 67.

MAURITIUS; Nouvelle Découverte and Piton du Milieu du l'Ile, *Bojer! Meller!* Also Bourbon.

10. **A. aphyllum,** *Thouars, Orch. Afr. t.* 73. A scrambling leafless epiphyte. Stem as thick as a crow-quill, terete, flexuous, clothed with brown scarious sheaths (the rudiments of lost leaves), bearing long, whip-like, sometimes branching aerial roots. Racemes 1 in. long; flowers crowded, minute, reddish; bracts setaceous; pedicel and ovary about $\frac{1}{12}$ in. long. Perianth-segments spreading, the petals a little shorter and narrower than the ovate-oblong sepals and labellum; spur clavate, almost straight, $\frac{1}{12}$ in. long. Column long for the genus; anther-cap with a long, obtuse, downward-reaching membranous appendage in front; caudicle oblong; gland subtriangular; rostellum of two narrow lobes projecting forwards over the entrance to the spur. *Rchb. f. in Walp. Ann.* vi. 907. Gussonea aphylla, *Rich. Orch. Maur.* 76, *t.* 11, f. 1. Saccolabium aphyllum, *Lindl. Gen. and Sp. Orch.* 223.

MAURITIUS, sea-shore round Flacq and on Montagne Longue, *Bojer! Bouton!* Possibly a distinct genus, owing to its habit and column. The plant is said by Richard to be a parasite, but I think erroneously. Lindley's *Microcœlia exilis* is evidently a congener.

The following are indeterminable :—

A. yuccæfolium, Bojer, Hort. Maur. p. 318, of which I have seen neither description nor specimen.

A. ramosum, Thouars, Orch. Afr. t. 59, the figure of a plant without flowers.

Apparently a new species near *A. caulescens*, Thouars, from Rodrigues (Balfour), unfortunately rather too far advanced for description.

19. EULOPHIA, *R. Br.*

Sepals and petals free, spreading, usually equal and similar. Labellum free from the column, generally 3-lobed, crested or bearded on the inner face, spurred or saccate at base. Column elongate, winged at the sides. Anther 1- or 2-celled. Pollen-masses 2 ; caudicle short ; gland transverse. —Terrestrial (occasionally epiphytical ?), usually pseudobulbous herbs. Leaves usually large, membranous and many-nerved, or long narrow and grass-like. Flowers small or large, in racemes or panicles. DISTRIB. A genus of many species, natives for the most part of tropical and subtropical Africa, India, and the Malayan Archipelago, and very sparingly represented in Australia and the tropics of the New World.

Leaves membranous, two or more to each pseudobulb.
Flowers about 1 in. diam.
  Leaves subdistichous, several together sheathing the pseudobulb, 1 in. (or less) broad. Flowers panicled. Mid-lobe of labellum papillose ; spur $\frac{1}{3}$ in long, entire . . . . 1. E. SCRIPTA.
  Leaves twin, crowning the pseudobulb, 2 in. broad. Flowers racemed. Mid-lobe of labellum glabrous ; spur $\frac{1}{12}$ in. long, bifid . . . . 2. E. PULCHRA.
Leaves fleshy, solitary. Flowers $\frac{1}{2}$ in. diam. . . . . 3. E. MONOPHYLLA.

1. **E. scripta,** *Lindl. Gen. and Sp. Orch.* p. 182. Pseudobulbs oblong-ovoid, clothed with the sheaths of the leaves, at length 3 in. long. Leaves several to each pseudobulb, subdistichous, narrow oblong, acute, many-nerved, $6\frac{1}{2}$ in. long, $\frac{1}{3}$ in. broad, ("8–9 in. long. 1 in broad," *Richard*) ; sheaths with membranous edges. Scape erect from the side of the base of the pseudobulb, bearing a lax panicle of monœcious flowers ; bracts oblong, $\frac{1}{4}$ in. in length ; pedicels patent, $\frac{3}{4}$ in. long. Sepals and petals subequal, ovate-oblong, obtuse or acute, $\frac{1}{2}$ in. long, yellowish-green with large purple or brown spots. Labellum nearly $\frac{1}{2}$ in. long, yellow with purple-brown spots, with two longitudinal raised lines expanding into flat plates near the centre ; lateral lobes embracing the sides of the column, rotundate, glabrous or with few papillæ near the end ; mid-lobe obovate, crenulate or emarginate, papillose towards the end ; spur at right angles to the labellum, entire, $\frac{1}{3}$ in. long. Column of the ♂ fl. slender, incurved, $\frac{1}{4}$ in. long, with two basal folds overlapping in the middle line ; stigmatic rudiment subtriangular ; of the ♀ fl. stout, straight, nearly $\frac{1}{3}$ in. long

bearing a small terminal rudiment of an anther. Capsule ovoid, crowned by the persistent perianth, 1 in. long. Limodorum scriptum, *Thouars, Orch. Afr. tt.* 46, 47; *Rich. Orch. Maur.* 48 (*excl. syn.*); *Bojer, Hort. Maur.* 313.

MAURITIUS, forest on high mountains near the centre of island, *Bojer.* Also Bourbon and Madagascar. Bojer is the only authority for its recurrence in Mauritius.

Var.? CONCOLOR. Sheathing leaf bases broader. Bracts ¼ in. long. Lateral lobes of labellum shorter. Sepals and petals without the purple spotting. E. concolor, *Lindl. Gen. and Sp. Orch.* 181. Limodorum concolor, *Thouars, Orch. Afr. t.* 45; *Bojer, Hort. Maur. p.* 313. Possibly the hermaphrodite form, though Thouars' figure does not decide the point. I have seen no specimen.

2. **E. pulchra,** *Lindl. Gen. and Sp. Orch.* 182. Pseudobulbs oblong-ovoid, laterally compressed, 1¾ in. long. Leaves twin, crowning the naked pseudobulbs, broadly ovate-lanceolate, narrowed towards the base, membranous, many-nerved 10 in. long, 2 in. broad. Flowers in a rather close raceme, erect from the side of the base of the pseudobulb; bracts ½ in. long; pedicels ascending, ¼ in. in length. Sepals and petals as in *E. scripta*, but smaller. Lateral lobes of the labellum almost obsolete; mid-lobe ovate, crenulate, glabrous; spur inflated, bifid, 1/12 in. long. Column stout, ¼ in. in length. Capsule narrowly obovoid, 1 in. long. Limodorum pulchrum, *Thouars, Orch. Afr. tt.* 43, 44; *Rich. Orch. Maur.* 49; *Bojer, Hort. Maur.* 313.

MAURITIUS, in forests on high mountains near centre of the island, *Bojer.* Also Bourbon. Given as Mauritian on Bojer's authority only.

3. **E. monophylla,** *S. Moore.* Pseudobulbs oblong, completely sheathed by persistent scales, ¾ in. long, borne on a stout creeping rootstock giving off numerous thick corky rootlets below. Leaves solitary, crowning the pseudobulb, oblong-lanceolate, 3–5 in. long, ¾–1 in. broad, fleshy. Scape stout, erect from the side of the base of the pseudobulb, 7–9 in. high, bearing a few loose sheathing scales up to the few-flowered, dense, corymbose raceme. Flowers purplish, about ½ in. diam. Sepals oblong-spathulate, ¼ in. long. Petals a little longer, oblong, obtuse. Labellum prominently veined, its inner surface with two rectangular flat plates near the centre; lateral lobes broad, truncate; mid-lobe obcordate; spur obtuse ¼ in. long, almost at right angles to labellum. Column incurved, ¼ in. long. Angræcum monophyllum, *Rich. Orch. Maur.* 66, *t.* 9; *Bojer, Hort. Maur.* 315. Œceoclades maculata, *Lindl. Gen. and Sp. Orch.* 237.

MAURITIUS, the Pouce, *Ayres*! Endemic.

20. CYRTOPERA, Lindl.

Sepals spreading, equal or the upper a little the shorter, the lateral ones inserted in the sides of the produced column-base. Petals ascending, equal to or smaller than the sepals and similar to or unlike them. Labellum adnate to the end of the base of the column, more or less deeply 3-lobed, usually crested or fringed with rows of hairs on the inner face. Column elongate, semiterete, winged at the sides; pollen-masses 2; caudicle short; gland transverse.—Terrestrial (sometimes leafless?) herbs, with fleshy or bulbous stems. Leaves usually broad, membranous, many-nerved, often appearing after the racemes of flowers. DISTRIB. A small genus widely dispersed over tropical and subtropical regions, but absent from Australia and Polynesia.

1. **C. plantaginea,** *Lindl. Gen. and Sp. Orch.* 189. Stems creeping, fleshy, occasionally producing small bulbous enlargements. Leaves three to each plant, ovate-lanceolate, many-nerved, 7 in. long, nearly 1½ in. broad, invested below by a scarious sheath. Scape erect, terete, 15 in. high, sparsely clothed with scales below the flowers; bracts linear, acuminate, ¾–1¼ in. in long; pedicels ascending, slender, together with the ovary 1 in. length. Sepals spathulate-oblong, obtuse, the lateral ¾ in. long, the upper ⅛ in. shorter. Petals ascending, broader and shorter than the sepals. Lateral lobes of the labellum rotundate, subentire; mid-lobe ovate-oblong, obtuse, crisply undulate; inner face with two central longitudinal raised lines developing into broad flat plates near the centre and becoming vermiculate on the mid-lobe. Produced base of column ⅓ in. long, broadly channelled; pollen-masses subtriangular. Limodorum plantagineum, *Thouars, Orch. Afr. tt.* 41, 42; *Bojer, Hort. Maur.* 313.

MAURITIUS, the Pouce, Quartier Militaire, and Nouvelle Découverte, *Bojer*. Known only from Bourbon and Madagascar, but inserted on Bojer's authority.

21. POLYSTACHYA, Hook.

Sepals erect, the lateral larger than the lower and adnate to the produced base of the column. Petals smaller than the sepals, erect. Labellum posterior, adnate to the end of the column-base, more or less deeply 3-lobed. Column semiterete, much shorter than its horizontal produced portion; pollen-masses 4, cohering in pairs, united by a linear caudicle to, or sessile on a small gland.—Caulescent or subacaulescent epipyhytes, the stem sometimes becoming bulbous. Leaves imbricate, scattered or solitary, fleshy or membranous. Flowers in terminal racemes or panicles, small. DISTRIB. The genus is represented by a considerable number of species in the tropics (and occasionally subtropics) of both worlds, with the exception of Australia and the Pacific Islands.

Leaves solitary, crowning the bulbiform stem.
  Panicle loosely divaricate. Labellum obovate . . . . 1. P. CULTRATA.
Leaves more or less imbricate.
  Leaves 4–6 in. long. Panicle stiff, ½–1 foot long. . . . 2. P. ZEYLANICA.
  Leaves 1½–3 in. long. Panicle rather lax, less than 2 in. long . . . . 3 P. FUSIFORMIS.

1 **P. cultrata,** *Lindl. Bot. Reg. sub. t.* 851; *Gen. and Sp. Orch.* 73. Stem 4–6 in. high, bulbiform, partially clothed with a single loose persistent scale. Leaves solitary, crowning the stem, broadly lanceolate,

subcordate at the base, membranous, 5½–10 in. long, 1–1½ in. broad. Panicle as long as the leaf, loosely divaricate, usually with one long, sheathing scale; bracts ⅛–¼ in. long. Lateral sepals broadly triangular-ovate, acuminate; lower a little shorter, lanceolate. Petals oblong-spathulate, ⅙ in. long. Labellum as long as the lateral sepals, ovate, papillose on the inner face; lateral lobes rounded, about as long as the ovate-oblong, cuspidulate mid-lobe. Pollen-masses sessile, ovoid. Capsule oblong, 1 in. long. Dendrobium cultriforme, *Thouars, Orch. Afr. t.* 87; *Rich. Orch. Maur* 59, *t.* 8, *f.* 3.

MAURITIUS; the Pouce, Peter Both, Quartier Militaire, and Nouvelle Découverte, *Bojer! Bouton! Ayres!* Endemic.

Var. NANA. Stem 1–1½ in. high. Leaf 3–4 in. long. MAURITIUS, *Bouton! Bojer.*

2. **P. zeylanica,** *Lindl. Bot. Reg.* 1844, *Misc.* no. 144. Leaves oblong or oblanceolate, fleshy, 4–6 in. long, about ¾ in. broad, imbricate on a short, erect stem and articulated on their loose, persistent, at length scarious sheaths. Panicle ascending, stiff, ½–1 foot high, sheathed with long loose scales; bracts ovate-lanceolate, about ½ in. long, but diminishing upwards; bracteoles $\frac{1}{12}$ in. in length. Lateral sepals triangular-ovate, ⅙ in. long; lower sepal a little shorter and narrower. Petals oblong-spathulate, about $\frac{1}{12}$ in. long. Labellum obovate, crenulate, papillose on the inner face; lateral lobes very short, obtuse; mid-lobe rotundate, entire or emarginate. Pollen-masses sessile, subpyriform. Capsule narrow-obovoid, nearly ½ in. long. *Rchb. f. in Walp. Ann.* vi. 639. Dendrobium polystachys, *Thouars, Orch. Afr. t.* 85; *Rich. Orch. Maur.* 57, *t.* 8, *f.* 4 (*excl. syn*).

MAURITIUS, the Pouce and Peter Both, *Bojer! Ayres!* etc. SEYCHELLES, *Horne!* Found also in Ceylon and the Indian Archipelago. The pedicels are of two kinds, some are short and slender, others long and stout.

Var. RACEMIFER. Flowers in racemes which are never more than ½ foot long. MAURITIUS. *Bouton!*

3. **P. fusiformis,** *Lindl. Bot. Reg. sub. t.* 851, *and Gen. and Sp. Orch.* 73. Stem erect, about 4 in. high, giving off occasionally a bulbiform appendage from the lower axils. Leaves subimbricate at the top of the stem, oblong, emarginate, 1½–3 in. long, ⅓–½ in. broad. Panicle nodding, about 2 in. long; bracts and bracteoles ovate, acute $\frac{1}{12}$–⅙ in. long. Sepals broadly ovate, acuminate, the lower a little the smaller. Petals oblong. Lateral lobes of labellum rotundate, almost as long as the broadly oblong, obtuse mid-lobe. Dendrobium fusiforme, *Thouars, Orch. Afr. t.* 86.

MAURITIUS, in sunny places on high mountains, *Bojer.* SEYCHELLES? *Wright!* I have seen no specimen unless Prof. Wright's plant, unfortunately only a scrap, is rightly referred here.

22. AGROSTOPHYLLUM, Bl.

Sepals usually free, spreading, the lateral more or less produced at base. Petals generally narrower and longer than the sepals. Labellum adnate to the lower part of the column, constricted in the middle, its limb short, truncate, the base developed into a saccate pouch. Column erect, clavate. Anther 2-celled; pollen-masses 8, pyriform; gland oval; rostellum elongate.—Leafy caulescent nonbulbous epiphytes, with grass-like, broadly, sheathing, distichous leaves. Flowers inconspicuous, in a terminal sessile capitulum. DISTRIB. A small genus, found in India, the Malayan Peninsula and Archipelago and the Pacific Islands; the following species, its western outlier, can be but partially described, owing to the absence of specimens in flower.

1. *A. sp. nov?* Stems more than 1 foot high, leafy from the base. Limb of leaf linear-oblong, obliquely emarginate, mucronulate, 2–4 in. long; sheaths tough, smooth, membranous at the margin. Capitulum subglobose, 1 in. diam. Capsule narrowly obovoid, ¼ in. long.

SEYCHELLES. Mahé, *Barkly! Horne!* Also Madagascar. The Seychelles specimens bear ripe fruits, those from Madagascar very young buds.

23. CALANTHE, R. Br.

Sepals and petals spreading, the latter usually the smaller and occasionally filiform. Labellum adnate to the column, entire or lobed, appendaged on the inner face and usually giving off below a long, slender, curving spur. Column erect, clavate, generally latterly compressed; pollen-masses 8, in two pairs; caudicles usually 2, short (often absent or single); gland oblong or ovoid; rostellum of two broad lobes, each shelving towards the stigmatic mass on its own side. —Terrestrial herbs with large membranous leaves, and long racemes of conspicuous flowers. DISTRIB. A genus of several species, natives for the most part of India and its Archipelago; one species is found in Australia, four or five occur in Polynesia, and about the same number in Tropical America.

1. **C. sylvatica,** *Lindl. Gen. and Sp. Orch.* 250. Leaves broadly ovate-lanceolate, when full-grown 1–1½ foot long, 2–3 in. broad, imbricate on a short stem clothed below the leaves with a few scarious sheathing scales. Racemes as long as the leaves; bracts lanceolate, about ½ in. long; pedicel and ovary nearly 1½ in. in length; flowers more than ½ in. diam., white (or the lip purple), at length orange. Sepals ovate-oblong, ½ in. long. Petals a little shorter and narrower. Labellum about the same length as the sepals, obovate, tubercled at base, 4-lobed; lobes ovate-oblong, obtuse, crenulate, the proximal pair much the smaller; spur ¾ in. long, arching forwards. Pollen-masses pyriform. *Rchb. f. in Walp. Ann.* vi. 914. C. versicolor, *Lindl. Sert. Orchid. t.* 42. Centrosis sylvatica, *Thouars, Orch. Afr. tt.* 35 and 36. Centrosia Auberti, *Rich. Orch. Maur.* 45, *t.* 7, *f.* 3. Bletia sylvatica, *Bojer, Hort. Maur.* 318.

MAURITIUS, forests on the Pouce and other woody places, *Bojer! Gardner!* etc. SEYCHELLES? Horne! No. 601 (specimen in fruit). Also Bourbon and East Indies.

ORDER XCIV*. IRIDACEÆ.

Perianth superior, corolline, the 6 divisions free or more or less joined above the ovary. Stamens 3, perigynous or epigynous; filaments free or monadelphous; anthers extrorse. Ovary 3-celled; placentation axile; style single; stigmas 3, filiform or petaloid. Capsule 3-celled, with loculicidal dehiscence. Seeds globose or discoid; embryo in the centre of abundant firm albumen. — Herbs with persistent ensiform or linear leaves and showy regular or irregular flowers in spikes or clusters, single or several together included in a couple of firm bracts (spathe-valves.) DISTRIB. Cosmopolitan. Species 500.

Rootstock not bulbous.
  Stamens monadelphous . . . . * SISYRINCHIUM.
  Stamens free. Stigmas petaloid . . . . * DIETES.
  Stamens free. Stigmas cuneate . . . . * BELEMCANDA.
Rootstock bulbous.
  Tube straight and limb regular . . . . * MORPHIXIA.
  Tube curved and limb regular . . . . * WATSONIA.
  Tube curved and limb irregular . . . . * ANTHOLYZA.

None of the plants of this order are wild in Mauritius, but the following are more or less established.

* *Sisyrinchium Bermudiana*, Linn.; (S. gramineum, *Lam.; Bot. Mag. tab.* 464), a native of North America, on the shoulder of the Pouce and hills about Moka. Roots fibrous. Leaves narrow, grass-like. Stems a foot high, flattened and winged. Flowers small, blue, regular, with a pilose yellow throat, 4–6 together, enclosed in two sharply keeled spathe-valves, from which they appear in succession. Stamens monadelphous. Capsule globose, the size of a pea.

* *Dietes iridifolia*, Salisb. in Trans. Hort. Soc. i. 307 (Moræa iridoides, *Gawl; Bot. Mag.* t. 693. M. catenulata. *Bojer, Hort. Maur.* 334, *non Ker*) a native of the Cape, in fields near Moka and Bois Chéri. Rhizomatous. Leaves large, ensiform, distichous. Inflorescence an ample few-flowered corymb; spathe-valves tight-clasping. Ovary cylindrical, on a pilose pedicel. Perianth large, whitish, slit down to the ovary, with falcate unequal divisions, the outer obovate and furnished with a beard of bright yellow hairs down the claw. Stigmas petaloid. Very near the European genus *Iris*.

* *Belemcanda chinensis*, Leman in Red. Lil. tab. 121 (Ixia chinensis, *Linn; Bot. Mag. tab.* 171; Pardanthus chinensis, *Ker*), a native of China, in fields near Port Louis. Rhizomatous. Leaves large, ensiform, distichous. Flowers in an ample corymb, in clusters of 5–6 together, on pedicels longer than the short clustered spathe-valves. Ovary fusiform; perianth slit down to the ovary into six oblanceolate divisions, coloured reddish orange with deeper spots, spirally twisted after flowering. Stamens rather shorter than the limb. Stigmas small, cuneate, like those of *Gladiolus*.

* *Morphixia paniculata*, Baker, (Ixia paniculata, *De la Roche Diss* 26; *tab.* 1; Tritonia longiflora, *Gawl. in Bot. Mag. tab.* 1502), a native of the Cape, in fields round Bois Chéri. Bulb small, globose, with membranous tunics. Leaves narrow, linear, small. Spike usually simple, few-flowered; spathe-valves small, membranous, truncate and toothed at the tip. Flowers whitish, with a very long (2–3 inch) cylindrical tube, dilated at the top and six oblong uniform oblong lobes under an inch long. Stamens not emerging from the tube. Capsule small, globose.

* *Watsonia Meriana*, Ker; Bot. Mag. tab. 418, a native of the Cape, in fields near Moka and Réduit, and on the shoulder of the Pouce. Bulb globose, surrounded and crowned by a network of coarse fibres. Leaves hard, dry, linear. Flowers few, in a lax simple spike; spathe-valves moderately large, lanceolate, entire, coriaceous. Perianth bright scarlet, 2–3 inches long, with lanceolate equal segments reaching down a third of its length, and the curved tube filiform in the lower and broadly cylindrical in the upper half. Stamens reaching the mouth of the limb, the style cut into 6 subulate falcate stigmatose divisions. *Lis du Cap à fleurs roses.*

* *Antholyza æthiopica*, Linn.; Bot. Mag. tab. 561, a native of the Cape, in fields near Moka. Rootstock bulbous. Leaves large, thin, ensiform, distichous. Flowers few or many in a simple spike; spathe-valves small, lanceolate, entire. Perianth red and yellow, 2–3 in. long, with a limb of six very unequal oblanceolate spathulate lobes and a curved cylindrical tube, narrow and slender at the base. Stamens reaching to the tip of the limb. Style cleft into three subulate forks at the tip. *Lis du Cap.*

ORDER XCV. AMARYLLIDACEÆ.

Perianth superior, corolline, the six subequal lobes free down to the ovary or more or less joined above it. Stamens 6, perigynous or epigynous; filaments free or united in a corona; anthers versatile, introrse. Ovary inferior, 3-celled; placentation axile; style simple; stigma capitate. Fruit usually a capsule with loculicidal dehiscence. Seeds with an embryo in the centre of abundant albumen.—Bulbous herbs, or shrubby, with fleshy leaves; flowers usually large and showy. DISTRIB. Cosmopolitan, mainly warm temperate. Species 500.

Bulbous herbs.
  Flowers small, with lobes free down to the ovary . . . . * NERINE.
  Flowers large, with a long tube above the ovary . . . . 1. CRINUM.
Shrubby, not bulbous.
  Perianth with a tube above the ovary and ascending limb . . . . * AGAVE.
  Perianth with 6 lobes spreading from the top of the ovary . . . . * FOURCROYA.

* *Nerine sarniensis*, Herb.; Kunth, Enum. v. 617 (Amaryllis sarniensis, *Linn.; Bot. Mag. tab.* 294), the so-called Guernsey Lily, a native of the Cape, is naturalised in Mauritius on the banks of the Moka river near the church. It has an ovoid bulb with membranous tunics, several glabrous fleshy lorate leaves a foot or more long, a naked scape as long as the leaves, bright red flowers 6–8 in an umbel, long pedicels, a globose deeply-grooved ovary, limb cut down to the ovary into oblanceolate divisions and more or less exserted stamens and style. *Petit Lis rouge.*

1. CRINUM, Linn.

Perianth superior, with a long funnel-shaped tube above the ovary, the 6 subequal segments spreading or permanently ascending. Stamens 6, inserted at the throat of the perianth-tube, declinate, shorter than the segments. Ovary inferior, 3-celled; style long, filiform, declinate; stigma capitate. Capsule globose, bursting irregularly, the seeds often bulbiform.—Very handsome bulbous plants with lorate leaves and large fragrant white or reddish flowers in umbels. DISTRIB. Cosmopolitan in the tropics. Species 30.

Flowers stalked, with a space between the perianth-segments when they are expanded.
  Segments ¼–⅓ in. broad . . . . 1. C. ASIATICUM.
  Segments ¾ in. broad . . . . 2. C. AUGUSTUM.
Flowers sessile, with perianth-segments edge to edge when expanded . . . . 3. C. CAREYANUM.

1. **C. asiaticum,** *Linn.; Kunth, Enum.* v. 547. Bulb ovoid, a foot long. Stem short. Leaves green, lorate, 3–4 feet long, 4–5 inches broad, rather fleshy. Peduncle lateral, slightly compressed, shorter than the leaves. Flowers 20–30 in an umbel, distinctly stalked, erect, white, scarcely at all scented, with a tube 3–4 inches long above the ovary and 6 rather shorter equally spreading strap-shaped segments ¼–⅓ in. broad. Filaments as long as the segments of the limb, with yellow anthers ¾ inch long. Capsule depresso-globose, 1½ in. broad. *Bot. Mag. tab.* 1073. C. toxicarium, *Roxb. Fl. Ind.* ii. 134.

Var. C. BRACTEATUM, *Willd.; Jacq. Hort. Schoen. tab.* 495. Smaller in all its parts, with leaves 12–18 inches long and tube and limb of the flower each only 2–2½ inches. *Gawl. in Bot. Reg. tab.* 179.

The type a native of tropical Asia, naturalised in Mauritius and Rodrigues. The *var. bracteatum*, common in the Seychelles, in some parts of Mahé, especially on the sandy beaches of the western coast, *Horne! Lis sauvage* and var. bracteatum *Lis à petites feuilles.*

2. **C. augustum,** *Roxb. Fl. Ind.* ii. 136. Bulb conical, 8–9 inches long and half a foot thick, with dull brown tunics. Leaves about half a dozen, contemporary with the flowers, lorate, bright green, 2–3 feet long, 3–4 inches broad, smooth at the edge. Scape lateral from the rosette of leaves, compressed, 2 feet high, an inch thick, much tinged with purple in the upper half. Spathes deltoid, bright red, 3–4 inches long; flowers 12–30 in an umbel, distinctly stalked, with a bright red tube 3–4 inches long, and segments of equal length, erecto-patent in full expansion, $\frac{3}{4}$ inches broad, bright red all down the back, paler red down the face, passing to pink at the edge. Stamens reaching about halfway up the limb, with anthers $\frac{1}{2}$ inch long. Scent strong. *Bot. Mag. tab.* 2397.

MAURITIUS, in marshes at Flacq and Pamplemousses and the border of the Rivière des Citroniers. SEYCHELLES, in poor light sandy soils in Mahé and Curieuse, *Horne*, 398! Described from a living plant sent to Kew by Mr. Horne. *C. mauritianum*, Lodd., known only from an imperfect figure in the Botanical Cabinet, tab. 650, may be this species. Endemic. *Lis du Pays.*

3. **C. Careyanum,** *Herbert in Bot. Mag. tab.* 2466. Bulb subglobose, with reddish tunics. Leaves bright green, spreading, 2–3 feet long, 2 inches broad, scabrous at the edge. Scape slightly compressed, green, as long as the leaves; spathe-valves 4 inches long; flowers 6–10 in an umbel, fragrant, sessile, with a slender tube 3–4 inches long and oblanceolate-oblong ascending segments of equal length about an inch broad, placed edge to edge when expanded, with a rose-coloured stripe down the middle on the outside. Filaments declinate, nearly as long as the limb. Style as long as the limb.

MAURITIUS, in damp places of the heights of the Quartier of Plaines-Wilhelms. SEYCHELLES, plentiful in Mahé on the beach at Port Victoria. Endemic, but scarcely more than a variety of *C. zeylanicum*, Linn. (Amaryllis ornata, Bot. Mag. tab. 1171. Crinum ornatum, Herb.; Kunth, Enum. v. 573), which is wild both in Tropical Asia and Tropical Africa, and is a stronger plant with broader leaves and a more decided band of red down the outside of the perianth-segments. The typical variety is commonly cultivated and is naturalized in some parts of Mauritius, as at Flacq and Pamplemousses. *Lis blanc.*

* *Agave americana*, Linn.; Kunth, Enum. v. 819, the common American Aloe, is often subspontaneous in hedgerows and on dry banks. It has a sessile rosette of few glaucous toothed oblanceolate leaves 6–8 feet long, very thick in texture, from which arises a stem 20–40 feet high which forms a lax thyrsoid panicle at the top, with flowers in crowded clusters. The flowers are yellowish-green, 3–4 inches long, with a cylindrical ovary as long as the limb, a short cup-shaped tube above it and ascending oblong segments, exserted stamens and very large (an inch long) yellow versatile anthers. *Aloes.* The plant called by Bojer *A. angustifolia*, Haworth, I have no means of identifying.

* *Fourcroya gigantea*, Vent.; Kunth, Enum. v. 841; Bot. Mag. tab. 2250 (Agave fœtida, *Linn.*), a native of Tropical America, is

established in Mauritius and Rodriguez. It has a short woody trunk, crowned by a rosette of 40–50 oblanceolate rigidly coriaceous sub-carnose bright green usually spineless leaves 4–5 feet long, from which arises a scape 20–30 feet high, forming in the upper half a lax panicle with rotate greenish-white flowers 2 inches broad with oblong segments, spreading from the top of a cylindrical ovary and stamens shorter than the limb with filaments strumose at the middle. Var. *Willemetiana*, Roemer, is a Mauritian form, with a few spines on the border of the lower part of the leaf. *Aloes vert.*

Order XCVI. HYPOXIDACEÆ.

Perianth superior; divisions 6, regular, free or united above the ovary, the three outer mostly hairy on the outside. Stamens 6, included, epigynous or perigynous; filaments subulate, short; anthers basifixed or versatile. Ovary inferior, 3-celled; placentation axile; ovules crowded; style cylindrical; stigmas 3, free or consolidated. Fruit capsular or baccate. Seeds turgid, copiously albuminous, with a crustaceous testa.—Perennial or annual herbs, with narrow persistent dry mostly pilose leaves and yellow stellate flowers variously arranged. Distrib. Tropical and warm temperate regions, especially of the southern hemisphere. Species 60–70.

Perianth with a long tube above the ovary . . . . 1. Curculigo.
Perianth cleft down to the ovary . . . . 2. Hypoxis.

1. CURCULIGO, Gærtn.

Perianth with a long tube above the ovary. Stamens inserted at the throat of the tube; filaments short, subulate; anthers basifixed or obscurely versatile. Ovary 3-celled; stigmas free or consolidated. Fruit baccate.—Annual or perennial herbs, with the habit of *Hypoxis*, the flowers sometimes solitary, sometimes densely clustered. Distrib. Tropics of the Old World, Cape, and one species American. Species 10–12.

1. **C. seychellensis,** *Bojer*, *Hort. Maur.* 342 (name only). Rootstock a perennial tuber. Petiole 1–1½ foot long, armed with spreading prickles; blade cuneate, coriaceous, strongly ribbed, bifid or simple, 1–5 feet long. Flowers 50 or more in a dense nearly sessile head; bracts 2–3 in. long, lanceolate, densely pilose. Ovary cylindrical, densely pilose; perianth tube filiform, pilose, 2–3 in. long; limb ½–¾ in., with lanceolate yellow segments, nearly naked on the outside. Stamens half as long as the limb; anthers linear, basifixed. Stigmas consolidated.

Seychelles, frequent in damp shady forests in several of the islands. The strong fibrous leaves are used for wrapping plugs of tobacco. Endemic. *Coco marron.*

2. HYPOXIS, Linn.

Perianth slit down to the ovary into 6 oblong-lanceolate segments. Stamens epigynous; filaments short, subulate; anthers basifixed or versatile. Ovary 3-celled, the septa sometimes evanescent; style cylindrical; stigmas free or consolidated. Fruit capsular.—Annual or perennial herbs, the flowers usually yellow and corymbose and leaves and outer perianth-segments on the outside and ovary hairy. DISTRIB. Of the order. Species about 50.

Expanded flower ½–¾ in. broad . . . . 1. H. ANGUSTIFOLIA.
Expanded flower 3 in. broad . . . . 2. H. RHIZOPHYLLA.

1. **H. angustifolia,** *Lam. Encycl.* iv. 182. Rootstock barrel-shaped, perennial, often bearing more than one rosette of leaves. Leaves linear, persistent, dry, 4–8 in. long, obscurely pilose. Peduncles several to a tuft, 1–6 in. long, 2–3-flowered, silky; bracts small, linear; pedicels ¼–1½ in. long. Ovary oblong. Perianth-segments lanceolate, ¼ in. long, silky on the outside. Stamens half as long as the limb; anthers sagittate, versatile. Capsule oblong, ¼ in. long, with 3–4 seeds in each cell.

MAURITIUS, frequent on dry hills. Also Madagascar and Tropical Africa.

2. **H. rhizophylla,** *Baker*. Rootstock a perennial tuber. Petiole ½–1 foot long; blade ligulate, 2–3 feet long, ¼–4 inches broad, often rooting at the tip, narrowed from the middle to both ends, plicate, not pilose. Flowers few, subspicate on a short densely pilose scape; bracts lanceolate, amplexicaul, acute, scariose, 1–1½ in. long. Ovary oblong, densely pilose, shortly stalked. Perianth-segments lanceolate, 1½ in. long.

SEYCHELLES, frequent amongst rocks and stones in the beds of the streams, *Horne*, 240! 609! Endemic.

ORDER XCVI*. DIOSCOREACEÆ.

Flowers polygamo-dioicous. Perianth superior, in the males cut down to the base, in the females to the ovary, into 6 subequal segments. Stamens 6, included; filaments short; anthers 2-celled. Ovary inferior, 3-celled; ovules 1–2 in a cell, anatropous; style 0 or short; stigmas 3. Fruit capsular or baccate. Seeds with a small embryo in the axis of abundant albumen. — Twining herbs or shrubs, with large tuberous rootstocks, broad sometimes compound leaves with reticulate venation and minute flowers in simple or panicled spikes. DISTRIB. Tropics of both hemispheres. Species 150.

2 B

* DIOSCOREA, Linn.

Male flower campanulate Three inner stamens sometimes imperfect. Fruit a loculicidal 3-winged capsule. DISTRIB. Of the order. Species 120–130.

Glabrous, with oblong capsule . . . . * D. SATIVA.
Pubescent, with obovate-cuneate capsule . . . . * D. SPINOSA.

* *D. sativa*, Linn. Hort. Cliff. 459, t. 28; Benth. Fl. Austral. vi. 461, (D. bulbifera, *Wight, Icon. t.* 878; Helmia bulbifera, *Kunth, Enum.* v. 435), the most commonly cultivated of the Yams, a native of Tropical Asia, is cultivated and subspontaneous in Mauritius, Seychelles, and Rodriguez. It has large tuberous rootstocks, slender terete unarmed wide-climbing stems, long-petioled cordate-ovate membranous 7–9-nerved simple leaves often bearing bulbillæ in their axils, simple female spikes fascicled in the axils of the leaves, male spikes simple or panicled, and an oblong 3-winged smooth shining capsule about an inch long and half as broad. *Cambare marron.*

In Dr. Balfour's Rodriguez collection there is a plant not in flower differing from this by its acutely tetragonous stems, which may be *D. alata*, Linn.

Mr. Horne has once gathered in a subspontaneous state in the Seychelles *D. spinosa*, Roxb.; Wall, Cat. No. 5103. a native of Tropical Asia, marked by its prickly stems, large round-cordate 11-nerved acute leaves tomentose beneath when young, simple lax female spikes, panicled male spikes, densely pilose ovaries and capsule twice as broad as long.

ORDER XCVI*. TACCACEÆ.

* *Tacca pinnatifida*, Forst.; Kunth, Enum. v. 459, a native of Tropical Asia and Polynesia, is commonly cultivated and casually subspontaneous in Mauritius and the Seychelles. It is a tall acaulescent perennial with a tuberous rhizome, long-petioled large 3-partite leaves with forked divisions pinnatifid down to a narrow wing with irregular ovate acute segments, flowers in a dense umbel subtended by several ovate spathulate leafy bracts and numerous long filiform barren pedicels, perianth superior funnel-shaped with six subequal segments, six stamens placed at the throat of the perianth, with hooded petaloid filaments, a mushroom-like stigma, a 1-celled ovary with three parietal placentas bearing numerous ovules and a globose baccate fruit as large as a plum. *Tavoul.*

ORDER XCVI*. MUSACEÆ.

Flowers hermaphrodite. Perianth superior, corolline, irregular, with 6 divisions free or variously combined above the ovary. Stamens 6 or some abortive; anthers 2-celled, basifixed. Ovary 3-celled; placenta-on axile; ovules many in a cell; style simple. Fruit capsular or accate. Seeds copiously albuminous. — Gigantic herbs or trees, with petioled large oblong leaves with parallel veins diverging from a stout midrib. DISTRIB. Tropics of both hemispheres. Species 50.

Perianth-limb 2-lobed; fruit fleshy . . . . * MUSA.
Perianth-limb 6-lobed; fruit capsular . . . . * RAVENALA.

* MUSA, Linn.

Perianth spathaceous, marcescent, slit down to the ovary into two unequal lobes, one representing 5 segments. Stamens epigynous, the linear basifixed anther as long as the filiform filament, 6 or one abortive. Style filiform; stigma obtusely 3-lobed. Fruit fleshy, indehiscent, oblong-cylindrical. DISTRIB. Tropics of the Old World. Species 20.

The Plantain, *Musa paradisaica*, Linn.; Trew, Ehret. tab. 18–20; Red. Lil. tab. 443, a native of Tropical Asia, but now universally cultivated through the torrid zone, is casually subspontaneous. It has a green trunk 10–20 feet high, oblong leaves 4–5 feet long, a nodding spike 3 or 4 feet long with 4 to 8 half-whorls of fertile flowers subtended by oblong acute violet purple bracts, a perianth-limb about an inch long with two unequal lobes, and a curved cylindrical-trigonous fruit 6–12 inches long, at first green, afterwards becoming yellow with a tough skin and not fit to eat without cooking. The Banana, *Musa sapientum*, Linn.; Trew, Ehret. tab. 21–23, which is not more than a variety of the same species, has usually a stem variegated with purple, leaves often edged with a purple line, lower bracts green on the inside, and a shorter straighter less angular fruit 3–6 inches long with yellowish-red flesh, a thinner skin, a more fragrant odour and fit to eat without cooking. Bojer, Hort. Maur. p. 332, describes ten varieties of *M. paradisaica* which are grown in Mauritius.

* *Ravenala madagascariensis*, Sonnerat Voy. ii. 223, tab. 124–6; Jacq. Hort. Schoen. t. 93 (Urania speciosa, *Willd.*; *Bojer, Hort. Maur.* 333), the Travellers' tree of Madagascar, is subspontaneous in Mauritius about the Mare aux Vacouas, and occurs also in Rodriguez. It differs from *Musa* in habit by having a tall simple woody trunk and distichous leaves. It has axillary solitary spreading distichously-branched clusters of flowers, ovate acute navicular coriaceous spathes, containing about ten flowers each, an oblique perianth-limb 6–8 inches long slit down to the base into six linear segments of which one is smaller than the rest, six very long basifixed anthers, a cylindrical style as long as the limb with a clavate stigma, an elliptic capsule 3–4 inches long with loculicidal dehiscence, and umbilicate seeds enveloped in a blue pulpy arillus. *Ravenal* or *Arbre du voyageur*.

ORDER XCVII. LILIACEÆ.

Perianth inferior, corolline, the six subequal lobes free or more or less united. Stamens 6, hypogynous or perigynous; filaments various; anthers usually versatile, introrse. Ovary superior, 3-celled; placentation axile; ovules anatropous; style simple or trifid. Fruit capsular or baccate. Seeds copiously albuminous.—Herbs or shrubs, the rootstock often bulbous, the leaves fleshy or thin, the flowers in racemes or umbels. DISTRIB. Cosmopolitan. Species 1800.

Fruit capsular (*Liliaceæ proper.*)
  Perianth gamophyllous.
    Roots fibrous.
      Leaves thin . . . . * HEMEROCALLIS.
      Leaves very thick and fleshy . . . . 1. ALOE.
    Roots bulbous . . . . 2. MILLA.
  Perianth polyphyllous. . . . . 3. ASPHODELUS.
Fruit baccate (*Asparagaceæ*).
  Perianth gamophyllous.
    Leaves fleshy, as in Aloe . . . . 4. LOMATOPHYLLUM.
    Leaves firm, thin . . . . 5. DRACÆNA.
  Perianth polyphyllous.
    Climbing shrub with white flowers and large lanceolate leaves . . . . 6. COHNIA.
    Herb with linear leaves and blue flowers . . . . 7. DIANELLA.
    Climbing shrubs with copious leaf-like sterile branchlets (cladodia) . . . . 8. ASPARAGUS.

* *Hemerocallis fulva*, Linn.; Bot. Mag. t. 64, a native of the north temperate zone of the Old World, an old garden favourite, is established in the Mauritius near Moka and on the heights of Nouvelle Découverte. It has fibrous roots, large ensiform leaves of grass-like texture, a scape 2–3 feet high with a few corymbose flowers, a funnel-shaped gamophyllous inodorous fulvous-red perianth 3–4 inches long with broad veined segments much longer than the tube. *Lis jaune.*

1. ALOE, Linn.

Perianth gamophyllous, tubular, bright red, with 6 equal ligulate permanently connivent lobes. Stamens 6, hypogynous; filaments filiform, as long as or longer than the perianth; anthers linear, versatile. Ovary oblong, 3-celled; style long, simple; stigma capitate. Fruit capsular.—Undershrubs, shrubs or rarely trees, with thick fleshy leaves, the flowers in crowded often panicled racemes. DISTRIB. Cape and a few in Tropical Africa. Species about 40.

1. **A. lomatophylloides**, *Baker*. Stemless. Leaves few in a rosette, ensiform, $1\frac{1}{2}$ feet long, 3 inches broad, narrowed gradually from the base to the apex, armed with small spreading deltoid teeth. Scape $\frac{1}{2}$ ft. long, with 2–3 ascending forks bearing dense racemes 3–6 in. long;

pedicels ⅙ in., finally ¾ in. long, articulated at the tip; bracts lanceolate, ⅛–⅙ in. long. Perianth ¾ in. long, the segments twice as long as the oblong tube. Stamens as long as the perianth. Style slightly exserted. Capsule oblong, ½ in. long.

RODRIGUEZ, common throughout the island, *Balfour*, 1306! Endemic. *Ananas marron.*

2. MILLA, Cav.

Perianth funnel-shaped, with a distinct tube and 6 subequal oblong spreading or ascending lobes. Stamens 6, included, uniseriate or biseriate near the throat of the tube; anthers versatile. Ovary sessile or stipitate; ovules many and superposed in a cell; style simple; stigma capitate. Fruit a membranous capsule. Seeds small, black, triquetrous. — Bulbous herbs, with narrow rather fleshy leaves and flowers in umbels. DISTRIB. All the other 25 species American.

1. **M. borbonica**, *Baker.* Leaves under a foot long, fleshy, ⅛ in. broad. Scape fragile, glabrous, above a foot long. Flowers 6–10 in an umbel, with two small lanceolate spathe-valves, on pedicels 1–1½ in. long. Perianth white, under ½ in. long, the oblong lobes twice as long as the broadly funnel-shaped tube. Stamens included, uniseriate at the throat of the tube; filaments lanceolate. Ovary subsessile; ovules 9–10 in a cell; style exserted, ⅛ in. long. Nothoscordum borbonicum, *Kunth, Enum.* iv. 462. Allium fragrans, *Bojer, Hort. Maur.* 348, *not Vent.*

MAURITIUS, in plenty in cultivated places and fields in the quarters of Plaines-Wilhelms and Pamplemousses. Also Bourbon.

3. ASPHODELUS, Linn.

Perianth polyphyllous, rotate when expanded, with six subequal 1-nerved oblanceolate segments. Stamens almost hypogynous, included; filaments flattened at the base; anthers versatile. Ovary sessile, globose; ovules 2, in a cell, collateral; style filiform; stigma capitate. Fruit a globose capsule. Seeds often solitary in the cells.—Annual or perennial herbs, with leaves in a basal rosette and white flowers in panicled racemes. DISTRIB. Old World, mainly in the north temperate zone. Species 5.

1. **A. fistulosus,** *Linn.;* var. A. TENUIFOLIUS, *Cav.; Kunth, Enum.* iv. 558. A glabrous annual, with fibrous roots. Leaves half a foot long, terete. Flowers in lax copiously panicled racemes 2–8 inches long; pedicels ¼ in., ascending, solitary, articulated at the middle, with a small lanceolate basal bract. Perianth ¼ in. long. Capsule globose, the size of a pea, the valves strongly ribbed horizontally.

MAURITIUS, in dry ground at various elevations. RODRIGUEZ, on the coral islets of Gombrani and Pierrota, *Balfour!* Also Mediterranean region and East Indies.

4. LOMATOPHYLLUM, Willd.

Perianth gamophyllous, tubular, greenish-red, the ligulate imbricated segments much exceeding the campanulate tube. Stamens hypogynous, included or exserted; filaments filiform, slightly declinate; anthers oblong, versatile. Ovary sessile, obovoid, with many superposed ovules in each cell; style filiform; stigma capitate. Fruit a globose berry.—Succulent shrubs, with the leaves and flowers of *Aloe*, from which they differ by their baccate fruit. DISTRIB. Endemic in the Mascarene Isles, a third species known in cultivation only.

Tall, with leaves 2–3 feet long . . . . 1. L. BORBONICUM.
Dwarf, with leaves a foot long . . . . 2. L. MACRUM.

1. **L. borbonicum,** *Willd.; Baker in Journ. Linn. Soc.* xiv. 550. Stem reaching a height of 6 or 8 feet and the thickness of a man's leg. Leaves 12–20 in a dense rosette, ensiform, 2–3 feet long, 3–4 inches broad at the base, narrowed gradually to the point, green, with a distinct red border and copious small, deltoid horny teeth. Racemes 6–9 inches long, several in an irregular panicle with a stout terete peduncle; pedicels ascending, $\frac{1}{2}$ inch long, with a minute deltoid bract at the base. Perianth $\frac{3}{4}$ in. long, the divisions 3–4 times as long as the the tube. Stamens included, but the style considerably exserted. Berry as large as a cherry. Phylloma aloiflorum, *Gawl. in Bot. Mag. tab.* 1585; *Bojer, Hort. Maur.* 349.

MAURITIUS, in dry mountainous situations; Round Island, *Sir H. Barkly*! Coin de Mire, *Horne*, 108! Also Bourbon.

2. **L. macrum,** *Salm-Dyck; Baker in Journ. Linn. Soc.* xiv. 551. Stem short. Leaves 10–12, lax, spreading, or the lower ones recurved, ensiform, a foot long, $\frac{3}{4}$–1 inch broad at the base, narrowed gradually to the point, with a red border and copious minute teeth. Scape lateral or terminal, a foot long, simple or forked. Racemes moderately dense, 4–6 in. long; pedicels ascending, $\frac{1}{4}$–$\frac{1}{2}$ in. long, with a lanceolate scariose bract half as long at the base. Perianth $\frac{1}{3}$–$\frac{3}{4}$ in. long, with included stamens. Aloe macra, *Haworth; Bojer, Hort. Maur.* 345.

MAURITIUS, on dry, hilly banks, specially of the hills of the Rivière Noire, and Montagne Longue. Also Bourbon. *Socotrine du pays.*

5. DRACÆNA, Vand.

Perianth gamophyllous, tubular, greenish-white with a cylindrical tube and 6 equal strap-shaped obtuse lobes. Stamens 6, inserted at the throat of the tube and nearly as long as the lobes; anthers oblong, versatile. Ovary sessile; ovules solitary in the cells; style filiform; stigma capitate. Fruit a globose berry, often by abortion

1-2-celled and 1-2-seeded.—Shrubs, with subcoriaceous sessile or petioled leaves and copious flowers in simple or panicled racemes. DISTRIB. Warmer regions of the Old World. Species 40.

Leaves in a dense rosette, ascending.
Leaves 1-1½ in. broad, without a red border.
Limb much longer than the tube . . . . 1. D. ANGUSTIFOLIA.
Tube much longer than the limb . . . . 2. D. UMBRACULIFERA.
Leaves 2-3 in. broad, with a distinct red border . . 3. D. CONCINNA.
Leaves spreading, laxly disposed on the branches . . 4. D. REFLEXA.

1. **D. angustifolia,** *Roxb.; Baker in Journ. Linn. Soc.* xiv. 526. Trunk reaching a height of 10–12 feet, crowned with a dense rosette of ascending subcoriaceous ensiform leaves 1–2 feet long, 1–1½ inch broad, not petioled, but narrowed to half an inch above the clasping base. Panicle erect, with several dense spreading racemes ¼–½ foot long; pedicels 1–4-nate, ¼ in. long, articulated above the middle; bracts small, deltoid. Perianth ¾ in. long, greenish-white, the divisions twice as long as the cylindrical tube. Stigma exserted. Berry 3-lobed, orange-red, depresso-globose, ½–¾ in. broad. D. ensifolia, *Wall.*

SEYCHELLES, frequent in the forests, *Horne*, 612! RODRIGUEZ, *Balfour !* Spread through Tropical Asia to North Australia; not African.

2. **D. umbraculifera,** *Jacq. Hort. Schoenb. t.* 95. Trunk several feet high, crowned with a dense rosette of ascending ensiform subcoriaceous leaves 3–3½ feet long, 1½–2 inches broad at the middle, not petioled, but narrowed to ½ in. above the clasping base. Panicles short, erect, corymbose, with flowers in short dense capitate racemes; pedicels simple or geminate, ascending ¼–½ in. long, with a small deltoid bract at the base, not distinctly articulated. Perianth 1⅓–1¾ in. long, with divisions not more than half as long as the cylindrical tube. Stigma much exserted. Lomatophyllum umbraculiferum, *Bojer, Hort. Maur*, 349.

MAURITIUS, in the dense forests of the interior of the island, *Bojer !* Endemic.

3. **D. concinna,** *Kunth; Baker in Journ. Linn. Soc.* xiv. 530. Trunk reaching 6 or 8 feet high, crowned with a dense rosette of very coriaceous lanceolate leaves 2–3 feet long, 2–3 inches broad at the middle, narrowed to an inch above the clasping base, bright green with a distinct red border. Flowers unknown. Cordyline Betschleriana, *Göppert in Nova Act. Nat. Cur.* xxv. 55.

MAURITIUS, on the Coin de Mire Island, *Horne*, 106! Endemic.

4. **D. reflexa,** *Lam.; Baker in Journ. Linn. Soc.* 530. xvi. Trunk reaching 10–15 feet high, slender, furnished in the upper part with comparatively lax spreading oblanceolate green shining acute sub-

coriaceous leaves 6–8 inches long, $\frac{3}{4}$–$1\frac{1}{2}$ in. broad at the middle, narrowed to $\frac{1}{8}$ inch above the dilated clasping base. Panicle erect, with several dense spreading racemes 3–6 inches long; pedicels $\frac{1}{8}$–$\frac{1}{4}$ inch long, articulated at the tip, the lower bracts lanceolate. Perianth greenish-white, $\frac{1}{2}$–$\frac{3}{4}$ in. long, with segments 3–4 times as long as the tube. Style exserted. Berry red, depresso-globose, $\frac{1}{2}$ in. broad. Lomatophyllum reflexum, *Bojer, Hort. Maur.* 349.

Var. CERNUA, *Baker, loc. cit.* Leaves the same size and shape as those of the type, bordered with a red line. Panicles deflexed, copiously branched. Dracæna cernua, *Jacq. Hort. Schoenb.* i. 50, *t.* 96. Lomatophyllum cernuum, *Bojer, Hort. Maur.* 349.

Var. ANGUSTIFOLIA, *Baker, loc. cit.* Panicle less compound, erect. Leaves narrower and longer, 1–2 in. long by under $\frac{1}{2}$ in. broad.

Var. LINEARIFOLIA, *Baker.* Panicle less compound, cernuous. Leaves 6–8 inches long by $\frac{1}{4}$ inch broad at the middle. D. linearifolia, *Ayres, MSS.*

The two first varieties common in the woods of MAURITIUS; the third gathered by Dr. Balfour in RODRIGUEZ; and the fourth by Dr. Ayres in the woods of the Pouce. Also Tropical Africa and Madagascar. *Bois de Chandelle.*

6. COHNIA, Kunth.

Perianth campanulate, 6-partite, with 6 equal ligulate divisions, spreading when fully expanded. Flowers polygamous; stamens included, surrounding a rudimentary ovary in the male flowers, with oblong versatile anthers. Ovary ovoid, with a peltate sessile stigma; ovules 4–6 in a cell. Fruit a small globose berry.—Climbing shrubs, with the leaves of *Cordyline* and copious small fragrant white flowers in panicles with racemose branches. DISTRIB. Polynesia and Mascarene Isles. Species 3.

1. **C. floribunda,** *Kunth, Enum.* v. 36. A climbing shrub, with stout terete woody branches. Leaves crowded at the top of the branchlets, lanceolate, subcoriaceous, $1\frac{1}{2}$–2 feet long, 2–3 inches broad at the middle, narrowed to the point and with a distinct channelled sheathing petiole. Flowers in a very compound panicle a foot or more long, with racemose branchlets; pedicels $\frac{1}{12}$–$\frac{1}{8}$ in. long, articulated at the tip, with three minute deltoid bracteoles at the base. Perianth campanulate, as long as the pedicel, white or tinged with red, the ligulate divisions obscurely 3-nerved. C. parviflora, *Kunth, loc. cit.* Dracæna mauritiana, *Bojer, Hort. Maur.* 348, *non Lam.*

MAURITIUS, in the dense woods of the centre of the island. Endemic. *Bois de Chandelle.*

7. DIANELLA, Lam.

Perianth 6-partite, normally blue, with subequal oblong divisions with several close or lax ribs on the back. Stamens 6, hypogynous, included; filaments short, geniculate, with a yellow struma; anthers dehiscing by terminal pores. Ovary globose, sessile; ovules several in a cell; style filiform, simple. Fruit a bright blue globose berry.—Herbs or undershrubs, with linear rigid clasping leaves and copious flowers in corymbose panicles. DISTRIB. Warmer regions of Old World, especially Australia. Species 11.

1. **D. ensifolia,** *Red. Lil. tab.* 1. A caulescent glabrous perennial, 3–6 feet high. Leaves 1–2 feet long, coriaceous, green, smooth on the keel and edges, clasping the stem at the base. Panicle obversely deltoid, lax, a foot or more long; pedicels $\frac{1}{4}$–$\frac{3}{4}$ in. long, articulated at the tip; bracts small, linear. Perianth $\frac{1}{4}$–$\frac{1}{3}$ in. long, blue, or rarely white. Anthers $\frac{1}{8}$–$\frac{1}{6}$ in. long, twice as long as the filament. Berry the size of a pea. Dracæna ensifolia, *Linn.* Dianella nemorosa, *Lam.; Bojer, Hort. Maur.* 348.

MAURITIUS and SEYCHELLES, frequent in woods. Also Madagascar, Bourbon, Tropical Asia and Polynesia, not Continental Africa. *Reine des bois.*

8. ASPARAGUS, Linn.

Flowers hermaphrodite or polygamous. Perianth small, white, campanulate, with 6 equal obtuse divisions free down to the base. Stamens included, inserted at the base of the segments; anthers round or oblong, versatile. Ovary globose, sessile; ovules 2 or several in a cell; style cylindrical, obscurely tricuspidate at the tip. Fruit a globose berry, often by abortion 1-celled and 1-seeded.—Herbs or shrubs, often scandent, with leaves reduced down to membranous scales, often spiny at the base and their function fulfilled by copious usually fascicled sterile branches (cladodes.) DISTRIB. Everywhere in the Old World. Species 90–100.

Stems not spiny. Flowers in axillary umbels . . . . 1. A. UMBELLULATUS.
Stems spiny. Flowers in racemes . . . . 2. A. RACEMOSUS.

1. **A. umbellulatus,** *Sieber; Baker in Journ. Linn. Soc.* xiv. 611. A scandent shrub, with firm slender woody stems and deflexed branchlets. Leaves not distinctly spiny at the base. Cladodes 1–3 together in the axillary clusters, angular or slightly compressed, $\frac{3}{4}$–1 in. long. Flowers hermaphrodite, in dense axillary umbels, on pedicels $\frac{1}{8}$–$\frac{1}{6}$ in. long, which are articulated at the middle. Perianth $\frac{1}{8}$ in. long, the divisions spreading when fully expanded. Anthers oblong, $\frac{1}{4}$ the length of the subulate filament. Ovules several in a cell. Asparagopsis umbellulata, *Kunth, Enum.* v. 81. Asparagus crispus, *Bojer, Hort. Maur.* 350, *not Lam.*

MAURITIUS and RODRIGUEZ, frequent in thickets. Endemic. *A. crispus*, Lam., though attributed by the author to Mauritius, is really a Cape species.

2. **A. racemosus,** *Willd.; Baker in Journ. Linn. Soc.* xiv. 623. A climbing shrub, with slender terete woody stems. Leaves of main stems produced at the base into a distinct spine $\frac{1}{4}$–$\frac{1}{2}$ in. long. Cladodes 3–6 in axillary clusters, falcate, angular or slightly compressed, $\frac{1}{2}$–$\frac{3}{4}$ in. long. Flowers in dense racemes 1–2 in. long from the nodes of the main branches, white, $\frac{1}{8}$ in. long, on pedicels as long as themselves, which are articulated at the middle. Anthers very small, globose, red. Ovules several in a cell.

RODRIGUEZ, *Dr. Balfour !* There is a specimen from Mauritius from Bojer in the Kew herbarium, but in Hort. Maur., it is disclaimed as native. It is spread through from the tropics from North Australia to Angola.

There are two other species in a state too incomplete for determination in Dr. Balfour's Rodriguez collection.

ORDER XCVIII. SMILACEÆ.

Flowers polygamo-dioicous, rarely hermaphrodite, arranged in umbels, rarely in racemes. Perianth inferior, subcorolline, with 6 subequal oblanceolate segments, Stamens 6, hypogynous; filaments subulate; anthers basifixed. Ovary sessile, free, surrounded by rudimentary stamens; cells 3; ovules solitary or geminate, orthotropous; stigmas 3, short. Fruit a berry, often 1-celled and 1-seeded by abortion.—Climbing shrubs, often prickly, with simple leaves with reticulated venation and a pair of stipulary tendrils, the small flowers arranged in simple or panicled racemes, the pedicels articulated at the base into a hollow of the receptacle like a ball into its socket. DISTRIB. Tropical and warm temperate regions of both hemispheres. Species 150.

1. SMILAX, Linn.

Flowers umbellate, polygamo-dioicous.—Habit and distribution as in the order.

1. **S. anceps,** *Willd.; Kunth, Enum.* v. 244. An unarmed climbing glabrous shrub. Young branches acutely tetragonous, old terete, both zigzag. Leaves ovate, slightly cordate, obtuse or subacute, rigidly coriaceous, 3–5 in. long, 5-nerved from the base, with raised reticulated veinlets between the main ribs; petiole under an inch long, channelled at the base and giving out at the top of the wing a pair of long firm spiral tendrils. Peduncles simple, axillary, rather longer than the petioles, jointed at the middle. Umbels 30–60-flowered, the flower-pedicels $\frac{1}{4}$–$\frac{1}{2}$ in., and those of the fruit nearly an inch long. Perianth $\frac{1}{8}$ in. long, with oblanceolate segments. Stamens nearly as long as the perianth. Berry the size of a large pea.

Var. SEMIAMPLEXICAULIS, *Bojer, Hort. Maur.* 353 (sp.) Stems more slender. Leaves smaller, more deeply cordate, more rigid in texture, with more distinctly raised venation. Flowers fewer in an umbel. Fruit pedicels ½ in. long. S. pseudo-china, *Sieber, Herb. Maur.* 195.

Var. BOUTONI, *Baker.* Leaves ovate, acute, 1½–2 in. long, rounded or slightly cordate at the base; petiole ¼ in. long. Stem much more slender than in the type, and flowers not more than 20 in an umbel on ⅛–¼ in. pedicels.

MAURITIUS, the type in woods; the two varieties in more open situations. Also Bourbon and Madagascar and very near the Australian *S. latifolia* R. Br. *Salsepareille indigène.*

ORDER XCIX. PALMÆ.

(By DR I. B. BALFOUR, F.L.S.)

Flowers polygamo-monoicous or dioicous. Perianth 6-partite, persistent. Stamens 6 or many, rarely 3, frequently monadelphous, often represented in the female flower by a toothed cup; anthers 2-celled. Ovary free, represented by a rudiment in the male flower; carpels 3, united or distinct; ovules usually solitary in the cells; style and stigma simple. Fruit indehiscent, dry or succulent. Seed more or less adherent to the endocarp, with a small embryo near the outside of a mass of cartilaginous often ruminate albumen. —Stems woody, frequently of great height, unbranched, usually marked round with the scars of fallen leaves, often spiny; leaves in a terminal cluster, entire or flabellately or pinnately cut, with sheathing petioles; flowers on usually branching spadices, enclosed in spathes. DISTRIB. Round the world in the warmer zones. Species about 1000.

Leaves palmatifid.
  Drupe over 1 foot long. Pyrene usually 2-lobed . . 1. LODOICEA.
  Drupe under 3 in. long. Pyrenes 3 . . . . 2. LATANIA.
Leaves pinnatisect.
  Leaves equally pinnatisect.
    Flowers in 6-7-flowered clusters . . . . 3. HYOPHORBE.
    Flowers in 3-flowered clusters.
      Stigma apical . . . . 4. DICTYOSPERMA.
      Stigma subbasilar.
        Fruit globose . . . . 5. ACANTHOPHŒNIX.
        Fruit compressed . . . . 6. DECKENIA.
  Leaves unequally pinnatisect.
    Fruit globose; stigma lateral . . . . 7. NEPHROSPERMA.
    Fruit elliptical; stigma subbasilar . . . . . 8. ROSCHERIA.
Leaves entire or not pinnatisect.
  Endocarp furrowed . . . . 9. VERSCHAFFELTIA.
  Endocarp not furrowed . . . . 10. STEVENSONIA.

1. LODOICEA, Comm.

Dioicous. Flowers in axillary spadices, surrounded at the base by several obliquely truncate spathes. MALE. Spikes cylindrical, the flowers in subreniform clusters in hollows of the axis, imbricated in two rows, each flower subtended by a bracteole. Outer segments of the perianth spathulate-cucullate; inner obcuneate. Stamens about 36; filaments monadelphous; anthers linear. Rudimentary pistil represented by 1–3 subulate processes. FEMALE. Flowers fewer than in the male spikes, contained in cups formed by a pair of bracteoles. Ovary ovoid, 3- rarely 2- or 4-celled; stigmas sessile. Stamens represented by minute staminodes. Drupe large, olive-green, usually 1-seeded; mesocarp thick, fibrous; pyrene large, bony, firmly attached to the mesocarp, usually 2-lobed. Albumen homogeneous, cartilaginous; embryo placed between the lobes. A single endemic species.

1. **L. sechellarum,** *Labill. in Ann. Mus.* ix. 140, *t.* 13. Palm 50 or even 100 feet high, with a stem thickened at the base. Leaves spreading, 15–20 feet long; petiole 8–10 feet long, dilated into an ample sheath; blade obovate-subrhomboid, cuneate at the base, 6 feet broad, flabellately cut, with bifid segments. Male spadix 5–6 feet long, with a few obliquely truncate spathes at the base; spikes 2–6 feet long, 4–5 in. thick, sheathed by basal spathes, female spikes 4–6 feet long, pendulous, on a 1-foot peduncle. Perianth ½ in. long, Drupe 1½ foot long, broadly ovoid, obtuse or acute, sessile in a large persistent perianth; pyrene a foot long. *Bot. Mag. t.* 2734–8. Cocos maldivica, *Willd. Sp. Plant.* iv. 402.

SEYCHELLES, especially abundant in Praslin. Endemic. *Coco de Mer, Double Coco Nut.*

2. LATANIA, Comm.

Dioicous. Flowers in distichously-branched axillary spadices, each branch sheathed by an obliquely truncate spathe. MALE. Spikes cylindrical, with pits formed by the union of imbricating bracts, each pit containing a single flower. Perianth-lobes imbricate. Stamens 15–30, exserted; filaments connate at the base. Rudimentary pistil a triquetrous column or of 3 or more subulate processes. FEMALE. Bracts toothed on their outer edge, combined in pairs to form a cup for each flower. Flowers fewer than in the male spikes. Stamens represented by a toothed cup. Ovary 3-celled; stigmas 3, distinct. Drupes containing 3 or, by abortion, 1–2 pyrenes; mesocarp succulent; pyrenes convex and sculptured externally. Seed with a testa which adheres completely to the endocarp, homogeneous albumen and an apical embryo.—Palms of moderate height, with long-petioled palmate-flabelliform leaves, the blade deeply laciniated. DISTRIB. These 3 the only species; confined to the Mascarene isles.

Male spikes under a foot long.
  Pyrene grooved longitudinally . . . . 1. L. COMMERSONII.
  Pyrene with tree-like branching ridges in the upper third . . . . 2. L. LODDIGESII.
Male spike under a foot long.
  Pyrene with a central crest and two smaller processes at the top . . . . 3. L. VERSCHAFFELTII.

1. **L. Commersonii,** *Gmel. Syst.* viii. 1035. Palm 40 feet high. Petiole 4–6 feet long, slightly tomentose, the margins smooth, spiny in young plants; blade 5–5½ feet long, dark green above, paler beneath; the segments lanceolate, acuminate, 2 feet long, 3¼–3½ in. broad, their margins entire, spiny in young plants; veins and margins tinged with red. Male spadix 3–6 feet long, with 9–16 branches; spikes 7–10 in. long, ¼–⅓ in. broad, arising in clusters of 4 to 20 from the end of the branch within the mouth of the spathe. "Perianth ⅛ in. long; margin of segments fringed. Stamens 28–32. Rudimentary pistil small, pyramidal-trigonous" (*Mart.*) Female spadix 3–6 feet long, with 8 or more branches, each bearing 3 spikes. Free portion of bracts deltoid. Drupe globose, 1½–1¾ in. diam.; pyrenes obovoid, 1⅛–1½ in. long, marked with numerous ridges which pass from the base to the apex and then curve down again, a central ridge always most prominent. Seed with a light brown testa. *Mart. Hist. Palm.* iii. 223, *t.* 142, 154, 161, ii. *figs.* 1–9. L. plagæcoma, *Comm. MSS.* L. rubra, *Jacq. Fragm. t.* 8. L. borbonica, *Lam. Encycl.* iii. 427. Cleophora lontaroides, *Gærtn. Fruct.* ii. 185, *tab.* 120, *fig.* 1.

MAURITIUS, in various parts of the island, but not abundant, *Horne!* SEYCHELLES, but not indigenous, *Horne!* Also Bourbon. *Latanier* or *latanier rouge.*

2. **L. Loddigesii,** *Mart. Hist. Palm.* 224, *t.* 161, *fig.* ii. 10–14. Palm 50 feet high. Petiole 3–4½ feet long, tomentose, the margins entire in the mature, spiny in the young plant; blade 3–5 feet long, very glaucous, the primary veins beneath slightly tomentose, and tinged with red, especially in young plants, the segments 2 feet long, under 3 in. broad, unequally acuminate, the edges spiny in young plants. Male spadix 5½ feet long, with 8-12 branches; spikes 8–10 in long, ⅜–$\frac{7}{12}$ in. broad, arising in clusters of 3 to 9 from the end of the branches on a level with the mouth of the spathe. Perianth ⅜ in. long; segments not fringed. Stamens 16 to 20 or more. Rudimentary pistil of 3–5 grooved filaments nearly as long as the stamens. Female spadix 3½–4 feet long, with 5–6 branches, each bearing 1 or 2 spikes. Drupe obovoid or pyriform, trigonous, 2½ in long, 1¾ in. broad; pyrenes elongate-obovoid, faintly mucronate at the apex, 1¾–2¼ in. long, ¾–⅝ in. broad, with a central ridge along the convex face with tree-like branching in the upper third, the inner surface furnished with a central crest, usually for only a part of its length. Seed with a dark brown testa. L. glaucophylla, *Hort.* Cleophora dendriformis, *Lodd. MSS.*

MAURITIUS, on Round Island, Flat Island, and Coin de Mire,. Indigenous only in these islets, but introduced on the main land, *Horne!* Endemic.

3. **L. Verschaffeltii,** *Lemaire, Ill. Hort.* vi. *t.* 229. Palm 40 feet high. Petiole 5–8 feet long, densely tomentose, with entire orange margins, spiny in young plants; blade pale green, 4½–5 feet long, the divisions 2½ feet long, above 2 in. broad, acuminate, the entire margins and veins beneath slightly tomentose. Male spadix 4–8 feet long, with 5–10 branches exceeding the spathes in length; spikes 1¼–2 feet long, ⅜ in.

broad, arising singly or in clusters of 2–3 on each branch. Perianth $\frac{1}{12}$–$\frac{1}{4}$ in. long. Stamens 20–30. Rudimentary pistil a triquetrous column, shorter than the stamens. Female spadix 3–5 feet long, with 1–4 branches bearing usually solitary spikes. Staminodes forming a minute cup with 6–8 teeth. Drupe obovoid, slightly trigonous, 2 in. long, $1\frac{1}{2}$ in. broad; pyrenes oblong, $1\frac{1}{3}$–$1\frac{3}{4}$ in. long, $\frac{5}{8}$ in. broad, the convex surface marked by many hard prominences and a medial ridge continued from the base to form a prominent apical crest and thence passing a short way down the inner face and ending abruptly; on each side also a deep groove separates the apical crest from a sharp process, whence one or more ridges run downwards. Seed with a light brown testa. L. aurea, *Duncan, Cat. Hort. Maur.* 52 (name only.)

RODRIGUEZ, abundant over the island, *Balfour!* Endemic.

3. HYOPHORBE, Gærtn.

Monoicous. Flowers superposed in linear spirally-arranged 3–7-flowered clusters on the branches of a compound spadix, the females 1 or 2 at the base of the cluster. Spathes many, distichous, imbricated. Inner segments of the perianth valvate, twice as long as the outer. MALE FLOWER. Stamens 6, included; filaments connate at the base. Rudimentary pistil a triquetrous or conical column, shorter than the stamens. FEMALE. Stamens represented by a cup with 6 teeth. Fruit a purplish drupe; scar of the stigma subbasal; mesocarp succulent and fibrous; endocarp chartaceous. Seed solitary, ascending; albumen homogeneous; raphe branching, but not anastomosing; embryo subapical or medial.—Palms of considerable height, the stem often very thick, the petiole subterete on the back, grooved or flat on the face, with a large complete basal sheath, the leaves pinnate with slightly reduplicate subopposite pinnæ. DISTRIB. Confined to the Mascarene group; only these three species known.

Pinnæ with prominent lateral nerves; no yellow line on back of petiole.
  Male spadix laxly branched; seed globose, $\frac{3}{4}$–$\frac{11}{12}$ in. long . . . 1. H. INDICA.
  Male spadix, subfastigiately branched; elliptical seed $\frac{5}{12}$–$\frac{7}{12}$ in. long . . . . 2. H. AMARICAULIS.
Pinnæ with no prominent lateral nerves; a yellow line on back of petiole . . . . 3. H. VERSCHAFFELTII.

1. **H. indica,** *Gærtn. Fruct.* ii. 186. Palm 40–50 feet high, with a slender cylindrical tapering stem 4–6 in. diameter. Leaf-sheaf cylindrical; petiole 1–$2\frac{1}{3}$ ft. long; pinnæ in 40–60 pairs, lanceolate, acuminate, 2 feet long, $2\frac{1}{2}$ in. broad; upper surface with a prominent central and two lateral veins; under surface with several secondary veins also slightly prominent, all clothed towards the base with linear white twisted fimbriated scales. Spadix laxly branched; peduncle 3–6 in. long. Perianth white or slightly yellow. Rudimentary pistil of male flower a triquetrous column dilated at the base and pyramidal at the tip. Fruit pyriform. Seed elliptico-globose, $\frac{3}{4}$–$\frac{11}{12}$ in. long, with the

branches of the raphe diverging from near the hilum and a subapical embryo. H. Commersoniana, *Mart. Hist. Palm.* iii. 164, *t.* 143, *fig.* 1, 154. Areca lutescens, *Bory. Voy.* ii. 296. Sublimia vilicaulis, *Comm. MSS.*

MAURITIUS, in shady vallies, rare, *Horne! Barkly!* Also Bourbon.

2. **H. amaricaulis,** *Mart. Hist. Palm.* iii. 309. Palm 60 feet high, with a bottle-shaped stem 15–24 in. diameter, near the base, slightly diminishing upwards to the base of the leaf-sheaths, and there abruptly constricted. Leaf-sheath cylindrical; petiole 12–18 in. long, somewhat trigonous, grooved on the face; pinnæ in 40–60 pairs, lanceolate, acuminate, 18 in. long, 2 in. broad, with the central and one lateral vein on each side prominent on the upper surface, and several secondary veins also prominent beneath, which are clothed towards the base with subrigid adpressed lanceolate scales. Spadix with clustered branches; peduncle a foot long. Rudimentary pistil of the male flower elongated, grooved. Fruit elliptic-oblong. Seed elliptical, $\frac{5}{12}$–$\frac{7}{12}$ in. long, with the branches of the raphe diverging a little above the hilum and the embryo either subapical or medial. Areca speciosa, *Hort.*; *Ill. Hort.* xiii. 462. Sublimia amaricaulis, *Comm. MSS.*

MAURITIUS; common in Round Island, *Barkly! Horne!* Endemic. *Palmiste Gargoulette.*

3. **H. Verschaffeltii,** *Wendl. in Ill. Hort.* xiii. *t.* 462–3. Palm 25–30 feet high, with a stem 6–12 in. diameter at the base, bulging after a few feet, reaching 12–24 in. in the middle, thence contracting upwards, rarely again bulging. Petiole about 3 in. long, subterete, slightly grooved on the upper surface, with a yellow band extending from the upper part of the leaf-sheath along the face of the petiole to the extremity of the blade; pinnæ in 30–50 pairs, acuminate, 20–30 inches long, an inch broad, the central vein alone prominent, clothed on the under surface towards the base with short linear scales, which are often subrigid at the base. Spadix with clustered branches; peduncle 8–14 in. long. Perianth orange. Rudimentary pistil of the male flower elongated, conical. Fruit cylindrical-oblong. Seed subcylindrical, $\frac{7}{12}$–1 in. long, $\frac{1}{8}$–$\frac{1}{4}$ in. broad, the branches of the raphe diverging from the middle of the seed, the embryo medial and horizontal. Areca Verschaffeltii *Hort.*

RODRIGUEZ, on the hill slopes, not uncommon, *Balfour!* Endemic. *Palmiste marron.*

4. DICTYOSPERMA, Wendl.

Monoicous. Flowers in spirally-disposed 3-flowered clusters on the branches of a simply subfastigiately branched spadix, the female flower between and below two males. MALE. Inner segments of perianth valvate, thickened, ovate-oblong, acute. Stamens 6, included. Rudimentary pistil a terete column, shorter than the stamens. FEMALE. Segments of perianth imbricate. Staminodes forming a ring with 6 linear teeth. Fruit olive-like, persistent; scar of the stigma exactly apical; mesocarp fibrous; endocarp slender, crustaceous. Seed attached to the endocarp on one side throughout its whole length; raphe forming a loose network; albumen ruminate; embryo subbasilar.—A non-spiny palm of moderate height, with equally pinnate leaves; petiole with a complete basal sheath; pinnæ strongly reduplicate at the base, 1-nerved, with a few scales beneath, the terminal pinnæ confluent. DISTRIB. The only species.

1. **D. alba,** *Wendl. in Linnæa,* xxxix. 181. Palm 40–50 feet high, with a stem 8–9 in. diameter, dilated at the base. Leaves 8–12 feet long; petiole semiterete, 6–18 in. long, grooved down the face; pinnæ $2\frac{1}{2}$–3 feet long, 2–3 in. broad, lanceolate acuminate, cuneate at the base, widely reduplicate, with one prominent medial nerve, and 3 lateral secondary nerves on each side, all bearing a few medially-attached scales, especially towards the base of the pinnæ; veins and margins of pinnæ green or reddish. Spadix 2 feet long, with a very short often tomentose peduncle; branches erect or slightly reflexed, 6–18 in. long, very zigzag when young; flowers often distichous at the base of the branches; spathes 1–$1\frac{1}{2}$ feet long. Inner segments of male perianth $\frac{1}{4}$ in. long, three times as long as the outer. Fruit ovoid-oblong, pointed, about $\frac{1}{2}$ in. long, purplish. Areca alba, *Bory, Voy.* i. 306; *Bojer, Hort. Maur.* 305.

MAURITIUS, common, *Horne! Balfour!* SEYCHELLES, not indigenous, *Horne!* Also Bourbon. In a plant from Round Island, Mr. Horne says one or two of the lower branches of the spadix are subtended by membranous bracts. *Palmiste blanc.* A very variable palm, of which the following are the principal forms.

D. (*Areca*) *rubra,* Hort., sent by Mr. Horne. This in its young state has darker green leaves, with primary veins and margins dark red, the redness disappearing very much in adult plants. Branches of the spadix longer and more reflexed than in the type. *Palmiste rouge.*

D. (*Areca*) *furfuracea,* Hort, differs from the last by the tomentose character of the petiole and leaf-sheath of the young plant.

Var. aurea, Balf. fil. Stem about 30 feet high, smaller and more slender than in the type. Leaves 4–8 feet long; petiole 8 in. long; leaf-sheath 1–2 ft. long; pinnæ $1\frac{1}{2}$–2 feet long, an inch broad; secondary veins scarcely visible. Branches of the spadix rigidly erect, 9–11 in. long. Flowers half the size of those of the type. Fruit cylindrico-conic, $\frac{3}{8}$–$\frac{1}{2}$ in. long. Young plants bright orange. *Areca aurea,* Hort. RODRIGUEZ, common. *Palmiste bon.*

5. ACANTHOPHŒNIX, Wendl.

Monoicous. Flowers in spirally-disposed 3-flowered clusters, slightly immersed in the branches of a twice-branching slightly drooping spadix, the female flower below and between two males. Spathes 2. MALE. Inner segments of the perianth valvate, linear, acute, two or three times the length of the outer. Stamens 12 or fewer, exserted; filaments long, twisted; anthers linear-sagittate. Rudimentary pistil elongated, deeply bifid. FEMALE. Perianth-segments imbricate. Staminodes forming a minute ring. Fruit small, globose; scar of the stigma subbasal; mesocarp thin, fibrous; endocarp crustaceous. Seed ascending, slightly compressed laterally; branches of the raphe spreading from the hilum, and anastomosing on the opposite side of the seed; albumen homogeneous; embryo basilar.—Palms of moderate height, with stems dilated at the base, leaves equally pinnate, with complete basal spiny sheaths, midrib grooved on each side above the attachment of the pinnæ, strongly reduplicate many-nerved pinnæ with scales and fine bristles on the under surface and midvein with a few bristles on the upper surface. DISTRIB. The only species.

Leaves glaucous beneath. Fruit globose . . . . 1. A. RUBRA.
Leaves silver white beneath. Fruit ovoid-oblong . . . . 2. A. CRINITA.

1. **A. rubra,** *Wendl. in Fl. des Serres*, xvi. 181. Palm 60 feet high. Leaf 6–12 feet long; petiole glabrous, 2–4 in. long; leaf-sheath 2½–4½ ft. long, thickly covered with long brown-black spines; pinnæ slightly glaucous beneath. Spadix 2½–3½ ft. long; peduncle 6–10 in. long, like the lower part of the branches, armed with straight spines; branches stout, subtended by linear-lanceolate bracts; spathes 1½–2½ ft. long, with a few straight spines on the inside near the base. Perianth reddish-brown (Horne). Fruit globose, ⅓–⅜ in. diameter, with a prominent ridge extending from the stigma to the base. Areca rubra, *Bory, Voy.* i. 306; *Mart. Hist.* iii. 180 (excl. descr. fruit). Calamus Verschaffeltii, *Hort.*

MAURITIUS, rare, *Horne!* Also Bourbon. Young plants have dark green leaves with red veins. *Palmiste rouge.*

2. **A. crinita,** *Wendl. in Fl. des Serres*, xvi. 181. Palm 50-60 feet high. Leaf 7–13 feet long; petiole densely tomentose, 4–8 in. long; leaf-sheath 2½–4½ feet long, thickly covered with short brown bristles and spines; pinnæ silver-white beneath. Spadix 1–2 feet long; peduncle 4–6 in. long, like the lower part of the slender branches armed with flexuose spines and clothed with dense brown tomentum; spathes tomentose, 1–1½ ft. long. Perianth pinkish-white. Fruit ovoid-oblong, ⅓–5/12 in. long, ⅛ in. broad, with a very slight swelling between the stigma and base. Areca crinita, *Bory, Voy.* i. 307.

MAURITIUS, common in the forests. Also Bourbon. Young plants have pale yellowish-green leaves. *Palmiste épineux.*

6. DECKENIA, Wendl.

Monoicous. Flowers in 3-flowered clusters, one female between and below two males, arranged spirally on the pendulous branches of a twice or thrice-branching spadix. Spadix shortly peduncled, slightly amplexicaul; branches very slender, spiny at the base. Spathes 2, complete, densely covered with flexuose yellow black-tipped spines. MALE. Perianth minute, the inner segments ovate, acute, valvate. Stamens 9, connate, equal in length to the inner segments; anthers globose. Rudimentary pistil an angular trifid column. FEMALE. Segments of perianth imbricate. Stamens represented by a minute toothed cup. Fruit ovoid-deltoid, greatly compressed; stigma subbasilar; mesocarp fibrous; endocarp crustaceous. Seed erect; raphe with 3–5 branches, which ascend from the hilum and then spread over the surface; albumen homogeneous; embryo erect, basilar. DISTRIB. The only species.

1. **D. nobilis,** *Wendl. MSS.* Palm 80–120 feet high, with a stem 10–14 in. in diameter. Leaf 9–14 feet long; petiole a foot long, pale green, smooth; leaf-sheath 3–6 feet long, usually spiny; pinnæ hairy beneath, bristly when young on both surfaces; midrib yellow. Spadix 2–6 feet long, slightly amplexicaul; branches very slender, pendulous; peduncle vertically compressed, much thickened at the base. Spathes seldom over a foot long. Perianth yellow, $\frac{1}{12}$–$\frac{1}{4}$ in. long. Fruit $\frac{1}{2}$ in. long, $\frac{1}{8}$ in. thick, black (Horne), straw-coloured when dried.

SEYCHELLES, now becoming scarce, *Horne!* Endemic. I have to thank M. Wendland for the description of the fruit and seed. *Chou palmiste.*

7. NEPHROSPERMA, Balf. fil.

Monoicous. Flowers in 3-flowered clusters, one female between and below two males, spirally disposed and slightly immersed on the branches of a simply-branching long-peduncled spadix in the axil of a leaf. Peduncle compressed, not amplexicaul. "Spathes 2, complete: outer spiny; three hairy bracts surrounding the spadix within." (Horne) MALE. Outer segments of perianth imbricate; inner valvate, thickened, thrice as long as the outer. Stamens 40–50, included, connate at the base; outer shorter, with adnate erect anthers; inner with horizontal anthers. Rudimentary pistil undivided. FEMALE. Perianth-segments imbricate. Staminodes forming a cup with many short toothed lobes. Fruit globular, slightly flattened on one side; stigma subapical on the flattened side; mesocarp fibrous; endocarp thin, crustaceous. Seed ascending, reniform; raphe spreading from the base and anastomosing at the apex; albumen densely ruminate; embryo basal. DISTRIB. The only species.

1. **N. Van Houtteana,** *Balf. fil.* Palm 20–35 feet high, with a stem 4–6 in. diameter. Leaf 5–7 feet long; petiole under a foot long, green, smooth; leaf-sheath $1\frac{1}{2}$–$2\frac{1}{2}$ feet long, woolly and sparsely spiny, with thin coriaceous edges; blade unequally pinnate; pinnæ 3–$3\frac{1}{2}$ feet long, glabrous; broad segments alternating irregularly with narrow ones, the latter with a single primary vein; veins bearing a few scales towards the base beneath; terminal segments confluent. Spadix 4–8 feet long; peduncle 3–$5\frac{1}{2}$ feet long; branches $2\frac{1}{4}$–$3\frac{1}{4}$ feet long, compressed at the base. "Basal spathe attached to the stem." (Horne) Fruit orange-red, about $\frac{1}{2}$ in. long. Oncosperma Van Houtteana, *Wendl. MSS.*

SEYCHELLES; not uncommon in open places and by the side of streams, up to 1000 feet, *Kirk! Horne!* Endemic.

8. ROSCHERIA, Wendl.

Monoicous. Flowers in 2-flowered clusters, one female below and slightly on one side of one male, spirally arranged on the very slender branches of a compoundly-branching spadix in the axil of a leaf with a long compressed glabrous peduncle. Spathes several, smooth, complete. MALE. Perianth very minute. Stamens 6, included, united into a ring. Rudimentary pistil a column as long as the stamens, capped by a triquetrous disk. FEMALE. Staminodes forming a minutely-toothed cup. Fruit small, black, elliptical; stigma subbasilar; mesocarp thin, fibrous; endocarp crustaceous. Seed ascending, elliptical, slightly oblique; raphe spreading from the base, its branches anastomosing on the side opposite the hilum; albumen loosely ruminate; embryo basal. DISTRIB. The only species.

1. **R. melanochœtes,** *Wendl. MSS.* Palm 15–25 feet high, with many aerial roots and a stem 2–3 in. in diameter, with a ring of spines when young below each leaf-scar. Leaf 4½–7 feet long; petiole 1½–2½ feet long, smooth, subtriquetrous, grooved down the face with a pale band running from the top of the sheath down the back of the petiole; leaf-sheath 1½–2½ feet long, with a few fine black spines rising from a compressed cushion; blade pale green, 3–5 feet long, 2–3 feet broad, entire when young, unequally pinnate; pinnæ 1–1½ feet long, bifid at the apex, with many primary veins ½–1 in. apart, clothed on the under side with medially-attached scales. Spadix 2½–6 feet long; peduncle 1–3 feet long, compressed, an inch thick; branches very slender, flattened at their insertion. Spathes marginate. Fruit ⅛–¼ in. long; scar of stigma very prominent. Seeds sometimes 2 (Horne). Verschaffeltia melanochœtes, *Wendl. in Ill. Hort.* 1871, *t.* 54.

SEYCHELLES, in shaded forests above 1000 feet in elevation, common, *Kirk! Horne!* Endemic. *Latanier Haubaum.*

3. VERSCHAFFELTIA, Wendl.

Monoicous. Flowers in 3-flowered clusters, one female between and below two males, spirally arranged on the short branches of a doubly-branched slightly amplexicaul slender drooping spadix with a glabrous compressed peduncle. Spathes 3. Perianth very minute, not seen in the flowering stage. Staminodes forming a ring with 6 short 2-lobed teeth. Fruit globular; scar of the stigma subbasal; mesocarp spongy; endocarp thick, woody, brittle, with vertical ridges reaching from base to apex. Seed ascending, globular, umbilicate at the base, marked with ridges corresponding to the grooves of the endocarp; raphe branching from the hilum and anastomosing freely over the surface; albumen deeply ruminate; embryo subbasal. DISTRIB. The only species.

1. **V. splendida,** *Wendl. in Ill. Hort.* xii. *Misc.* 5. Palm 80 feet high, with many aerial roots and a stem 6–12 in. in diameter, which, like the leaf-sheaths and petiole, is very spiny when young. Leaf 5–8 feet long; petiole ½–1 foot long, pale green, semiterete, grooved down

the face; leaf-sheath 2½–3½ feet long, white-granular; blade cuneate obovate, bright green, 4–7 feet long, 3–5 feet broad, bifid, the edges deeply incised, the primary veins prominent on both surfaces, furnished with a few medially-attached scales on the lower one, each primary nerve bordered by two inconspicuous veinlets. Spadix 3–6 feet long; peduncle compressed, 3–4 feet long; flowering-branches 7–8 inches long. Fruit ⅞–1 in. diam. Regelia magnifica, princeps, and majestica, *Hort.* Stevensonia viridifolia, *Duncan*, *MSS.*

SEYCHELLES, very common amongst rocks in all the islands, *Horne!* Endemic. *Latte.*

10. STEVENSONIA, Duncan.

Monoicous. Flowers in 3-flowered clusters, one female between and below two males, spirally arranged on the thick branches of a doubly-branched erect long-peduncled spadix in the axil of a leaf. Spathes 2; outer persistent, covered with bristles; inner woody, deciduous. (Horne.) MALE. Inner segments of perianth valvate, many times longer than the outer ones. Stamens 15–20, connate at the base, included. Rudimentary pistil a subulate grooved column. FEMALE. Staminodes forming a shortly-toothed cup. Fruit a small ovoid drupe, flattened on the side on which the subbasilar stigma is placed, furnished with a ridge on the convex side when dry; mesocarp thin fibrous; endocarp crustaceous, not grooved. Seed ascending, cordate-ovoid, flattened on the side on which it is attached; branches of the raphe spreading from the base and anastomosing near the apex; albumen deeply ruminate; embryo basilar. DISTRIB. The only species.

1. **S. grandifolia,** *Duncan, Cat. Hort. Maur.* 87 (name only). Palm 40–50 feet high, the stem very spiny when young, less so when old. Petiole 9–18 in. long, glabrous, pale green, convex below; leaf-sheath 2–3 feet long, hoary, scaly and spiny; blade cuneate-obovate, bifid, oblique at the base, deeply laciniated down the side, with incised segments; primary veins prominent, bordered with two secondary veinlets on each side, clothed with a few medially-attached brown scales beneath. Spadix 3–6 feet long; peduncle 1½–3 feet long, compressed at the base; branches 1–1¼ foot long. Lower spathes 15 in. long; upper club-shaped, smooth, 2–3½ feet long (Horne). Fruit orange-red, ½–⅝ in. long. Seed ¼ in. long. Phœnicophorium sechellarum, *Wendl. in Ill. Hort.* xii. 433, *Misc.* 5. Astrocaryum pictum and Borsigianum, *Hort.* Areca sechellarum, *Hort.*

SEYCHELLES, common in all the islands, *Horne!* Endemic. *Latanier feuillé.*

We retain the name given to this plant by its discoverer, and published by him, though without description. The name *Phœnicophorium*, subsequently given, and invented for the purpose of commemorating the disgraceful fact of a specimen of this Palm having been stolen from Kew by a foreign employé, should surely be suppressed.

ORDER C. JUNCACEÆ.

Flowers regular, usually hermaphrodite. Perianth inferior, of 6 subequal free dry subcoriaceous segments. Stamens 6, hypogynous or deeply perigynous; filaments subulate; anthers 2-celled, basifixed. Ovary free, mostly 3-celled, sometimes 1-celled; style subulate; stigmas 3, distinct. Fruit usually a 3-valved capsule with loculicidal dehiscence. Seed with a small embryo at the base of abundant albumen.—Herbs, mostly perennial, with rigid persistent leaves and copious small inconspicuous flowers. DISTRIB. Cosmopolitan, but scarcely at all tropical. Species 150.

Fruit capsular, with abundant 2-tailed seeds . . . . . . 1. JUNCUS.
Fruit baccate, 1-seeded . . . . 2. FLAGELLARIA.

1. JUNCUS, Linn.

Perianth with 6 lanceolate glumaceous equal acute free segments. Stamens 6 or reduced to 3, inserted at the base of the segments, included. Ovary 3-celled, with axile placentation and numerous superposed ovules; style short; stigmas 3, subulate. Capsule 3-celled, or 1-celled by the obliteration of the septa; seeds numerous, tailed at both ends by the loose cellular testa.—Perennial rarely annual tufted herbs, with abundant small brown flowers, the leaves developed or reduced to mere sheaths. DISTRIB. Everywhere in the temperate and Arctic-alpine zones. Species 100.

1. **J. effusus,** *Linn. Sp.* 464. Stems densely tufted, erect, terete, 3–4 feet long, filled with continuous soft pith, green, finely striated. Leaves reduced to mere sheaths at the base of the stem. Flowers in a lax lateral panicle some distance from the top of the stem. Perianth-segments $\frac{1}{12}$ in. long, lanceolate-acuminate. Capsule bright brown, obovoid, obtuse, mucronate, as long as the perianth. J. mauritianus, *Bojer, Hort. Maur.* 360. J. communis *var.* effusus, *E. Meyer.*

MAURITIUS, in hill swamps at the Mare aux Vacouas, etc. Cosmopolitan in the two colder zones.

2. FLAGELLARIA, Linn.

Perianth of 6 membranous free oblong obtuse much imbricated greenish-white segments. Stamens 6, hypogynous; filaments very short; anthers ligulate, basifixed. Ovary 3-celled; ovule in each cell solitary, basilar; style very short, conical; stigmas 3, subulate. Fruit a globose berry, 1-celled by abortion and 1-seeded. DISTRIB. The only species.

1. **F. indica,** *Linn.; Kunth, Enum.* iii. 370. A climbing perennial herb, with stems reaching a length of 10 feet or more, clothed in the lower part by the withered leaves. Leaves glossy, subcoriaceous,

lanceolate acuminate, spreading, ending in a spiral tendril, ½–1 foot long, ½–¾ in. broad. Flowers in a sessile terminal panicle 3–9 inches long and broad, with compound branches, in sessile clusters. Perianth $\frac{1}{12}$ in. long. Berry red, the size of a small pea.

Mauritius and Seychelles, common in woods. Spread through the tropics of the Old World. *Flagellaire. Rotin du pays.* There are two varieties: one, *glauca*, Bojer, with large glaucous leaves, and the other, *angustifolia*, Bojer, with green leaves ½ foot long, ¼ inch broad and smaller panicles.

Order CI. ERIOCAULONEÆ.

Flowers monoicous, membranous, arranged in a dense head in the axils of imbricated bracts, the inner males, the outer females. Male perianth double; outer of 2–3 free segments; inner of the same number, connate in a funnel-shaped tube. Stamens inserted at the throat of the tube, as many or twice as many as the lobes of inner perianth. Female flowers of two rows of 2–3 free segments. Ovary superior; cells 2–3, with a single ovule in each; stigmas subulate, as many as the cells. Fruit a loculicidal capsule. Seed with embryo outside the albumen.—Acaulescent or caulescent herbs, with minute flowers. Distrib. Warmer regions of both hemispheres. Species 300.

1. ERIOCAULON, Linn.

Flowers 2-merous or 3-merous, in our plant (§ *Nasmythia*, Mart.) the former, with sepals and petals 2 each, the latter joined in a slender tube in the males. Male flower with 2 rudimentary carpels and 4 stamens inserted at the summit of the tube. Female Flower. Ovary 2-celled, with subulate simple stigmas. Capsule subglobose, membranous.—Usually stemless herbs with leaves in a dense basal rosette and minute flowers in a globose head at the top of a naked scape, each subtended by a coriaceous bract. Distrib. Mainly tropics of Old World. Species 50.

1. **E. repens,** *Lam.; Kunth, Enum.* iii. 569. Densely tufted, with abundant root-fibres. Leaves linear, glossy, erect, crowded in a basal rosette, 3–6 in. long, closely ribbed. Scape very slender, ½–1 foot long, with 5 deep ribs, sheathed at the base with a leaf free at the top. Flowers in a dense globose head ¼ in. diam.; outer bracts glossy, round-deltoid; inner cuneate, matted at the top with a patch of white tomentum. Flowers flattened, finally protruded from the bracts. E. quinquangulare, *Bojer, Hort. Maur.* 361, *non Linn.* E. longifolium, *Nees; Kunth, Enum.* iii. 567.

Mauritius, on the banks of the streams of Grand Bassin. Also Bourbon and Madagascar.

ORDER CII. NAIADACEÆ.

Flowers monochlamydeous or achlamydeous, hermaphrodite or monoicous. Perianth when present herbaceous and inferior. Stamens 1–4, hypogynous; anthers 1–2- rarely 4-celled; pollen globose or tubular. Ovary of 1–4 1-celled carpels; ovules except in *Halophila* solitary in the cells; style often oblique; stigma usually peltate, oblique. Fruit indehiscent, dry or rather fleshy. Seed usually exalbuminous.—Water plants, with various foliage and inflorescence, the flowers always minute. DISTRIB. Cosmopolitan. Species 100.

Ovules solitary. Special spathe none.
  Flowers in spikes . . . . 1. POTAMOGETON.
  Flowers 1–2, sessile or stalked in the axils of the leaves.
    Flowers hermaphrodite, without any perianth . . . . 2. RUPPIA.
    Flowers monoicous, the female with a perianth . . . . 3. ZANNICHELLIA.
Ovules numerous. Flowers in a special spathe . . . . 4. HALOPHILA.

1. POTAMOGETON, Linn.

Flowers hermaphrodite, monochlamydeous, in dense peduncled spikes. Perianth herbaceous, of 4 valvate free inferior segments. Stamens 4; anthers nearly sessile, 2-celled. Ovary of 4 free sessile carpels; ovule solitary in each carpel, ascending; stigma oblique, peltate, nearly or quite sessile. Fruit drupaceous, indehiscent, with a tough pericarp.—Aquatic herbs, with leaves mostly alternate, all alike membranous and submerged, or some floating different in shape and firmer in texture. DISTRIB. Cosmopolitan. Species 50.

Stipules free. Leaves many-nerved.
  Upper leaves floating, subcoriaceous . . . . 1. P. NATANS.
  All the leaves submerged and membranous.
    Leaves large, lanceolate. . . . . 2. P. LUCENS.
    Leaves small, ligulate . . . . 3. P. CRISPUS.
Stipules adnate to the mostly 1-nerved leaf . . . . 4. P. PECTINATUS.

1. **P. natans,** *Linn.*; *Kunth, Enum.* iii, 127. Stems comparatively stout, reaching a length of several feet. Submerged leaves petiole-like, channelled, alternate. Floating leaves many, upper opposite, long-petioled, oblong, 2–4 in. long, 1–1½ in. broad, rounded to both ends, subcoriaceous, brownish-green, with 6–12 arching ribs on each side, connected by distinct transverse veinlets; stipules 1–1½ in. long, free, lanceolate. Peduncle ⅛ in. thick, longer than the spike. Spike dense, 1–1½ in. long. Drupes ⅛ in. long, oblique obovoid, keeled, with a short beak from the ventral angle. P. indicum, *Roxb. Fl. Ind.* i. 452.

MAURITIUS and SEYCHELLES, common in ponds and still waters. Cosmopolitan.

2. **P. lucens,** *Linn.*; *Kunth, Enum.* iii. 132. Stems $\frac{1}{12}$ in. thick,

reaching a length of several feet. Leaves alternate, lanceolate, narrowed gradually from the middle to both ends, all submerged, very thin, bright green, 3-6 in. long, $\frac{3}{4}$–1 in. broad, with 3–6 veins on each side of the midrib, connected by distinct transverse veinlets, the edge minutely crispato-denticulate; stipules above 1 in. long, free, lanceolate. Peduncle stout, 2–4 in. long. Spikes dense, 1–1$\frac{1}{2}$ in. long. Drupes smaller than in *P. natans* and not keeled.

MAURITIUS, in inland lakes and slow streams. Cosmopolitan.

3. **P. crispus,** *Linn.*; *Kunth*, *Enum.* iii. 133. Stems slender, copiously branched. Leaves alternate, ligulate, obtuse, sessile, all submerged and very thin, bright green, 1–2 in. long, $\frac{1}{8}$–$\frac{1}{4}$ in. broad, with a single intra-marginal nerve, the edge crisped and denticulate; stipules small, free, obtuse, evanescent. Peduncle slender, curved, 1–1$\frac{1}{2}$ in. long. Spike $\frac{1}{4}$–$\frac{1}{2}$ in. long, rather lax. Drupes $\frac{1}{8}$ in. long, oblique ovoid, with a distinct beak. P. tuberosus, *Roxb.*; *Bojer*, *Hort. Maur.* 358.

MAURITIUS, in inland streams. Cosmopolitan.

4. **P. pectinatus,** *Linn.*; *Kunth*, *Enum.* iii. 137. Stems slender, several feet long, copiously branched, forming dense masses. Leaves sessile, narrow ligulate, 1-nerved, 4–8 in. long, $\frac{1}{48}$–$\frac{1}{24}$ in. broad; stipules $\frac{1}{2}$–1 in., adnate to the edge of the blade. Peduncle slender, an inch long. Spike as long as the peduncle, interrupted. Drupes $\frac{1}{8}$ in. long, nearly globose, with a short central beak.

MAURITIUS, in inland streams and in the sea at Fort William and Canonier Point. Cosmopolitan.

2. RUPPIA, Linn.

Flowers hermaphrodite, 2 or more on a peduncle which at first is enclosed in a sheath formed by the stipules connate with the base of the leaf. Perianth 0. Stamens 2; filaments very short; anthers 2-celled. Ovary of 4 free carpels; ovules solitary in each carpel, pendulous; style 0 or short; stigma peltate, oblique. Drupes oblong, long-stalked.—Salt-water herbs, with slender branched stems forming dense masses and filiform 1-nerved leaves. DISTRIB. Cosmopolitan. Species, or rather subspecies, 3.

1. **R. rostellata,** *Koch in Reich. Ic.* ii. 66, *t.* 174. Stems very slender, rooting at some of the joints and sometimes forming tubercles from which new plants spring. Leaves 1–3 in. long, $\frac{1}{72}$ in. broad, with a narrow stipular sheath about $\frac{1}{2}$ in. long. Pedunoles short, not spirally twisted. Drupe $\frac{1}{16}$ in. long, oblique globose, narrowed into a distinct beak. R. maritima, *Kunth*, *Enum.* iii. 123, in part; *Bojer*, *Hort. Maur.* 358.

MAURITIUS and RODRIGUEZ, in the sea and brackish ditches. Cosmopolitan.

3. ZANNICHELLIA, Linn.

Flowers usually monoicous, a male and female in the same spathe-like leaf-sheath. Male achlamydeous, consisting of a single stamen, with a filiform filament and 2–4-celled sagittate anther; pollen sub-globose. Female flower with a minute campanulate perianth; 2–6 finally pedicellate carpels; ovule solitary, pendulous; style long or short, with an oblique peltate stigma. Fruit of 2–6 minute achenes.—A single cosmopolitan species with 3 or 4 varieties or subspecies,

1. **Z. palustris,** *Linn.;* var. **Z. brachystemon,** *Gay.* Stems wide-creeping, filiform. Leaves 1–2 inches long, bright green, all submerged, $\frac{1}{48}$ in. broad. Filament short; anther 2-celled. Achene oblong, $\frac{1}{12}$ in. long, with a distinctly crenate keel, a short pedicel, a style half as long as itself, and a large white papillose stigma. Z. repens, *Bonng.* Z. dentata, *Lloyd.*

RODRIGUEZ, in streams and estuaries, *Balfour!* Cosmopolitan.

4. HALOPHILA, Thouars.

Flowers monoicous, solitary in the axils of the leaves, enclosed in a 2-leaved membranous spathe. Perianth membranous, tubular. Male flowers with 3 stamens; filaments short, monadelphous; anther 2-celled; pollen confervoid. Female flower with a single ovary, with 3 parietal placentas, bearing numerous ascending anatropous ovules; style long; stigmas 3–4, subulate, jointed at the base. Fruit indehiscent. Seed with copious albumen.—Submarine herbs with creeping stems and opposite petioled stipulate membranous leaves. The only species.

Leaves oblong, long-petioled . . . . 1. H. OVATA.
Leaves ligulate, short-petioled . . . . 2. H. STIPULACEA.

1. **H. ovata,** *Gaud. in Freyc. Voy.* 430, *tab.* 40, *fig.* 1. Stems very slender, wide-creeping; nodes distant, bearing a pair of erect leaves. Stipules membranous, obtuse, much shorter than the petioles, which are sometimes above an inch long; blade $\frac{1}{2}$–1 in. long, oblong or obovate-oblong, obtuse, the ascending veins connected by a distinctly intramarginal line. Spathes membranous, ovate, acute, $\frac{1}{12}$ in. long, solitary, sessile or on short pedicels from the leaf-bearing nodes. *Hook. fil. Fl. Tasm.* ii. 45.

Shores of MAURITIUS, RODRIGUEZ, and SEYCHELLES. Spread through the tropics of the Old World.

2. **H. stipulacea,** *Aschers. in. Linnæa,* xxxv. 172. Stems wide-creeping, stouter than in *H. ovata.* Stipules $\frac{1}{4}$–$\frac{1}{3}$ in., white, membra-

nous, obtuse, longer than the short petioles; blade ligulate, pale green, membranous, denticulate, 1–2 inches long, $\frac{1}{12}$–$\frac{1}{6}$ in. broad, with a distinct midrib and submarginal nerve. Flowers not seen. Thalassia stipulacea, *König*; *Kunth*, *Enum*. iii. 120.

Gathered on the shores of MAURITIUS by Col. Pike, and of RODRIGUEZ, by Dr. Balfour. Australia to Africa.

ORDER CIII. TYPHACEÆ.

Flowers monoicous, in globose or cylindrical heads, the male heads uppermost. Perianth of minute capillary or membranous scales. Stamens 2 or many; filaments subulate, free, or monadelphous; anthers 2-celled, basifixed. Ovary usually 1-celled, sessile or stalked; ovule solitary, pendulous from the apex; style simple; stigma oblique. Fruit dehiscent or indehiscent. Seed albuminous.—Swamp plants, with abundant densely packed small flowers and narrow persistent leaves. DISTRIB. Cosmopolitan. Species 10–12.

1. TYPHA, Linn.

Spikes cylindrical, usually one male and one female. Perianth of the male of two or three brown subulate scales; filaments short, monadelphous; anthers ligulate, 2–4 in a bundle, crested by the produced brown connective. Ovaries stalked, mostly imperfect, with a perianth of dense white silky threads like a pappus; style produced; stigma lanceolate, oblique. Fruit minute, with a hyaline pericarp.—Gregarious swamp-loving perennials, with grass-like leaves and tall stems. DISTRIB. Cosmopolitan. Species 6–8.

1. **T. angustata,** *Bory and Chaub.*; *Rohrb. in Verhand. Bot. Verein Brand.* 1869, 87. Stems 6–8 feet long. Leaves nearly or quite as long as the stem, bright green, sheathing it for the lower foot or more, $\frac{1}{4}$–$\frac{3}{8}$ in. broad after they leave it, nearly flat on the face, rounded on the back. Female spikes rarely two, varying from 3 inches to a foot in length. Brown stigmas just protruding from the hairs, which before they become detached are $\frac{1}{12}$ in. long. Male spike as long as the female, with a space of about an inch between them. Anthers $\frac{1}{12}$ in. long, 2–4 in a bundle. T. angustifolia, *Bojer*, *Hort. Maur*. 357.

MAURITIUS and SEYCHELLES, everywhere common in marshes. Warmer regions of the Old World. *Voundre*.

ORDER CIV. PANDANEÆ.

(By DR. I. B. BALFOUR.)

Flower dioicous, on simple or branching spadices, enclosed by persistent or deciduous spathes. Perianth 0. Stamens many, the filaments often connate; anthers 2-celled, basifixed, dehiscing longitudinally. Ovary 1- or many-celled; ovules in our genus solitary, on a parietal placenta; stigmas sessile or stalked, distinct. Fruits drupaceous, many aggregated into a head; endocarp bony. Seeds oblong; testa membranous; embryo straight, basal, in abundant fleshy albumen.—Trees or shrubs, usually with a branching stem supported by strong adventitious roots and simple long narrow firm spiny leaves imbricated in three spiral rows. DISTRIB. Tropical regions of the Old World. Species 70.

1. PANDANUS, Linn.

MALE. Spadix compound, thyrsoid, borne at the extremity of a branch, the lateral spikes each in the axil of a leafy often-coloured spathe, which is often longer than the spike. Stamens many, usually connate in bundles. FEMALE. Spadix usually simple, borne at the end of a branch, surrounded by many spathes. Ovaries, fruit, and habit as described under the order.

Heads solitary.
  Drupes typically 1-celled.
    Heads erect; drupes $1\frac{1}{4}$–$1\frac{1}{2}$ in. long . . . . 1. P. SPHÆROIDEUS.
    Heads pendulous; drupes under an inch long . . . 2. P. MICROCARPUS.
  Drupes typically 2- or many-celled.
    Cells of drupe 2. . . . . 3. P. HORNEI.
    Cells of drupe 3 or more, rarely 1–2.
      Drupes greatly compressed, with carpels in a single row.
        Apex of drupe deeply cleft between the prominent stigmas . . . . 4. P. BARKLYI.
        Apex of drupe shallowly cleft between the immersed stigmas . . . . 5. P. CONOIDEUS.
      Drupes not greatly compressed, with carpels not in a single row.
        Stigmas flat; free portion of the drupe narrowed upwards.
          Stigmas less than $\frac{1}{12}$ in. broad, sessile.
            Endocarp basal . . . . 6. P. VANDERMEESCHII.
            Endocarp medial . . . . * P. UTILIS.
          Stigmas above $\frac{1}{12}$ in. broad, sessile.
            Stigmas not placed in a depressed areole . 7. P. PYRAMIDALIS.
            Stigmas placed in a depressed central areole.
              Mesocarp spongy when dry.
                Drupe free in the upper sixth or eighth 8. P. HETEROCARPUS.
                Drupe free in the upper third or quarter 9. P. TENUIFOLIUS.
              Mesocarp laminated when dry . . . . 10. P. ICERYI.

Stigmas stipitate . . . . 11. P. DRUPACEUS.
Stigmas flat; free portion of drupe not narrowed upwards . . . . 12. P. EYDOUXIA.
Stigmas oblique, mucronate.
Summit of drupe shallowly channelled; mesocarp septate . . . . * P. ODORATISSIMUS.
Summit of drupe deeply channelled; mesocarp not septate.
Stigmas $\frac{1}{6}$ in. broad, with a short mucro. . 13. P. PALUSTRIS.
Stigmas $\frac{1}{12}$ in. broad, with a long mucro . 14. P. SECHELLARUM.
Heads numerous.
Stigmas flat, reniform . . . . 15. P. MULTISPICATUS.
Stigmas oblique, ovate . . . . 16. P. CONGLOMERATUS.

1. **P. sphæroideus**, *Thouars; Kunth, Enum.* iii. 97. A low tree 8–12 feet high, with a slender decumbent light dun-coloured freely-branching stem, the branches decumbent and aerial roots descending freely from all parts. Leaves firm in texture, 3–5 feet long, 2–3$\frac{1}{2}$ in. broad, pale green, the edges irregularly armed with short finally reddish spines; midrib not very prominent, spiny towards the tip, with the blade reduplicate on each side; lateral veinlets inconspicuous beneath. Female heads containing above 100 drupes, globose, slightly trigonous, 4$\frac{1}{2}$ in. in diam.; peduncle erect, 9 in. long, with numerous persistent leafy bracts, adnate by their face to the peduncle and densely spiny at the tip, enveloping and concealing the head. Drupes *regularly hexagonal, usually 1-celled, 1$\frac{1}{4}$–1$\frac{1}{2}$ in. long, pink at the base when ripe, free in the upper fifth or sixth, $\frac{1}{2}$–$\frac{3}{4}$ in. broad at the top, tapering to $\frac{1}{4}$ in. at the base, the apex regularly pyramidal, pale blue-green, marked with 5 or 6 ridges; stigma umbilicate, subpeltate, $\frac{1}{8}$ in. broad; endocarp smooth at the sides, depressed at the apex, with a circle of fibres passing upwards from the edges and penetrating the spongy mesocarp, which is thin round the endocarp. Seed $\frac{1}{2}$–$\frac{3}{4}$ in. long. P. globuliferus, *Thouars, loc. cit.*

MAURITIUS, in clumps on the higher part of the island, usually in moist soil. *Barkly! Horne! Bouton! Balfour!* Endemic.

2. **P. microcarpus**, *Balf. fil.* A small tree or shrub, with a light dun-coloured smooth stem 3–4 in. in diameter, branching freely at an acute angle. Leaves thin, coriaceous, 1–2 feet long, $\frac{7}{12}$–$\frac{3}{4}$ in. broad, dark green on the upper surface, slightly glaucous beneath, the margins armed throughout with short sharp red spines; midrib spiny only at the tip and base; lateral veinlets distinct on the under surface. Female heads containing 50–90 drupes, globose, 2$\frac{1}{2}$ in. in diameter, pendulous; peduncle 5–6 in. long, frequently recurved, with several persistent leaf-like bracts, which overtop the head. Drupe purple with a slight bloom, orange at the base when ripe,

* The description of the drupes must always be understood as applying to those of the middle of the head, the form of the others being usually much distorted.

usually 1- rarely 2–3-celled, irregularly 5–6-angled, $\frac{3}{4}$–$1\frac{1}{4}$ in. long, $\frac{1}{3}$–$\frac{7}{12}$ in. broad and deep, free in the upper quarter; apex flatly pyramidal, marked with 5 or 6 faint ridges; stigma subreniform, slightly umbilicate, $\frac{1}{12}$ in. broad, prominent, endocarp smooth at the sides, filling up nearly the whole drupe; apex depressed, a circlet of fibres piercing the succulent mesocarp. Seed above $\frac{1}{4}$ in. long.

MAURITIUS, not uncommon on the banks of streams at Vacoa and Curepipe, *Barkly! Horne! Balfour!* Endemic.

3. **P. Hornei,** *Balf. fil.* A large tree, often 60 feet high, with a smooth stem a foot in diameter, branching freely. Leaves thin, coriaceous, 6–10 feet long, 3 in. broad, tapering to a long point, dark green on the upper surface, the edges armed throughout with short dense red adpressed spines; midrib spiny from the middle to the tip; lateral veinlets invisible beneath. Female heads containing 80–100 drupes, globose, a foot in diameter, pendulous; peduncle $1\frac{1}{2}$–$2\frac{1}{2}$ feet long, with several leafy persistent bracts. Drupe 2-celled, purple, slightly glaucous, 3–5 in. long, 2–$2\frac{1}{2}$ in. broad, $1\frac{1}{2}$–2 in. deep, regu- regularly 5–6-angled, free in the upper third; apex dome-like, with faintly-marked ridges; stigmas reniform, $\frac{1}{2}$ in. broad, sessile, slightly prominent; endocarp inversely mitræform, sending out many fibres into the thick spongy mesocarp, covered with downwardly-directed deltoid prominences, the apex deeply excavated, with two conical processes arising from the base of the hollow. Seed $1\frac{1}{4}$ in. long.

SEYCHELLES, very common in Mahé, Praslin, and Silhouette, *Horne!* Endemic.

4. **P. Barklyi,** *Balf. fil.* A small tree, 5–8 feet high, with slender decumbent stems and branches, with adventitious roots from all parts. Leaves 1–3 feet long, $\frac{3}{4}$–2 in. broad; blade reduplicate on on each side of the midrib, tapering to a long point, dark green above, glaucescent beneath, the margins and midrib armed throughout or at the base and tip only with short spines, green at first, but turning red. Female heads containing 70–100 drupes, elliptical or ovoid, slightly flattened at the base, 6–8 in. long. 4–5 in. broad, drooping; peduncle long, with 3–5 deciduous bracts. Drupes purple, compressed, 4–6-celled, $1\frac{1}{2}$–2 in. long, free in the upper two-fifths, 1–2 in. broad, $\frac{3}{4}$–$1\frac{1}{2}$ in. deep, the united part tapering rapidly downwards; apex a tranversely elongated ridge deeply cleft between the prominent stigmas; stigmas deeply reniform, sessile, $\frac{1}{8}$–$\frac{1}{6}$ in. broad; endocarp smooth, transversely elongated, very short. slightly depressed at the apex, with processes that pass up to each of the stigmas, surrounded by many fibres which pierce the spongy mesocarp, which is very thin round the endocarp. Seed $\frac{1}{4}$ in. long. Vinsonia sylvestris, *Gaudich. Atl. Bonite, tab.* 17, *fig.* 16–17.

MAURITIUS, common near marshes and on flat open plains in the higher part of the island, *Horne! Barkly!* Endemic.

5. **P. conoideus,** *Thouars, Kunth, Enum.* iii. 97. A small tree, about 14 feet high, the slate-grey stem frequently decumbent, covered with many short sharp warts, branching freely. Leaves thick, coriaceous, 4–5 feet long, 2–4 in. broad, dark green, the margins irregularly spiny, the spines near the base being close and spreading, those higher up incurved or adpressed, all green, the midrib spiny in the upper half, the blade reduplicate on each side of it: lateral veinlets obscure beneath. Female heads globose, 5–6 in. diameter, containing above 100 drupes; peduncle above a foot long, slightly drooping, with many long linear-lanceolate leafy deciduous bracts, which much exceed the head. Drupes greatly compressed, 3–7-celled, 1$\frac{3}{8}$ in. long, free in the upper fifth, $\frac{3}{4}$–1 in. broad, $\frac{7}{12}$–$\frac{11}{12}$ in. deep, the united portion lemon-yellowwhen ripe, cuneato-hexagonal; apex green, very narrow, shallowly cleft between the stigmas; stigmas deeply reniform, $\frac{1}{12}$–$\frac{1}{8}$ in. broad, immersed, slightly umbilicate; endocarp smooth at the sides, tranversely elongated, very short, not depressed at the apex, with a process passing up to each stigma through the spongy mesocarp, which is thin round the endocarp. Seed $\frac{1}{3}$ in. long.

MAURITIUS, common in the higher parts of the island in damp soil in open places growing in clusters. *Barkly! Bouton! Horne! Balfour!* Endemic. *Vacoa marron.*

6. **P. Vandermeeschii,** *Balf. fil.* A tree about 20 feet high, with a light-coloured stem 5–6 in. in diameter, branching freely, the branches often twisted. Leaves stiff, suberect, 2$\frac{1}{2}$–3 feet long, 1$\frac{1}{2}$–2 in. broad, very glaucous on both surfaces, the thickened red margins armed throughout with strong red pungent spines, and the prominent red midrib also spiny from the base to the tip; lateral veinlets distinctly visible on the under surface. Heads trigono-globose. 4–5 in. in diameter, containing over 100 drupes; peduncle straight, drooping, 8–9 in. long, often red, with several short deciduous leafy bracts. Drupes fusiform, 2–6-celled, rarely 1-celled, free in the upper two-thirds, 1 in. long, $\frac{1}{3}$–$\frac{1}{2}$ in. broad and deep; free apex faintly angled, subterete, red or streaked with transverse bands of red and green; base strongly, but irregularly 5–6-angled; stigmas flat, reniform, $\frac{1}{16}$–$\frac{1}{12}$ in. broad, crowded substipitate, often oblique; epicarp very hard; endocarp placed at the base of the drupe, sending up processes to its tip, and a few fibres through the spongy mesocarp, which fills up the upper part of the drupe, but is thin round the endocarp. Foullioya maritima, *Gaudich. Atl. Bonite, tab.* 26, *fig.* 21–24.

MAURITIUS, on Round Island, Amber Island, Flat Island, and Coin de Mire, not on the main land, *Barkly! Horne! Balfour!* Endemic.

* *P. utilis,* Bory, Voy. ii. 3, a native of Madagascar, is commonly planted in Mauritius for the sake of its leaves. It is a tree 60 feet high, with firm glaucous erect leaves 1–2$\frac{1}{2}$ feet long with sharp red spines, trigono-globose long-peduncled pendulous heads about half a foot in diameter, containing above 100 drupes 3–8-celled 1$\frac{1}{4}$–1$\frac{1}{2}$ in. long free in the upper half 5–6-angled in the lower half and yellow when ripe, the apex

domelike and faintly 5–6-angled, stigmas small reniform crowded, and an endocarp flattened at the apex with a short process passing to each stigma and a few fibres piercing the spongy mesocarp. Here belong *P. nudus* and *sativus* of Thouars, *P. Candelabrum*, Bot. Mag. t. 5014, and *Vinsonia stephanocarpa, utilis, Thouarsii, propinqua, striata, consanguinea, and media* of Gaudichaud. *P. maritimus*, Thouars, and *Vinsonia palustris*, Gaudich, are merely a variety in which the drupe is compressed, with the apex appreciably cleft. *Vacoa sac.*

7. **P. pyramidalis,** *Barkly, MSS.* A tree 30 feet high, with a straight dark brown stem 8–10 in. in diameter, with horizontal or slightly deflexed branches ending in drooping tufts of leaves. Leaves thick, coriaceous, 2–5 feet long, 1–2 in. broad, tapering to a long point, dark green, slightly glaucescent on both surfaces; margins red, armed throughout or except at the middle with short red-tipped spines; midrib prominent, spiny in the upper half, with the blade reduplicate on each side of it; lateral veinlets distinct beneath. Female heads trigono-globose, pendulous, 6–8 in. in diameter, containing above 100 drupes; peduncle $1\frac{1}{3}$ ft. long, with many bracts, which much overtop the head. Drupes 4–6-celled, slightly compressed, $1\frac{1}{2}$–2 in. long, $1\frac{1}{4}$–$1\frac{1}{2}$ in. broad, free in the upper quarter; connate portion orange when ripe, 5–6-angled; apex pyramidal, marked with a circular groove, above which is an irregularly polygonal flattened space, on which are placed the sessile reniform prominent stigmas, which are $\frac{1}{8}$–$\frac{1}{6}$ in. broad; endocarp smooth at the sides, truncate at the apex, with 4–6 hard processes passing upwards, many fibres passing up through the spongy mesocarp, which is very thin round the endocarp. Seed $\frac{1}{3}$–$\frac{1}{2}$ in. long.

MAURITIUS, at Curepipe, *Barkly! Horne! Balfour!* Endemic.

8. **P. heterocarpus,** *Balf. fil.* An erect tree, about 20 feet high, with a light brown stem 5–7 in. in diameter, which branches freely so as to form a regular dome-like head, the tufts of leaves either erect or drooping. Leaves firm, $1\frac{1}{2}$–3 feet long, $1\frac{1}{2}$–$2\frac{1}{2}$ in. broad, pale or dark green, often glaucescent at the base, the pink edges armed throughout or except at the middle with very sharp red spines; midrib slightly tinged with red, spiny above the middle, the blade not reduplicate; lateral veinlets distinct beneath. Female heads globose and slightly compressed vertically or oblong, containing usually 60–70 drupes, $4\frac{1}{2}$–6 in. long, pendulous; peduncle 3–15 in. long, with several short deciduous bracts. Drupes 2–5-celled, obversely pyramidal, about an inch long, 1–$1\frac{1}{4}$ in. broad, $\frac{3}{4}$–1 in. deep, free in the upper sixth or eighth, not compressed 5–6-angled; connate portion red or yellow when ripe; apex shortly pyramidal, usually flattened and depressed, more rarely rounded and convex in the centre, with a rugulose border, the summit a distinctly-bordered areole enclosing the reniform sessile prominent stigmas, which are $\frac{1}{8}$–$\frac{1}{4}$ in. broad; endocarp smooth at the sides, flattened at the top, with a prominence running

to each stigma and few fibres piercing the spongy mesocarp, which is thick round the endocarp. Seed $\frac{1}{3}$ in. long.

RODRIGUEZ, abundant over the island, *Barkly! Horne! Balfour!* Endemic. A very variable plant, assuming marked forms in the individual drupes and shape of the heads. According to these variations it is known as *Vacoa calé rouge, Vacoa calé blanc, Vacoa poteau, Vacoa parasol, Vacoa Sac,* and *Vacoa mâle. P. ornatus*, Hort. of which a young flowerless plant is figured by André in the Illustration Horticole, vol. xix. t. 97. and in Journ. Hort. Soc. Lond. Misc. I. 1866, is probably the same species.

9. **P. tenuifolius,** *Balf. fil.* A small tree, about 15 feet high, growing usually in clumps, with a light brown smooth stem about 3 in. in diameter, branching freely at an acute angle, the thick erect branches ending abruptly in tufts of reflexed drooping leaves. Leaves coriaceous, dilated and widely amplexicaul at the base, narrowed to a long point, 8–24 in. long, $\frac{1}{4}$–$\frac{1}{2}$ in. broad, dark green, often very glaucous at the base; margins thickened, slightly tinged with red, armed throughout or except at the middle with sharp red spines; blade not reduplicate; midrib red, spiny above the middle; lateral veinlets distinct beneath. Female heads subglobose, 3–5 in. in diameter, containing 20–40 drupes, pendulous from a curved peduncle 5–11 in. long. Drupes 2–5-celled, shortly pyriform, $1\frac{1}{2}$ in. long, $1\frac{1}{3}$–$1\frac{5}{6}$ in. broad, $1\frac{1}{4}$–$1\frac{1}{2}$ in. deep, free in the upper third or quarter, not compressed; connate portion 5–6-angled, obversely pyramidal; apex dome-shaped, faintly 5–6 angled, with a somewhat flattened summit with a distinctly-bordered areole in the centre containing the flat sessile reniform stigmas, which are $\frac{1}{8}$–$\frac{1}{4}$ in. broad; endocarp smooth, more or less rounded, flattened at the top, with a prominence running to each stigma and sending out few fibres to pierce the mesocarp, which is thick round the endocarp. Seed $\frac{1}{3}$ in. long.

RODRIGUEZ, only in the higher parts of the island, *Balfour!* Endemic. *Vacoa Chevron.*

10. **P. Iceryi,** *Horne, MSS.* A tree 20–30 feet high, with an unbranched stem terminating in an erect tuft of leaves. Leaves 2–6 feet long, 3–6 in. broad, narrowed suddenly to the point, bright green above, glaucous beneath; the margins armed except at the middle with closely-set white spines; blade reduplicate on each side of the midrib, with a tendency to split at the top. Female heads ovoid, 3–4 in. long, containing about 40 drupes, cernuous; peduncle arising from the main trunk, under a foot long, with numerous small leafy bracts. Drupes 2–5-rarely 1-celled, 1–$1\frac{1}{4}$ in. long, $\frac{5}{8}$–$\frac{3}{4}$ in. broad, free in the upper third, slightly compressed, regularly 5–6-angular; apex dome-shaped, with a depressed areole in the centre, enclosing the crowded flat sessile prominent, reniform stigmas, which are $\frac{1}{8}$ in. broad; endocarp medial, sending out few fibres into the mesocarp, which is thin round the endocarp. Seed $\frac{1}{3}$ in. long.

MAURITIUS, in forests between the Piton de Milieu de l'Isle and Cent Gaulettes Mountain; also near Fresanges, *Horne!* Endemic.

11. **P. drupaceus,** *Thouars; Kunth, Enum.* iii. 96. A low tree, about 12 feet high, with a light grey stem about 8 in. in diameter,

which is at first decumbent and branches freely. Leaves firm, pale green, 8–6 feet long, 5–6 in. broad, the thickened red margins armed with red closely-set strongly incurved spines from the middle to the tip; midrib very prominent, spiny at the tip, with the blade reduplicate on each side of it; lateral veinlets conspicuous on the under surface. Female heads globose, 8–12 in. in diameter, containing 30–40 drupes; peduncle cernuous, 8–15 in. long, with many short persistent bracts. Drupes 9–20-celled, 3–3½ in. long, 1½–2½ in. broad and deep, irregularly 4–6-angled, slightly compressed, free in the upper two-thirds; united portion narrowing downwards; apex purple, slightly glaucous; free portion little narrowed to the top; summit broad, flattened and slightly depressed; stigmas scattered, angular-reniform, shortly pedicellate, ⅛–⅙ in. broad. Endocarp hard, urnshaped, the apex divided into many sharp prominences, with many fibres passing out on all sides into the thick spongy mesocarp. Seed above an inch long.

MAURITIUS, common at Fresanges, and more rarely at Curepipe, *Bouton! Barkly! Horne!* Endemic. *Vacoa marron.*

12. **P. Eydouxia,** *Balf. fil.* A flat-topped tree 20 feet high, with a slate-coloured stem 8–9 in. in diameter, with many short spiny knobs, the numerous branches ending in tufts of drooping leaves. Leaves very firm in texture, tapering to a long point, dark green, glaucous, 5–7 feet long, 3-5 in. broad, the slightly thickened margins irregularly armed with red-tipped spines; midrib prominent on the under surface, spiny above the middle, with the blade reduplicate on each side of it; lateral veinlets inconspicuous on the under surface. Female heads globose, 9 in. in diameter, containing 20–30 drupes, slightly cernuous; peduncle 9 in. long, furnished with many persistent bracts, which enwrap the head. Drupes 20–30-celled, 3–5 in. long, irregularly 5–6-angled, 3–4 in. broad, 1¾–3½ in. deep, free in the upper half, usually compressed, tapering from the apex to the base, which is orange-yellow when ripe; flat summit marked with as many broad areoles as there are cells; stigmas reniform, sessile, $\frac{1}{24}$–⅙ in. broad. Endocarp transversely elongated, short, the apex marked with as many prominences as there are stigmas, many fibres passing upwards through the spongy mesocarp, which is thin round the endocarp. Seed ½ in. long. Eydouxia macrocarpa, *Gaudich. Atl. Bonite, tab.* 18, *fig.* 1–6.

MAURITIUS, in damp soil on the banks of streams in the higher part of the island, *Bouton! Barkly! Horne! Balfour!* Endemic.

* *P. odoratissimus*, Linn. fil. Suppl. 424, a native of Tropical Asia, is common in the Seychelles, but most likely introduced, rare in Mauritius, and is reported by Sir H. Barkly from Rodriguez. It is a slender tree, about 20 feet high, with short branches ending in drooping tufts of leaves, coriaceous, bright green leaves 3–5 feet long, 3–3½ in. broad, armed throughout on the edge and wholly or partially on the midrib with short white spines, oblong-elliptical drooping heads 6–10 in. long, containing 70–90 turbinate regularly 5–6-

angled 5–9-celled drupes 2 in. long free in the upper three-eighths, yellow at the base and often red upwards, the free apex truncate and divided by shallow grooves into spaces, each of which is capped by a hard subreniform oblique stigma $\frac{1}{8}$ in. broad, with the outer edge produced into a short mucro, the endocarp at the base of the drupe with the apex prolonged into as many septa as there are carpels. Seed $\frac{1}{2}$ in. long. Here apparently belong *P. Rumphii, Boryi, Chamissonis, Douglasii, Menziesii. Loureiri, Linnæi*, and *Rheedii* of Gaudichaud, and probably his *Eydouxia Delessertii*, Atlas Bonite, tab. 18, fig 7–8, is only a monstrosity with a doubled drupe.

13. **P. palustris,** *Thouars ; Kunth, Enum.* iii. 96. An erect tree, about 20 feet high, with a slate-grey stem about 8 in. in diameter, with short spiny knobs, not branching freely, with many aerial roots, the branches ending in tufts of drooping very persistent leaves. Leaves firm in texture, tapering very gradually to a point, $4\frac{1}{2}$–6 feet long, $4\frac{1}{2}$–6 in. broad, the margins armed, usually throughout, with small sharp black-tipped spines; midrib prominent, spiny throughout; lateral veinlets inconspicuous beneath. Female heads globose, a foot in diameter, containing 50–60 drupes, cernuous; peduncle above a foot long, furnished with many persistent bracts, which almost conceal the head. Drupes 4–6-celled, 5–6-angled, 4–$5\frac{1}{2}$ in. long, $2\frac{1}{2}$–$2\frac{3}{4}$ in. broad, $1\frac{3}{4}$–2 in. deep, free in the upper quarter, tapering to the base, which is yellow when ripe, the truncate apex divided by deep grooves into as many conical prominences as there are cells; stigmas hard, oblique, irregularly angular, shortly mucronate, $\frac{1}{4}$ in. broad. Endocarp with a convex apex sending out from all sides copious fibres into the spongy mesocarp which is not septate. Seed nearly an inch long.

MAURITIUS, in moist places, especially at the Mare aux Vacouas, *Barkly! Horne! Balfour!* Endemic.

14. **P. sechellarum,** *Balf. fil.* A pyramidally-headed tree, reaching a height of 40 feet, with a trunk 3–5 in. in diameter, and copious aerial roots passing down even from the branches. Leaves coriaceous, tapering to a long point, 4–8 feet long, $2\frac{1}{2}$–3 in. broad, pale glaucous green, the margins armed throughout with minute suberect pungent pinkish straight spines; midrib prominent, spiny throughout; lateral veinlets conspicuous beneath, Female heads subglobose, 6–12 in. in diameter, containing 50–70 drupes; peduncle above a foot long; bracts few, deciduous. Drupes 4–6-celled, 2–4 in. long, 1–2 in. broad and deep, regularly 5–6-angled, free in the upper third; united portion narrowing rapidly downwards; apex pyramidal, summit green, dark purple below, divided by deep grooves into as many prominences as there are cells; stigmas hard, oblique, $\frac{1}{12}$ in. broad, with a mucro $\frac{1}{8}$–$\frac{1}{6}$ in. long. Endocarp irregular in outline, the apex with as many prominences as there are stigmas, many fibres passing into the spongy mesocarp, which is not septate. Seed $\frac{1}{4}$–$\frac{1}{2}$ in. long.

SEYCHELLES, common in nearly all the islands in rocky and mountainous parts, usually on moss-covered granite boulders, *Kirk! Horne!* Endemic. *Vacoa marron.*

15. **P. multispicatus,** *Balf. fil.* A shrub 6–12 feet high, branching freely, sometimes decumbent. Leaves bright green, 1–5 feet long, 1–1½ in. broad, tapering to a long point, densely spiny on the margins and midrib beneath. Female heads 6–8 in a dense spike, oblong-trigonous, 2 inches long, an inch broad, each containing 200–400 drupes and placed in the axis of a persistent leaflike bract. Drupes 1-celled, ¼ in. long, ⅛ in. broad, free in the upper third, each surrounded by a whorl of filaments; apex pyramidal; stigma reniform, stipitate, $\frac{1}{24}$ in. broad. Endocarp smooth, occupying nearly the whole of the drupe; mesocarp thin, fibrous.

SEYCHELLES, on the banks of streams and frequently on the tops of hills, especially in Mahé, *Horne!* Endemic. *Vacoa du Rivière.*

16. **P. conglomeratus,** *Balf. fil.* A small tree, 12–15 feet high, with a slender trunk, semi-decumbent and sparingly branched. Leaves 3–12 feet long, 2–5 inches broad, narrowed gradually to a point, pale green, with the midrib and edges armed with long white unequal ascending spines; blade slightly reduplicate on each side of the midrib. Female heads above ten on the same peduncle, all sessile except the lowest, oblong, 6–8 in. long, 2½–3½ in. broad, the uppermost smaller, globose. Drupes 3–6-celled, 1–1½ in. long, ¾ in. broad, regularly 5–6-angled, slightly compressed, free in the upper third; free portion regularly dome-shaped, slightly flattened at the top; stigmas distant, ovoid, oblique, $\frac{1}{12}$ in. broad, obscurely mucronate; endocarp medial, sending out copious fibres into the mesocarp. Seed ½ in. long.

MAURITIUS, on the banks of streams at Midlands and Beau Bassin, *Bouton! Horne!* Endemic.

ORDER CIV*. AROIDEÆ.

Flowers sessile on a cylindrical spadix, either covering the whole or leaving the top part and sometimes the centre naked, monochlamydeous or achlamydeous, unisexual or hermaphrodite or some neuter. Perianth when present of 4–8 valvate segments. Stamens free or connate; filaments 0 or very short; anthers 2-celled, opening by slits or pores. Ovary 1- or more-celled; placentation various; ovules various in number and structure; style simple, often absent; stigma capitate. Fruit baccate. Seed albuminous.—Herbs usually with creeping or tuberous rootstocks; leaves net-veined, often hastate; the spadices enclosed in persistent or deciduous spathes. DISTRIB. Mainly tropical in both hemispheres. Species 1000.

The three genera naturalised in our bounds all belong to the tribe *Caladieæ,* marked by achlamydeous monoicous flowers and many-celled anthers with a columnar connective.

Placentas parietal . . . . * COLOCASIA.
Placentas basilar . . . . * ALOCASIA.
Placentas axile . . . . * XANTHOSOMA.

* *Colocasia antiquorum*, Schott, Prod. 138 (Arum Colocasia, *Linn.; Wight. Ic. t.* 786. Caladium esculentum and nympheifolium, *Vent.*), a native of the tropics of the Old World, long-cultivated for the sake of the farina of its caudex, is commonly naturalised in marshes and by streamsides both in Mauritius, Rodriguez, and the Seychelles. It has an erect oblong-cylindrical caudex, bearing 3–6 ovate membranous leaves 1–3 feet long deeply lobed at the base, with a petiole much longer than the blade inserted a third of the way up, tufted slender peduncles bearing a spathe 6–9 inches long with a short oblong tube and an open lanceolate yellow limb, containing a cylindrical spadix which is barren at the top and bears next a mass of male flowers, at the bottom a mass of female flowers and a quantity of neuter ones on the constricted intermediate part. *Songe.*

* *Alocasia macrorhiza*, Schott, Prod. 146 (Arum macrorhizum, *Linn.; Bojer, Hort. Maur.* 356), a native of Tropical Asia, is naturalised in Mauritius, Rodriguez, and the Seychelles, by streamsides. It has a tall stout caudex, very large deltoid-sagittate leaves with long petioles inserted at the base of the sinus, short stout clustered peduncles, spathes a foot long with an oblong tube and a hooded glaucous-green finally yellowish limb, containing a free cylindrical spadix with a rugulose barren tip, bearing few female flowers at the base, many crowded male ones above and neuter ones on the constricted intermediate part. *Songe blanc.*

* *Xanthosoma sagittifolium*, Schott, Prod. 179; Bot. Mag. t. 4989, (Caladium sagittifolium, *Vent.; Bojer, Hort. Maur.* 356), a native of the West Indies, is naturalised in Mauritius by streamsides in several places. It has a short erect caudex, large membranous deltoid-hastate leaves with the petiole inserted at the base of the sinus, short stout clustered peduncles, a spathe ½–1 foot long with an oblong tube and an oblong-greenish-white lamina, containing a cylindrical spadix with flowers quite continuous from base to tip, a few females at the base, numerous males at the top and neuter flowers in the constricted intermediate part.

ORDER CV. LEMNACEÆ.

Flowers very minute, hermaphrodite, achlamydeous, 1–3 together in a spathe produced from the edge or, without a spathe, from the middle of the frond. Stamens solitary; filaments subulate; anthers 1–2-celled. Ovary 1-celled; ovules 1 or many, various in structure; style short; stigma hollow, capitate. Fruit a bottle-shaped utricle. Seed albuminous. —Small or minute floating fronds, with roots simple or absent, propagated usually by budding and almost destitute of vascular tissue. DISTRIB. Cosmopolitan. Species 10–12.

1. LEMNA, Linn.

Flowers with a spathe produced from a cleft at the edge of the frond, which possesses a capillary root. Anthers 2-celled. Ovule solitary, semi-anatropous. Seed horizontal, with copious albumen. DISTRIB. Cosmopolitan. Species 5–6.

1. **L. minor,** *Linn.*; *Kunth, Enum.* iii. 4. Fronds obovate or oblong, thin, green, or tinged with purple, $\frac{1}{12}$–$\frac{1}{8}$ in. long, with a single long capillary root, the young ones sessile on the edges of the old. Spathe marginal, 2-lipped, containing one female and two male flowers, which expand one after the other. Style distinct. L. obcordata, *Bojer, Hort. Maur.* 358, *not Vahl.*

MAURITIUS, frequent in ponds and swamps. Cosmopolitan. Vahl's plant is a *Riccia*. *Goemon*, or *Lenticule*.

ORDER CVI. CYPERACEÆ.

Flowers hermaphrodite or unisexual, each placed in the axis of a single small imbricating bract (glume). Perianth usually 0; if present, composed of hypogynous bristles or scales. Stamens 1–6, usually 3, hypogynous; filaments filiform; anthers 2-celled, basifixed, pendulous, dehiscing longitudinally. Ovary 1-celled; ovule solitary, erect, anatropous; style 1; stigmas 2–3, subulate. Fruit a minute hard lenticular or triquetrous achene, in *Carex* enclosed in a bottle-like sac (perigyne). Seed with abundant farinaceous albumen, at or near the outside of which at the base the minute embryo is placed.—Herbs of various habit, with grass-like leaves, clasping the often triquetrous stem by a closed sheath. Glumes distichous or multifarious, several forming a spikelet, nearly all or only one or two fertile. DISTRIB. Cosmopolitan. Species 2000.

Tribe I. CYPEREÆ. Glumes distichous. Flowers all hermaphrodite. Achene naked.

Glumes completely distichous.
  Flowers many in a spikelet . . . . 1. CYPERUS.
  Flowers few in a spikelet.
    Inflorescence a sessile head . . . . 2. KYLLINGA.
    Infloresence an umbel of spikelets . . . . 3. MARISCUS.
Glumes incompletely distichous.
  Rachis twisted as it matures . . . . 4. ABILGAARDIA.
  Rachis straight.
    Hypogynous bristles 0 . . . . 5. ARTHROSTYLIS.
    Hypogynous bristles present . . . . 6. ASTEROCHÆTE.

Tribe II. Scirpeæ. Glumes multifarious. Flowers many in a spikelet, hermaphrodite. Achenes naked.

Hypogynous bristles 0.
  Spikelets solitary. . . . . 7. Isolepis.
  Spikelets panicled . . . . 8. Fimbristylis.
Perianth of bristles.
  Spikelets solitary . . . . 9. Eleocharis.
  Spikelets clustered . . . . 10. Scirpus.
Perianth of navicular scales.
  Spikelets in a sessile head. Stamen 1 . . . . 11. Lipocarpha.
  Spikelets crowded in heads, mostly panicled . . . . 12. Fuirena.
  Spikelets in a lax corymbose panicle . . . . . . 13. Hypolytrum.

Tribe III. Rhynchosporeæ. Glumes multifarious. Flowers 1–2 in a spikelet, usually hermaphrodite. Achenes naked.

Some of the flowers hermaphrodite. Achenes minute.
  Hypogynous bristles 0. Style trifid . . . . . . 14. Cladium.
  Hypogynous bristles present. Style bifid . . . . 15. Rhynchospora.
All the flowers unisexual. Achenes large, glossy . . . 16. Scleria.

Tribe IV. Caricineæ. Glumes multifarious. Flowers all unisexual. Achenes enclosed in a bottle-shaped utricle.

The only genus . . . . 17. Carex.

1. CYPERUS, Linn.

Flowers hermaphrodite, arranged in distichous many-flowered spikelets. Glumes boat-shaped, usually much imbricated, all except the lowest fertile. Hypogynous bristles 0. Stamens usually 3, rarely 1 or 2. Style trifid and achene triquetrous (*Eucyperus*), or style bifid and achene plano-convex (*Pycreus*).—Perennial or annual herbs, with sheathing grass-like leaves (sheaths rarely not produced into a blade), usually triquetrous stems, spikes usually very numerous, arranged in simple or compound umbels, rarely congested into a single head. Distrib. Cosmopolitan in the tropical and warmer temperate zones. Species 300.

Subgenus Pycreus. Stigmas 2. Achenes plano-convex.

Spikelets in a dense simple lateral head . . . . . . 1. C. lævigatus.
Spikelets in a dense simple terminal head . . . . . 2. C. pygmæus.
Spikelets in a simple terminal umbel.
  Glumes drab-brown.
    Annual; involucre 3-leaved . . . . 3. C. globosus.
    Perennial; involucre 5–6-leaved . . . . 4. C. polystachyus.
  Glumes bright red-brown.
    Involucre about 3-leaved, short. Glumes obtuse . 5. C. cruentus.
    Involucre 6–8-leaved, long. Glumes subacute . 6. C. ferrugineus.
Spikelets in compound terminal umbels.
  Glumes drab-brown; spikelets $\frac{1}{8}$–$\frac{1}{4}$ in. long . . . 7. C. alopecuroides.
  Glumes bright red-brown; spikelets $\frac{1}{8}$–$\frac{3}{4}$ in. long . 8. C. tremulus.

Subgenus Cyperus proper. Stigmas 3. Achenes triquetrous.

Spikelets sessile in a single terminal head.
  Spikelets 3–5. Glumes dark-brown. . . . . 9. C. exilis.
  Spikelets 20–40. Glumes drab . . . . 10. C. dubius.
Spikelets in a simple umbel.
  Annual. Glumes drab-brown.
    Glumes small, obtuse. Leaves setaceous . . . 11. C. microlepis.
    Glumes large, acute. Leaves linear . . . . . . 12. C. compressus.
  Perennial, stoloniferous. Glumes bright red-brown.
    Spikelets $\frac{3}{8}$–$\frac{1}{2}$ in. long . . . . 13. C. tuberosus.
    Spikelets $\frac{1}{3}$–1 in. long . . . . 14. C. rotundus.
Spikelets in a compound umbel.
  Glumes bright reddish-brown.
    Annual, with imbricated glumes . . . . 15. C. amabilis.
    Perennial, with imbricated glumes . . . . . 16. C. longus.
    Perennial, with distant glumes . . . . 17. C. distans.
  Glumes drab- or greenish-brown, rarely darker.
    Glumes $\frac{1}{48}$–$\frac{1}{36}$ in. long.
      Spikelets in globose heads . . . . 18. C. difformis.
      Spikelets not congested in heads . . . . . 19. C. Iria.
    Glumes $\frac{1}{24}$–$\frac{1}{12}$ in. long.
      Rays of primary umbel equal . . . . 20. C. æqualis.
      Rays of primary umbel very unequal.
        Stems leafless, distinctly articulated. . . . . 21. C. articulatus.
        Stems leafy, not articulated.
          Leaves $\frac{1}{8}$–$\frac{1}{4}$ in. broad.
            Spikelets 6–10-flowered.
              Glumes ribbed on the sides . . . . . 22. C. pennatus.
              Glumes ribbed on the keel only . . 23. C. pilosus.
            Spikelets 25–30-flowered . . . . 24. C. Gardneri.
          Leaves $\frac{1}{4}$–$\frac{1}{2}$ in. broad . . . . 25. C. longifolius.
          Leaves an inch or more broad . . . . . . 26. C. latifolius.

1. **C. lævigatus,** *Linn. Mant.* 179. Stems close or a space apart on a creeping rhizome, 6–18 inches high, terete, clasped by two membranous sheaths at the base, the top one usually produced into a short blade. Spikelets 6–20 in a dense sessile lateral cluster some distance from the top of the stem, bracteated by a single small linear leaf $\frac{1}{4}$–$\frac{3}{8}$ in. long, 12–30-flowered. Glumes ovate-deltoid, $\frac{1}{24}$ in. long, subobtuse, whitish, much imbricated. Achene plano-convex, bright brown, half as long as the glume. C. mucronatus, *Rottb.; Kunth, Enum.* ii. 17.

Mauritius and Rodriguez, in swamps through the islands. Warmer regions of both hemispheres. There is a very depauperated form in Dr. Balfour's Rodrigues collection with solitary spikelets and stems 2–3 inches long.

2. **C. pygmæus,** *Rottb.; Kunth. Enum.* ii. 18. Annual. Stems densely tufted, 2–3 in. long, triquetrous. Leaves linear, acutely keeled, as long as the stems. Spikelets very numerous, $\frac{1}{6}$ in. long, crowded into a globose terminal head, bracteated by 6–8 linear leaves 1–3 in. long, 20–30-flowered. Glumes lanceolate, acuminate, greenish,

rather squarrose, much imbricated. Achene oblong, plano-convex, brownish, half as long as the glume.

MAURITIUS, in swamps at Flacq and Pamplemousses, *Bojer*. Tropical Asia and Nile country.

3. **C. globosus**, *All. Auct. Fl. Ped.* 49. Annual, densely tufted. Stems slender, erect, triquetrous, $\frac{1}{3}$–1 foot long. Leaves linear-subulate, nearly as long as the stems. Umbel of 1–4 clusters, each containing several spreading spikelets, if more than one the others shortly peduncled; bracts usually 3, linear-subulate, unequal. Flowers 20–40 in a spikelet. Glumes $\frac{1}{24}$ in. long, oblong-navicular, obtuse, much imbricated, drab with a green keel. Achene oblong, opaque, brown, a third as long as the glume. C. capillaris, *Roxb.; Bojer, Hort. Maur.* 379. C. divaricatus, *Lam.* C. vulgaris, *Sieber; Kunth, Enum.* ii. 4. C. lanceolatus, *Sieber, Herb. Maur. No.* 32, *not Poir.*

MAURITIUS and SEYCHELLES, common in damp soil. Through the tropics of the Old World. Not Bojer's *flavidus*, which is *C. polystachyus*, Rottb.

4. **C. polystachyus**, *Rottb.; Kunth, Enum.* ii. 13. Perennial. Stems densely tufted, triquetrous, much stouter than in the last, 1–2 feet high. Leaves linear, much shorter than the stem, sheathing it for some distance above the base, $\frac{1}{4}$ in. broad. Spikelets in many dense clusters, all nearly sessile, or outer shortly peduncled, $\frac{1}{4}$–$\frac{1}{3}$ in. long, 15–20-flowered; involucre of 5–6 unequal linear leaves 2–3 times as long as the heads. Glumes greenish-brown, $\frac{1}{24}$ in. long, acute, much imbricated. Achene oblong, castaneous, opaque, half as long as the glume. C. flavidus, *Bojer, Hort. Maur.* 380, *not Retz.*

MAURITIUS, RODRIGUEZ, and SEYCHELLES, one of the commonest species. Round the world in the tropics.

5. **C. cruentus**, *Retz. Obs.* v. 13. Perennial. Stems from a wide-trailing rhizome, triquetrous, $\frac{1}{4}$–1 foot long. Leaves several, short, linear, $\frac{1}{8}$ in. broad. Clusters of spikelets several in an umbel, the outer ones shortly peduncled; involucre of about 3 short linear leaves; spikelets $\frac{1}{4}$–$\frac{1}{3}$ in. long, 15–30-flowered. Glumes $\frac{1}{24}$ in. long, much imbricated, oblong-navicular, obtuse, dark shining red-brown. Style much exserted from the glume, bifid. Achene subglobose, dark brown, a quarter as long as the glume. C. Eragrostis, *Vahl; Kunth. Enum.* ii. 7. C. sanguinolentus, *Vahl.*

MAURITIUS, in sandy soil. Tropics of the Old World.

6. **C. ferrugineus**, *Poir.; Kunth, Enum.* ii. 19. Perennial. Stems tufted, erect, triquetrous, a foot or more long. Leaves several, linear, as long as the stem, $\frac{1}{8}$–$\frac{1}{6}$ in. broad. Clusters numerous, in a simple umbel, bracteated by 6–8 long linear leaves, the outer ones on peduncles 1–2 in. long; spikelets $\frac{1}{4}$–$\frac{1}{3}$ in. long, 15–20-flowered. Glumes $\frac{1}{12}$ in. long,

oblong-navicular, subacute, much imbricated, bright red-brown, with a green keel. Achene elliptic, dark brown, half as long as the glume. C. foliosus, *Willd.; Kunth, Enum.* ii. 11. C. Thouarsii, *Kunth, Enum.* ii. 12.

MAURITIUS, in woods at the foot of the mountains. Also Bourbon and Madagascar.

7. **C. alopecuroides,** *Rottb.; Kunth, Enum.* ii. 19. Perennial. Stem 3–4 feet long, acutely triquetrous. Leaves linear, ¼–½ in. broad. Clusters of spikelets very numerous, cylindrical, in compound umbels bracteated by about a dozen linear leaves that reach a length of a foot or more, the outer umbels on 6–9 in. peduncles; spikelets ⅙–¼ in. long, 10–20-flowered. Glumes drab, oblong-navicular, subacute, much imbricated $\frac{1}{16}$ in. long. Achene obovoid, smooth, shining nearly as long as the glume.

SEYCHELLES, in damp woods of Mahé, *Horne*, 221! Through the tropics of the Old World.

8. **C. tremulus,** *Poir.; Kunth, Enum.* ii. 16. Perennial. Stems 2–3 feet long, stout, triquetrous. Leaves nearly as long as the stem, linear, ¼–⅓ in. broad. Clusters very numerous, in a very compound umbel, the outer peduncles half a foot long; spikelets ½–¾ in. long, 20–40-flowered. Glumes $\frac{1}{16}$–$\frac{1}{12}$ in. long, much imbricated, bright reddish-brown, with a green keel, and a distinct hyaline border at the top, obtuse. Achene oblong, dark brown, half as long as the glume. C. expansus, *Bojer, Hort. Maur.* 380, *not Kunth.*

MAURITIUS, in swamps and by the side of streams. Also Madagascar, Tropical Africa and Asia, and probably conspecific with the American *C. flavicomus*, Michx.

9. **C. exilis,** *Willd.; Kunth, Enum.* ii. 50. Annual, densely tufted. Stems 2–3 in. long, slender, triquetrous. Leaves subulate, shorter than the stems. Spikelets 3–5 in a sessile head, bracteated by 2–3 linear-subulate leaves ½–1½ in. long, each ¼–⅓ in. long, lanceolate, 15–20-flowered. Glumes $\frac{1}{24}$ in. long, ovate-navicular, subacute, dark-brown, much imbricated, closely distinctly many-ribbed. Achene obovoid-triquetrous, half as long as the glume.

MAURITIUS, on the Pouce, *Sieber, Herb.* ii. No. 29! *Gardner!* Also Madagascar.

10. **C. dubius,** *Rottb. Gram.* 20, *t.* 4, *fig.* 5. Perennial. Stems densely tufted, rather thickened at the base, 4–12 in. long, triquetrous. Leaves linear, shorter than the stems. Spikelets 20–40, lanceolate, all sessile in a single dense globose terminal head, bracteated by 2–3 linear leaves 1–4 in. long, each ⅛ in. long, 6–8-flowered. Glumes brownish-drab, $\frac{1}{24}$ in. long, much imbricated, ovate-deltoid, subacute, wiih several distinct ribs. Achene obovoid-triquetrous, dark glossy brown, half as long as the glume. C. kyllingioides, *Vahl; Kunth, Enum.* ii. 94. C.

capitatus, *Poir. Encycl.* vii. 246, *an Bojer, Hort. Maur.* 379? Mariscus Kraussii, *Hochst.*

MAURITIUS, *Sieber, Herb.* ii. No. 67. RODRIGUEZ, *Bouton! Balfour!* Natal, Madagascar, Tropical Africa, Tropical Asia.

11. **C. microlepis,** *Baker.* Annual, densely tufted. Stems 4–6 in. long, very slender, triquetrous. Leaves filiform, nearly as long as the stem. Clusters 3–6, simple or forked, crowded in a terminal umbel, bracteated by one short and one long filiform leaf; spikelets $\frac{1}{8}$–$\frac{1}{4}$ in. long, 6–12-flowered. Glumes oblong, obtuse, pale brown, glossy, obscurely cuspidate, little imbricated, $\frac{1}{36}$ in. long, furnished with a distinctly 3-ribbed green keel. Achene obovoid-triquetrous, nearly as long as the glume.

MAURITIUS, *Grey!* Rivière de Moka, *Horne!* Endemic. Glumes very like those of *C. Iria;* but habit very different.

12. **C. compressus,** *Linn.; Kunth, Enum.* iii. 23. Annual, densely tufted. Stems 3–12 in. long, triquetrous. Leaves linear, $\frac{1}{8}$ in. broad, shorter than the stems. Clusters several in a simple umbel, bracteated by 4–6 long linear leaves, the outer clusters on 1–3 in. peduncles; spikelets lanceolate, $\frac{1}{2}$–$\frac{3}{4}$ in. long, 10–30-flowered. Glumes greenish-drab or tinged with brown, ovate-navicular, acute, much imbricated, $\frac{1}{12}$ in. long, with numerous ribs on the broad green keel. Achene globose-triquetrous, bright-brown, a third as long as the glume. C. brachiatus, *Poir. Encycl.* vii. 259.

MAURITIUS and SEYCHELLES, common in damp places. Spread through the tropics of both hemispheres.

13. **C. tuberosus,** *Rottb. Gram.* 98, *t.* 7, *fig.* 1. Perennial, stoloniferous, the stems tuberous at the base, triquetrous, $\frac{1}{2}$–1 foot long. Leaves linear, as long as the stem. Clusters 6–10 in a simple umbel, subtended by 3–4 long linear leaves, the outer clusters on 1–2 in. peduncles; spikelets $\frac{1}{3}$–$\frac{1}{2}$ in. long, 15–20 flowered. Glumes bright red-brown, much imbricated, subacute, with a greenish border and narrow green keel, $\frac{1}{14}$–$\frac{1}{18}$ in. long. Achene obovoid-triquetrous, dark brown, half as long as the glume. *Kunth, Enum.* ii. 50. C. stoloniferus, *Vahl.*

MAURITIUS, in sands of the shore, near Fort George, etc. Also Tropical Asia and Tropical Africa.

14. **C. rotundus,** *Linn.; Kunth, Enum.* ii. 59. Perennial, abundantly stoloniferous, the stems tuberous at the base, triquetrous, $\frac{1}{2}$–1$\frac{1}{2}$ ft. long. Leaves linear, $\frac{1}{8}$ in. broad, shorter than the stem. Clusters 4–6 in a simple umbel, bracteated by 2–3 linear leaves, the outer clusters on 1–2 in. peduncles; spikelets $\frac{1}{2}$–1 in. long, 20–30-flowered. Glumes ovate-navicular, $\frac{1}{12}$ in. long, bright red-brown, obtuse, much imbricated, showing 5–7 distinct ribs. Stigmas much protruded from the glumes.

Achene brown, obovoid-triquetrous, a third as long as the glume. C. bicolor, *Vahl; Bojer, Hort. Maur.* 379. C. maritimus, *Bojer, Hort. Maur.* 378.

MAURITIUS, in damp places and a troublesome weed in cultivated ground. Round the world in the tropical and warm temperate zone. *Herbe à Oignon.*

15. **C. amabilis,** *Vahl; Kunth, Enum.* ii. 108. Annual, densely tufted. Stems 3–6 in. long, slender, triquetrous. Leaves linear-subulate, as long as the stem. Clusters numerous, in a slightly compound umbel bracteated by 4–6 subulate leaves, the outer clusters on 2–3 in. peduncles; spikelets 20–30-flowered, $\frac{1}{4}$–$\frac{1}{2}$ in. long. Glumes ovate-navicular, $\frac{1}{12}$ in. long, much imbricated, obtuse, bright red-brown, with a narrow 3-nerved green keel. Achene bright brown, obovoid-triquetrous, a third as long as the glume.

SEYCHELLES, common in damp place, *Horne*, 634! Through the tropics of the Old World.

16. **C. longus,** *Linn.; Kunth, Enum.* ii. 60. Perennial, with a creeping aromatic rootstock. Stems 2–3 feet long, moderately stout, triquetrous. Leaves narrow linear, shorter than the stem. Clusters numerous, arranged in a compound umbel, bracteated by 4–5 $\frac{1}{4}$–$\frac{1}{2}$ ft. linear leaves, the outer clusters on 3–4 in. peduncles; spikelets $\frac{1}{2}$–$\frac{3}{4}$ in. long, 20–30-flowered. Glumes $\frac{1}{12}$ in. long, ovate-navicular, bright red, with a distinct 5-nerved green keel, subobtuse, much imbricated. Achene oblong-triquetrous, a third as long as the glume. C. pertenius, *Bojer, Hort. Maur.* 379.

MAURITIUS, in swamps of the Trou Fanfaron, etc. Through the warmer regions of the Old World.

17. **C. distans,** *Linn.; Kunth, Enum.* ii. 93. Perennial. Stems stout, tufted, triquetrous, 2–4 feet long. Leaves $\frac{1}{4}$–$\frac{1}{2}$ in. broad, nearly as long as the stem. Clusters very numerous, arranged in a very compound umbel often a foot long, on long peduncles, bracteated by 6–12 long linear leaves; spikelets very slender, $\frac{3}{4}$–1 in. long, 10–15-flowered. Glumes oblong-navicular, $\frac{1}{12}$ in. long, obtuse, not at all imbricated, dark reddish-brown, with a 5-nerved green keel. Achene oblong-triquetrous, nearly as long as the glume. C. laxus, *Vahl, Enum.* ii. 362. C. nutans, *Sieber, Herb. Maur.* No. 34.

MAURITIUS, RODRIGUEZ, and SEYCHELLES, common in swampy places. Spread through the warmer regions of the Old World.

18. **C. difformis,** *Linn.; Kunth, Enum.* ii. 38. Annual, tufted. Stems 1–2 feet high, weak, angular at the top. Leaves narrow linear, flaccid, shorter than the stem. Involucre of 2–3 linear leaves, one

much longer than the others. Spikelets capitate in globose clusters $\frac{1}{4}$–$\frac{1}{3}$ in. broad, arranged in compound umbels, the outer on peduncles an inch or more long, each $\frac{1}{12}$–$\frac{1}{8}$ in. long, 10–20-flowered. Glumes roundish, obtuse, very small ($\frac{1}{24}$ in. long) with a 3-nerved green keel and drab border, much imbricated. Achene obovoid, nearly as long as the glume.

MAURITIUS, frequent in swamps. Spread through the warmer zones of both hemispheres.

19. **C. Iria,** *Linn.; Kunth, Enum.* ii. 38. Annual. Stems densely tufted, $\frac{1}{2}$–1 foot long, sharply triquetrous. Leaves narrow linear, as long as the stem. Spikelets copiously panicled, the panicles arranged in a compound umbel bracteated by 4–5 linear leaves, the outer umbels on 1–2 in. peduncles, each $\frac{1}{8}$–$\frac{1}{4}$ in. long, 10–15-flowered. Glumes $\frac{1}{18}$ in. long, roundish-navicular, obtuse, little imbricated, drab, with a distinctly 5-nerved green keel. Achene oblong-triquetrous, nearly as long as the glume. C. Santonici, *Rottb. Descr.* 41, *tab.* 9, *fig.* 4.

MAURITIUS, in swamps at Fort George, etc. Also Madagascar and Tropical Asia.

20. **C. æqualis,** *Vahl; Kunth, Enum.* ii. 37. Perennial. Stems densely tufted, terete, 2–3 feet long, with 2–3 large clasping brown sheaths at the lower part not produced into leaves. Involucral bracts 2–3, small, lanceolate; rays of the umbel 50–100 or more, slender, 2–4 in. long, subequal, bearing simple or slightly compound heads; spikelets $\frac{1}{4}$–$\frac{1}{2}$ in. long, 10–30 flowered. Glumes deltoid-navicular, $\frac{1}{24}$ in. long, much imbricated, obtuse. Achene ovoid-triquetrous, $\frac{1}{3}$–$\frac{1}{2}$ as long as the glume. Papyrus æqualis, *Bojer, Hort. Maur.* 581. Cyperus madagascariensis, *Kunth, Enum.* ii. 64.

MAURITIUS, by streamsides at Flacq and Pamplemousses, and at the Mare aux Vacouas. Also Madagascar, Bourbon, and Natal.

21. **C. articulatus,** *Linn.; Kunth, Enum.* ii. 53. Rhizome creeping. Stems terete, stout, 3–5 feet long, containing numerous septa visible on the outside in dried specimens, but not when fresh, the scariose basal sheaths not produced into leaves. Umbel very compound, bracteated by 2–3 small lanceolate leaves, the outer umbels on 2–3 in. peduncles; spikelets $\frac{1}{2}$–$\frac{3}{4}$ in. long, 20–30-flowered. Glumes deltoid-navicular, subobtuse, drab or tinged with brown, $\frac{1}{12}$ in. long, with a distinctly 3-nerved green keel. Achene obovoid-triquetrous, glossy, dark brown, half as long as the glume.

MAURITIUS and SEYCHELLES, common in swamps. Spread through the tropics of both hemispheres.

22. **C. pennatus,** *Lam.; Kunth, Enum.* ii. 80. Perennial. Stems 2–3 feet long, triquetrous. Leaves coriaceous, linear, ¼ in. broad, as long as the stem. General involucre of 6–8 linear leaves 1–2 feet long. Spikelets panicled, arranged in a very compound umbel, the outer peduncles 3–4 in. long, each ¼–⅜ in. long, 6–10-flowered. Glumes oblong-navicular, $\frac{1}{12}$ in. long, much imbricated, distinctly nerved all over the back, subobtuse, drab-brown. Achene castaneous, glossy, obovoid, half as long as the glume. C. canescens, *Vahl, Enum.* ii. 355.

SEYCHELLES, common in swamps, *Horne*, 219! 648! Spread through the tropics of the Old World.

23. **C. pilosus,** *Vahl; Kunth, Enum.* ii. 80. Perennial, tufted. Stems 1–2 feet long, triquetrous. Leaves ⅛ in. broad, sheathing the base of the stem for some distance, reaching a foot long. Spikelets laxly panicled, arranged in a compound umbel, bracteated by 3–4 long linear leaves, the lower peduncles 1–2 in. long; each ¼–½ in. long, 6–10-flowered. Glumes nearly $\frac{1}{12}$ in. long, deltoid-navicular, subobtuse, much imbricated, greenish-drab, with a distinct 3-nerved green keel and drab sides. Achene triquetrous, half as long as the glume. C. obliquus, *Nees; Kunth, Enum.* ii. 69.

MAURITIUS, *Bouton!* Spread through the tropics of the Old World.

24. **C. Gardneri,** *Baker.* Perennial Stem triquetrous, 1½ ft. long. Leaves narrow linear, nearly as long as the stem. Spikelets crowded into globose heads, arranged in a compound umbel, bracteated by 5–6 long linear leaves. the outer peduncles 1½–2 in. long, each ⅓–½ in. long, 30-flowered. Glumes $\frac{1}{24}$ in. long, deltoid-navicular, cuspidate, green or tinged with brown, much imbricated, many-nerved, with a distinct acute green keel. Achene oblong, glossy, nearly black, half as long as the glume.

MAURITIUS, *Gardner!* Endemic.

25. **C. longifolius,** *Poir.; Kunth, Enum.* ii. 30. Perennial, tufted. Stem 1½–2 feet long, triquetrous. Leaves 2–3 feet long, thin but firm, glossy, ½–¾ in. broad. Umbel thrice compound, 6–9 in. long and broad, bracteated by 6–9 linear leaves ½–1 foot long, the outer peduncles 3–4 in. long; spikelets solitary or few together, ¼–⅓ in. long, 8–10 flowered. Glumes deltoid-cuspidate, $\frac{1}{24}$ in. long, much imbricated, with a 5–7-ribbed distinct green keel and drab sides. Achene nearly black, oblong-triquetrous, nearly as long as the glume.

MAURITIUS, in woods of the Pouce, etc. Also Bourbon and Madagascar.

26. **C. latifolius,** *Poir.; Kunth, Enum.* ii. 75. Perennial. Stem stout, 3–4 feet long, acutely triquetrous. Leaves rigidly coriaceous, strongly keeled, 2–3 feet long, an inch or more broad. Umbel very

compound, nearly a foot long and broad, bracteated by 5–6 broad linear leaves 1–2 feet long; spikelets crowded, ½–1 in. long, 30–40-flowered. Glumes oblong-rhomboidal-navicular, $\frac{1}{12}$ in. long, brown-drab, much imbricated, obtuse, with 3–5 ribs on the back. Achene obovoid, nearly black, half as long as the glume.

MAURITIUS, in marshes through the island. Also Madagascar and the Cape. *Horne.*

2. KYLLINGA, Rottb.

Flowers hermaphrodite, usually one, sometimes two fertile in a spikelet of 4 ovate-lanceolate much imbricated distichous glumes. Hypogynous bristles 0. Style bifid, deciduous, not bulbous at the base. Achene minute, lenticular.—Perennial herbs, with short creeping rhizomes, narrow grass-like leaves and minute spikelets congested into a terminal head, bracteated as in *Cyperus* and *Mariscus* by several leaves reduced in size, but unaltered in texture. DISTRIB. Warmer zones of both hemispheres. Species about 10.

One flower in the spikelet fertile. Involucre 3–4 leaved.
  Head globose . . . . 1. K. MONOCEPHALA.
  Head with usually two accessory ones at the side . . . . 2. K. TRICEPS.
Two flowers in the spikelet fertile. Involucre 4–8 leaved . . . . 3. K. POLYPHYLLA.

1. **K. monocephala,** *Rottb.; Kunth, Enum.* ii. 129. Rhizome short-creeping. Stem ½–1 foot long, slender, triquetrous. Leaves 3–4 to a stem, $\frac{1}{12}$ in. broad, as long as the stem. Spikelets in a single globose terminal head, bracteated by 3–4 narrow linear leaves 2–4 in. long; each $\frac{1}{12}$ in. long, with only a single flower fertile. Glumes greenish-white, ovate-lanceolate, acute, 5–7-nerved, often scabrous on the edge, and distinct green keel. Achene elliptical, yellowish-brown, half as long as the fertile glume. Stamens 2, rarely 1 or 3. K. sororia, *Kunth, Enum.* ii. 131. K. cruciformis, *Schrad.; Kunth, Enum.* ii. 131 (monandrous form).

Var. K. CYLINDRICA, *Nees; Kunth, Enum.* ii. 133. Heads oblong. Spikes ½ in. long. Glumes whitish. Stamens 2.

Var. K. BREVIFOLIA, *Rottb.; Kunth, Enum.* ii. 130. A more robust variety, with broader leaves than in the type, larger spikes and stamens usually 3.

MAURITIUS, RODRIGUEZ, and SEYCHELLES, common in swampy places. Round the world in the Tropics.

2. **K. triceps,** *Rottb.; Kunth Enum.* ii. 133. Rhizome short-creeping. Stems ½–1 foot long, triquetrous. Leaves 3–5 to a stem,

shorter than the stem, thin, but firm, $\frac{1}{8}$–$\frac{1}{6}$ in. broad. Heads ternate when the plant is properly developed, one central and a smaller one at each side, $\frac{3}{8}$–$\frac{1}{2}$ inch long, bracteated by 3–4 linear leaves, 2–5 inches long; spikelets $\frac{1}{8}$ in. long. Glumes greenish-drab, 5–7-ribbed, ovate-lanceolate, acute, only one fertile, often scabrous on the keel and edge. Stamens usually 2. Achene oblong, brownish, smooth, half as long as the fertile glume. K. vaginata, *Bojer, Hort. Maur.* 381, *not Lam.* K. odorata, *Vahl; Kunth, Enum.* ii. 132.

MAURITIUS, frequent in swamps. Tropics of both hemispheres.

3. **K. polyphylla,** *Willd.; Kunth Enu.* ii. 134. Stems crowded on a short thickened rhizome, rigid, triquetrous, distinctly striated, a foot or more long. Leaves much shorter than the stem, firmer in texture and more rigid than in *K. monocephala* and *triceps*, $\frac{1}{8}$–$\frac{1}{6}$ in. broad. Heads ternate when fully developed, $\frac{3}{4}$ in. broad and long, bracteated by 4–8 reflexed or ascending firm linear leaves 2–4 inches long; spikelets $\frac{1}{8}$ in. long, usually 2-flowered. Glumes brownish-drab, ovate-lanceolate, acute, 7–9-nerved. Stamens 3. Achene dark-brown, half as long as the fertile glume. K. involucrata, *Bojer, MSS.*

MAURITIUS and SEYCHELLES, frequent in swamps. Also Madagascar, Comoros, and Tropical Africa, I cannot clearly distinguish from this *K. macrantha*, Boeckl. in Linnæa xxxv, 420, from th Seychelles.

3. MARISCUS, Vahl.

Flowers hermaphrodite, in distichous 1–2-flowered spikelets. Glumes boat-shaped much imbricated. Hypogynous bristles 0. Stamens 3. Style trifid, deciduous. Achene minute, triquetrous.—Habit of *Cyperus* § *Eucyperus*, from which it differs only by its few-flowered spikes. DISTRIB. As in *Cyperus*. Species 40.

1. **M. umbellatus,** *Vahl; Kunth, Enum.* ii. 118. Perennial, densely tufted. Stems 1–1$\frac{1}{2}$ ft. long, triquetrous. Leaves narrow linear, sometimes as long as the stem. Umbel simple, 10–15-rayed, bracteated by 8–10 linear leaves; peduncles 1–2 in. long; spikelets arranged in dense oblong clusters, $\frac{1}{4}$–$\frac{1}{3}$ in. long, 1–2- rarely 3-flowered. Glumes drab, elliptic, obtuse, with a green keel, much imbricated. Achene oblong, brown-black, $\frac{1}{3}$–$\frac{1}{2}$ the length of the glume. M. Sieberianus, *Nees in Sieber, Herb. Maur.* ii. No. 3.

MAURITIUS and SEYCHELLES, common in damp woods. Spread through the tropics of the Old World, and united by Boeckler with the American *Cyperus ovularis*, Torrey.

4. ABILGAARDIA, Vahl.

Flowers hermaphrodite, in many-flowered spikelets. Glumes imbricated in two regular rows, but the rachis twisting as the flowers mature. Hypogynous bristles 0. Stamens 1–3. Style trifid, breaking away above the thickened base. Achene triquetrous.—Perennial herbs, with stems leafy at the base only, and solitary or umbellate spikes. DISTRIB. Tropics of both hemispheres. Species 10.

1. **A. monostachya,** *Vahl*; *Kunth, Enum.* ii. 247. Perennial, densely tufted. Stems slender, $\frac{1}{2}$–1 foot long. Leaves subulate, rigid, much shorter than the stem. Spikelets solitary, terminal, ovate, $\frac{1}{4}$–$\frac{1}{2}$ in. long, 8–10-flowered. Glumes deltoid, compressed laterally, $\frac{1}{8}$ in. long, acute, coriaceous, with a green keel and whitish sides. Stamens 3 Style long, ciliated, trifid. Achene white, rugose, turbinate. Cyperus monostachyus, *Linn.*; *Rottb. Descr.* 18, *tab.* 13, *fig.* 3.

MAURITIUS, in dry soil near Port Louis and the lower part of the Pouce range. Tropics of both hemispheres.

5. ARTHROSTYLIS, R. Br.

Glumes 4–6, subdistichous, much imbricated, the two inner enclosing the single hermaphrodite flower, the rest barren. Hypogynous bristles or scales 0. Stamens 3; filaments long. Style deeply trifid, falling away and leaving its bulbous base at the top of the trigonous achene.—Densely-tufted leafless perennials, with the spikelets congested into a single terminal head. DISTRIB. Three other species, severally Ceylonese, Chinese, and Australian.

1. **A. Thouarsii,** *Kunth, Enum.* ii. 284. Perennial, densely tufted. Stems above a foot long, very slender, wiry, triquetrous, deeply sulcate. Spikelets 4–10, sessile in a single terminal head, bracteated by 2 very minute linear leaves, each lanceolate, acuminate, under $\frac{1}{4}$ in. long. Two inner glumes distichous, firm in texture, glossy, lanceolate, acuminate, with a 3-nerved green keel and pale brown sides, the outer much smaller, linear acuminate. Achene glossy, greenish, triquetrous.

MAURITIUS, *Du Petit Thouars.* Also Madagascar, *Gerrard.*

6. ASTEROCHŒTE, Nees.

Flowers 2, both hermaphrodite, in a spikelet of about half a dozen subdistichous lanceolate glumes. Hypogynous bristles about 6, ciliated, persistent. Stamens 3. Style trifid, breaking off above the base. Achene triquetrous, beaked with the persistent base of the style.—Coarse perennials, with leafy triquetrous stems, the spikelets usually crowded and arranged in ample panicles. DISTRIB. Cape and Polynesia. Species 6.

Spikelets solitary . . . . 1. A. ELONGATA.
Spikelets crowded . . . . 2. A. NITENS.

1. **A. elongata,** *Kunth, Enum.* ii. 312. A coarse erect perennial, several feet high. Leaves in a dense basal tuft, linear, coriaceous, 3 feet long, ½ in. broad, denticulate on the edge. Panicle 1½ ft. long, with many distant ascending decompound branches, the lower bracteated by linear coriaceous leaves 3–4 in. long; pedicels often as long as the spikelets, with small subulate bracts at the base; spikelets ¼ in. long, with one or two perfect flowers. Outer glumes minute, deltoid, cuspidate; fertile glume lanceolate, brown, membranous, ¼ in. long; rachis flexuose, flattened, 3-ribbed; two upper glumes smaller, empty. Achene minute, oblong-triquetrous, rostrate, surrounded by 7–8 flattened pubescent bristles, several times longer than itself. Carpha elongata, *Bœckl. in Linnæa*, xxxviii. 273.

SEYCHELLES, common in open places on the mountains of Mahé, *Horne*, 626! MAURITIUS, *Thouars*. Endemic. My description is taken entirely from the Seychelles plant.

2. **A. nitens,** *Kunth, Enum.* ii. 313. Leaves coriaceous, a foot or more long, ¼–⅙ in. broad. Stem 1½–3 feet long, slender, leafy, obsoletely trigonous. Panicle 1–1½ ft. long, with many decompound rather drooping branches, the lowest the longest, bracteated by linear leaves. Spikelets clustered, ¼ in. long, 2-flowered. Glumes 6, oblong-lanceolate, subacute, pale reddish brown. Achene under $\frac{1}{12}$ in. long, ferruginous, ellipsoid-triquetrous, strongly reticulated, surrounded by 6 longer unequal scabrous bristles. Carpha Aubertii, *Nees in Linnæa*, ix. 300.

MAURITIUS, *Du Petit Thouars*. Endemic. I have not seen specimens.

7. ISOLEPIS, R. Br.

Flowers hermaphrodite, arranged in many-flowered spikelets. Glumes multifarious. Hypogynous bristles 0. Stamens usually 3. Style trifid, not swollen at the base. Achene triquetrous.—Swamp annuals, or perennials, with the habit of *Scirpus*, from which they only differ by the want of hypogynous bristles. DISTRIB. Cosmopolitan. Species 50 or more.

Leaves none. Head of spikelets lateral . . . . 1. I. SUPINA.
Leaves subulate. Head of spikelets terminal . . . . 2. I. BARBATA.

1. **I. supina,** *R. Br.; Kunth, Enum.* ii. 196. Stems densely tufted, erect, slender, terete, ½–1 foot long, with only a basal sheath, not produced into any lamina. Spikelets 2–6, all sessile in a single lateral cluster, usually above the middle of the stem, ¼–⅓ in. long, 10–15-flowered. Glumes much imbricated, oblong-navicular, strongly mucronate, ⅛ in. long, green or tinged with brown. Stamens 3. Achene

globose-triquetrous, shining, nearly black, rugose, tipped with the persistent base of the style. Scirpus natans, *Thunb.*; *Bojer, Hort. Maur.* 383.

MAURITIUS, at the Mareaux Vacouas, etc. Spread through the tropics of the Old World.

2. **I. barbata,** *R. Br.*; *Kunth, Enum.* ii. 208. A minute annual, 3–4 inches high, with densely tufted erect stems, and abundant capillary basal leaves. Spikelets 3–6, congested into a single terminal head, bracteated by 3–4 small subulate leaves, each $\frac{1}{8}$ in. long, 6–10-flowered. Glumes much imbricated, $\frac{1}{12}$ in. long, lanceolate, acuminate, green or castaneous. Stamen 1. Nut pale, very minute, globoso-trigonous, mucronate with the persistent base of the style. Scirpus tristachya, *Bojer, Hort. Maur.* 383, *not Rottb.* (*which is a Ficinia*).

MAURITIUS, in the damp alleys of the Pamplemousses garden, etc. Spread through the tropics of the Old World.

8. FIMBRISTYLIS, Vahl.

Flowers hermaphrodite, arranged in many-flowered spikelets. Glumes multifarious, nearly all fertile. Hypogynous bristles 0. Style bifid or trifid, usually pilose. Achene lenticular, with a minute disk.—Tufted perennial herbs, with stems leafy at the base only and small brown usually numerous spikelets arranged in simple or compound umbels. Scarcely differs from *Isolepis* by any technical characters, but taking the Mauritian species alone there is an umbel of spikelets here and only a head at the end of the stem in *Isolepis*. DISTRIB. Warmer zones of both hemispheres. Species 30 or 40.

FIMBRISTYLIS PROPER. Style bifid.
Annual, with filiform leaves and 2–4 spikelets . . . 1. F. SECHELLENSIS.
Perennial, with flat leaves and many spikelets.
Glumes obtuse, $\frac{1}{12}$ in. long . . . . 2. F. GLOMERATA.
Glumes mucronate, glabrous, $\frac{1}{12}$ in. long . . . . 3. F. DIPHYLLA.
Glumes mucronate, hoary $\frac{1}{8}$ in. long . . . . . . 4. F. FERRUGINEA.
TRICHELOSTYLIS (Nees). Style trifid.
The only species . . . . 5. F. MILIACEA.

1. **F. sechellensis,** *Baker.* Annual, densely tufted. Stems 6–9 in. long, very slender, acutely angular. Leaves as long as the stem, filiform, pilose. Spikelets 2–4 in a close simple umbel, subtended by two subulate leaves, one of which much overtops it, each oblong, $\frac{1}{6}$ in. long, 10–12-flowered. Glumes $\frac{1}{12}$ in. long, scariose, greenish, oblong-lanceolate, acute. Style bifid, pilose. Achene pale, turbinate, striated.

SEYCHELLES, in dry ground, *Horne*, 635! Endemic. Habit of *Isolepis pubernla*, Kunth, Enum. ii. 213 and *Fimbristylis hispidula*, Kunth.

2. **F. glomerata,** *Nees, Cyper. Bras.* 77. Perennial, densely

tufted. Stems 6–18 in. long, erect, stiff, subterete, striated. Leaves in a dense tuft, rigid, coriaceous, narrow ligulate, obtuse, 3–6 in. long, $\frac{1}{12}$–$\frac{1}{8}$ in. broad. Spikelets numerous, arranged in a compound umbel, which is often congested into a globose head, bracteated by 2–3 short rigid leaves, each oblong, $\frac{1}{8}$ in. long. Glumes oblong, obtuse, glabrous, $\frac{1}{24}$ in. long, with a green keel, brown sides and a hyaline border. Stamens 2. Style shortly bifid, not pilose. Achene turbinate, glossy, striated, brown-black. Scirpus glomeratus, *Retz.; Bojer, Hort. Maur.* 384. F. rigida, *Kunth, Enum.* ii. 231. F. Wightiana, *Nees; Kunth, Enum.* ii. 241.

Mauritius, Rodriguez, and Seychelles, in dry places, often near the sea, common. Coin de Mire, *Horne!* Spread through the tropics of both hemispheres.

3. **F. diphylla,** *Vahl, Enum.* ii. 289. Perennial, densely tufted. Stems 1–2 feet long, slender, wiry, angular. Leaves numerous, narrow linear, glabrous, $\frac{1}{2}$–1 foot long, $\frac{1}{24}$–$\frac{1}{8}$ in. broad. Spikelets numerous, arranged in a lax compound umbel, bracteated by 4–6 very unequal short linear leaves, each oblong, $\frac{1}{8}$–$\frac{1}{4}$ in. long. Glumes ovate, $\frac{1}{12}$ in. long, glabrous, brown, scariose, obtuse, tipped with a mucro formed by the distinct green keel. Style long, bifid, pilose. Achene obovoid-lenticular, brown, glossy, striated. F. communis, *Kunth, Enum.* ii. 235. F. marginata, ovalis, and Royeniana, *Nees.* F. polymorpha, *Bæckl. in Linnæa,* xxxvi. 14. Very variable in the size of its spikelets and vestiture and size of its leaves. The following are the principal forms.

1. F. rigidula, *Nees in Wight, Cont. Bot.* 99. Umbel and spikelets of the type, but leaves short, rigid, obtuse, 2–4 in. long, like those of *F. glomerata.* F. marginata, and striata, *Labill. Fl. Nov. Cal. t.* 16.

2. F. pilosa, *Vahl; Bojer, Hort. Maur.* 383. Spikelets $\frac{1}{4}$–$\frac{1}{3}$ in. long. Leaves a foot long, $\frac{1}{8}$ in. broad, pilose. F. tomentosa, *Vahl.*

3. F. glauca, *Vahl; Kunth, Enum.* ii. 234. Leaves narrower than in the last and spikelets smaller.

Mauritius, Rodriguez, and Seychelles, common. Spread through the tropics of both hemispheres.

4. **F. ferruginea,** *Vahl; Kunth, Enum.* ii. 236. Perennial, tufted. Stems 1–2 feet long, wiry, ancipitous, glabrous, striated. Leaves much shorter than the stems, narrow linear, coriaceous, glabrous, $\frac{1}{12}$ in. broad. Umbels lax, compound, bracteated by 3–4 short linear rigid leaves; spikelets oblong, $\frac{1}{4}$–$\frac{1}{3}$ in. long. Glumes oblong, $\frac{1}{8}$ in. long, obtuse, brown, scariose, tipped with a minute mucro formed by the strong green keel and hoary with thin grey tomentum in the exposed portion. Style long, pilose, bifid. Achene obovoid-lenticular, shining, dark brown, strongly ribbed. F. arvensis, *Vahl; Kunth, Enum.* ii. 237. F. mauri-

tiana, *Tausch in Sieber, Herb. Maur.* No. 28. F. Sieberiana, *Kunth, Enum.* ii. 237.

MAURITIUS and SEYCHELLES, in swamps. Spread through the tropics of both hemispheres.

5. **F. miliacea,** *Vahl; Kunth, Enum.* ii. 230. Perennial, densely tufted. Stems $1\frac{1}{2}$–2 feet long, glabrous, acutely tetragonous. Leaves much shorter than the stem, narrow linear, glabrous, $\frac{1}{2}$–1 foot long, 1–$1\frac{1}{2}$ in. broad. Spikelets very numerous, arranged in a lax umbel bracteated by several minute subulate leaves, each ovate, obtuse, $\frac{1}{12}$ in. long. Glumes oblong, brown, with a green keel, $\frac{1}{24}$ in. long, obtuse, glabrous. Stamens 3. Style trifid, pilose. Achene very minute, obovoid, lenticular, whitish. Scirpus miliaceus, *Linn.; Rottb. Descr.* 57, *t.* 5, *fig.* 2. Scirpus tetragonus, *Poir.; Bojer, Hort. Maur.* 383. Trichelostylis miliacea and tetragona, *Nees.*

MAURITIUS and SEYCHELLES, frequent in swamps. Also Madagascar, and spread through the tropics of the Old World.

9. ELEOCHARIS, R. Br.

Flowers hermaphrodite, arranged in solitary many-flowered cylindrical or oblong spikelets. Glumes multifarious. Hypogynous bristles 3–8. Stamens usually 3. Style usually trifid. Achene usually triquetrous, crowned with the deltoid white persistent base of the style.—Swamp herbs, usually leafless, with terminal spikelets. DISTRIB. Cosmopolitan. Species about 50.

Glumes membranous.
  Style bifid. Flowers 50 or more in a spikelet . . . 1. E. CAPITATA.
  Style trifid. Flowers 8–12 in a spikelet . . . . . 2. E. CHÆTARIA.
Glumes coriaceous (*Limnocharis*, Nees).
  Stem furnished with transverse septa . . . . 3. E. PLANTAGINEA.
  Stem without transverse septa . . . . 4. E. VARIEGATA.

1. **E. capitata,** *R. Br.; Kunth, Enum.* ii. 150. Stems densely tufted, slender, angular, erect, striated, 3–12 in. long, leafless except a short basal sheath. Spikelets oblong, obtuse, $\frac{1}{8}$–$\frac{1}{4}$ in. long; flowers 50 or more. Glumes much imbricated, $\frac{1}{24}$ in. long, very obtuse, with a brown keel and scariose sides. Bristles 4–8, brown. Style bifid. Achene obovoid, smooth, glossy, castaneous, $\frac{1}{2}$ as long as the glume. Scirpus cariboeus, *Rottb. Descr.* 46, *t.* 15, *fig.* 3.

A plant of MAURITIUS, according to Kunth, but I have not seen specimens. Spread through the tropics of both hemispheres.

2. **E. chætaria,** *Rœm. and Schult.*; *Kunth, Enum.* ii. 140. Stems 3–6 in. long, very slender, densely tufted, with a leafless sheath at the base. Spikelets $\frac{1}{8}$–$\frac{1}{6}$ in. long, ovate or oblong, subacute, 8–12-flowered. Glumes oblong, $\frac{1}{12}$ in. long, scariose, obtuse or the upper subacute, with a green keel and brown scariose sides and a

hyaline edge. Bristles 6, whitish. Style trifid. Achene round-obovoid, glossy, castaneous, tipped with the white deltoid base of the style. Cyperus setaceus, *Retz*, *Obs*. v. 10. E. acicularis, *Bojer*, *Hort. Maur*. 384.

MAURITIUS, frequent in swamps and ponds. Also East Indies and Madagascar. I cannot from the description, distinguish from this *E. radicans*, Kunth, Enum. ii. 142, said to be a plant of Mauritius and Peru.

3. **E. plantaginea,** *R. Br.*; *Kunth*, *Enum*. ii. 158. Densely tufted. Stems stout, erect, terete, 2–3 feet high, $\frac{1}{8}$–$\frac{1}{4}$ in. thick, with copious transverse septa visible only when the plant is dried, with a leafless sheath at the base. Spikelets cylindrical, 1–2 in. long; flowers 50 or more. Glumes coriaceous, persistent, $\frac{1}{8}$–$\frac{1}{6}$ in. long, oblong, obtuse, emarginate, green with a brown and membranous border. Bristles 6–8, exceeding the achene. Achene subglobose, under $\frac{1}{12}$ in. long, green at first, finally brown, lenticular, ribbed. Style deeply trifid. E. interstincta, *R. Br.*; *Kunth*, *Enum*. ii. 154.

MAURITIUS and SEYCHELLES, frequent in ponds. Tropics of both hemispheres.

4. **E. variegata,** *Kunth*, *Enum*. ii. 153. Densely tufted. Stems erect, terete, $\frac{1}{8}$–$\frac{1}{4}$ in. thick, without transverse septa, with a leafless sheath at the base. Spikelets cylindrical, 1–2 in. long; flowers 30–50 in a spike. Glumes ovate-oblong, coriaceous, $\frac{1}{8}$ in. long, with a green keel, and dark brown border edged with membrane. Bristles 3–6, brown, longer than the achene. Achene subglobose, $\frac{1}{24}$ in. long, greenish at first, finally brown, strongly ribbed vertically, tipped with the persistent brown base of the 2–3-fid style. E. Sieberi, *Kunth*, *loc. cit.*

MAURITIUS, in swamps, *Sieber*, ii. 19! Also Madagascar, Tropical Asia and N. America.

10. SCIRPUS, Linn.

Flowers hermaphrodite, arranged in many-flowered spikelets. Glumes imbricated all round the rachis. Hypogynous bristles 6 or fewer, smooth or ciliated or plumose. Stamens usually 3. Style usually trifid. Achene triquetrous or plano-convex.—Perennial herbs, leafy or leafless, the spikes nearly always clustered or panicled. DISTRIB. Cosmopolitan. Species 50 or more.

I have no means of identifying *S. pungens*, *tranquebarensis*, and *Willemsti* of Bojer, Hort. Maur. 383.

1. **S. mucronatus,** *Linn.*; *Kunth*, *Enum*. ii. 161. Perennial, densely tufted. Stems 2–3 feet long, sharply triquetrous at the top, the large basal sheath not produced into any lamina. Spikelets 2–20, in a sessile lateral cluster near the top of the stem, each about $\frac{1}{2}$ in. long, 20–30-flowered. Glumes much imbricated, broad ovate, cuspidate, $\frac{1}{8}$ in. long, green or brown, ribbed all over the back. Bristles 6, longer

than the achene, armed with reflexed spines. Achene plano-convex, $\frac{1}{24}$ in. long, shining, nearly black. S. triangulatus, *Roxb.* S. javanus, *Nees*; *Kunth, Enum. loc. cit.*

MAURITIUS and SEYCHELLES, common in standing waters. Tropics of both hemispheres.

11. LIPOCARPHA, R. Br.

Flowers hermaphrodite, arranged in many-flowered spikelets. Glumes multifarious. Perianth of two navicular membranous scales. Stamens 1, rarely 2. Style 2–3-fid, articulated and falling away above the base. Achene plano-convex, enclosed in the perianth-scales.—Perennial herbs, with a tuft of narrow leaves at the base and a few small spikelets congested into a single terminal head. DISTRIB. Tropics of both hemispheres. Species 5 or 6.

1. **L. argentea,** *R. Br.*; *Kunth, Enum.* ii. 266. Perennial, densely tufted. Stems 1–2 feet long, slender, terete. Leaves 5–6, narrow linear, $\frac{1}{12}$–$\frac{1}{8}$ in. broad, much shorter than the stem, glabrous. Spikelets 4–8, ovoid, sessile or nearly so, congested into a single terminal head bracteated by 2–3 long linear-leaves, each 50–100-flowered. Glumes oblanceolate, obtuse, whitish, coriaceous, $\frac{1}{12}$ in. long. Scales of perianth lanceolate-navicular, acute, twice as long as the oblong pale brown achene. Scirpus senegalensis, *Lam. Ill.* i. 140.

MAURITIUS, in swamps of the Pouce, Pieter Both, etc. Tropics of both hemispheres.

12. FUIRENA, Rottb.

Flowers hermaphrodite, arranged in many-flowered cylindrical spikelets. Glumes inserted all round the axis, much imbricated. Hypogynous scales 3, minute, elliptic, membranous, usually alternating with 3 bristles. Stamens 3, with long filaments. Style trifid. Achene triquetrous, tipped with the persistent base of the style.—Perennial herbs, with distantly leafy stems, and many-flowered spikelets congested into heads, which are usually arranged in panicles. DISTRIB. Warmer zones of both hemispheres. Species about 10.

1. **F. umbellata,** *Rottb.*; *Kunth, Enum.* ii. 185, var. F. CAPITATA, *Willd.*; *Kunth, Enum.* ii. 186. Perennial, tufted. Stems 2–3 feet long, 5-angular, densely pilose upwards. Leaves 4–5 below the inflorescence, with pentagonal sheaths and a linear glabrous 5-nerved lamina $\frac{1}{4}$–$\frac{1}{3}$ in. broad, 3–6 inches long. Heads 6–15, arranged in a lax panicle, the upper ones crowded; spikelets 6–15 in globose heads $\frac{1}{3}$–$\frac{1}{2}$ in. broad, each $\frac{1}{6}$–$\frac{1}{4}$ long, sessile, 10–20-flowered. Glumes oblong-navicular, $\frac{1}{12}$ in. long, 3-nerved on the back, strongly ciliated at the top and tipped with a mucro as long or half as long as the glume, which

is usually ascending, but in the lower part of the spikelet sometimes spreading. Bristles 0 or very minute. Achene brown, smooth, ½ as long as the glume. F. glomerata, *Bojer, Hort. Maur.* 382, *not Lam.*

MAURITIUS, in swamps at Pamplemousses, etc. *F. mauritiana*, Nees; Kunth, Enum. iii. 186, is apparently a form without the awn to the glumes. Our specimen of Sieber, Herb. Maur. ii. No. 1, has it as usual. *F. Thouarsiana*, Kunth, iii. 186, is probably another variety in which the bristles are developed. The Indian *F. pentagona*, Wight, appears another variety of the same species, which is spread through the tropics of both hemispheres.

13. HYPOLYTRUM, Rich.

Flowers hermaphrodite, in many-flowered terete spikelets. Glumes multifarious. Perianth of 2, rarely 3, oblong-navicular membranous scales. Stamens 2–3. Style bifid, swollen at the base. Achene bony, lenticular.—Perennial herbs, with leafy stems and small brown spikelets in an ample corymbose panicle, rarely congested. DISTRIB. Tropics in both hemispheres. Species 10.

1. **H. latifolium**, *Rich.; Kunth, Enum.* ii. 271. Perennial. Stems triquetrous, 2–4 feet long. Leaves subcoriaceous, 2–3 feet long, strongly ribbed, with serrulate edges. Spikelets very numerous, arranged in a corymbose terminal panicle sometimes 6–9 inches broad, the lower branches bracteated by large and the upper by small leaves; unexpanded spikelets fusiform, ¼–⅓ in. long. Glumes much imbricated, oblong, obtuse, brown, with a scariose border. Hypogynous scales two, rarely three, oblong-navicular, at first connate. Achene ovoid-lenticular, narrowed to the point, rugose. H. nemorum, *Beauv. Flor. Owar.* ii. 13, *t.* 67. H. trinervium, *Kunth, Enum.* ii. 272. H. mauritianum, *Nees; Kunth, Enum.* ii. 272. Rhynchospora binervis, *Nees in Sieb. Herb. Maur.* ii. 51. Albikia scirpoides, *Presl in Rel. Haenk. t.* 34–35.

MAURITIUS and SEYCHELLES, in dry places on the hill-sides. Spread through the tropics of the Old World.

14. CLADIUM, P. Br.

Flowers usually one perfect and fruit-bearing and another imperfect, in a spikelet of 5–6 multifarious glumes. Hypogynous bristles or scales 0. Stamens 2–3. Style trifid, the lower part remaining as a beak to the bony triquetrous nut.—Coarse perennials, with rigid leaves, leafy stems and very abundant small spikelets arranged in ample panicles. DISTRIB. Cosmopolitan. Species 30–40.

Stems terete; leaves deeply channelled down the face.
Glumes acute, brown to the tip . . . . 1. C. MARISCUS.
Glumes with a distinct green cusp . . . . 2. C.? XIPHOLEPIS.
Stems ancipitous; leaves distichous, (*Vincentia*, Kunth).
The only species . . . . 3. C. IRIDIFOLIUM.

1. **C. Mariscus,** *R. Br.; Kunth, Enum.* ii. 303. Rootstock wide-creeping. Leaves in a dense basal tuft, 2–3 feet long, rigid, linear, acutely keeled, distinctly serrulate on the edge. Stem terete, 3–5 feet long, with many narrow linear leaves. Panicle lax, a foot or more long, the branches corymbose, the spikelets crowded at the end of the short branchlets, each ⅛–¼ in. long. Glumes 5–6, unequal, scariose, lanceolate, acute, not distinctly keeled. Stamens 2. Style long, deeply trifid. Achene oblong, castaneous, glossy, mucronate. C. occidentale, *Sieber, Herb. Maur.* 27.

MAURITIUS, on the banks of the stream at Moka, etc. Tropical and temperate zones of both hemispheres.

2. **C.? xipholepis,** *Baker*. Leaves many, in basal tufts, edged with red-brown at the base, narrow linear, ¼–⅓ in. broad, 1½–2 feet long, rigid in texture, scabrous on the edges, deeply channelled all down the face. Stem terete, 1½-2 feet long, with a few narrow linear leaves, the sheaths glossy, castaneous. Panicle lax, above a foot long, the spikelets contiguous, but not crowded, the end one distinctly peduncled, seen only in a young state. Glumes 5–6, lanceolate, acuminate, glossy, brown with a green cusp, the outer one the largest, and its cusp the longest. Achene not seen.

SEYCHELLES, *Dr. Wright!* Endemic. Requires re-examination in a more mature state.

3. **C. iridifolium,** *Baker*. Tufts of leaves and stem crowded. Basal leaves 6–8, ensiform, flat, distichous, 1½–2 feet long, ½–1 inch broad, sheathing at the base by their inner borders. Stem 2–3 feet long, compressed, furnished with a few similar leaves. Spikelets ¼ in. long, arranged in a lax panicle ½–1 ft. long, in clusters of 2–3 together at the end and sides of the slender flexuose branchlets. Glumes lanceolate, acute, brown, membranous. Achene triquetrous, with a pyramidal beak as long as itself. Scirpus iridifolius, *Bory Iter.* ii. 34, *t.* 22, 23. S. lavarum, *Poir. Encycl.* vi. 738. Machærina anceps and lavarum, *Bojer, Hort. Maur.* 385. Vincentia latifolia, *Kunth, Enum.* ii. 314.

MAURITIUS, in swamps both of the hills and plains. Also Bourbon. *Machærina restioides*, Vahl, to which this has been referred, is a West Indian plant of similar habit, but with a perianth of bristles.

15. RHYNCHOSPORA, Vahl.

Flowers usually one hermaphrodite, and one above it with stamens only, in a spikelet of 5–6 multifarious unequal glumes. Hypogynous bristles about 6, persistent. Stamens usually 3. Style bifid, the lower part remaining as a persistent beak to the lenticular achene. —Perennials, with the stems mostly more or less leafy, with varied inflorescence. DISTRIB. Cosmopolitan. Species 50.

Spikelets in a single globose terminal head . . . . . . 1. R. HÆNKEI.
Spikelets in 2–8 globose heads . . . . 2. R. POLYCEPHALA.
Spikelets in corymbose panicles.
Dwarf, with narrow leaves . . . . 3. R. LAXA.
Tall, with broad leaves . . . . 4. R. AUREA.

1. **R. Hænkei,** *Presl.; Kunth, Enum.* ii. 290. Perennial. Stem slender, terete, 1–2 ft. long, leafless. Leaves in a dense basal tuft, narrow linear, $\frac{1}{12}$–$\frac{1}{8}$ in. broad, rigid, much shorter than the stem. Spikelets under $\frac{1}{4}$ in. long, 50 or more in a single globose terminal head bracteated by 3–4 rigid linear leaves. Glumes rigid, glossy, pale brown, acute. Bristles shorter than the achene. Achene obovoid, glossy, brown, the beak reduced to a minute mucro. R. Wallichiana, *Kunth, Enum.* ii. 289. Morisia Wallichii and capitata, *Nees.*

MAURITIUS, teste *Kunth.* Spread through the tropics of the Old World.

2. **R. polycephala,** *Wydl.; Kunth Enum.* ii. 291. Perennial, tufted. Stems triquetrous upwards, 2–3 feet long, sparingly leafy. Leaves shorter than the stems, narrow linear, convolute. Spikelets 30–50, $\frac{1}{8}$–$\frac{1}{6}$ in. long, arranged in a globose head; heads 2–8, one terminal and the rest peduncled, often 3–4 in an end umbel. Glumes pale brown, acute, the outer ovate, the inner lanceolate. Bristles longer than the achene. Achene pale brown, obovoid-lenticular; beak as long as the achene, subulate, with a broad base. R. sparganioides, *Bojer, Hort. Maur.* 386. Schœnus triceps, *Vahl, Ecl.* ii. 4.

MAURITIUS, in marshes of Grandport, Savanne, etc. Also Cape, Madagascar, Bourbon, and Tropical America.

3. **R. laxa,** *R. Br.; Kunth, Enum.* ii. 298. A tufted perennial, with slender wiry subterete sparingly leafy stems 1–2 feet long. Leaves $\frac{1}{12}$ in. broad, firm in texture, nearly or quite as long as the stem. Spikelets $\frac{1}{8}$ in. long, congested in small heads, which are arranged in simple or distantly-panicled corymbs. Glumes dark brown, moderately firm, lanceolate, acute. Bristles longer than both achene and beak. Achene subglobose, brown; beak minute. R. Brownei, gracilis, sinensis, and Thouarsii, *Nees.* R. lavarum, *Gaudich.*

MAURITIUS, in hill swamps. Spread through the tropics of the Old World.

4. **R. aurea,** *Vahl; Kunth, Enum.* ii. 293. Radical leaves ensiform, acuminate, 2–3 feet long, an inch broad at the base, flat, scabrous on the edge and acute keel. Stem stout, triquetrous, distantly leafy, 3–4

feet long. Spikelets $\frac{1}{4}$ in. long, a few together in a lax head, the heads arranged in an ample panicle with distant corymbose divisions. Glumes pale brown, the inner lanceolate, acute. Bristles longer than the achene. Achene globose, brown, with a hard narrow-conical beak longer than itself. Scirpus corymbosus, *Linn. Sp. Plant.* i. 76. Schœnus surinamensis. *Rottb. Descr.* 68, *t.* 21, *fig.* 1.

MAURITIUS, in swamps at the source of the Moka river at the base of Pieter-Both, etc. Spread through the tropics of both hemispheres.

16. SCLERIA, Linn.

Spikelets monoicous, male and female mixed in the same cluster. Glumes multifarious, one flower-bearing in the female spikelet in our plant, and two or three in the male. Hypogynous bristles 0. Stamens 3. Style trifid. Achene glossy, globose, seated on a distinct disk. — Perennials, with leafy stems, the inflorescence variously arranged, DISTRIB. Warmer zones of both hemispheres. Species 50 or more.

1. **S. Sieberi,** *Nees; Kunth, Enum.* ii. 345. Stems sharply triquetrous, 3–6 feet long, copiously leafy. Leaves reedy, a foot or more long, $\frac{1}{2}$–$\frac{3}{4}$ in. broad, with three strong ribs. Inflorescence an ample terminal rhomboid panicle and smaller ones peduncled from the axils of large leaves for some distance down the stem. Male spikelets copious, oblong, $\frac{1}{8}$ in. long, the glumes pale brown, the inner ones lanceolate. Female spikelets sessile in the axils of the branchlets, with only small deltoid glumes, from which the achene protrudes. Achene glossy, ovoid, $\frac{1}{12}$ in. long, minutely cuspidate, usually white, sometimes brown, girt at the base by the lacerated scales of the narrow disk. S. racemosa, *Bojer, Hort. Maur.* 385, *not Poir.*

MAURITIUS and SEYCHELLES, common in mountain bogs. Endemic.

17. CAREX, Linn.

Flowers all unisexual, usually monoicous, arranged in many-flowered spikelets. Glumes multifarious. Hypogynous bristles 0. Stamens usually 3. Achene triquetrous or lenticular, enclosed in a sac (perigyne) with a bidentate beak, from which the 2–3 stigmas are protruded.—Perennial herbs, with triquetrous leafy stems, the spikes remote or aggregated in bisexual heads. DISTRIB. Mainly in the Arctic-alpine and temperate zones. Species about 1000. The second or third largest of known genera.

Spikelets many, sessile, forming lax panicles.
  Side spikelets erecto-patent . . . . 1. C. WAHLENBERGIANA.
  Side spikelets spreading . . . . 2. C. RAMOSA.
Spikelets few, long, cylindrical.
  Spikelets small, with stiffly erect peduncles. Stigmas 2, 3. C. BRUNNEA.
  Spikelets larger, cernuous. Stigmas 3.
    Spikelets few, towards the top of the stem . . 4. C. BORBONICA.
    Spikelets many, laxly disposed . . . . 5. C. BORYANA.

1. **C. Wahlenbergiana,** *Boott, Ill. Gen. Car.* ii. 101, *t.* 301–5. Stems slender, triquetrous, 2–4 feet long, bearing usually two leaves below the inflorescence. Leaves 1–3 feet long, scabrous, flaccid, $\frac{1}{8}$–$\frac{3}{8}$ in. broad. Panicles lax, rhomboid, 2–3 in. long, the side ones distinctly peduncled and bracteated by long leaves; spikelets sessile, cylindrical, about $\frac{1}{2}$ inch long, crowded, all male at the top and female below, the side ones ascending. Female glumes $\frac{1}{8}$–$\frac{1}{6}$ in. long, ovate with a distinct cusp, all green, or brown with a green keel. Perigyne green, narrow, elliptical, strongly ribbed, with a distinctly bifid beak, both together as long as the glume. Stigmas 3. C. indica. *Schk. Car. fig.* 206; *Kunth, Enum.* ii. 509, in part; *Bojer, Hort. Maur.* 387, *not Linn.*

Mauritius, frequent in woods, ascending to the top of the Pouce. Also Bourbon, Madagascar, Natal, and Tropical Africa.

2. **C. ramosa,** *Schk. Car. tab.* 204. Stems about 2 feet long, slender, triquetrous, with 2–3 leaves below the inflorescence. Leaves $\frac{1}{8}$–$\frac{1}{4}$ in. broad. Panicles lax, deltoid, 1–3 in. long, the side ones distinctly peduncled and bracteated by long leaves; spikelets about $\frac{1}{2}$ in. long, all sessile, male at the top, female below, the side ones spreading from the rachis at a right angle. Female glumes ovate, acute, pale brown, $\frac{1}{8}$ in. long. Perigyne curved, narrow elliptical, rostrate, with a bifid beak $\frac{1}{12}$ in. long, which is protruded beyond the glume. Stigmas 3. *Kunth, Enum.* ii. 507; *Boott, Ill. Gen. Car.* iii. 106, *tab.* 322.

Mauritius, in woods, *Bojer!* Also East Indies.

3. **C. brunnea,** *Thunb. Fl. Jap.* 58. Densely tufted. Stems slender, triquetrous, 1–2 feet long, with a single leaf below the inflorescence. Leaves about a foot long, firm, very narrow, rigid, striated. Spikelets 6–20 on the upper $\frac{1}{4}$–$\frac{1}{2}$ foot of the stem, all stiff, erect, $\frac{1}{2}$–1 in. long, the uppermost often all male, the rest male at the tip and female below, the peduncles all simple, or the lowest compound. Female glumes $\frac{1}{12}$–$\frac{1}{8}$ in. long, ovate, acute, with brown sides and green keel, with several distinct ribs, and green edge. Perigyne elliptical-lenticular, with a short bifid beak and many distinct ribs. Stigmas 2. C. gracilis, *R. Br.*; *Kunth, Enum.* ii. 513. *Boott, Ill. Gen. Car.* i. 59, *t.* 154–156. C. Commersoniana, *Kunth, Enum.* ii. 391. C. lenta, *D. Don*; *Kunth, Enum.* ii. 418. C. lachnosperma, *Wall.*; *Kunth, Enum.* ii. 505, *in part.*

Mauritius and Rodriguez, in woods. Also Tropical Asia and Australia.

4. **C. borbonica,** *Lam.*; *Kunth, Enum.* ii. 522. Stems triquetrous, slender, 1–$1\frac{1}{2}$ foot long, with usually two leaves below the inflorescence. Basal leaves firm, $\frac{1}{8}$–$\frac{1}{4}$ in. broad, shorter than the stem. Spikelets about 4, cylindrical, 1–2 in. long, crowded near the top of the stem, the end one all male, the others cernuous on short peduncles, all female, or male at the very tip. Female glumes nearly $\frac{1}{4}$ in. long, ovate-lanceolate, with a long cusp, brown on the sides, green and 3-ribbed on the keel. Perigyne elliptic, scabrous, with a distinctly bifid

beak $\frac{1}{3}$–$\frac{1}{4}$ as long as the body of the perigyne, both together as long as the glume. Stigmas 3. *Boott, Ill. Gen. Carex*, iii. 109, *tab*. 338–340.

MAURITIUS, in dense forests of the Rivière Noire and Grand Bassin, *Bojer*. Also Bourbon, *Boivin !* I have not seen Mauritian specimens.

5. **C. Boryana,** *Schk. Car. fig*. 121. Stems 3–4 feet long, triquetrous, with 2–3 leaves below the inflorescence. Leaves as long as the stem, stiff, scabrous, $\frac{1}{4}$–$\frac{1}{2}$ in. broad. Spikelets 6–10 on the upper half foot of the stem, cylindrical, 1–4 in. long, the upper 2–3 all male, the rest all female or male at the very tip only, cernuous, distinctly peduncled. Female glumes $\frac{1}{6}$ in. long, ovate-lanceolate, cuspidate, with brown black sides and a distinct 1-nerved green keel. Perigyne elliptical, as long as the glume, with a protruded deeply bifid beak $\frac{1}{12}$ in. long. Stigmas 3. *Kunth, Enum*. ii. 506 ; *Boott, Ill. Gen. Car*. iii. 110, *tab*. 345–9.

MAURITIUS, in the damp woods and meadows of the Pouce and Quartier Militaire, *Bojer*. Also Bourbon and Tropical Africa.

ORDER CVII. GRAMINEÆ.

Flowers usually some hermaphrodite, often accompanied by others more or less imperfect sexually, each placed in the axis of a membranous bract (pale), which with the flower is enclosed in another boat-shaped bract of firmer texture (flowering glume). Flowers one or more in a spikelet, which has a pair of similar bracts (empty glumes) at the base. Perianth of two or more minute hypogynous scales, which are sometimes absent. Stamens hypogynous, usually 3; filaments long, thread-like ; anthers pendulous. Ovary 1-celled; ovule 1, basal, anatropous; styles 2, long or short; stigmas feathery or hairy. Fruit a caryopsis (grain), free or sometimes adhering to one or both of its enfolding bracts. Seed adnate to the pericarp, containing abundant floury albumen, with the embryo on one side at the base.—Herbs, rarely shrubs, with distinctly-jointed hollow stems, narrow leaves with open sheaths split to the base, and panicled racemose or spicate inflorescence. DISTRIB. One of the most cosmopolitan of orders. Species 4000–5000.

Series I. **Clisantheæ.** Spikelets closed in flower. Styles elongated. Stigmas protruded at the top of the flower.

Tribe I. OLYREÆ. All the flowers unisexual.

The only genus . . . . 1. COIX.

Tribe II. PANICEÆ. Empty glumes smaller than the coriaceous flowering glume. Flowers 2 in a spikelet, the lower imperfect.

Involucre 0.
 Outer empty glume not developed . . . . 2. PASPALUM.
 Empty glumes both present.
  Rachis not hollowed out against the spikelets . . . 3. PANICUM.
  Rachis hollowed out against the spikelets . . . . 4. STENOTAPHRUM.

Spikelets one or more subtended by an involucre of bristles or scales.
  Hypogynous scales 0 or very minute.
    Involucre of united lanceolate scales . . . . 5. CENCHRUS.
    Involucre of plumose bristles . . . . 6. PENNISETUM.
  Hypogynous scales distinct.
    Involucre falling with the spikelet . . . . 7. GYMNOTHRIX.
    Involucre not falling with the spikelet . . . . . . 8. SETARIA.

Tribe III. ANDROPOGONEÆ. Empty glumes firm in texture and enclosing the membranous flowering glume and pale. Flowers usually 2 in the most complete spikelets, the lower imperfect.

Inner empty glume abortive . . . . 9. ZOYSIA.
Both the empty glumes present.
  Flowers in pairs, both perfect . . . . * SACCHARUM.
  Flowers in pairs, the pale of the imperfect one absent.
    Grain small . . . . 10. ANDROPOGON.
    Grain comparatively large . . . . * SORGHUM.
  Flowers in pairs, the pale of the imperfect one present . 11. ISCHÆMUM.
  Flowers many in a cluster, only one perfect . . . . . 12. ANTHISTIRIA.

Series II. Euryantheæ. Spikelets open in flower. Styles short Rudimentary flowers, if present, placed usually above the perfect ones.

Tribe IV. ORYZEÆ. Empty glumes absent. Spikelets 1-flowered, panicled.

The only genus . . . . 13. LEERSIA.

Empty glumes 2. (Tribes v–ix).

Tribe V. AGROSTIDEÆ. Spikelets 1-flowered, panicled.

Awn 0 . . . . 14. VILFA.
Awn simple, dorsal . . . . 15. AGROSTIS.
Awn trifid, terminal . . . . 16. ARISTIDA.

Tribe VI. CHLORIDEÆ. Spikelets 2- or many-flowered, arranged in secund simple or digitate spikes.

Glumes all without awns.
  Obvious flower one only, the other represented by a pedicel . . . . 17. CYNODON.
  Obvious flowers several . . . . 18. ELEUSINE.
Some of the glumes awned.
  Spikes solitary . . . . 19. CTENIUM.
  Spikes two or more.
    Spikelets very dense, spreading . . . . 20. DACTYLOCTENIUM.
    Spikelets less dense, erecto-patent . . . . . . 21. CHLORIS.

Tribe VII. FESTUCEÆ. Spikelets many-flowered, panicled. Herbs.

Flowers placed in a tuft of hair . . . . 22. PHRAGMITES.
Flowers not placed in a tuft of hair.
  Grain free from the pale.
    Flowers webbed . . . . * POA.
    Flowers not webbed . . . . 23. ERAGROSTIS.
  Grain adhering to the pale . . . . * BRIZA.

Tribe VIII. Bambuseæ. Spikelets many-flowered, panicled. Arborescent.

Fruit a small dry grain . . . . * Bambusa.
Fruit often fleshy, comparatively large.
  Flowering glume spiny-tipped . . . . * Dendrocalamus.
  Flowering glume not spine-tipped . . . . * Melanocanna.

Tribe Rottbœllieæ. Spikelets placed in the hollows of a simple jointed rachis.

The only genus . . . . 24. Rottbœllia.

1. COIX, Linn.

Spikelets monoicous, 1–2 females at the bottom of each branch of the panicle, enclosed in a hard bottle-shaped glossy white involucre, from which the long stigmas protrude; upper spikelets many, male, 2-flowered. Empty glumes large, muticous, the outer one winged at the edge. Flowering glume and pale membranous, enclosed within the empty glumes, lanceolate, acute. Hypogynous scales 2, fleshy. Stamens 3.—A single species, cosmopolitan in the tropics.

1. **C. Lachryma,** *Linn.*; *Kunth, Enum.* i. 20. Erect, glabrous in all its parts. Stems stout, terete, much-branched, 3–5 feet long. Leaves a foot long, lanceolate, firm in texture, with a distinct midrib. Panicles lax, leafy to the top, with many erecto-patent, simple branches, which break away after flowering above the female spikelets. Male spikelets imbricating, erecto-patent, ¼–⅓ in. long. *Bot. Mag. t.* 2479.

Mauritius, Rodriguez, and Seychelles, frequent by roadsides, etc., ascending nearly to the summit of the Pouce. Spread through the tropics of both hemispheres. *Larmes de Job.*

2. PASPALUM, Linn.

Outer empty glume present, the inner abortive. Spikelets 2-flowered, the lower flower neuter, minute, the upper one hermaphrodite. Flowering glume flattish, clasping the narrower pale by its edges, both muticous. Hypogynous scales glabrous, entire, truncate. Stamens 3. Stigmas protruded from the top of the flower. Grain oblong or round, plano-convex.—Stems leafy; spikelets arranged in two rows in spikes with a more or less decidedly flattened rachis; pedicels very short, articulated at the tip. Distrib. Tropics of both hemispheres, especially the New World. Species 200.

Nodes of the stem usually one or two . . . . 1. P. platycaule.
Nodes of stem three or more.
  Spike solitary . . . . 2. P. heteropodium.
  Spikes two or more.
    Spikelets acute.
      Spikelets $\frac{1}{12}$ in. long . . . . 3. P. longiflorum.
      Spikelets ⅛ in. long . . . . 4. P. distichum.
    Spikelets obtuse . . . . 5. P. scrobiculatum.

1. **P. platycaule,** *Poir.*; *Kunth, Enum.* i. 48. Stems tufted, 1–1½ foot long, flattened, with 1–2 densely pubescent nodes. Sheaths flattened, ⅛–⅙ in. broad, glabrous, 4–6 in. long; lamina, in our plant, pilose, obtuse, 2–3 in. long, ¼–⅜ in. broad. Spikes 2–3, with a very narrow glabrous rachis, erect or erecto-patent, if more than two alternate, on a wiry naked peduncle emerging 2–3 inches from the top sheath, 2–3 in. long; spikelets laxly disposed, $\frac{1}{12}$ in. long, oblong, glabrous, acute, on very short ascending pedicels. *Trin. Ic. t.* 118. P. platyculmum, *Thouars*; *Kunth, Enum.* i. 49. P. compressum and complanatum, *Nees.* P. macropodium, *Steud.*

MAURITIUS, in fields through the island. Common in Tropical America. Also Guinea.

2. **P. heteropodium,** *Steud. Gram.* 19. Stems slender, terete, densely tufted, 1½–2 feet high, with several glabrous nodes. Sheaths glabrous, 1½–2 in. long, with a tuft of hairs at the throat; lamina glabrous, lanceolate, acuminate, 3–4 in. long, ⅜–½ in. broad. Spikes always solitary at the end of the branches on long slender erect peduncles, ½–2 in. long, with a narrow zigzag glabrous rachis; spikelets erecto-patent, oblong, glabrous, obtuse, $\frac{1}{16}$ in. long; pedicel half as long as the spikelet. P. capillare, *Bojer, Hort. Maur.* 362, *not Lam.* P. Boivini, *Steud. Gram.* 416. P. supinum, *Sieber.*

MAURITIUS, near Moka, etc., *Bojer! Sieber,* ii. 29! *Boivin! Ayres!* etc. Endemic.

3. **P. longiflorum,** *Retz. Obs.* iv. 15, *not Trin.* Stems very slender, ½–1 foot high, from a wide-creeping rhizome; nodes many pilose; uppermost sheath 1–2 in. long; lamina ½–2 in. long, glabrous, linear or lanceolate, acute. Spikes 2–3 on a very slender erect wiry peduncle, sometimes sheathed to the top, 1–1½ in. long, with a very narrow glabrous rachis; spikelets imbricated, oblong, acute, glabrous, $\frac{1}{14}$ in. long, with a very short pedicel. P. brevifolium, *Flugge; Kunth Enum.* i. 48. P. pseudo-duroa, *Nees.*

MAURITIUS, in hilly fields through the island. Also Comoros, Natal, Tropical Asia and Africa.

4. **P. distichum,** *Burm.*; *Kunth, Enum.* i. 52. Rhizome wide-creeping and sending out roots from the nodes. Stem ½–1 foot long, terete, often decumbent, with numerous nodes. Leaves a dozen or more to a stem, glabrous, narrow-linear, often folded together, 1–3 in. long, the sheaths much imbricating. Spikes 2, rarely 3, at the end of a peduncle sometimes not exserted from the upper sheath, 1–2 in. long, erecto-patent, with a glabrous rachis under $\frac{1}{12}$ in. broad; spikelets imbricating, ⅛ in. long, oblong, glossy, glabrous, acute, on very short pedicels. P. vaginatum, *Sw.*; *Bojer, Hort. Maur.* 362; *Trin. Ic. t.* 120. P. littorale, *R. Br.*; *Trin. Ic. t.* 112.

MAURITIUS, in swamps, especially round the coast. Spread through the warmer regions of both hemispheres.

P. Michauxianum, Kunth, (P. Digitaria, *Poir.*), said by Kunth to be a Mauritian species, is very near this, but differs by its taller and more erect habit, broader leaves and larger spikelets.

5. **P. scrobiculatum,** *Linn.; Kunth, Enum.* i. 53. Stems tufted, 2–3 feet long, with 3–4 glabrous black nodes. Sheaths terete, nearly as long as the internodes, pilose at the throat; central leaves half a foot long, acute, $\frac{1}{4}$–$\frac{1}{3}$ in. broad, glabrous. Spikes usually about 3, but varying from 1 to 9, ascending, 1–4 in. long, with a keeled channelled rachis $\frac{1}{12}$–$\frac{1}{8}$ in. broad; spikelets imbricated, glabrous, on very short pedicels, broad-oblong, obtuse, $\frac{1}{12}$ in. long, arranged in two regular rows. *Trin. Ic. t.* 143. P. Commersoni, *Lam.* P. Kora, *Willd.* P. mauritanicum, *Nees.*

MAURITIUS, RODRIGUEZ, and SEYCHELLES, frequent in inundated places. *P. firmum,* Trin. Ic. t. 125 (figured from a Mauritian specimen) and *P. longifolium,* Trin. Ic. t. 138, are luxuriant forms with several long spikes. Spread through the tropics of the Old World. *Herbe à épée.*

3. PANICUM, Linn.

Empty glumes 2, unequal, muticous. Spikelets 2-flowered, the top flower hermaphrodite and seed-bearing, the lower one minute, staminate or entirely abortive. Flowering glume coriaceous, nearly flat on the back, clasping the pale, which is similar in texture but narrower, muticous or in one group awned. Hypogynous scales 2, fleshy, truncate. Stamens 3. Stigmas protruded from the top of the closed glumes. Grain plano-convex, clasped tightly and permanently by its glumes.—Annuals or perennials, with leafy stems and varied inflorescence. DISTRIB. All tropical and warm temperate regions. Much the largest genus of grasses, the species 500 or more

Subgenus PANICUM PROPER. None of the glumes distinctly awned.

Spikelets in a single congested spike . . . . 1. P. CONGLOMERATUM.
Spikelets secund, nearly sessile on the simple flattened branches of the panicle.
  Panicle narrow.
    Spikelets glabrous.
      Leaves rather obtuse . . . . 2. P. BRIZOIDES.
      Leaves acuminate . . . . 3. P. FLUITANS.
    Spikelets pilose . . . . 4. P. ERUCIFORME.
  Panicle rhomboid.
    Spikelets $\frac{1}{8}$ in. long.
      Spikelets glabrous . . . . 5. P. AMBIGUUM.
      Spikelets pilose . . . . 6. P. JAVANICUM.
    Spikelets $\frac{1}{12}$ in. long . . . . 7. P. PETIVERII.
    Spikelets $\frac{1}{24}$ in. long . . . . 7. P. PROSTRATUM.
  Panicle more or less digitate.
    Spikelets 2–3 . . . . 8. P. DIDACTYLUM.
    Spikelets 5–9 . . . . 9. P. SANGUINALE.
Branches of panicle distinctly compound.
  Spikelets large, $\frac{1}{12}$ in. or more long.
    Nodes of stem with a dense tuft of hairs . . . * P. MOLLE.
    Nodes of stem glabrous . . . . * P. MAXIMUM.
  Spikelets small, obtuse.

Pedicels short . . . . 10. P. MULTINODE.
Pedicels reaching 1/6–1/4 in. long . . . . 11. P. BIFLORUM.
Spikelets small, acute.
Tall, with large broad leaves.
Leaves plicate, narrowed to base . . . . 12. P. PLICATUM.
Leaves flat, rounded at base . . . . * P. ACARIFERUM.
Middle sized, with linear leaves.
Pedicels very short . . . . 13. P. AURITUM.
Pedicels longer than the spikelets . . . . . . 14. P. MADAGASCARIENSE.
Dwarf, procumbent, with small spreading lanceolate leaves . . . . 15. P. PARVIFOLIUM.

Subgenus OPLISMENUS. Some of the glumes distinctly awned.

Awns only on the glume of the lower barren flower and sometimes not developed (*Echinochloa*).
Spikelets 1/12 in. long . . . . 16. P. COLONUM.
Spikelets 1/8 in. long . . . . * P. CRUS-GALLI.
Awns always distinct on the empty glumes (*Orthopogon*).
Spikes simple . . . . 17. P. BALFOURII.
Spikes panicled.
Spikes dense, 1/4 in long . . . . 18. P. BURMANNI.
Spikes lax, 1–2 in. iong . . . . 19. P. COMPOSITUM.
Spikes lax, 1/2 foot long . . . . 20. P. BENTHAMI.

1. **P. conglomeratum,** *Bojer, Hort. Maur.* 364, *vix Linn.* Annual, forming a dense intertangled mass half a foot broad. Stems 1–1½ in. long, with 3–4 nodes. Sheaths 1/8–1/6 in. long, finely pilose; blade linear, acute, glabrous, 1/2–3/4 in. long. Spikelets 6–8 in a congested equilateral deltoid spike under 1/4 in. long, each ovate, acute, finely pubescent, 1/24 in. long; pedicels not more than half as long as the spikelets.

MAURITIUS, a weed in the streets of Port Louis, etc. I have failed to identify this with any extra-Mauritian species.

2. **P. brizoides,** *Linn.; Kunth, Enum.* i. 79. Annual, tufted, glabrous throughout. Stems 1–2 feet long, with 4–5 nodes and leaves. Sheaths compressed, the upper ones 2–3 in. long; blade 3–6 in. long, linear, obtuse. Panicle half a foot long, with 6–10 alternate dense spikes 1/2 in. long erect and adpressed to the rachis; spikelets secund, biserial on a narrow flattened naked rachis, glossy, greenish-white, oblong, subacute. *Jacq. Eclog. Gram.* i. *t.* 2; *Trin. Ic. t.* 158—9. P. flavidum, *Retz.; Bojer, Hort. Maur.* 364. P. granulare, *Lam. not Bojer.*

MAURITIUS, RODRIGUEZ, and SEYCHELLES, common in waste places and fields. Spread through the tropics of both hemispheres. *Herbe de Riz petite espèce.*

3. **P. fluitans,** *Retz.; Kunth, Enum.* i. 78. Tufted, perennial. glabrous in all its parts. Stems 2–5 feet long, geniculate and rooting at the lower nodes. Upper sheaths half a foot long; blade linear, 1/2–1 ft. long, acute. Panicle 1/3–1/2 ft. long, with 10–15 erect spikes 1/2–1 in. long; spikelets just like those of *P. brizoides.* P.

granulare, *Bojer*, *Hort. Maur.* 364, *not Lam.* P. truncatum, *Trin. Ic. t.* 168. P. paspaloides, *Pers.*; *Kunth*, *Enum.* i. 77.; *Webb*, *Phyt. Can. t.* 245. P. affine, *Nees*. P. brizæforme, *Presl*; *Kunth*, *Enum.* i. 78. Digitaria appressa, *Pers. not Bojer*.

MAURITIUS and RODRIGUEZ, abundant in swamps. Tropics of both hemispheres. *Herbe de Riz.*

4. **P. eruciforme,** *Sibth. and Sm. Fl. Græc. t.* 59. Stems trailing at the base, tufted, much branched, pilose, 1–1½ ft. long; nodes numerous, hairy. Sheaths 1–2 in. long, pilose; blade linear, acuminate, pilose, 1–2 in. long. Panicle 2–3 in. long, with 6–8 erect spikes ½ in. long adpressed to the main rachis; spikelets secund, biserial, much imbricated, oblong, acute, densely pilose, $\frac{1}{12}$ in. long. *Kunth*, *Enum.* i. 78. P. caucasicum, *Trin. Ic. t.* 268. Echinochloa eruciformis, *Reich.* Panicum Wightii, *Nees*.

MAURITIUS, in waste ground, *Bojer! Bouton!* Spread through the warmer regions of the Old World.

5. **P. ambiguum,** *Trin.*; *Steud. Gram.* 61. Much branched, glabrous in all its parts. Stems 1½–2 feet long, slender, terete, with 4–6 naked nodes. Upper sheaths 3–4 in. long; blade linear, acuminate, 4–6 in. long, $\frac{1}{8}$–$\frac{1}{6}$ in. broad. Panicle rhomboid, 2–3 in. long, with 1–4 ascending branches 1–2 in. long; rachis narrow, flexuose, naked; spikelets secund, $\frac{1}{8}$ in. long, oblong, acute, laxly disposed. Urochloa paspaloides, *Presl*; *Kunth*, *Enum.* i. 75. Digitaria adpressa, *Bojer*, *Hort. Maur.* 363, *not Pers.*

MAURITIUS, in waste ground near Pamplemousses, etc. Also Tropical Asia. Closely allied to *P. numidianum*, Trin. Ic. t. 174.

6. **P. javanicum,** *Poir. Encycl. Suppl.* iv. 274. Stems tufted, much-branched, geniculate at the base, 1–3 feet long, clothed with fine soft spreading hairs; nodes many, densely pilose. Sheaths 2–3 in. long; blade lanceolate, acuminate, pilose, cordate at the base, 3–4 in. long, $\frac{1}{3}$–$\frac{1}{2}$ in. broad. Panicle rhomboid, 2–4 in. long, with 3–10 erecto-patent branches 1–2 in. long; rachis of spikes flattened, flexuose, usually beset with a few long fine hairs like those of the stem, sometimes naked; spikelets oblong, acute, imbricated, pilose, nearly $\frac{1}{8}$ in. long. Urochloa panicoides, *Beauv. Agrost.* 52, *t.* 11, *fig.* 1; *Kunth*, *Enum.* i. 74. U. pubescens, *Kunth*, *loc. cit.* U. mauritiana, *Bojer*, *Hort. Maur.* 363. Panicum hirsutum, *Kœnig in Roxb. Fl. Ind.* i. 303. P. Helopus, *Trin. Ic.* ii. 148, *t.* 123. P. trichopus, *Hochst.*

MAURITIUS, common in marshes and cultivated ground. Spread through the tropics of the Old World. *Herbe à Cornets.*

7. **P. Petiverii,** *Trin. Ic. t.* 176; *Kunth*, *Enum.* i. 91. Annual, densely tufted, nearly glabrous. Stems a foot or more long, ascending, with 6–8 glabrous nodes. Upper sheaths 1½–2 in. long; blade lanceo-

late, acuminate, 2–3 in. long, $\frac{1}{4}$–$\frac{1}{2}$ in. broad. Panicle rhomboid, 2–3 in. long, with several erecto-patent branches on each side, the lower 1–1$\frac{1}{2}$ in. long; spikelets sessile or shortly pedicelled, equilateral, oblong, acute, $\frac{1}{12}$ in. long, finely hairy. P. pygmæum, *Bojer, Hort. Maur.* 365. P. patens, *Bojer, loc. cit.*

MAURITIUS, in the low country round St. Louis. Spread through the tropics of the Old World.

7. **P. prostratum,** *Lam.; Kunth, Enum.* i. 89. Annual. Stems slender, tufted, much-branched, procumbent, $\frac{1}{2}$–1 ft. long; nodes numerous, glabrous or pilose. Sheaths $\frac{1}{2}$–1 in. long, pilose at the throat; blade spreading, lanceolate, acute, cordate at the base, 1–2 in. long, glabrous or finely pilose. Panicle rhomboid, 1–2 in. long, with 6–12 erecto-patent branches, the lower ones 1–2 in. long; rachis of spikes flattened, naked or beset with a few long white bristly hairs; spikelets secund, irregularly imbricated, oblong, acute, $\frac{1}{24}$ in. long. *Trin. Ic. t.* 184–5. P. setigerum, *Retz.; Kunth, Enum.* i. 90; *Bojer, Hort. Maur.* 364. P. umbrosum, *Retz.; Kunth, Enum. loc. cit.* P. repens, *Burm. Ind. tab.* xi. *fig.* 1; *Bojer, Hort. Maur.* 364, *not Linn.* P. barbatum, *Lam. Encycl.* iv. 475. P. procumbens, *Nees.*

MAURITIUS, common in waste and cultivated ground. Spread through the tropics of both hemispheres. *Herbe à Matelas, Herbe à Cornets.*

8. **P. didactylum,** *Kunth, Enum.* i. 84. Annual, tufted. Stems slender, under a foot long, geniculate at the base, then erect. Leaves 5–6; sheath 1–2 in. long, glabrous; blade the same length, narrow linear, acute. Spikes 2–3, ascending, 1–1$\frac{1}{2}$ in. long; rachis flexuose, glabrous, flattened and narrowly bordered; spikelets closer than in *P. sanguinale*, oblong, acute, glossy, $\frac{1}{14}$ in. long. Glumes ciliated at the edge. Digitaria didactyla, *Willd. Enum.* 91. D. distachyum, *Bojer, Hort. Maur.* 363, *not Pers.* (*Lam. Ill. t.* 43, *fig.* 2). Panicum bicorne, *Sieb.; Steud. Gram.* 41.

MAURITIUS, in waste ground, *Sieber*, ii. 42! etc. Also Bourbon and Madagascar.

9. **P. sanguinale,** *Linn.; var.* P. CILIARE, *Retz.; Kunth, Enum.* i. 82. Annual, tufted. Stems slender, a foot or more long, decumbent at the base, then erect. Leaves few, distant; sheath 2–3 in. long, furnished with fine spreading hairs; blade linear, acute, 3–4 in. long, usually glabrous. Spikes 5–9, usually in two whorls with a short internode, ascending, 4–5 in. long; rachis flattened, flexuose, bordered: spikelets laxly disposed, glossy, oblong, acute, $\frac{1}{12}$ in. long. Outer glume with 7 strong ribs, and usually ciliated with short bristly hairs. *Trin. Ic. t.* 144. Digitaria ciliaris, *Pers.; Bojer, Hort. Maur.* 362. D. biformis, *Willd.; Bojer, loc. cit.* D. setigera, *Roth.* D. ægyptiaca, *Willd.* Panicum horizontale, *Meyer; Kunth, Enum.* i. 81. P. commutatum, *Nees in Linnæa*, vii. 274.

MAURITIUS and SEYCHELLES, common in waste places and cultivated ground. Tropics of both hemispheres.

* *P. molle*, Swartz; Kunth, Enum. i. 92 (P. barbinode, Trin. Ic. t. 318), a native of the West Indies, now widely spread in the Old World, is naturalised in Mauritius and Seychelles. It is a perennial, with stems reaching a height of 6 or 8 feet, with nodes clothed with a dense tuft of spreading white hairs, sheaths half a foot long, linear leaves ½–1 foot long, an ample rhomboid panicle 6–9 in. long with decompound ascending branches, rachis rather flattened and often furnished with a few long white hairs, crowded sessile oblong acute glabrous spikelets $\frac{1}{12}$ in. long pale green or tinged with purple. In Ceylon Dr. Thwaites says it is grown under the name of Mauritius grass.

* *P. maximum*, Jacq. Ic. t. 13 (P. jumentorum, Pers.; P. polygamum, Sw; P. læve, Lam.; P. altissimum, DC), a native of Guinea, now everywhere cultivated in the tropics of both hemispheres, was introduced many years ago by Governor Labourdonnais into Mauritius as a forage grass, and is now plentifully established both there and also in Rodriguez and the Seychelles. It has glabrous stems, which reach a height of 6 or 8 feet, linear leaves 1–2 feet long narrowed gradually to both ends, a panicle a foot or more long, with very numerous ascending branches, the lower ones in a dense whorl, pedicels ⅛–¼ in. long and oblong acute glossy glabrous spikelets above $\frac{1}{12}$ in. long. Judging from the description, *P. pamplemoussense*, Steud. Gram. 71, is this species. *Fataque. Herbe de Guinée.*

10. **P. multinode,** *Lam.; Kunth, Enum.* i. 116. Perennial. Stems tufted, geniculate and rooting from the lower nodes, then ascending, a foot or more long. Leaves 6–8; upper sheaths 1–2 in. long, glabrous or pilose with a dense tuft of hairs at the throat; blade linear, acute, glabrous, 2–4 in. long. Panicle rhomboid, 2–4 in. long, with numerous slender erecto-patent decompound pubescent branches; spikelets shortly pedicellate, oblique oblong, obtuse, glabrous, brownish, $\frac{1}{12}$ in. long. P. pilipes, *Nees.*

SEYCHELLES, common by roadsides and in waste ground, *Pervillé*, 157! *Horne*. 629! MAURITIUS, according to Lamarck. Also Madagascar and East Indies. Near *P. trigonum*, Retz. (P. patens, Burm. Fl. Ind. tab. 10, fig. 2), and *P. radicans*, Retz (Kunth, Enum. i. 126). Dr. Thwaites regards them as three varieties of a single species.

11. **P. biflorum,** *Lam. Ill.* i. 174. A much-branched annual, with slender stems a foot or more long. Leaves 6–8; upper sheaths 1½–2 in. long, glabrous or pilose; blade linear, acuminate, glabrous, 3–6 in. long. Panicle rhomboid, 2–4 in. long, with numerous erecto-patent decompound capillary branches; pedicels reaching ⅛–¼ in. long; spikelets $\frac{1}{14}$ in. long, obovate, obtuse, glossy, glabrous. Isachne mauritiana, *Kunth, Enum.* i. 136. Neurachne meneritana, *Bojer, Hort. Maur.* 366, *not R. and S.*

MAURITIUS, frequent by roadsides and in cultivated fields. Also Tropical Africa.

12. **P. plicatum,** *Lam.; var.* P. COSTATUM, *Roxb.; Kunth, Enum.* i. 93.

Perennial. Stems 3–4 feet long, decumbent at the base. Upper sheaths 4–5 in. long, densely clothed with conspicuous spreading hairs; blade lanceolate, acuminate, ½–1 foot long, 1–1½ in. broad at the middle, conspicuously plicate, more or less hairy, narrowed to the base. Panicle ½–1 foot long, the branches short, ascending or spreading; pedicels very short; spikelets oblong, acute, $\frac{1}{14}$ in. long, many subtended by a single long flexuose bristle. *A. Braun in Walp. Ann.* vi. 947. P. Thouarsianum, *Nees in Steud. Gram.* 62. Setaria mauritiana, *Spreng.; Kunth, Enum.* i. 156?

MAURITIUS, RODRIGUEZ, and SEYCHELLES, common in fields and woods. Round the world in the tropics under many varieties, for an account of which A. Braun's paper above quoted may be consulted. *Herbe aux Anes.*

* *P. acariferum*, Trin. Ic. t. 87; Kunth, Enum. i. 125 (Thysanolæna acarifera, Arn. and Nees in Nova Acta, xvii. Suppl. i. 180; Melica latifolia, Roxb. Fl. Ind. i. 330; Bojer, Hort. Maur. 368), a native of the East Indies is naturalised in Mauritius, at Plaines Wilhelms and Moka. It is a perennial, 6–10 feet high, with terete woody stems, leaves a foot or more long lanceolate reedy 1½–2 in. broad rounded at the base, panicle above a foot long, with very numerous ascending slender decompound branches, spikelets glabrous oblong acute $\frac{1}{24}$ in. long in dense deltoid heads on short branchlets. *Bambou naine, Bambou de Chine.*

13. **P. auritum,** *Presl; Kunth, Enum.* i. 113. Perennial, glabrous in all its parts. Stems erect, 2–3 feet long. Leaves about half a dozen; upper sheaths 3–4 in. long; blade 4–6 in. long, linear, acute. Panicle ½–1 foot long, rhomboid or deltoid, with numerous ascending or spreading decompound branches; pedicels very short; spikelets oblong, acute, pale green, under $\frac{1}{12}$ in. long. P. patens, *Bojer, Hort. Maur.* 365, *not Linn.*

MAURITIUS, in the damp forests of the Pouce range, etc. Tropical Asia, not Africa. Allied to *P. antidotale*, Retz.

14. **P. madagascariense,** *Spreng.; Kunth, Enum.* i. 131. Stems 2 feet long, geniculate at the base, then ascending. Sheaths terete, glabrous; blade linear, glabrous, 4–6 in. long, ⅛–⅙ in. broad. Panicle 8–10 in. long, the branches spreading and decompound; pedicels exceeding the oblong acute glabrous obsoletely nerved spikelets. *Steud. Gram.* 85. P. airoides, *Flugge; Nees in Mart. Bras.* ii. 175.

MAURITIUS. Also Madagascar. I have not seen this species.

15. **P. parvifolium,** *Lam.; Kunth, Enum.* i. 109. Perennial, with wide-trailing much-branched stems, ascending at the end; nodes very numerous. Sheaths about half an inch long, pilose at the throat, usually glabrous on the outside; blade lanceolate, acute, spreading, ½–¾ in. long, ⅙ in. broad, rounded at the base, glabrous. Panicle rhomboid, about an inch long, with several slender slightly compound

ascending capillary branches; pedicels at most not longer than the spikelet; spikelets glossy, oblong, subacute, glabrous, $\frac{1}{12}$ in. long. *Trin. Ic. t.* 236. P. brevifolium, *Bojer, Hort. Maur.* 365, *not Linn.*

Var. P. SERPENS, *Kunth, Enum.* i. 117. Sheaths, leaves and spikelets pilose. P. repens, *Nees in Mart. Bras.* 236, *not Linn.* P. umbellatum, *Trin. Diss.* ii. 238. P. pygmæum, *Spreng.; Bojer, Hort. Maur.* 365, *not R. Br.*

MAURITIUS, SEYCHELLES, and RODRIGUEZ, frequent in dry soil. Sieber, ii. 34, referred by Kunth to *P. repens*, Linn., belongs here. Also Guinea and Tropical America. *Gros Chiendent.*

16. **P. colonum,** *Linn. Sp. Plant.* 84. Annual, densely tufted, glabrous. Stems terete, 1–2 feet high, bearing several leaves. Upper sheaths 2–3 in. long; blade linear, acuminate, glabrous, 4–6 in. long, $\frac{1}{4}$ in. broad. Panicle 2–4 in. long, formed of 5–9 dense ascending spikes $\frac{1}{2}$–$\frac{3}{4}$ in. long; rachis narrow, flattened, glabrous or pilose; spikelets crowded, ovoid, acute, $\frac{1}{12}$ in. long, pale green or purplish, finely pilose. Awn of the empty flower very short. *Trin. Ic. t.* 160. Oplismenus colonus, *H. B. K.*; *Kunth, Enum.* i. 142.

MAURITIUS and SEYCHELLES, common in marshes and damp fields, *Sieber*, ii. 31, etc. Cosmopolitan in the tropics. Resembles *Paspalum brizoides* in habit.

* *P. Crus-galli*, Linn. Sp. 83; Trin. Ic. 161–163 (Oplismenus, *Kunth*; Echinochloa, *Beauv.*), a common weed through the warmer zones of both hemispheres, occurs casually in Mauritius. It is like *P. colonum*, but more robust, with rather broader leaves, a panicle half a foot long with many ascending branches reaching 1–1$\frac{1}{2}$ in. long, oblong acute, spikelets $\frac{1}{8}$ in. long, glume of the lower flower furnished with an awn $\frac{1}{8}$–$\frac{1}{4}$ in. long, which is sometimes abortive.

17. **P. Balfourii,** *Baker.* Annual, tufted, glabrous. Stems slender, trailing, a foot long. Leaves numerous; upper sheaths imbricated, $\frac{1}{2}$–2 in. long; blade lanceolate, acuminate, glabrous, 2–3 in. long, $\frac{1}{4}$–$\frac{1}{3}$ in. broad at the middle. Spikelets solitary, laxly disposed on a glabrous simple rachis, oblong, acute, glabrous, $\frac{1}{6}$ in. long. Awn twice as long as the spikelet. Oplismenus acuminatus, *Nees.*

RODRIGUEZ, *Dr. Balfour!* Also Tropical Asia. Closely allied to *P. undulatifolium*, Ard.

18. **P. Burmanni,** *Retz.*; *Trin. Ic. t.* 193. Annual, tufted. Stems slender, trailing, a foot or more long, many-leaved; upper sheaths an inch long, pilose or glabrous; blade 1–1$\frac{1}{2}$ in. long, lanceolate, acute, $\frac{1}{4}$–$\frac{1}{3}$ in. broad, often pilose. Panicle 2–3 in. long, composed of 4–8 ascending spikes $\frac{1}{3}$–$\frac{1}{2}$ in. long, with a densely pilose rachis; spikelets crowded, pale green, oblong, acute, $\frac{1}{12}$ in. long, densely pilose. Awn 2–3 times as long as the empty glume. Oplismenus Burmanni, *Beauv.*; *Kunth, Enum.* i. 139. Panicum hirtellum, *Burm. Fl. Ind.* 24, *t.* 12,

fig. 1, *not Linn.* P. bromoides, *Lam. Ill.* 170. Oplismenus bromoides, *Bojer, Hort. Maur.* 366.

MAURITIUS, in cultivated ground. Round the world in the tropics.

19. **P. compositum,** *Linn. Sp. Plant.* 84. Perennial, tufted, nearly glabrous. Stems slender, trailing and rooting at the base, then erect for a foot or more, many-leaved; upper sheaths 2–3 in. long, glabrous or finely pilose, especially at the edge in the upper part; blade lanceolate, acute, glabrous, 2–4 in. long, ⅓–½ in. broad. Panicle 6–9 in. long, composed of 6–8 ascending spikes 2–3 in. long, with a finely pilose rachis; spikelets laxly disposed, oblong, acute, greenish, nearly glabrous, ⅛ in. long. Awn of the outer empty glume ¼–½ in. long. *Trin. Ic. t.* 187–189. Oplismenus compositus, *Rœm. and Schult.*; *Kunth, Enum.* i. 141. Panicum sylvaticum, *Lam. Encycl.* iv. 473. Oplismenus sylvaticus, *R. and S.*; *Kunth, Enum.* i. 139. Andropogon undatus, *Jacq. Ic. t.* 631. Oplismenus Jacquini, *Kunth, Enum.* i. 140. O. lanceolatus, *Kunth, Enum.* i. 146. Panicum undatum, *Steud. Gram.* 45.

MAURITIUS and SEYCHELLES, in woods, not common. Also Madagascar, Comoros, and Tropical Asia.

20. **P. Benthami,** *Steud. Gram.* 48. Annual, tufted, subglabrous. Stems erect, 3–4 feet high, glabrous, or with a few spreading hairs. Leaves 5–6; sheath very scabrous, upper 3–6 in. long; blade lanceolate, membranous, acute, 3–6 in. long, ½–¾ in. broad, rounded at the base, glabrous on the face, ciliated on the edge. Panicle half a foot long, on a long naked peduncle, composed of a dozen or more ascending branches half a foot long with a very slender glabrous rachis; spikelets shortly pedicellate, oblong, acute, glabrous, ⅛ in. long. Outer empty glume with an awn as long as or longer than itself. Urochloa paniculata, *Benth. in Hook. Fl. Nigr.* 558.

MAURITIUS, in cultivated fields, *Bouton!* Also Zambesi-land and Guinea.

I have not identified *P. rarisetum*, Steud. Gram. 52, said to be a plant of Mauritius (Sieber, Herb. Mixt. 144) and Bourbon, and to have a creeping stoloniferous rootstock, a glabrous stem a foot high geniculate at the base, sheaths pilose at the edge and throat, linear leaves 2–4 in. long, ⅛–¼ in. broad, with a few long scattered hairs, panicle contracted, racemes distichous at the base and confluent above, and spikelets subtended as in *P. costatum*, with a single scabrous flexuose bristle.

4. STENOTAPHRUM, Trin.

Spikelets 2-flowered, the upper flower hermaphrodite, the lower male or neuter, arranged in one or few-flowered crowded spikes pressed against the hollows of a thick common rachis. Empty glumes 2, membranous, the outer one small. Flowering glume and pale large, oblong, acute. Stamens 3. Styles 2, long; stigmas protruded from the top of the flower. Hypogynous scales truncate. Grain plano-convex, free inside the indurated wrappers. — Trailing perennials, differing from the rest of the *Paniceæ* by the thickened excavated main rachis of the inflorescence. DISTRIB. Everywhere in the tropics. Species 2.

Rachis jointed. Leaves obtuse . . . . 1. S. COMPLANATUM.
Rachis unjointed. Leaves acute . . . . 2. S. SUBULATUM.

1. **S. complanatum,** *Schrank; Kunth, Enum.* i. 137. Perennial, glabrous, with a wide-creeping rhizome, rooting and bearing tufts of leaves at the nodes, from which the flowering stems ascend to a height of a foot or more. Upper sheaths 3–4 in. long; blade ligulate, obtuse, 1–4 in. long, $\frac{1}{4}$–$\frac{1}{2}$ in. broad. Panicle 3–4 in. long, with a flat jointed rachis $\frac{1}{8}$–$\frac{1}{4}$ in. broad, deeply excavated against the spikes; upper spikes 2–3-, lower 5–6-flowered; spikelets oblong, glossy, acute, straw-coloured, $\frac{1}{4}$ in. long. Rottboellia complanata, *Sw.; Bojer, Hort. Maur.* 372. Panicum dimidiatum, *Linn.* S. americanum, *Kunth, Enum.* i. 138. S. madagascariense, *Kunth, Enum.* i. 524. Panicum poæformis, *Bojer, Hort. Maur.* 365.

MAURITIUS, RODRIGUEZ, and SEYCHELLES, everywhere common, ascending to the very summit of the Pouce. Tropics of both hemispheres. *Gros Chiendent.*

2. **S. subulatum,** *Trin.; Steud. Gram.* 18. Habit of the last. Assurgent flowering stems with much shorter internodes and copiously-branched. Upper sheaths 1–1$\frac{1}{2}$ in. long; blade linear, acute, 1–3 in. long, $\frac{1}{8}$–$\frac{1}{4}$ in. broad, sometimes densely hairy. Rachis of inflorescence 1–4 in. long, oblong in section, $\frac{1}{8}$ in. thick; upper spikes 1–2-, lower 3–4-flowered, almost hidden in the hollows of the unjointed rachis; spikelets $\frac{1}{12}$ in. long, glabrous, oblong-lanceolate, acute. Lepturus repens, *Bojer, Hort. Maur.* 372, *not R. Br.*

MAURITIUS, in sandy soil on the seashore, *Bojer!* RODRIGUEZ, not uncommon on Ile Gombrain, *Balfour!* Also Galega Island, *Bojer!* and Philippines.

5. CENCHRUS, Linn.

Spikelets 2-flowered, the upper flower hermaphrodite, the lower male or neuter, several together enclosed in a fimbriated rigid involucre, which falls with them. Empty glumes membranous, oblong, acute; flowering glume and pale oblong, acute, coriaceous. Stamens 3. Hypogynous scales 0. Styles 2, long; stigmas plumose, protruded from the top of the flower. Grain compressed, free within its rigid wrappers.—Annuals, with the clusters of spikelets in dense spikes. DISTRIB. Tropics of both hemispheres. Species about 10.

1. **C. echinatus,** *Linn.; Kunth, Enum.* i. 166. Annual, glabrous in all its parts, with tufted trailing stems a foot or more long. Leaves several; upper sheaths 2–3 in. long; blade linear, acute, $\frac{1}{4}$–$\frac{1}{2}$ ft. long. Spikes dense, 2–3 in. long, with a flexuose rachis. Involucres campanulate, stramineous, with about ten lanceolate divisions and many

rigid spreading bristles outside. Spikelets 3–6 in an involucre, under ¼ in. long, oblong, acute.

MAURITIUS and RODRIGUEZ, in dry soil. Round the world in the tropical zone. *Racle. Herbe à cateaux.*

6. PENNISETUM, Rich.

Spikelets 2-flowered, solitary in an involucre of plumose bristles, that falls with them; upper flower hermaphrodite; lower male or neuter. Empty glumes unequal. Flowering glume and pale coriaceous, concave, awnless. Stamens 3. Hypogynous scales 0 or very minute. Style elongated, free or connate in the lower part; stigmas protruded from the top of the flower. Grain compressed, free within its coriaceous wrappers.—Tall grasses, with dense simple terminal spikes. DISTRIB. Warmer regions of both hemispheres. Species about 20.

Annual, with ascending spikelets . . . . 1. P. CENCHROIDES.
Perennial, with spreading spikelets . . . . * P. SETOSUM.

1. **P. cenchroides,** *Rich.; Kunth, Enum.* i. 162. A tufted glabrous annual, with ascending branched stems 1–2 feet long. Upper sheaths 2–3 in. long, pilose at the throat; blade linear, glabrous, acute, 4–6 in. long. Spikes 1–3 in. long; spikelets ascending, sessile, crowded, oblong, acute, ⅛ in. long, included in an involucre of numerous bristles, densely plumose in the lower part, unequal and much longer than themselves, greenish or tinged with purple.

SEYCHELLES, common in dry soil, *Horne*, 633! Warmer regions of both hemispheres.

* *P. setosum*, Rich.; Trin. Ic. t. 20 (P. purpurascens, *H. B. K.; Kunth, Enum.* i. 160), a native of Tropical America, sometimes cultivated in the Old World, is established in the Seychelles. It is an erect perennial, with stems 3–4 feet long, linear acute glabrous or pilose leaves, a very dense purple spike half a foot long, and spreading sessile oblong acute spikelets $\frac{1}{12}$ in. long, enclosed in an involucre of a dozen or more fine bristles densely plumose in the lower part, one much longer (½ inch) and stronger than the rest.

7. GYMNOTHRIX, Beauv.

Spikelets solitary, 2-flowered, enclosed in an involucre of bristles that falls with them; upper flower hermaphrodite, the lower male or neuter. Empty glumes unequal, membranous, concave. Flowering-glume and pale awnless, coriaceous. Stamens 3. Hypogynous scales distinct. Styles 2, elongated, in our plant united above the base; stigmas plumose. Grain compressed.—Tall grasses, with dense long simple terminal spikes. DISTRIB. Cape and tropical zone of both hemispheres. Species about 20.

1. **G. hordeiformis,** *Nees in Linnæa*, vii. 276. A glabrous perennial, 3–4 feet high, with stout erect terete firm glossy stems. Sheaths pilose at the throat, upper 6–9 in. long; upper leaves a foot long, linear, acute, firm in texture, with crowded scabrous ribs. Spike ½–1 foot long, ½ inch thick; spikelets crowded, ascending, lanceolate, acute, straw-coloured, sessile, glabrous, ¼ in. long. Involucre of a dozen or more unequal simple straw-coloured bristles, some twice as long as the spikelet. G. cenchroides, *Ræm. and Schult.*; *Kunth. Enum.* i. 158. G. caudata, *Schrad.*

MAURITIUS, according to *Kunth.* Cape, Tropical Africa, Tropical Asia.

* *G Thouarsii*, Beauv. Agrost. 59, t. 13, fig. 6, said to have been gathered in Mauritius by Du Petit Thouars, has a much laxer spike and a larger spikelet and involucre, the longest bristle of the latter being an inch long. If the figure be correct, it differs from *G. japonica*, Kunth, by its sessile spikelets and free styles.

8. SETARIA, Beauv.

Spikelets like those of *Panicum*, but subtended by a unilateral cluster of bristles. Glumes and pale awnless. Style elongated.—Annual grasses, with linear leaves and abundant minute flowers in dense spikes or narrow panicles. DISTRIB. Warmer regions of both hemispheres.

1. **S. glauca,** *Beauv.*; *Kunth, Enum.* i. 149. Annual, tufted, glabrous, very various in stature, 1–5 feet high. Leaves many, narrow linear; upper ½ foot long, with sheaths nearly as long. Spikelets in a cylindrical spike 1–3 in. long, oblong, obtuse, $\frac{1}{12}$ in. long, pale green, subtended on the outside by a tuft of yellow bristles, variable in length, in our specimens ¼ in. long. Panicum glaucum, *Linn.* P. flavescens, *Moench.* Setaria aurea, *Hochst.*

MAURITIUS, in cultivated ground, *Bouton!* Everywhere within the tropics. *Millet.*

9. ZOYSIA, Willd.

Spikelets 1-flowered, arranged in a simple spike with a flexuose jointless rachis, on very short pedicels. Empty glume single, coriaceous, convolute, acute or shortly awned. Flowering glume membranous, boat-shaped. Pale the same texture, smaller, sometimes absent. Stamens 3. Hypogynous scales absent. Styles elongated; stigmas plumose. Grain oblong, compressed, free.—Shore perennials, with a creeping rootstock and small spikes. DISTRIB. Warmer regions of the Old World on the seashore. Species 1 or 2.

1. **Z. pungens,** *Willd.*; *Kunth, Enum.* i. 471. Perennial, with a wide-creeping wiry rhizome, from which the erect stems arise to the height of a few inches above the soil. Leaves crowded, erecto-patent, linear-subulate, glabrous. Spikes ½–1 in. long, distinctly peduncled; rachis slender, very flexuose, not jointed; spikelets adpressed to

the rachis, glossy, oblong, acute, $\frac{1}{12}$ in. long. Agrostis Matrella, *Linn.*

MAURITIUS and RODRIGUEZ, common on sandy shores, Flat Island, and Coin de Mire, *Horne!* Spread through the warmer regions of the Old World. *Z. tenuifolia*, Willd. (Sieber, ii. 40.) is a variety, with longer more slender leaves 1½–2 in. long, and fewer smaller spikelets than usual. *Chiendent gazon.*

* The Sugar-cane, *Saccharum officinale*, Linn.; Kunth, Enum. i. 474, easily recognisable by its large firm thin leaves, very numerous flowers arranged in a regular ample panicle and each enveloped in a dense tuft of silky hairs, is often found about abandoned plantations. *Canne à Sucre.*

10. ANDROPOGON, Linn.

Spikelets arranged in simple or panicled spikes, usually in pairs, one pedicellate and sterile, the other sessile, with 2 flowers, the lower imperfect without any pale, the upper hermaphrodite, sometimes in threes. Empty glumes coriaceous, the outer enfolding the inner, not usually awned. Flowering glume smaller, membranous, furnished usually with a stout twisted terminal awn. Pale like the flower-glume in texture, both of them smaller than the empty glumes and enclosed in them. Stamens usually 3. Hypogynous scales present. Styles elongated; stigmas protruded from the top of the flower. Grain free. — Annual or perennial grasses, of very various habit, the leaves usually linear, the spikelets narrow and acute, and the axis of the inflorescence pilose. DISTRIB. Spread through the two warmer zones of both hemispheres. Species 300.

Spikes simple.
  Annual; awn short . . . . 1. A. PEDUNCULARIS.
  Perennial; awn very long . . . . 2. A. CONTORTUS.
Spikes few, crowded into an almost digitate panicle.
  Trailing, with lanceolate leaves (*Batratherum*, Nees). 3. A. LANCEOLATUS.
  Erect, with linear leaves (*Gymnandropogon*, Nees).
    Spikelets oblong-lanceolate, acute . . . . 4. A. PERTUSUS.
    Spikelets oblong, obtuse . . . . 5. A. ARISTATUS.
Spikes many, arranged in an ample rhomboid panicle without bracts (*Chrysopogon*, Trin).
  Empty glumes not muricated on the back.
    Branches of panicle glabrous . . . . 6. A. ACICULARIS.
    Branches of panicle pilose . . . . 7. A. VERTICILLATUS.
  Empty glumes muricated on the back . . . . * A. MURICATUS.
Spikes many, arranged in an ample panicle, the branches of which bear abundant boat-shaped bracts (*Cymbopogon*, Nees).
  Bracts springing from just below the pairs of spikes.
    Rachis of spikes densely pilose . . . . 8. A. SCHŒNANTHUS.
    Rachis of spikes thinly pilose . . . . 9. A. FOLIATUS.
  Bracts springing from some distance below the pairs of spikes.
    Panicle lax . . . . 10. A. HIRTUS.
    Panicle dense . . . . 11. A. FINITIMUS.

1. **A. peduncularis,** *Kunth*, *Enum*. i. 509. Annual. Stems slender, glabrous, a foot long. Leaf-sheaths 1½–2 in. long; blade narrow linear, glabrous, ½ ft. long. Spike simple, cylindrical, 2–3 in. long, clasped at the base by the uppermost sheath; spikelets glabrous, in pairs, laxly disposed on a densely pilose rachis, the upper one perfect, ⅛ in. long, with an awn nearly as long as itself, 3 stamens, and an outer glume emarginate at the tip, the lower reduced to a single glume with a densely pilose flattened pedicel as long as itself. Pollinia monandra, *Spreng.*; *Bojer*, *Hort. Maur.* 374.

MAURITIUS, in stony ground on the crest of Montagne Longue. Also said to be East Indian. General Munro, who has kindly examined for me our single specimen, places the plant in *Schizachyrium*, near *Andropogon zeylanicum*, Arnott.

2. **A. contortus,** *Linn.*; *Kunth*, *Enum*. i. 486. Perennial, with densely tufted two-edged stems 1–2 feet long. Leaves linear, glaucous, usually glabrous, ¼–½ ft. long. Spikes many, simple, cylindrical, 2–3 in. long, on crowded stiffly erect peduncles; spikelets much imbricated, several of the lower awnless and with both flowers imperfect. Outer empty glume lanceolate, acute, ¼ in. long, usually densely pilose. Hermaphrodite flowers with an awn 2–3 in. long to the flowering glume, which is very robust, geniculate at the middle, and conspicuously pubescent in the lower half. Heteropogon contortus, *Ræm. and Schult.*; *Bojer*, *Hort. Maur.* 375. H. hirtus, *Pers.*

MAURITIUS, RODRIGUEZ, and SEYCHELLES, common at all elevations; Coin de Mire, *Horne!* Spread through the warmer zones of both hemispheres.

3. **A. lanceolatus,** *Roxb.*; *Kunth*, *Enum*. i. 498. Annual. Stems slender, diffuse, trailing, much branched. Sheaths glabrous, 1–1½ in. long; blade lanceolate, acuminate, 1–1½ in. long, ½ in. broad, conspicuously ciliated at the edge in the lower part. Spikes 3–6, close, subdigitate, 1–2 in. long; rachis finely pilose; spikelets lanceolate, acute, ⅛–¼ in. long. Outer empty glume finely ribbed, glabrous on the back, conspicuously ciliated. Awn slender, twice as long as the spikelet. Batratherum lanceolatum, *Nees*.

MAURITIUS, in dry soil. Also Tropical Asia.

4. **A. pertusus,** *Willd.*; *Kunth*, *Enum*. i. 498. Annual. Stems glabrous, tufted, geniculate at the base, then erect, above a foot high. Sheaths 1½–2 in. long, with a tuft of hairs at the throat; blade linear, glabrous, acuminate, 3–6 in. long. Spikes 4–8, crowded in an almost digitate panicle with a slender stiffly erect peduncle, 1½–2 in. long; rachis densely clothed with white hairs shorter than the spikelets. Spikelets ⅙ in. long, glossy, green or purple, oblong-lanceolate, acute. Outer empty glume with 11–13 distinct ribs. Awn 2–3 times as long as the spikelet. Gymnandropogon pertusus, *Nees*. A. punctatus

and fascicularis, *Roxb.*; *Kunth*, *Enum.* i. 506. A. fasciculatus, *Steud. Gram.* 382? A. galloinsulanus, *Steud. Gram.* 371?

MAURITIUS, common in dry soil at all elevations. Spread through the tropics of the Old World.

5. **A. aristatus,** *Poir.*; *Kunth*, *Enum.* i. 498. Perennial. Stems firm, glabrous, erect, 2–3 feet long. Sheaths glabrous; upper 3–5 in. long; blade 6–9 in. long, glabrous, narrow linear, acuminate. Spikes 2–4, crowded in an almost digitate panicle, 2–3 in. long, flexuose, on short densely pilose peduncles; spikelets imbricated all round the slender rachis and completely hiding it; rachis and pedicel of the imperfect spikelet shortly pilose. Outer empty glume of the hermaphrodite flower $\frac{1}{6}$ in. long, oblong, obtuse, finely pubescent on the back and edge, marked with very numerous distinct ribs. Awn purple, $\frac{1}{2}$–$\frac{3}{4}$ in. long. A. molliconius, *Kunth*, *Gram.* i. 365, *t.* 96; *Enum.* i. 497. Lepeocęrcis mollissimus, *Nees.*

MAURITIUS, frequent in dry soil at all elevations, *Sieber*, ii. 48! etc. Also Tropical Asia.

6. **A. acicularis,** *Retz.*; *Kunth*, *Enum.* i. 505. Perennial Stems tufted, glabrous, decumbent at the base, then erect, a foot or more high. Leaves many, crowded near the base of the stem, the rest few, distant; blade linear, acute, 2–3 in. long, glabrous, like the sheath. Panicle dense, rhomboid, 2–4 in. long, with numerous very slender ascending branches with the spikelets at the end in threes, two pedicellate and imperfect, one sessile and containing a hermaphrodite flower; branches scabrous, like the spikelets, quite glabrous; spikelets glossy, lanceolate, acute, $\frac{1}{8}$ in. long. Awn variable in length, sometimes shorter than its glume, sometimes twice as long. Chrysopogon aciculatus, *Trin.* Rhaphis trivalvis, *Lour.*; *Trin. Ic. t.* 8–9. Andropogon aciculatus, *Roxb.*

MAURITIUS, on the heights of Flacq, Quartier Militaire, etc., *Sieber*, ii. 49! etc. Spread through the tropics of the Old World.

7. **A. verticillatus,** *Roxb.*; *Kunth*, *Enum.* i. 506. A robust erect glabrous perennial, several feet high. Leaves linear, the lower ones reaching a length of $1\frac{1}{2}$–2 feet, $\frac{1}{4}$–$\frac{1}{3}$ in. broad, scabrous on the edges and keel. Panicle dense, rhomboid, 4–8 in. long, the spikelets laxly placed in threes on the slender glabrous ascending branches, two of the three usually fertile, immersed in a short tuft of brown hairs, $\frac{1}{4}$ in. long, awnless or shortly awned, the barren glumes scabrous on the keel, the third spikelet pedicellate and rudimentary.

MAURITIUS, on the banks of the Moka River, *Bojer!* Also East Indies.

* *A. muricatus*, Retz.; Kunth, Enum. i. 505 (Anatherum muricatum *Beauv.*; *Bojer*, *Hort. Maur.* 373), a native of Tropical Asia, is now established copiously in Mauritius and Rodriguez. It is a perennial, 4–6 feet high, with an aromatic rootstock, firm terete culm, long linear

glabrous leaves, a dense stiff panicle ½–1 ft. long with very numerous whorled slender ascending branches, spikelets in pairs, one sessile with a hermaphrodite and male flower, the other pedicellate with both the flowers imperfect, subcoriaceous equal acute empty glumes ⅛ in. long covered on the back with minute prickles, flowering glume of the perfect floret without any awn. *Vetivert.*

8. **A. Schœnanthus,** *Linn.; Vent. Hort. Cels. t.* 89. Perennial tufted. Stems erect, glabrous, 2–3 feet long. Leaves linear, glabrous, acuminate, ½ foot or more long, ¼ in. broad, fragrant. Spikes in a dense subsecund panicle 3–6 in. long; bracts lanceolate-boatshaped, ¾–1 in. long, springing from near the base of a pair of spikes and hiding them till they are fully expanded; rachis densely clothed with white silky hairs. Outer empty glume oblong-lanceolate, ⅙ in. long, with 7 strong ribs. Awn twice as long as the glume. A. pruinosus, *Nees.* A. connatus. *Hochst.* A. Martini, *Roxb.; Kunth, Enum.* i. 494. A. pachnodes, *Trin.* Cymbopogon elegans, *Spreng.; Bojer, Hort. Maur.* 374.

MAURITIUS and RODRIGUEZ, common in dry soil, *Sieber* ii. 45! etc.; Flat Island and Coin de Mire, *Horne!* Spread through the tropics of the Old World. *Citronelle.*

9. **A. foliatus,** *Steud. Gram.* 389. Perennial. Stems glabrous, a foot long. Leaves glabrous, linear, 6–9 in. long. Spikes few, in pairs in a small contracted panicle, mixed with many lanceolate-boatshaped bracts, which spring from just below them; rachis of the spikes very slightly pilose; spikelets green, glabrous, oblong-lanceolate, ⅙ in. long. Awn twice as long as the spikelets.

MAURITIUS and RODRIGUEZ, in dry soil. Also Bourbon. Probably a mere variety of *A. Schœnanthus.*

10. **A. hirtus,** *Linn.; Kunth, Enum.* i. 492. Perennial. Stems glabrous, 2–4 feet high. Leaves linear, glabrous, acuminate, 6–9 in. long. Spikes 1–1½ in. long, arranged in pairs in a very lax panicle, the lanceolate-boatshaped bracts often 1½ in. long and springing from some distance below the pairs of spikes; rachis of spikes clothed with short brown silky hairs. Outer empty glume lanceolate, ⅙–¼ in. long, glabrous. Awn twisted, ¾–1 in. long. Cymbopogon hirtus, *Nees.* Andropogon pubescens, *Vis.*; *Kunth, Enum. loc. cit.* A. fulvicomus, *Hochst.*

MAURITIUS, frequent in dry soil. Widely spread through the warmer regions of the Old World.

11. **A. finitimus,** *Hochst.; Steud. Gram.* 385. Perennial, tufted. Stems glabrous, 3–4 feet long. Leaves linear, acuminate, glabrous, 6–9 in. long. Spikes ½–1 in. long, arranged in ample panicles, mixed with linear-boatshaped long-pointed bracts often 1½–2 in. long, which are inserted some distance below the pairs of spikes; rachis of spikes shortly finely pilose. Outer empty glume lanceolate, ⅙ in. long. Awn strong, purple, twisted, often an inch long. A. filipendulinus, *Hochst.*

MAURITIUS, RODRIGUEZ, and SEYCHELLES, frequent. Also Tropical Africa.

* SORGHUM, Pers.

Of the genus *Sorghum*, Pers., which includes the Millets commonly cultivated in the two warmer zones and differs from *Andropogon* mainly by its larger grains and the more rigid texture of its empty glumes, two species are planted and casually subspontaneous.

* *S. saccharatum*, Pers. (S. caffrorum, *Beauv.*) Leaves firm, glabrous, 1–3 inches broad; panicle dense, $\frac{1}{2}$–1 foot long, with very silky branches; outer glume of the hermaphrodite spikelet obovate-oblong, $\frac{1}{6}$ in. long by half as broad; grain subglobose, the size of a small pea.

* *S. halepense*, Pers., with narrower leaves, a laxer panicle, oblanceolate glumes and smaller grains.

11. ISCHÆMUM, Linn.

Spikelets in pairs, arranged in simple or panicled spikes, one pedicellate and imperfect, the other sessile, with 2 flowers, the upper flower hermaphrodite, with an awned flowering glume, the other male or neuter, but furnished with both flower-glume and pale. Empty glumes coriaceous, awnless. Flowering glume and pale smaller and membranous. Stamens 3. Hypogynous scales present. Styles produced; stigmas protruded from the top of the flower. Grain small, free.—Grasses with the habit of *Andropogon*, from which they only differ by possessing a pale in the imperfect flower. DISTRIB. Tropics of the Old World. Species 30.

1. **I. barbatum,** *Retz.; Kunth, Enum.* i. 513. Perennial, tufted. Stems slender, erect, glabrous, 1–2 feet high. Upper sheaths 2–3 in. long, hairy at the edge and throat; blade linear-acuminate, 4–6 in. long, $\frac{1}{4}$–$\frac{1}{3}$ in. broad, glabrous or finely pilose on the face. Spikes 2–4, crowded in a digitate panicle, 2–3 in. long; rachis densely clothed with conspicuous white hairs; spikelets $\frac{1}{6}$ in. long, oblong-lanceolate, acute. Outer empty glume with 7–9 prominent ribs on the back, glabrous. Awn purplish, twisted, $\frac{1}{2}$ in. long. Meoschium barbatum, *Beauv.*; *Bojer, Hort. Maur.* 376.

MAURITIUS and SEYCHELLES, in cultivated ground, not common. Also Tropical Asia.

12. ANTHISTIRIA, Linn.

Spikelets in clusters of 7, arranged in an ample panicle and each bracteated by a keeled lanceolate leaf, 4 sessile, similar, neuter, surrounding the other three, of which two are imperfect and pedicellate, and only one perfect and sessile. Empty glumes coriaceous, convolute, muticous. Flowering glume of the perfect flower furnished with a long scabrous awn. Pale membranous, muticous. Stamens 3, exserted. Hypogynous scales present. Styles elongated; stigmas plumose. Grain free, cylindrical.—Tall annual grasses, with the habit of

Andropogons of the section *Cymbopogon*. Distrib. Warmer regions of both hemispheres. Species 10.

1. **A. ciliata,** *Linn.*; *Kunth, Enum.* i. 481. An erect annual, 3–6 feet high. Leaves linear, glabrous, $\frac{1}{2}$–$\frac{3}{4}$ foot long. Spikelets in a long nodding panicle, the distant ascending dense branches of which are bracteated by large linear leaves, one special membranous boatshaped bract an inch or more long with a long point subtending each cluster of spikelets. Glumes of the four outer flowers $\frac{1}{4}$ in. long, oblanceolate, clothed with conspicuous spreading bristly hairs. Fertile flower sessile in the centre of these four, with two other minute naked shortly-stalked glumes by its side and a scabrous awn from its tip protruded sometimes a couple of inches. A. barbata, *Desf.*; *Kunth, Enum. loc. cit.*

Mauritius, common at all elevations. Spread through the warmer regions of both hemispheres. *Esquine.*

13. LEERSIA, Soland.

Spikelets 1-flowered. Empty glumes both obsolete. Flowering glume rigidly coriaceous, flat, awnless. Pale just like the flowering glume in texture, but narrower. Hypogynous scales 2, ovate, entire. Stamens in our plant 6. Ovary glabrous; style short; stigmas plumose, protruded from the side of the spikelet. Grain laterally compressed, enclosed in the indurated glume and pale.—Slender grasses, with long stems, narrow leaves and panicled spikes. Distrib. Cosmopolitan in the tropical and warm temperate zones. Species about 10.

1. **L. hexandra,** *Sw.*; *Kunth, Enum.* i. 6. Glabrous in all its parts. Rootstock wide-creeping. Stem slender, terete, 2–3 feet long; nodes and leaves 4–6 to a stem. Blade linear, acute, 3–6 in. long, $\frac{1}{4}$–$\frac{1}{2}$ in. broad. Panicle rhomboid, 2–4 in. long, with many simple or compound ascending branches; rachis filiform, flexuose; spikelets $\frac{1}{8}$ in. long, oblong, acute, strongly ribbed, imbricated, whitish or tinged with purple. L. australis, *R. Br.* L. mexicana, *Kunth.* Asprella hexandra, *R. and S.* A. purpurea, *Bojer, Hort. Maur.* 376.

Mauritius, in swamps by the Moka River, etc. Warmer regions of both hemispheres.

14. VILFA, Adans.

(*Sporobolus*, R. Br.)

Spikelets 1-flowered, minute, arranged in lax or dense panicles. Empty glumes 2, equal or unequal, at most as long as the spikelet, often shorter. Flowering glume lanceolate or oblong, similar in texture to the empty glumes. Stamens 2–3. Hypogynous scales 2, glabrous. Styles short; stigmas plumose, protruded from the side of the flower. Grain free, large for the size of the spikelet, with a loose crustaceous pericarp.—Annuals or perennials, with narrow leaves and very numerous minute muticous spikelets. DISTRIB. Both hemispheres, mainly tropical. Species about 50.

Empty glumes much shorter than the flowering glume.
  Panicle narrow, spike-like . . . . 1. V. INDICA.
  Panicle lax, diffuse . . . . 2. V. MINUTIFLORA.
Empty glumes about as long as the flowering glume . . . . 3. V. VIRGINICA.

1. **V. indica,** *Steud. Gram.* 162. Perennial, densely tufted, erect, glabrous, 2–3 feet high. Stems firm, terete, with few nodes. Leaves narrow linear, convolute, often a foot long. Panicle $\frac{1}{2}$–1 foot long, narrow and spike-like, with very numerous short laxly-placed branches adpressed to the rachis; pedicels none or very short; spikelets $\frac{1}{12}$ in. long, glossy, oblong, acute. Empty glumes unequal and much shorter than the flowering glume. Grain terete, oblong-cylindrical, more than half as long as the flowering glume. Agrostis indica, *Linn.* A tenacissima, *Jacq. Ic. t.* 26. A. minutiflora, *Steud. Gram.* 170. Sporobolus indicus, tenacissimus, capensis, and elongatus, *Kunth, Enum.* i. 211–2.

MAURITIUS, in dry soil at Plaines Wilhelms, and on the shoulder of the Pouce. Warmer regions of both the Old and New World.

2. **V. minutiflora,** *Trin. Agrost.* i. 63. Stems densely tufted, erect, 1–2 feet high, glabrous, with 4–5 nodes. Leaves 3–9 in. long, $\frac{1}{8}$ in. broad, acuminate, flat or convolute. Panicle very lax, often a foot or more long, 2–3 in. broad, with distant laxly-panicled branches; pedicels capillary, $\frac{1}{8}$–$\frac{1}{4}$ in. long. Empty glumes oblong, obtuse, subequal, half as long as the spikelet. Flowering glume and pale oblong-lanceolate, $\frac{1}{24}$ in. long. Grain oblong, truncate, as long as the glume and pale and clasped by them. V. mangalorica, *Hochst.; Steud. Gram.* 159. Sporobolus minutiflorus, *Link; Kunth, Enum.* i. 214.

MAURITIUS, in cultivated fields and shady places. Tropics of both hemispheres.

3. **V. virginica,** *Beauv.; Trin. Ic. t.* 48. Perennial, glabrous. Stems trailing, $\frac{1}{2}$–1 foot long, with short internodes, imbricated sheaths and 10–20 erecto-patent linear-convolute leaves $1\frac{1}{2}$–2 inches long. Panicle $1\frac{1}{2}$–2 in. long, dense and narrow; pedicels at most as long as the spikelets, which are pale green, glossy and about $\frac{1}{12}$ in. long. Empty glumes lanceolate-navicular, acute, nearly as long as the flowering glume and pale, which are like them in shape and texture. Grain oblong. Agrostis virginica, *Linn.* Sporobolus tremulus and virginicus, *Kunth, Enum.* i. 210.

MAURITIUS and RODRIGUEZ, in dry soil, especially sands of the shore. Warmer zones of both hemispheres.

15. AGROSTIS, Linn.

Spikelets 1-flowered, arranged in a lax panicle. Empty glumes 2, subequal, boat-shaped, awnless, usually longer than the flower. Flowering glume usually awned on the back; pale minute, sometimes absent. Hypogynous scales 2, entire. Stamens 1–3. Stigmas nearly sessile, plumose, protruded from the side of the spikelet. Grain free, minute, terete.—Tufted grasses with slender leaves and minute flowers in lax panicles. Distrib. Nearly all in the temperate zone of both hemispheres. Species 50.

1. **A. tropica,** *Beauv. Fl. Owar.* ii. 37, *t.* 80. Root and leaves not known. Culm slender, finely pilose. Panicle lax, 3–4 in. long; branches short, ascending, decompound; pedicels exceeding the spikelets. Empty glumes $\frac{1}{12}$ in. long, lanceolate, subequal, pilose. Flowering glume much shorter, oblong, tricuspidate, with an awn from the back twice as long as itself. Pale minute, oblong. *Kunth, Enum.* i. 222.

Mauritius, *Du Petit Thouars.* Description taken entirely from Beauvois' figures above quoted. Endemic.

16. ARISTIDA, Linn.

Spikelets 1-flowered, laxly panicled. Empty glumes 2, membranous, lanceolate, unequal, sometimes shortly awned. Flowering glume coriaceous, lanceolate, involute, with a trifid awn; pale minute, membranous. Hypogynous scales entire. Stamens 3; filaments adnate to the stalk of the ovary. Ovary stipitate; styles short; stigmas plumose, protruded from the side of the spikelet. Grain terete, free inside the convolute flower-glume.—Tufted slender grasses, with narrow leaves and narrow spikelets, with very prominent awns. Distrib. Cosmopolitan, but scarcely European.

Spikelet $\frac{1}{4}$–$\frac{1}{3}$ in. long . . . . 1. A. adscensionis.
Spikelet $\frac{1}{2}$–$\frac{2}{3}$ in. long . . . . 2. A. hystrix.

1. **A. adscensionis,** *Linn.; Kunth, Enum.* i. 190. Perennial, erect, tufted, a foot or more high, glabrous. Stems very slender. Leaves $\frac{1}{4}$–$\frac{1}{2}$ ft. long, linear-subulate, involute. Panicle 3–4 in. long, with numerous distant short slender ascending branches; pedicels very short. Spikelets $\frac{1}{4}$–$\frac{1}{3}$ in. long, green or bright purple. Empty glumes lanceolate, acute, not awned, the inner one nearly as long as the spikelet, and the outer a third shorter. Awns trifid, scabrous. $\frac{1}{2}$–$\frac{3}{4}$ in. long. A. depressa, *Retz.; Kunth, Enum.* i. 190. A. mauritiana, *Kunth, Gram.* i. 265, *t.* 44. A. vulgaris, *Trin.; Steud. Gram.* 138. A festucoides. *Poir.*

Mauritius, Rodriguez, and Seychelles, frequent in dry soil. Spread through the tropics of the Old World.

2. **A. Hystrix,** *Linn. fil.; Kunth, Enum.* i. 191. Perennial, tufted, $1\frac{1}{2}$–2 feet high. Stem much stronger than in the last, terete. Leaves 6–9 in. long, $\frac{1}{8}$ in. broad at the base, convolute. Panicle half a foot long, with short distant ascending branches; spikelets $\frac{1}{2}$–$\frac{3}{5}$ in. long. Inner empty glume as long as the spikelet; outer shorter, with a short awn. Awn of flowering glume trifid, the central branch an inch or more long. A. Sieberiana, *Trin.; Kunth, Enum.* i. 191.

MAURITIUS, *Boivin!* Also Bourbon, *Commerson!*, Orient and East Indies.

17. CYNODON, Rich.

Spikelets arranged in unilateral digitate spikes, each containing a single perfect flower and above it the obscure rudiment of a second. Empty glumes lanceolate, subequal, persistent. Flowering glume similar in texture to the empty glumes, oblong, deeply boat-shaped; pale straight, narrow-oblong, nearly as long. Hypogynous scales 2. Stamens 3. Styles short; stigmas spreading, plumose. Grain free, glabrous.—Small perennial trailing grasses, with linear leaves. DISTRIB. All tropical and warm temperate regions. Species about 10.

1. **C. Dactylon,** *Pers.; Kunth, Enum.* i. 259. Perennial, tufted, glabrous. Stems trailing, $\frac{1}{2}$–1 ft. long, the lower internodes short and numerous. Leaves 1–3 in. long, narrow linear, acute. Spikes 5–9, 1–3 in. long, with a slender quadrangular rachis; spikelets $\frac{1}{12}$ in. long, unilateral, much imbricated, pale green, oblong, acute, finally deciduous. Empty glumes a third shorter than the spikelet, persistent, the outer one with a strong green keel. C. linearis, *Willd.* Panicum Dactylon, *Linn.*

MAURITIUS, RODRIGUEZ, and SEYCHELLES, common in dry soil. All round the world in the two warmer zones. *Chiendent.*

18. ELEUSINE, Gærtn.

Spikelets many-flowered, arranged in digitate or panicled long secund spikes. Empty glumes 2, firm, persistent, not awned; outer largest, 3–5-nerved on the keel. Flowering glume oblong, not awned, the same texture as the others; pale much smaller. Hypogynous scales 2, fimbriated. Stamens 3. Styles short; stigmas spreading, plumose. Grain free, oblong-trigonal, with a loose membranous pericarp.—Glabrous annual grasses, with linear leaves and many dense spikes. DISTRIB. All warm regions. Species about 10.

1. **E. indica,** *Gærtn.; Kunth, Enum.* i. 272. Annual, glabrous, with densely tufted erect stems 1–2 feet long. Leaves few, linear, acute, glabrous, $\frac{1}{2}$–1 foot long. Spikes 3–6 in. long, 4–6, all digitate from the tip of the stem or 1 or more placed lower on the culm; rachis slender, straight, triquetrous; spikelets 5-flowered, much compressed laterally, $\frac{1}{6}$–$\frac{1}{4}$ in. long. Outer empty glumes $\frac{1}{8}$ in. long, im-

bricated, erecto-patent. *Trin. Ic. t.* 71, and a short-spiked variety, *Trin. Ic. t.* 72.

MAURITIUS, RODRIGUEZ, and SEYCHELLES, common at all elevations. Everywhere in the two warmer zones. *Chiendent patte de poules.*

19. CTENIUM, Panz.

Spikelets 3–4-flowered, densely crowded in secund usually solitary spikes. Lowest flower of the spikelet in our plant alone hermaphrodite, the three upper more or less imperfect. Empty glumes unequal, lanceolate, membranous. Flowering glume firm in texture, lanceolate, strongly keeled, the keel running out below the tip into a long awn; pale smaller and less firm in texture. Hypogynous scales 2. Stamens 3. Stigmas plumose, spreading laterally. Grain small, free.—Tufted erect grasses, with narrow leaves and long flexuose tightly-packed usually solitary spikes. DISTRIB. Tropical America and Tropical Africa, not Asia. Species 10.

1. **C. sechellense,** *Baker.* Densely tufted, with erect glabrous slender stems 2 feet high. Leaves few; upper sheaths 4–5 in. long, with a tuft of hairs at the throat; blade narrow linear, acuminate, glabrous, glaucous, ½ foot long. Spikes solitary, 5–6 in. long; spikelets erecto-patent, much imbricated, biserial on a slender triquetrous straight rachis. Outer empty glume ¼ in. long, cuspidate; inner much smaller. Flowers with a tuft of hairs at the base. Flowering glume of hermaphrodite flower ⅛ in. long, the awn 2–3 times its length. Awns of imperfect flowers shorter and of the uppermost not developed.

SEYCHELLES, common, *Horne,* 632! Endemic.

20. DACTYLOCTENIUM, Willd.

Spikelets densely packed in digitate unilateral spikes, 3–5-flowered, the upper flowers imperfect. Empty glumes unequal, the inner ovate, minute, the outer coriaceous, linear-subulate, nearly as long as the spikelet. Flowering glume oblong, deeply boat-shaped, with a hairy keel, which runs out into a point; pale much narrower. Hypogynous scales glabrous. Stamens 3. Stigmas spreading, plumose; styles short. Grain small, free, angular.—Small annual grasses, with linear leaves. DISTRIB. Spread through all warm regions. Species perhaps one only.

1. **D. ægyptiacum,** *Willd.; Kunth, Enum.* i. 261. Annual, with often a creeping rootstock, rooting at the nodes. Stems ascending, ½–2 feet long. Upper sheaths 1–2 in. long, densely pilose at the throat; blade linear, acute, 1–6 in. long, often loosely pilose. Spikes 4–8, 1–2 in. long, the spikelets spreading horizontally from a slender rigid triquetrous rachis, usually produced into a sharp point at the top.

Flowering glume acute, pale green, pilose on the mucronate keel, $\frac{1}{8}$ in. long. D. mucronatum, *Willd.; Trin. Ic. t.* 69.

MAURITIUS and SEYCHELLES, common at all elevations. Spread round the world in the two warmer zones. *D. distachyum*, Bojer, Hort. Maur. 370, is *D. prostratum*, Willd.; Kunth, Enum. t. 261, a dwarf variety, with the spikes reduced to two or three. *Chiendent patte de poules.*

21. CHLORIS, Sw.

Spikelets few-flowered, the lowest flower alone perfect, arranged in secund digitate spikes. Empty glumes lanceolate, acute, persistent. Flowering glume firmer in texture, awned from the tip, boat-shaped; pale smaller. Hypogynous scales 2, entire. Stamens 3. Styles short; stigmas plumose, spreading. Grain free, trigonous, with a membranous pericarp.—Tropical grasses, with few linear leaves. DISTRIB. Warmer zones of both hemispheres. Species 50.

Flowering glume densely bearded, and furnished with a long awn . . . . 1. C. BARBATA.
Flowers glume glabrous, with a short awn . . . . . . 2. C. MONOSTACHYA.

1. **C. barbata,** *Sw.; Kunth, Enum.* i. 264. Annual, with stems and leaves in tufts from a rooting rhizome. Stems slender, 1–2 feet long, with few nodes in the ascending portion. Leaves narrow linear, acuminate, 3–6 in. long, glabrous or pilose. Spikes 10–15, 2–3 inches long; spikelets 3–4-flowered, the lowest flower awned, hermaphrodite, the two next awned, imperfect, the uppermost a mere rudiment. Flowering glume $\frac{1}{12}$ in. long, densely ciliated, with a scabrous awn three times its length. Outer empty glume as long as the spikelet. *Jacq. Eclog. Gram. t.* 8. Andropogon barbatus, *Linn. Mant.* 302.

MAURITIUS, RODRIGUEZ, and SEYCHELLES, common. Coin de Mire, *Horne!* Tropics of both hemispheres.

2. **C. monostachya,** *Poir. Encycl. Suppl.* ii. 238. Annual, glabrous, with a very slender rhizome. Leaves in dense basal tufts, linear-subulate, 1–1½ in. long. Flowering-stem erect, very slender, 6–9 in. long, with a single small leaf below the middle. Spikes 1–2, ½–1½ in. long; spikelets $\frac{1}{12}$ in. long, 2–3-flowered. Outer empty glume acute, shorter than the spikelet. Flowering glume lanceolate, glabrous, with a short awn. C. distachya, *Bojer, Hort. Maur.* 371; *Kunth, Gram.* i. 291, *t.* 57; *Enum.* i. 266.

MAURITIUS, on the crest of Montagne Longue. Also East Indies and Bourbon.

22. PHRAGMITES, Trin.

Spikelets 4–6-flowered, arranged in very ample lax panicles. Empty glumes much shorter than the spikelet, membranous, the inner one lanceolate, the other very small, ovate. Flowers distinctly spaced on the rachis, all except the lowest hermaphrodite and enveloped in a dense tuft of hairs, the lowest imperfect and sessile inside the empty glumes. Flowering glume like the empty ones in texture, lanceolate, with a long point; pale small, included. Hypogynous scales large. Stamens 3. Styles short; stigmas plumose, protruded from the side of the spikelet. Grain free, cylindrical.—Tall swamp-grasses, with many broad leaves and very ample panicles. DISTRIB. Cosmopolitan. Perhaps one species only.

1. **P. communis,** *Trin.* var. *P. mauritianus, Kunth, Gram.* i. 80, 277, *t.* 50. Stem 10–12 feet long, erect, terete, hollow, $\frac{1}{4}$–$\frac{1}{2}$ in. thick, with numerous nodes. Leaves linear, subcoriaceous, acuminate, 1–2 feet long, $\frac{1}{2}$–$\frac{3}{4}$ in. broad, scabrous and cartilaginous at the edge. Panicle a foot or more long, with very numerous ascending decompound slender branches in half-whorls; spikelets $\frac{1}{2}$ inch long, 5–6-flowered. Outer empty glume lanceolate, $\frac{1}{8}$ in. long; inner ovate, half as long. Flowering glume $\frac{1}{4}$ in. long, lanceolate, with a long point. *Kunth, Enum.* i. 251. Arundo bengalensis, *Bojer, Hort. Maur.* 368, *not Retz.*

MAURITIUS and RODRIGUEZ, frequent in lakes and swamps. Cosmopolitan in the temperate and warm temperate zones. *Arundo bengalensis*, Retz., with which Bojer confounded the plant, is *A. Donax*, Linn., of similar general habit, but with empty glumes as long as the spikelet, and all the florets fertile and enveloped in tufts of hairs.

* Of the genus *Poa*, Linn, which includes many of the staple grasses of the greensward of the temperate zone in both the northern and southern hemispheres, and which differs from *Eragrostis* mainly by its webbed and usually 5-ribbed flowering glumes and deciduous pale, two of the common northern species occur casually in Mauritius, viz.—

* *P. annua*, Linn.; Kunth, Enum. i. 349; annual, stems a span high with few nodes, panicle lax with 1–2-nate finally horizontal or even deflexed branches and 3–7-flowered spikelets.

* *P. compressa*, Linn.; Kunth Enum. i. 355; perennial, with a creeping rootstock, stems 1–2 feet high compressed with many nodes, panicle contracted with short ascending 2–3-nate branches and flowers 4–9 to a spikelet.

23. ERAGROSTIS, Beauv.

(*Megastachya*, Beauv.; Bojer.)

Spikelets many-flowered, arranged in ample panicles. Empty glumes chartaceous, unequal, or subequal. Flowering glume oblong, similar to the empty glumes in texture, usually 3-nerved, not webbed. Pale persistent, 2-ribbed. Hypogynous scales 2. Stamens 3. Styles short; stigmas plumose, protruded from the side of the spikelet. Grain oblong, brown, free.—Annual or perennial densely-tufted grasses with narrow leaves and small laterally-compressed spikelets. DISTRIB. Warmer zones of both hemispheres. Species 100.

Panicle lax, oblong-rhomboid; pedicels sometimes longer than the spikelets.
Spikelets lanceolate. Flowering glumes remote on the rachis . . . . 1. E. PILOSA.
Spikelets oblong. Flowers crowded on the rachis.
Flowering glume not ciliated.
Spikelets $\frac{1}{8}$–$\frac{1}{4}$ in. long . . . . 2. E. POÆOIDES.
Spikelets $\frac{1}{12}$ in. long. Pale ciliated. . . . . 3. E. TENELLA.
Spikelets under $\frac{1}{12}$ in. long. Pale not ciliated . . 4. E. LAXA.
Flowering glume ciliated . . . . 5. E. MAURITII.
Panicle long and dense; pedicels none or very short.
Flowering glume ciliated . . . . 6. E. CILIARIS.
Flowering glume not ciliated . . . . 7. E. INTERRUPTA.

1. **E. pilosa,** *Beauv. Agrost.* 71. Annual, densely tufted. Stems $\frac{1}{2}$–1 ft. long, geniculate at the base, then ascending. Sheaths with a dense tuft of hairs at the throat; upper $1\frac{1}{2}$–2 in. long; blade narrow linear, glabrous, 2–3 in. long. Panicle 3–6 in. long, lax, oblong-rhomboid; branches erecto-patent, lower densely whorled, $1\frac{1}{2}$–2 in. long; pedicels often equalling or exceeding the spikelets; spikelets lanceolate, $\frac{1}{8}$ in. long, 8–10-flowered, glabrous, glossy, ascending, rather laxly placed on the rachis. Empty glumes membranous, unequal. Flowering glume $\frac{1}{30}$ in. long, 1-nerved, oblong, acute, neither it nor the pale ciliated. Poa pilosa, *Linn.; Kunth, Enum.*, i. 329. P. verticillata, *Cav. Ic. t.* 93; *Kunth, loc. cit.* P. punctata, *Linn.; Kunth, Enum.* i. 330.

MAURITIUS, in dry soil, *Sieber*, ii. 43! etc. SEYCHELLES, common, *Horne*, 622! Warmer zones of both hemispheres.

2. **E. poæoides,** *Beauv. Agrost.* 71. Annual, tufted. Stems a foot or more long, stronger than in any of the others, ascending. Sheaths with a tuft of hairs at the throat; upper $1\frac{1}{2}$–2 in. long; blade linear, glabrous, acuminate, 3–4 in. long, $\frac{1}{8}$–$\frac{1}{6}$ in. broad. Panicle lax, oblong-rhomboid, 3–4 in. long; branches erecto-patent; side pedicels shorter than the spikelets; spikelets $\frac{1}{8}$–$\frac{1}{4}$ in. long, oblong, glossy, 8–16-flowered. Flowering glume oblong, 3-nerved, $\frac{1}{12}$ in. long, cuspidate, both it and the pale glabrous on both back and edges. Poa Eragrostis, *Linn.; Knuth, Enum.*, i. 332. Megastachya brizoides, *Bojer, Hort. Maur.* 369.

MAURITIUS, in sandy ground near the sea. Spread through the two warmer zones of both hemispheres.

3. **E. tenella,** *Beauv. Agrost.* 71. Annual, densely tufted. Stems erect or geniculate at the base, $\frac{1}{2}$–$1\frac{1}{2}$ ft. long. Sheaths with a conspicuous tuft of hairs at the throat; upper an inch or less long; blade linear, glabrous, 2–3 in. long. Panicle lax, oblong, 2–4 in. long; branches erecto-patent, lower an inch or less long; pedicels sometimes longer than the spikelets; spikelets oblong, $\frac{1}{12}$ in. long, 6–10-flowered. Flowering glume erecto-patent, oblong, obtuse, $\frac{1}{30}$ in. long, with 3 distinct green ribs, glabrous, not ciliated. Pale oblong, conspicuously ciliated. Poa tenella, *Linn.; Kunth, Enum.* i. 338. Mega-

stachya tenella, *Bojer*, *Hort. Maur.* 369. P. plumosa, *Retz.*; *Kunth*, *Enum. loc. cit.* Eragrostis plumosa, *Link.*; *Steud. Gram.* 266.

MAURITIUS and SEYCHELLES, common in dry soil at all elevations. Also Madagascar and Tropical Asia.

4. **E. laxa,** *Baker*. Densely tufted. Stems very slender, ¼–½ ft. long, geniculate at the base. Sheaths with a dense tuft of hair at the throat; upper ½–¾ in. long; blade narrow linear, glabrous, convolute, 1½–2 in. long. Panicle 1½–2 in. long, lax, oblong-rhomboid; branches erecto-patent; pedicels sometimes 3–4 times the length of the spikelets; spikelets oblong, under $\frac{1}{12}$ in. long, 6–8-flowered. Flowering glume erecto-patent, dense, oblong, 3-nerved, glabrous, obtuse, like the pale, glabrous on both surface and edges.

SEYCHELLES, *Pervillé*, 118! Endemic.

5. **E. Mauritii,** *Steud. Gram.* 272. Tufted. Stems slender, glabrous, ¼–½ ft. long. Sheaths densely pilose at the throat; blade glabrous, narrow linear, 1–1½ in. long. Panicle lax, 1½–3 in. long, the lower branches whorled; pedicels longer than the spikelets; spikelets 5–10-flowered. Flowering glume strongly ciliated.

MAURITIUS, *D'Urville*. Also Bourbon. I have not seen this.

6. **E. ciliaris,** *Link, Hort. Berol.* i. 192. Annual, densely tufted. Stems trailing in the lower part, a foot or more long. Sheaths with a tuft of hairs at the throat; upper 2–3 in. long; blade narrow linear, glabrous, acuminate, 3–4 in. long. Panicle 3–4 inches long, narrow, dense; branches erecto-patent, lower an inch or less long; pedicels none or very short. Spikelets $\frac{1}{12}$ in. long and nearly as broad. Flower-glume $\frac{1}{12}$ in. long, densely ciliated with strong hairs, 3-nerved. Pale also ciliated. Poa ciliaris, *Linn.*; *Jacq. Ic. t.* 304; *Kunth, Enum.* i. 337. P. Boryana, *Willd.*; *Kunth, loc. cit.* Megastachya ciliaris and Boryana, *Bojer, Hort. Maur.* 369.

MAURITIUS, frequent in dry soil at all elevations, *Sieber*, ii. 24, etc. Warmer zones of both hemispheres.

7. **E. interrupta,** *Beauv. Agrost.* 71. Densely tufted, 1½–2 feet high. Sheaths without a tuft of hairs at the throat; upper 2–3 in. long; blade narrow linear, glabrous, 3–4 in. long. Panicle narrow, ½–1 ft. long, with numerous short branches in distant ascending fascicles; pedicels usually very short; spikelets oblong, $\frac{1}{12}$ in. long, 8–12-flowered. Flowering glume erecto-patent, oblong, obtuse, $\frac{1}{16}$ in. long, glabrous, like the pale, on the back and edges or the pale indistinctly ciliated. Poa interrupta, *Lam.*; *Kunth. Gram.* ii. 547. *tab.* 118. P. elongata, *Kunth, Enum.* i. 334. Megastachya elongata, *Beauv.*; *Bojer, Hort. Maur.* 369. Eragrostis propinqua, *Steud. Gram.* 271. P. nutans, *Retz.*; *Kunth, Enum.* i. 332.

MAURITIUS, in dry soil at all elevations. Spread through the tropics of the Old World.

* *Briza minor*, Linn.; Kunth, Enum. i. 372, a grass widely-spread through the southern half of Europe and now naturalised at the Cape and in South America, has been gathered in Mauritius by Bojer and Dr. Ayres on hills of the Pouce range near Moka. It is a tufted erect annual, a foot high, glabrous in all its parts, with linear leaves and a very compound panicle 3–4 in. long with slender ascending branches, capillary pedicels, deltoid spikelets ⅛ in. broad and long, with very obtuse many-nerved deeply boat-shaped flowering glumes much imbricated and spreading from the rachis almost horizontally.

Of the Bamboos none are native within the limits of our flora, but three of the tropical Asiatic species are now naturalised in Mauritius viz.:—

* *Bambusa arundinacea*, Retz.; Roxb. Cor. Pl. t. 79; Munro in Trans. Linn. Soc. xxvi. 103. Spinose, with stems 20–50 feet high, leaves glabrous lanceolate ½–1 ft. long, panicle with very long distant branches, spikelets few together in distant clusters lanceolate ½–1 in. long, acute flowering glumes and a linear-oblong grain. *Bambou.*

* *Dendrocalamus strictus*, Nees; Munro in Trans. Linn. Soc. xxvi. 147, (Bambusa stricta, *Roxb.; Bojer*, *Hort. Maur.* 377). Stems 10–100 feet high spinose or unarmed, leaves lanceolate rough-pubescent, spikelets 50–100 or more in dense globes 1–1½ in. in diam., flowering glume spiny at the tip, fruit ovoid baccate beaked ¼–⅓ in. in diam. *Bambou gaulette.*

* *Melanocanna bambusoides*, Trin.; Munro in Trans. Linn. Soc. xxvi. 132. Stems 50 feet long unarmed branched at the top only, leaves lanceolate acuminate glabrous ½–1 ft. long, spikelets lanceolate 3–4 together in close unilateral clusters enveloped each in a large coriaceous bract, flowering glume acute but not spine-tipped, fruit fleshy globose 3–5 in. in diameter.

24. ROTTBOELLIA, Linn.

Spikelets arranged in the hollows of a terete jointed simple rachis, compressed from the back, in pairs, one abortive, the other consisting of one hermaphrodite and one imperfect flower. Empty glumes similar in size and shape, but the outer one coriaceous and many-ribbed and the inner one membranous. Flowering glume and pale similar to one another in shape and both membranous. Hypogynous scales 2. Stamens 3. Stigmas plumose, protruded from the side of the spikelet. Grain free.—Tall, much-branched erect grasses, with flat rather firm leaves and distant simple spikes. DISTRIB. Tropics of both hemispheres. Species 20.

1. **R. exaltata,** *Linn. fil.; Kunth, Enum.* i. 466. An erect annual 3–4 feet high. Stems stout, with numerous erect branches. Sheaths 3–5 in. long, loosely hairy on the outside; blade above a foot long,

acuminate, glabrous, $\frac{1}{2}$–$\frac{3}{4}$ in. broad. Spikes distant, simple, lateral and terminal, $\frac{1}{4}$–$\frac{1}{2}$ ft. long, the lower ones more or less wrapped in a leaf-sheath; rachis terete, $\frac{1}{6}$ in. thick; joints $\frac{1}{6}$–$\frac{1}{4}$ in. long. Spikelets oblong, acute, glabrous, usually rather longer than the joints. R. arundinacea, *Hochst.*

SEYCHELLES, in the northern part of the island of Mahé. *Horne*, 625! Spread through the tropics of the Old World.

The Maize, **Zea Mays**, Linn., is cultivated in Mauritius and Seychelles, and is in Dr. Balfour's Rodriguez collection as a subspontaneous species.

The Rice, **Oryza sativa**, Linn., is also cultivated abundantly and casually subspontaneous.

ORDER CVIII. FILICES.

Fructification consisting of minute 1-celled stalked or sessile capsules (sporangia), which dehisce vertically or laterally and are usually surrounded by an incomplete or a complete ring and aggregated in clusters (sori) on the back or edge of leafy fronds. These sori sometimes form spikes or panicles or become connate in a mass (synangia), and when dorsal or marginal on the frond are either naked or covered from above or below with a scale (involucre). The spores which they contain are very minute, uniform, and without spiral threads (elaters), and after falling to the ground give rise to a leafy expansion (prothallus), on the lower surface of which are developed cellular sacs which open at their mouth (archegonia) and contain a single germ-cell, and other cellular hollows (antheridia), each of which holds several sperm-cells (antherozoids) which possess the power of motion and fertilise the archegonia.—Rootstock erect (caudex) rarely produced above ground, or creeping at or below the surface (rhizome), more or less scaly; leaves (fronds) very various in texture and cutting, usually furnished with a petiole (stipe), always abundantly veined. DISTRIB. Cosmopolitan. Species 3000.

Suborder I. GLEICHENIACEÆ. Capsules few, sessile on a depressed receptacle, with a complete horizontal ring, splitting vertically.

The only genus . . . . 1. GLEICHENIA.

Suborder II. HYMENOPHYLLACEÆ. Capsules many, sessile on a subulate receptacle, with a complete oblique ring, splitting vertically. Texture of frond filmy.

Involucre deeply 2-valved . . . . 2. HYMENOPHYLLUM.
Involucre truncate at the mouth or shallowly 2-valved . . . . 3. TRICHOMANES.

Suborder III. CYATHEACEÆ. Capsules usually sessile on a barrel-shaped receptacle, with a rather oblique incomplete vertical ring, splitting transversely. Tree-ferns.

The only genus . . . . 4. CYATHEA.

Suborder IV. POLYPODIACEÆ. Capsules stalked, on a depressed receptacle, with an incomplete vertical ring, splitting transversely.

Involucre placed beneath the sorus.
  Sori globose or oblong, dorsal or marginal.
    Involucre cup-shaped, entire or 2-valved . . . . 5. DICKSONIA.
    Involucre adpressed to the surface of the frond.
      Sori placed at the tip of veins . . . . 6. DAVALLIA.
      Sori placed on the back of veins . . . . 7. CYSTOPTERIS.
  Sori linear, marginal.
    Frond simple . . . . 8. VITTARIA.
    Frond compound . . . . 9. LINDSAYA.
Involucre placed above the sorus.
  Sori marginal.
    Involucre bearing the capsules on its under surface . . . . 10. ADIANTUM.
    Involucre wrapped over the capsules.
      Sori placed in the final sinuses.
        Sori round . . . . 11. HYPOLEPIS.
        Sori crescent-shaped . . . . 12. LONCHITIS.
      Sori placed along the edge of the final segments.
        Sori round or oblong . . . . 13. OCHROPTERIS.
      Sori linear, not filling up the whole of the segments.
        Sori at first in dots, soon confluent in a line . 14. PELLÆA.
        Sori linear from the first . . . . 15. PTERIS.
      Sori linear, filling up the whole of the segments of a special frond . . . . 16. LOMARIA.
  Sori dorsal.
    Sori linear or oblong . . . . 17. ASPLENIUM.
    Sori round.
      Involucre peltate . . . . 18. ASPIDIUM.
      Involucre reniform.
        Frond simple . . . . 19. OLEANDRA.
        Frond compound, with pinnæ articulated at the base . . . . 20. NEPHROLEPIS.
        Frond compound, with pinnæ not articulated at the base . . . . 21. NEPHRODIUM.
Involucre none.
  Sori placed on the veins only.
    Sori confined to the midrib . . . . 22. MONOGRAMME.
    Sori dorsal on secondary veins.
      Sori round or rarely oblong . . . . 23. POLYPODIUM.
      Sori linear, not anastomosing . . . . 24. GYMNOGRAMME.
      Sori linear, anastomosing . . . . 25. ANTROPHYUM.
  Sori occupying both veins and interspaces.
    Sori occupying the whole surface . . . . 26. ACROSTICHUM.
    Sori forming partial patches . . . . 27. PLATYCERIUM.

Suborder V. OSMUNDACEÆ. Capsules stalked, with a short horizontal ring, splitting vertically.

The only genus . . . . 28. OSMUNDA.

Suborder VI. SCHIZÆACEÆ. Capsules sessile, crowned with a complete ring, splitting vertically.

The only genus . . . . 29. SCHIZÆA.

Suborder VI. MARATTIACEÆ. Capsules sessile, without any ring, usually concrete in masses, splitting vertically. Stems articulated on a tuberous rootstock, furnished at the base with two large auricles.

Capsule concrete in masses . . . . 30. MARATTIA.
Capsules not concrete in masses . . . . 31. ANGIOPTERIS.

Suborder VII. OPHIOGLOSSACEÆ. Capsules sessile, without any ring arranged in spikes or panicles, splitting laterally.

The only genus . . . . 32. OPHIOGLOSSUM.

1. GLEICHENIA, Smith.

Capsules sessile, splitting from top to bottom into halves, girt by a broad complete oblique transverse ring. Sori globose, without any involucre, consisting of very few comparatively large capsules, placed on a depressed receptacle on the back or at the base of the veins.—Large coriaceous dichotomously-forked ferns, with wiry wide-creeping rootstocks, the ultimate segments in our plants linear. DISTRIB. Tropical and warm temperate regions, especially of the southern hemisphere. Species 20–30.

Only the ultimate branches of the frond leaf-bearing . . 1. G. DICHOTOMA.
All the branches of the frond leaf-bearing . . . . . . 2. G. FLAGELLARIS.

1. **G. dichotoma,** *Willd.; Hook. and Baker, Syn. Fil.* 15. Rootstock woody, wide-creeping, the thickness of a quill. Fronds reaching a height of 10 or 15 feet, 1–4 times dichotomously forked, with a pair of large erecto-patent pinnæ with a scaly bud in their axil from the end of each branch and a pair of smaller deflexed pinnæ also from each fork, the texture rigidly subcoriaceous, the surfaces naked, or the lower with a little ferruginous down on the midrib of the segments. End-pinnæ lanceolate, 6–12 in. long, 1–2½ in. broad, cut down to the rachis into close-spreading entire obtuse linear segments. Veins close, distinct, mostly trifurcate. Sori nearer the midrib than the edge. G. Hermanni, *R. Br.; Bojer. Hort. Maur.* 420.

MAURITIUS and SEYCHELLES, common on dry hills. Cosmopolitan in tropical and subtropical countries.

2. **G. flagellaris,** *Spreng.; Hook. and Baker, Syn. Fil.* 14. Fronds 3 or 4 times dichotomously forked, leafy from the first forking continuously to the top of the ultimate branchlets, the texture rigidly subcoriaceous, the upper surface dark green and naked, the lower glaucous and with a little ferruginous down on the midrib of the segments. Pinnæ lanceolate, 1–2 in. broad, cut down to the rachis into close adnate entire linear ultimate segments. Veins fine, distinct, once forked near the base. Sori on the back of the veins, nearer the edge than the

midrib, consisting of not more than 4 or 5 capsules. G. muricata, *Bojer, Hort. Maur.* 421.

MAURITIUS, in woods at Moka, Savanne, Grandport, etc. Also Bourbon, Madagascar, and the Malayan and Polynesian islands.

2. HYMENOPHYLLUM, Linn.

Capsules sessile, densely crowded on a subulate receptacle, broader than long, furnished with a broad transverse ring and opening irregularly from the top. Sori marginal on the segments, terminating on the veins, enclosed in a persistent cup-shaped involucre, which is split into two valves to below the middle.—Small ferns of filmy texture, various in cutting, with wide-creeping thread-like rootstocks, usually forming dense masses. DISTRIB. All tropical and warm temperate regions. Species 80.

Fronds glabrous. Segments not toothed.
  Fronds small, bipinnatifid, with rachis not winged in the lower half . . . . 1. H. RARUM.
  Fronds small, tripinnatifid, with rachis winged throughout . . . . 2. H. TENELLUM.
  Fronds middle-sized, 3-4-pinnatifid.
    Segments few, not crowded . . . . 3. H. INÆQUALE.
    Segments many, crowded . . . . 4. H. POLYANTHOS.
Fronds hairy. Segments not toothed.
  Fronds lanceolate, under an inch broad . . . . . . 5. H. BOUTONI.
  Fronds oblong-deltoid, 1-4 in. broad.
    Main rachis winged throughout . . . . 6. H. CILIATUM.
    Main rachis winged only at the very top . . . . 7. H. HYGROMETRICUM.
Fronds glabrous. Segments distinctly toothed . . . . 8. H. TUNBRIDGENSE.

1. **H. rarum,** *R. Br.; Hook. and Baker, Syn. Fil.* 58. Stipe slender, wiry, $\frac{1}{2}$-1 in. long. Frond flaccid, pendulous, glabrous, 1-2 in. long, $\frac{1}{3}$ in. broad, lanceolate, narrowed to the base, bipinnatifid, the rachis winged in the upper half; the most compound pinnæ with very few segments and a broadly winged rachis. Ultimate segments $\frac{1}{8}$-$\frac{1}{6}$ in. long, $\frac{1}{24}$ in. broad, quite entire. Sori few to a frond, the involucre as broad as the segments, with an immersed base and semicircular valves. H. fumarioides, *Bory; Bojer, Hort. Maur.* 411.

MAURITIUS, damp rocks and trees of Savanne, Grand Bassin, and Pouce ranges. Round the world, principally in the southern hemisphere.

2. **H. tenellum,** *Kuhn; Hook. and Baker, Syn. Fil. edit.* ii. 57. Stipe $\frac{1}{2}$-1 in. long, winged in the upper half. Frond glabrous, 1-2 in. long, $\frac{3}{4}$-1 in. broad, oblong, 2-3-pinnatifid. Pinnæ few, only the lowest divisions forked. Main rachis distinctly winged throughout. Ultimate segments $\frac{1}{12}$-$\frac{1}{8}$ in. long, $\frac{1}{24}$ in. broad, entire, much more numerous than in *H. rarum*. Sori few to a frond, terminal on the upper segments. Involucre immersed at the base, with semicircular valves, as broad as the segments, the receptacle sometimes protruded.

H. emersum, *Baker*, *Syn. Fil. edit.* i. 457. H. ricciæfolium, *Bory*; *Bojer*, *Hort. Maur.* 411.

MAURITIUS, in forests of the Savanne range, *Lady Barkly*! Freanges on the base of mossy trees, *Cattell*. Also Ceylon, Bourbon, and Madagascar.

3. **H. inæquale,** *Desv.*; *Kuhn*, *Fil. Afr.* 40. Stipe 2–3 in. long, wiry, subulate. Frond oblong-lanceolate, 3–4-pinnatifid, 3–6 in. long, 1–2 in. broad, glabrous, with distant ascending pinnæ and pinnules. Rachis winged only towards the top of the frond. Ultimate segments ligulate, entire, $\frac{1}{8}$–$\frac{1}{6}$ in. long, $\frac{1}{36}$ in. broad. Sori many to a frond, terminal on the lower segments of the upper pinnæ. Involucre as broad as the segments, with an immersed deltoid base and semicircular valves. H. gracile, *Bory*; *Hook. and Grev. Ic. Fil. t.* 198; *Hook. and Baker*, *Syn. Fil.* 58.

MAURITIUS, in forests of the Pouce range and Quartier Militaire. Also Bourbon, Madagascar, and Natal.

4. **H. polyanthos,** *Sw.*; *Hook. and Baker*, *Syn. Fil.* 60. Stipe wiry, 1–2 in. long. Frond oblong-lanceolate, glabrous, 4-pinnatifid 3–6 in. long, 1–2 in. broad, flaccid, pendulous, the main rachis winged throughout. Pinnæ lanceolate, the divisions of all grades more numerous and closer than in *H. inæquale*, the final segments $\frac{1}{12}$–$\frac{1}{8}$ in. in. long by $\frac{1}{36}$ in. broad, entire. Sori often several to a pinna, terminal on the lower segments. Involucre broader than the segments, the base very slightly immersed, the valves semicircular.

SEYCHELLES, common in the woods of Mahé, *Horne*, 146! Cosmopolitan in the tropics, but rare in Africa.

5. **H. Boutoni,** *Baker*. Stipe under an inch long, winged at the top. Frond lanceolate, bipinnatifid, 2–3 in. long, $\frac{3}{8}$–$\frac{1}{2}$ in. broad, thinly pilose, with the main rachis distinctly winged throughout. Pinnæ cuneate-deltoid, the lower consisting of 4–6 ascending entire segments, which are $\frac{1}{8}$–$\frac{1}{6}$ in. long by $\frac{1}{24}$ in. broad. Sori many to a pinna, terminal on all the segments, and broader than they are. Involucre immersed at the base, densely matted with ferruginous hairs; valves semicircular.

MAURITIUS, *Bouton*! Endemic. Intermediate between *H. ciliatum* and *lineare*, with the narrow frond and cutting of the latter, and the winged main rachis and large involucre of the former.

6. **H. ciliatum,** *Sw.*; *Hook. and Baker*, *Syn. Fil.* 63. Stipe 1–2 in. long, pilose, distinctly winged in the upper half. Frond oblong-deltoid, 2–4 in. long, 1–2 in. broad, 2–3-pinnatifid, densely clothed with short brown hairs, the main rachis winged throughout. Pinnæ crowded, lanceolate, cut away on the lower side at the base; segments entire, contiguous, reaching $\frac{1}{8}$–$\frac{1}{6}$ in. long by $\frac{1}{24}$ in. broad. Sori many to a pinna, terminal on any of the segments, and as broad as they are. Involucre immersed at the base, densely tomentose;

valves semicircular. H. Boryanum, *Willd.*: *Bojer, Hort. Maur.* 111. H. Arbuscula, *Desv.*

MAURITIUS, in the damp forests of the Pouce range, etc. SEYCHELLES, *Ward!* Cosmopolitan in tropical and sub-tropical regions.

7. **H. hygrometricum,** *Desv.*; *Kuhn, Fil. Afr.* 89. Stipe wiry, dark brown, 2–4 in. long, not at all winged. Frond oblong-deltoid, 6–12 in. long, 2–4 in. broad, 3–4-pinnatifid, very elastic in texture and sensitive to moisture, so that it curls up when the air is dry, thinly covered with stellate hairs, the main rachis winged only at the top. Pinnæ lanceolate-deltoid, cut away on the lower side at the base. Ultimate segments close, erecto-patent, entire, $\frac{1}{8}$–$\frac{1}{4}$ in. long, $\frac{1}{18}$ in. broad. Sori minute, many to a pinnule. Involucre immersed at the base; valves semicircular, conspicuously ciliated. H. elasticum, *Bory*; *Hook. and Grev. Ic. Fil. t.* 135; *Hook. and Baker, Syn. Fil.* 64.

MAURITIUS, in woods of the Pouce range, etc. SEYCHELLES, common in Mahé, *Pervillé, Horne*, 149! Also Bourbon and Madagascar. Very near *H. hirtellum*, Sw., of Tropical America.

8. **H. Tunbridgense,** *Smith*; *Hook. and Baker, Syn. Fil.* 67. Stipe wiry, $\frac{1}{2}$–1 in. long, not winged. Frond lanceolate, 2–3 in. long, under an inch broad, 2–3-pinnatifid, the main rachis winged only at the top. Pinnæ ascending, close, cuneate-deltoid, the lower made up of 6–10 distinctly-toothed segments, which are $\frac{1}{8}$–$\frac{1}{4}$ in. long by $\frac{1}{24}$ in. broad. Sori only one to a pinna, terminal on a short basal anterior lobe. Involucre free; valves obovate, distinctly toothed.

MAURITIUS, *Carmichael!* According to Bojer, *H. unilaterale*, Willd., which is a variety with entire involucral-valves, is found in the woods of Savanne and Grand Bassin, but we have not seen any specimen. Widely spread in Tropical and Temperate regions of the Old and New World.

3. TRICHOMANES, Smith.

Capsules, position of the sori, texture, and general habit just as in *Hymenophyllum*, but the involucre cylindrical or funnel-shaped, with a truncate mouth, or two shallow valves. Receptacle usually longer than in *Hymenophyllum* and protruded from the involucre. DISTRIB. All damp, tropical and warm temperate countries. Species 80.

Fronds very small, entire or slightly lobed.
  Sorus solitary, terminal . . . . 1. T. BARKLIANUM.
  Sori several to a frond.
    Midrib distinct at the base only . . . . 2. T. CUSPIDATUM.
    Midrib distinct nearly to the top . . . . 3. T. EROSUM.
Fronds very small, digitately pinnatifid.
  Segments few, obscurely flabellate . . . . 4. T. DIGITATUM.
  Segments many, distinctly flabellate.
    Vein of segments solitary . . . . 5. T. FLABELLATUM.
    Veins of segments three . . . . 6. T. TRINERVE.

Fronds middle-sized, tripinnatifid.
  Involucre with two large valves . . . . 7. T. BIPUNCTATUM.
  Involucre with a spreading collar-like limb . . . . 8. T. PYXIDIFERUM.
Fronds large and firm in texture, decompound.
  Ultimate segments ligulate, very short . . . . . 9. T. RIGIDUM.
  Ultimate segments very narrow, linear-subulate . . 10. T. PARVIFLORUM.

1. **T. Barklianum,** *Baker; Hook. and Baker, Syn. Fil.* 74. Rootstock thread-like. Stipe $\frac{1}{12}$–$\frac{1}{8}$ in. long, filiform. Frond linear-oblong, entire, $\frac{1}{6}$–$\frac{1}{3}$ in. long, with a distinct midrib from base to apex and 6–10 parallel erecto-patent veins on each side of it, without any faint intermediate veinlets. Sori one to a frond, terminal. Involucre cylindrical, immersed, with a broad spreading faintly two-lipped mouth. *Baker in Journ. Linn. Soc.* ix. 338, *tab.* 8, *fig. D.*

MAURITIUS, at the falls of the Tamarin River, *Sir Henry and Lady Barkly!* Endemic.

2. **T. cuspidatum,** *Willd.; Hook. and Baker, Syn. Fil.* 73. Rootstock thread like. Stipe $\frac{1}{4}$–$\frac{1}{2}$ in. long, filiform. Frond rhomboid, deltoid or semicircular, $\frac{1}{4}$–$\frac{1}{2}$ in. broad, entire or slightly lobed, the veins radiating like a fan through the upper half or two-thirds, with copious faint veinlets between them. Sori many to a frond, placed round the upper half. Involucre cylindrical, quite immersed, with a spreading collar-like entire mouth. T. adiantinum, *Bory; Bojer, Hort. Maur.* 409. T. Bojeri, *Hook and Grev. Ic. Fil. t.* 155; *Bojer, Hort. Maur.* 409.

MAURITIUS, in the forests of the Savanne and Grand Bassin hills. SEYCHELLES, teste *Kuhn*. RODRIGUEZ, *Balfour!* Also Bourbon, Madagascar, and the Comoros.

3. **T. erosum,** *Willd.; Kuhn. Fil. Afr.* 34. Rootstock thread-like. Stipe filiform, $\frac{1}{4}$–$\frac{1}{2}$ in. long. Frond very variable in shape, lanceolate, oblong, deltoid or semicircular, entire or repand-pinnatifid, 1–2 in. long, with very abundant ascending fine distinct veins, a zigzag central one distinct nearly to the top, accompanied by abundant faint intermediate veinlets. Sori one or many placed along the upper margin of the frond. Involucre immersed, cylindrical, with a large spreading collar-like nearly entire limb. T. muscoides, *Hook. and Baker, Syn. Fil.* 75.

SEYCHELLES, common in the mountain forests, *Horne*, 147! 672! 673! Cosmopolitan in the tropics.

4. **T. digitatum,** *Sw.; Hook. and Baker, Syn. Fil.* 76. Rootstock wide-creeping, filiform. Stipe wiry, $\frac{1}{4}$–$\frac{1}{2}$ in. long. Frond 1–$1\frac{1}{2}$ in. long, with 4–10 distant deep ascending flabellate strap-shaped segments $\frac{1}{16}$–$\frac{1}{12}$ in. broad, each with a distinct midrib and no other veinlets. Sori few to a frond, terminal on the segments. Involucre funnel-shaped, with an immersed tube, and two obscure valves. T. lanceum, *Bory; Hook. and Grev. Ic. Fil. t.* 33; *Bojer, Hort. Maur.* 409.

MAURITIUS, on trees and rocks of the Pouce and Savanne ranges. Also Asia, Polynesia, and Cape.

5. **T. flabellatum,** *Bory; Hook. and Baker, Syn. Fil.* 76. Rootstock filiform. Stipe wiry, $\frac{1}{2}$–$\frac{3}{4}$ in. long. Frond semicircular or cuneate-deltoid, $\frac{1}{4}$–$\frac{3}{4}$ in. broad, flabellately cut into many close dichotomous segments $\frac{1}{18}$ in. broad, which have a distinct midrib, but no veinlets. Sori 2–4 to a frond, at the end of central segments. Involucre immersed, turbinate, with two distinct semicircular denticulate lips. T. sibthorpioides, *Bory.* Hymenophyllum sibthorpioides. *Mett.; Kuhn, Fil. Afr.* 41.

MAURITIUS, teste *Kuhn.* We have it from Bourbon, Madagascar, and Johanna Island, but not from Mauritius. Probably this is Bojer's *T. parvulum*, found at the cascades of the Black River and the wood of Savanne, but we have not authentic specimens. The true *T. parvulum*, which is found in Bourbon, has shorter stipes and an involucre with a broad spreading collar-like limb.

6. **T. trinerve,** *Baker.* Rootstock filiform. Stipe terete, $\frac{1}{4}$–$\frac{1}{2}$ in. long. Frond $\frac{1}{4}$ in. broad, bright green, cuneate-deltoid, cut into 4–6 close ligulate lobes $\frac{1}{24}$ in. broad, each with a distinct midrib and distinct vein on each side. Sori 1–3 to a frond, placed at the end of the central lobes. Involucre funnel-shaped, immersed at the base only, with a large spreading obscurely two-lipped collar-like limb.

MAURITIUS, at the Tamarin cascade, with *T. Barklianum, Sir H. and Lady Barkly! Dr. Meller!* Endemic. Closely allied to the West African *T Mannii.*

7. **T. bipunctatum,** *Poir.; Kuhn, Fil. Afr.* 32. Rootstock filiform, wide-creeping, tomentose. Stipe $\frac{1}{2}$–1 in. long, winged at the top. Frond oblong-lanceolate or oblong-deltoid, 2–3 in. long, about an inch broad, tripinnatifid, with the rachis winged throughout. Pinnæ lanceolate, cut away on the lower side at the base. Ultimate segments close, erecto-patent, strap-shaped, $\frac{1}{8}$–$\frac{1}{6}$ in, long, $\frac{1}{36}$ in. broad, with a central midrib and usually no other vein. Sori 1 or more to a pinna, especially on the lowest lobe. Involucre funnel-shaped, winged, with two very distinct lips. T. Filicula, *Bory; Hook. and Baker, Syn. Fil.* 81.

MAURITIUS, in woods of the Savanne and Pouce ranges. *T. depauperatum*, Bojer, Hort. Maur. 410, probably belongs here, but I have not seen authentic specimens. Through the tropics, principally of the Old World.

8. **T. pyxidiferum,** *Linn.; Hook. and Baker, Syn. Fil.* 81. General habit and cutting exactly of *T. bipunctatum*, but the involucre with a spreading subentire collar-like limb. T. borbonicum, *V. D. B.; Kuhn, Fil. Afr.* 33. T. melanotrichum, *Schlecht.; Kuhn, Fil. Afr.* 35.

Gathered in MAURITIUS, according to Kuhn, but I have not seen a specimen. Round the world in tropical and subtropical regions. We have it from Bourbon and Johanna Island.

9. **T. rigidum,** *Swartz; Hook. and Baker, Syn. Fil.* 86. Rootstock woody, suberect or short-creeping, densely clothed with minute

subulate dark brown scales. Stipe wiry, ¼–½ ft. long, naked except near the base. Frond oblong-lanceolate, 6–12 in. long, 3–4 in. broad, quadripinnatifid, firmer in texture than in almost any other of the filmy-ferns, the rachis winged at the top only. Pinnæ and pinnules crowded, lanceolate. Ultimate segments under 1/12 in. long, with only a narrow wing to the stout rigid midrib. Involucre minute, more or less exserted, the mouth faintly two-lipped and not expanded into a collar; receptacle much exserted. T. stylosum, *Poir.; Kuhn, Fil. Afr.* 37. T. obscurum, *Blume; Kuhn, Fil. Afr.* 35. T. tamarisciforme, *Jacq.; Kuhn, Fil. Af.* 38; *Bojer, Hort. Maur.* 410. T. achilleæfolium, *Willd.; Bojer, Hort. Maur.* 410. T. longisetum, *Bojer, Hort. Maur.* 410, *not Bory.*

MAURITIUS and SEYCHELLES, common in the hillwoods. Round the world in the tropical and sub-tropical zone. I have not seen an authentic example of *T. meifolium*, Bojer, Hort. Maur. 410, from the forests of Savanne.

10, **T. parviflorum,** *Poir.; Kuhn, Fil. Afr.* 35. Closely allied to *T. rigidum*, with which it quite agrees in general habit, but from which it differs by its much longer narrower ultimate segments, which are almost reduced to the vein, and by its still smaller involucre, which is quite exserted from the lamina and not more than 1/36 in. long by half as broad. T fœniculaceum, *Bory; Hook. and Baker, Syn. Fil.* 88; *Bojer, Hort. Maur.* 411.

MAURITIUS, in the woods of the Savanne and Grandport ranges. Also Bourbon, Madagascar, the Malay isles and Australia.

4. CYATHEA, Sm.

Capsules with an incomplete slightly oblique vertical ring, forming dense globose sori, placed on an elevated receptacle, and often mixed with jointed filaments, included in a complete membranous cup, which is placed on the middle of a vein on the under surface of the frond.—Treeferns, with ample bipinnate or tripinnate fronds, the stipes and rachises often prickly. DISTRIB. Cosmopolitan in tropical and subtropical regions, few African. Species 70–80.

Frond bipinnate . . . . 1. C. CANALICULATA.
Frond tripinnate.
  Involucre regularly truncate . . . . 2. C. SECHELLARUM.
  Involucre breaking up irregularly . . . . 3. C. EXCELSA.

1. **C. canaliculata,** *Willd.; Hook. and Baker, Syn. Fil.* 23. Frond bipinnate, 1–2 feet or more broad, membranous or subcoriaceous, green and quite naked on both surfaces, with pale or dark brown unarmed rachises, usually quite naked, rarely with a thin coating of tomentum on the under side. Pinnæ lanceolate, ½–1 ft. long, 1–2½ in. broad. Pinnules close, lanceolate, adnate, toothed in the upper half, ¾–1½ in. long, ⅓–⅜ in. broad. Veins fine, distinct, slightly ascending, 15–40-jugate, forked. Sori in a long row at the forking of the veins, near the midrib.

Involucre thin, breaking up irregularly. C. borbonica, *Desv.; Bojer, Hort. Maur.* 388. C. robusta, *Bojer; Wall. Cat.* 182. Alsophila Telfairiana, *Wall.; Hook. Sp. Fil.* i. 56.

MAURITIUS, in the forests of Grandport and Savanne. Also Bourbon and Madagascar. *C. lævigata*, Willd. and *C. Percilléana* and *Commersoniana* of Fée, are varieties with large pinnules, like the form figured in Hook. Sp. Fil. vol. i. t. 13 A.

2. **C. sechellarum,** *Mett.; Hook. and Baker, Syn. Fil.* 22. Trunk reaching a height of 40–50 feet. Stipe 1–2 feet long, pale or dark brown, armed with small prickles, which extend to the rachises. Fronds 4–9 feet long, 2–4 feet broad, deltoid, tripinnate, dark green above, pale green or faintly glaucous beneath, minutely scaly on the midrib of the segments on the under side. Pinnæ and pinnules both lanceolate, the latter 3–4 in. long, $\frac{3}{8}$–$\frac{1}{2}$ in. broad, cut down to the rachis into close lanceolate distinctly-toothed tertiary segments $\frac{1}{12}$ in. broad. Veins 10–12-jugate, distinct, deeply forked. Sori crowded close to the midrib, confined to the lower half of the segments. Involucre a firm distinct hemispherical cup with an entire rim, like that of the American *C. arborea.*

SEYCHELLES, common in the hill-forests of Mahé. Endemic.

3. **C. excelsa,** *Swartz; Hook. and Baker, Syn. Fil.* 22. Fronds tripinnate, reaching 6–8 feet long, moderately firm in texture, green and glabrous on both surfaces, with pale brown more or less prickly rachises. Pinnæ and pinnules both lanceolate, the latter acuminate, 3–4 in. long, $\frac{3}{4}$–1 in. broad, cut down to the rachis into lanceolate distinctly-toothed tertiary segments $\frac{1}{8}$–$\frac{1}{6}$ in. broad. Veins 10–15-jugate, deeply forked. Sori at the forking of the veins, forming a row close to the midrib. Involucre membranous, breaking up irregularly. C. arborea, *Bory, Voy.* i. 179, *not Smith.*

MAURITIUS, in the forests of the Savanne and Black River ranges. Also Bourbon. *C. glauca*, Bory, which differs from *C. excelsa* by its tomentose rachises and glaucous under surface, is given by Bojer as Mauritian, but I have seen it from Bourbon only.

5. DICKSONIA, Smith.

Capsules stalked, splitting transversely, with an incomplete vertical ring. Sori globose, placed at the tip of a vein, either at or just within the margin. Involucre inferior, cup- or plate-shaped or furnished with two distinct lips.—Ferns of very various size and cutting, some arborescent, some dwarf with creeping rootstocks. DISTRIB. Tropical and warm temperate regions of both hemispheres. Species 30–35.

Frond simply pinnate. Involucre marginal, two-lipped . . 1. D. ABRUPTA.
Frond decompound. Involucre intra-marginal, plate-shaped . . . . 2. D. ANTHRISCIFOLIA.

1. **D. abrupta,** *Bory; Hook. and Baker, Syn. Fil.* 32. Stipes short, tufted. Fronds lanceolate, simply pinnate, 2–3 feet long, 3–5

in. broad, glossy, green, subcoriaceous, with a rather tomentose stout stiff rachis channelled down the front. Pinnæ crowded, lanceolate, articulated at the base and falling away readily, the barren ones $\frac{1}{2}$–$\frac{3}{4}$ in. broad, finely toothed, the fertile ones narrower, usually confined to the upper half of the frond. Veins except the midrib of the pinnæ fine and indistinct. Involucre forming little round marginal lobes along both borders of the fertile pinnæ, the outer lip formed by the indurated edge of the frond, the inner one also rigid and semicircular, rather smaller. Nephrolepis abrupta, *Mett.; Kuhn, Fil. Afr.* 154. Leptopleuria, *Presl.*

MAURITIUS, on decayed timber in the forests of Plaines Wilhelms, *Sir Henry and Lady Barkly!* Also Bourbon and Madagascar.

2. **D. anthriscifolia,** *Kaulf.; Hook. and Baker, Syn. Fil.* 53. Fronds ample, decompound, membranous, quadripinnatifid, $\frac{3}{4}$–1 foot broad, with a pale brown rachis; the ribs of the under side of the frond more or less bristly. Pinnæ and pinnules lanceolate, cut away on the lower side at the base. Ultimate segments oblong, obtuse, adnate, inciso-crenate, $\frac{1}{12}$ in. broad. Veinlets free, distant, distinct, erecto-patent. Sori minute, placed just within the margin at the tip of a veinlet. Involucre plate-like, pale, membranous. Adiantum fragile, *Bojer, Hort. Maur.* 405, *not Sw.*

MAURITIUS, in the woods of Grandport and Savanne. Also Bourbon and Madagascar, and scarcely distinct specifically from *D. rubiginosa* of America.

6. DAVALLIA, Smith.

Capsules stalked, splitting transversely, with an incomplete vertical ring. Sori marginal or intramarginal, placed at the tip of a vein, globose or oblong. Involucre adpressed to the surface of the frond, oblong or round or broader than long, persistent, free or open at the sides.—Habit and cutting very various. Texture coriaceous or membranous. Veins free in all the Mauritian species. DISTRIB. Tropical regions, principally of Asia. Species 30.

Frond coriaceous, glabrous.
  Rootstock wide-creeping, with distant fronds.
    Frond small, simply pinnate . . . . 1. D. PEDATA.
    Frond large, decompound . . . . 2. D. ELATA.
  Rootstock short-creeping, with close fronds, with cuneate segments . . . . 3. D. TENUIFOLIA.
Frond membranous, pilose . . . . 4. D. SPELUNCÆ.
Frond membranous, glabrous, with segments truncate, as in *Lindsaya*, on the lower and inner edge.
  Frond simply pinnate, with a very short stipe . . . 5. D. REPENS.
  Frond bipinnate, with a produced stipe . . . . 6. D. HORNEI.

1. **D. pedata,** *Sw.; Hook. and Baker, Syn. Fil.* 89. Rootstock wide-creeping, superficial, $\frac{1}{12}$ in. thick, clothed with small lanceolate adpressed ferruginous scales. Stipe 1–3 in. long, with a few scattered minute

scales. Frond deltoid, coriaceous, glabrous, 2–3 in. long, the upper pinnæ simple, close, erecto-patent, those of the fertile frond distinctly toothed, the lowest pair much larger, deltoid, distinctly lobed on the lower side. Veins fine, close, erecto-patent. Sori minute, marginal, oblique. Involucre twice as broad as long, free at the sides. *Hook. Sp. Fil.* i. 54, *t.* 45. D. repens, *Kuhn, Fil. Afr.* 158. (Adiantum, *Linn.*)

MAURITIUS and SEYCHELLES, common on rocks and old trunks. Tropical Asia and Polynesia, not Continental Africa.

2. **D. elata,** *Sw.; Hook. and Baker, Syn. Fil.* 95. Rootstock woody, wide-creeping above ground, densely clothed with linear-subulate bright brown scales. Stipe ½ to 1 foot long, glossy, naked, pale brown. Frond deltoid, coriaceous, glabrous, quadripinnatifid, ½–1½ foot long and broad. Pinnæ and pinnules deltoid, the lowest the longest, distinctly stalked. Ultimate segments erecto-patent, linear or lanceolate, $\frac{1}{12}$–$\frac{1}{24}$ in. broad. Veins fine, close, ascending. Sori minute, copious, marginal, oblong, the sides of the coriaceous involucre attached to the frond. D. mauritiana, *Hook.; Hook. and Baker, Syn. Fil.* 26. D. Vogelii, *Hook.* D. denticulata, *Mett.; Kuhn, Fil. Afr.* 157.

MAURITIUS, RODRIGUEZ, and SEYCHELLES, common on old trunks in shaded places. Spread through the warmer zones of the Old World.

3. **D. tenuifolia,** *Swartz; Hook. and Baker, Syn. Fil.* 102. Rootstock short-creeping, clothed with minute subulate brown scales. Stipe naked, glossy, pale brown, ½–1 foot long. Frond ½–2 feet long, oblong-lanceolate, subcoriaceous, naked, decompound. Pinnæ and pinnules deltoid. Ultimate segments cuneate, ⅛–⅙ in. long, narrowed from the tip to the base. Veins distinct, one or two to each segment. Sori marginal, confined to the tip of the segments. Involucre firm, persistent, often broader than long. Lindsaya chinensis, *Mett.; Kuhn, Fil. Afr.* 67.

MAURITIUS and SEYCHELLES, frequent in woods and ravines. Spread through the tropics of the Old World.

4. **D. speluncæ,** *Baker; Hook. and Baker, Syn. Fil.* 100. Rootstock short-creeping, subterranean. Stipe 1 ft. or more long, straw-coloured, naked. Frond ample, deltoid, decompound, membranous, pilose. Pinnæ and pinnules oblong-lanceolate, cut away on the lower side at the base. Ultimate entire segments oblong, obtuse, adnate, $\frac{1}{12}$ in. broad. Veinlets fine, forked, erecto-patent. Sori distinctly intramarginal. Involucre minute, pale, membranous, half cup-shaped, attached at the sides. D. polypodioides, *Hook. Syn. Fil.* i. 181. Microlepia speluncæ, *Moore; Kuhn, Fil. Afr.* 159.

SEYCHELLES, frequent in the forests. Gathered in MAURITIUS by Thouars, but unknown to recent collectors. Cosmopolitan in the Tropics.

5. **D. repens,** *Desv.; Hook. and Baker, Syn. Fil.* 93. Rootstock woody, wide-creeping above ground, $\frac{1}{12}$–$\frac{1}{8}$ in. thick, thinly clothed with small brown lanceolate scales. Stipe under an inch long. Frond linear, a foot long, 1–1½ in. broad, simply pinnate, membranous, glabrous, pale green. Pinnæ sessile, half ovate, cut away in a straight line on the inner and lower borders, rounded and toothed on the upper. Veins fine, radiating from the lower border, all free. Sori globose, submarginal, placed in a row in the teeth of the upper edge. Involucre broader than long, membranous, free at the sides. D. Boryana, *Presl; Bojer, Hort. Maur.* 408. D. hemiptera, *Bory.* Lindsaya repens, *Kunze; Kuhn, Fil. Afr.* 68.

MAURITIUS, in the forests of Grand Bassin and Trou aux Cerfs. Also Bourbon, Tropical Asia, and Polynesia, not Continental Africa.

6. **D. Hornei,** *Baker.* Rootstock subterranean, short-creeping. Stipes contiguous, 2–3 in. long, pale-brown or straw-coloured, naked, broadly grooved down the face. Frond deltoid or rhomboid, bipinnate, 3–4 in. long, Lindsaya-like in texture, subcoriaceous, glabrous, pale green, the main rachis furnished with one or two linear erecto-patent forks from the lower half on each side. Segments sessile, obversely deltoid, $\frac{1}{6}$ in. broad, with an upcurved lower and truncate inner border, the upper border erecto-patent as regards the rachis and toothed. Veins close, fine, free, flabellato-dichotomous. Sori globose, placed at the tip of the teeth of the upper edge. Involucre broader than long, membranous, free at the sides.

SEYCHELLES, common between rocks in the bed of streams, *Horne*, 677! Endemic.

7. CYSTOPTERIS, Bernh.

Capsules stalked, splitting transversely, with an incomplete vertical ring. Sori globose, placed on the back of the veins. Involucre deltoid, membranous, free at the sides, inserted by its base under the sorus and at first folded over it.—Small membranous decompound ferns, with free veins. DISTRIB. Everywhere in temperate and subtemperate regions. Species 5.

1. **C. fragilis,** *Bernh.; Hook. and Baker, Syn. fil.* 103. Rootstock suberect; scales lanceolate, red-brown, membranous. Stipe straw-coloured, 2–4 in. long, slightly scaly. Frond oblong-lanceolate, membranous, glabrous, tripinnatifid, 4–12 in. long, 2–3 in. broad. Pinnæ and pinnules lanceolate, cut away on the lower side at the base, the former with the rachis winged all through, the latter deeply pinnatifid with sharply-toothed segments. Veins fine, erecto-patent. Sori many to a full-sized pinnule, medial on the veins.

Gathered in MAURITIUS by Thouars, according to Kuhn, but not seen by recent collectors. We have it from Bourbon, from Lady Barkly. Everywhere in the temperate zone.

8. VITTARIA, Smith.

Capsules stalked, with an incomplete vertical ring, splitting transversely. Sori linear, marginal or just intramarginal, immersed in a groove, the two more or less prominent edges of which are quite similar in texture to the rest of the frond.—Ferns with entire grass-like fronds, simple veining, and membranous,blackish reticulate scales. DISTRIB. Warmer zones of both hemispheres. Species about 10. A genus doubtful in position between the involucrate and ex-involucrate series.

Sori sunk in a deep groove with distinct lips.
  Lips of groove equal . . . . 1. V. ELONGATA.
  Outer lip of groove broadest . . . . 2. V. LINEATA.
Sori sunk in a groove without distinct lips . . . . 3. V. SCOLOPENDRINA.

1. **V. elongata,** *Sw.; Hook. and Baker, Syn. Fil.* 395. Rootstock short-creeping, $\frac{1}{8}$–$\frac{1}{6}$ in. thick. Frond sessile or narrowed to a short flattened stipe, 1–2 feet long, $\frac{1}{4}$–$\frac{3}{8}$ in. broad at the middle, narrowed gradually to both ends. Veins long, parallel, distinct, ascending. Sorus continuous along the very edge of the back of the frond in a deep groove, the outer valve of which is scarcely broader than the inner. V. plantaginea, ensifolia, isoetifolia, and zosteræfolia, *Bojer, Hort. Maur.* 403.

MAURITIUS and SEYCHELLES, common on old trunks in the forests. Spread through the tropics of the Old World.

2. **V. lineata,** *Sw.; Hook. and Baker, Syn. Fil.* 396. Rootstock short-creeping, $\frac{1}{8}$–$\frac{1}{6}$ in. thick. Frond shorter, narrower, and thicker in texture than in *V. elongata*, with the sorus just within the edge, the outer valve of the deep groove broader than the inner and rolled over the sorus till it fully matures. V. isoetifolia, *Bory; Kuhn, Fil. Afr.* 55, *not Bojer*.

SEYCHELLES, on trees in the forests, *Pervillé*, 94! *Horne*, 162! Spread through the warmer zones of both hemispheres.

3. **V. scolopendrina,** *Thwaites; Hook. and Baker, Syn. Fil.* 396. Rootstock much thicker than in the two other species. Frond 1–2 feet long, $\frac{3}{4}$–1 in. broad at the middle, narrowed gradually to an acute point and a short flattened stipe, the parallel erecto-patent veins distinctly visible. Sorus distinctly intramarginal, sunk in a shallow groove, with no distinct lip on the inner side, the frond produced about half the breadth of the groove outside it. V. zeylanica and latipes, *Fée*.

SEYCHELLES, on trees in the thick forests of Mahé, *Kirk! Horne*, 159! MAURITIUS, at Camisard, *Lady Barkly!* Mozambique to Samoa.

9. LINDSAYA, Dryand.

Capsules stalked, splitting transversely, with an incomplete vertical ring. Sori marginal, linear, uniting two or more of the veins. Involucre with two lips, both opening towards the outside.—Generally small subcoriaceous bright green ferns, with free veining and ultimate segments truncate on the lower and inner side. DISTRIB. Tropics of both hemispheres. Species 50.

Frond simply pinnate.
Frond membranous, glabrous . . . . 1. L. ENSIFOLIA.
Frond subcoriaceous, tomentose . . . . 2. L. ACUTIFOLIA.
Frond bipinnate.
Pinnules obovate-cuneate . . . . 3. L. CUNEATA.
Pinnules oblong-trapezoid . . . . 4. L. KIRKII.

1. **L. ensifolia,** *Swartz; Hook. and Baker, Syn. Fil.* 112. Rootstock woody, short-creeping above ground, as thick as a quill, clothed with minute lanceolate bright brown scales. Stipe $\frac{1}{4}$–$\frac{1}{2}$ ft. long, glossy, naked, chestnut-brown. Frond membranous, bright green, naked, rhomboid, simply pinnate, $\frac{1}{2}$–1 ft. long. Pinnæ 2–12 pairs, distant, ligulate, erecto-patent, 2–6 in. long, $\frac{1}{4}$–$\frac{1}{2}$ in. broad, cuneate at the base, the barren ones faintly crenate. Veins fine, distinct, lax, ascending from a distinct central midrib, joining mainly in costal arches. Sori continuous along both sides of the pinnæ. Involucre pale, narrow, membranous.

MAURITIUS and SEYCHELLES, frequent in the forests. Spread through the tropics of the Old World. Also Cape.

2. **L. acutifolia,** *Desv.; Hook. Sp. Fil.* i. 209. Rootstock woody, short-creeping, clothed with minute bright brown linear-subulate scales. Stipe naked, stout, greenish, $\frac{1}{4}$–$\frac{1}{2}$ ft. long. Frond simply pinnate, subcoriaceous, lanceolate, narrowed gradually to the base, 2–3 ft. long, 4–6 in. broad, densely clothed with brown tomentum, soon glabrescent on the upper surface. Pinnæ very numerous, crowded, sessile, the fertile ones lanceolate, 2–3 in. long, $\frac{1}{4}$–$\frac{1}{2}$ in. broad, often rather falcate, the barren ones shorter, broader and more obtuse, margined with a row of white dots, articulated at the base and easily falling. Veins fine, immersed, erecto-patent from a distinct central midrib. Sori forming a narrow line along both edges of the pinnæ. Involucre firm, brown, glabrous. L. lanuginosa, *Wall.; Hook. and Baker, Syn. Fil.* 109.

MAURITIUS, near Bon Amour, *Gardner!* RODRIGUEZ, *Bouton!* New Guinea to Zambesi-land. Resembles *Nephrolepis acuta* in general habit and texture.

3. **L. cuneata,** *Willd.; Bojer, Hort. Maur.* 403. Stipe slender, angular, naked, dark chestnut-brown, 4–5 in. long. Frond membranous, bright green, naked, rhomboid, bipinnatifid, 5–6 in. long and broad. Pinnæ erecto-patent, 5–6 on a side, linear, 3–4 in. long, ending in a long point at the tip, the rest cut down to a narrow wing into obtuse obovate-cuneate segments $\frac{1}{8}$ in. broad. Veins fine, free, erecto-

patent. Sori placed on both sides of the tip of the pinnæ and round the outer border of the segments. Involucre narrow, firm, greenish.

MAURITIUS, in the woods of Grand Bassin, *Bojer !* Also Bourbon. Probably a variety of *L. heterophylla*, Dry., of Tropical Asia.

4. **L. Kirkii,** *Hook.; Hook. and Baker, Syn. Fil.* 108. Rootstock woody, creeping, clothed with minute lanceolate dark brown scales. Stipe a foot or more long, terete, naked, greenish. Frond bipinnate, 1–2 feet long, $\frac{3}{4}$–1 foot broad, bright green, naked, membranous. Pinnæ crowded, numerous, erecto-patent, 6–9 in. long, 1–1$\frac{1}{4}$ in. broad, with a terete wingless rachis. Segments sessile, close, oblong-trapezoid, truncate in a straight line on the lower and inner border. Veins close, distinct, radiating from the lower border, casually anastomosing. Sorus a narrow line round the upper and outer edge of the segments. *Wright, in Trans. Roy. Irish Acad.* vol. xxv. *t.* 28. L. Pervillei, *Mett.; Kuhn, Fil. Afr.* 17 and 68.

SEYCHELLES, one of the commonest ferns of the forests. Endemic.

10. ADIANTUM, Linn.

Capsules stalked, splitting transversely, with an incomplete vertical ring. Sori marginal, varying in shape from globose-reniform to linear. Involucre the same shape as the sorus, formed of the reflexed edge of the frond indurated in texture, bearing the capsules on its under side. —Small ferns, very various in cutting, with dark brown glossy rachis, usually naked, with free veining. DISTRIB. All tropical and subtropical regions, mainly of America. Species 60–70.

Fronds simple, orbicular . . . . 1. A. RENIFORME.
Fronds compound, with segments cut away in a straight line on the inner and lower borders.
  Simply pinnate, rooting at the tip . . . . 2. A. CAUDATUM.
  Pedate, with pinnate divisions . . . . 3. A. HISPIDULUM.
Fronds compound; segments stalked, cuneate at the base
  Segments $\frac{1}{4}$–$\frac{1}{2}$ in. broad . . . . 4. A. ÆTHIOPICUM.
  Segments $\frac{1}{8}$–$\frac{1}{4}$ in. broad . . . . 5. A. CAPILLUS-VENERIS.

1. **A. reniforme,** *Linn.;* var. A. ASARIFOLIUM, *Willd.; Hook. and Baker, Syn. Fil.* 114. Rootstock erect; scales lanceolate, dark-brown. Stipes densely tufted, wiry, nearly black, scaly at the base, 2–12 in. long. Frond orbicular or broader than long, entire, 2–4 in. broad, with a deep sinus and rounded lobes that open or overlap and embrace the top of the stipe, rigidly coriaceous, glabrous. Veins fine, distinct, close, radiating from the top of the stipe. Sori placed all round the entire border of the frond except in the sinus, orbicular or oblong, $\frac{1}{12}$–$\frac{1}{4}$ in. long, crowded.

MAURITIUS, on rocks of the Pouce range, etc. Also Bourbon and Natal, and the type in Madeira and the Canaries.

2. **A. caudatum,** *Linn.; Hook. and Baker, Syn. Fil.* 115. Rootstock erect; scales very minute, linear, dark brown. Stipes densely tufted, slender, wiry, chestnut-brown, 1–4 in. long. Frond lanceolate, simply pinnate, often drawn out and rooting at the tip, 4–9 in. long, 1–1½ in. broad, subcoriaceous, varying from densely pilose to glabrous. Segments sessile, trapezoid, straight and entire on the inner and lower side, deeply lobed on the upper and outer. Veins fine, close, radiating from the basal inner corner of the segments. Sori orbicular or oblong-reniform, confined to the tip of the lobes. A. hirsutum, *Bory; Bojer, Hort. Maur.* 404. A. rhizophorum, *Sw.; Bojer, loc. cit.*

MAURITIUS, RODRIGUEZ, and SEYCHELLES, frequent in the crevices of rocks. Round Island, *Sir H. Barkly!* Flat Island and Coin de Mire, *Horne!* Spread through the tropics of the Old World. *A. hirsutum* is the pilose and *A. rhizophorum* the subglabrous form of the species.

3. **A. hispidulum,** *Sw.; Hook. and Baker, Syn. Fil.* 126. Rootstock short-creeping; scales very minute, brown, linear. Stipe glossy, slender, naked, castaneous, 4–9 in. long. Frond deltoid, 6–9 in. long, bright green, finely pubescent, pedate, the central division simply pinnate, the outside ones forked 2–3 times from the lower side at the base. Segments close, sessile, trapezoid, ½ in. broad, cut away in a straight line on the inner and lower edge, crenate on the upper and outer. Veins very fine and close, radiating from the point of attachment of the segments. Sori many, small, orbicular-reniform, confined to the upper and outer edges of the segments. A. pubescens, *Schk.; Bojer, Hort. Maur.* 404.

MAURITIUS, and RODRIGUEZ, in crevices of rocks. Spread through the warmer regions of the Old World.

5. **A. Capillus-veneris,** *Linn.; Hook. and Baker, Syn. Fil.* 123 Rootstock creeping, as thick as a quill. Scales very minute, brown. linear. Stipe nearly black, slender, glossy, naked, 3–9 in. long, Frond deltoid, ½–1 ft. long, bright green, membranous, glabrous, 3–4-pinnate. Pinnæ and pinnules deltoid, the lowest much the largest. Segments deltoid. stalked, erecto-patent. ½–¾ in. broad, deeply lobed from the upper border only. Veins fine, close, radiating from the base of the segments. Sori oblong-reniform, several to each segment. Involucre firm, broad, persistent $\frac{1}{12}$–⅛ in. broad.

MAURITIUS and RODRIGUEZ, in caves and by streamsides. Everywhere in the tropical and warm temperate zones of both hemispheres.

4. **A. æthiopicum,** *Linn.; Hook. and Baker, Syn. Fil.* 123. Rootstock slender, wide-creeping. Scales very minute, linear, dark brown. Stipe naked, wiry, glossy, nearly black, ½–¾ ft. long. Frond deltoid, glabrous, bright green, ½–1 ft. long, 4-pinnate. Pinnæ and pinnules stalked, deltoid, the lowest much the largest. Segments orbicular, with a truncate or broad-cuneate base, ¼–⅓ in. broad, crenate round the upper border. Veins fine, close, radiating from the base. Sori

oblong-reniform, several to a segment, absent from its lower half. Involucre firm, broad, persistent. A. emarginatum, *Bory; Bojer, Hort. Maur.* 404. A. fumarioides, *Willd.; Bojer, Hort. Maur.* 405.

MAURITIUS, on the banks of the Black River and at the Tamarin Cascade, etc. Spread through the warmer regions of both hemispheres, especially Cape and Australia.

11. HYPOLEPIS, Bernh.

Capsules stalked, splitting transversely, with an incomplete vertical ring. Sori marginal, globose, placed in sinuses of the ultimate lobes of the frond. Involucre reniform, membranous, formed of the modified margin of the frond wrapped over the sorus.—Large decompound ferns, with free veins and wide-creeping rootstocks. DISTRIB. Tropical and south-temperate regions. Species 11.

1. **H. anthriscifolia,** *Presl.; Hook. and Baker, Syn. Fil.* 129. Rootstock stout, wide-creeping clothed with minute linear-subulate brown scales. Stipes distant, pale bright brown, like the rachises slightly pubescent and scabrous. Frond 6–10 feet long, deltoid, 4-pinnatifid, membranous, bright green, with minute linear scales on the ribs beneath. Pinnæ deltoid, the lowest the largest, 1–2 feet long. Ultimate segments lanceolate, ¼–⅜ in. long, deeply pinnatifid, with upcurved adnate oblong lobes, each bearing a small round sorus in a hollow of its upper margin. Involucre narrow, membranous. H. sparsisora, *Kuhn, Fil. Afr.* 120. Adiantum altissimum, *Bojer, Hort. Maur.* 405.

MAURITIUS, in the gorges of the Black River and Savanne ranges. Also Bourbon, and widely-spread through Tropical Africa and the Cape.

12. LONCHITIS, Linn.

Capsules stalked, splitting transversely, with an incomplete vertical ring. Sori marginal, half-moon-shaped, confined to the ultimate sinuses. Involucre membranous, narrow, formed of the modified edge of the frond reflexed and wrapped over the sorus.—Large ferns of membranous texture, with broad leafy segments and anastomosing veins. DISTRIB. One other species in West Africa.

1. **L. pubescens,** *Willd.; Hook. and Baker, Syn. Fil.* 128. Rootstock erect. Stipe stout, 1–2 feet long, densely clothed, like the rachises, with short spreading ferruginous hairs. Frond deltoid, 3–4 feet long, membranous, pubescent, bipinnate. Pinnæ oblong-lanceolate, the lowest the longest, 1–1½ foot long, its lower pinnules free, spreading from the rachis at a right angle, ¾–1 in. broad, with broad obtuse shallow or deep lobes, and one semicircular sorus at the bottom of each of the narrow sinuses. Veins uniting in one or two rows of broad areolæ between midrib and edge, which do not contain any free veinlets.

Involucre narrow, membranous, soon disappearing. Pteris pubescens, *Kuhn, Fil. Afr.* 88.

MAURITIUS, in the forests of the Pouce, Grand Bassin, etc. SEYCHELLES, *Dr. Kirk!* Africa and America, principally the former, reaching far down south and into the Cape territory.

13. OCHROPTERIS, J. Sm.

Capsules stalked, splitting transversely, with an incomplete vertical ring. Sori marginal, oblique, varying in shape from orbicular to oblong. Involucre formed of the reflexed edge of the frond modified in texture and wrapped over the sorus. A single species.

1. **O. pallens,** *J. Smith; Hook. and Baker, Syn. Fil.* 127. Rootstock like that of a hare's-foot *Davallia*, stout, wide-creeping, densely clothed with linear-subulate bright reddish-brown scales. Stipe a foot or more long, straw-coloured, glossy, naked. Frond 1–2 feet long, deltoid, glabrous, rigidly subcoriaceous, 4-pinnate. Pinnæ and pinnules deltoid, the lowest the largest. Final entire lobes erecto-patent, close, oblong-trapezoid, acute, $\frac{1}{12}$–$\frac{1}{8}$ in. broad. Sori placed at the tip of the lobes, $\frac{1}{24}$–$\frac{1}{8}$ in. long, Involucre firm, broad, persistent, at first pale, finally brown. Adiantum pallens, *Sw.; Bojer, Hort. Maur.* 405. Pteris pallens, *Mett.; Kuhn, Fil. Afr.* 86.

MAURITIUS, in the forests of the Pouce, Grand Bassin, and other hill ranges. Also Bourbon and Madagascar.

14. PELLÆA, Link.

Capsules stalked, with an incomplete vertical ring, splitting transversely. Sori marginal, at the first in dots, soon confluent into irregular lines. Involucre the same shape as the sorus, narrow or broad, formed of the modified edge of the frond wrapped over the sorus.—Generally small or middle-sized ferns of subcoriaceous or membranous texture, with free veins and glossy dark brown or black rachises. DISTRIB. Tropical and warm temperate regions of both hemispheres. Species 45.

Frond small, with the main rachis winged all through.
- Frond densely pilose . . . . 1. P. PILOSA.
- Frond glabrous . . . . 2. P. GERANIÆFOLIA.

Frond large, decompound, with small ultimate segment and a broad involucre . . . . 3. P. BARKLYÆ.

Frond large 1–3-pinnate, with large ultimate segments and a narrow involucre.
- Veins free.
  - Frond simply pinnate . . . . 4. P. DONIANA.
  - Frond 2–3 pinnate, with segments cuneate at the base . . . . 5. P. HASTATA.
  - Frond 2–3-pinnate, with segments cordate at the base 6. P BOIVINI.
- Veins anastomosing. Frond bipinnate with cordate segments . . . . 7. P ANGULOSA.

1. **P. pilosa,** *Hook.; Hook. and Baker, Syn. Fil.* 145. Fronds

distinctly dimorphous, the barren ones less cut, with broader divisions and shorter stipes than the fertile ones. Stipe wiry, glossy, dark chestnut-brown, 4–9 in. long, clothed with small spreading deciduous linear scales. Frond deltoid, 1½–3 in. long and broad, thinly clothed with brown pubescence above, densely clothed with brown pubescence beneath, the lower pinnæ much the largest, unequal-sided, with the basal fork on the lower side much larger than the rest. Barren fronds with a broad wing to the rachis all through, and oblong or round lobes ⅙ in. broad. Fertile fronds with rachis winged at the top only and lanceolate segments. Veins fine, immersed, obscure. Sori continuous from the base to the tip of the segments. Involucre broad, distinct, persistent. Cheilanthes heterophylla, *Willd.; Bojer, Hort. Maur.* 405. Pteris pilosa, *Lam.; Kuhn, Fil. Afr.* 87.

MAURITIUS, on rocks of the hills of Corps de Garde and Trois Mamelles. Also Bourbon.

2. **P. geraniæfolia,** *Fée; Hook. and Baker, Syn. Fil.* 146. Rootstock suberect; scales minute, brown, lanceolate. Stipes tufted, 3–9 in. long, slender, wiry, glossy, nearly black, with a few spreading deciduous scales. Frond deltoid, membranous, glabrous, 3–4 in. long and broad, with the main rachis winged all through. Central pinnæ lanceolate, deeply pinnatifid, with ascending lanceolate lobes $\frac{1}{12}$–⅙ in. broad; lowest pinnæ very unequal-sided, with deeply pinnatifid pinnules from the lower side. Veins fine, free, immersed. Involucre narrow, membranous, irregular, sometimes all broken up into small rounded lobes, as in *Cheilanthes.* Pellæa concolor, *Baker.* Pteris Pohliana, *Presl; Kuhn, Fil. Afr.* 88. P. pedata, *Bojer, Hort. Maur.* 399, *not Linn.*

MAURITIUS, on high rocks of the Pouce range, etc. Spread through the warmer regions of both hemispheres.

3. **P. Barklyæ,** *Baker; Hook. and Baker, Syn. Fil.* 151. Rootstock suberect. Stipes tufted, naked, glossy, chestnut-brown, often above a foot long. Frond deltoid, 4-pinnatifid, rigidly subcoriaceous, green and glossy on both sides, often a foot long and broad. Pinnæ close, deltoid, stalked, cut away on the lower side at the base, the lowest much the largest. Ultimate segments erecto-patent, lanceolate-trapezoid, narrowly adnate, with a cuneate base, acute, $\frac{1}{12}$ in. broad. Veins fine, immersed, free, erecto-patent. Sori absent from the tip and base of the segments. Involucre moderately broad, firm, persistent. *Wright, in Trans. Roy. Irish Acad. vol.* XXV. *tab.* 29. Pteris Barklyæ, *Mett.; Kuhn Fil. Afr.* 77.

SEYCHELLES, in the woods of Praslin and Mahé. Endemic.

4. **P. Doniana,** *Hook.; Hook. and Baker, Syn. Fil.* 152. Rootstock suberect; scales small, bright brown, linear-subulate. Stipes tufted, glossy, nearly black, 3–9 in. long. Frond lanceolate, simply pinnate,

rigidly subcoriaceous, glabrous, 6–18 in. long, 4–6 in. broad; rachis stiff, finely pilose on the upper surface. Pinnæ 5–20 pairs, distinctly stalked, the petiole articulated at the top, lanceolate, cordate at the base, 1½–3 in. long, ½–¾ in. broad. Veins fine, immersed, free, erecto-patent. Sorus continuous from the base of the pinnæ to the tip. Involucre narrow, soon flattened out and hidden by the sorus. Pteris Doniana, *Kuhn*, *Fil. Afr.* 83.

SEYCHELLES, in the woods of Félicité, *Horne*, 187! Spread through Tropical Africa.

5. **P. hastata,** *Link.; Hook. and Baker*, *Syn. Fil.* 152. Rootstock woody, suberect; scales minute, brown, linear. Stipes tufted, naked, glossy, dark chestnut-brown, 3–9 in. long. Frond deltoid, glabrous, membranous, 2–3-pinnate, ½–1 ft. long. Segments sessile or shortly petioled, very variable in size and shape, lanceolate or deltoid, cuneate at the base, ½–1½ in. long, those that are terminal on the main rachis and pinnæ usually hastate. Veins distinct, fine, close, free, ascending, dichotomously forked. Sori continuous from the base to the tip of the segments. Involucre narrow, membranous, soon flattened out and hidden by the sorus. Pteris viridis, *Forsk.; Kuhn*, *Fil. Afr.* 89.

MAURITIUS, RODRIGUEZ, and SEYCHELLES, frequent in rocky woods Cape and through Tropical Africa. A variety with small tripinnate fronds and segments not more than ¼–½ in. long, closely resembling *P. consobrina* in cutting, was gathered in Mauritius by Mrs. Higginson, at Baie du Cap.

6. **P. Boivini,** *Hook.; Hook. and Baker*, *Syn. Fil.* 149. Rootstock suberect; scales dense, linear-subulate, bright reddish-brown. Stipes tufted, glossy, nearly black, ½ ft. long, slightly scaly at first. Fronds deltoid, rigidly subcoriaceous, glabrous, 2–3-pinnate, 6–9 in. long; rachises finely pilose on the upper surface. Segments lanceolate, ½–¾ in. long, the upper ones adnate, the lower ones shortly petioled, truncate or slightly cordate at the base. Veins fine, hidden, immersed, ascending, free. Sori continuous from the base to the tip of the segments. Involucre narrow, soon hidden by the sorus. Pteris Boivini, *Moore; Kuhn*, *Fil. Afr.* 78. P. dura, *Bojer*, *Hort. Maur.* 400.

MAURITIUS, on dry rocks on the banks of the Grand Rivière and Moka River. Also Madagascar, Tropical Africa and East Indies.

7. **P. angulosa,** *Baker.; Hook. and Baker*, *Syn. Fil. edit.* 2, 153. Rootstock suberect; scales minute, brown, linear. Stipes tufted, ½–1 ft., long, glossy, black-brown, slightly, scaly at the first. Frond deltoid, rigidly subcoriaceous, glabrous, pale green on both sides, 2–3-pinnate, ½–1 ft. long; rachises finely pilose on the face. Segments shortly petioled, lanceolate, 1–2 in. long, cordate or rounded at the base. Veins obscure, fine, immersed, anastomosing in rhomboid areolæ. Sori continuous from the base to the tip of the segments. Involucre narrow,

soon hidden by the sorus. P. angulosa, *Bory; Bojer, Hort. Maur.* 400. P. articulata, *Kaulf.; Bojer, Hort. Maur.* 402.

MAURITIUS, on rocks in the ravines of the hilly tracts. Also Bourbon and Madagascar.

15. PTERIS, Linn.

Capsule stalked, splitting transversely, with an incomplete vertical ring. Sorus marginal, linear, continuous. Involucre linear, formed of the modified edge of the frond rolled over the sorus.—Usually large ferns, of various habit and cutting; rootstock suberect or creeping; veins free or variously anastomosing. DISTRIB. One of the most cosmopolitan of fern-genera. Species about 100.

Subgenus I. EUPTERIS. Fronds large. Veins pinnate, all free.

Frond simply pinnate, with all the pinnæ simple . . 1. P. LONGIFOLIA.
Frond simply pinnate, with the lowest pinnæ forked 2. P. CRETICA.
Frond regularly bipinnatifid, with only the lowest pinnæ once forked.
  Texture membranous . . . . 3. P. QUADRIAURITA.
  Texture rigidly coriaceous . . . . 4. P. SCABRA.
Frond regularly bipinnatifid, with the lowest pinnæ compound . . . . 5. P. FLABELLATA.
Frond decompound, with a wide-creeping rootstock . . . . 6. P. AQUILINA.

Subgenus II. ACTINIOPTERIS. Fronds small. Veins flabellate, all free.

The only species . . . . 7. P. DICHOTOMA.

Subgenus II. CAMPTERIA. Veins next the midrib of the pinnæ anastomosing in a series of arches, the rest free.

The only species . . . . 8. P. BIAURITA.

Subgenus III. LITOBROCHIA. Veins of the ultimate segments more or less uniting in areolæ.

Rootstock suberect; stipes tufted.
  Frond small, bipinnatifid, with few large segments . . . . 9. P. PEDATA.
  Fronds large, bipinnatifid, with forked lower pinnæ.
    Stipe prickly; texture firm . . . . 10. P. ATROVIRENS.
    Stipe unarmed; texture very thin . . . . . 11. P. WOODWARDIOIDES.
  Frond 5-partite, with bipinnatifid divisions . . . 12. P. MARGINATA.
Rootstock wide-creeping; stipes solitary . . . . . 13. P. INCISA.

1. **P. longifolia,** *Linn.; Hook. and Baker, Syn. Fil.* 153. Rootstock stout, short-creeping; scales dense, linear-subulate, spreading, pale brown. Stipes contiguous, 3–12 in. long, naked or scaly. Frond oblong-lanceolate, narrowed gradually from the middle to both ends,

1–2 ft. long, 6–12 in. broad, subcoriaceous, naked, simply pinnate. Fertile pinnæ 20–30 on a side, linear, acuminate, sessile, adnate to the rachis on the lower side; central ones 3–6 in. long, ¼–⅜ in. broad; lowest reduced to mere auricles; barren pinnæ shorter, broader and less pointed, finely serrated. Veins fine, crowded, ascending, free. Involucre narrow, soon hidden by the sorus. P. costata, *Bory*; *Bojer*, *Hort. Maur.* 399.

MAURITIUS, on the banks of streams. Cosmopolitan in the tropical and warm temperate zones.

2. **P. cretica,** *Linn.*; *Hook. and Baker*, *Syn. Fil.* 154. Rootstock short-creeping. Stipes contiguous, 1–2 ft. long, naked, glossy, straw-coloured, except at the base, where they are brown. Frond deltoid, ½–1 ft. long, naked, subcoriaceous, simply pinnate, but the lowest pair of pinnæ forked at the base. Pinnæ sessile, 3–9 on a side, linear, acuminate, 3–6 in. long, the fertile ones ¼–⅓ in. broad, the barren ones twice as broad, with sharply-toothed edges. Veins crowded, distinct, spreading from the midrib almost at a right angle. Involucre narrow, soon hidden by the sorus.

MAURITIUS, in the woods of Savanne and Grand Bassin. Tropical and warm temperate zones, principally of the Old World.

3. **P. quadriaurita,** *Retz.*; *Hook. and Baker*, *Syn. Fil.* 158. Rootstock suberect. Stipes naked, tufted, 1–2 ft. long, generally straw-coloured, except at the base. Frond deltoid, 1–2 ft. long and broad, membranous, naked, bright green on both sides, regularly deeply bipinnatifid, except that the lowest pair of pinnæ are forked at the base. Central pinnæ lanceolate, 6–12 in. long, 1½–3 in. broad, cut down to a narrow wing into obtuse ascending ligulate segments ⅙–¼ in. broad. Veins free, distinct, erecto-patent, forked at the base. Involucre narrow, membranous, glabrous. Barren segments entire or obscurely serrated. P. nemoralis, *Bojer*, *Hort. Maur.* 401. P. pyrophylla, *Blume*; *Kuhn*, *Fil. Afr.* 89.

MAURITIUS and SEYCHELLES, in woods. Common in the tropical and warm temperate zones of both hemispheres.

4. **P. scabra,** *Bory*; *Hook. and Baker*, *Syn. Fil.* 159. Rootstock suberect. Stipes tufted, naked, a foot or more long, dark glossy chestnut-brown, as is also the rachis. Frond deltoid, 1–2 ft. long and broad, glabrous, rigidly coriaceous, regularly deeply pinnatifid, except that the lowest pair of pinnæ are forked at the base. Central pinnæ lanceolate, 6–9 in. long, 1–2 in. broad, cut down to a narrow wing into close ligulate obtuse ascending segments ⅛–¼ in. broad, the barren ones minutely serrated. Veins forked, erecto-patent, very distinct. Involucre narrow, distinct, persistent. P. angusta, *Bojer*, *Hort. Maur.* 401.

MAURITIUS, in woods of the Black River, Grand Bassin, Trou aux Cerfs, etc. Also Bourbon and Madagascar.

5. **P. flabellata,** *Thunb.; Hook. and Baker, Syn. Fil.* 161. Rootstock suberect. Stipes 1–2 ft. long, tufted, naked, glossy, straw-coloured, chestnut-brown at the base. Frond deltoid, bright green, membranous, glabrous, 1–2 ft. long and broad, regularly deeply bipinnatifid, except that the lowest pair of pinnæ are copiously compound on both sides, and the next one or two pairs usually but not always forked at the base. Central pinnæ lanceolate, 2–2½ in. broad, cut down to a narrow wing into linear ascending segments ⅛–¼ in. broad, the barren ones distinctly serrated. Veins fine, erecto-patent, deeply forked. Sori not reaching to the tip of the segments. Involucre narrow, membranous. P. pseudo-lonchitis, *Bojer, Hort. Maur.* 401. P. arguta, *var.* flabellata, *Mett.; Kuhn, Fil. Afric.* 76.

MAURITIUS, in the woods of Savanne and Grandport. RODRIGUEZ, *Bouton! Balfour!* Also Tropical Africa and Cape Colony, and scarcely more than a variety of the Mediterranean *P. arguta*, Ait.

6. **P. aquilina,** *Linn.; var.* P. LANUGINOSA, *Bory.* Rootstock wide-creeping. Stipes stout, scabrous, 1–2 ft. long. Frond ample, decompound, subcoriaceous, 3–4 ft. long and broad, densely pilose on the lower surface with brown or straw-coloured pilose and glandular-scabrous rachises. Ultimate segments linear, adnate, ¼–½ in. long. Veins free, obscure, forked, immersed, erecto-patent. Involucre firm, ciliated, with an obscure membranous second inner valve.

MAURITIUS, on dry exposed parts of the Pouce range, etc. One of the most widely-spread ferns of both the Old and the New Worlds.

7. **P. dichotoma,** *Kuhn, Fil. Afric.* 79. Rootstock erect. Stipes densely tufted, naked, wiry, ¼–½ ft. long, brown at the base, green above it. Frond fan-like, glabrous, coriaceous, 1–3 in. long, composed of several dichotomously-forked narrow linear segments with revolute edges, which are so near one another that their sori seem to coalesce. Veins few, distinct, nearly vertical. P. radiata and australis, *Bojer, Hort. Maur.* 399. Actiniopteris radiata, *Link; Hook. and Baker, Syn. Fil.* 246.

MAURITIUS and SEYCHELLES, on dry hills. Also Tropical Asia and Tropical Africa.

8. **P. biaurita,** *Linn.; Hook. and Baker, Syn. Fil.* 164. Rootstock suberect. Stipes naked, tufted, not prickly, 1–2 ft. long, generally straw-coloured unless towards the base. Frond deltoid, 1–2 ft. long and broad, membranous, naked, bright green on both sides, regularly deeply bipinnatifid, except that the lowest pair of pinnæ is forked at the base. Central pinnæ lanceolate, 6–12 in. long, 1½–3 in. broad, cut down to a broad wing into ligulate rather ascending obtuse segments ⅛–¼ in. broad, the barren ones entire or obscurely toothed. Veins free, except that there is a series of arches against the midrib of

the pinnæ. Involucre narrow, membranous, glabrous. P. geminata, *Wall.*; *Kuhn, Fil. Afric.* 80.

MAURITIUS and SEYCHELLES, frequent in the woods. Round the world in the warmer zones. Only differs from *P. quadriaurita* in the broader wing of the pinnæ and arching of the veins nearest their midrib.

9. **P. pedata,** *Linn.*; *Hook. and Baker, Syn. Fil.* 167. Stipes densely tufted, black, glossy, naked, 3–6 in. long. Frond deltoid, membranous, naked, 2–3 in. long and broad; fertile one deeply bipinnatifid, only the lowest pair of pinnæ compound, very unequal-sided, deltoid, deeply pinnatifid with a few close large lanceolate segments; barren frond less deeply cut with fewer broader obtuse segments. Veins fine, immersed, uniting in abundant oblique areoles. Involucre narrow, glabrous, evanescent. P. pedatoides, *Desv.*; *Kuhn, Fil. Afric.* 87.

MAURITIUS, on Corps de Garde mountain, *Lady Barkly!* Signal Mountain, *Cattell.* Also Bourbon, Madagascar, and Tropical America.

10. **P. atrovirens,** *Willd.*; *Hook. and Baker, Syn. Fil.* 170. Rootstock suberect. Stipes tufted, naked, a foot or more long, generally brown at the base, straw-coloured upwards, armed with a few obscure distant prickles. Frond deltoid, 1–2 feet long and broad, bright green and glabrous on both sides, moderately firm in texture, regularly deeply bipinnatifid, except that the lowest pair of pinnæ are forked at the base. Central pinnæ lanceolate, 6–12 in. long, 2–3 in. broad, cut down to a broad wing into ascending lanceolate segments ¼–⅓ in. broad, those of the barren frond toothed. Veins uniting to form one or two rows of areoles between the midrib and edge of the final segments. Involucre narrow, glabrous.

SEYCHELLES, in the Cascade woods, Mahé, *Horne,* 652! Spread through Tropical Africa. General habit exactly of *P. quadriaurita* and *P. biaurita.*

11. **P. woodwardioides,** *Bory*; *Hook. and Baker, Syn. Fil.* 170. Rootstock suberect. Stipes tufted, naked, unarmed, straw-coloured, a foot or more long. Frond deltoid, 1–2 feet long and broad, bright green and glabrous on both sides, very thin and membranous in texture, regularly deeply bipinnatifid, except that the lowest pair of pinnæ are forked at the base. Central pinnæ lanceolate, ½–1 foot long, 1½–2 in. broad, cut down to a narrow wing into ligulate obtuse segments ¼–⅓ in. broad. Veins distinct, uniting to form one or two rows of areoles between the midrib and edge of the final segments. P. pellucida, *Kaulf.*; *Bojer, Hort. Maur.* 400.

MAURITIUS, common in the mountain woods. Also Bourbon. Very near the last.

12. **P. marginata,** *Bory*; *Hook. and Baker, Syn. Fil.* 172. Rootstock erect. Stipes naked, straw-coloured, unarmed, a foot or more long.

Frond 5-partite, deltoid, reaching a length and breadth of several feet, membranous, green and glabrous on both sides, the five divisions all bipinnatifid, with lanceolate pinnules cut down to a narrow wing into ligulate entire lobes $\frac{1}{8}$–$\frac{1}{6}$ in. broad. Veins fine, immersed, forming usually a single row of areoles against the midrib of the final segments. Involucre narrow, membranous, glabrous. P. tripartita, *Sw.*

MAURITIUS and SEYCHELLES, frequent in woods. Spread through the warm regions of the Old World.

13. **P. incisa,** *Thunb.; Hook. and Baker, Syn. Fil.* 172. Rootstock slender, wide-creeping. Stipes brown or straw-coloured, glossy, naked, unarmed. Frond deltoid, often several feet long and broad, 3- or 4-pinnatifid, membranous, green above, glaucous beneath, the penultimate divisions lanceolate with deep oblong obtuse segments $\frac{1}{4}$–$\frac{1}{3}$ in. broad. Lowest pinnules of the pinnæ often contracted, and less deeply cut. Veins fine, immersed, sometimes but not always forming long narrow areoles against the midrib of the final segments, always against the midrib of those of a higher grade. Involucre firm, narrow, glabrous. P. vespertilionis, *Labill.; Bojer, Hort. Maur.* 402.

MAURITIUS and SEYCHELLES, common amongst the hills. Spread through the tropical and south temperate zone of both hemispheres.

16. LOMARIA, Willd.

Capsules stalked, splitting transversely, with an incomplete vertical ring. Sori linear, continuous, occupying the whole space between the midrib of the segments and their margins. Involucre linear, formed of the modified edge of the frond rolled over the sorus.—Large or middle-sized ferns, usually simply pinnate, with dimorphic fronds, the pinnæ of the barren ones much broader than those of the fertile ones, and simple close veining. DISTRIB. Both hemispheres, nearly all south temperate or tropical. Species 40.

Barren pinnæ dilated at the base . . . . 1. L. ATTENUATA.
Barren pinnæ narrowed at the base . . . . 2. L. BORYANA.

1. **L. attenuata,** *Willd.; Hook. and Baker, Syn. Fil.* 176. Rootstock woody, subscandent, densely clothed with linear dark-brown scales. Stipes contiguous, naked, $\frac{1}{2}$–1 foot long. Barren frond 1–2 feet long, rigidly subcoriaceous, green and glabrous on both sides, usually simply pinnate to the tip, sometimes simple or pinnate only in the lower half. Pinnæ adnate by the whole of the dilated base, linear, narrowed to a long point, the central ones 3–4 in. long, $\frac{1}{2}$–$\frac{3}{4}$ in. broad, the lower ones growing gradually smaller. Fertile pinnæ distant, not more than $\frac{1}{12}$ in. broad. Veins fine, close, obscure. L. circinata, *Bojer, Hort. Maur.* 406. Blechnum polypodioides, *Kuhn, Fil. Afric.* 92.

MAURITIUS, common on old trunks in the forests. Tropical and south temperate regions of the Old and New World.

2. **L. Boryana**, *Willd.; Hook. and Baker, Syn. Fil.* 180. Rootstock erect, 1–2 feet high, clothed with rigid linear-subulate dark-brown scales above an inch long. Stipes short, stout, scaly at the base only. Barren frond 1–2 feet long, rigidly coriaceous, green and glabrous on both sides, simply pinnate. Pinnæ very numerous, ligulate, obtuse, 2–4 in. long, $\frac{3}{8}$–$\frac{1}{2}$ in. broad, cuneately narrowed to the base, the lower ones distant and growing gradually smaller. Veins fine, close, distinct. Fertile pinnæ distant, not more than $\frac{1}{8}$ in. broad. Blechnum tabulare, *Kuhn, Fil. Afric.* 94.

MAURITIUS, at the Mare aux Vacoas and Trou aux Cerfs. Principally in the south temperate zone of both hemispheres.

17. ASPLENIUM, Linn.

Capsules stalked, splitting transversely, with an incomplete vertical ring. Sori dorsal, running down the veins, oblique with regard to the midrib and edge of the segments, single or double, usually linear. Involucre the same shape as the sorus and rolled over it.—Ferns of very various size, shape, and texture, some of the species running through a wide range of variety in cutting; veining simple or compound. DISTRIB. Cosmopolitan. Species 300.

Subgenus I. ASPLENIUM PROPER. Veins free. Sori single.

Frond simply pinnate (in the typical form).
  Pinnæ rhomboid.
    Frond $\frac{3}{4}$–1 in. broad . . . . 1. A. SANDERSONI.
    Frond 2–4 in. broad . . . . 2. A. RESECTUM.
  Pinnæ linear, equal-sided . . . . 3. A. LONGISSIMUM.
  Pinnæ linear or lanceolate, unequal-sided in the lower half.
    Frond membranous.
      Sori oblong, medial . . . . 4. A. LUNULATUM.
      Sori linear, nearly reaching both edge and midrib.
        Frond 2–3 in. broad . . . . 5. A. TENERUM.
        Frond 4–6 in. broad . . . . 6. A. LINEATUM.
    Frond subcoriaceous.
      Frond about an inch broad . . . . 7. A. ÆQUABILE.
      Frond 4–10 inches broad.
        Rachis very furfuraceous . . . . 8. A. PELLUCIDUM.
        Rachis nearly or quite naked.
          Sori reaching from the midrib halfway to the edge . . . . 9. A. NITENS.
          Sori nearly touching both edge and midrib . 10. A. FALCATUM.
Frond bipinnatifid or bipinnate.
  Large; none of the secondary segments free.
    Frond membranous . . . . 11. A. PROTENSUM.
    Frond subcoriaceous . . . . 12. A. CAUDATUM.
  Small; 1–3 secondary segments free . . . . . . 13. A. BIPARTITUM.
Frond tripinnatifid or decompound.
  Ultimate segments cuneate-deltoid or rhomboid.
    Teeth of segments sharp and long.
      Frond coriaceous; rachis fibrillose . . . . 14. A. FURCATUM.

Frond membranous; rachis naked . . . . . . 15. A. BULBIFERUM.
Teeth of segments small . . . . 16. A. CUNEATUM.
Ultimate segments very narrow, linear or ligulate.
Segments ligulate, obtuse . . . . 17. A. BORBONICUM.
Segments linear, acute . . . . 18. A. VIVIPARUM.

Subgenus II. DIPLAZIUM. Veins free. Some of the sori double, placed back to back.

Frond simply pinnate . . . . 19. A. SYLVATICUM.
Frond tripinnatifid.
Rachises unarmed . . . . 20. A. ARBORESCENS.
Rachises prickly . . . . 21. A. SECHELLARUM.

Subgenus III. THAMNOPTERIS. Veins uniting in an arch just within the edge.

The only species . . . . 22. A. NIDUS.

Subgenus IV. ANISOGONIUM. Veins uniting. Some of the sori double.

The only species . . . . 23. A. PROLIFERUM.

1. **A. Sandersoni,** *Hook.; Hook. and Baker, Syn. Fil.* 196. Rootstock erect; scales minute, brown, lanceolate. Stipes tufted, green, naked, 1–2 in. long. Frond lanceolate, membranous, glabrous, simply pinnate, 4–6 in. long, ½–1 in. broad, often rooting at the tip. Pinnæ 12–20 on a side, deltoid or square, nearly sessile, cut away in a straight line on the inner and lower sides, deeply crenated on the upper and outer. Veins few, flabellate, one running up the centre of each lobe. Sori oblong, medial on the veins. Involucre pale, ciliated.

MAURITIUS, between Grand Bassin and Petrin, *Sir H. Barkly!* Also Madagascar, Natal, and Tropical Africa.

2. **A. resectum,** *Smith; Hook. and Baker, Syn. Fil.* 210. Rootstock slender, wide-creeping; scales very minute. Stipes ½ ft. long, distant, slender, naked, bright brown. Frond lanceolate, bright green, membranous, simply pinnate, ½–1 foot long, 2–4 in. broad; rachis quite naked. Pinnæ numerous, nearly sessile, rhomboid, 1–2 in. long, ¼–⅓ in. broad, faintly or deeply toothed down the upper and outer edges, parallel with the rachis on the upper side at the base, truncate at a right angle with the rachis on the lower side. Veins fine, distinct, very oblique. Sori medial on the veins, $\frac{1}{12}$–⅙ in. long. Involucre membranous, glabrous.

MAURITIUS and SEYCHELLES, in damp ravines. Spread through the tropics of the Old World.

3. **A. longissimum,** *Blume; Hook. and Baker, Syn. Fil.* 199. Rootstock erect; scales linear, small, bright brown. Stipes naked, reaching a length of nearly a foot. Frond 1–3 feet long, 2–4 in. broad at the

middle, simply pinnate, glabrous, moderately firm in texture. Pinnæ very numerous, linear, sessile, entire or faintly toothed, subequally cuneate at the base, the central ones 1–2 in. long, ¼–⅓ in. broad. Rachis slightly scaly. Veins erecto-patent, moderately close. Sori numerous, parallel, nearly reaching both edge and midrib. Involucre pale, glabrous.

MAURITIUS, rare. Diego Garcia, *Bouton!* Tropical Asia, not African.

4. **A. lunulatum,** *Sw.; Hook. and Baker, Syn. Fil.* 202. Rootstock erect; scales minute, linear, brown. Stipes 3–6 in. long, slender. naked, green or brownish. Frond lanceolate, green, membranous, simply pinnate, ½–1 ft. long, 1–2 in. broad; rachis slender, naked. Pinnæ numerous, sessile, oblique lanceolate, distinctly toothed all down the margin, parallel with the rachis on the upper side at the base, cuneate on the lower; central ones ¾–1 in. long, ¼–⅓ in. broad; lower ones little smaller. Veins fine, distant, erecto-patent, forked. Sori oblong, medial, 1/12–⅛ in. long. Involucre glabrous, membranous. A. stoloniferum, *Bory; Kuhn, Fil. Afric.* 117. A. pulchrum, *Thouars; Kuhn, Fil. Afric.* 118.

Var. A. MACRÆI, *Hook. and Grev.* Pinnæ smaller, obtuse, more deeply toothed, with a free deltoid lobe on the upper side at the base.

MAURITIUS, in damp woods of Grandport and Grand Bassin. SEYCHELLES, in the woods of Mahé, *Horne*, 404! Cosmopolitan in tropical and subtropical regions. We have a single Mauritian specimen from Bojer of the var. *Macræi.*

5. **A. tenerum,** *Forst.; Hook. and Baker, Syn. Fil.* 201. Rootstock suberect; scales small, lanceolate, brown-black. Stipes contiguous, green, naked, ¼–½ foot long. Frond lanceolate, green, glabrous, membranous, simply pinnate, under a foot long, 2–3 in. broad. Rachis naked. Pinnæ numerous, nearly sessile, oblique lanceolate, crenate throughout the sides, the central ones 1½ in. long, ⅓–½ in. broad, parallel with the rachis on the upper side at the base, and often a little auricled, cuneate on the lower side. Veins distinct, erecto-patent, simple, except the lowest on the upper side. Sori copious, parallel, nearly reaching both edge and midrib. Involucre glabrous, persistent.

SEYCHELLES, in the woods of Mahé, not common, *Horne*, 684! Spread through the tropics of the Old World, but rare in Africa; gathered only by Livingstone.

6. **A. lineatum,** *Sw.; Hook. and Baker, Syn. Fil.* 202. Rootstock woody, short-creeping; scales linear, dark brown. Stipes contiguous, ½ foot long, greenish, slightly scaly. Frond oblong-lanceolate, bright green, glabrous, membranous, simply pinnate, 1–2 feet long, 4–6 in, broad; rachis furfuraceous. Pinnæ very numerous, subsessile, oblique, linear, acuminate, the central ones 3–4 in. long, ⅓–¼ in. broad, dentate, parallel with the rachis on the upper side at the base, cuneate on the lower. Veins moderately close, fine, forked, erecto-patent. Sori copious, parallel, nearly reaching both midrib and margin. Involucre glabrous, persistent. A. nodulosum, *Kaulf.; Bojer, Hort. Maur.* 395.

Var. INÆQUALE. Frond bipinnate, with linear pinnules entire or toothed at the tip. Cænopteris inæqualis and intermedia, *Bojer, Hort. Maur.* 393–4.

Var. BIFIDUM. Frond bipinnate, with linear, cuneate deeply bifid lower pinnules. Cænopteris bifida, *Bojer, Hort. Maur.* 394.

Var. TRIPINNATIFIDUM. Frond tripinnatifid, with the lower pinnules cut into ligulate erecto-patent tertiary segments. Cænopteris violascens, *Bojer, Hort. Maur.* 394. Asplenium palmatifidum, *Moore; Kuhn, Fil. Afric.* 110.

MAURITIUS, common in the forests. Also Bourbon. *A. obliquum*, Bojer, Hort. Maur. 395, not Forst., is a form of this with proliferous pinnæ, so that we unite here as one what Bojer has treated as seven species.

7. **A. æquabile,** *Baker; Hook. and Baker, Syn. Fil. edit.* ii. 485. Rootstock and scales not seen. Stipe short, naked, straw-coloured. Frond lanceolate, glabrous, subcoriaceous, simply pinnate, 5–6 in. long, an inch broad; rachis naked. Pinnæ numerous, close, subsessile. oblong-quadrate, obtuse, crenate all down the margins, ½ in. long, ⅓ in. broad, parallel with the rachis and rather auricled on the upper side at the base, cuneate on the lower. Veins distant, erecto-patent, simple except the lowest on the upper side. Sori oblong, nearly reaching the edge, but distant from the midrib.

Island of Diego Garcia, a single specimen sent by Lady Barkly. Endemic.

8. **A. pellucidum,** *Lam.: Bojer, Hort. Maur.* 395. Rootstock woody, erect; scales dense, linear, brown or nearly black. Stipes tufted, 1–4 in. long, naked or finely scaly. Frond lanceolate, glabrous, subcoriaceous, simply pinnate, 1–3 feet long, 4–8 in. broad; rachis dark-coloured and conspicuously furfuraceous throughout. Pinnæ very numerous, close, sessile, the central ones oblique linear, acute, 1–4 in. long, ⅓–½ in. broad, toothed all down the edges, parallel with the rachis on the upper side at the base, cuneate on the lower, many lower ones growing gradually smaller and more obtuse. Veins fine, erecto-patent, branched. Sori linear, reaching from near the midrib more than halfway to the edge. Involucre narrow, glabrous. A. hirtum, *Kaulf.; Hook. and Baker, Syn. Fil.* 205. A. plumosum, *Bory; Bojer, Hort. Maur.* 396.

MAURITIUS, SEYCHELLES, and RODRIGUEZ, frequent in shady ravines. Also Bourbon, Madagascar, Tropical Asia, and Polynesia.

9. **A. nitens,** *Sw.: Hook. and Baker, Syn. Fil.* 206. Rootstock creeping, as thick as a man's finger; scales brown, linear. Stipes distant, naked, brownish. Frond oblong-lanceolate, glabrous, subcoriaceous, simply pinnate, 1–1½ ft. long, 6–10 in. broad; rachis naked. Pinnæ numerous, subsessile, oblong-lanceolate, acuminate, 3–4 in. long, ½–¾ in. broad, toothed all down the edges, parallel with the rachis on the upper side at the base, cuneate on the lower. Veins fine, close, forked, erecto-patent, very oblique. Sori linear, reaching from the midrib halfway to the edge. Involucre narrow, persistent, glabrous.

MAURITIUS, frequent on fallen trunks in the forests. Also Bourbon and Comoros.

10. **A. falcatum,** *Lam.; Hook. and Baker, Syn. Fil.* 208. Rootstock woody, suberect; scales small, linear, dark brown. Stipes contiguous, naked, dark-green, ½ ft. long. Frond oblong-lanceolate, glabrous, subcoriaceous, simply pinnate, ½–1 foot long, 4–6 in. broad; rachis nearly naked. Pinnæ numerous, nearly sessile, oblique lanceolate, acuminate, 2–3 in. long, ¾–1 in. broad, sharply toothed all down the edges, parallel with the rachis and often auricled on the upper side at the base, cuneate on the lower. Veins fine, close, erecto-patent, very oblique. Sori reaching from the midrib nearly to the edge. Involucre narrow, glabrous, persistent. A. macrophyllum, *Bojer, Hort. Maur.* 394, *not Sw.*

MAURITIUS and RODRIGUEZ, frequent in the forests. Spread through the warmer regions of the Old World. Passes into *A. macrophyllum*, Sw., by gradual intermediate stages.

11. **A. protensum,** *Schrad.; Hook. and Baker, Syn. Fil.* 211. Rootstock suberect or short-creeping; scales minute, brown, lanceolate. Stipes contiguous, brownish, slightly scaly, 2–4 in. long. Frond lanceolate, bipinnatifid, membranous, bright green, glabrous, 1–2 feet long, 3–4 in. broad; rachis furfuraceous. Pinnæ very numerous, oblique lanceolate, sessile, 1½–2 in. long, ½ in. broad, parallel with the rachis on the upper side at the base, cuneate on the lower, cut about halfway down to the rachis into sharply-toothed erecto-patent lobes. Veins fine, close, erecto-patent. Sori reaching from the midrib about halfway to the edge. Involucre narrow, glabrous, evanescent.

MAURITIUS, in the woods of the Pouce and Pieterboth. Also Bourbon, Cape, and Tropical Africa.

12. **A. caudatum,** *Forst.; Hook. and Baker, Syn. Fil.* 209. Rootstock suberect; scales linear, dark brown. Stipes contiguous, naked, greenish, 6–9 in. long. Frond oblong-lanceolate, glabrous, subcoriaceous, bipinnatifid, 1–2 feet long, 6–10 in. broad; rachis naked. Pinnæ very numerous, nearly sessile, oblique lanceolate, acuminate, 3–5 in. long, ¾–1 in. broad, deeply cut into erecto-patent sharply-toothed lobes all down the margins, parallel with the rachis and often auricled on the upper side at the base, cuneate on the lower. Veins close, fine, distinct, forked, very oblique. Sori linear, irregular, reaching about halfway from the midrib to the edge. Involucre firm, glabrous, persistent.

SEYCHELLES, frequent in the forest, *Horne*, 174! 668! Warmer zones, principally of Africa and Polynesia.

13. **A. bipartitum,** *Bory; Hook. and Baker, Syn. Fil.* 212. Rootstock erect; scales minute, lanceolate. Stipes tufted, slender, greenish, naked, ¼–½ ft. long. Frond lanceolate, bipinnate, subcoriaceous, glabrous, 6–8 in. long, 2–3 in. broad; rachis naked. Pinnæ distinctly stalked, oblique lanceolate, 1–1½ in. long, ½ in. broad, parallel with the rachis on the upper side at the base, cuneate on the lower, shallowly

lobed in the upper part; 1–3 lowest lobes free, cuneate-deltoid, the rest erecto-patent, ligulate. Veins distinct, erecto-patent. Sori reaching from the midrib nearly to the edge. Involucre glabrous, persistent. A. auritum, *Sieber, not Sw.*

MAURITIUS, frequent in woods. Also Nissobé and Bourbon, where Dr. Balfour found a Dareoid form.

14. **A. furcatum,** *Thunb.; Hook. and Baker, Syn. Fil.* 214. Rootstock suberect; scales linear-subulate, dark bright brown. Stipes contiguous, brown, ½–1 foot long, scaly in the lower part. Frond oblong-lanceolate, subcoriaceous, tripinnatifid, ½–2 feet long, 3–6 in. broad, glabrous; rachises fibrillose. Pinnæ lanceolate-deltoid, parallel with the rachis on the upper side at the base, cuneate on the lower; ultimate segments cuneate-deltoid, ⅛–¼ in. broad, sharply toothed through the upper half. Veins close, distinct, flabellate. Sori reaching from the base of the segments nearly into the teeth. Involucre glabrous, persistent. A. præmorsum, *Sw.; Bojer, Hort. Maur.* 348.

MAURITIUS, on dry hills. Cosmopolitan in the tropical and warm temperate zones.

15. **A. bulbiferum,** *Forst.; Hook. and Baker, Syn. Fil.* 218. Rootstock erect; scales small, brown, linear. Stipes contiguous, naked, green, ½–1 ft. long. Frond oblong-lanceolate, green, glabrous, membranous, tripinnatifid, 1–2 feet long, 6–8 in. broad, often viviparous; rachis naked. Pinnæ deltoid, parallel with the rachis on the upper side at the base, cuneate on the lower; ultimate segments oblong-rhomboid, ⅛–¼ in. broad, cuneate at the base, sharply toothed in the upper half. Veins fine, immersed, distant. Sori medial, $\frac{1}{12}$–⅛ in. long. Involucre pale, broad, glabrous.

SEYCHELLES, rare, *Dr. Kirk!* Also Comoros, Himalayas, Australia, Polynesia, and Central Africa.

16. **A. cuneatum,** *Lam.; Hook. and Baker, Syn. Fil.* 214. Rootstock erect; scales minute, linear, dark brown. Stipes contiguous, naked, greenish, 4–6 in. long. Frond oblong-lanceolate, bright green, glabrous, membranous, bipinnate or tripinnatifid, ½–1½ foot long, 3–6 in. broad. Pinnæ deltoid, stalked, parallel with the rachis on the upper side at the base, cuneate on the lower; ultimate segments cuneate-deltoid, ⅛–¼ in. broad, inciso-crenate round the upper half. Veins fine, immersed, flabellate. Sori linear, reaching from the base nearly to the summit of the segments. Involucre glabrous, persistent.

Var. A. AFFINE, *Sw.; Hook. and Baker, Syn. Fil.* 215. More robust, with a larger tripinnate frond 1½–2 feet long, of stouter texture, with broader ultimate segments. A. nitidum, *Bojer, Hort. Maur.* 397, *not Sw.*

MAURITIUS, RODRIGUEZ, and SEYCHELLES, the typical form rare, the variety common in forests. Cosmopolitan in the tropics. Lady Barkly has shown conclusively, by tracing out the intermediate stages, that *A. pygmæum*, Bojer, Hort. Maur. 395, is merely an undeveloped form of this species.

17. **A. borbonicum**, *Hook.; Hook. and Baker, Syn. Fil.* 222. Rootstock erect; scales small, brown, lanceolate. Stipes contiguous, green, naked, 4–6 in. long. Frond lanceolate, subcoriaceous, glabrous, tripinnatifid, ½–1 foot long, 3–4 in. broad; rachis naked. Pinnæ lanceolate, ½–¾ in. broad, parallel with the rachis on the upper side at the base, cuneate on the lower, many upper segments simple, parallel, ligulate, obtuse, the lowest on the upper side usually deltoid and deeply flabellately lobed. Veins solitary in the centre of the segments, which are so narrow that the medial solitary sorus seems marginal. Cænopteris furcata, *Bojer, Hort. Maur.* 393. A. rutæfolium, var., *Kuhn, Fil. Afric.* 115.

MAURITIUS, in the mountain forests of Grandport. Also Bourbon.

18. **A. viviparum**, *Presl; Hook. and Baker, Syn. Fil.* 228. Rootstock erect; scales large, linear, brownish-black. Stipes contiguous, green, naked, 4–6 in. long. Frond oblong-lanceolate, moderately firm in texture, bright green, glabrous, ½–1½ foot long, 6–8 in. broad, 3–4-pinnate, usually copiously viviparous. Pinnæ close, lanceolate, 1–1½ in. broad, parallel with the rachis on the upper side at the base, cuneate on the lower; ultimate segments linear, acute, erecto-patent, $\frac{1}{16}$–$\frac{1}{12}$ in. broad. Veins single in the centre of the segments, which are so narrow that the short sorus seems quite marginal. Cænopteris vivipara, *Bojer, Hort. Maur.* 394.

MAURITIUS, common in the forests. Also Bourbon and Madagascar.

19. **A. sylvaticum**, *Presl; Hook. and Baker, Syn. Fil.* 232. Rootstock erect; scales dark-brown, lanceolate. Stipes tufted, ½–1 ft. long, scaly towards the base. Frond oblong-lanceolate, membranous, 1–1½ ft. long, 6–8 in. broad, glabrous, simply pinnate; rachis naked. Pinnæ lanceolate, sessile or the lower ones stalked, 3–4 in. long, ¾–1 in. broad, acute, shallowly lobed down the edges, parallel with the rachis on both sides at the base. Veins in a pinnate group opposite each lobe, with several ascending distinct free veinlets. Sori reaching along nearly the whole length of the veinlets, only the lowest double. Involucre narrow, glabrous, membranous. Diplazium sylvaticum and humile, *Bojer, Hort. Maur.* 398.

MAURITIUS, in forests. Cosmopolitan in the Tropics.

20. **A. arborescens**, *Mett.; Hook. and Baker, Syn. Fil.* 240. Rootstock arborescent; scales not seen. Frond ample, deltoid, tripinnatifid, glabrous, moderately firm in texture; rachis straw-coloured, naked, unarmed. Lower pinnæ oblong-lanceolate, 1–1½ foot long,

about half a foot broad; pinnules lanceolate, sessile or the lower ones shortly stalked, cut down to a narrow wing into close ligulate subentire or finely toothed tertiary segments ⅛ in. broad. Veins copiously pinnate in the tertiary segments, with 7–8 pairs of distinct parallel simple or forked veinlets. Sori reaching from the midrib to within a short distance of the edge, rarely double. Involucre narrow, membranous, persistent. Diplazium arborescens, *Sw.; Bojer, Hort. Maur.* 398.

MAURITIUS, in the thick forests of Savanne and Grandport. Also Bourbon.

21. **A. sechellarum,** *Baker; Hook. and Baker, Syn. Fil.* 491. Rootstock arborescent, reaching a height of 5–6 feet; basal scales large, brown, lanceolate. Stipe and rachises muricated. Frond ample, deltoid, tripinnatfid, glabrous, moderately firm in texture. Lower pinnæ oblong-lanceolate. 1½–2 feet long; pinnules lanceolate, sessile, ½–1 in. broad, cut down to a narrow wing into ligulate obtuse subentire or inciso-crenate tertiary segments $\frac{1}{12}$–⅛ in. broad. Veins copiously pinnate in the tertiary segments, with 8–12 pairs of distinct erecto-patent usually simple veinlets. Sori reaching from the midrib three quarters of the way to the edge. Involucre narrow, membranous, persistent.

SEYCHELLES, common in the damp shady forests of Mahé, *Bouton! Horne!* Also Madagascar.

22. **A. Nidus,** *Linn.; Hook. and Baker, Syn. Fil.* 190. Rootstock erect. Fronds forming a dense ring round a vacant centre, on very short stout stipes, simple, lanceolate, subcoriaceous, glabrous, green on both sides, 1–4 feet long, 4–8 in. broad, narrowed gradually to both ends. Veins close, distinct, parallel, erecto-patent, connected by a transverse vein just within the edge. Sori 1–3 in. long, beginning near the midrib. Involucre firm, narrow, persistent.

MAURITIUS, SEYCHELLES, and RODRIGUEZ, common in the forest on old trunks. Tropical regions of the Old World. *Langue de Bœuf.*

23. **A. proliferum,** *Lam.; Kuhn, Fil. Afr.* 112. Rootstock erect, subarborescent. Stipes 1–2 feet long, naked, sometimes prickly. Frond oblong-lanceolate, 3–4 feet long, glabrous, simply pinnate. Pinnæ sessile, lanceolate, 6–12 in. long, 1–2 feet broad, acute, broadly shallowly lobed down the edges, often bulbiferous in their axils. Veins in abundant spreading pinnate groups in the pinnæ, with 6–8 pairs of erecto-patent parallel distinct veinlets, which unite at their tips. Sori produced along the whole length of the veinlets, many double. Involucre narrow, persistent. Diplazium proliferum, *Kaulf.; Bojer, Hort. Maur*, 397. Asplenium decussatum, *Sw.; Hook. and Baker, Syn. Fil.* 248.

MAURITIUS and RODRIGUEZ, frequent in the denser forests. Spread through the tropics of the Old World.

No. 689 of Mr. Horne's Seychelles collection may be *Asplenium* (*Athyrium*) *nigripes*, Blume; Hook. and Baker, Syn. Fil. 227, a species common to Tropical Asia and Madagascar, but in the absence of fructification this is quite uncertain.

18. ASPIDIUM, Sw.

Capsules stalked, splitting transversely, with an incomplete vertical ring. Sori round, dorsal, covered with a peltate superior involucre. —Fronds of various cutting, mostly coriaceous in texture; veins rarely anastomosing, free in both the Mauritian species. Distrib. Cosmopolitan. Species 50–60.

Stipes tufted; ultimate lobes with cuspidate teeth . . . 1. A. aculeatum.
Stipes distant; cuspidate teeth none . . . . 2. A. capense.

1. **A. aculeatum,** *Sw.; Hook. and Baker, Syn. Fil.* 252. Rootstock erect; basal scales large, bright pale brown, membranous, linear, and subulate intermixed. Stipes tufted, ½–1 foot long, densely clothed with large lanceolate pale brown scales. Frond oblong-lanceolate, subcoriaceous, glabrous, tripinnatifid, 1–2 foot long; rachis slightly furfuraceous. Pinnæ lanceolate, truncate on the upper side at the base, cuneate on the lower; pinnules obliquely rhomboid, sessile, deeply lobed and sharply toothed. Veinlets forked, erecto-patent. Sori small, medial, many to each tertiary segment. Involucre firm, glabrous, persistent. A. stramineum, *Kaulf.; Bojer, Hort. Maur.* 391. A. ammifolium, *Desv.; Kuhn, Fil. Afric.* 125.

Mauritius, frequent in the hill-woods. One of the most cosmopolitan of all ferns.

2. **A. capense,** *Willd.; Hook. and Baker, Syn. Fil.* 254. Rootstock stout, creeping; scales large, dense, membranous, lanceolate acuminate, reddish-brown. Stipes distant, a foot or more long, scaly in the lower part or throughout. Frond deltoid, coriaceous, 1–2 feet long and broad, tripinnatifid or tripinnate; rachis naked or slightly furfuraceous. Lower pinnæ deltoid; divisions of all grades cuneate on the lower side at the base; ultimate segments oblong, obtuse. Veinlets fine, immersed. Sori medial, much larger than in *A. aculeatum*. Involucre glabrous, persistent. A. coriaceum, *Sw.; Bojer, Hort. Maur.* 391.

Mauritius and Seychelles, frequent. Round the world, especially in the south temperate zone.

19. OLEANDRA, Cav.

Capsules stalked, splitting transversely, with an incomplete vertical ring. Sori round, placed on the back of the veins distant from the margin of the frond, covered with a reniform superior involucre.— Ferns with a wide-spreading rootstock, distinctly-articulated stipes, simple fronds and fine simple or forked transverse veins. Distrib. Species 7. Tropics of both hemispheres.

1. **O. articulata,** *Cav.; Hook. and Baker, Syn. Fil.* 302. Rootstock stiff, slender, woody, wide-creeping, clothed with adpressed linear reddish-brown scales. Stipes 1–2 in. long, naked, jointed above the base. Frond simple, lanceolate, membranous, glabrous, 9–15 in. long, 1–1½ in. broad at the middle, narrowed gradually to both ends. Veins fine, transverse, simple or forked. Sori small, forming a single irregular row some distance from the midrib. Involucre membranous, glabrous, persistent. Aspidium articulatum, *Sw.; Bojer, Hort. Maur.* 389.

MAURITIUS and SEYCHELLES, frequent in woods. Also Madagascar, Bourbon, Tropical Africa and Natal.

20. NEPHROLEPIS, Schott.

Capsules stalked, splitting transversely, with an incomplete vertical ring. Sori round, placed near the margin of the segments at the end of a vein, covered with a reniform superior involucre.—Fronds simply pinnate; pinnæ articulated at the base, very deciduous in dried specimens; veins free. DISTRIB. Warmer zones of both hemispheres. Species 6.

Involucre with a broad open basal sinus . . . . 1. N. CORDIFOLIA.
Involucre with a deep narrow basal sinus . . . . 2. N. EXALTATA.

1. **N. cordifolia,** *Presl; Hook. and Baker, Syn. Fil.* 300. Rootstock erect, sending out long wiry stolons, which bear globose scaly tubers; scales small, linear, pale reddish-brown. Stipes tufted, 2–3 in. long, glossy, naked. Frond lanceolate, membranous, glabrous, simply pinnate, 1–2 feet long, 1½–2 in. broad; rachis furfuraceous. Pinnæ crowded, sessile, lanceolate, obtuse, ¼–⅓ in. broad, obscurely toothed, with an auricle imbricating over the rachis on the upper side at the base. Veins erecto-patent, fine, immersed, forked. Sori in a long row, almost transverse as regards the pinnæ. Involucre firm in texture, with a broad open basal sinus. Aspidium tuberosum, *Bory; Bojer, Hort. Maur.* 390. Nephrodium imbricatum, *Bojer, Hort. Maur.* 392.

MAURITIUS and SEYCHELLES, on trees in the hill-forests. Cosmopolitan in the tropical zone.

2. **N. exaltata,** *Schott; Hook. and Baker, Syn. Fil.* 301. Rootstock erect, the wiry stolons not bearing tubers; scales small, linear, reddish-brown. Stipes tufted, 3–4 in. long, usually naked. Frond lanceolate, membranous, glabrous, simply pinnate, 1–2 feet long, 4–6 in. broad; rachis more or less densely furfuraceous. Pinnæ crowded, sessile, acute, about ½ in. broad, crenate towards the tip, truncate at the base. Veins erecto-patent, fine, immersed, forked. Sori placed obliquely as regards the pinnæ, in a long row a little within the margin. Involucre thinner than in *N. cordifolia*, with a deep narrow basal sinus.

Var. N. BISERRATA, *Schott*. Frond broader, with pinnæ reaching a length of 5 or 6 inches, more acuminate and more distinctly toothed.

Aspidium biserratum, *Sw.*; *Bojer*, *Hort. Maur.* 390. A. mauritianum, *Desv.*; *Bojer*, *Hort. Maur.* 389. Nephrodium splendens, *Bojer*, *Hort. Maur.* 392.

MAURITIUS, RODRIGUEZ, and SEYCHELLES, common in woods, both in the plains and amongst the hills. Cosmopolitan in the warmer zones.

21. NEPHRODIUM, Rich.

Capsules stalked, splitting transversely, with an incomplete vertical ring. Sori round, placed on the back of the segments generally on the middle of a vein covered with a reniform superior involucre.—Fronds of very various texture and cutting, the veins free or variously anastomosing. DISTRIB. Cosmopolitan. Species 250.

Subgenus LASTREA. Veins all free.

Frond oblong-lanceolate, bipinnatifid.
  Rootstock wide-creeping . . . . 1. N. ALBO-PUNCTATUM.
  Rootstock erect.
    Lower pinnæ not dwarfed . . . . 2. N. CRINITUM.
    Lower pinnæ much dwarfed.
      Frond obscurely pilose . . . . 3. N. PROLIXUM.
      Frond densely pilose . . . . 4. N. TOMENTOSUM.
Frond deltoid, tripinnatifid or still more compound.
  Rachises not scaly.
    Frond glabrous.
      Sori medial
        Frond tripinnatifid.
          Tertiary segments symmetrical at the base 5. N. FILIX-MAS. var. ELONGATUM.
          Tertiary segments unsymmetrical at the base 6. N. SPARSUM.
        Frond quadripinnatifid . . . . 7. N. WARDII.
      Sori nearly marginal . . . . 8. N. HORNEI.
    Frond pubescent.
      Frond ½-1 foot long . . . . 9. N. CRENATUM.
      Frond several feet long . . . . 10. N. LANUGINOSUM.
  Rachises densely scaly . . . . 11. N. OPPOSITUM.

Subgenus EUNEPHRODIUM. Veins in regular pinnate groups, one or a few of the lower ones in each group uniting by their tips.

Rootstock wide-creeping.
  Lowest pinnæ not dwarfed . . . . 12. N. UNITUM.
  Lowest pinnæ much and suddenly dwarfed.
    Pinnæ ½-¾ in. broad . . . . 13. N. CUCULLATUM.
    Pinnæ ¾-1¼ in. broad . . . . 14. N. ELATUM.
Rootstock suberect or short-creeping.
  Pinnæ shallowly lobed . . . . 15. N. ARBUSCULA.
  Pinnæ deeply lobed.
    Frond more or less pilose . . . . 16. N. MOLLE.
    Frond glabrous . . . . 17. N. TRUNCATUM.

Subgenus SAGENIA. Veins uniting copiously in hexagonal areolæ.

Involucre minute, fugacious.
Stipe and rachis brown . . . . 18. N. SUBTRIPHYLLUM.
Stipe and rachis black . . . . 19. N. PLEIOTOMUM.
Involucre large, persistent . . . . 20. N. PICA.

1. **N. albo-punctatum,** *Desv.; Hook. and Baker, Syn. Fil.* 264. Rootstock slender, wide-trailing; scales peltate, with a brown middle and pale border. Stipes distant, brown, naked, glossy, articulated above the base. Frond oblong-lanceolate, $\frac{3}{4}$–1 foot long, membranous, bipinnatifid, glabrous or slightly pilose, dotted with white along the edge of the segments on the upper surface. Pinnæ sessile, $\frac{3}{8}$–$\frac{1}{2}$ in. broad, cut down to a broad wing into oblong subentire segments $\frac{1}{12}$–$\frac{1}{8}$ in. broad. Veins pinnate in the segments, with 3–4 pairs of simple erecto-patent veinlets. Sori submarginal, terminal on the veinlets. Involucre ciliated, evanescent. Polypodium sarmentosum, *Bojer, Hort. Maur.* 419.

MAURITIUS, on Long Mountain, Trois Mamelles, and Corps de Gard Mountain, on trees and trailing on the ground. Also Natal, and spread through the tropics of the Old World.

2. **N. crinitum,** *Desv.; Hook. and Baker, Syn. Fil.* 265. Rootstock erect; scales brown-black, linear-subulate. Stipes tufted, $\frac{1}{2}$–1 ft. long, densely scaly throughout. Frond oblong-lanceolate, 1–1$\frac{1}{2}$ ft. long, 8–10 in. broad, moderately firm in texture, glabrous, bipinnatifid; rachis densely clothed throughout with spreading brown-black subulate scales. Pinnæ lanceolate, sessile, 1–1$\frac{1}{4}$ in. broad, cut down to a narrow wing into entire ligulate segments $\frac{1}{8}$–$\frac{1}{6}$ in. broad. Veins pinnate in the secondary segments, with 10–12 simple distinct ascending veinlets on each side. Sori small, medial. Involucre minute, evanescent. Polypodium crinitum, *Poir.; Bojer, Hort. Maur.* 418. P. thelypteroides, *Desv.; Bojer, loc. cit.* Aspidium strigosum, *Mett.*

Var. PAUCIFLORUM. Stipe densely scaly at the base only, and rachis clothed only with minute ascending linear scales. Aspidium sulcatum and pauciflorum, *Kaulf.* A. nitidum, *Bory.*

Var. NUDATUM. Stipe scaly at the base only, the rest of it and the rachis glossy, glabrous and quite free from scales. Nephrodium humidum, *Cordemoy.*

MAURITIUS and RODRIGUEZ, common. Also Bourbon. A very variable species in the character and abundance of its scales, but fairly uniform in other respects.

3. **N. prolixum,** *Baker; Hook. and Baker, Syn. Fil.* 268. Rootstock erect; scales not seen. Stipes tufted, naked, $\frac{1}{2}$ ft. long. Frond oblong-lanceolate, 2–3 feet long, a foot broad, moderately firm in texture, bipinnatifid, obscurely pilose; rachis square, pale brown, scaleless. Pinnæ lanceolate, sessile, $\frac{3}{4}$–1 in. broad, cut down to a narrow wing into entire ligulate segments $\frac{1}{12}$ in. broad, the lower pinnæ much dwarfed and distant. Veins pinnate in the secondary segments, with 10–15 pairs of simple veinlets. Sori medial. Involucre minute, persistent,

glabrous. N. tetragonum, *Bojer, Hort. Maur.* 398. Aspidium mascaranense, *Bojer. Hort. Maur.* 390, in part. A. heteropteron, *Mett.; Kuhn, Fil. Afr.* 134.

MAURITIUS, in woods. Also Bourbon, Madagascar, and Tropical Asia, not African.

4. **N. tomentosum,** *Desv.; Hook. and Baker, Syn. Fil.* 269. Rootstock erect; scales lanceolate, dull brown. Stipes short, tufted, pilose, scaleless. Frond oblong-lanceolate, bipinnatifid, 1–2 feet long 8–10 in. broad, moderately firm in texture, densely finely pilose; rachis pilose, scaleless. Pinnæ lanceolate, sessile, $\frac{3}{4}$ in. broad, cut down to a narrow wing into ligulate entire segments $\frac{1}{8}$ in. broad, the lower pinnæ much dwarfed. Veins pinnate in the secondary segments, with 8–12 pairs of simple distinct veinlets. Sori small, medial. Involucre minute, membranous, fugacious. Polypodium tomentosum and nervosum, *Bojer, Hort. Maur.* 419. Aspidium riparium, *Bory; Kuhn, Fil. Afr.* 140. A. strigosum, *Willd.*

MAURITIUS and SEYCHELLES, in rocky woods. Also Bourbon and Tristan d'Acunha, and probably a variety of the American *N. conterminum.*

5. **N. Filix-mas,** *Rich.*; var. N. ELONGATUM, *Hook. and Grev.; Hook and Baker, Syn. Fil.* 280. Rootstock erect; scales lanceolate, reddish-brown. Stipes tufted, straw-coloured, a foot long, with a few scales above the base. Frond deltoid, glabrous, moderately firm in texture, tripinnatifid, 1–2 feet long; rachis straw-coloured, naked. Pinnæ oblong-lanceolate; pinnules lanceolate; tertiary segments oblong, toothed, $\frac{1}{8}$–$\frac{1}{4}$ in. broad. Veins pinnate in the tertiary segments, with erecto-patent forked veinlets. Sori medial. Involucre firm, glabrous, persistent. N. Bojeri, *Hook. and Baker, Syn. Fil.* 280. Aspidium Boryanum, *Bojer, Hort. Maur.* 391, *not Willd.*

MAURITIUS, in woods of the Pouce, Black River, and Quartier Militaire. The variety spread through the tropics of the Old World; the type cosmopolitan.

6. **N. sparsum,** *Don; Hook. and Baker, Syn. Fil.* 276. Rootstock erect; scales brown, lanceolate. Stipes tufted, $\frac{1}{2}$–1 foot long, naked in the upper part, straw-coloured. Frond deltoid, moderately firm in texture, 1–1$\frac{1}{2}$ foot long, tripinnatifid, glabrous. Pinnæ cuneate on the lower side at the base, the lower ones deltoid, stalked, the upper ones sessile, lanceolate; tertiary segments oblong, obtuse, toothed, $\frac{1}{12}$–$\frac{1}{8}$ in. broad. Veins pinnate in the tertiary segments, with erecto-patent forked veinlets. Sori medial. Involucre firm, glabrous, persistent.

MAURITIUS; two sheets in the Kew herbarium without special station. There may be some mistake, as otherwise the species is not known beyond Tropical Asia.

7. **N. Wardii,** *Baker; Hook. and Baker, Syn. Fil. edit.* ii. 500. Rootstock and scales not seen. Stipes glossy, naked, straw-coloured. Frond deltoid, membranous, fragile, glabrous, 4-pinnatifid, 1$\frac{1}{2}$–2 feet long; rachis straw-coloured, naked. Pinnæ stalked, oblong-lanceolate;

tertiary segments deltoid, parallel with the rachis on the upper side at the base, cuneate on the lower, deeply pinnatifid, with obtuse entire or toothed lobes. Veins pinnate or forked in the final lobes. Sori medial. Involucre glabrous, persistent. *Wright in Trans. Roy. Irish Acad.* xxv. *t.* 30.

SEYCHELLES, common in the woods of Mahé, first sent to Kew by Swinburne Ward, Esq. Endemic.

8. **N. Hornei,** *Baker; Hook. and Baker, Syn. Fil. ed.* ii. 500. Rootstock and basal scales not seen. Stipes naked, glossy, straw-coloured. Frond very large, deltoid, decompound, glabrous, moderately firm in texture; rachises glabrous, straw-coloured. Lowest pinnæ deltoid, produced on the lower side, attaining a length of 2 or 3 feet; ultimate segments oblong-lanceolate, with oblong obtuse lobes, produced on the upper side and parallel at the base with the winged rachis, cuneate on the lower. Veins pinnate or forked opposite the final lobes. Sori small, nearly marginal. Involucre firm, glabrous, persistent.

SEYCHELLES, common in the shady forests of Mahé and Silhouette, *Horne*, 182! 685! Endemic.

9. **N. crenatum,** *Baker.* Rootstock erect; scales very dense, large, lanceolate, bright reddish-brown. Stipes tufted, naked, straw-coloured, 6–9 in. long. Frond deltoid, membranous, tripinnatifid, densely pilose, $\frac{1}{2}$–1 foot long; rachis naked, pilose. Pinnæ truncate at the base, the lowest much the largest, deltoid, produced on the lower side; tertiary segments oblong, obtuse, crenate. Ultimate veinlets distant, erecto-patent, forked. Sori medial, filling up nearly the whole segment. Involucre pale, persistent, densely pilose. N. odoratum, *Hook. and Baker, Syn. Fil.* 280. Aspidium odoratum and lanuginosum, *Bojer, Hort. Maur.* 391.

MAURITIUS, in ravines at Grand Bassin and Trou aux Cerfs. Spread through the warmer regions of the Old World.

10. **N. lanuginosum,** *Desv. Ann. Linn.* vi. 262. Rootstock and basal scales not seen. Stipes 2–3 feet long, pilose in the upper, scaly in the lower part. Frond very large, deltoid, decompound, membranous, pilose; rachis scaleless, finely pilose. Lower pinnæ reaching a length of $1\frac{1}{2}$–2 feet, oblong-lanceolate, or the lowest deltoid, produced on the lower side; ultimate segments adnate, oblong, obtuse, crenate or pinnatifid, $\frac{1}{8}$–$\frac{1}{6}$ in. broad. Veins pinnate in the ultimate segments; veinlets erecto-patent, the lower forked. Sori medial. Involucre membranous, densely pilose, fugacious. N. catopteron, *Hook. and Baker, Syn. Fil.* 284.

MAURITIUS, *Sieber*, 48! Escalier woods, *Lady Barkly!* Also Bourbon, the Cape, and through Tropical Asia.

11. **N. oppositum,** *Hook.; Hook. and Baker, Syn. Fil.* 283. Rootstock and basal scales not seen. Stipes above a foot long, densely clothed throughout with large linear brown scales. Frond deltoid, moderately firm in texture, glabrous, tripinnatifid or tripinnate; rachises pubescent and densely scaly. Pinnæ oblong-lanceolate, reaching a foot long, the lowest sometimes deltoid, produced on the lower side; pinnules lanceolate, cut down nearly or quite to the rachis into oblong obtuse entire tertiary segments 1/8–1/6 in. broad. Veins pinnate in the tertiary segments, with simple or forked distinct veinlets. Sori medial. Involucre small, glabrous. Aspidium crinitum, *Bojer, Hort. Maur.* 391.

MAURITIUS, in Trou Kanaka and the woods of the Savanne district. Also Bourbon and Madagascar.

12. **N. unitum,** *R. Br.; Hook. and Baker, Syn. Fil.* 289. Rootstock wide-creeping; scales minute, lanceolate, dark brown. Stipes 2–3 feet long, brown or straw-coloured, glossy, naked. Frond oblong-lanceolate, bipinnatifid, 1–2 feet long, 6–8 in. broad, subcoriaceous, glabrous or minutely pubescent; rachis naked. Pinnæ lanceolate, sessile, 1/2–3/4 in. broad, cut down to a broad wing into oblong obtuse entire lobes 1/6–1/4 in. broad; lower pinnæ not dwarfed. Veins pinnate in the secondary lobes, with 10–12 pairs of distinct simple veinlets, 3 or 4 of which join at the tip. Sori copious, minute, medial. Involucre minute, persistent, glabrous or pilose.

MAURITIUS, in damp plains at Moka, Plaines Wilhelms, and Savanne; Diego Garcia, *Bouton!* Tropical and subtropical zones of both hemispheres.

13. **N. cucullatum,** *Baker; Hook. and Baker, Syn. Fil.* 290. Rootstock wide-creeping; scales small, brown, lanceolate. Stipes 1/2–1 foot long, brownish, pubescent, naked above the base. Frond oblong-lanceolate, bipinnatifid, 1–1½ foot long, 6–10 in. broad, rigidly coriaceous, densely pilose, especially on the under surface; rachis scaleless, densely pubescent. Pinnæ lanceolate, sessile, 3/8–1/2 in. broad, cut about a third of the way down to the midrib into oblong obtuse entire lobes 1/12 in. broad; lower pinnæ suddenly very much dwarfed. Veins pinnate in the secondary lobes, with 8–10 pairs of distinctly-raised pilose simple veinlets. Sori copious, minute, medial. Involucre glabrous, firm, persistent. Aspidium obtusatum, *Bojer, Hort. Maur.* 390.

MAURITIUS, RODRIGUEZ, and SEYCHELLES, frequent in swamps at a low level. Spread through the tropics of the Old World.

14. **N. elatum,** *Baker; Hook. and Baker, Syn. Fil. ed.* ii. 502. Rootstock wide-creeping; scales lanceolate, dark brown. Stipes pubescent, scaleless, a foot long. Frond oblong-lanceolate, bipinnatifid, membranous, minutely pubescent, reaching, according to Bojer, a length of 6 or 8 feet and a breadth of 2½–3 feet; rachis scaleless, pubescent. Pinnæ lanceolate, sessile, 1½ in. broad, cut about halfway down to the

midrib into ligulate ascending entire lobes $\frac{1}{8}$ in. broad; lower pinnæ distant and suddenly very much dwarfed. Veins pinnate in the secondary lobes, with 12–16 pairs of simple veinlets. Sori medial. Involucre membranous, ciliated. Aspidium elatum, *Bojer, Hort. Maur.* 390.

Var. N. MAURITIANUM, *Fee, Gen. Fil.* 305. Pinnæ narrower ($\frac{3}{4}$–1 inch). Veinlets closer and more distinct. N. procerum, *Baker in Hook. and Baker, Syn. Fil. edit.* ii. 502.

The typical form in MAURITIUS, in dense forests at Curepipe and Grand Bassin, *Lady Barkly!* Also Natal. Of the variety we have a Mauritian specimen from Bojer, and Dr. Balfour has found it in RODRIGUEZ. Also Bourbon.

15. **N. Arbuscula**, *Desv.; Hook. and Baker, Syn. Fil.* 292. Rootstock suberect; scales linear, dark brown. Stipes tufted, very short, scaleless, pubescent. Frond oblong-lanceolate, simply pinnate, membranous, finely pilose, 1–1$\frac{1}{2}$ foot long, 6–10 in. broad. Pinnæ sessile, lanceolate, $\frac{3}{8}$–$\frac{1}{2}$ in. broad, shallowly obtusely lobed, parallel with the rachis, and auricled on the upper side at the base, cuneate on the lower side, many lower ones more distant and gradually dwarfed. Veins in pinnate groups, with 3–4 or in the auricle 5–6 pairs of simple veinlets. Sori minute, medial. Involucre membranous, fugacious.

MAURITIUS, frequent in damp woods. Also Bourbon and Tropical Asia.

16. **N. molle**. *R. Br.; Hook. and Baker. Syn. Fil.* 293. Rootstock short-creeping; scales small, brown, lanceolate. Stipes a foot long, scaleless, pubescent. Frond oblong-lanceolate, bipinnatifid, 1–2 feet long, 6–10 in. broad, membranous, more or less pilose; rachis pubescent, scaleless. Pinnæ sessile, lanceolate, cut generally about half way down to the midrib into oblong obtuse entire lobes $\frac{1}{8}$ in. broad; many lower pinnæ usually gradually dwarfed. Veins pinnate in the secondary lobes, with 6–8 pairs of simple distinct veinlets. Sori medial. Involucre membranous, pilose.

Var. N. HILSENBERGII, *Presl Tent.* 81. A very membranous small pilose form, with acuminate pinnæ under $\frac{1}{2}$ in. broad, cut nearly down to the rachis into lobes $\frac{1}{12}$ in. broad, the lowest pinnæ deflexed, but hardly at all dwarfed.

MAURITIUS, RODRIGUEZ, and SEYCHELLES, common in woods Very variable both in vestiture and the extent to which the lower pinnæ are dwarfed. In Mauritius there is every range from densely pilose to nearly glabrous forms. Spread through the warmer zones of both hemispheres.

17. **N. truncatum**, *Presl; Hook. and Baker, Syn. Fil.* 294. Rootstock suberect. Stipes naked, a foot or more long. Frond oblong-lanceolate, bipinnatifid, glabrous, membranous, 2–3 feet long, often a foot or more broad; rachis glabrous, scaleless. Pinnæ lanceolate, sessile, $\frac{3}{4}$–1 in. broad, cut about halfway down to the midrib into entire oblong obtuse or truncate lobes $\frac{1}{8}$ in. broad; lowest pinnæ suddenly dwarfed. Veins pinnate in the secondary lobes, with 6–8 pairs of

simple distinct veinlets. Sori medial. Involucre membranous, glabrous, fugacious. Aspidium caudiculatum, *Sieber*. A. mascaranense, *Kaulf*.

MAURITIUS, in woods. Also Bourbon, Madagascar, and Tropical Asia.

18. **N. subtriphyllum,** *Baker; Hook. and Baker, Syn. Fil.* 296. Rootstock short-creeping; scales small, brown, linear. Stipes brown, glossy, naked, a foot long. Frond deltoid, bipinnate, about a foot long and broad, glabrous except the main ribs on the lower surface. Free pinnæ about 3 pairs, the upper lanceolate, the lowest pair much the largest, deltoid, produced on the lower side, with the lowest pinnule usually free. Main veins distinct from the midrib to the edge, with intermediate veins anastomosing in copious irregular areolæ with free included veinlets. Sori small, scattered irregularly. Involucre minute, fugacious. Polypodium reticulatum, *Bojer, Hort. Maur.* 419. Phegopteris triphylla, *Kuhn, Fil. Afric.* 124.

MAURITIUS, in the woods of Anse Courtois. Through Tropical Asia, not African.

19. **N. pleiotomum,** *Baker; Hook. and Baker, Syn. Fil. ed.* ii. 297. Rootstock and basal scales not seen. Stipes 1–1½ foot long, black, glossy, naked. Frond membranous, glabrous, deltoid, bipinnate, 1–1½ foot long and broad. Free pinnæ 2–3 pairs, the upper ones lanceolate, the lowest pair deltoid, distinctly stalked, much produced on the lower side, the lowest pinnule nearly or quite free. Main veins distinct from the midrib to the edge, with intermediate veins anastomosing in copious small areolæ with free included veinlets. Sori small, scattered irregularly. Involucre minute, fugacious. *Wright in Trans. Roy. Irish Acad.* xxv. *t.* 31 B.

SEYCHELLES, common in the woods of Mahé, *Ward! Wright! Horne!* Also Madagascar.

20. **N. Pica,** *Baker; Hook, and Baker, Syn. Fil.* 298. Rootstock suberect; scales lanceolate, dark brown. Stipes contiguous, black, glossy, naked, ½–1 foot long. Frond deltoid, deeply pinnatifid or the lowest one or two pairs of primary segments free, 6–15 in. long and broad, membranous, glabrous except the main veins on the under surface. Central segments lanceolate, acute; lowest pair largest, deltoid, produced and deeply pinnatifid on the lower side. Main veins distinct from the midrib to the edge, the intermediate veins anastomosing in copious areolæ with free included veinlets. Sori large, arranged in regular rows near the main veins. Involucre membranous, glabrous. Aspidium trifoliatum, *Sw. in part; Bojer, Hort. Maur.* 392.

MAURITIUS, frequent in woods. Also Bourbon and Madagascar. *Capillaire à grandes feuilles.*

22. MONOGRAMME, Schk.

Capsules stalked, splitting transversely, with an incomplete vertical ring. Sori linear, running down the midrib of the frond, without any involucre.—Minute ferns, with narrow grass-like fronds. DISTRIB. Tropics of both hemispheres. Species 9.

1. **M. graminea,** *Schk.; Hook. and Baker, Syn. Fil.* 375. Rootstock slender, wide-creeping; scales linear-subulate, spreading, blackish, clathrate. Fronds sessile, membranous, green, glabrous, 2–4 in. long, $\frac{1}{24}$ in. broad, with a distinct midrib, but no other veins, the sorus confined to the tip in a channel formed by its reduplicate margins. M. linearis, *Kaulf.; Bojer, Hort. Maur.* 407.

MAURITIUS, on old trunks in the woods of the Pouce range, etc. SEYCHELLES, *Pervillé!* Also Bourbon and perhaps also Cape.

23. POLYPODIUM, Linn.

Capsule stalked, splitting transversely, with an incomplete vertical ring. Sori round, placed on the back of the frond either at the tip of or on the back of a vein, without any involucre.—Ferns of every variety of cutting, texture, and veining. DISTRIB. Cosmopolitan, mainly tropical. Species 400.

Series I. Habit of *Nephrodium*, with stipes continuous with the rootstock.

Subgenus I. PHEGOPTERIS. Veins free.

Frond bipinnatifid.
  Ultimate veinlets simple . . . . 1. P. OBTUSILOBUM.
  Ultimate veinlets forked . . . . 2. P. CYATHEÆFOLIUM.
Frond large, tripinnatifid . . . . 3. P. CRUCIATUM.

Subgenus II. GONIOPTERIS. Veins in pinnate groups, with many veinlets joining at their tips with those of the next group.

Rachis naked . . . . 4. P. PROLIFERUM.
Rachis densely scaly . . . . 5. P. TOMENTOSUM.

Series II. Stipes jointed at their point of junction with the rootstock.

Subgenus III. EUPOLYPODIUM. Veins free.

Frond simple.
  Frond entire.
    Sori small, remaining distinct . . . . 6. P. PERVILLEI.
    Sori large, becoming confluent . . . . 7. P. MULTIFIDUM.
  Frond crenate . . . . 8. P. BARBATULUM.

Frond pinnatifid.
  Lobes very short, 1-veined . . . . 9. P. SERRULATUM.
  Lobes oblong or lanceolate, with pinnate veining.
    Frond membranous, pendulous . . . . 10. P. SECHELLARUM.
    Frond coriaceous, erect.
      Frond naked . . . . 11. P. LEUCOSORUM.
      Frond pubescent and white farinose . . . . 12. P. ALBOBRUNNEUM.
Frond simply pinnate.
  Frond flaccid, pendulous, pubescent . . . . . . 13. P. CULTRATUM.
  Frond stiff, erect, glabrous.
    Frond $\frac{3}{8}$–$\frac{3}{4}$ in. broad.
      Not coriaceous ; veins distinct . . . . . . 14. P. PARVULUM.
      Coriaceous ; veins hidden . . . . 15. P. RIGESCENS.
    Frond 1–3 in. broad . . . . 16. P. ARGYRATUM.

Subgenus IV. NIPHOBOLUS. Veins anastomosing copiously ; under surface of the frond densely tomentose.

The only species . . . . 17. P. ADNASCENS.

Subgenus V. PHYMATODES. Veins anastomising copiously. Fronds all of one kind, not tomentose beneath.

Frond entire.
  Sori forming a single row between the midrib and edge.
    Stipes very short . . . . 18. P. LYCOPODIOIDES.
    Stipes 1–2 in. long.
      Frond naked beneath . . . . 19. P. LINEARE.
      Frond with scattered peltate scales beneath . . 20. P. LANCEOLATUM.
  Sori copious, scattered . . . . 21. P. IRIOIDES.
Frond pinnatifid . . . . 22. P. PHYMATODES.

Subgenus VI. DRYNARIA. Veins anastomosing copiously. Fronds naked beneath, the barren one very different from the fertile one.

The only species. . . . . 23. P. WILLDENOVII.

1. **P. obtusifolium,** *Desv.*; *Hook. and Baker*, *Syn. Fil.* 305. Rootstock erect; scales brown, membranous, lanceolate. Stipes tufted, naked, slightly pilose, $\frac{1}{2}$–1 ft. long. Frond oblong-lanceolate, bipinnatifid, membranous, finely pilose on the ribs beneath, 1–2 feet long, 6–10 in. broad at the middle, narrowed gradually to the base; rachis scaleless, finely pubescent. Pinnæ lanceolate, sessile, $\frac{1}{2}$–$\frac{3}{4}$ in. broad, cut down to a narrow wing into oblong obtuse entire segments $\frac{1}{12}$ in. broad. Veins pinnate in the secondary segments, with 8–12 pairs of simple veinlets. Sori small, medial. Aspidium Desvauxii, *Mett.*; *Kuhn*, *Fil. Afric.* 131.

MAURITIUS, in woods of the Pouce range, etc., *Bojer!* Also Natal, Madagascar, and Tropical Africa. I have not seen an involucre, and so leave this here, but have great doubt whether it be not a variety of *Nephrodium conterminum*.

2. **P. cyatheæfolium,** *Desv.*; *Hook. and Baker*, *Syn. Fil. ed.* ii. 306. Rootstock erect; scales dull brown, lanceolate, membranous

Stipes tufted, straw-coloured, naked, a foot or more long. Frond oblong-deltoid, bipinnatifid, membranous, glabrous, 1–2 feet long, reaching a foot or more broad; rachis straw-coloured, naked. Pinnæ lanceolate, sessile, 1½ in. broad, cut down to a broad wing, into lanceolate entire falcate segments ¼–⅓ in. broad; lowest pair dwarfed, deflexed and produced on the lower side. Veins pinnate in the secondary segments, with very numerous ascending forked veinlets, which casually anastomose. Sori small, medial. P. Sieberianum, *Kaulf.; Bojer, Hort. Maur.* 418. Phegopteris cyatheæfolia, *Mett.; Kuhn, Fil. Afric.* 122.

MAURITIUS, in the woods of Pamplemousses and Poudre d'Or. Endemic.

3. **P. cruciatum,** *Baker.* Rootstock and basal scales not seen. Stipes glossy, naked, straw-coloured, slightly pilose. Frond ample, deltoid, tripinnatifid, membranous, with a few long hairs on the ribs of the under surface; rachises pale, naked. Lower pinnæ oblong-lanceolate, a foot long; pinnules lanceolate, sessile, cut down to a narrow wing into oblong obtuse entire or toothed segments. Veins pinnate in the tertiary segments, with many simple or forked veinlets. Sori small, medial. P. Bojeri, *Hook. and Baker, Syn. Fil.* 311. P. ammifolium, *Bojer, Hort. Maur.* 420. P. sessilifolium, *Hook. Sp. Fil.* iv. 251. Phegopteris cruciata, *Mett.; Kuhn, Fil. Afric.* 122.

MAURITIUS, in the dense woods of the Pouce range, etc. Also Bourbon.

4. **P. proliferum,** *Presl; Hook. and Baker, Syn. Fil.* 315. Rootstock erect; scales small, dull brown, lanceolate. Stipes ¼–½ ft. long, naked, straw-coloured. Frond oblong-lanceolate, simply pinnate, moderately firm in texture, subglabrous, 1–3 feet long, 6–12 in. broad; rachis naked, often irregularly proliferous. Pinnæ sessile, lanceolate, with many shallow obtuse lobes. Veins in a pinnate group opposite each lobe, with 8-12 pairs of simple veinlets, most of which anastomose at the tip. Sori small, those of the upper veins medial, of the lower apical. Phegopteris luxurians, *Mett.*

MAURITIUS, at Baie du Cap, *C. H. Higginson!* Also Natal, Zambesi-land and Tropical Asia.

5. **P. tomentosum,** *Bory; Hook. and Baker, Syn. Fil. ed.* ii. 315. Rootstock and stipes not seen. Frond oblong-lanceolate, simply pinnate, about a foot long, 6–7 in. broad, membranous, finely pubescent all over; rachis densely clothed with brown subulate scales. Pinnæ lanceolate, acute, ½–¾ in. broad, entire or shallowly lobed, the lower ones stalked. Veins in transverse pinnate groups, with few distant pairs of fine obscure veinlets. Sori small, medial. P. arthothrix, *Hook. Sp. Fil.* v. 14. Phegopteris tomentosa, *Mett.; Kuhn, Fil. Afric.* 123.

MAURITIUS, gathered by Belanger, according to Kuhn, but I have seen only Madagascar specimens.

6. **P. Pervillei,** *Mett.; Hook. and Baker, Syn. Fil. ed.* ii. 321. Rootstock slender, creeping; scales very minute, brown, lanceolate. Stipes distant, very short. Frond ligulate, entire, membranous, bright green, glabrous, 1–2 in. long, $\frac{1}{12}$–$\frac{1}{8}$ in. broad, obtuse, narrowed gradually from the middle to the base. Veins simple, erecto-patent, not reaching the edge. Sori oblong, superficial, dorsal on the veins, forming a row close to the midrib on each side. *Wright in Trans. Roy. Irish Acad.* xxv. *t.* 31, *A.*

SEYCHELLES, on mossy rocks amongst the hills, *Pervillé! Wright! Horne,* 195! Endemic.

7. **P. multifidum,** *Bory; Hook. and Baker, Sp. Fil.* 322. Rootstock slender, wide-creeping; basal scales minute, brown, linear. Stipes tufted, naked, $\frac{1}{4}$–$\frac{1}{2}$ in. long. Frond ligulate, entire, coriaceous, bright green, glabrous, 1–2 in. long, $\frac{1}{12}$–$\frac{1}{6}$ in. broad, obtuse, cuneate at the base. Veins simple, erecto-patent, not reaching the edge. Sori round, or the lower ones oblong, superficial, when mature filling up the whole space between the edge and midrib. Pleopeltis angusta, *Bojer, Hort. Maur.* 389, *non H.B.K.* Grammitis obtusa, *Willd.; Bojer, Hort. Maur.* 414.

MAURITIUS, on mossy rocks of the Pouce range, etc. Also Bourbon. The plant was named by Bory upon a cristate monstrosity, but the frond is properly simple.

8. **P. barbatulum,** *Baker, in Hook. and Baker, Syn. Fil.* 323. Rootstock short-creeping; scales minute, linear, brown. Stipes contiguous, wiry, brown, $\frac{1}{2}$–1 in. long, clothed with fine long spreading brown hairs. Frond linear, simple, 1$\frac{1}{2}$–2 in. long, $\frac{1}{4}$–$\frac{1}{3}$ in. broad, shallowly obtusely lobed, cuneate at the base, subcoriaceous, thinly clothed on both sides with fine brown hairs. Veins 2–3-furcate opposite each lobe, not reaching the edge. Sori round, superficial, forming a single row midway between the midrib and edge. P. ciliatum, *Bojer, Hort. Maur.* 416, *not Willd.* P. Beaumontii, *Leperv.; Kuhn, Fil. Afric.* 209.

MAURITIUS, on rocks and trees in the forests of Grandport and Savanne. Also Bourbon.

9. **P. serrulatum,** *Mett.; Hook. and Baker, Syn. Fil.* 323. Rootstock creeping, clothed with minute adpressed brown lanceolate scales. Stipes very short, tufted, slender, naked. Frond linear, rigidly subcoriaceous, glabrous, the lower part cut about halfway down to the midrib into obliquely deltoid teeth, the upper part when fertile subentire. Veins distant, simple, distinct, erecto-patent, one running into each tooth and reaching the edge. Sori oblong, superficial, soon confluent and filling up the whole of the upper third or half of the frond, except the edge. Xiphopteris serrulata, *Kaulf.; Bojer, Hort. Maur.* 415.

MAURITIUS and SEYCHELLES, on mossy rocks and old trunks. Cosmopolitan in the Tropics.

10. **P. sechellarum,** *Baker; Hook and Baker, Syn. Fil. ed.* ii. 508. Rootstock short. Stipes tufted, wiry, brown, 1–1½ in. long, slightly pubescent. Frond pendulous, lanceolate, membranous, ½ foot long, ½ in. broad, thinly clothed with fine brown spreading hairs, cut down to a broad wing into oblong obtuse lobes ⅛–⅙ in. broad. Veins distinct, pinnate in the lobes, with 4–5 pairs of branched veinlets. Sori round, superficial, forming a row midway between the midrib and edge of the lobes terminal on the anterior fork of the veinlets.

SEYCHELLES, on trunks of trees in the hill-woods of Mahé, *Horne*, 194! MAURITIUS, *Lady Barkly!* Endemic.

11. **P. leucosorum,** *Bojer; Hook. and Baker, Syn. Fil.* 324. Rootstock stout, short-creeping; basal scales dense, linear, spreading, dark brown. Stipes contiguous, wiry, erect, bright brown, naked, 3–6 in. long. Frond lanceolate, coriaceous, glabrous, 6–9 in. long, 1–2 in. broad, cut down nearly to the midrib into spreading entire lanceolate acute or oblong obtuse lobes ¼–½ in. broad. Veins fine, obscure, immersed, copiously pinnate in the lobes, with two branches to most of the veinlets. Sori large, round, superficial, forming a single row midway between the midrib and edge, placed on the tip of the lowest branch of each veinlet.

MAURITIUS, on mossy trunks in the woods of Nouvelle Découverte and Grandport. Also Bourbon.

12. **P. albobrunneum,** *Baker.* Rhizome stout, short-creeping; basal scales very dense, linear, bright brown, spreading. Stipes contiguous, wiry, erect, brown, 1–2 in. long, densely clothed with short fine spreading brown hairs. Frond lanceolate, coriaceous, 4–6 in. long, ¾–1 in. broad, white-farinose and thinly clothed with fine spreading brown hairs, cut down nearly to the midrib into lanceolate obtuse lobes ⅛ in. broad, the lower ones shorter and broader. Veins copiously pinnate in the lobes, with erecto-patent forked veinlets. Sori round, superficial, forming a row close to the edge, terminal on the anterior fork of the veinlets.

SEYCHELLES, in the hill-woods of Mahé, *Horne*, 681! 682! Endemic.

13. **P. cultratum,** *Willd.; Hook. and Baker, Syn. Fil.* 327. Rootstock erect; basal scales hair-like. Stipes densely tufted, under an inch long, densely clothed with short spreading soft brown hairs. Frond flaccid, pendulous, lanceolate, ½–1 foot long, ½–¾ in. broad, clothed with fine soft-spreading brown hairs, cut down to the rachis into very numerous adnate oblique-lanceolate obtuse pinnæ $\frac{1}{12}$–⅛ in. broad. Veins pinnate in the pinnæ, with distant erecto-patent simple

veinlets which do not reach the edge. Sori round, superficial, 4–6 to a pinna, placed at the tip of the veinlets. P. elasticum, *Bory*. P. asplenifolium, *Bojer*, *Hort. Maur.* 418, *not Linn.*

MAURITIUS and SEYCHELLES, on mossy trunks in the woods, frequent. Also Bourbon, Guinea, and common in Tropical America.

14. **P. parvulum,** *Bory; Hook. and Baker, Syn. Fil.* 326. Root-stock short-creeping; scales brown, lanceolate, imbricated. Stipes close, very short, wiry, naked. Frond lanceolate, erect, moderately firm in texture, glabrous, 4–6 in. long, $\frac{1}{2}$–$\frac{3}{4}$ in. broad, cut down to the rachis into numerous linear entire subacute adnate pinnæ $\frac{1}{12}$ in. broad, the lower ones gradually dwarfed. Veins pinnate in the pinnæ, with distant simple erecto-patent veinlets, which do not reach the edge. Sori round, superficial, 4–6 to each pinna, placed at the tip of the veinlets. P. Filicula, *Bojer*, *Hort. Maur.* 418, *non Kaulf.*

MAURITIUS, on old trunks in woods of the Pouce range, etc. Also Bourbon.

15. **P. rigescens,** *Bory; Hook. and Baker, Syn. Fil.* 331. Root-stock wide-creeping, as thick as a quill, clothed with imbricated lanceolate dull brown scales. Stipes wiry, erect, naked, 1–2 in. long. Frond lanceolate, erect, coriaceous, glabrous, 3–6 in. long, $\frac{1}{4}$–$\frac{1}{2}$ in. broad, cut down to the rachis into very numerous adnate entire lanceolate obtuse pinnæ $\frac{1}{12}$ in. broad. Veins pinnate in the pinnæ; veinlets quite hidden. Sori round, superficial, 4–6 to a pinna, finally filling up the whole space between the midrib and edge.

MAURITIUS, in woods of the Pouce and Quartier Militaire, *Bojer*. Also Bourbon, Guinea, and Tropical America.

16. **P. argyratum,** *Bory; Hook. and Baker, Syn. Fil.* 331. Root-stock woody, short-creeping; scales dense, linear, bright brown. Stipes close, wiry, naked, 2–3 in. long. Frond lanceolate, coriaceous, white-mealy on the under surface, 6–10 in. long, $1\frac{1}{2}$–3 in. broad, cut down to the rachis into very numerous close aduate entire linear pinnæ $\frac{1}{8}$–$\frac{1}{4}$ in. broad at the base, narrowed gradually to the point. Veins copiously pinnate in the pinnæ; veinlets forked. Sori round, forming a row close to the edge of the pinniæ. P. argyrophanes, *Bory*; *Bojer*, *Hort. Maur.* 418.

MAURITIUS, in the woods of Grandport and Bel Ombre. Also Bourbon.

17. **P. adnascens,** *Sw.; Hook. and Baker, Syn. Fil.* 349. Root-stock slender, wide-creeping; scales bright brown, linear, acuminate. Stipes distant, naked, $\frac{1}{2}$–1 in. long. Fronds linear, simple, coriaceous, nearly naked on the upper, densely clothed with pale-brown tomentum made up of stellate hairs on the under surface, the fertile ones linear, 4–6 in. long, $\frac{1}{4}$–$\frac{1}{3}$ in. broad, the barren ones as broad, but much shorter, with a shorter stipe. Veins fine, quite hidden. Sori small, round,

immersed in the tomentum, filling up the whole of the upper half or three-quarters of the frond. P. spissum, *Bory; Kuhn, Fil. Afric.* 153. Niphobolus spissus, *Kaulf.; Bojer, Hort. Maur.* 415.

MAURITIUS, RODRIGUEZ, and SEYCHELLES, on mossy rocks. Spread through the tropics of the Old World.

18. **P. lycopodioides,** *Linn.; Hook. and Baker, Syn. Fil.* 357. Rootstock wide-creeping, about $\frac{1}{8}$ in. thick, often much branched; scales lanceolate, bright brown. Stipes distant, very short. Frond lanceolate, entire, subcoriaceous, glabrous, 3–4 in. long, $\frac{1}{2}$–$\frac{3}{4}$ in. broad, acute, cuneate at the base. Veins fine, immersed, anastomosing copiously. Sori round, immersed, forming a single row midway between the midrib and edge. P. lagopodioides, *Desv.; Bojer, Hort. Maur.* 416.

MAURITIUS, on rocks of the Pouce, Pieterboth, etc. Cosmopolitan in the tropics.

19. **P. lineare,** *Thunb.; Hook. and Baker, Syn. Fil.* 354. Rootstock woody, wide-creeping, glaucous, $\frac{1}{8}$–$\frac{1}{6}$ in. thick; scales brown, lanceolate, deciduous. Stipes distant, naked, straw-coloured, 1–2 in. long. Frond lanceolate, entire, subcoriaceous, green and glabrous on both surfaces, 6–12 in. long, $\frac{1}{3}$–1 in. broad at the middle, narrowed gradually to both ends. Veins fine, immersed, anastomosing copiously. Sori large, round, immersed, mixed with peltate scales, forming a single row nearer the midrib than the margin. P. excavatum, *Bory; Bojer Hort. Maur.* 416. P. simplex, *Sw.; Bojer, loc. cit.*

MAURITIUS, on rocks and trees. Spread through the two warmer zones of the Old World.

20. **P. lanceolatum,** *Linn.; Hook. and Baker, Syn. Fil.* 356. Rootstock slender, woody, wide-creeping; scales small, brown, lanceolate. Stipes distant, naked, 1–2 in. long. Frond lanceolate, entire, 4–6 in. long, $\frac{1}{2}$–$\frac{3}{4}$ in. broad at the middle, narrowed gradually to both ends, coriaceous, glabrous above, clothed beneath with scattered peltate scales brown in the middle and pale at the edge. Veins fine, immersed, anastomosing copiously. Sori large, round, slightly immersed, forming a single row midway between the midrib and edge. Pleopeltis macrocarpa and marginalis, *Kaulf.; Bojer, Hort. Maur.* 389.

MAURITIUS, on exposed mountain rocks, rare. Spread through the two warmer zones of both hemispheres.

21. **P. irioides,** *Lam.; Hook. and Baker, Syn. Fil.* 360. Rootstock stout, woody, short-creeping; scales few, minute, brown, lanceolate. Fronds tufted, sessile, simple, entire, lanceolate, glabrous, membranous or subcoriaceous, 1–3 feet long, 1–3 in. broad above the middle acute, narrowed very gradually to the base. Veins fine, immersed, anastomosing copiously, the main ones erecto-patent, distinct nearly to

the edge. Sori round, superficial, scattered, minute, very abundant. P. punctatum, *Sw.*, *non Thunb.* P. altum, *Bojer*, *Hort. Maur.* 417. P. sessile, *Kaulf.*; *Bojer*, *Hort. Maur.* 416.

MAURITIUS and SEYCHELLES, on old trunks in the forests. Spread through the tropical zone of the Old World.

22. **P. Phymatodes,** *Linn.*; *Hook. and Baker*, *Syn. Fil.* 364. Rootstock woody, wide-creeping, ¼–½ in. thick; scales linear-subulate, nearly black. Stipes distant, naked, straw-coloured, ½–1 foot long. Frond rhomboid or deltoid, ½–1 foot long, membranous, green and naked on both surfaces, cut down to a broad wing into lanceolate acute entire segments ½–1 in. broad. Veins fine, immersed, anastomosing copiously. Sori round, moderately large, scattered, distinctly immersed. P. scutifrons, *Bojer*, *Hort. Maur.* 417.

MAURITIUS, RODRIGUEZ, and SEYCHELLES, common on old trunks in the forests. Spread through the tropics of the Old World.

23. **P. Willdenovii,** *Bory*; *Hook. and Baker*, *Syn. Fil.* 367. Rootstock thick, woody, wide-creeping; scales dense, linear, bright reddish-brown. Barren fronds sessile, oblong, brown, rigidly coriaceous, 6–9 in. long, shallowly pinnatifid, with oblong obtuse lobes. Fertile frond much larger (1–2 feet long) subcoriaceous, naked, on a short naked stipe, cut down nearly or quite to the rachis into lanceolate entire pinnæ 1–1¼ in. broad. Veins prominently raised, the main ones erecto-patent, distinct nearly to the edge. Sori round, distinctly immersed, forming a single row near the midrib of the pinnæ.

MAURITIUS, on old trees at Quartier Militaire and on the Pouce range. Also Madagascar, Bourbon, and Tropical Africa.

24. GYMNOGRAMME, Desv.

Capsules stalked, splitting transversely, with an incomplete vertical ring. Sori dorsal, linear, simple or forked, not anastomosing, without any involucre.—Ferns of very various habit and cutting, with simple or compound veining. DISTRIB. Tropical and warm temperate zones of both hemispheres. Species 90.

1. **G. lanceolata,** *Hook.*; *Hook. and Baker*, *Syn. Fil.* 387. Rootstock slender, wide-creeping; scales linear, dull brown. Frond simple, lanceolate, coriaceous, glabrous, 9–18 in. long, ¾–1¼ in. broad at the middle, narrowed to an acute point and short flattened stipe. Veins fine, immersed, anastomosing copiously. Sori simple, linear, ½–1 in. long, parallel to one another in a row on each side of the midrib. Grammitis lanceolata, *Sw.*; *Bojer*, *Hort. Maur.* 415. Polypodium Loxogramme, *Mett.*; *Kuhn*, *Fil. Afric.* 149.

MAURITIUS, on rocks and old trunks in the forests of the Pouce, etc. Spread through the tropics of the Old World.

G. cheilanthoides, Kaulf.; Hook. and Baker, Syn. Fil. 382 (G. filipendulæfolia, *Desv.*,) a plant of Tristan d'Acunha, is given by Swartz as a Mauritian species, probably in error. It has a brown stipe and rachis, and a lanceolate membranous pilose frond 6-9 inches long, with deltoid pinnæ cut up into small ligulate 1-nerved tertiary segments.

25. ANTROPHYUM, Kaulf.

Capsules stalked, splitting transversely, with an incomplete vertical ring. Sori dorsal, linear, anastomosing copiously, scattered over the whole under surface of the frond, without any involucre.—Fronds simple, coriaceous or membranous, rather fleshy, tufted, sessile or stipitate, the veins always immersed and anastomosing copiously, the basal scales dull brown and clathrate, like those of Vittaria. DISTRIB. Tropics of both hemispheres. Species 15.

Sori entirely immersed . . . . 1. A. IMMERSUM.
Sori half immersed . . . . 2. A. RETICULATUM.
Sori superficial . . . . 3. A. BORYANUM.

1. **A. immersum**, *Mett.; Hook and Baker, Syn. Fil.* 393. Fronds oblanceolate, coriaceous, 3–5 in. long, ¾–1 in. broad at the middle, sessile or narrowed gradually to a short stipe; midrib visible at the base only. Sori slender, completely immersed in a deep groove. A. pumilum, *Kaulf.; Bojer, Hort. Maur.* 398. A. Hookerianum, *Fée.*

MAURITIUS and SEYCHELLES, on old trunks in the forests. Also Bourbon and Java.

2. **A. reticulatum**, *Kaulf.; Hook. and Baker, Syn. Fil.* 393. Fronds oblanceolate, subcoriaceous, 9–12 in. long, 1½ in. broad above the middle, narrowed gradually to the base, the broad midrib visible in the lower half. Sori stouter than in *A. immersum*, not more than half immersed in the shallower groove. A. callæfolium, *Blume.*

SEYCHELLES, in the woods of Mahé and Silhouette, not common, *Horne*, 688! Tropical Asia, not African.

3. **A. Boryanum,** *Kaulf; Hook. and Baker, Syn. Fil.* 394. Fronds broad oblanceolate, membranous or coriaceous, 1–1½ foot long, 2½–4 in. broad above the middle, acute in the typical form, narrowed gradually from the middle to the base or a short stipe; midrib visible near the base only. Sori much more abundant than in the other two species, very slender, anastomosing more copiously, hardly at all immersed. A. giganteum, *Bory; Hook. and Baker, loc. cit.* A. obtusum, *Kaulf.; Bojer, Hort. Maur.* 398.

MAURITIUS, frequent in the mountain forests. Also Bourbon and Comoros. *A. obtusum* is a variety with a narrower and more obtuse frond than in the type, and *A. giganteum* a large coriaceous form.

26. ACROSTICHUM, Linn.

Capsules stalked, splitting transversely, with an incomplete vertical ring. Sori spread in a regular stratum over the whole surface of the frond or of the upper pinnæ, without any involucre.—Ferns of very various texture, cutting and veining, the fertile fronds or segments often different from the barren in shape and size. DISTRIB. Both hemispheres, principally within the tropics. Species 140.

Subgenus ELAPHOGLOSSUM. Veins free. Fronds simple.

Sterile frond naked.
  Marginal scales none.
    Sterile frond linear, $\frac{1}{3}$–$\frac{1}{2}$ in. broad . . . . 1. A. LINEARE.
    Sterile frond lanceolate or oblong-lanceolate.
      Sterile frond 4–6 in. long . . . . 2. A. CONFORME.
      Sterile frond 6–12 in. long.
        Basal scales lanceolate . . . . 3. A. LATIFOLIUM.
        Basal scales linear-subulate . . . . 4. A. SIEBERI.
  Marginal scales few . . . . 5. A. HYBRIDUM.
Sterile frond obscurely minutely scaly.
  Basal scales linear-subulate, dark brown . . . . . . 6. A. VISCOSUM.
  Basal scales lanceolate, light brown . . . . 7. A. BOIVINI.
Sterile frond densely conspicuously scaly.
  Sterile frond oblong or obovate-oblong, 1–2 in. long . 8. A. SPATHULATUM.
  Sterile frond lanceolate, 4–6 in. long . . . . 9. A. SQUAMOSUM.
  Sterile frond lanceolate, 1–1½ ft. long . . . . . . 10. A. TOMENTOSUM.

Subgenus STENOCHLÆNA. Veins free. Fronds compound. Fertile frond with narrow linear segments.

Fertile frond simply pinnate . . . . 11. A. SORBIFOLIUM.
Fertile frond bipinnate . . . . 12. A. TENUIFOLIUM.

Subgenus GYMNOPTERIS. Veins anastomosing, unequal, the main ones distinct to the edge. Fertile frond soriferous all over the under surface.

Frond simply pinnate . . . . 13. A. PUNCTATUM.
Frond bipinnatifid . . . . 14. A. REPANDUM.

Subgenus CHRYSODIUM. Veins anastomosing, equal. Fertile frond soriferous all over the upper pinnæ.

The only species . . . . 15. A. AUREUM.

Subgenus HYMENOLEPIS. Veins anastomosing. Frond simple, soriferous only on the contracted tip.

The only species . . . . 16. A. SPICATUM.

1. **A. simplex**, *Sw.; Hook. and Baker, Syn. Fil.* 400; *var.* A. MARTINICENSE, *Desv.* Rootstock woody, short-creeping; scales minute, brown, lanceolate. Sterile frond linear, 6–8 in. long, $\frac{1}{3}$–$\frac{1}{2}$ in. broad, naked, rigidly coriaceous, obtuse or subacute, narrowed very

gradually to the base or a very short stipe. Veins immersed, quite invisible. Fertile frond shorter, with a stipe 2–3 in. long.

SEYCHELLES, not uncommon in Mahé and Silhouette, *Horne*, 676! Also Tropical America, Guinea, and perhaps Madagascar.

2. **A. conforme,** *Sw.; Hook and Baker, Syn. Fil.* 401. Rootstock thick, woody, short-creeping; scales large, brown, lanceolate. Sterile frond lanceolate or oblong-lanceolate, 4–6 in. long, 1–2 in. broad at the middle, acute, deltoid at the base, rigidly coriaceous, naked, with a naked straw-coloured stipe 1–3 in. long. Veins fine, close, rather ascending, usually forked. Fertile frond smaller, with a longer stipe. A. macropodium, *Fée, Acrost.* 30, *tab.* vi. *fig.* 2. A. ovalifolium, *Bojer, Hort. Maur.* 414.

Var. CARMICHAELII, *Baker.* Sterile frond lanceolate, 8–9 in. long, 1½ in. broad, narrowed gradually to both ends, with a stipe 1½–2 in. long. Fertile frond smaller, on a stipe 3–8 in. long, scaly near the base.

MAURITIUS and SEYCHELLES, in woods; the variety, which recedes from the type towards *A. latifolium*, gathered in Mauritius by Captain Carmichael. Tropical and warm temperate zones of both hemispheres.

3. **A. latifolium,** *Sw.; Hook. and Baker, Syn. Fil.* 403. Rootstock thick, woody, short-creeping; scales dense, lanceolate, bright brown. Sterile frond lanceolate or oblong-lanceolate, 6–12 in. long, 1½–3 in. broad at the middle, naked, rigidly coriaceous, acute, deltoid at the base, with a naked straw-coloured stipe 3–6 in. long. Veins fine, close, rather ascending, usually forked. Fertile frond narrower, on a stipe of about equal length. A. callæfolium, *Blume.*

SEYCHELLES, in the woods of Mahé, *Ward! Horne*, 172! Warmer zones of both hemispheres.

4. **A. Sieberi,** *Hook. and Grev.; Hook. and Baker, Syn. Fil.* 403. Rootstock thick, woody, short-creeping; scales dense, linear-subulate, dark brown. Sterile frond lanceolate or oblong-lanceolate, 8–12 in. long, 1½–3 in. broad at the middle, naked, rigidly coriaceous, acute, cuneate at the base, with a naked stipe 4–5 in. long. Veins fine, close, ascending, usually forked. Fertile frond narrower, on a longer stipe. A. ellipticum, *Fée, Acrost.* 30, *t.* 4.

MAURITIUS, in the woods of the Black River, etc. Also Bourbon.

5 **A. hybridum,** *Bory; Hook. and Baker, Syn. Fil.* 403. Rootstock thick, woody, short-creeping; scales dense, linear, dark bright brown. Sterile frond lanceolate, subcoriaceous, with a few spreading linear scales on the edges and midrib beneath, 6–9 in. long, 1½–2 in. broad, acute, deltoid or rather rounded at the base, with a straw-coloured stipe 3–6 in. long, furnished with a few spreading deciduous scales.

Veins distinct, rather ascending, $\frac{1}{12}$–$\frac{1}{8}$ in. apart, usually forked. Fertile frond the same shape, but much smaller.

MAURITIUS, forests of the Pouce, etc. Also Madagascar, Bourbon, Natal, Tropical Africa and Tropical America.

6. **A. viscosum**, *Sw.; Hook. and Baker, Syn. Fil.* 406. Rootstock short-creeping; scales minute, dense, linear-subulate, dark chestnut-brown. Sterile frond linear or lanceolate, moderately firm in texture, 6–12 in. long, $\frac{1}{2}$–$\frac{3}{4}$ in. broad, narrowed very gradually to the base and an acute point, slightly furfuraceous beneath, especially on the midrib and furnished with scattered sessile glands; stipe slender, 2–4 in. long, thinly minutely scaly. Veins distinct, ascending, simple or forked, $\frac{1}{24}$–$\frac{1}{16}$ in. apart. Fertile frond narrower, on a longer stipe. A. salicifolium, *Willd.* A. neriifolium, *Wall.*

Var. GLABRESCENS, *Baker.* Sterile frond larger, 1–1$\frac{3}{4}$ in. broad, nearly or quite naked.

Var. LANATUM, *Bojer, MSS.* Sterile frond 6–8 in. long, $\frac{5}{8}$–$\frac{3}{4}$ in. broad, sometimes obtuse, most narrowed in the lower half, thinly matted on both sides all over when young with delicate lanceolate ciliated ferruginous scales.

MAURITIUS, frequent on old trunks in the hill woods. Var. *glabrescens*; SEYCHELLES, in the woods of Mahé, *Ward! Horne!* Var. *lanatum*; in Mauritius at Bois Chéri, *Bojer!* Warmer zones of both hemispheres.

7. **A. Boivini**, *Mett.; Kuhn, Fil. Afric.* 43. Rootstock short-creeping; scales dense, lanceolate, acuminate, membranous, bright reddish-brown. Sterile frond lanceolate, $\frac{1}{2}$ foot long, $\frac{3}{4}$ in. broad, membranous, thinly scattered over with minute ovate acuminate scales; stipe 3 in. long, densely clothed with spreading linear-subulate scales; veins ascending, forked, $\frac{1}{16}$ in. apart, thickened at the tip. Fertile frond shorter and rather narrower, on a slightly longer stipe.

MAURITIUS, *Boivin*, according to Dr. Kuhn. Endemic, if it be not, as I suspect, a variety of *A. Aubertii*, Desv.

8. **A. spathulatum**, *Bory; Hook. and Baker, Syn. Fil.* 408. Rootstock slender, short-creeping or suberect; scales minute, brown, linear. Sterile frond oblong or obovate-oblong, moderately firm in texture, obtuse or subacute, 1–2 in. long, cuneate at the base, densely clothed when young with brown linear or subulate scales. Stipe about as long as the frond, densely clothed with spreading similar scales; veins erecto-patent, distant, forked. Fertile frond smaller, more rounded at the ends, on a longer stipe. A. piloselloides, *Presl.*

MAURITIUS, at Grand Port and Savanne, *Bojer.* SEYCHELLES, on trunks in the mountain woods of Mahé, *Horne!* Warmer zones of both hemispheres.

9. **A. squamosum**, *Sw.; Hook. and Baker, Syn. Fil.* 411. Root-

stock short-creeping; scales dense, lanceolate, bright dark brown. Sterile frond lanceolate, 4–6 in. long, ¾–1 in. broad, thick but not rigid in texture, acute, densely clothed on both sides with imbricated lanceolate bright brown densely ciliated membranous scales; stipe 1–2 in. long, densely clothed with similar scales; veins close, distinct, rather ascending. Fertile frond rather smaller, on a longer stipe. A. splendens, *Bory*.

MAURITIUS, on rocks and old trees in the hill-forests, *Bojer!* Warmer zones of both hemispheres.

10. **A. tomentosum,** *Bory; Hook. and Baker, Syn. Fil.* 51. Rootstock thick, woody, short-creeping; scales dense, small, black with a sudden pale edge, rigid, linear. Sterile frond lanceolate, 1–1½ ft. long, 1–1½ in. broad, acute, rigidly coriaceous, clothed with minute adnate lepidote scales mixed irregularly with larger linear pale brown or whitish ones, which are fixed at the base only; stipe 3–4 in. long, clothed with small lanceolate scales black in the middle and pale brown at the edges; veins rather ascending, distinct, moderately close, usually forked. Fertile frond smaller, on a much longer stipe. A. heterolepis, *Fée, Acrost.* 56, *tab.* 15, *fig.* 1.

Var. A. OBDUCTUM, *Kaulf.; Hook. and Baker, Syn. Fil.* 410. All the scales minute and lepidote.

Var. A. GLABRESCENS, *Kuhn, Fil. Afric.* 45. Frond quite denuded of scales when mature.

MAURITIUS, in woods of the Pouce, etc. Also Bourbon.

11. **A. sorbifolium,** *Linn.; Hook. and Baker, Syn. Fil.* 412. Rootstock woody, wide-scandent, ¼–½ in. thick; scales brown, lanceolate. Stipe 3–6 in. long, naked or scaly. Sterile frond simply pinnate, 1–2 feet long, 6–10 in. broad, glabrous, subcoriaceous; rachis naked. Pinnæ lanceolate, acute, entire, ¾–1 in. broad, cuneate and articulated at the base, the lower ones shortly petioled. Veins close, distinct, rather ascending, simple or forked. Fertile frond simply pinnate, with distant narrow linear pinnæ 3–4 in. long. Lomaria elliptica and fraxinea, *Bojer, Hort. Maur.* 406–7. Lomariopsis Pervillei, pollicina and sorbifolia, *Kuhn. Fil. Afric.* 54.

MAURITIUS and SEYCHELLES, on old trunks in the forests. Spread round the world in the tropics. *Lomaria variabilis*, Willd.; Bojer, Hort. Maur. 407, is an abnormal form with small subsessile lanceolate fronds entire at the top, pinnatifid or pinnate downwards with irregular rounded segments.

12. **A. tenuifolium,** *Baker; Hook. and Baker, Syn. Fil.* 412. Rootstock woody, wide-scandent, ¼–½ in. thick; scales minute, linear, dark brown. Stipes naked, ½–1 foot long. Sterile frond simply pinnate, 1–4 feet long, 1–2 foot broad, glabrous, subcoriaceous; rachis naked. Pinnæ lanceolate, acute, ¾–½ in. broad, sharply serrated, not articulated, cuneate at the base, the lower shortly petioled. Veins very

close, fine, distinct, mostly simple. Fertile frond bipinnate, with narrow linear secondary segments 2–4 in. long. A. Meyerianum, *Hook, Sp. Fil.* v. 250. Lomaria tenuifolia, *Desv.; Bojer, Hort. Maur.* 407. L. grandis, *Bojer, loc. cit.*

MAURITIUS, and SEYCHELLES, on old trunks in the forests. Also Natal, Madagascar, and East Tropical Africa.

13. **A. punctatum,** *Linn. Suppl.* 444. Rootstock wide-creeping; scales few, linear, dark brown. Stipe of sterile frond ½–1 foot long, slightly scaly. Sterile frond simply pinnate, membranous, glabrous, 9–18 in. long. Pinnæ few or many, lanceolate, acute, entire or obscurely lobed, 1–2 in. broad, the upper ones adnate to the rachis, the lower ones free, sessile. Veins unequal; main ones distinct nearly to the edge, with abundant fine intermediate veinlets anastomosing in hexagonal areolæ. Fertile frond with a longer stipe and smaller pinnæ, all fertile. A. punctulatum, *Sw.; Hook. and Baker, Syn. Fil.* 419. A. mascarenense, *Spreng.; Bojer, Hort. Maur.* 414.

MAURITIUS, in dense forests. Also Bourbon, the Comoros, Madagascar, and Tropical Africa.

14. **A. repandum,** *Blume.; Hook. and Baker, Syn. Fil.* 419. Rootstock short-creeping; scales few, brown, lanceolate. Stipe of sterile frond ½–1 ft. long, naked or slightly scaly. Sterile frond bipinnatifid, membranous, glabrous, 1–2 feet long, 9–18 in. broad; rachis naked. Pinnæ numerous, lanceolate, acute, 1–1½ in. broad, cut down to the middle or beyond into obtuse dentate segments ⅛–¼ in. broad. Veins unequal; main ones distinct to the edge, one running down the centre of each lobe; intermediate veinlets anastomosing in copious hexagonal areoles. Fertile frond with a longer stipe and smaller pinnæ, all fertile. Chrysodium bipinnatifidum, *Mett.; Kuhn, Fil. Afric.* 50.

SEYCHELLES, one of the commonest species in the mountain-woods of Mahé. Also Bourbon, Tropical Asia, and Polynesia.

15. **A. aureum,** *Linn.; Hook. and Baker, Syn. Fil.* 423. Rootstock erect; scales few, brown, lanceolate. Stipes very long, naked. Frond simply pinnate, 1–4 feet long, the same one fertile in the upper, sterile in the lower part, coriaceous, usually glabrous; rachis naked. Pinnæ lanceolate, acute or obtuse, 6–12 in. long, 1–2 in. broad, the lower ones shortly stalked. Veins fine, close, equal, anastomosing copiously in narrow areoles. A. speciosum, *Bojer, Hort. Maur.* 414.

MAURITIUS and SEYCHELLES, common in lowland swamps and salt marshes. Cosmopolitan in the tropical and warm temperate zones.

16. **A. spicatum,** *Linn.; Hook. and Baker, Syn. Fil.* 424. Rootstock short-creeping; scales few, minute, lanceolate. Stipe 1–2 in. long, articulated above the base. Frond simple, lanceolate, glabrous, subcoriaceous, 6–12 in. long, ¾–1 in. broad, narrowed very gradually

to the base, contracted at the tip into a fertile linear spike 3–4 in. long. Veins fine, immersed; the main ones erecto-patent, distinct more than halfway to the edge, the veinlets anastomosing in copious, hexagonal areoles. Hymenolepis ophioglossoides, *Bojer, Hort. Maur.* 407.

MAURITIUS and SEYCHELLES, frequent in the mountain forests. Also Madagascar, Bourbon, Comoros, Tropical Asia, and Polynesia, not African.

A. succisæfolium, Thouars; Hook. and Baker, Syn. Fil. 408, a plant of Tristan d'Acunha is said by Bojer, probably in error, to have been found in Mauritius amongst the Savanné mountains. It is one of the simple-fronded free-veined species, with a wide-creeping rootstock, dark brown linear scales, an obtuse lanceolate sterile frond 5–6 in. long densely clothed on the under surface with lanceolate bright brown shortly ciliated scales, with a long scaly stipe and a narrower fertile frond with a longer stipe.

27. PLATYCERIUM, Desv.

Capsules stalked, splitting transversely, with an incomplete vertical ring. Sori forming large irregularly-shaped patches on the upper part of the fertile frond, without any involucre.—Fronds of two kinds, the barren ones short and rounded, the fertile ones dichotomously forked, with broad segments; veins anastomosing copiously. DISTRIB. Warmer regions of the Old World, one also American. Species 7.

1. **P. alcicorne,** *Desv.; Hook. and Baker, Syn. Fil.* 425. Barren frond sessile, suborbicular, ½–1 ft. broad, with prominent veins radiating from the base. Fertile frond cuneate-deltoid, 1–2 feet long, coriaceous, clothed beneath with thin white tomentum, two or three times dichotomously forked, with obtuse lanceolate ultimate segments ½–1 in. broad. Sori forming patches at the base of the ultimate segments, extending from edge to edge.

MAURITIUS and SEYCHELLES, on old trunks in the forests. Also East Tropical Africa, Madagascar, Comoros, Australia, and Peru.

28. OSMUNDA, Linn.

Capsules short-stalked, splitting vertically, furnished with a short broad horizontal ring about the middle, aggregated into leafless spikes or panicles.—Large compound ferns, with free veining, the fertile segments usually terminal or central on leafy fronds. DISTRIB. Temperate zone and mountains of the tropics in both hemispheres. Species 7.

1. **O. regalis,** *Linn.; Hook. and Baker, Syn. Fil.* 427. Rootstock erect. Stipes tufted, naked, 1–1½ ft. long. Fronds bipinnate, membranous, glabrous, 2–4 feet long; rachises naked. Pinnæ oblong-lanceolate; pinnules lanceolate, obtuse, 1–2 in. long. Veins distinct, erecto-patent, forked. Fertile segments forming a regular bipinnate terminal panicle about half a foot long. O. obtusifolia, *Willd.; Bojer, Hort. Maur.* 421. O. Hilsenbergii, *Hook. and Grev.*

MAURITIUS, at the Mare aux Vacoas, etc. Cosmopolitan in temperate and warm temperate regions.

29. SCHIZÆA, Smith.

Capsules sessile, splitting vertically, crowned by a complete transverse ring, aggregated in 2–4 rows in spikes that form a close terminal panicle or digitate cluster.—Coriaceous tufted ferns of very characteristic habit, with the sterile part of the frond stem-like and simple or flattened and dichotomously forked. DISTRIB. Tropical and warm temperate zones of both hemispheres. Species about 20.

Capsules biserial. Fertile spikes pinnate . . . . 1. S. DICHOTOMA.
Capsules 4-serial. Fertile spikes digitate . . . . 2. S. DIGITATA.

1. **S. dichotoma,** *Sw.; Hook. and Baker, Syn. Fil.* 430. Stipes wiry, angular, densely tufted, naked, 4–12 in. long. Frond cuneate-deltoid, $\frac{1}{4}$–$\frac{1}{2}$ foot long and broad, several times dichotomously forked, with flattened 1-nerved ultimate segments 1–3 in. long, about $\frac{1}{24}$ in. broad. Fertile segments pinnate, reduplicate, forming a recurved deltoid terminal panicle $\frac{1}{4}$–$\frac{1}{3}$ in. long.

MAURITIUS, on old trunks in the woods of Flacq and round the Grand Bassin. Also Bourbon, Madagascar, and tropical and warm temperate regions of both hemispheres, but not African.

2. **S. digitata,** *Sw.; Hook. and Baker, Syn. Fil.* 430, var. S. INTERMEDIA, *Mett.* Rootstock short-creeping, with minute brown linear scales. Fronds simple, without any distinct stipe, 2–18 in. long, $\frac{1}{12}$ in. broad, flat, with the midrib prominently raised on the under surface. Spikes 1–1$\frac{1}{2}$ in. long, arranged 6–12 together in a close terminal digitate cluster.

SEYCHELLES, frequent in the woods of Mahé, *Wright! Horne,* 184! 653! Madagascar, Tropical Asia, and Polynesia.

30. MARATTIA, Smith.

Capsules in our plant sessile, slit down the side, without a ring, placed in two divaricating rows, many connate into an oblong boat-shaped mass (synangium), which is decurrent on the veins and furnished with an obscure inferior fimbriated involucre.—Fronds large, compound, glabrous, rather fleshy in texture, with stipes and pinnæ swollen at the base and free veining. DISTRIB. Tropical and warm temperate regions of both hemispheres.

1. **M. fraxinea,** *Smith: Hook. and Baker Syn. Fil.* 440. Stipes 1–2 feet long. Frond deltoid, 6–15 feet long, bipinnate, bright green, glabrous. Pinnæ oblong-lanceolate, 1$\frac{1}{2}$–2 feet long; pinnules sessile, lanceolate, acuminate, serrated, 5–6 in. long, $\frac{3}{4}$–1 in. broad. Veins distinct, spreading, not nearly so numerous and close as in *Angiopteris*. Sori $\frac{1}{12}$ in. or less long, oblong, slightly intramarginal. M. sorbifolia, *Sw.; Bojer, Hort. Maur.* 422. M. macrophylla, *De Vriese.*

MAURITIUS, in the dense forests of the hill-ranges. Spread through the two warmer zones of the Old World.

31. ANGIOPTERIS, Hoffm.

Capsules sessile, slit down the side, without any ring, forming oblong sori decurrent on the veins, not connate into a mass, as they are in the other genera of *Marattiaceæ*, furnished with an obscure plate-shaped inferior involucre. The only species.

1. **A. evecta,** *Hoffm.; Hook. and Baker, Syn. Fil.* 440. Rootstock erect, reaching a height of several feet. Stipes and pinnæ swollen at the base. Frond deltoid, bipinnate, 6–15 feet or more long, bright green, glabrous, rather fleshy in texture. Pinnæ oblong-lanceolate, 2–3 feet long; pinnules sessile, lanceolate, acuminate, 5–6 in. long, ¾–1 in. broad, serrated at the tip. Veins fine, distinct, free, spreading, simple or forked. Sori small, oblong, crowded, consisting each of 6–10 capsules, placed on each vein near the margin of the pinnules.

MAURITIUS, *Bojer!* SEYCHELLES, common in the shady woods of Mahé on the banks of streams, *Horne*, 199! 650! Spread through the tropics of the Old World.

32. OPHIOGLOSSUM, Linn.

Capsules 2-valved, splitting down the side, without any ring or involucre, confluent into distichous spikes.—Rootstock cylindrical or tuberous; fronds rather fleshy in texture, consisting usually of a sterile simple leafy segment, with a peduncled simple spike arising from its base or surface. Veins fine, anastomosing copiously. Vernation not circinate, as it is in all the other genera of Mauritian Filices. DISTRIB. Cosmopolitan. Species 10.

Fertile spike slender, arising from the base of the sterile segment . . . . 1. O. RETICULATUM.
Fertile spike stout, arising from the surface of the sterile segment . . . . 2. O. PENDULUM.

1. **O. reticulatum,** *Linn.; Hook. and Baker, Syn. Fil.* 446. Rootstock suberect, not tuberous. Stipe slender, 3–6 in. long. Sterile segment cordate-ovate, 2–3 in. long, membranous in texture, with distinct fine veins forming minute hexagonal areoles with free included veinlets. Fertile spikes slender, erect, 1–2 in. long, with a slender peduncle much longer than itself, arising from the base of the sterile segment.

MAURITIUS, and RODRIGUEZ, in grassy places. Warmer zones of both hemispheres. *O. ovatum*, Bory; Bojer, Hort. Maur. 422, is a variety with the sterile segment ovate, but not cordate at the base.

2. **O. pendulum,** *Linn.; Hook. and Baker, Syn. Fil.* 446. Sterile segment riband-shaped, often several feet long, narrowed gradually to a short obscure stout stipe, simple or shallowly forked upwards, stouter

and more fleshy in texture than in *O. reticulatum*, with much longer areolæ without any included free veinlets. Fertile stout, 2–6 in. long, with a short peduncle, arising from the surface of the sterile segment.

MAURITIUS and SEYCHELLES, in the hill-forests, rare. Also Bourbon, Madagascar, Tropical Asia, and Polynesia, not African.

ORDER CIX. EQUISETACEÆ.

Fructification consisting of minute 1-celled capsules (sporangia), which dehisce by a vertical slit and are placed 6–9 together round the under surface of stalked peltate scales, of which many are crowded on the end of the stem to form a bractless terminal cone. Spores numerous, uniform, very minute, each furnished with 4 spiral threads thickened at the tip (elaters) and falling to the ground to give rise to a prothallus, which bears antheridia and archegonia as in Filices.—Rootstock wide-creeping, subterranean; stems cylindrical, distinctly jointed, hollow except at the nodes, distinctly ribbed, each rib ending at the node in the tooth of a sheath, simple or bearing whorls of the branches, the fruit cones solitary and terminal. DISTRIB. Cosmopolitan. Species 25.

1. EQUISETUM, Linn.

The only genus. Characters and distribution of the order.

1. **E. ramosissimum,** *Desf. Fl. Atlant.* ii. 398. Very variable in stature and habit. Stems densely tufted, scabrous, firm in texture, erect or decumbent, 1–3 feet long, simple or furnished with few or many solitary or whorled branches. Ribs of the main stem 6–20, of the branches 4–6. Sheaths dilated; teeth linear-cuspidate, with a deciduous point, nearly black. Cone of fruit oblong, apiculate, about ½ in. long. E. elongatum, *Willd.; Bojer, Hort. Maur.* 426.

MAURITIUS, on the borders of the Grand Rivière and at the Réduit cascade. Cosmopolitan in the tropical and warm temperate zones.

ORDER CX. LYCOPODIACEÆ.

Fructification consisting of small uniform 1–3-celled 2–3-valved capsules (sporangia), which are solitary and sessile in the axils of the leaves, and contain copious minute spores without elaters, which give rise to a prothallus which bears antheridia and archegonia, as in *Filices*.—Stems with a vascular axis, erect or trailing, branched dichotomously or pinnately, bearing usually crowded multifarious small 1-nerved leaves, the capsules placed either in the axils of ordinary leaves all down the stem or in the axils of modified upper leaves (bracts) so as to form a special terminal spike; vernation not circinate. DISTRIB. Cosmopolitan. Species 100.

Capsule 1-celled, 2-valved . . . . 1. LYCOPODIUM.
Capsule 3-celled, 3-valved . . . . 2. PSILOTUM.

I. LYCOPODIUM, Linn.

Capsules 1-celled, 2-valved, scattered or crowded into a terminal spike. Spores marked with 3 radiating lines.—Leaves in all the Mauritian species multifarious and uniform. DISTRIB. Cosmopolitan. Species about 100.

Capsules placed in the axils of unaltered leaves all down the stem.
  Stems stiffly erect, stout, simple, or once forked . . 1. L. SAURURUS.
  Stems pendulous, slender, many times forked . . . . 2. L. VERTICILLATUM.
Capsules placed in the axils of little altered leaves so as to form an indistinct spike.
  Leaves linear . . . . 3. L. SQUARROSUM.
  Leaves lanceolate . . . . 4. L. GNIDIOIDES.
Capsules forming a distinct spike.
  Branching of the main stem dichotomous.
    Leaves ovate or ovate-lanceolate acute . . . . . . 5. L. PHLEGMARIA.
    Leaves obovate, obtuse . . . . 6. L. OBTUSIFOLIUM.
  Branching of the main stem pinnate.
    Spikes $\frac{1}{4}$–$\frac{1}{2}$ in. long, sessile . . . . 7. L. CERNUUM.
    Spikes 1–2 in. long, peduncled.
      Spikes simple . . . . 8. L. CAROLINIANUM.
      Spikes panicled . . . . 9. L. CLAVATUM.

1. **L. Saururus,** *Lam.*; *Spring*, *Monog. Lycop.* i. 21. Stems densely tufted, stout, stiffly erect, $\frac{1}{2}$–1 foot long, simple or once forked, with erect branches. Leaves lanceolate, acute, $\frac{1}{8}$–$\frac{1}{2}$ in. long, bright green and glossy, all ascending, very thick and rigid in texture, wrinkled, with an obscure midrib. Capsules hidden in the axils of unaltered leaves all down the stem.

MAURITIUS, on the mountains, *Thouars*, *Bojer*. Also Cape, Bourbon, and hills of Tropical Africa and America. I have not seen a Mauritian specimen.

2. **L. verticillatum,** *Linn.*; *Spring*, *Monog. Lycop.* i. 46. Stems densely tufted, slender, pendulous, 1–2 feet long, many times equally dichotomously forked. Leaves linear-subulate, $\frac{1}{8}$–$\frac{1}{4}$ in. long, all ascending, furnished with a distinct midrib. Capsules hidden in the axils of unaltered leaves in the upper half of the stem. L. acerosum, *Sw.*; *Bojer*, *Hort. Maur.* 423.

MAURITIUS, in dense forests of the Savanne range, *Bojer* ! Also Bourbon, Natal, and Tropical America.

3. **L. squarrosum,** *Forst.*; *Spring*, *Monog. Lycop.* i. 52. Stems 1–2 feet long, suberect in the lower, pendulous in the upper half, several times dichotomously forked. Leaves linear, acute, with a distinct midrib, the lower ones spreading, $\frac{1}{2}$–$\frac{5}{8}$ in. long, the upper ones erecto-patent. Capsules placed regularly in the axils of lanceolate leaves $\frac{1}{8}$–$\frac{1}{4}$ in. long in the upper 6–9 in. of the stem so as to form an indistinct spike. L. verticillatum, *Willd.*; *Bojer*, *Hort. Maur.* 423, *not Linn.* L. epiceæfolium, *Desv.*; *Bojer*, *Hort. Maur.* 423.

L. ulicifolium, *Vent.; Bojer, Hort. Maur.* 424. L. Hippuris, *Desv.* L. proliferum, *Blume.*

MAURITIUS and SEYCHELLES, frequent in the hill-forests. Spread through the tropics of the Old World.

4. **L. gnidioides,** *Linn.; Spring, Monog. Lycop.* i. 55. Stems 1–2 feet long, suberect in the lower, pendulous in the upper part, several times dichotomously forked. Leaves ⅜–½ in. long, lanceolate, subacute, all ascending, very thick and rigid in texture, with a distinct midrib. Capsules placed regularly in the axils of lanceolate acute leaves about ⅛ in. long in the upper 3–6 in. of the stem so as to form an indistinct spike.

MAURITIUS, frequent in the hill-forests. Also Bourbon and Cape.

5. **L. Phlegmaria,** *Linn.; Spring, Monog. Lycop.* i. 63. Stems pendulous, 1–2 feet long, once or twice dichotomously forked. Leaves moderately dense, ovate or ovate-lanceolate, acute, ½ in. long, spreading or rather ascending, bright green, broadly rounded at the base, furnished with a distinct midrib. Spikes slender, 3–6 in. long, sessile, 2–4 times dichotomously forked; bracts deltoid, the upper ones obscurely pointed, not longer than the capsules, the lower more distinctly pointed and a little longer.

MAURITIUS, RODRIGUEZ, and SEYCHELLES, frequent in woods. Cosmopolitan in the Tropics.

6. **L. obtusifolium,** *Sw.; Spring, Monog.* i. 67. Stems pendulous, 1–2 feet long, once or twice dichotomously forked. Leaves obovate, obscurely pointed, ¼–⅓ in long, narrowed to the base, subsecund, rigid in texture, with an indistinct midrib. Spikes slender, 3–4 in. long, sessile, once or twice dichotomously forked; bracts minute, deltoid, obscurely pointed.

MAURITIUS, in the forests, *Bory, Bojer.* Also Bourbon, and may be conspecific with the Malayan *L. nummularifolium,* Blume.

7. **L. cernuum,** *Linn.; Spring, Monog. Lycop.* i. 79. Main stem stiffly erect, reaching a height of one or two feet, unbranched in the lower part, copiously furnished in the upper part with spreading or decurved very compound branches. Leaves dense, linear-subulate, 1/12–⅛ in. long, spreading in the lower, curved upwards in their upper half. Spikes sessile, simple, ¼–½ in. long; bracts deltoid-cuspidate, exceeding the very minute capsules.

MAURITIUS and SEYCHELLES, common in woods. Cosmopolitan in the tropical and warm temperate zones.

8. **L. carolinianum,** *Linn.; Spring, Monog. Lycop.* 98. Main stem trailing to a length of ½–1 foot, with a few short distant spreading

branches. Leaves moderately dense, spreading, secund, lanceolate, acute, 1/8–1/4 in. long, with a distinct midrib. Spikes cylindrical, 1–2 in. long, erect, simple, with a stiffly-erect peduncle much longer than themselves; bracts deltoid-cuspidate, 2–3 times the length of the capsules.

MAURITIUS, in damp woods at Savanne and Grand Bassin. Cosmopolitan in the tropical and warm temperate zones.

9. **L. clavatum,** *Linn.; Spring, Monog. Lycop.* i. 89. Stem trailing to a length of several feet, with distant spreading dichotomously-forked branches. Leaves 1/4 in. long, linear, hair-tipped, erecto-patent, furnished with a distinct midrib. Spikes cylindrical, 1–2 in. long, 1–5 together panicled at the top of a stiffly erect peduncle 2–4 in. long. L. inflexum, *Sw.*; *Bojer, Hort. Maur.* 424.

MAURITIUS, on plateaux at Nouvelle Découverte, *Bojer*. Cosmopolitan in temperate regions.

We have at Kew a specimen of *L. rigidum*, Willd. (L. Sieberianum, *Spring*) in Sieber's Synopsis Filicum, No. 148, labelled as Mauritian, doubtless in error, as it is otherwise known only in Tropical America. It has stiffly erect stems under a foot long once or twice equally forked, rigid linear spreading or ascending leaves 1/4–1/3 in. long and capsules hidden in the axils of unaltered leaves all down the stem.

2. PSILOTUM, Sw.

Capsules depresso-globose, 3-celled, 3-valved, scattered down the branches in the axils of the very minute leaves. Spores marked with a single line.—Stems glabrous, coriaceous, simple in the lower part, copiously dichotomously branched upwards. The only species.

Branchlets triquetrous . . . . 1. P. NUDUM.
Branchlets flat . . . . 2. P. COMPLANATUM.

1. **P. nudum,** *Griseb. Flor. Brit. West Ind.* 130. Stems 1–2 feet long, erect, the ultimate branchlets triquetrous, not more than 1/24 in. thick. Leaves at most as long as the thickness of the branches, shorter than the capsules. P. triquetrum, *Sw.; Bojer, Hort. Maur.* 428.

MAURITIUS and RODRIGUEZ, frequent in the forests, both on rocks and trees. Cosmopolitan in the tropics.

2. **P. complanatum,** *Sw.; Spring, Monog. Lycop.* ii. 271. Stems 1–2 long, pendulous except near the base, the ultimate branchlets flat, 1/12–1/8 in. broad, with a distinct midrib, distantly alternately toothed, the capsules placed in the teeth, and leaves represented only by a minute cusp to each tooth. P. flaccidum, *Wall.; Kuhn. Fil Afric.* 187.

SEYCHELLES, frequent in the forests. Cosmopolitan in the tropics, but much less frequent than *P. nudum*.

ORDER CXI. SELAGINELLACEÆ.

Fructification consisting of naked solitary 1-celled sporangia of two kinds, sessile in the axils of ordinary or modified leaves, which are crowded so as to form a special terminal spike in all the Mauritian species. Macrosporangia one or few, placed in the axils of the lower bracts of the spike, containing each 4 macrospores, which give rise to a prothallus, which bears several archegonia, of which one only is fertilised. Microsporangia numerous, placed in the axils of the upper bracts of the spike, containing each numerous very minute microspores, from which the antheridia are emitted.—Stems procumbent or erect, with a vascular axis, dichotomously forked, with small crowded oblique leaves of two kinds (the smaller ones sometimes called stipules) spreading distichously; vernation not circinate. DISTRIB. Cosmopolitan, mainly in the warmer zones of both hemispheres.

1. SELAGINELLA, Beauv.

The only genus. Characters and distribution of the order.

Spikes slender, tetragonous; bracts all uniform.
  Stems decumbent, branched throughout.
    Leaves oblong, obtuse.
      Stems not more than an inch long . . . . . 1. S. BARKLYI.
      Stems 3–4 in. long.
        Leaves pale green, $\frac{1}{16}$ in. long . . . . . 2. S. BALFOURII.
        Leaves bright green, $\frac{1}{12}$ in. long . . . . . 3. S. OBTUSA.
      Stems a foot or more long . . . . 4. S. RODRIGUESIANA.
    Leaves oblong-lanceolate, acute.
      Bracts lanceolate . . . . 5. S. SECHELLARUM.
      Bracts deltoid.
        Stems about ½ foot long, branches close . . 6. S. FISSIDENTOIDES.
        Stems a foot or more long; branches distant.
          Leaves entire . . . . 7. S. CONCINNA.
          Leaves denticulate . . . . 8. S. SERRULATA.
  Stems erect, simple in the lower half or third . . 9. S. FALCATA.
Spikes distichous; bracts, like the leaves, of two kinds 10. S. BRACHYSTACHYA.

1. **S. Barklyi**, *Baker*. Stems decumbent, densely tufted, not more than an inch long, several times dichotomously forked. Larger leaves oblique oblong, obtuse, spreading, much imbricating, firm in texture, not ciliated; smaller leaves half as long as the larger, obovate, with a distinct mucro. Spikes ⅛–¼ in. long, tetragonous; bracts uniform, deltoid, cuspidate.

MAURITIUS, Round Island, *Sir H. Barkly!* and what is probably a more robust form of the same species with larger leaves from Coin de Mire, *Horne!* Endemic.

2. **S. Balfourii**, *Baker*. Stems decumbent, densely tufted, trailing to a length of 3–4 inches, with many short ascending compound branches. Larger leaves oblique oblong, obtuse, spreading, $\frac{1}{16}$ in. long, pale green, membranous, distinctly ciliated, those of the final branchlets placed

edge to edge; smaller leaves a third as long as the larger, obovate, with a long mucro. Spikes ¼–½ in. long, tetragonous; bracts uniform, deltoid, cuspidate.

RODRIGUEZ, on the coralline limestone, *Balfour!* Endemic.

3. **S. obtusa,** *Spring, Monog. Lycop.* ii. 201. Stems decumbent, trailing to a length of 3–4 inches, with many short spreading compound branches. Larger leaves oblique, oblong, obtuse, spreading, $\frac{1}{12}$ in. long, bright green, moderately firm in texture, obscurely ciliated, those of the final branchlets slightly imbricated; smaller leaves a third as long as the larger, obovate with a long mucro. Spikes ¼–½ in. long, tetragonous; bracts uniform, deltoid, cuspidate. Lycopodium pusillum, *Desv.; Bojer, Hort. Maur.* 426.

MAURITIUS, in shady damp places on the slopes of the Pouce, etc. Also Bourbon and Madagascar.

4. **S. rodriguesiana,** *Baker.* Stems decumbent, not articulated, trailing to a length of a foot, with many distant ascending compound branches. Larger leaves oblique, oblong, obtuse, falcate, $\frac{1}{12}$ in. long, bright green, membranous, entire, obscurely ciliated, those of the final branchlets placed edge to edge; smaller leaves a third as long as the larger, obovate with a long mucro. Spikes ¼–½ in. long, tetragonous; bracts uniform, deltoid, strongly cuspidate.

RODRIGUEZ, common on damp grassy banks, *Balfour!* Endemic.

5. **S. sechellarum,** *Baker.* Stems decumbent, not articulated, trailing to a length of a foot, with short distant ascending compound branches. Larger leaves oblique oblong-lanceolate, rather curved upwards, acute, with the point at the upper corner, $\frac{1}{12}$ in. long, bright green, membranous, not ciliated, those of the final branchlets slightly imbricated; smaller leaves a third as long as the larger, oblique oblong, with a distinct mucro. Spikes ¼–½ in. long, tetragonous; bracts uniform, lanceolate, twice as long as the microsporangia.

SEYCHELLES, in Mahé, *Horne*, 157! General habit very like that of *S. Kraussiana*, but the stem not articulated.

6. **S. fissidentoides,** *Spring, Monog. Lycop.* ii. 111. Stems decumbent, not articulated, trailing to a length of half a foot, with many close ascending compound branches. Larger leaves oblique oblong-lanceolate, rather curved upwards, acute, with the point at the upper corner, $\frac{1}{12}$ in. long, moderately firm in texture, entire, obscurely ciliated, those of the final branchlets placed edge to edge; smaller leaves a third as long as the larger, oblique oblong, with a long mucro. Spikes ½–1 in. long, tetragonous; bracts uniform, deltoid, cuspidate.

SEYCHELLES, common in damp grassy places, *Pervillé*, 76! *Horne*, 166! 666! Also Bourbon and Madagascar.

7. **S. concinna,** *Spring, Monog. Lycop.* ii. 199. Stems decumbent, not articulated, trailing to a length of a foot or more, with many distant short more or less ascending compound branches. Larger leaves oblique oblong-lanceolate, rather curved upwards, with the point at the upper corner, $\frac{1}{12}$–$\frac{1}{8}$ in. long, bright green, moderately firm in texture, entire, obscurely ciliated, those of the final branchlets imbricated; smaller leaves a third as long as the larger, oblique obovate, with a long mucro. Spikes $\frac{1}{2}$–1 in. long, tetragonous; bracts uniform, deltoid, strongly cuspidate. Lycopodium concinnum, *Sw.; Bojer, Hort. Maur.* 425.

MAURITIUS, common in damp grassy places. Also Bourbon, Madagascar, and Tropical Asia.

8. **S. serrulata,** *Spring, Monog. Lycop.* ii. 202. Stems decumbent, not articulated, trailing to a length of a foot or more, the fertile branches short and cernuous, the sterile longer and more compound Larger leaves oblique oblong-lanceolate, rather curved upwards, with the point at the upper corner, $\frac{1}{8}$ in. long, firm in texture, ciliated and denticulate, those of the final branchlets imbricated; smaller leaves a third as long as the outer, oblique, obovate, with a mucro. Spikes $\frac{1}{2}$–$\frac{3}{4}$ in. long, tetragonous; bracts uniform, deltoid, cuspidate. Lycopodium serrulatum, *Desv.; Bojer, Hort. Maur.* 425.

MAURITIUS, on mossy rocks of the high mountains, *Commerson, Bojer.* Also Bourbon.

9. **S. falcata,** *Spring, Monog. Lycop,* ii. 181. Stems 1–1$\frac{1}{2}$ foot high, erect, not articulated, simple in the lower half, copiously branched with crowded erecto-patent branches and branchlets in the upper half. Larger leaves oblique oblong-lanceolate, acute, with the point placed at the upper corner, slightly ascending, $\frac{1}{12}$–$\frac{1}{8}$ in. long, moderately firm in texture, those of the final branchlets slightly imbricated; smaller leaves a third as long as the larger, oblique oblong, cuspidate. Spikes $\frac{1}{4}$–$\frac{1}{2}$ in. long, slender, tetragonous; bracts uniform, deltoid, cuspidate. S. membranacea, deliquescens and tereticaulis, *Spring, Monog. Lycop.* ii. 178–180. Lycopodium canaliculatum and fruticulosum, *Bojer, Hort. Maur.* 425.

MAURITIUS, in woods of the Pouce range, etc., frequent. Also Bourbon and Madagascar.

10. **S. brachystachya,** *Spring, Monog. Lycop,* ii. 256. Stems 1–1$\frac{1}{2}$ foot long, decumbent and sending out roots in the lower half, ascending and copiously branched in the upper half. Larger leaves oblique oblong, $\frac{1}{8}$ in. long, obtuse, spreading or rather ascending, dark green, membranous, those of the final branchlets placed edge to edge; smaller leaves a third as long as the larger, oblique, obovate, with a mucro, distichous. Spikes $\frac{1}{4}$–$\frac{1}{2}$ in. long, $\frac{1}{12}$ in. broad, with the ligulate obtuse larger bracts three times as long as the microsporangia.

MAURITIUS, in shady places, *Bojer!* Also Ceylon and East Himalayas.

There is a specimen in Sieber's Flora Mixta, No. 326, localised as Mauritian, of *S. mnioides*, A. Braun (which includes *S. ciliauricula*, *S. cirrhipes*, and in part *S. mnioides* of Spring's Monograph). This is an American species, with wide-trailing articulated stems, and no doubt, as in the case of *Lycopodium Sieberianum*, the assigned locality is a mistake.

ORDER CXII. MARSILEACEÆ.

Fructification consisting of 2–4-celled 2–4-valved receptacles (sporocarps), which contain both macrosporangia and microsporangia. Macrosporangia containing each a single spore (macrospore), which gives rise to a prothallus, which bears a single archegonium, which is fertilised by the antherozoids, of which many are contained in each microsporangium.—Water or swamp plants with wide-creeping thread-like rootstocks, the fronds circinate in vernation, either consisting of 4 simple flabellately veined leaflets or reduced to a mere rachis. DISTRIB. Cosmopolitan. Species 50.

1. MARSILEA, Linn.

Receptacles 2-celled, 2-valved, the parietal placentas protruded when they burst in the form of gelatinous cylinders, which bear membranous sacs containing both oophoridia and antheridia.—Fronds consisting of 4 flabellately-veined small simple leaflets, at the summit of a common petiole, from at or near the base of which 1 or more receptacles arise on separate or more or less thoroughly connate peduncles. DISTRIB. Tropical and warm temperate regions. Species 40–50.

1. **M. crenulata,** *Desv.; A. Br. in Kuhn, Fil. Afr.* 198. Rootstock thread-like, wide-creeping. Petiole many times longer than the glabrous leaflets, which are usually toothed round their outer border, except in large sterile aquatic forms of the plant. Receptacles several to a node, pilose when immature, glabrescent, horizontal, $\frac{1}{8}$ in. long, half as long again as broad, obliquely broad oblong, neither distinctly veined nor bordered, furnished with a single distinct or obscure tooth on the side to which the peduncle is attached; peduncle free, basal, $\frac{1}{8}$–$\frac{1}{4}$ in long. M. vulgaris and coromandelina, *Bojer, Hort. Maur.* 426.

MAURITIUS, in ponds and swamps of the low country. Spread through the tropics of the Old World. According to A. Braun, *M. diffusa*, Leprieur, which mainly differs by having a couple of distinct teeth on the margin of the receptacle above the attachment of the peduncle, has been gathered in Mauritius by Perottet.

ADDITIONS AND CORRECTIONS.

Page 7. For *Nasturtium indicum*, Linn., read *N. indicum*, DC.

Page 9. *Thylachium panduriforme*, Juss, given by De Candolle as Mauritian and included in Sieber's herbarium, is only known in the island as a cultivated plant.

Page 17. Through the exertions of Mr. Horne flowers and fruit of the Seychelles Dipterocarp have now been procured, from which Mr. Thistleton Dyer, who monographed the order in the Flora of British India, has kindly drawn up the following diagnosis.

1. VATERIA, Linn.

Calyx-tube very short, adnate to the receptacle; sepals persistent, scarcely augmented in fruit. Stamens 15, rarely indefinite; anthers with an apiculate connective. Fruit baccate, globose, leathery, 1-seeded.—Trees with entire coriaceous feather-veined leaves and lax terminal and lateral panicles or short few-flowered lateral racemes. Distrib. Tropical Asia and Indian Archipelago. Species about 20.

1. **V. seychellarum,** *Dyer*. A tree 80–100 feet high, with lepidote branches. Leaves long-petioled (2–3 in.) elliptic, 6–8 in. long by 4–6 in. broad, shortly apiculate, glabrous on both sides. Flowers ¾ in. in diameter; few-flowered lateral racemes 1½–2 in. long; pedicels about ⅓ in. Calyx ¼ in. deep, glabrous; sepals ovate, obtuse, not reflexed in fruit. Petals ¼ in. long, obovate; margins erose. Stamens indefinite; external valves of the anther much the longer. Fruit globose, slightly depressed, about 1½ in. diam; pericarp leathery, irregularly dehiscing on germination; cotyledons fleshy, plano-convex radiately-sulcate at the attachment of the petioles.

Seychelles, *Horne!* The calyx unreflexed in fruit departs from the general character of the genus. The general habit closely agrees with that of *V. ceylanica*, from which however it is easily distinguished by the longer petioles, indefinite stamens and unreflexed fruit-calyx.

Page 18. Under Malvastrum tricuspidatum "*Pl. Fendl.*" should be "*Pl. Wright.*'

Page 35. The authority "*Planch.*" refers to Reinwardtia trigyna.

Page 40. Under T. aculeata for "*T. lanceolata,*" read "*T. angustifolia.*"

Page 91. *T. officinalis*, Hook. is figured Bot. Mag. t. 4563 not 4363.

Page 111. *Terminalia Catappa*. The citation of Bot. Mag. should be t. 3004.

Page 186. In the general character of the order Rutaceæ for "stamens numerous," read "*isomerous.*"

Page 145. According to Mr. Hiern genus 13 is *Plectronia*, DC., not Linn., and the name that should stand is *Canthium*, Lam.

Page 171. Dr. Balfour, who has seen type specimens at Paris, identifies my *Psiadia trinervia*, var. *macrodon*, with *Sarcanthemum Coronopus*, Cass., which disposes satisfactorily of one of the doubtful genera of our flora.

Page 298. Peperomia No. 7 Dr. Balfour has named *P. Rodriguesii*, and No. 8 *P. hirta*.

Page 339. An additional synonym for *Platylepis goodyeroides*, Rich., is *P. occulta*, Rchb. f. (in Linnæa. vol. VII. pt. I. 1876) p. 62.

Page 340. *Goodyera nuda*, Thouars. The citation of Richard's work should be erased, Richard's plant having been distinguished from Thouars' by Prof. Reichenbach (l. c. p. 60) as *Monochilus Boryi*. This species has not been found in Mauritius.

Page 341. The following genus was inadvertently omitted.

10* VANILLA, Plum.

Sepals and petals subequal, patent. Labellum adnate to the column, usually entire, concave, with a median bearded or pubescent ridge or plate, usually slightly gibbous at the base. Column elongated, terete; anther terminal, appendaged at each side; pollen-masses 2, 2-lobed, mealy, without prolongations. Capsule large, fleshy, aromatic.—Scandent herbs with stout, flexuous stems. Leaves fleshy or absent. Flowers conspicuous, usually clustered on stout axillary or terminal peduncles.—Distrib. The genus is found in the tropics of both worlds.

1. **V. Phalænopsis,** *Rchb. f. in Flore des Serres, tt.* 1769–70. A scandent leafless herb. Stem stout, longitudinally grooved, dark green, articulate at the nodes and giving off there a single unbranched aerial root. Peduncles very thick, the axillary ones more than 2 in. long, the terminal apparently much longer; bracts deltoid, acute, ¼ in. long; pedicel and ovary about 1½ in. in length, terete, longitudinally grooved; flowers nearly 3 in. diam., crowded. Sepals ovate-oblong, subacute, entire, about 2½ in. long, white with faint yellow suffusion below. Petals like the sepals, but cuneate-ovate and somewhat undulated. Labellum entire, widening upwards, obtuse, undulated, with two median longitudinal pilose ridges reaching to the middle on the inner face, bright yellow inside, pinkish outside, 1½ in. long. Lateral lobes of the anther rotundate, crenulate. Capsule linear, subterete, about 4 inches long. *Rchb. f. in Linnæa*, 1876, p. 66.

Seychelles, common in all the islands, *Horne! Bernard.* Closely connected with *V. Walkeriæ*, Wight, of Ceylon and *V. aphylla*, Bl. of Java.

Page 345. *Bulbophyllum sechellarum* has lately been described by Reichenbach (l. c. p. 93).

INDEX OF VERNACULAR NAMES.

INDEX OF GENERA AND SPECIES.

Names of Synonyms and Varieties are printed in Italics.

COLONIAL AND FOREIGN FLORAS.

FLORA OF BRITISH INDIA. By Dr. J. D. HOOKER, F.R.S., and others. Parts I. to IV., 10*s.* 6*d.* each. Vol. I., 32*s.*

FLORA CAPENSIS; a Systematic Description of the Plants of the Cape Colony, Caffraria, and Port Natal. By WILLIAM H. HARVEY, M.D., F.R.S., Professor of Botany in the University of Dublin, and OTTO WILHELM SONDER, Ph.D. Vols. I. and II., each 12*s.*, Vol. III. 18*s.*

FLORA OF TROPICAL AFRICA. By DANIEL OLIVER, F.R.S., F.L.S. Vols. I. and II., each 20*s.* Published under the authority of the First Commissioner of Her Majesty's Works. [*Vol. III. in the press.*

FLORA AUSTRALIENSIS; a Description of the Plants of the Australian Territory. By G. BENTHAM, F.R.S., P.L.S., assisted by F. MUELLER, F.R.S., Government Botanist, Melbourne, Victoria. Vols. I. to VI., 20*s.* each. Published under the auspices of the several Governments of Australia. [*Vol. VII., completing the work, in the press.*

HANDBOOK OF THE NEW ZEALAND FLORA; ; a Systematic Description of the Native Plants of New Zealand, and the Chatham, Kermadec's, Lord Auckland's, Campbell's, and Macquarries Islands. By Dr. J. D. HOOKER, F.R.S. Complete in one Vol., 30*s.* Published under the auspices of the Government of that Colony.

FLORA OF THE BRITISH WEST INDIAN ISLANDS. By Dr. GRISEBACH, F.L.S. 37*s.* 6*d.* Published under the auspices of the Secretary of State for the Colonies.

FLORA HONGKONGENSIS; a Description of the Flowering Plants and Ferns of the Island of Hongkong. By GEORGE BENTHAM, P.L.S. With a Map of the Island and Supplement by Dr. HANCE, 18*s.* Published under the authority of Her Majesty's Secretary of State for the Colonies. The Supplement separately, 2*s.* 6*d.*

FLORA VITIENSIS; a Description of the Plants of the Viti or Fiji Islands, with an Account of their History, Uses, and Properties. By Dr. BERTHOLD SEEMANN, F.L.S. Royal 4to, 100 Coloured Plates, complete in one Vol., cloth, 8*l.* 5*s.*

FLORA OF TASMANIA. By Dr. J. D. HOOKER, F.R.S., Royal 4to, 2 vols., 200 Plates, 17*l.* 10*s.* coloured. Published under the authority of the Lords Commissioners of the Admiralty.

ON THE FLORA OF AUSTRALIA; its Origin, Affinities, and Distribution. By Dr. J. D. HOOKER, F.R.S. 10*s.*

CONTRIBUTIONS TO THE FLORA OF MENTONE, and to a Winter Flora of the Riviera, including the Coast from Marseilles to Genoa. By J. TRAHERNE MOGGRIDGE. Royal 8vo. Parts I. to IV., each, with 25 Coloured Plates, 15*s.*, or complete in one Vol., 63*s.*

OUTLINES OF ELEMENTARY BOTANY, as Introductory to Local Floras. By G. BENTHAM, F.R.S., President of the Linnean Society. New Edition, 2*s.* 6*d.*

LAWS OF BOTANICAL NOMENCLATURE adopted by the International Botanical Congress, with an Historical Introduction and a Commentary. By ALPHONSE DE CANDOLLE. 2*s.* 6*d.*

L. REEVE & Co., 5, Henrietta Street, Covent Garden.

WORKS ON BOTANY.

THE NATURAL HISTORY OF PLANTS. By H. BAILLON. Superior-royal 8vo. Vols. I. to IV., with 1800 Wood-Engravings, 25*s.* each. [*Vol. V. in the press.*

HANDBOOK OF THE BRITISH FLORA; a Description of the Flowering Plants and Ferns indigenous to, or naturalized in, the British Isles. By G. BENTHAM, F.R.S. New Edition, 12*s.*

THE ILLUSTRATED BRITISH FLORA, a Description (with a Wood-Engraving, including dissections, of each species) of the Flowering Plants and Ferns indigenous to, or naturalized in, the British Isles. By G. BENTHAM, F.R.S., 2 vols., 1295 Wood-Engravings, 70*s.*

GENERA PLANTARUM, AD EXEMPLARIA IMPRIMIS IN HERBARIIS KEWENSIBUS SERVATA DEFINITA. By G. BENTHAM, F.R.S., F.L.S., and Dr. J. D. HOOKER, Pres. R.S. Vol. I. Part I. Royal 8vo, 21*s.* Part II. 14*s.*; Part III., 15*s.*; or Vol. I. complete, 50*s.* Vol. II. Part I., 24*s.*; Part II. 32*s.*; or Vol. II. complete, 56*s.*

THE BRITISH FERNS; Coloured Figures and Descriptions, with Analysis of the Fructification and Venation of the Ferns of Great Britain and Ireland. By Sir W. J. HOOKER, F.R.S. Royal 8vo, 66 Coloured Plates, 2*l.* 2*s.*

FILICES EXOTICÆ; Coloured Figures and Description of Exotic Ferns. By Sir W. J. HOOKER, F.R.S. Royal 4to, 100 Coloured Plates, 6*l.* 11*s.*

HANDBOOK OF BRITISH MOSSES. By the Rev. M. J. BERKELEY, M.A., F.L.S. 24 Coloured Plates, 21*s.*

BRITISH FUNGOLOGY. By the Rev. M. J. BERKELEY, M.A., F.L.S. 24 Coloured Plates, 30*s.*

THE ESCULENT FUNGUSES OF ENGLAND. Containing an Account of their Classical History, Uses, Characters, Development, Structure, Nutritous Properties, Modes of Cooking and Preserving, &c. By C. D. BADHAM, M.D. Second Edition. Edited by F. CURREY, F.R.S. 12 Coloured Plates, 12*s.*

PHYCOLOGIA BRITANNICA: or, History of British Seaweeds. By Dr. W. H. HARVEY, F.R.S. New Edition. Royal 8vo, 4 vols, 360 Coloured Plates, 7*l.* 10*s.*

PHYCOLOGIA AUSTRALICA: a History of Australian Seaweeds. By Dr. HARVEY, F.R.S. Royal 8vo, 5 vols, 300 Coloured Plates, 7*l.* 13*s.*

THE RHODODENDRONS OF SIKKIM-HIMALAYA; being an Account, Botanical and Geographical, of the Rhododendrons recently discovered in the Mountains of Eastern Himalaya by Dr. J. D. Hooker, F.R.S. By Sir W. J. HOOKER, F.R.S. Folio, 30 Coloured Plates, 4*l.* 14*s.* 6*d.*

REVISION OF THE NATURAL ORDER HEDERACEÆ, By BERTHOLD SEEMANN, Ph. D., F.L.S. 7 Plates, 10*s.* 6*d.*

ELEMENTARY LESSONS IN BOTANICAL GEOGRAPHY. By J. G. BAKER, F.L.S., 3*s.*

THE BOTANICAL MAGAZINE; Figures and Descriptions of New and Rare Plants. By Dr. J. D. HOOKER, C.B., Pres. R.S., Director of the Royal Gardens, Kew. Royal 8vo. Published Monthly, with 6 coloured Plates, 3*s.* 6*d.* Annual Subscription, 42*s.*

RE-ISSUE of the THIRD SERIES in monthly vols., 42*s.* each; to Subscribers for the entire series, 36*s.* each.

L. REEVE & Co., 5, Henrietta Street, Covent Garden.

LIST OF WORKS

PUBLISHED BY

L. REEVE & CO.,

5, Henrietta Street, Covent Garden, W.C.

NEW SERIES OF NATURAL HISTORY FOR BEGINNERS.

*** A good introductory series of books on Natural History for the use of students and amateurs is still a *desideratum*. Those at present in use have been too much compiled from antiquated sources; whilst the figures, copied in many instances from sources equally antiquated, are far from accurate, the colouring of them having become degenerated through the adoption, for the sake of cheapness, of mechanical processes.

The present series will be entirely the result of original research carried to its most advanced point; and the figures, which will be chiefly engraved on steel, by the artist most highly renowned in each department for his technical knowledge of the subjects, will in all cases be drawn from actual specimens, and coloured separately by hand.

Each work will treat of a department of Natural History sufficiently limited in extent to admit of a satisfactory degree of completeness.

The following are now ready:—

British Insects; a Familiar Description of the Form, Structure, Habits, and Transformations of Insects. By E. F. Staveley. Crown 8vo, 16 Coloured Steel Plates, engraved from Natural Specimens expressly for the work by E. W. Robinson, and numerous Wood-Engravings by E. C. Rye, 14*s*.

British Butterflies and Moths; an Introduction to the Study of our Native Lepidoptera. By H. T. Stainton. Crown 8vo, 16 Coloured Steel Plates, containing Figures of 100 Species, engraved from Natural Specimens expressly for the work by E. W. Robinson, and Wood-Engravings, 10*s*. 6*d*.

British Beetles; an Introduction to the Study of our Indigenous Coleoptera. By E. C. Rye. Crown 8vo, 16 Coloured Steel Plates, comprising Figures of nearly 100 Species, engraved from Natural Specimens, expressly for the work, by E. W. Robinson, and 11 Wood-Engravings of Dissections by the Author, 10*s*. 6*d*.

British Bees; an Introduction to the Study of the Natural History and Economy of the Bees indigenous to the British Isles. By W. E. Shuckard. Crown 8vo, 16 Coloured Steel Plates, containing nearly 100 Figures, engraved from Natural Specimens, expressly for the work, by E. W. Robinson, and Woodcuts of Dissections, 10*s*. 6*d*.

British Spiders; an Introduction to the Study of the Araneidæ found in Great Britain and Ireland. By E. F. Staveley. Crown 8vo, 16 Plates, containing Coloured Figures of nearly 100 Species, and 40 Diagrams, showing the number and position of the eyes in various Genera, drawn expressly for the work by Tuffen West, and 44 Wood-engravings, 10*s*. 6*d*.

British Grasses; an Introduction to the Study of the Grasses found in the British Isles. By M. Plues. Crown 8vo, 16 Coloured Plates, drawn expressly for the work by W. Fitch, and 100 Wood-Engravings, 10*s*. 6*d*.

British Ferns; an Introduction to the Study of the Ferns, Lycopods, and Equiseta indigenous to the British Isles. With Chapters on the Structure, Propagation, Cultivation, Diseases, Uses, Preservation, and Distribution of Ferns. By M. Plues. Crown 8vo, 16 Coloured Plates, drawn expressly for the work by W. Fitch, and 55 Wood-Engravings, 10*s*. 6*d*.

British Seaweeds; an Introduction to the Study of the Marine Algæ of Great Britain, Ireland, and the Channel Islands. By S. O. Gray. Crown 8vo, 16 Coloured Plates, drawn expressly for the work by W. Fitch, 10*s*. 6*d*.

Other Works in preparation.

BOTANY.

The Narcissus, its History and Culture, with Coloured Figures of all known Species and principal Varieties. By F. W. BURBIDGE, and a Review of the Classification by J. G. BAKER, F.L.S. Super-royal 8vo. 48 Coloured Plates, 32*s*.

The Young Collector's Handybook of Botany. By the Rev. H. P. DUNSTER, M.A., 66 Wood-Engravings, 3*s*. 6*d*.

The Natural History of Plants. By H. BAILLON, President of the Linnæan Society of Paris, Professor of Medical Natural History and Director of the Botanical Garden of the Faculty of Medicine of Paris. Super-royal 8vo. Vols. I. to IV., with 1800 Wood-Engravings, 25*s*. each.

Domestic Botany; an Exposition of the Structure and Classification of Plants, and of their uses for Food, Clothing, Medicine, and Manufacturing Purposes. By JOHN SMITH, A.L.S., ex-Curator of the Royal Botanic Gardens, Kew. Crown 8vo, 16 Coloured Plates and Wood-Engravings, 16*s*.

Handbook of the British Flora; a Description of the Flowering Plants and Ferns indigenous to, or naturalized in, the British Isles. For the Use of Beginners and Amateurs. By GEORGE BENTHAM, F.R.S., President of the Linnæan Society. New Edition, Crown 8vo, 12*s*.

The Illustrated British Flora, a Description (with a Wood-Engraving, including dissections, of each species) of the Flowering Plants and Ferns indigenous to, or naturalized in, the British Isles. By GEORGE BENTHAM, F.R.S., President of the Linnæan Society. Demy 8vo, 2 vols., 1295 Wood-Engravings, from Original Drawings by W. FITCH, 70*s*.

British Wild Flowers, Familiarly Described in the Four Seasons. A New Edition of "The Field Botanists' Companion." By THOMAS MOORE, F.L.S. Demy 8vo, 24 Coloured Plates, by W. FITCH, 16*s*.

Outlines of Elementary Botany, as Introductory to Local Floras. By GEORGE BENTHAM, F.R.S., President of the Linnæan Society. Second Edition, 2*s.* 6*d.*

British Grasses; an Introduction to the Study of the Gramineæ of Great Britain and Ireland. By M. PLUES. Crown 8vo, with 16 Coloured Plates by W. FITCH, and 100 Wood-Engravings, 10*s.* 6*d.*

The Botanical Magazine; Figures and Descriptions of New and Rare Plants of Interest to the Botanical Student, and suitable for the Garden, Stove, or Greenhouse. By Dr. J. D. HOOKER, C.B., Pres.R.S., Director of the Royal Gardens, Kew. Royal 8vo. Published Monthly, with 6 Plates, 3*s.* 6*d.* coloured. Annual Subscription, 42*s.*

RE-ISSUE of the THIRD SERIES in monthly vols., 42*s.* each; to Subscribers for the entire series, 36*s.* each.

The Floral Magazine; New Series, enlarged to Royal 4to. Figures and Descriptions of the choicest New Flowers for the Garden, Stove, or Conservatory. Monthly. with 4 beautifully Coloured Plates, 3*s.* 6*d.* Annual Subscription, 42*s.*

First series complete in 10 vols., with 560 beautifully Coloured Plates, £18 7*s.* 6*d.*

Laws of Botanical Nomenclature adopted by the International Botanical Congress, with an Historical Introduction and a Commentary. By ALPHONSE DE CANDOLLE. 2*s.* 6*d.*

Contributions to the Flora of Mentone, and to a Winter Flora of the Riviera, including the Coast from Marseilles to Genoa. By J. TRAHERNE MOGGRIDGE F.L.S. Royal 8vo. In 4 parts, each with 25 Coloured Plates, 15*s.*, or complete in one vol., 63*s.*

Flora Vitiensis; a description of the Plants of the Viti or Fiji Islands, with an Account of their History, Uses, and Properties. By Dr. BERTHOLD SEEMANN, F.L.S. Royal 4to, Coloured Plates, £8 5*s.*

Flora of British India. By Dr. J. D. HOOKER, C.B., F.R.S., &c.; assisted by various Botanists. Parts I. to IV., each 10*s.* 6*d.* Vol. I. (Parts I. to III.), cloth, 32*s.* Published under the Authority of the Secretary of State for India in Council.

Flora of Tropical Africa. By DANIEL OLIVER, F.R.S., F.L.S. Vols I. and II., 20*s.* each. Published under the authority of the First Commissioner of Her Majesty's Works.

Handbook of the New Zealand Flora; a Systematic Description of the Native Plants of New Zealand, and the Chatham, Kermadec's, Lord Auckland's, Campbell's, and Macquarrie's Islands. By Dr. J. D. HOOKER, F.R.S. Complete in one vol., 30*s.* Published under the auspices of the Government of that colony.

Flora Australiensis; a Description of the Plants of the Australian Territory. By GEORGE BENTHAM, F.R.S., President of the Linnean Society, assisted by FERDINAND MUELLER, F.R.S.. Government Botanist, Melbourne, Victoria. Vols. I. to VI., 20*s.* each. Published under the auspices of the several Governments of Australia.

Flora of the British West Indian Islands. By Dr. GRISEBACH, F.L.S. 37*s.* 6*d.* Published under the auspices of the Secretary of State for the Colonies.

Flora Hongkongensis; a Description of the Flowering Plants and Ferns of the Island of Hongkong. By GEORGE BENTHAM, F.L.S. With a map of the Island, and a Supplement by Dr. HANCE. 18*s.* Published under the authority of Her Majesty's Secretary of State for the Colonies. The Supplement separately, 2*s.* 6*d.*

Flora Capensis: a Systematic Description of the Plants of the Cape Colony, Caffraria, and Port Natal. By WILLIAM H. HARVEY, M.D., F.R.S., Professor of Botany in the University of Dublin, and OTTO WILHEM SONDER, Ph.D. Vols. I and II., 12*s.* each. Vol. III., 18*s.*

Elementary Lessons in Botanical Geography. By J. G. Baker, F.L.S., 3*s*.

On the Flora of Australia, its Origin, Affinities and Distribution; being an Introductory Essay to the "Flora of Tasmania." By Dr. J. D. HOCKER, F.R.S., 10*s*.

Genera Plantarum, ad Exemplaria imprimis in Herbariis Kewensibus servata definita. By GEORGE BENTHAM, F.R.S., F.L.S., and Dr. J. D. HOOKER, Pres.R.S., Director of the Royal Gardens, Kew. Vol. I. Part I. Royal 8vo, 21*s*. Part II., 14*s*.; Part III., 15*s*; or Vol. I. complete, 50*s*. Vol. II. Part I. 24*s*.; Part II. 32*s*.; or Vol. II. complete, 56*s*.

Illustrations of the Genus Carex. By FRANCIS BOOTT, M.D. Folio, 600 Plates. Part I., 10*l*. Parts II. and III., each 5*l*. Part IV., 10*l*.

Illustrations of the Nueva Quinologia of Pavon, with Observations on the Barks described. By J. E. HOWARD, F.L.S. With 27 coloured Plates by W. FITCH. Imperial folio, half morroco, gilt edges, 6*l*. 6*s*.

The Quinology of the East Indian Plantations. By J. E. HOWARD, F.L.S. Folio, 3 Coloured Plates, 21*s*. Parts II. and III., with 10 Coloured and 2 Plain Plates, and 2 Photo-prints, cloth 63*s*., or complete in one Vol., 84*s*.

Revision of the Natural Order Hederaceæ, being a reprint, with numerous additions and corrections, of a series of papers published in the "Journal of Botany, British and Foreign." By BERTHOLD SEEMANN, Ph. D., F.L.S. 7 Plates, 10*s*. 6*d*.

Icones Plantarum. Figures, with Brief Descriptive Characters and Remarks, of New and Rare Plants selected from the Author's Herbarium. By Sir W. J. HOOKER, F.R.S. New Series, Vol. V. 100 Plates, 31*s*. 6*d*.

Orchids: and How to Grow them in India and other Tropical Climates. By SAMUEL JENNINGS, F.L.S., F.R.H.S., late Vice-President of the Agri-Horticultural Society of India. Royal 4to. Complete in 1 Vol., cloth, gilt edges, 63*s*.

A Second Century of Orchidaceous Plants, selected from the Subjects published in Curtis's "Botanical Magazine" since the issue of the "First Century." Edited by JAMES BATEMAN, Esq., F.R.S. Complete in 1 Vol. royal 4to, 100 Coloured Plates, 5*l*. 5*s*.

Dedicated by Special Permission to H.R.H. the Princess of Wales.

Monograph of Odontoglossum, a Genus of the Vandeous Section of Orchidaceous Plants. By JAMES BATEMAN, Esq., F.R.S. Imperial folio, complete in 6 Parts, each with 5 Coloured Plates, and occasional Wood-Engravings, 21*s*., or in one vol., half morocco, gilt edges, 7*l*. 7*s*.

Select Orchidaceous Plants. By ROBERT WARNER, F.R.H.S. With Notes on Culture by B. S. WILLIAMS. Folio, with 40 Coloured Plates, cloth gilt, 7*l*. 7*s*.
Second Series, complete, with 39 Coloured Plates, 7*l*. 7*s*.

The Rhododendrons of Sikkim-Himalaya; being an Account, Botanical and Geographical, of the Rhododendrons recently discovered in the Mountains of Eastern Himalaya, by Dr. J. D. Hooker, F.R.S. By Sir W. J. HOOKER, F.R.S. Folio, 30 Coloured Plates, 4*l*. 14*s*. 6*d*.

Botanical Names for English Readers. By RANDAL H. ALCOCK. 8vo, 6*s*.

FERNS.

British Ferns; an Introduction to the Study of the FERNS, LYCOPODS, and EQUISETA indigenous to the British Isles. With Chapters on the Structure, Propagation, Cultivation, Diseases. Uses, Preservation, and Distribution of Ferns. By M. PLUES. Crown 8vo, with 16 Coloured Plates by W. FITCH, and 55 Wood-Engravings, 10*s*. 6*d*.

The British Ferns; Coloured Figures and Descriptions, with Analysis of the Fructification and Venation of the Ferns of Great Britain and Ireland. By Sir W. J. HOOKER, F.R.S. Royal 8vo, 66 Coloured Plates, 2*l*. 2*s*.

Garden Ferns; Coloured Figures and Descriptions, with Analysis of the Fructification and Venation, of a Selection of Exotic Ferns, adapted for Cultivation in the Garden, Hothouse, and Conservatory. By Sir W. J. HOOKER, F.R.S. Royal 8vo, 64 Coloured Plates, 2*l*. 2*s*.

Filices Exoticæ; Coloured Figures and Description of Exotic Ferns. By Sir W. J. HOOKER, F.R.S. Royal 4to, 100 Coloured Plates, 6*l*. 11*s*.

Ferny Combes; a Ramble after Ferns in the Glens and Valleys of Devonshire. By CHARLOTTE CHANTER. *Third Edition.* Fcap. 8vo, 8 Coloured Plates by FITCH, and a Map of the County, 5*s*.

MOSSES.

Handbook of British Mosses, containing all that are known to be natives of the British Isles. By the Rev. M. J. BERKELEY, M.A., F.L.S. Demy 8vo, 24 Coloured Plates, 21*s*.

Synopsis of British Mosses, containing Descriptions of all the Genera and Species (with localities of the rarer ones) found in Great Britain and Ireland. By CHARLES P. HOBKIRK, President of the Huddersfield Naturalist's Society. Crown 8vo, 7*s*. 6*d*.

SEAWEEDS.

British Seaweeds; an Introduction to the Study of the Marine Algæ of Great Britain, Ireland, and the Channel Islands. By S. O. GRAY. Crown 8vo, with 16 Coloured Plates, drawn expressly for the work by W. FITCH, 10*s*. 6*d*.

Phycologia Britannica; or, History of British Seaweeds, containing Coloured Figures, Generic and Specific Characters, Synomyms and Descriptions of all the Species of Algæ inhabiting the Shores of the British Islands. By Dr. W. H. HARVEY, F.R.S. New Edition. Royal 8vo, 4 vols. 360 Coloured Plates, 7*l.* 10*s.*

Phycologia Australica: a History of Australian Seaweeds, comprising Coloured Figures and Descriptions of the more characteristic Marine Algæ of New South Wales, Victoria, Tasmania, South Australia and Western Australia, and a Synopsis of all known Australian Algæ. By Dr. HARVEY, F.R.S. Royal 8vo, 5 vols, 300 Coloured Plates, 7*l.* 13*s.*

FUNGI.

Outlines of British Fungology, containing Characters of above a Thousand Species of Fungi, and a Complete List of all that have been described as Natives of the British Isles. By the Rev. M. J. BERKELEY, M.A., F.L.S. Demy 8vo, 24 Coloured Plates, 30*s.*

The Esculent Funguses of England. Containing an Account of their Classical History, Uses, Characters, Development, Structure, Nutritious Properties, Modes of Cooking and Preserving, &c. By C. D. BADHAM, M.D. Second Edition. Edited by F. CURREY, F.R.S. Demy 8vo, 12 Coloured Plates, 12*s.*

Illustrations of British Mycology, comprising Figures and Descriptions of the Funguses of interest and novelty indigenous to Britain. By Mrs. T. J. HUSSEY. Royal 4to. Second Series, 50 Coloured Plates, £4 10*s.*

Clavis Agaricinorum: an Analytical Key to the British Agaricini, with Characters of the Genera and Subgenera. By WORTHINGTON G. SMITH, F.L.S. Six plates. 2*s.* 6*d.*

SHELLS AND MOLLUSKS.

Elements of Conchology; an Introduction to the Natural History of Shells, and of the Animals which form them. By LOVELL REEVE, F.L.S. Royal 8vo, 2 vols. 62 Coloured Plates, £2 16*s*.

Conchologia Iconica; or, Figures and Descriptions of the Shells of Mollusks, with remarks on their Affinities, Synonymy, and Geographical Distribution. By LOVELL REEVE, F.L.S. Demy 4to, in double Parts, with 16 Coloured Plates. 20*s*.

A detailed list of Monographs and Volumes published may be had.

Conchologia Indica; Illustrations of the Land and Freshwater Shells of British India. Edited by SYLVANUS HANLEY, F.L.S., and WILLIAM THEOBALD, of the Geological Survey of India. 4to, Parts I. to VIII., each with 20 Coloured Plates, 20*s*., or complete in one vol., cloth, £8 5 .

The Edible Mollusks of Great Britain and Ireland, with the Modes of Cooking them. By M. S. LOVELL. Crown 8vo, with 12 Coloured Plates, 8*s*. 6*d*.

INSECTS.

Harvesting Ants and Trap-door Spiders; Notes and Observations on their Habits and Dwellings. By J. T. MOGGRIDGE, F.L.S. With a SUPPLEMENT of 160 pp. and 8 additional Plates, 17*s*. The Supplement separately, cloth, 7*s*. 6*d*.

British Insects. A Familiar Description of the Form, Structure, Habits, and Transformations of Insects. By E. F. STAVELEY, Author of "British Spiders." Crown 8vo, with 16 Coloured Steel Plates and numerous Wood-Engravings, 14*s*.

British Beetles; an Introduction to the Study of our Indigenous COLEOPTERA. By E. C. RYE. Crown 8vo, 16 Coloured Steel Plates, comprising Figures of nearly 100 Species, engraved from Natural Specimens, expressly for the work, by E. W. ROBINSON, and 11 Wood-Engravings of Dissections by the Author, 10*s*. 6*d*.

British Bees; an Introduction to the Study of the Natural History and Economy of the Bees indigenous to the British Isles. By W. E. SHUCKARD. Crown 8vo, 16 Coloured Steel Plates, containing nearly 100 Figures, engraved from Natural Specimens, expressly for the work, by E. W. ROBINSON, and Woodcuts of Dissections, 10*s*. 6*d*.

British Butterflies and Moths; an Introduction to the Study of our Native LEPIDOPTERA. By H. T. STAINTON. Crown 8vo, 16 Coloured Steel Plates, containing Figures of 100 Species, engraved from Natural Specimens expressly for the work by E. W. ROBINSON, and Wood-Engravings, 10*s*. 6*d*.

British Spiders; an introduction to the Study of the ARANEIDÆ found in Great Britain and Ireland. By E. F. STAVELEY. Crown 8vo. 16 Plates, containing Coloured Figures of nearly 100 species, and 40 Diagrams, showing the number and position of the eyes in various Genera, drawn expressly for the work by TUFFEN WEST, and 44 Wood-Engravings, 10*s*. 6*d*.

Curtis's British Entomology. Illustrations and Descriptions of the Genera of Insects found in Great Britain and Ireland, containing Coloured Figures, from Nature, of the most rare and beautiful Species, and in many instances, upon the plants on which they are found. 8 vols. Royal 8vo, 770 Coloured Plates. £28.

Or in Separate Monographs.

Orders.	*Plates.*	£	*s.*	*d.*	*Orders.*	*Plates.*	£	*s.*	*d.*
APHANIPTERA	2 ...	0	2	0	HYMENOPTERA	125 ...	6	5	0
COLEOPTERA	256 ...	12	16	0	LEPIDOPTERA.........	193 ...	9	13	0
DERMAPTERA.........	1 ...	0	1	0	NEUROPTERA	13 ...	0	13	0
DICTYOPTERA	1 ...	0	1	0	OMALOPTERA	6 ...	0	6	0
DIPTERA	103 ...	5	3	0	ORTHOPTERA	5 ...	0	5	0
HEMIPTERA	32 ...	1	12	0	STREPSIPTERA	3 ...	0	3	0
HOMOPTERA	21 ...	1	1	0	TRICHOPTERA	9 ...	0	9	0

"Curtis's Entomology," which Cuvier pronounced to have "reached the ultimatum of parfection," is still the standard work on the Genera of British Insects. The Figures executed by the author himself, with wonderful minuteness and accuracy, have never been surpassed, even if equal'ed. The price at which the work was originally published was £43 16*s*.

Insecta Britannica; Vol. III., Diptera. By FRANCIS WALKER, F.L.S. 8vo, with 10 Plates, 25*s*.

FINE ART.

The Royal Academy Album; a Series of Photographs from Works of Art in the Exhibition of the Royal Academy of Arts, 1875. Atlas 4to, with 32 fine Photographs, cloth, gilt edges, £6 6*s*. Half Morocco, £7 7*s*.

The same for 1876, with 48 beautiful Photo-prints, cloth £6 6*s*. Half Morocco £7 7*s*. Small Edition, Royal 4to, cloth, gilt edges, 63*s*.

Photographs from Modern Paintings by Eminent Artists. A New Copyright Series of Photographs, taken direct from the original paintings with the sanction of the Artists. Large size on Imperial India-tinted mounts, 9*s*. each. Smaller size on Atlas 4to, do., 4*s*. 6d. Lists of Subjects ready on application.

ANTIQUARIAN.

Sacred Archæology; a Popular Dictionary of Ecclesiastical Art and Institutions, from Primitive to Modern Times. Comprising Architecture, Music, Vestments, Furniture Arrangement, Offices, Customs, Ritual Symbolism, Ceremonial Traditions, Religious Orders, &c., of the Church Catholic in all Ages. By MACKENZIE E. C. WALCOTT, B.D., Oxon., F.S.A., Præcentor and Prebendary of Chichester Cathedral. Demy 8vo, 18*s*.

A Manual of British Archæology. By CHARLES BOUTELL, M.A. 20 Coloured Plates, 10*s*. 6*d*.

Man's Age in the World according to Holy Scripture and Science. By AN ESSEX RECTOR. 8*s*. 6*d*.

The Antiquity of Man; an Examination of Sir Charles Lyell's recent Work. By S. R. PATTISON, F.G.S. Second Edition. 8vo, 1*s*.

MISCELLANEOUS.

Natal; a History and Description of the Colony, including its Natural Features, Productions, Industrial Condition and Prospects. By HENRY BROOKS, for many years a resident. Edited by Dr. R. J. MANN, F.R.A.S., F.R.G.S., late Superintendent of Education in the Colony. Demy 8vo, with Maps, Coloured Plates, and Photographic Views, 21*s*.

St. Helena. A Physical, Historical, and Topographical Description of the Island, including its Geology, Fauna, Flora, and Meteorology. By J. C. MELLISS, A.I.C.E., F.G.S., F.L.S. In one large Vol. Super royal 8vo, with 56 Plates and Maps, mostly Coloured. 42*s*.

International Series of Elementary Text Books of Natural Science.

Zoology. By ADRIAN J. EBELL, Ph.B., M.D. Part I.: Structural Distinctions, Functions, and Classification of the Orders of Animals, 1*s*.

Lahore to Yarkand. Incidents of the Route and Natural History of the Countries traversed by the Expedition of 1870, under T. D. FORSYTH, Esq., C.B. By GEORGE HENDERSON, M.D., F.L.S., F.R.G.S., and ALLAN O. HUME, Esq., C.B., F.Z.S. With 32 Coloured Plates of Birds, 6 of Plants, 26 Photographic Views, Map, and Geological Sections, 42*s*.

On Intelligence. By H. Taine, D.C.L. Oxon. Translated from the French by T. D. HAYE, and revised, with additions, by the Author. Complete in One Volume, 18*s*.

The Young Collector's Handy Book of Recreative Science. By the Rev. H. P. DUNSTER, M.A. Cuts. 3*s*. 6*d*.

The Gladiolus: its History, Cultivation, and Exhibition. By the Rev. H. HONYWOOD DOMBRAIN, B.A. 1*s*.

The Birds of Sherwood Forest; with Observations on their Nesting, Habits, and Migrations. By W. J. STERLAND. Crown 8vo, 4 plates. 7*s.* 6*d.* coloured.

The Naturalist in Norway; or, Notes on the Wild Animals, Birds, Fishes, and Plants of that Country, with some account of the principal Salmon Rivers. By the Rev. J. BOWDEN, LL.D. Crown 8vo, 8 Coloured Plates. 10*s.* 6*d.*

The Zoology of the Voyage of H.M.S. *Samarang*, under the command of Captain Sir Edward Belcher, C.B. during the Years 1843–46. By Professor OWEN, Dr. J. E. GRAY, Sir J. RICHARDSON, A. ADAMS, L. REEVE, and A. WHITE. Edited by ARTHUR ADAMS, F.L.S. Royal 4to, 55 Plates, mostly coloured, £3 10*s.*

A Survey of the Early Geography of Western Europe, as connected with the First Inhabitants of Britain, their Origin, Language, Religious Rites, and Edifices. By HENRY LAWES LONG, Esq. 8vo, 6*s.*

The Geologist. A Magazine of Geology, Palæontology, and Mineralogy. Illustrated with highly-finished Wood Engravings. Edited by S. J. MACKIE, F.G.S., F.S.A. Vols. V. and VI., each, with numerous Wood-Engravings, 18*s.* Vol. VII. 9*s.*

The Stereoscopic Magazine. A Gallery for the Stereoscope of Landscape Scenery, Architecture, Antiquities, Natural History, Rustic Character, &c. With Descriptions. 5 vols., each complete in itself and containing 50 Stereographs, £2 2*s.*

Everybody's Weather-Guide. The Use of Metereological Instruments clearly Explained, with Directions for Securing at any time a probable Prognostic of the Weather. By A. STEINMETZ, Esq., Author of "Sunshine and Showers," &c. 1*s.*

The Artificial Production of Fish. By PISCARIUS. Third Edition. 1*s.*

Sunshine and Showers: their Influences throughout Creation. A Compendium ot Popular Meteorology. By ANDREW STEINMETZ, Esq. Crown 8vo, Cuts, 7*s.* 6*d.*

The Reasoning Power in Animals. By the REV. J. S. WATSON, M A. Crown 8vo, 9*s.*

Manual of Chemical Analysis, Qualitative and Quantitative; for the use of Students. By Dr. HENRY M. NOAD, F.R.S. New edition. Crown 8vo. 109 Wood-Engravings, 16*s.* Or, separately, Part I., 'QUALITATIVE,' New Edition, new Notation, 6*s.*; Part II., 'QUANTITATIVE,' 10*s.* 6*d.*

Phosphorescence; or, the Emission of Light by Minerals, Plants, and Animals. By Dr. T. L. PHIPSON, F.C.S. Small 8vo, 30 Cuts and Coloured Frontispiece, 5*s.*

Meteors, Aerolites, and Falling Stars. By Dr. T. L. PHIPSON, F.C.S. Crown 8vo, 25 Woodcuts and Lithographic Frontispiece, 6*s.*

Live Coals; or, Faces from the Fire. By L. M. BUDGEN, "Acheta," Author of 'Episodes of Insect Life,' etc., Dedicated, by Special Permission, to H.R.H. Field-Marshal the Duke of Cambridge. Royal 4to, 35 Original Sketches printed in colours, 21*s.*

Caliphs and Sultans; being Tales omitted in the ordinary English Version of "The Arabian Nights' Entertainments," freely rewritten and rearranged. By S. HANLEY, F.L.S. 6*s.*

PLATES.

Floral Plates, from the Floral Magazine. Beautifully Coloured, for Screens, Scrap-books, Studies in Flower painting. &c. 6*d.* and 1*s.* each. Lists of over 700 varieties.

Botanical Plates, from the Botanical Magazine. Beautifully Coloured Figures of New and Rare Plants. 6*d.* and 1*s.* each. Lists of over 2000.

SERIALS.

The Botanical Magazine. Figures and Descriptions of New and Rare Plants. By Dr. J. D. HOOKER, C.B., Pres.R.S. Monthly, with 6 Coloured Plates, 3*s*. 6*d*. Annual Subscription, post free, 42*s*.

Re-issue of the Third Series in monthly vols., 42*s*. each: to Subscribers for the entire Series, 36*s*. each.

The Floral Magazine. New Series, enlarged to Royal 4to. Figures and Descriptions of Select New Flowers for the Garden, Stove, or Conservatory. Monthly, with 4 Coloured Plates, 3*s*. 6*d*. Annual Subscription, post free, 42*s*.

Select Orchidaceous Plants. By ROBERT WARNER. 3 Coloured Plates, 10*s*. 6*d*.

Conchologia Iconica. By LOVELL REEVE, F.L.S., and G. B. SOWERBY, F.L.S. In Double Parts, with 16 Coloured Plates, 20*s*.

FORTHCOMING WORKS.

West Yorkshire: its Geology, Physical Geography and Botany. By JAMES W. DAVIS, F.G.S., F.L.S., and FREDERIC ARNOLD LEES, F.L.S.

The Food Plants of the British Lepidoptera. By OWEN WILSON.

Handbook to the Freshwater Fishes of India. By Captain R. BEAVAN.

Phalænopsis: a Genus of Orchidaceous Plants.

Genera Plantarum. By BENTHAM and HOOKER.

Flora of India. By Dr. HOOKER and others.

Natural History of Plants. By Prof. BAILLON.

Flora of the Mauritius. By J. G. BAKER, F.L.S.

Flora of Tropical Africa. By Prof. OLIVER.

Flora Australiensis. By G. BENTHAM. Vol. 7.